The Pepin Press

Visual Encyclopedia
Visuelle Enzyklopädie
Encyclopédie Visuelle
Enciclopedia Visuale
Enciclopedia Visual

ビジュアル百科事典
視覺百科全書

衣裳 服飾
Costume
Kostüm
Vêtement
Indumentaria
Costume

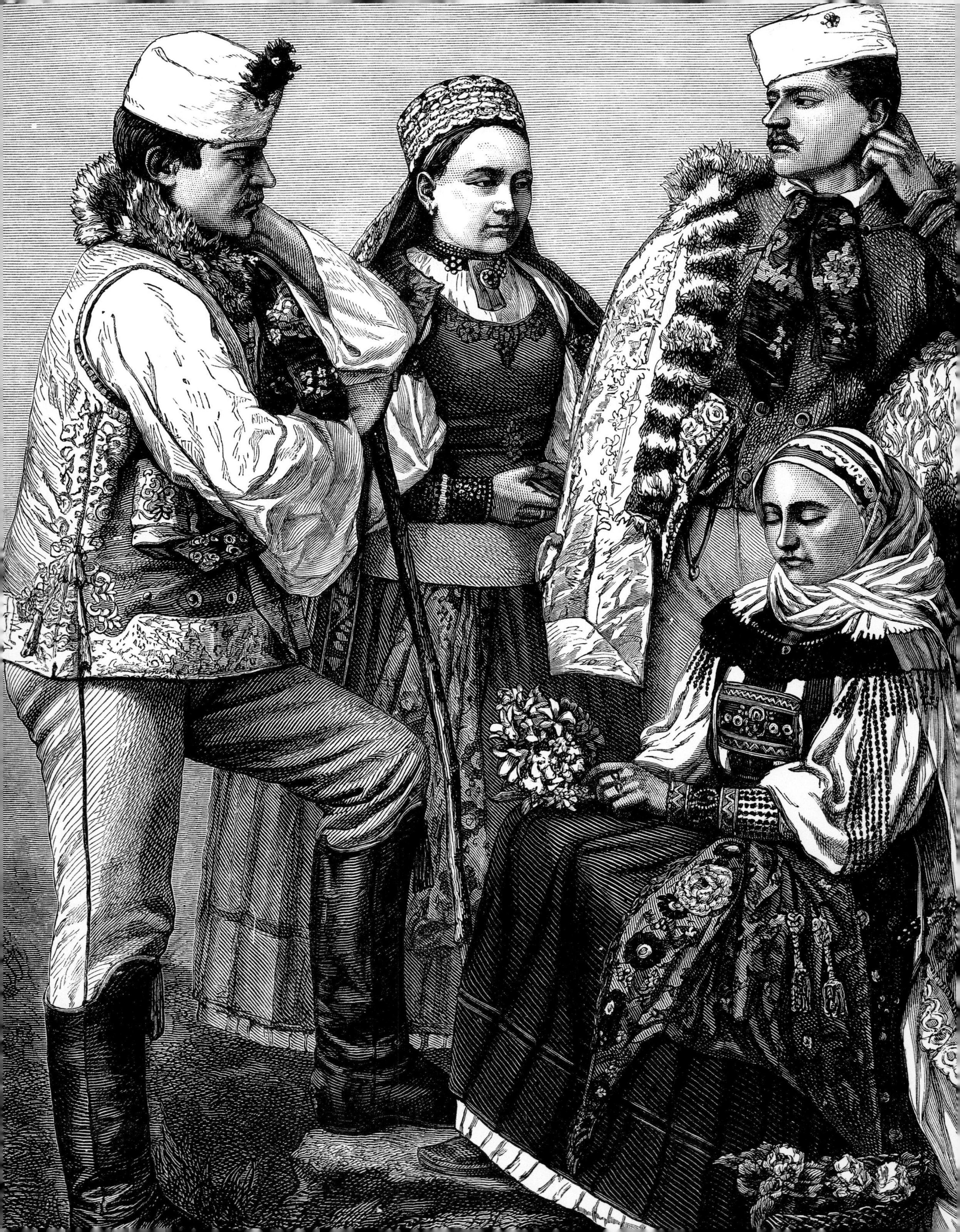

The Pepin Press

Visual Encyclopedia
Visuelle Enzyklopädie
Encyclopédie Visuelle
Enciclopedia Visuale
Enciclopedia Visual

ビジュアル百科事典
視覺百科全書

衣裳 服飾

Costume
Kostüm
Vêtement
Indumentaria
Costume

The Pepin Press publishes a wide range of books and book+CD-Rom sets
on architecture, ornament, costume, and various types of design.
For more information, please consult our website: www.pepinpress.com

Illustrations pages 2–13:

2	Hungarians, c. 1880
6	South African *Saqua*, or Bushmen, c. 1880
7	Persians, c. 1870
8–9	*Sohkalar* or *Yakut* people from Siberia, c. 1860
10	Bazar in Bahrein, c. 1890
11	Croat, c. 1880
12	Peruvian girl, c. 1850
13	Japanese, c. 1650

ISBN 90 5496 079 5

This book is produced by The Pepin Press in Amsterdam and Singapore.

Visual Encyclopædia design concept: Dorine van den Beukel and Pepin van Roojen
This volume is edited and designed by Pepin van Roojen
German, French, Italian and Spanish translations: LocTeam, Barcelona
Japanese and Chinese translations: Link-Up Mitaka, Leeds

The Pepin Press BV
P.O. Box 10349
1001 EH Amsterdam
mail@pepinpress.com
www.pepinpress.com

Printed and bound in Singapore

2005 04 03 02
10 9 8 7 6 5 4 3 2

Contents

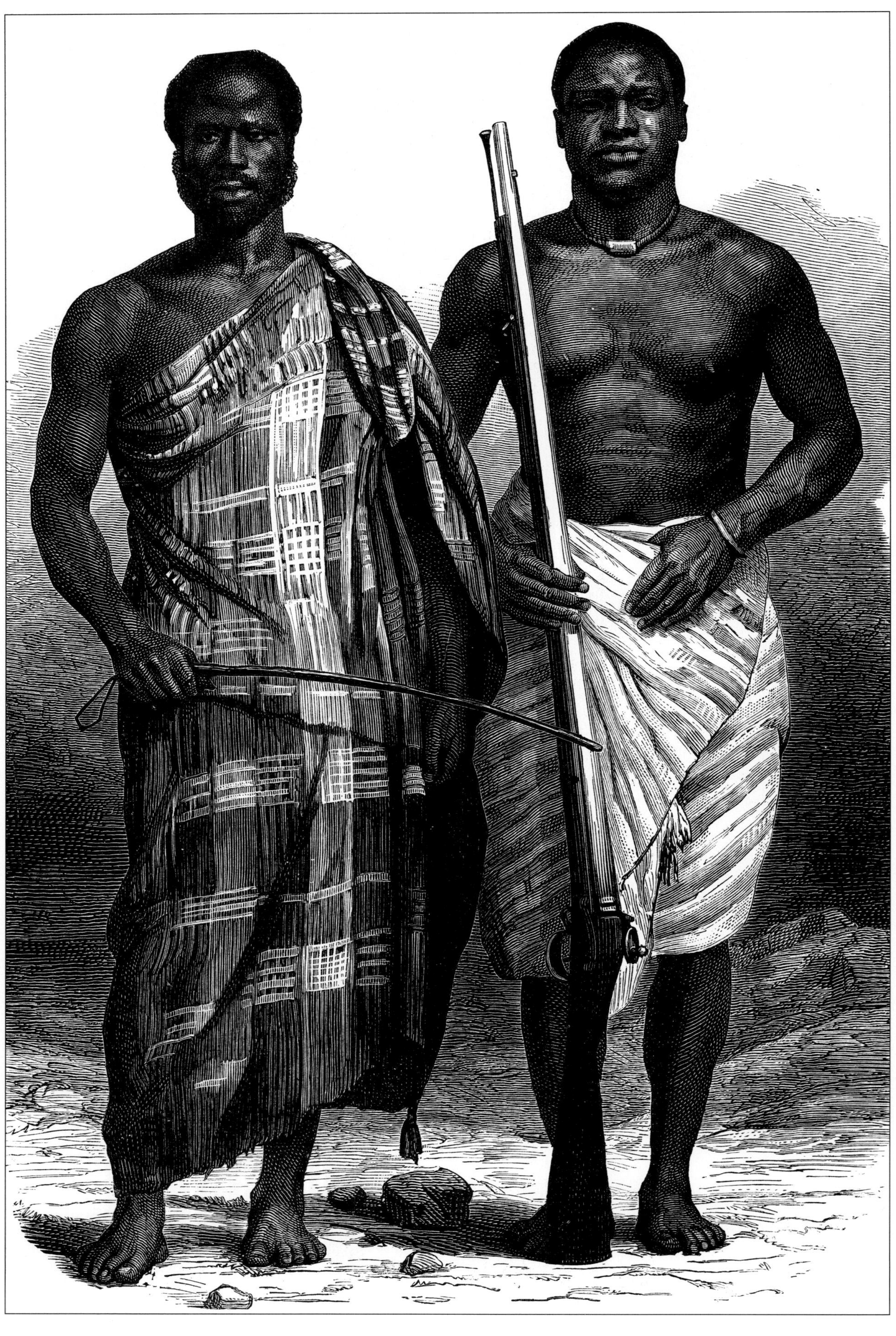

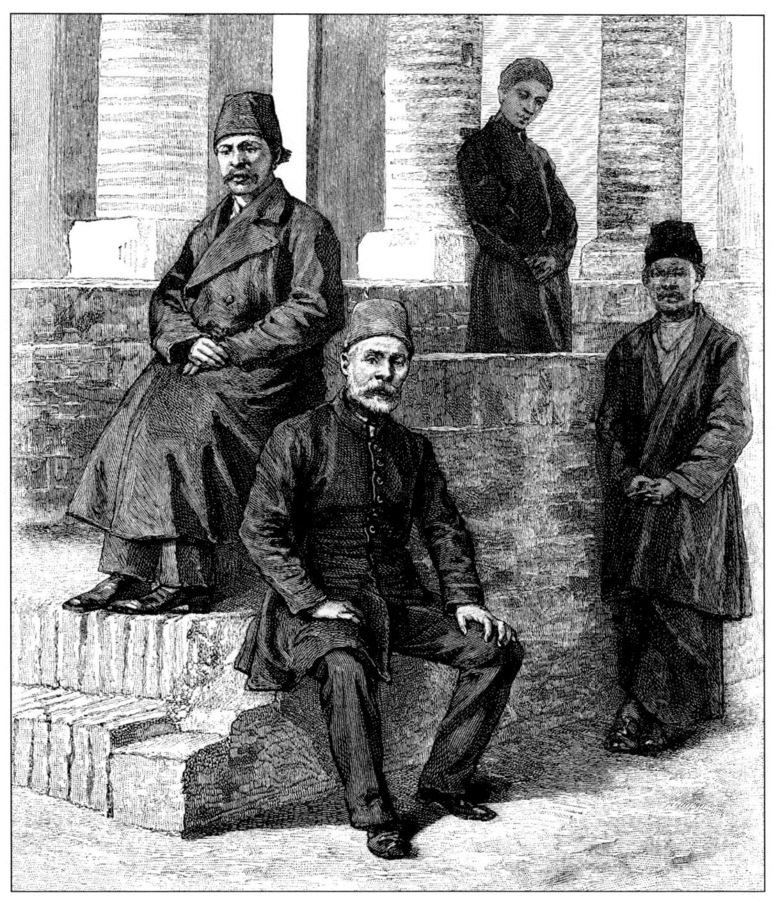

Introduction

THE PEPIN PRESS VISUAL ENCYCLOPÆDIAS are massive visual resources, containing thousands of high-quality line drawings per volume and featuring practically every country in the world. The following themes have been published or are in preparation: ARCHITECTURE, COSTUME, ORNAMENTAL DESIGN and FURNITURE. More volumes are to follow. Each book exhaustively covers the great cultures, such as Ancient Egypt, the Mayas, Persia, China, Japan, India, the Muslim World. For Europe, the usual chronology is followed: Prehistory and Classical Cultures, the Middle Ages, Renaissance, Baroque, etc. However, the focus is certainly not only on the established highlights; also less prominent, but equally interesting items are illustrated.
Much attention, too, is given to the cultural expressions of less documented regions. So in addition to classical themes such as Greek vases, Italian churches, and 18th-century fashion from Paris, in the Pepin Press Visual Encyclopaedias one can find, for example, constructions and designs from the Solomon Islands, costume from Friesland, Cabo Verde and Uzbekistan, Eskimo carvings, and ornaments from Benin.

The illustrations and captions on each page are ordered from left to right and from top to bottom.

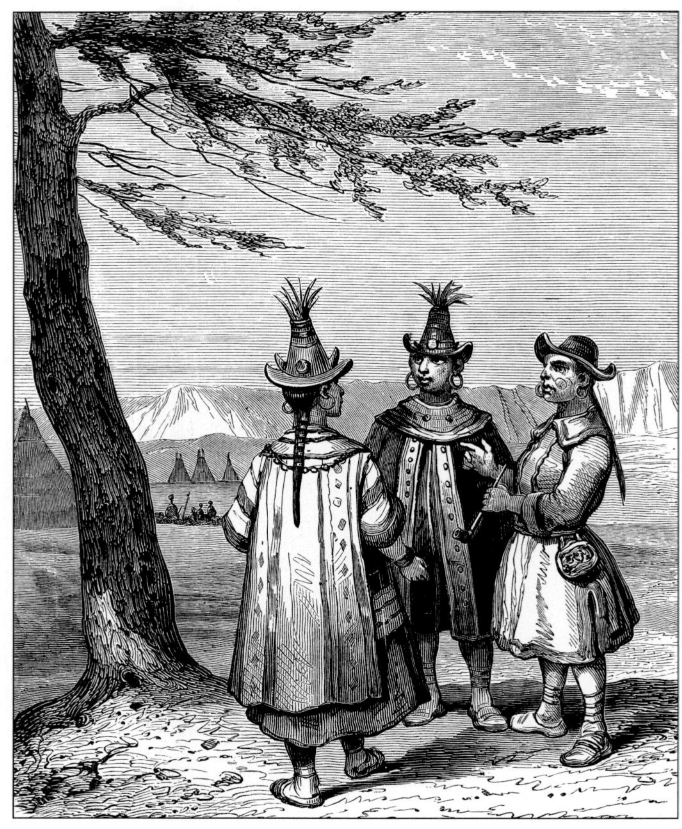

Einführung

DIE VISUELLEN ENZYKLOPÄDIEN VON PEPIN PRESS sind umfassende visuelle Ressourcen mit tausenden von qualitativ hochwertigen Linienzeichnungen in jedem Band, in denen praktisch jedes Land der Welt enthalten ist. Veröffentlicht oder in Vorbereitung sind die Themenbereiche ARCHITEKTUR, KOSTÜME, DEKORATIVE KUNST und MÖBEL; weitere Bände sind geplant. Jeder Band behandelt ausführlich die großen Kulturkreise wie Altägypten, die Mayas, Persien, China, Japan, Indien und die moslemische Welt. Für Europa wurde die übliche Zeitenfolge eingehalten, nämlich Vorgeschichte und klassische Kulturen, Mittelalter, Renaissance, Barock usw. Dennoch liegt der Schwerpunkt nicht ausschließlich auf den anerkannten kulturellen Höhepunkten; auch weniger bekannte, jedoch ebenso interessante Aspekte werden illustriert.
Sehr viel Aufmerksamkeit wurde auch den kulturellen Ausdrucksformen weniger dokumentierter Regionen zuteil. So findet der Leser in den Visuellen Enzyklopädien von Pepin Press neben klassischen Themen wie griechischen Vasen, italienischen Kirchen und Mode aus dem 18. Jahrhundert aus Paris beispielsweise auch Bauten und Gestaltungsformen von den Salomonen, Kostüme aus Friesland, Kap Verde und Usbekistan, Schnitzereien der Eskimos und Ornamente aus Benin.

Die Illustrationen und Bildunterschriften auf jeder Seite sind von links nach rechts und von oben nach unten geordnet.

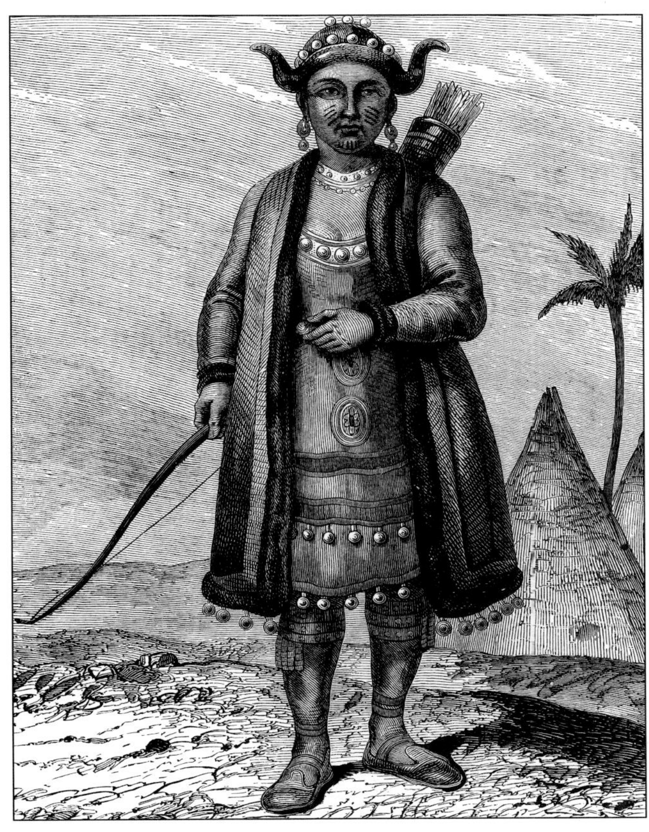

Introducción

LAS ENCICLOPEDIAS VISUALES DE PEPIN PRESS son fuentes documentales visuales de referencia. Cada volumen contiene miles de ilustraciones de calidad suprema y trazo elegante donde aparecen retratados prácticamente todos los países del mundo. A continuación incluimos una serie de títulos, algunos de los cuales ya están en el mercado, mientras que otros está previsto publicarlos próximamente: ARQUITECTURA, INDUMENTARIA, DISEÑO ORNAMENTAL y MOBILIARIO. Estos títulos se irán ampliando en el futuro con nuevas publicaciones. Cada volumen cubre exhaustivamente las principales culturas, como el antiguo Egipto, el Imperio Maya, Persia, China, Japón, el mundo árabe, etc. Por lo que respecta a Europa, las ilustraciones se presentan ordenadas cronológicamente: prehistoria y culturas clásicas, Edad Media, Renacimiento, Barroco, etc. Las enciclopedias de Pepin Press no se concentran exclusivamente en las piezas más célebres, sino que amplían su espectro para incluir también ilustraciones de objetcs y edificios menos prominentes, pero no por ello menos interesantes.
Por otro lado, se presta una atención especial a las manifestaciones culturales de las regiones del mundo menos documentadas. Por ello, además de las piezas clásicas por excelencia, como las vasijas griegas, las iglesias italianas y la moda decimonónica de París, en las enciclopedias de Pepin Press es posible encontrar, por ejemplo, construcciones y diseños procedentes de las islas Salomón, de Frisia, de Cabo Verde y de Uzbekistán; grabados esquimales, y piezas decorativas de Benín.

Las ilustraciones y los pies de fotografía que aparecen en cada página están ordenados de izquierda a derecha y de arriba abajo.

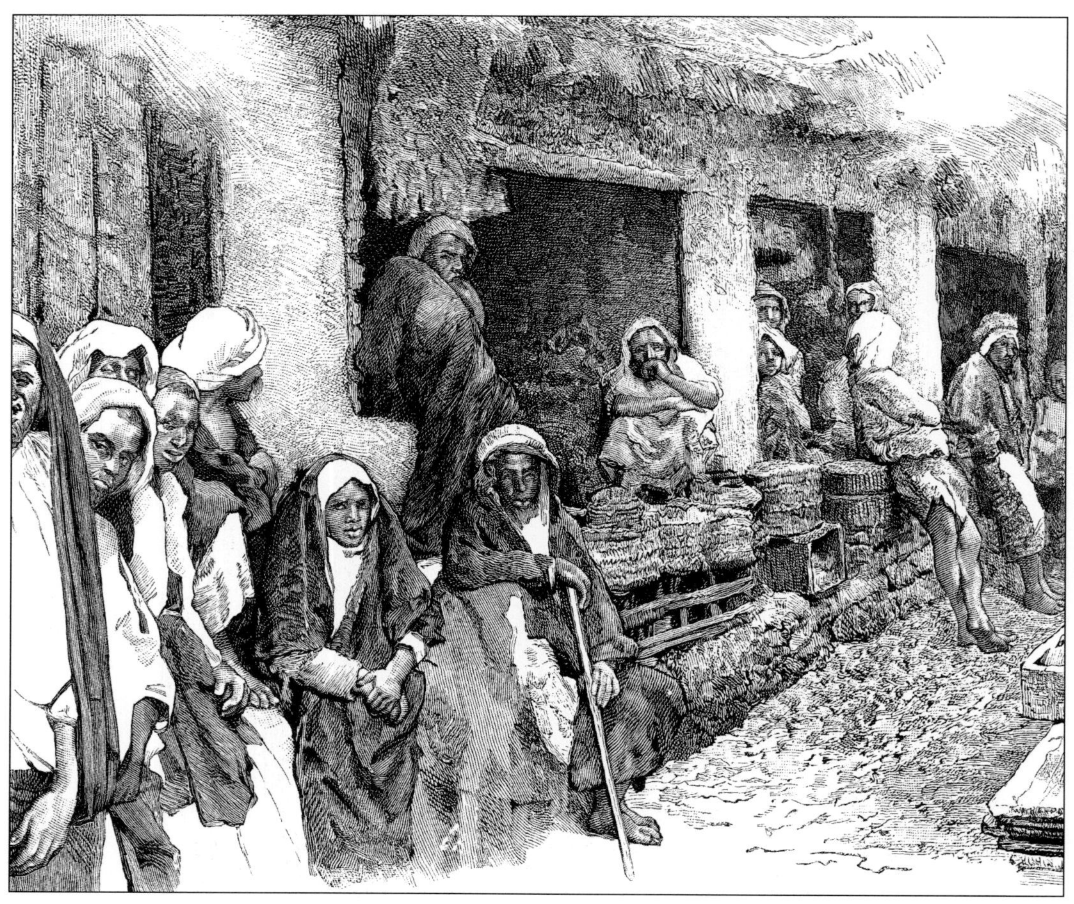

Introduzione

LE ENCICLOPEDIE VISUALI PEPIN PRESS sono delle grandi risorse visuali che contengono migliaia di disegni di alta qualità per ogni volume e abbracciano praticamente tutti i paesi del mondo. Gli argomenti elencati di seguito sono stati pubblicati o sono in corso di preparazione: ARCHITETTURA, COSTUME, DISEGNO ORNAMENTALE e ARREDAMENTO. Seguiranno altri volumi. Ogni libro tratta esaurientemente le grandi culture quali l'Antico Egitto, i Maya, la Persia, la Cina, il Giappone, l'India, il mondo musulmano, ecc. Per l'Europa è stata seguita la cronologia tradizionale: preistoria e culture classiche, Medioevo, Rinascimento, Barocco, ecc. Ad ogni modo, la nostra attenzione non si rivolge esclusivamente agli elementi più salienti: sono stati illustrati anche i punti meno rilevanti ma di altrettanto interesse. Grande attenzione viene inoltre dedicata alle espressioni culturali delle regioni delle quali si dispone di scarsa documentazione. Quindi, oltre agli argomenti classici come i vasi greci, le chiese italiane e la moda parigina del XVII secolo, nelle Enciclopedie visuali Pepin Press si possono trovare, ad esempio, costruzioni e progetti delle Isole Salomone, il costume della Frisia, di Capo Verde e dell'Uzbechistan, le sculture esquimesi e gli ornamenti del Benin.

Le illustrazioni e le didascalie su ogni pagina sono ordinate da sinistra verso destra e dall'alto verso il basso.

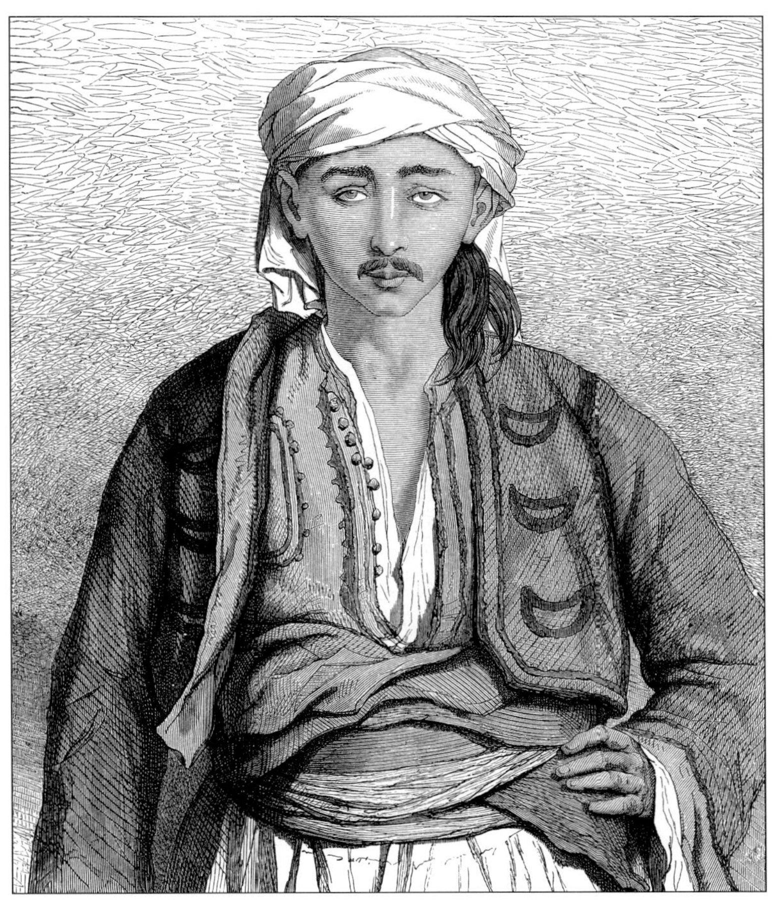

Introduction

LES ENCYCLOPÉDIES VISUELLES PEPIN PRESS sont richement illustrées. Chaque volume contient plusieurs milliers d'illustrations dont la qualité du trait est incomparable et où presque tous les pays du monde sont représentés. Les thèmes suivants ont été publiés ou sont en préparation : ARCHITECTURE, VÊTEMENT, MOTIFS ORNEMENTAUX et MOBILIER. D'autres volumes seront bientôt disponibles. Chaque ouvrage couvre de façon approfondie les grandes civilisations : l'Égypte antique, les Mayas, la Perse, la Chine, le Japon, les Indes, le monde musulman, etc. Pour l'Europe, la chronologie habituelle est suivie : la préhistoire, les cultures classiques, le Moyen Âge, la Renaissance, le baroque, etc. L'encyclopédie ne se limite pas aux faits marquants, loin s'en faut. Des sujets annexes mais tout aussi intéressants sont illustrés.
Une attention toute particulière est également portée sur les représentations culturelles des régions pour lesquelles il n'existe peu de documents. Ainsi, aux thèmes classiques, tels que les vases grecs, les églises italiennes et la mode parisienne du 18ème siècle, s'ajoutent par exemple dans les encyclopédies visuelles Pepin Press la construction et le design des îles Salomon, les habits en Friesland, aux îles Cap-Vert et en Ouzbékistan, les sculptures esquimaudes et les ornements du Bénin.

Les illustrations et les légendes sur chaque page commencent du haut vers le bas et de gauche à droite.

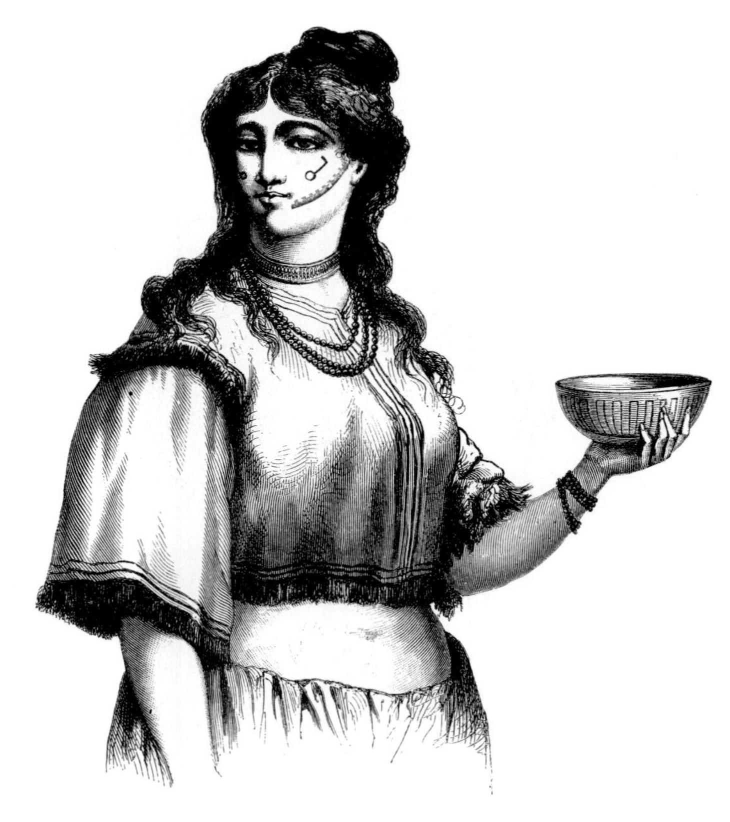

導 言

佩鵬出版社的視覺百科全書內容豐富，每一捲含有數以千計的優質線條畫，並包括了幾乎所有的國家。已譯出版或正準備出版的專題有：建築、服飾、裝飾設計及家具。今後將出版更多捲冊。每本書詳盡地收集了各主要文化，如古代埃及、馬雅、波斯、中國、日本、印度、伊斯蘭世界等等。就歐洲而言，一般的編年史為：史前、古典文化、中世紀、文藝複興、巴羅克等等。但內容並不僅僅限於重大事件，也包括不那麼重要但同樣有意義的項目。
此外還有較多篇幅涉及到其文化現象至今尚未詳細記錄闡述的地區。因此，在佩鵬出版社的視覺百科全書中，除了希臘花瓶、意大利教堂及十八世紀巴黎時裝等古典專題以外，您還會發現所羅門群島的建築和設計；荷蘭弗裡斯蘭省、卡博弗得及烏茲別克斯坦的服飾；愛斯基摩的雕刻品以及貝寧的裝飾物等等。

每一頁上插圖和說明的排列順序為從左到右，自上而下。

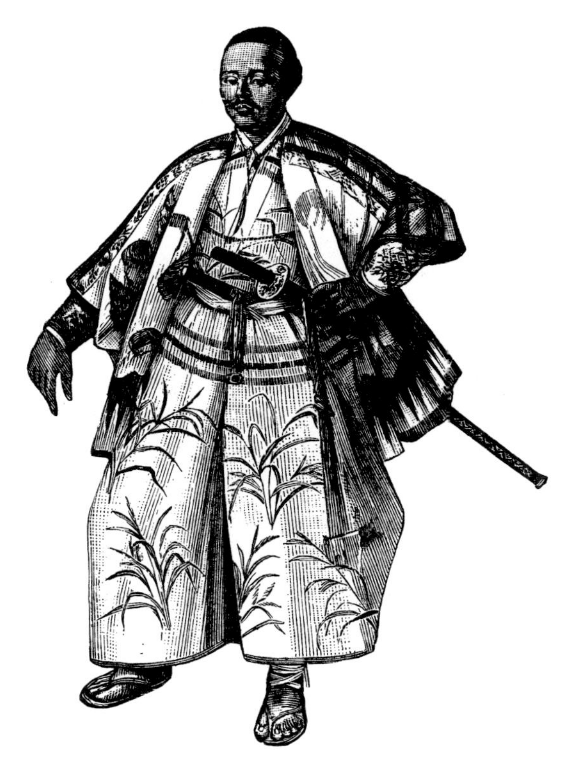

はじめに

PEPIN PRESSのビジュアル百科事典は充実したビジュアルリソースで、各巻に何千もの質の高い線画を用い、実際に世界中すべての国を取り上げています。以下のテーマはすでに出版されているか、あるいは出版予定の物です。「建築」「衣裳」「装飾デザイン」「家具」。さらに多くの巻が続きます。古代エジプト、マヤ、ペルシャ、中国、日本、インド、イスラム世界などの偉大な文化を各巻が網羅しています。ヨーロッパについては、通常の年代順に、有史前、古典文化、中世、ルネサンス、バロックなどと続きます。しかしすでに広く知られているようなできごとだけでなく、それほど有名ではないことにも焦点を当て、関心を引く項目は同等に図解しています。詳細な記録の少ない地域についての文化的表現にも、細心の注意を払っています。そのため、ギリシャの壷、イタリアの教会、18世紀のパリのファッションといった古典的なテーマに加え、この百科事典では、例えばソロモン諸島の建築やデザイン、フリースラントの衣裳、ヴェルデ岬やウズベキスタン、エスキモーの彫刻、ベニンの装飾なども収めています。

ページごとのイラストや注釈は左から右、上から下の順に並べられています。

Antiquity
Antike
Età antica
Antiquité
Antigüedad Clásica
古代
古 代

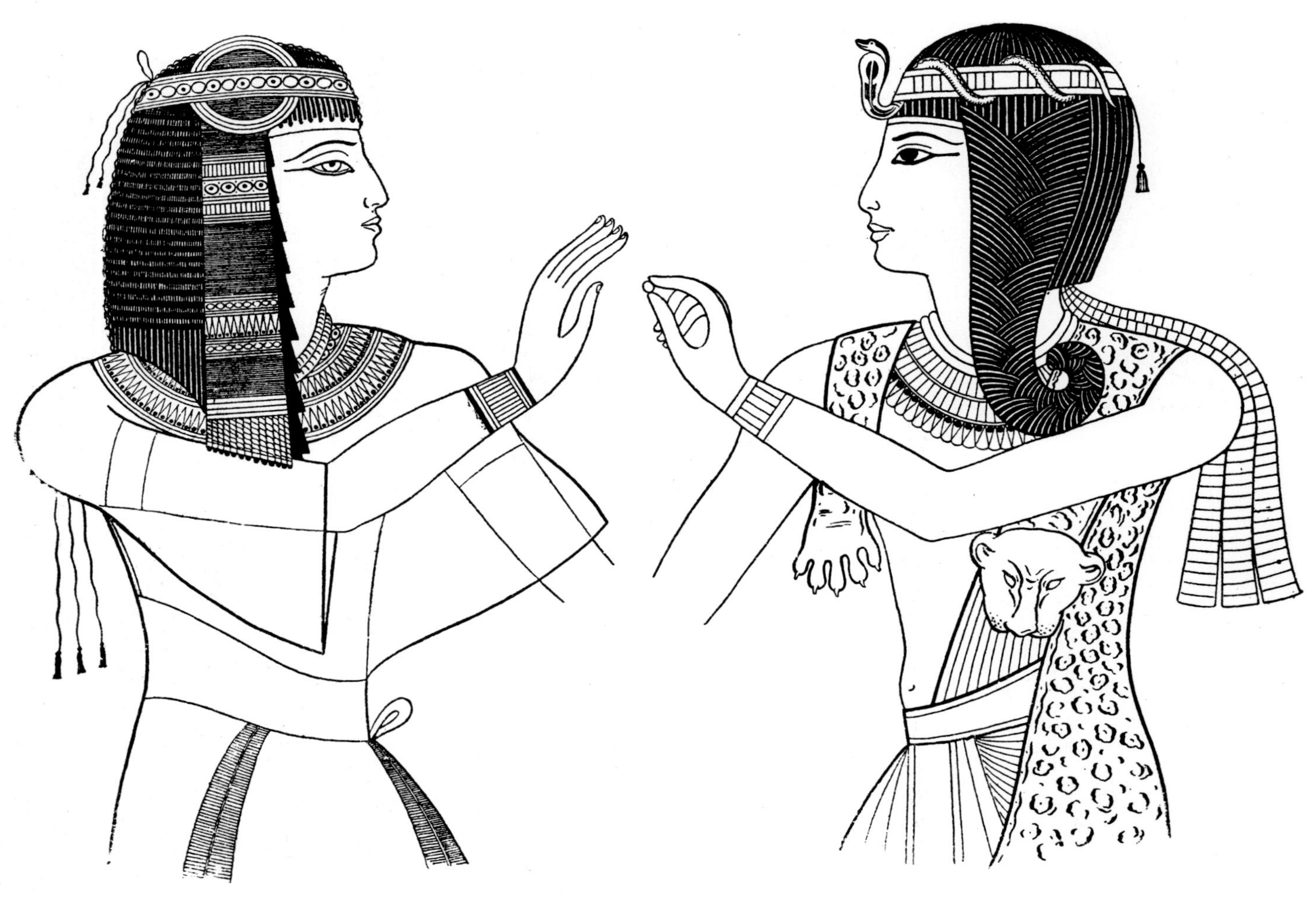

Ramses II (right) with one of his sons

Ramses II. (rechts) mit einem seiner Söhne

Ramsete II (destra) con uno dei suoi figli

Ramsès II (à droite) avec un de ses fils

Ramsés II (derecha) con uno de sus hijos

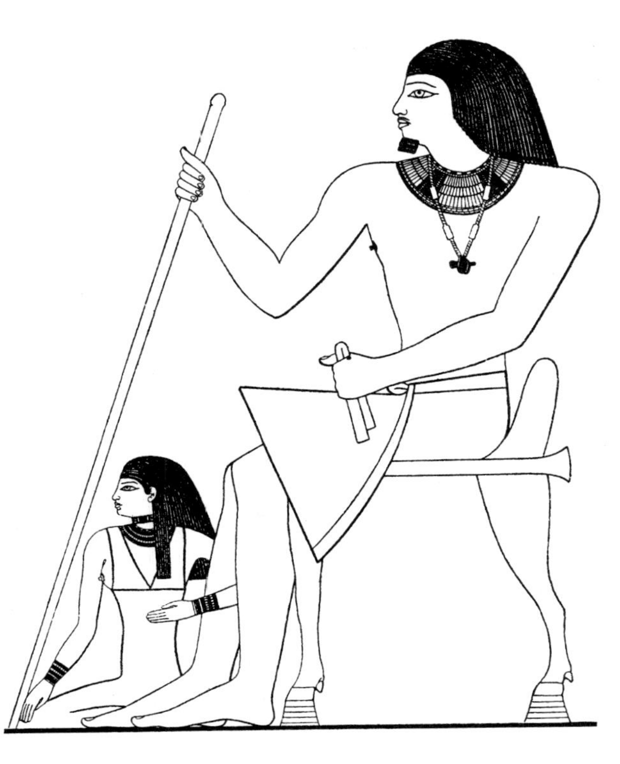

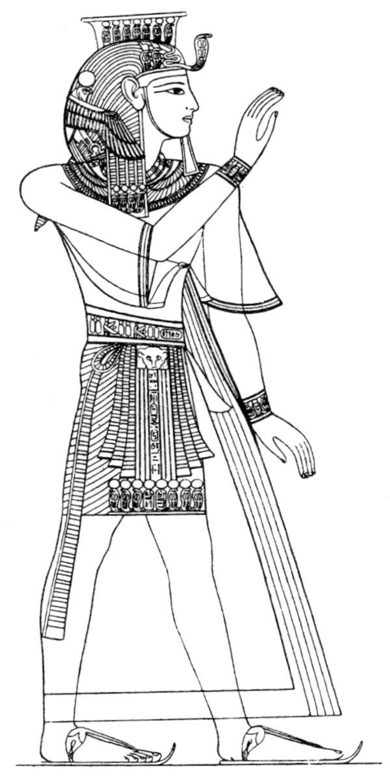

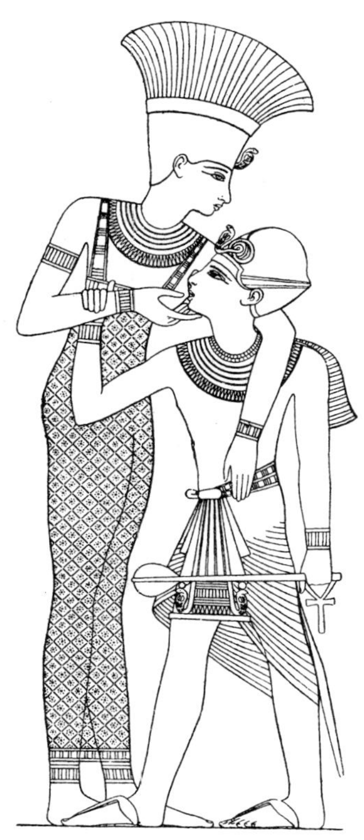

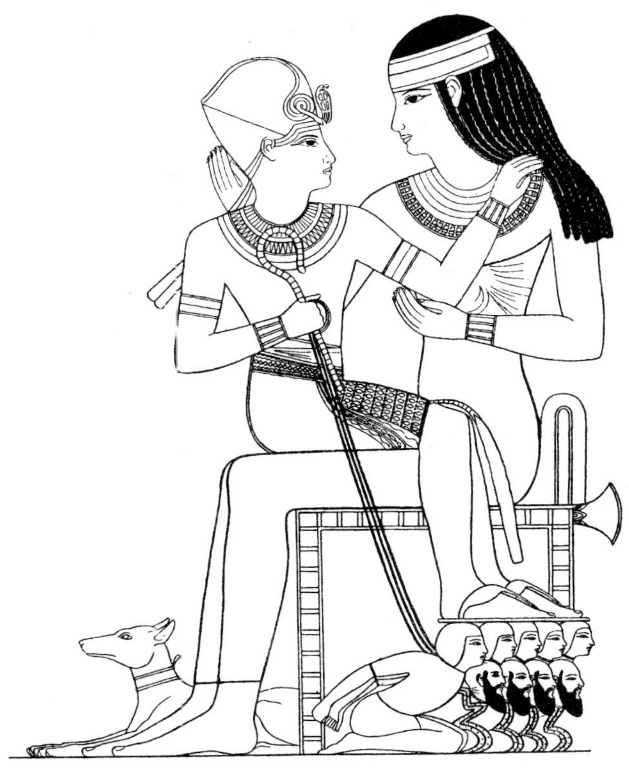

Various costumes from Dynastian Egypt

Verschiedene Gewänder aus der Zeit der Dynastien, Ägypten

Vari costumi dell'Egitto dinastico

Costumes divers de la dynastie égyptienne

Diversos trajes del Egipto dinástico

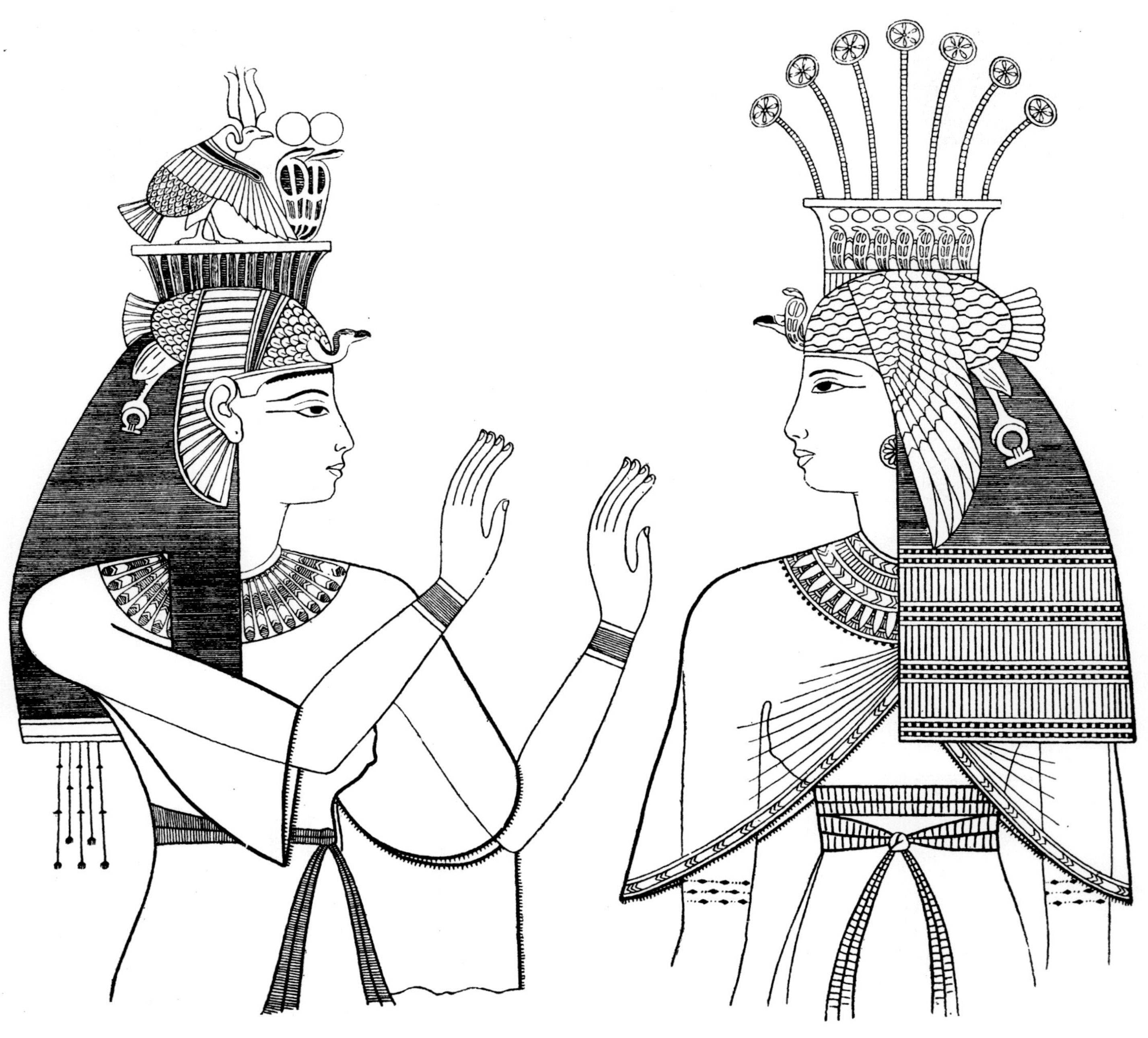

Egyptian queens Ägyptische Königinnen Regine egiziane Reines égyptiennes Reinas egipcias

Ancient Egypt

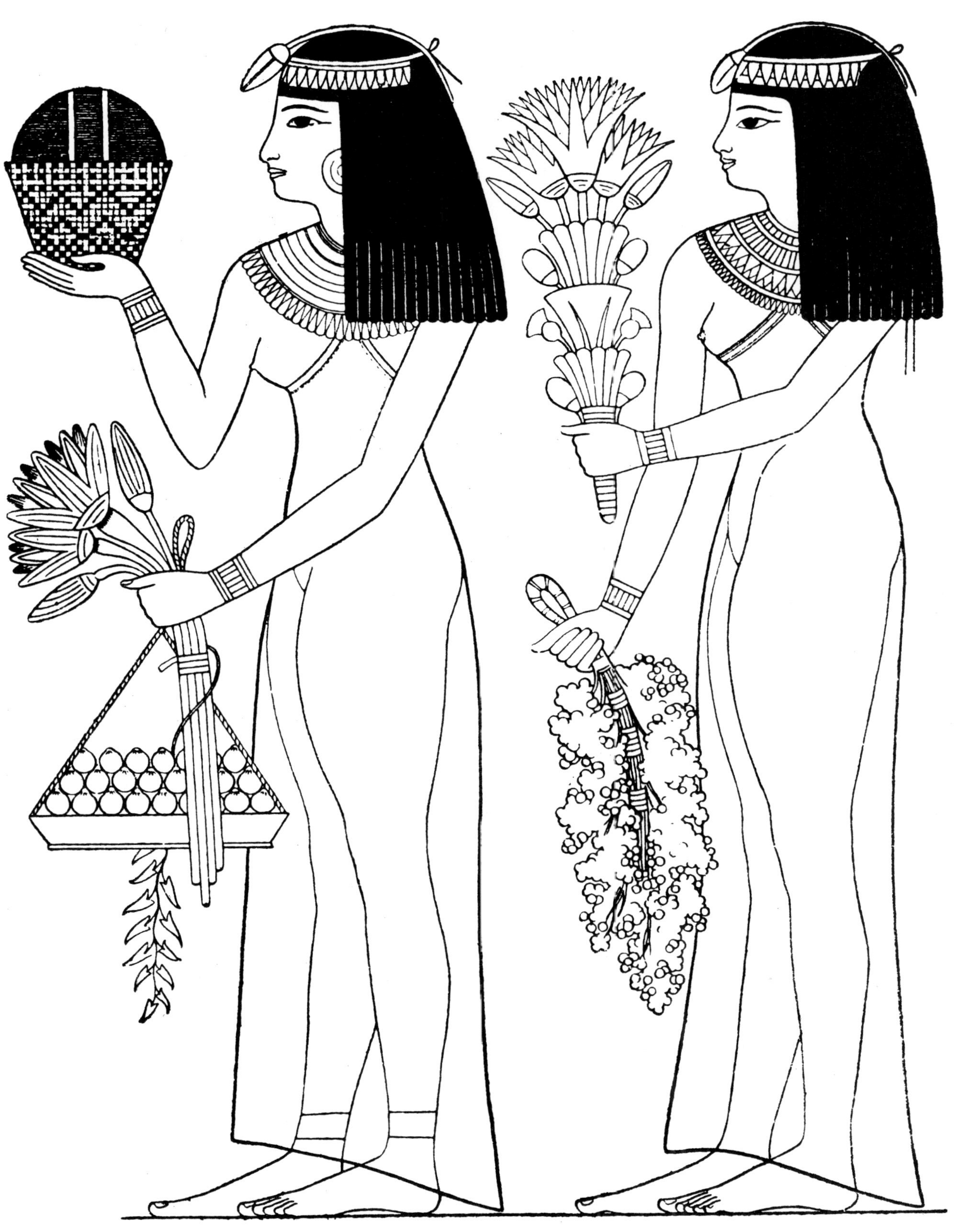

Women carrying offerings for the gods

Frauen mit Opfergaben für die Götter

Donne che portano offerte per gli dei

Femmes portant des offrandes pour les Dieux

Mujeres con ofrendas para los dioses

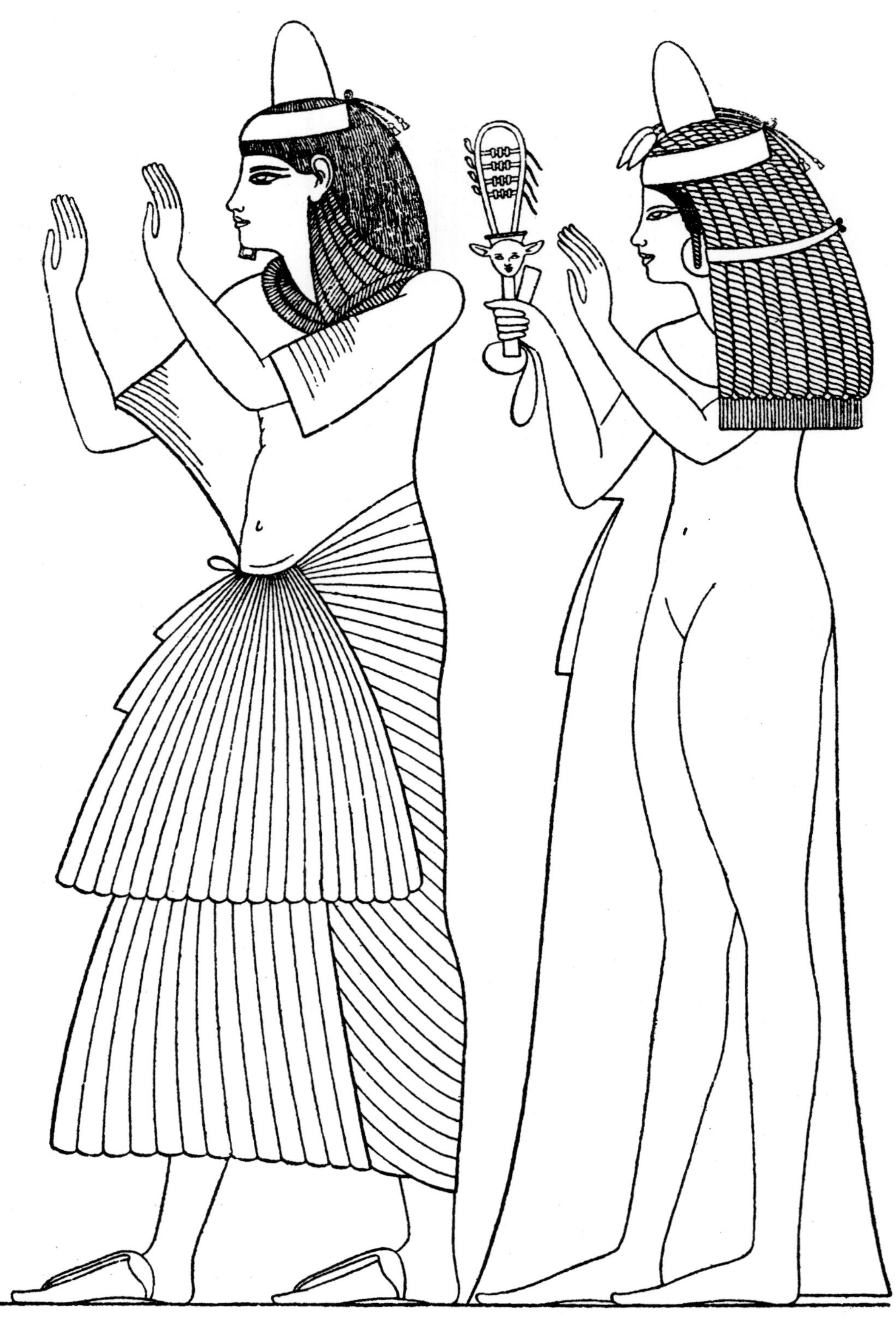

Man and woman, Thebes dynasty

Mann und Frau, Zeit der Dynastien, Theben

Uomo e donna, dinastia di Tebe d'Egitto

Homme et femme, dynastie Thèbes

Hombre y mujer, dinastía de Tebas

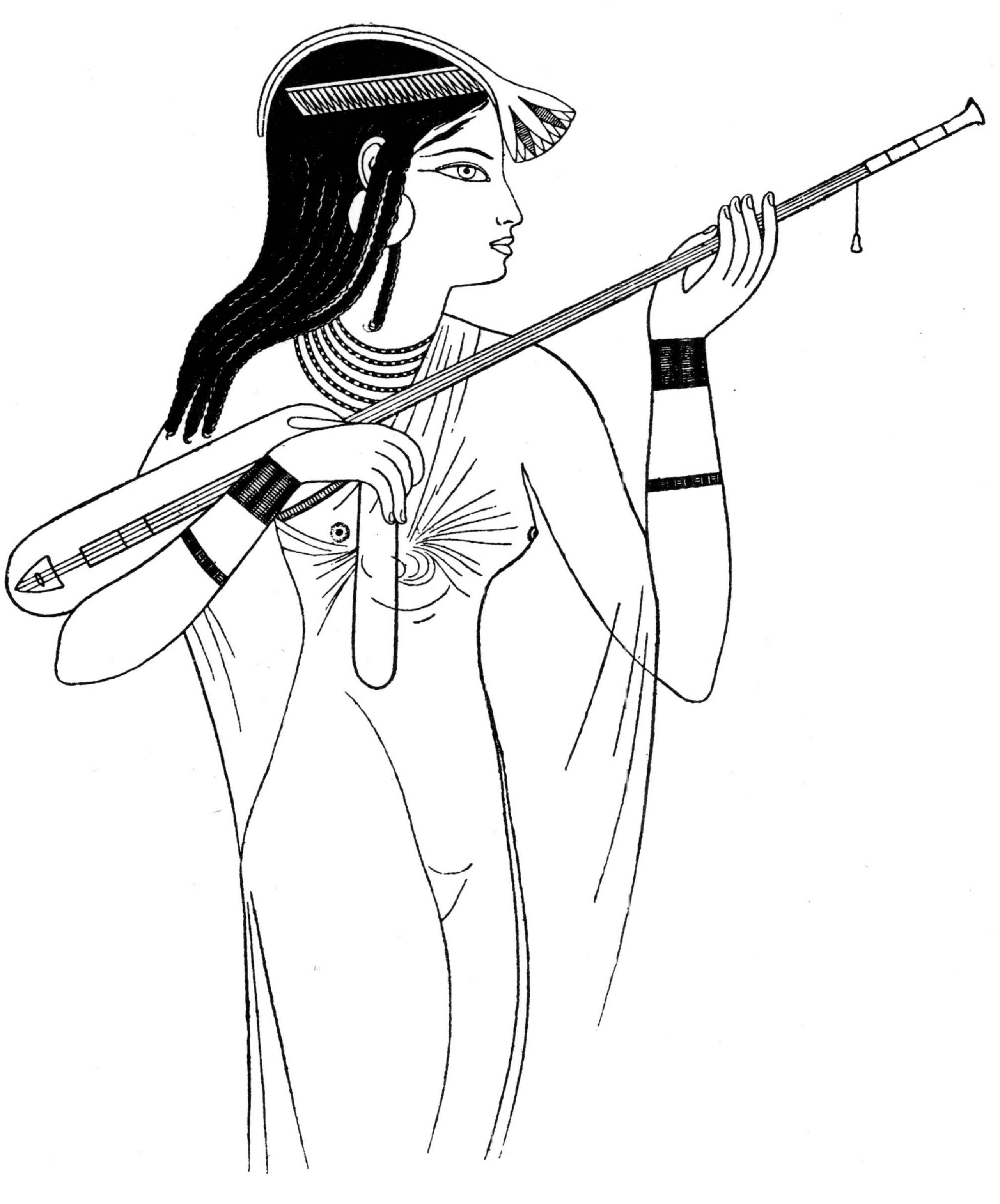

Female musician Musizierende Frau Musicista donna Musicienne Música

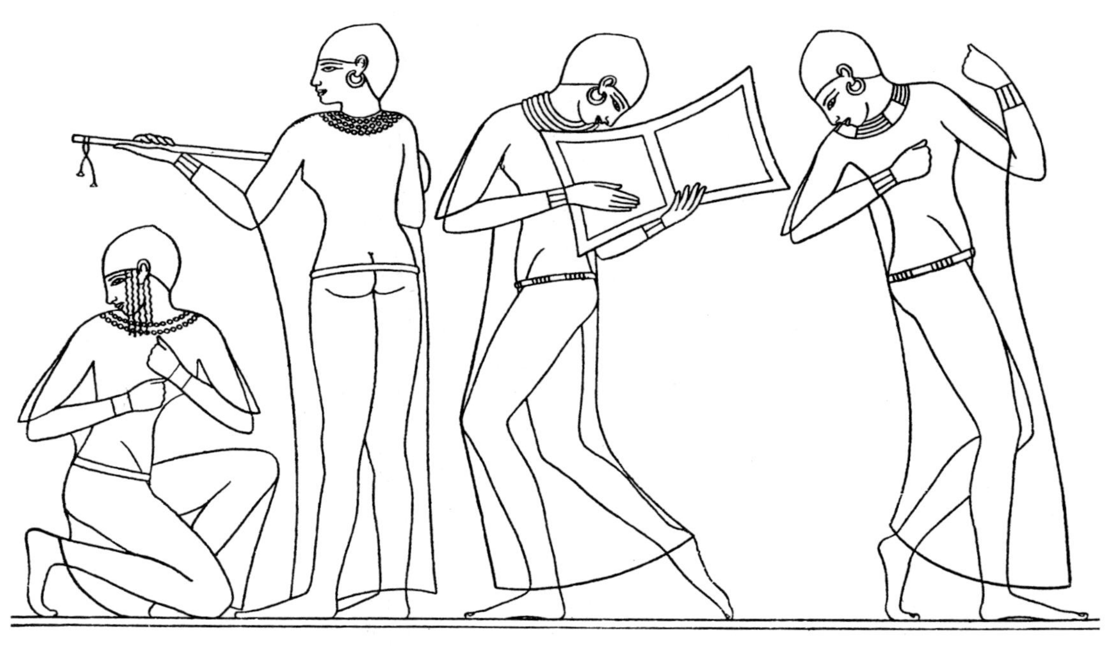

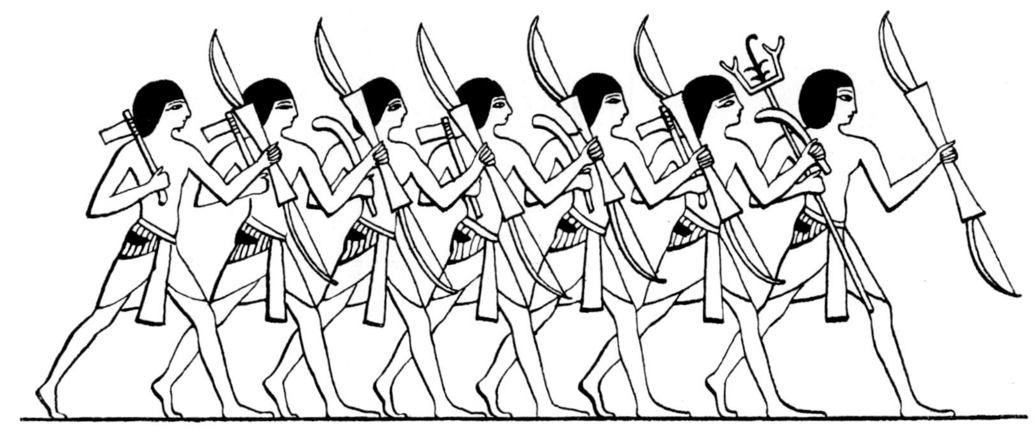

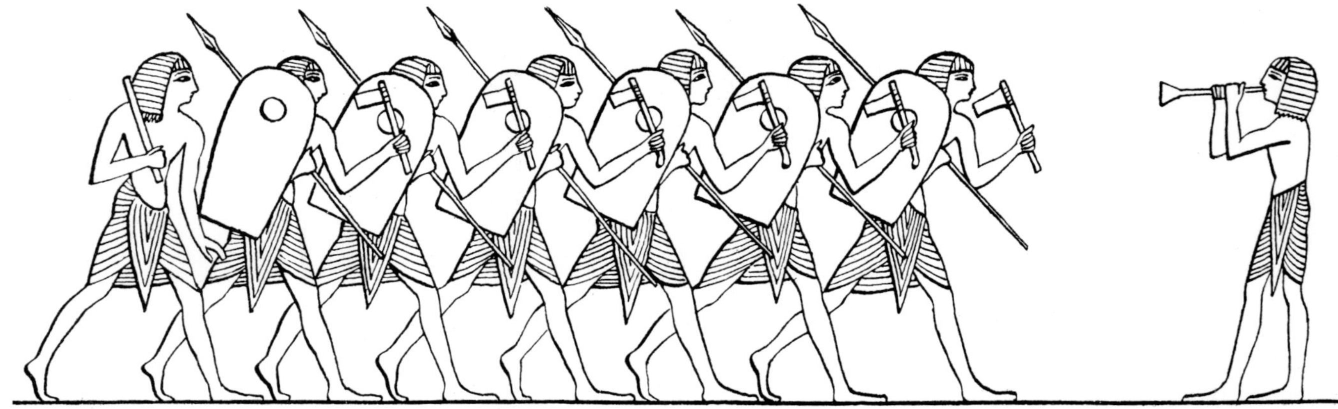

a	Musicians and dancers, Thebes dynasty	Musiker und Tänzer, Zeit der Dynastien, Theben	Musicisti e ballerini, dinastia di Tebe d'Egitto	Musiciens et danseurs de la dynastie Thèbes	Músicos y bailarines, dinastía de Tebas
b-c	Soldiers, Thebes dynasty	Soldaten, Zeit der Dynastien, Theben	Soldati, dinastia di Tebe d'Egitto	Soldats de la dynastie Thèbes	Soldados, dinastía de Tebas

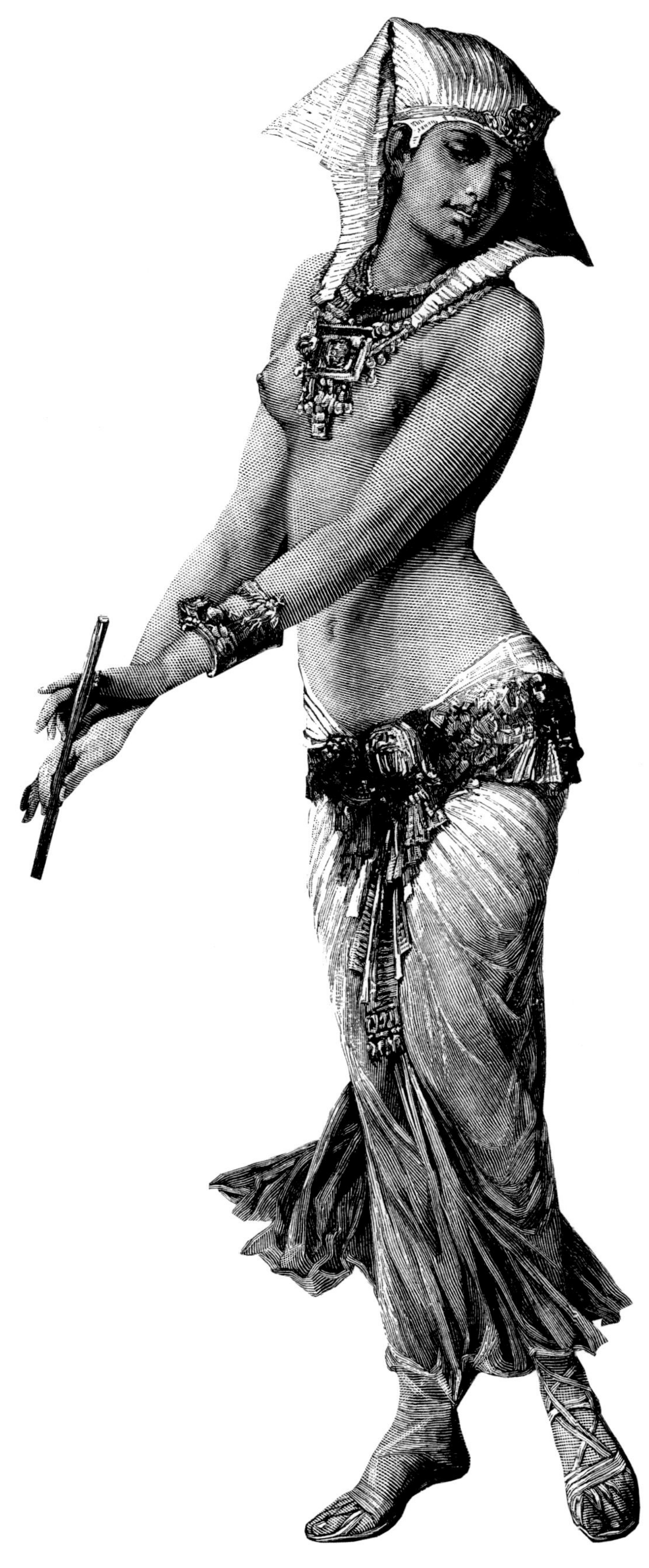

Dancing girl | Tanzendes Mädchen | Ragazza che balla | Danseuse | Bailarina

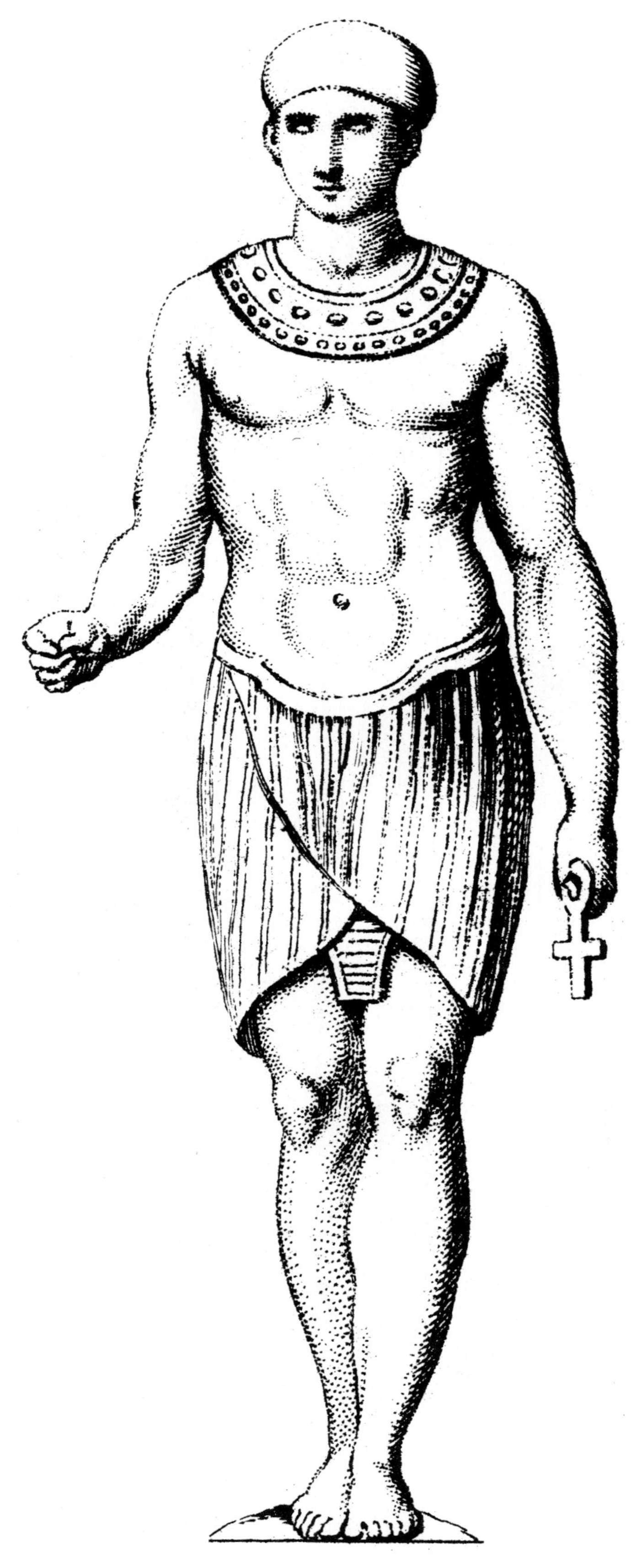

Young Egyptian Junger Ägypter Giovane egizio Jeune égyptien Joven egipcio

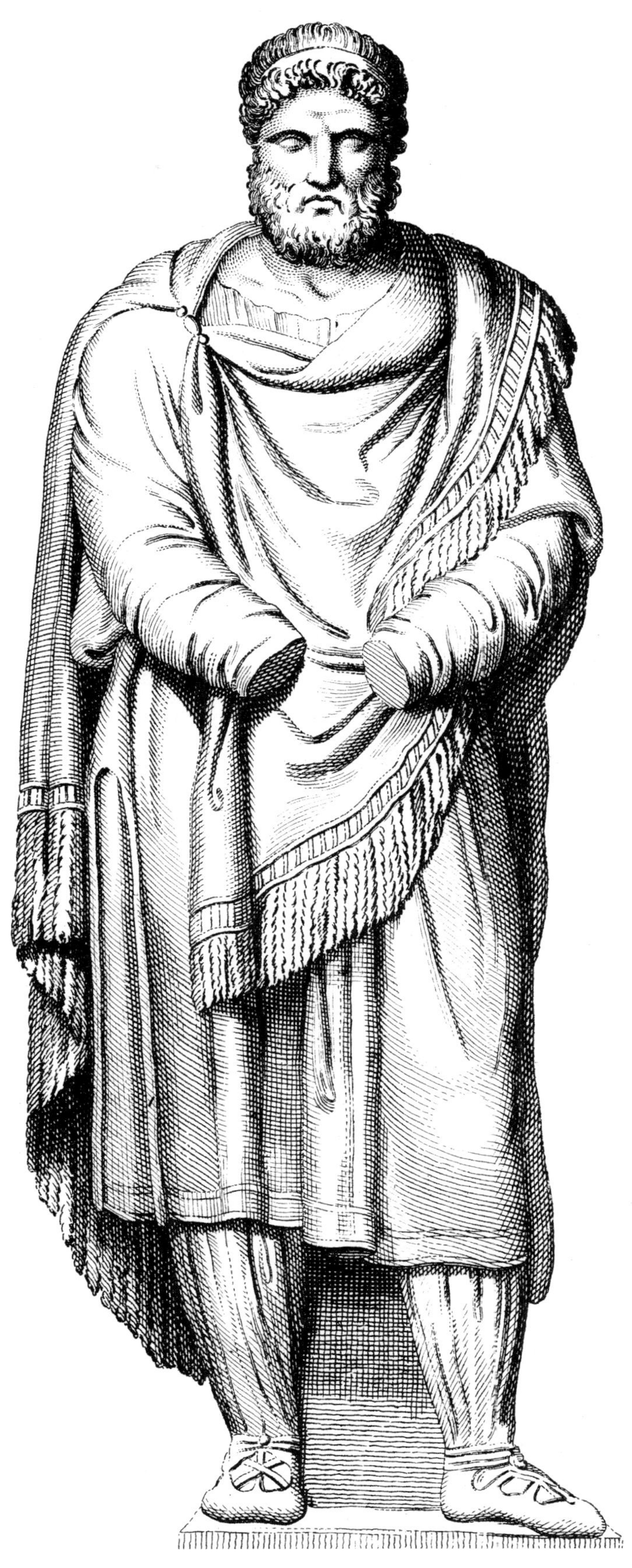

Assyrian men's dress

Assyrisches Männergewand

Abito da uomo assiro

Vêtement masculin assyrien

Traje asirio de hombre

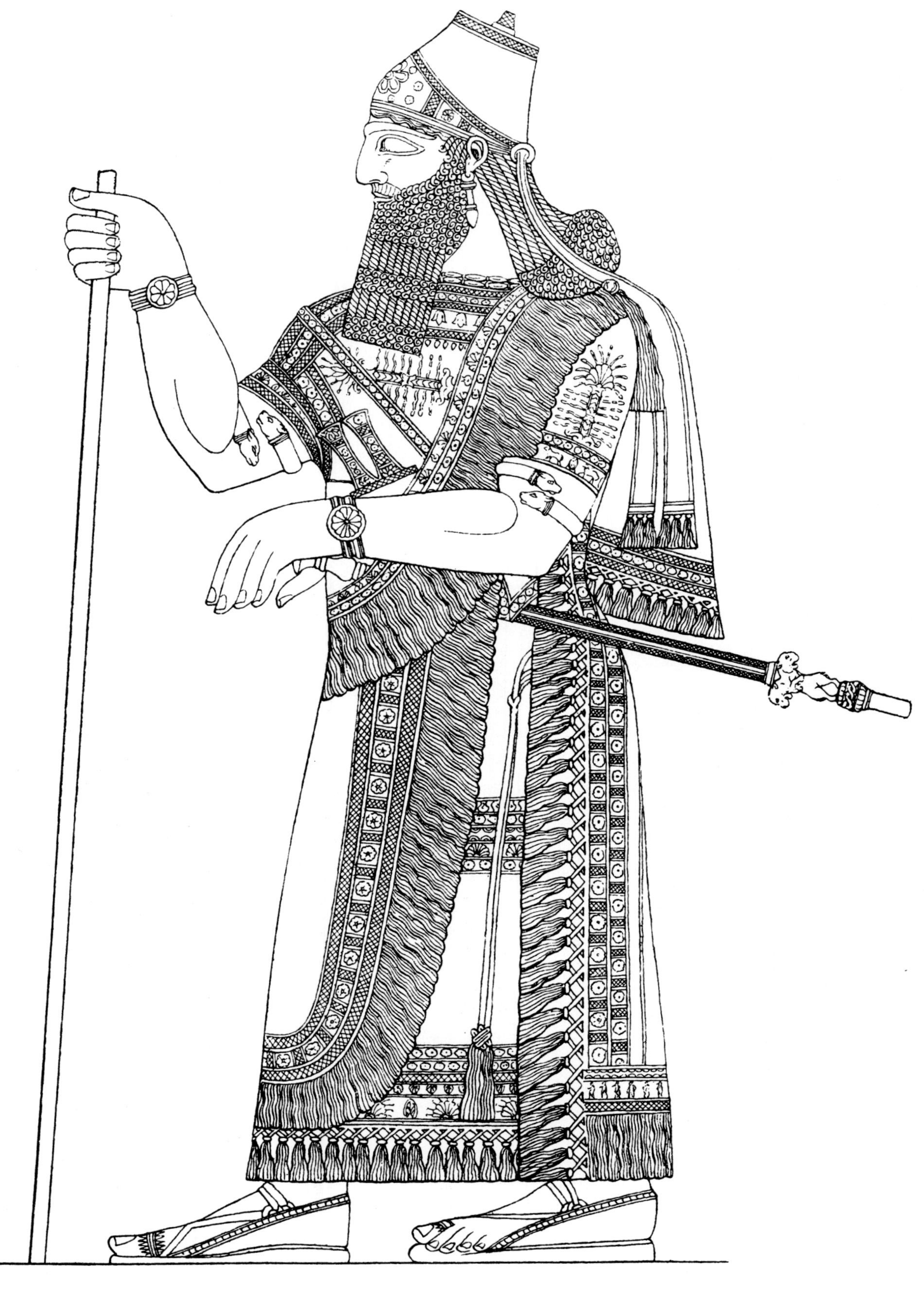

Assyrian king	Assyrischer König	Re assiro	Roi assyrien	Rey asirio

Assyria

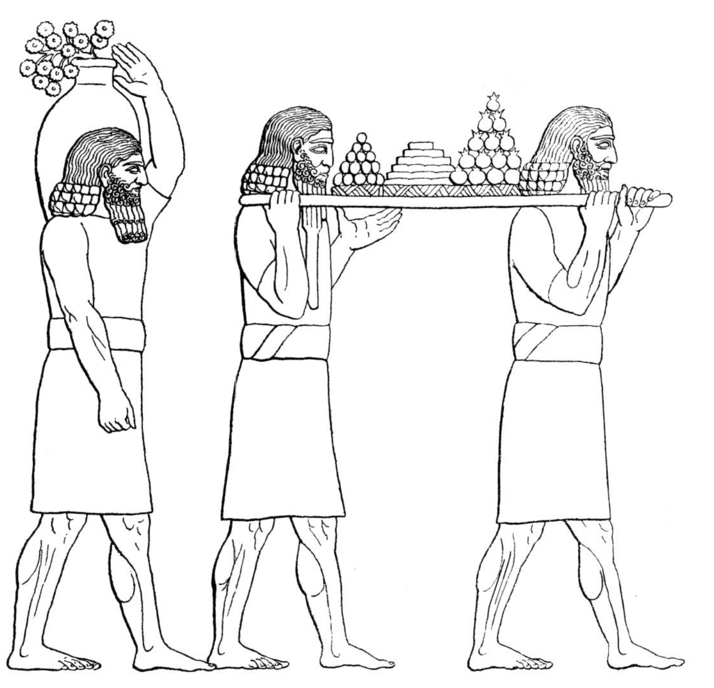

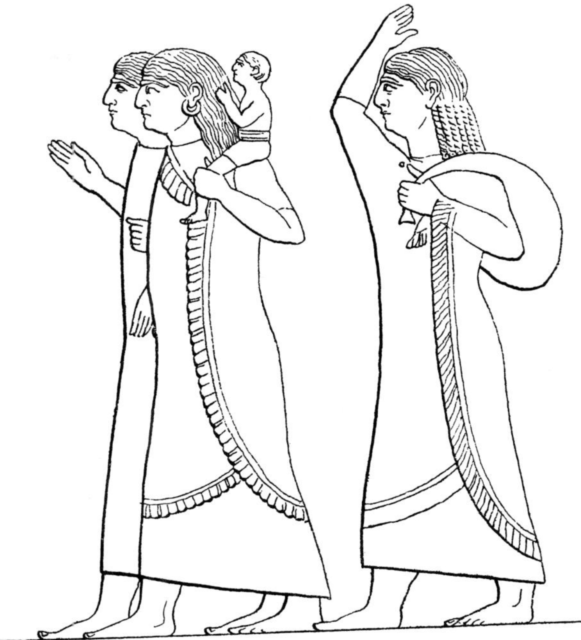

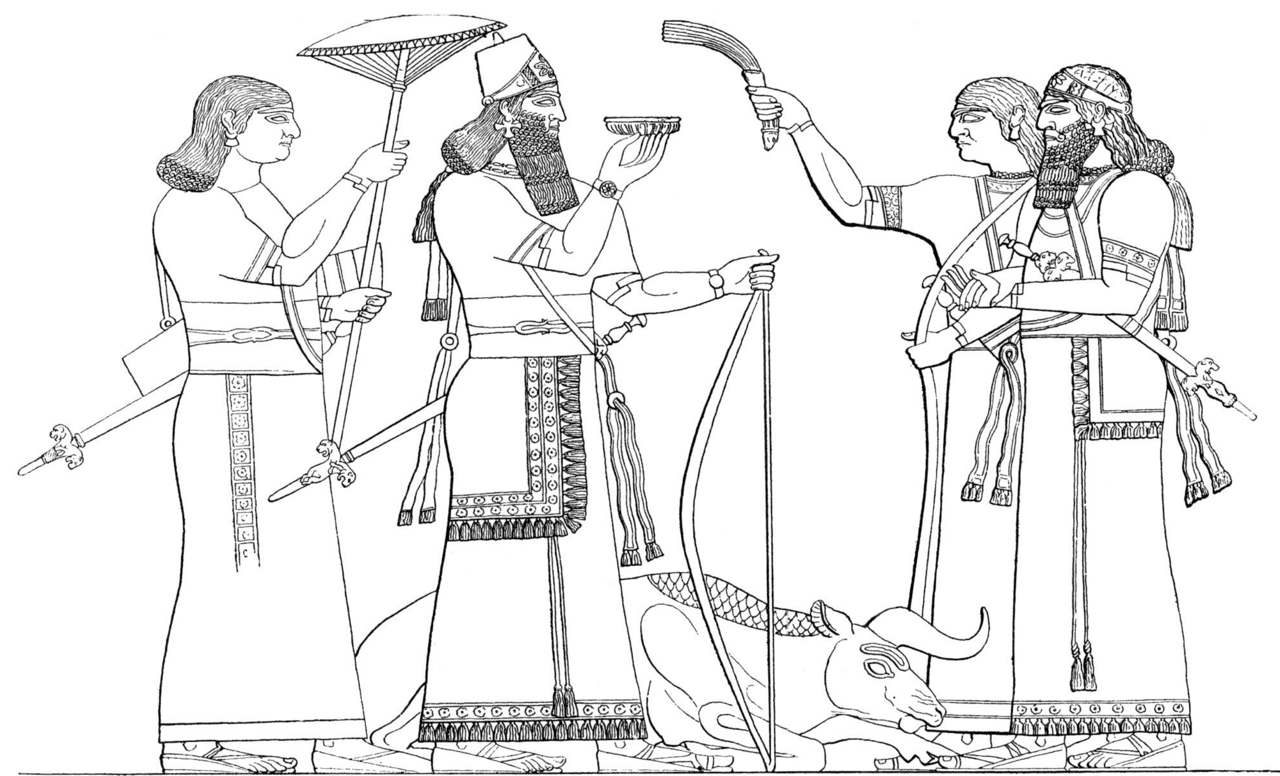

a	Assyrian men	Assyrischer Mann	Uomini assiri	Assyriens	Hombres asirios
b	Assyrian women	Assyrische Frau	Donne assire	Assyriennes	Mujeres asirias
c	Assyrian king with servants	Assyrischer König mit Dienern	Re assiro con domestici	Roi assyrien et ses serviteurs	Rey asirio con sirvientes

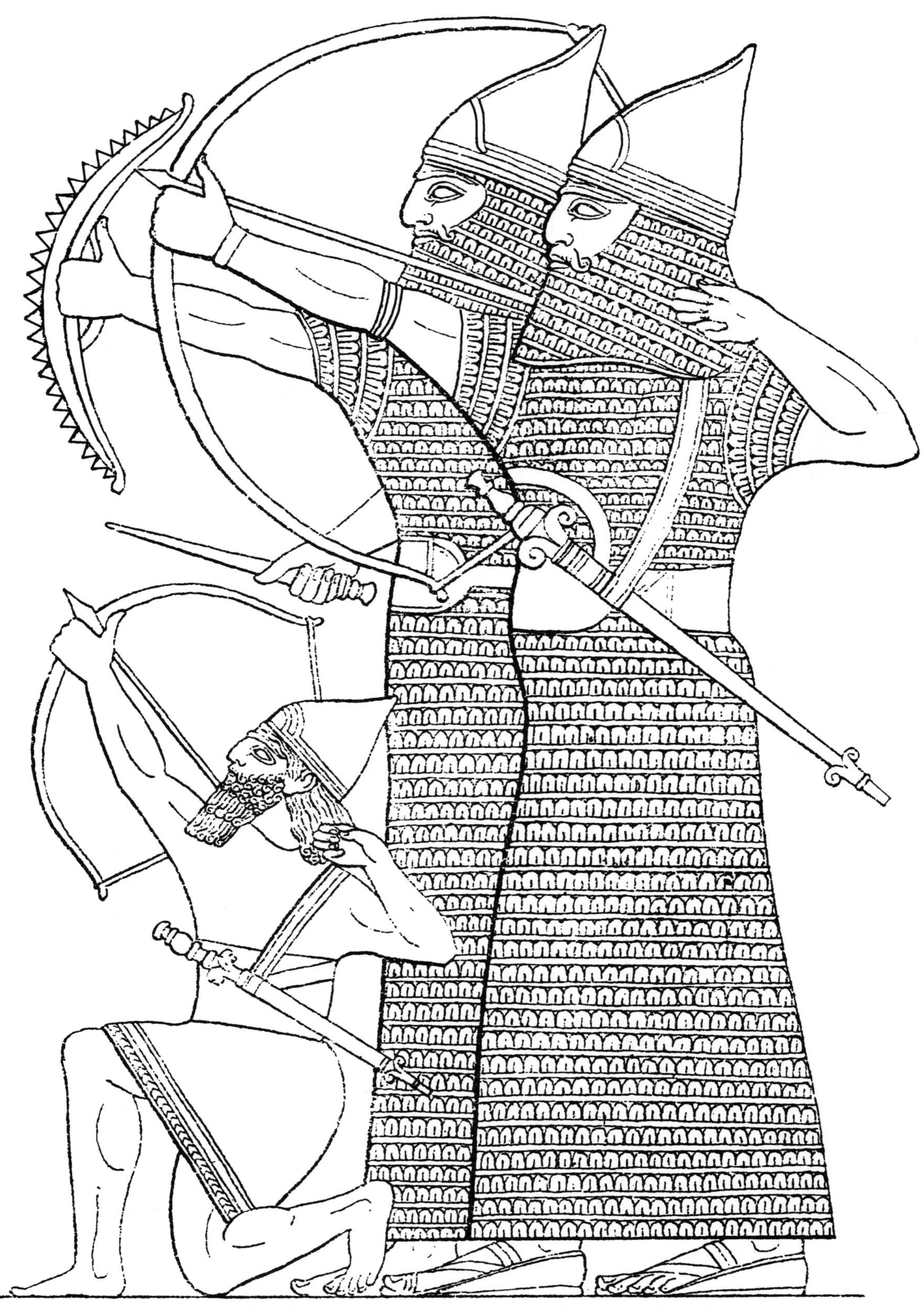

Assyrian soldiers in full armour

Assyrische Soldaten in voller Rüstung

Soldati assiri in armatura completa

Soldats assyriens armés de pied en cap

Soldados asirios con armaduras

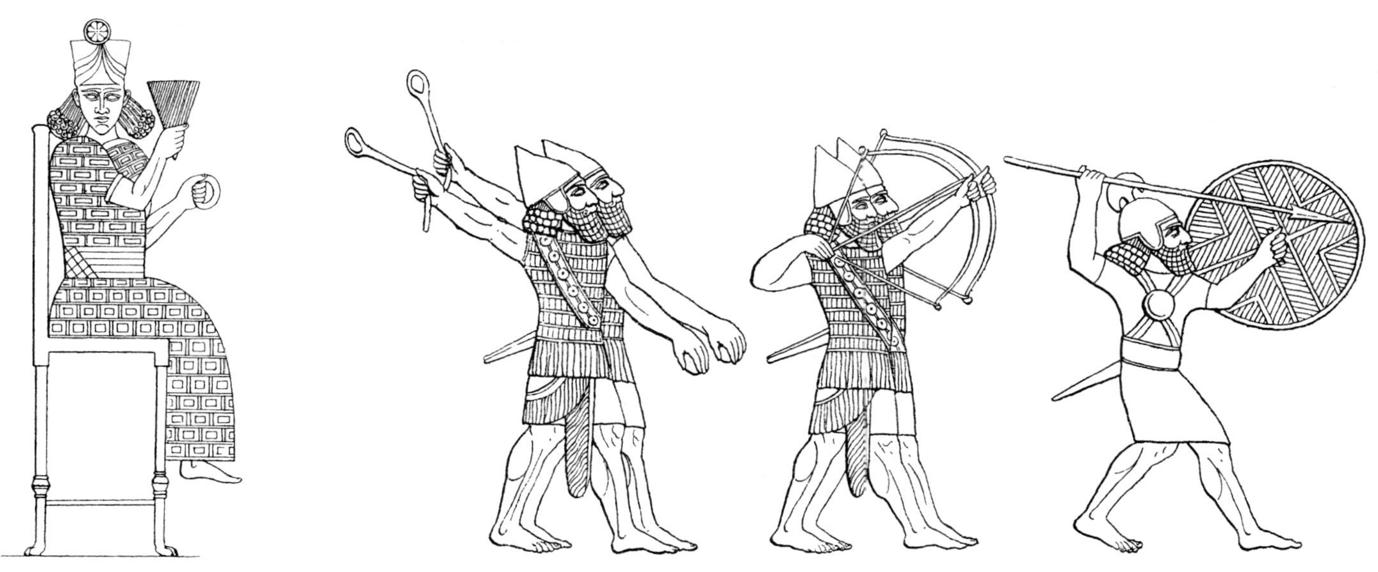

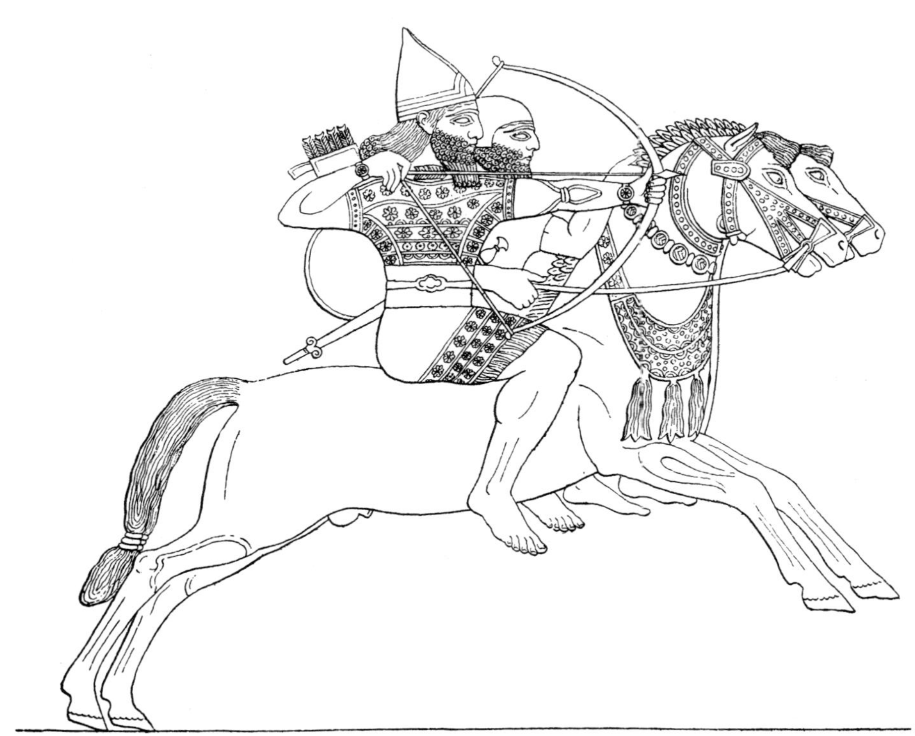

a	Assyrian Godess	Assyrische Göttin	Dea assira	Déesse asyrienne	Diosa asiria
b	Soldiers	Soldaten	Soldati	Soldats	Soldados
c	Assyrian horsemen	Assyrische Reiter	Cavallerizzi assiri	Cavaliers assyriens	Jinetes asirios

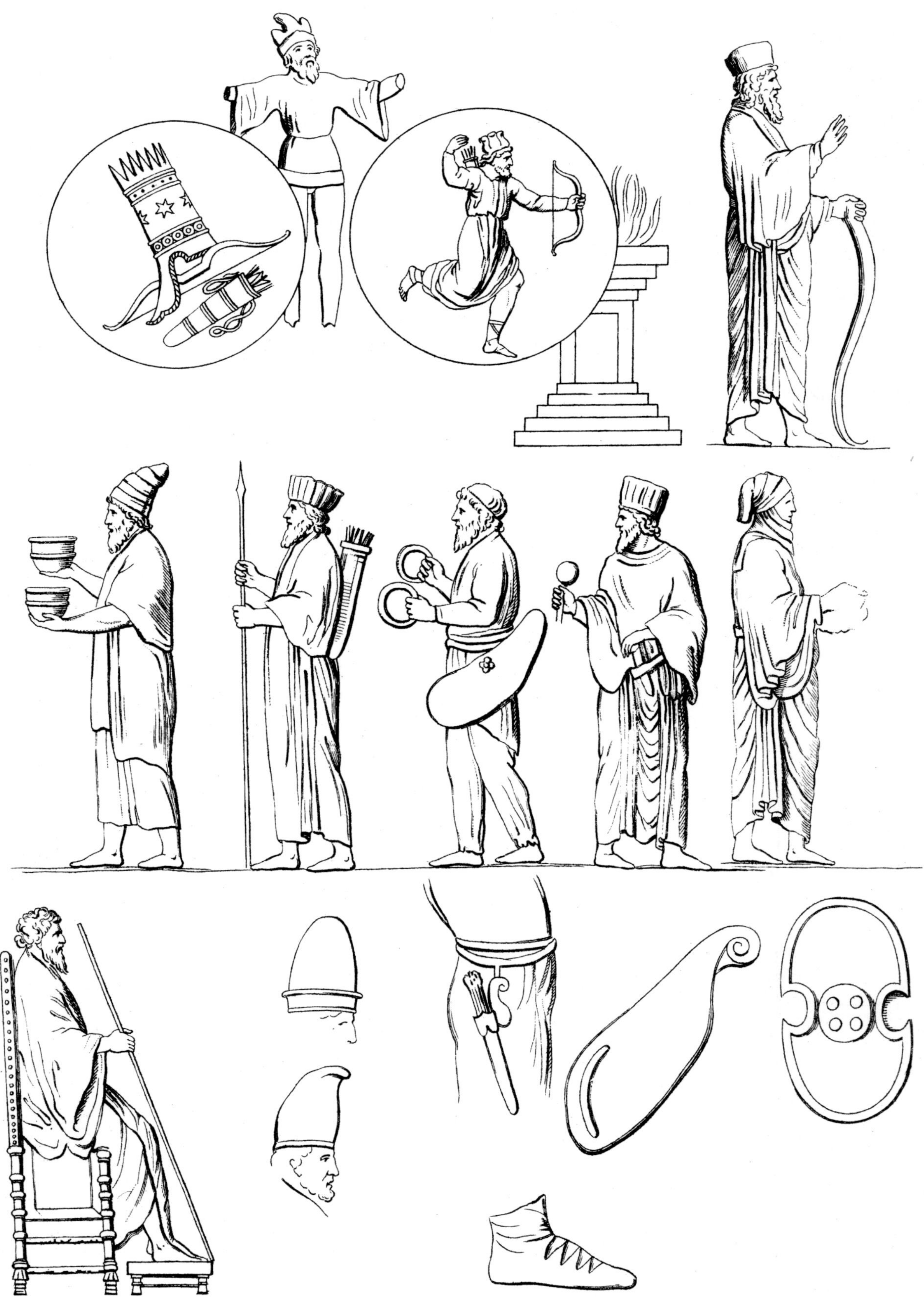

Mede dress (Ancient Media is in present-day north-west Iran)

Medische Gewänder (das Altmedische Reich lag im heutigen Nordwestiran)

Abito medo (l'antica Media è l'attuale Iran nord-occidentale)

Tenues Mède (l'ancien empire Mède correspond à présent au nord-ouest de l'Iran)

Trajes medos (la antigua Media corresponde al noroeste del actual Irán)

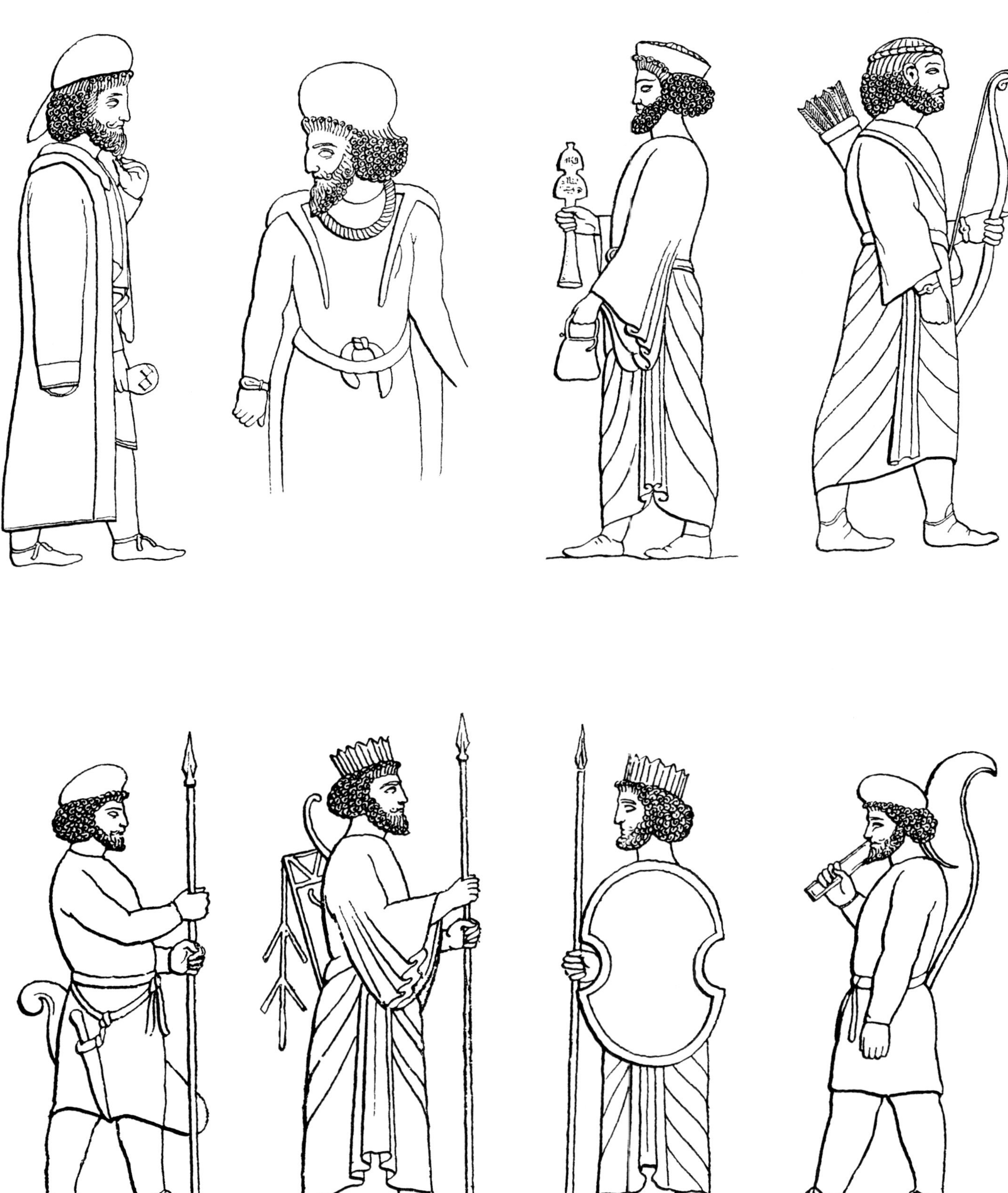

Medes and Persian soldiers

Medische und persische Soldaten

Soldati medi e persiani

Soldats Mèdes et Persans

Soldados medos y persas

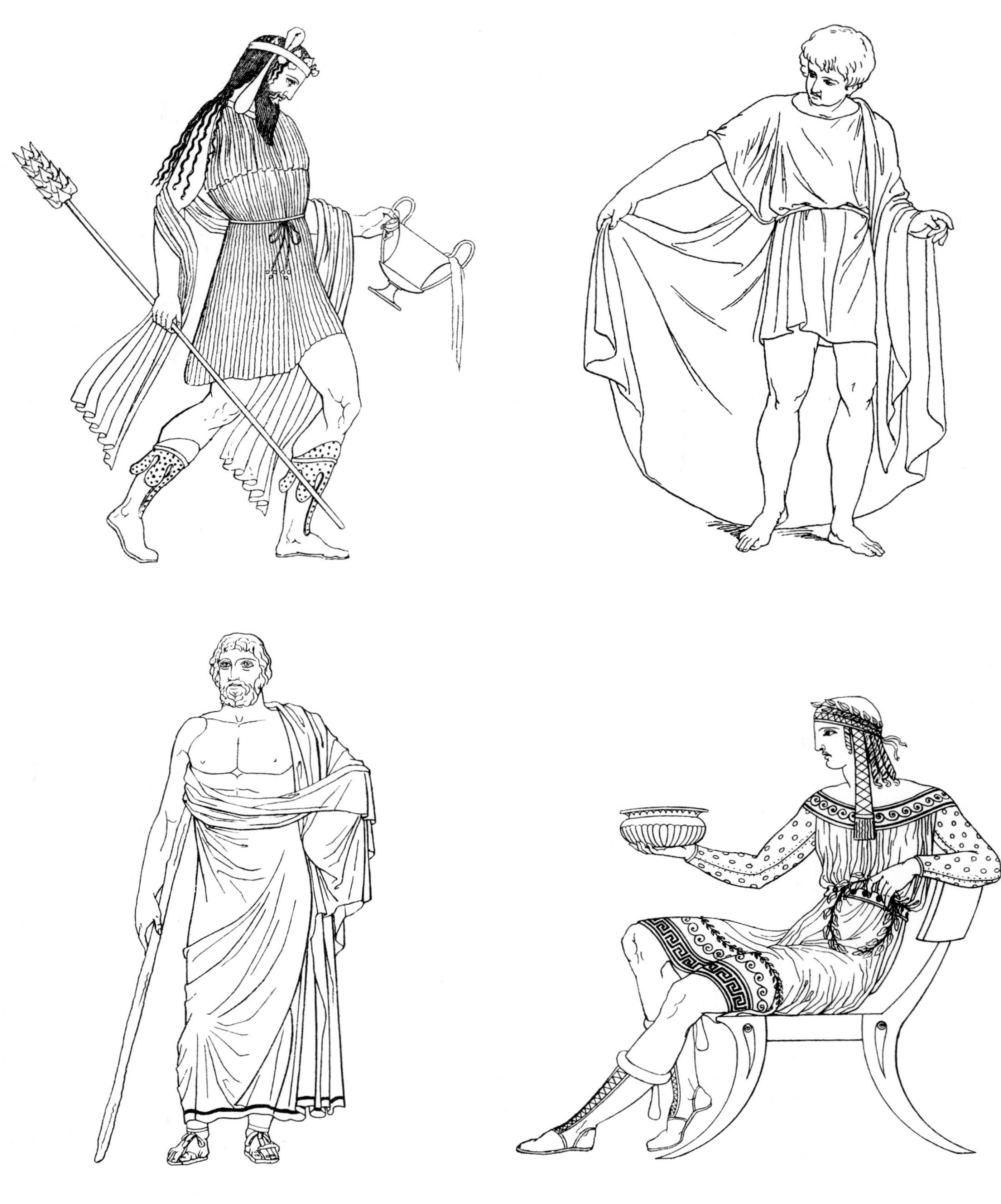

Ancient Greek male dress

Altgriechisches Männergewand

Abito maschile dell'antica Grecia

Vêtement masculin de la Grèce Ancienne

Trajes de hombre de la antigua Grecia

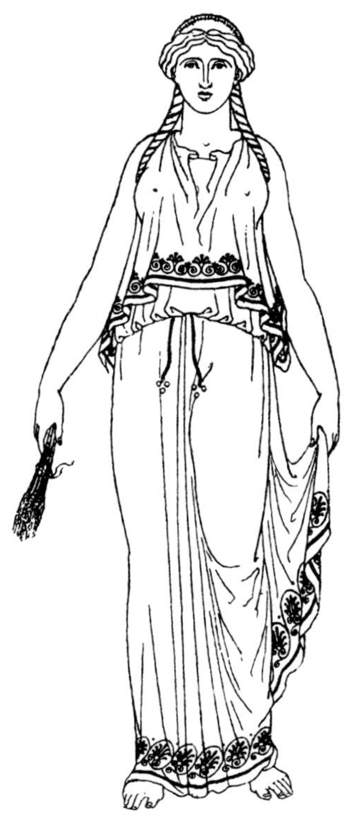
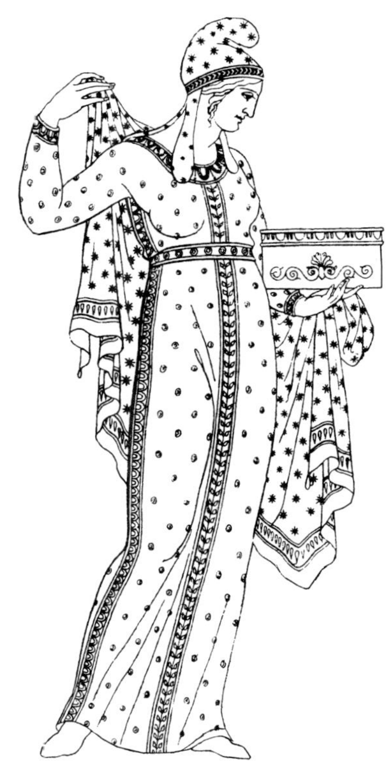
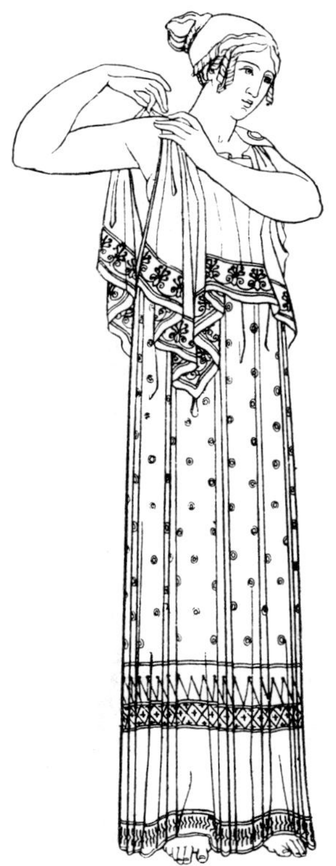
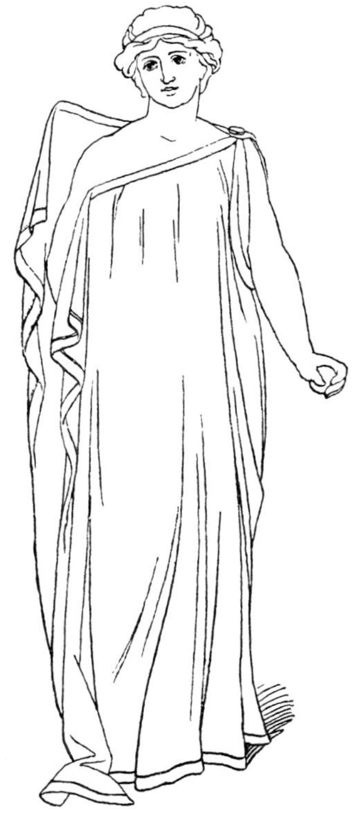

Ancient Greek female dress

Altgriechisches Frauengewand

Abito femminile dell'antica Grecia

Vêtement féminin de la Grèce Ancienne

Trajes de mujer de la antigua Grecia

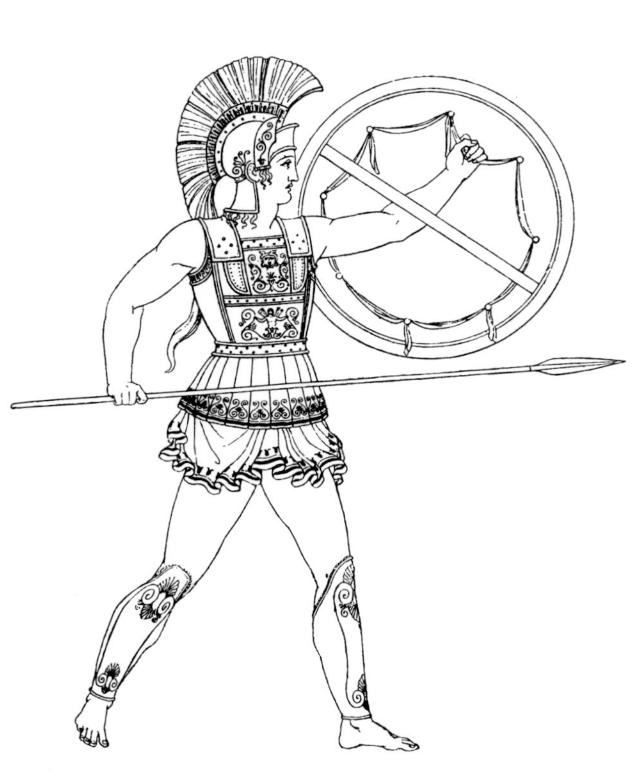

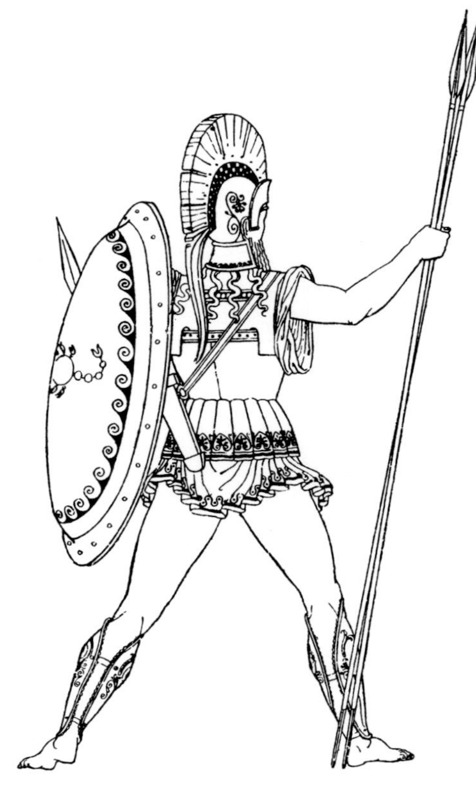

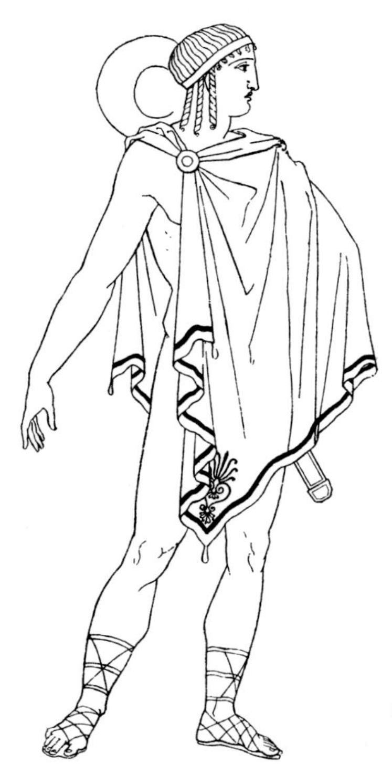

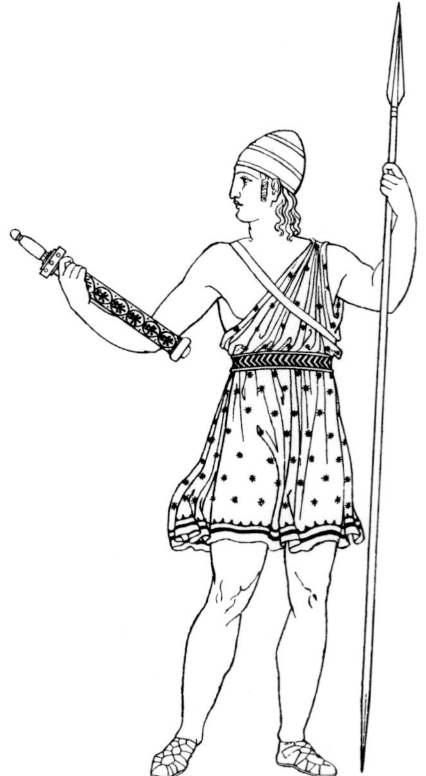

Greek soldiers

Griechische Soldaten

Soldati greci

Soldats grecs

Soldados griegos

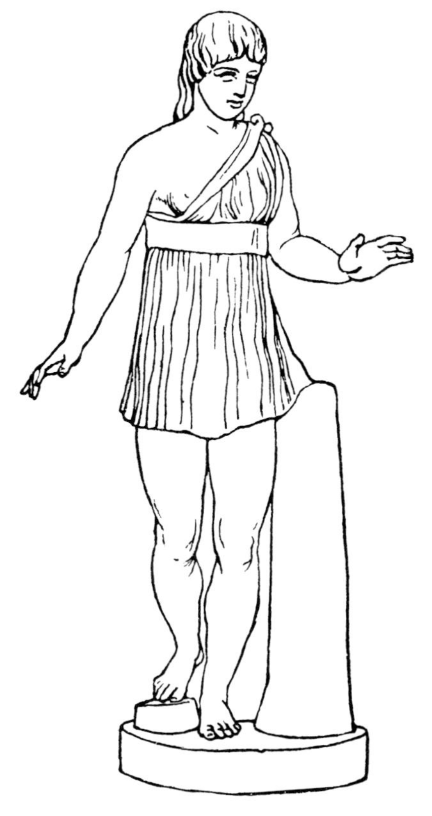

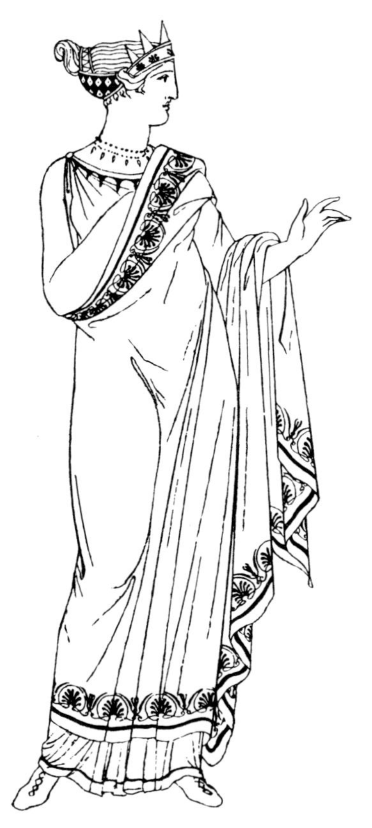

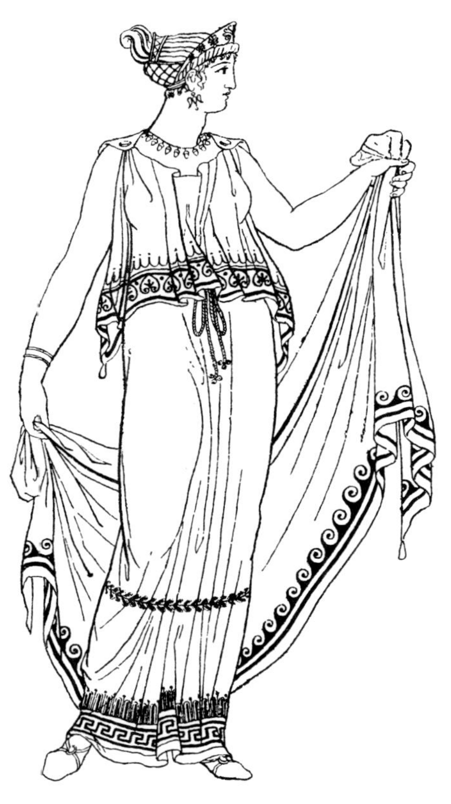

a	Girl from Sparta	Mädchen aus Sparta	Ragazza di Sparta	Jeune fille de Sparte	Muchacha de Esparta
b-c	Greek ladies	Griechische Damen	Donne greche	Femmes grecques	Damas griegas

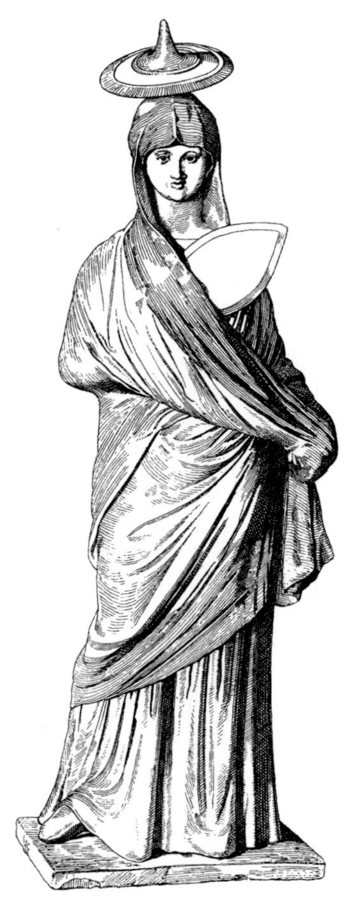

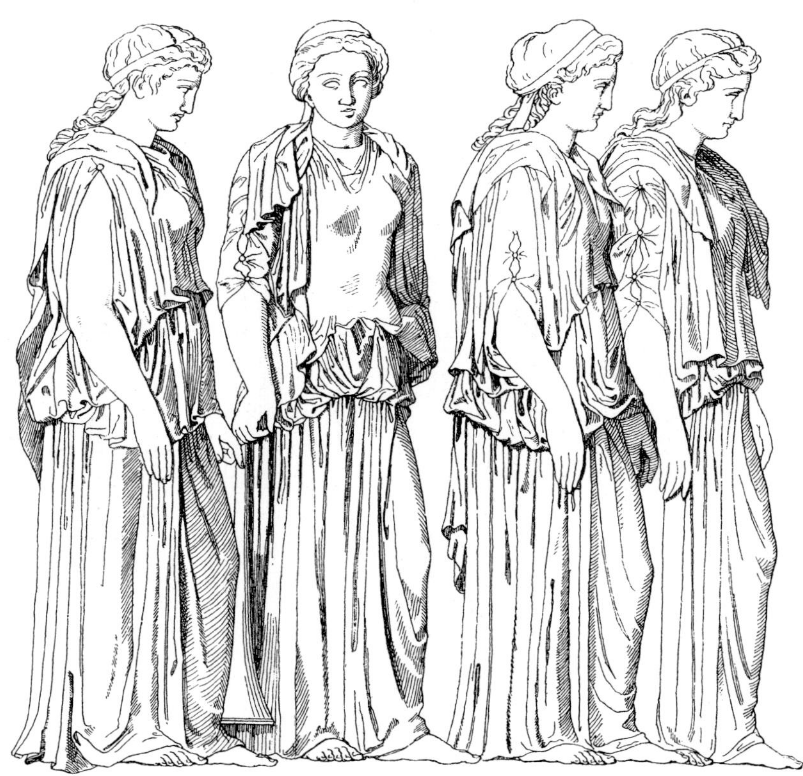

a	Greek lady	Griechische Dame	Donna greca	Femme grecque	Dama griega
b	Women from Athens in party dress	Frauen aus Athen in Festkleidung	Donne di Atene in abito da gala	Athéniennes en costume de fête	Mujeres de Atenas con vestidos de gala

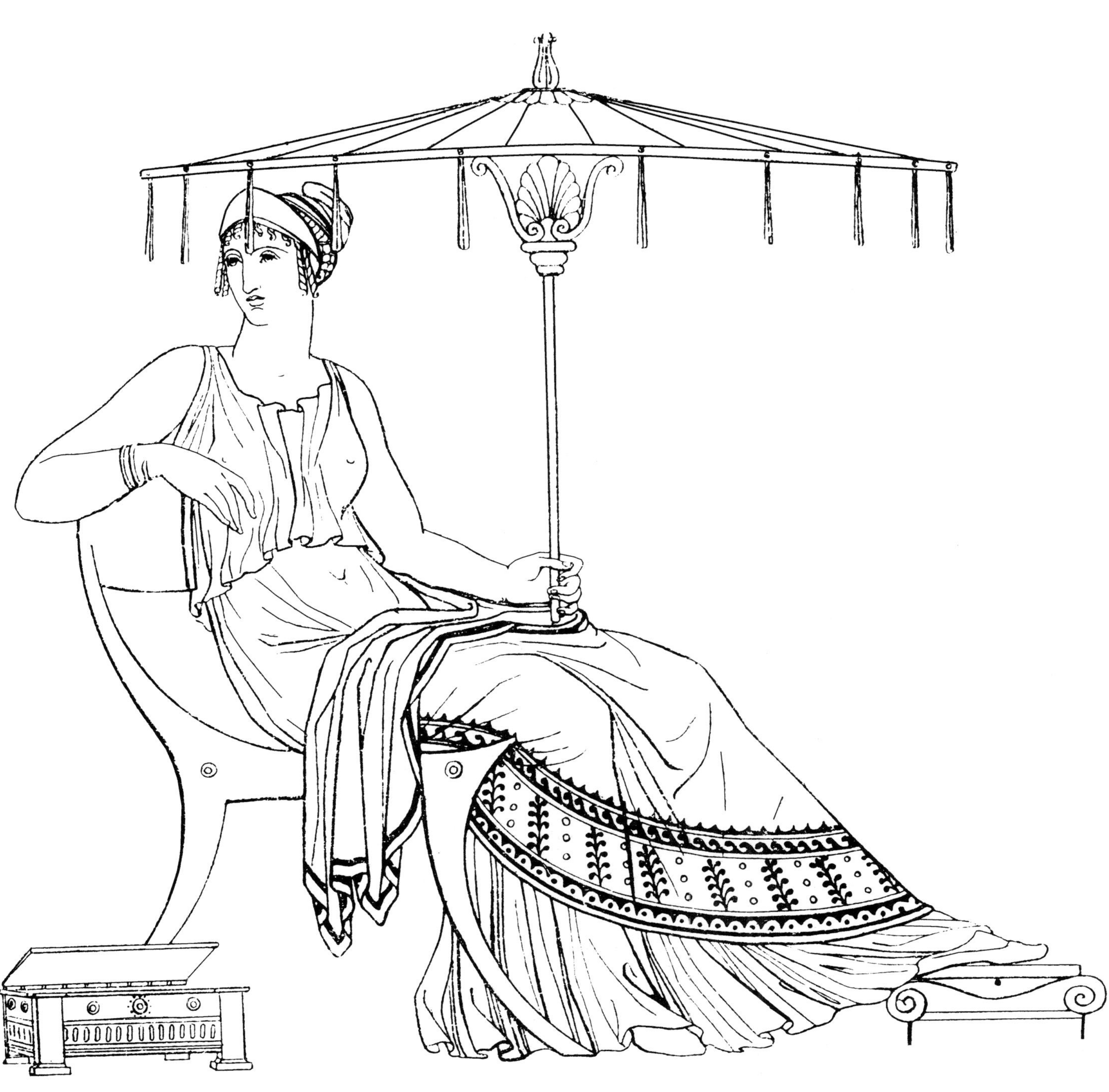

Ancient Greek female costume

Algriechisches Frauengewand

Costume femminile dell'antica Grecia

Costume féminin de la Grèce Ancienne

Traje de mujer de la antigua Grecia

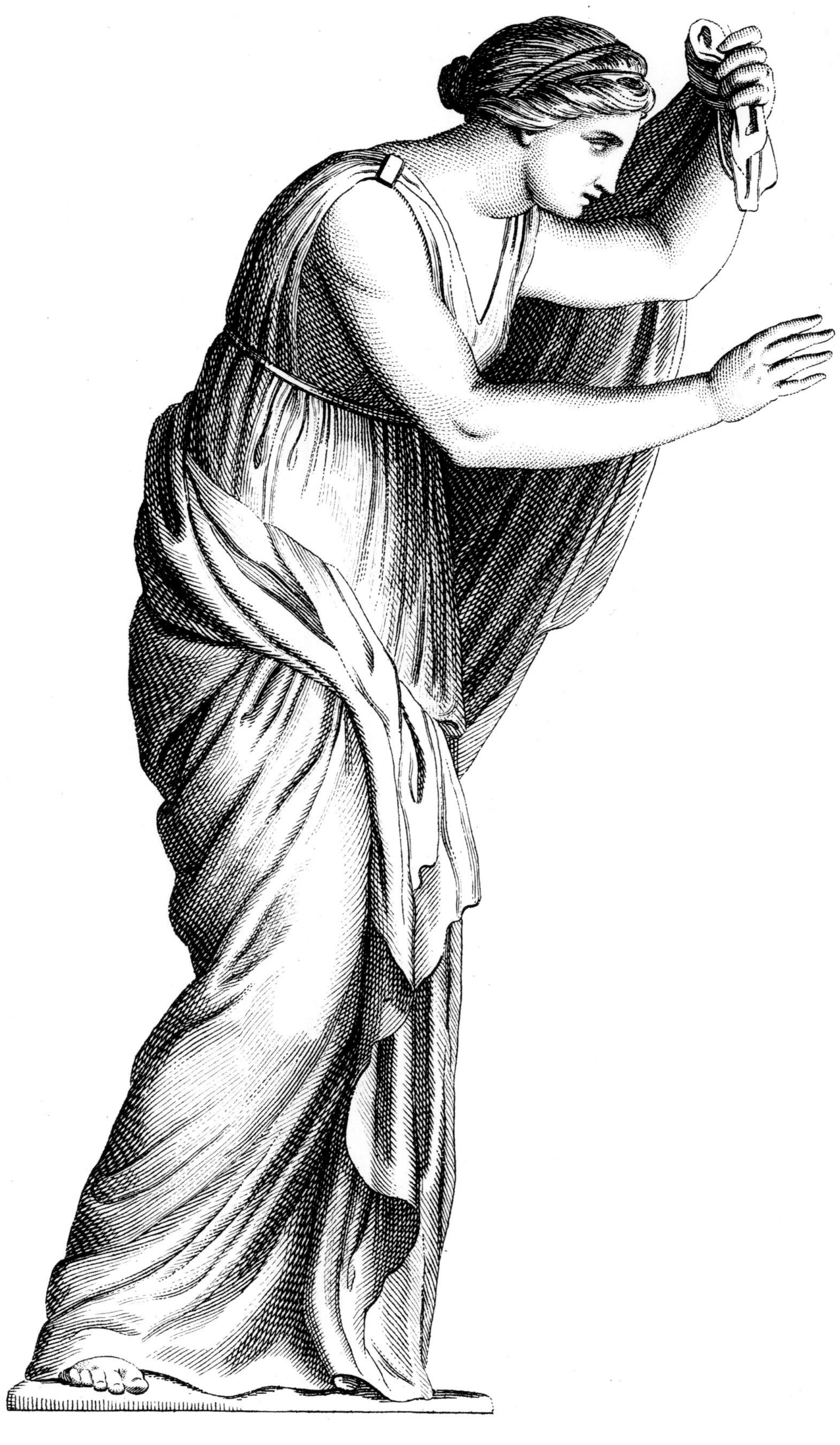

Greek female dress

Griechisches Frauengewand

Abito femminile greco

Vêtement grec féminin

Vestido griego de mujer

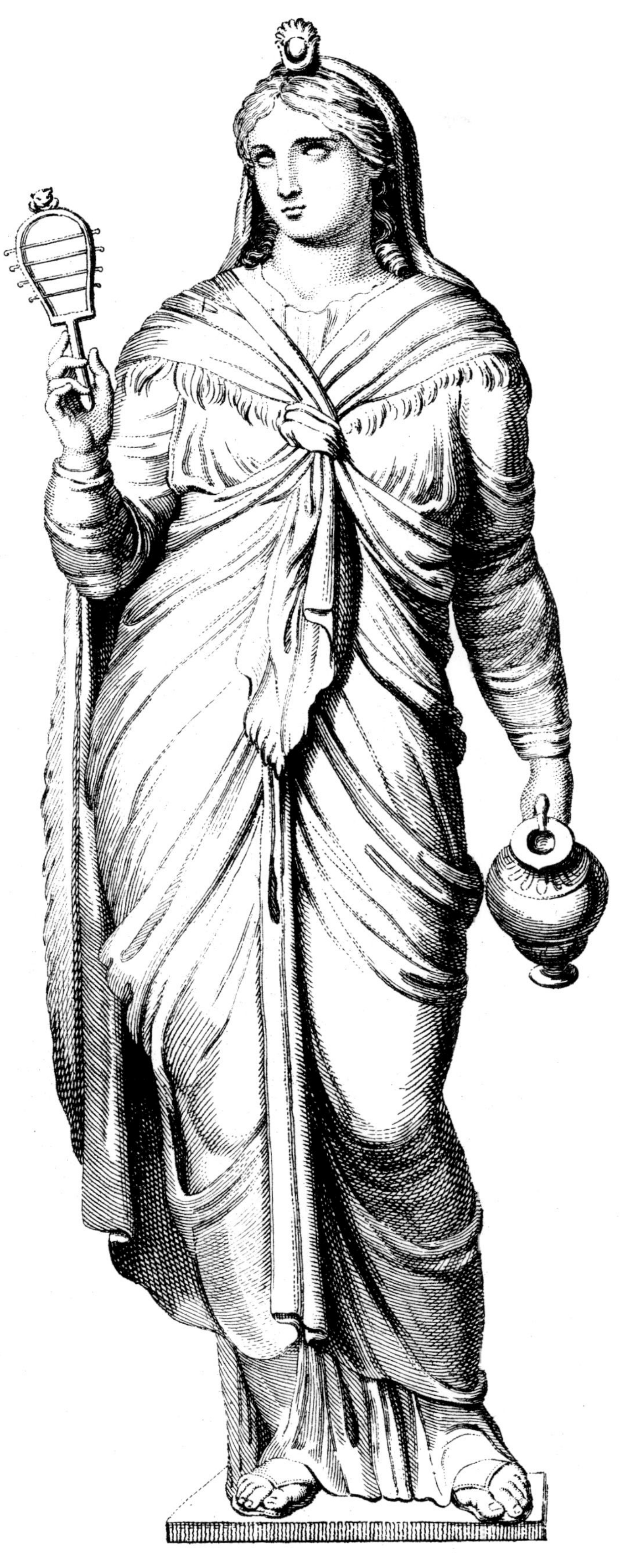

Greek female dress

Griechisches Frauengewand

Abito femminile greco

Vêtement grec féminin

Vestido griego de mujer

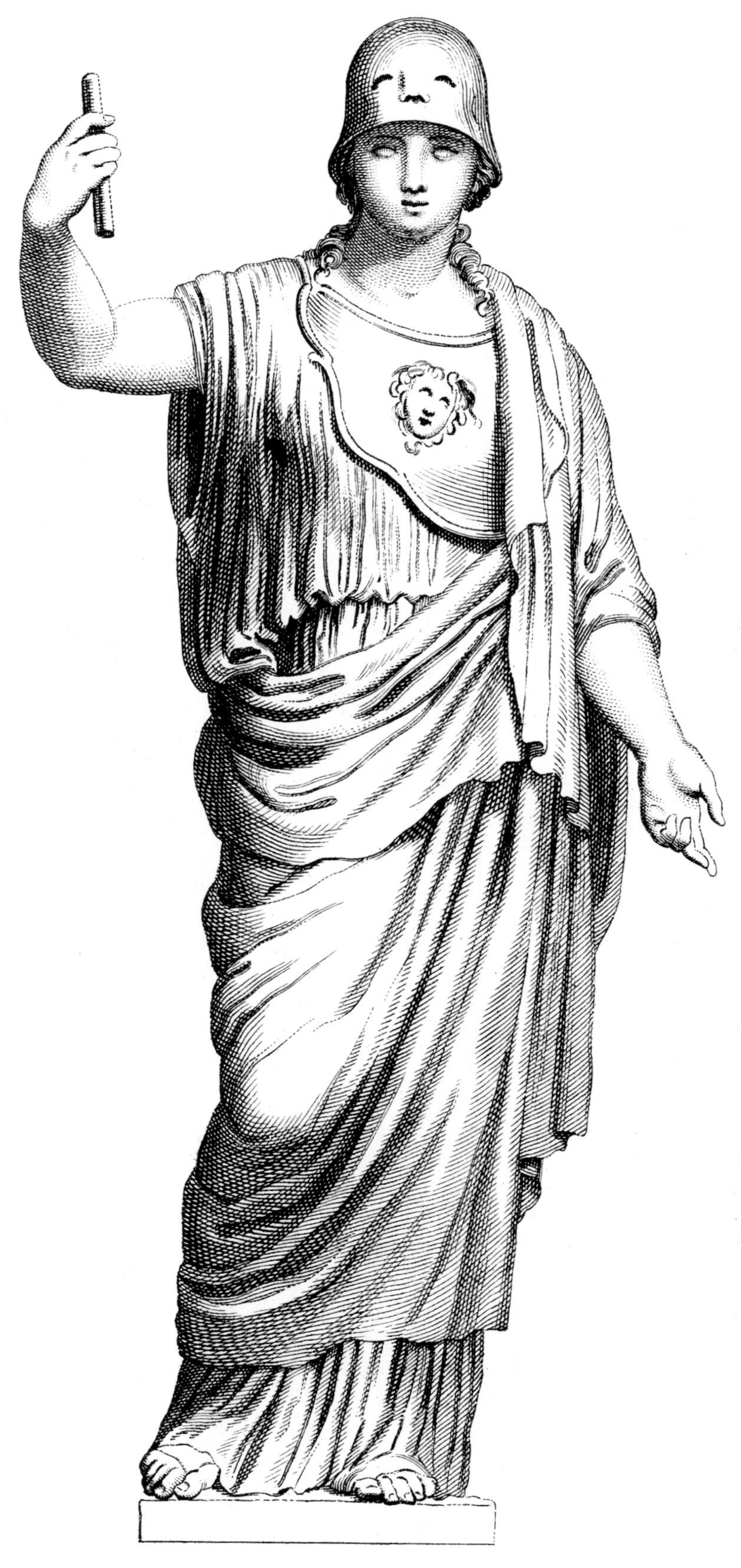

Greek female dress

Griechisches Frauengewand

Abito femminile greco

Vêtement grec féminin

Vestido griego de mujer

Ancient Egypt

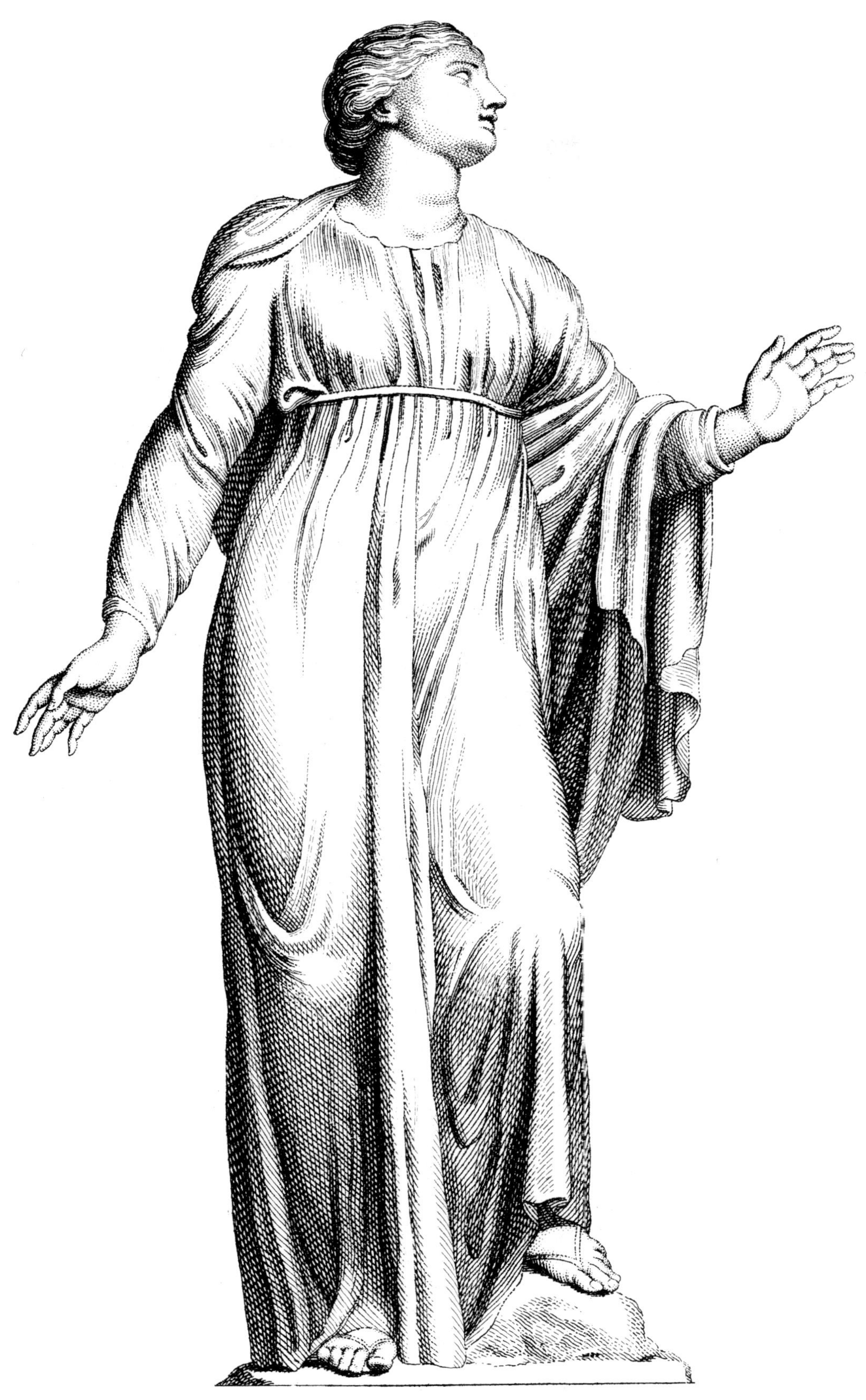

Greek female dress

Griechisches Frauengewand

Abito femminile greco

Vêtement grec féminin

Vestido griego de mujer

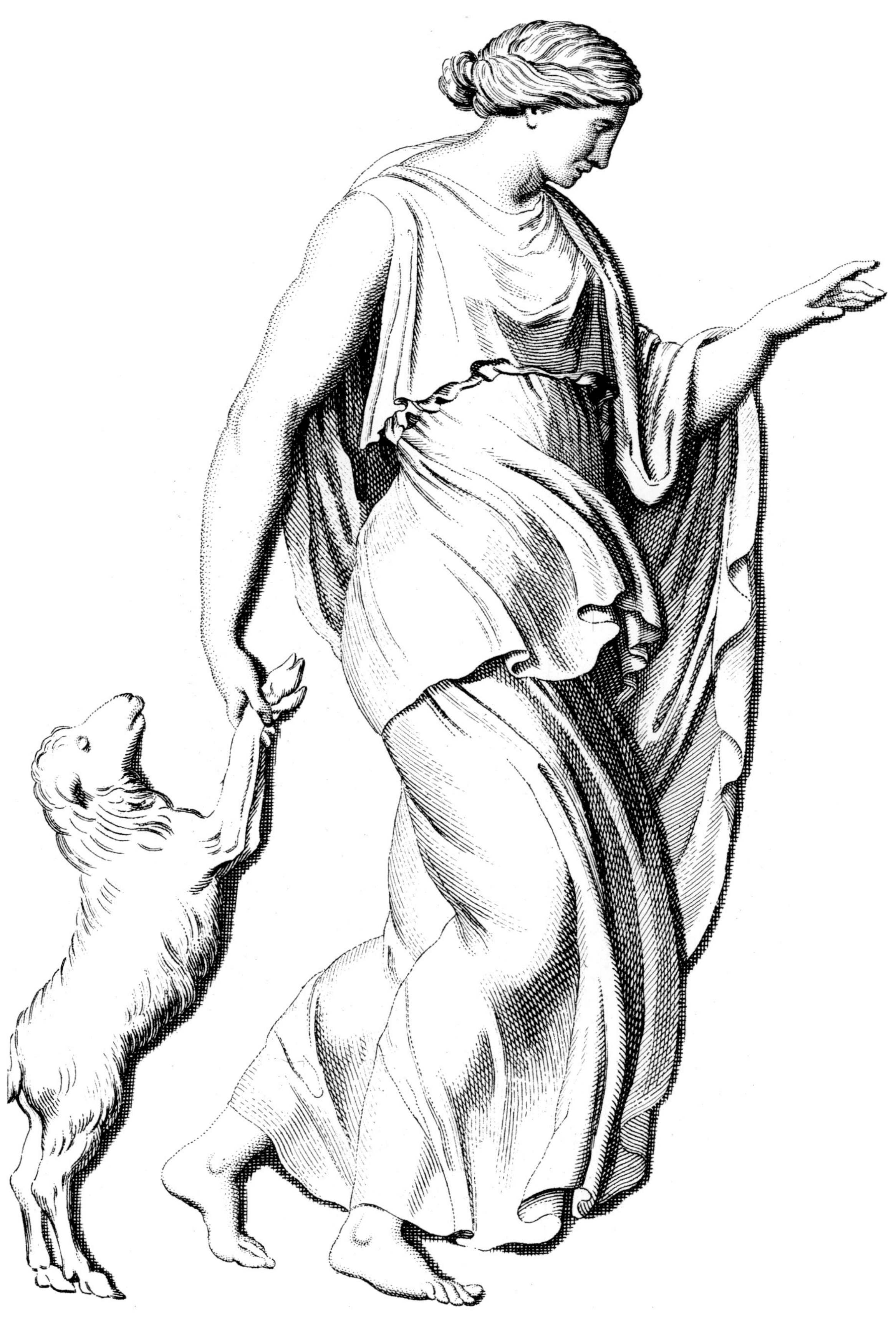

Greek female dress

Griechisches Frauengewand

Abito femminile greco

Vêtement grec féminin

Vestido griego de mujer

Ancient Greece

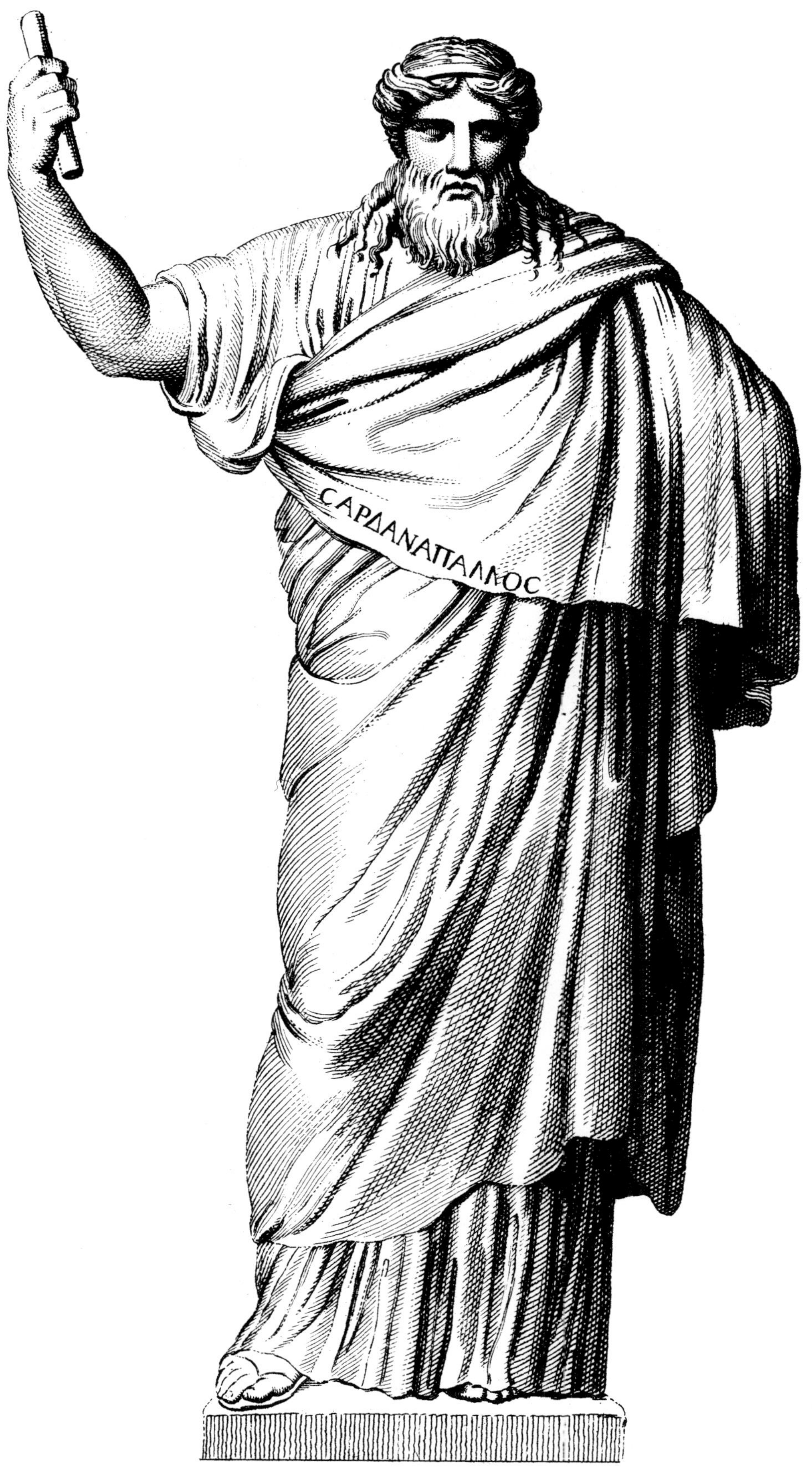

Greek toga | Griechische Toga | Toga greca | Toge grecque | Toga griega

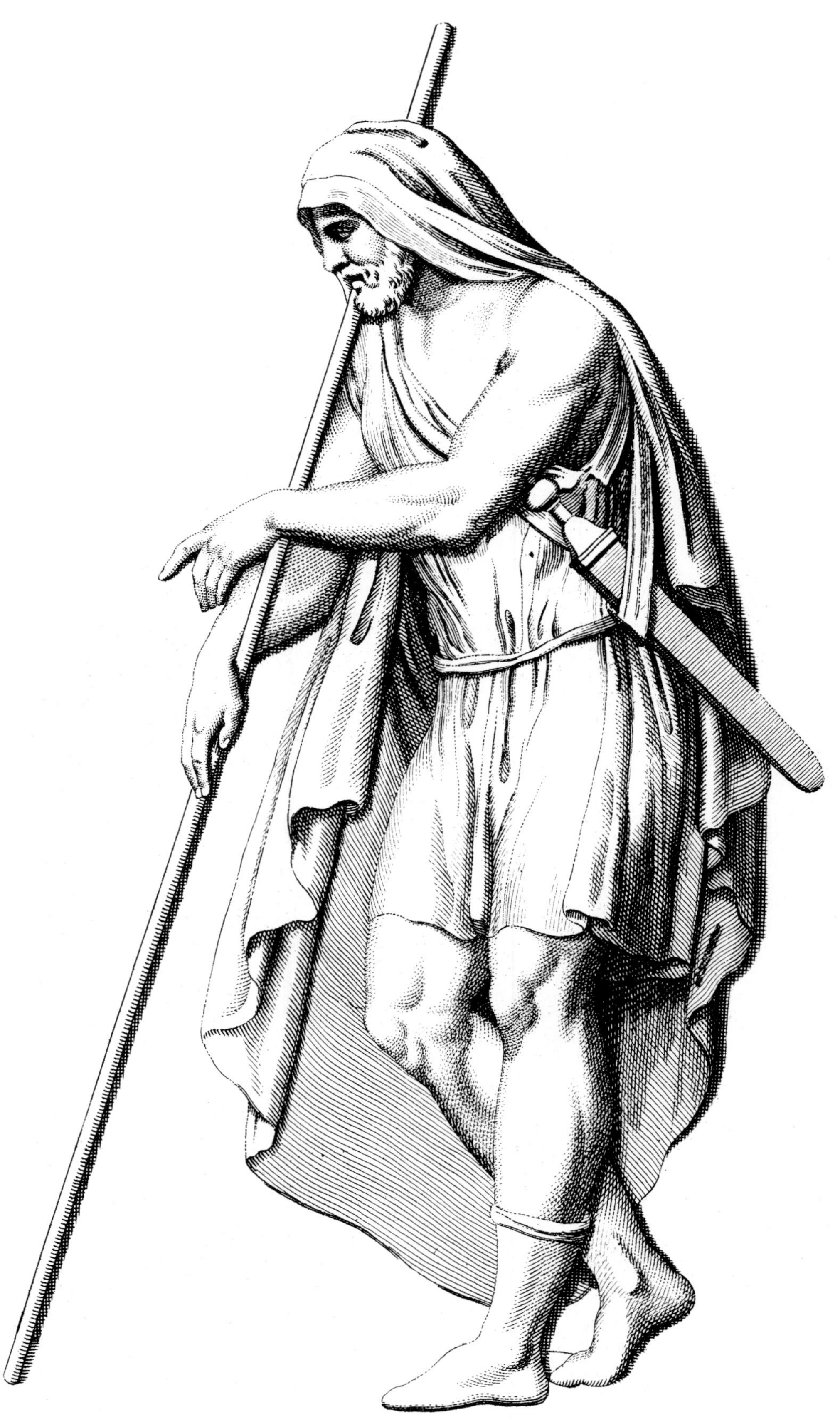

Greek men’s dress

Griechisches Männergewand

Abito maschile greco

Vêtement grec masculin

Traje griego de hombre

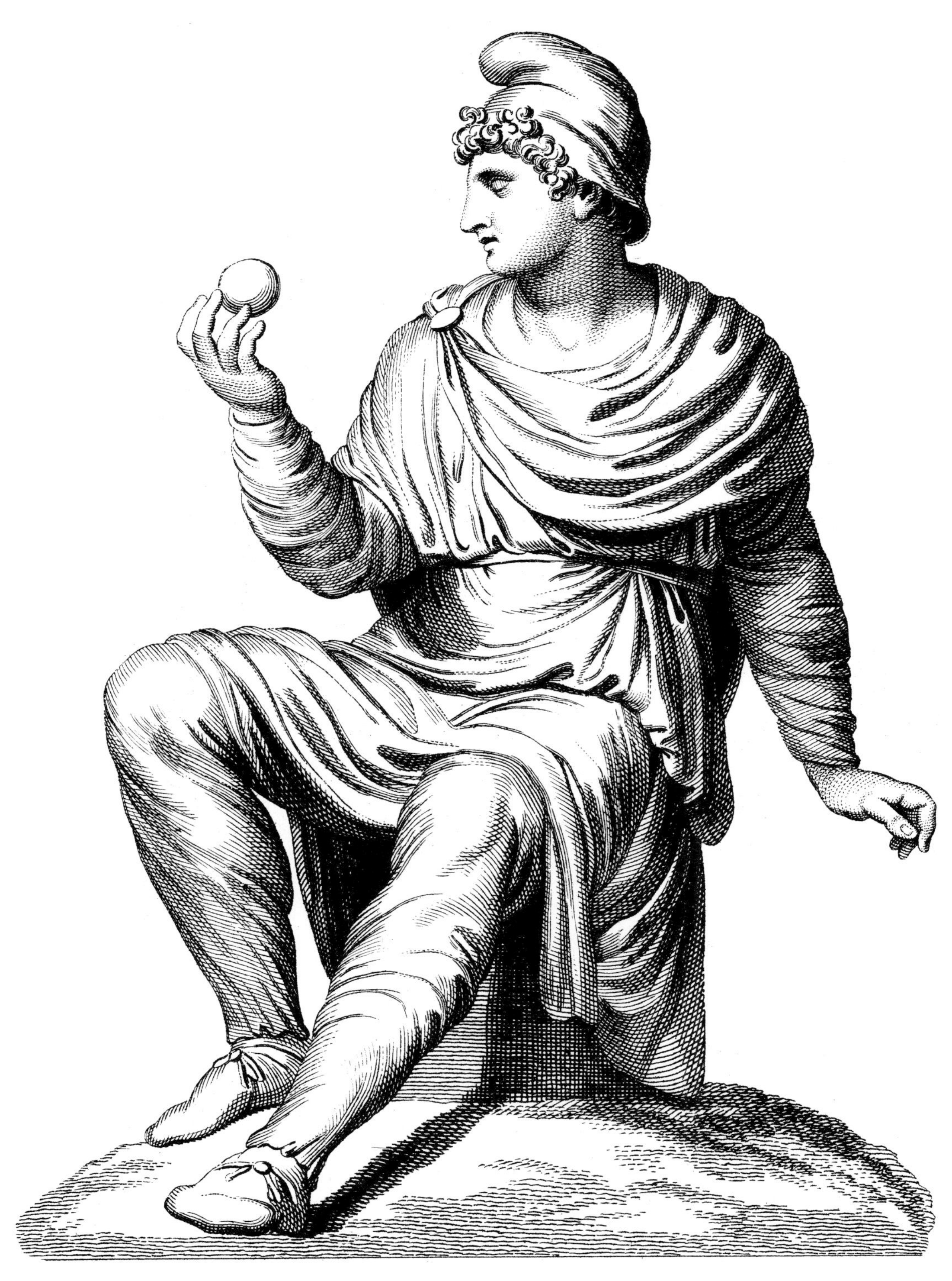

Greek men's dress | Griechisches Männergewand | Abito maschile greco | Vêtement grec masculin | Traje griego de hombre

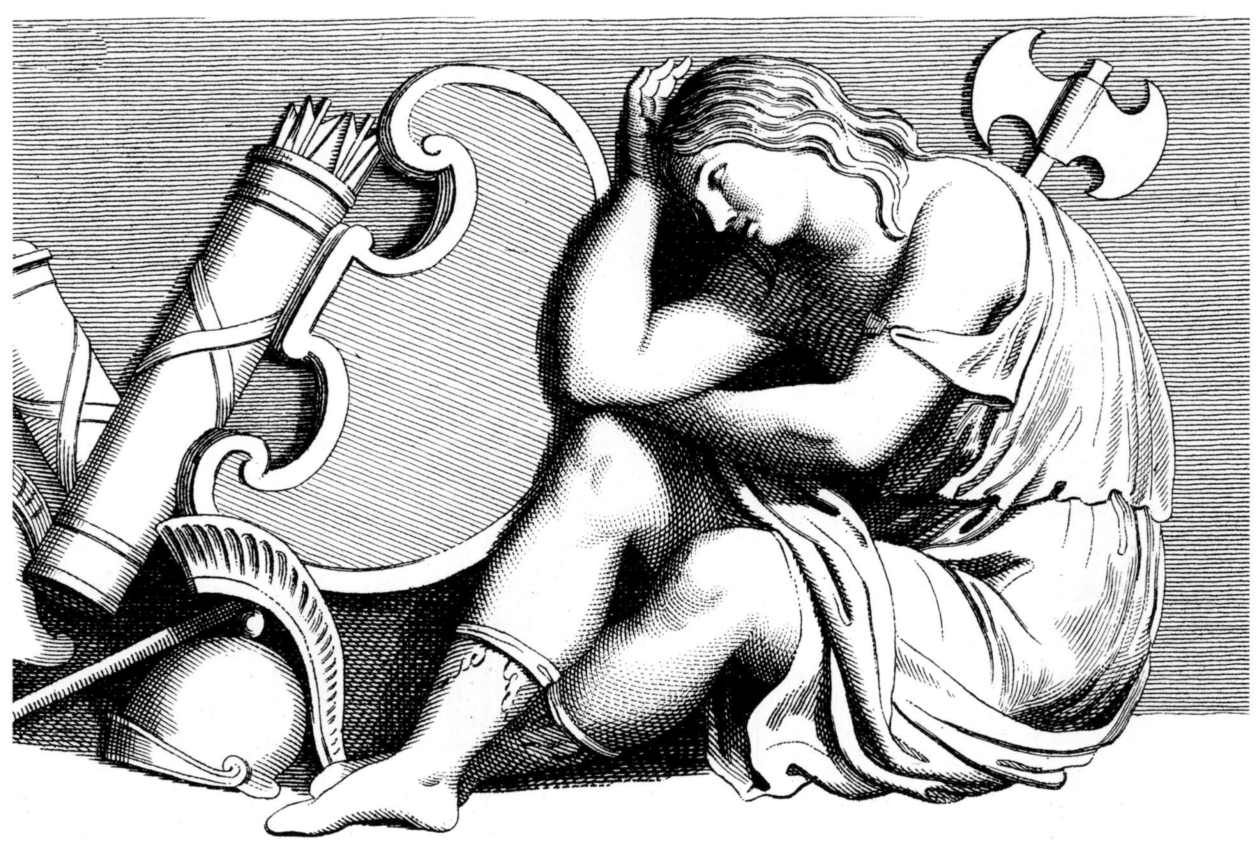

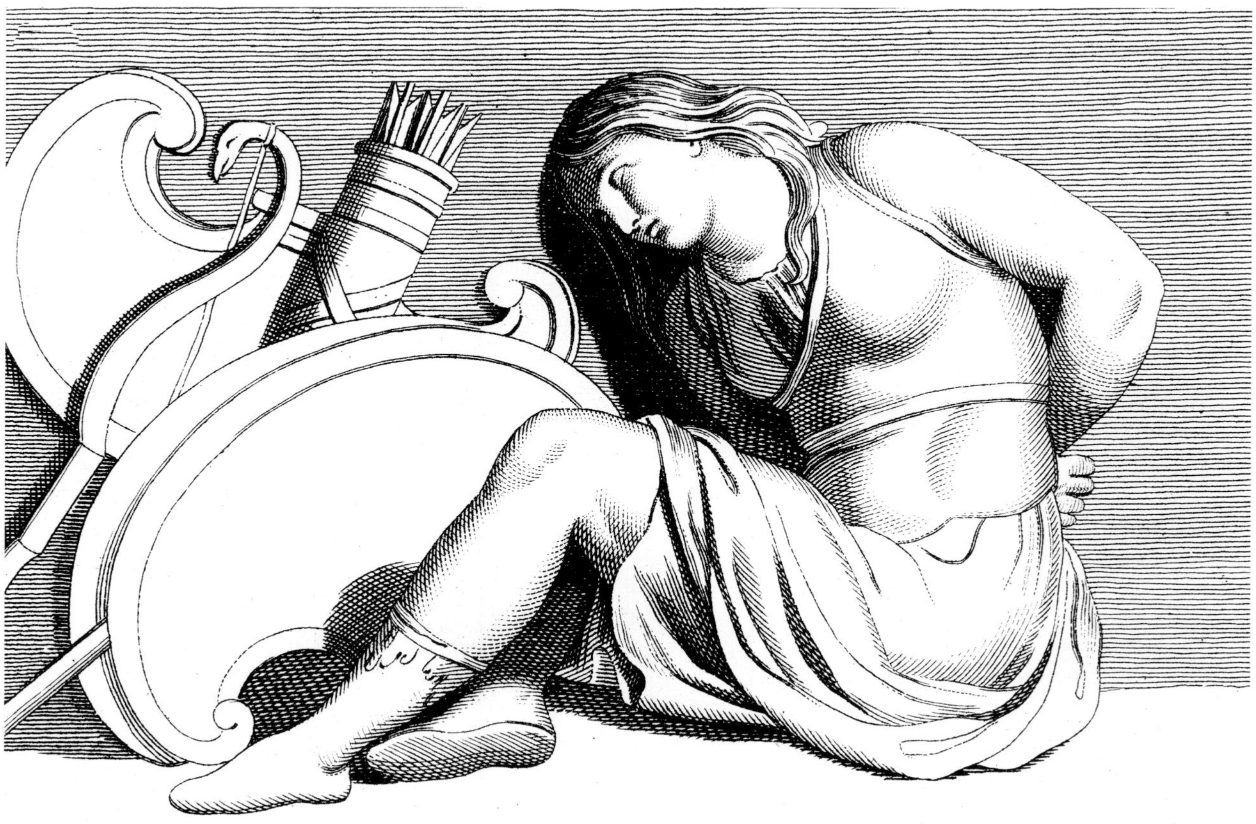

Female warriors from Greek mythology

Kriegerinnen aus der griechischen Mythologie

Guerriere femminili della mitologia greca

Guerrières de la mythologie grecque

Guerreras de la mitología griega

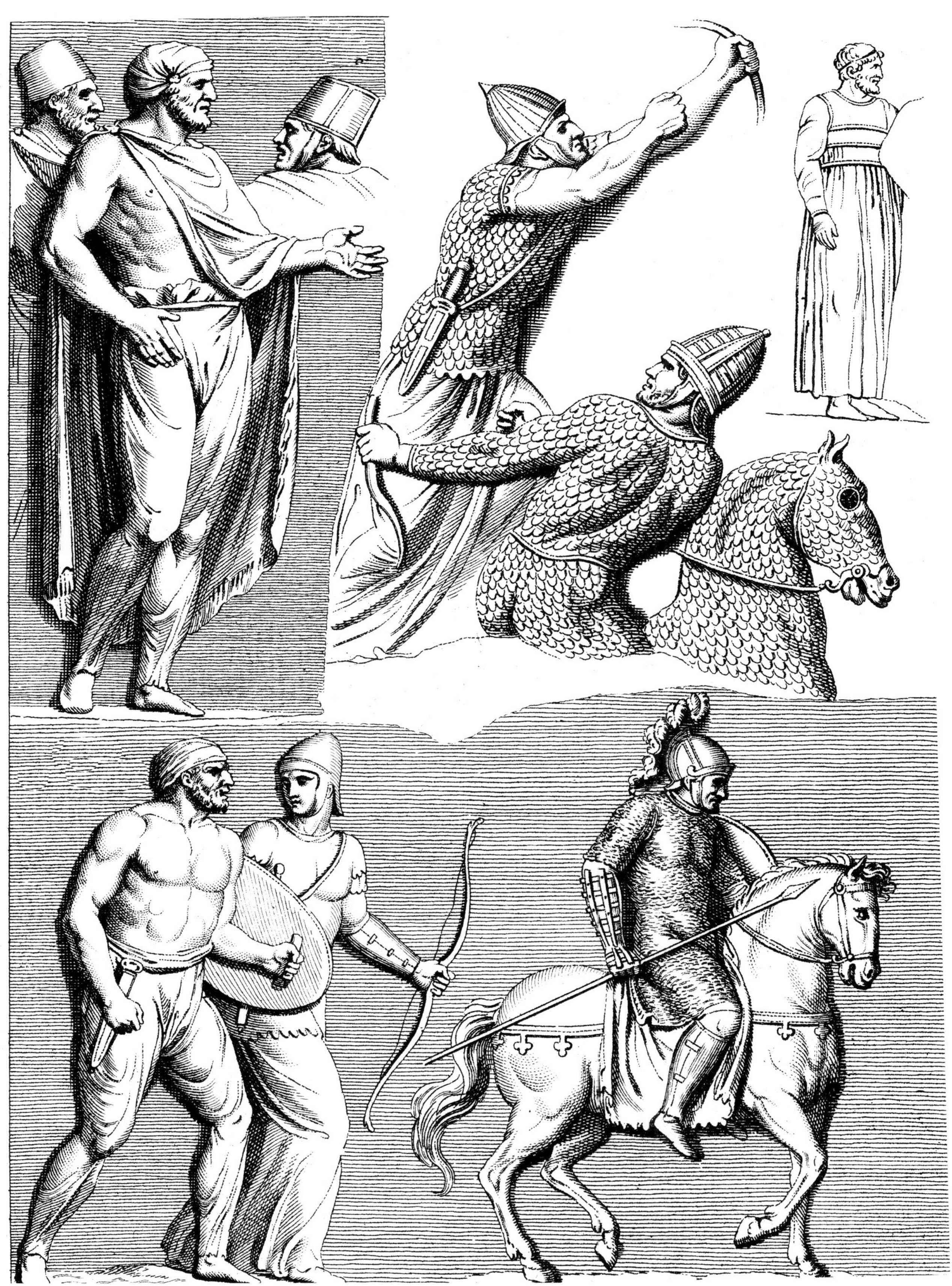

Costumes from various ancient cultures: Assyrians, Parthen and Gauls

Gewänder aus unterschiedlichen alten Kulturen: Assyrier, Parther und Gallier

Costumi di diverse culture antiche: assiri, parti e galli

Costumes de cultures anciennes diverses : assyriens, parthes et gaulois

Trajes de diversas culturas antiguas: asirios, partos y galos

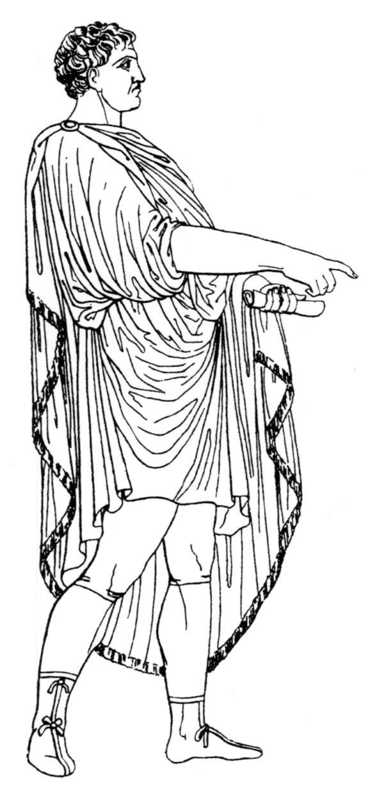

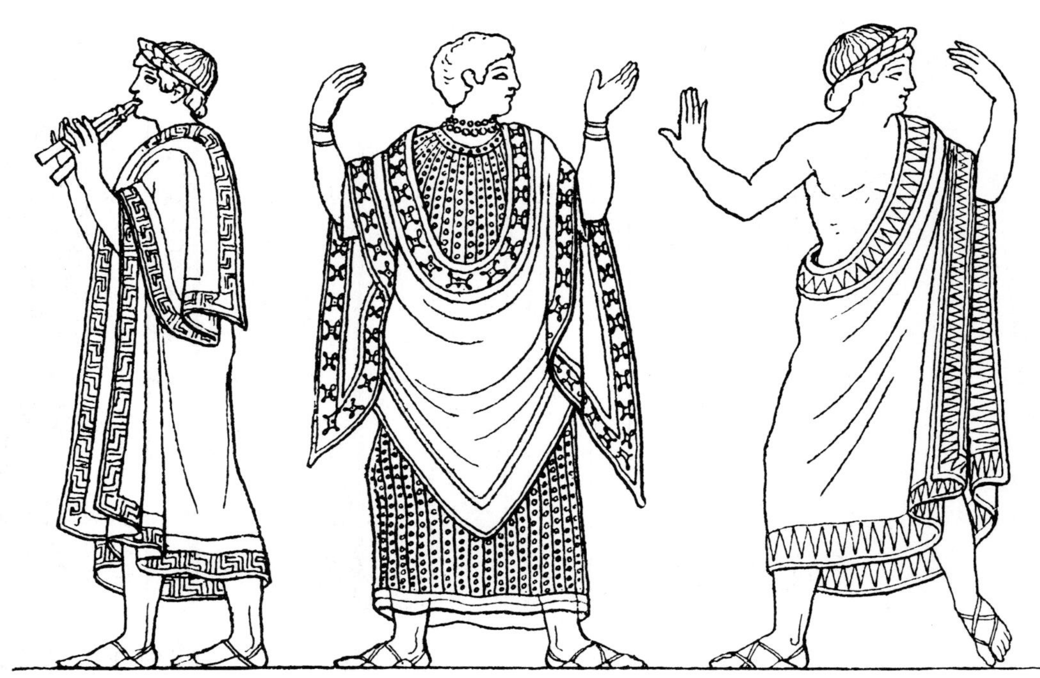

a	Roman Emperor in tunic	Römischer Kaiser mit Tunika	Imperatore romano con tunica	Empereur romain en tunique	Emperador romano con túnica
b	Etruscan costumes	Etruskische Tracht	Costumi etruschi	Costumes étrusques	Trajes etruscos

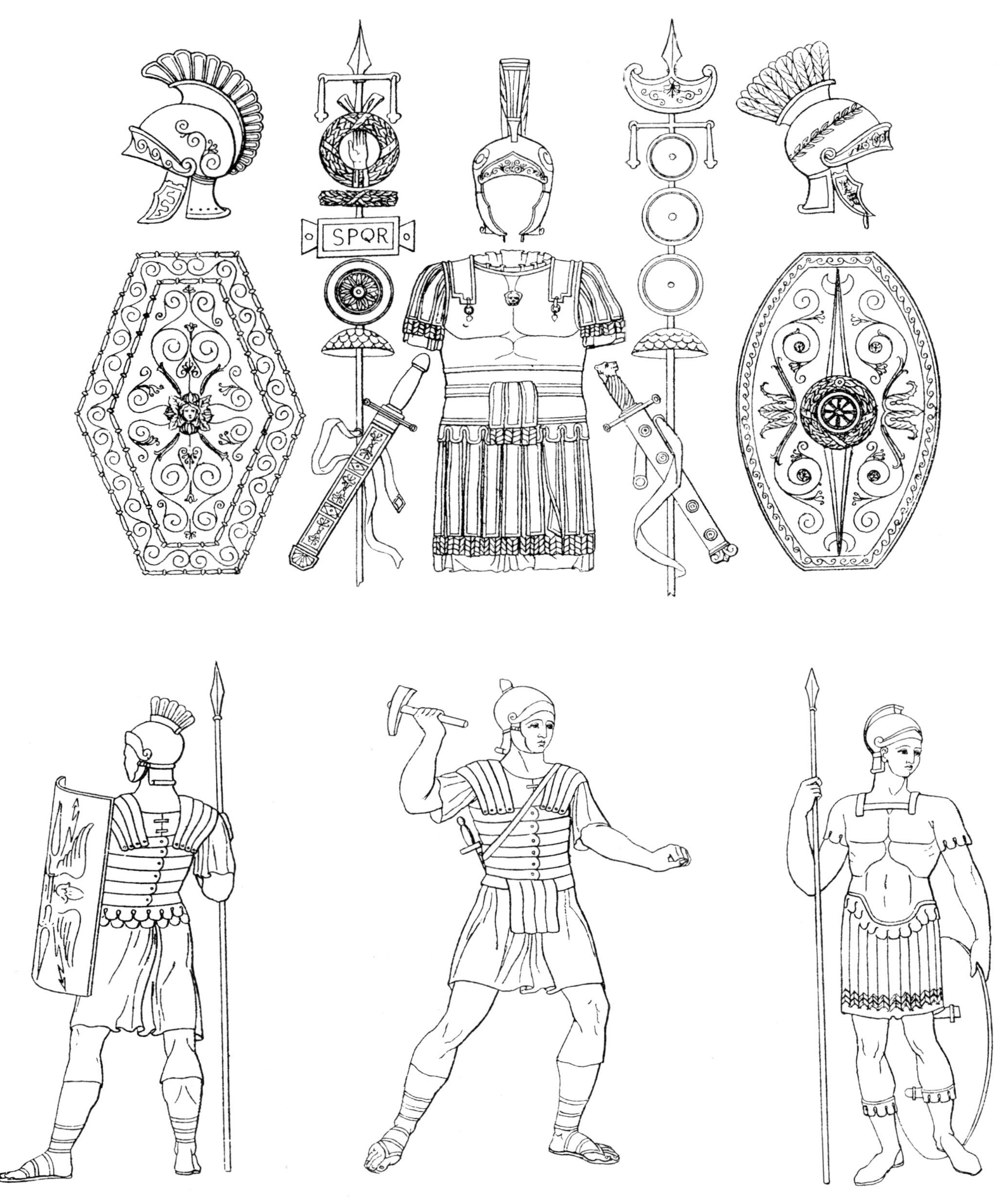

Roman armour, weapons and soldiers in uniform

Römische Rüstung, Waffen und Soldaten in Uniform

Armatura, armi e soldati in uniforme romani

Armure romaine, armes et soldats en uniforme

Armadura romana, armas y soldados de uniforme

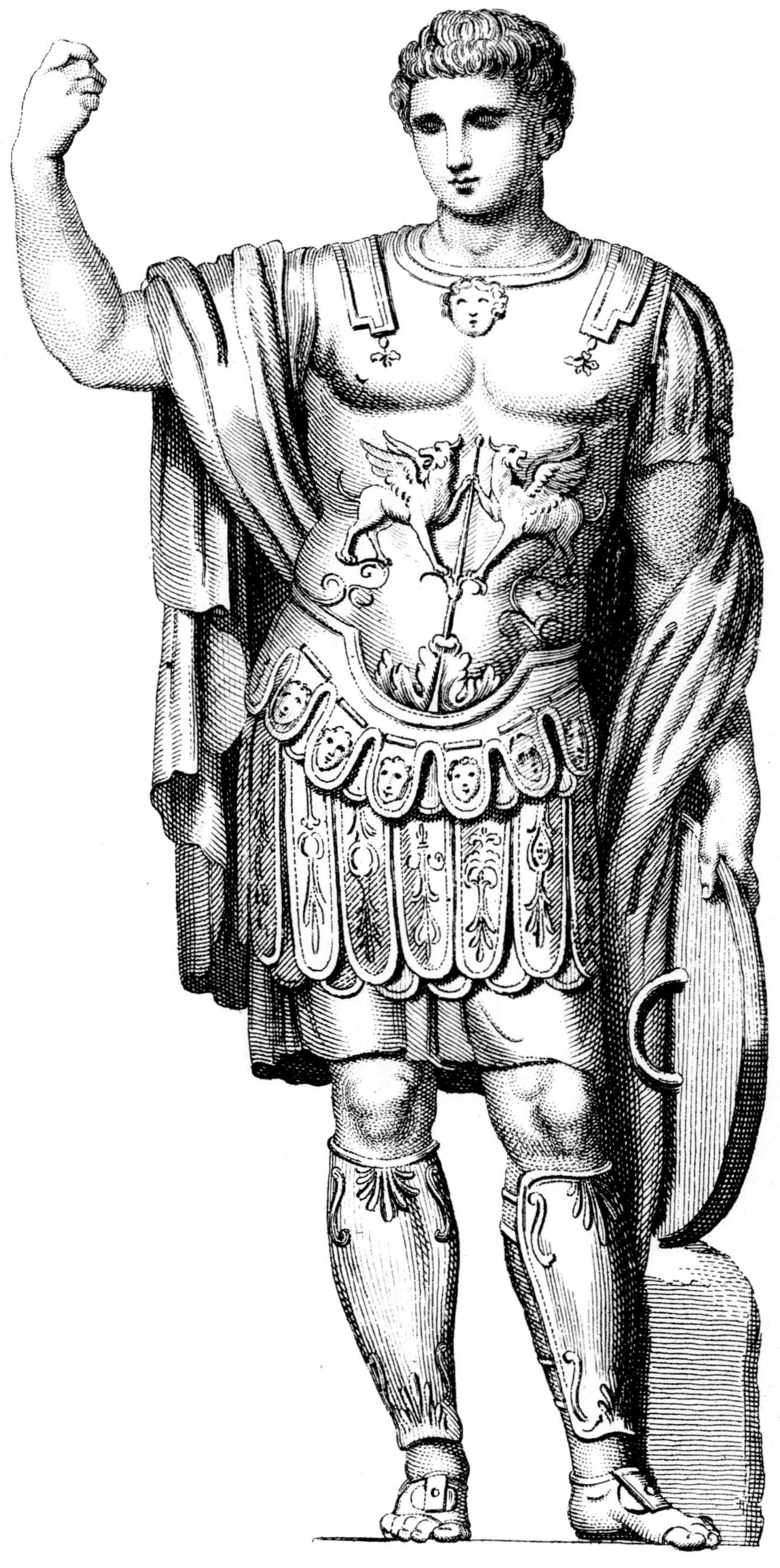

Roman soldier Römischer Soldat Soldato romano Soldat romain Soldado romano

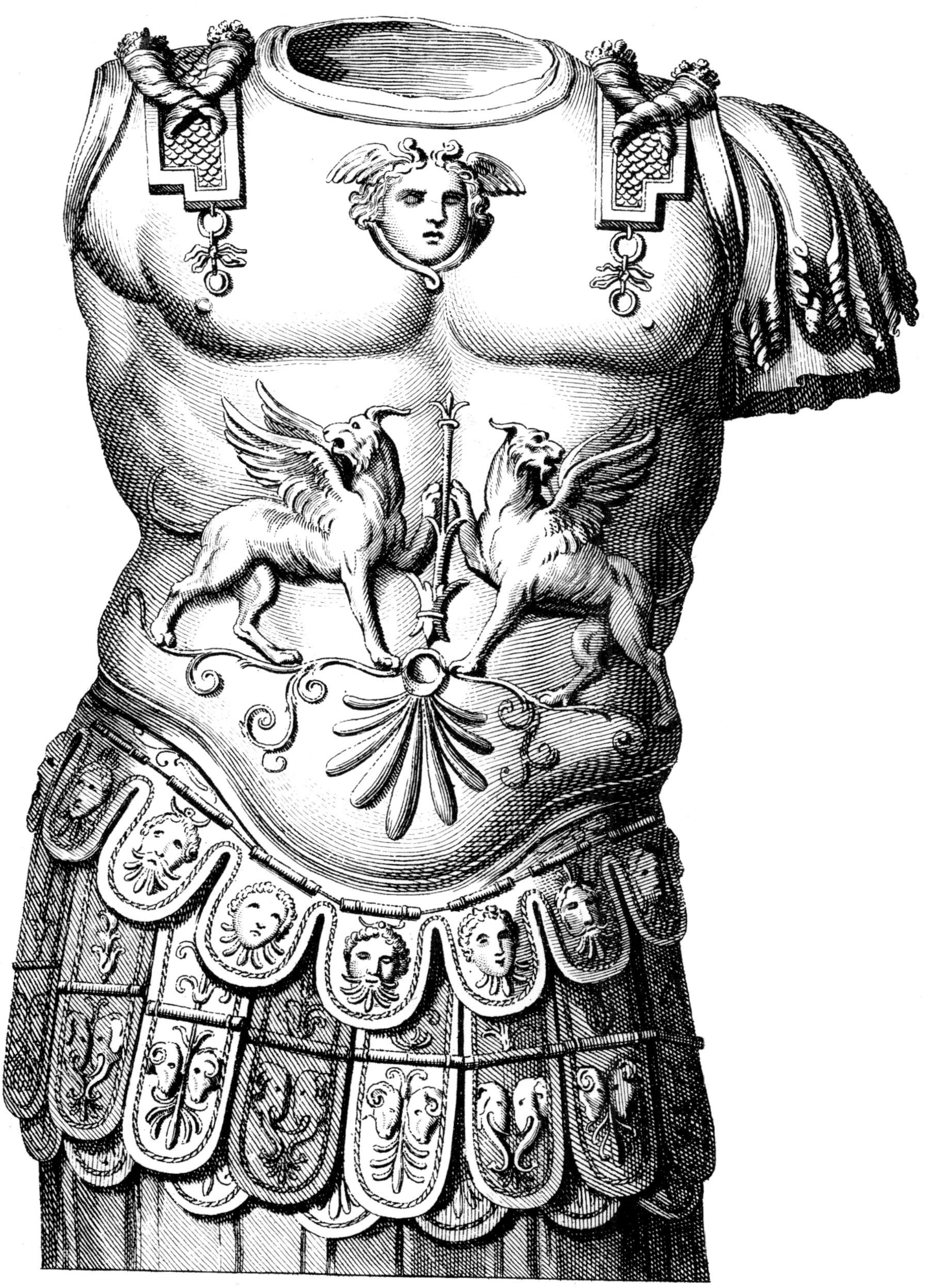

Roman armour Römische Rüstung Armatura romana Armure romaine Armadura romana

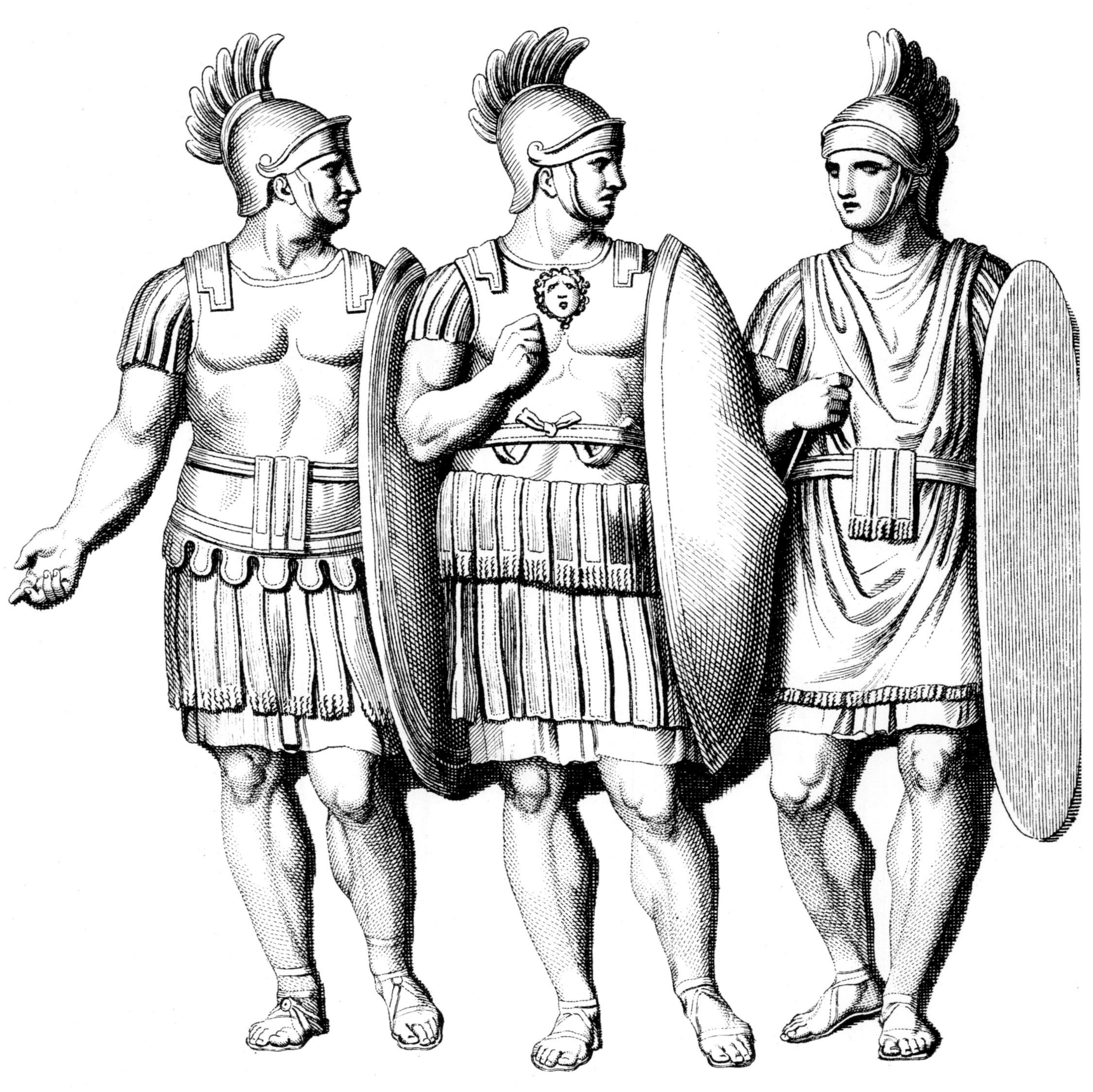

Roman soldiers Römische Soldaten Soldati romani Soldats romains Soldados romanos

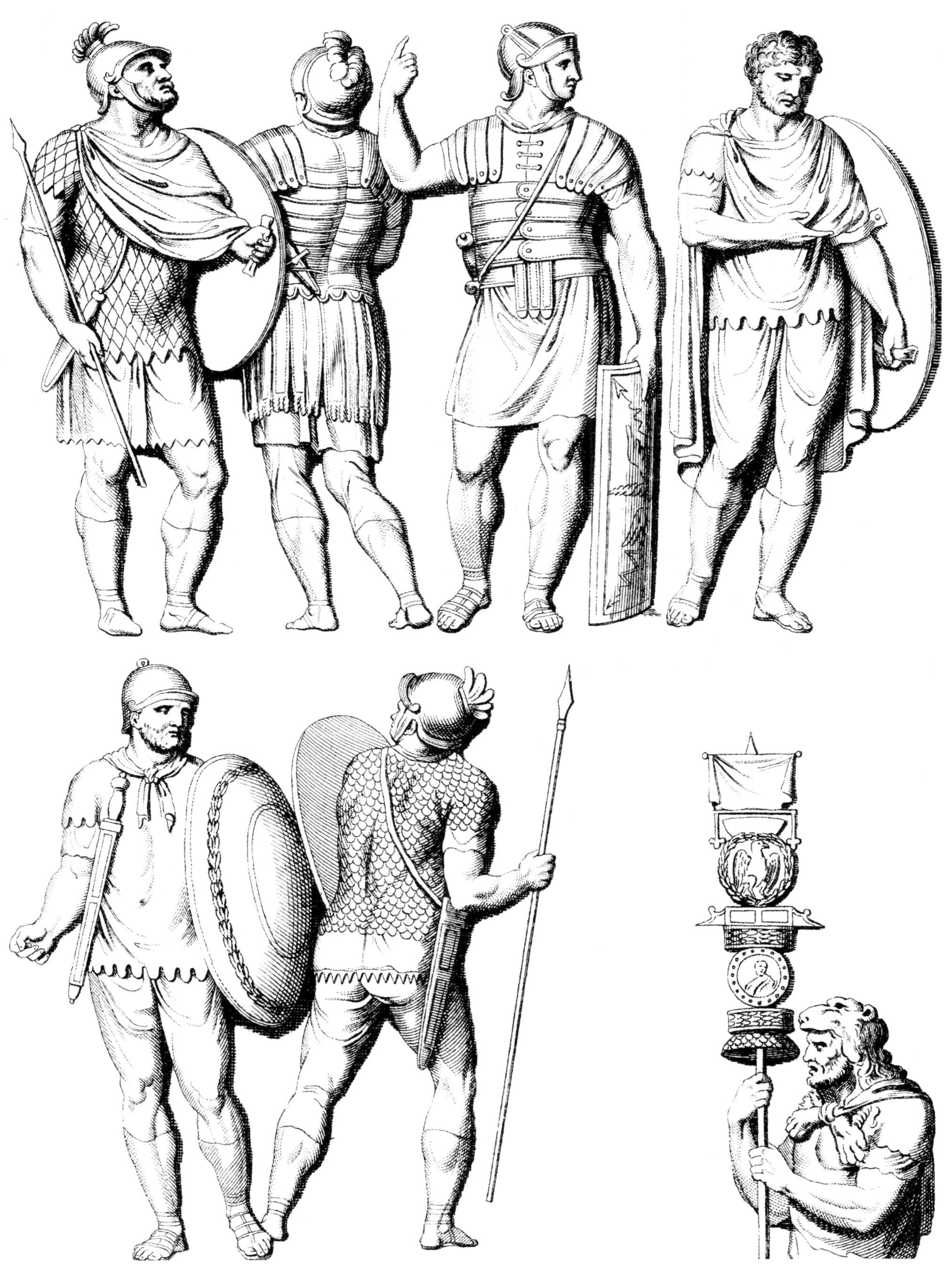

Roman soldiers Römische Soldaten Soldati romani Soldats romains Soldados romanos

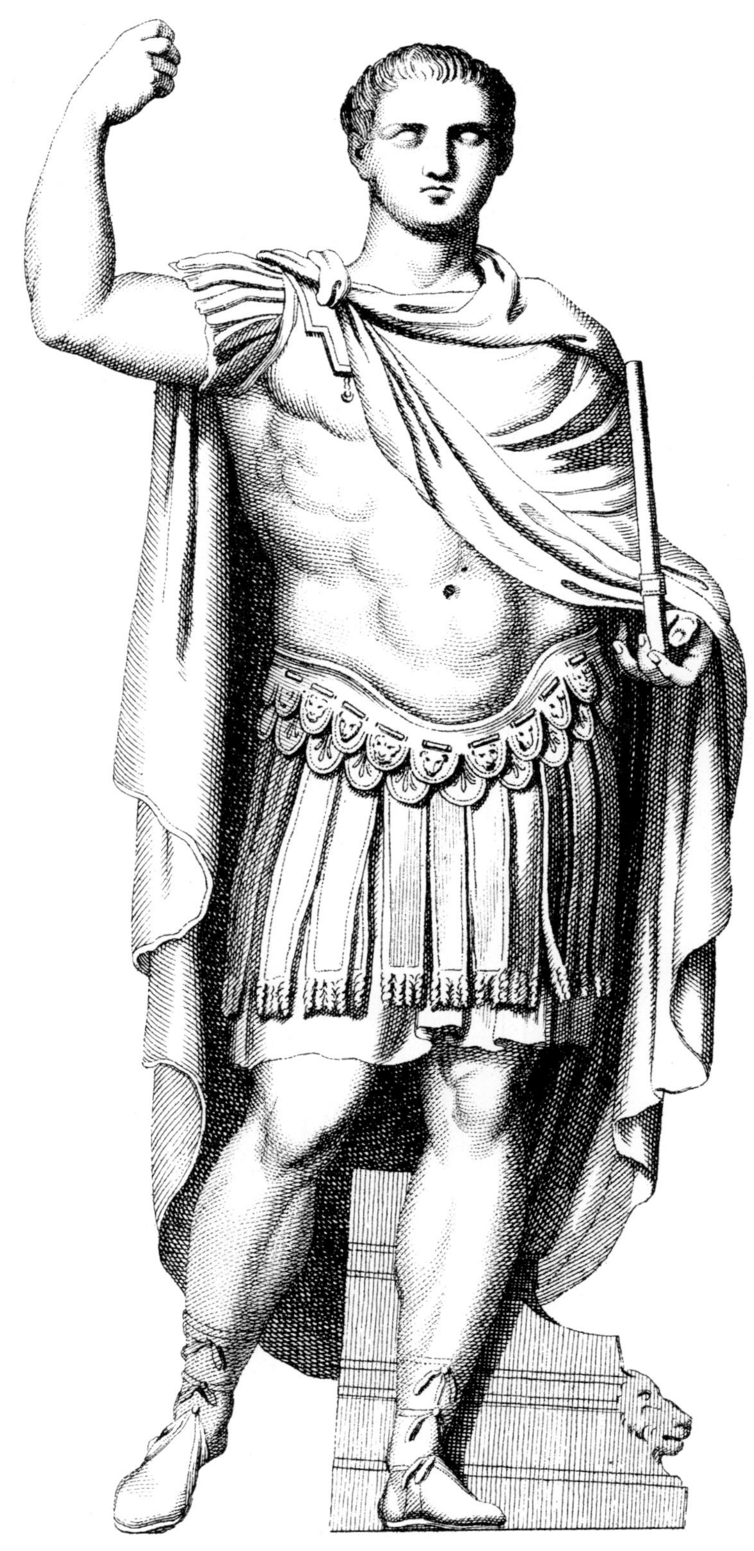

Roman soldier | Römischer Soldat | Soldato romano | Soldat romain | Soldado romano

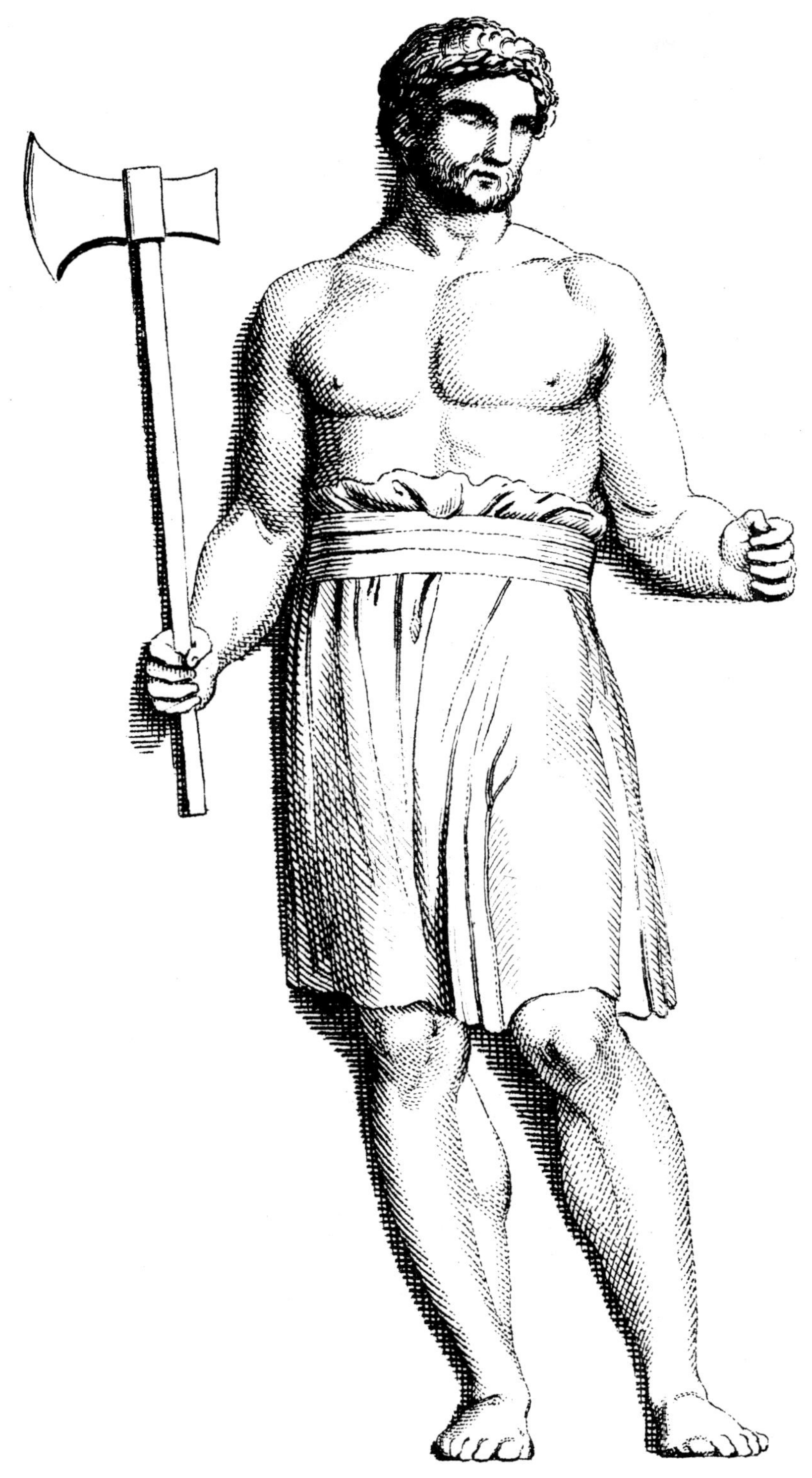

Roman gladiator Römischer Gladiator Gladiatore romano Gladiateur romain Gladiador romano

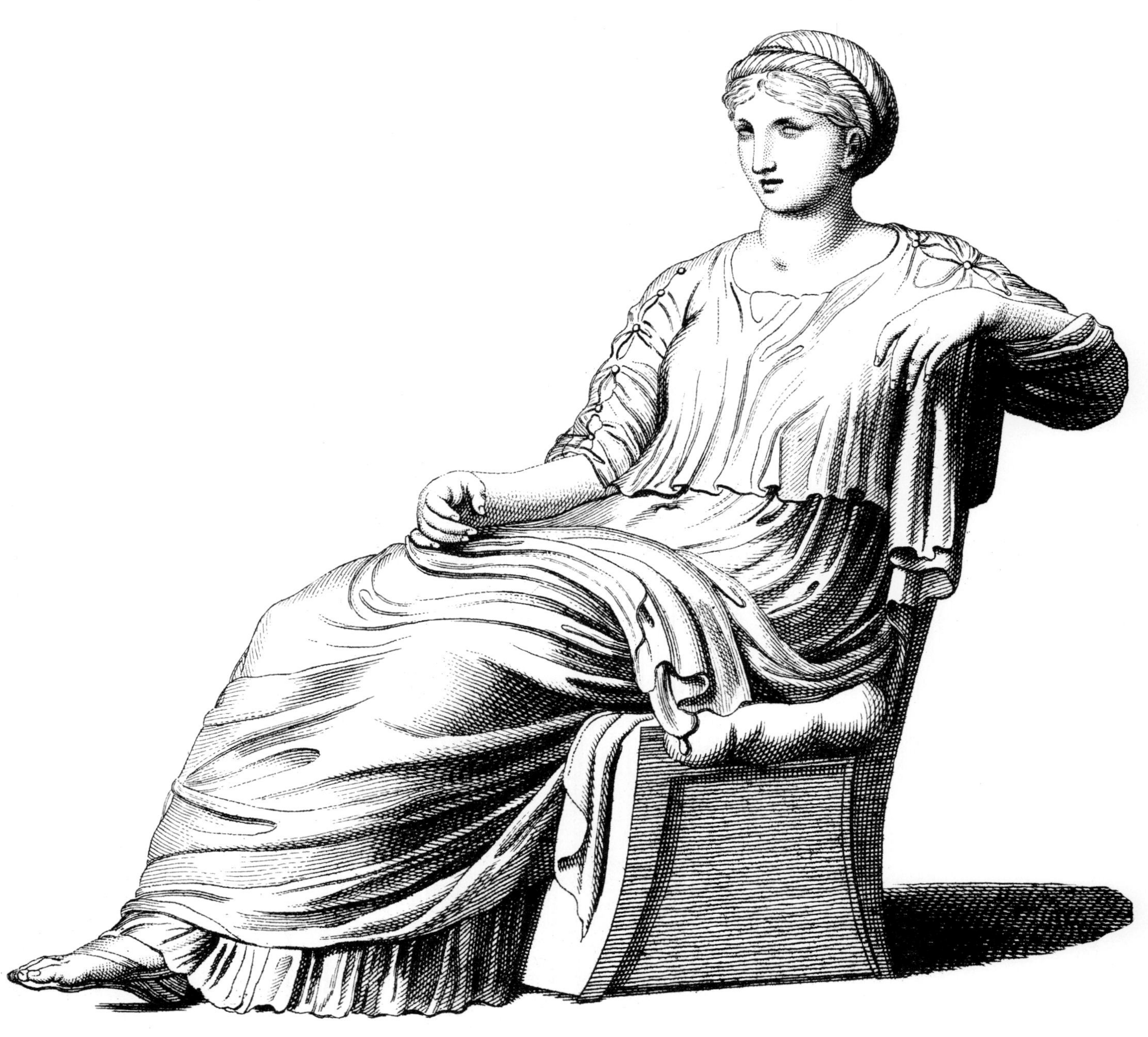

Roman female dress

Römisches Frauengewand

Abito femminile romano

Vêtement romain féminin

Vestido romano de mujer

Ancient Rome

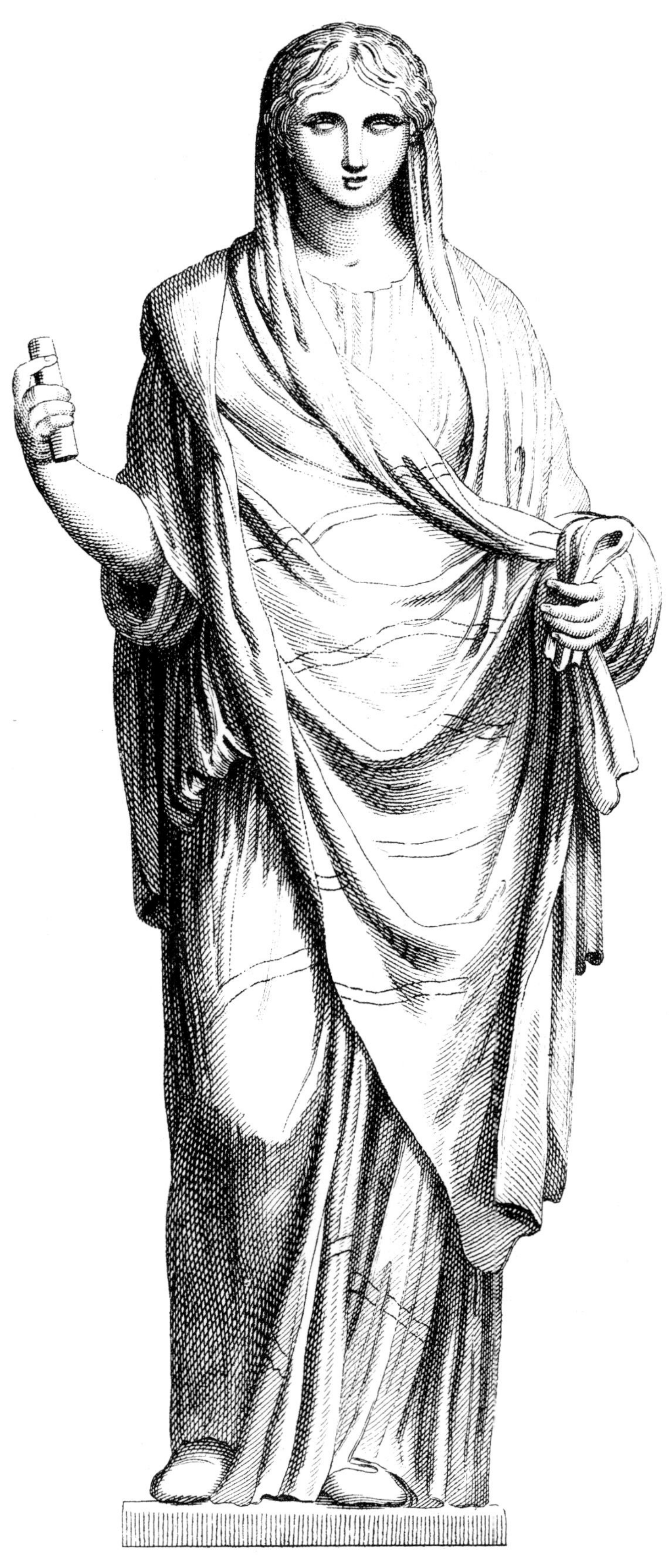

Roman female dress

Römisches Frauengewand

Abito femminile romano

Vêtement romain féminin

Vestido romano de mujer

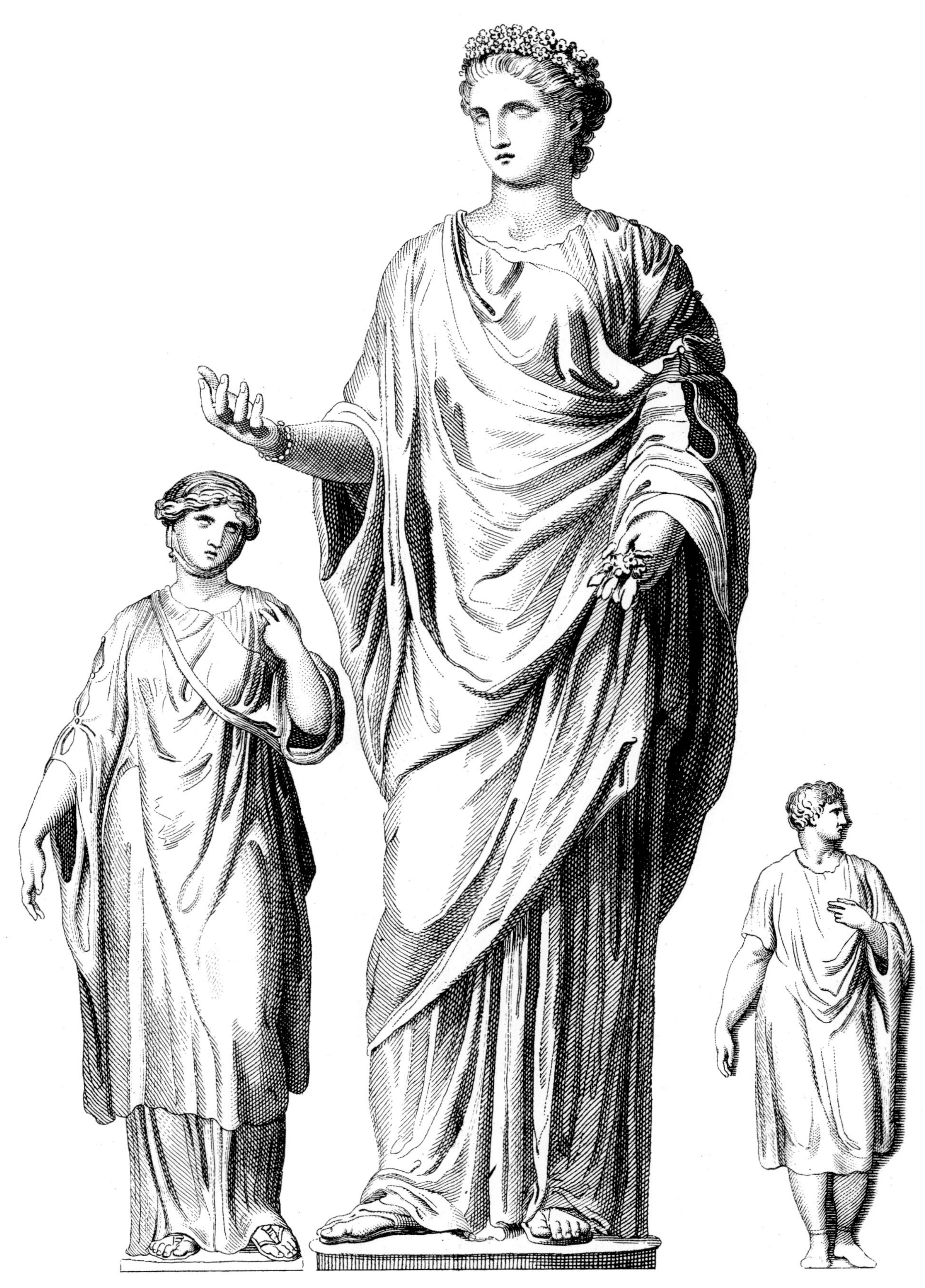

Roman female dress

Römisches Frauengewand

Abito femminile romano

Vêtement romain féminin

Vestidos romanos de mujer

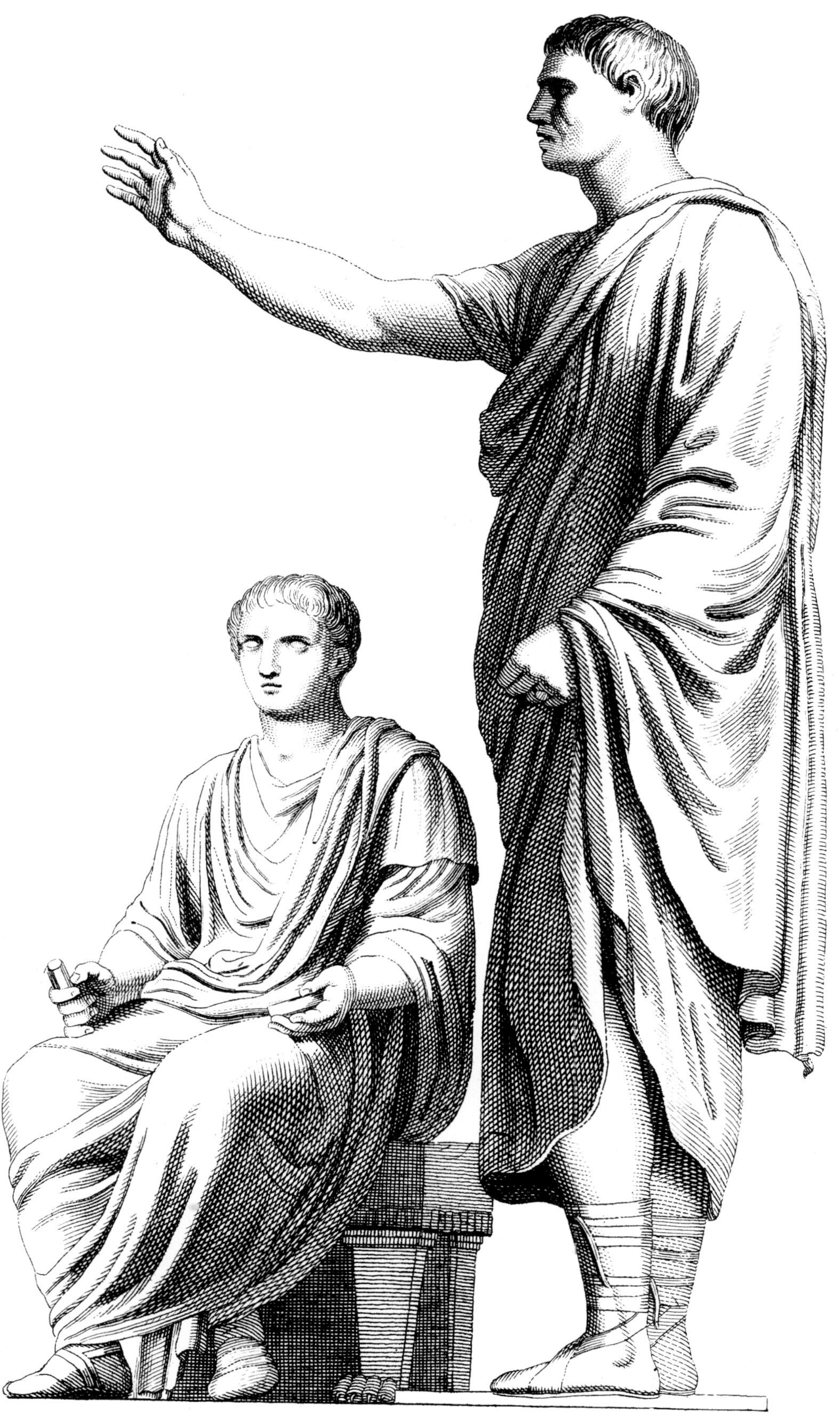

Romans in toga　Römer mit Toga　Romani in toga　Romains en toge　Romanos con togas

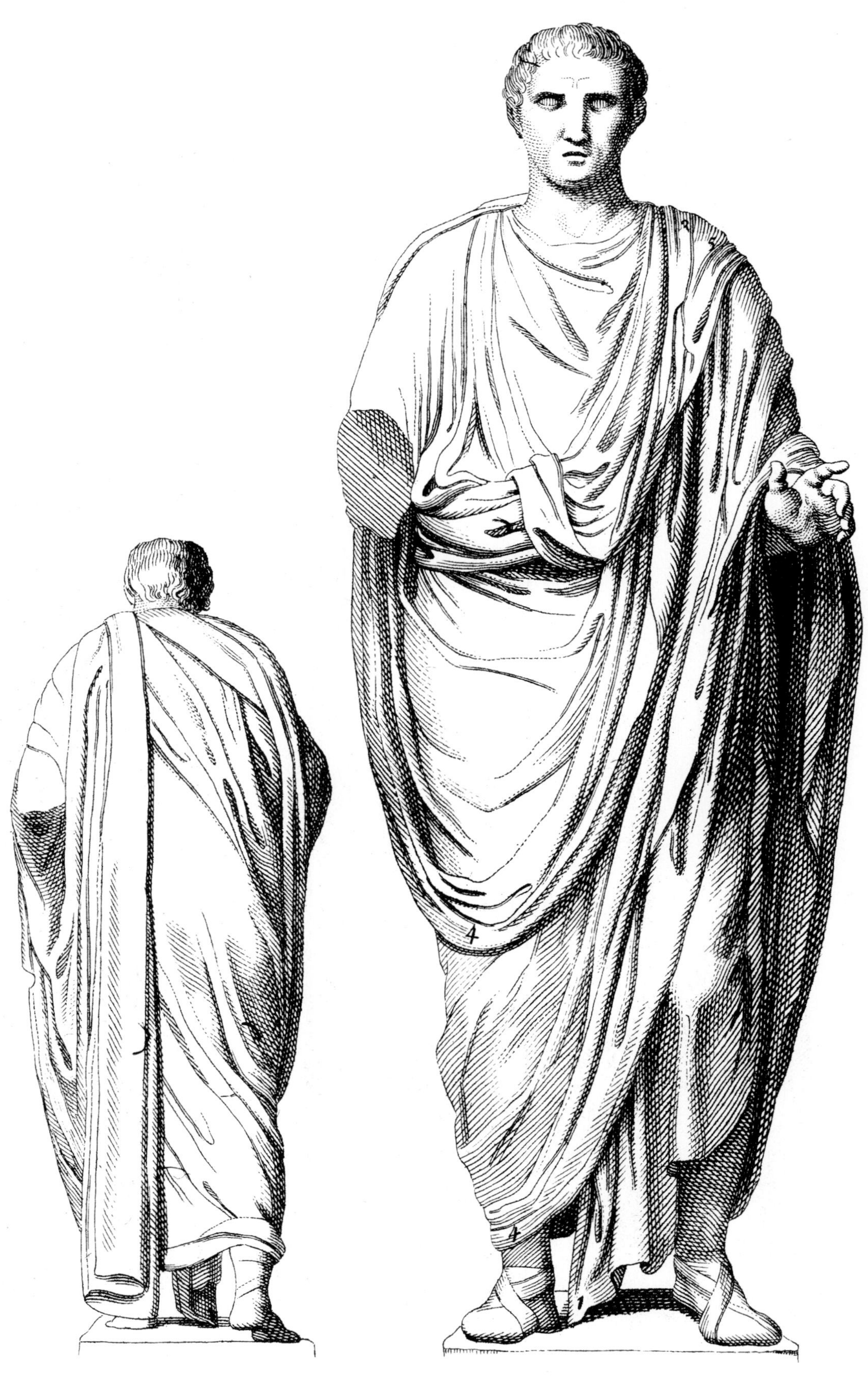

Roman toga Römische Toga Toga romana Toge romaine Toga romana

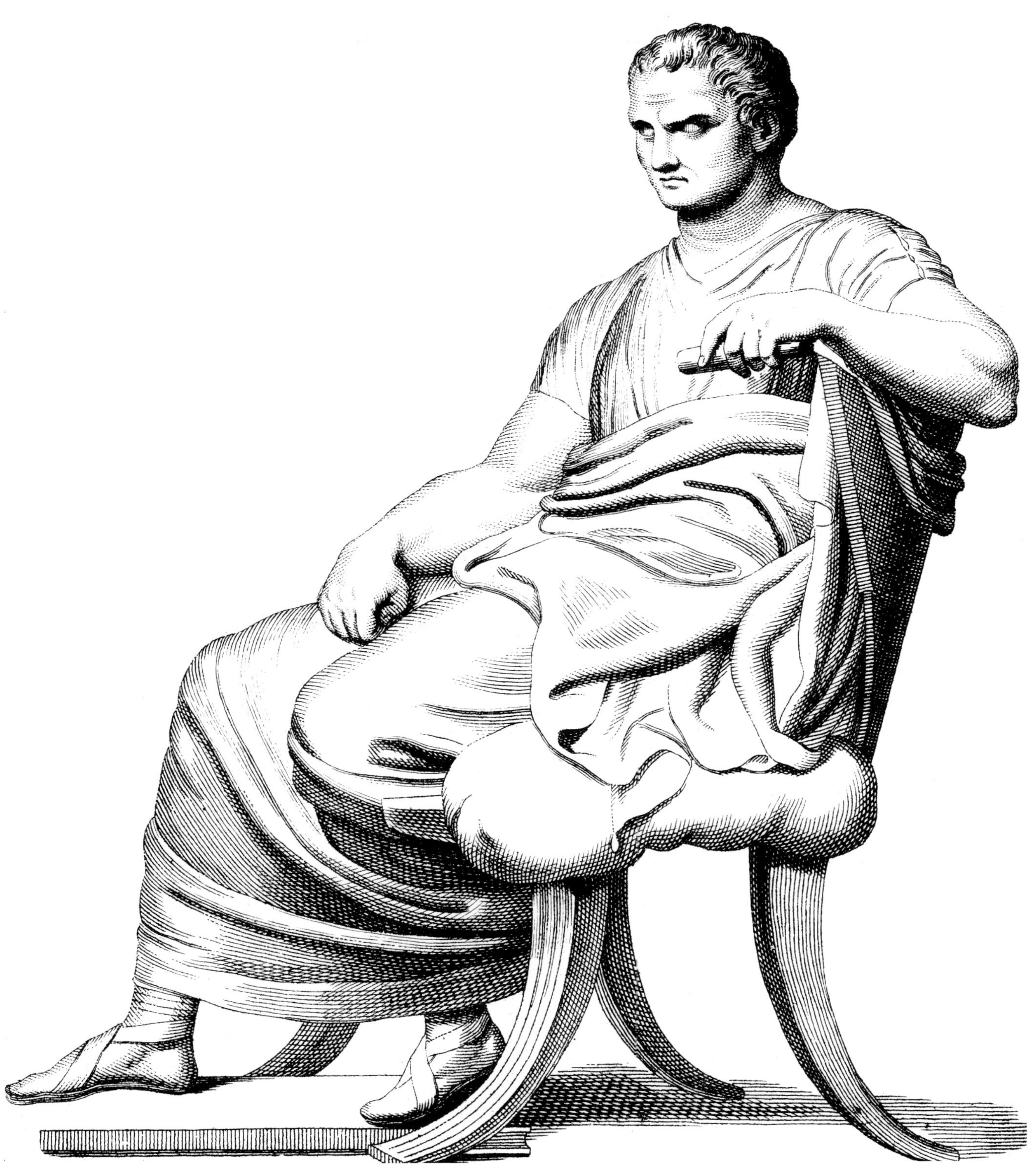

Roman toga Römische Toga Toga romana Toge romaine Toga romana

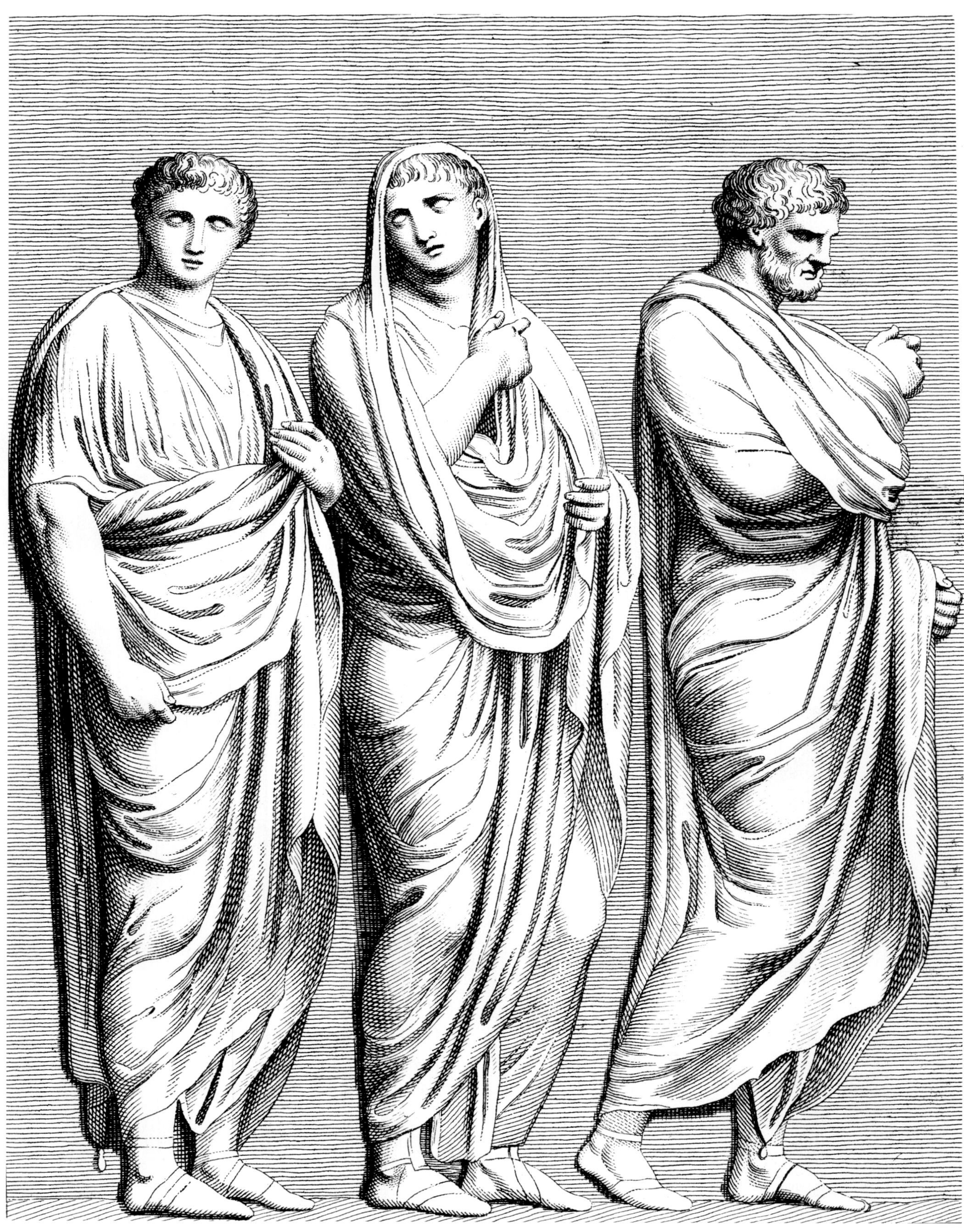

Roman togas Römische Toga Toghe romane Toges romaines Togas romanas

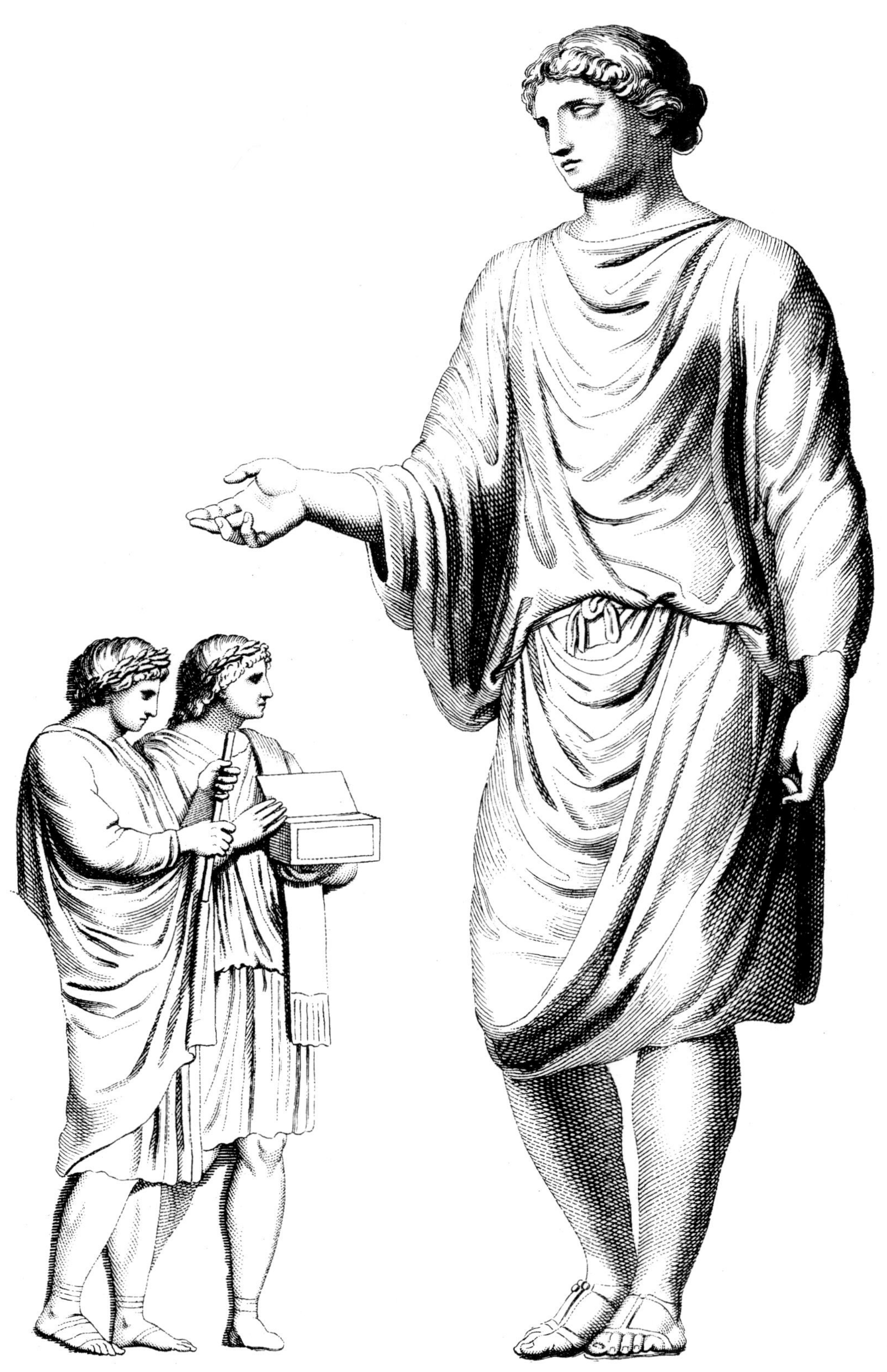

Roman female dress | Römisches Frauengewand | Abito femminile romano | Vêtement romain féminin | Vestido romano de mujer

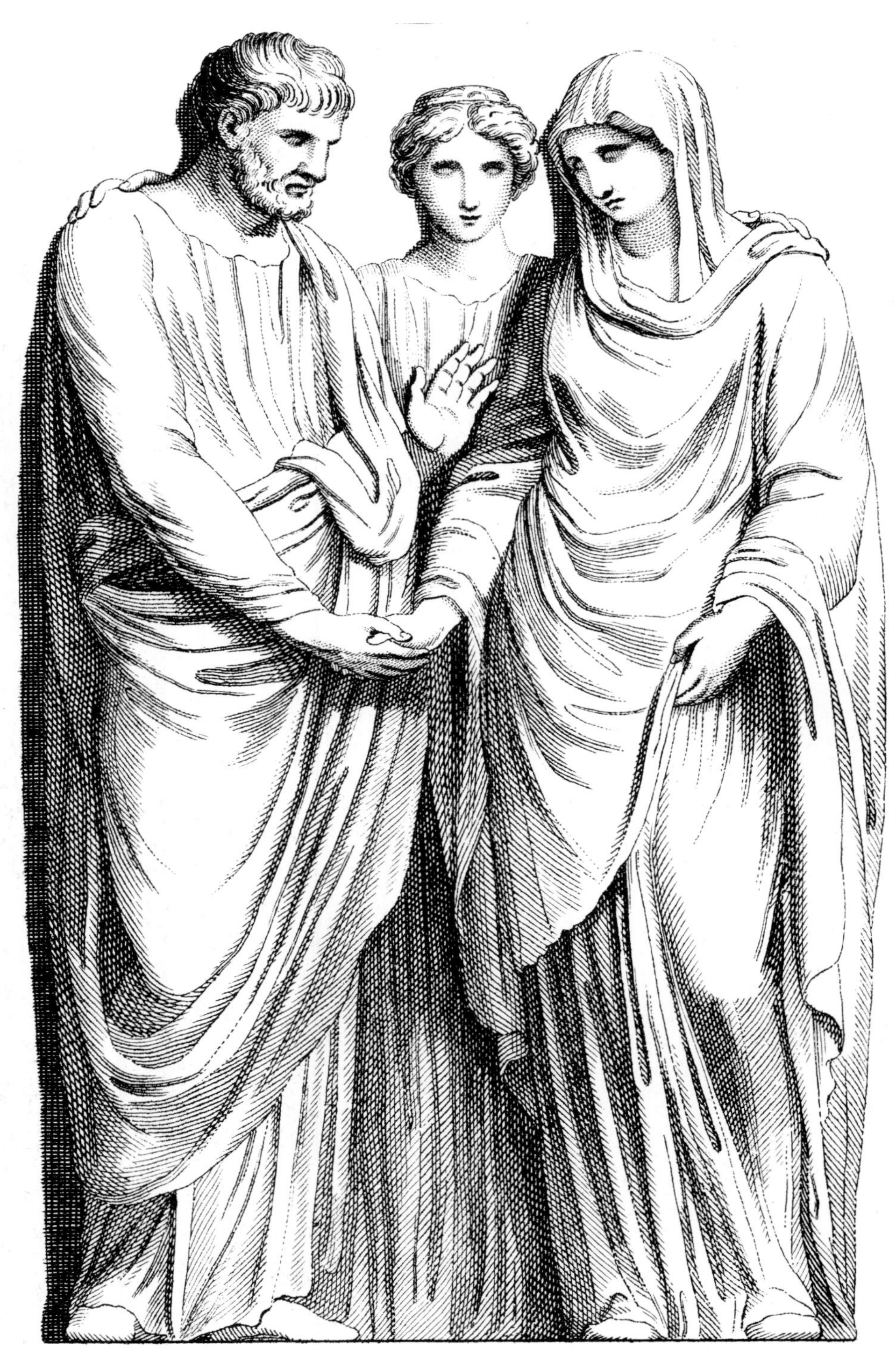

Roman male and female dress

Römisches Männer- und Frauengewand

Abito maschile e femminile romano

Vêtements romains masculin et féminin

Vestidos romanos de hombre y de mujer

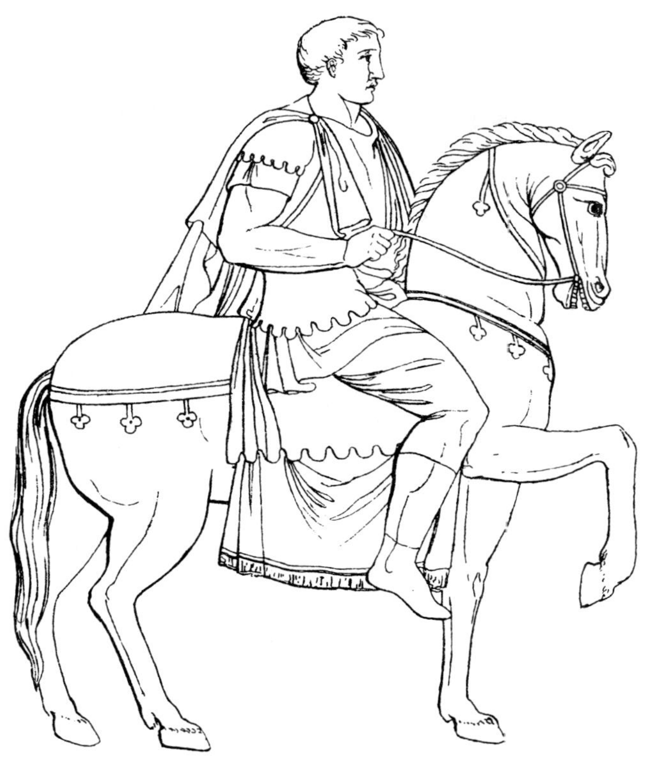

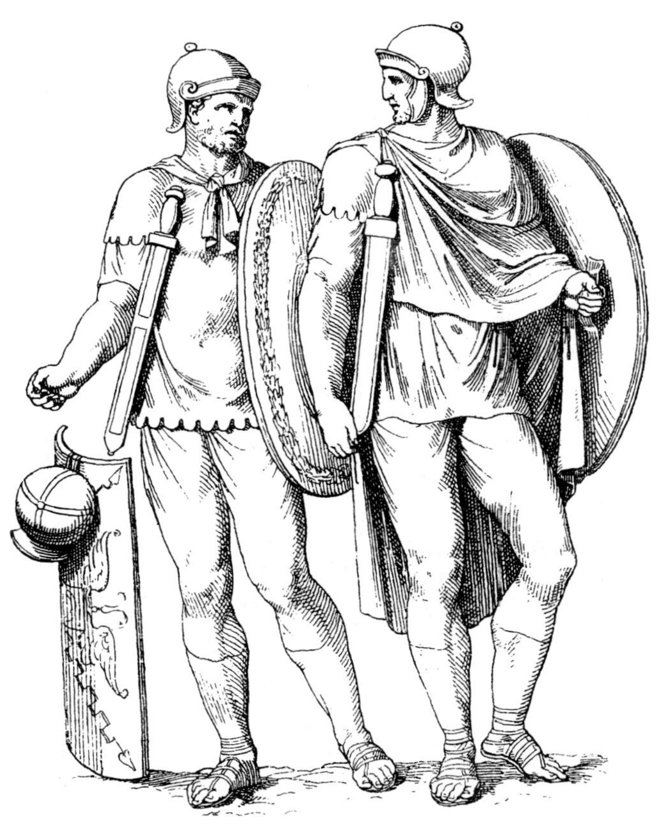

a	Roman Emperor	Römischer Kaiser	Imperatore romano	Empereur romain	Emperador romano
b	Roman soldiers, c. 400 AD	Römische Soldaten, um 400 n. Chr.	Soldati romani, ca. 400 d.C.	Soldats romains, vers 400 ap. J-C	Soldados romanos, hacia el año 400

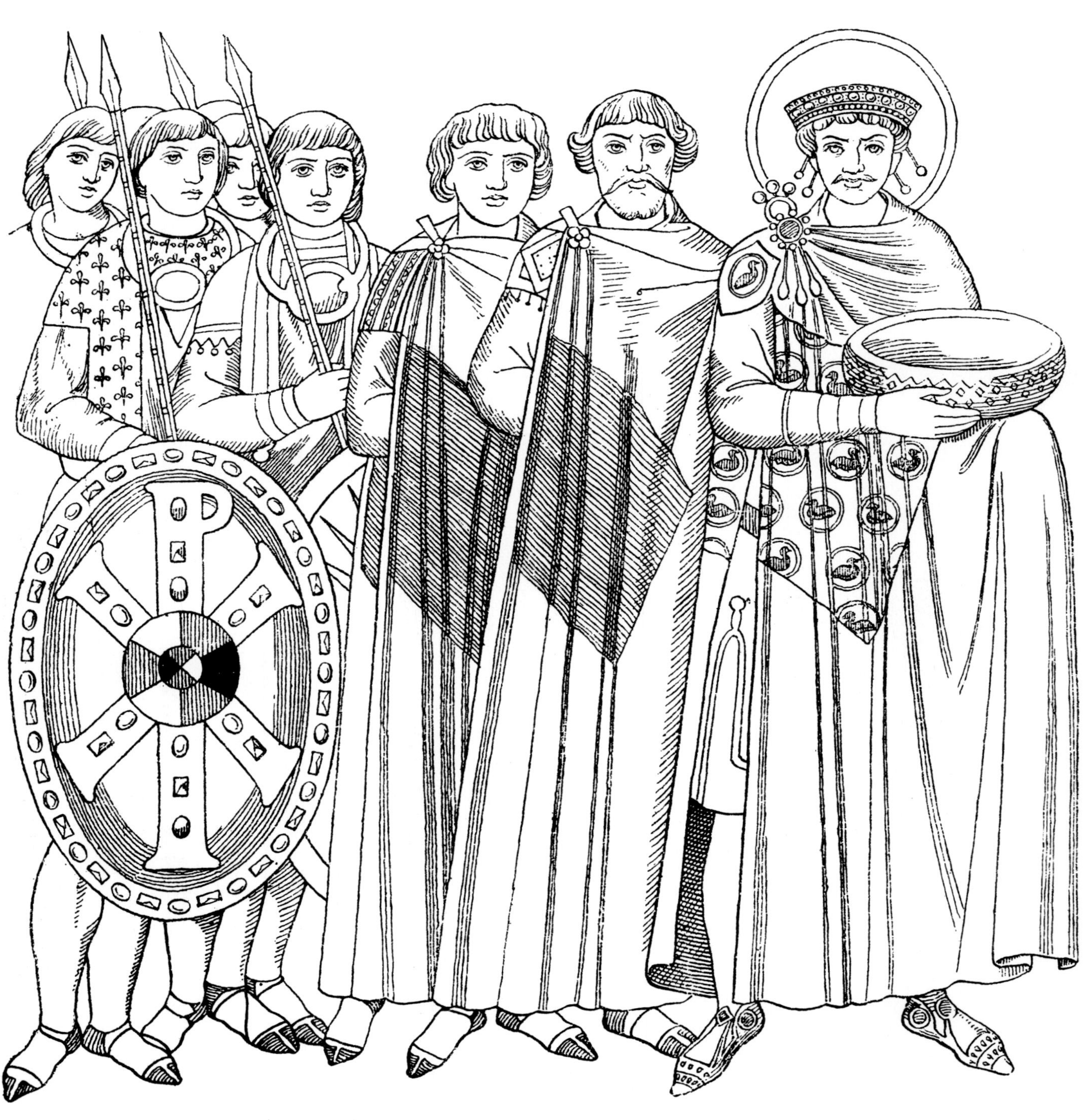

Byzanthine Emperor with his courtiers, 6th century AD

Byzantinischer Kaiser mit seinen Höflingen, 6. Jahrhundert n. Chr.

Imperatore bizantino con i suoi cortigiani, VI secolo d.C.

Empereur byzantin et sa Cour, VIe siècle ap. J-C

Emperador bizantino y cortesanos, siglo VI

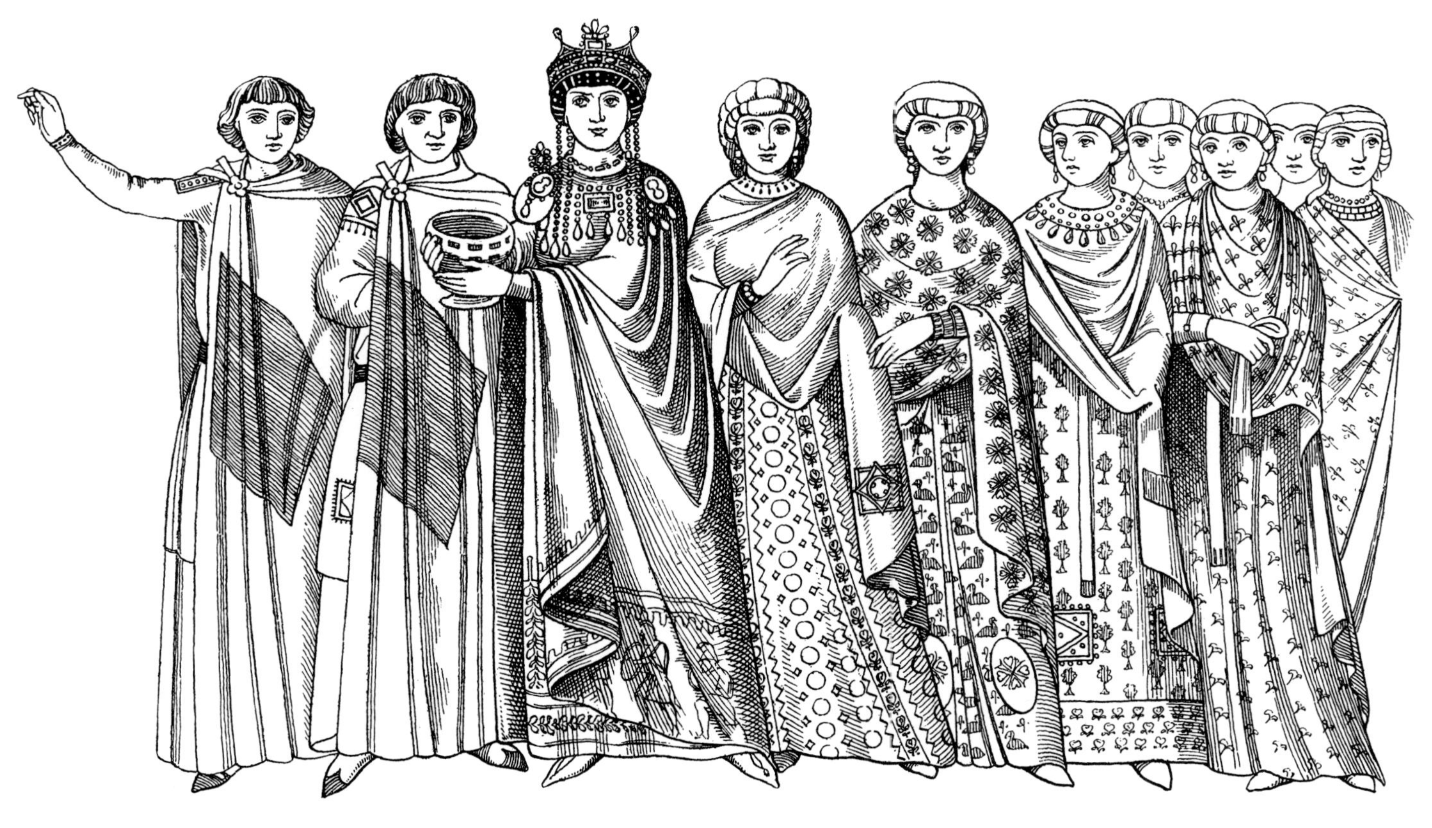

Byzanthine Empress with court ladies, 6th century AD

Byzantinische Kaiserin mit Hofdamen, 6. Jahrhundert n. Chr.

Imperatrice bizantina con le dame di corte, VI secolo d.C.

Impératrice byzantine avec les dames de la Cour, VIe siècle ap. J-C

Emperatriz bizantina y cortesanas, siglo VI

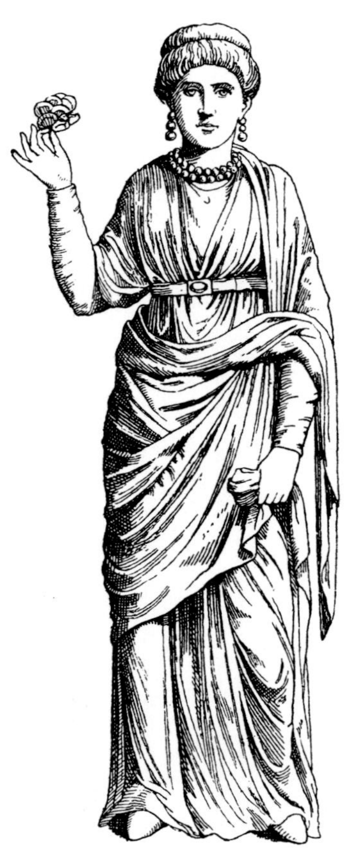

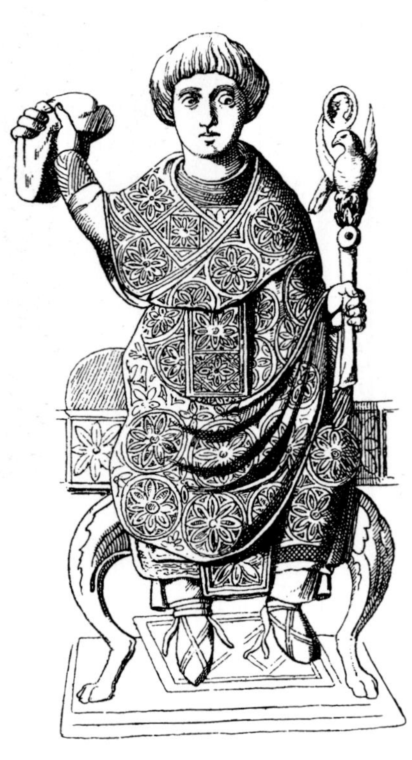

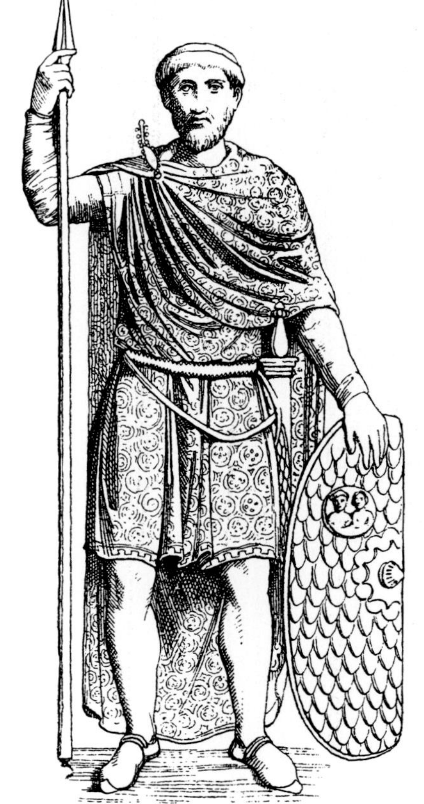

a	Byzantine Princess, 6th century AD	Byzantinische Prinzessin, 6. Jahrhundert n. Chr.	Principessa bizantina, VI secolo d.C.	Princesse byzantine, VIe siècle ap. J-C	Princesa bizantina, siglo VI
b	Emperor, 6th century AD	Kaiser, 6. Jahrhundert n. Chr.	Imperatore, VI secolo d.C.	Empereur, VIe siècle ap. J-C	Emperador, siglo VI
c	Nobleman, 5th century AD	Adliger, 5. Jahrhundert n. Chr.	Nobiluomo, V secolo d.C.	Noble, Ve siècle ap. J-C	Noble, siglo V

Byzanthium

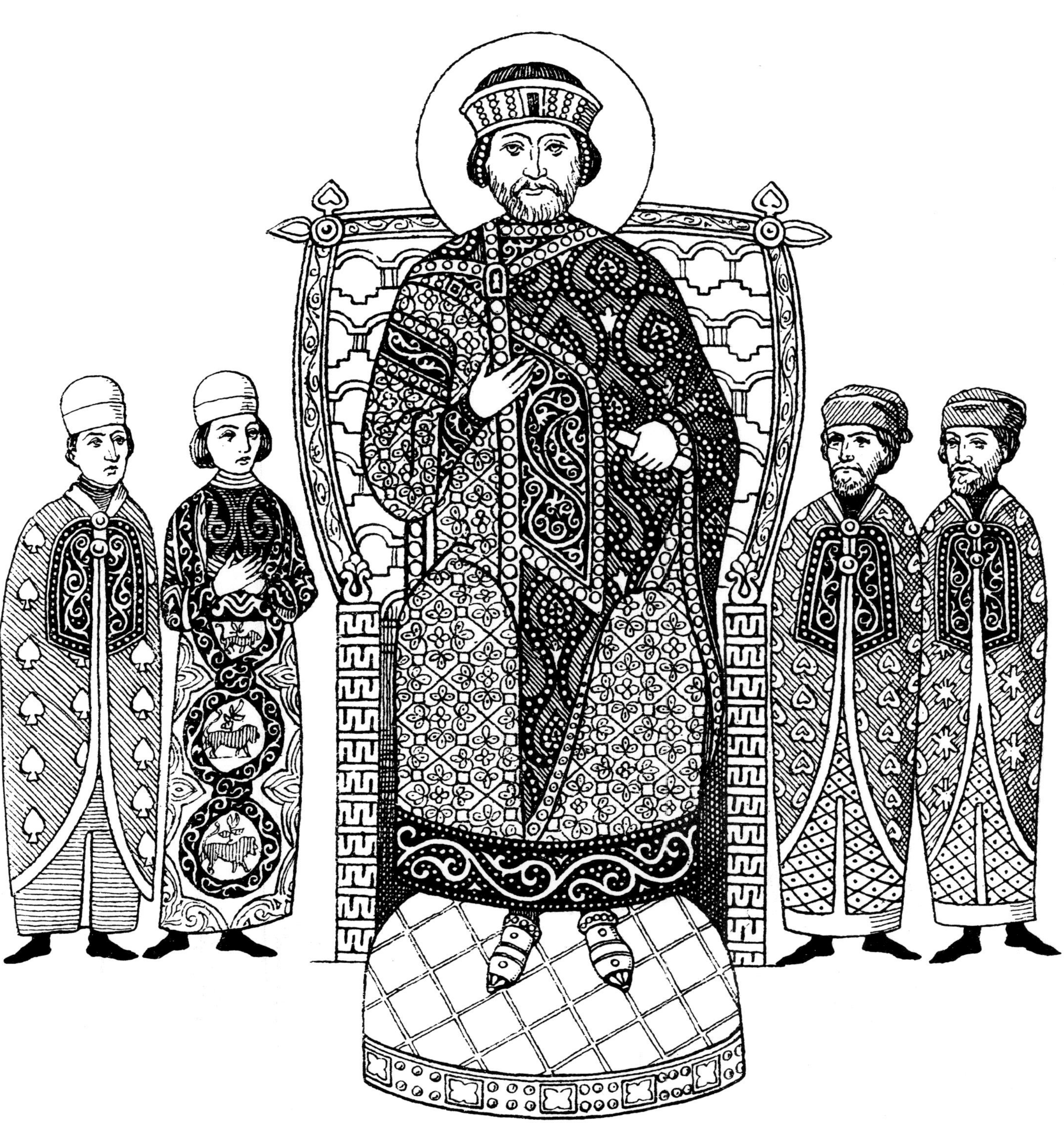

Byzanthine Emperor with courtiers, 11th century AD

Byzantinischer Kaiser mit Höflingen, 11. Jahrhundert n. Chr.

Imperatore bizantino con cortigiani, XI secolo d.C.

Empereur byzantin et sa Cour, XIe siècle ap. J-C

Emperador bizantino y cortesanos, siglo XI

Europe

Europa

Europa

Europe

Europa

ヨーロッパ

歐洲

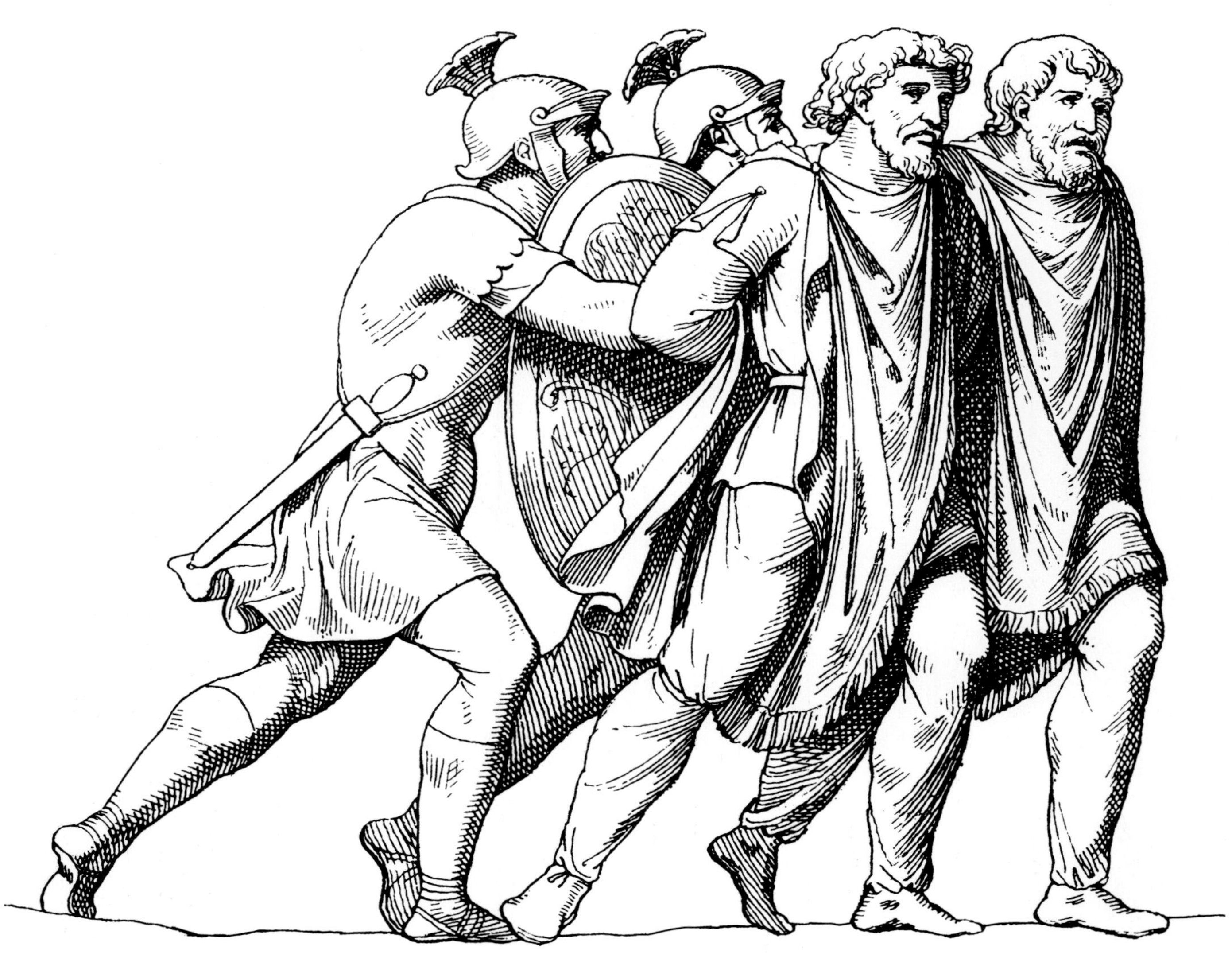

Germanic men with their Roman captors

Germanen mit ihren römischen Häschern

Uomini germanici catturati da romani

Germaniques capturés par les romains

Soldados romanos con prisioneros germánicos

200–300 AD

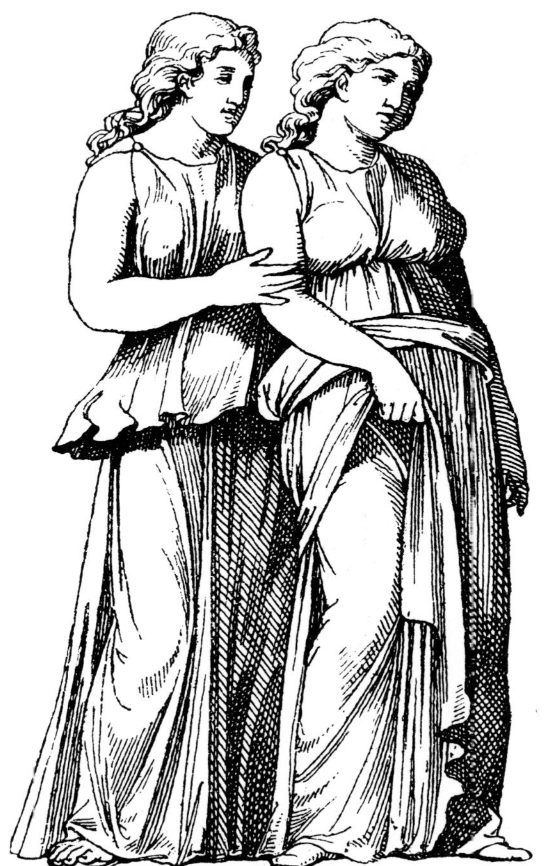

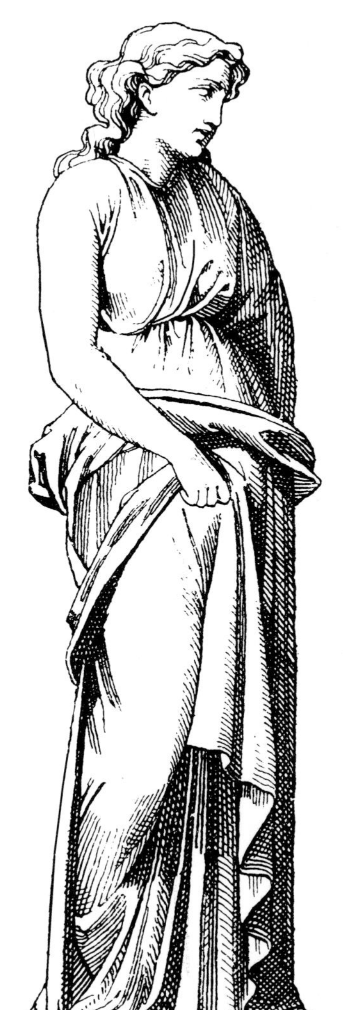

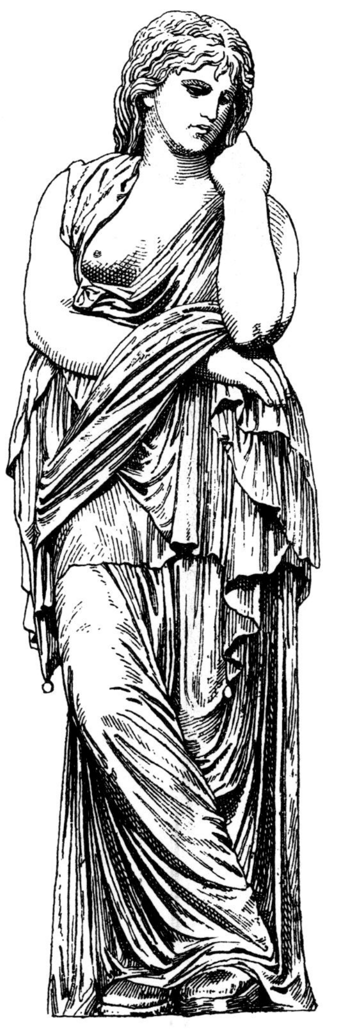

Germanic Female dress

Germanisches Frauengewand

Abito femminile germanico

Vêtement germanique féminin

Vestido germánico de mujer

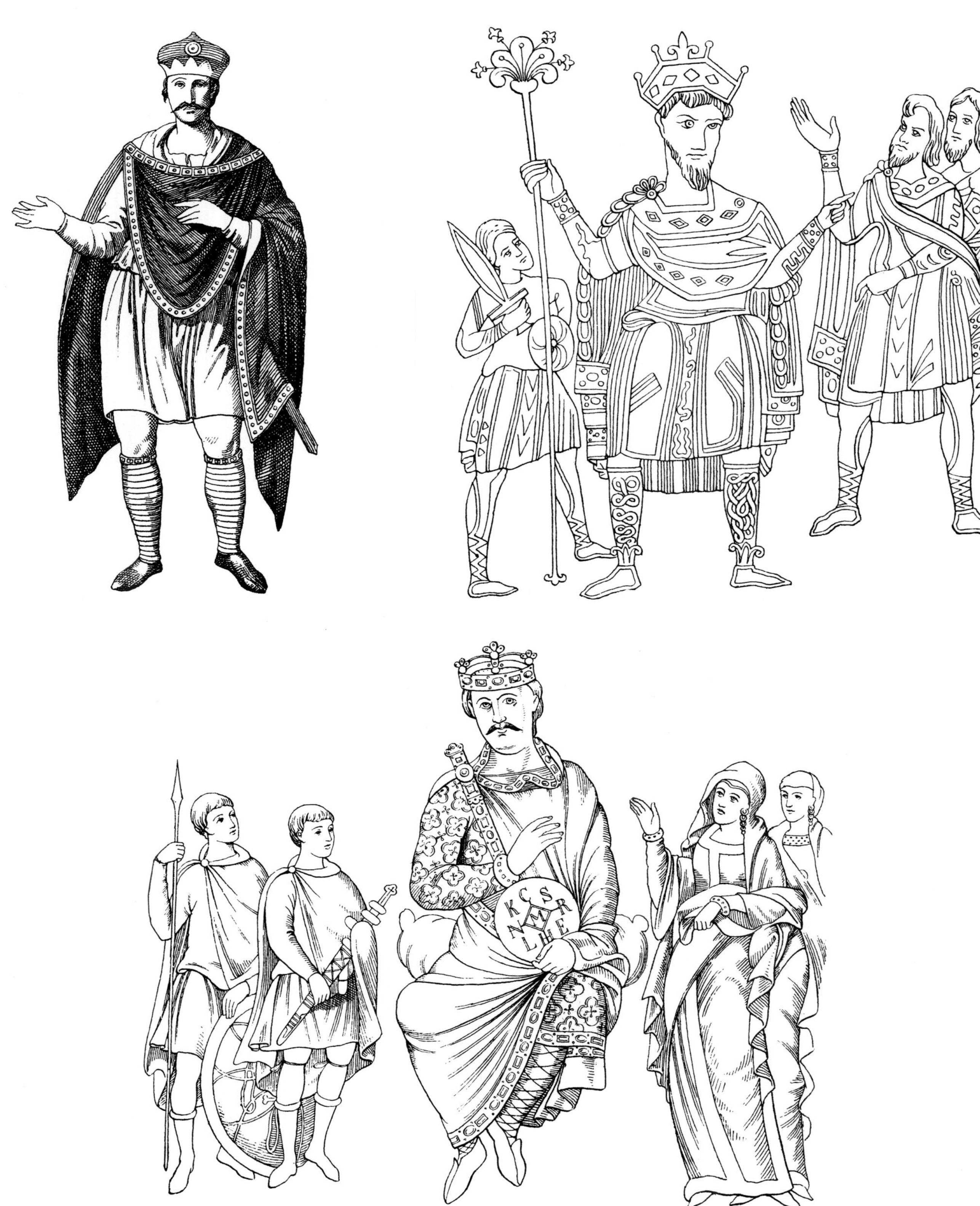

Charlemagne

Langobard King with courtiers, 7th century AD

Frankish King, 9th century AD

Karl der Große

Der König der Langobarden mit Höflingen, 7. Jahrhundert n. Chr.

Fränkischer König, 9. Jahrhundert n. Chr.

Carlo Magno

Re longobardo con cortigiani, VII secolo d.C.

Re franco, IX secolo d.C.

Charlemagne

Le Roi Langobard et sa Cour, VIIe siècle ap. J-C

Roi Franc, IXe siècle ap. J-C

Carlomagno

Rey lombardo y cortesanos, siglo VII

Rey franco, siglo IX

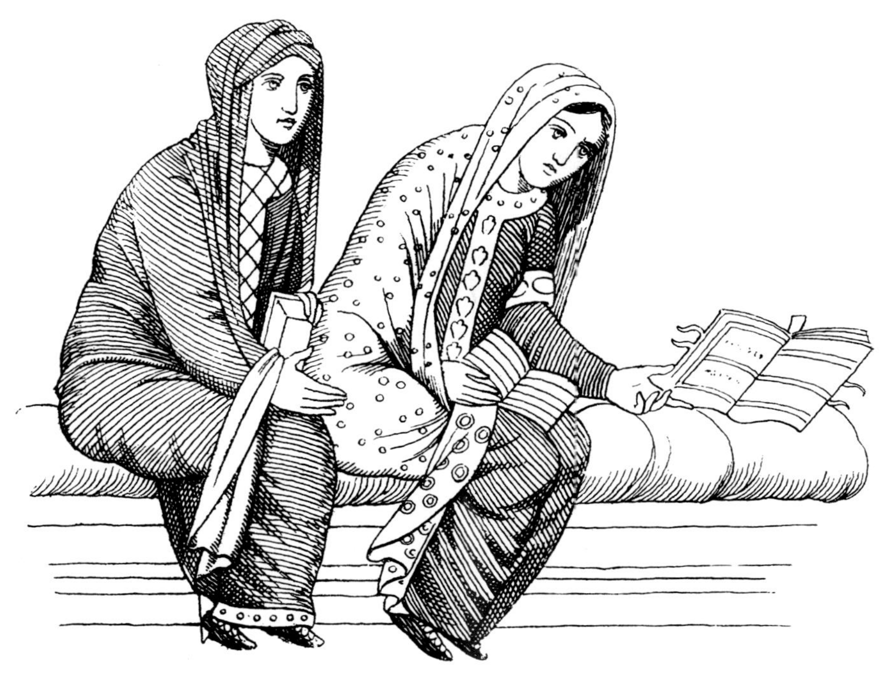

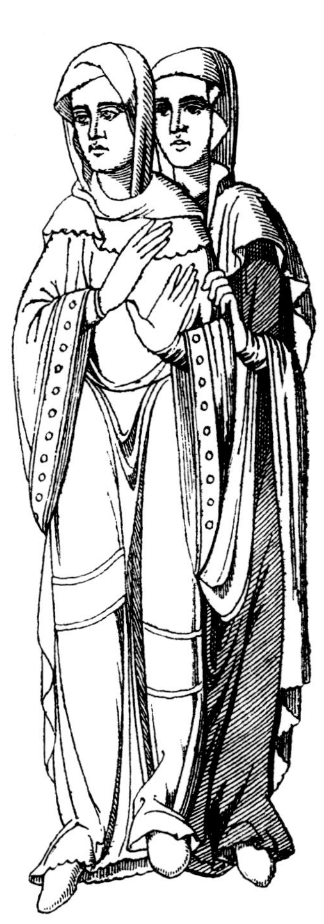

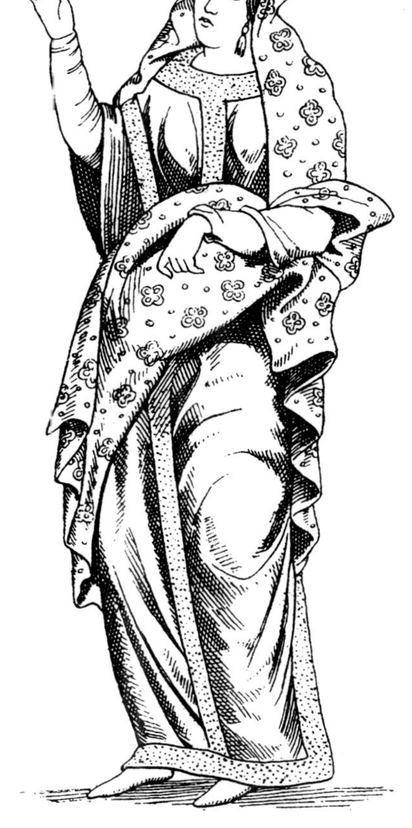

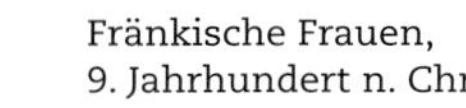

Frankish ladies, 9th century AD

Fränkische Frauen, 9. Jahrhundert n. Chr.

Donne franche, IX secolo d.C.

Femmes Franques, IXe siècle ap. J-C

Damas francas, siglo IX

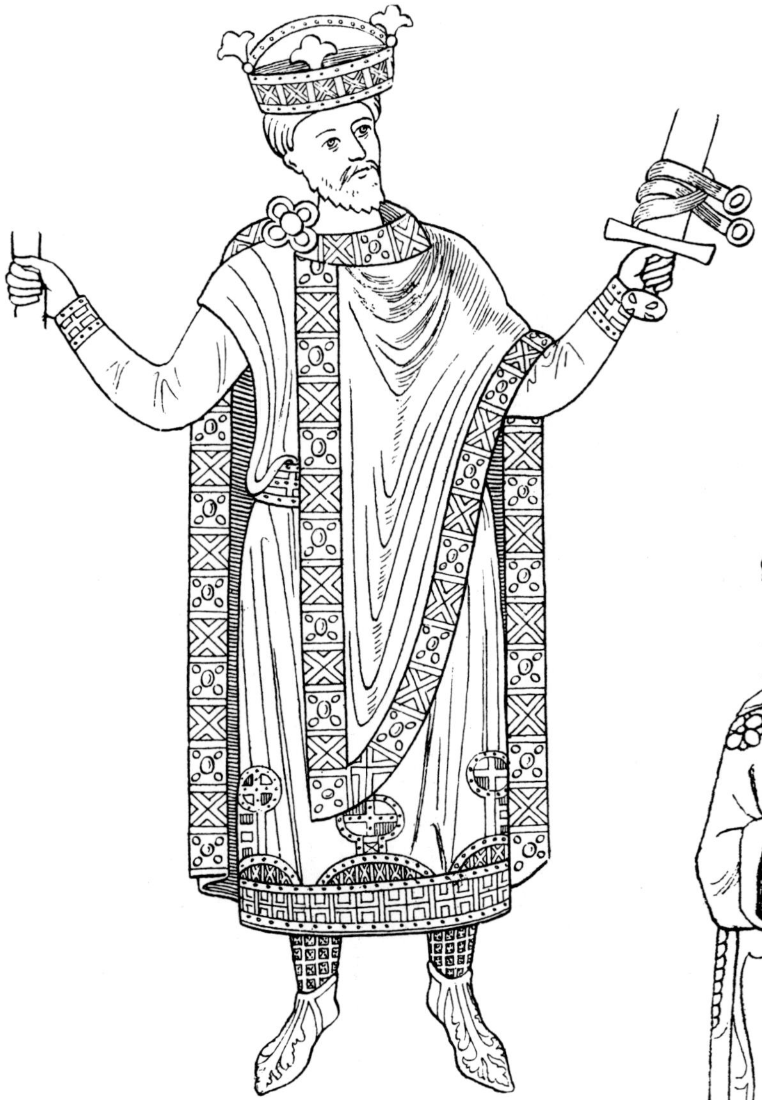

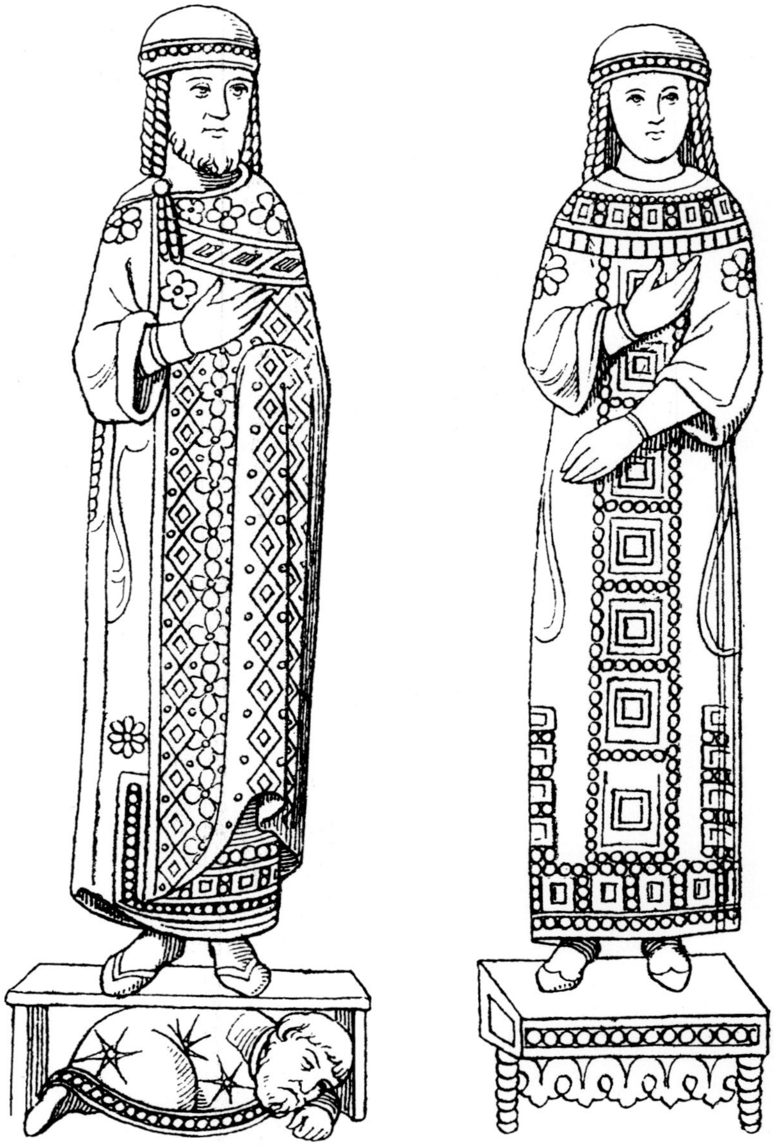

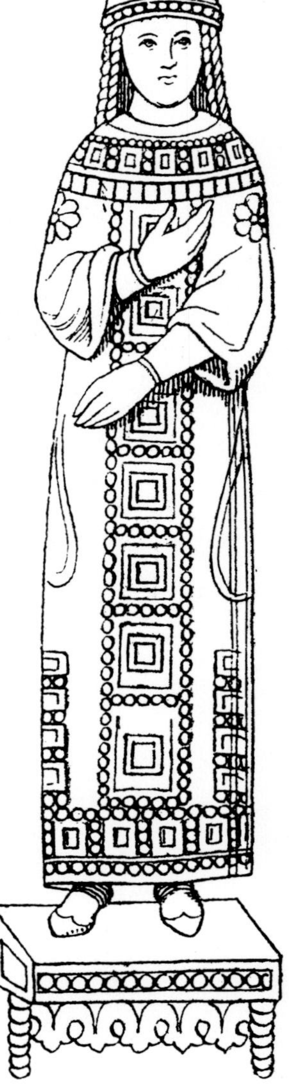

a	King Henry II, c. 1014	König Henry II., um 1014	Re Enrico II, ca. 1014	Roi Henry II, vers 1014	El rey Enrique II, en 1014
b	10th century Emperor and Empress in Greek dress	Kaiser und Kaiserin aus dem 10. Jahrhundert in griechischen Gewändern	Imperatore ed Imperatrice del x secolo in abito greco	Empereur et Impératrice du xe siècle en costume grec	Emperador y emperatriz con trajes griegos, siglo x

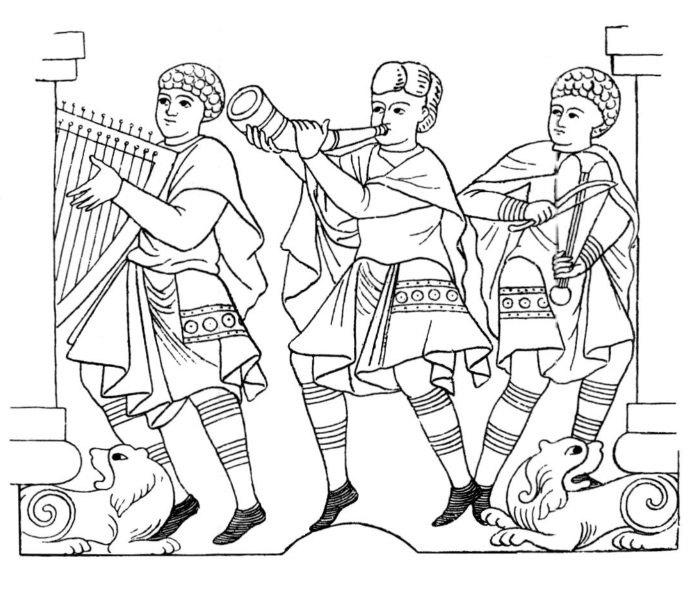

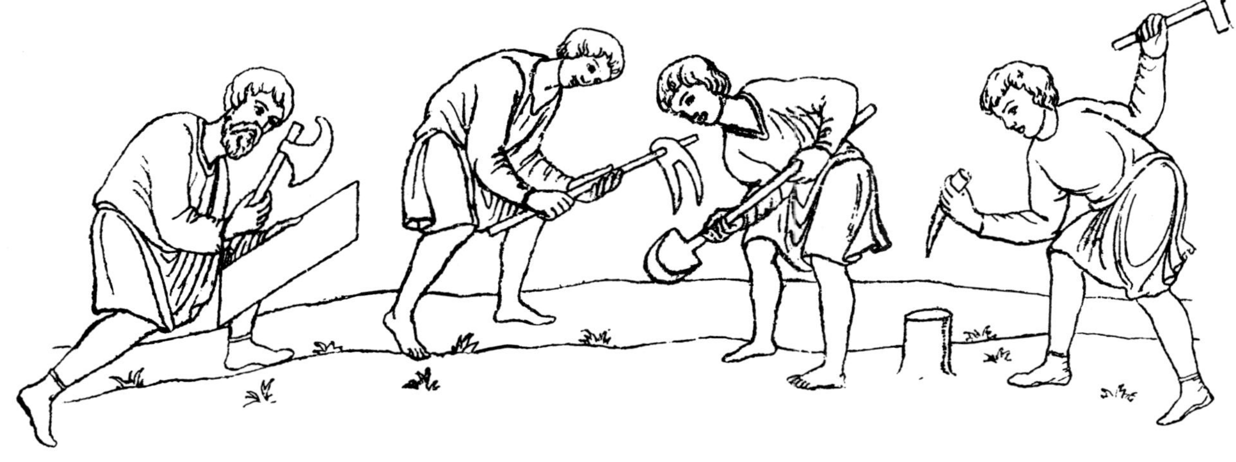

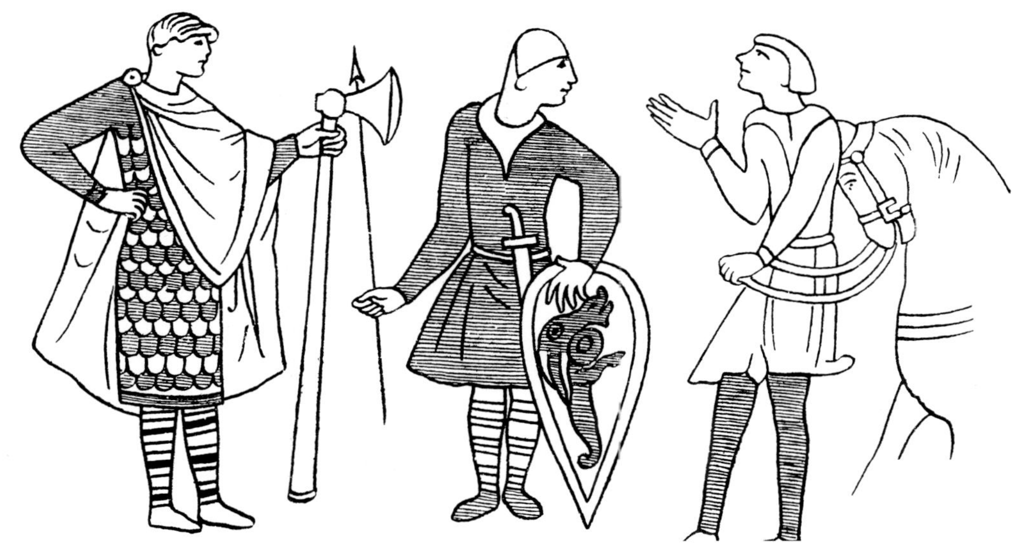

a	Germanic young men, c. 1000 AD	Junge Germanen, um 1000 n. Chr.	Giovani germanici, ca. 1000 d.C.	Jeunes gens germaniques, vers 1000 ap. J-C	Jóvenes germánicos, hacia el año 1000
b	North European workers, 11th century	Nordeuropäische Arbeiter, 11. Jahrhundert	Operai del nord d'Europa, XI secolo	Serfs d'Europe du Nord, XIe siècle	Trabajadores del norte de Europa, siglo XI
c	Norse men, c. 1070	Skandinavier, um 1070	Scandinavi, ca. 1070	Scandinaves, vers 1070	Escandinavos, hacia 1070

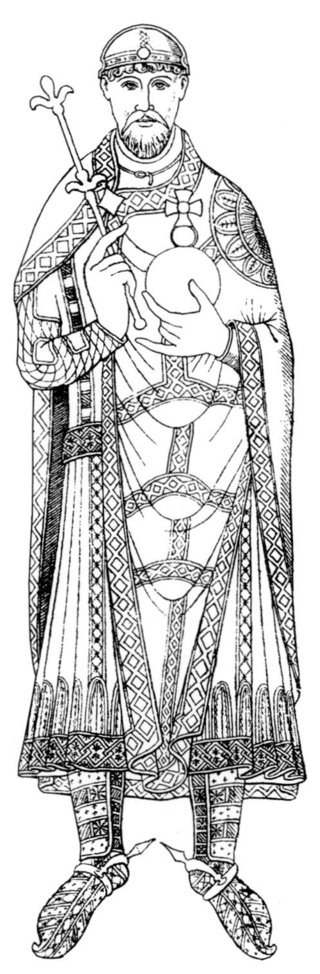

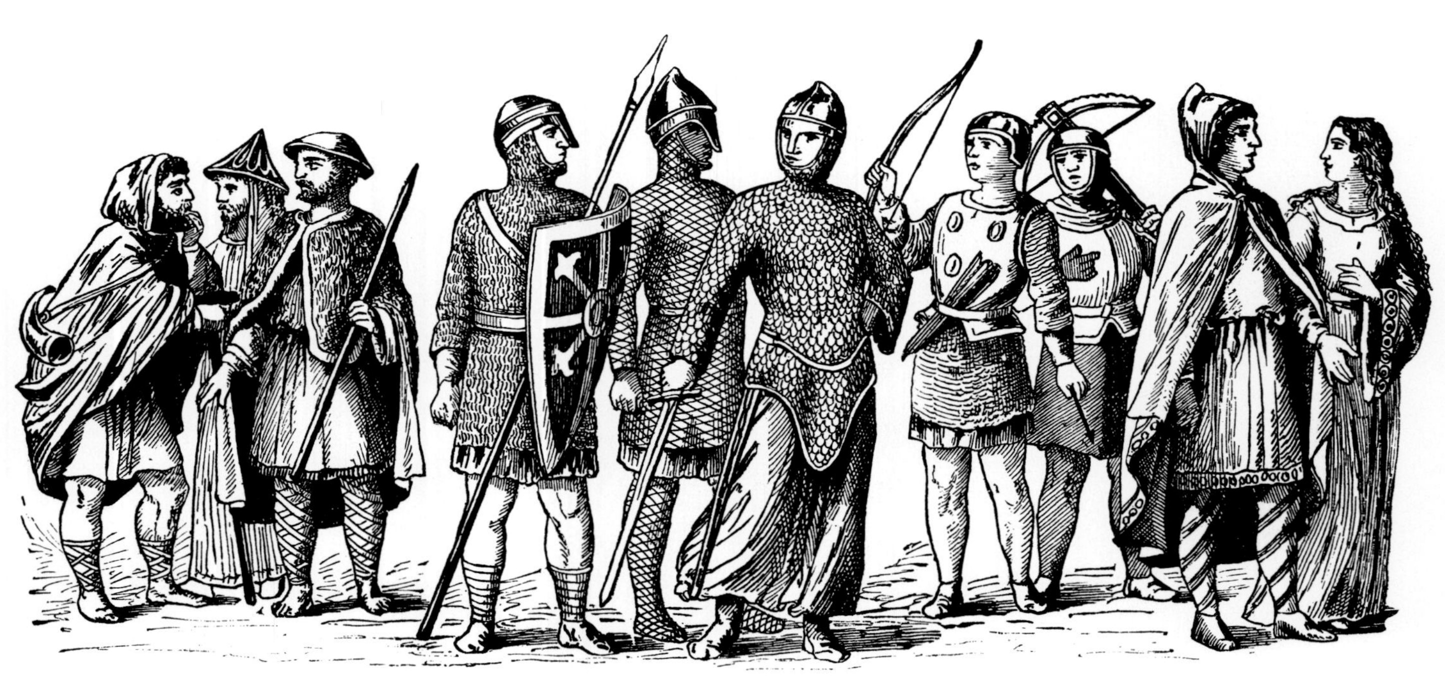

a	German King, c. 1070	Deutscher König, um 1070	Re tedesco, ca. 1070	Roi allemand, vers 1070	Rey alemán, hacia 1070
b	Norman Costumes	Normannische Trachten	Costumi normanni	Costumes normands	Trajes normandos

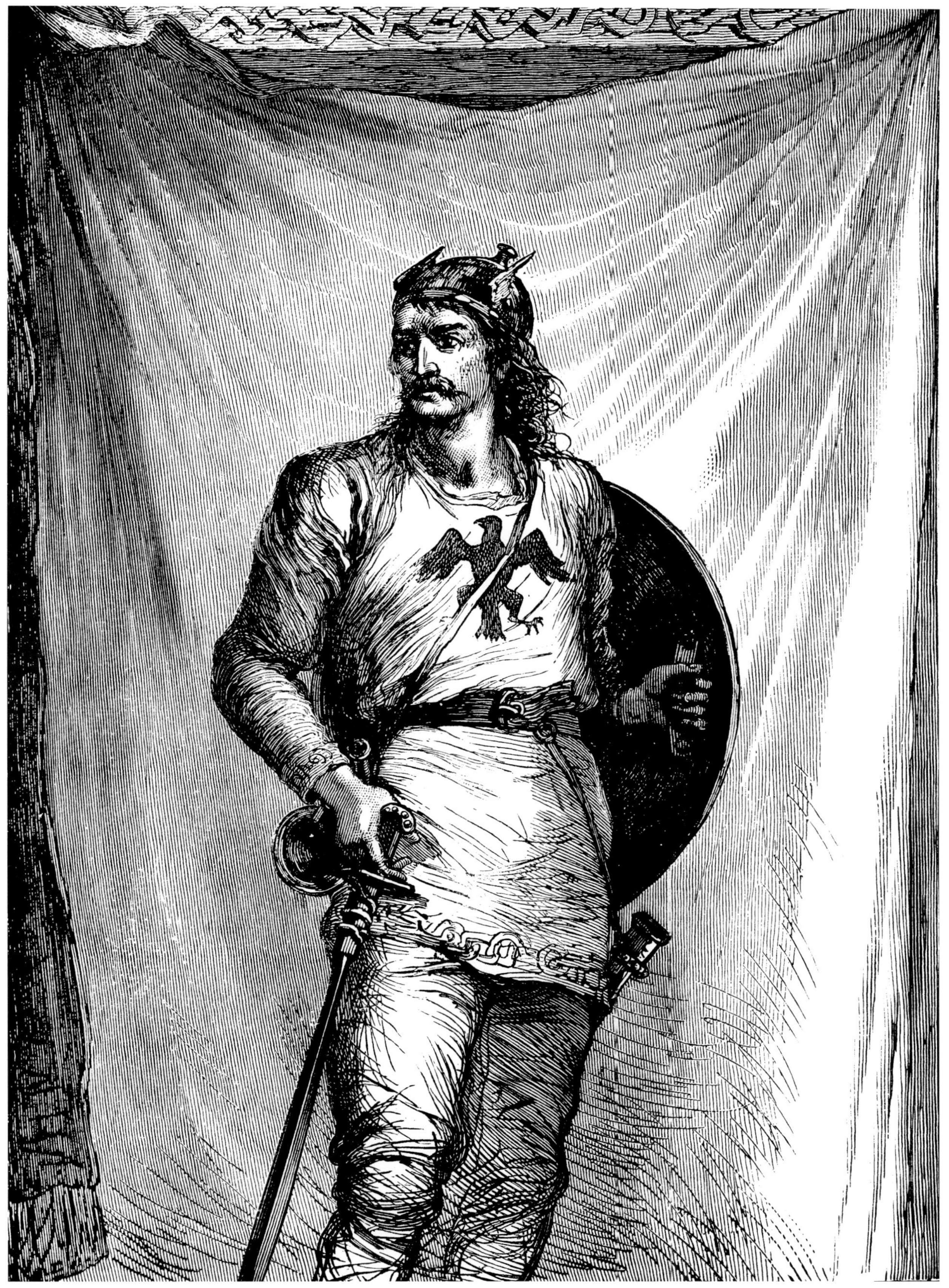

Viking Wikinger Vichingo Viking Víkingo

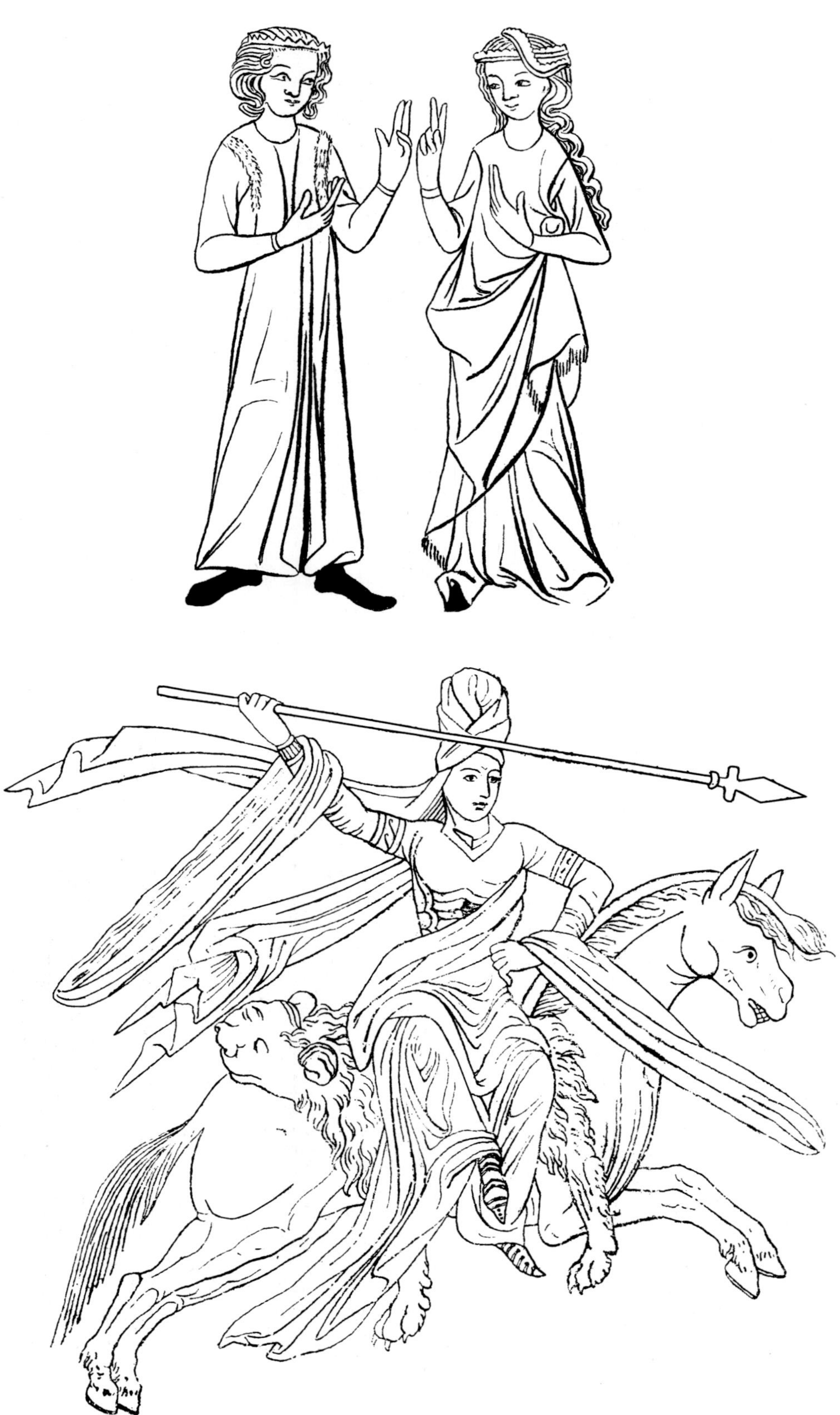

a	German noble couple, 13th century	Deutsches Adligenpaar, 13. Jahrhundert	Coppia di nobili tedeschi, XIII secolo	Couple de nobles allemands, XIIIe siècle	Pareja de nobles alemanes, siglo XIII
b	12th-century phantasy image	Fantasiebild aus dem 12. Jahrhundert	Immagine fantastica del XII secolo	Image fantaisiste du XIIe siècle	Imagen fantástica del siglo XII

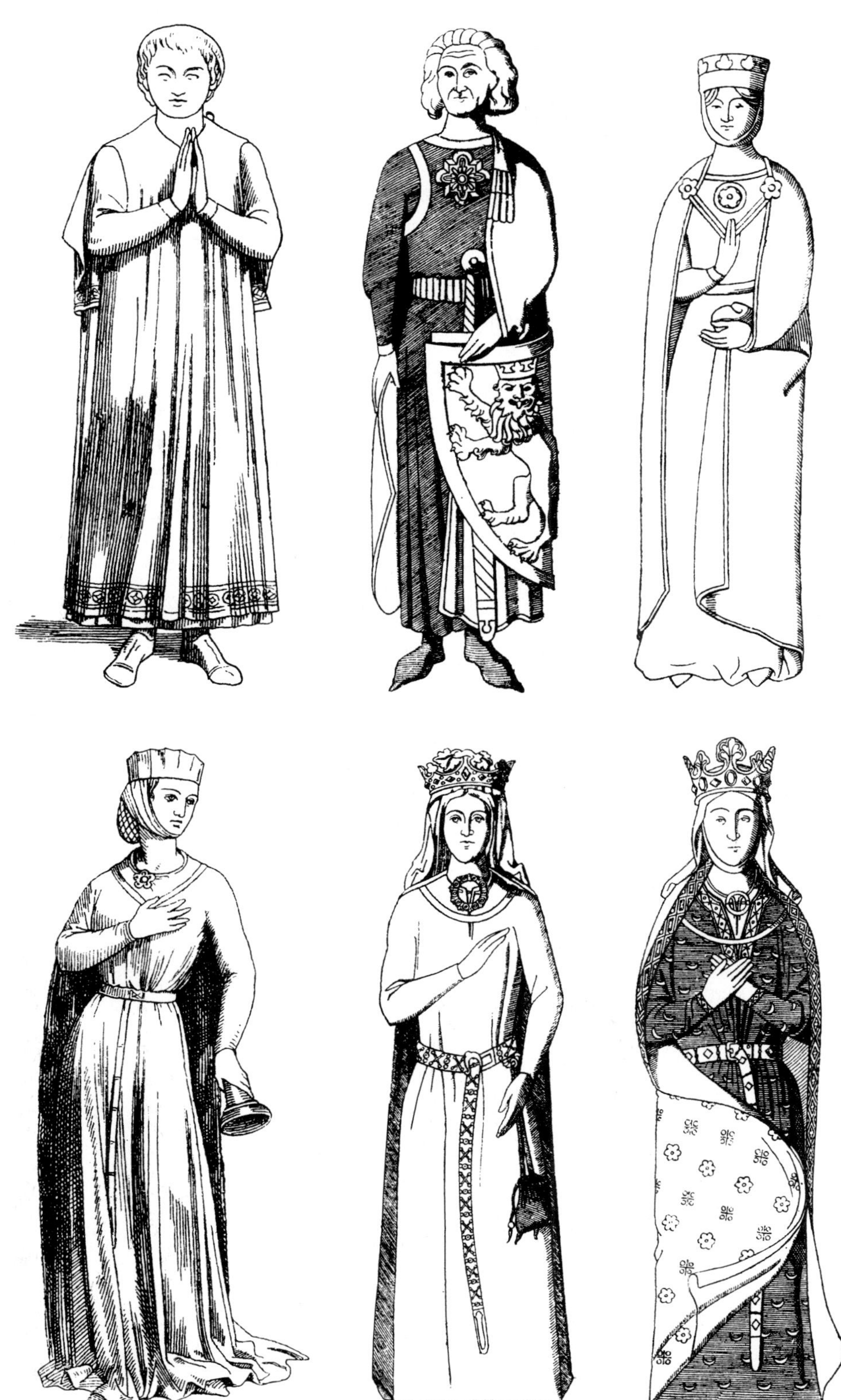

a	French and German nobles, early 13th century	Französische und deutsche Adlige, frühes 13. Jahrhundert	Nobili francesi e tedeschi, inizio del XIII secolo	Nobles français et allemands, début du XIIIe siècle	Nobles franceses y alemanes de principios del siglo XIII
b	French and English noblewomen, early 13th century	Französische und englische Frauen aus dem Adel, frühes 13. Jahrhundert	Nobildonne francesi ed inglesi, inizio del XIII secolo	Femmes de la noblesse française et anglaise, début du XIIIe siècle	Damas de la nobleza francesa e inglesa de principios del siglo XIII

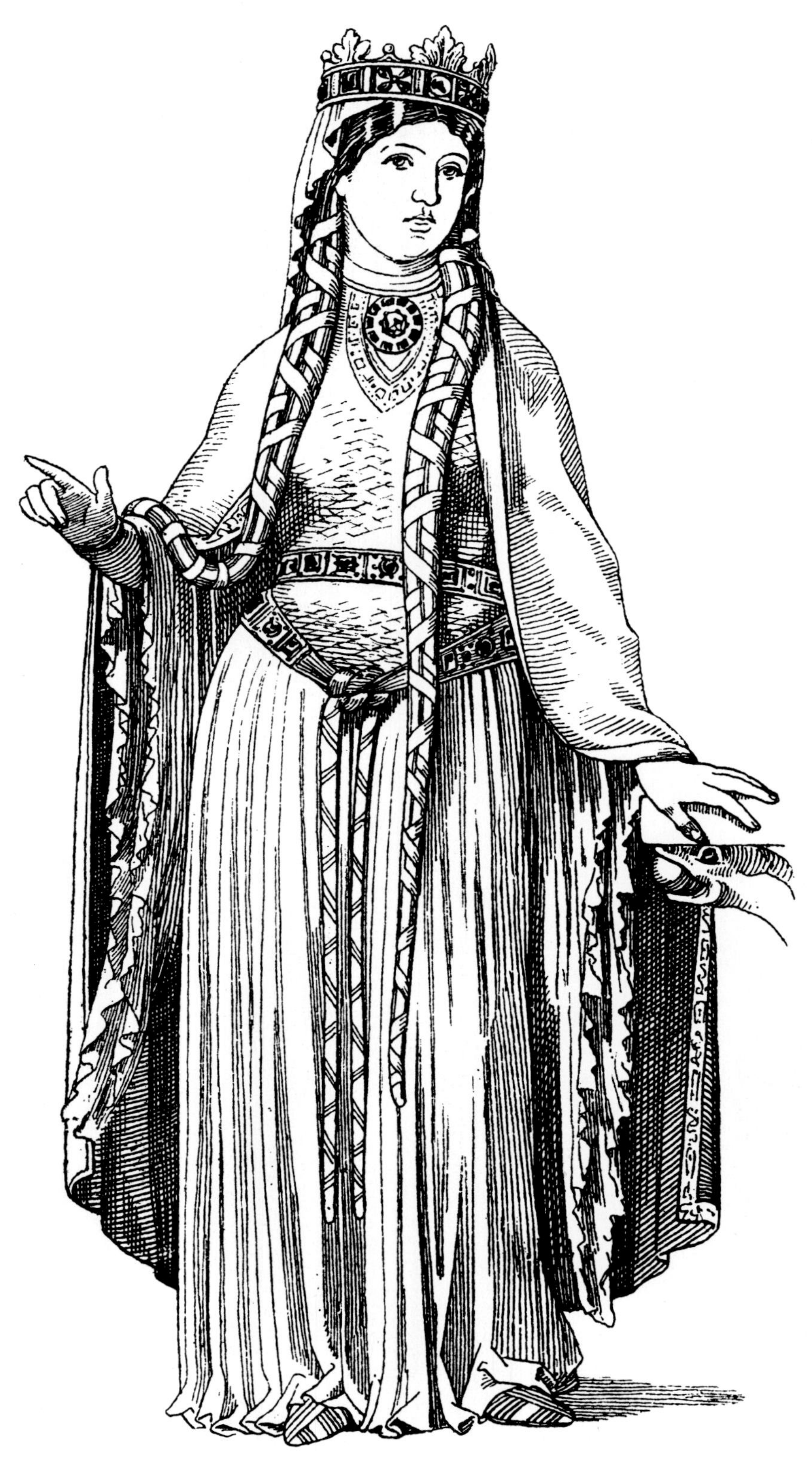

French lady, 12th century

Französische Dame, 12. Jahrhundert

Dama francese, XII secolo

Dame française, XIIe siècle

Dama francesa, siglo XII

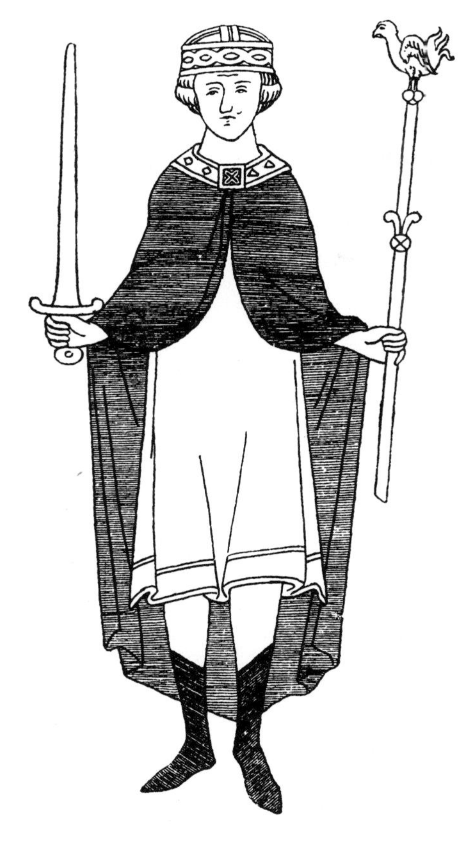

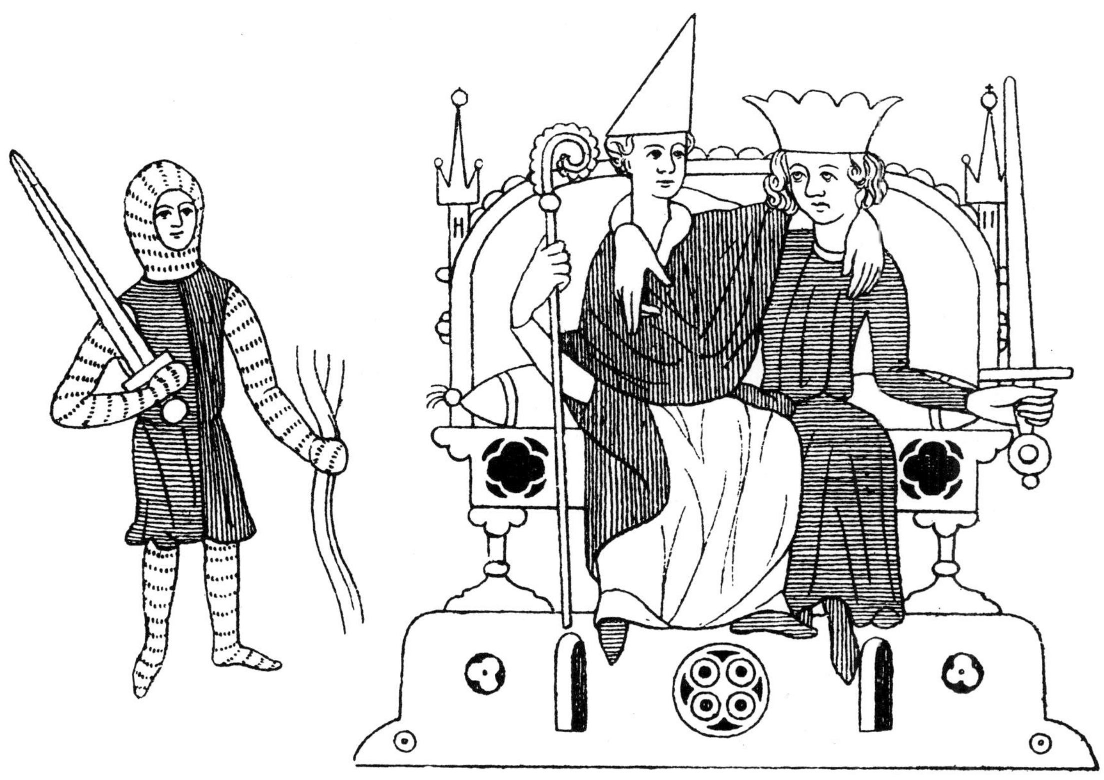

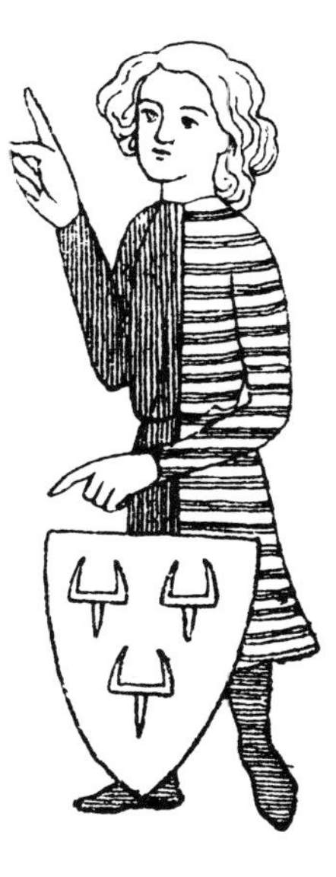

a	English King, c. 1090	Englischer König, um 1090	Re inglese, ca. 1090	Roi anglais, vers 1090	Rey inglés, hacia 1090
b	Pope, king and courtiers, c. 1200	Papst, König und Höflinge, um 1200	Papa, re e cortigiani, ca. 1200	Pape, Roi et courtisans, vers 1200	El Papa, el Rey y cortesanos, hacia 1200

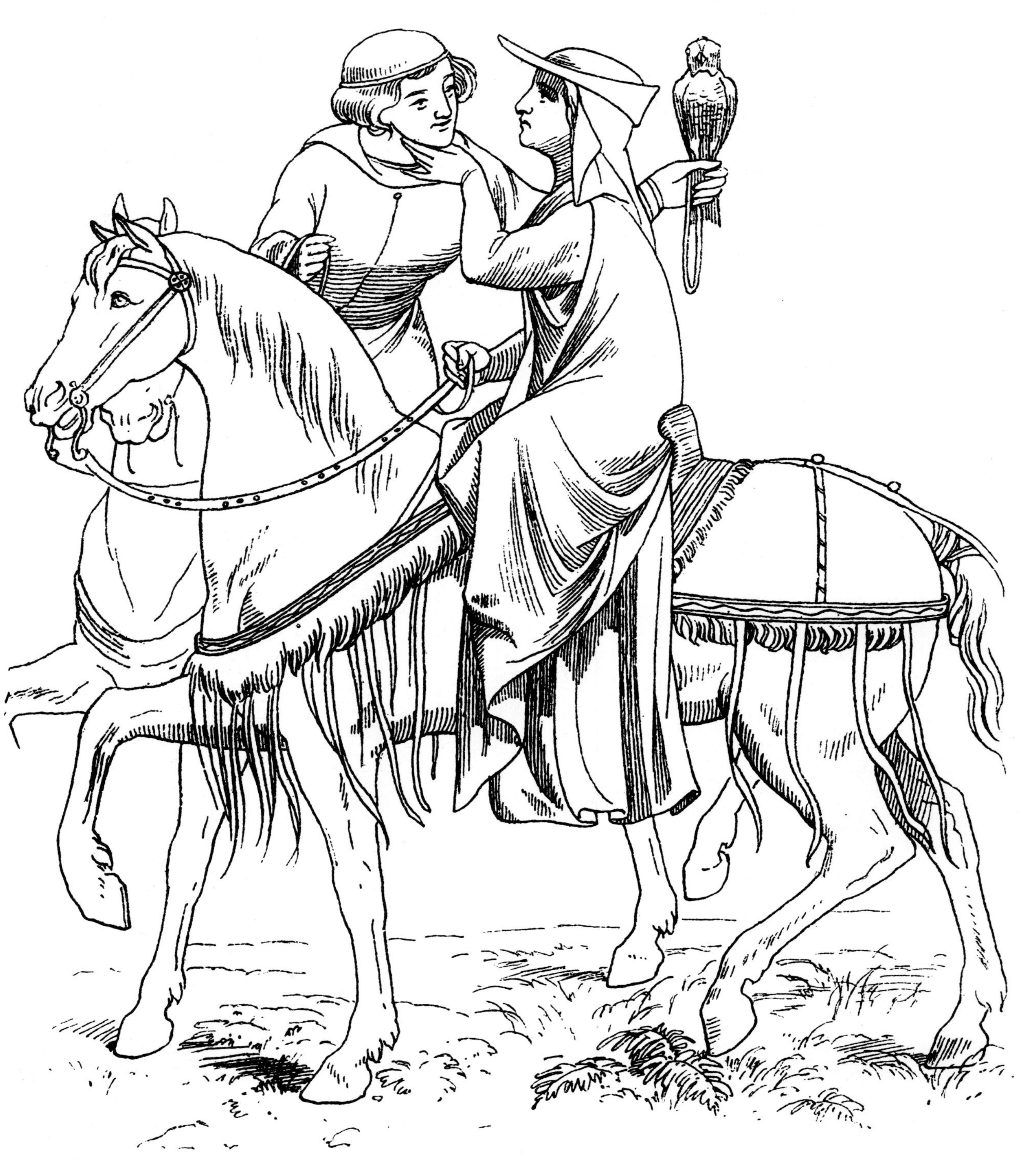

Hunting couple, early 14th century

Jagendes Paar, frühes 14. Jahrhundert

Coppia a caccia, inizio del XIV secolo

Couple de chasseurs, début du XIVe siècle

Pareja participando en una cacería a principios del siglo XIV

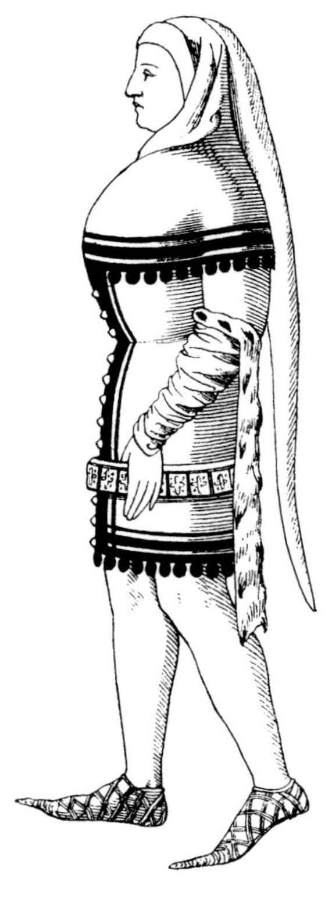

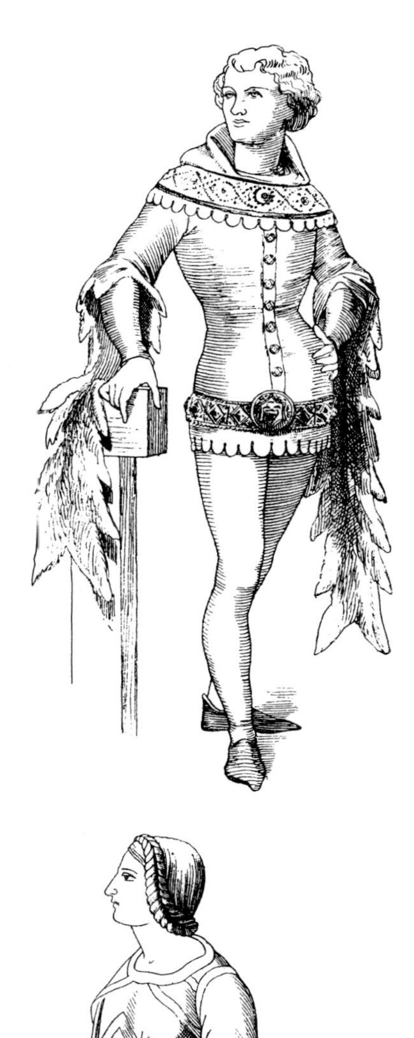

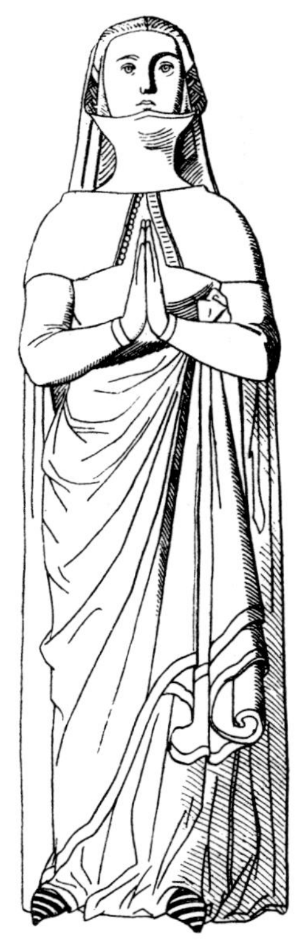

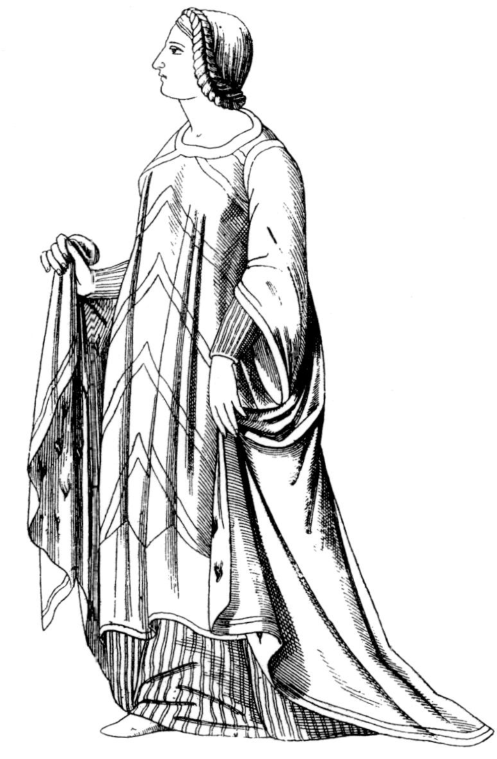

a	French nobleman, c. 1360	Französischer Adliger, um 1360	Nobiluomo francese, ca. 1360	Noble français, vers 1360	Noble francés, hacia el año 1360
b	Young French nobleman, c. 1380	Junger französischer Adliger, um 1380	Giovane nobile francese, ca. 1380	Jeune noble français, vers 1380	Joven noble francés, hacia 1380
c	Franch lady, c. 1350	Französische Dame, um 1350	Dama francese, ca. 1350	Dame française, vers 1350	Dama francesa, hacia el año 1350
d	Italian lady, c. 1350	Italienische Dame, um 1350	Dama italiana, ca. 1350	Dame italienne, vers 1350	Dama italiana, hacia 1350

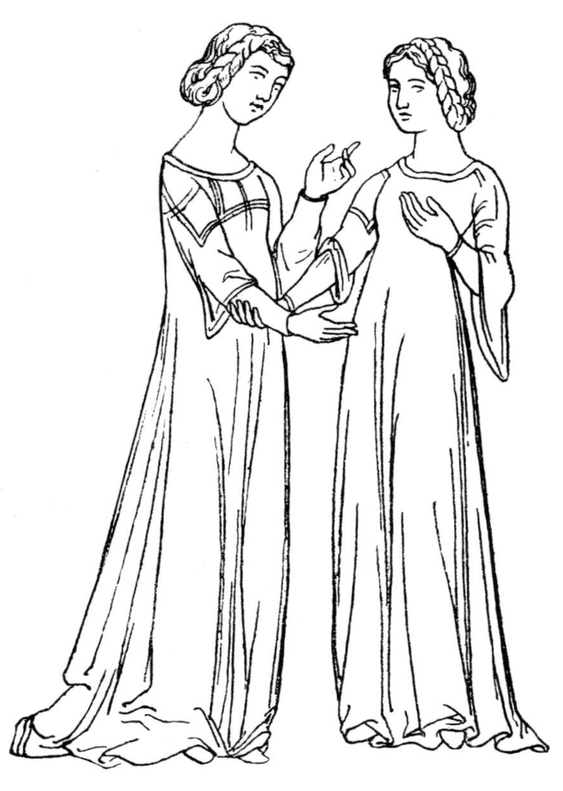

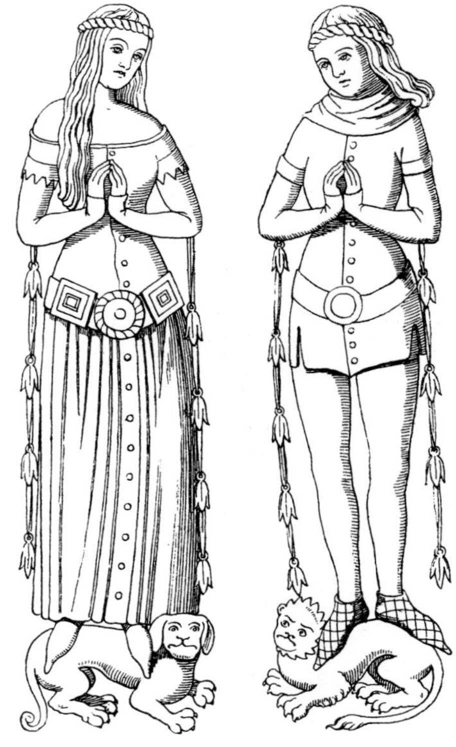

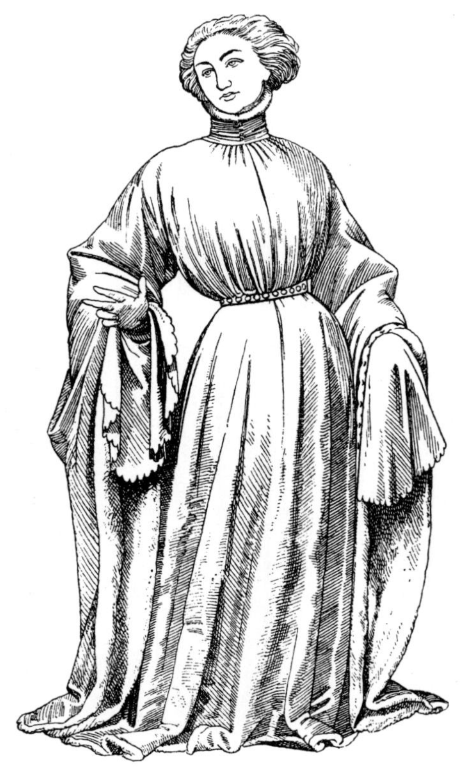

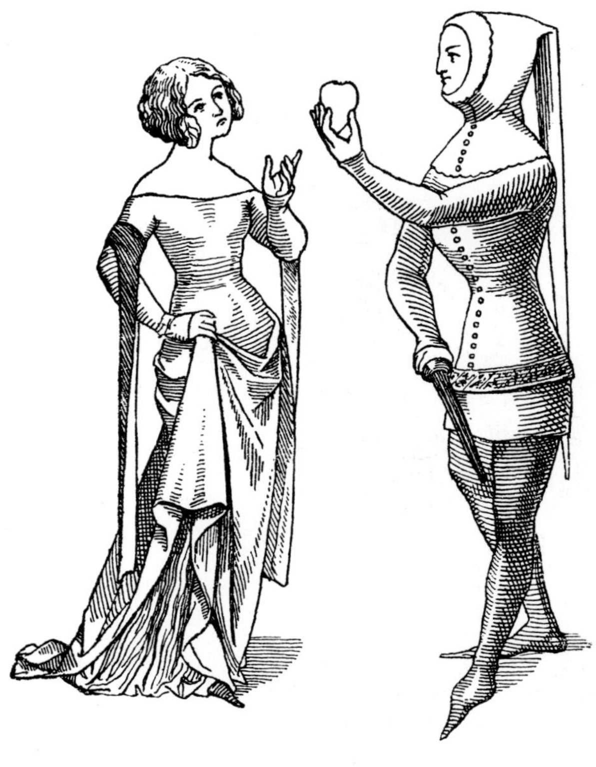

a	Italian ladies, c. 1350	Italienische Damen, 1350	Dame italiane, ca. 1350	Dames italiennes, 1350	Damas italianas, 1350
b	German couple, c. 1360	Deutsches Paar, 1360	Coppia tedesca, ca. 1360	Couple allemand, 1360	Pareja alemana, 1360
c	French aristocrat, 1380	Französische Aristokratin, 1380	Aristocratica francese, 1380	Aristocrate française, 1380	Aristócrata francesa, 1380
d	Aristocratic couple, c. 1360	Aristokratenpaar, um 1360	Coppia di aristocratici, ca. 1360	Couple d'aristocrates, vers 1360	Pareja aristocrática, hacia el año 1360

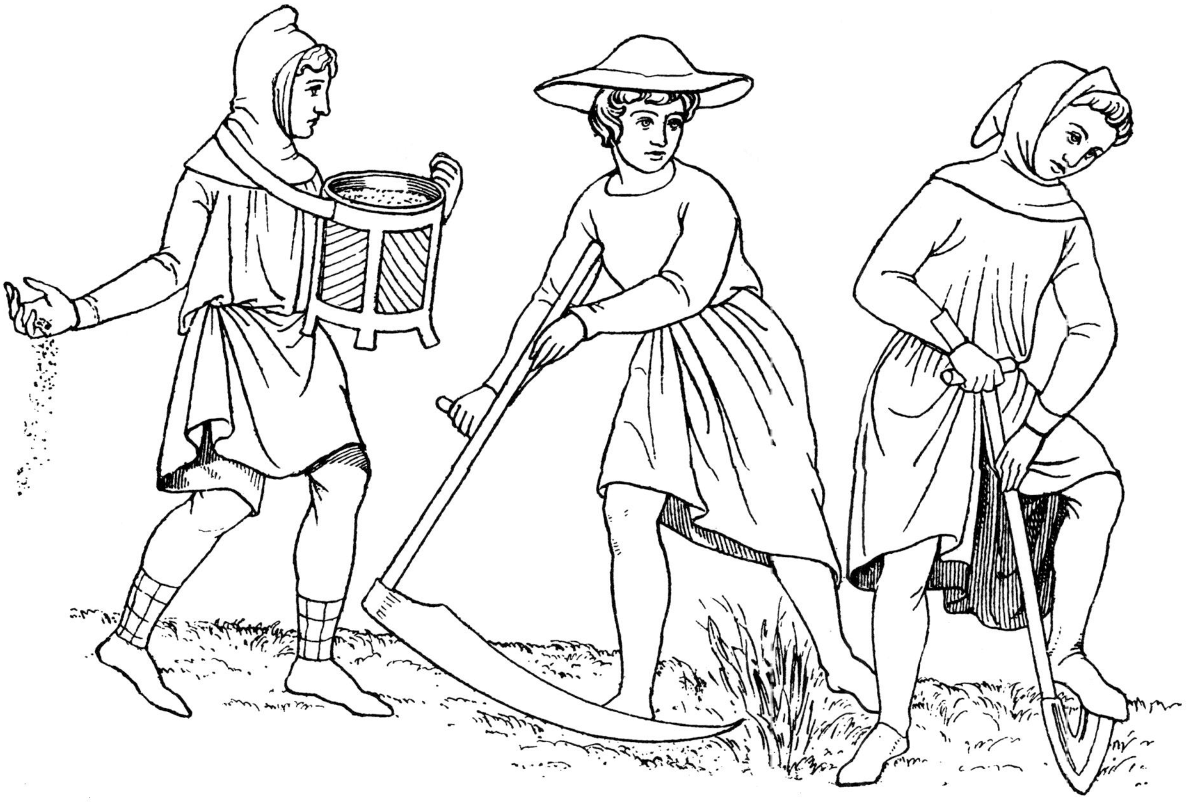

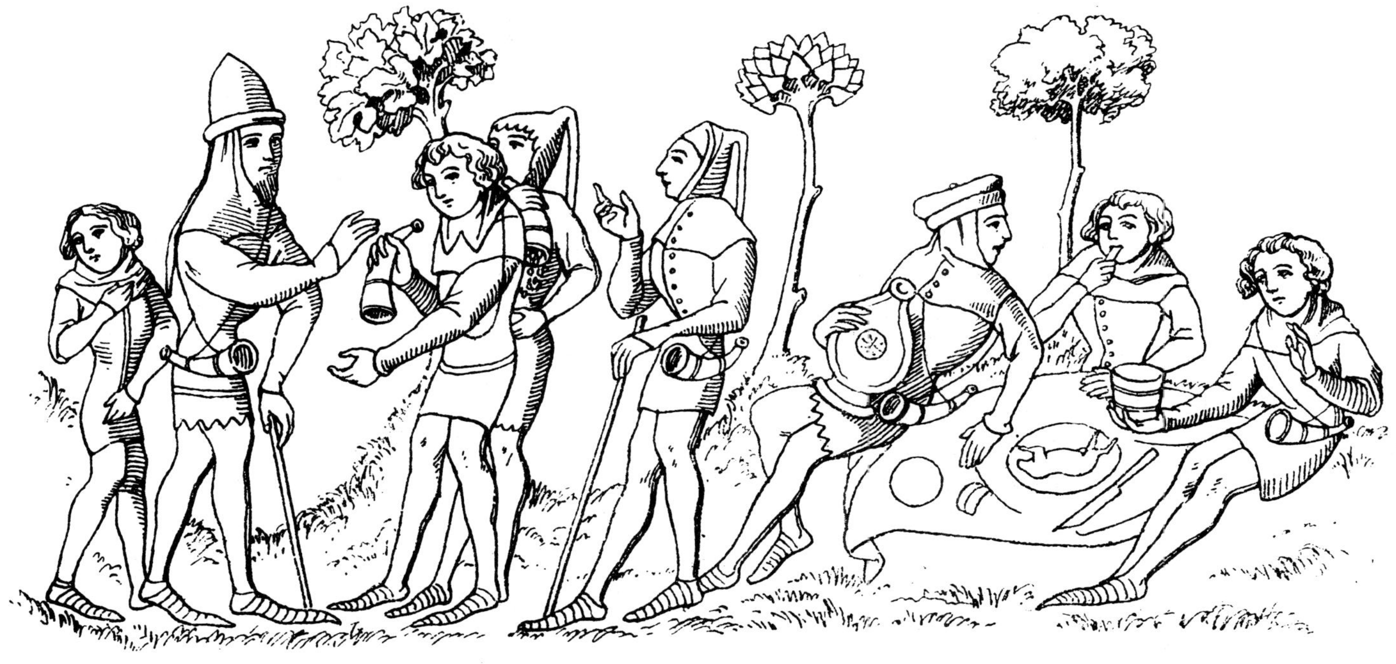

a	Field workers, c. 1350	Feldarbeiter, um 1350	Agricoltori, ca. 1350	Travailleurs aux champs, vers 1350	Campesinos, hacia el año 1350
b	Group of hunters, c. 1350	Jagdgesellsch aft, um 1350	Gruppo di cacciatori, ca. 1350	Groupe de chasseurs, vers 1350	Grupo de cazadores, hacia el año 1350

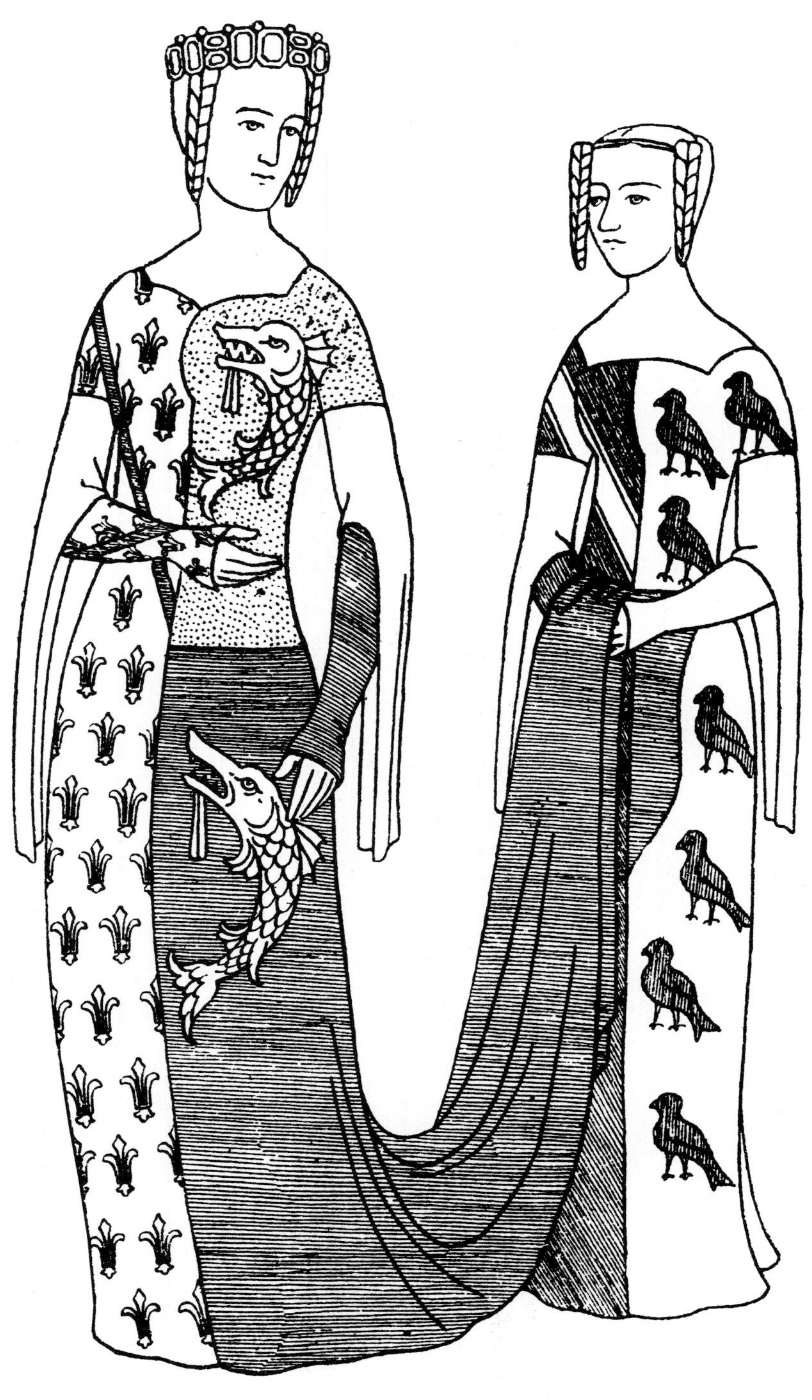

French ladies from the Auvergne, 1370

Französische Damen aus der Auvergne, 1370

Dame francesi di Auvergne, 1370

Dames françaises d'Auvergne, 1370

Damas francesas de Auvernia, 1370

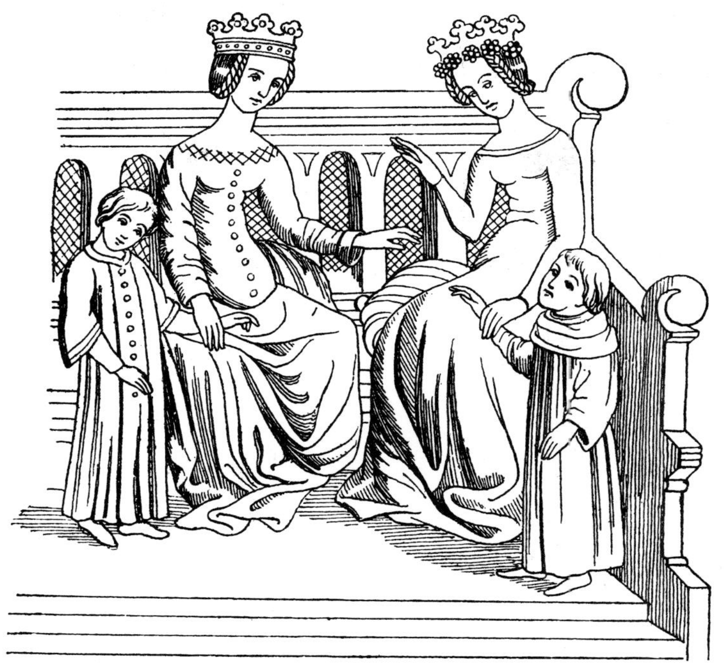

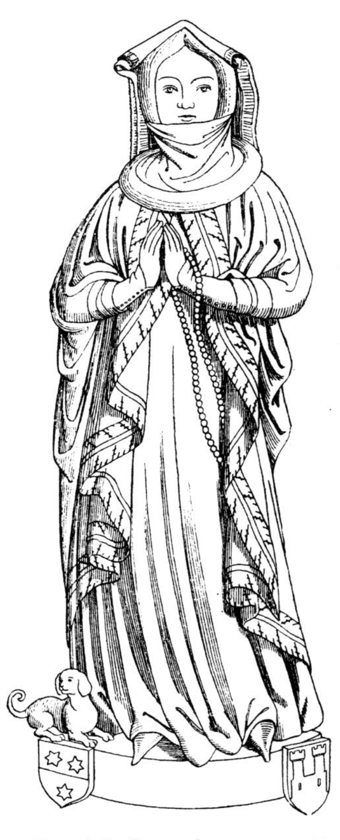

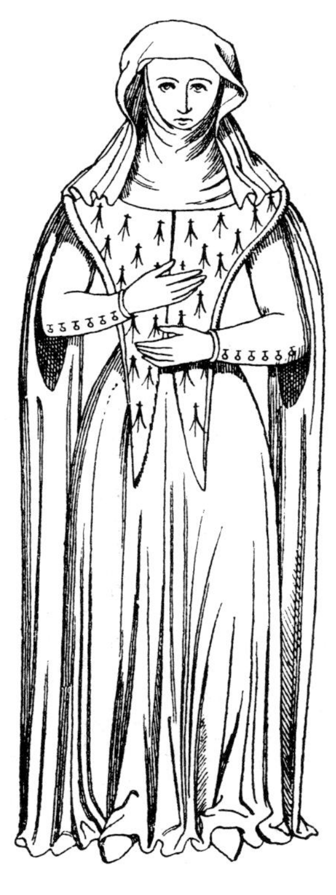

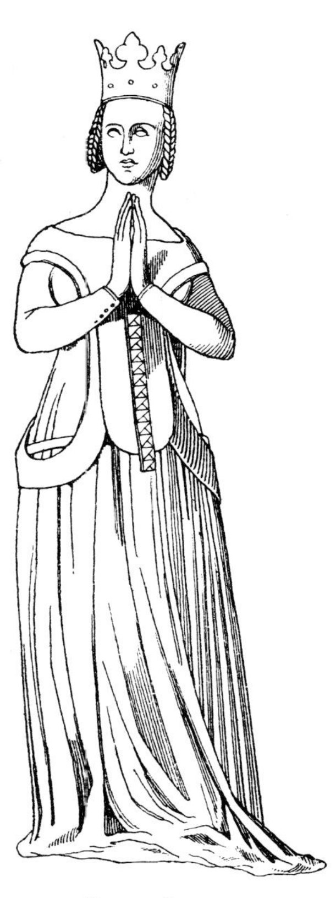

a	French ladies and children, c. 1360	Französische Damen mit Kindern, um 1360	Dame e bambini francesi, ca. 1360	Dames et enfants français, vers 1360	Damas francesas con sus hijos, hacia 1360
b	German aristocratic lady, c. 1380	Deutsche Aristokratin, um 1380	Dama aristocratica tedesca, ca. 1380	Dame de l'aristocratie allemande, vers 1380	Aristócrata alemana, hacia 1380
c	French lady, c. 1350	Französische Dame, um 1350	Dama francese, ca. 1350	Dame française, vers 1350	Dama francesa, hacia 1350
d	Wife of the King of France, 1360	Ehefrau des Königs von Frankreich, 1360	Moglie del re di Francia, 1360	Épouse du Roi de France, 1360	Esposa del rey de Francia, 1360

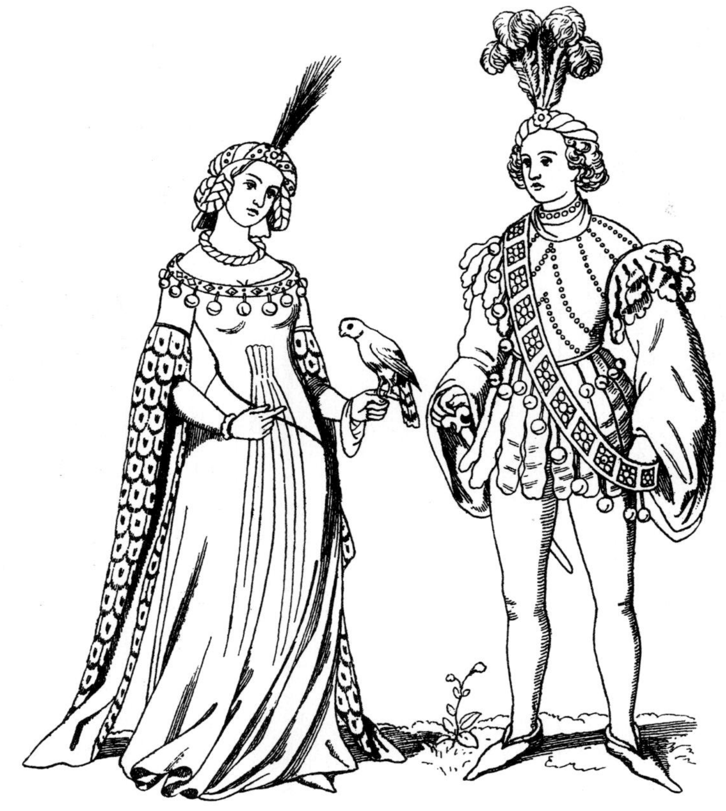

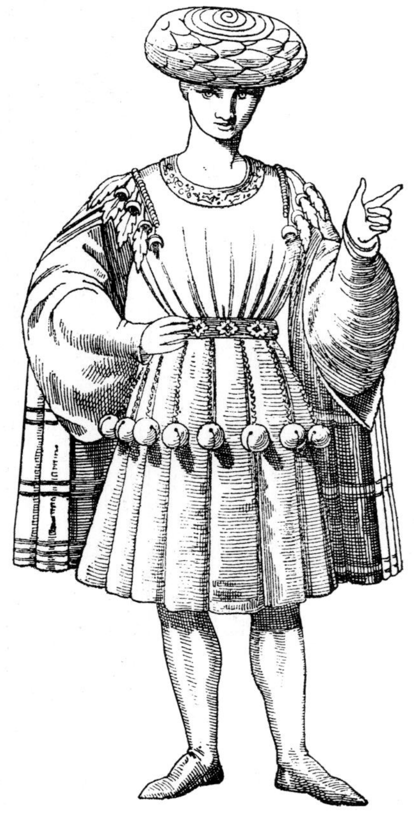

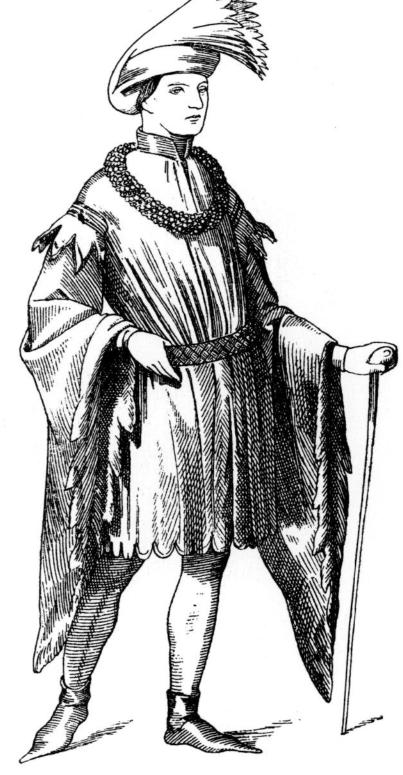

a	Aristocratic couple, early 15th century	Aristokratenpaar, frühes 15. Jahrhundert	Coppia aristocratica, inizio del XIV secolo	Couple de l'aristocratie, début du XVe siècle	Pareja aristocrática, principios del siglo XV
b+c	French noblemen, c. 1420	Französischer Adlige, um 1420	Nobiluomini francesi, ca. 1420	Nobles français, vers 1420	Nobles franceses, hacia el año 1420

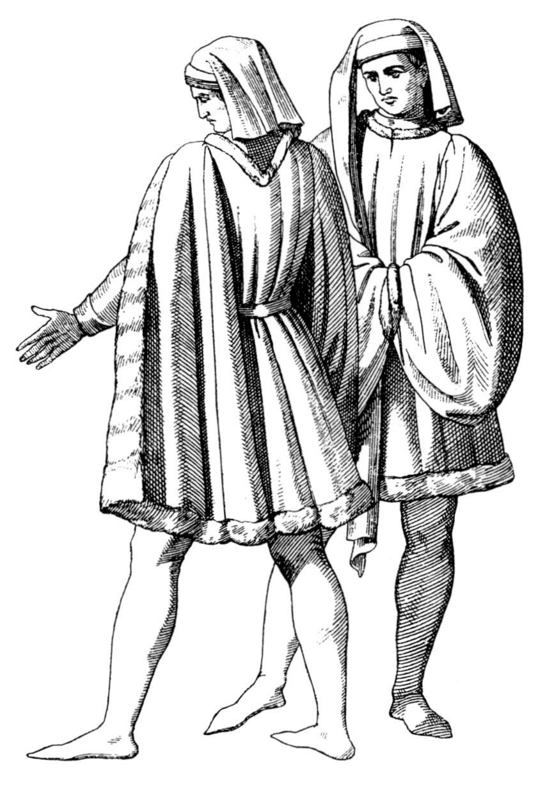

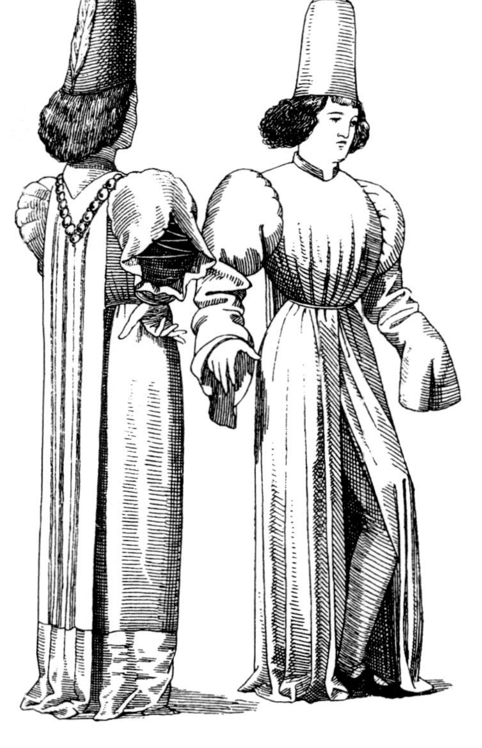

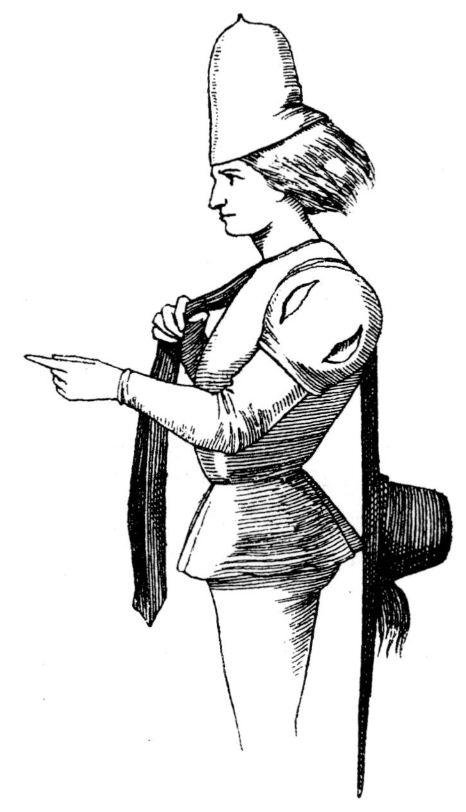

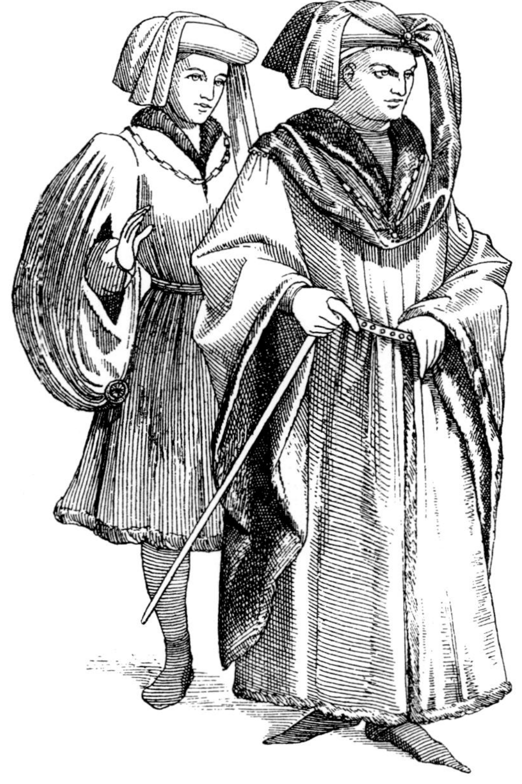

a	Florentine gentlemen, c. 1420	Florentinische Edelleute, um 1420	Gentiluomini fiorentini, ca. 1420	Gentilshommes florentins, vers 1420	Caballeros florentinos, hacia 1420
b+c	Noblemen from the Burgundy, c. 1465	Adlige aus Burgund, um 1465	Nobiluomini del Burgundy, ca. 1465	Nobles de Bourgogne, vers 1465	Nobles de Borgoña, hacia 1465
d	French traders, c. 1430	Französische Händler, um 1430	Commercianti francesi, ca. 1430	Marchands français, vers 1430	Comerciantes franceses, hacia 1430

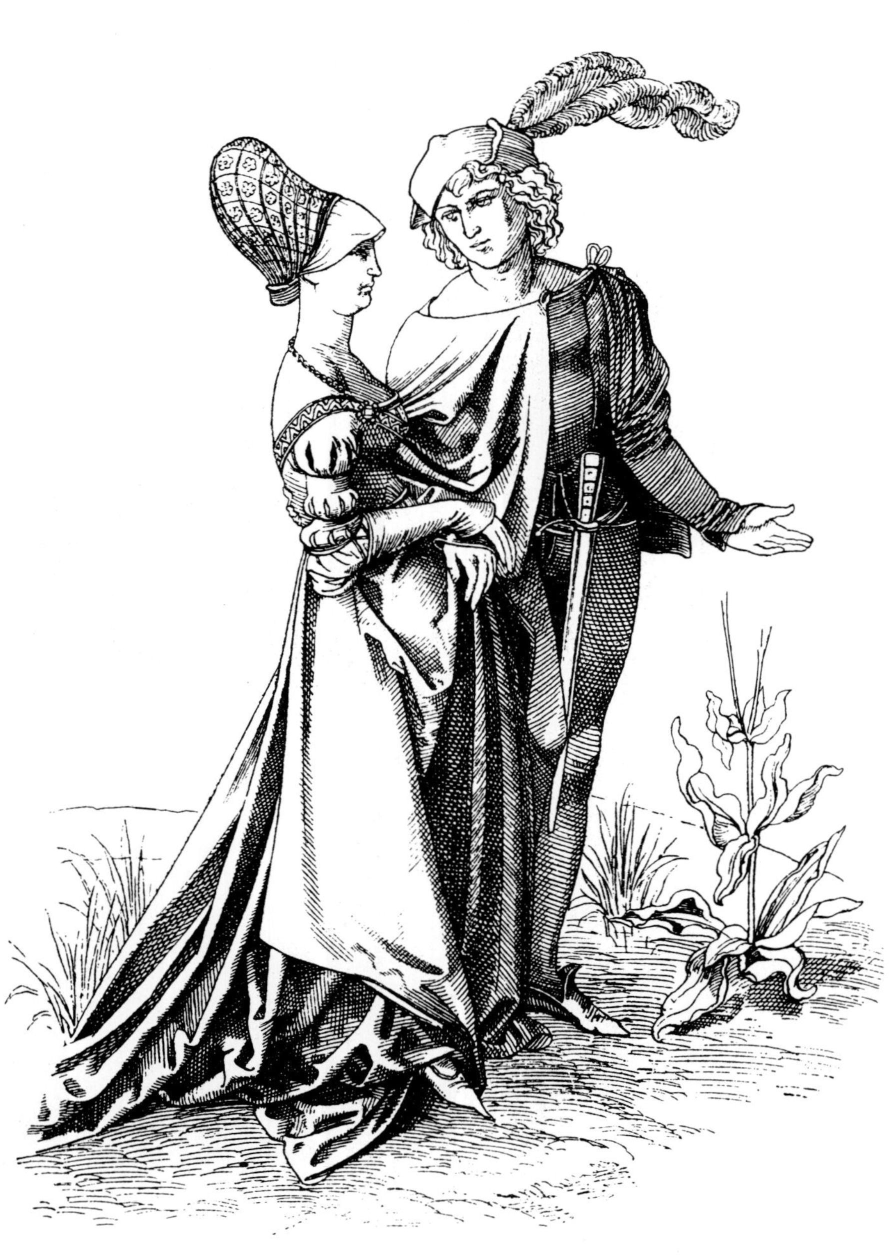

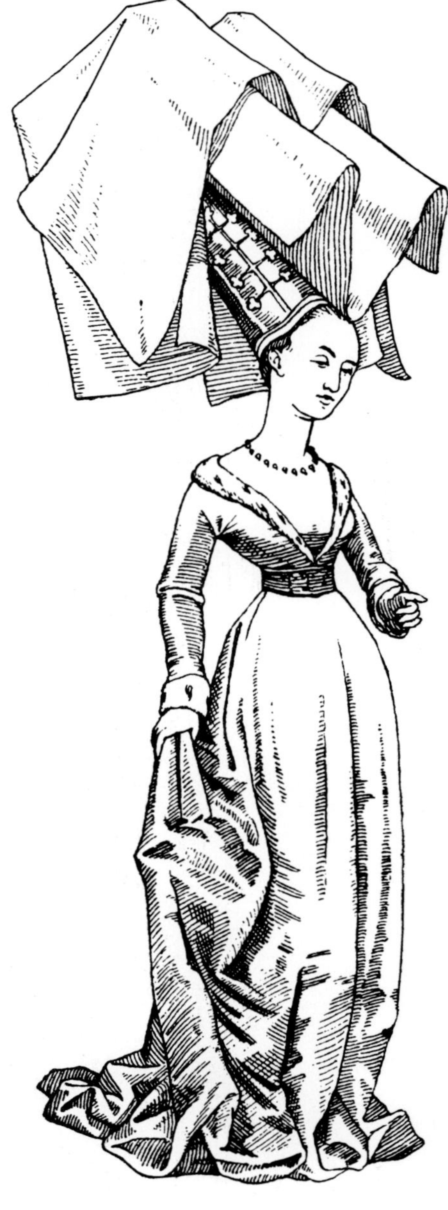

a	Dutch aristocrats, c. 1480	Holländische Aristokraten, um 1480	Aristocratici olandesi, ca. 1480	Aristocrates hollandais, vers 1480	Aristócratas holandeses, hacia 1480
b	French court lady, c. 1450	Französische Hofdame, um 1450	Dama di corte francese, ca. 1450	Dame de la Cour de France, vers 1450	Cortesana francesa, hacia 1450

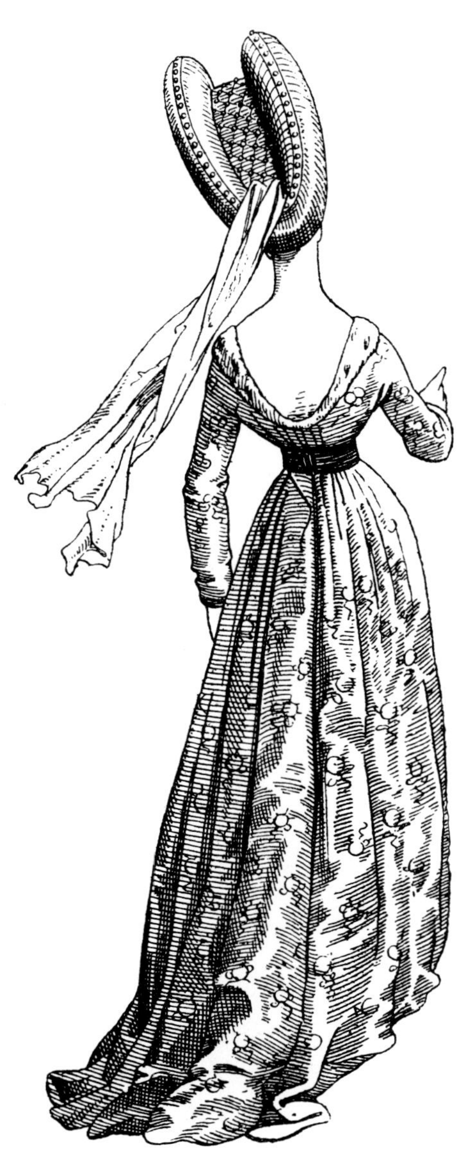

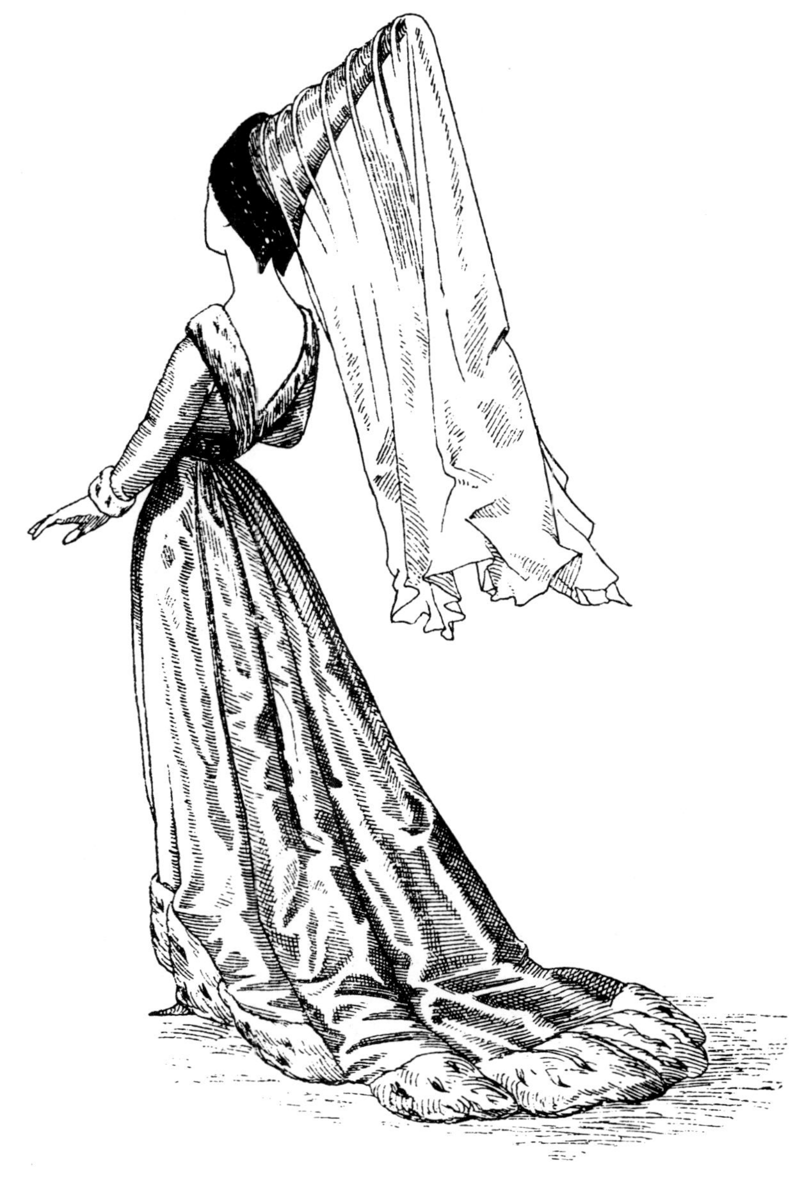

a	French court lady, c. 1450	Französische Hofdame, um 1450	Dama di corte francese, ca. 1450	Dame de la Cour de France, vers 1450	Cortesana francesa, hacia 1450
b	German lady, c. 1470	Deutsche Dame, um 1470	Dama tedesca, ca. 1470	Dame allemande, vers 1470	Dama alemana, hacia 1470

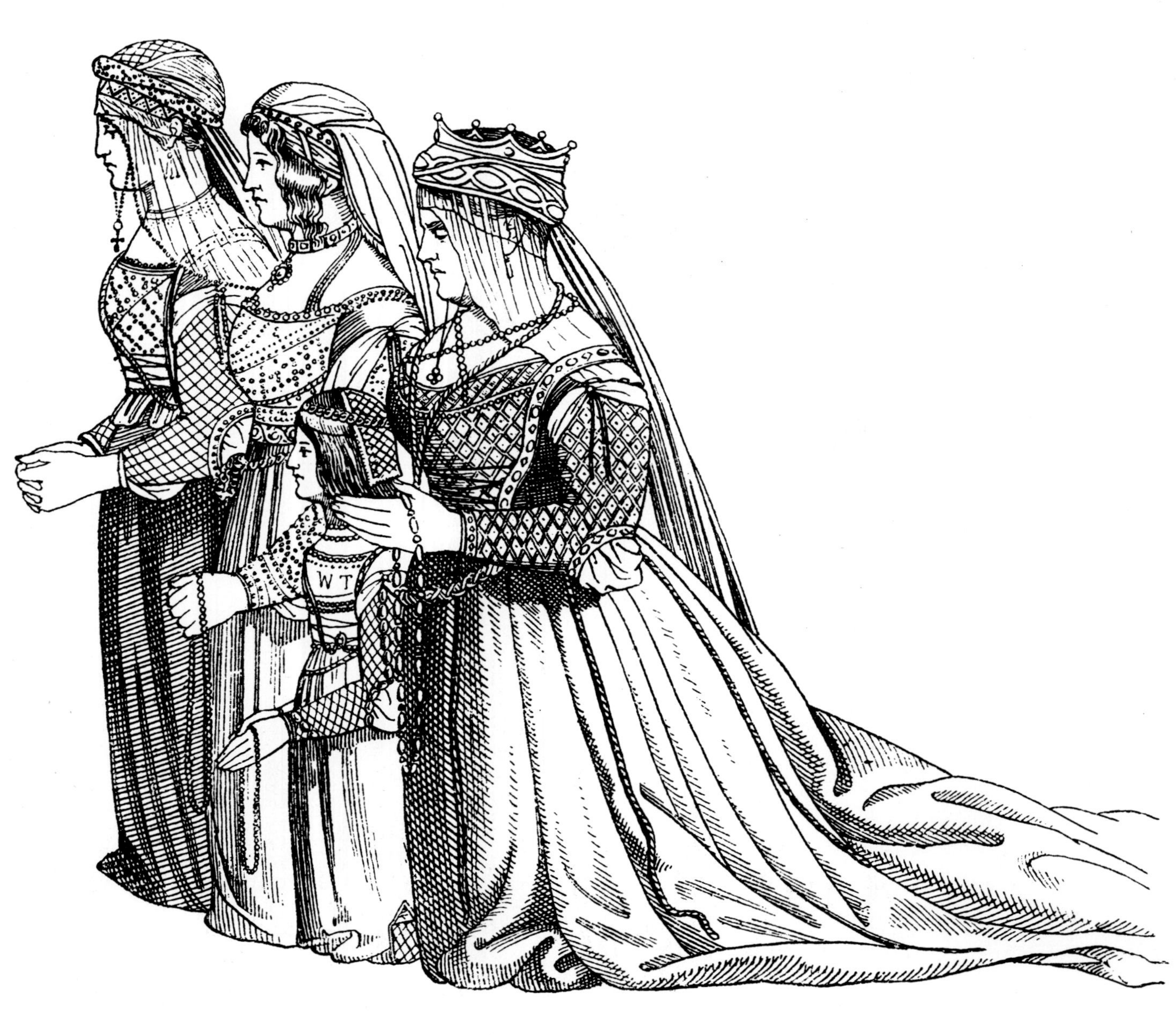

The Queen of Cyprus with court ladies in Venetian dress, c. 1480

Die Königin von Zypern mit Hofdamen in venezianischer Tracht, um 1480

La Regina di Cipro con le dame di corte in abito veneziano, ca. 1480

La Reine de Chypre avec des dames de la cour en costume vénitien, vers 1480

La reina de Chipre y cortesanas con vestidos venecianos, hacia 1480

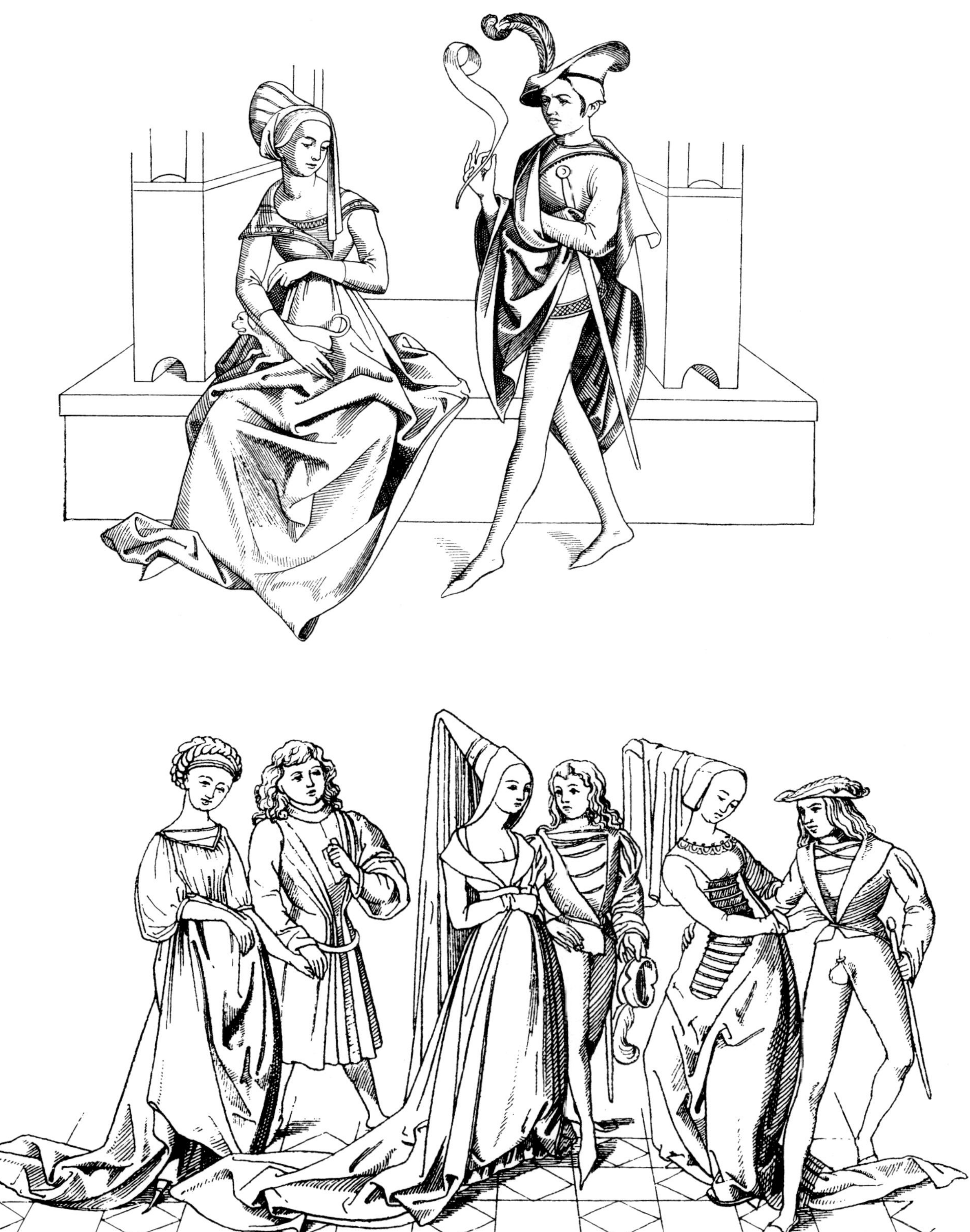

a	German dress, c. 1480	Deutsche Gewänder, um 1480	Abiti tedeschi, ca. 1480	Vêtements allemands, vers 1480	Trajes alemanes, hacia 1480
b	Dutch dress. c. 1480	Holländische Gewänder, um 1480	Abiti olandesi, ca. 1480	Vêtements hollandais, vers 1480	Trajes holandeses, hacia 1480

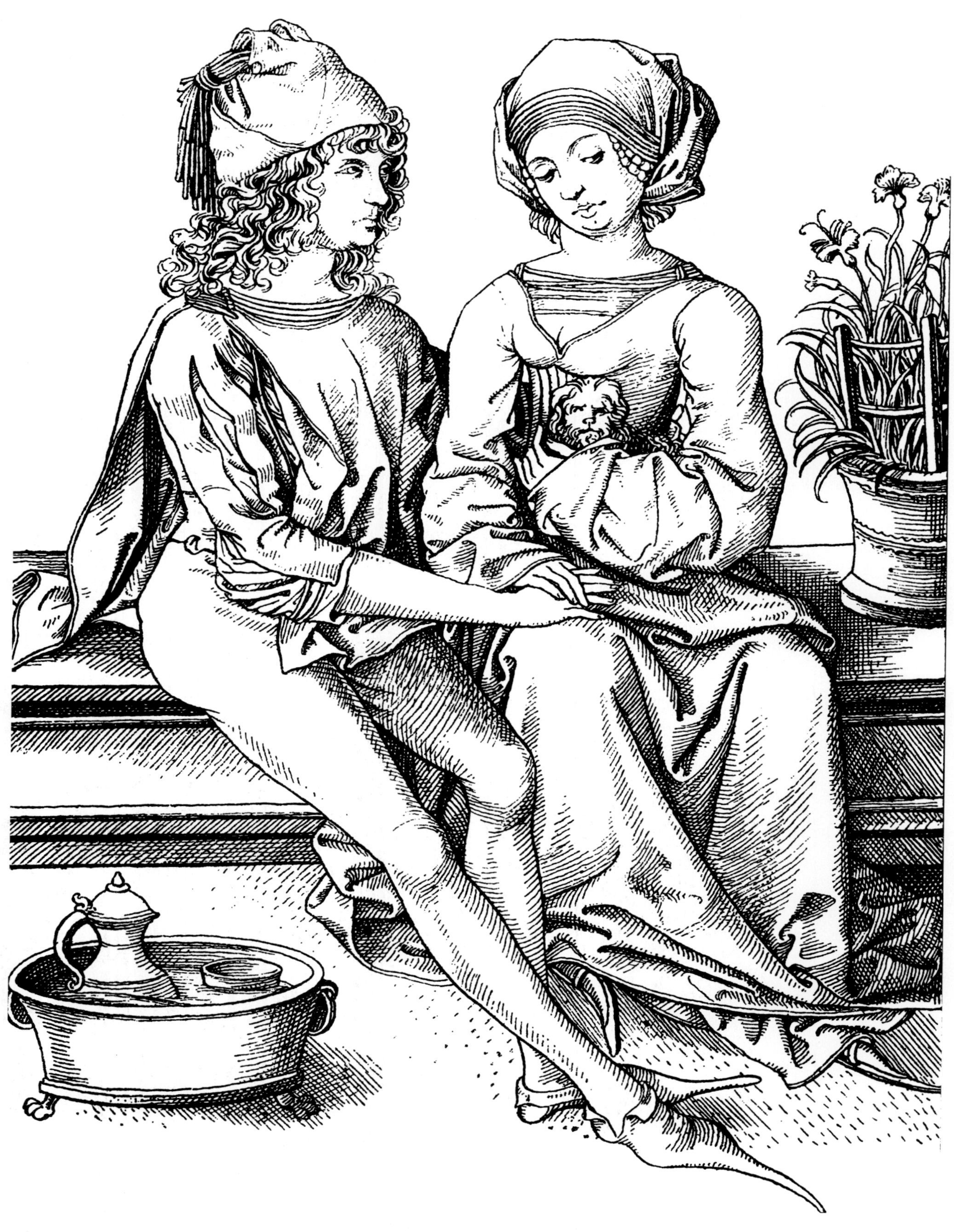

German couple, c. 1480

Deutsches Paar, um 1480

Coppia tedesca, ca. 1480

Couple allemand, vers 1480

Pareja alemana, hacia 1480

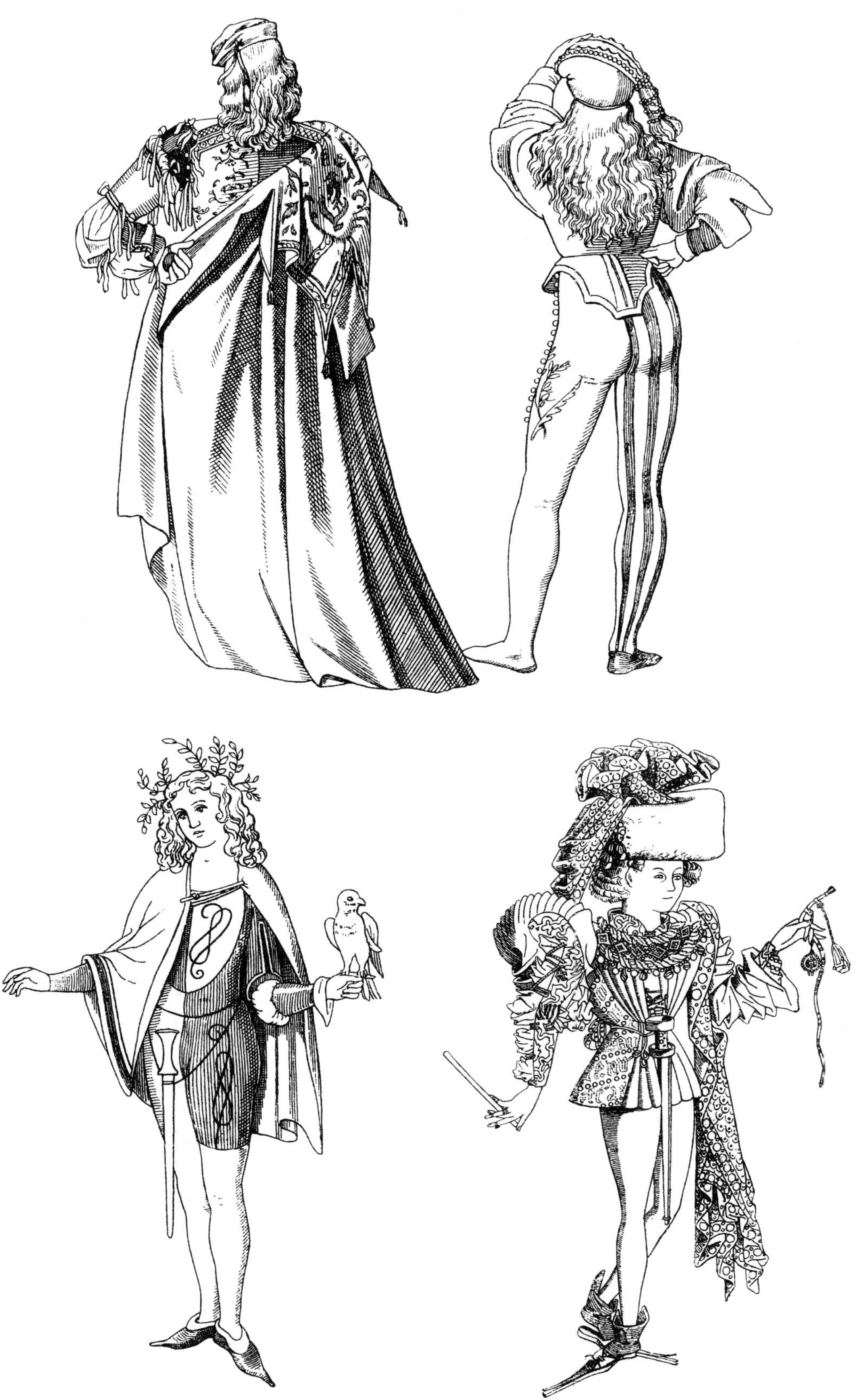

a	Venetian noblemen, c. 1480	Venezianische Adlige, um 1480	Nobiluomini veneziani, ca. 1480	Nobles vénitiens, vers 1480	Nobles venecianos, hacia el año 1480
b	Young noblemen. c. 1480	Junge Adlige, um 1480	Giovani nobiluomini, ca. 1480	Jeunes nobles, vers 1480	Jóvenes nobles, hacia el año 1480

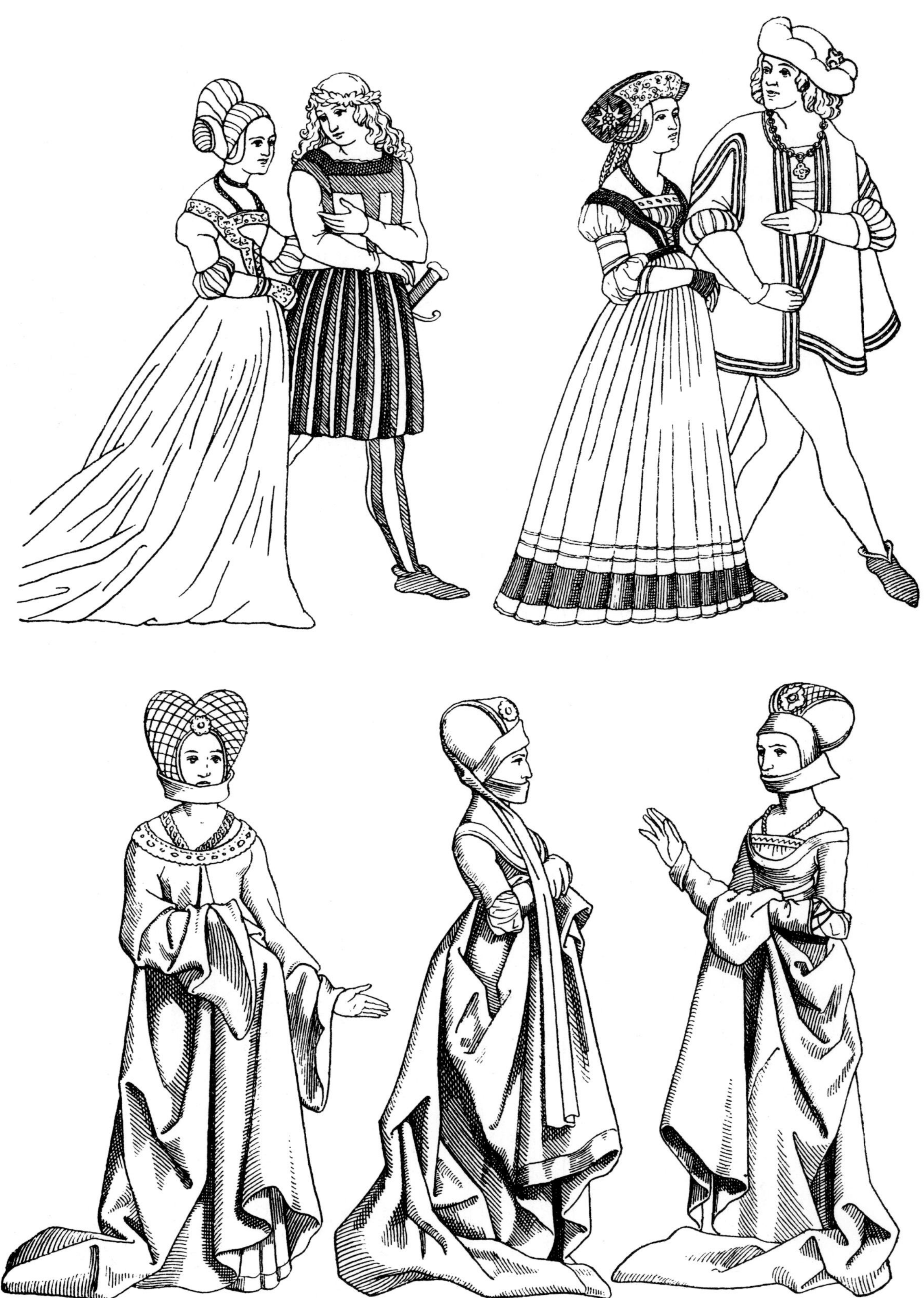

a	German party dress, Nürnberg	Deutsche Festgewänder, Nürnberg	Abiti da gala tedeschi, Norimberga	Vêtements de bal allemands, Nüremberg	Trajes de gala alemanes, Núremberg
b	German female dress	Deutsche Frauengewänder	Abiti femminili tedeschi	Vêtements féminins allemands	Vestidos alemanes de mujer

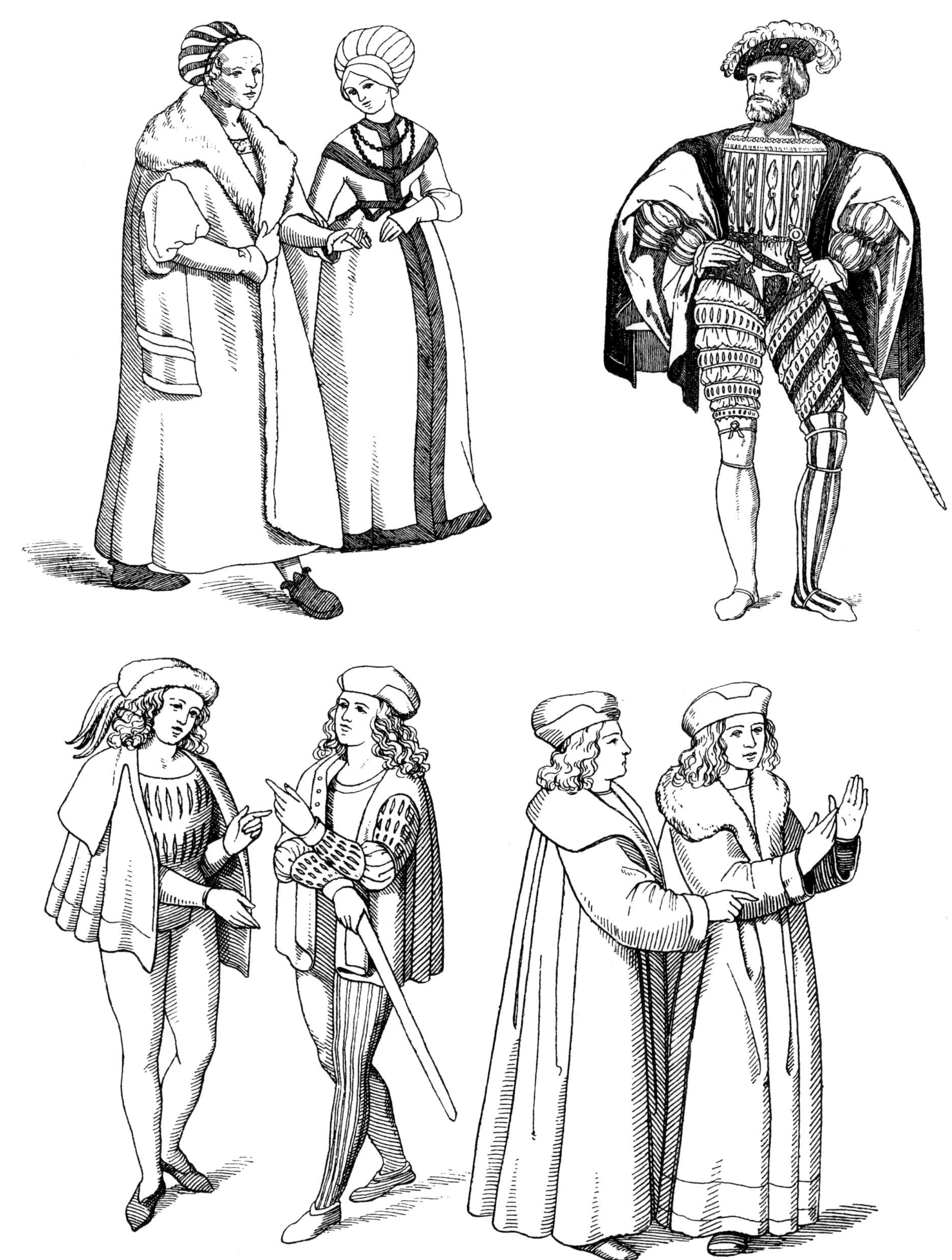

a	German middle-class couple	Deutsches Bürgerpaar	Coppia tedesca di ceto medio	Couple allemand de la classe moyenne	Pareja alemana de clase media
b	French nobleman	Französischer Adliger	Nobiluomo francese	Noble français	Noble francés
c	German students	Deutsche Studenten	Studenti tedeschi	Étudiants allemands	Estudiantes alemanes

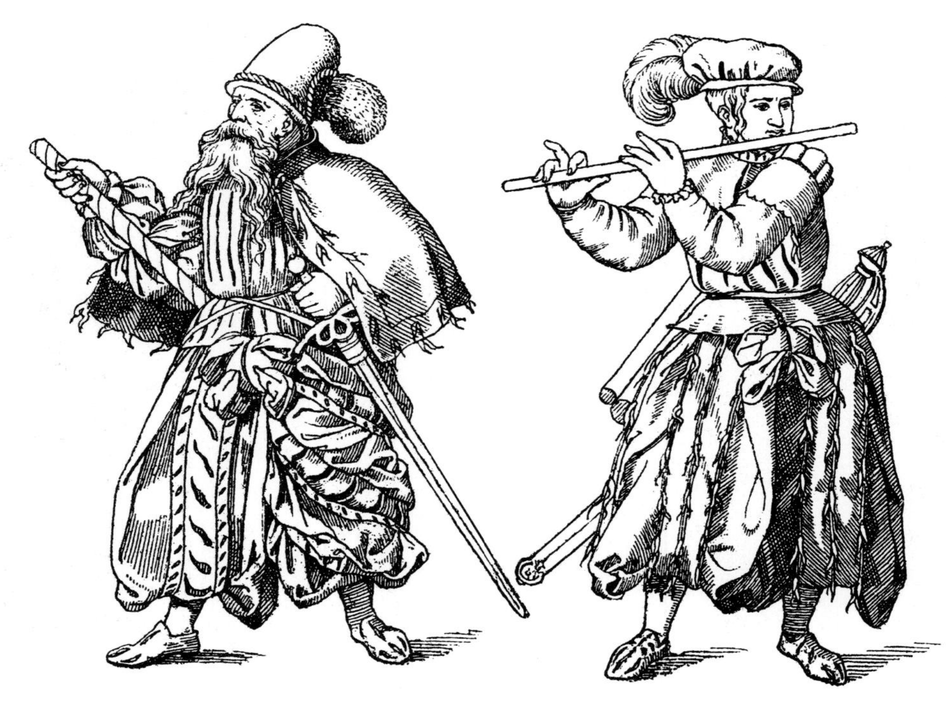

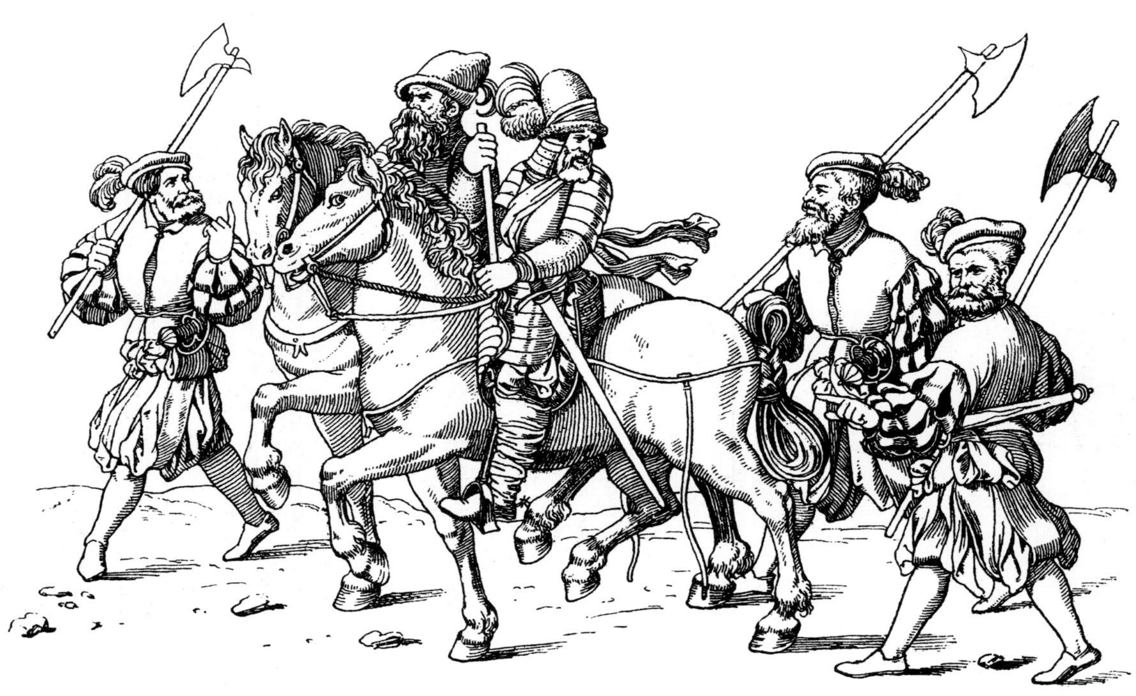

German foot soldiers and leaders on horse

Deutsche Fußsoldaten mit Anführern auf Pferden

Soldati tedeschi a piedi e capi a cavallo

Soldats à pied et chefs à cheval allemands

Soldados de infantería alemanes y capitanes a caballo

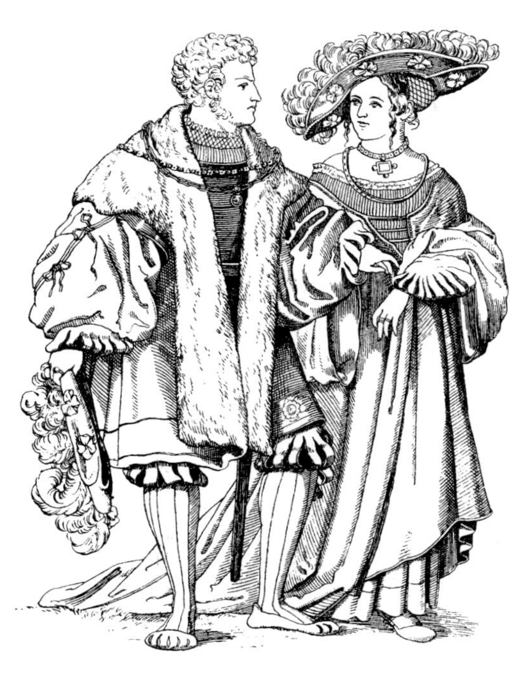

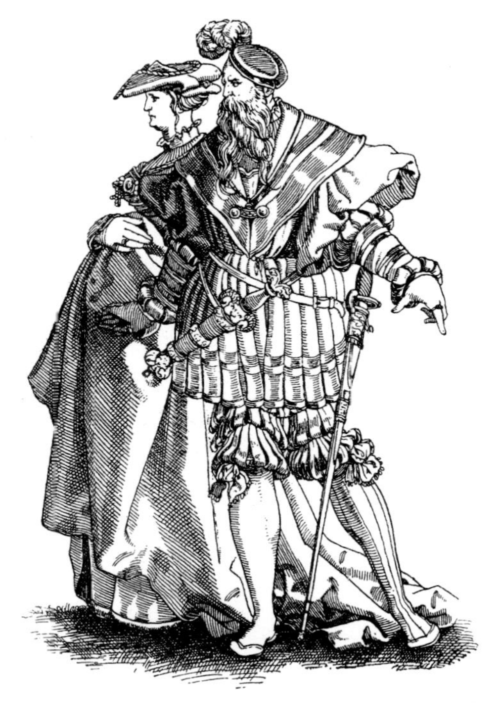

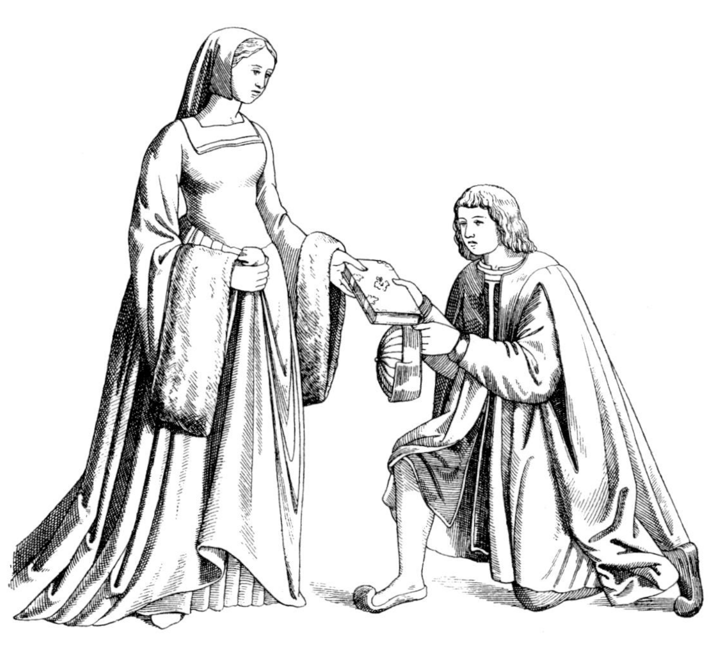

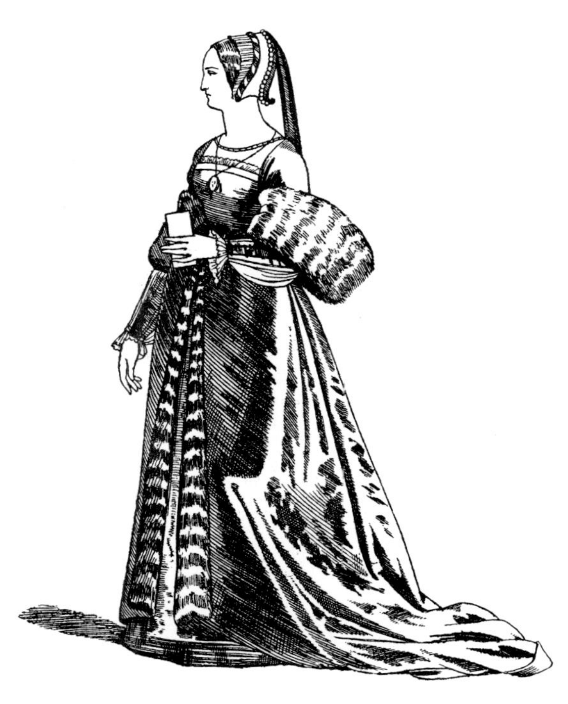

a+b	German noble couples	Deutsche adelige Ehepaare	Coppie nobili tedesche	Couples de nobles allemands	Parejas de nobles alemanes
c	French midle class dress	Französisches Bürgergewand	Abiti francesi del ceto medio	Vêtements de la classe moyenne française	Trajes de la clase media francesa
d	French court lady	Französische Hofdame	Dama di corte francese	Dame de la Cour de France	Cortesana francesa

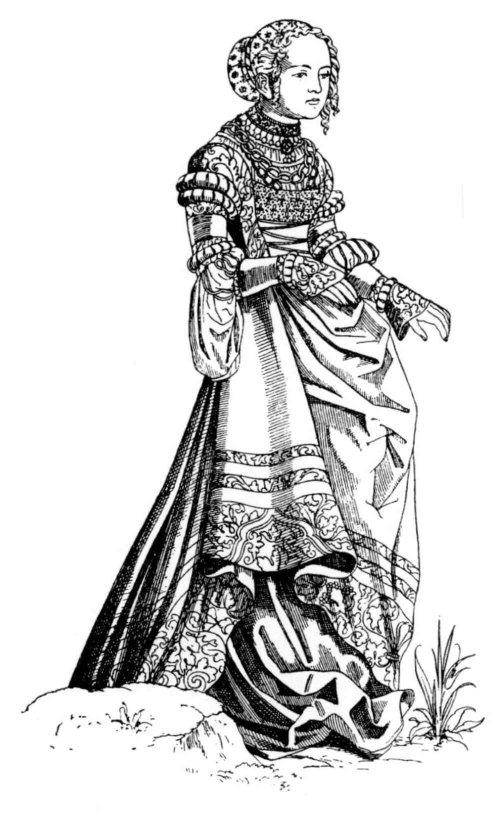

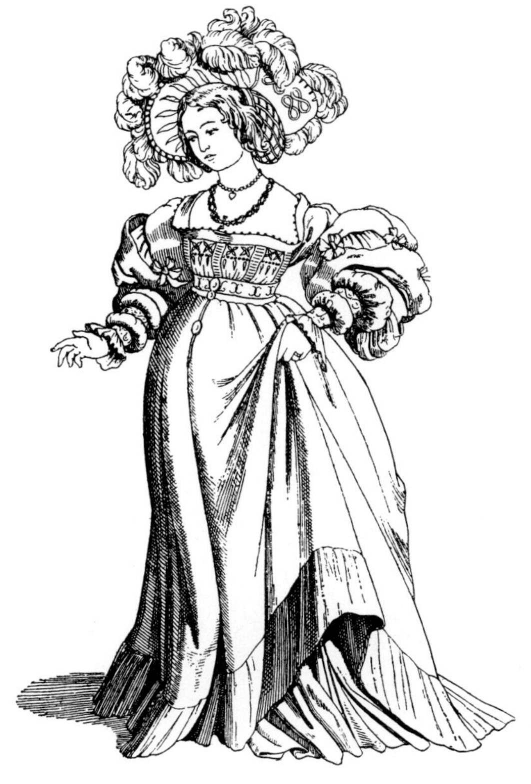

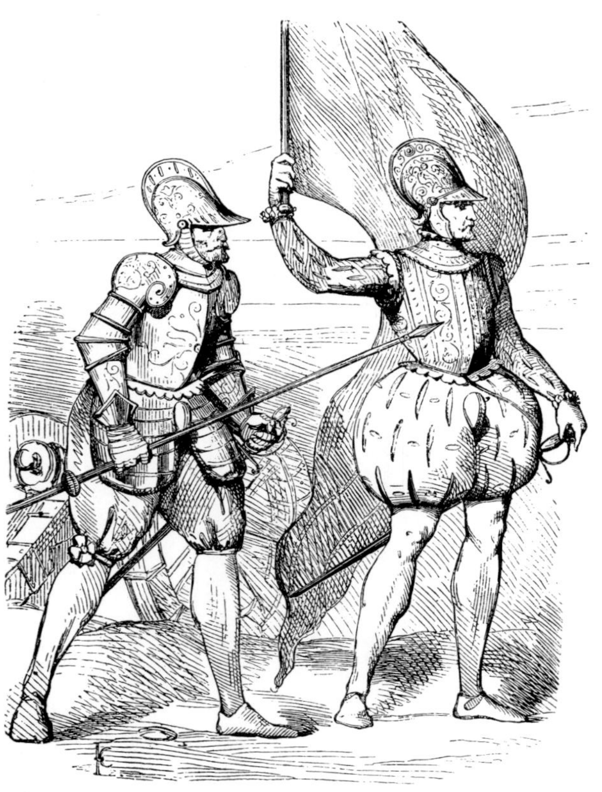

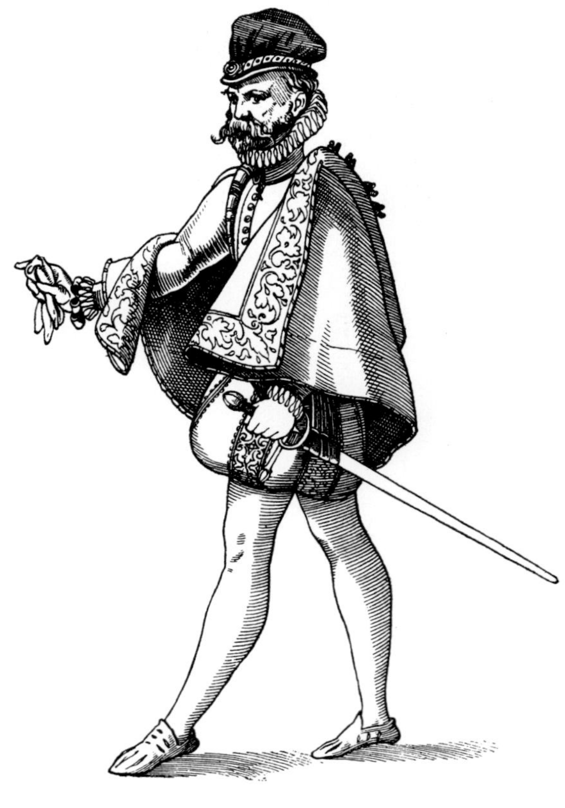

a+b	German ladies	Deutsche Damen	Dame tedesche	Dames allemandes	Damas alemanas
c	French soldiers	Französische Soldaten	Soldati francesi	Soldats français	Soldados franceses
d	Spanish nobleman	Spanischer Adliger	Nobiluomo spagnolo	Noble espagnol	Noble español

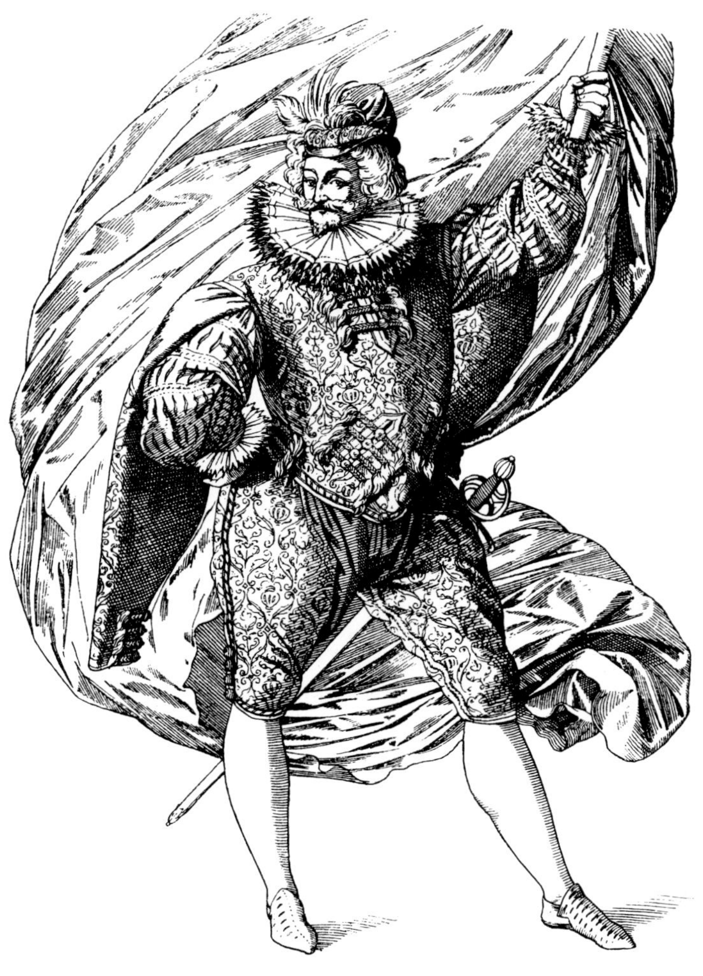

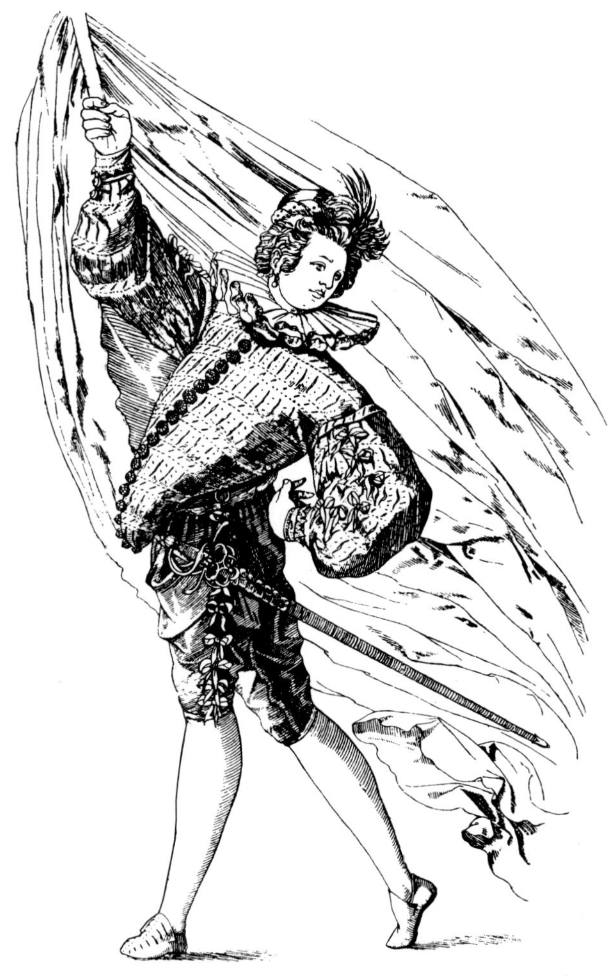

Noblemen from the Netherlands

Adlige aus den Niederlanden

Nobiluomini dei Paesi Bassi

Nobles des Pays-Bas

Nobles de los Países Bajos

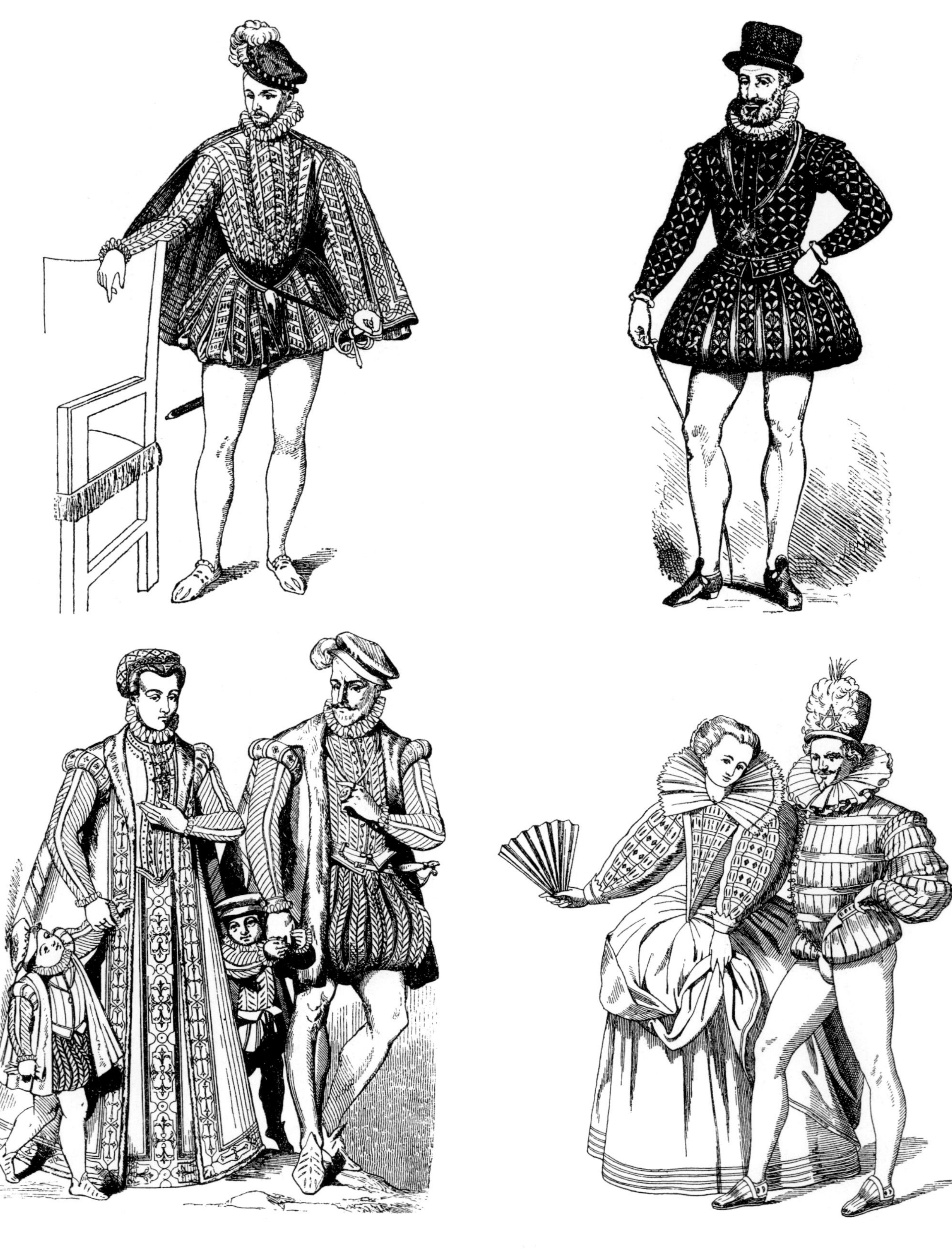

French nobles Französische Adlige Nobili francesi Nobles français Nobles franceses

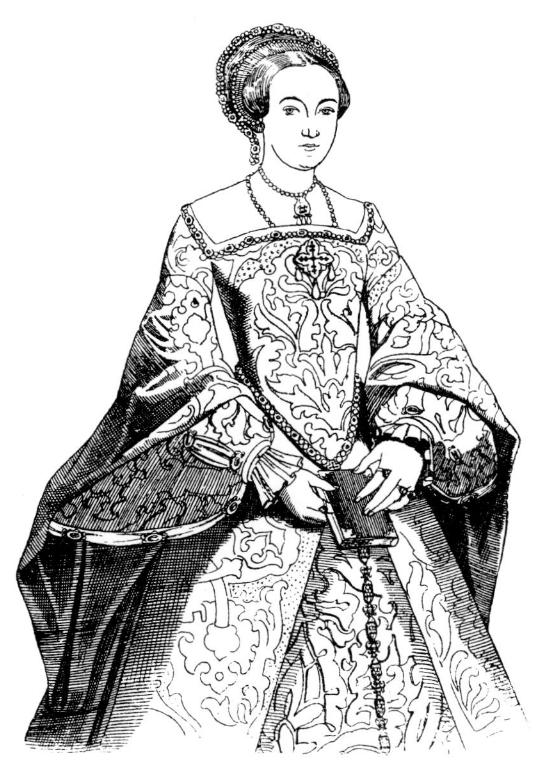
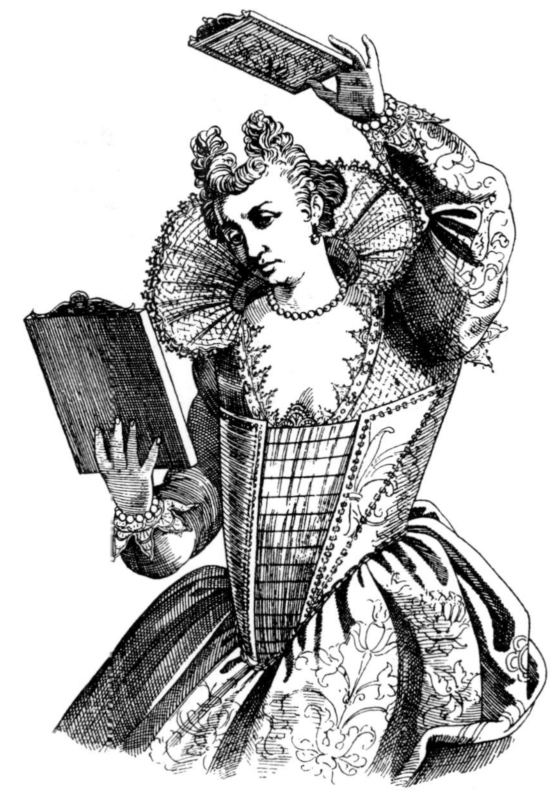
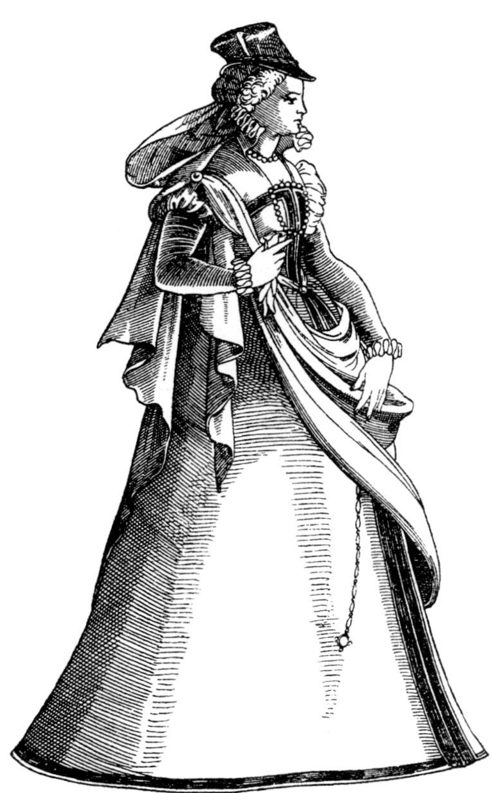
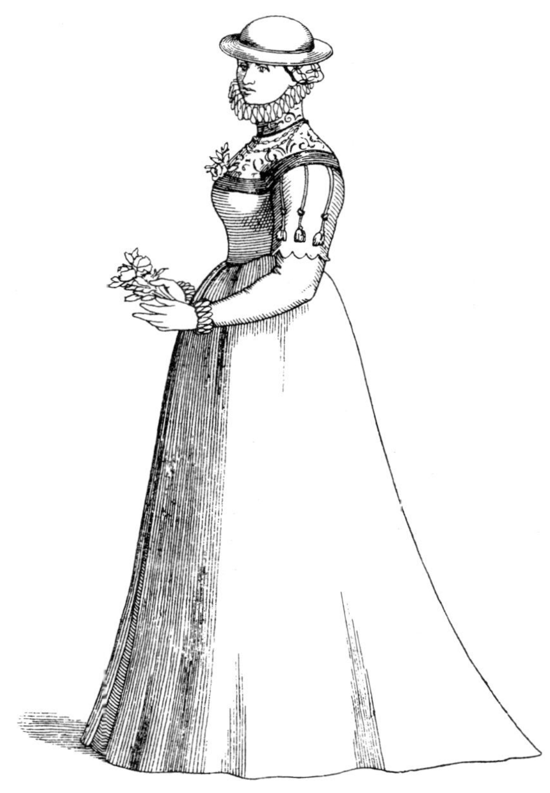

a	Queen Elisabeth of England	Königin Elisabeth von England	La Regina Elisabetta d'Inghilterra	Reine Elizabeth d'Angleterre	La reina Isabel de Inglaterra
b	Lady from Venice	Dame aus Venedig	Dama di Venezia	Dame vénitienne	Dama de Venecia
c	Lady from Siena	Dame aus Siena	Dama di Siena	Dame de Sienne	Dama de Siena
d	English lady	Englische Dame	Dama inglese	Dame anglaise	Dama inglesa

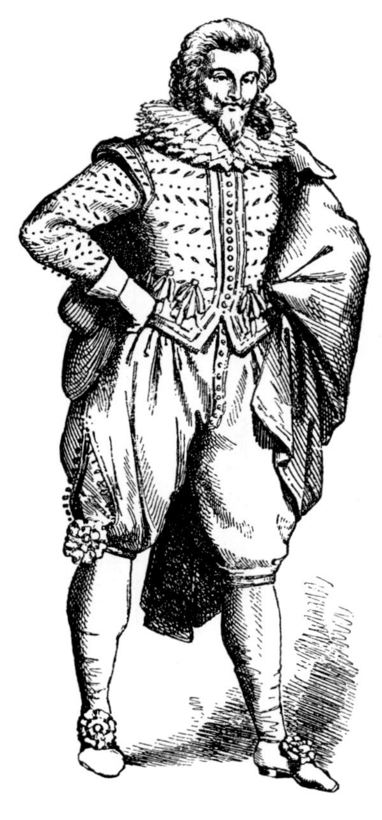

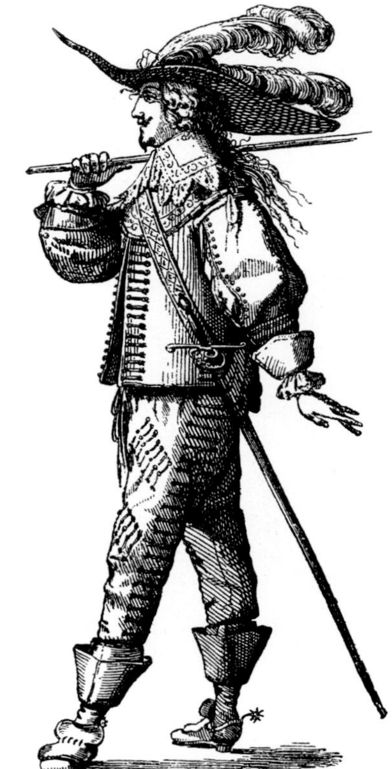

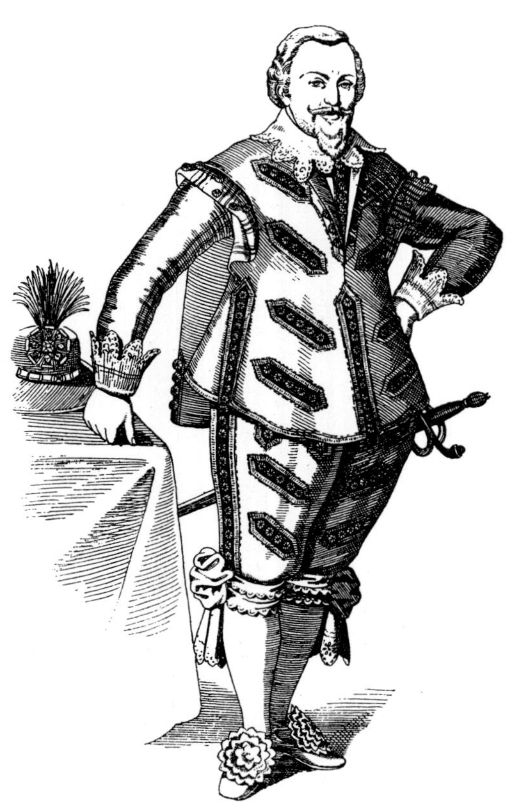

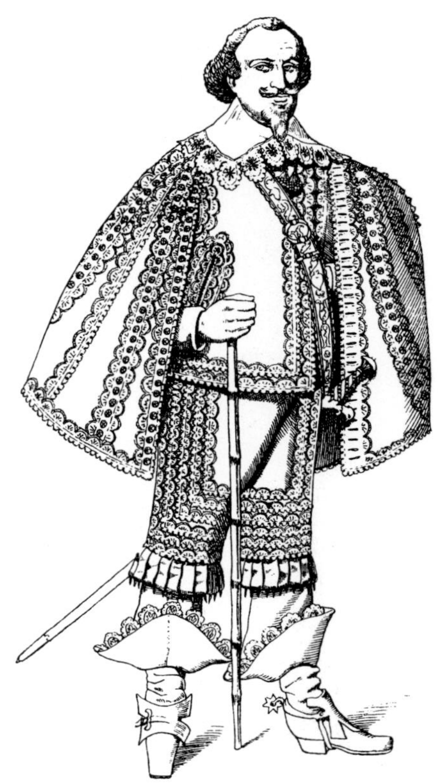

a	French Nobleman	Französischer Adliger	Nobiluomo francese	Noble français	Noble francés
b	French Officer	Französischer Offizier	Ufficiale francese	Officier français	Oficial francés
c	Dutch Prince	Holländischer Prinz	Principe olandese	Prince hollandais	Príncipe holandés
d	German count	Deutscher Graf	Conte tedesco	Comte allemand	Conde alemán

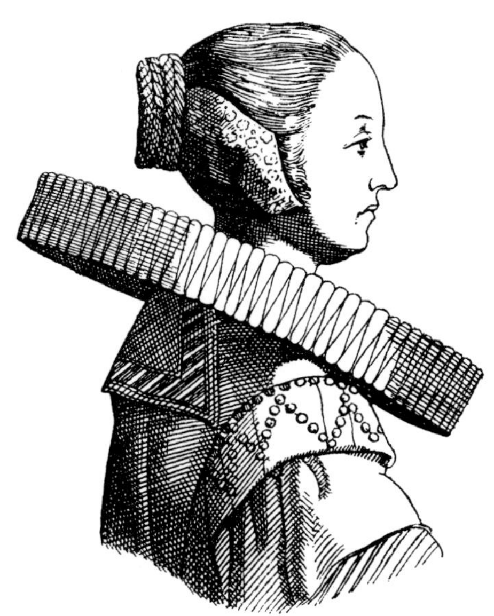

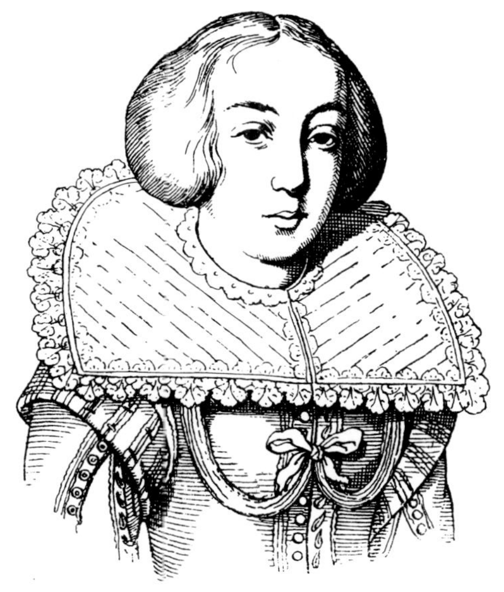

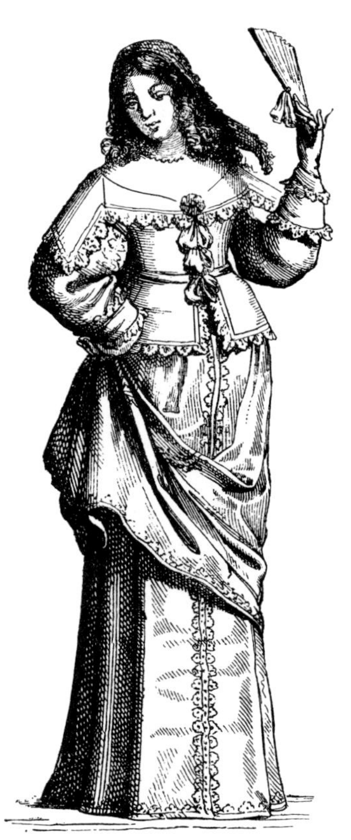

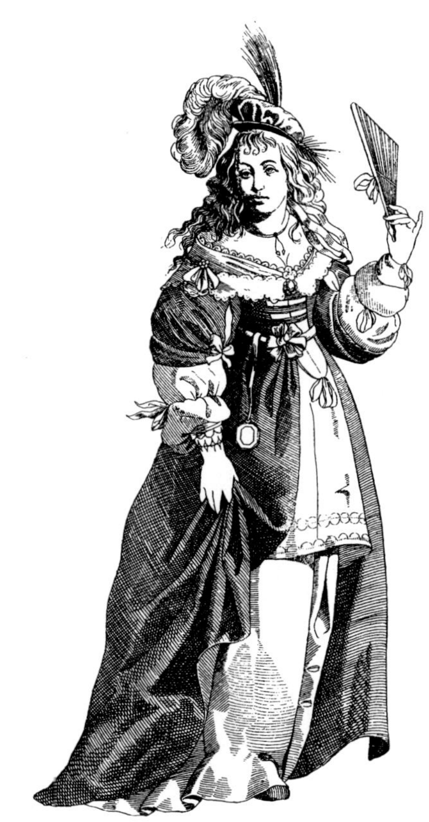

a+ b	17th-century collars	Kragen aus dem 17. Jahrhundert	Collare del XVII secolo	Collerettes du XVIIe siècle	Cuellos del siglo XVII
c	Spanish lady	Spanische Dame	Dama spagnola	Dame espagnole	Dama española
d	French lady	Französische Dame	Dama francese	Dame française	Dama francesa

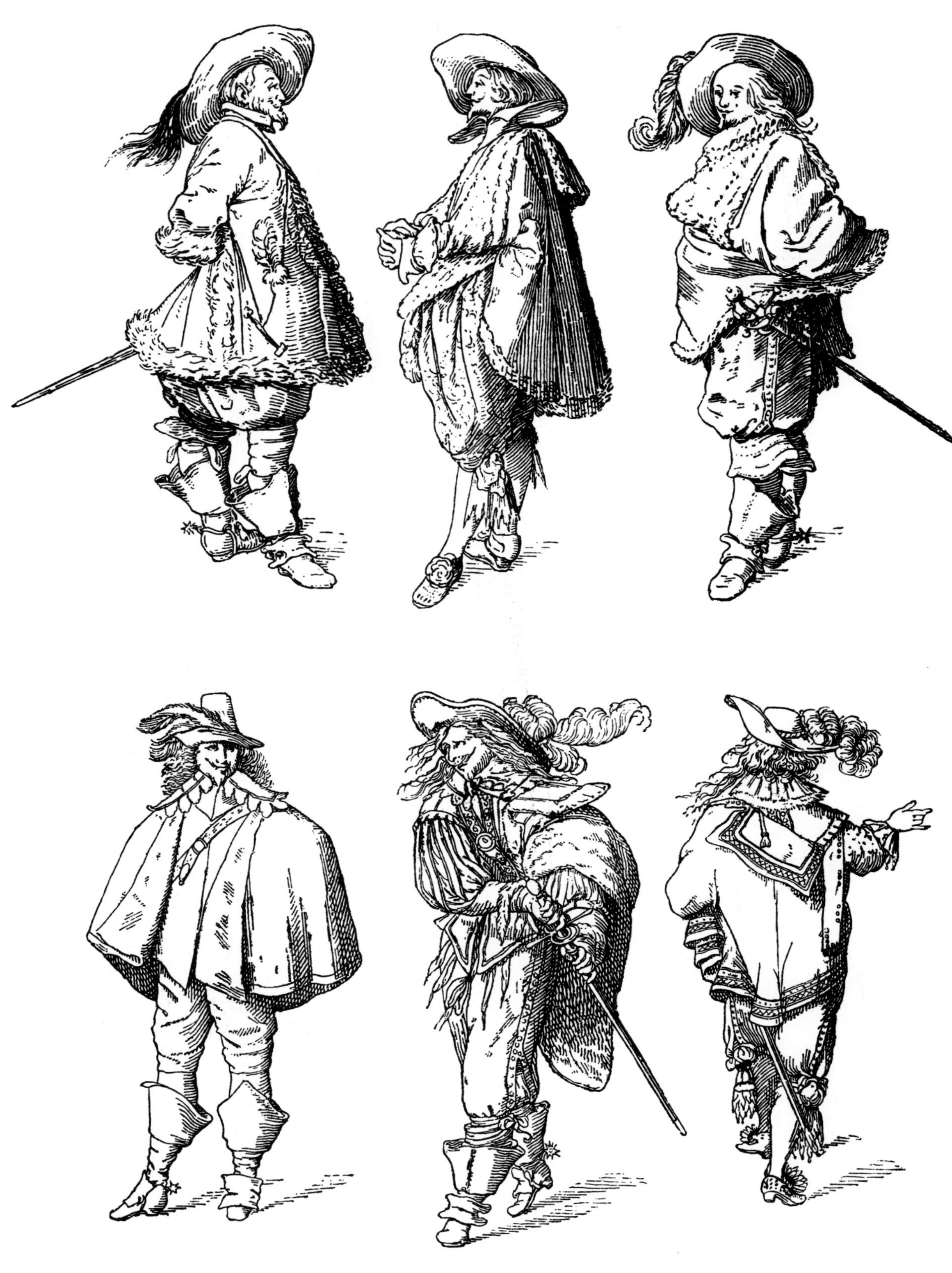

French and German noblemen in fashionable dress

Französische und deutsche Adlige in eleganter Kleidung

Nobiluomini francese e tedeschi in abiti alla moda

Nobles français et allemands à la mode de l'époque

Nobles franceses y alemanes con trajes de moda

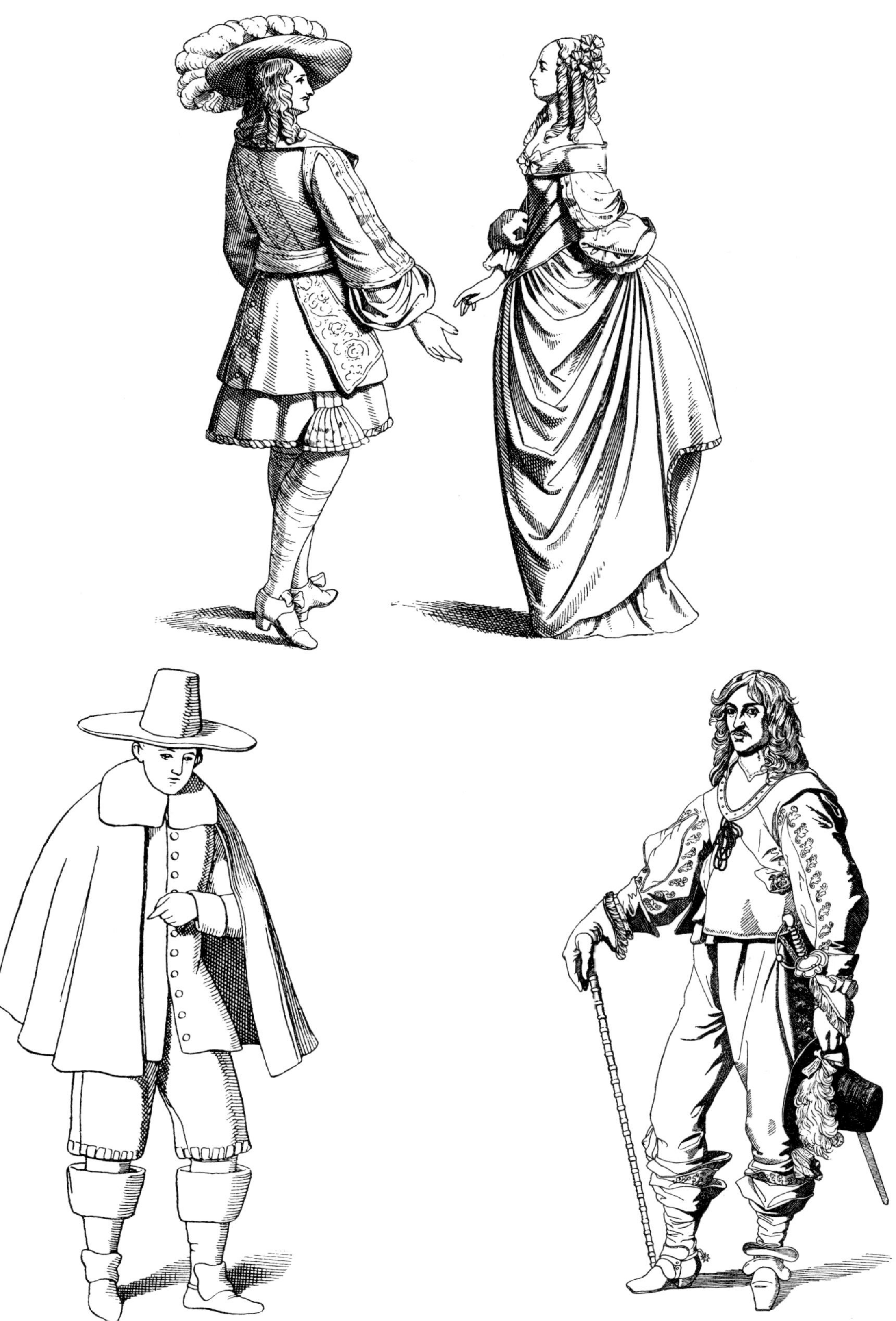

a	English noble couple	Englisches Adelspaar	Coppia di nobili inglesi	Couple de nobles anglais	Pareja de nobles ingleses
b	English puritan	Englischer Puritaner	Puritano inglese	Puritain anglais	Puritano inglés
c	English gentleman	Englischer Edelmann	Gentiluomo inglese	Gentilhomme anglais	Caballero inglés

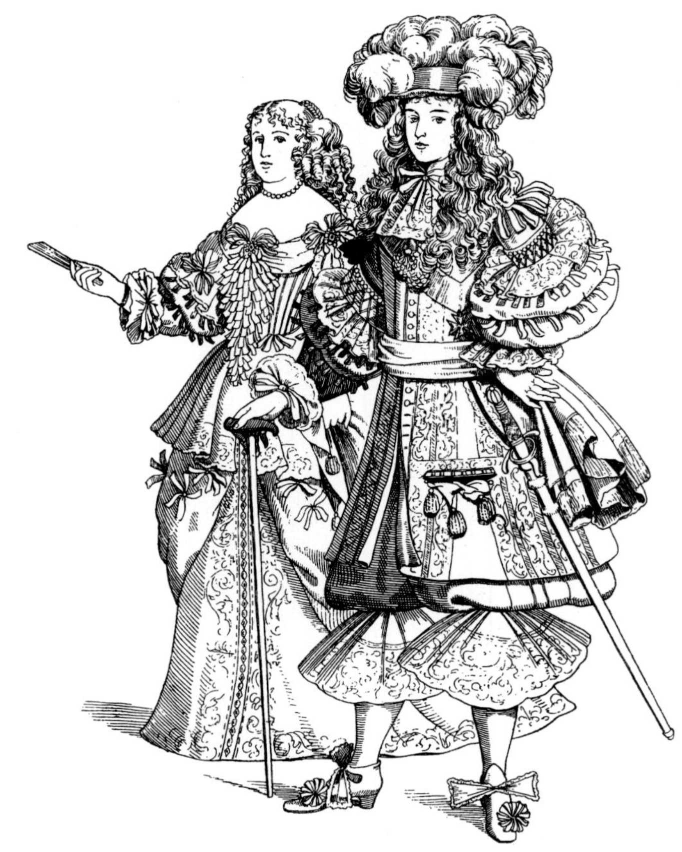

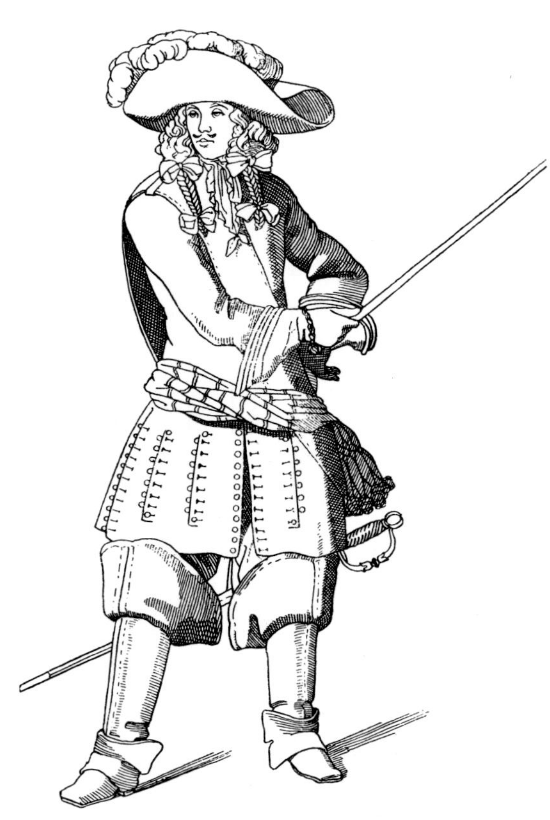

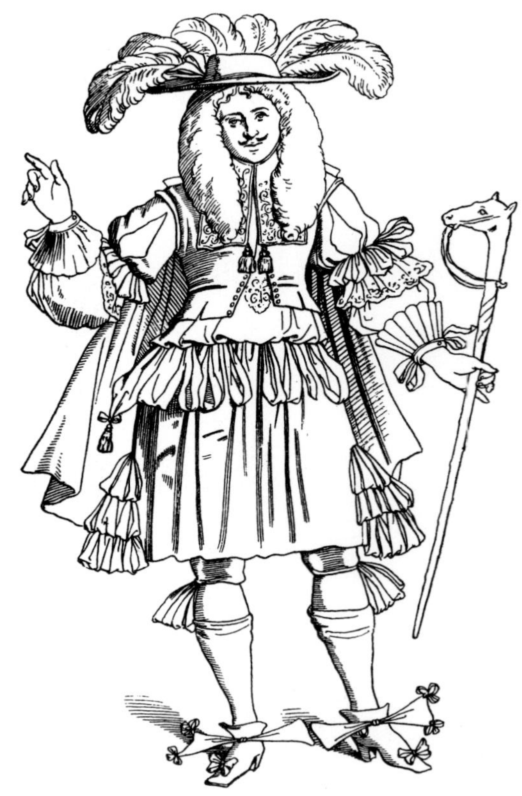

a	King Louis XIV of France	König Louis XIV. von Frankreich	Re Luigi XIV di Francia	Louis XIV, Roi de France	El rey Luis XIV de Francia
b+c	French noblemen	Französische Adlige	Nobiluomini francesi	Nobles français	Nobles franceses

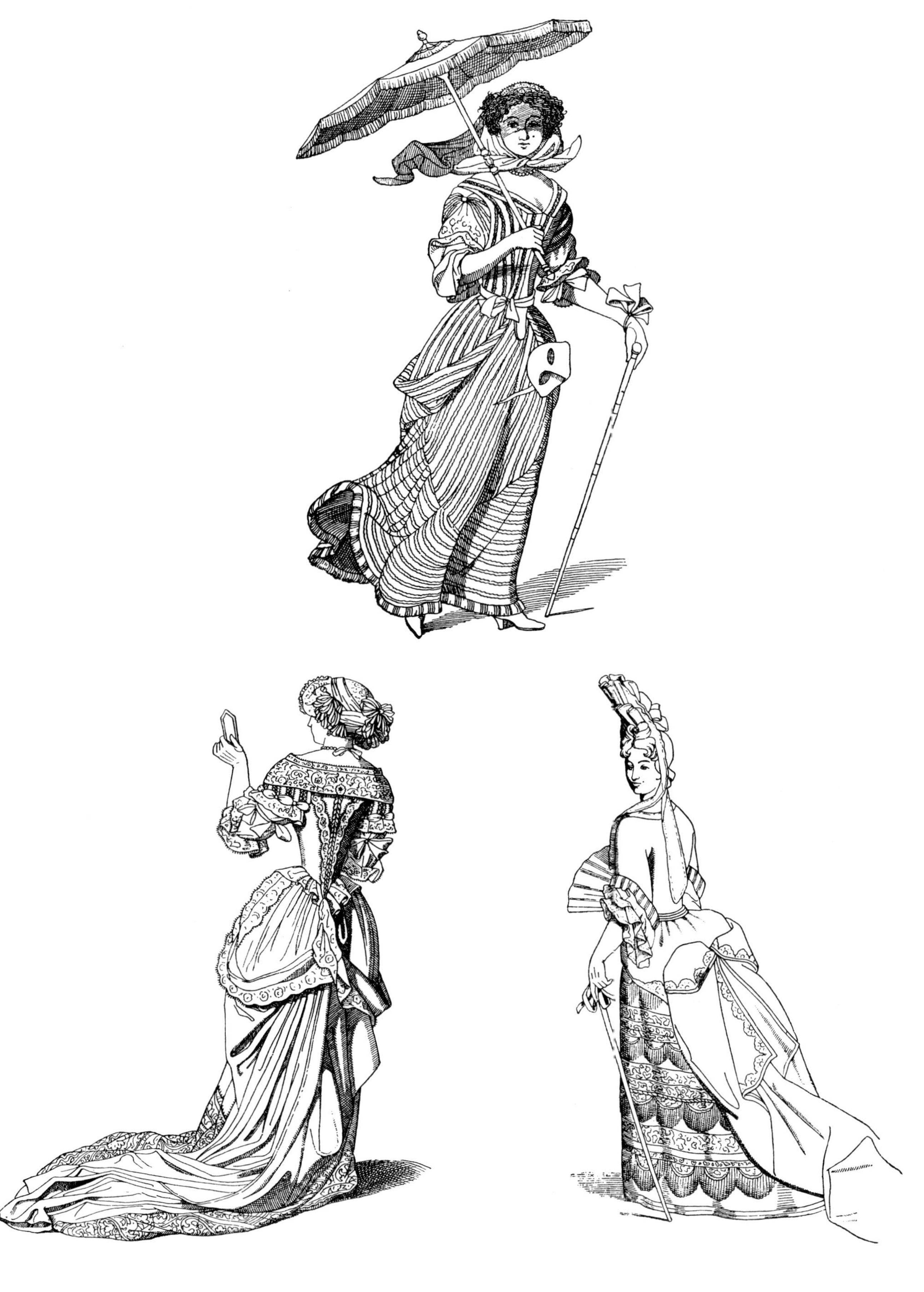

French ladies | Französische Damen | Dame francesi | Dames françaises | Damas francesas

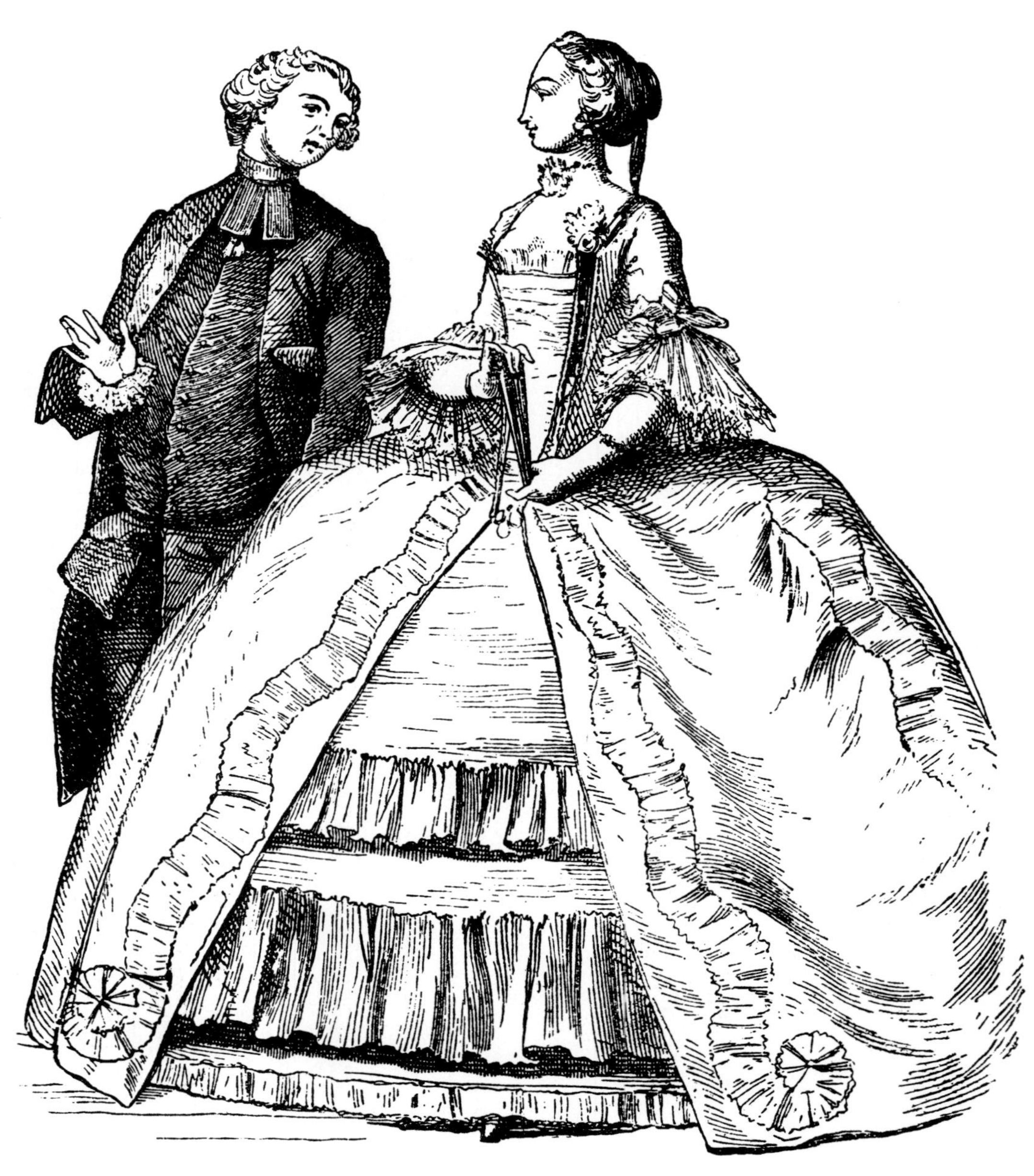

German couple — Deutsches Paar — Coppia tedesca — Couple allemand — Pareja alemana

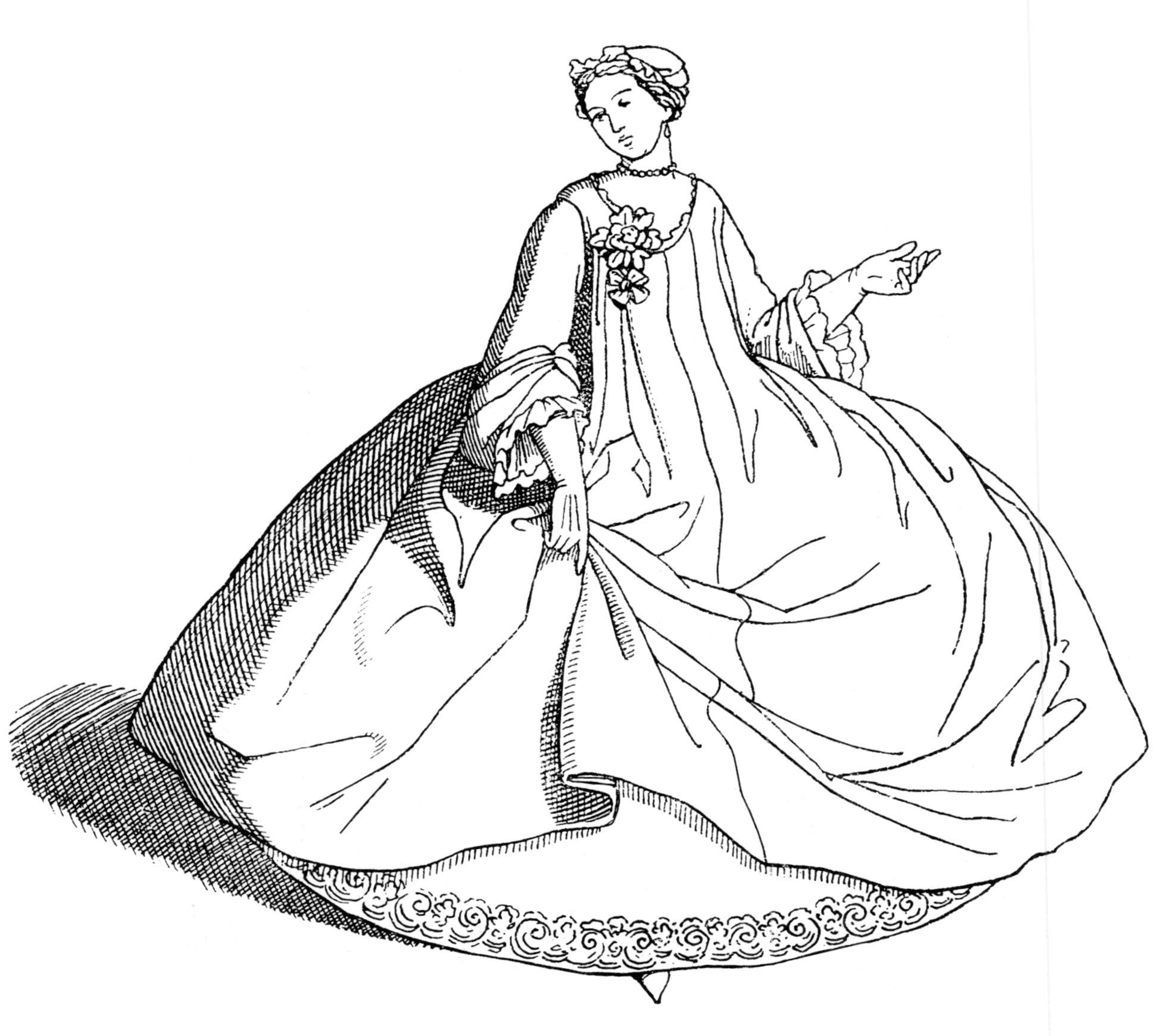

German lady | Deutsche Dame | Dama tedesca | Dame allemande | Dama alemana

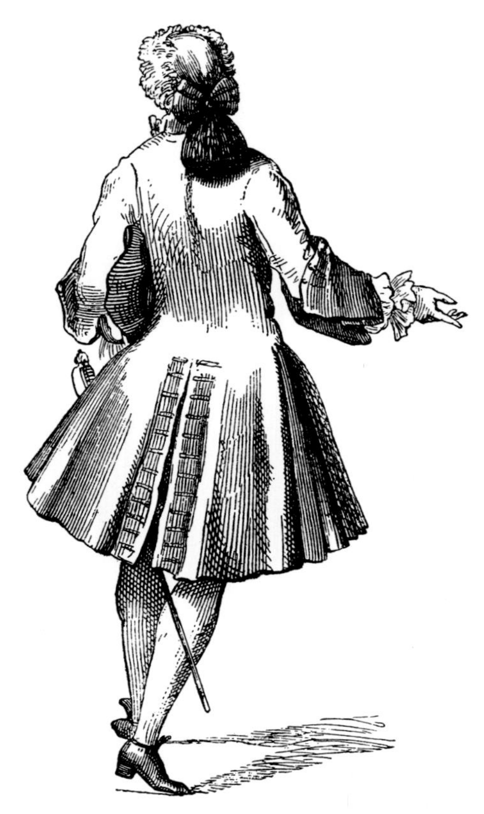

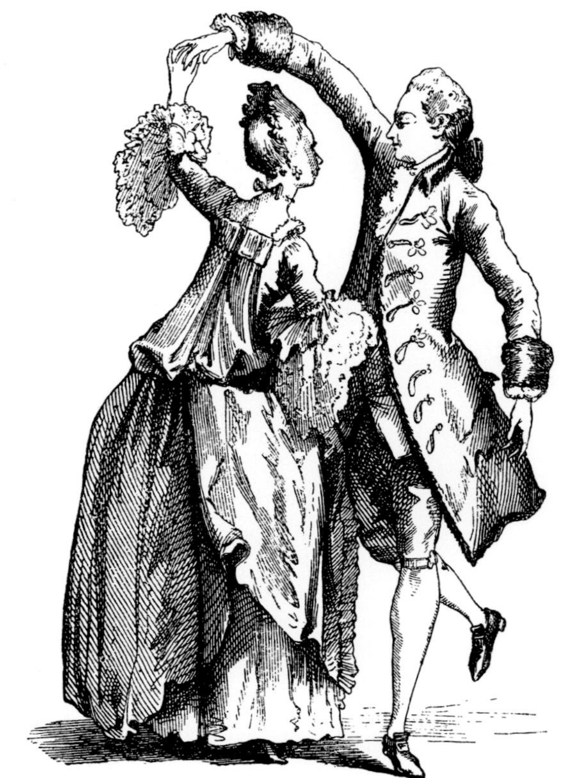

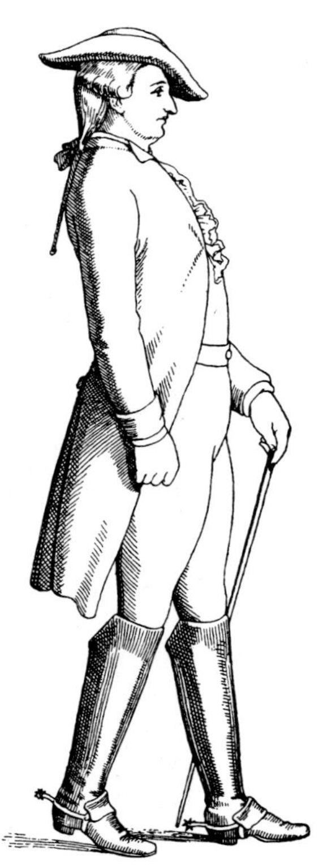

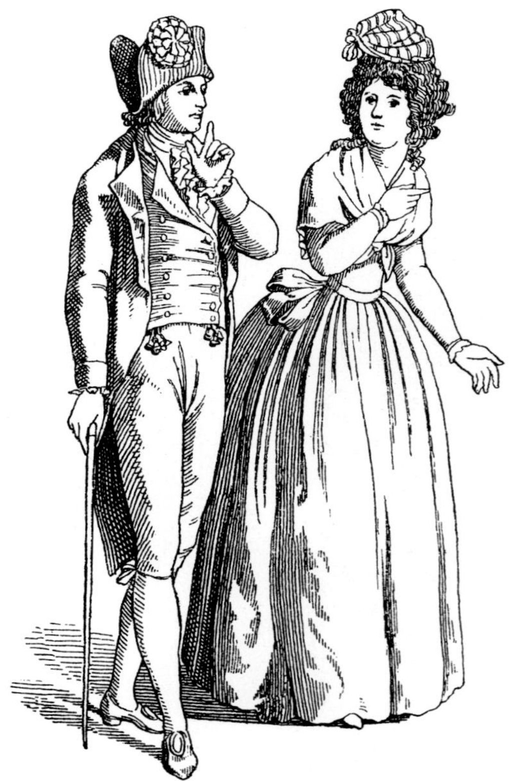

a	Men's coat, Germany	Herrenjacke, Deutschland	Cappotto da uomo, Germania	Habit masculin, Allemagne	Abrigo de hombre, Alemania
b	French couple	Französisches Paar	Coppia francese	Couple français	Pareja francesa
c	German man	Deutscher Mann	Uomo tedesco	Allemand	Hombre alemán
d	German couple	Deutsches Paar	Coppia tedesca	Couple allemand	Pareja alemana

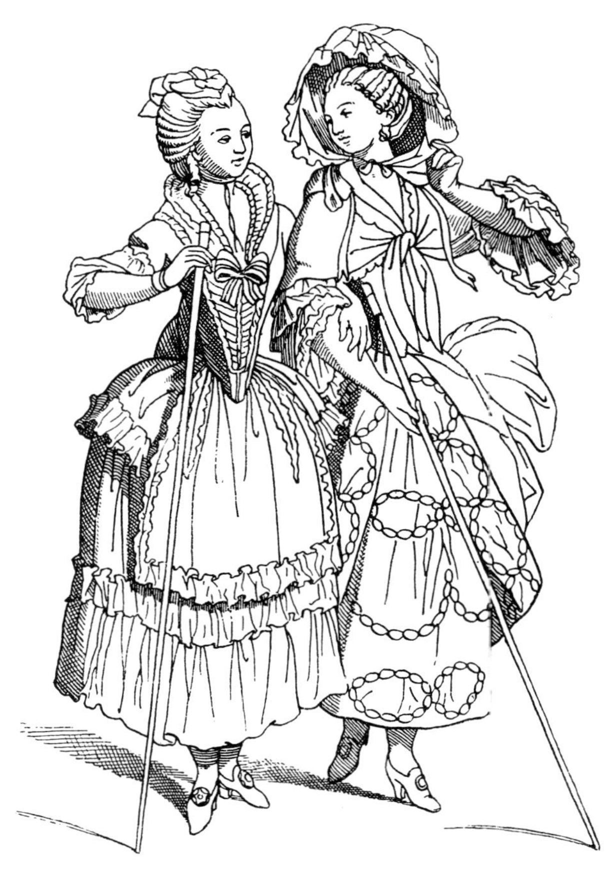

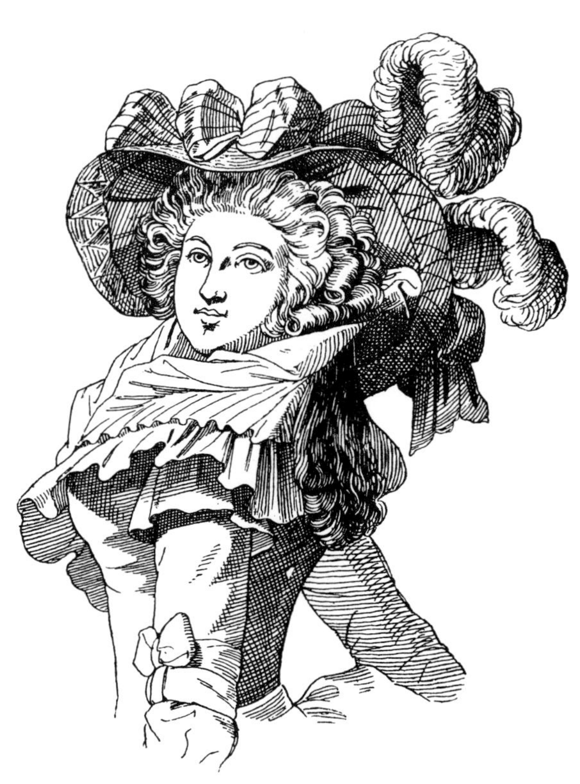

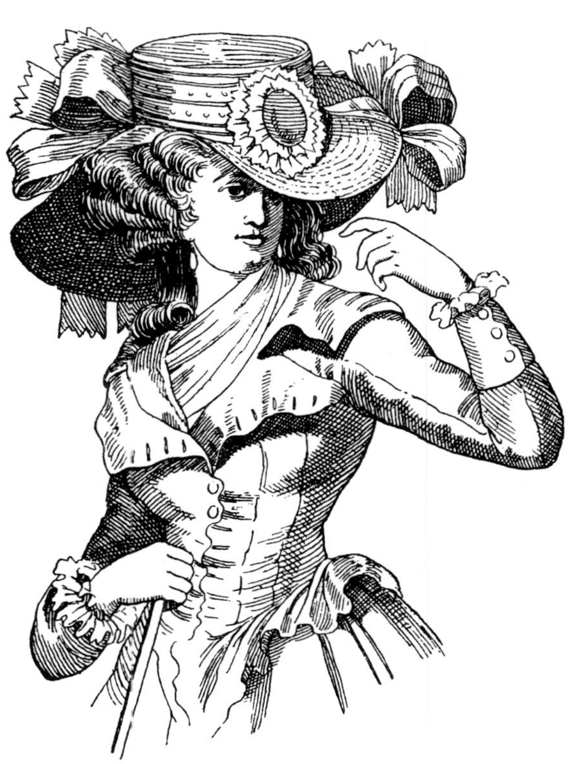

French ladies Französische Damen Dame francesi Dames françaises Damas francesas

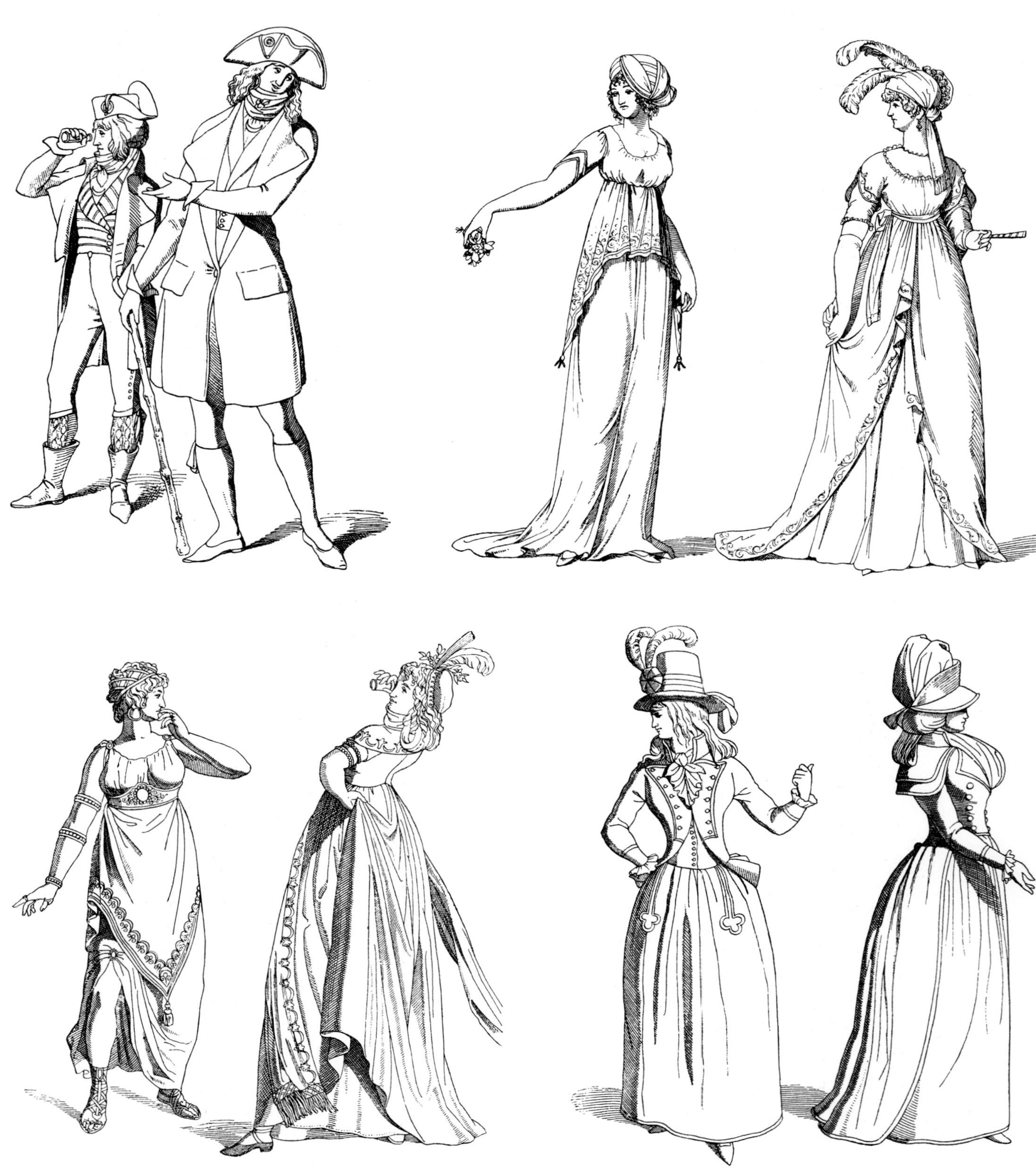

Late 18th-century men's and women's fashion

Elegante Kleidung für Männer und Frauen aus dem späten 18. Jahrhundert

Moda da uomo e da donna del tardo XVIII secolo

Mode homme et femme de la fin du XVIIIe siècle

Moda masculina y femenina de finales del siglo XVIII

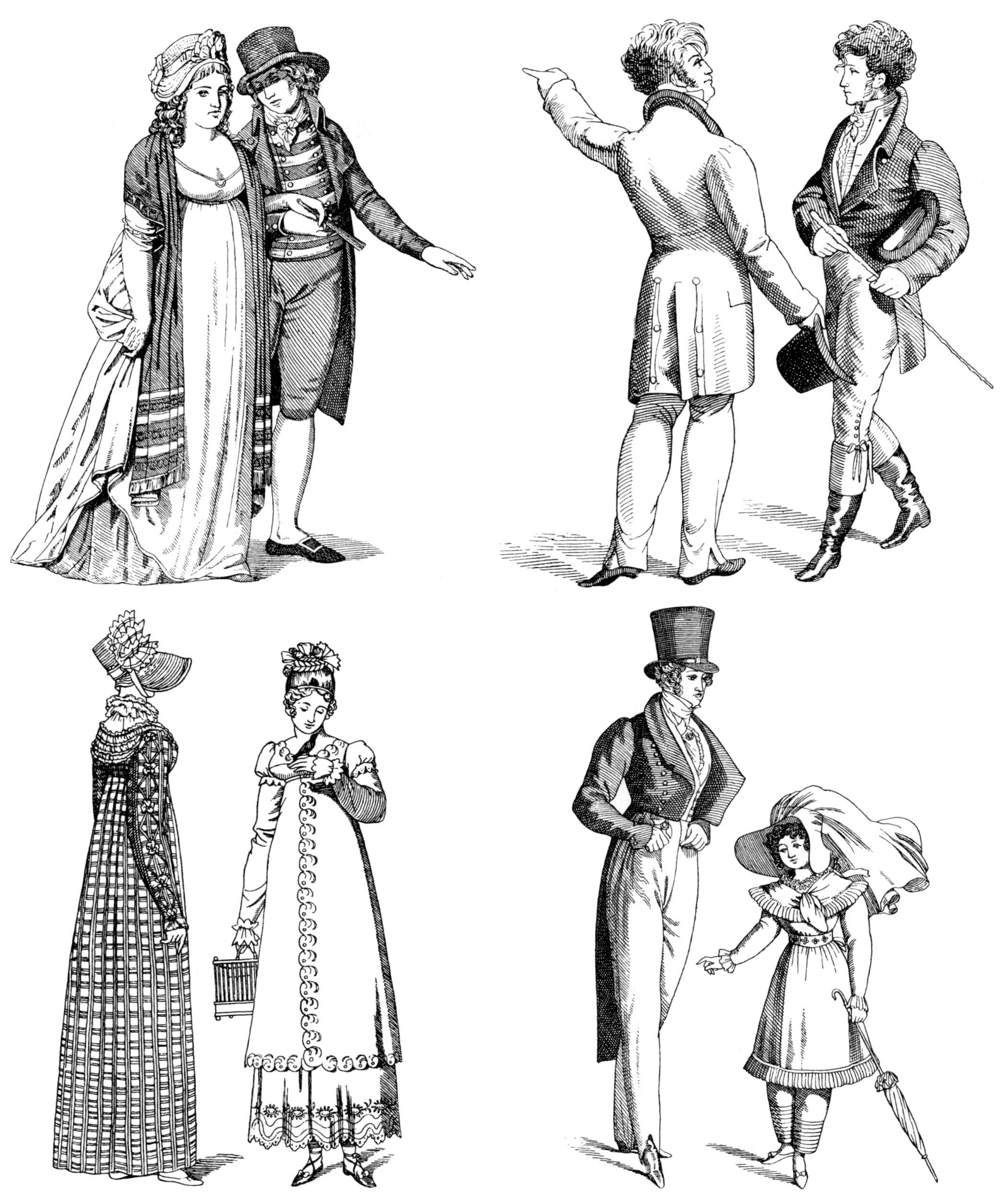

a	German couple	Deutsches Paar	Coppia tedesca	Couple allemand	Pareja alemana
b	Young men from Berlin	Junge Männer aus Berlin	Giovani di Berlino	Jeunes gens de Berlin	Jóvenes berlineses
c	French ladies	Französische Damen	Dame francesi	Dames françaises	Damas francesas
d	German man and girl	Deutscher Mann mit Mädchen	Uomo e ragazza tedeschi	Homme et petite fille allemands	Hombre y niña alemanes

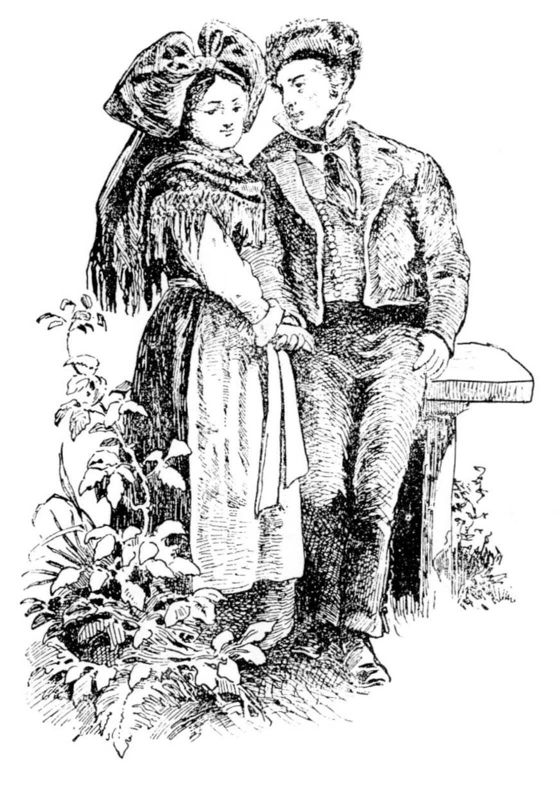

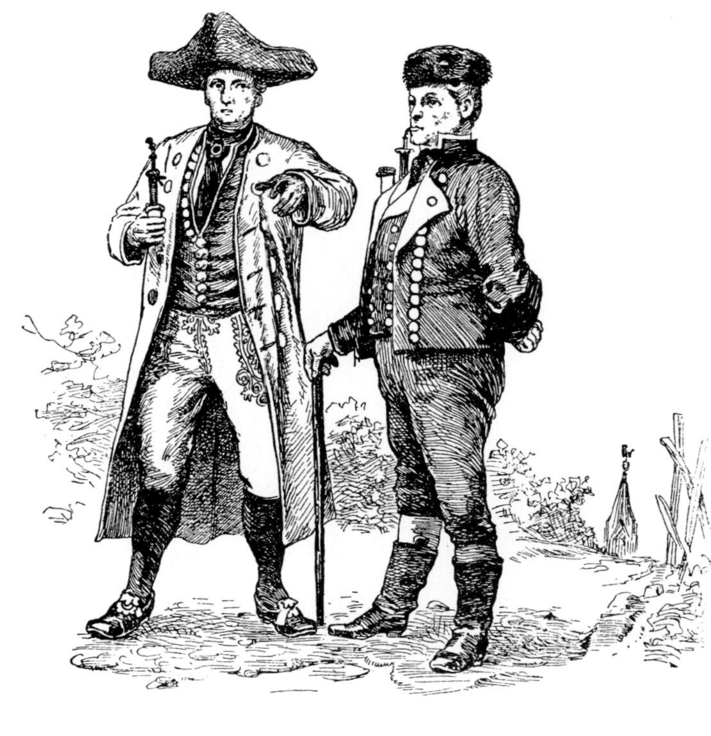

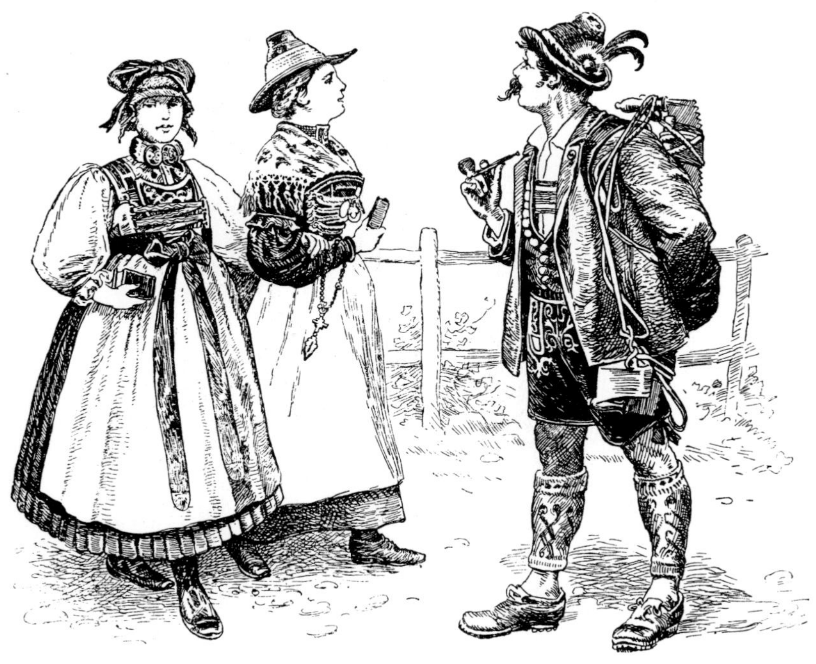

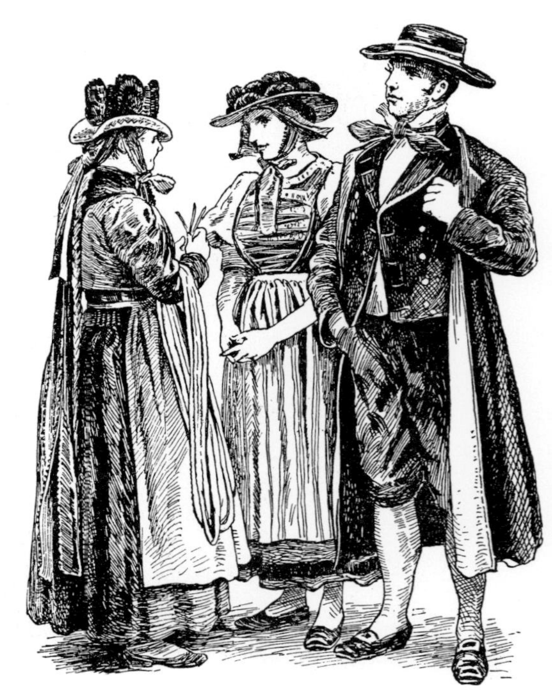

a	Alsace	Elsass	Alsazia	Alsace	Alsacia
b	Wurtemberg	Württemberg	Würtemberg	Würtemberg	Wurtemberg
c	Bavaria	Bayern	Baviera	Bavière	Bavaria
d	Baden	Baden	Baden	Baden	Baden

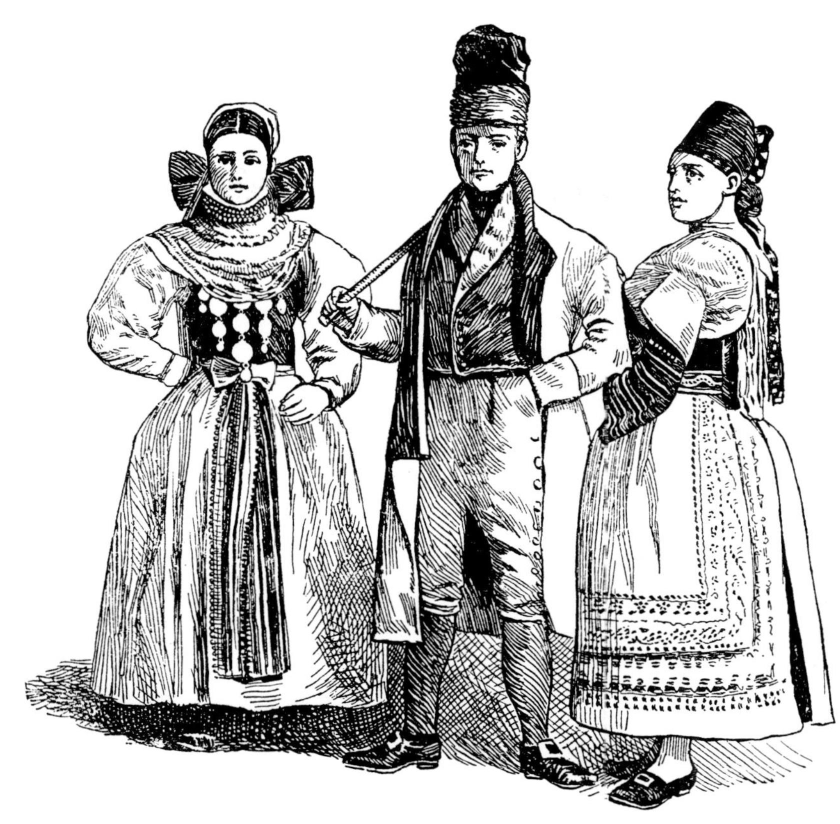

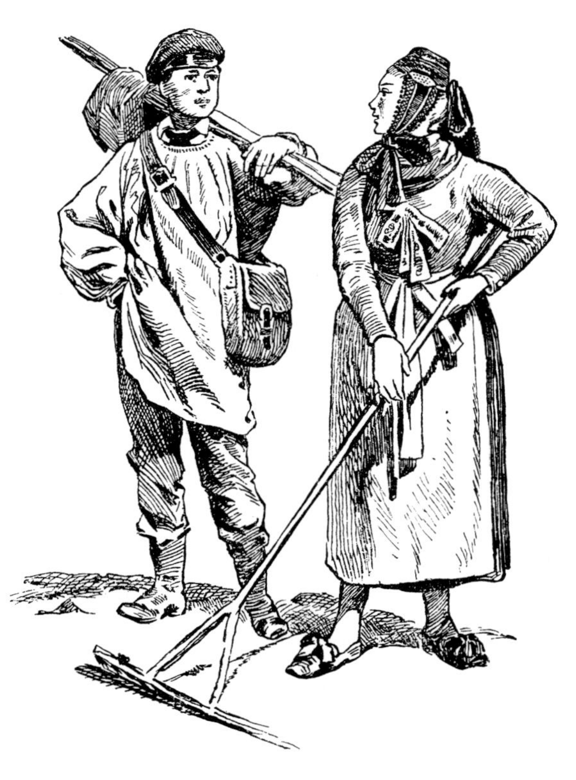

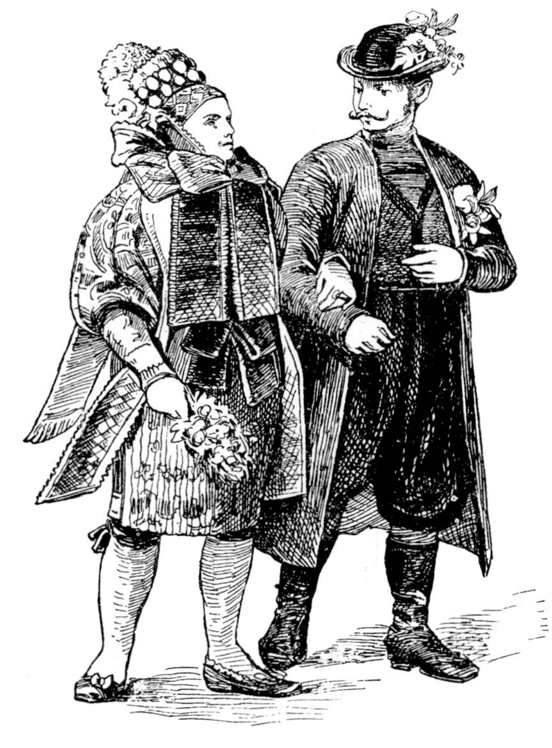

a	Polish dress	Polnische Trachten	Abiti polacchi	Vêtements polonais	Trajes polacos
b	Rhineland, Germany	Rheinland, Deutschland	Renania, Germania	Rheinland, Allemagne	Renania, Alemania
c	Thüringa, Germany	Thüringen, Deutschland	Turingia, Germania	Thüringa, Allemagne	Turingia, Alemania

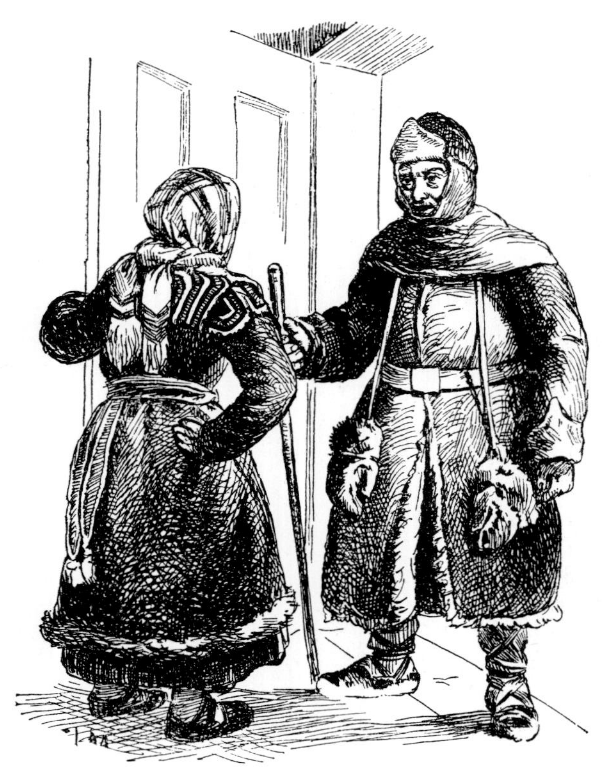

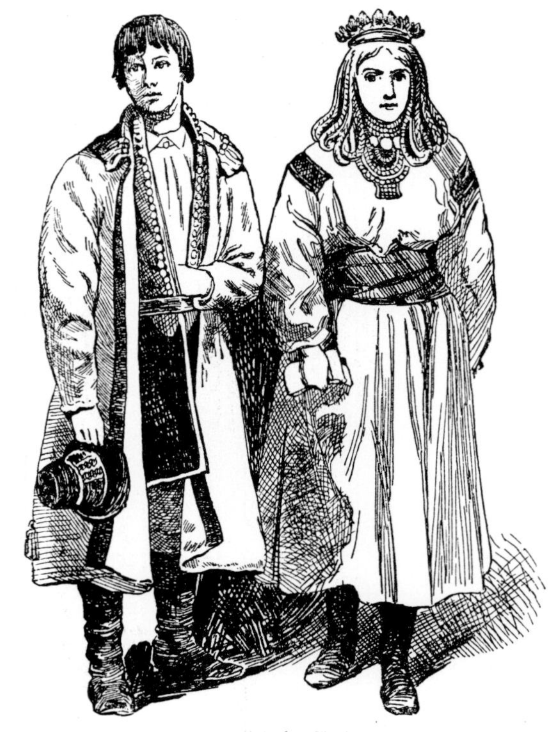

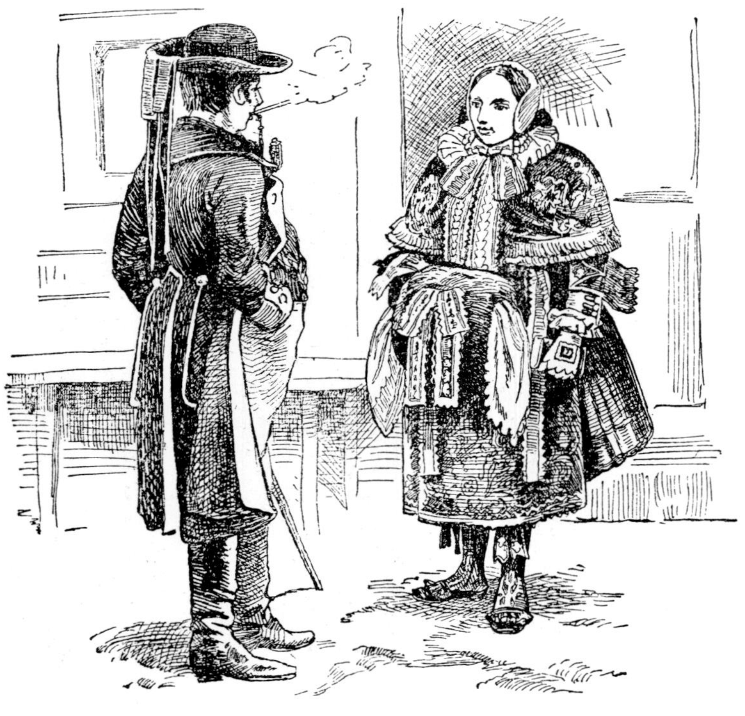

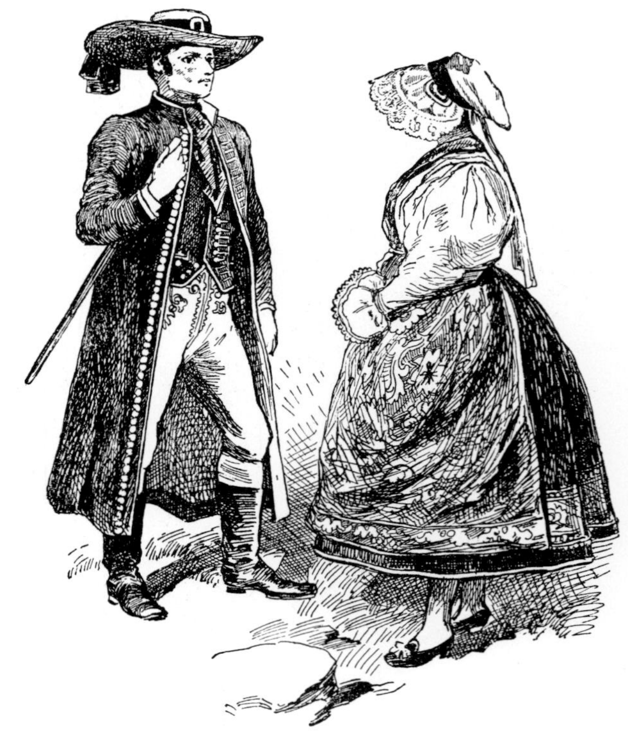

a	Lithuania	Littauen	Lituania	Lithuanie	Lituania
b+c	Poland	Polen	Polonia	Pologne	Polonia
d	Bohemia	Böhmen	Boemia	Bohème	Bohemia

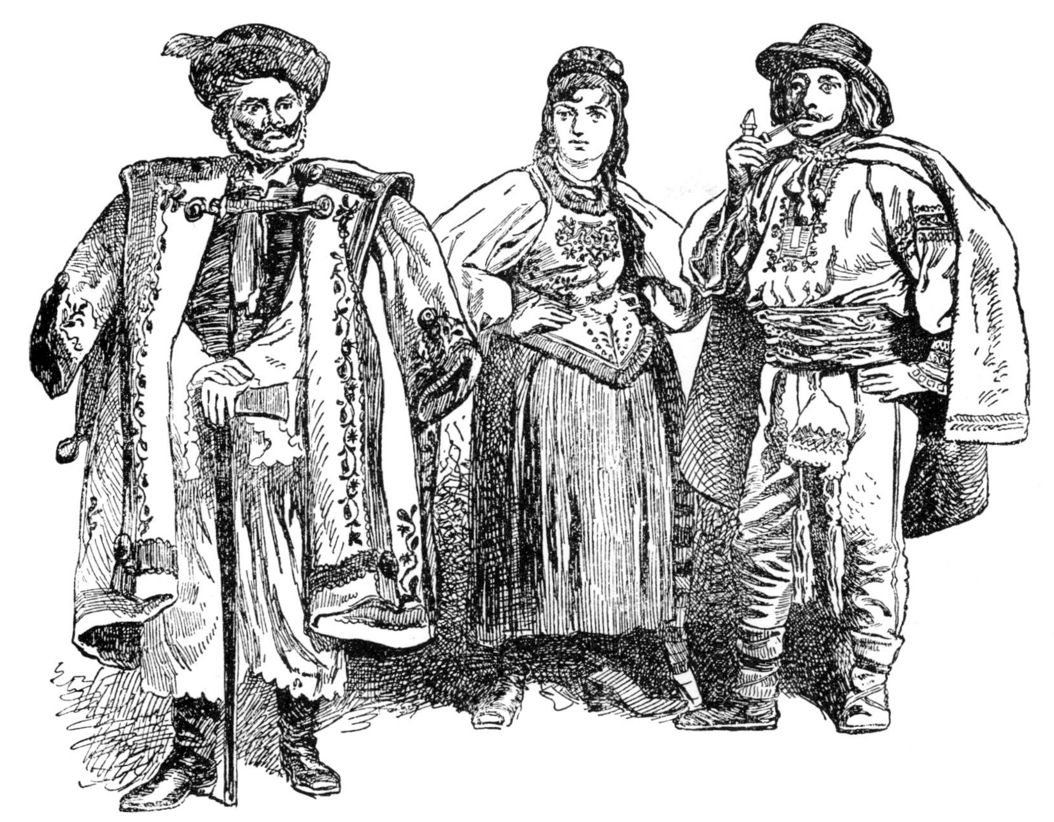

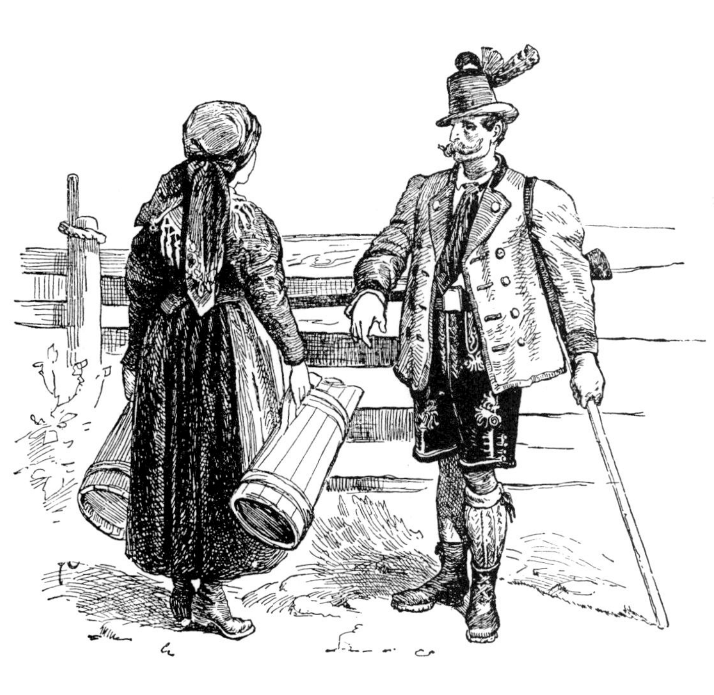

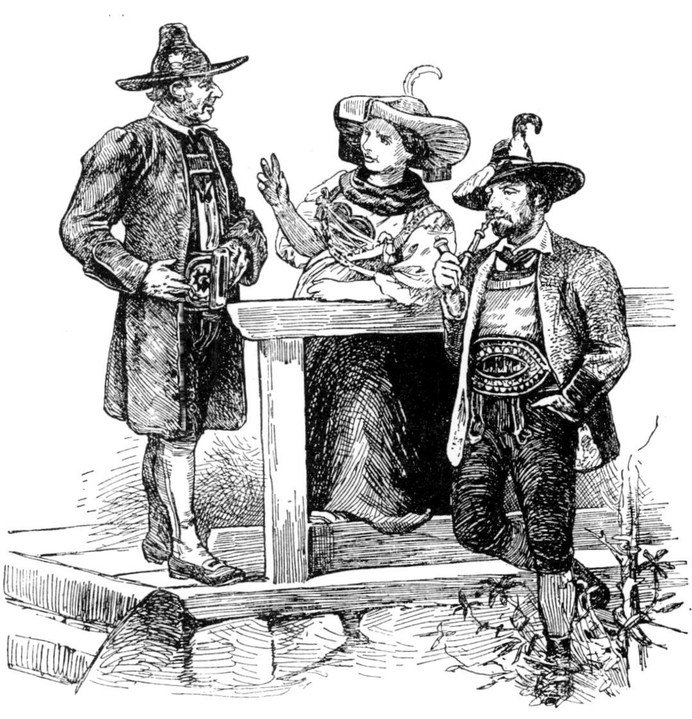

a	Hungary	Ungarn	Ungheria	Hongrie	Hungría
b+c	Austria	Österreich	Austria	Autriche	Austria

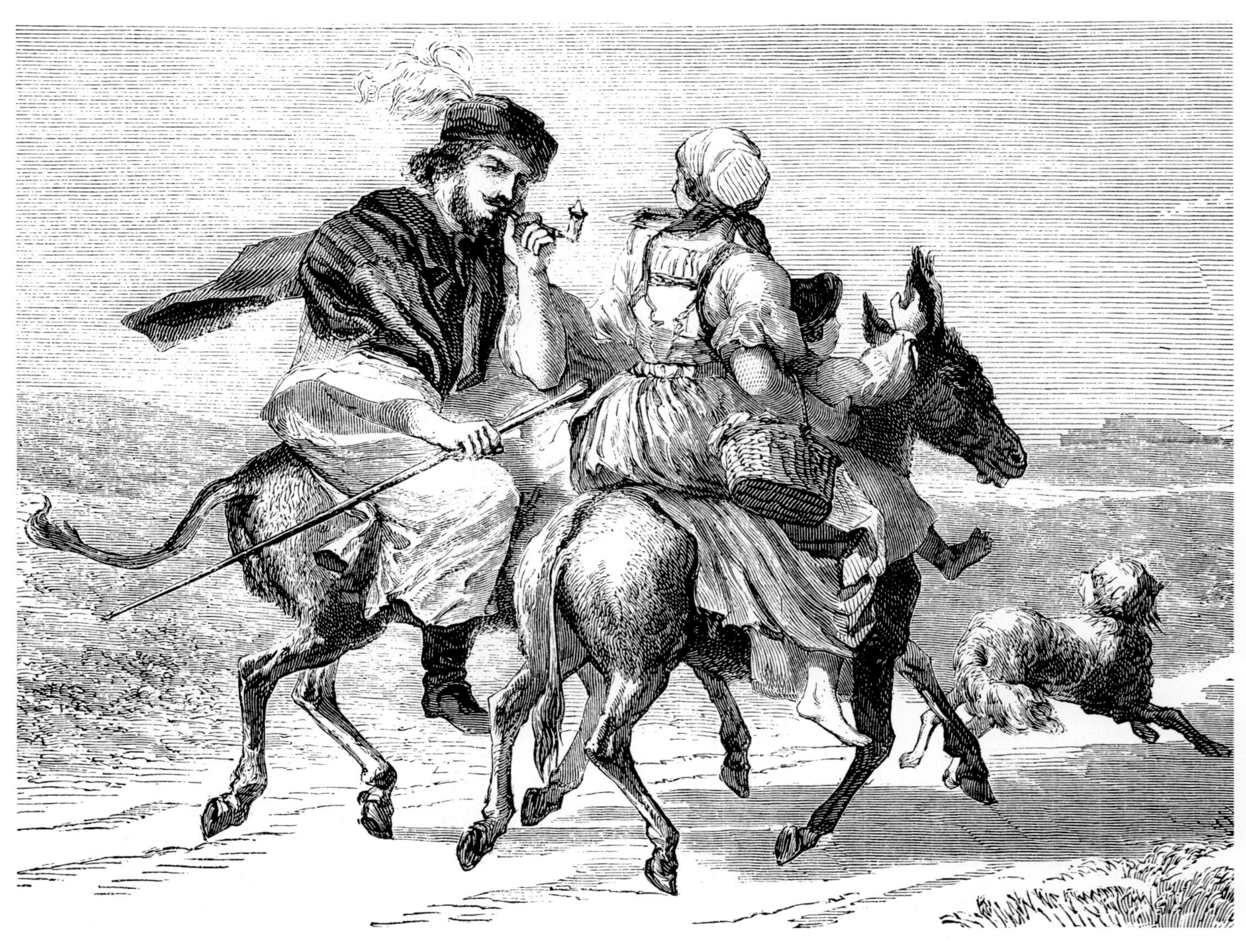

Hungary Ungarn Ungheria Hongrie Hungría

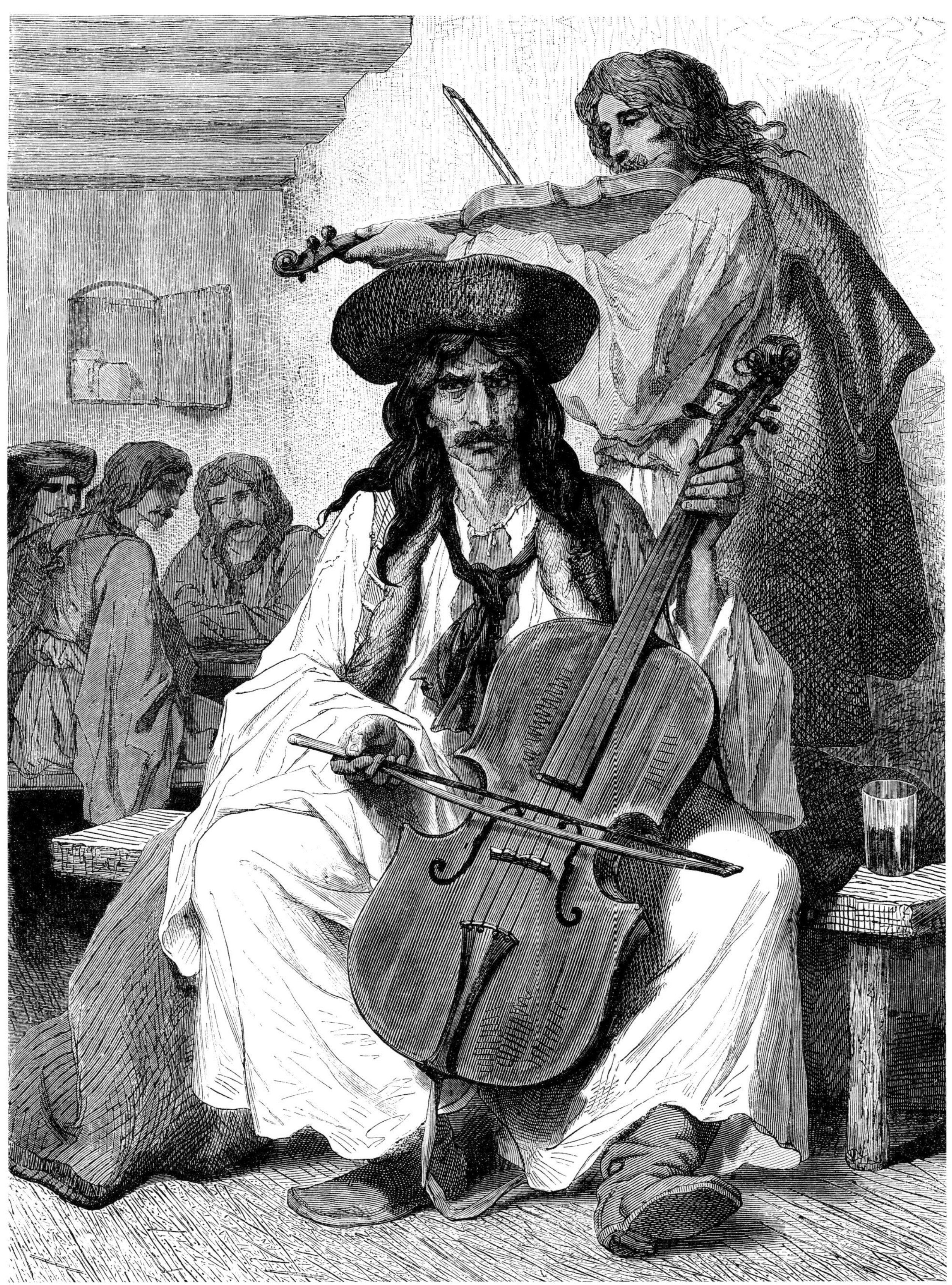

Gypsy musician in Hungary

Zigeunermusiker in Ungarn

Musicista gitano in Ungheria

Musicien Tzigane en Hongrie

Músico gitano en Hungría

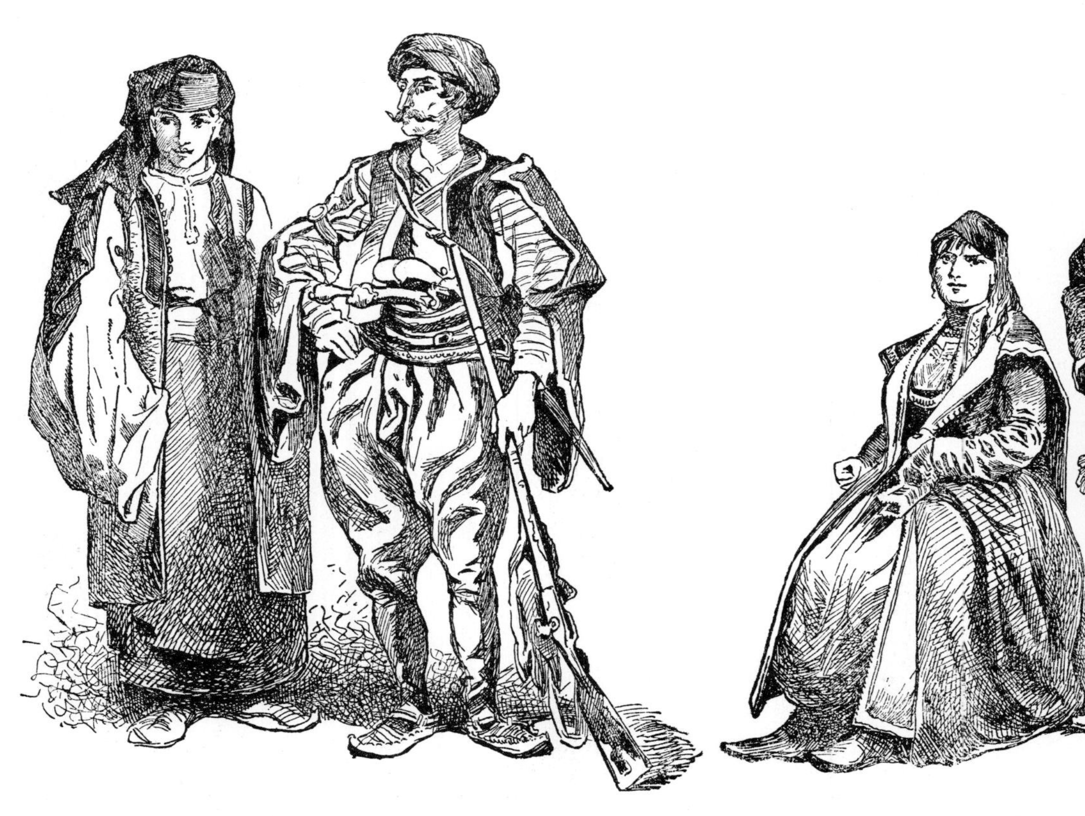

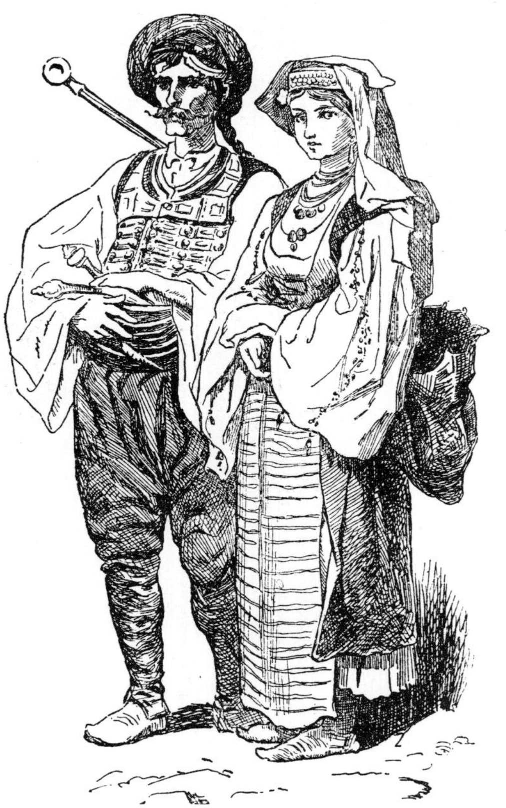

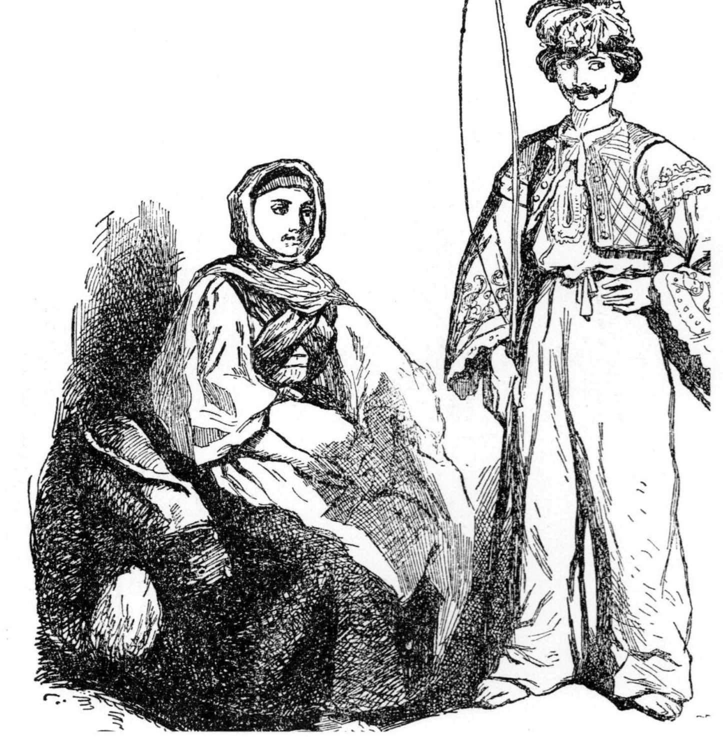

a	Hercogovinia	Herzegowina	Erzegovina	Herzégovine	Herzegovina
b	Bosnia	Bosnien	Bosnia	Bosnie	Bosnia
c	Dalmatia	Dalmatien	Dalmazia	Dalmatie	Dalmacia
d	Solovakia	Slowakei	Slovacchia	Slovaquie	Eslovaquia

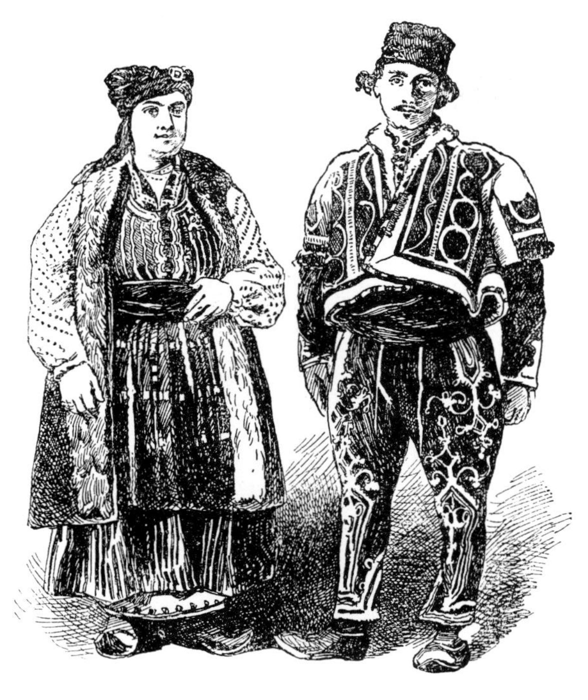

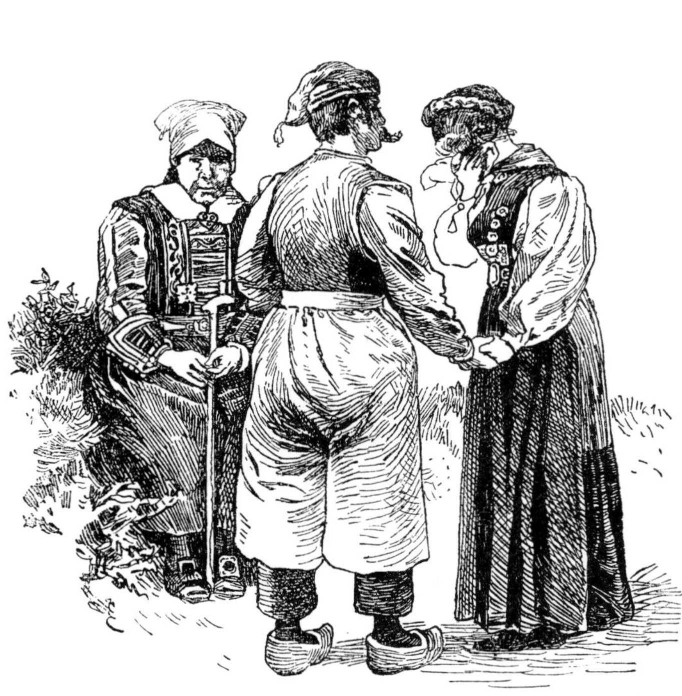

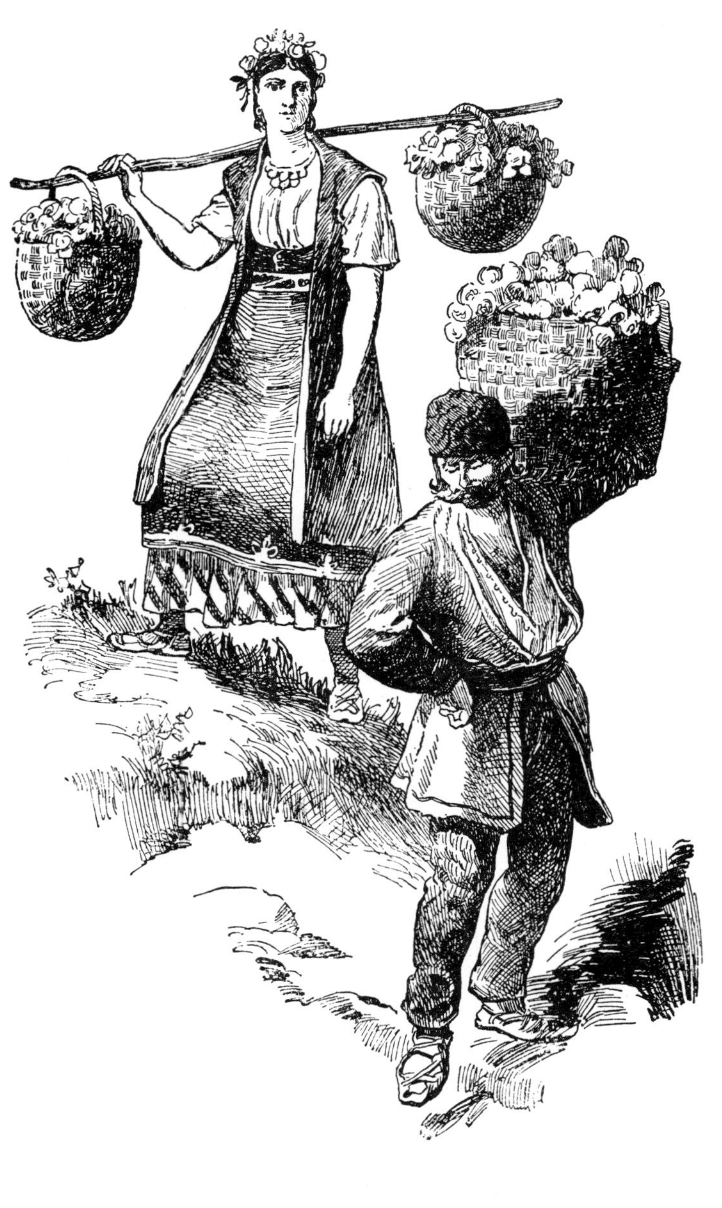

a+ b	Bulgaria	Bulgarien	Bulgaria	Bulgarie	Bulgaria
c	Greece	Griechenland	Grecia	Grèce	Grecia

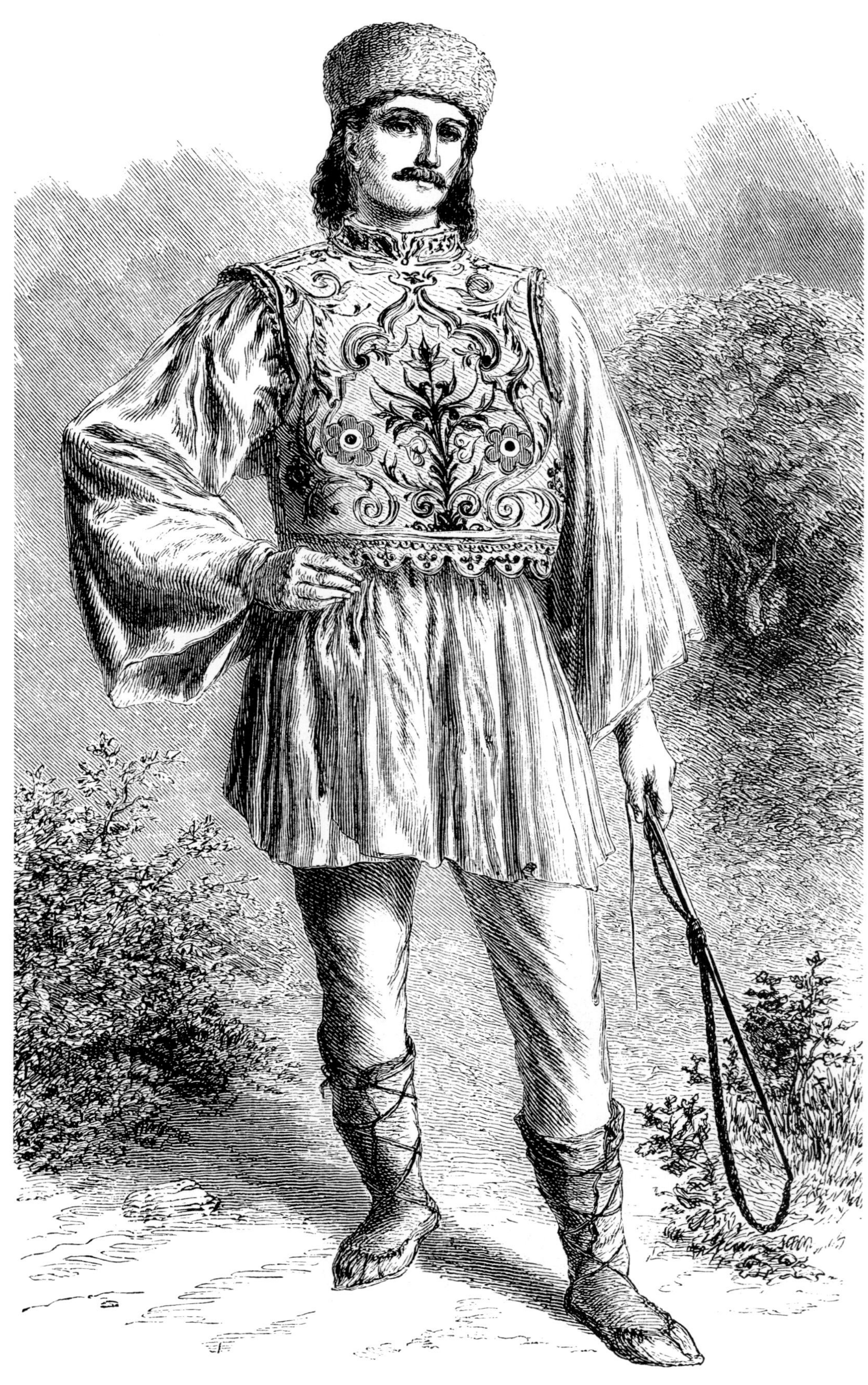

Rumanian man, c. 1860 Rumäne, um 1860 Uomo rumeno, ca. 1860 Roumain, vers 1860 Hombre rumano, hacia el año 1860

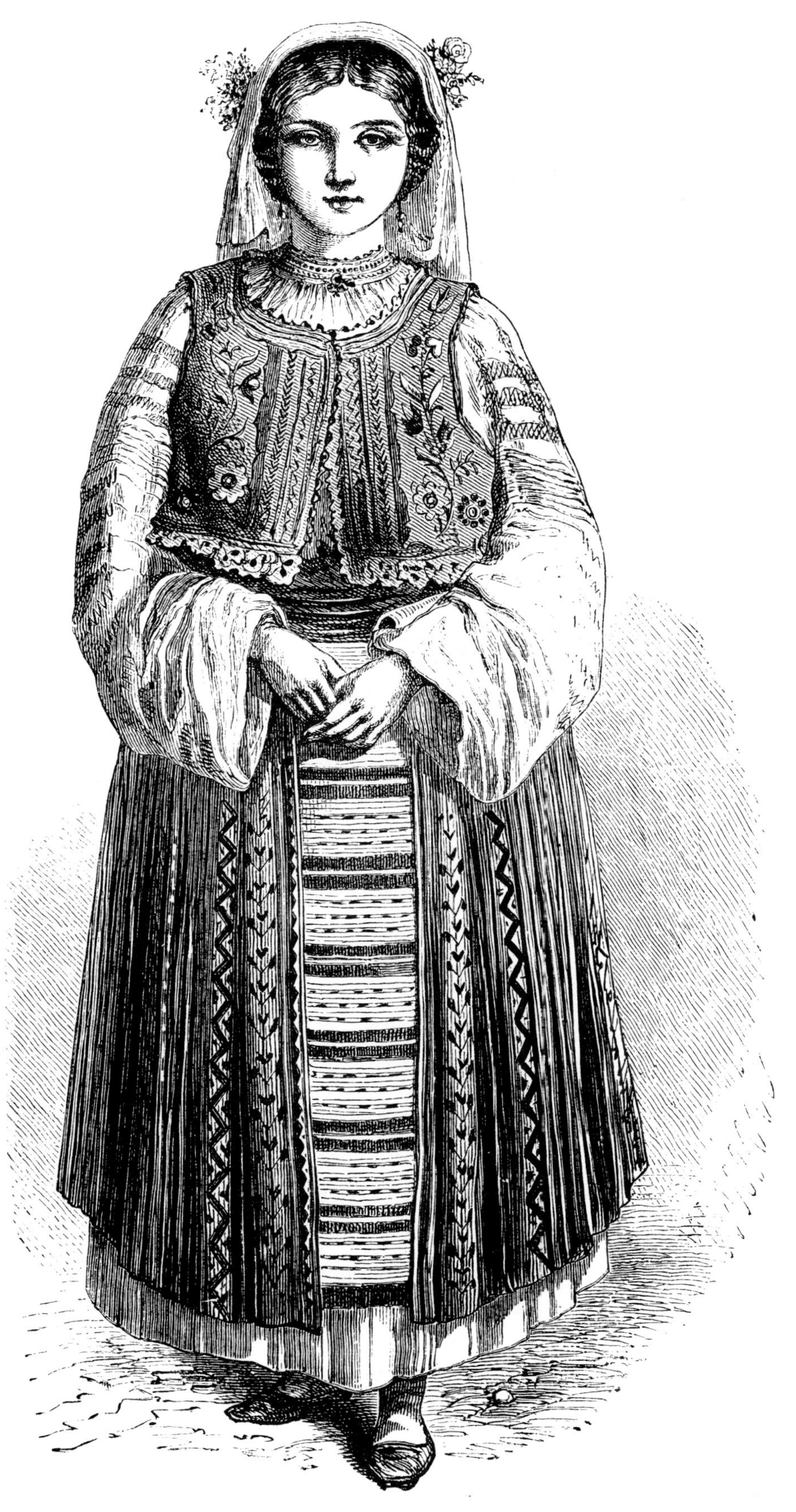

Rumanian woman, c. 1860

Rumänin, um 1860

Donna rumena, ca. 1860

Roumaine, vers 1860

Mujer rumana, hacia el año 1860

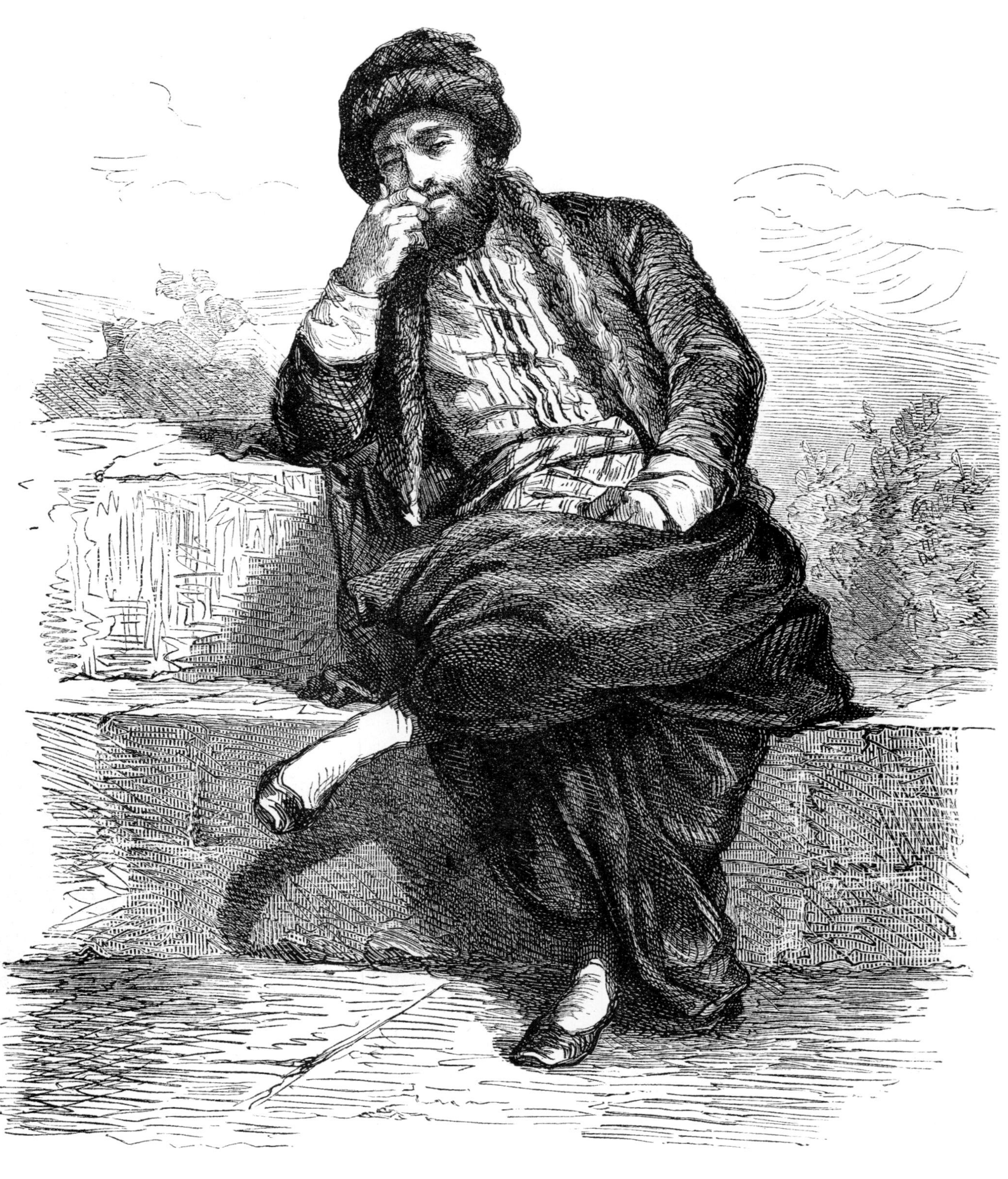

Jewish man from Thessaloniki, c. 1880

Jüdischer Mann aus Thessaloniki, um 1880

Ebreo di Tessalonica, ca. 1880

Juif de Thessalonique, vers 1880

Hombre judío de Salónica, hacia 1880

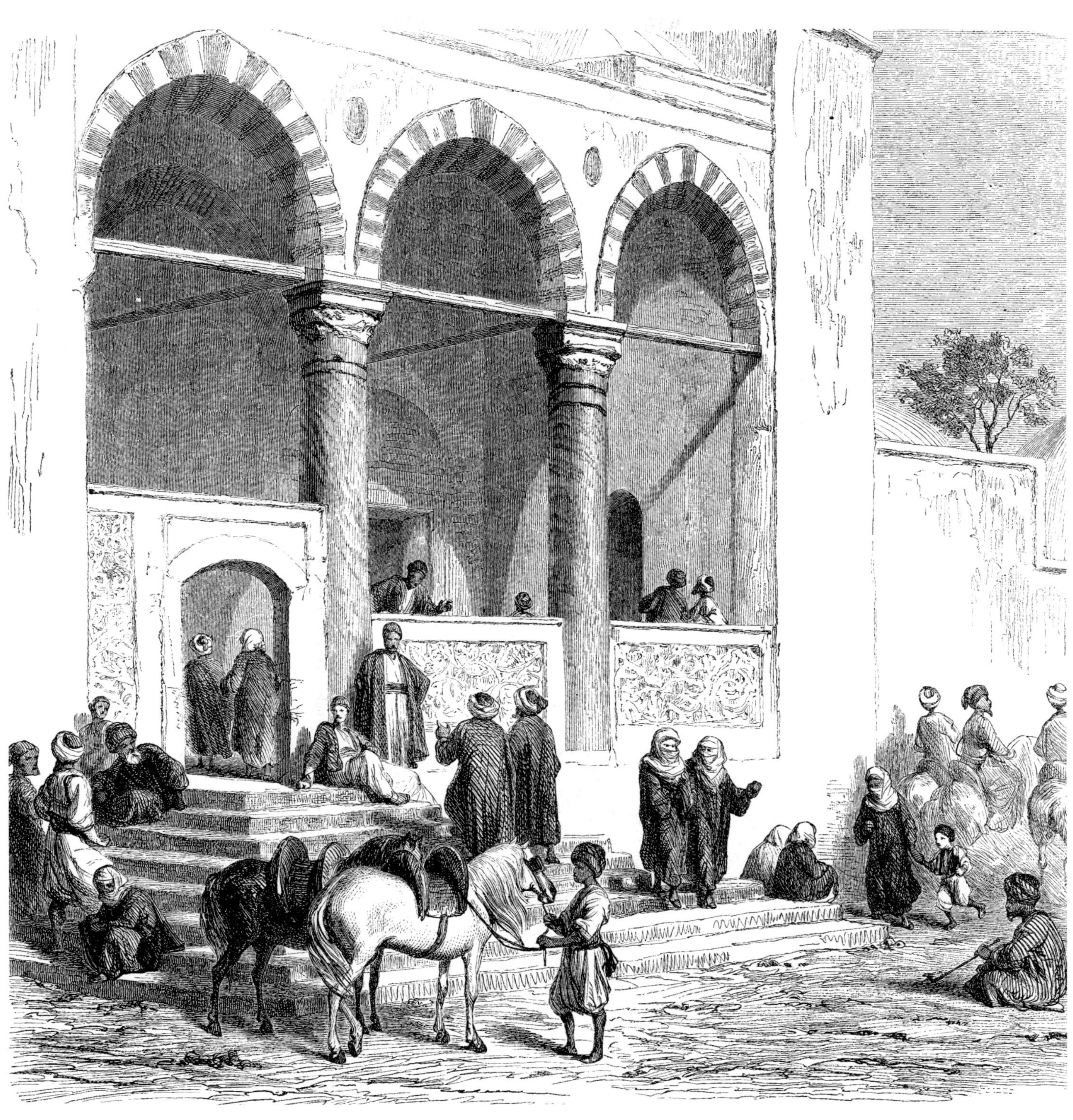

Muslims at the mosque of Thessaoloniki, c. 1880

Moslems vor der Moschee von Thessaloniki, um 1880

Musulmani alla moschea di Tessalonica, ca. 1880

Musulmans à la mosquée de Thessalonique, vers 1880

Musulmanes en la mezquita de Salónica, hacia el año 1880

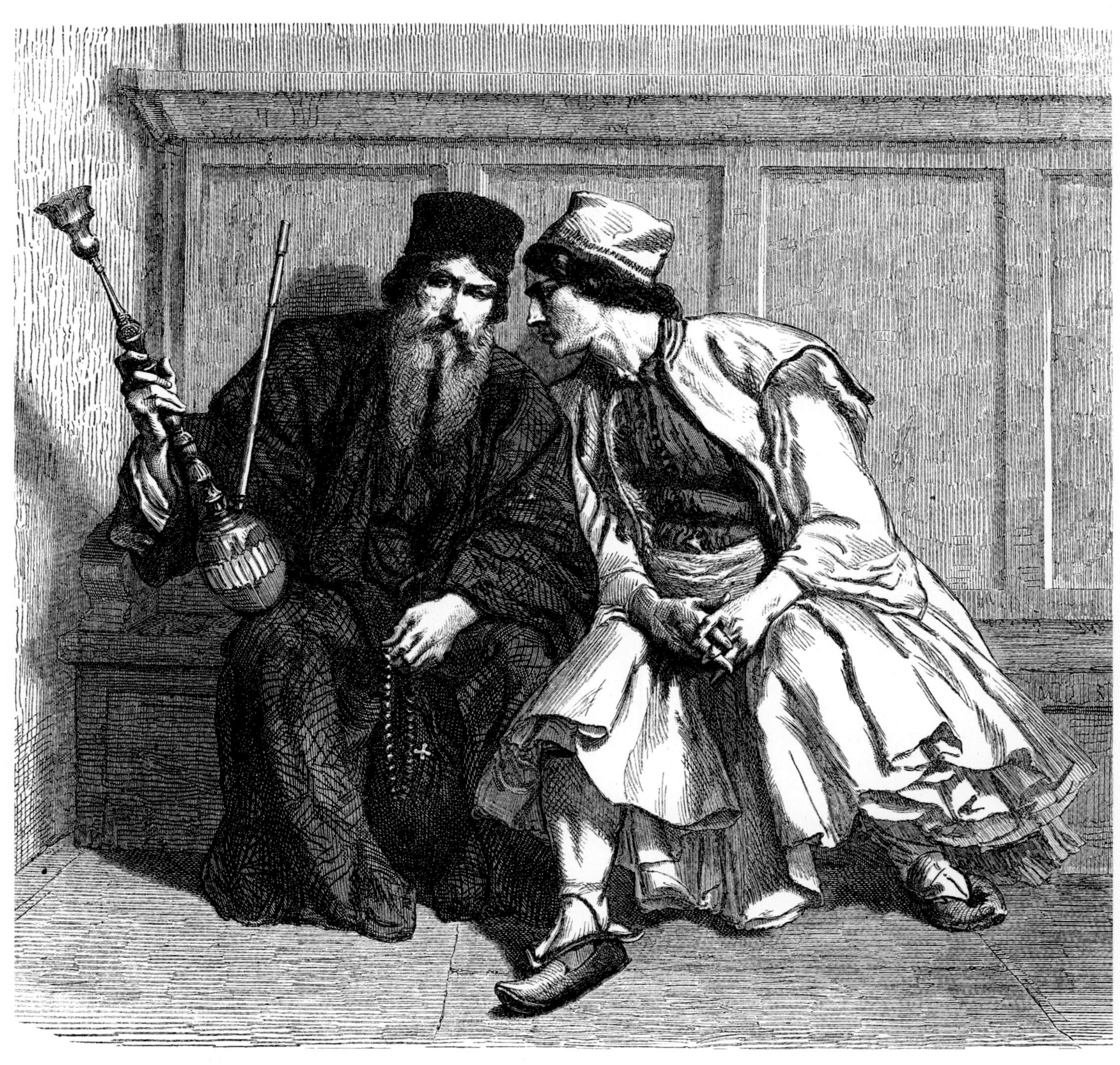

Orthodox cleric hearing confession, Greece, c. 1880

Orthodoxer Geistlicher beim Abnehmen der Beichte, Griechenland, um 1880

Sacerdote ortodosso in confessione, Grecia, ca. 1880

Ecclésiastique orthodoxe en confession, Grèce, vers 1880

Clérigo ortodoxo escuchando una confesión, Grecia, hacia 1880

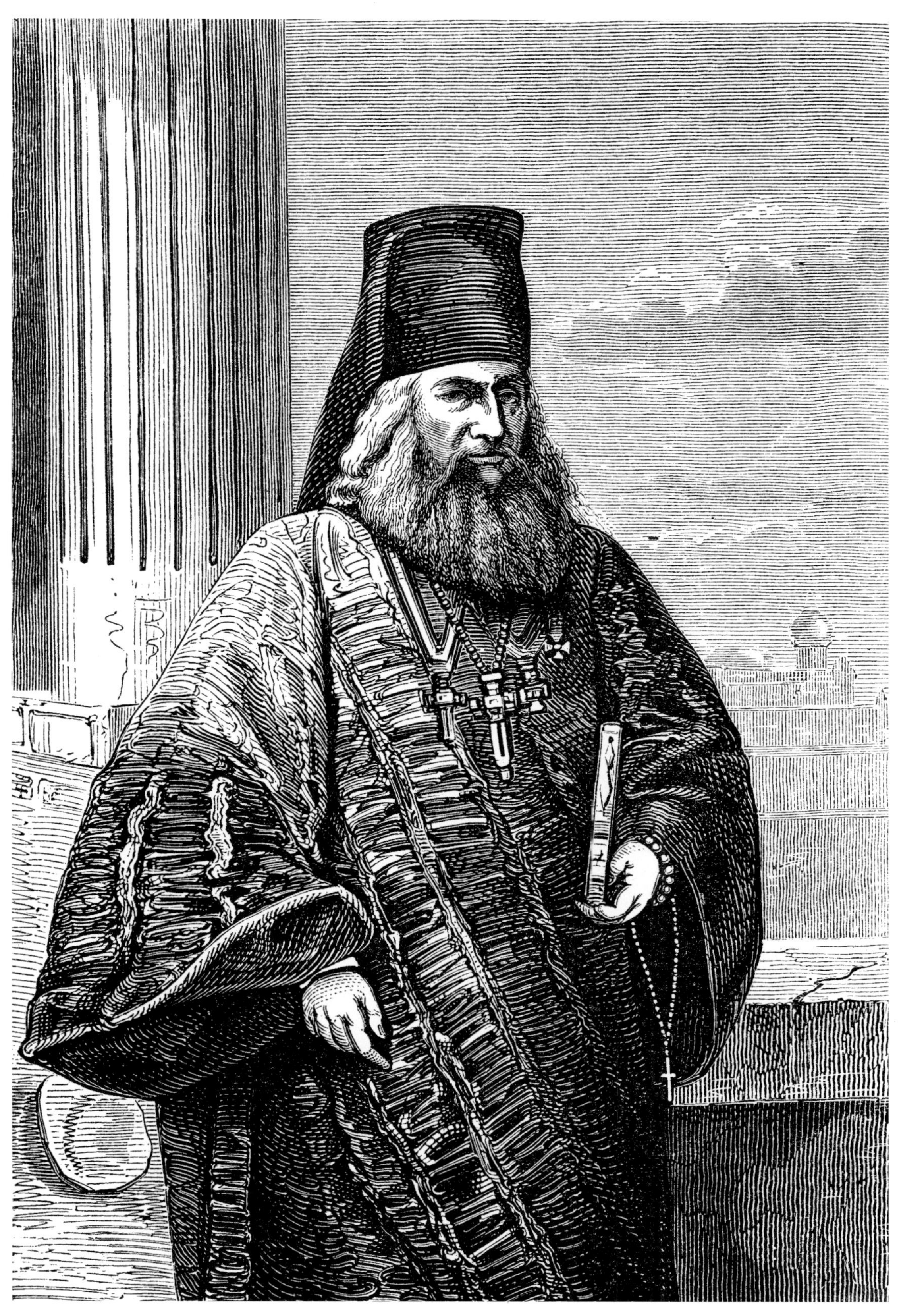

Greek Orthodox cleric, c. 1870

Griechisch-orthodoxer Geistlicher, um 1870

Sacerdote greco ortodosso, ca. 1870

Ecclésiastique grec orthodoxe, vers 1870

Clérigo ortodoxo griego, hacia 1870

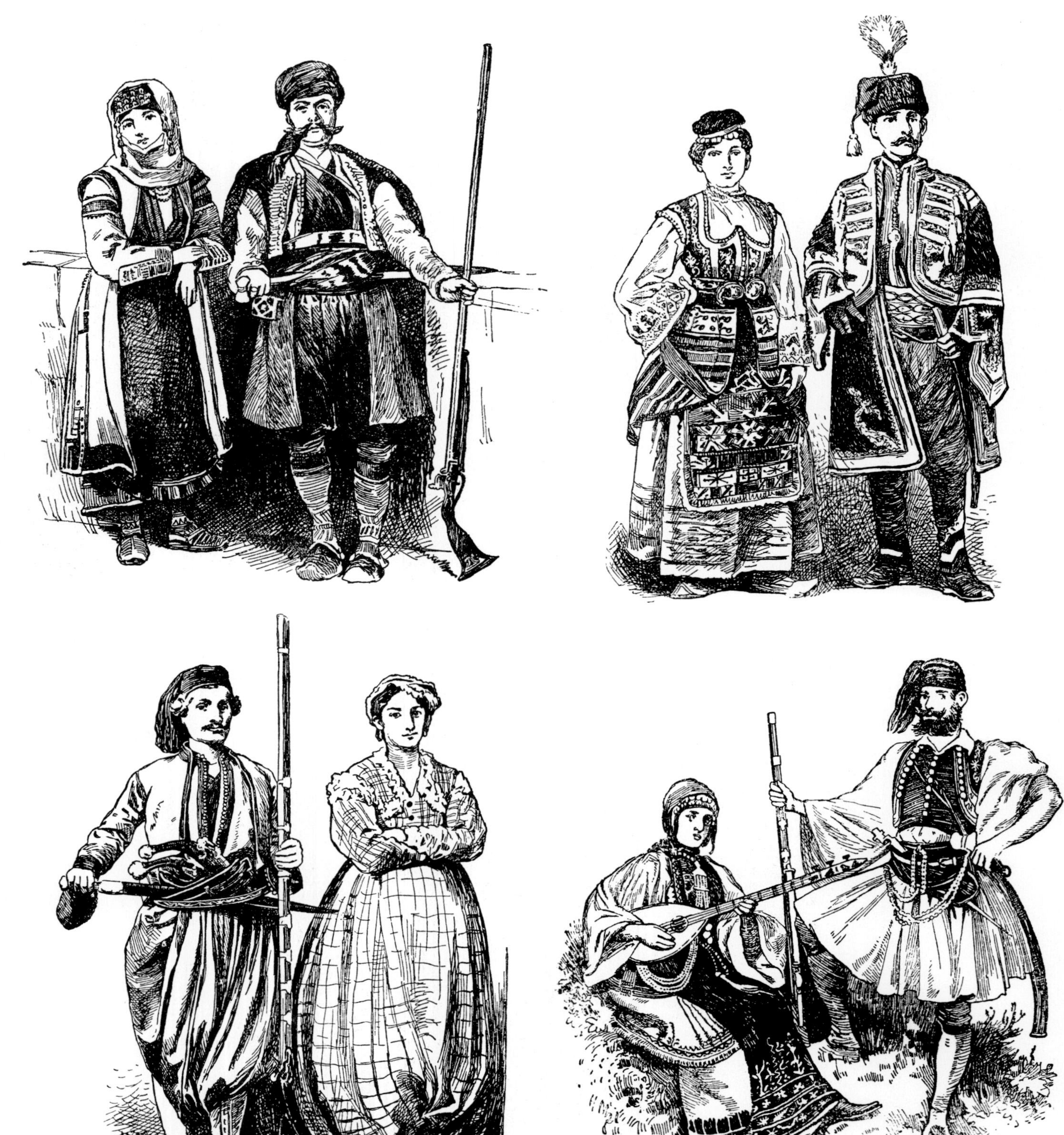

a	Montenegro	Montenegro	Montenegro	Montenegro	Montenegro
b	Serbia	Serbien	Serbia	Serbie	Serbia
c+d	Greece	Griechenland	Grecia	Grèce	Grecia

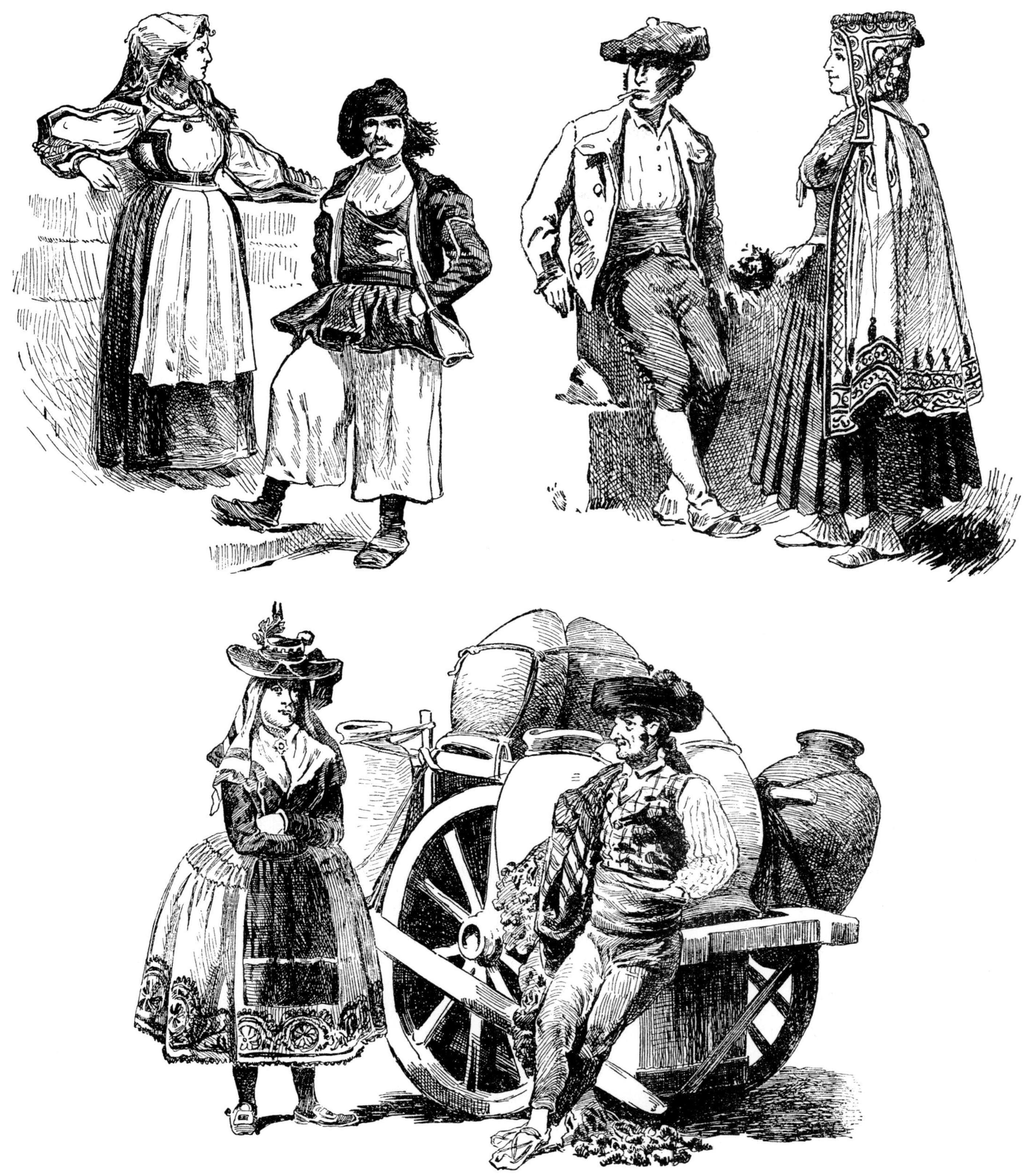

a	Sardinia, Italy	Sardinien, Italien	Sardegna, Italia	Sardaigne, Italie	Cerdeña, Italia
b	Basque country, Spain	Baskenland, Spanien	Paesi Baschi, Spagna	Pays Basque, Espagne	País Vasco, España
c	Aragon, Spain	Aragon, Spanien	Aragona, Spagna	Aragon, Espagne	Aragón, España

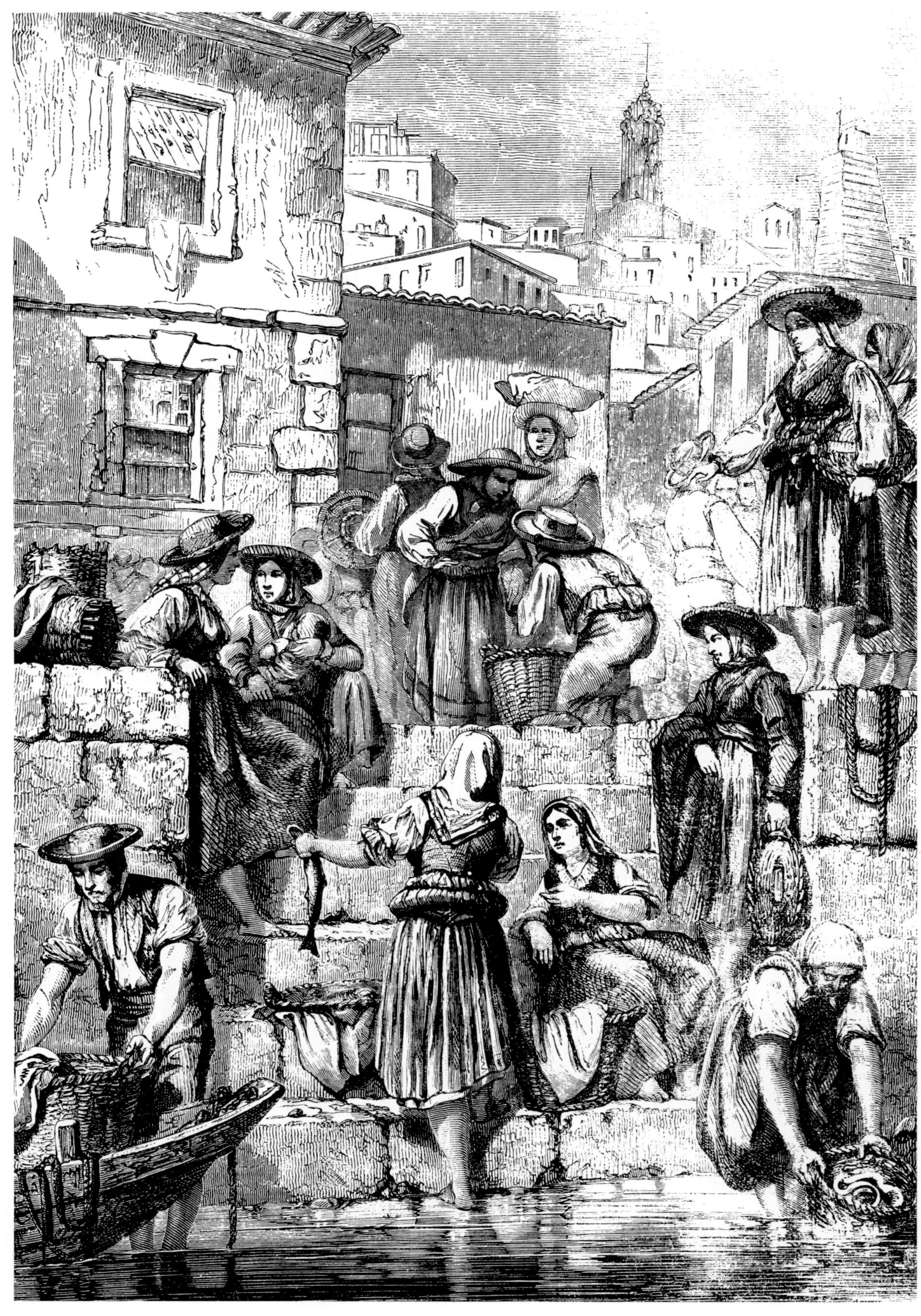

Fisherwomen of Oporto, Portugal, c. 1860

Fischersfrauen in Oporto, Portugal, um 1860

Pescatrice di Oporto, Portogallo, ca. 1860

Femmes pêcheurs de Porto au Portugal, vers 1860

Pescadoras de Oporto, Portugal, hacia 1860

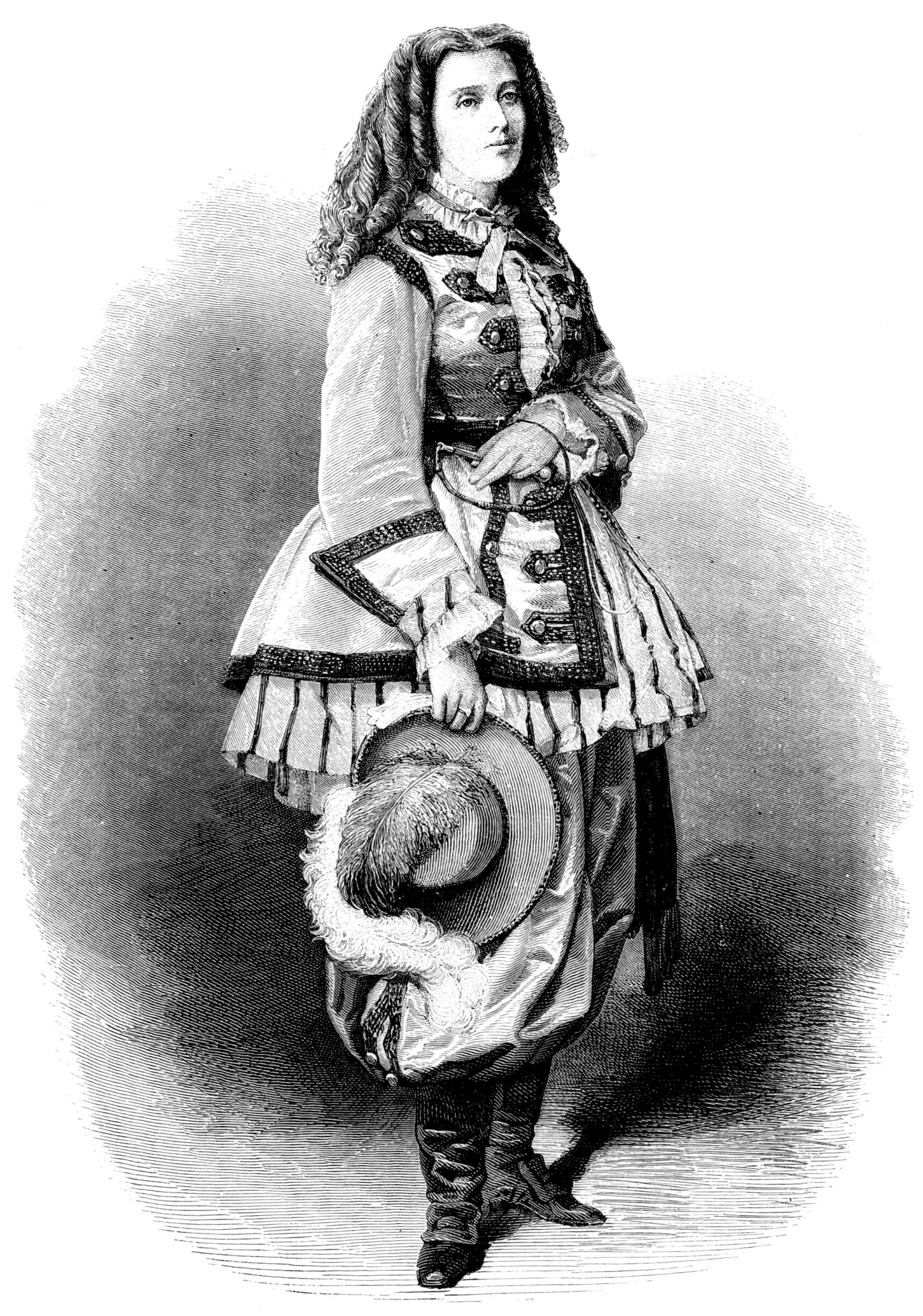

French lady in travel costume

Französische Dame in Reisekleidung

Dama francese in abito da viaggio

Dame française en costume de voyage

Mujer francesa con traje de viaje

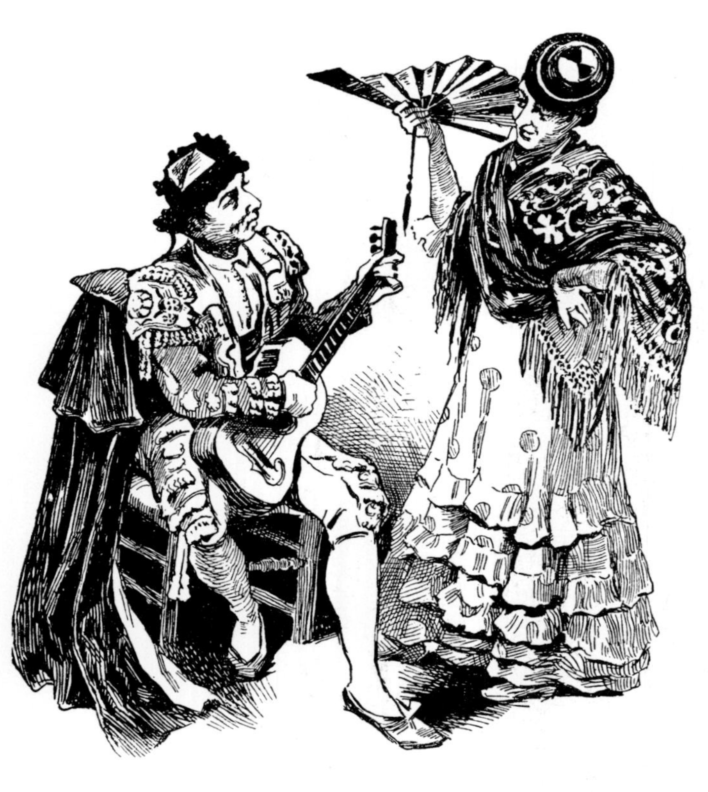

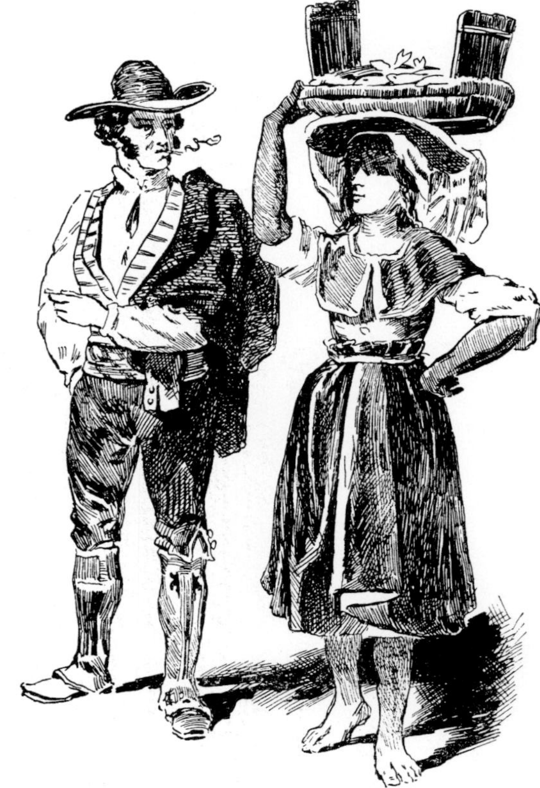

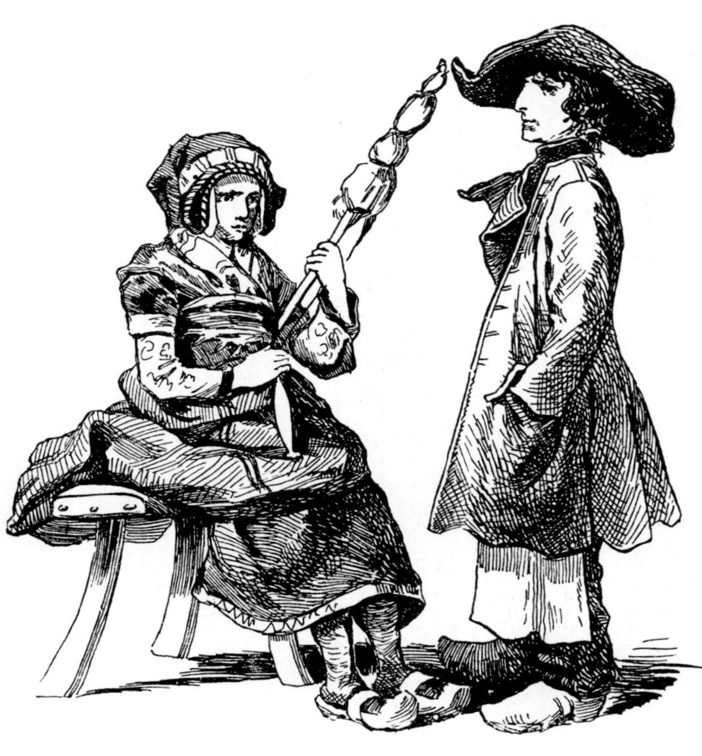

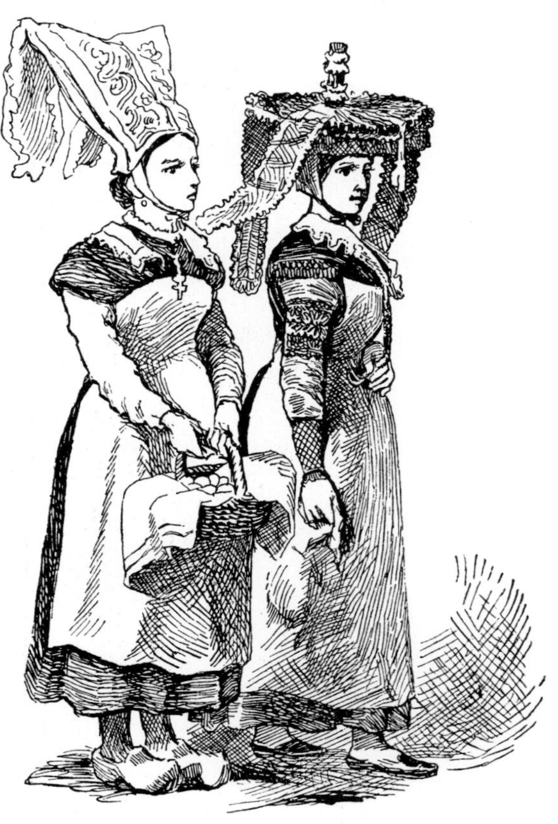

a	Andalucia, Spain	Andalusien, Spanien	Andalusia, Spagna	Andalousie, Espagne	Andalucía, España
b	Portugal	Portugal	Portogallo	Portugal	Portugal
c	Auvergne, France	Auvergne, Frankreich	Auvergne, Francia	Auvergne, France	Auvernia, Francia
d	Bourgogne, France	Bourgogne, Frankreich	Borgogna, Francia	Bourgogne, France	Borgoña, Francia

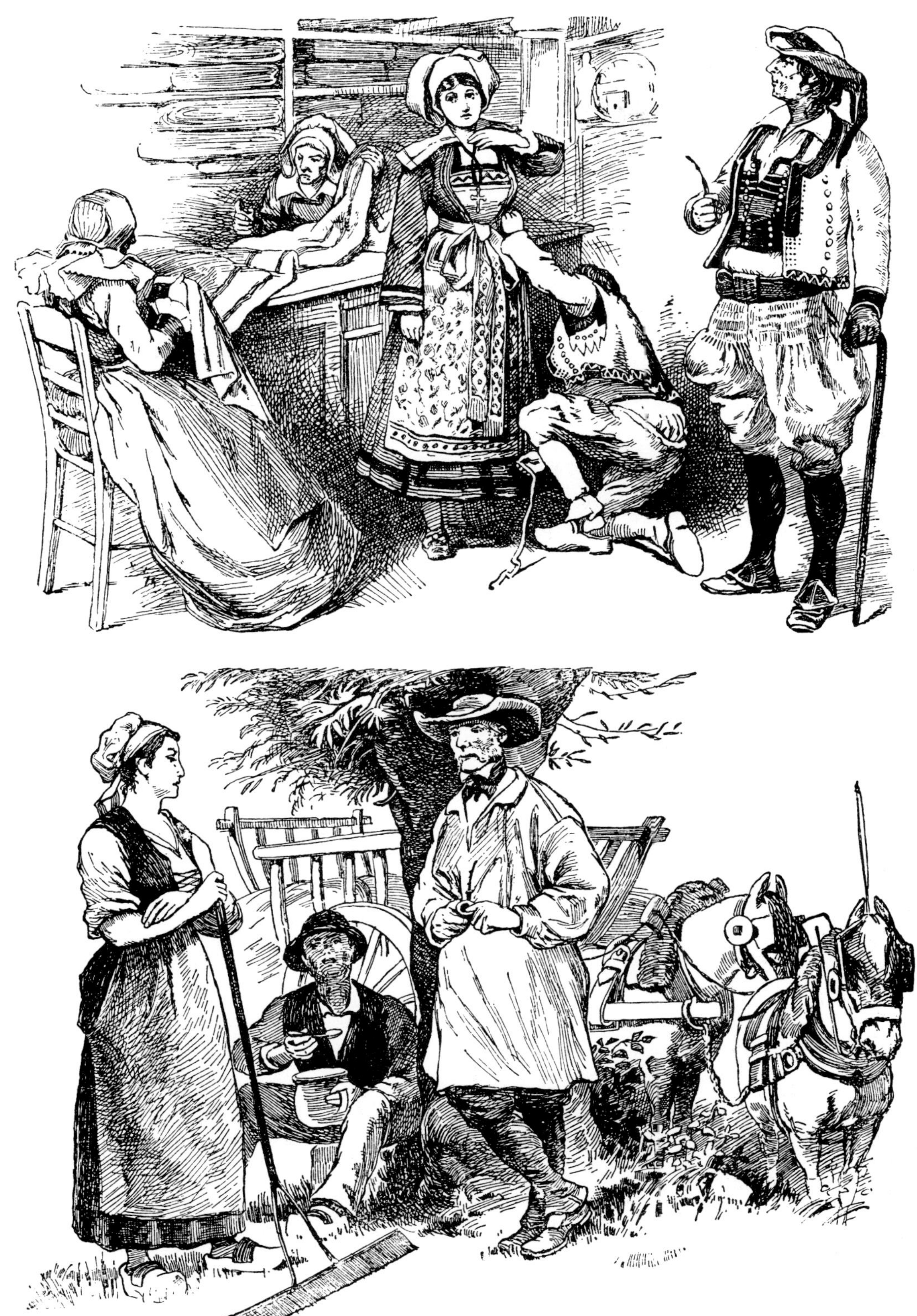

a	Britanny, France	Bretagne, Frankreich	Bretagna, Francia	Eretagne, France	Bretaña, Francia
b	Picardie, France	Picardie, Frankreich	Piccardia, Francia	Ficardie, France	Picardía, Francia

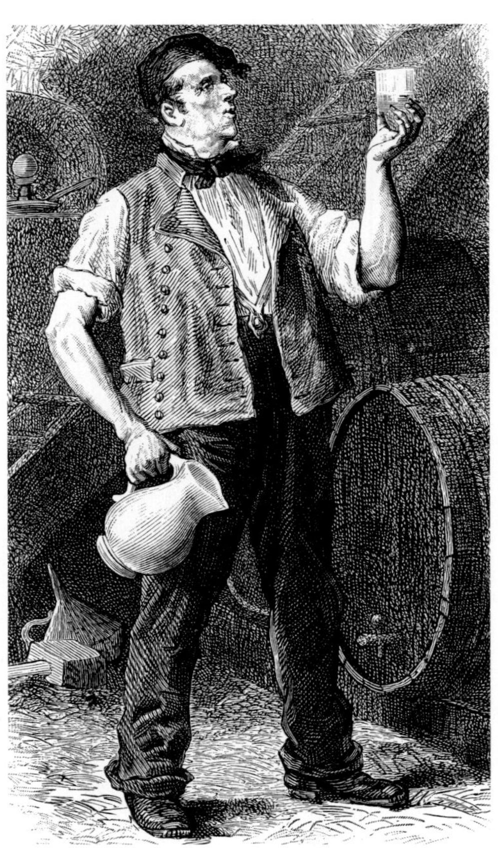

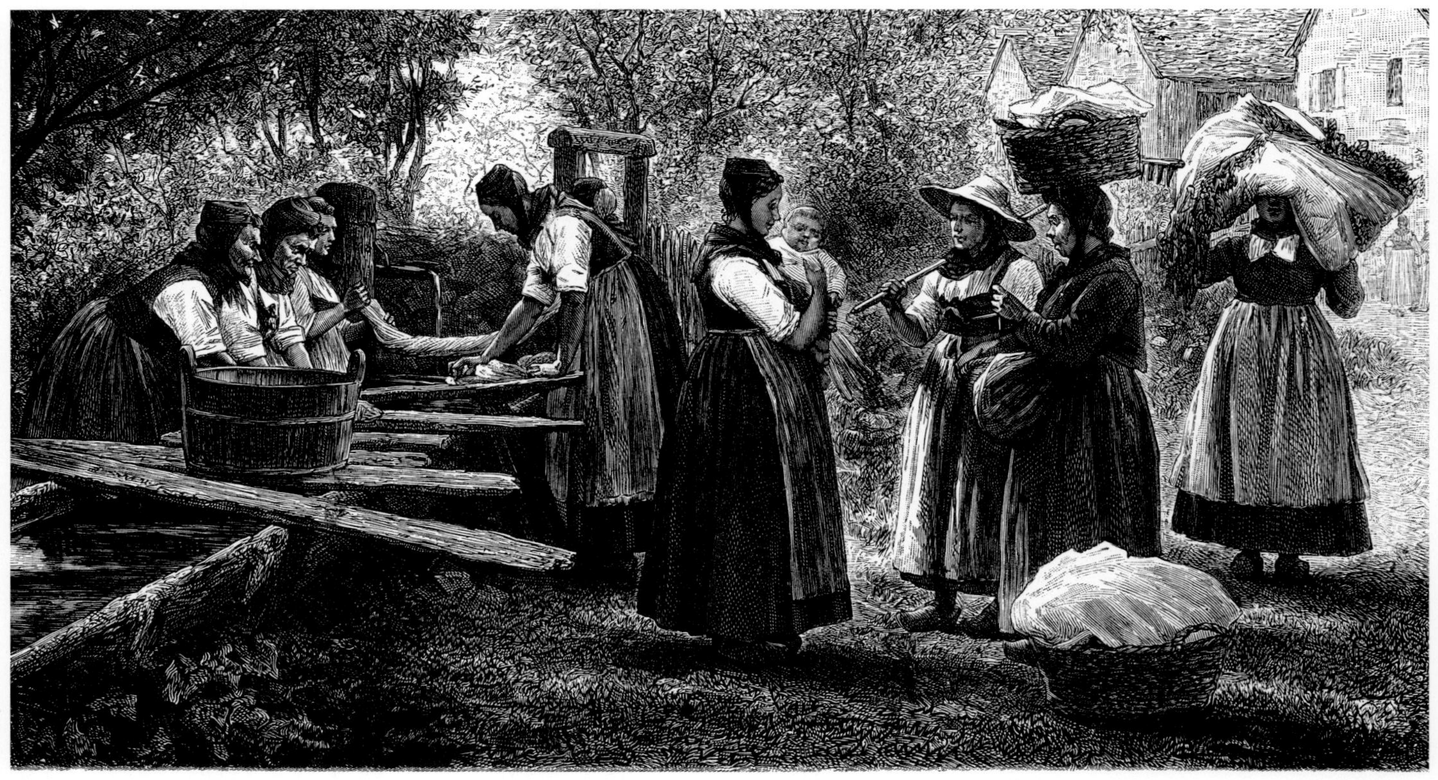

a	Vintner, Alsace, 1865	Weinhändler im Elsass, 1865	Vinaio, Alsazia, 1865	Vigneron, Alsace, 1865	Vinatero, Alsacia, 1865
b	Women washing, Alsace, c. 1860	Waschende Frauen, Elsass, um 1860	Donne al lavatoio, Alsazia, ca. 1860	Femmes au lavoir, Alsace, vers 1860	Mujeres lavando la colada, Alsacia, hacia 1860

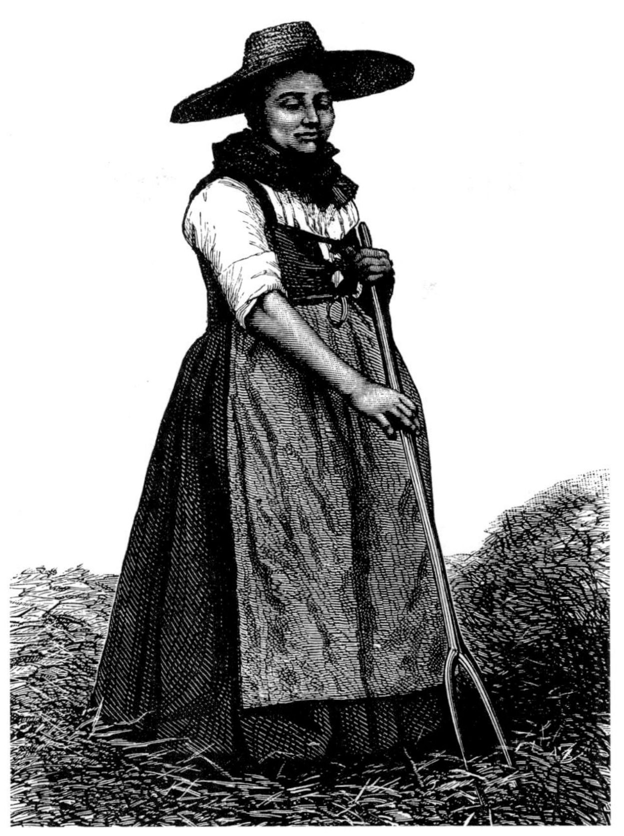

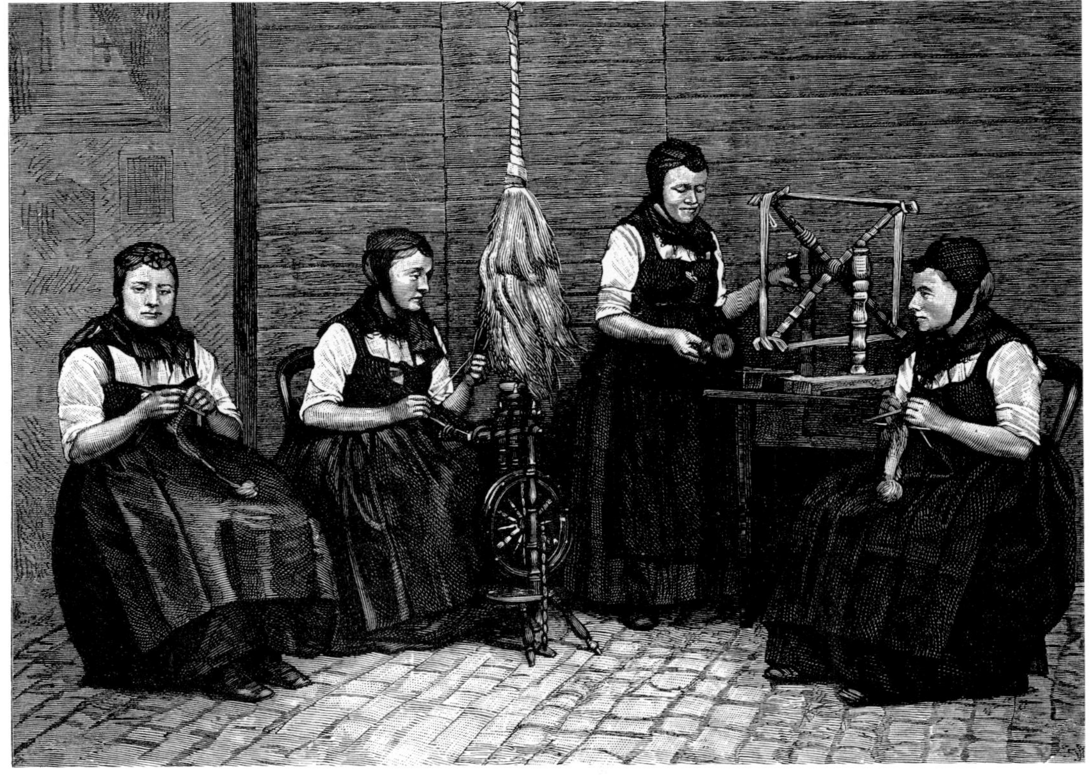

a	Female farmer, Alsace, c. 1890	Bäuerin, Elsass, um 1890	Contadina, Alsazia, ca. 1890	Paysanne, Alsace, vers 1890	Campesina, Alsacia, hacia el año 1890
b	Women spinning, Alsace, c. 1860	Spinnende Frauen, Elsass, um 1860	Donne che filano, Alsazia, ca. 1860	Fileuses, Alsace, vers 1860	Hilanderas, Alsacia, hacia el año 1860

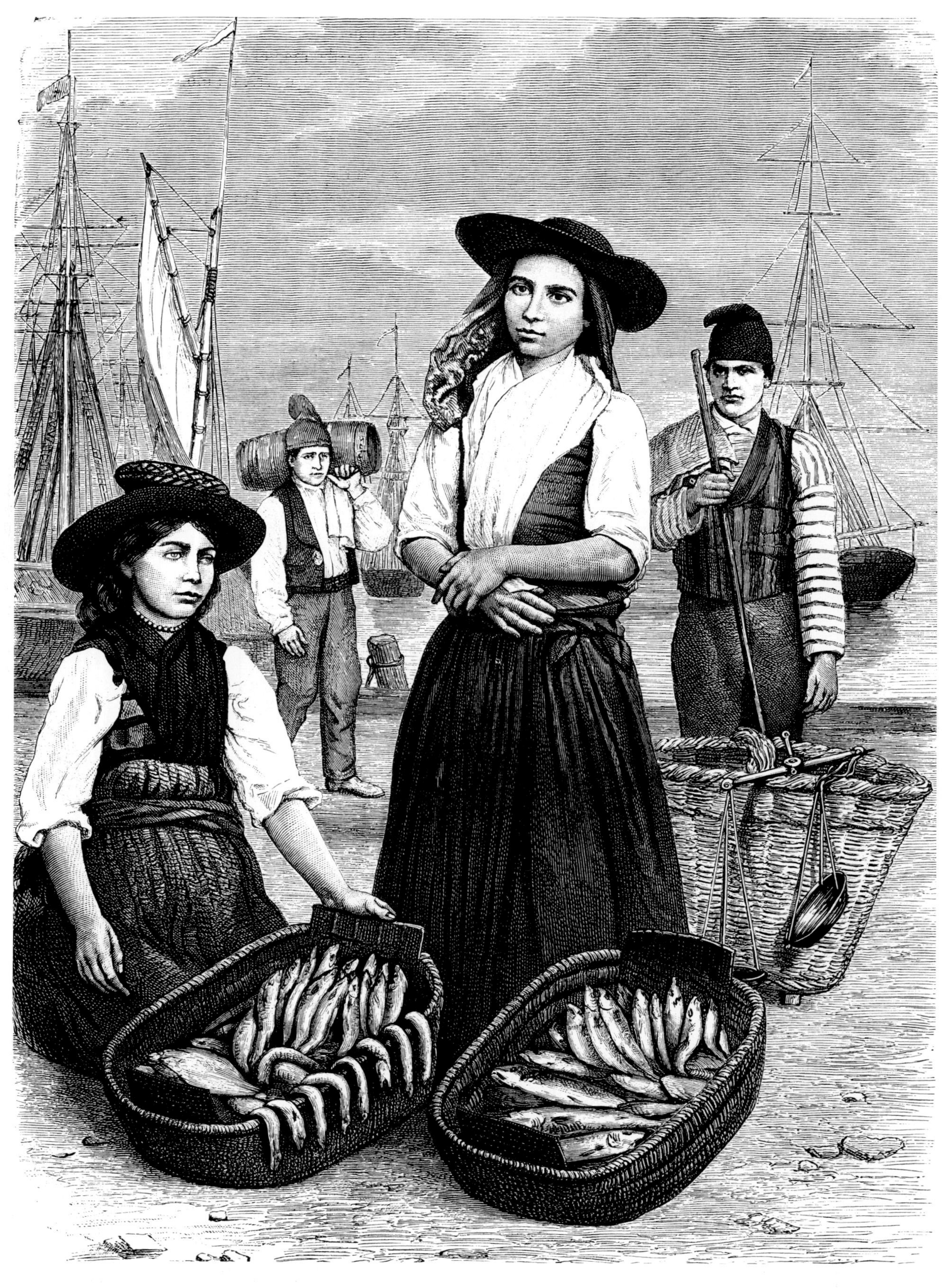

Fish sellers, Belgium, c. 1870

Fischverkäufer, Belgien, um 1870

Venditori di pesce, Belgio, ca. 1870

Vendeurs de poisson, Belgique, vers 1870

Vendedores de pescado, Bélgica, hacia 1870

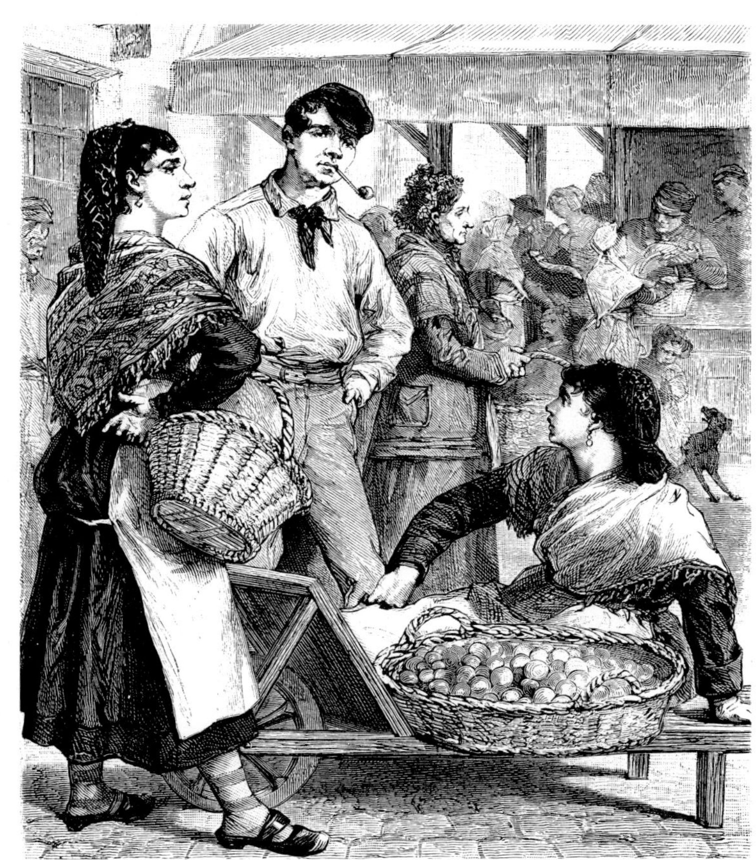

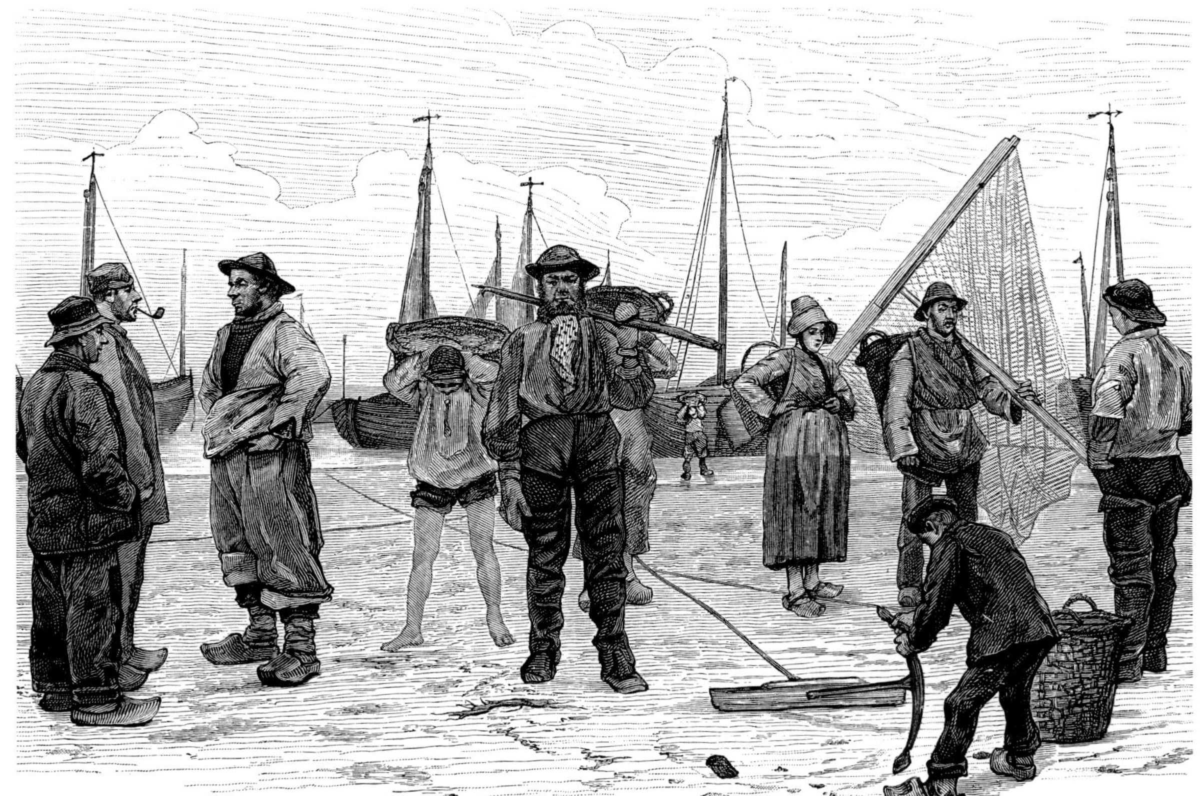

a	Street vendors, Brussels, Belgium, c. 1870	Straßenverkäufer, Brüssel, Belgien, um 1870	Venditori ambulanti, Bruxelles, Belgio, ca. 1870	Vendeurs de rue à Bruxelles, Belgique, vers 1870	Vendedores ambulantes, Bruselas, Bélgica, hacia 1870
b	Fishermen, Belgium, c. 1860	Fischer, Belgien, um 1860	Pescatori, Belgio, ca. 1860	Pêcheurs, Belgique, vers 1860	Pescadores, Bélgica, hacia 1860

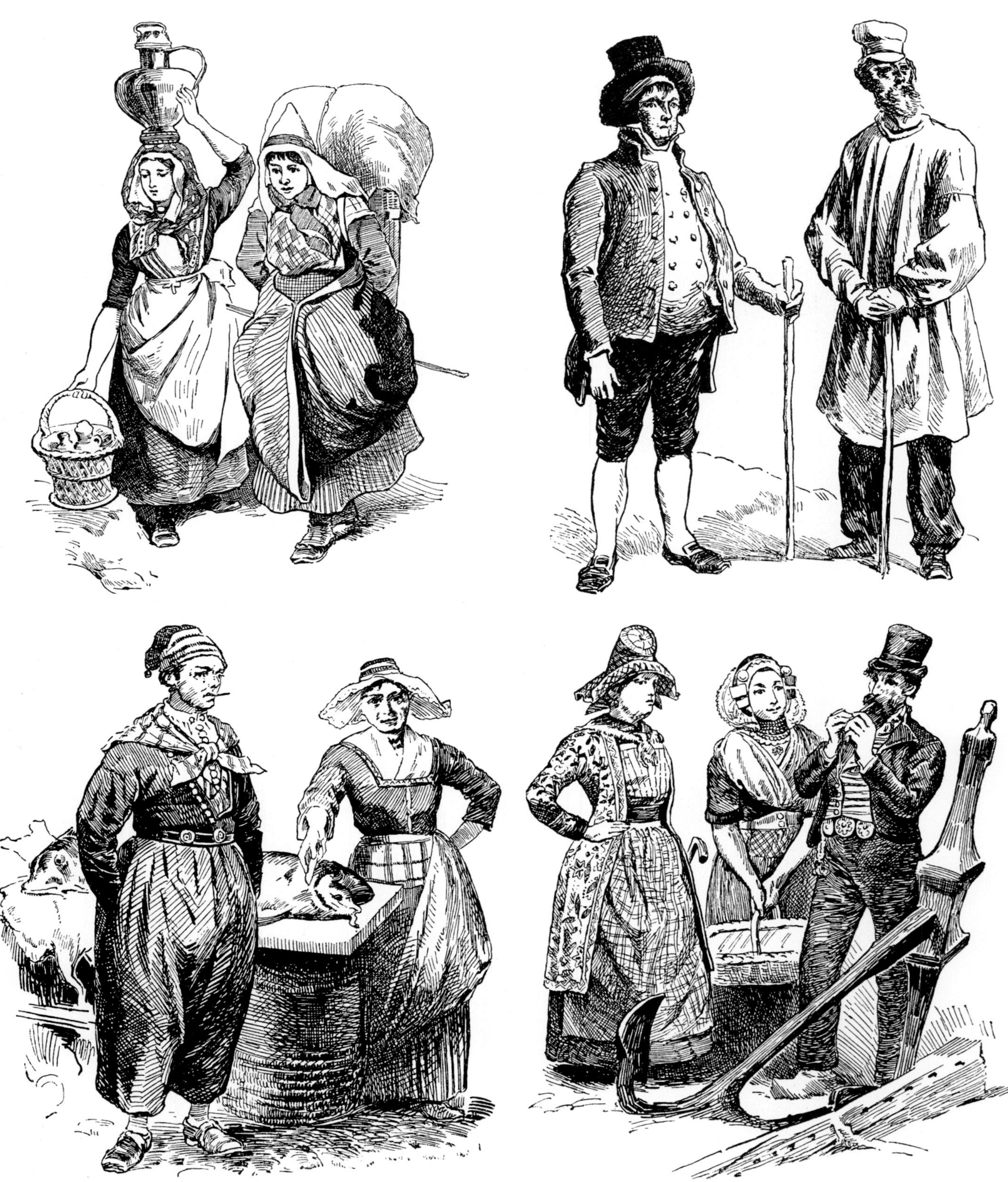

a	Antwerp, Belgium	Antwerpen, Belgien	Anversa, Belgio	Anvers, Belgique	Amberes, Bélgica
b	Brussels, Belgium	Brüssel, Belgien	Bruxelles, Belgio	Bruxelles, Belgique	Bruselas, Bélgica
c+d	The Netherlands	Die Niederlande	Paesi Bassi	Pays-Bas	Países Bajos

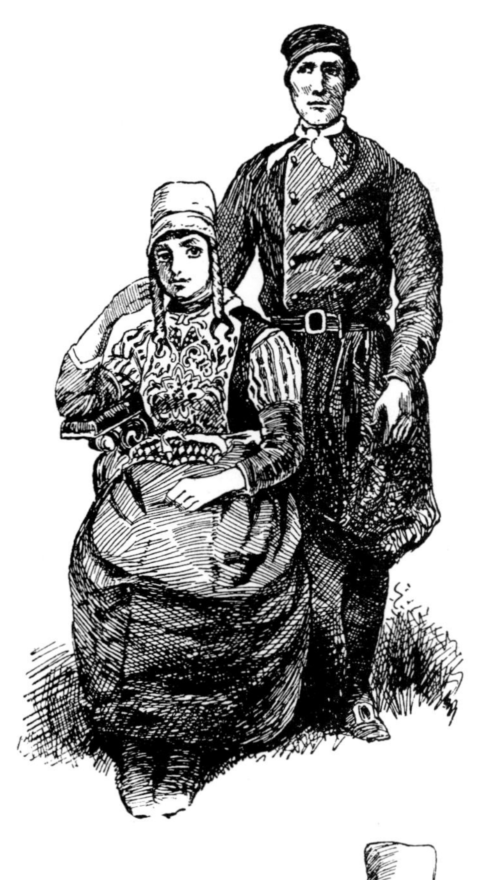

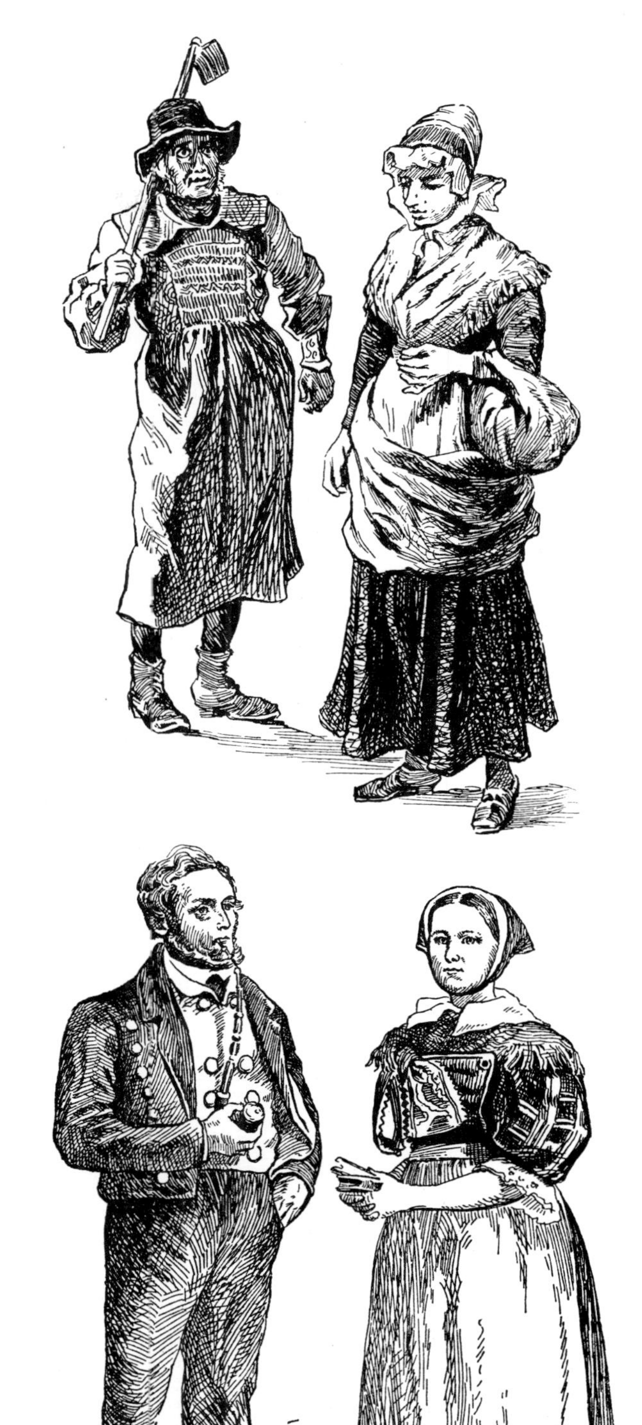

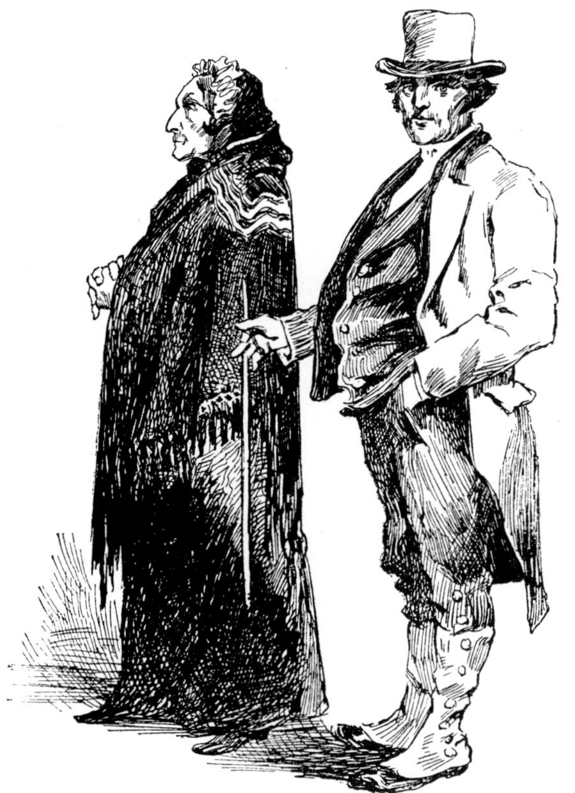

a	The Netherlands	Die Niederlande	Paesi Bassi	Pays-Bas	Países Bajos
b	Wales	Wales	Galles	Pays de Galles	Gales
c	Ireland	Irland	Irlanda	Irlande	Irlanda
d	Danmark	Dänemark	Danimarca	Danemark	Dinamarca

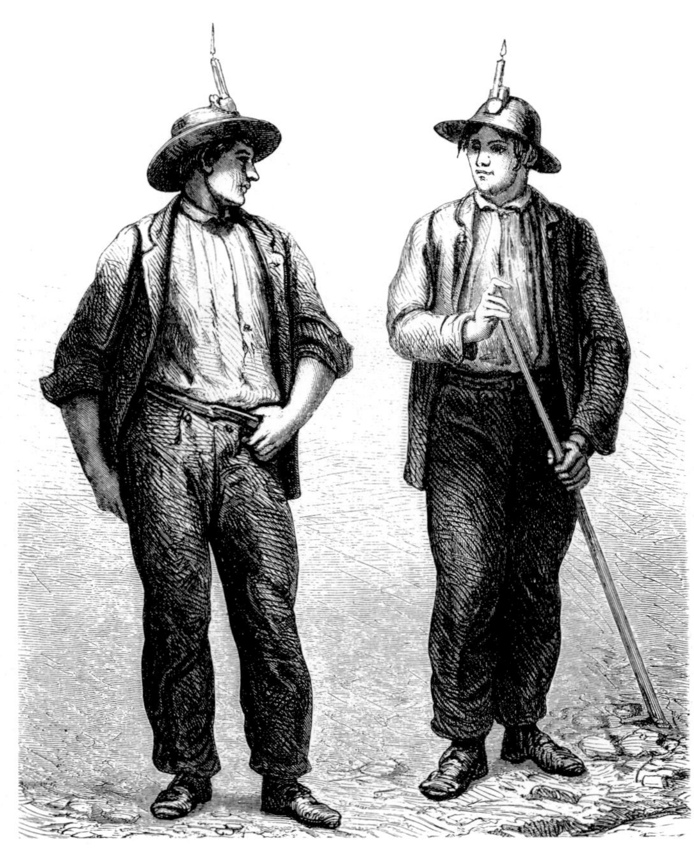

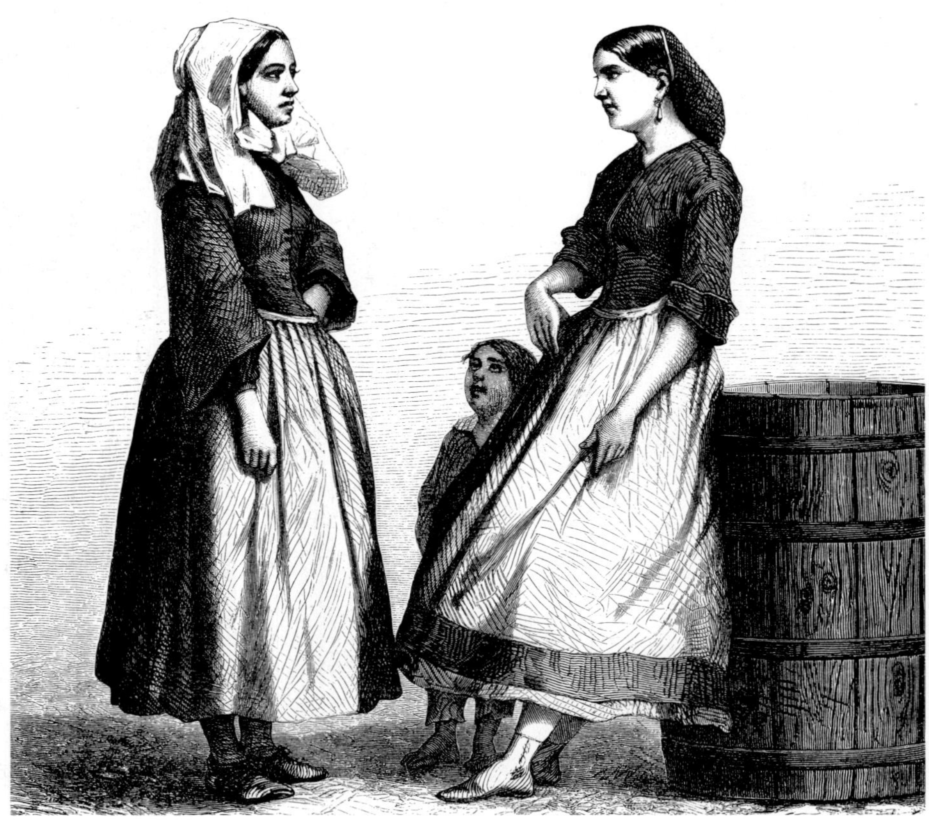

a	Miners from Cornwall, England	Bergarbeiter aus Cornwall, England	Minatori della Cornovaglia, Inghilterra	Mineurs de Cornouailles en Angleterre	Mineros de Cornwall, Inglaterra
b	Miners' wives, c. 1860	Bergarbeiterfrauen, um 1860	Mogli di minatori, ca. 1860	Femmes de mineurs, vers 1860	Esposas de mineros, hacia el año 1860

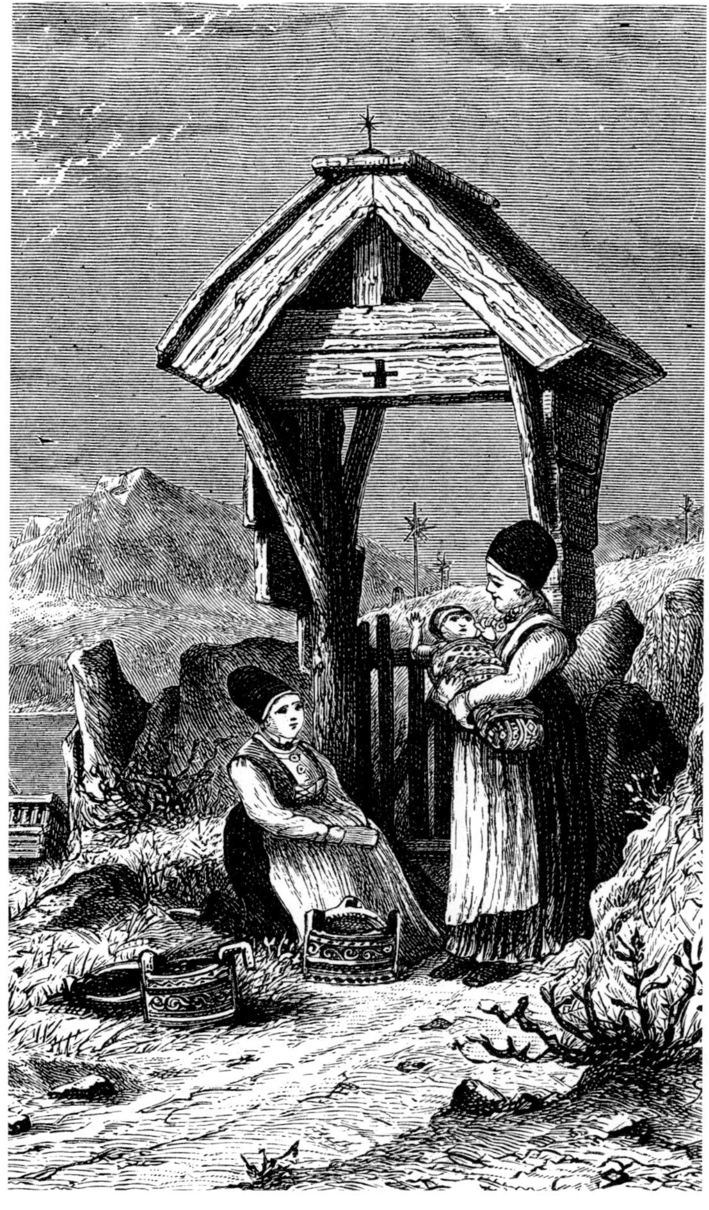

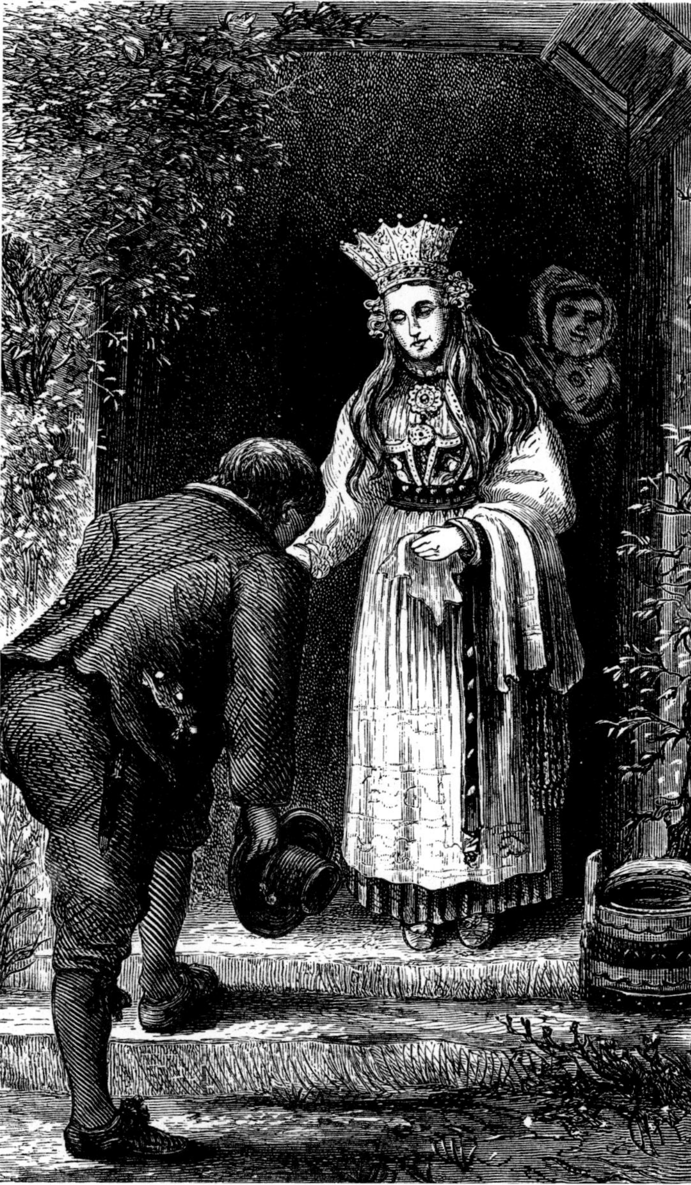

a	Norwegian women and baby, c. 1860	Norwegerinnen mit Kleinkind, um 1860	Donne e bambino norvegesi, ca. 1860	Femmes et enfant norvégiens, vers 1860	Mujeres y niño noruegos, hacia 1860
b	Norwegian bride, c. 1860	Norwegische Braut, um 1860	Sposa norvegese, ca. 1860	Mariée norvégienne, vers 1860	Novia noruega, alrededor de 1860

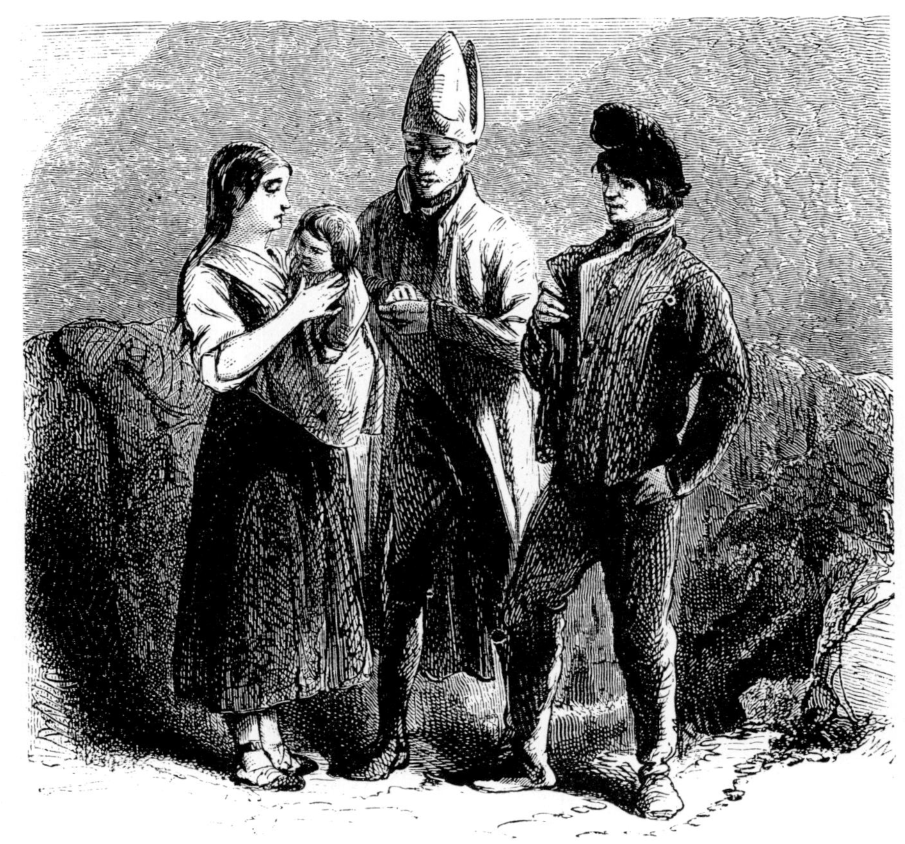

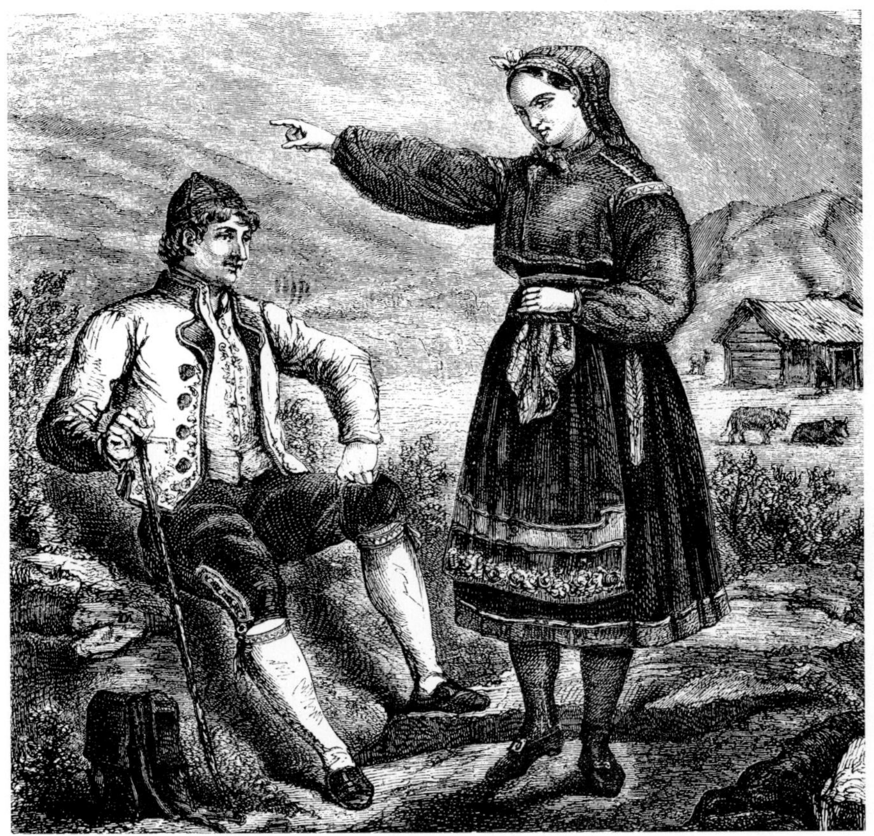

a	Iceland, c. 1860	Island, um 1860	Islanda, ca. 1860	Islande, vers 1860	Islandia, hacia 1860
b	Telemark, Norway, c. 1860	Telemark, Norwegen, um 1860	Telemark, Norvegia, ca. 1860	Telemark, Norvège, vers 1860	Telemark, Noruega, hacia 1860

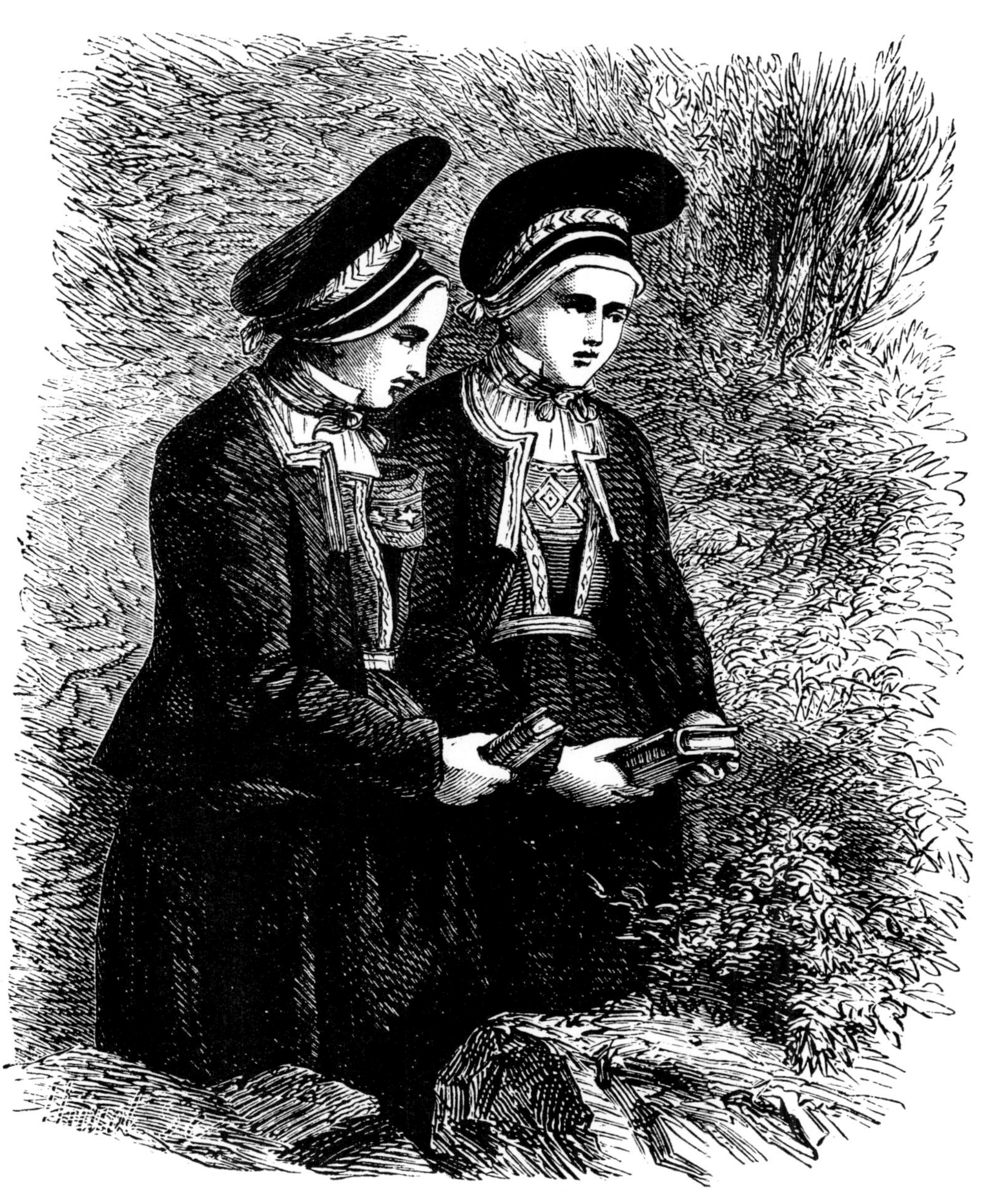

Rosendal, Norway, c. 1860

Rosendal, Norwegen, um 1860

Rosendal, Norvegia, ca. 1860

Rosendal, Norvège, vers 1860

Rosendal, Noruega, hacia 1860

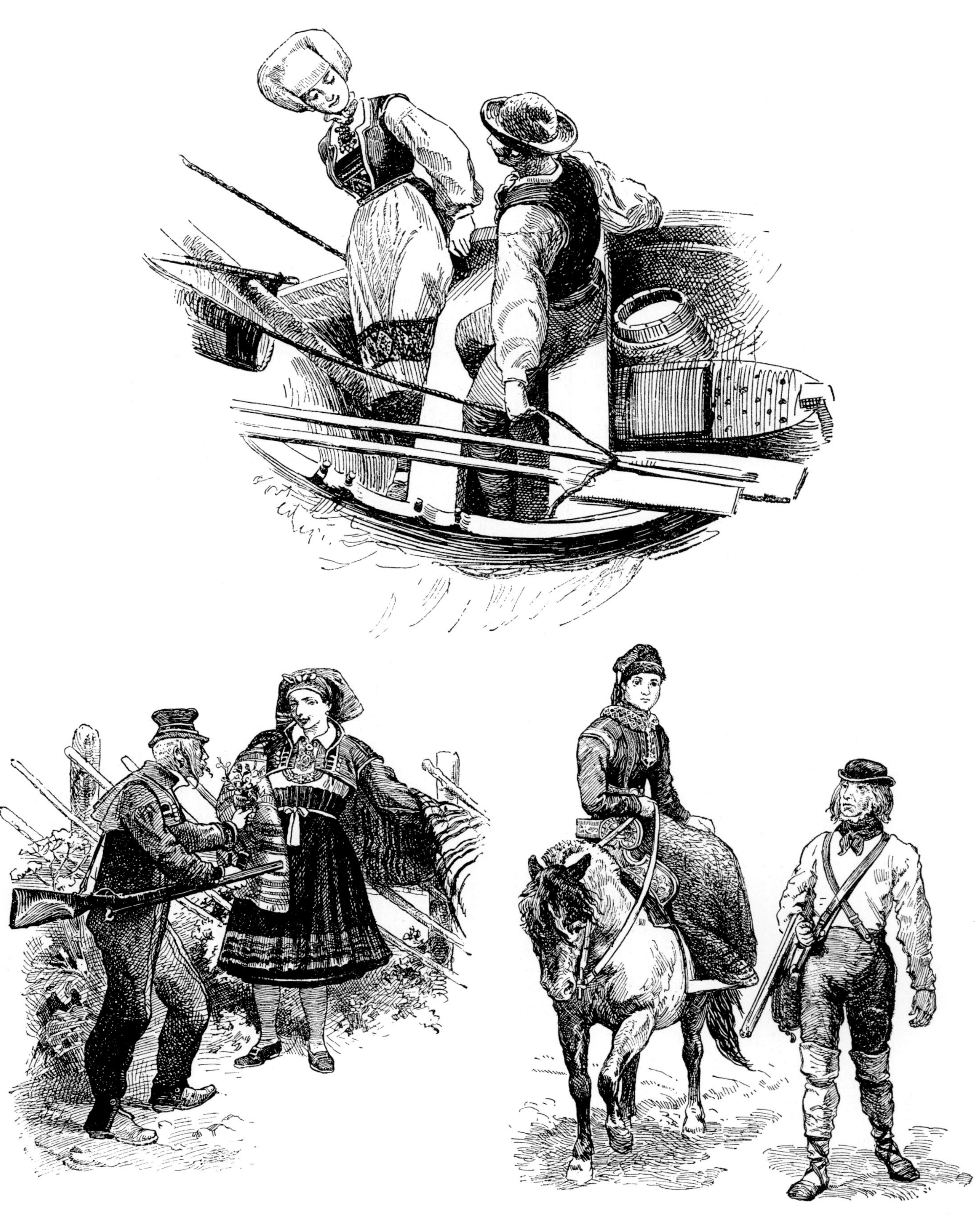

a+ b	Norway	Nowegen	Norvegia	Norvège	Noruega
c	Iceland	Island	Islanda	Islande	Islandia

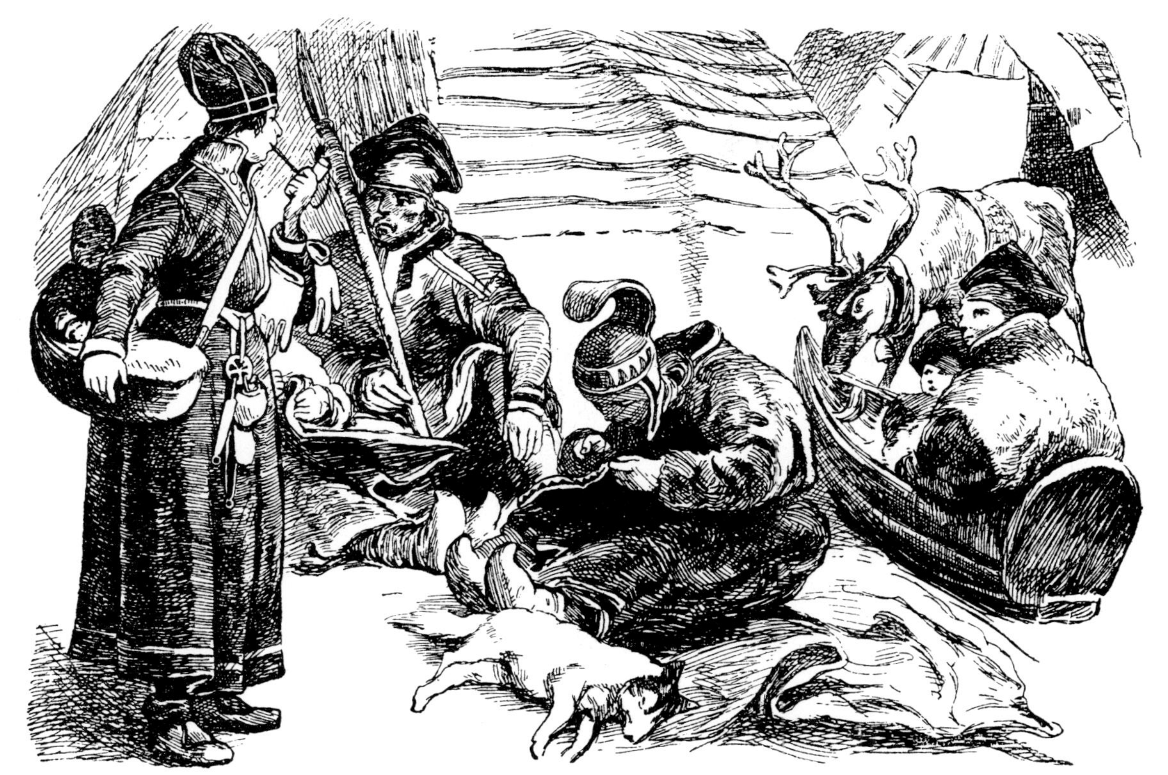

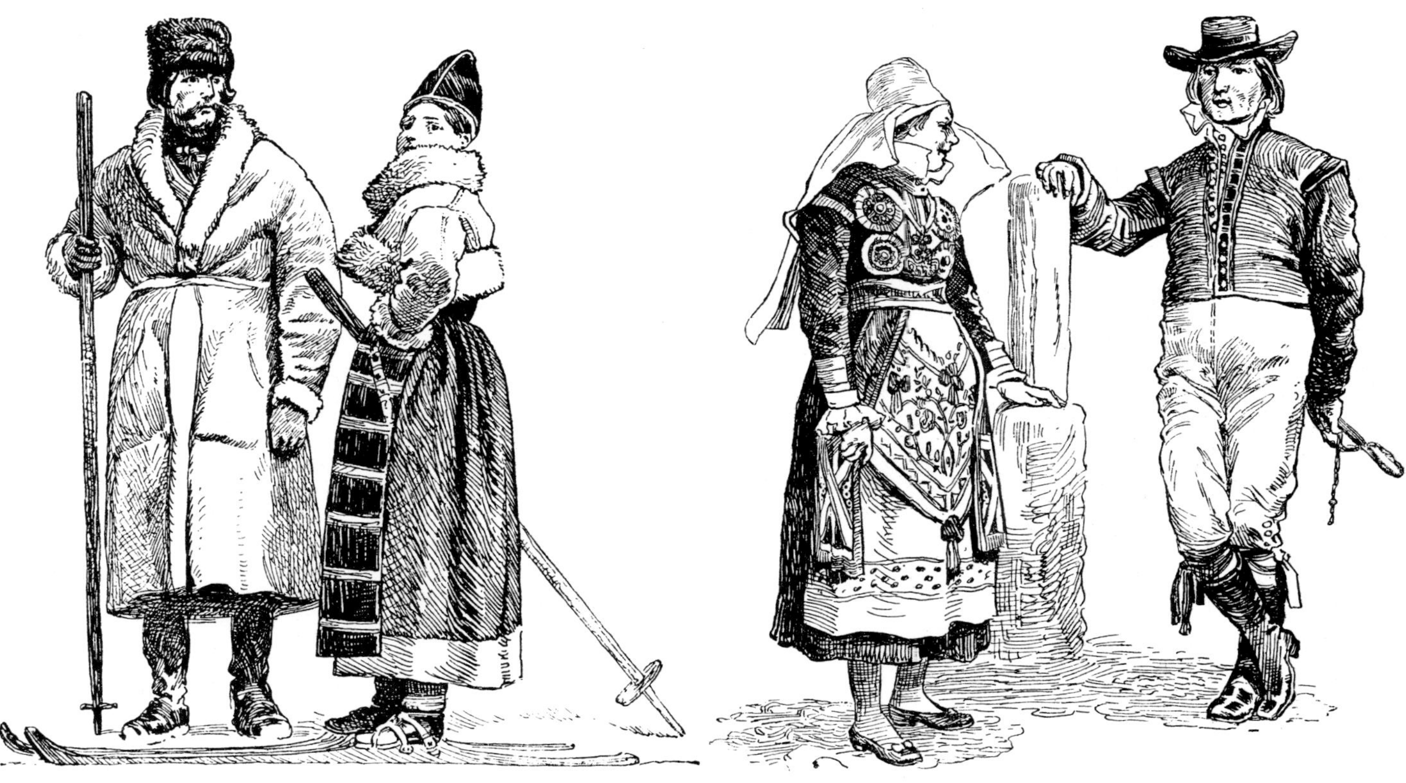

a	Lapland, Finland	Lappland, Finnland	Lapponia, Finlandia	Laponie, Finlande	Laponia, Finlandia
b+c	Sweden	Schweden	Svezia	Suède	Suecia

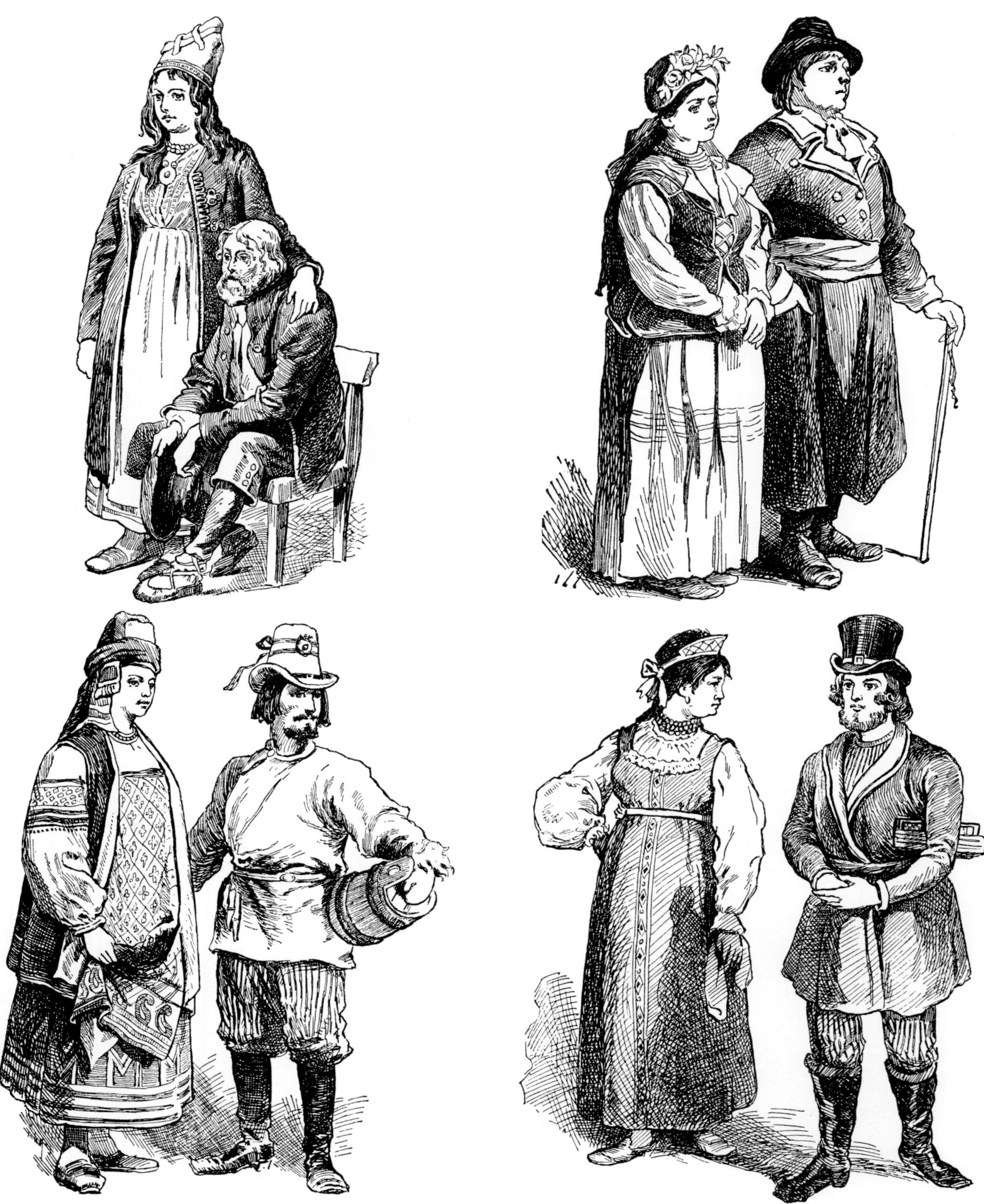

a	Estonia	Estland	Estonia	Estonie	Estonia
b	Poland	Polen	Polonia	Pologne	Polonia
c+d	Russia	Russland	Russia	Russie	Rusia

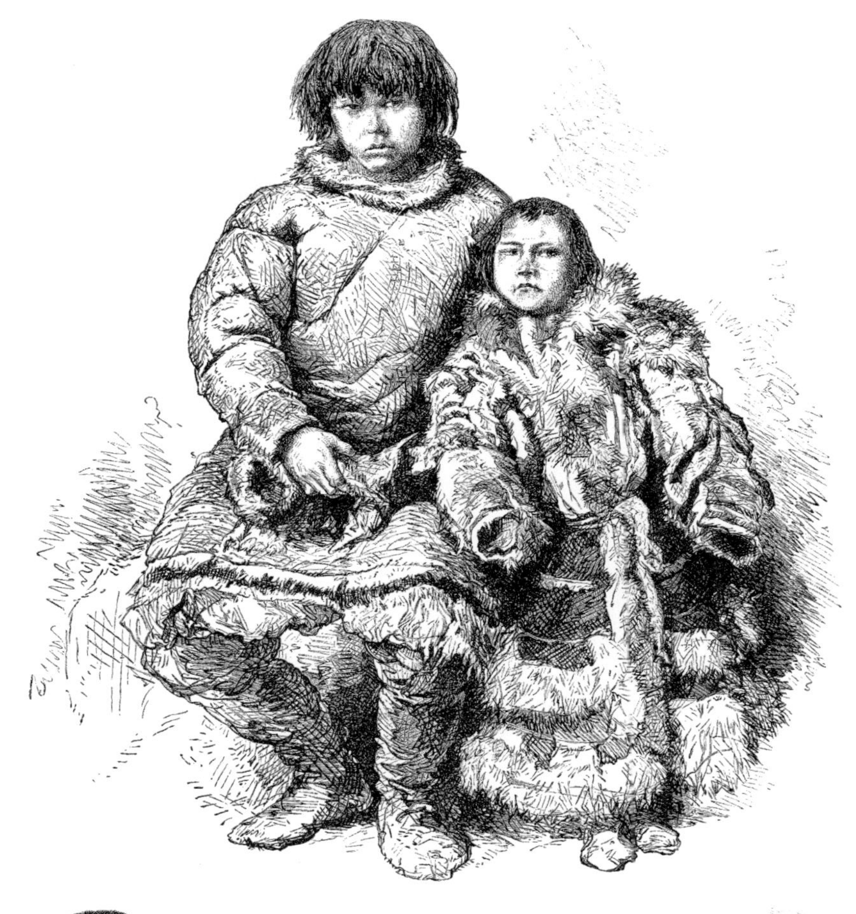

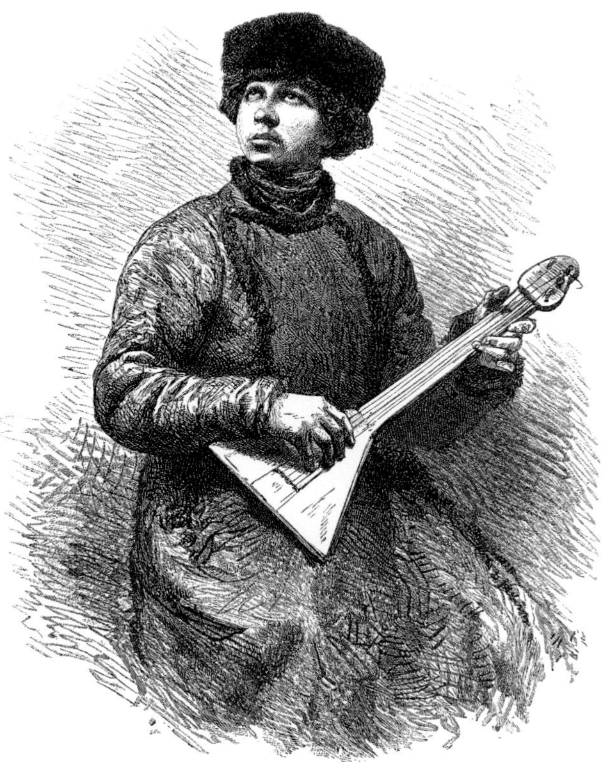

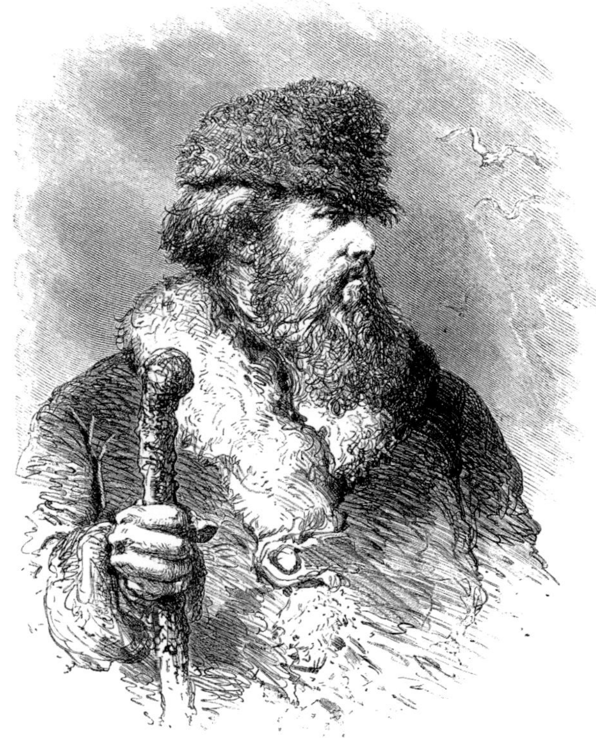

a	Northern Russia	Nordrussland	Russia settentrionale	Nord de la Russie	Norte de Rusia
b	Russian village musician	Russischer Dorfmusiker	Musicista di un villaggio russo	Musicien d'un village russe	Músico callejero ruso
c	Russian guide	Russischer Führer	Guida russa	Guide russe	Guía ruso

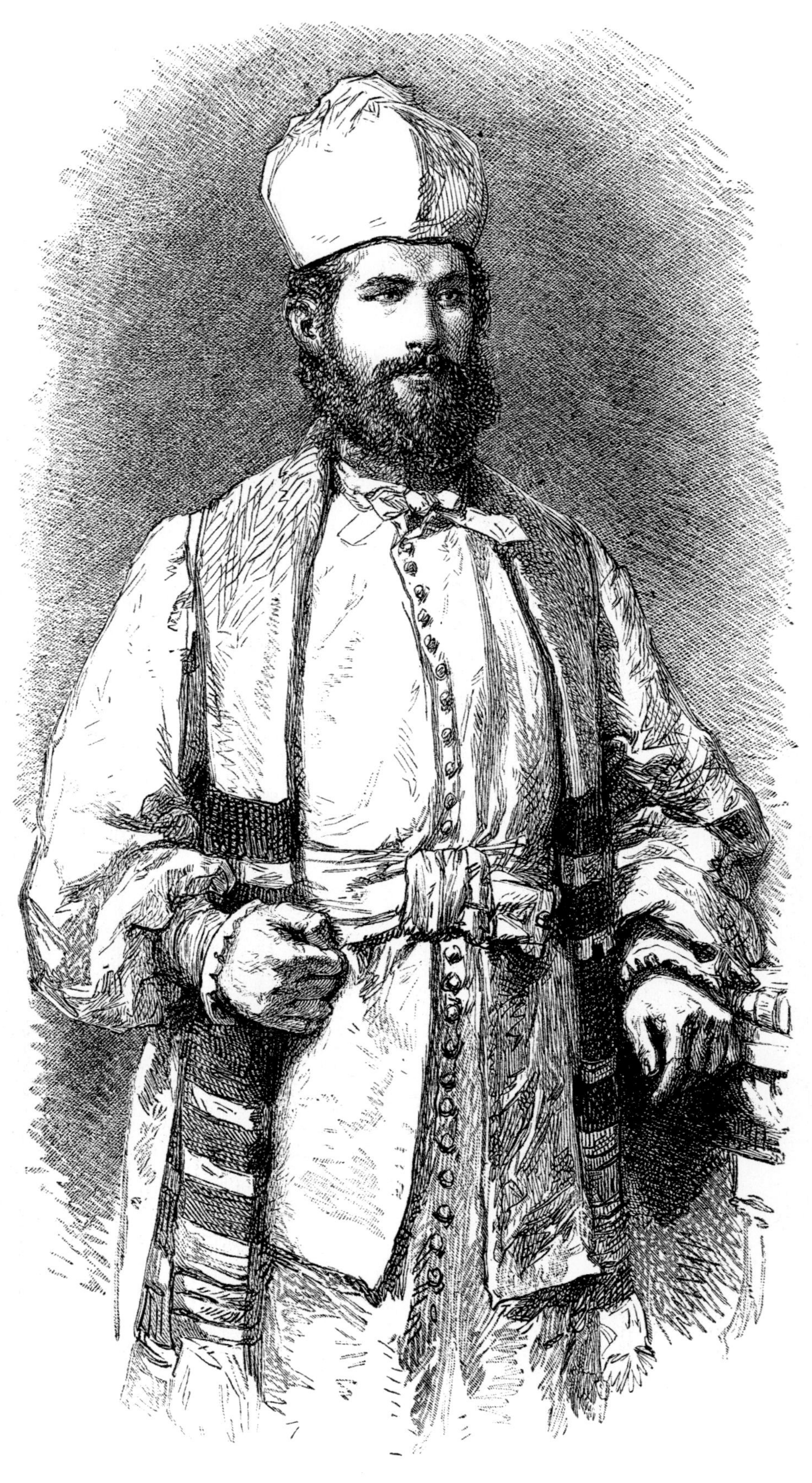

Jewish man in Moskou, c. 1870

Jüdischer Mann in Moskau, um 1870

Ebreo a Mosca, ca. 1870

Juif à Moscou, vers 1870

Hombre judío de Moscú, hacia 1870

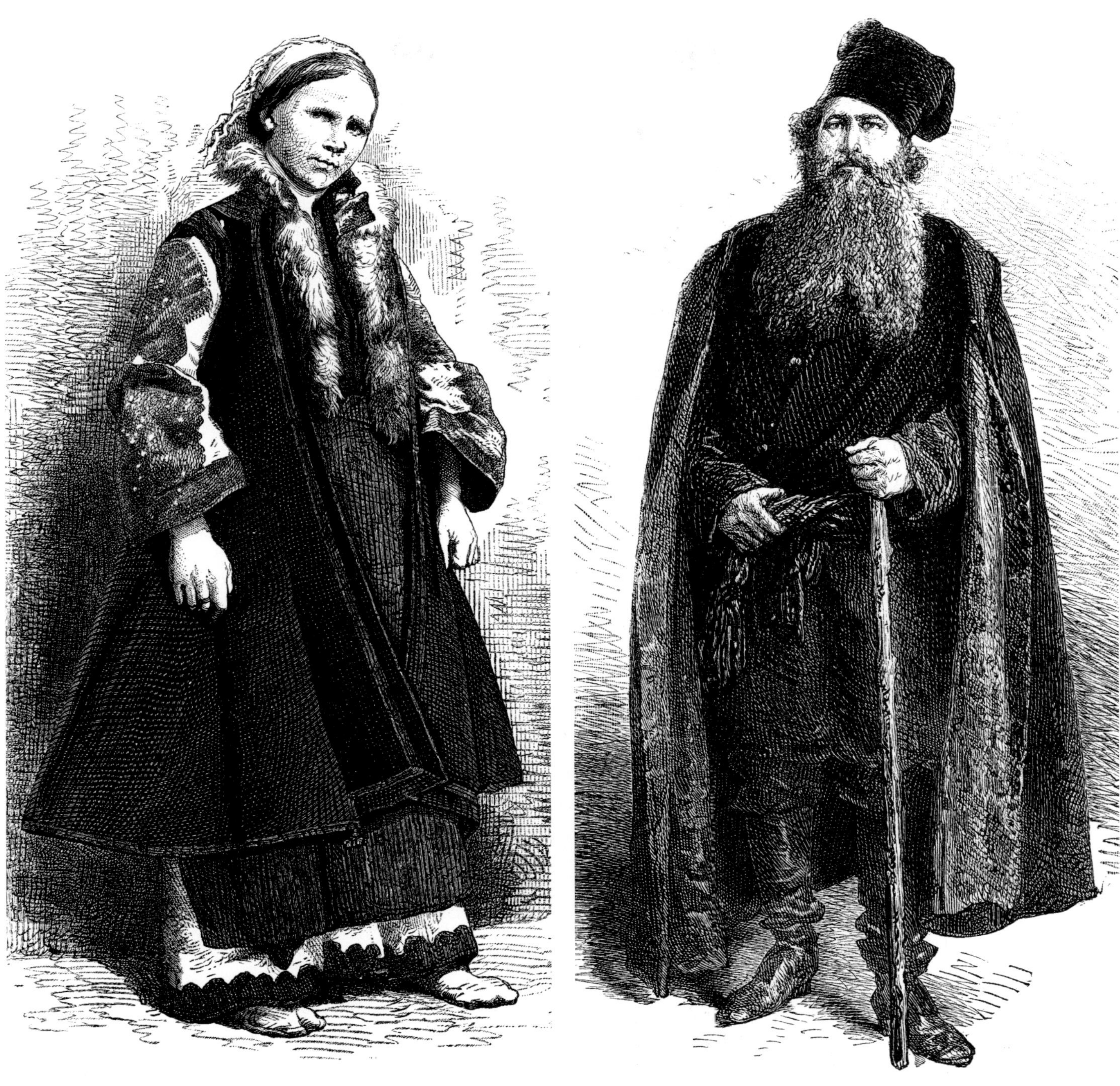

Muscovites, c. 1870 Moskowiter, um 1870 Moscoviti, ca. 1870 Moscovites, vers 1870 Moscovitas, hacia 1870

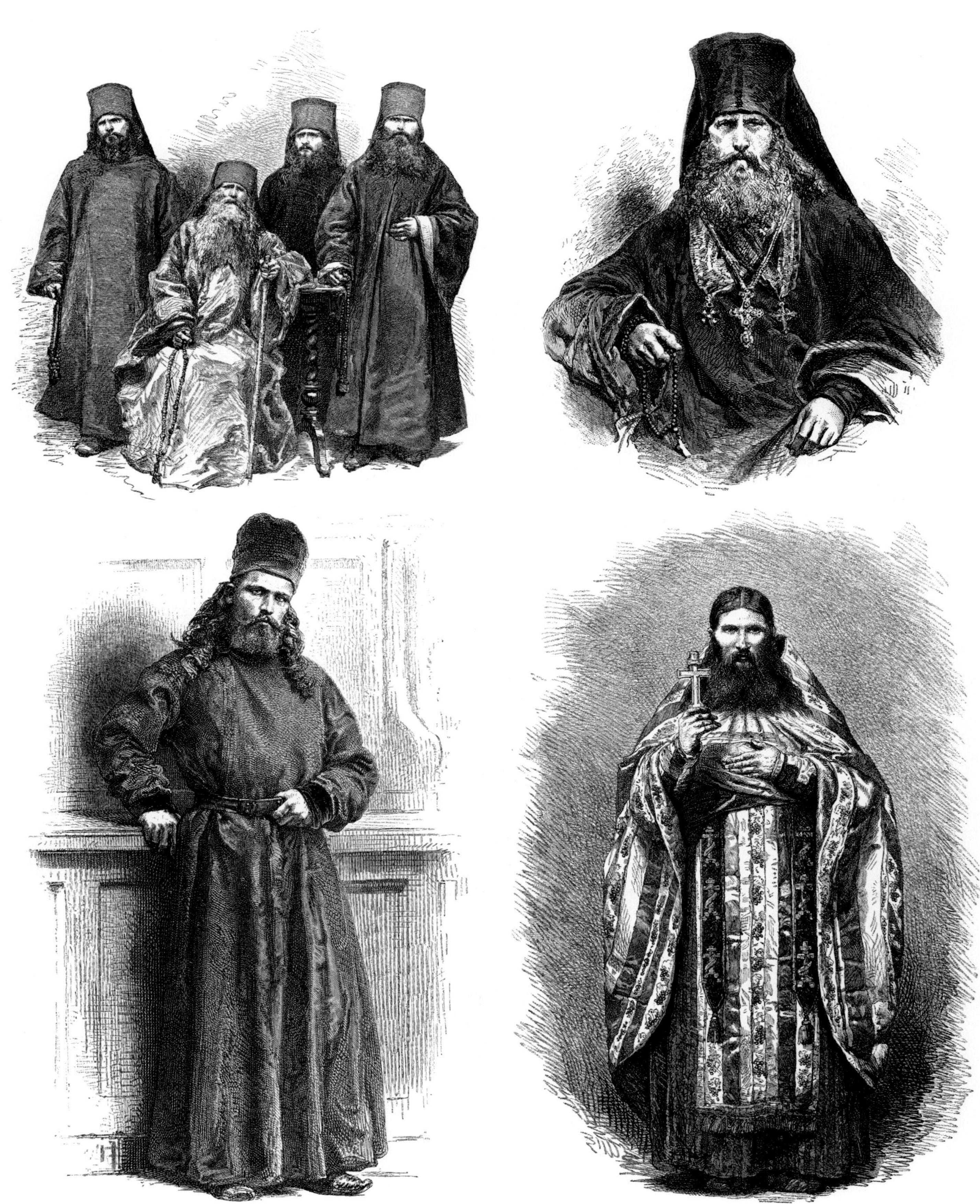

Russian Orthodox clerics and monks, c. 1870

Russisch-orthodoxe Kleriker und Mönche, um 1870

Sacerdoti e monaci greci ortodossi, ca. 1870

Ecclésiastiques et moines orthodoxes russes, vers 1870

Clérigos y monjes ortodoxos rusos, hacia 1870

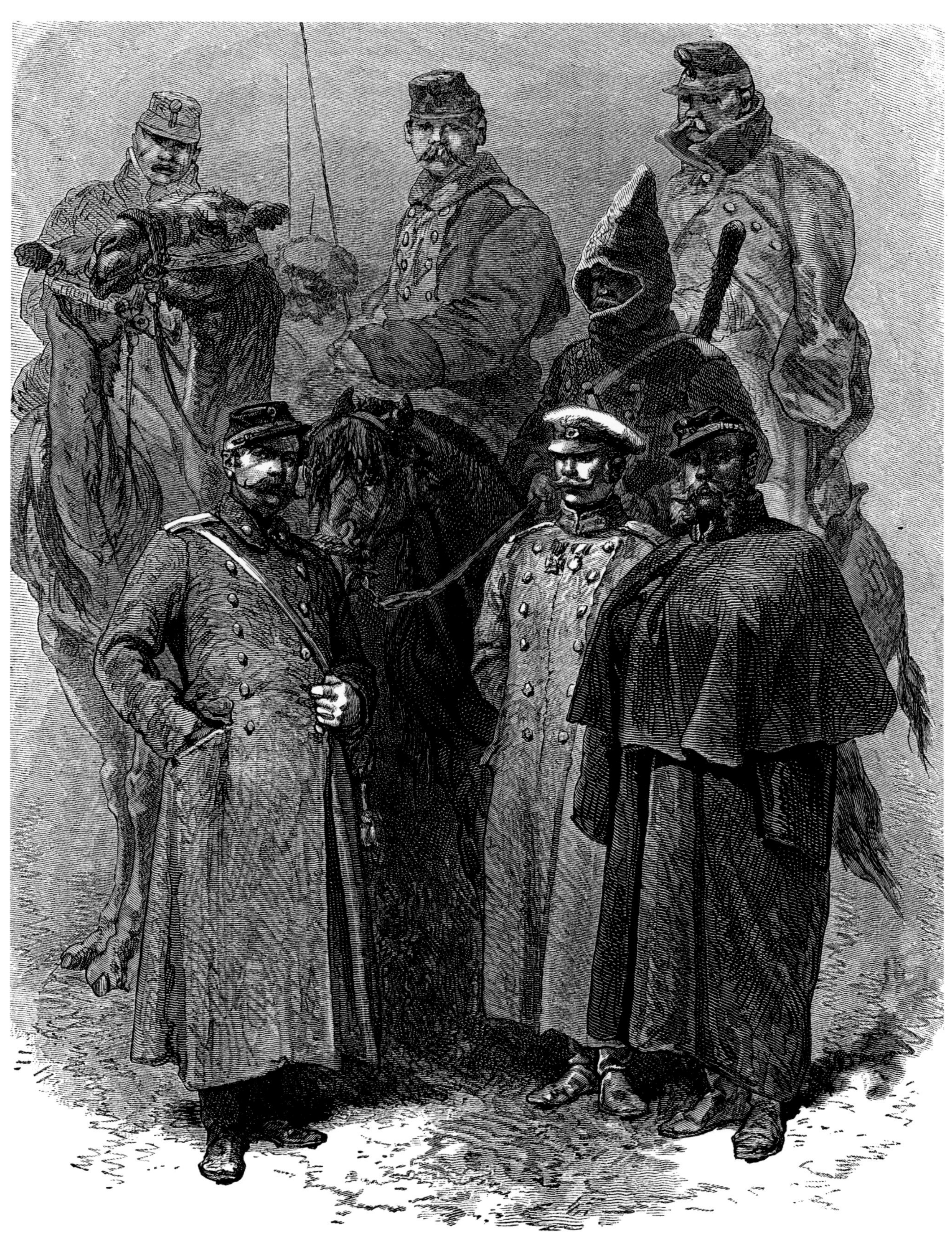

Russian soldiers, c. 1865

Russische Soldaten, um 1865

Soldati russi, ca. 1865

Soldats russes, vers 1865

Soldados rusos, hacia 1865

Africa
Afrika
Africa
Afrique
África
アフリカ
非洲

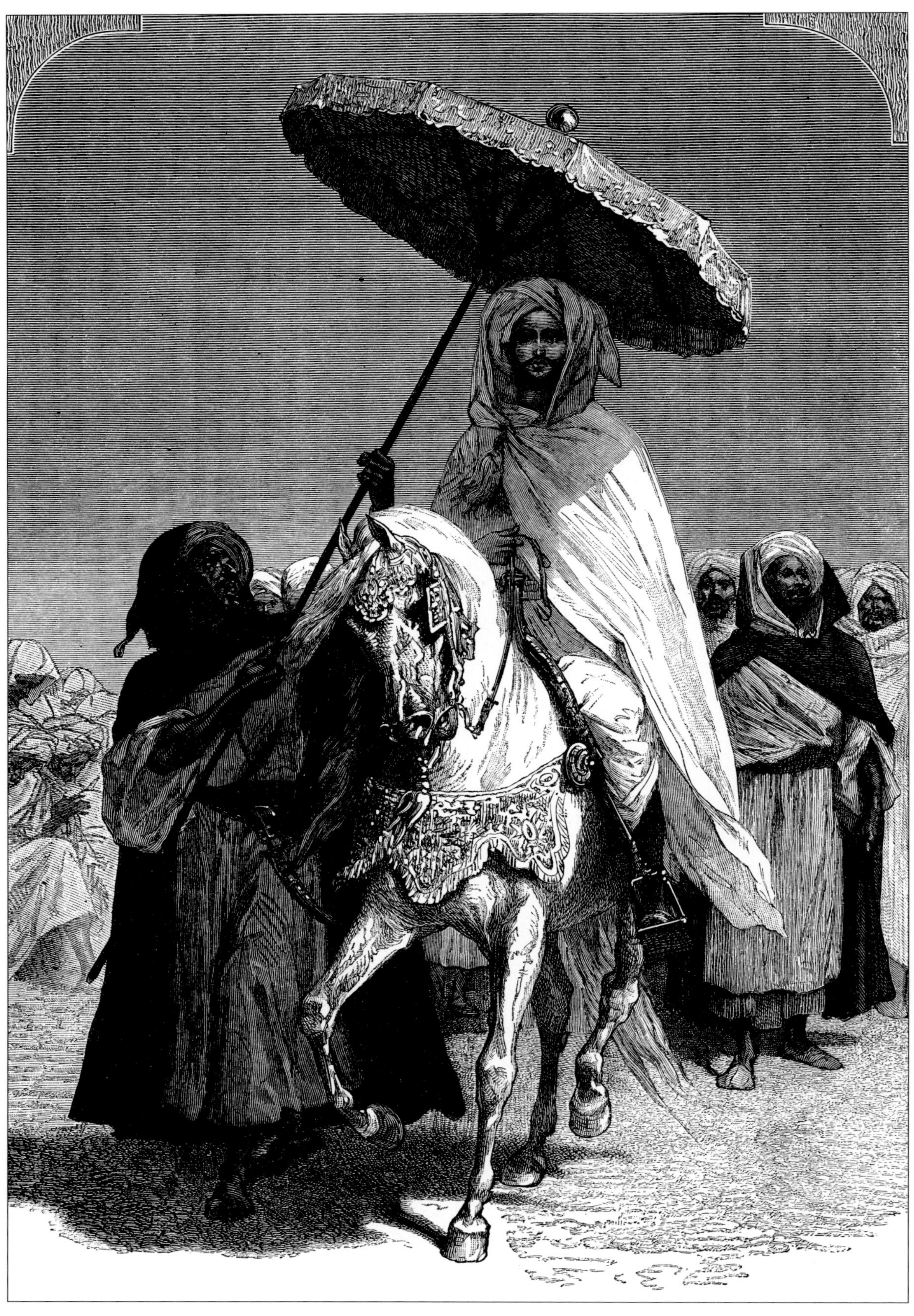

King Hassan of Morocco, c. 1890

König Hassan von Marokko, um 1890

Re Hassan del Marocco, ca. 1890

Roi Hassan du Maroc, vers 1890

El rey Hasán de Marruecos, hacia 1890

Morocco

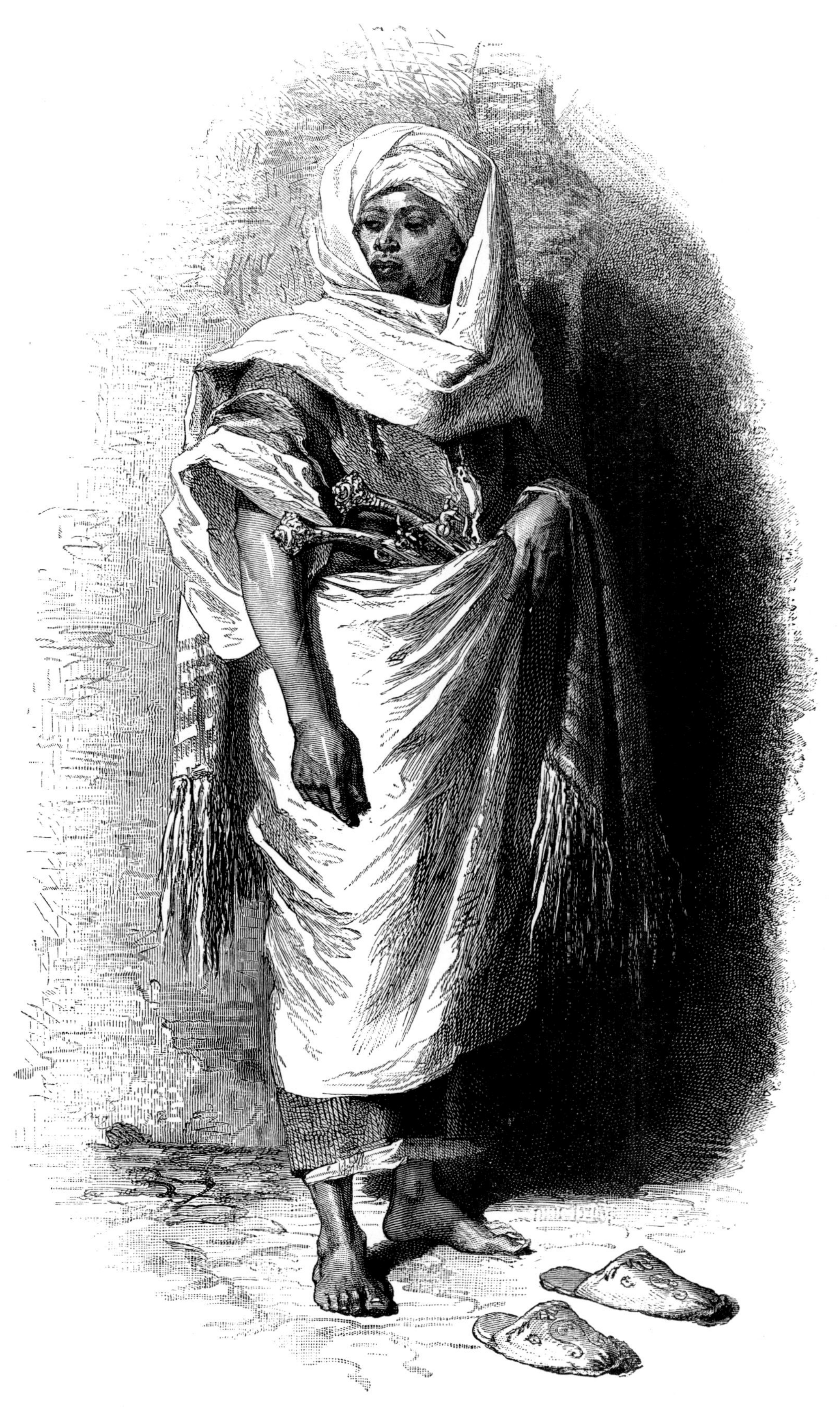

Moroccan man, c. 1900

Marokkaner, um 1900

Uomo marocchino, ca. 1900

Marocain, vers 1900

Marroquí, hacia 1900

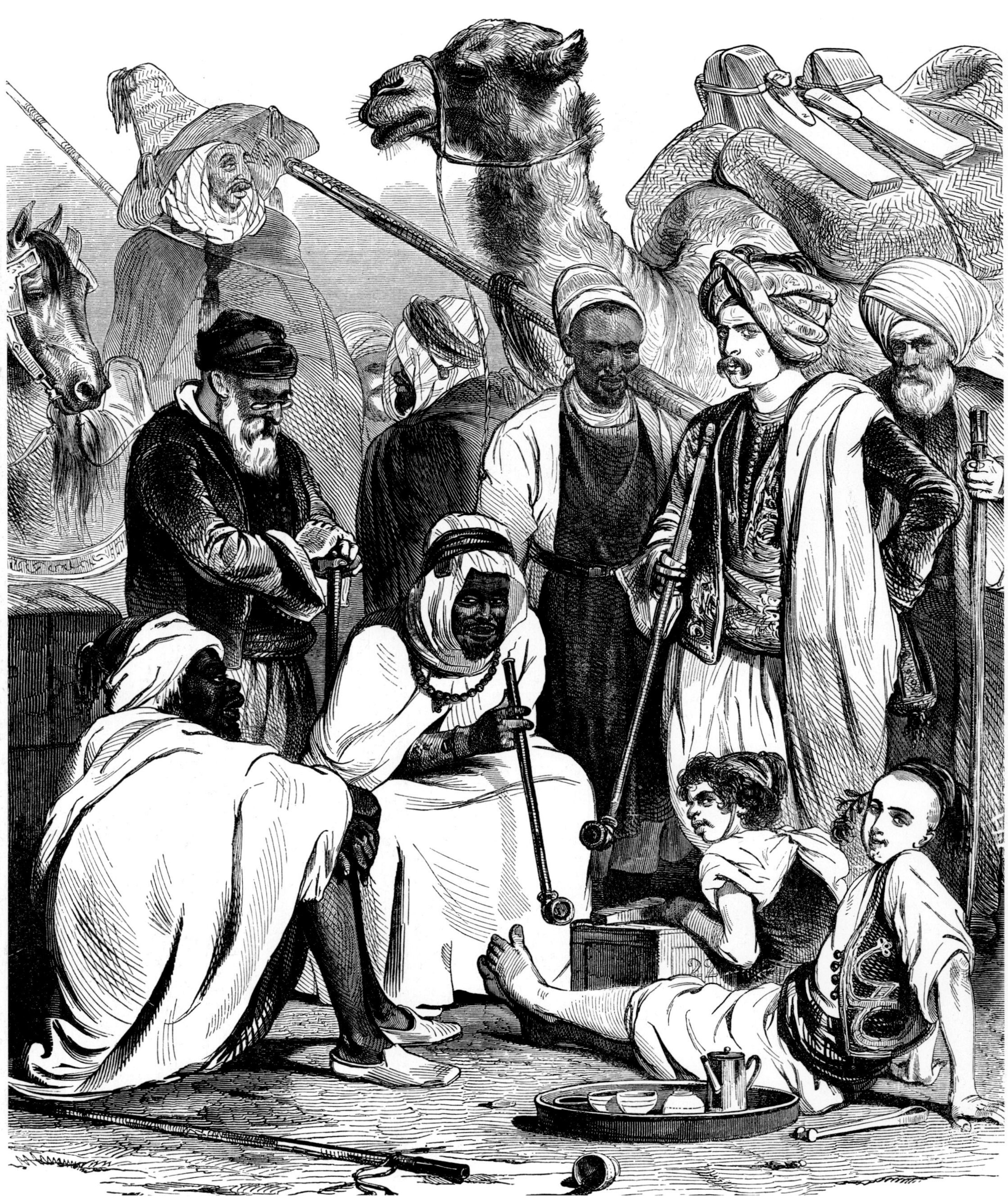

Arab, Jewish, Negro and Kabilyan inhabitants of Algiers, 1840

Arabische, jüdische, schwarze und kabylische Einwohner von Algier, 1840

Abitanti arabi, ebrei, negri e cabili di Algeri, 1840

Habitants arabes, juifs, noirs et kabyles d'Alger, 1840

Habitantes árabes, judíos, negros y cabilas de Argel, 1840

Algeria

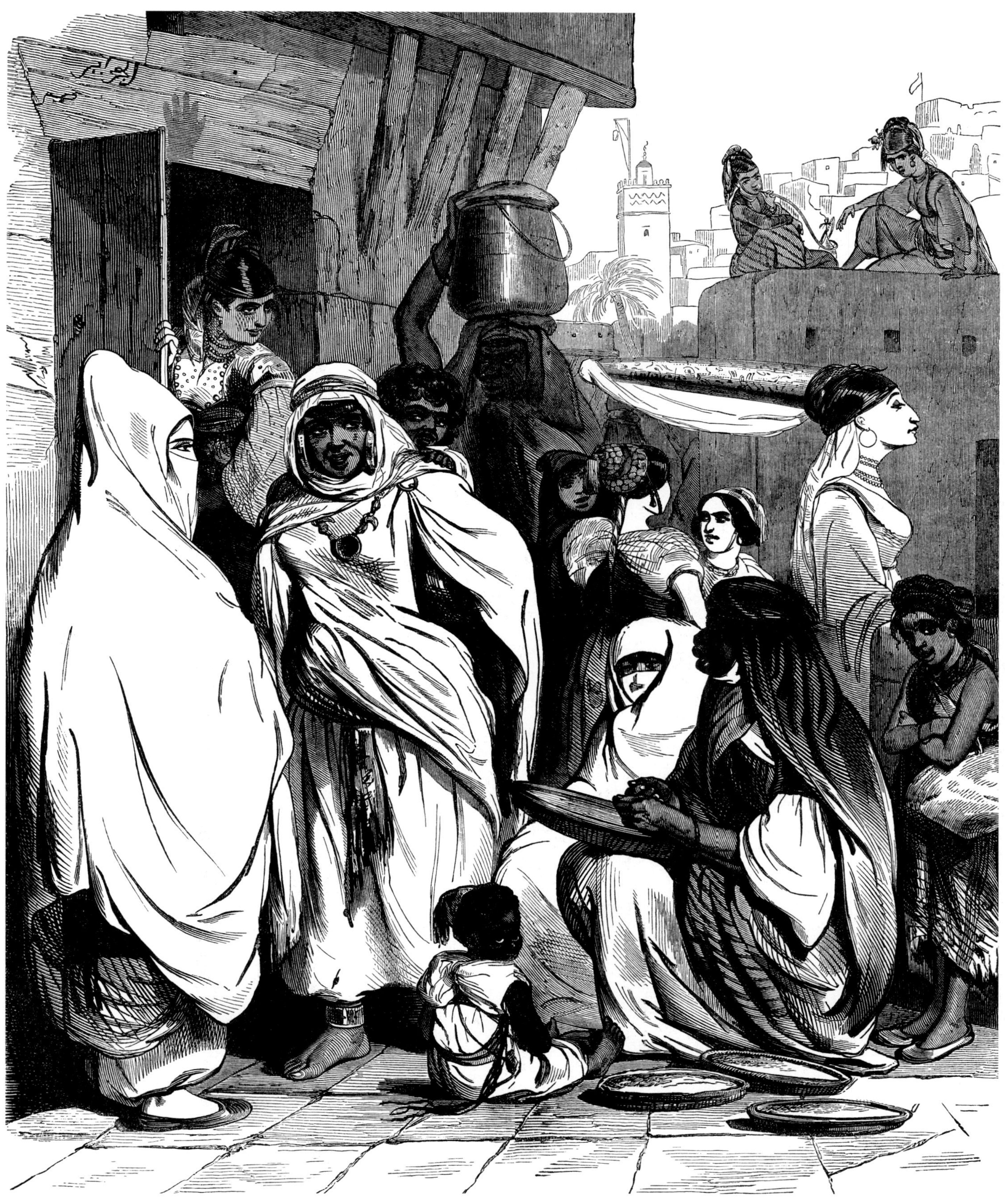

Arab, Bedouin and Jewish inhabitants of Algiers, 1840

Arabische, beduinische und jüdische Einwohner von Algier, 1840

Abitanti arabi, beduini ed ebrei di Algeri, 1840

Habitants arabes, bédouins et juifs d'Alger, 1840

Habitantes árabes, beduinos y judíos de Argel, 1840

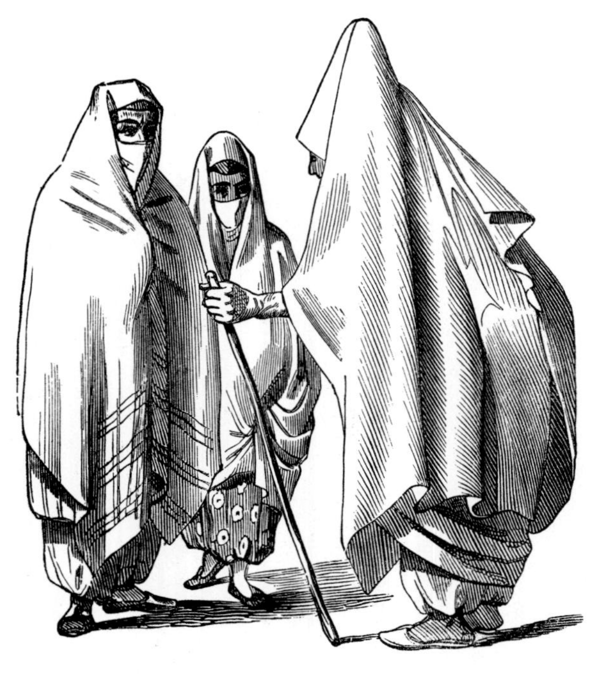

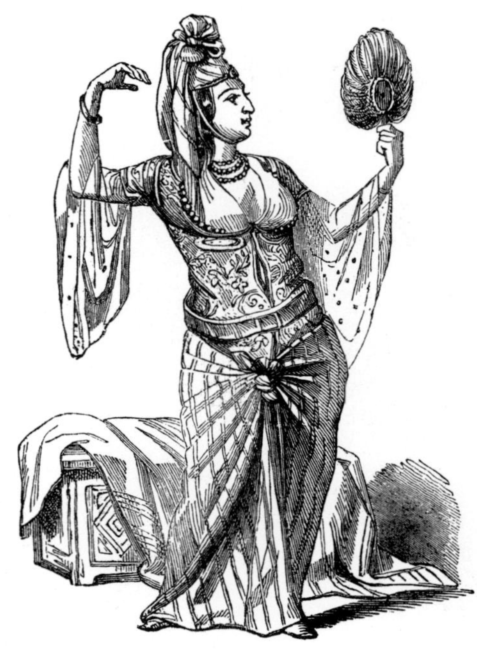

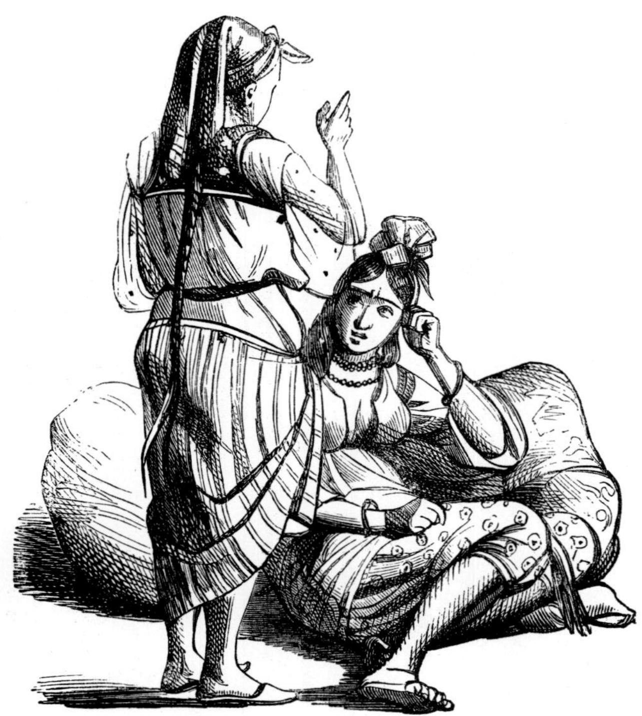

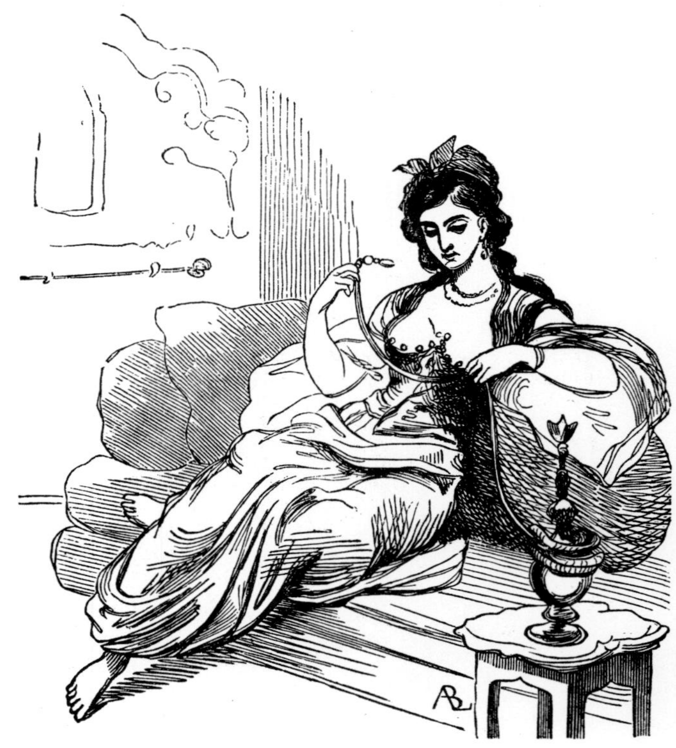

a	Algerian ladies in street dress, c. 1840	Algerische Damen in Straßenkleidung, um 1840	Donne algerine in abito per uscire, ca. 1840	Dames algériennes en tenue de rue, vers 1840	Damas argelinas en traje de calle, hacia el año 1840
b+c	Algerian ladies in house dress, c. 1840	Algerische Damen in Hauskleidung, um 1840	Donne algerine in abito da casa, ca. 1840	Dames algériennes en tenue d'intérieur, vers 1840	Damas argelinas en traje de casa, hacia el año 1840
d	Harem dress, c. 1840	Haremskleidung, um 1840	Abito da harem, ca. 1840	Robe de harem, vers 1840	Vestido del harén, 1840

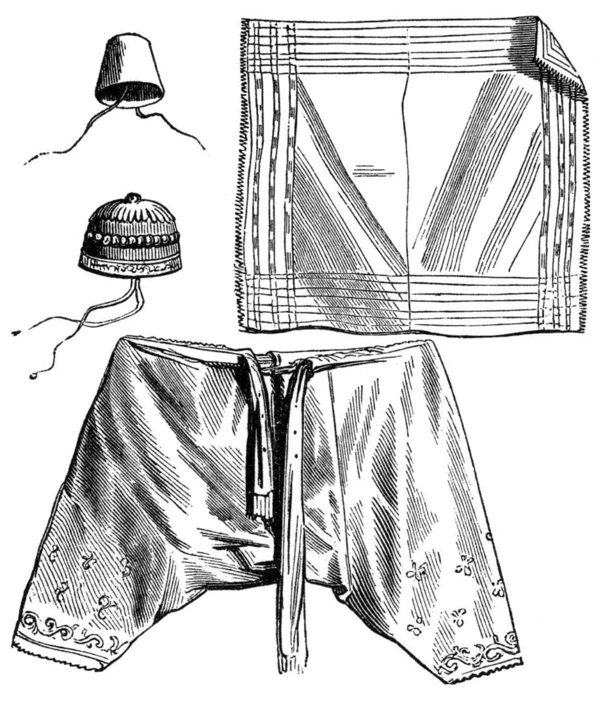

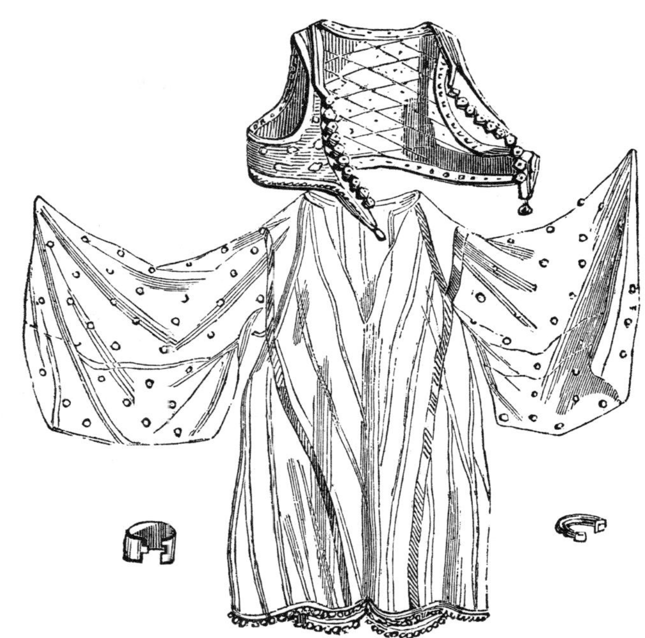

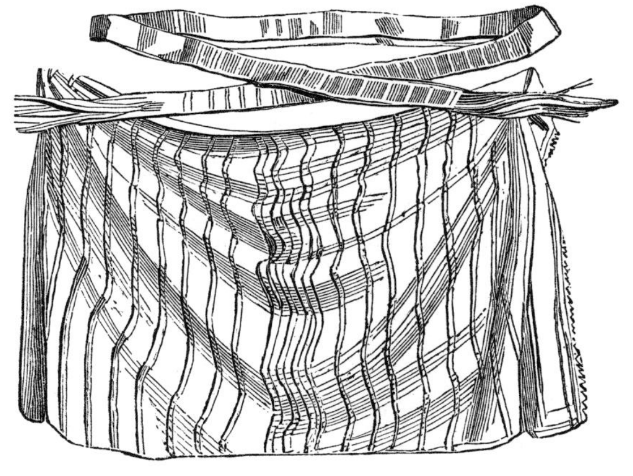

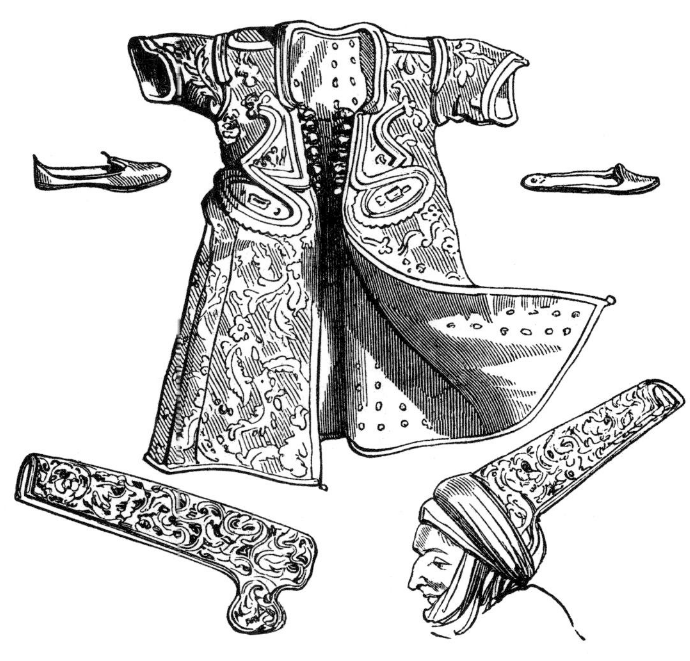

Algerian female dress items, 1845

Teile algerischer Frauenkleidung, 1845

Articoli di abito femminile algerino, 1845

Éléments de la garde-robe féminine algérienne, 1845

Prendas de vestir femeninas argelinas, 1845

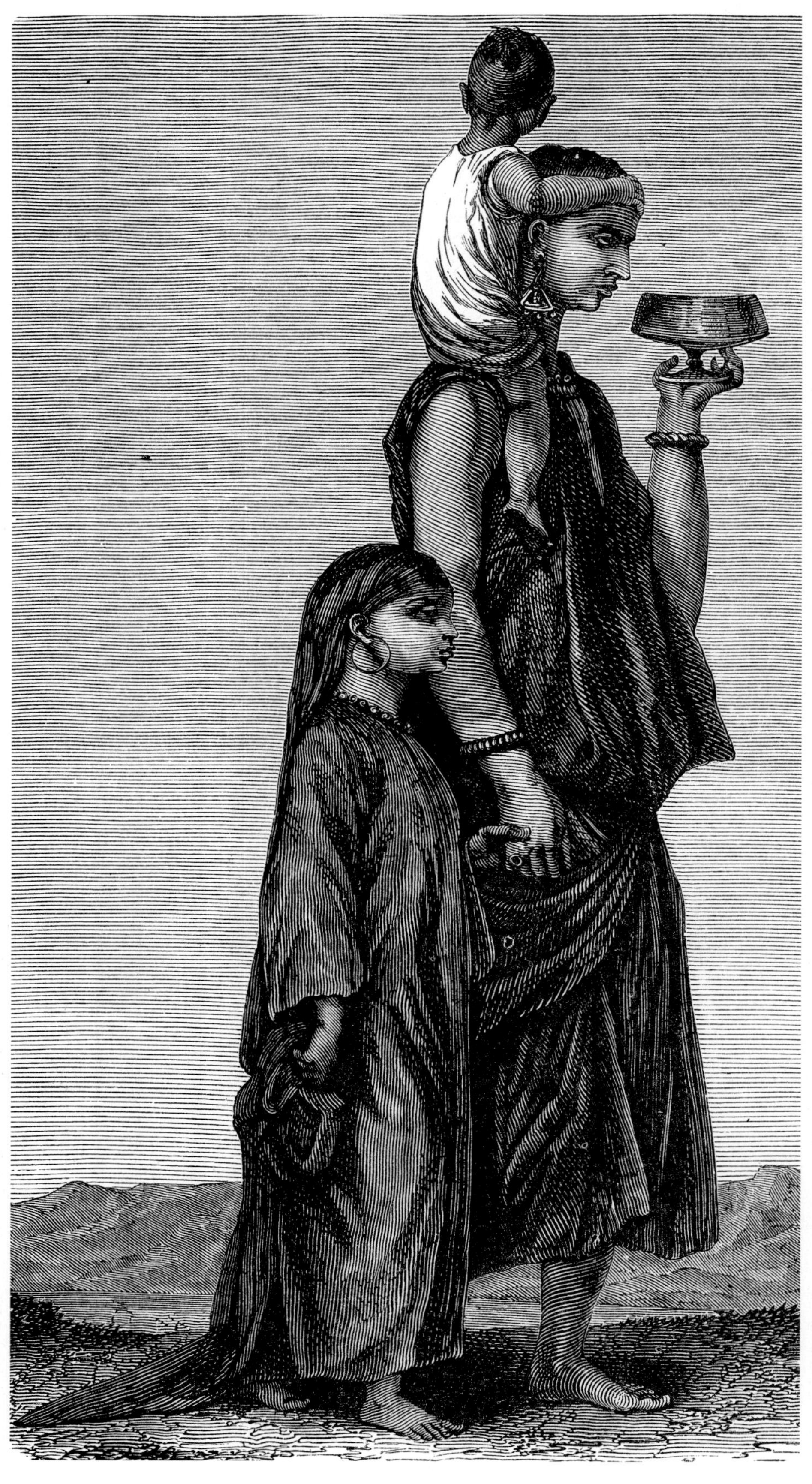

Berber lady with children, c, 1880

Berberfrau mit Kinder, um 1880

Donna berbera con bambini, ca. 1880

Femme berbère et ses enfants, vers 1880

Mujer beréber con sus hijos, hacia 1880

Algeria

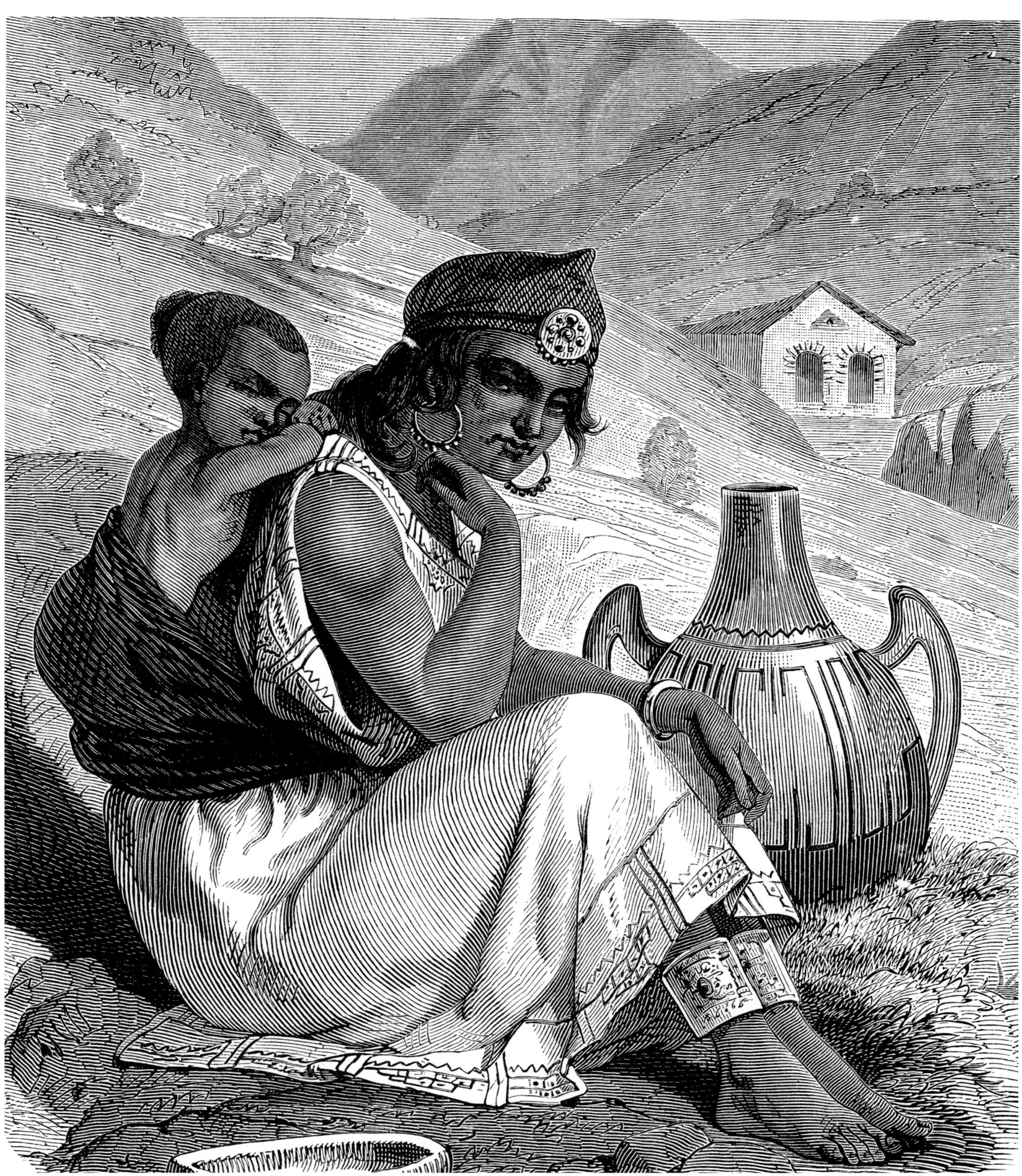

Kabyle lady, Atlas Mountains, c. 1880

Kabylenfrau, Atlasgebirge, um 1880

Donna cabila, Montagne dell'Atlante, ca. 1880

Femme kabyle, Montagnes de l'Atlas, vers 1880

Mujer cabila, cordillera del Atlas, hacia el año 1880

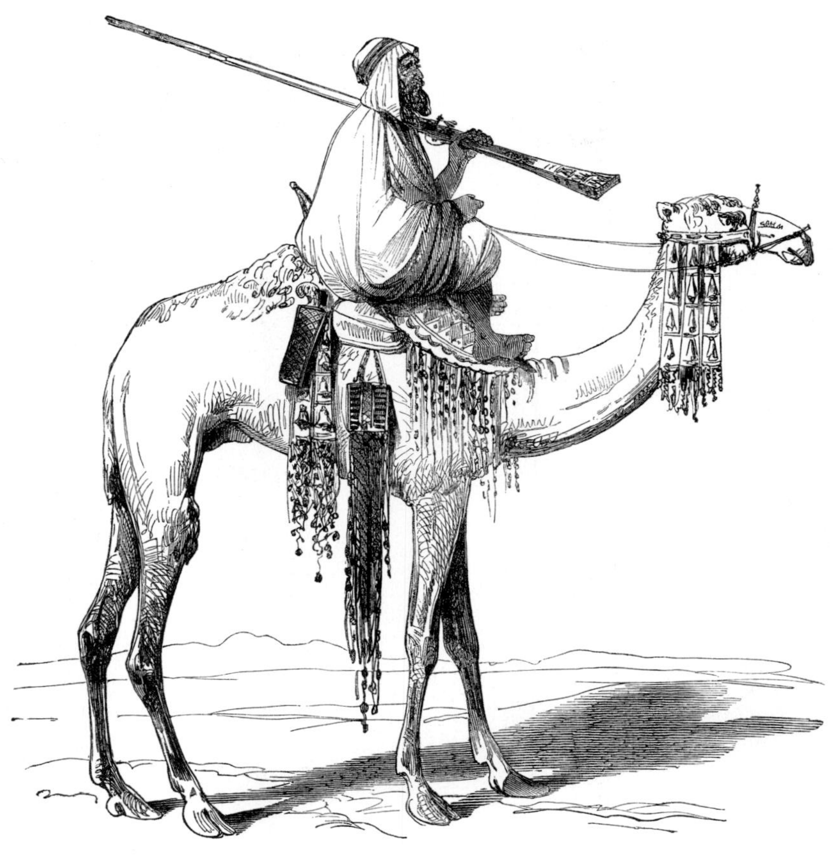

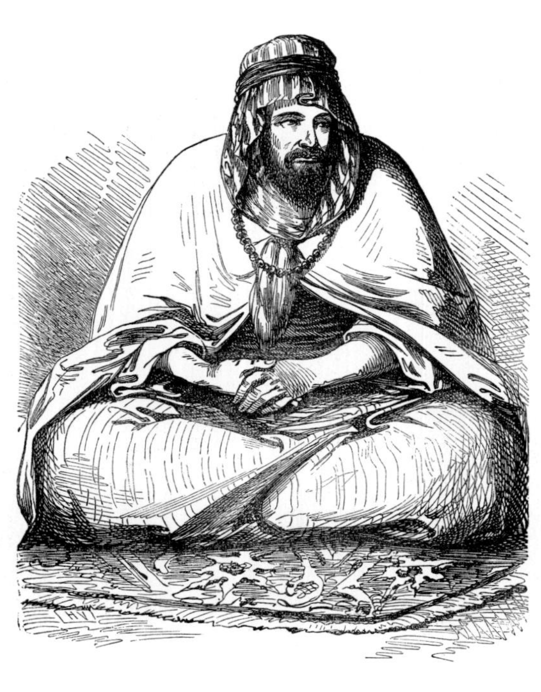

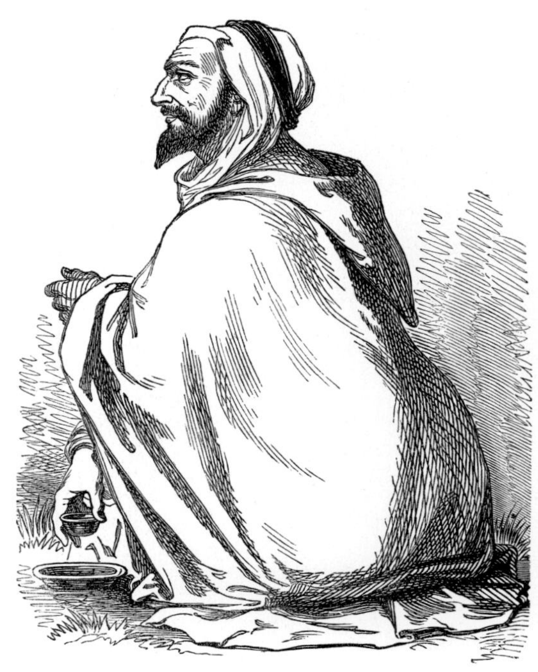

Men's dress, Algerian Sahara, c. 1845

Männerkleidung, algerische Wüste, um 1845

Abito maschile, Sahara algerino, ca. 1845

Vêtements masculins, Sahara algérien, vers 1845

Trajes de hombre, Sahara argelino, hacia 1845

Algeria

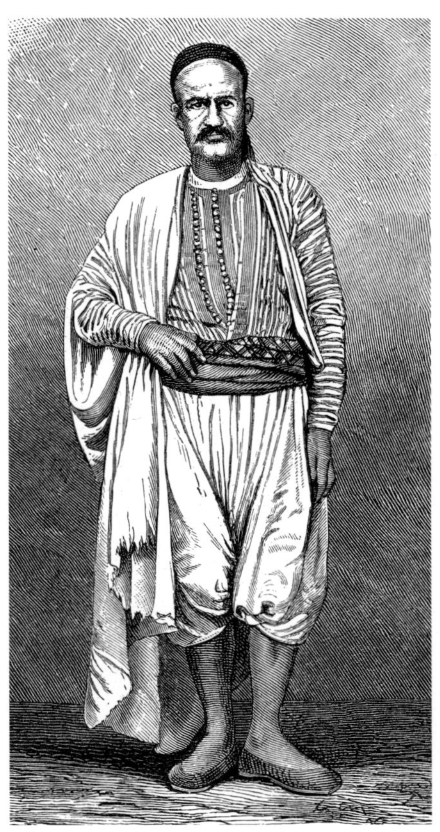

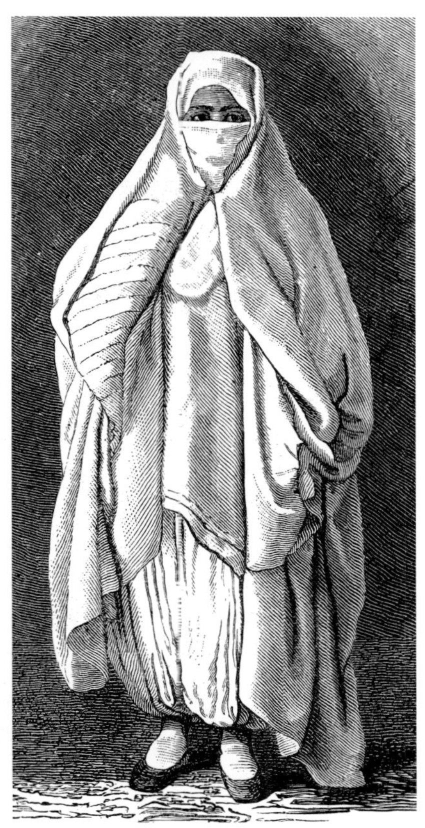

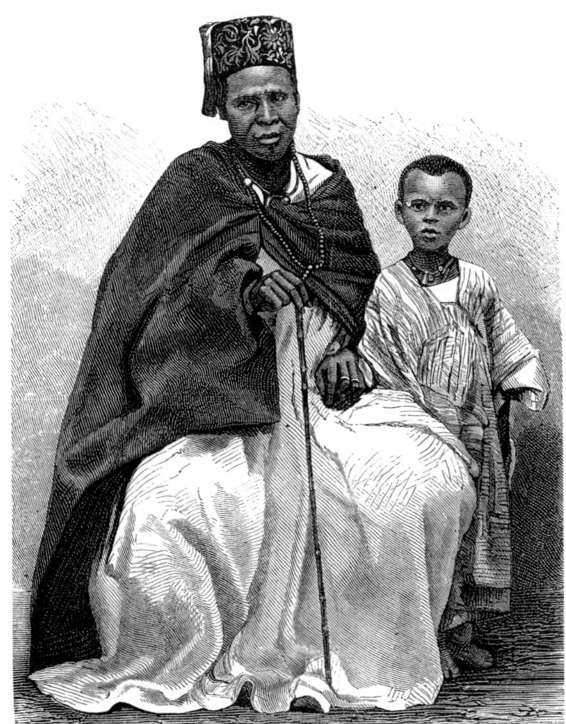

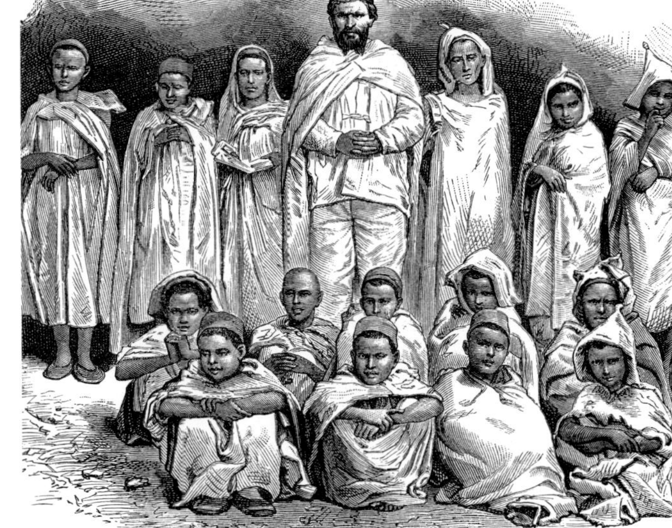

a+b	Man and woman from Constantine, c. 1890	Mann und Frau aus Constantine, um 1890	Uomo e donna di Constantine, ca. 1890	Homme et femme de Constantine, vers 1890	Hombre y mujer de Constantina, hacia 1890
c	Algerian Marabou	Algerischer Marabou	Marabù algerino	Marabout algérien	Morabito argelino
d	Kabilyan Children, c. 1900	Kabylenkinder, um 1900	Bambini cabili, ca. 1900	Enfants kabyles, vers 1900	Niños cabilas, hacia 1900

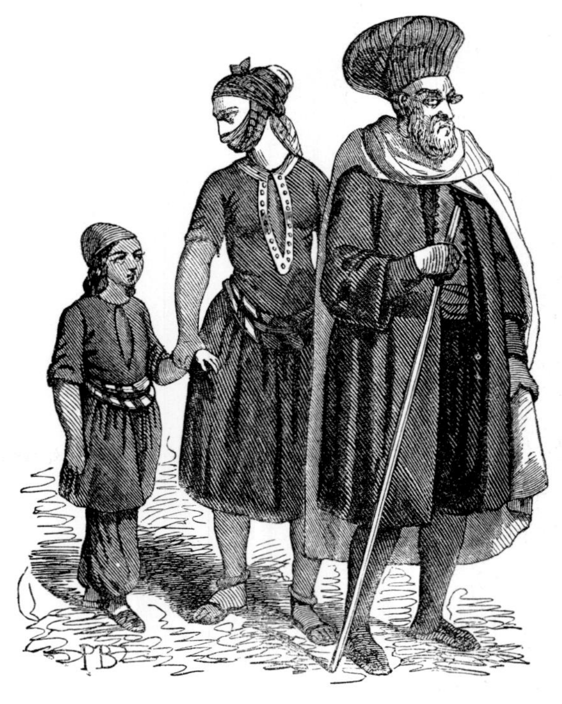

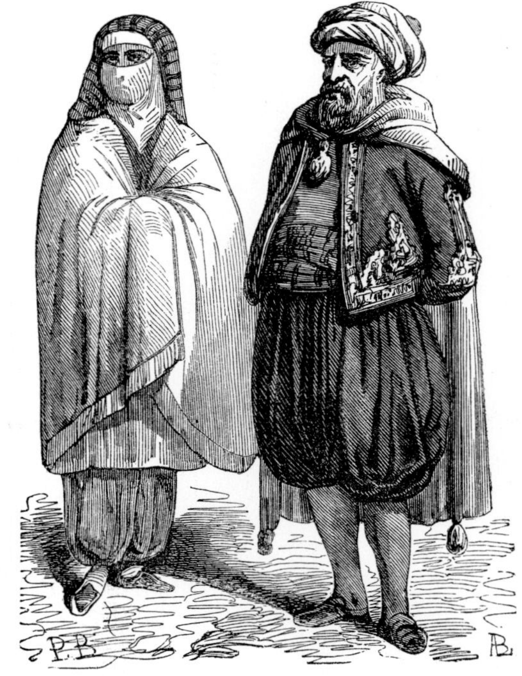

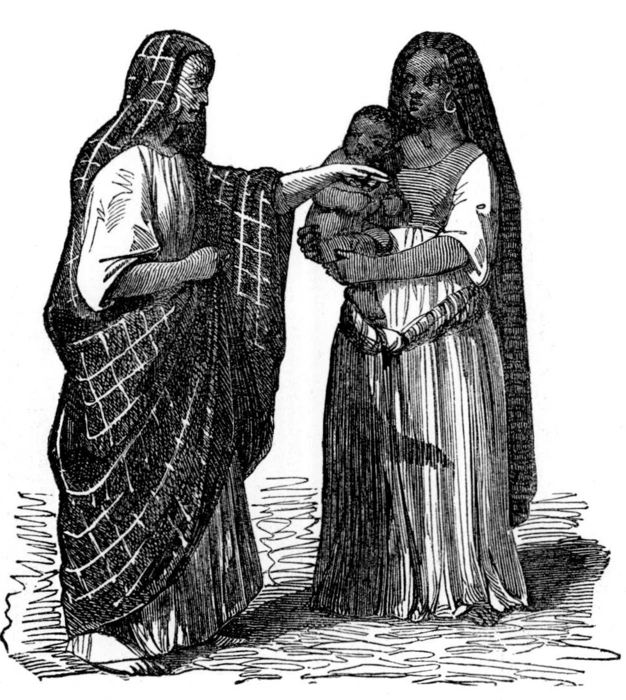

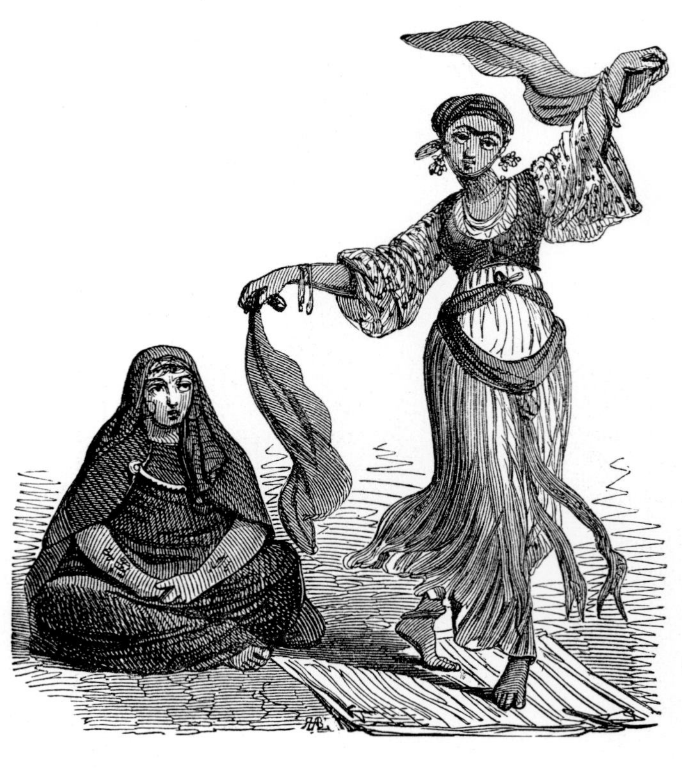

a	Jewish family, Tunis, 1840	Jüdische Familie, Tunis, 1840	Famiglia ebraica, Tunisi, 1840	Famille juive, Tunis, 1840	Familia judía, Túnez, 1840
b	Arab couple, Tunis, 1840	Arabisches Paar, Tunis, 1840	Coppia araba, Tunisi, 1840	Couple arabe, Tunis, 1840	Pareja árabe, Túnez, 1840
c	Arab lady with servant, Tunis, 1840	Arabische Dame mit Dienerin, Tunis, 1840	Donna araba con domestica, Tunisi, 1840	Femme arabe et sa servante, Tunis, 1840	Mujer árabe y su sirviente, Túnez, 1840
d	Dancing girl, Tunis, 1840	Tanzendes Mädchen, Tunis, 1840	Danzatrice, Tunisi, 1840	Danseuse, Tunis, 1840	Bailarina, Túnez, 1840

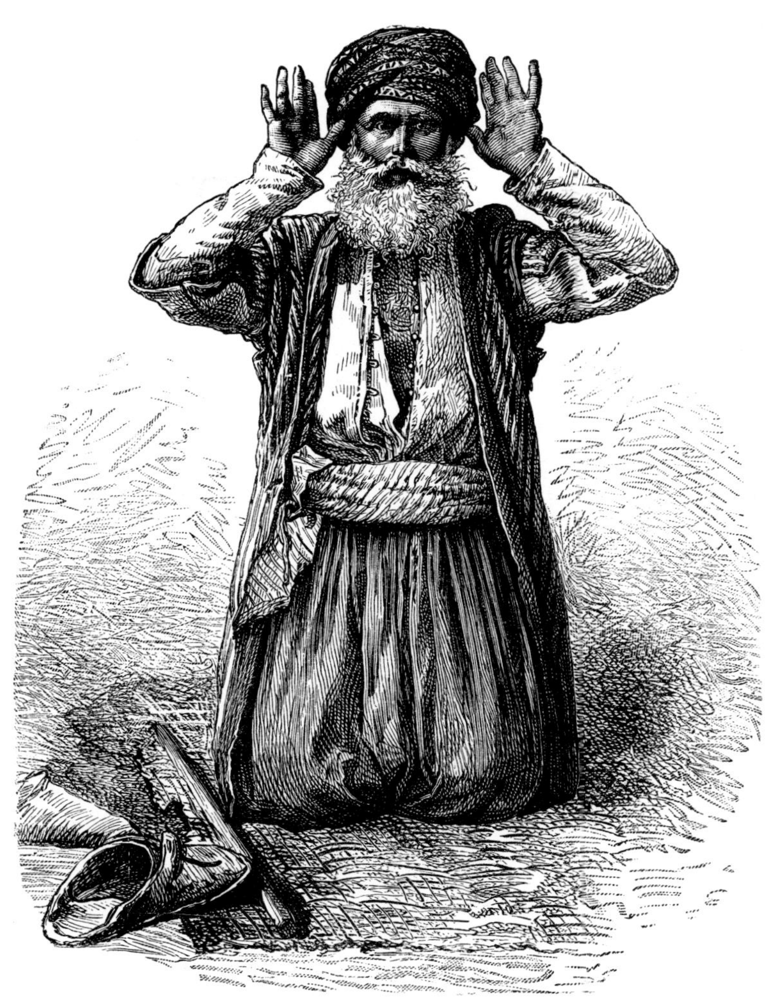

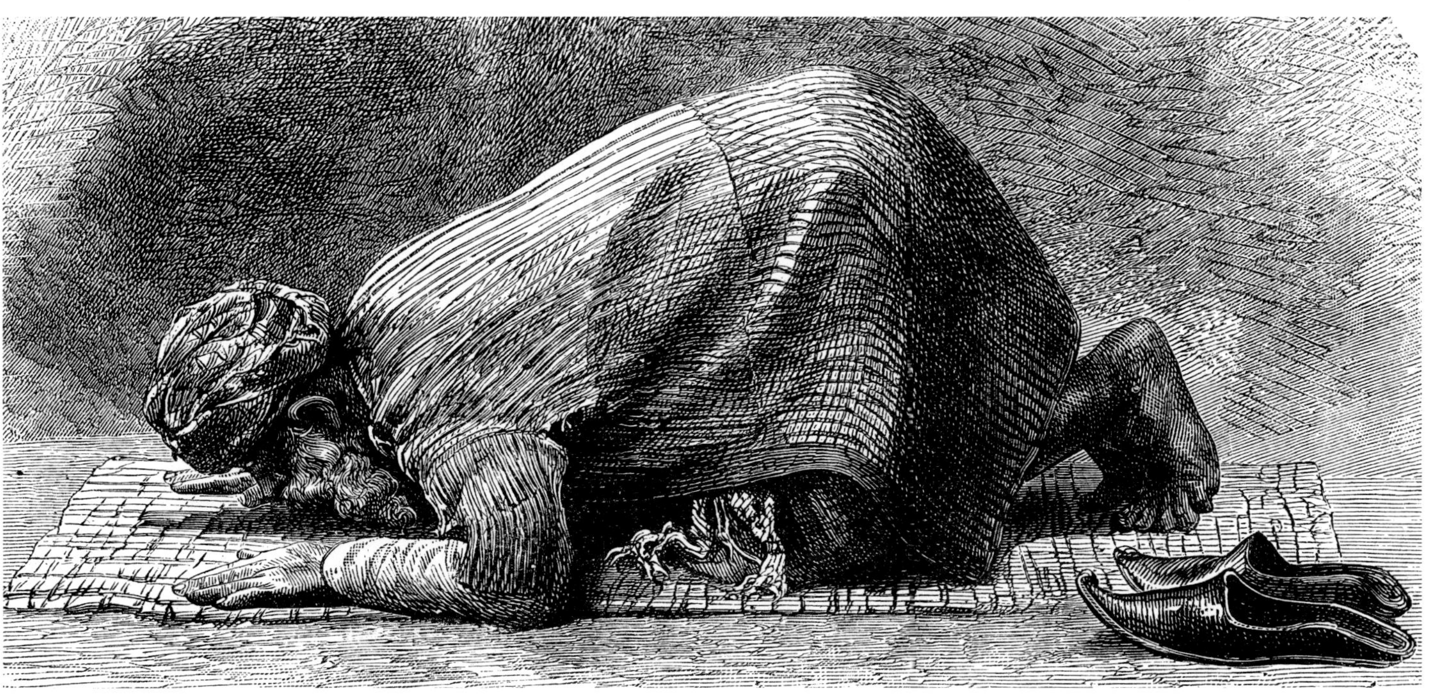

Tunisian man praying, c. 1890

Tunesischer Mann beim Gebet, um 1890

Tunisino in preghiera, ca. 1890

Tunisien à l'heure de la prière, vers 1890

Hombre tunecino orando, hacia 1890

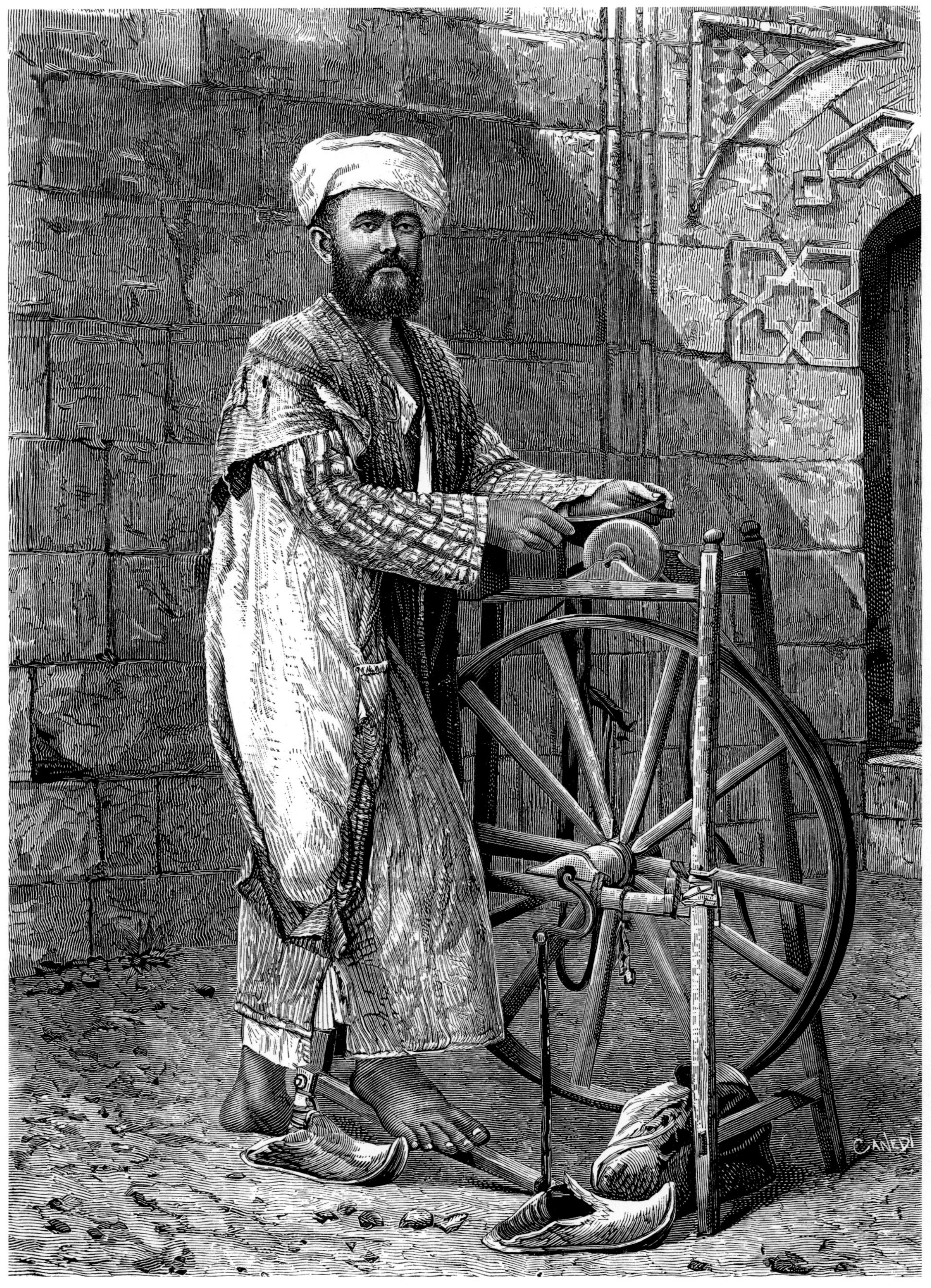

Tunisian, c. 1880 Tunesier, um 1880 Tunisino, ca. 1880 Tunisien, vers 1880 Tunecino, hacia 1880

Tunisia

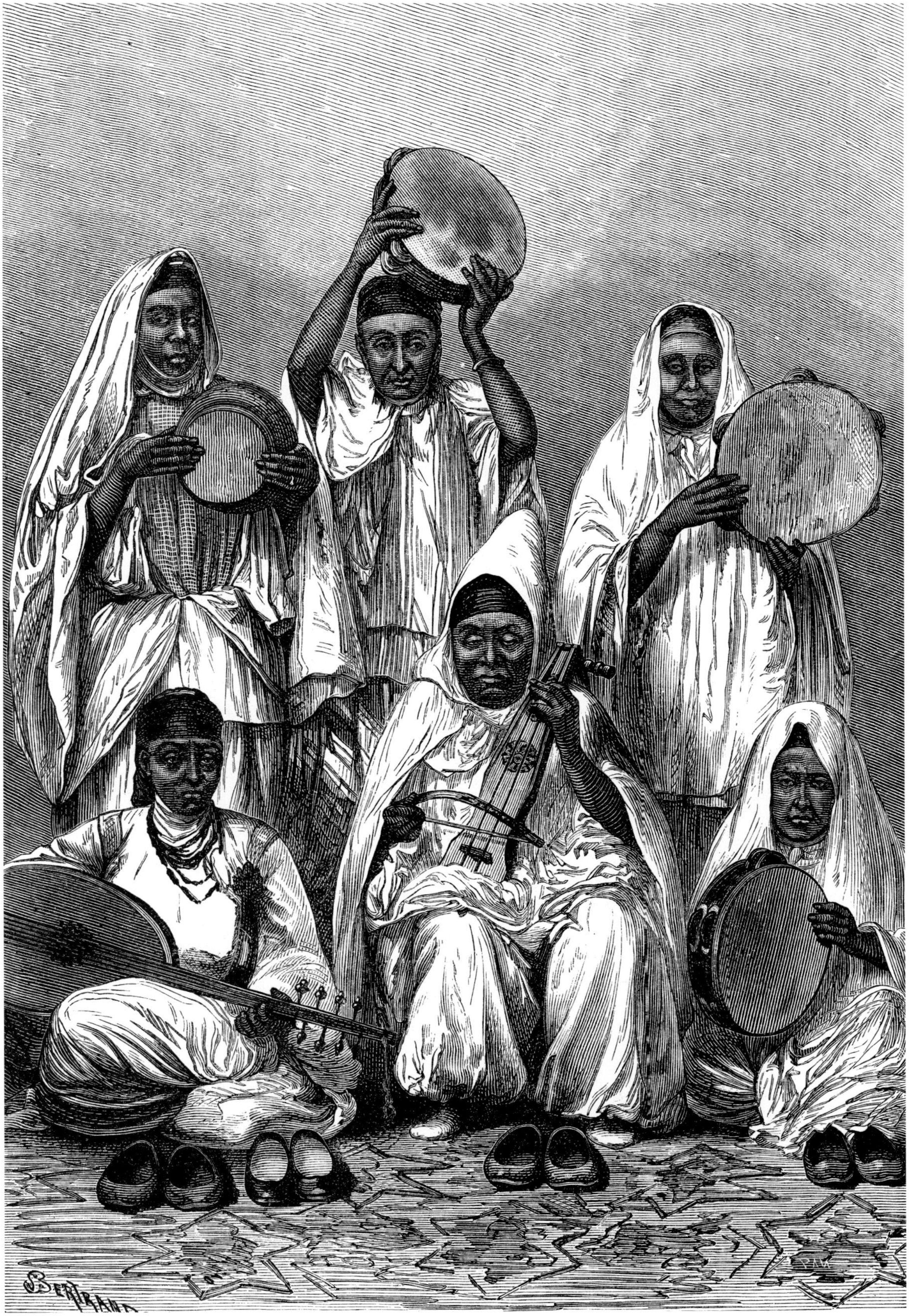

Tuareg Musicians, c. 1890

Tuareg-Musiker, um 1890

Musicisti tuareg, ca. 1890

Musiciens touaregs, vers 1890

Músicos tuaregs, hacia 1890

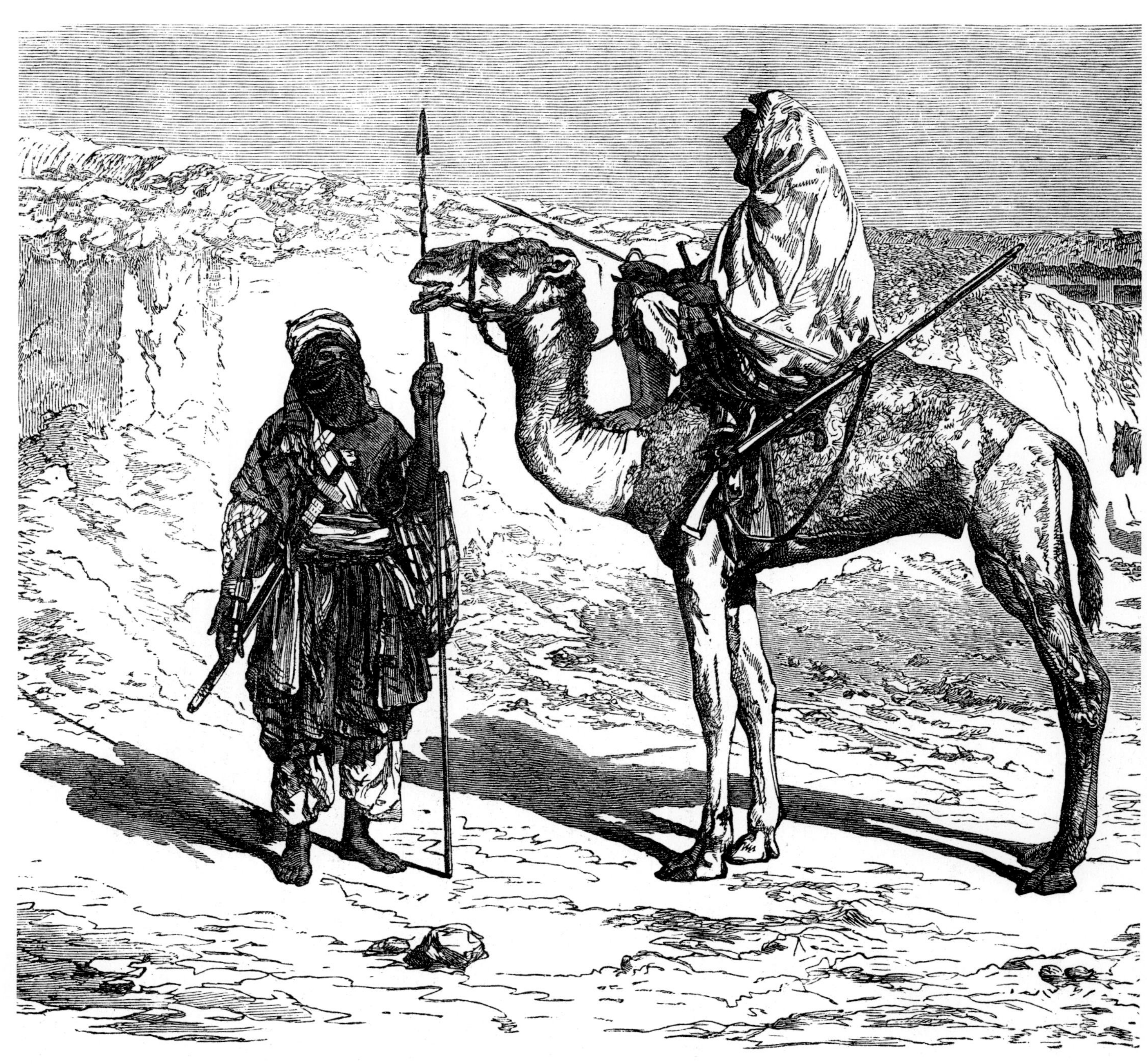

Tuareg men, 1850　Tuareg, 1850　Tuareg, 1850　Touaregs, 1850　Tuaregs, 1850

Tunisia/Algeria

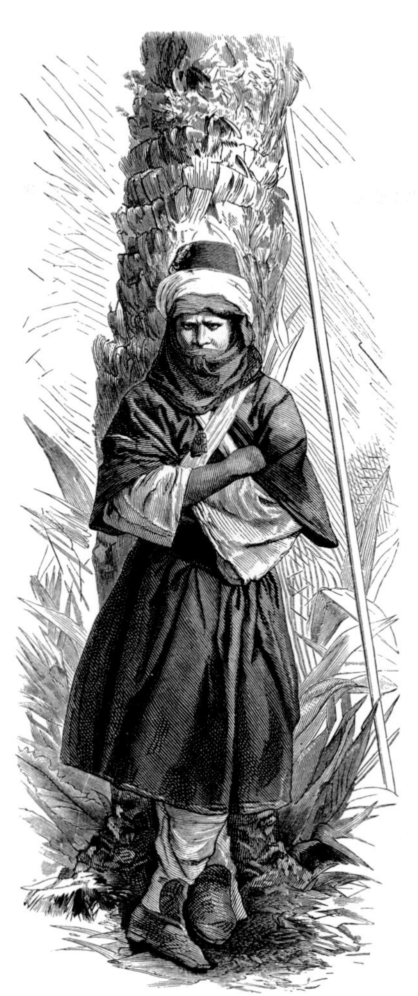

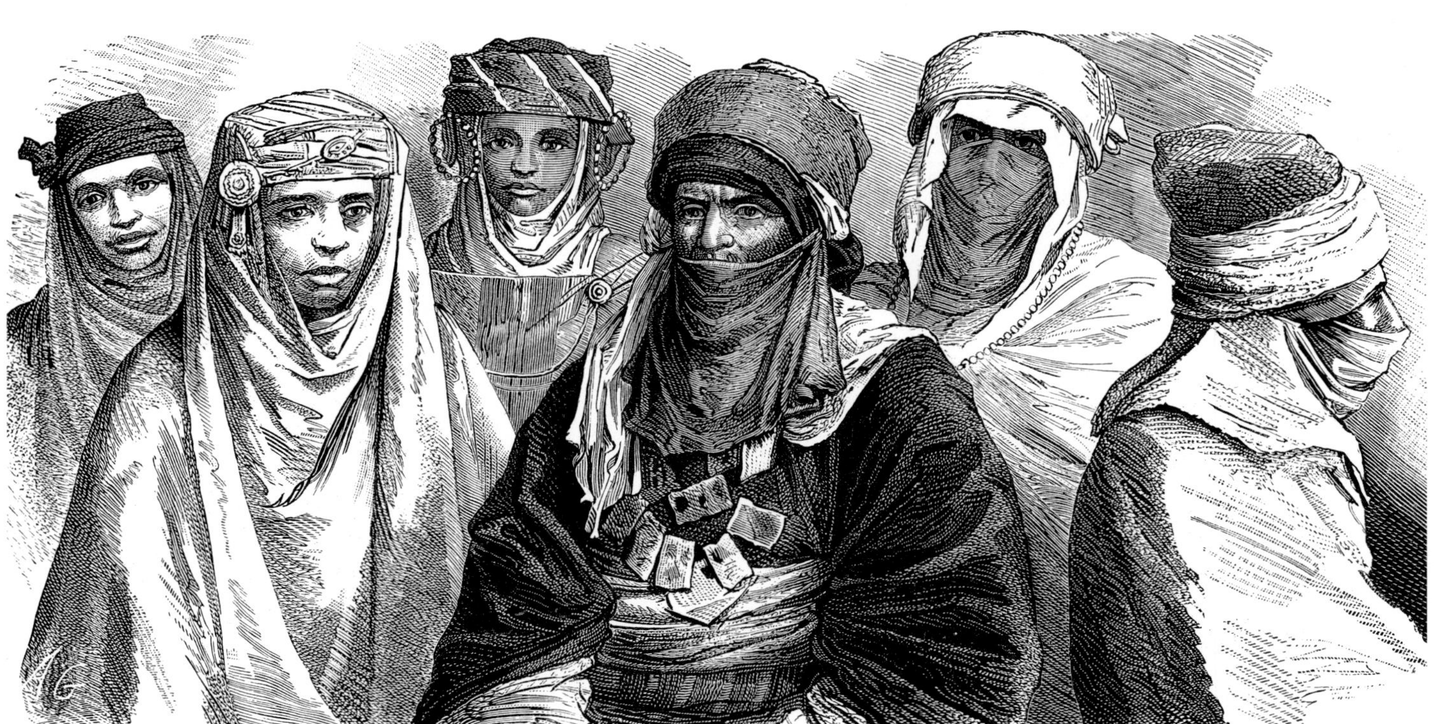

Saharan Tuareg, c. 1900. Typically, the men are veiled, the women not

Tuareg aus der Sahara, um 1900; die Männer sind normalerweise verschleiert, die Frauen nicht

Tuareg sahariano, ca. 1900. Generalmente gli uomini portano il velo e le donne no

Touaregs du Sahara, vers 1900. Les hommes sont généralement voilés, les femmes non

Tuareg sahariano, hacia 1900. Los hombres suelen cubrirse el rostro, las mujeres no

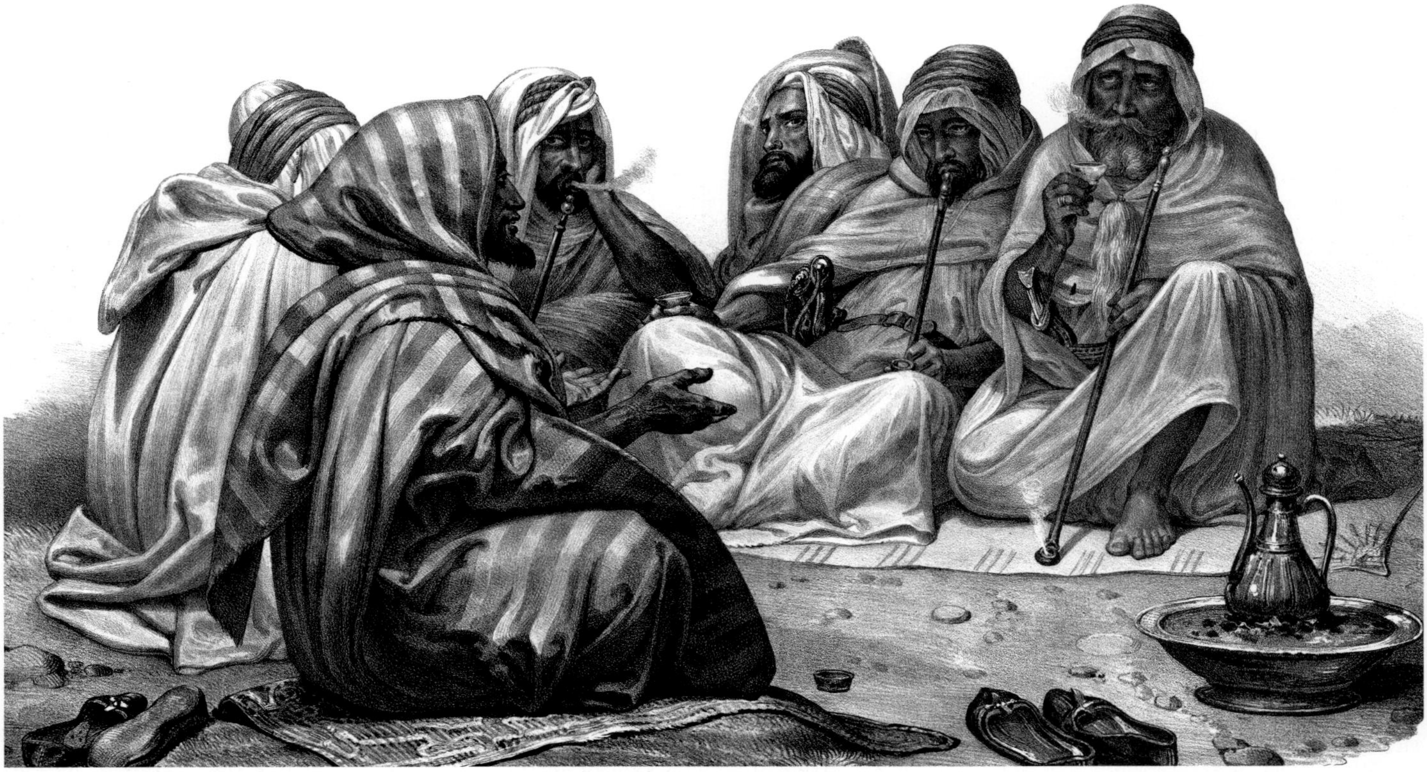

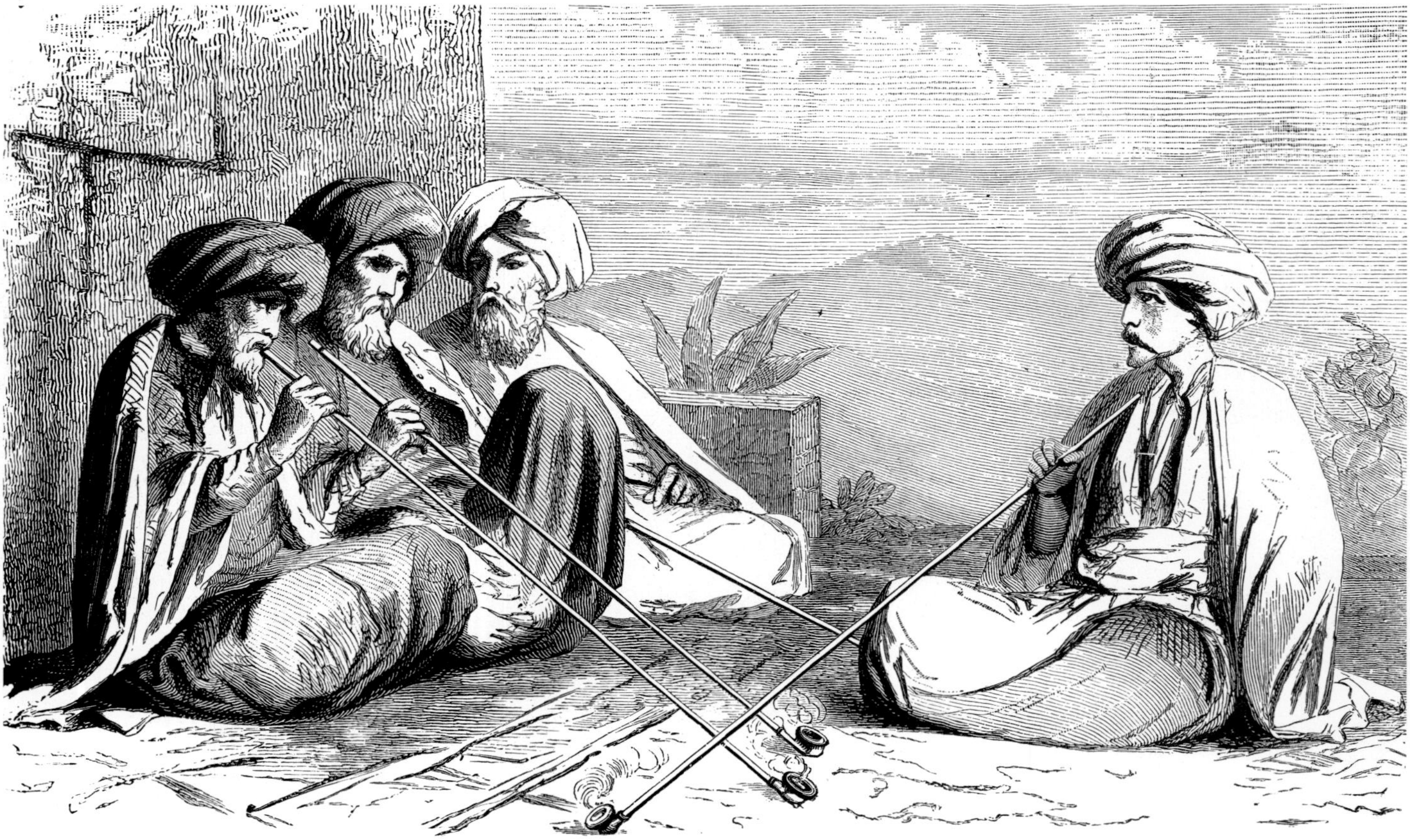

Tunisian men, c. 1850

Tunesische Männer, um 1850

Tunisini, ca. 1850

Tunisiens, vers1850

Tunecinos, hacia 1850

Tunisia

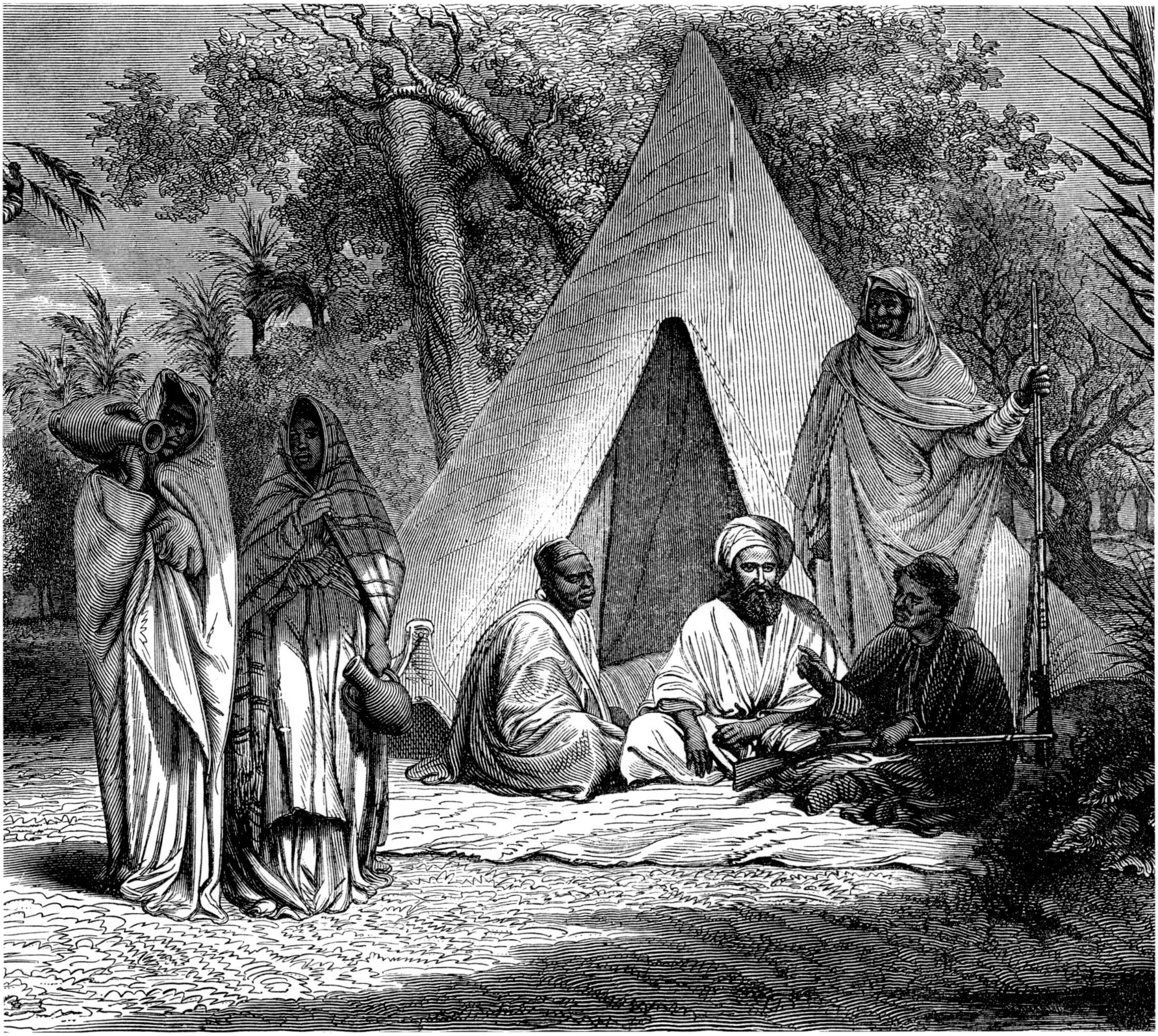

Arab Nomads, c. 1900

Arabische Nomaden, um 1900

Nomadi arabi, ca. 1900

Nomades arabes, vers 1900

Nómadas árabes, hacia el año 1900

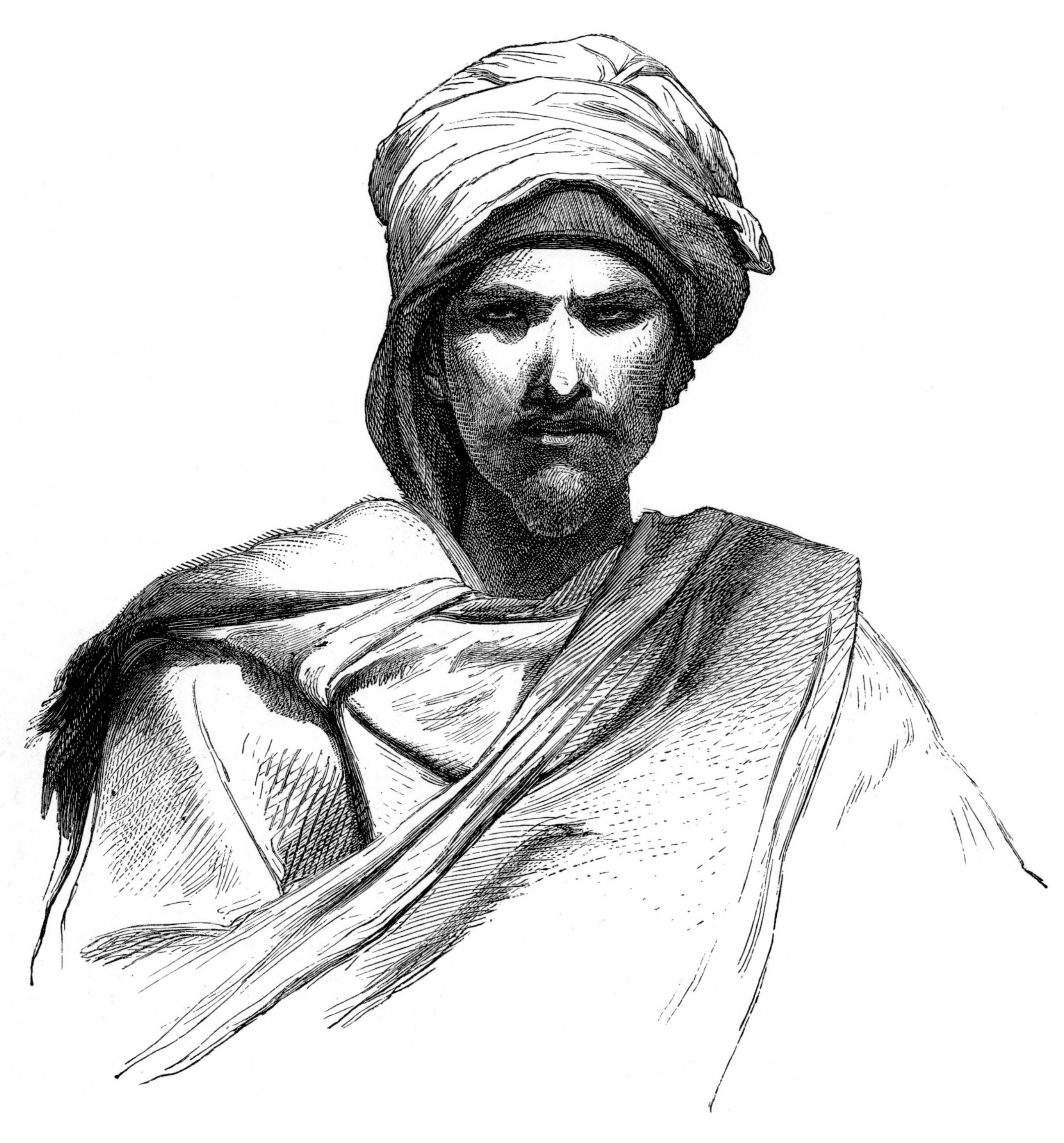

Bedouin from the Sinai dessert, c. 1860

Beduine aus der Wüste Sinai, um 1860

Beduino del deserto del Sinai, ca. 1860

Bédouin du désert du Sinaï, vers 1860

Beduino del desierto del Sinaí, alrededor de 1860

Egypt

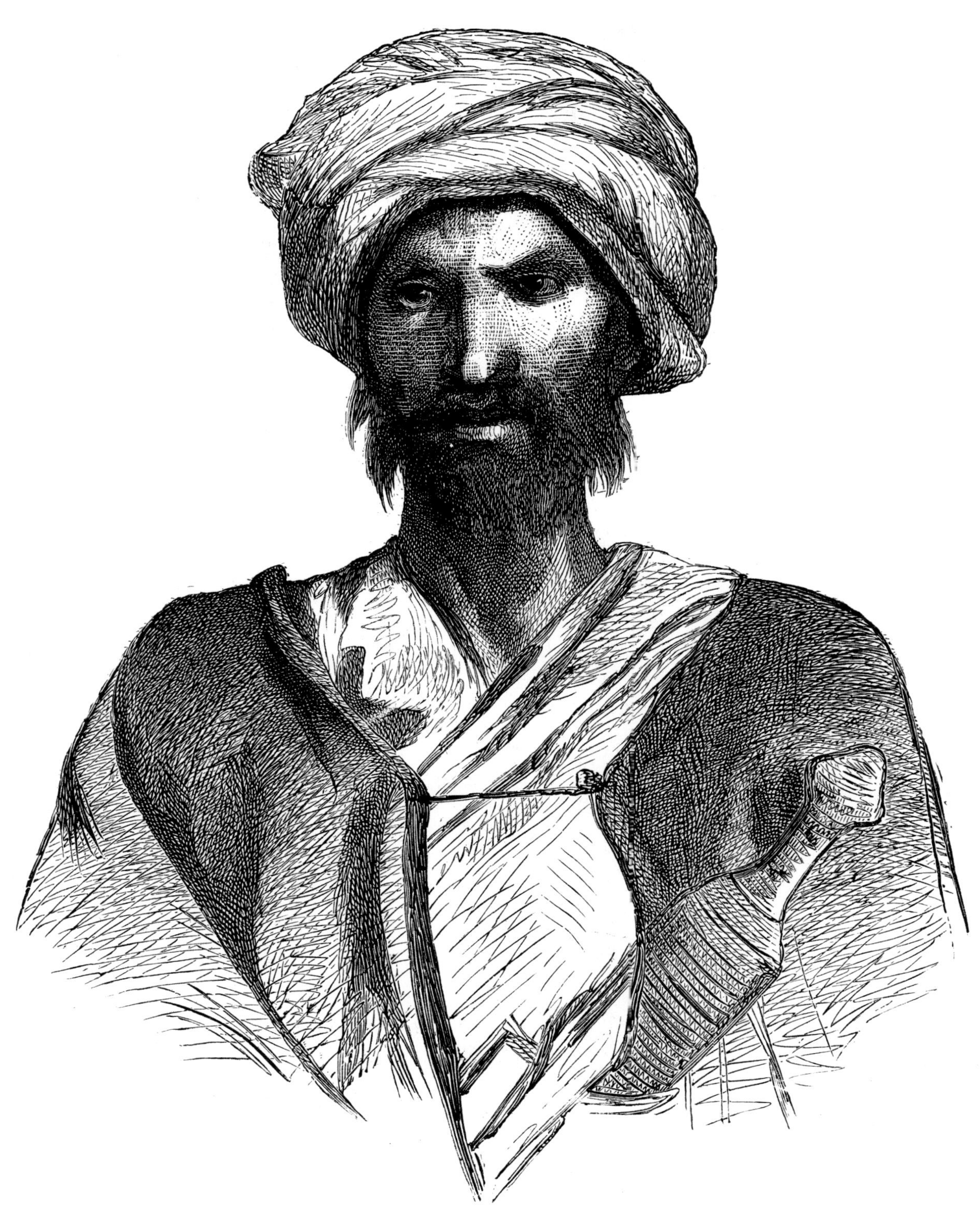

Bedouin from the Sinai dessert, c. 1860

Beduine aus der Wüste Sinai, um 1860

Beduino del deserto del Sinai, ca. 1860

Bédouin du désert du Sinaï, vers 1860

Beduino del desierto del Sinaí, alrededor de 1860

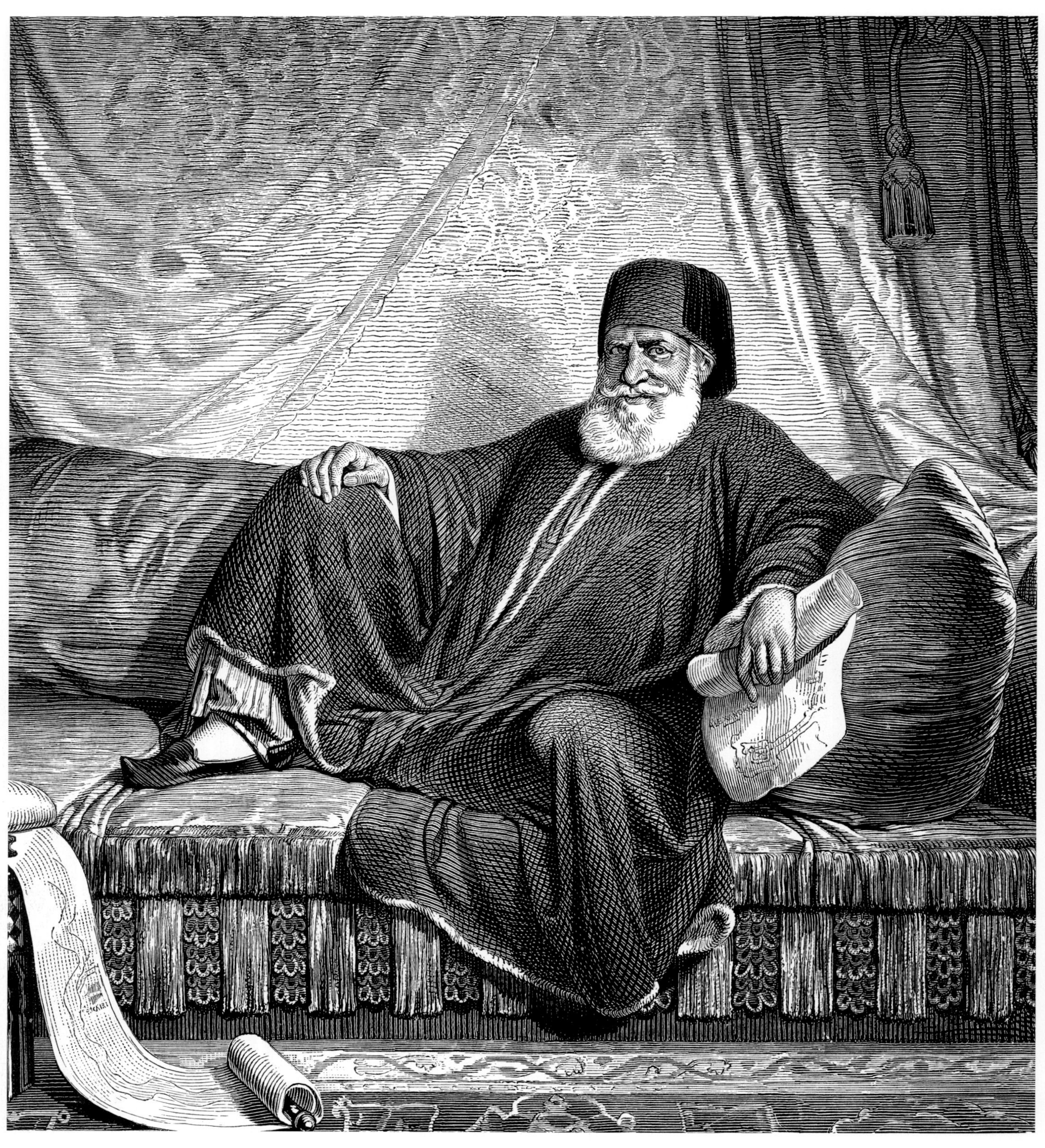

Sultan Mohemmed Ali Sultan Mohammed Ali Sultano Mohemmed Alì Sultan Mohemmed Ali Sultán Muhammad Ali

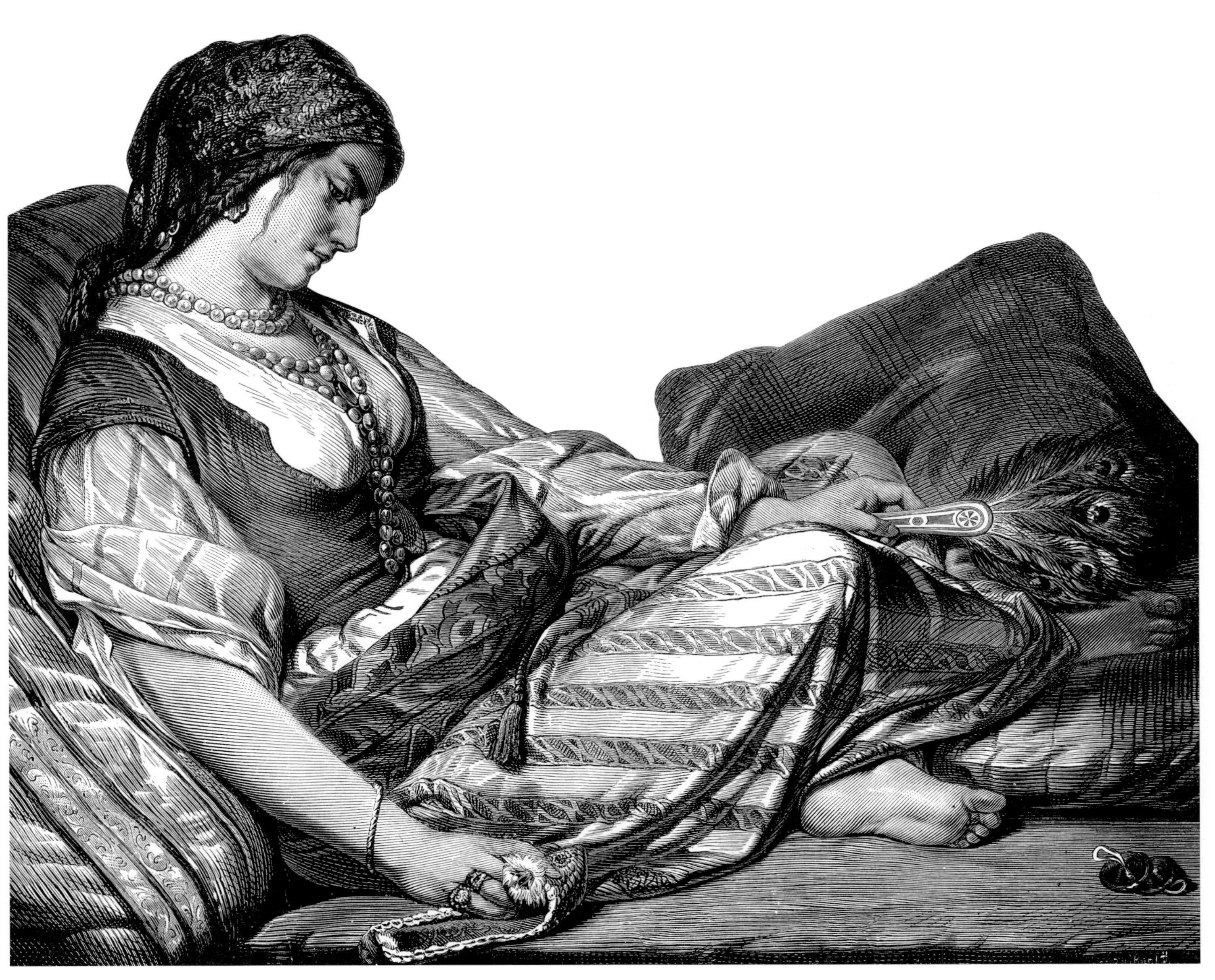

The consort of the Sultan, Cairo, 1895

La consorte del Sultano, Il Cairo, 1895

La consorte del Sultano, Il Cairo, 1895

Épouse du Sultan, Le Caire, 1895

Consorte del sultán, El Cairo, 1895

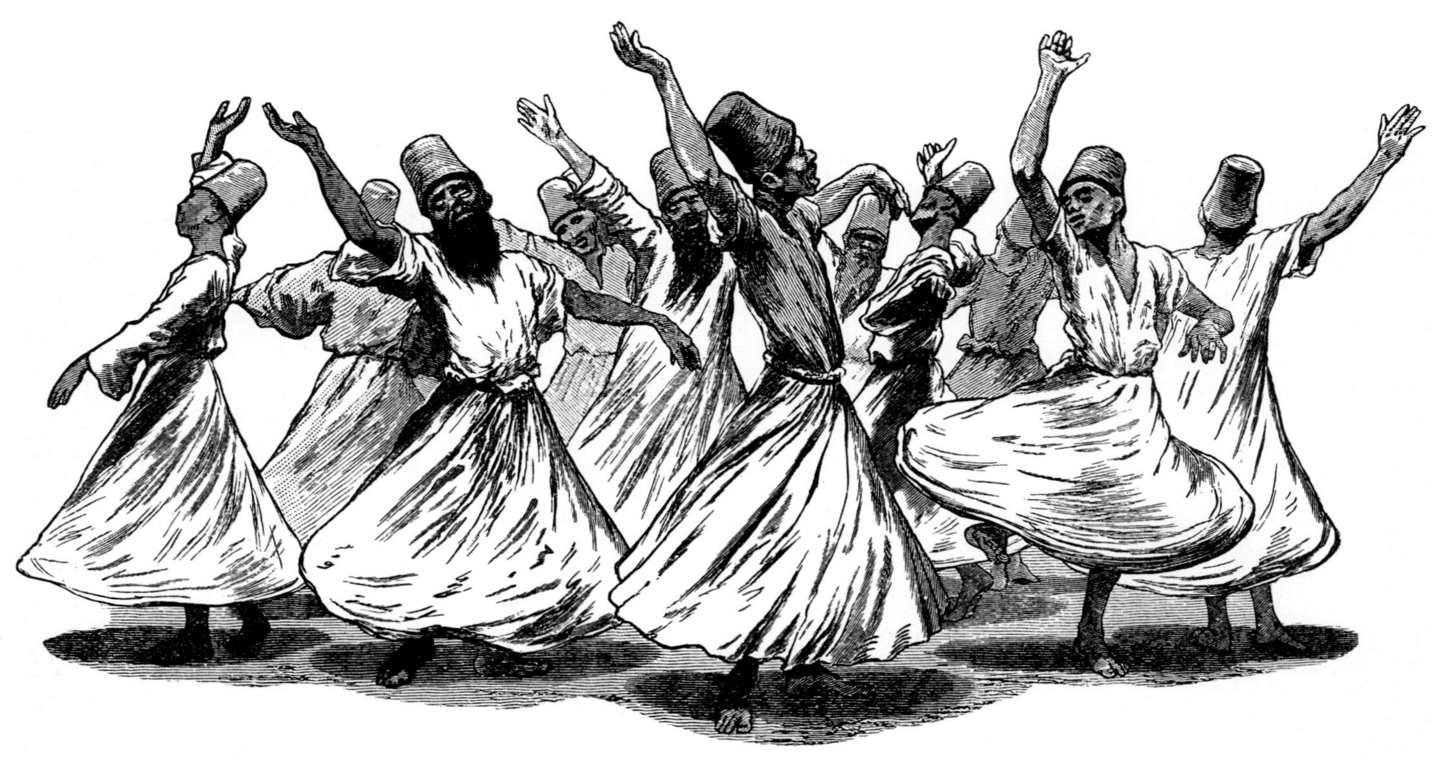

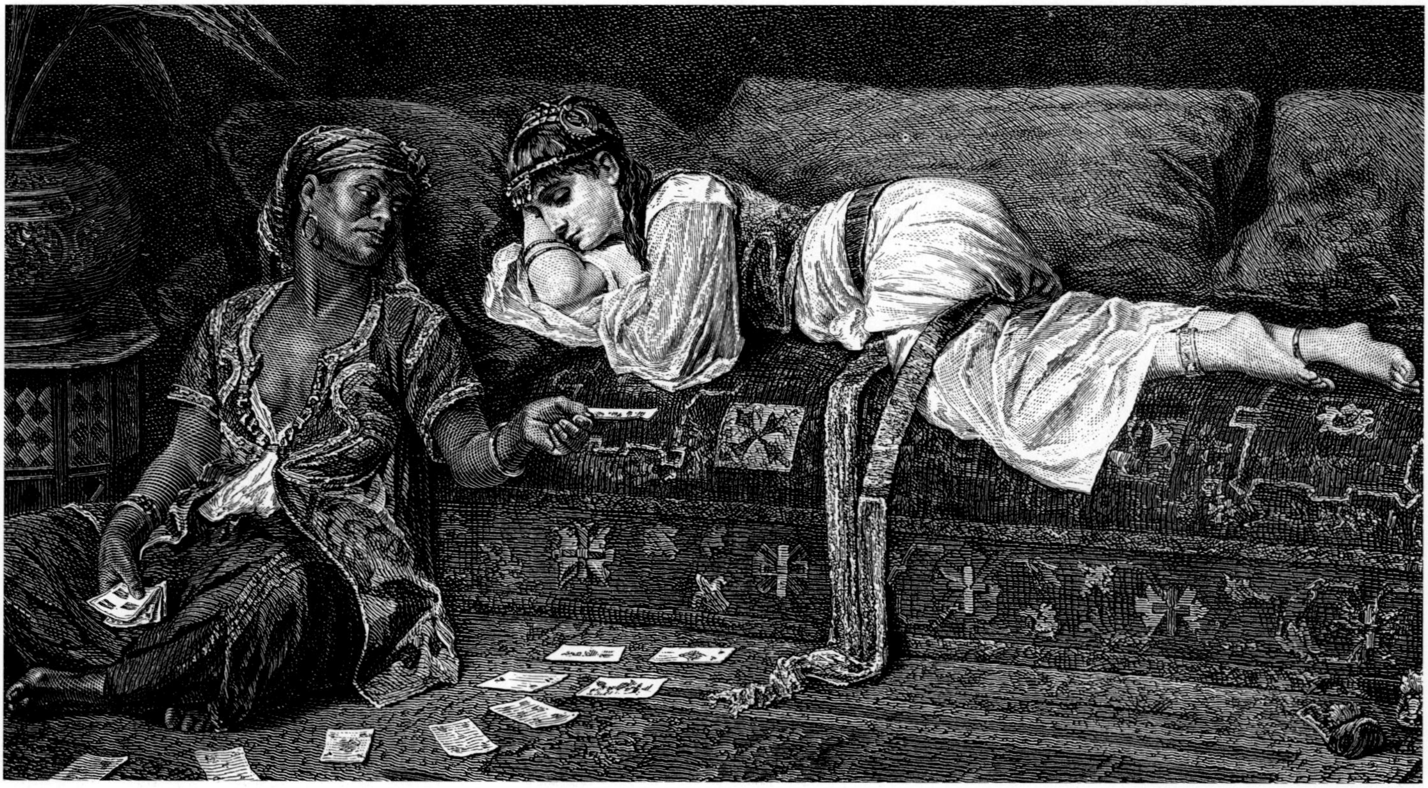

a	Dancing men, Cairo, 1890	Tanzende Männer, Kairo, 1890	Danzatori, Il Cairo, 1890	Danseurs, Le Caire, 1890	Bailarines, El Cairo, 1890
b	Harem scene, Cairo, 1890	Szene im Harem, Kairo, 1890	Scena di un harem, Il Cairo, 1890	Scène de harem, Le Caire, 1890	Escena de un harén, El Cairo, 1890

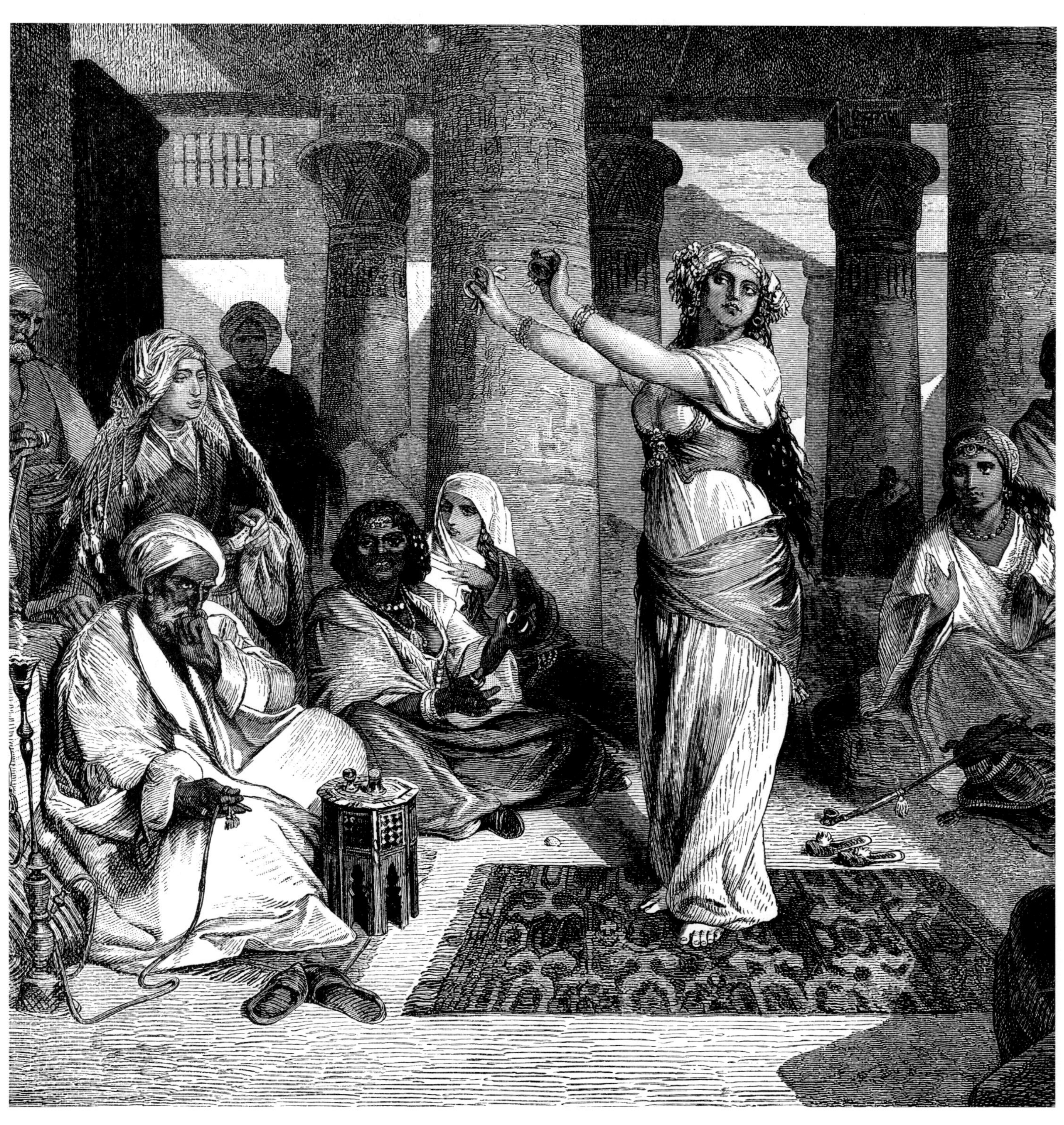

Dance in the ruins of Karnak, 1890

Tanz in den Ruinen von Karnak, 1890

Danza nelle rovine di Karnak, 1890

Danse dans les ruines de Karnak, 1890

Danza en las ruinas de Karnak, 1890

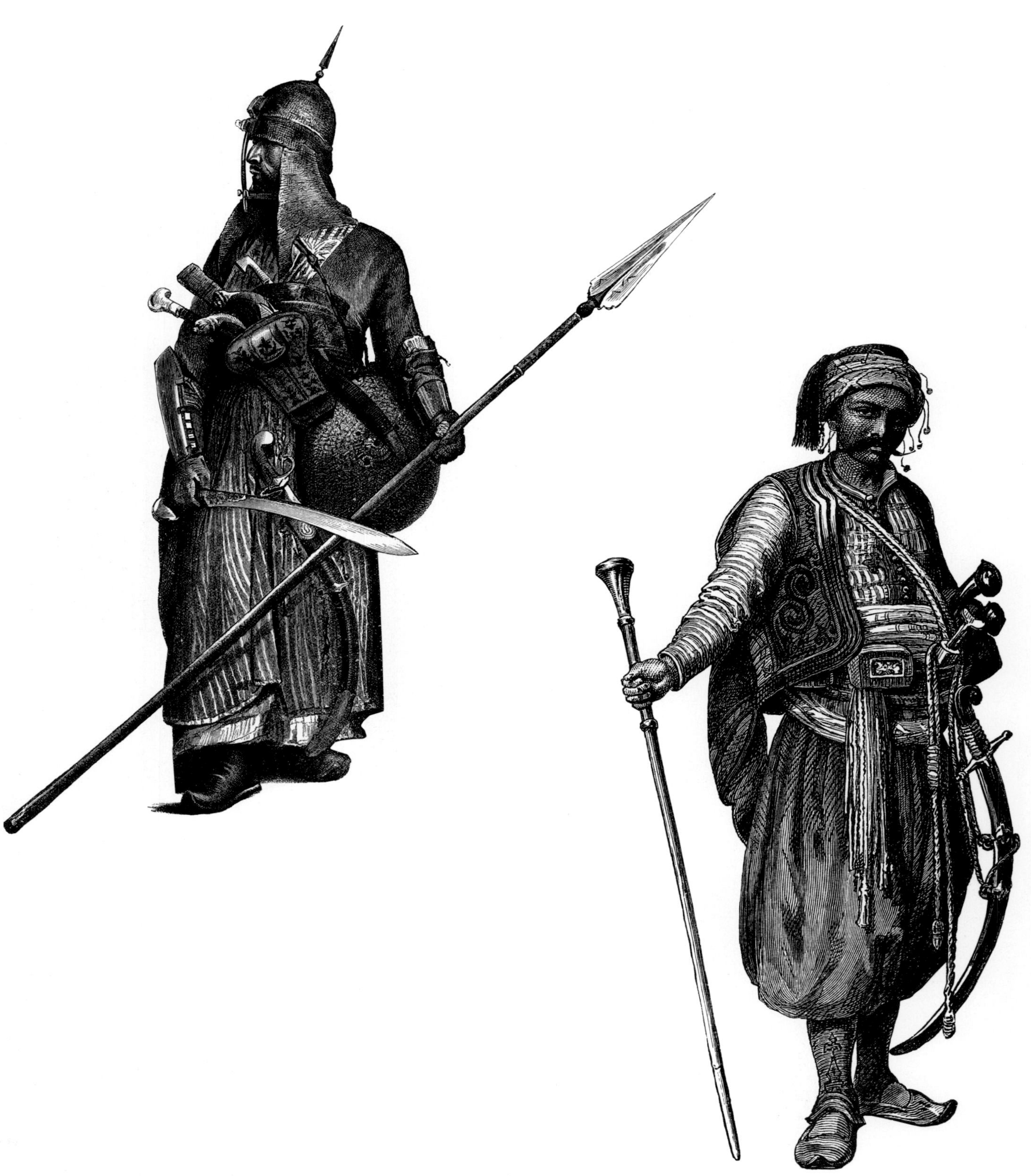

a	Memeluke in full armour, 1890	Mameluke in voller Rüstung, 1890	Mammalucco in armatura completa, 1890	Mamelouk armé de pied en cap, 1890	Mameluco con armadura, 1890
b	Egyptian guardsman, 1890	Ägyptischer Wächter, 1890	Guardie egizie, 1890	Soldat de la garde royale égyptienne, 1890	Guardia egipcio, 1890

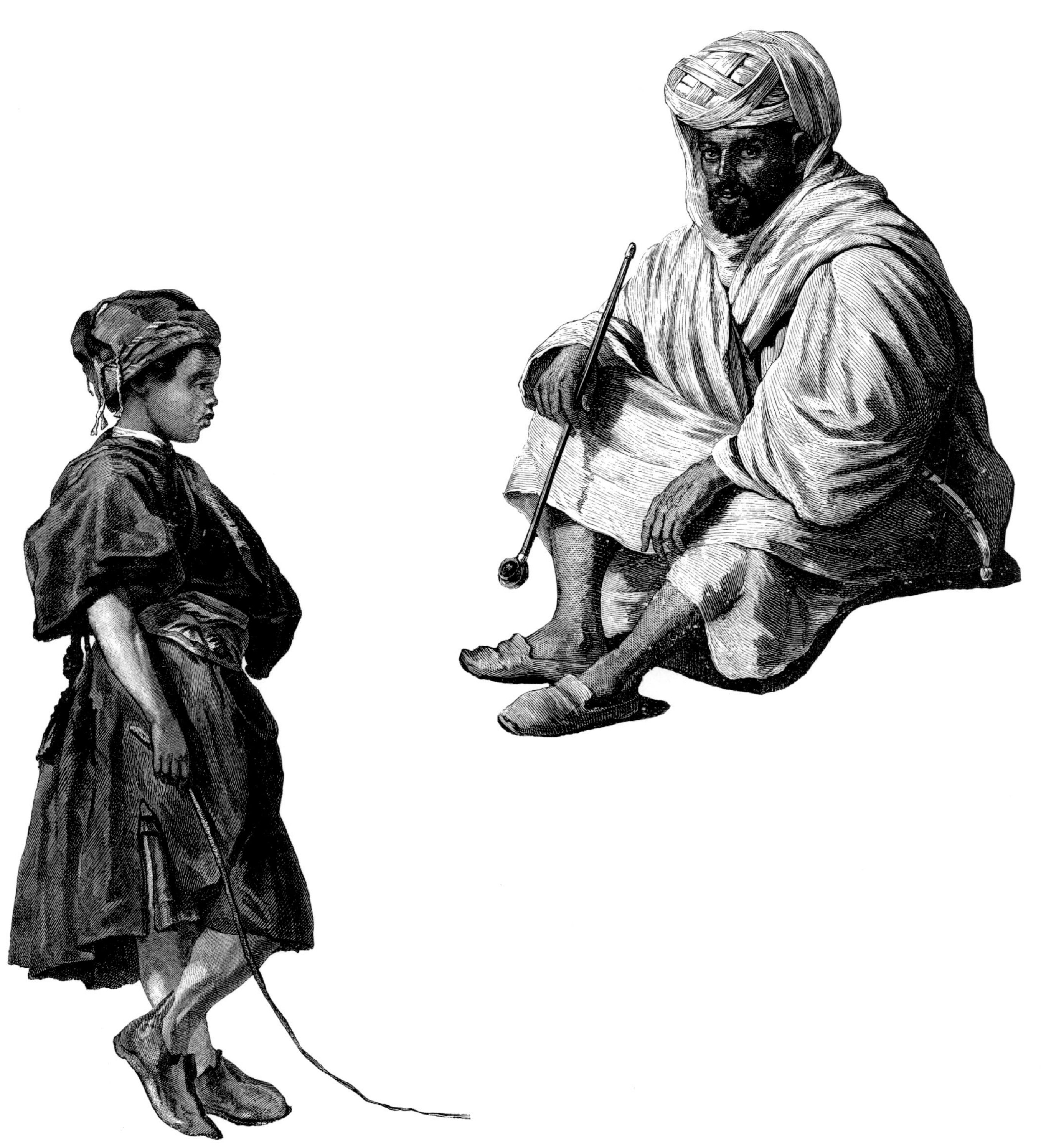

a	Egyptian boy, Cairo, 1890	Ägyptischer Junge, Kairo, 1890	Ragazzo egizio, Il Cairo, 1890	Enfant égyptien, , Le Caire, 1890	Muchacho egipcio, El Cairo, 1890
b	Tunisian pilgrim in Egypt, 1890	Tunesischer Pilger in Ägypten, 1890	Pellegrino tunisino in Egitto, 1890	Pèlerin tunisien en Égypte, 1890	Peregrino tunecino en Egipto, 1890

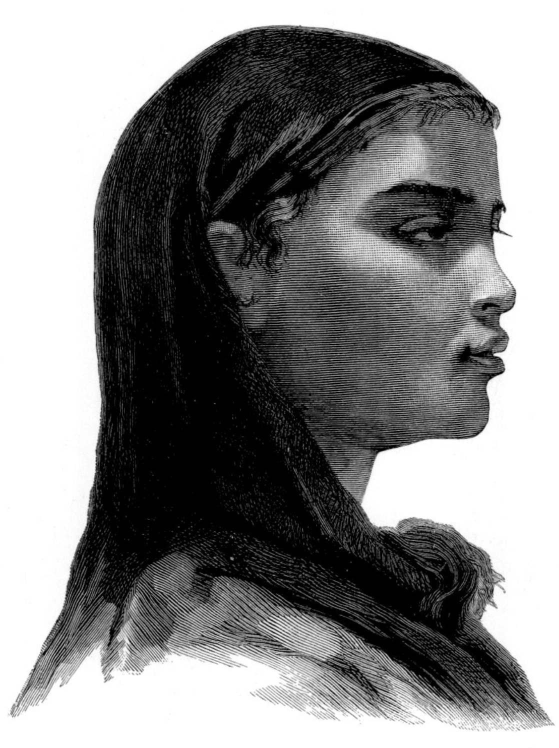

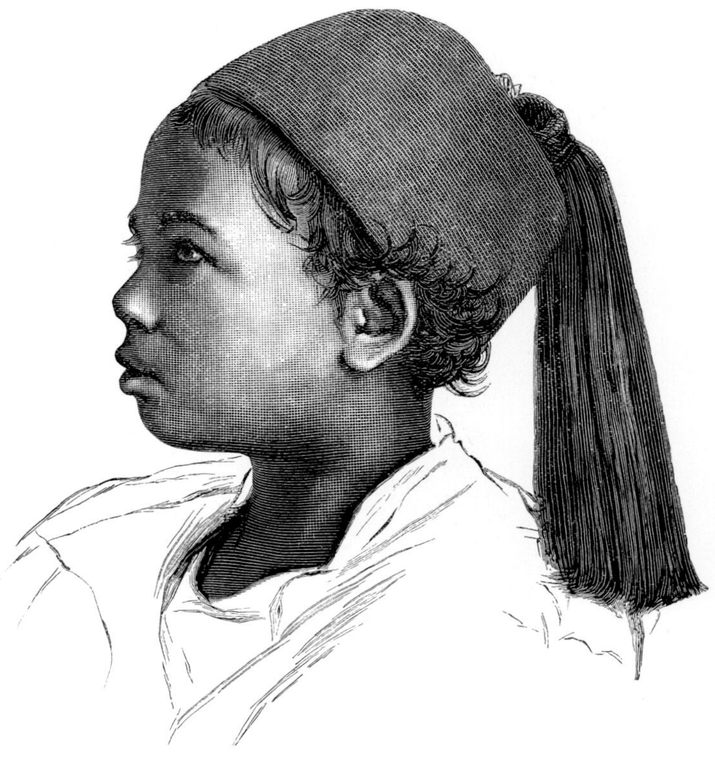

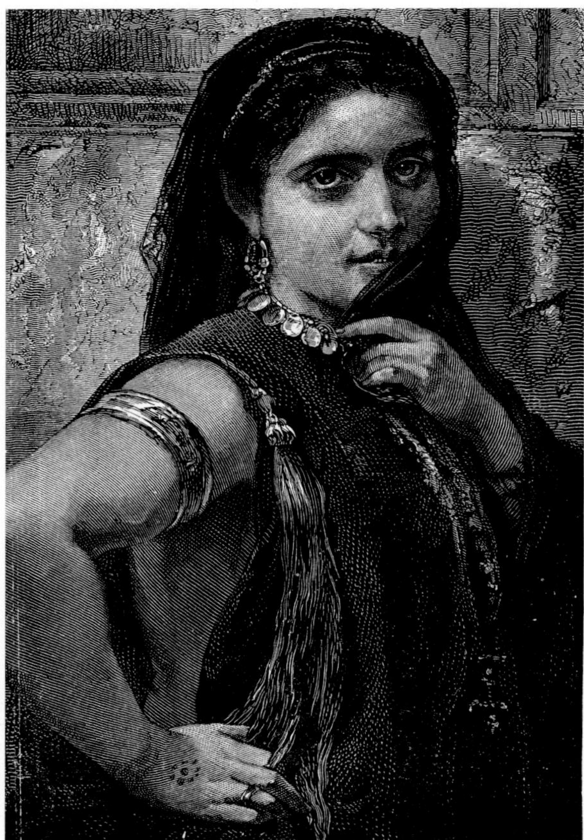

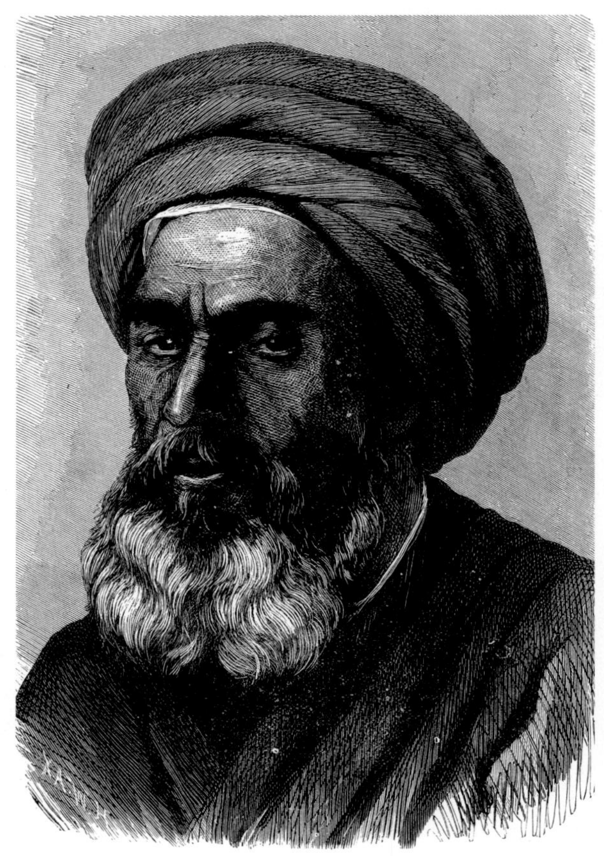

Egyptian women's and men's head-dresses

Ägyptische Haartrachten für Frauen und Männer

Copricapo maschili e femminili egiziani

Coiffures égyptiennes masculines et féminines

Tocados de mujeres y hombres egipcios

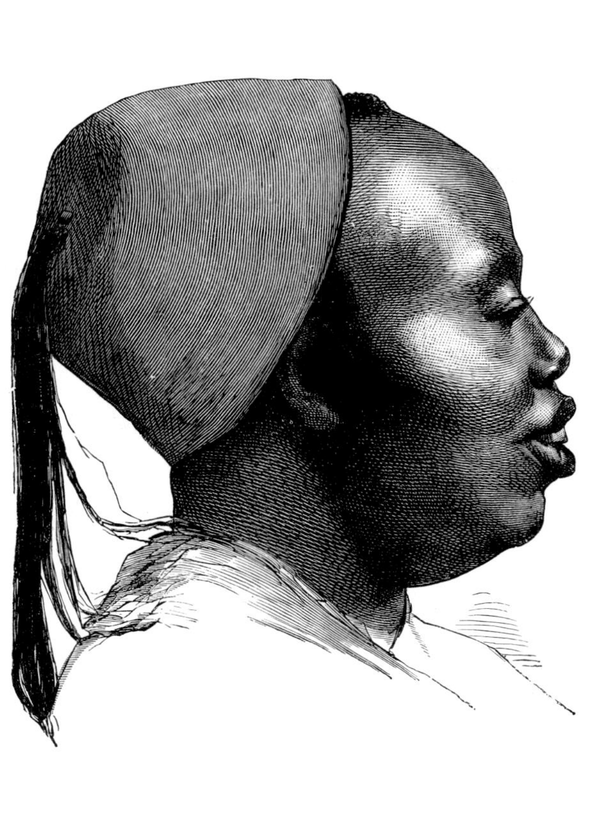

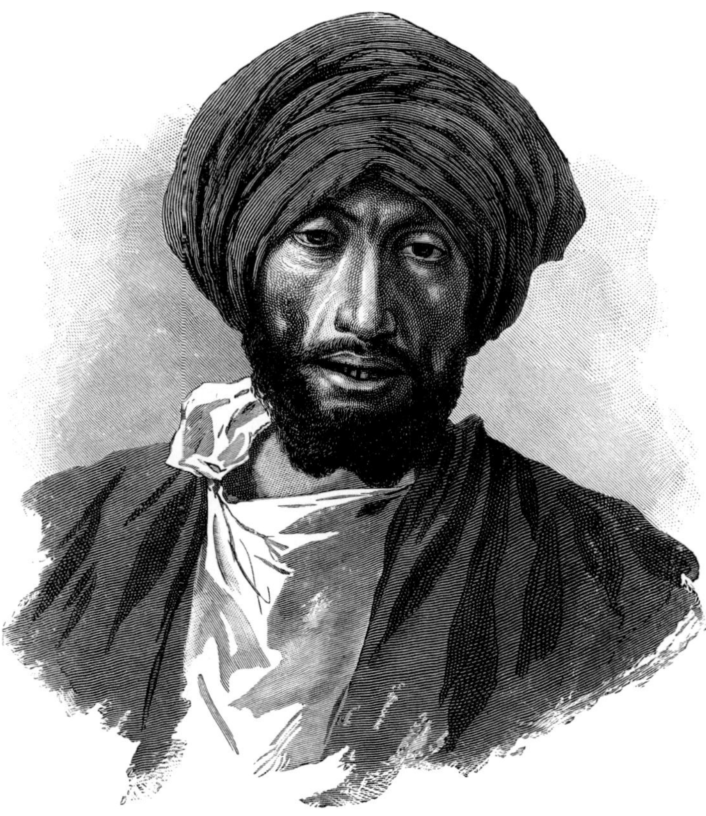

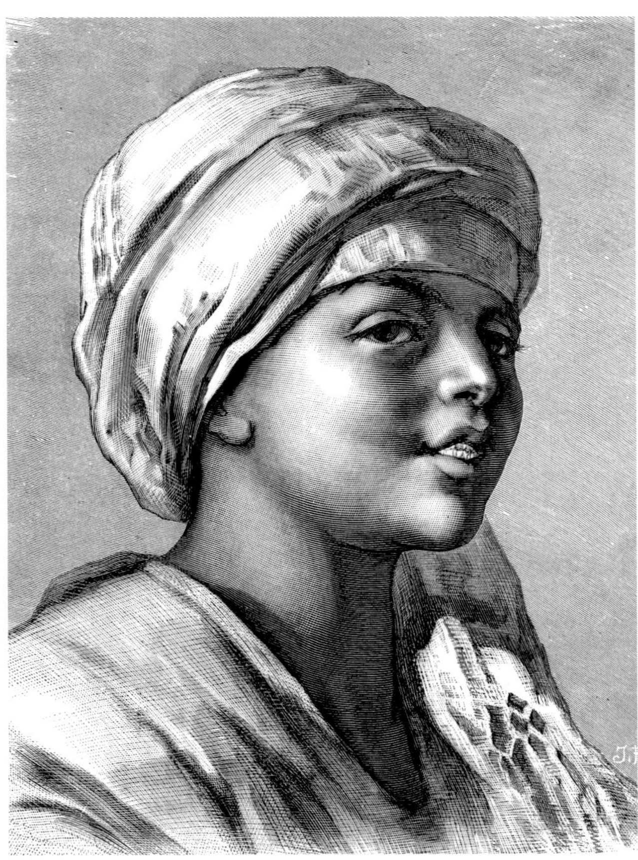

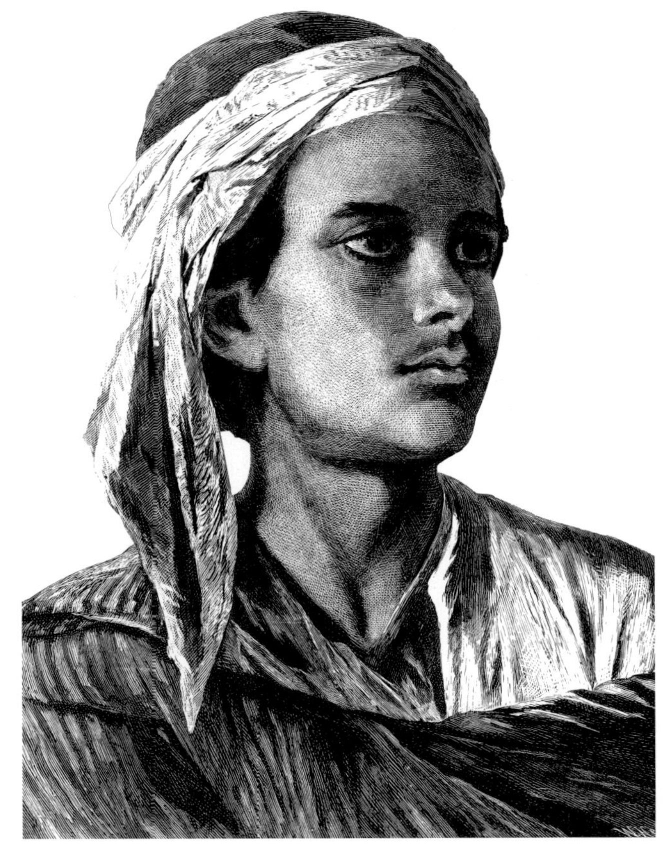

Egyptian men's head-dresses

Ägyptische Haartrachten für Männer

Copricapo maschili egiziani

Coiffures égyptiennes masculines

Tocados de hombres egipcios

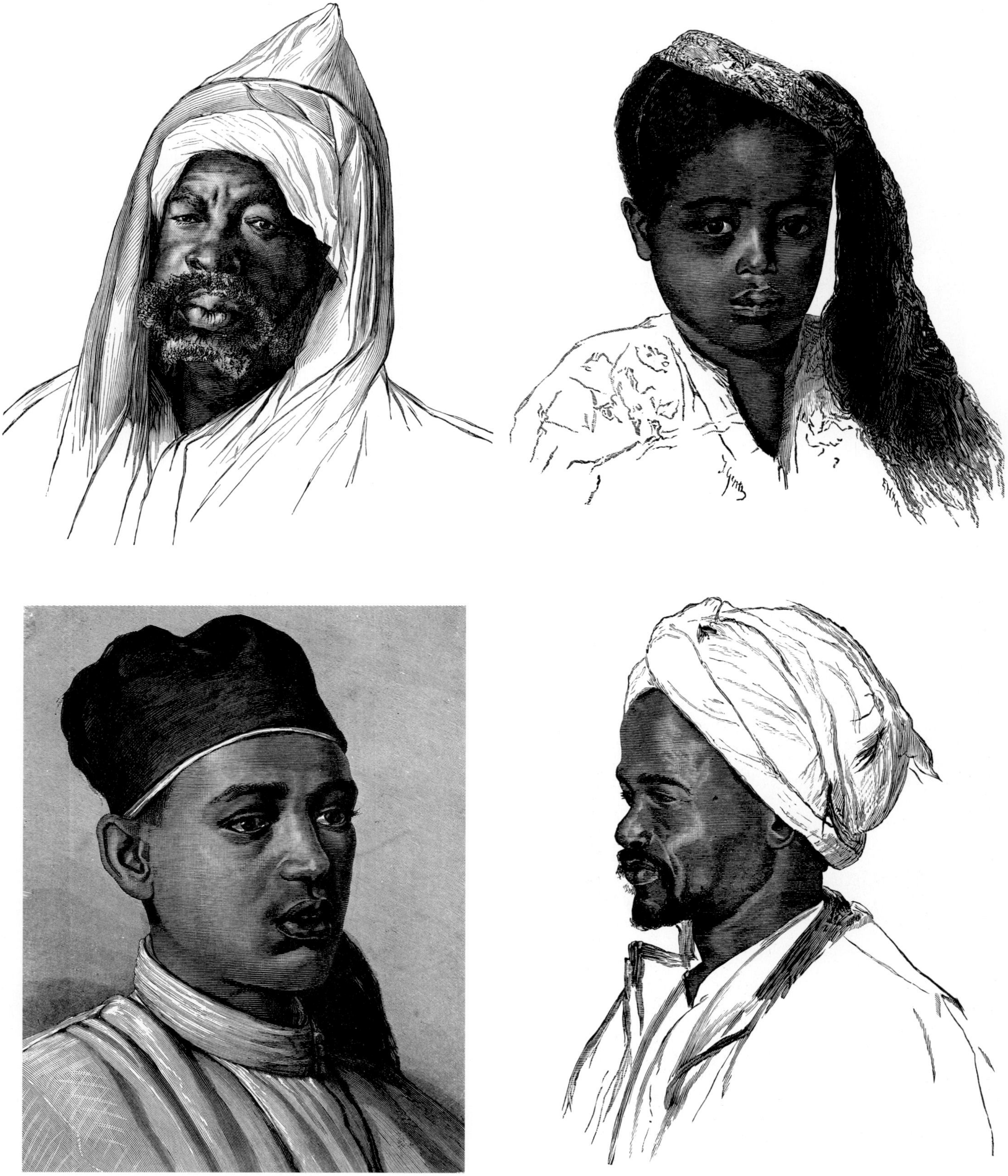

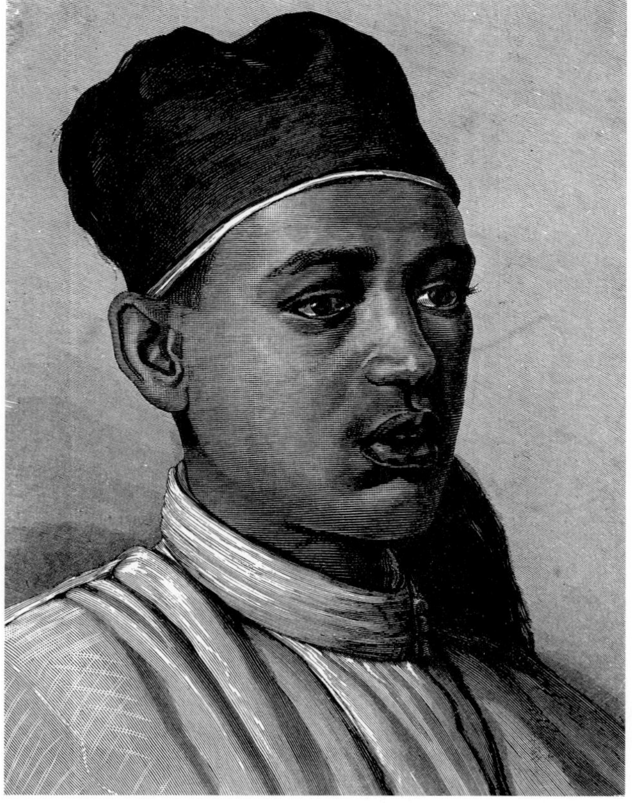

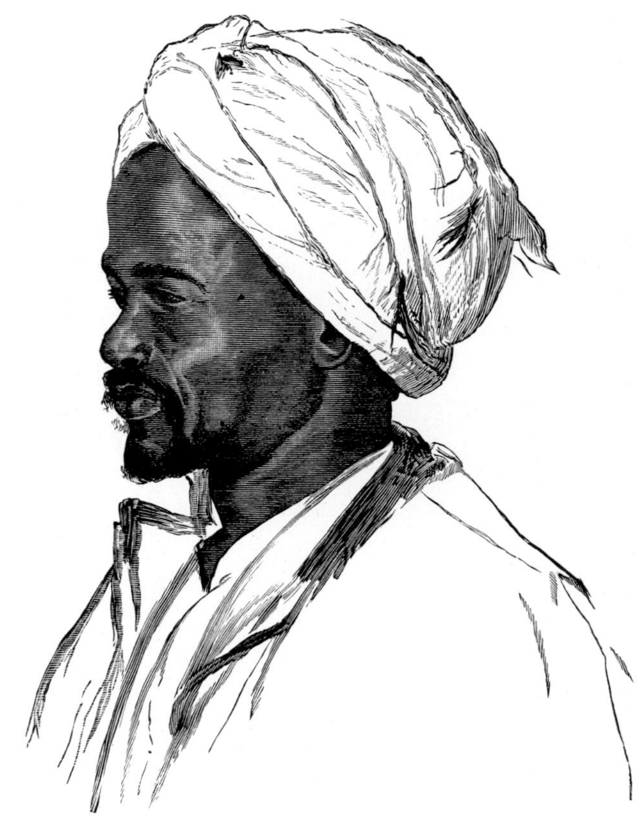

Egyptian men's head-dresses

Ägyptische Haartrachten für Männer

Copricapo maschili egiziani

Coiffures égyptiennes masculines

Tocados de hombres egipcios

Egypt

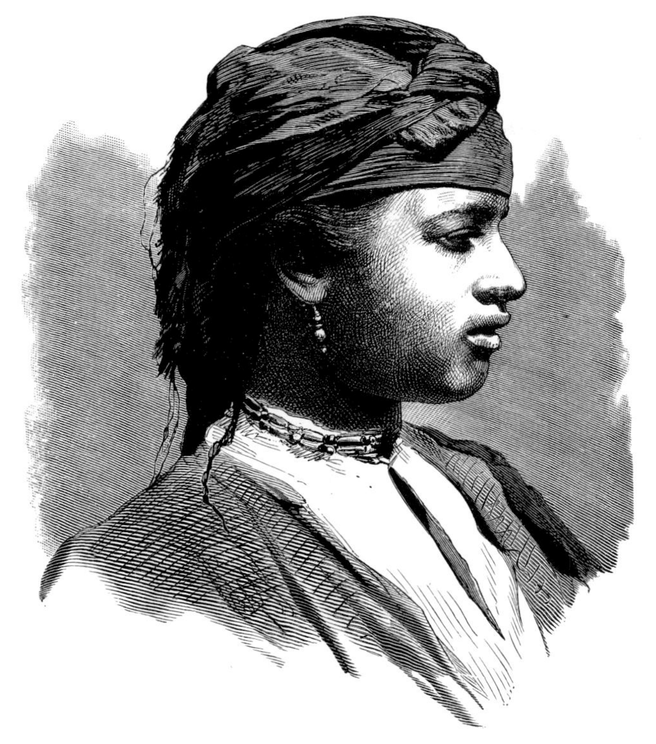

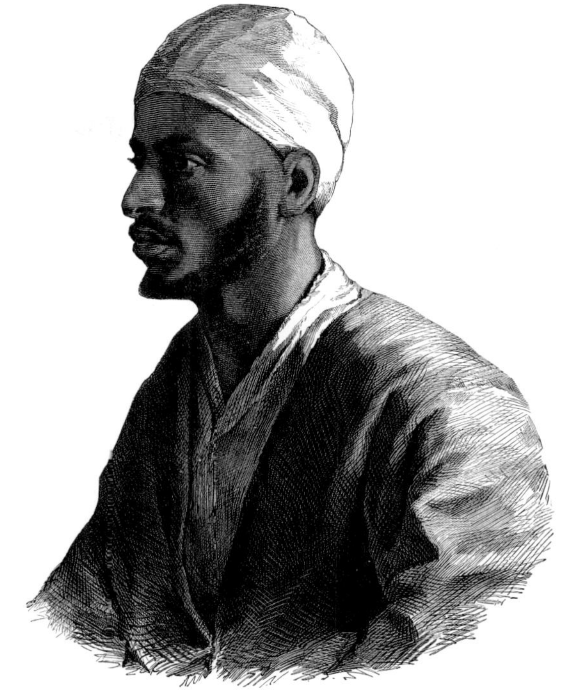

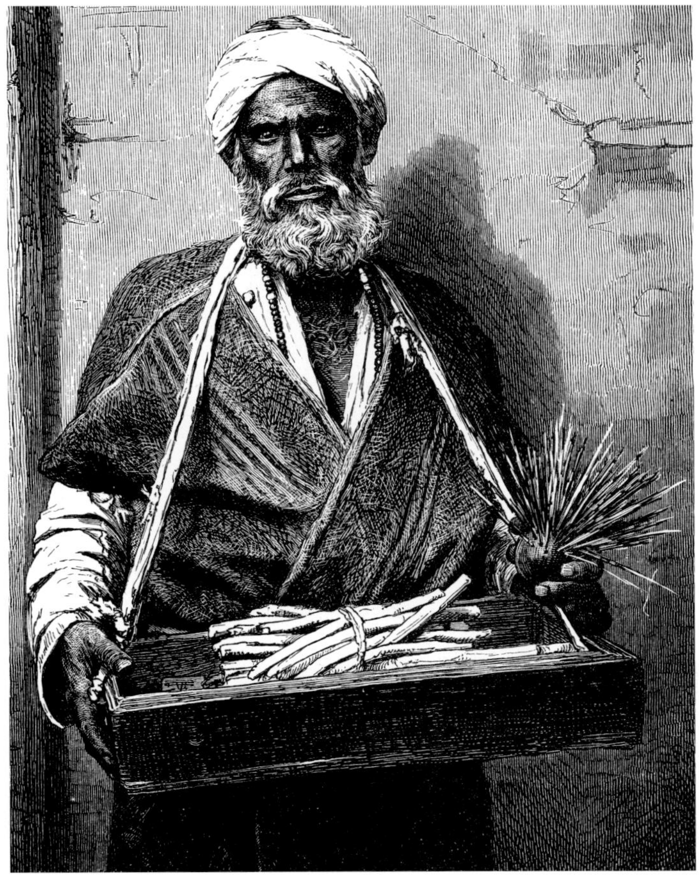

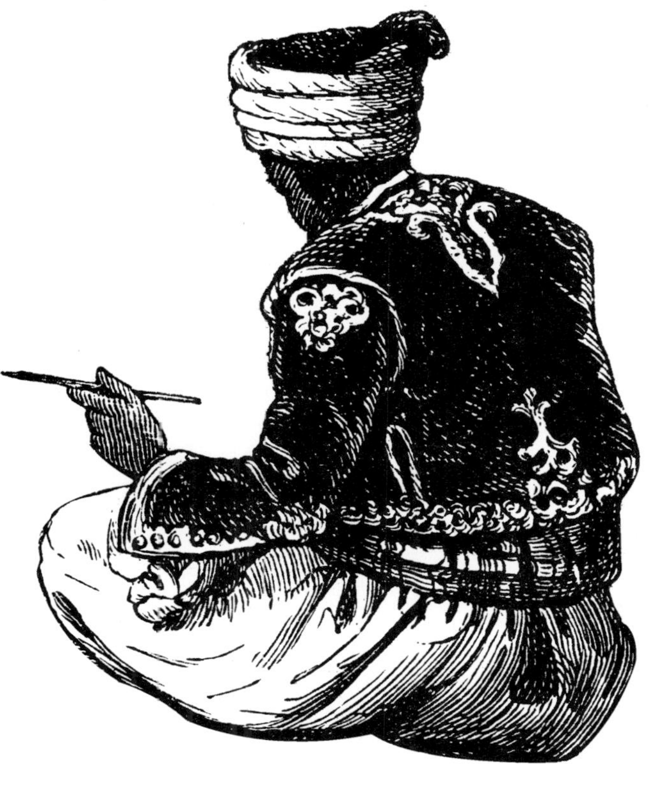

a+b	Head-dresses	Haartrachten	Copricapo	Coiffures	Tocados
c	Street vendor	Straßenverkäufer	Venditore ambulante	Vendeur de rue	Vendedor ambulante
d	Embroidered jacket	Bestickte Jacke	Giacca ricamata	Veste brodée	Chaqueta bordada

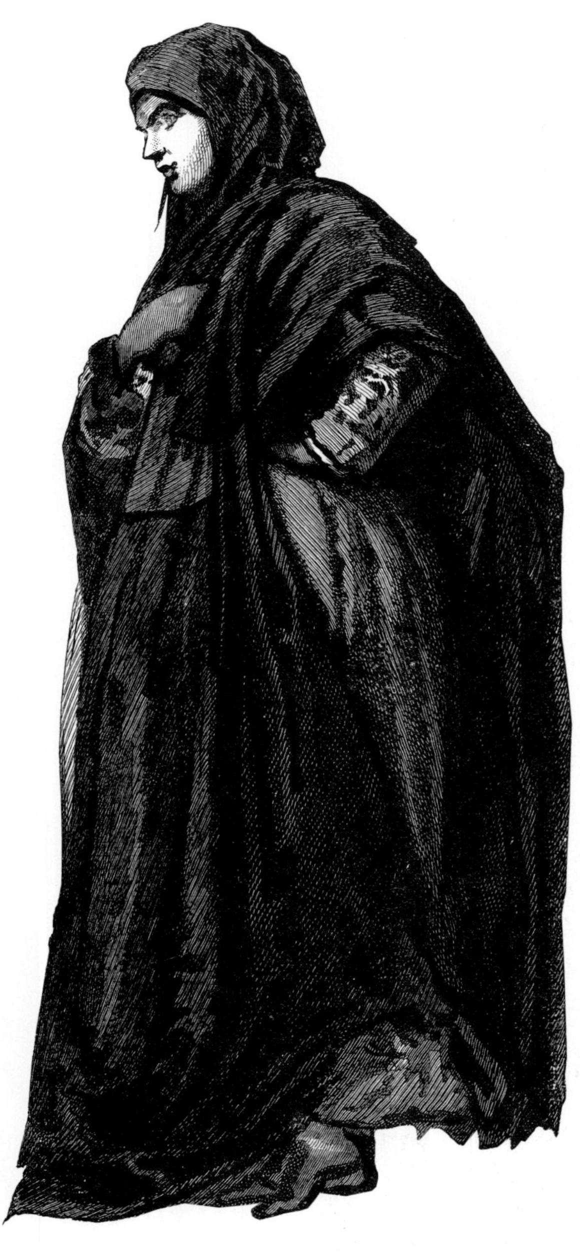

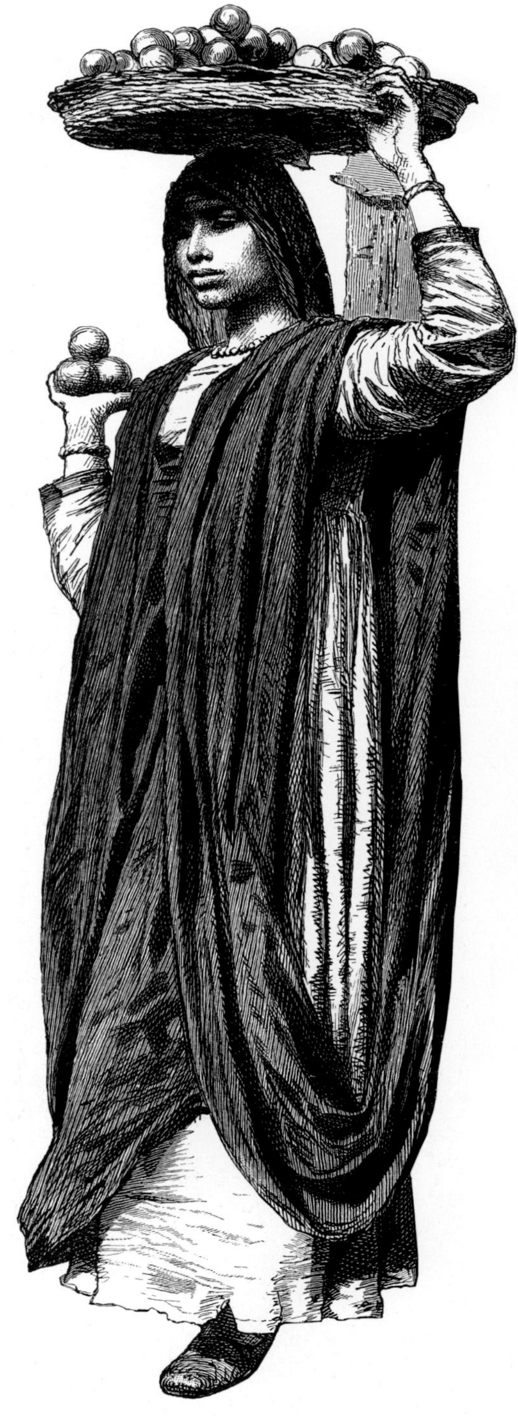

a	Coptic lady dressed to go to church, 1890	Koptische Frau, für den Kirchgang gekleidet, 1890	Donna copta vestita per andare in chiesa, 1890	Femme copte habillée pour se rendre à l'église, 1890	Dama copta vestida para acudir a la iglesia, 1890
b	Orange seller, Cairo, 1890	Orangenverkäufer, Kairo, 1890	Venditore di arance, Il Cairo, 1890	Vendeur d'oranges, Le Caire, 1890	Vendedor de naranjas, El Cairo, 1890

Egypt

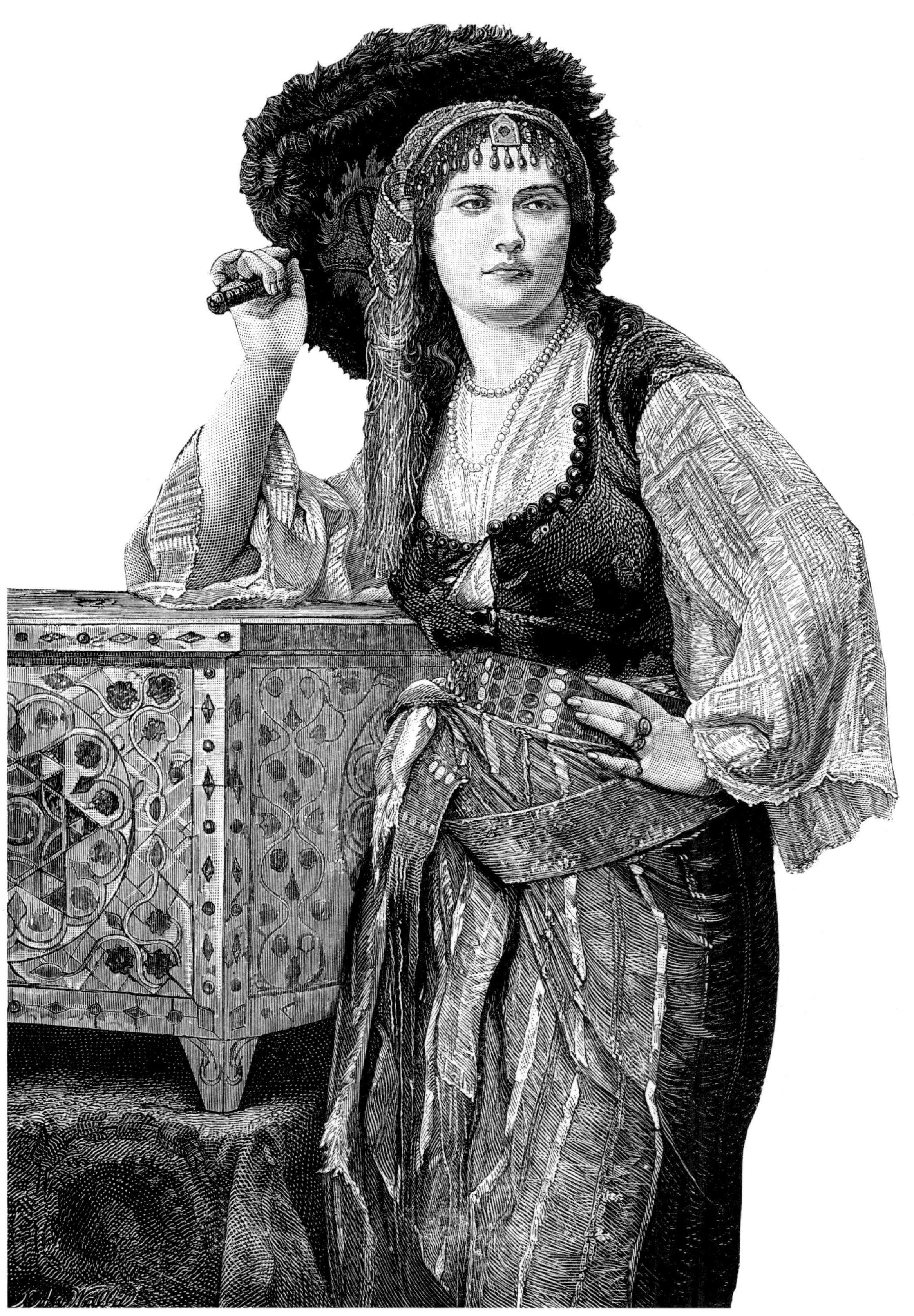

Egyptian lady in harem dress, Cairo, 1890

Ägyptische Frau in Haremskleidung, Kairo, 1890

Donna egiziana in abito da harem, Il Cairo, 1890

Femme égyptienne en robe de harem, Le Caire, 1890

Joven egipcia del harén, El Cairo, 1890

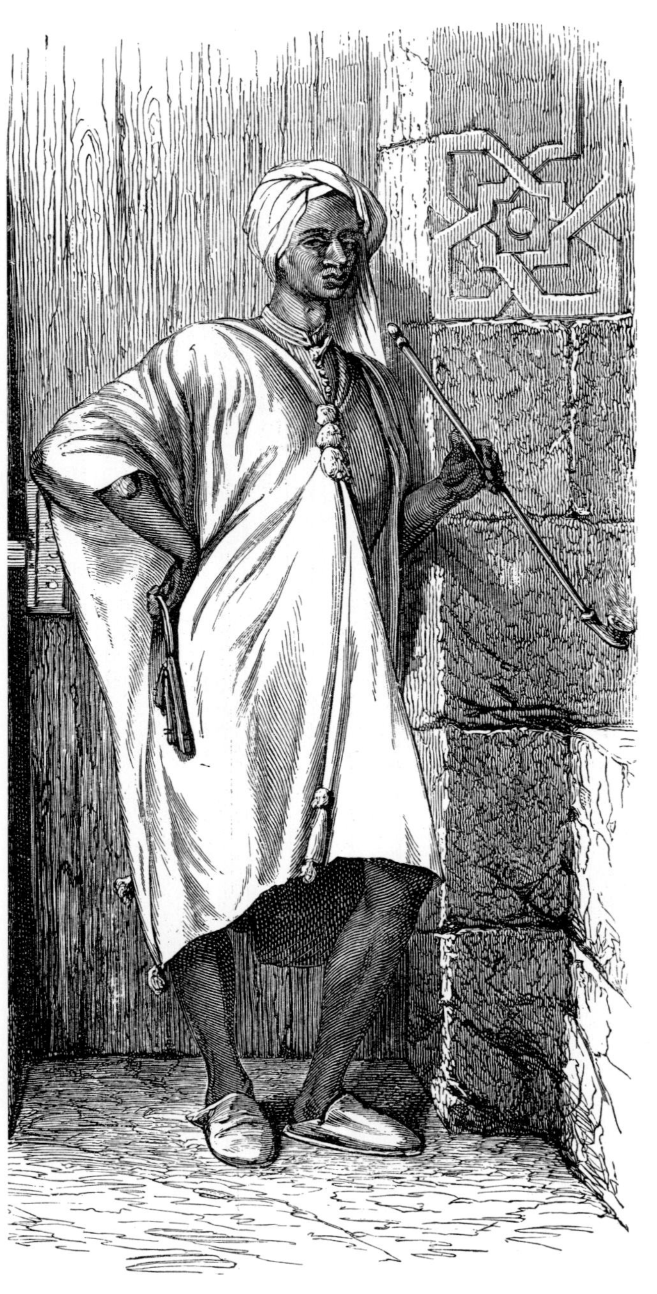

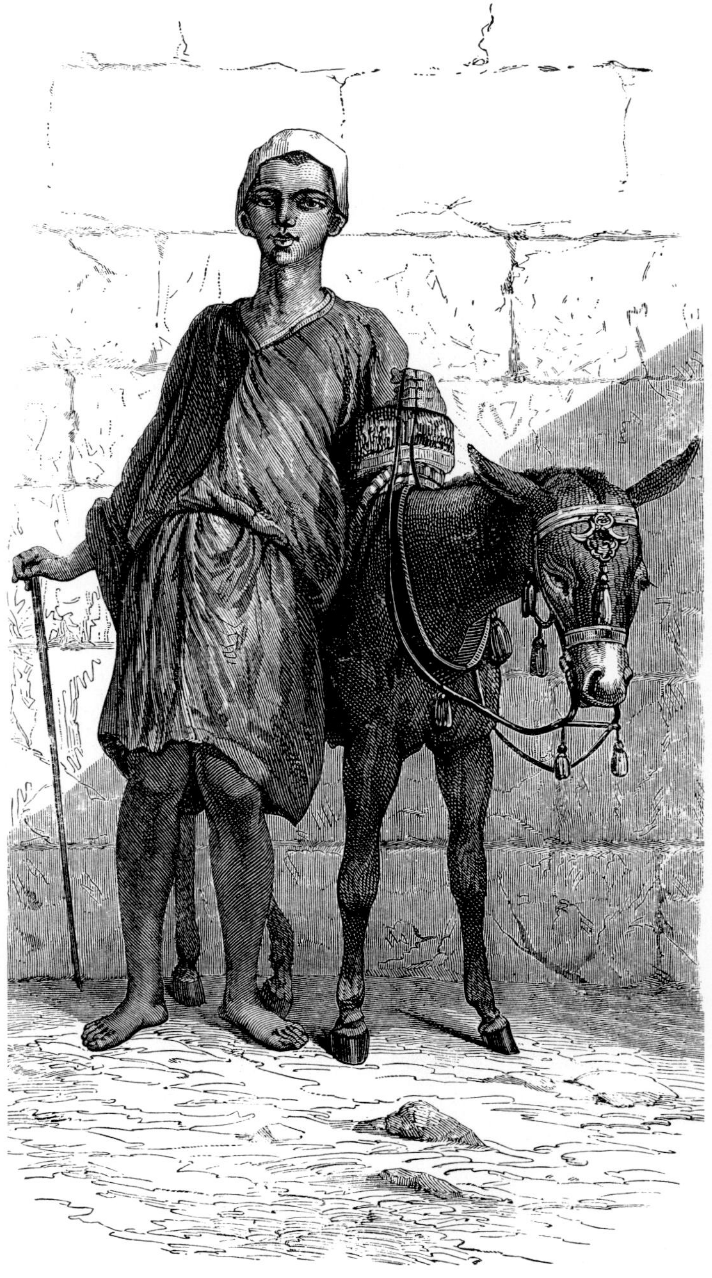

a	Nubian man from Cairo, c. 1890	Nubischer Mann aus Kairo, um 1890	Nubiano di Il Cairo, ca. 1890	Nubien du Caire, vers 1890	Hombre nubio de El Cairo, alrededor de 1890
b	Donkey driver, Cairo, c. 1900	Eselstreiber, Kairo, um 1900	Ragazzo con asino, Il Cairo, ca. 1900	Meneur d'âne, Le Caire, vers 1900	Trajinante con su burro, El Cairo, hacia 1900

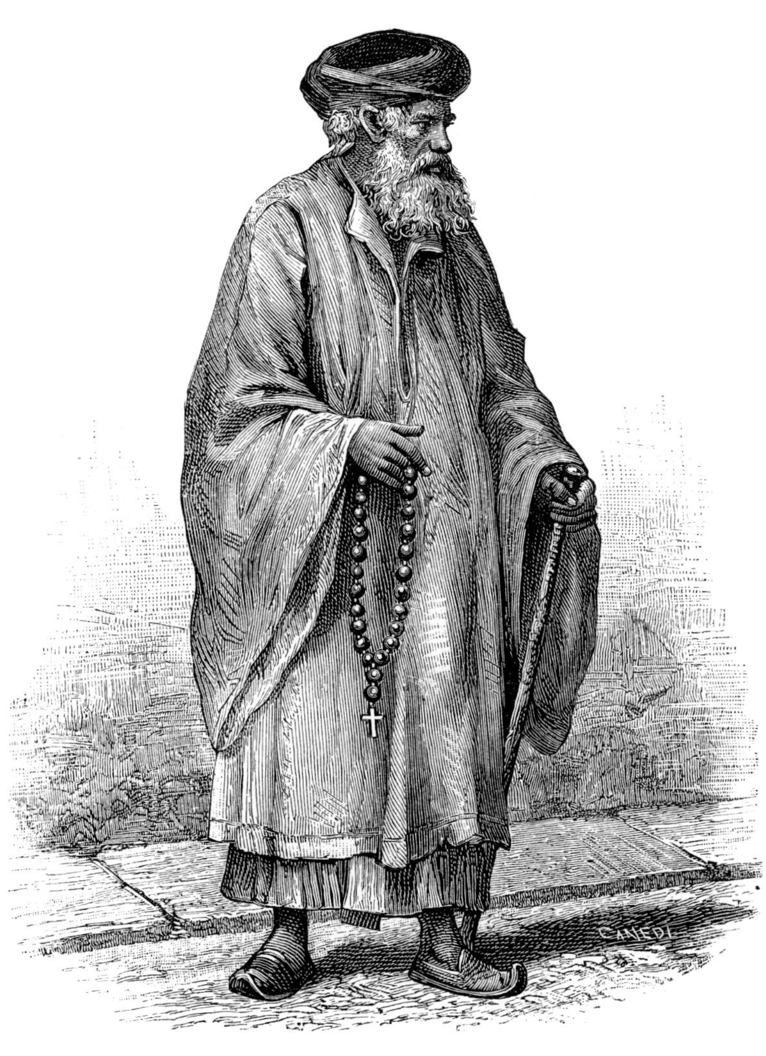

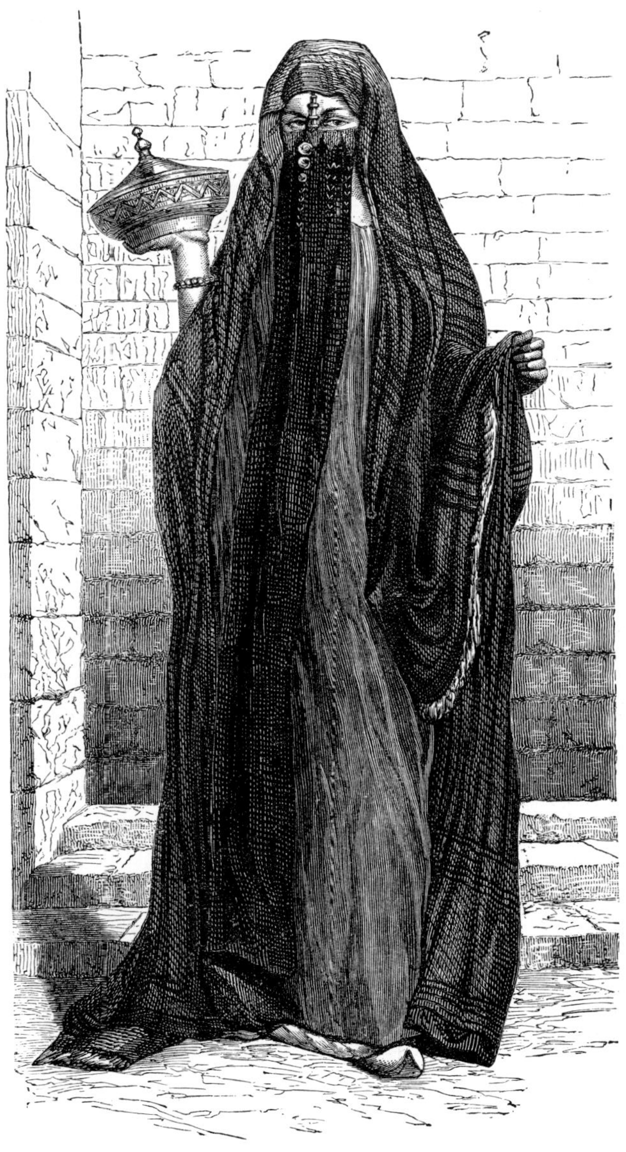

a	North Egyptian Copt, c. 1900	Koptischer Mann aus Nordägypten, um 1900	Copto dell'Egitto settentrionale, ca. 1900	Copte du Nord de l'Égypte, vers 1900	Copto del norte de Egipto, hacia 1900
b	Veiled Muslim lady, Cairo, c. 1890	Verschleierte Moslemfrau, Kairo, um 1890	Donna musulmana con velo, Il Cairo, ca. 1890	Femme musulmane voilée, Le Caire, vers 1890	Mujer musulmana con velo, El Cairo, hacia 1890

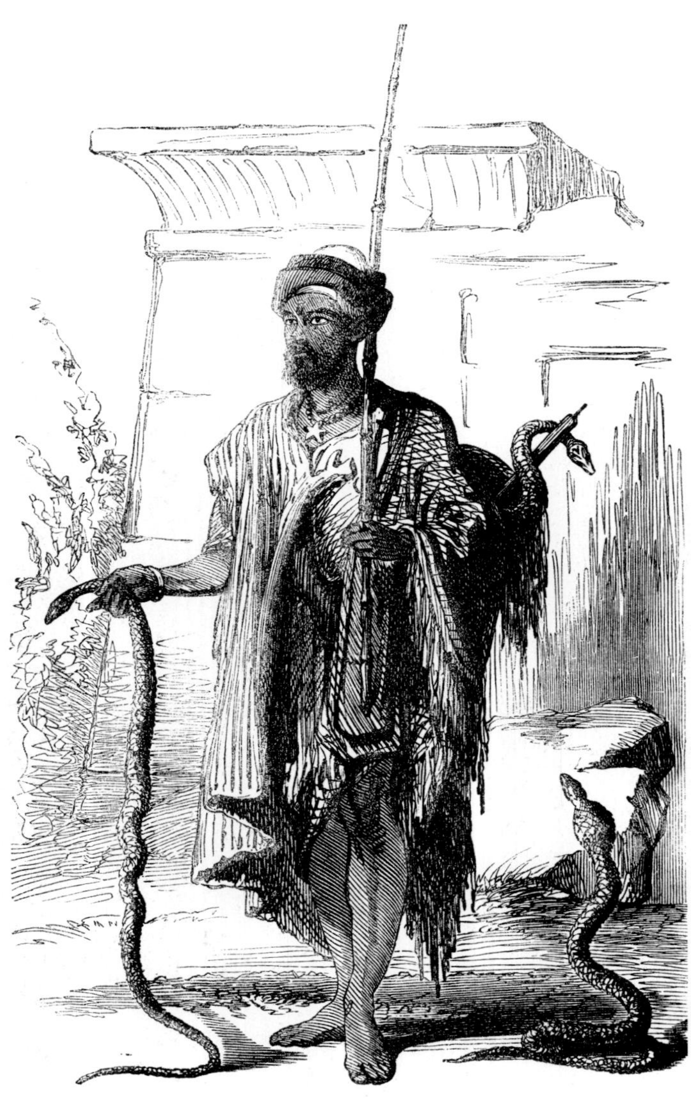

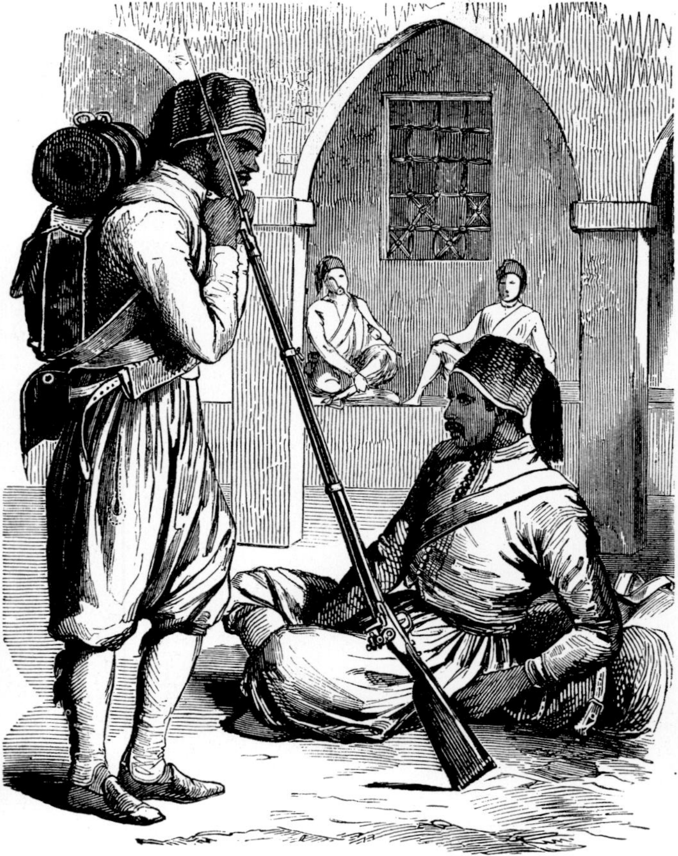

a	Snake charmer, Cairo, 1845	Schlangenbeschwörer, Kairo, 1845	Incantatore di serpenti, Il Cairo, 1845	Charmeur de serpents, Le Caire, 1845	Encantador de serpientes, El Cairo, 1845
b	Egyptian infantrymen, 1845	Ägyptische Infanteristen, 1845	Esponente di fanteria egiziana, 1845	Fantassins égyptiens, 1845	Soldados de infantería egipcios, 1845

Egypt

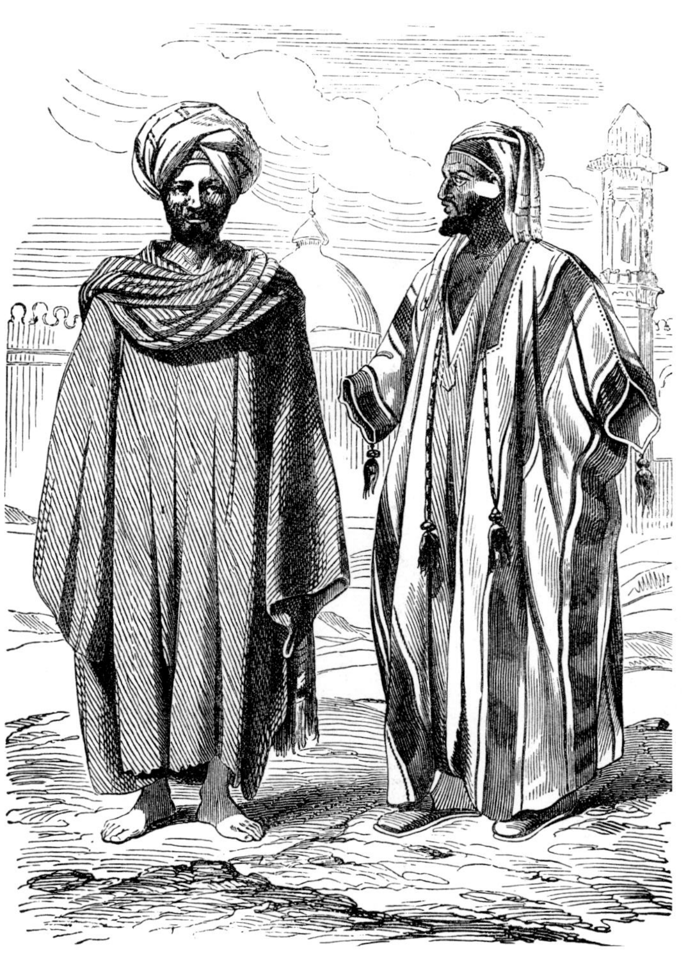

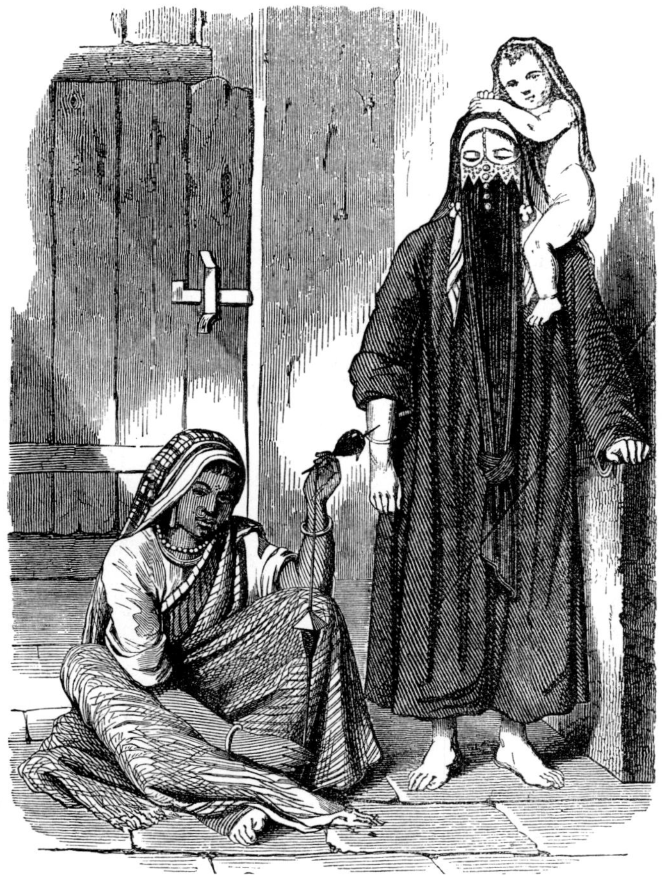

a	Fellah men, Cairo, c. 1845	Fellachen, Kairo, um 1845	Uomini fellah, Il Cairo, ca. 1845	Hommes Fellah, Le Caire, vers 1845	Hombres fellah, El Cairo, hacia el año 1845
b	Fellah ladies, Cairo, c. 1845	Fellachenfrauen, Kairo, um 1845	Donne fellah, Il Cairo, ca. 1845	Femmes Fellah, Le Caire, vers 1845	Mujeres fellah, El Cairo, hacia el año 1845

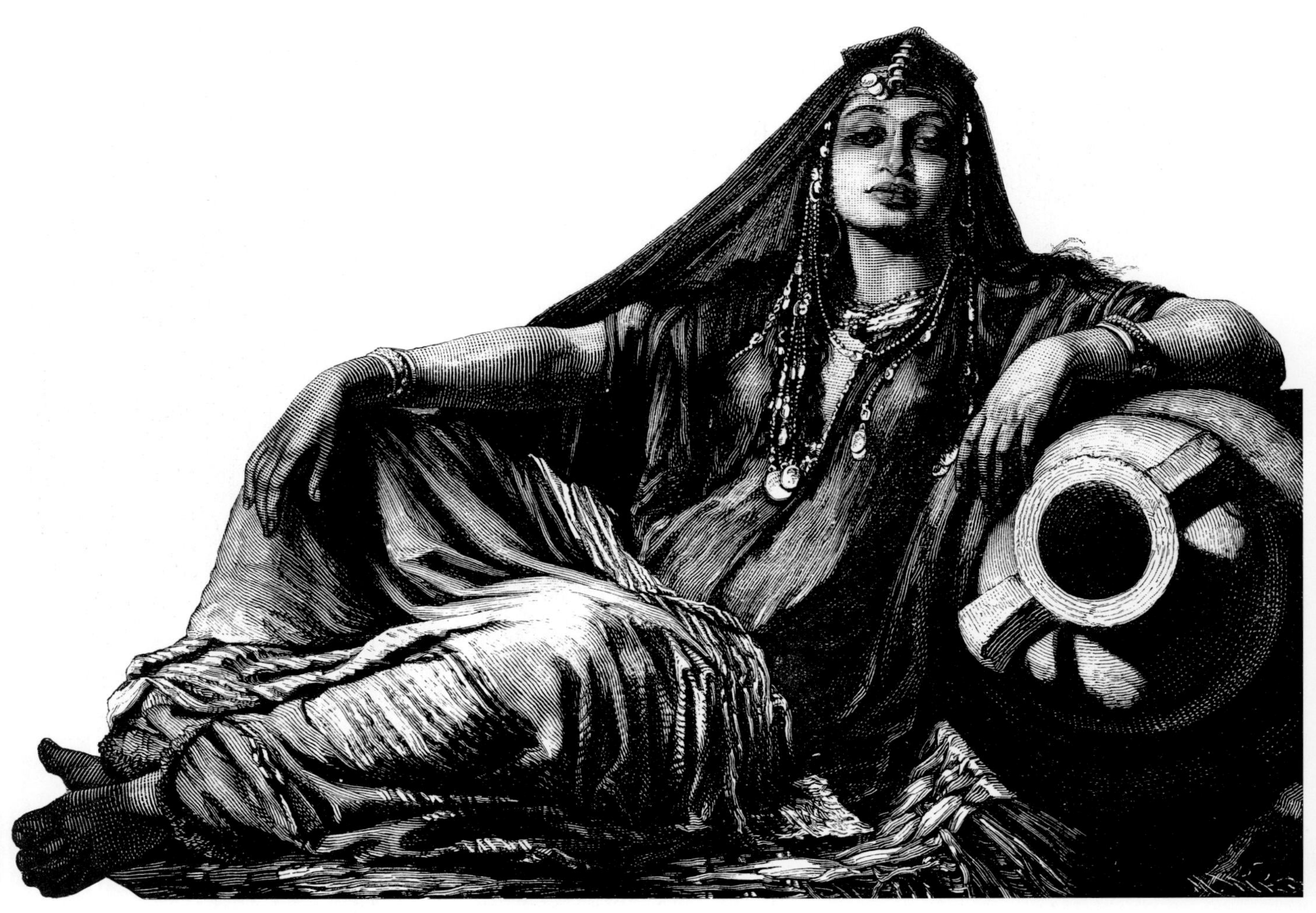

Egyptian lady, c. 1880

Ägyptische Dame, um 1880

Donna egiziana, ca. 1880

Femme égyptienne, vers 1880

Dama egipcia, hacia 1880

Egypt

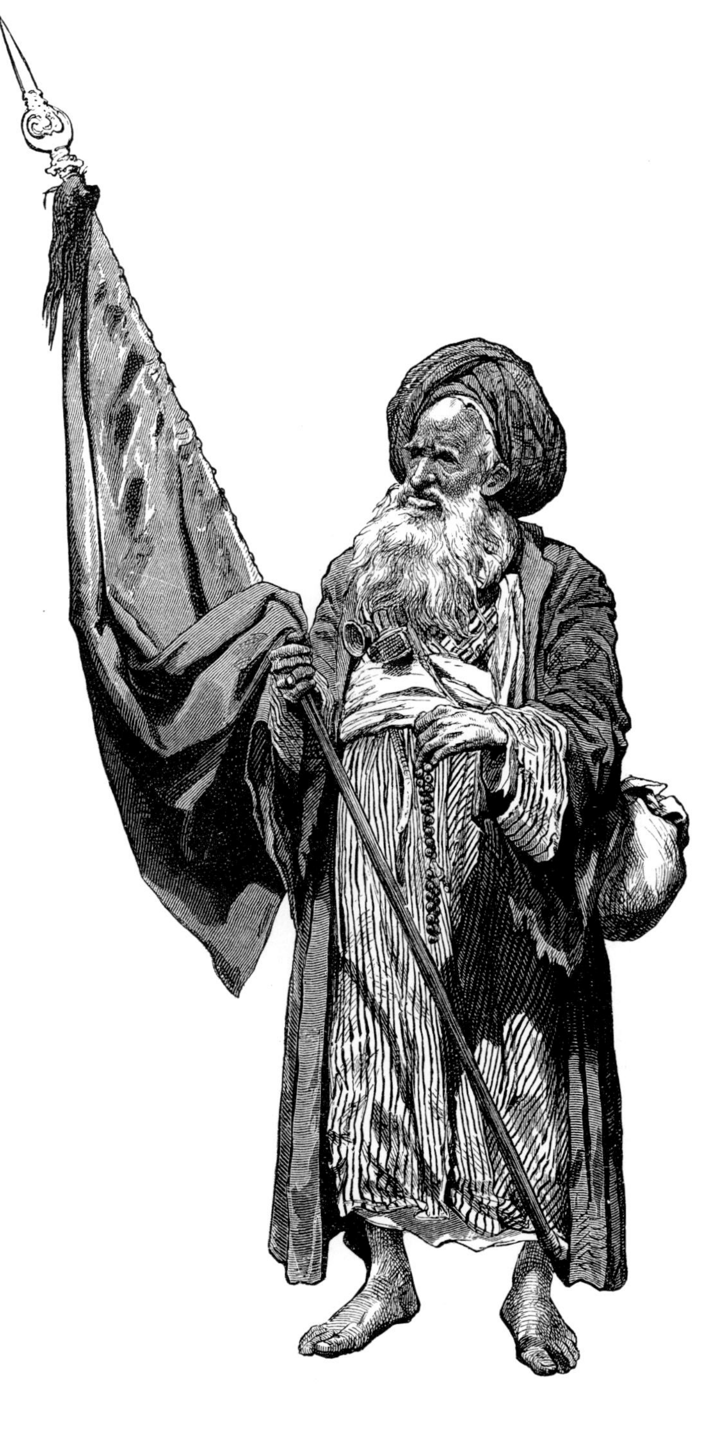

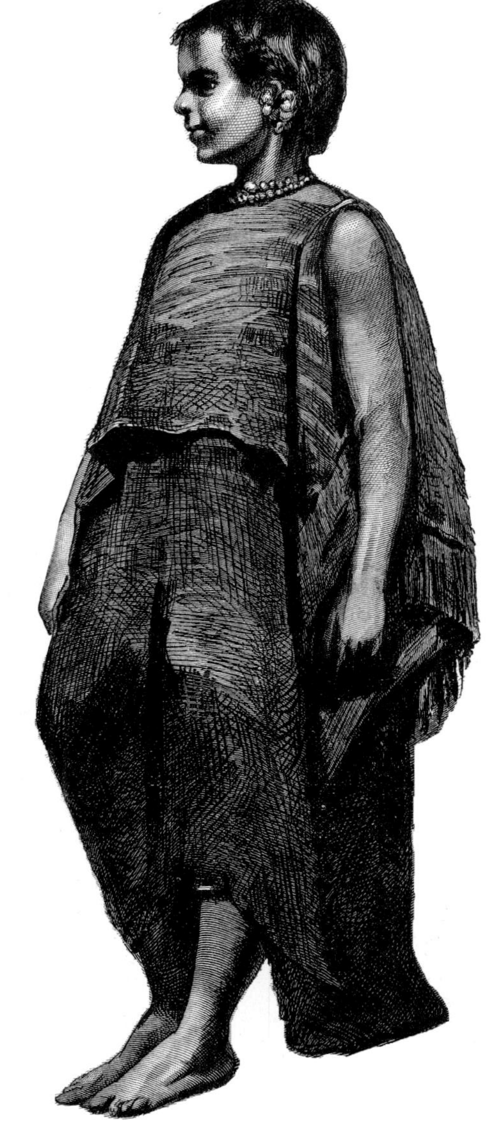

a	Egyptian dervish	Ägyptischer Derwisch	Dervis egiziano	Derviche égyptien	Derviche egipcio
b	Water carrier, c. 1880	Wasserträger, um 1880	Portatore di acqua, ca. 1880	Porteur d'eau, vers 1880	Aguador, hacia 1880

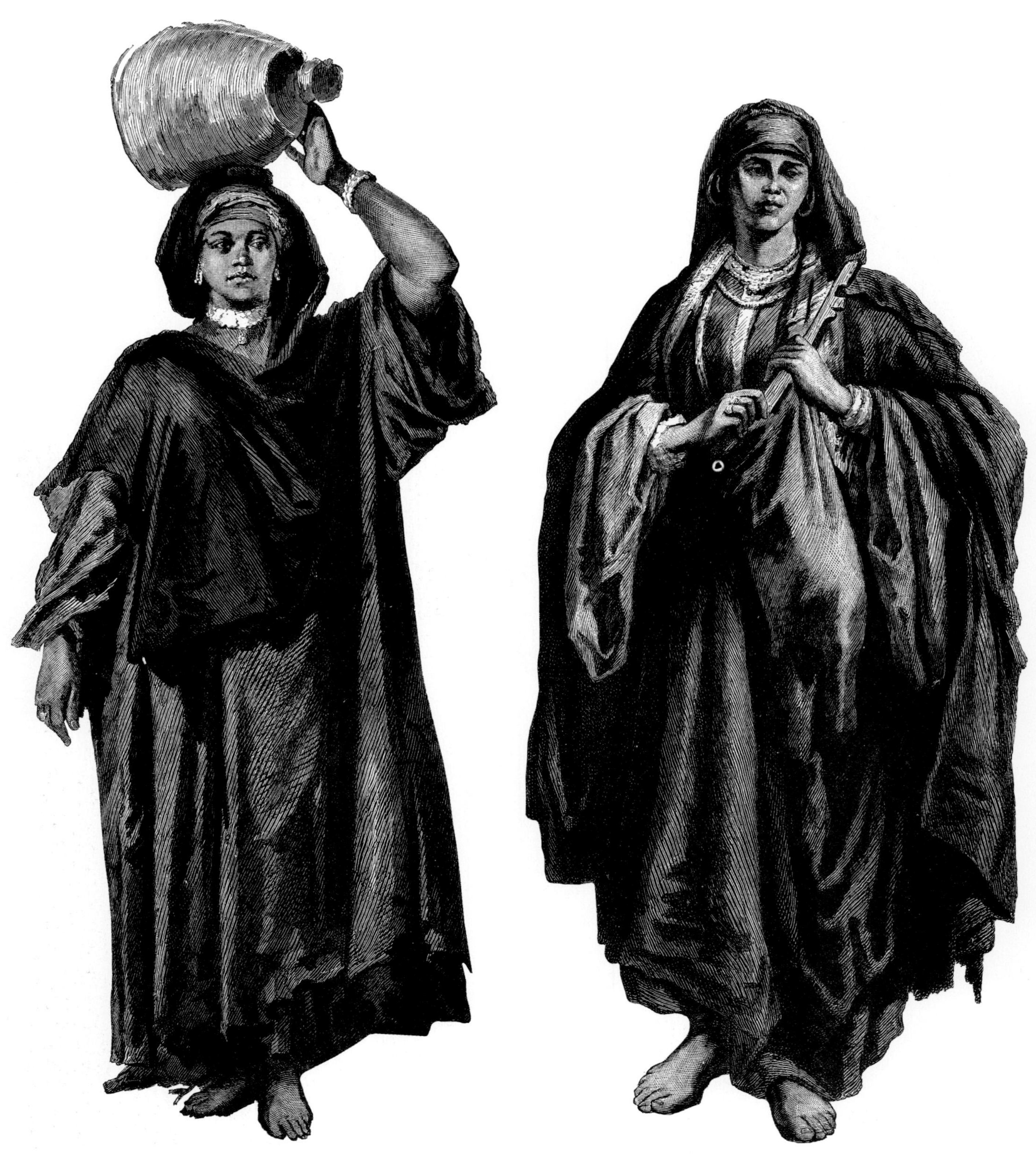

a	Fellah lady	Fellachendame	Donna fellah	Femme Fellah	Mujer fellah
b	Egyptian gypsy, c. 1890	Ägyptische Zigeunerin, um 1890	Zingara egiziana, ca. 1890	Tzigane égyptienne, vers 1890	Gitana egipcia, alrededor del año 1890

Egypt

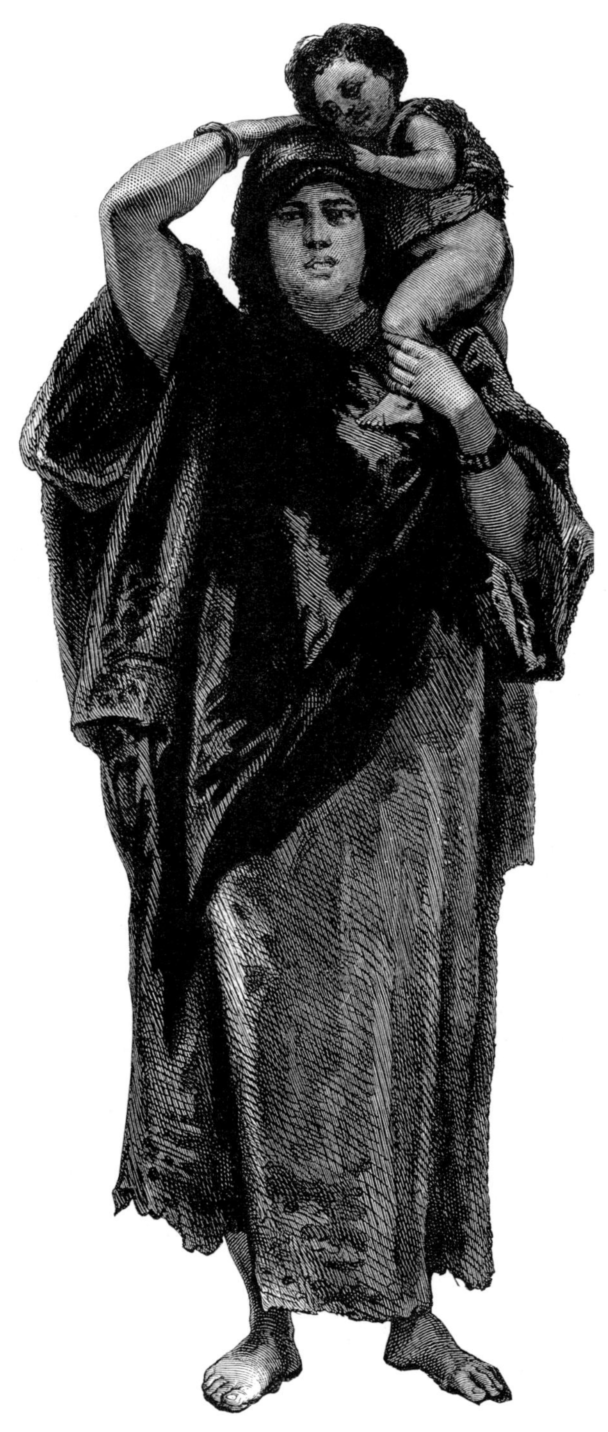

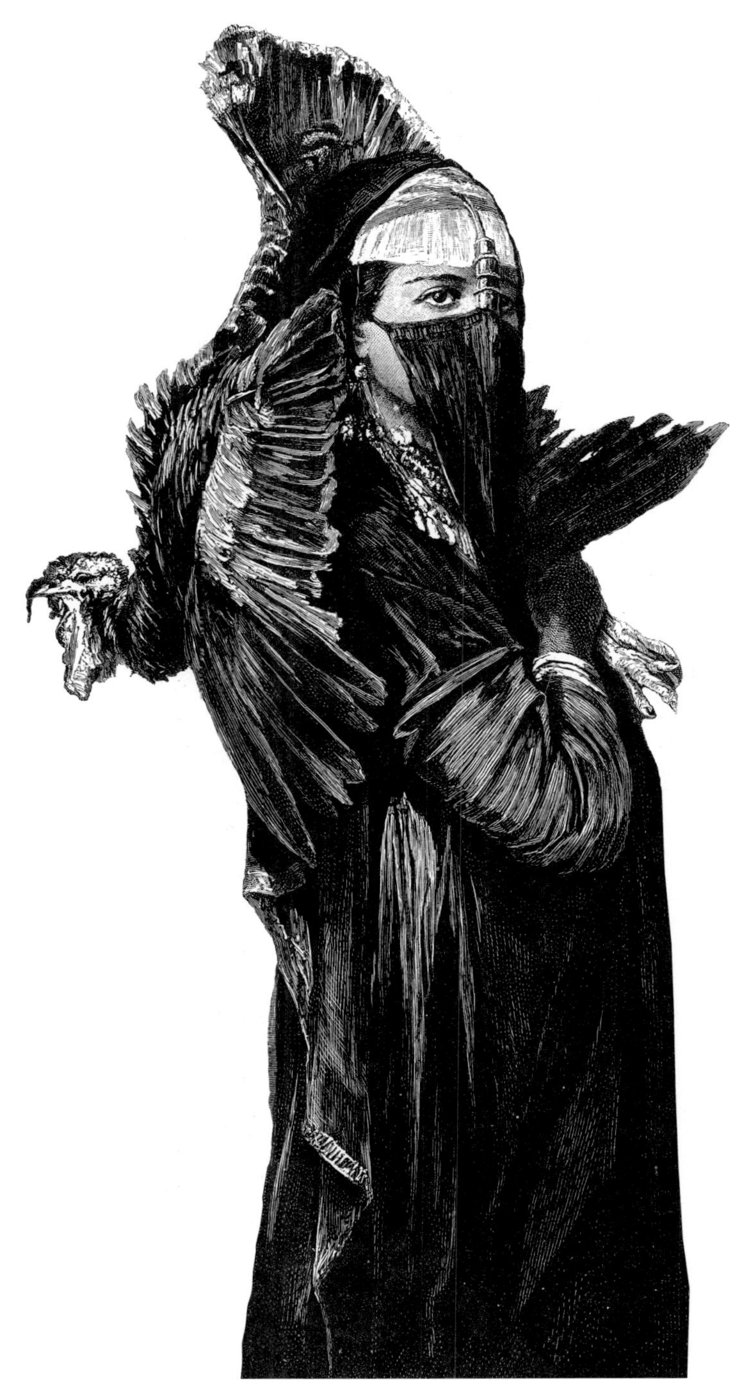

a	Fellah lady of Karnak, 1890	Fellachendame aus Karnak, 1890	Donna fellah di Karnak, 1890	Femme Fellah de Karnak, 1890	Mujer fellah de Karnak, 1890
b	Turkey seller, 1890	Truthahnverkäufer, 1890	Venditore de tacchini, 1890	Vendeur de dindes, 1890	Vendedor de pavos, 1890

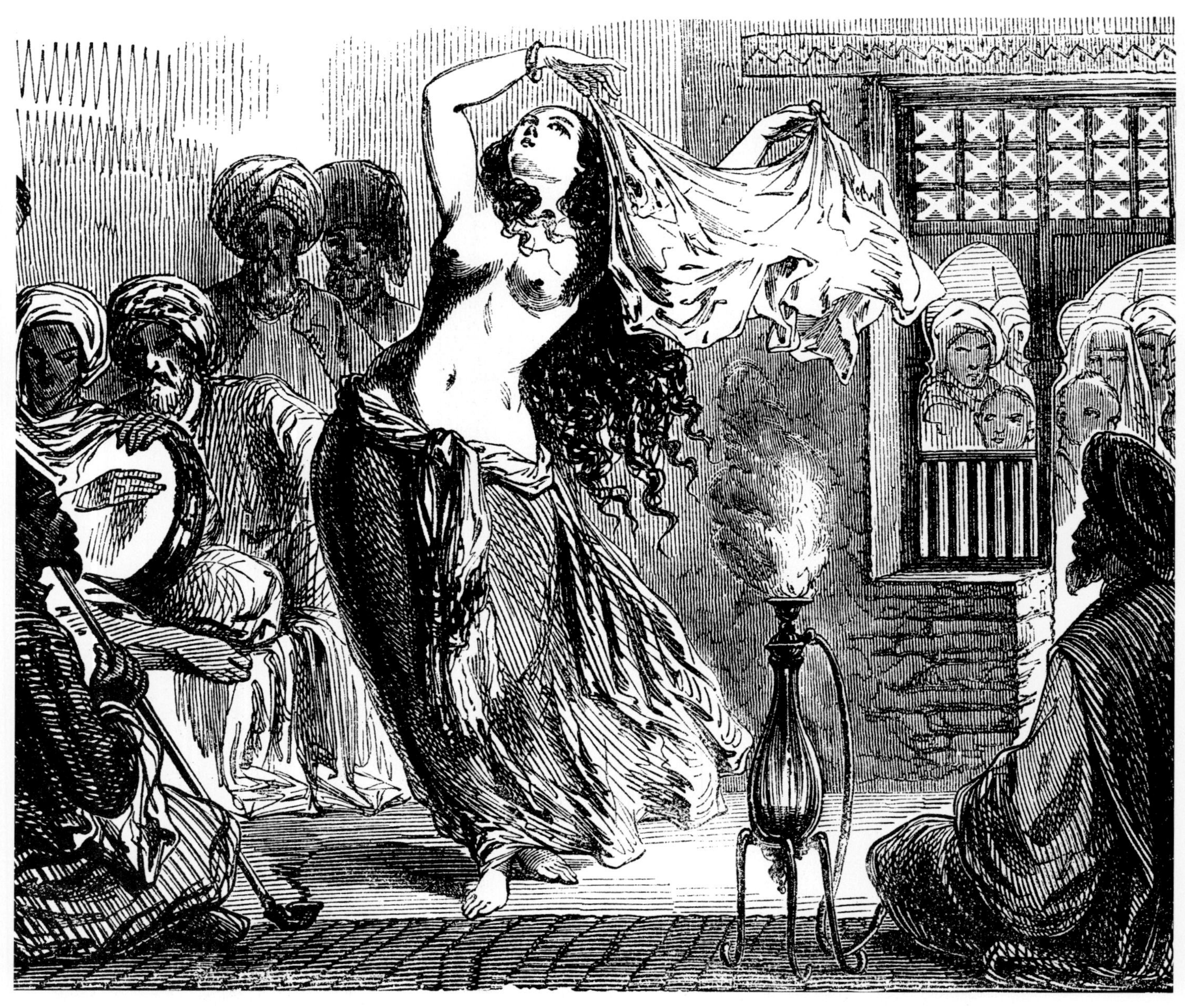

Belly dance, Cairo, 1845

Bauchtanz, Kairo, 1845

Danza del ventre, Il Cairo, 1845

Danse du ventre, Le Caire, 1845

Danza del vientre, El Cairo, 1845

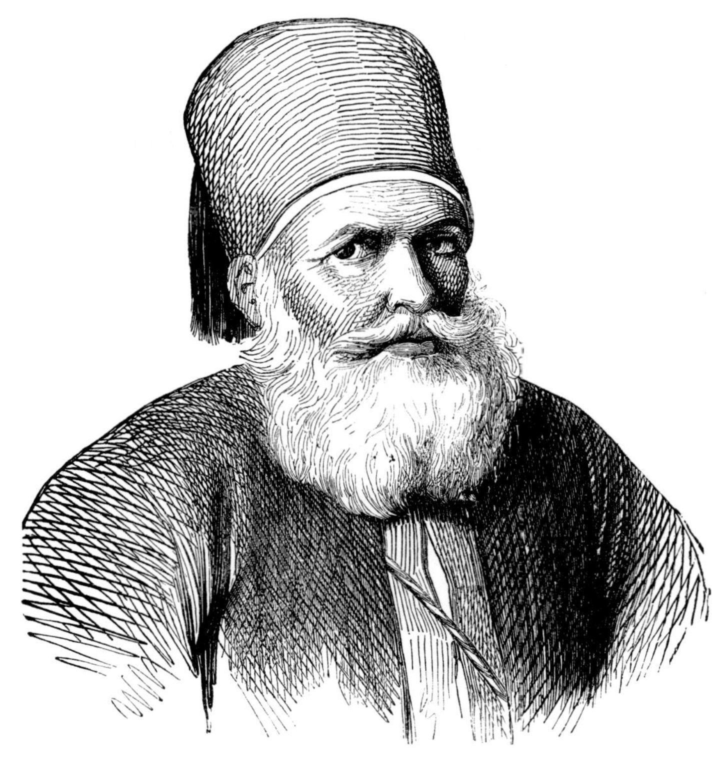

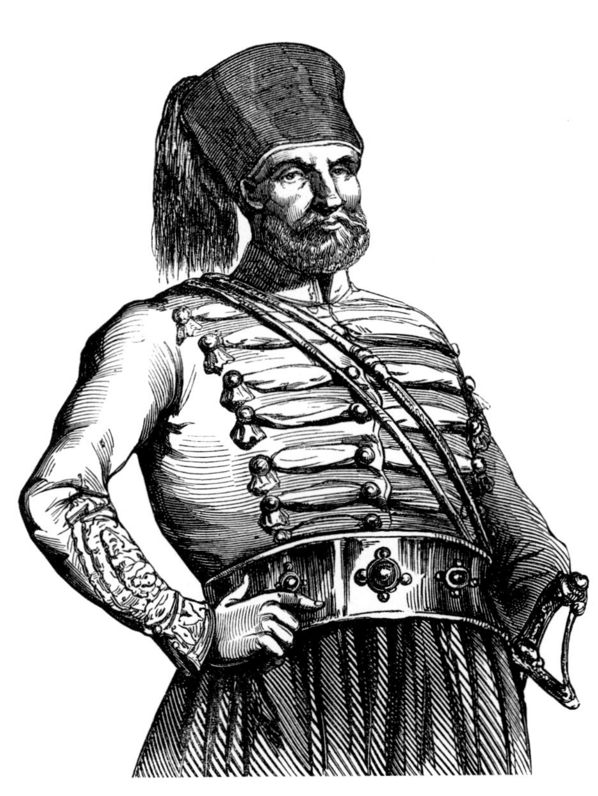

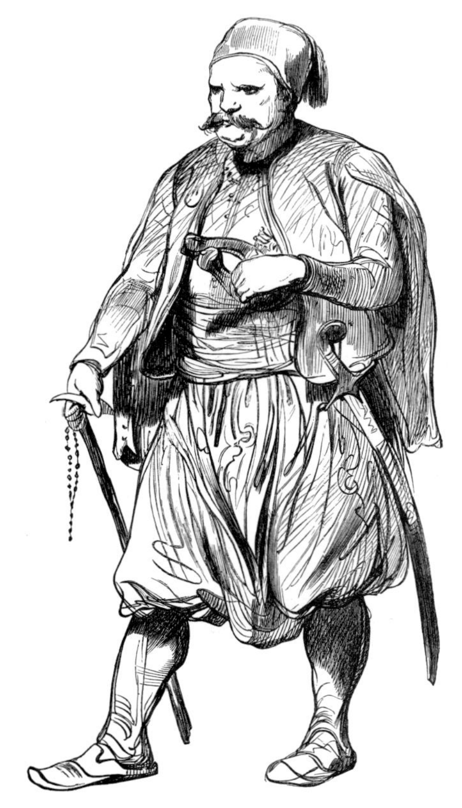

a	Vice-King of Egypt, 1840	Vizekönig von Ägypten, 1840	Viceré di Egitto, 1840	Vice-roi d'Égypte, 1840	Virrey de Egipto, 1840
b	Son of the vice-King in military uniform, 1840	Sohn des Vizekönigs in Militäruniform, 1840	Figlio del Viceré in uniforme militare, 1840	Fils du Vice-roi en uniforme, 1840	Hijo del virrey con uniforme militar, 1840
c	Egyptian colonel, 1840	Ägyptischer Oberst, 1840	Colonnello egiziano, 1840	Colonel égyptien, 1840	Coronel egipcio, 1840

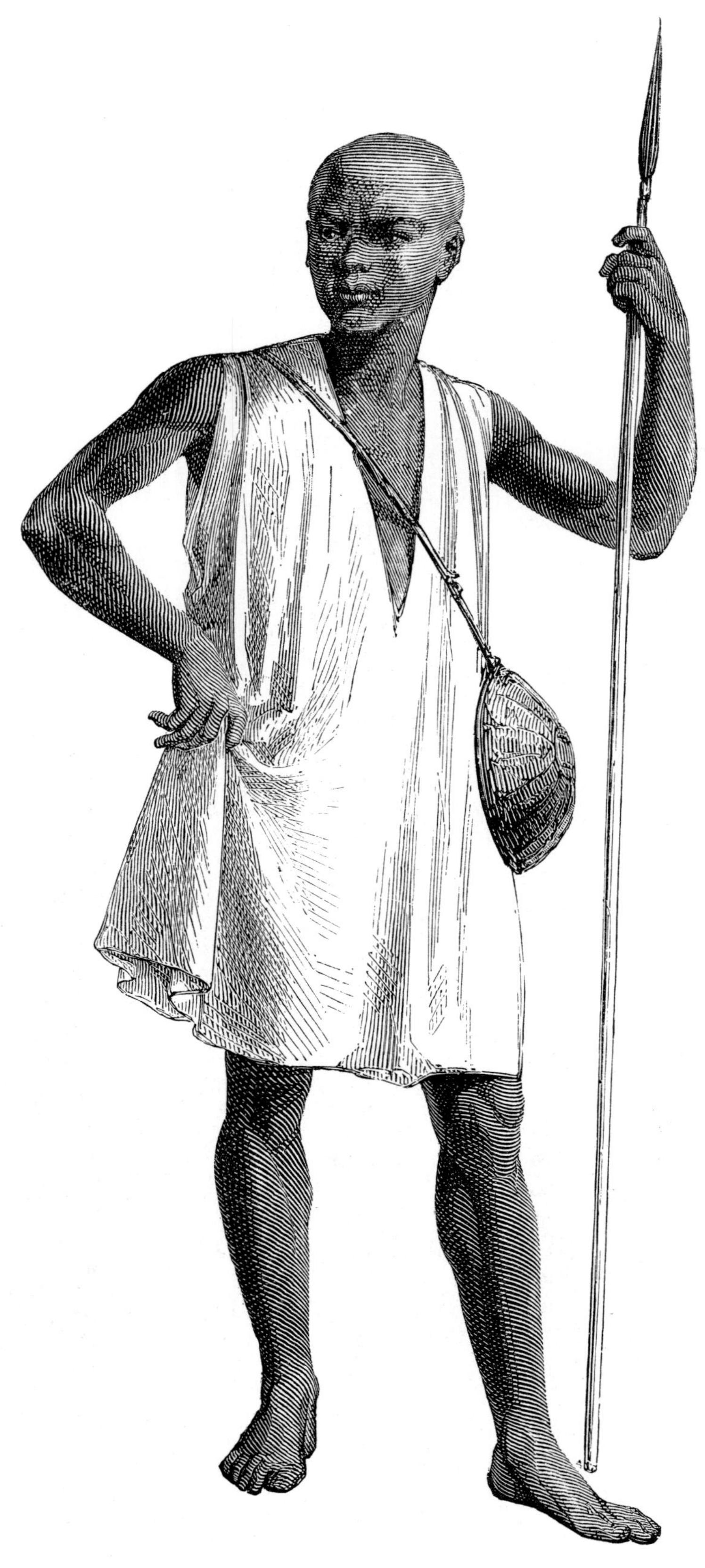

Nubian soldier, c. 1870

Nubischer Krieger, um 1870

Soldato nubiano, ca. 1870

Soldat nubien, vers 1870

Soldado nubio, hacia 1870

Sudan

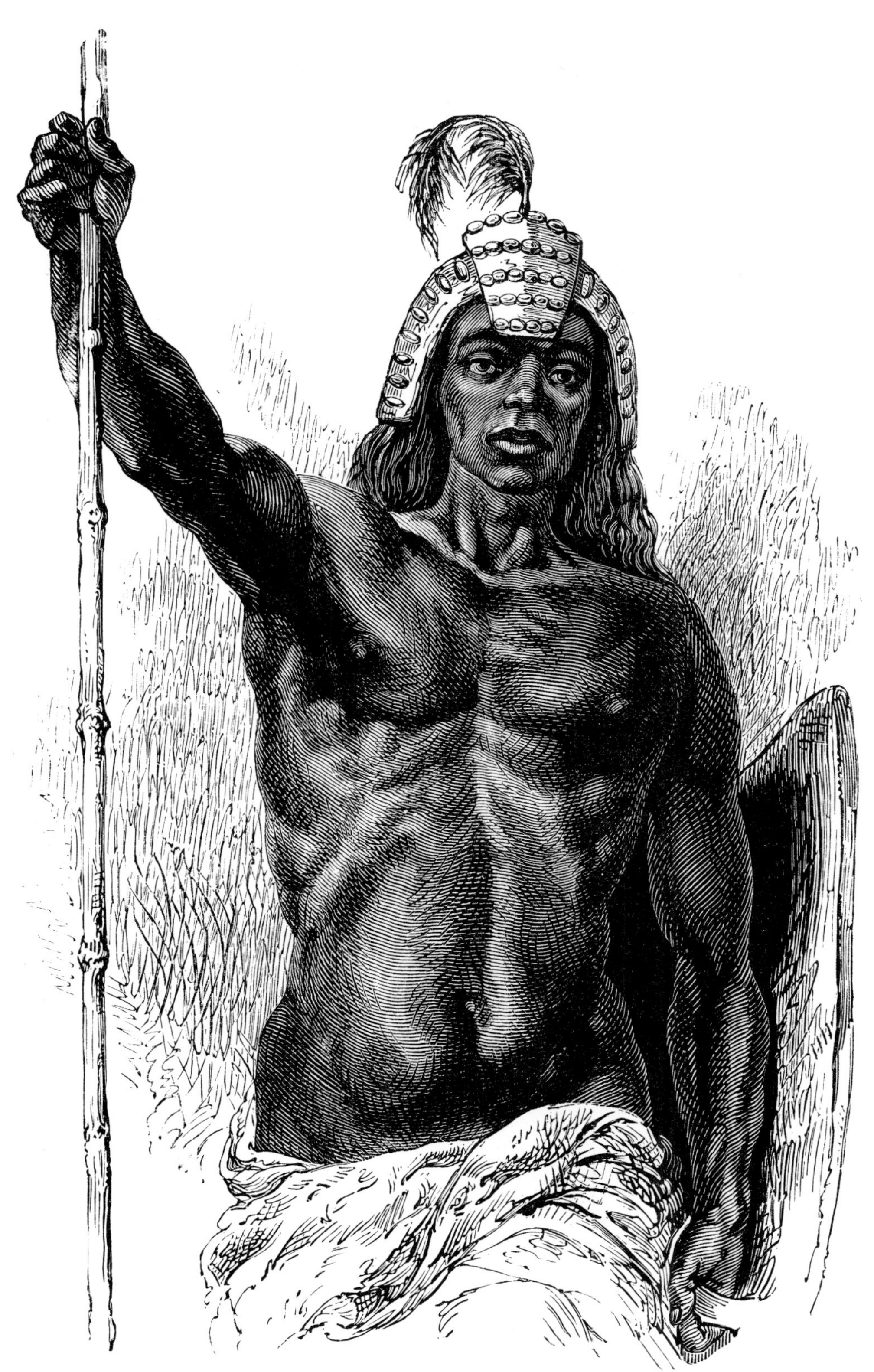

Nuba chief, c. 1880

Nubischer Häuptling, um 1880

Capo nuba, ca. 1880

Chef Nuba, vers 1880

Jefe nubio, hacia 1880

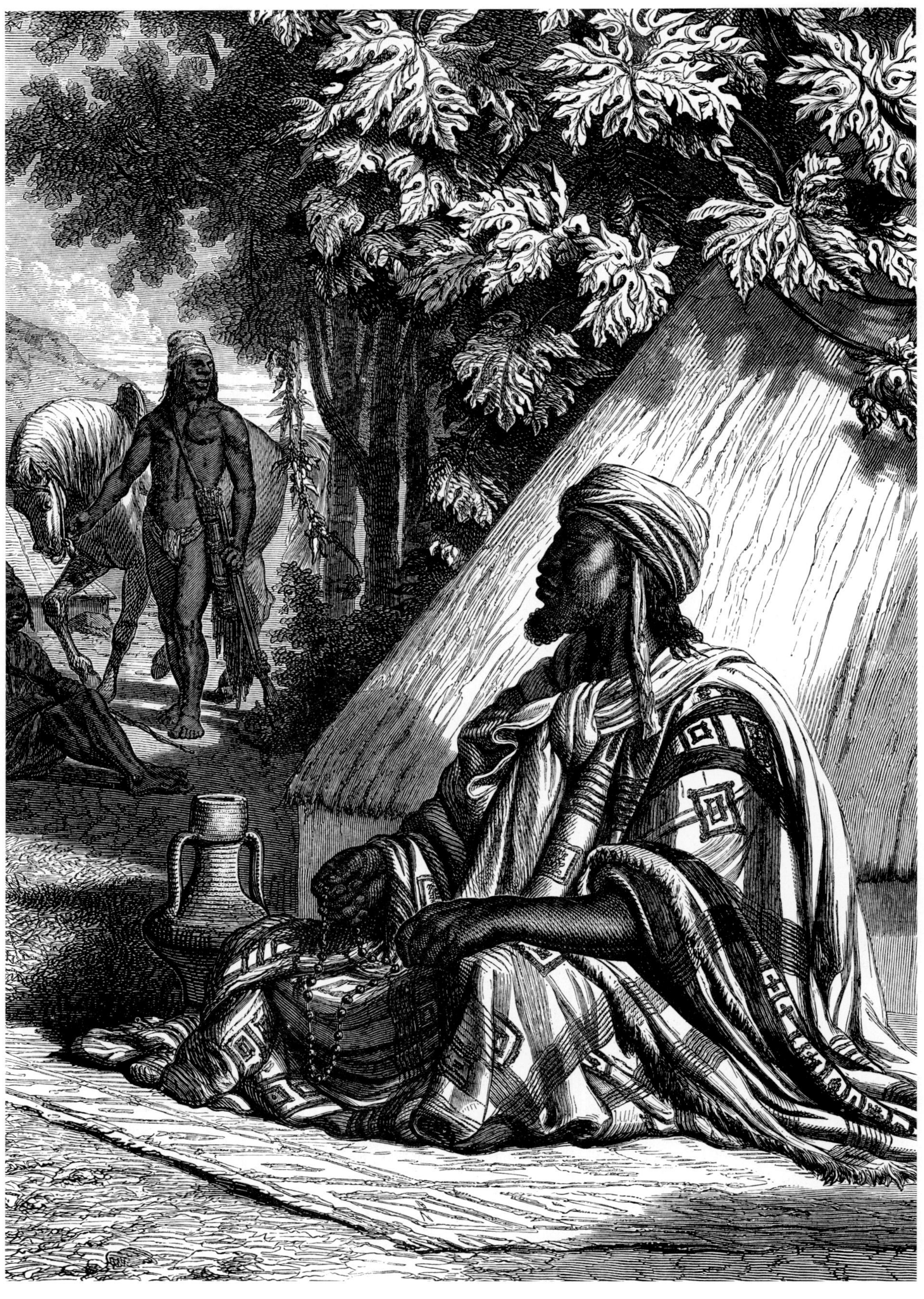

Nuba chief, c. 1880

Nubischer Häuptling, um 1880

Capo nuba, ca. 1880

Chef Nuba, vers 1880

Jefe nubio, hacia 1880

Sudan

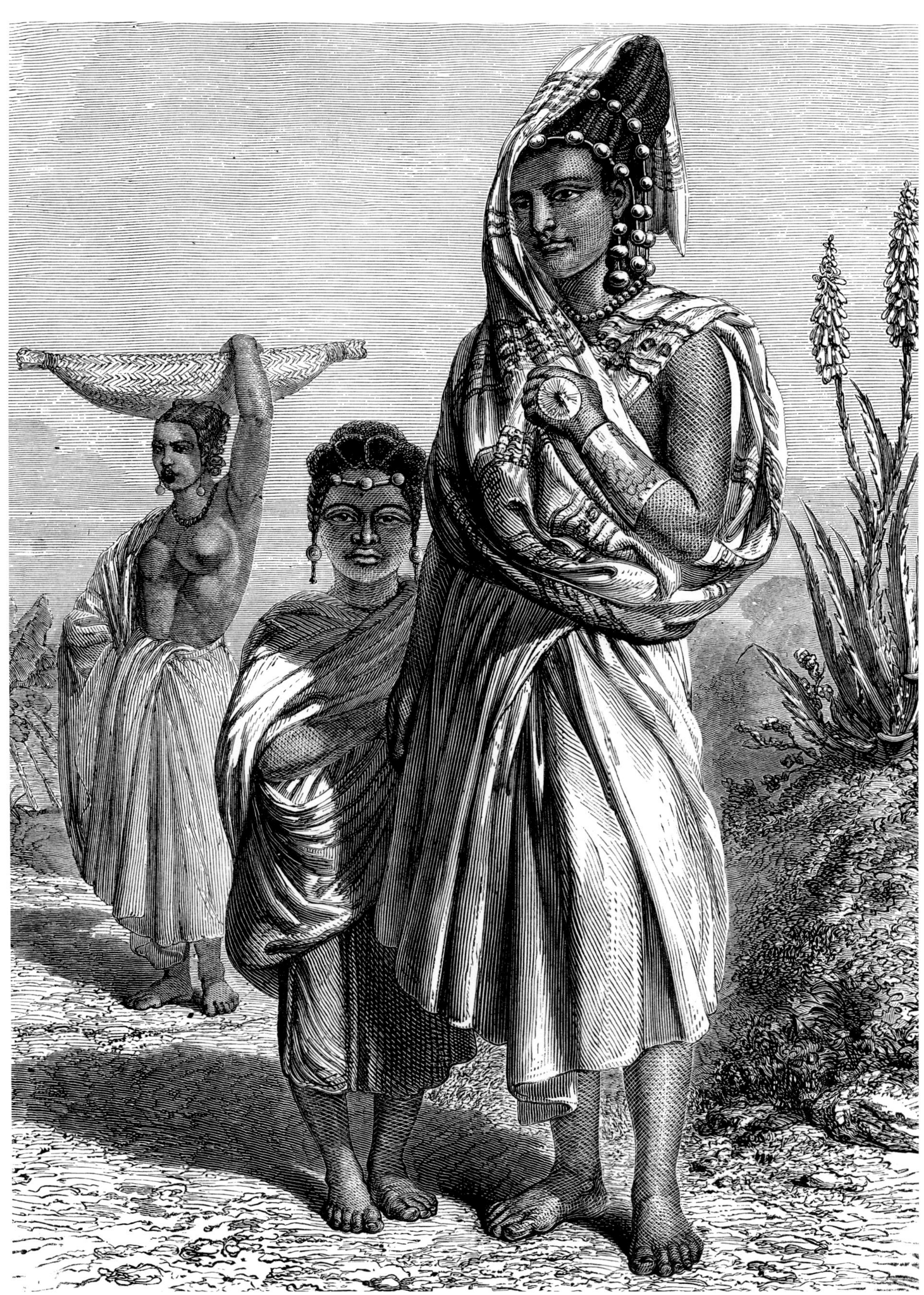

Nuba Lady with child and servant, c. 1880

Nubische Frau mit Kind und Dienerin, um 1880

Donna nuba con bambino e domestica, ca. 1880

Femme Nuba avec son enfant et une servante, vers 1880

Mujer nubia con su hijo y su sirviente, hacia 1880

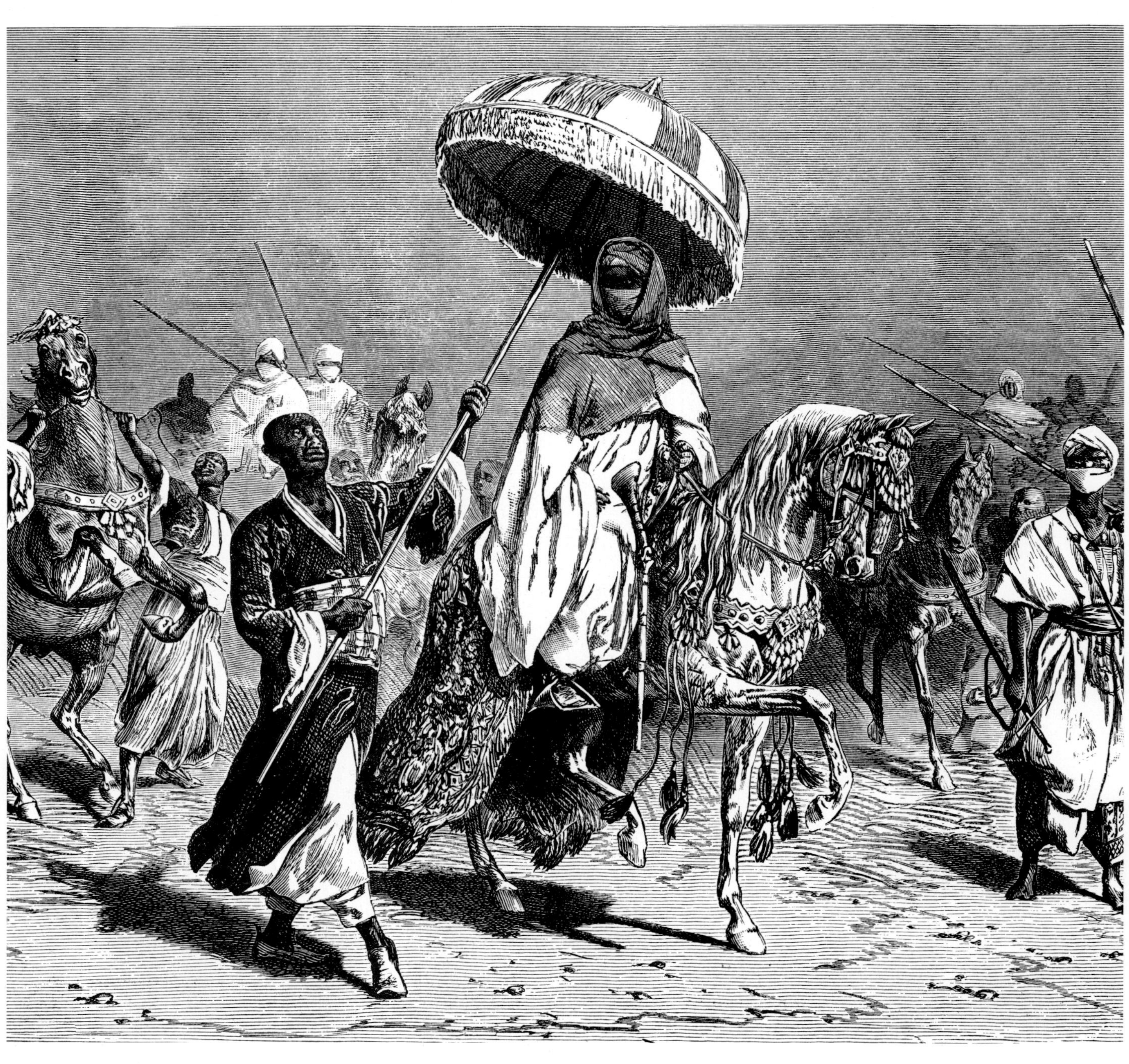

North Sudanese Sultan with his courtiers, c. 1880.

Nordsudanesischer Sultan mit Höflingen, um 1880

Sultano sudanese settentrionale con i suoi cortigiani, ca. 1880

Sultan du Nord du Soudan accompagné de sa Cour, vers 1880

Sultán del norte del Sudán y sus cortesanos, hacia 1880

Sudan

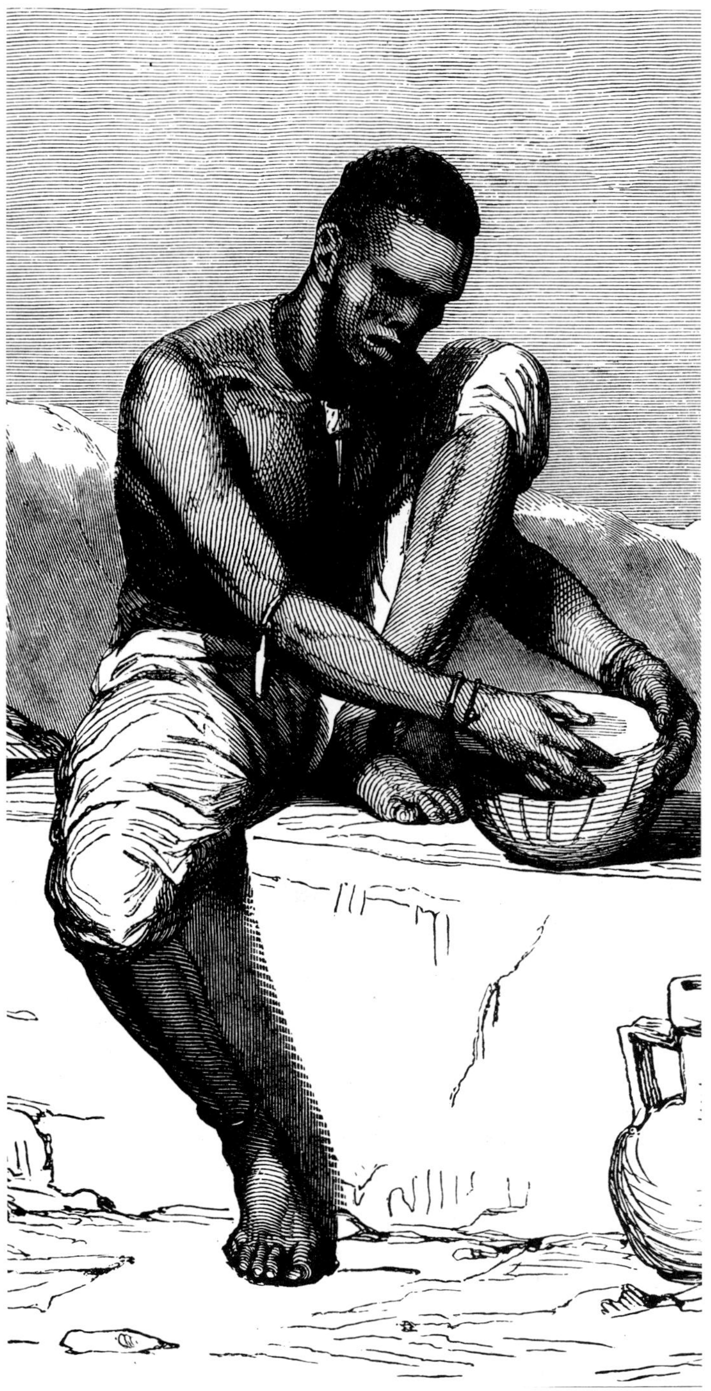

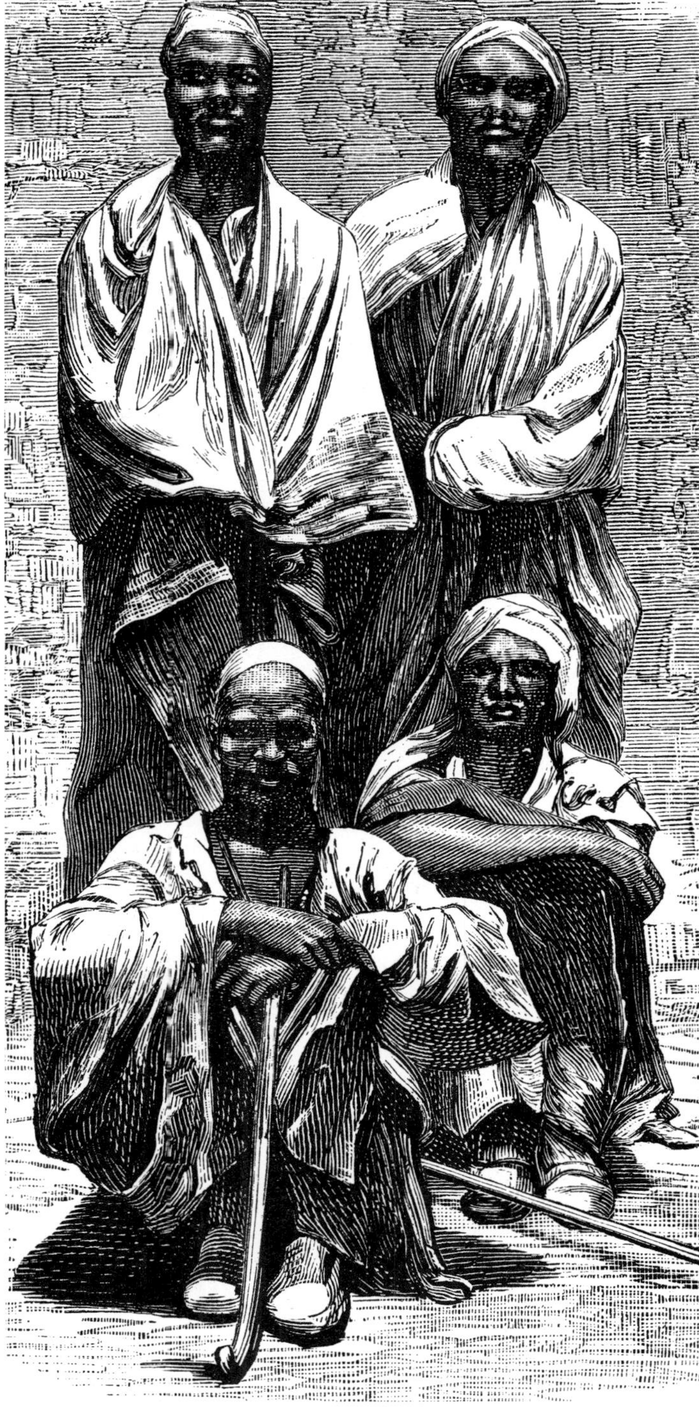

a Sudanese Dinka Man, c. 1880 | Dinka aus dem Sudan, um 1880 | Dinka sudanese, ca. 1880 | Dinka soudanais, vers 1880 | Hombre dinka sudanés, hacia 1880

b Camel drivers, Kharthoum, c. 1880 | Kameltreiber, Khartoum, um 1880 | Cammellieri, Kharthoum, ca. 1880 | Meneurs de chameaux, Khartoum, vers 1880 | Camelleros, Jartum, hacia 1880

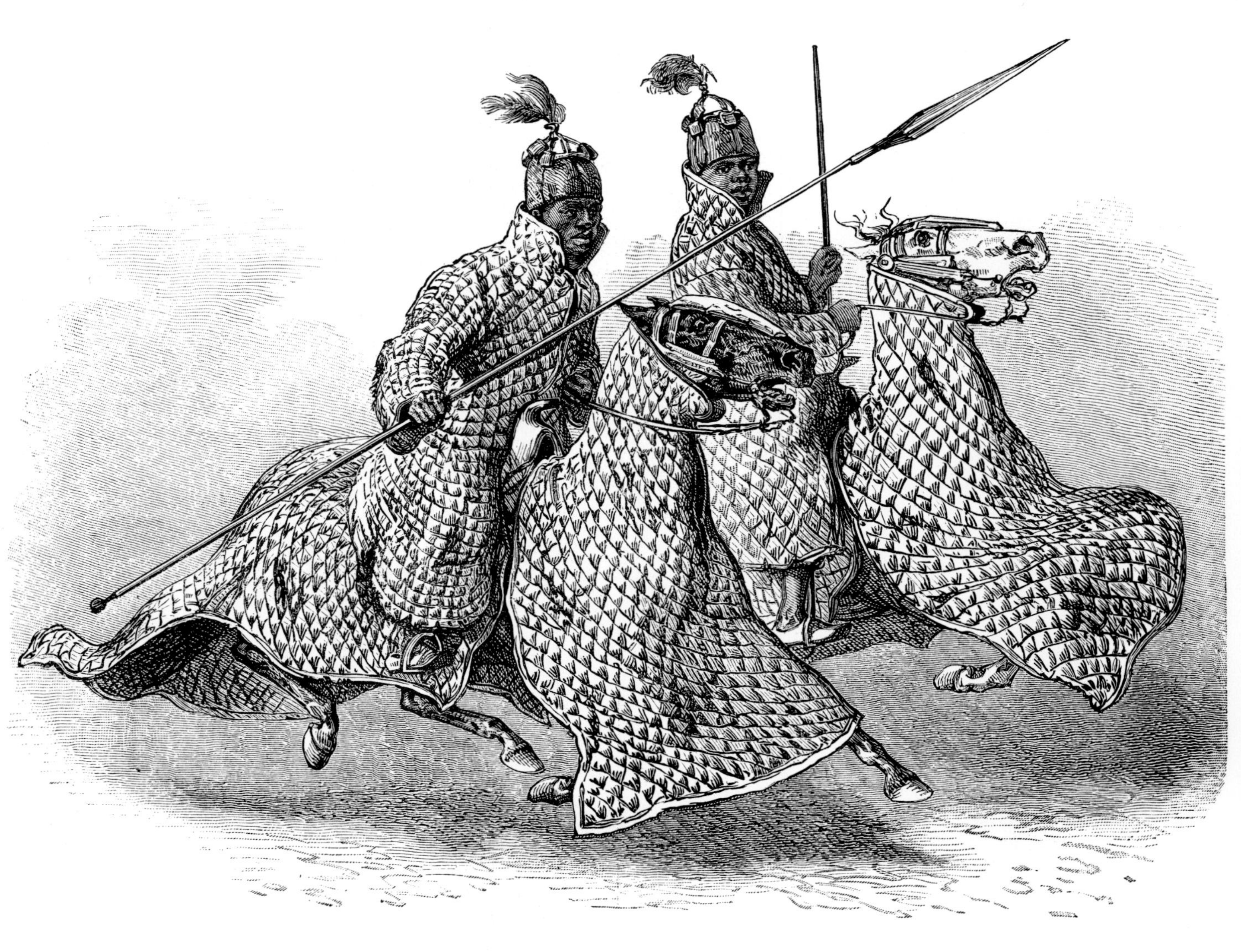

Sudanese warriors in padded armour, c. 1900

Sudanesische Krieger mit gefüttertem Panzer, um 1900

Guerrieri sudanesi in armatura imbottita, ca. 1900

Guerriers soudanais en armure matelassée, vers 1900

Guerreros sudaneses con armaduras acolchadas, hacia 1900

Sudan

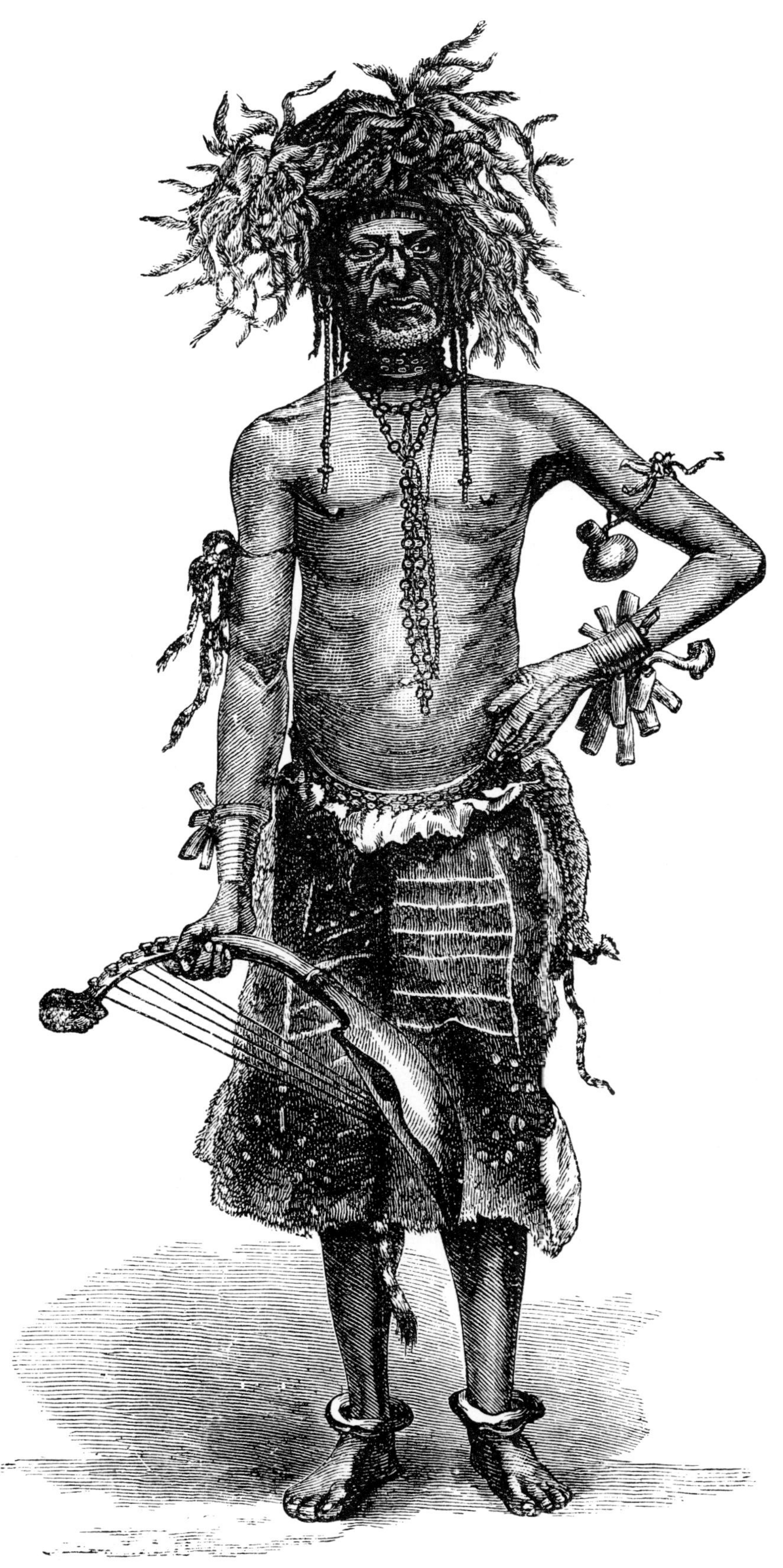

Musician, c. 1880 Musiker, um 1880 Musicista, ca. 1880 Musicien, vers 1880 Músico, hacia 1880

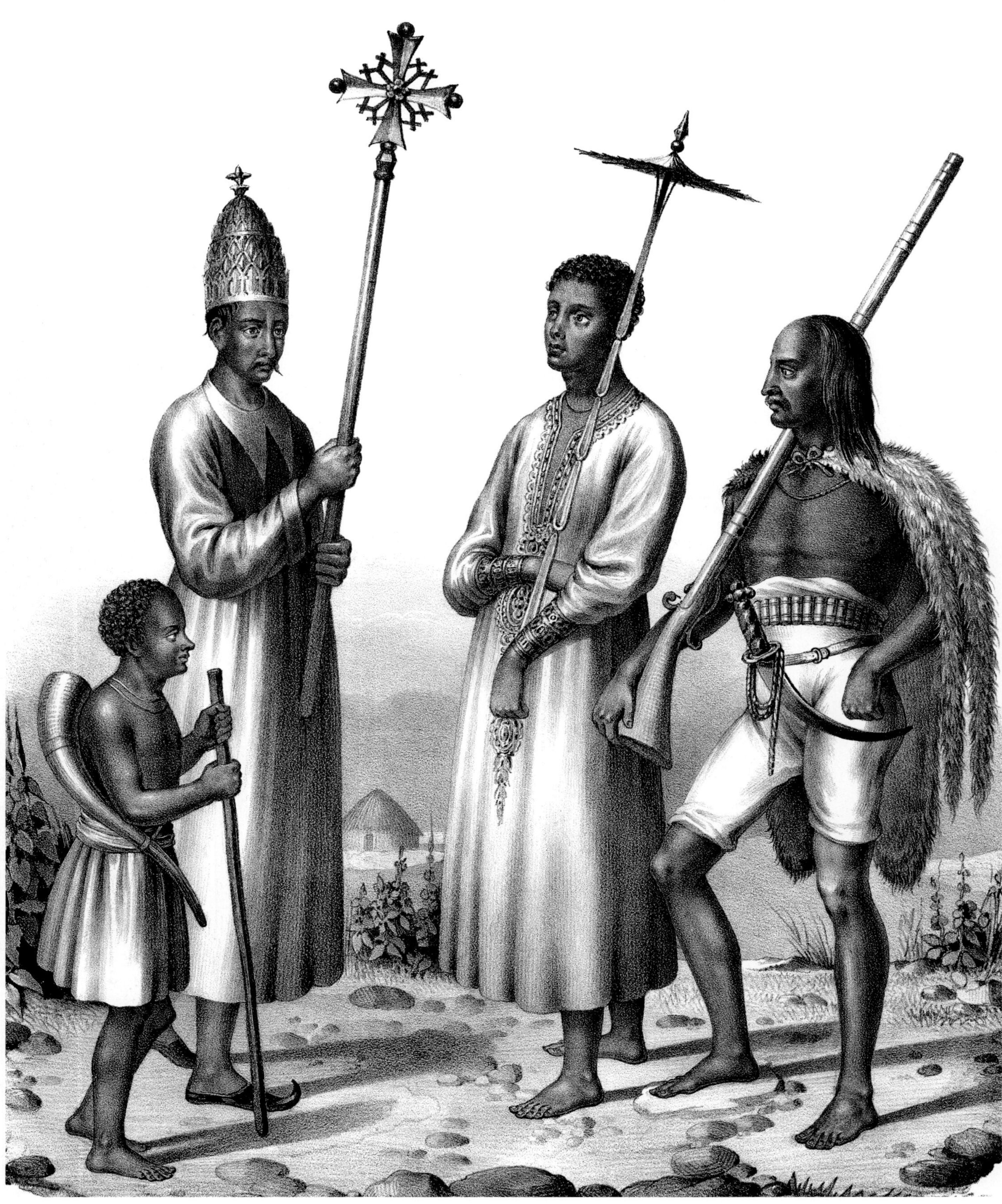

Christian converts, Abyssinia (present-day Ethiopia), c. 1880

Christliche Konvertiten, Abessinien (heute Äthiopien), um 1880

Convertiti cristiani, Abissinia (attualmente Etiopia), ca. 1880

Indigènes convertis au christianisme, Abyssinie (actuellement l'Éthiopie), vers 1880

Cristianos conversos, Abisinia (actual Etiopía), alrededor del año 1880

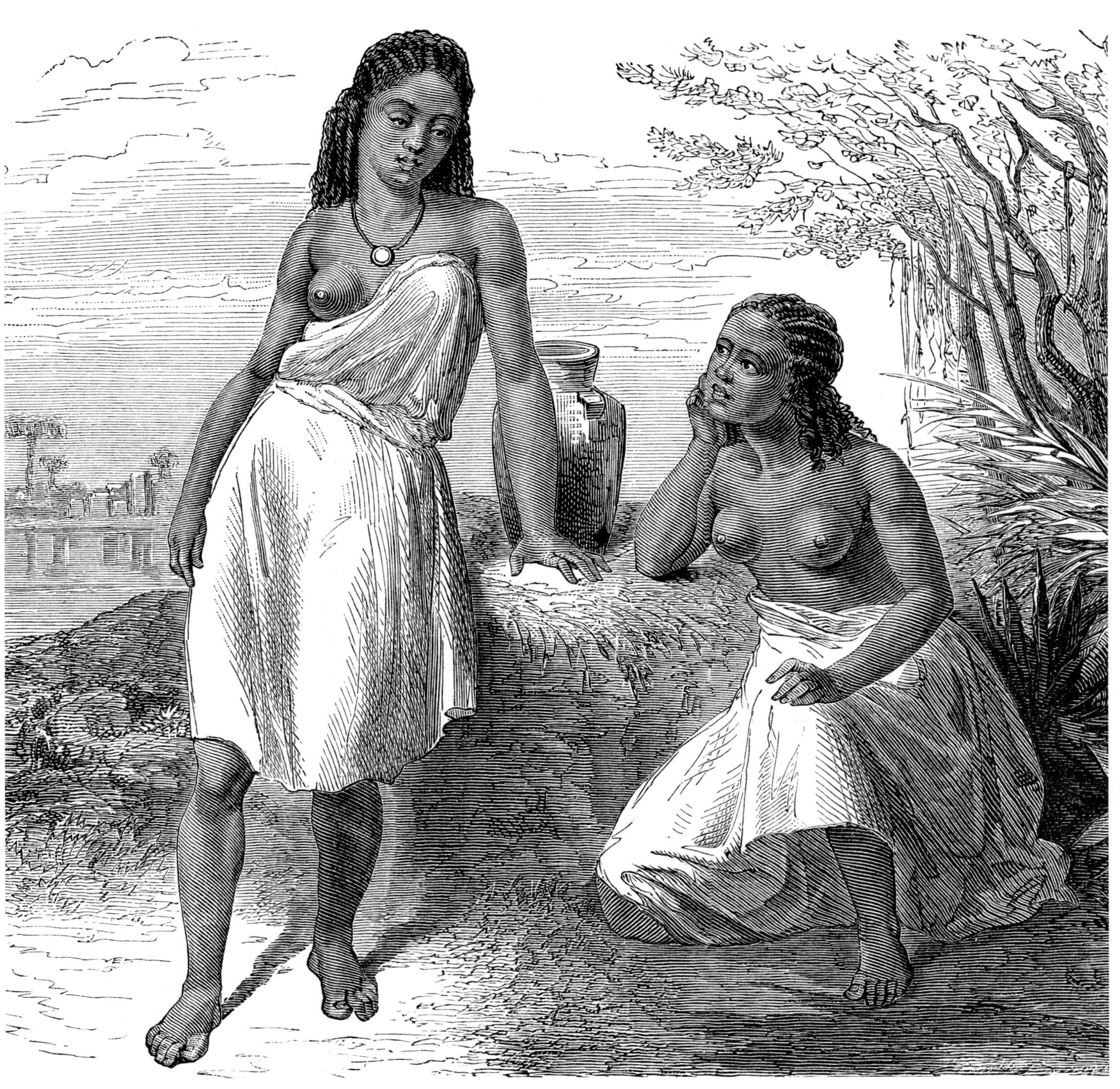

Abyssinian girls, c. 1880

Abessinische Mädchen, um 1880

Ragazze abissine, ca. 1880

Jeunes filles d'Abyssinie, vers 1880

Jóvenes abisinias, hacia el año 1880

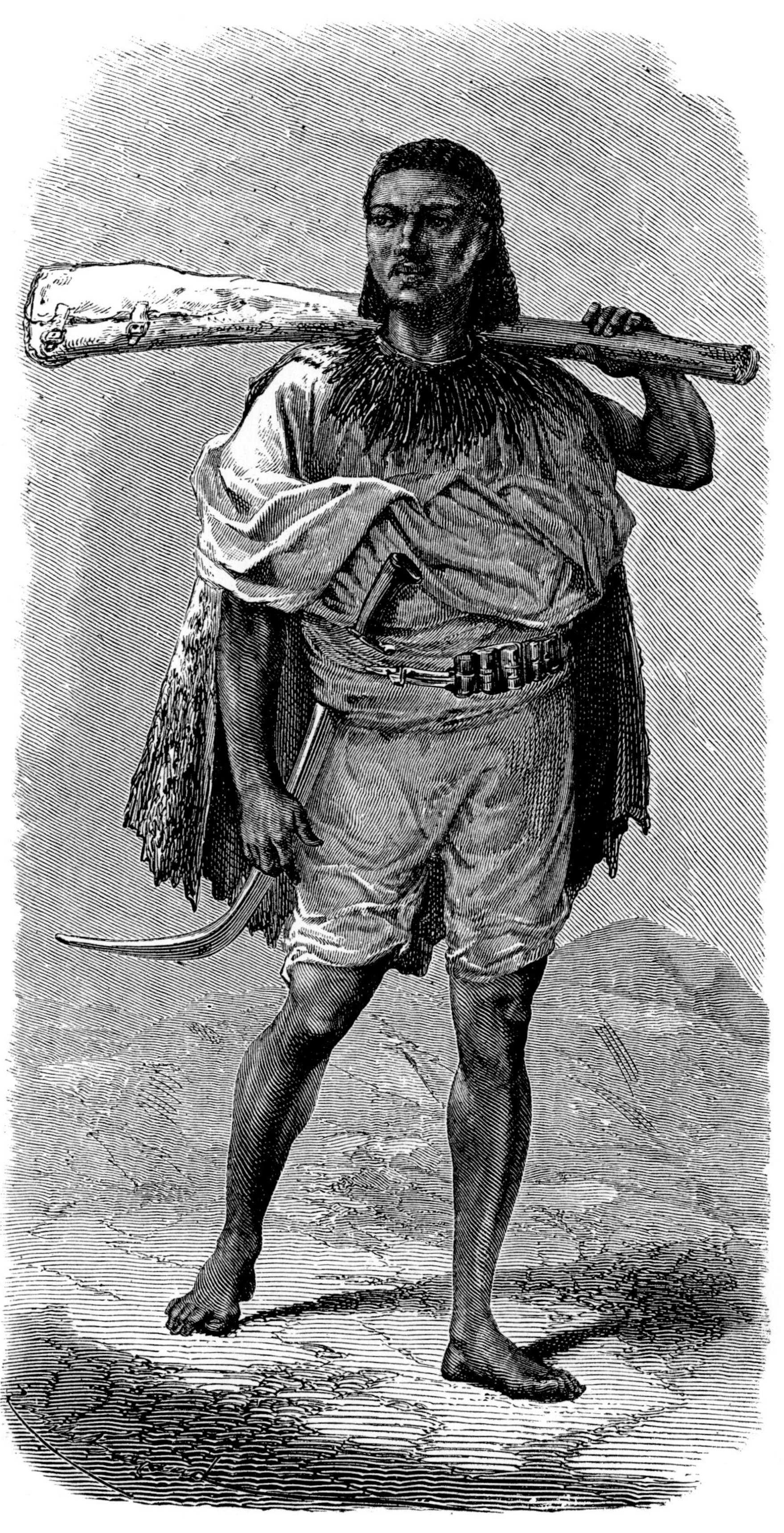

Abyssinian soldier, c. 1880

Abessinischer Krieger, um 1880

Soldato abissino, ca. 1880

Soldat abyssin, vers 1880

Soldado abisinio, alrededor del año 1880

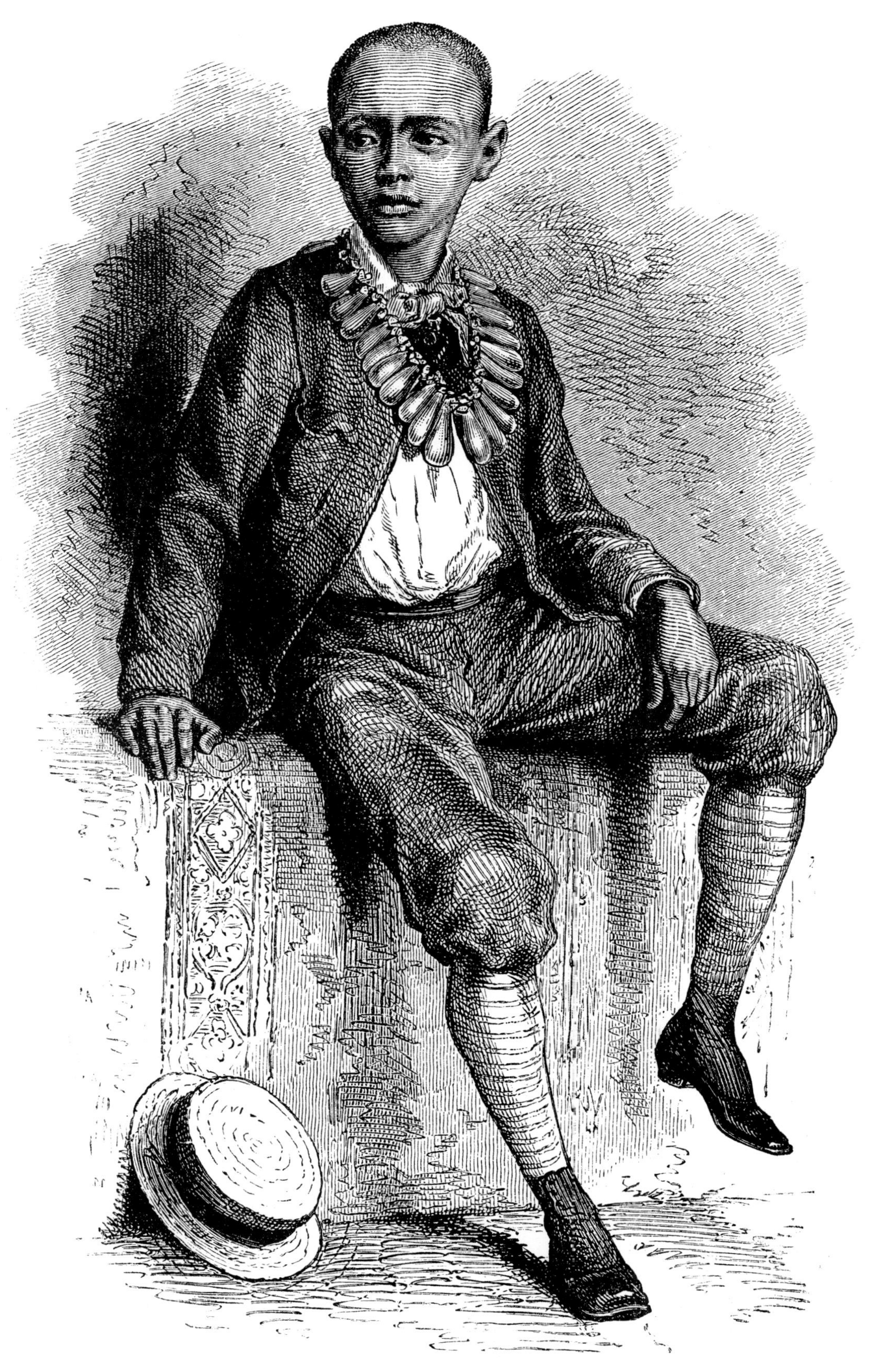

Abessinian Prince, 1875 Abessinischer Prinz, 1875 Principe abissino, 1875 Prince abyssin, 1875 Príncipe abisinio, 1875

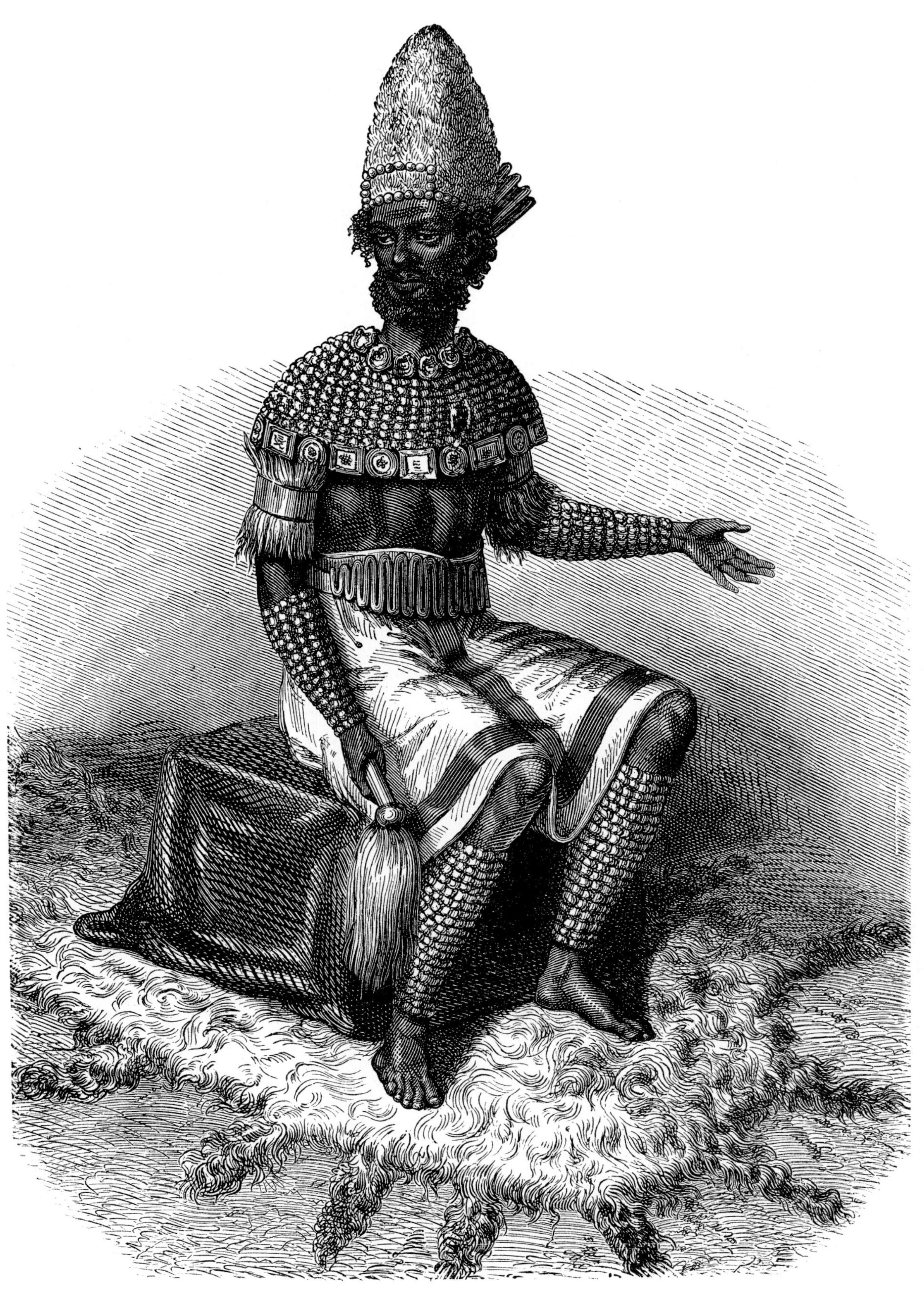

Abessinian King, c. 1900 (present-day Ethiopia)

Abessinischer König, um 1900 (heute Äthiopien)

Re abissino, ca. 1900 (attualmente Etiopia)

Roi abyssin, vers 1900 (actuellement l'Éthiopie)

Rey abisinio, hacia 1900 (actual Etiopía)

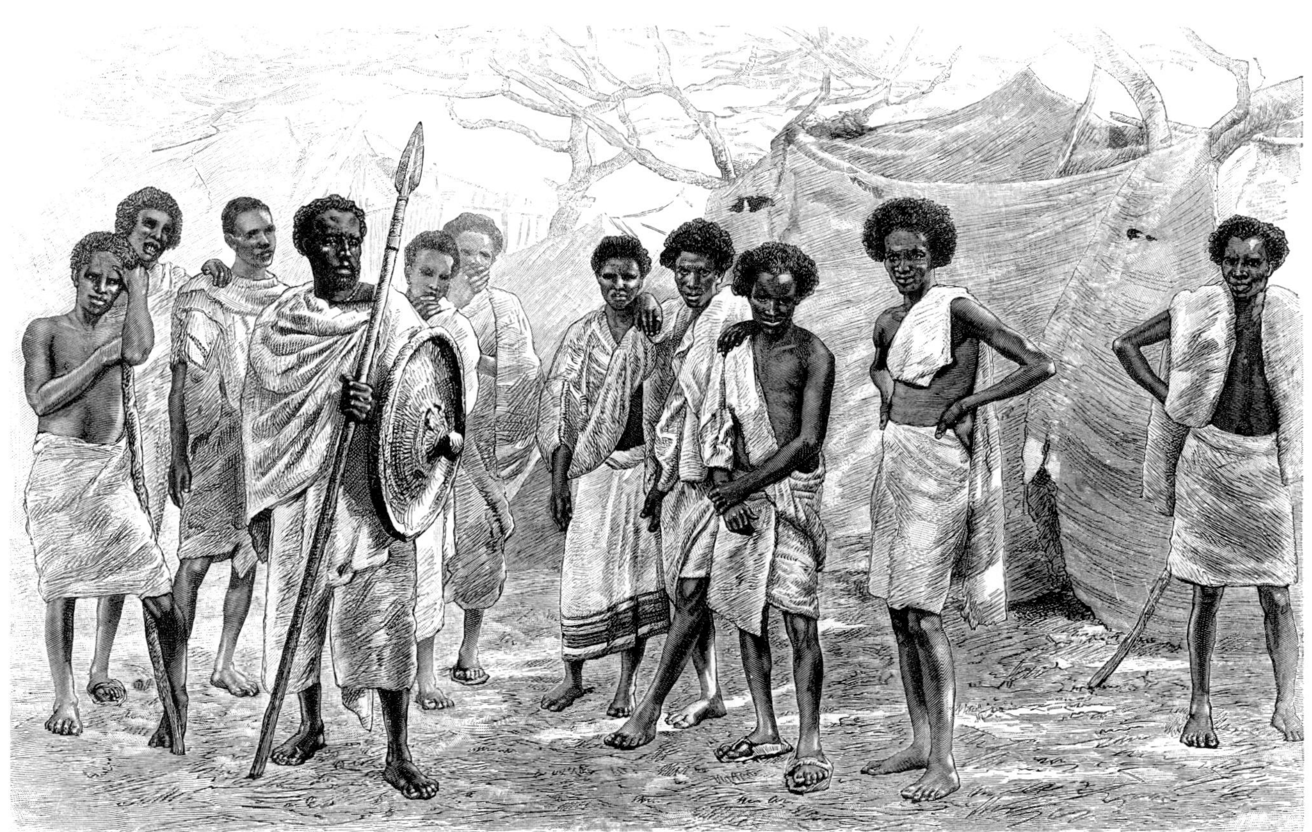

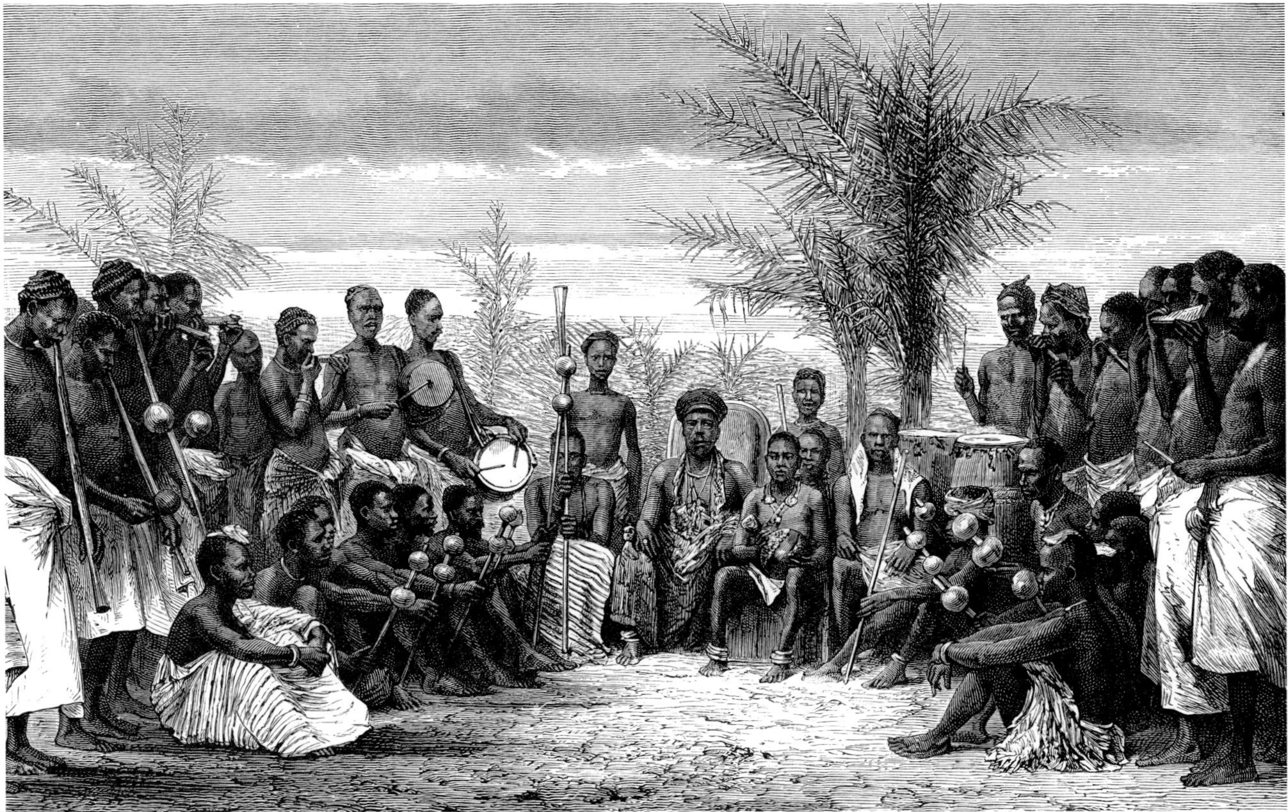

a	Djibouti headman with villagers, c. 1870	Dschibuti-Häuptling mit Dorfbewohnern, um 1870	Capotribù di Gibuti con abitanti del villaggio, ca. 1870	Chef djiboutien entouré de villageois, vers 1870	Jefe yibutiano y aldeanos, hacia 1870
b	Somali King with his courtiers, 1880	Somalischer König mit Höflingen, 1880	Re somalo con i suoi cortigiani, 1880	Roi somalien et sa Cour, 1880	Rey somalí y cortesanos, 1880

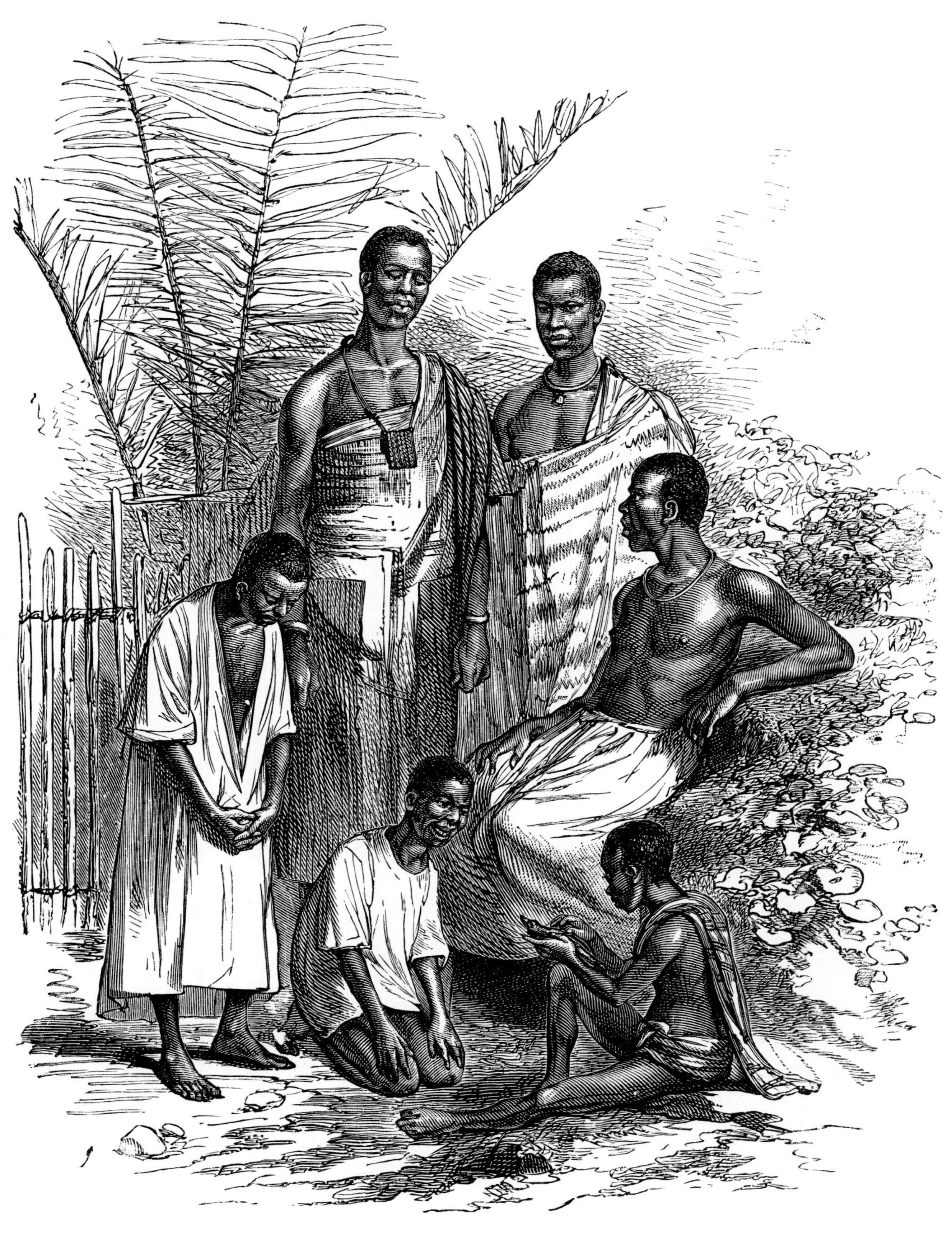

Ugandans, 1900 Ugander, 1900 Ugandesi, 1900 Ougandais, 1900 Ugandeses, 1900

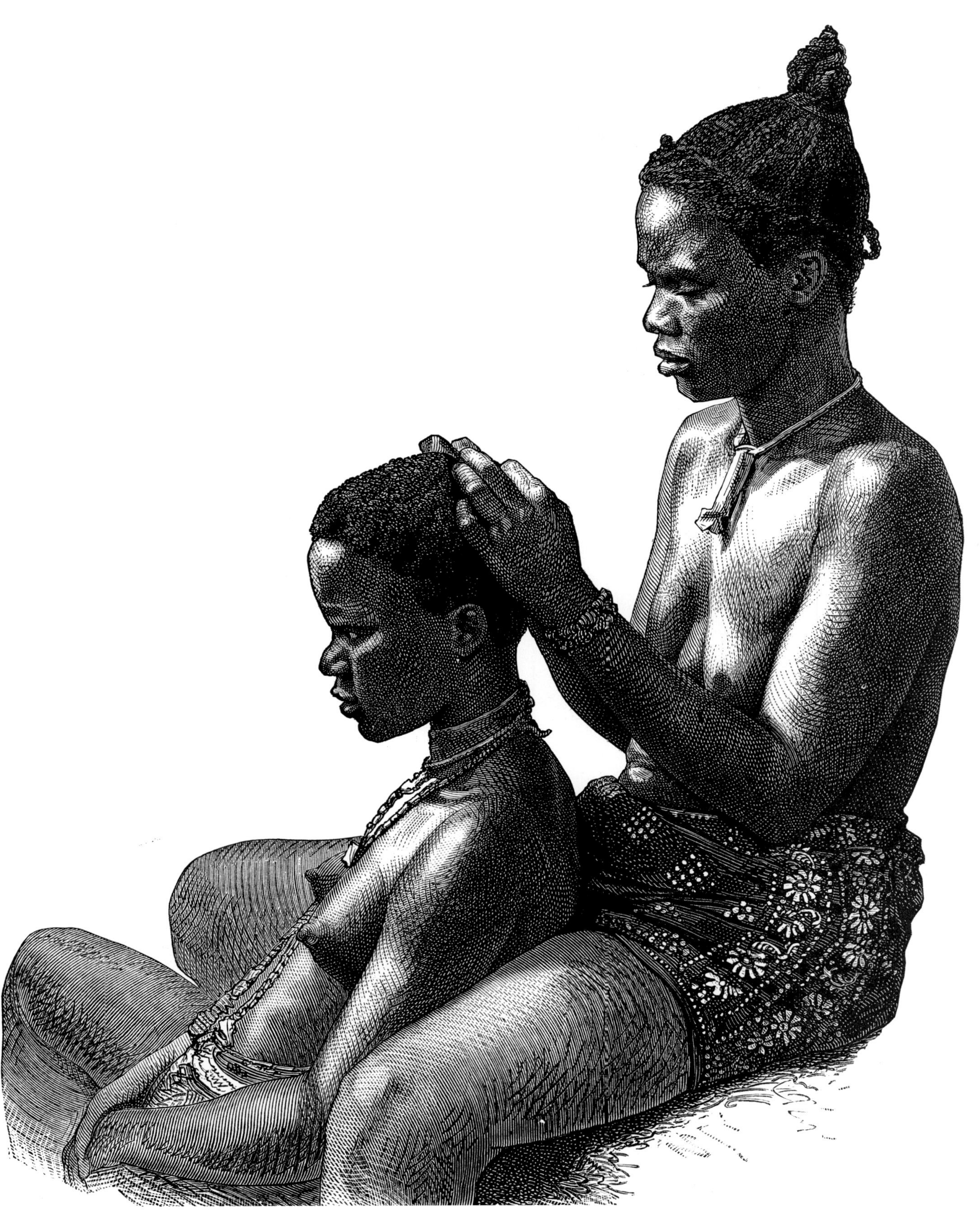

Ugandan women, 1880 Ugandische Frauen, 1880 Donne ugandesi, 1880 Ougandaises, 1880 Mujeres ugandesas, 1880

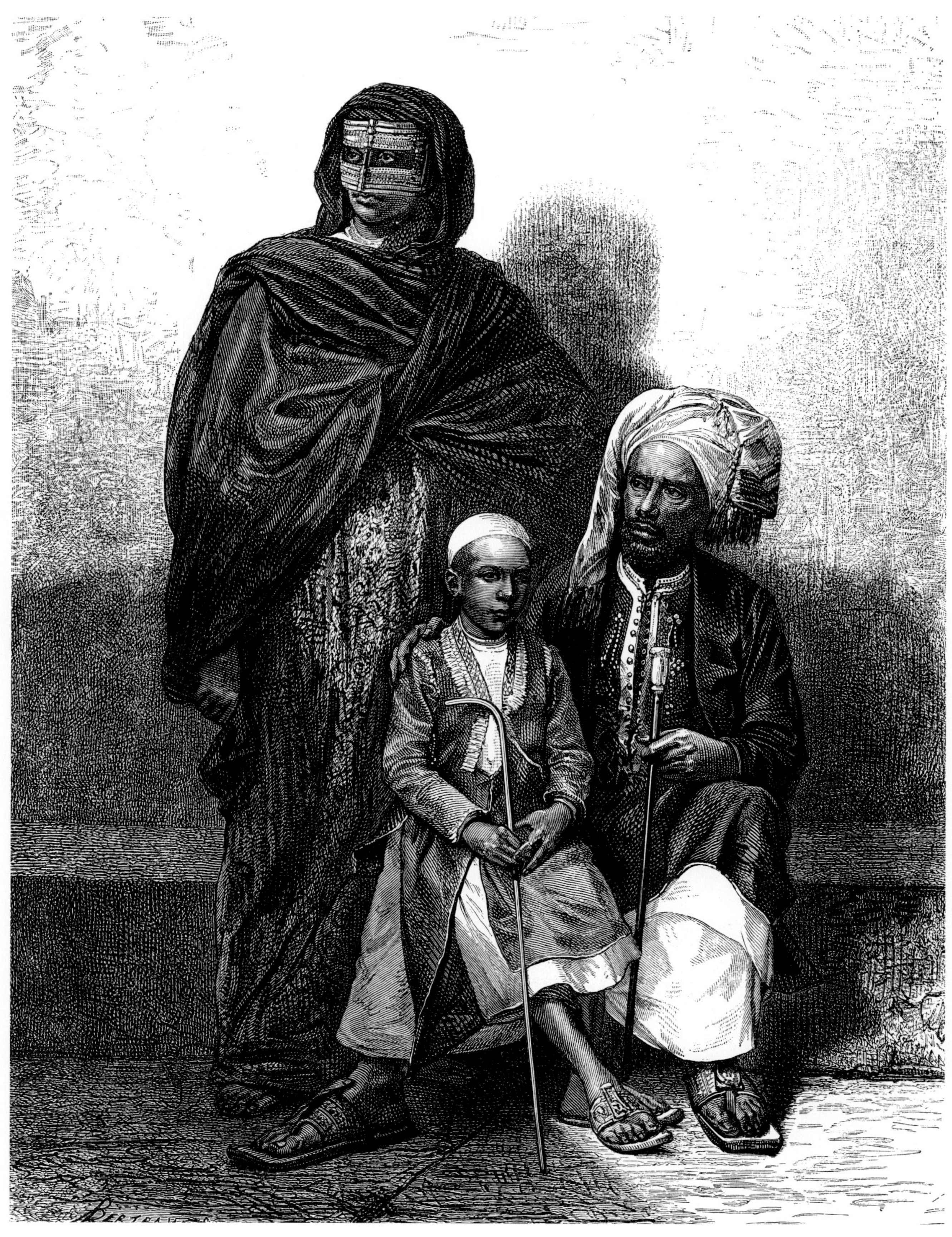

Arab family, Zanzibar, c. 1880

Arabische Familie, Sansibar, um 1880

Famiglia araba, Zanzibar, ca. 1880

Famille arabe, Zanzibar, vers 1880

Familia árabe, Zanzíbar, hacia el año 1880

Zanzibar

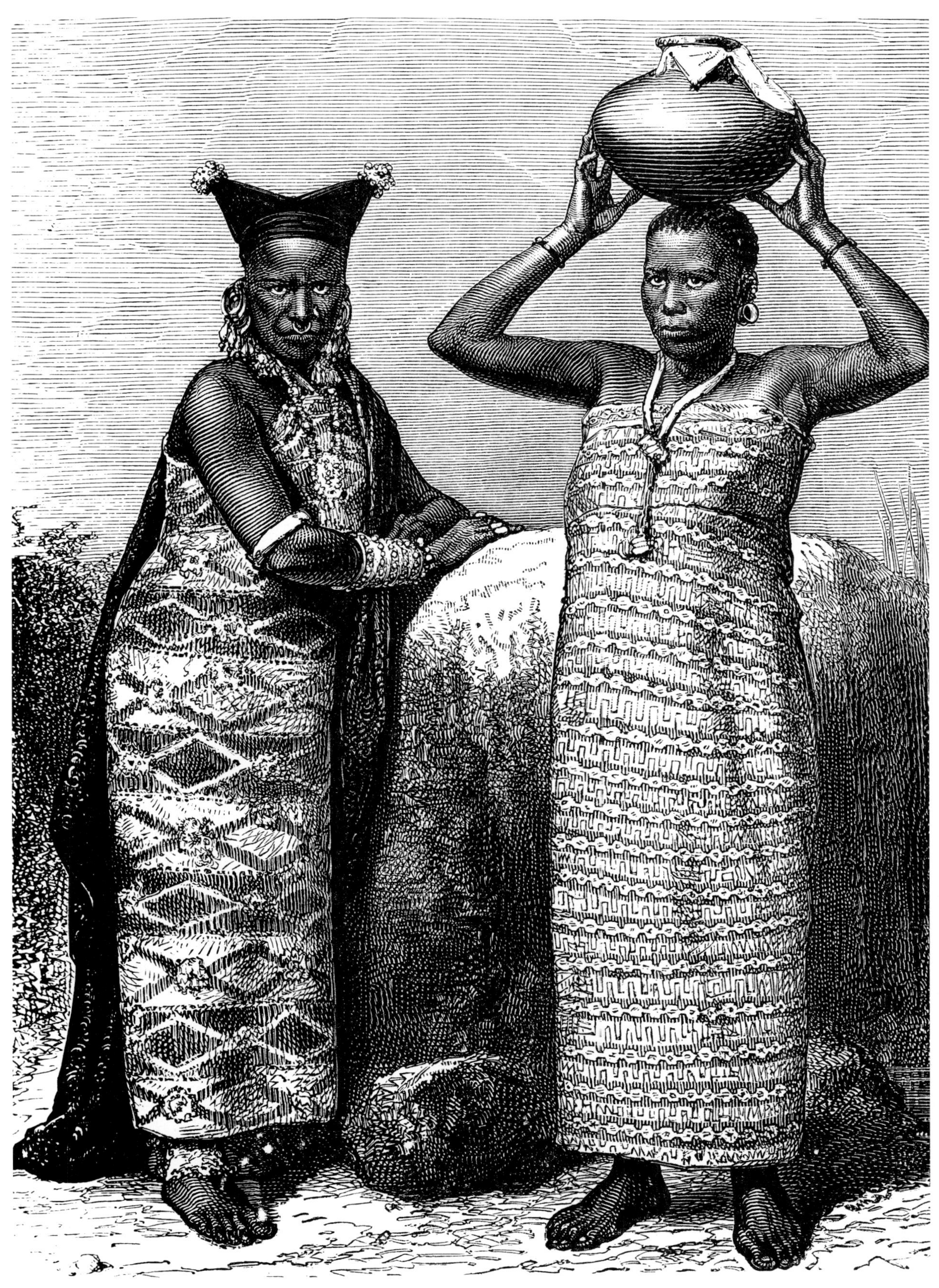

Servants, Zanzibar, 1875

Bedienstete, Sansibar, 1875

Domestiche, Zanzibar, 1875

Servantes, Zanzibar, 1875

Sirvientes, Zanzíbar, 1875

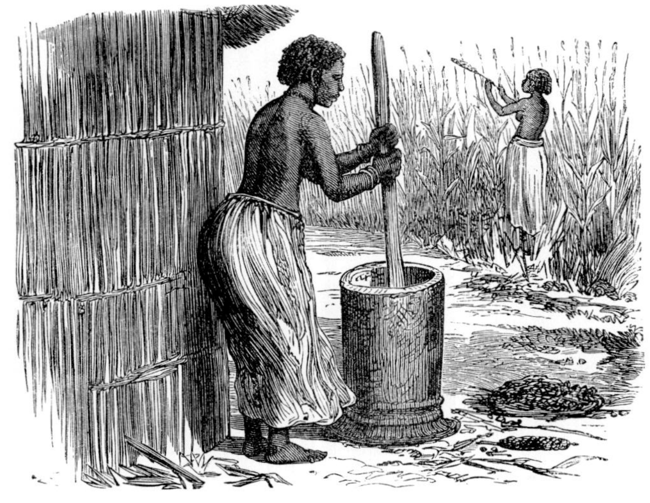

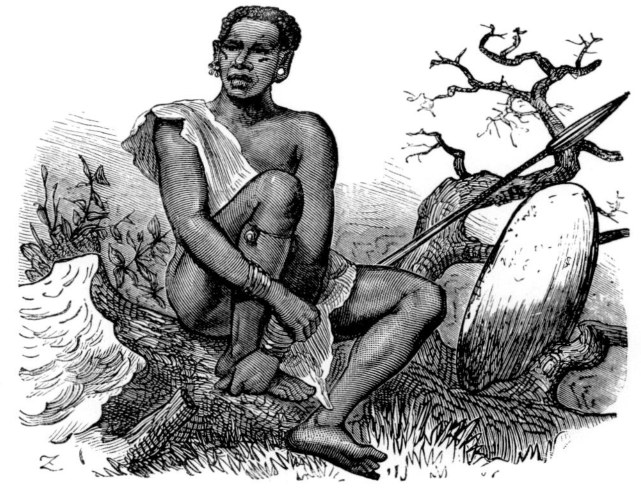

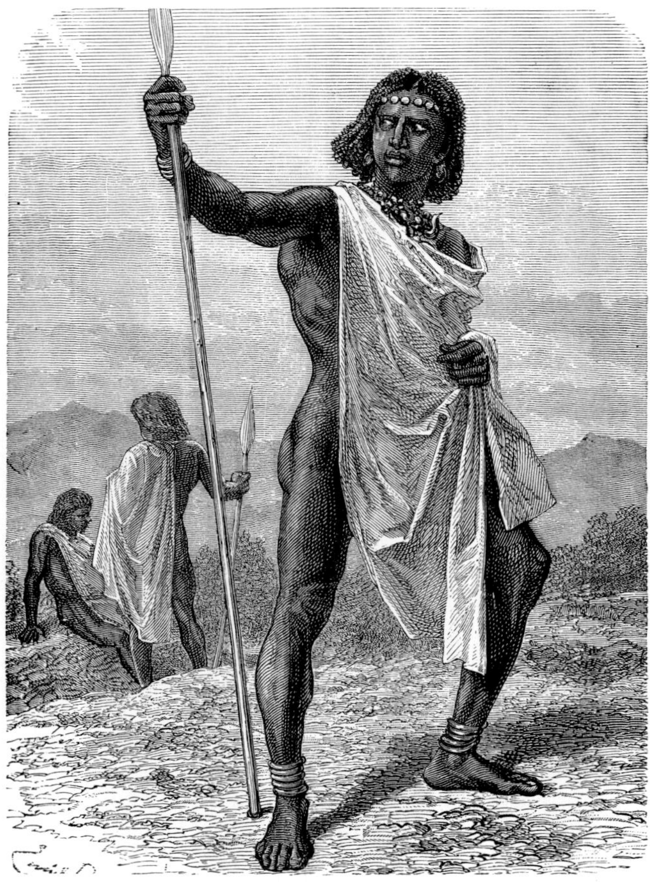

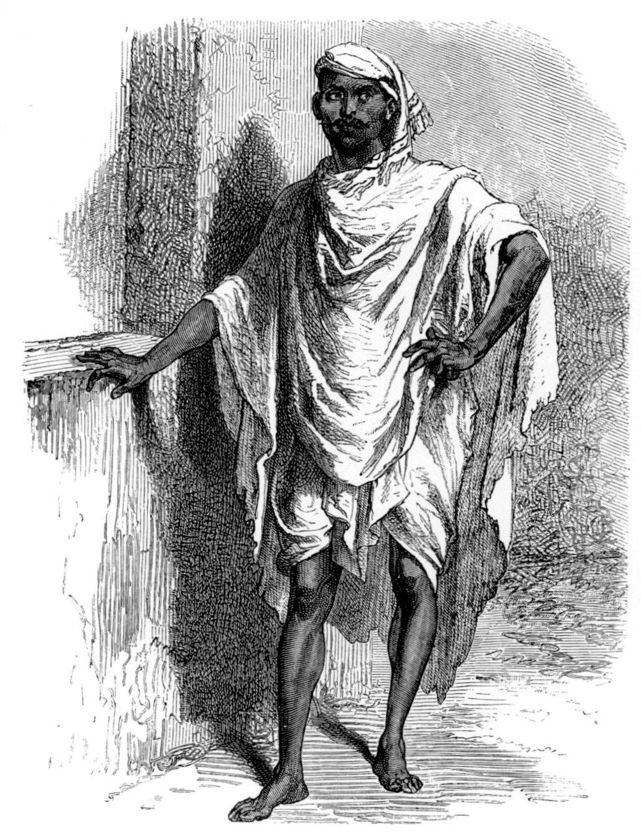

a	Kisemene woman pounding grain, 1875	Kisemene-Frau beim Mahlen von Getreide, 1875	Donna kisemene mentre frantuma cereali, 1875	Femme kisemène pilant du grain, 1875	Mujer kisemene moliendo grano, 1875
b	Man from the Tanzania coast, 1875	Mann von der Küsten Tansanias, 1875	Uomo della costa della Tanzania, 1875	Homme de la côte tanzanienne, 1875	Hombre de la costa de Tanzania, 1875
c	Ousagara man, 1875	Ousgara, 1875	Uomo di Ousagara, 1875	Homme ousagara, 1875	Hombre usagara, 1875
d	Young man from around Lake Tanganyika, 1875	Junger Mann aus der Umgebung des Tanganjika-Sees, 1875	Giovane dei dintorni del Lago Tanganica, 1875	Jeune homme des alentours du lac Tanganyika, 1875	Joven de la región del lago Tanganica, 1875

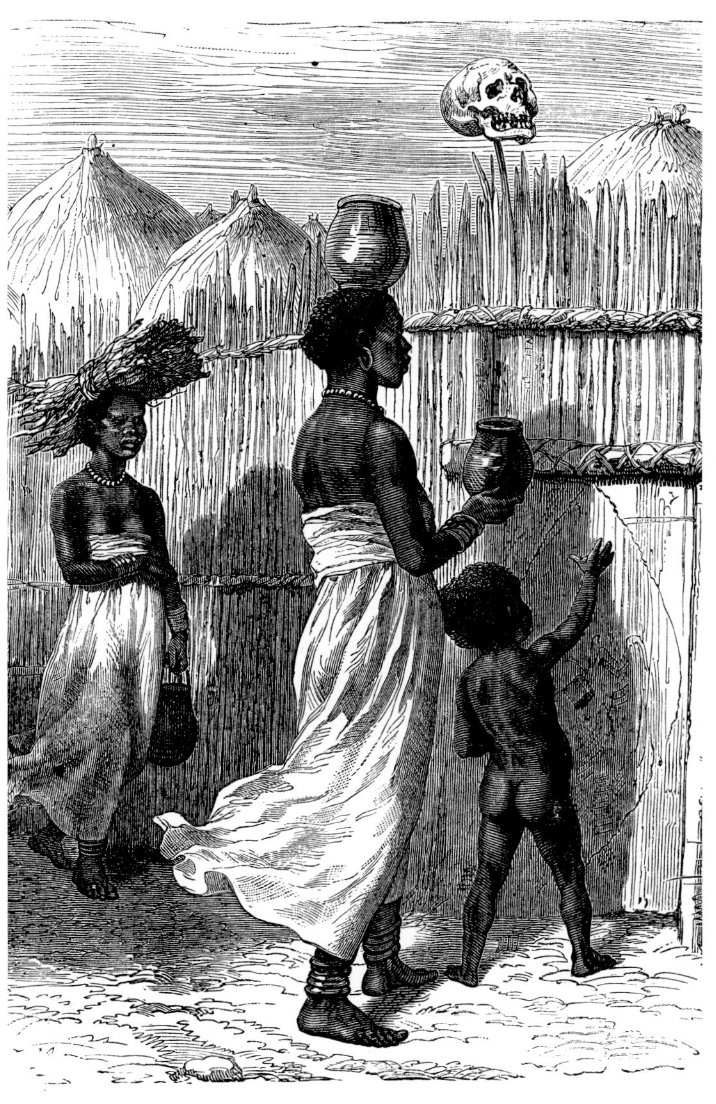

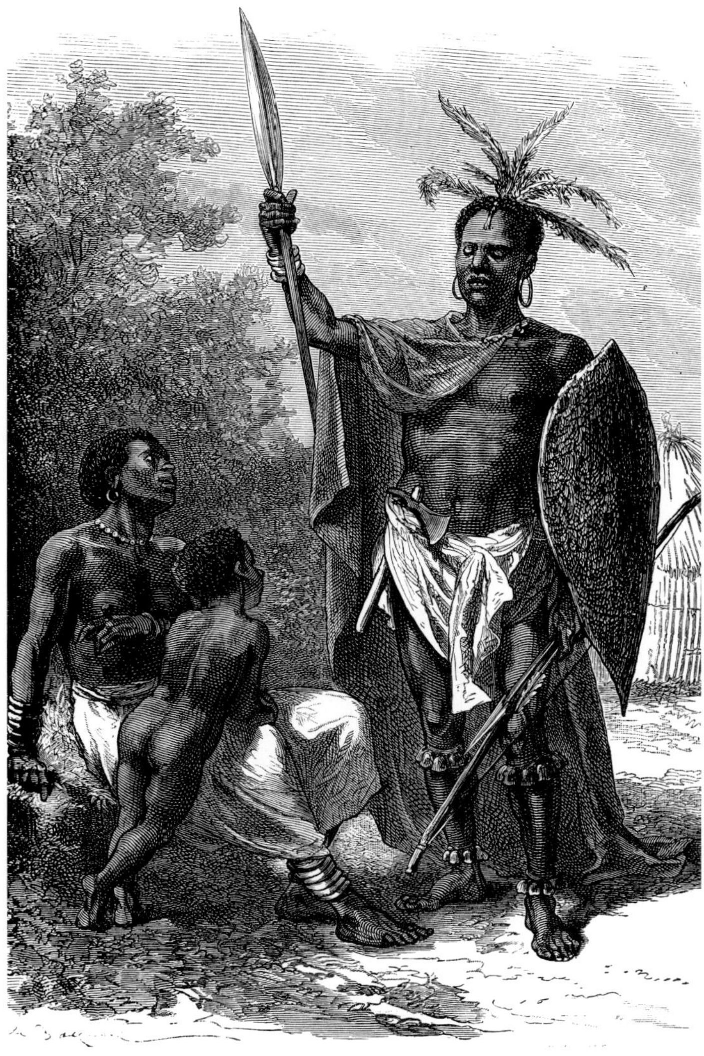

a	Vouakouere village, 1875	Vouakouere-Dorf, 1875	Villaggio vouakouere, 1875	Village de Vouakouere, 1875	Pueblo vouakouere, 1875
b	Ugogo family, 1875	Ugogo-Familie, 1875	Famiglia ugogo, 1875	Famille Ugogo, 1875	Familia ugogo, 1875

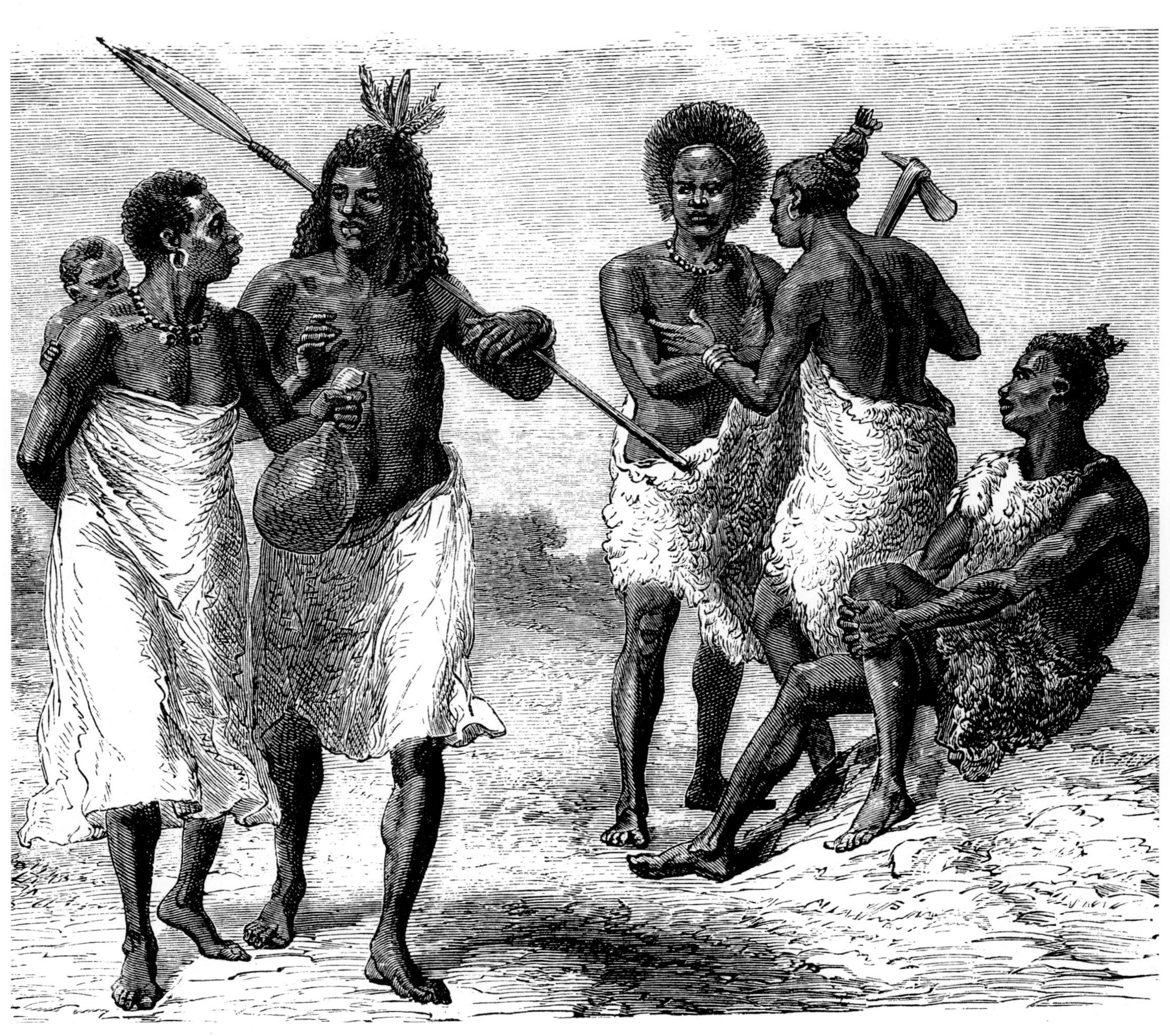

Villagers in Tanzania, 1875

Dorf in Tansania, 1875

Abitanti di un villaggio in Tanzania, 1875

Villageois de Tanzanie, 1875

Aldeanos tanzanos, 1875

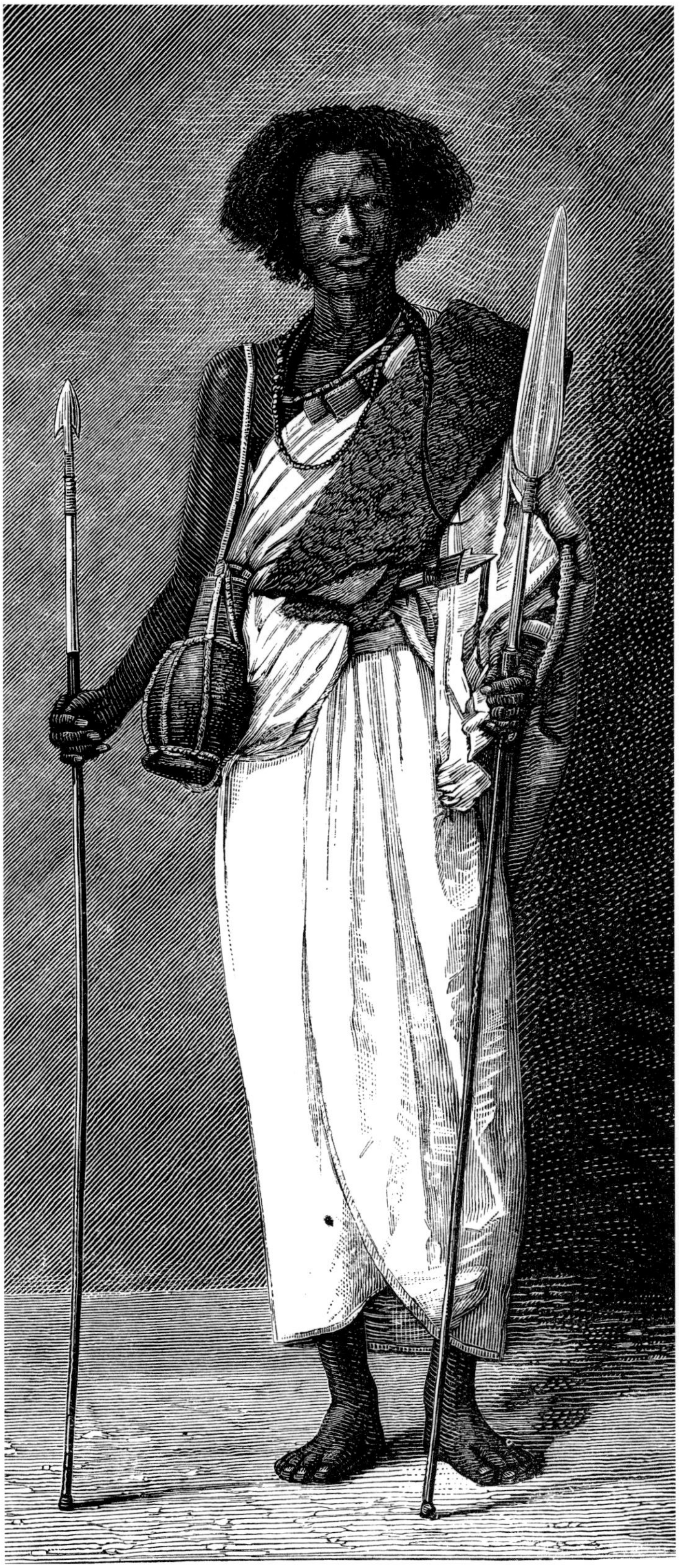

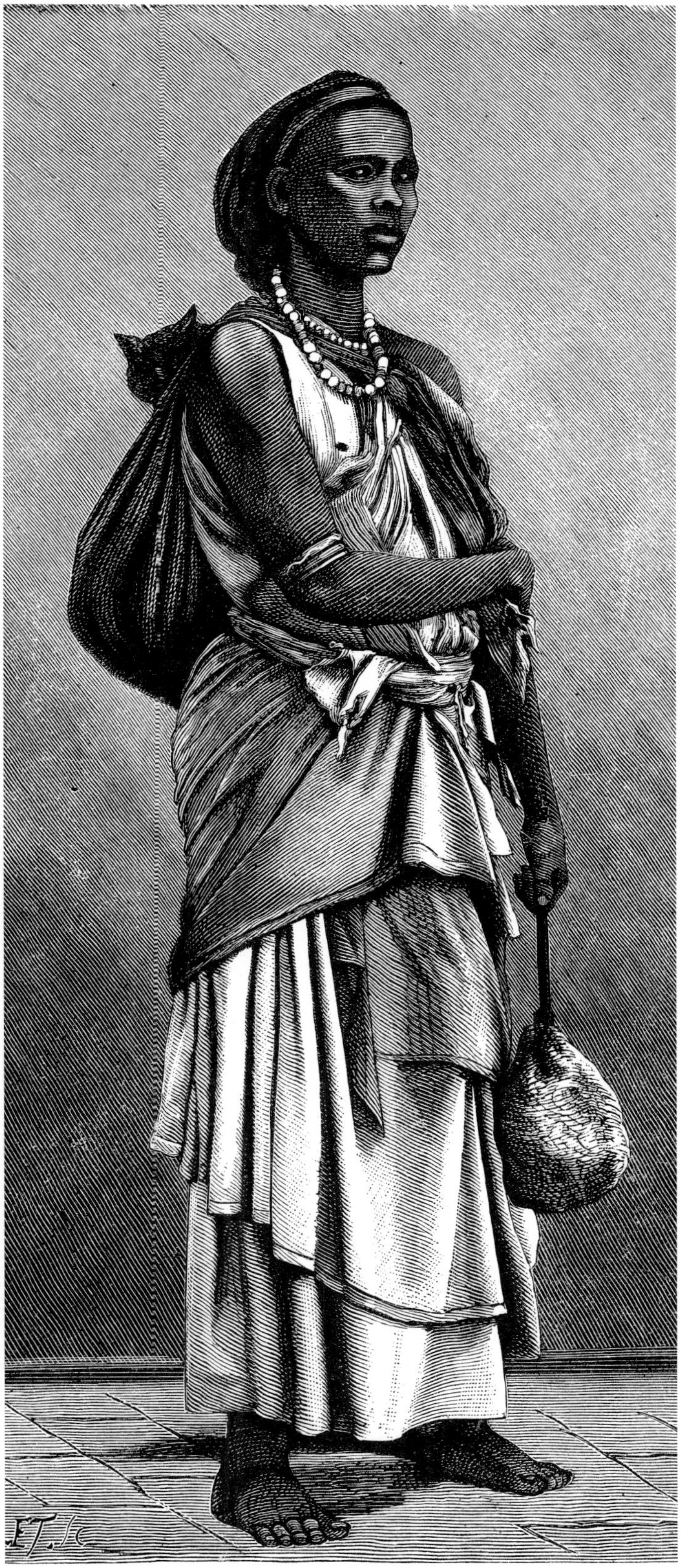

a	Somali warrior, c. 1890	Somali-Krieger, um 1890	Guerriero somalo, ca. 1890	Guerrier somalien, vers 1890	Guerrero somalí, alrededor del año 1890
b	Somali lady, c. 1890	Somalische Frau, um 1890	Donna somala, ca. 1890	Somalienne, vers 1890	Mujer somalí, alrededor del año 1890

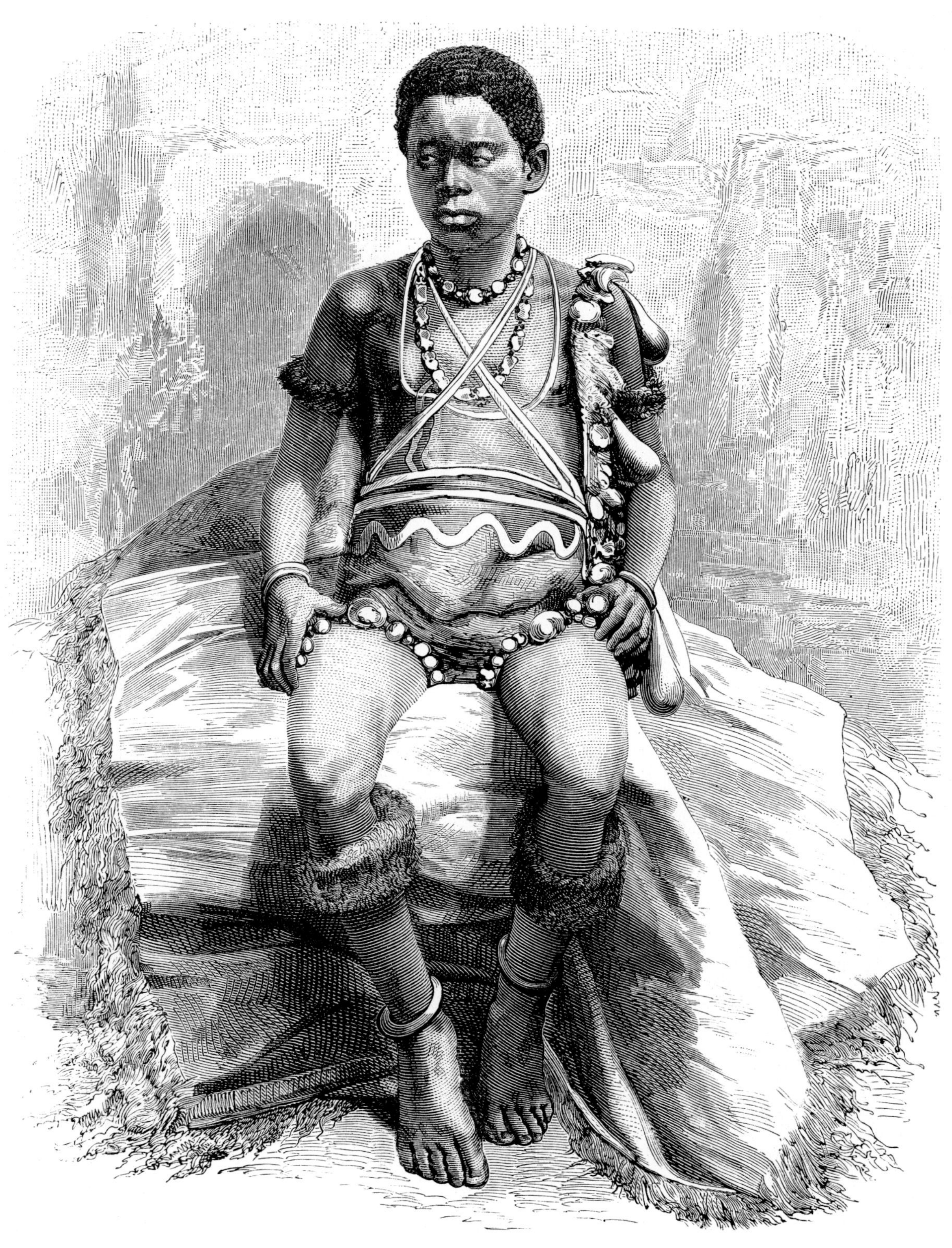

Boy from around Lake Tanganyika, 1880

Junge aus der Umgebung des Tanganjika-Sees, 1880

Ragazzo dei dintorni del Lago Tanganica, 1880

Enfant des alentours du lac Tanganyika, 1880

Muchacho de la región del lago Tanganica, 1880

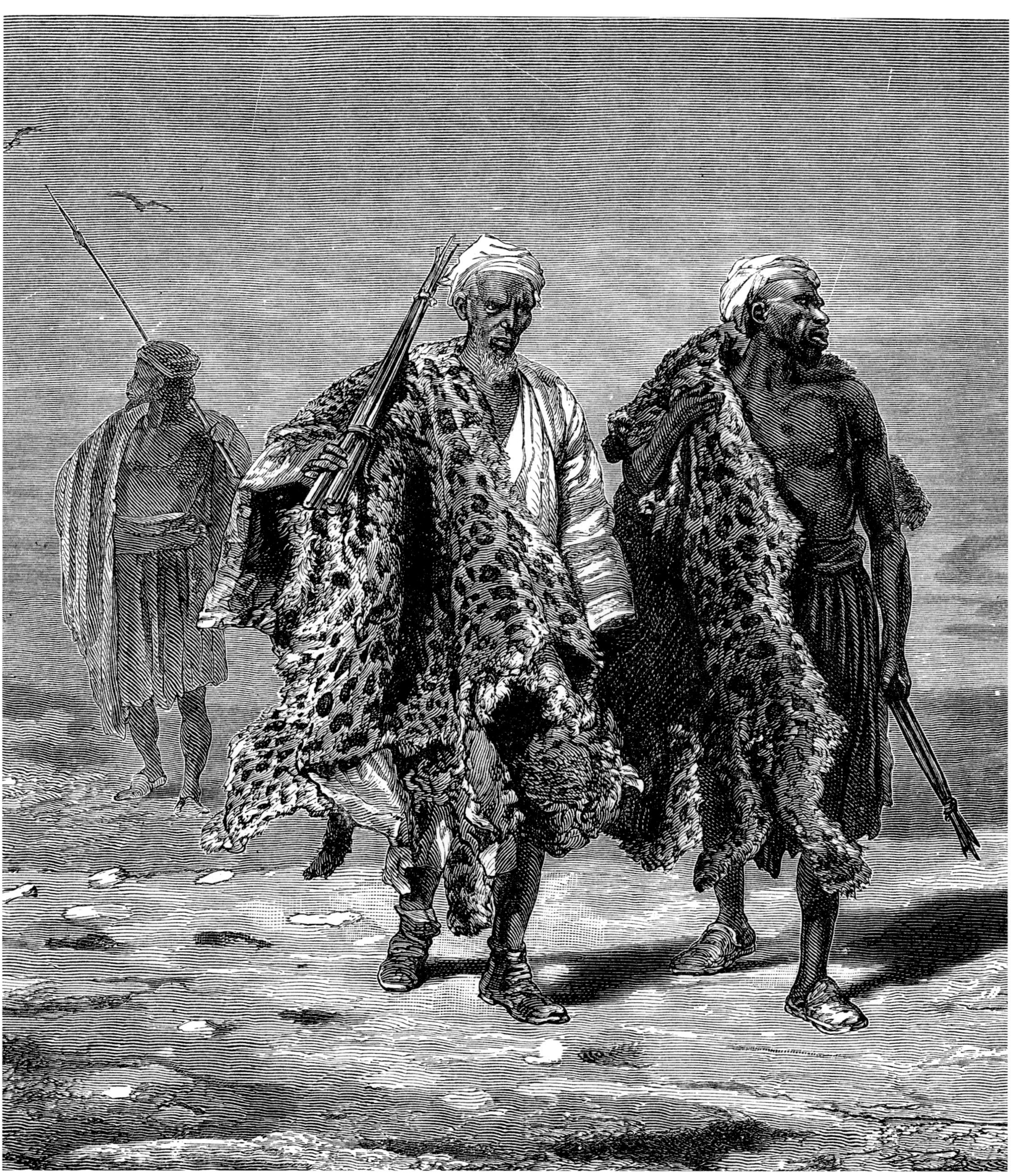

Arab skin traders, c. 1880

Arabische Fellhändler, um 1880

Commercianti di pelli arabi, ca. 1880

Vendeurs de peaux arabes, vers 1880

Comerciantes de pieles árabes, hacia 1880

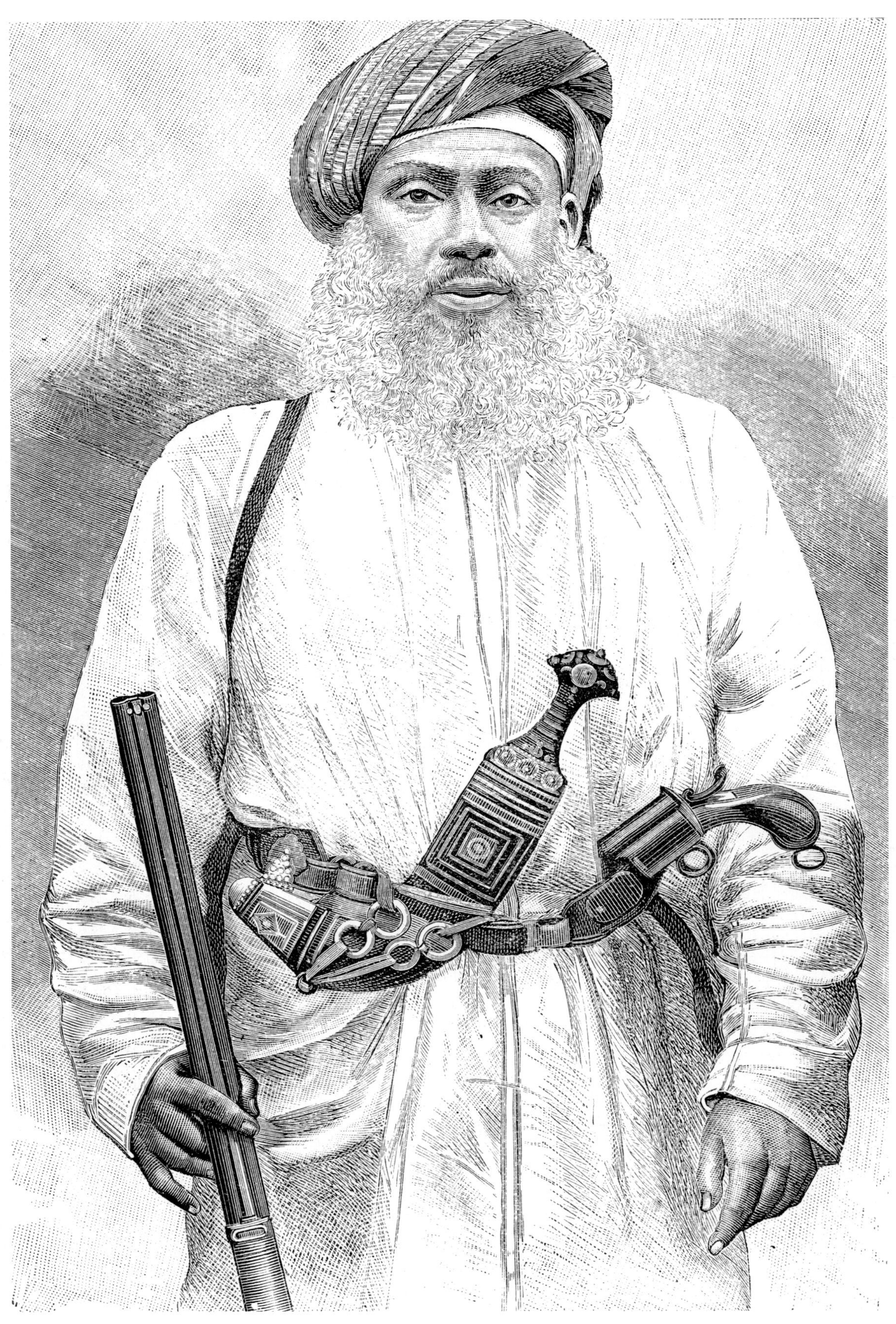

Arab Headman, 1888

Arabischer Anführer, 1888

Capo arabo, 1888

Chef arabe, 1888

Jefe árabe, 1888

Zanzibar

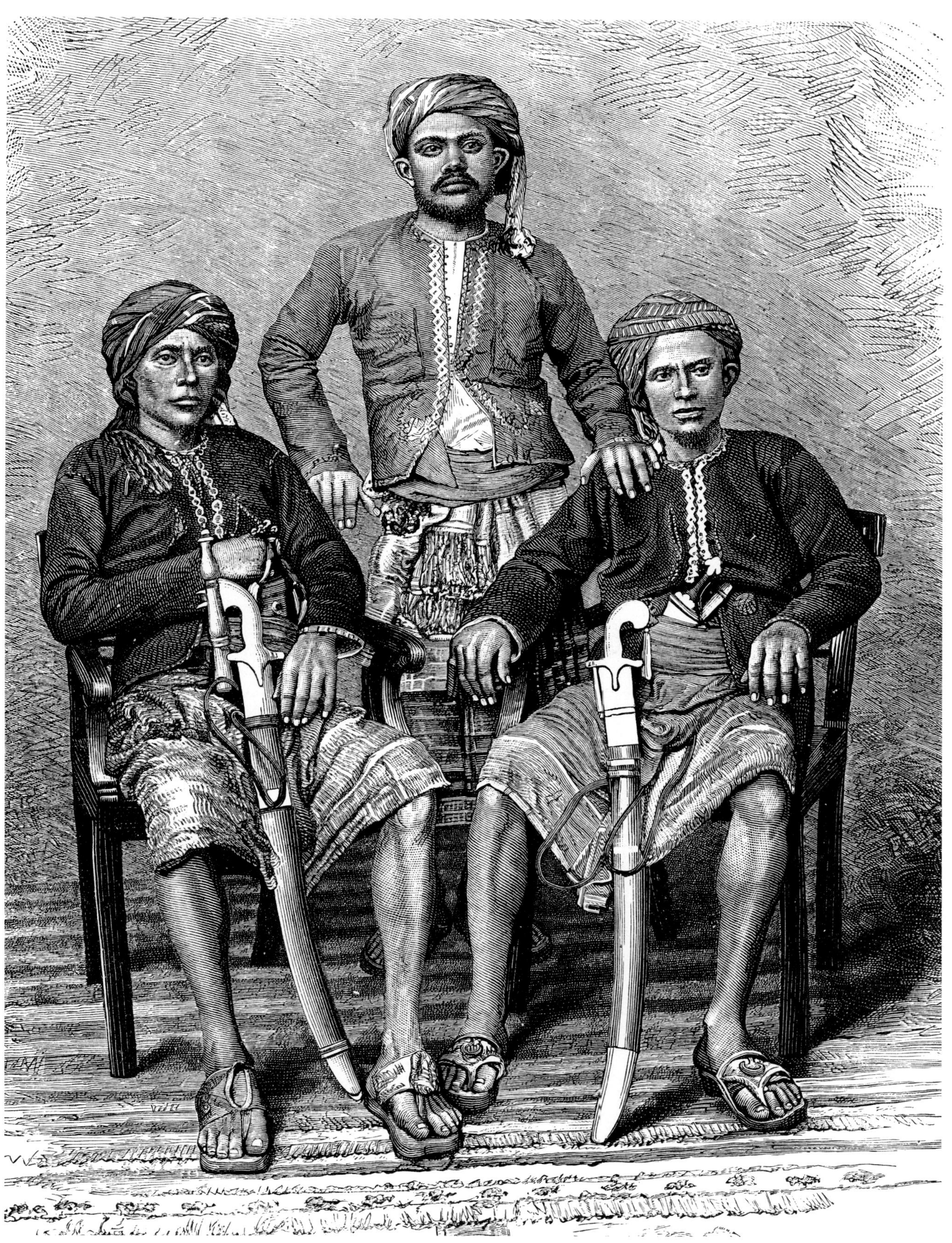

Arab Headmen, Tanzania Coast, 1889

Arabische Anführer, Tansania, Küste, 1889

Capi arabi, Costa della Tanzania, 1889

Chefs arabes, côte Tanzanienne, 1889

Jefes árabes de la costa de Tanzania, 1889

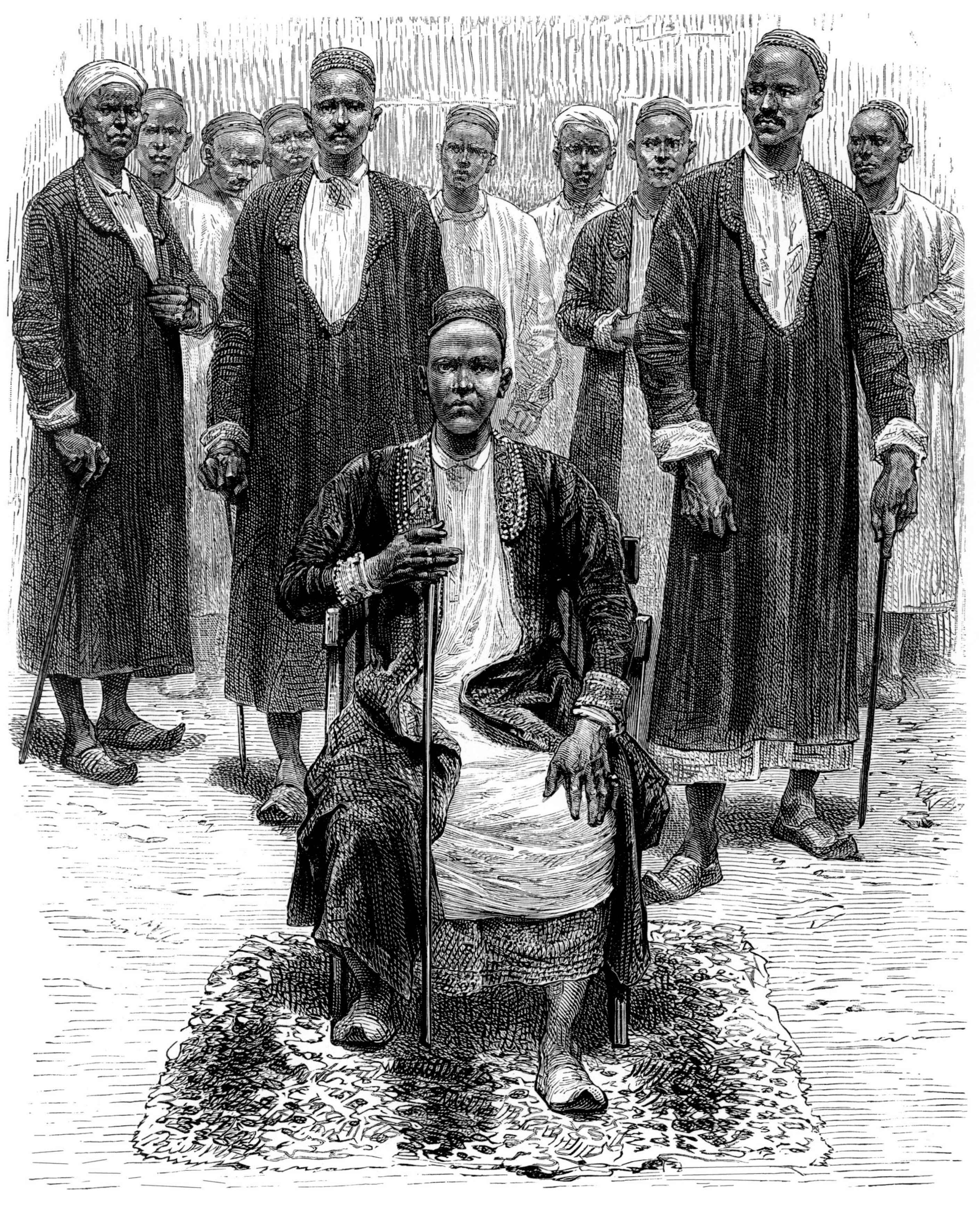

The King of Uganda and his Ministers, 1879

Der König von Uganda und seine Minister, 1879

Il Re di Uganda e i suoi ministri, 1879

Le Roi d'Ouganda et ses ministres, 1879

El rey de Uganda y sus ministros, 1879

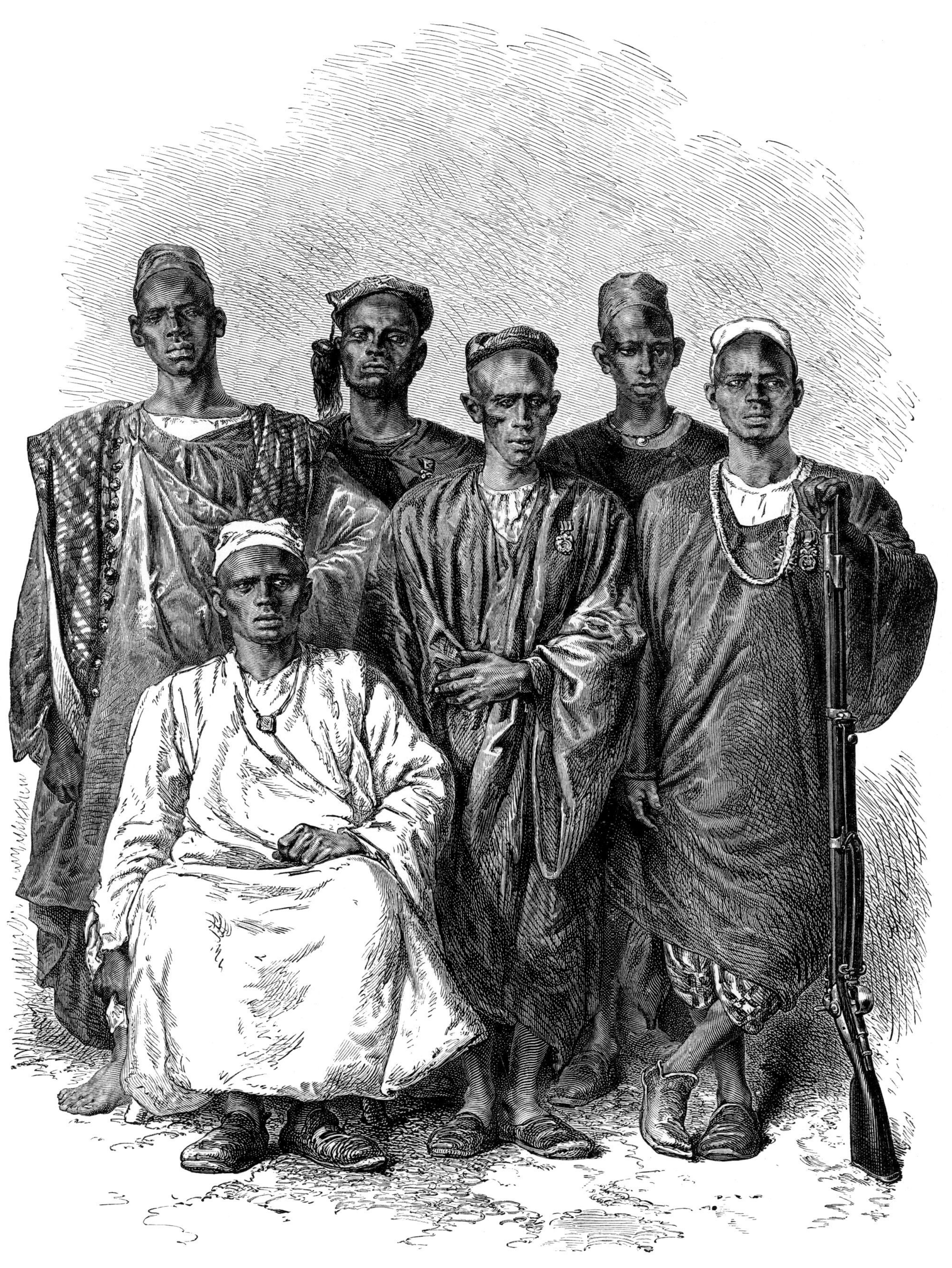

Muslim chiefs, Somalia, c. 1890

Moslemische Häuptlinge, Somalia, um 1890

Capi musulmani, Somalia, ca. 1890

Chefs musulmans, Somalie, vers 1890

Jefes musulmanes, Somalia, c 1890

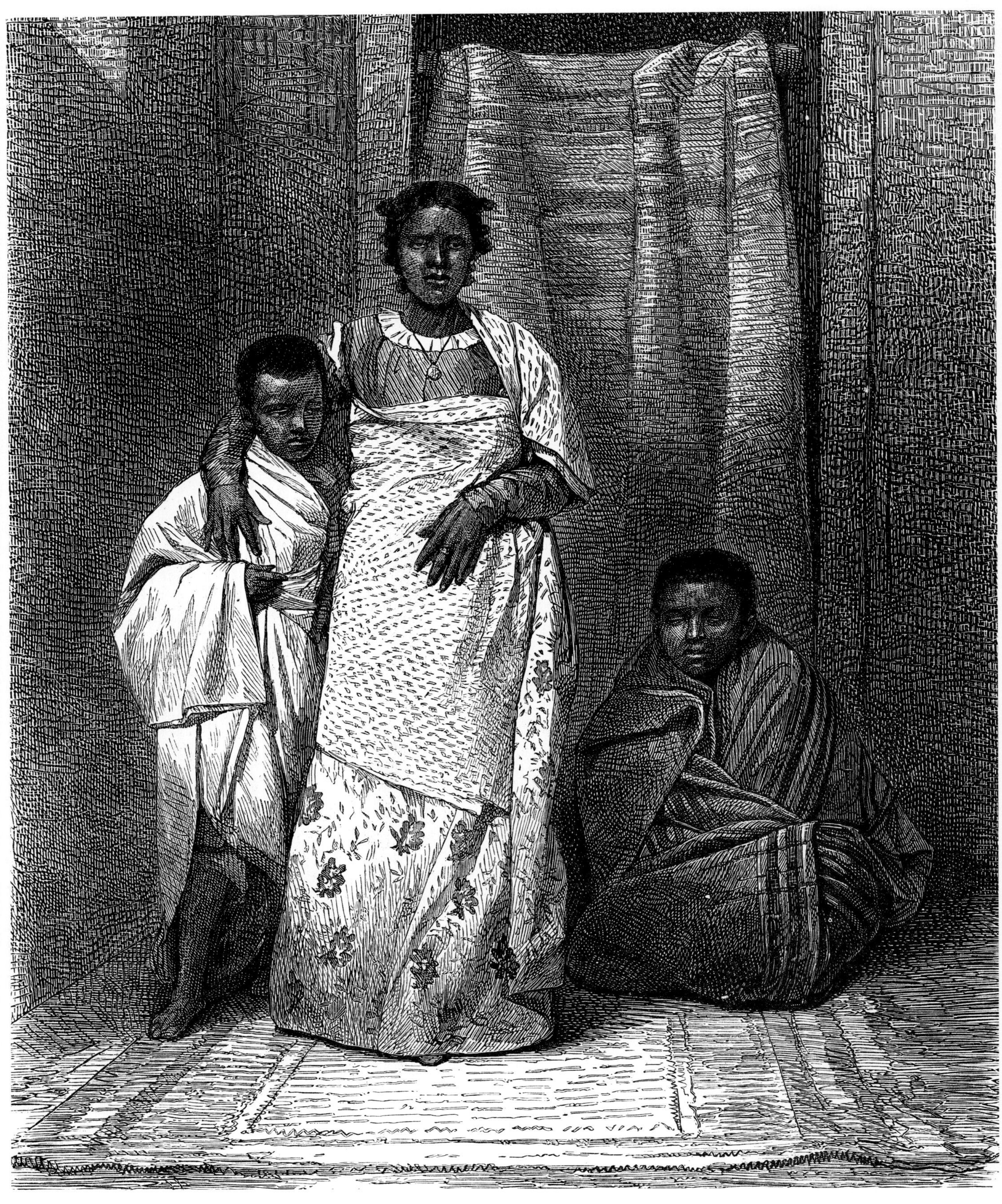

Malagassy woman and children, c. 1880

Madagassin mit Kind, um 1880

Donna e bambini malagasci, ca. 1880

Femme et enfant malgaches, vers 1880

Mujer y niños malgaches, alrededor del año 1880

Madagascar

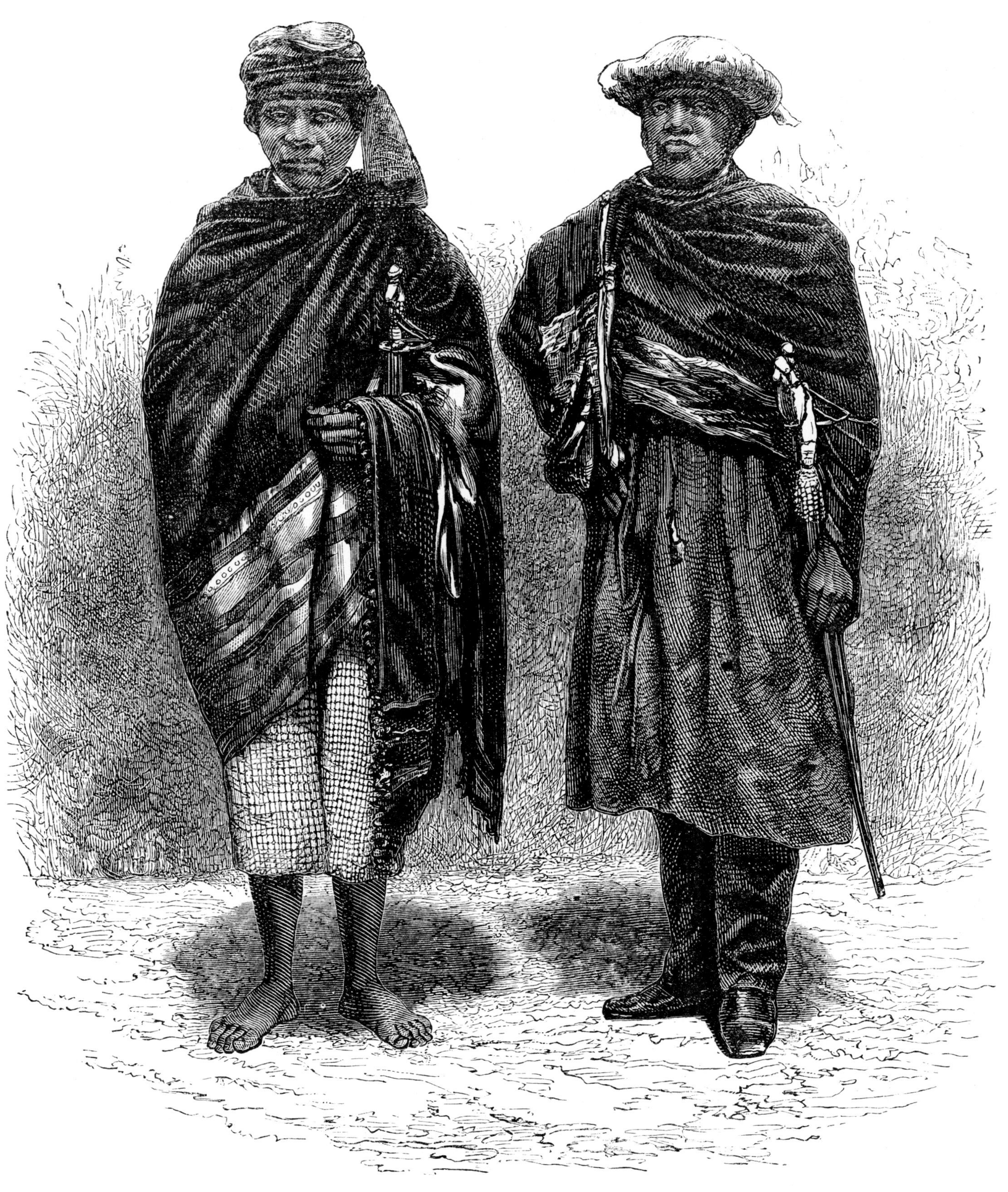

Malagassy officials, c. 1880

Madagassische Offiziere, um 1880

Ufficiali malagasci, ca. 1880

Fonctionnaires malgaches, vers 1880

Funcionarios malgaches, alrededor del año 1880

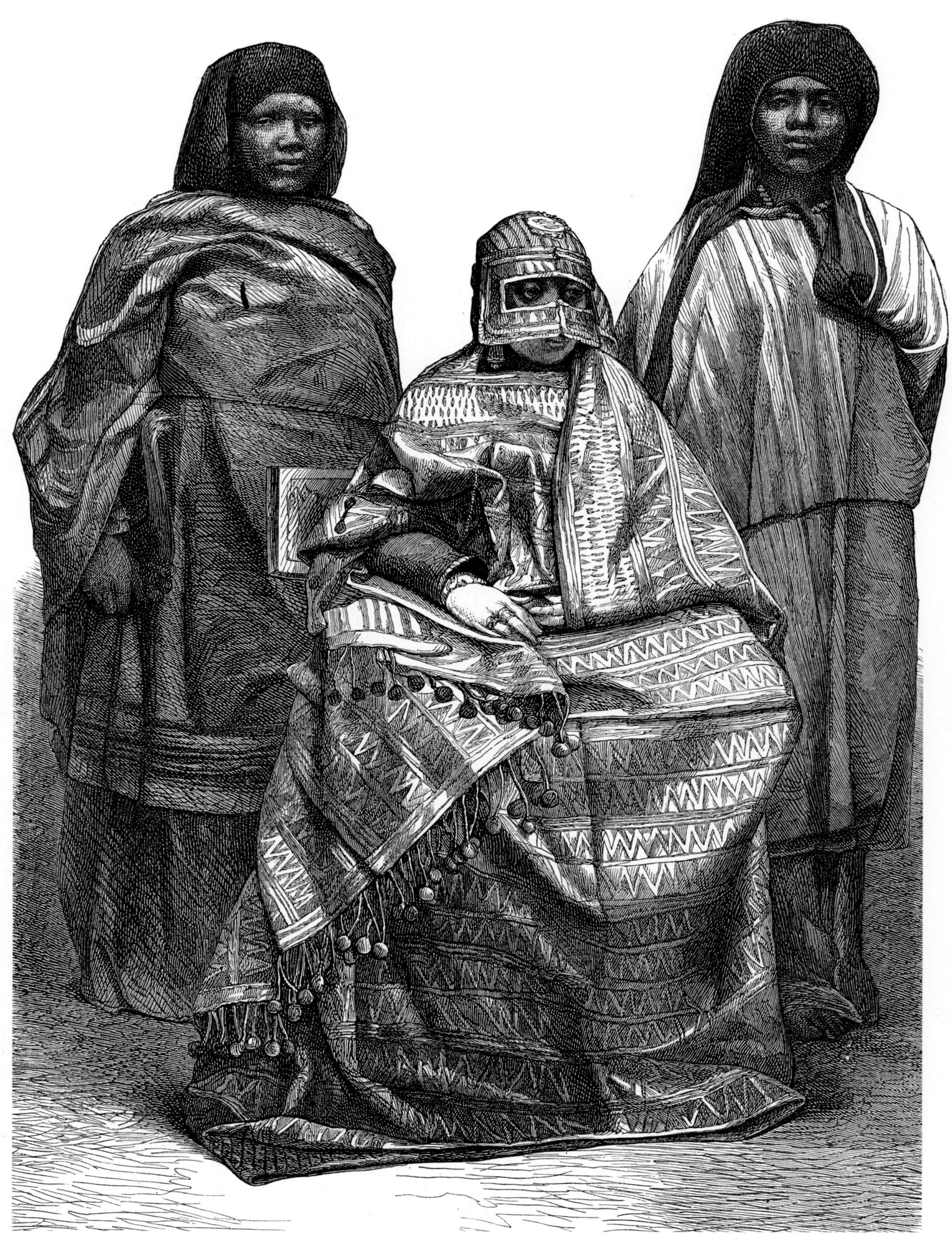

Queen Moheli of Madagascar, c. 1875

Königin Moheli von Madagaskar, um 1875

Regina Moheli del Madagascar, ca. 1875

Reine Moheli de Madagascar, vers 1875

Reina Moheli, Madagascar, hacia 1875

Madagascar

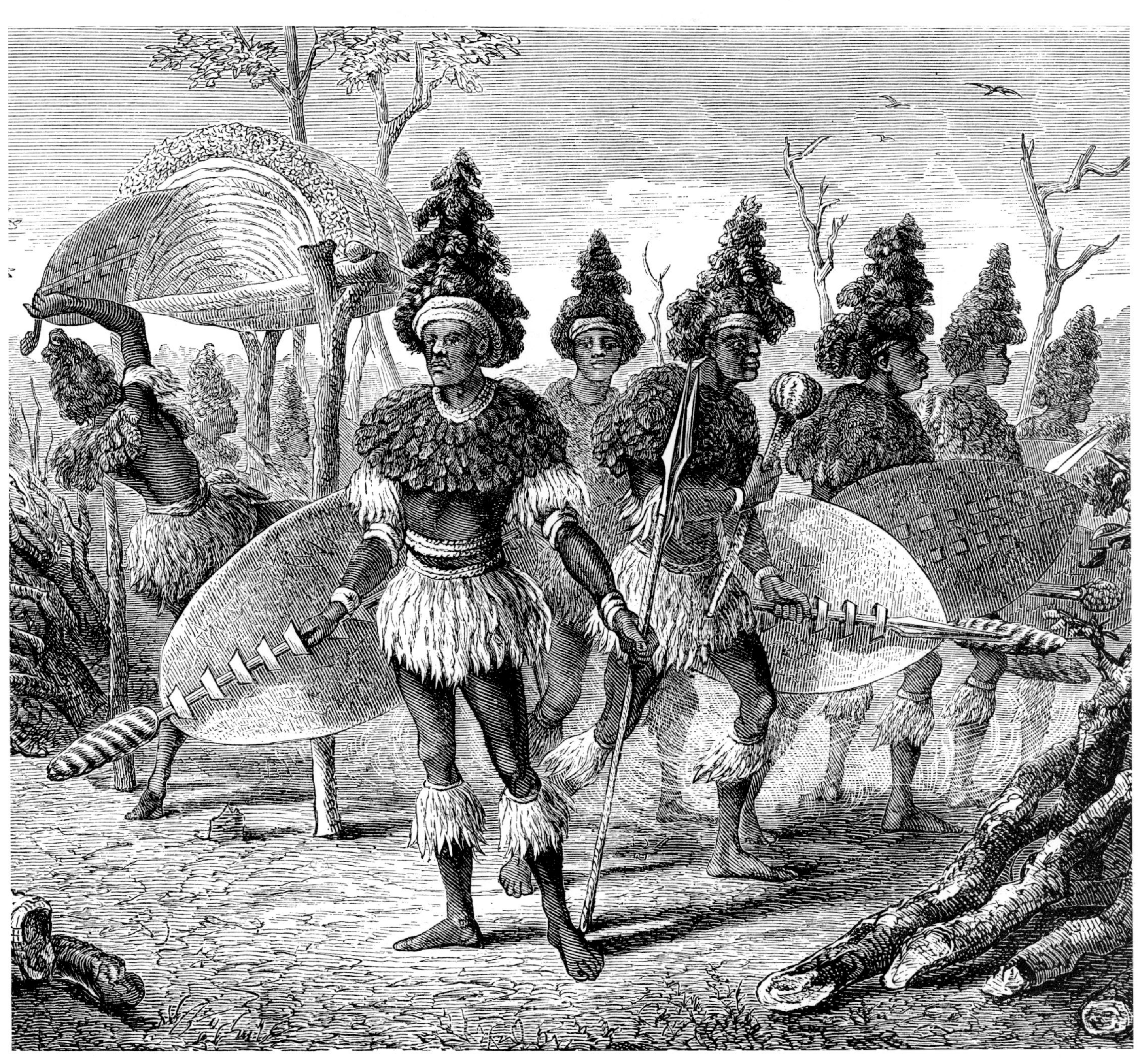

Matabele Warriors in what is present-day Zimbabwe, 1876

Matabele-Krieger im heutigen Simbabwe, 1876

Guerrieri matabele nell'attuale Zimbabwe, 1876

Guerriers matabele (actuel Zimbabwe), 1876

Guerreros matabelé en el actual Zimbabue, 1876

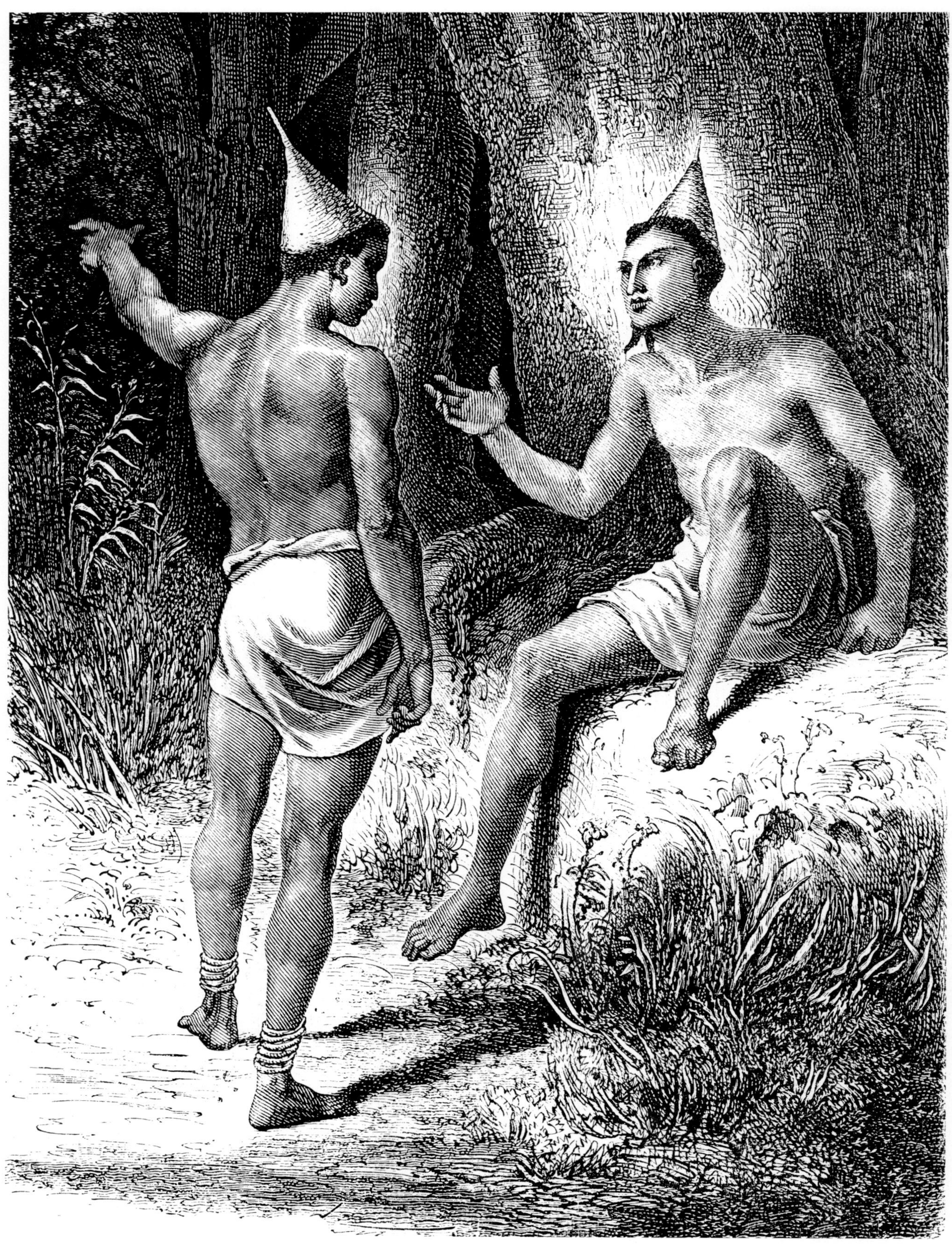

Men from along the Zambesi river, c. 1860

Männer vom Sambesi-Strom, um 1860

Abitanti della zona lungo il fiume Zambesi, ca. 1860

Hommes des rives du fleuve Zambesi, vers 1860

Hombres de la ribera del río Zambeze, hacia el año 1860

Mozambique

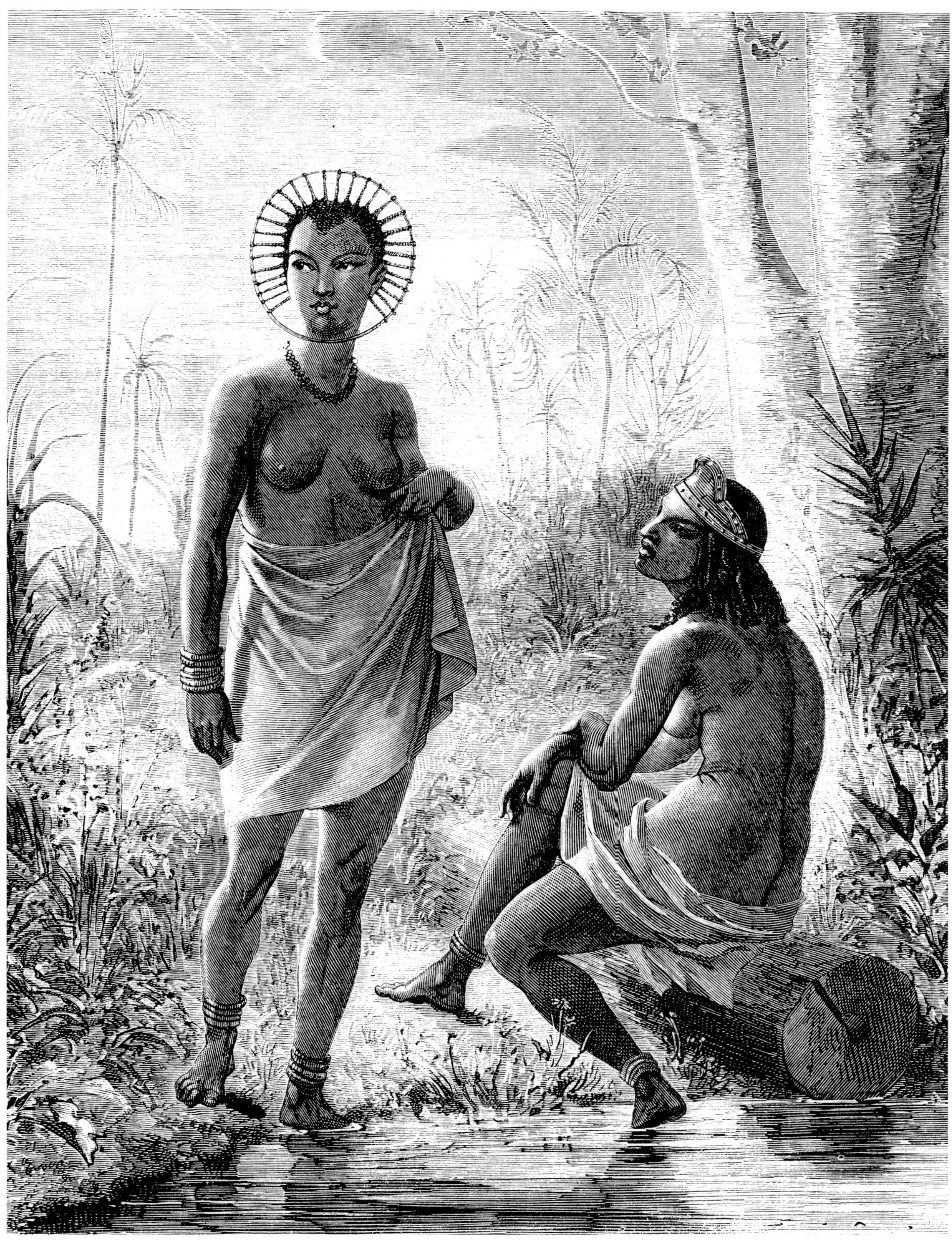

King's consorts, Zambesi river, c. 1860

Die Frauen des Königs, Sambesi-Strom, um 1860

Consorti del re, fiume Zambesi, ca. 1860

Épouses du roi, fleuve Zambesi, vers 1860

Consortes del rey, río Zambeze, hacia 1860

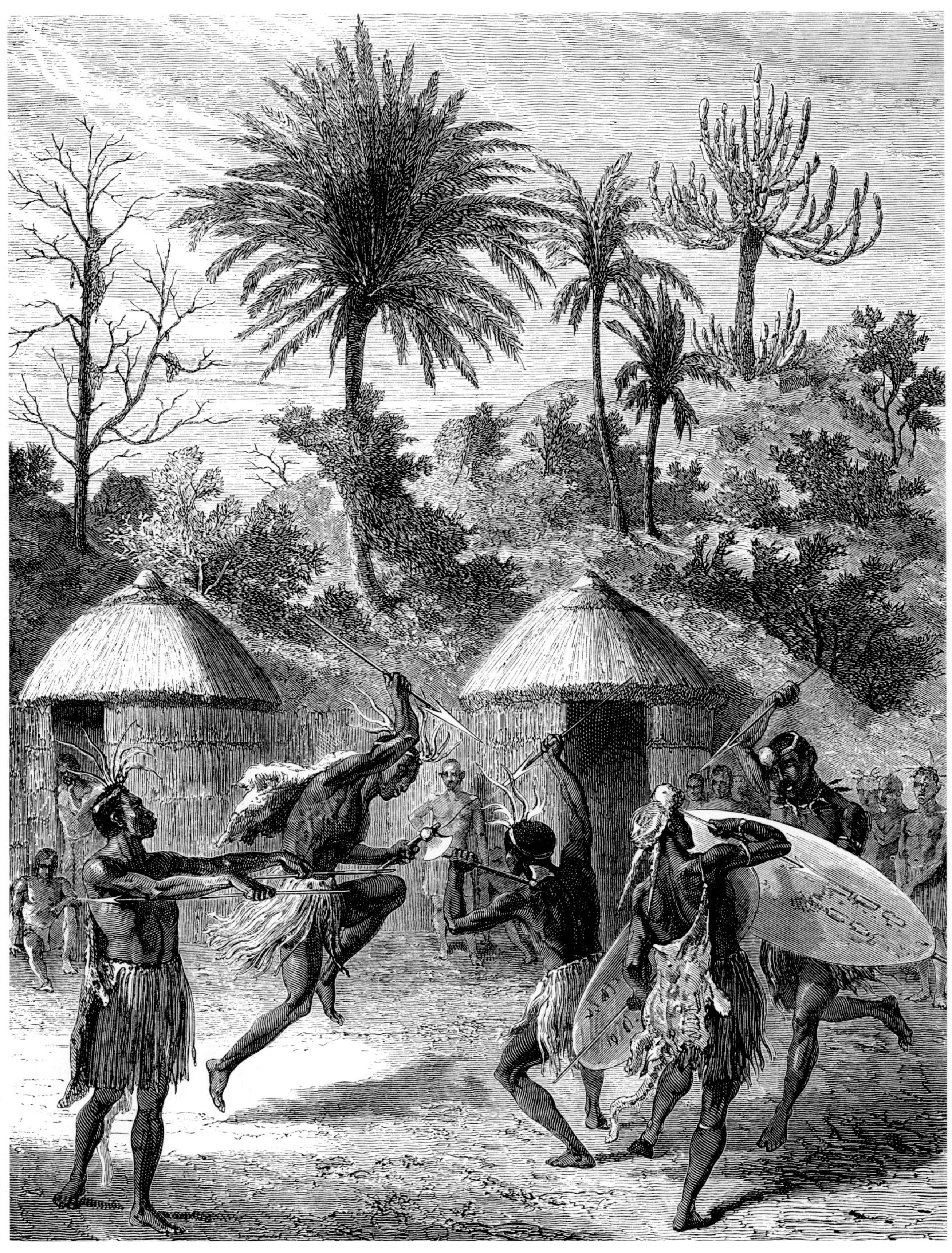

Zulu warriors, c. 1860

Zulu-Krieger, um 1860

Guerrieri zulu, ca. 1860

Guerriers zoulous, vers 1860

Guerreros zulúes, 1860

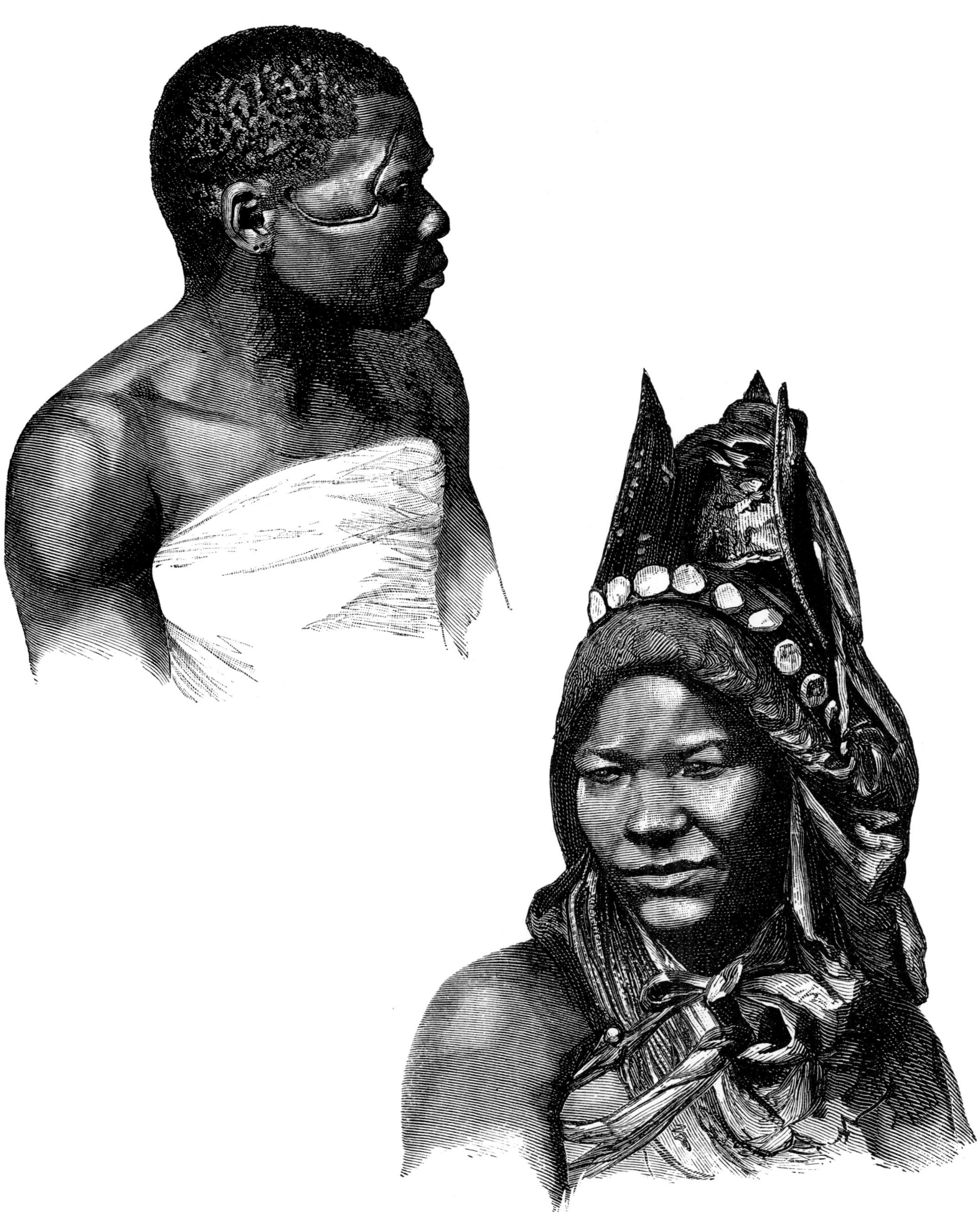

Bantu man and woman, c. 1890

Mann und Frau vom Bantu-Stamm, um 1890

Uomo e donna bantu, ca. 1890

Homme et femme bantous, vers 1890

Hombre y mujer bantúes, alrededor del año 1890

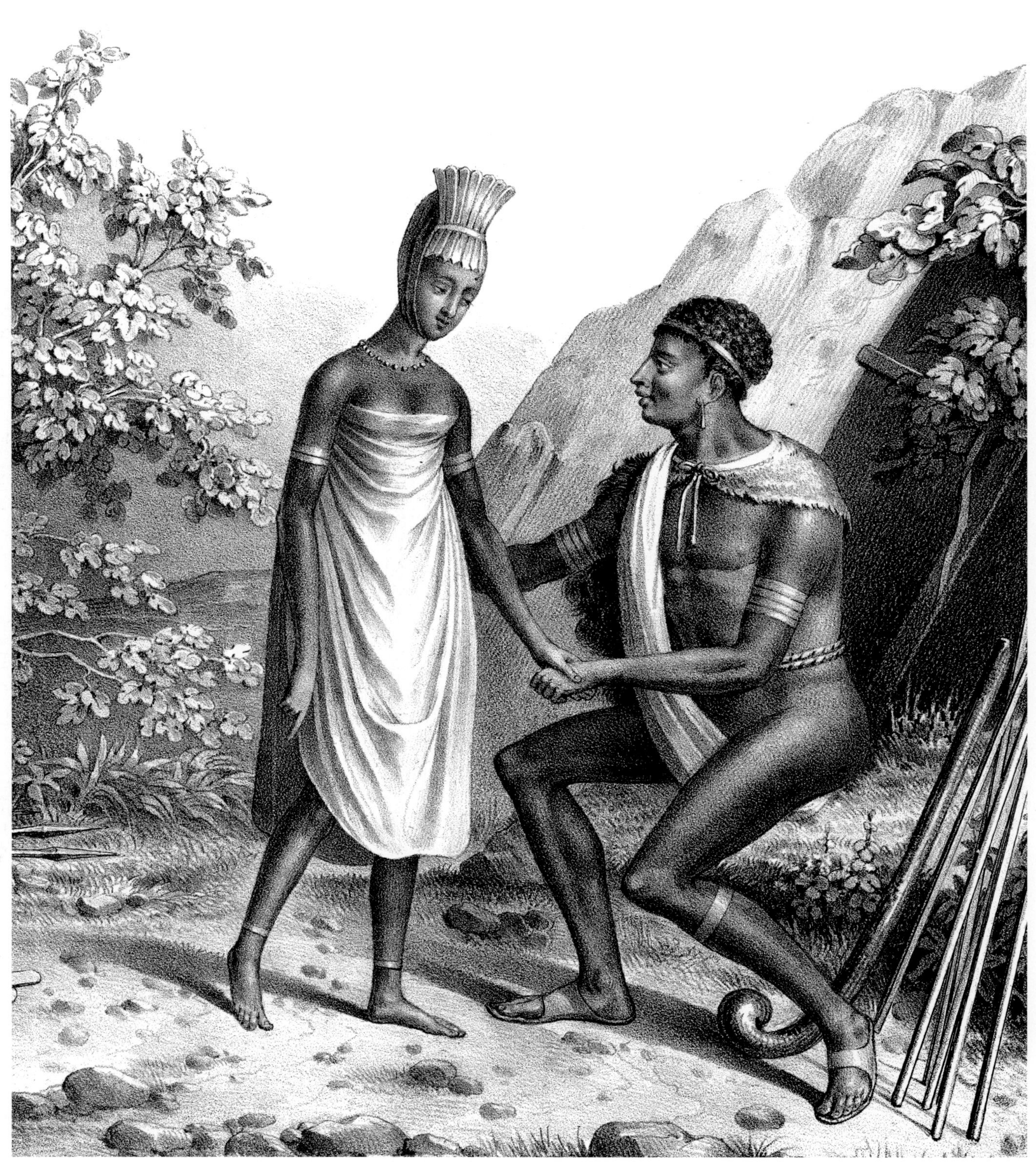

South african warrior and wife, c. 1880

Südafrikanischer Krieger mit Frau, um 1880

Guerriero e moglie sudafricani, ca. 1880

Guerrier sud-africain et sa femme, vers 1880

Guerrero sudafricano y su esposa, hacia 1880

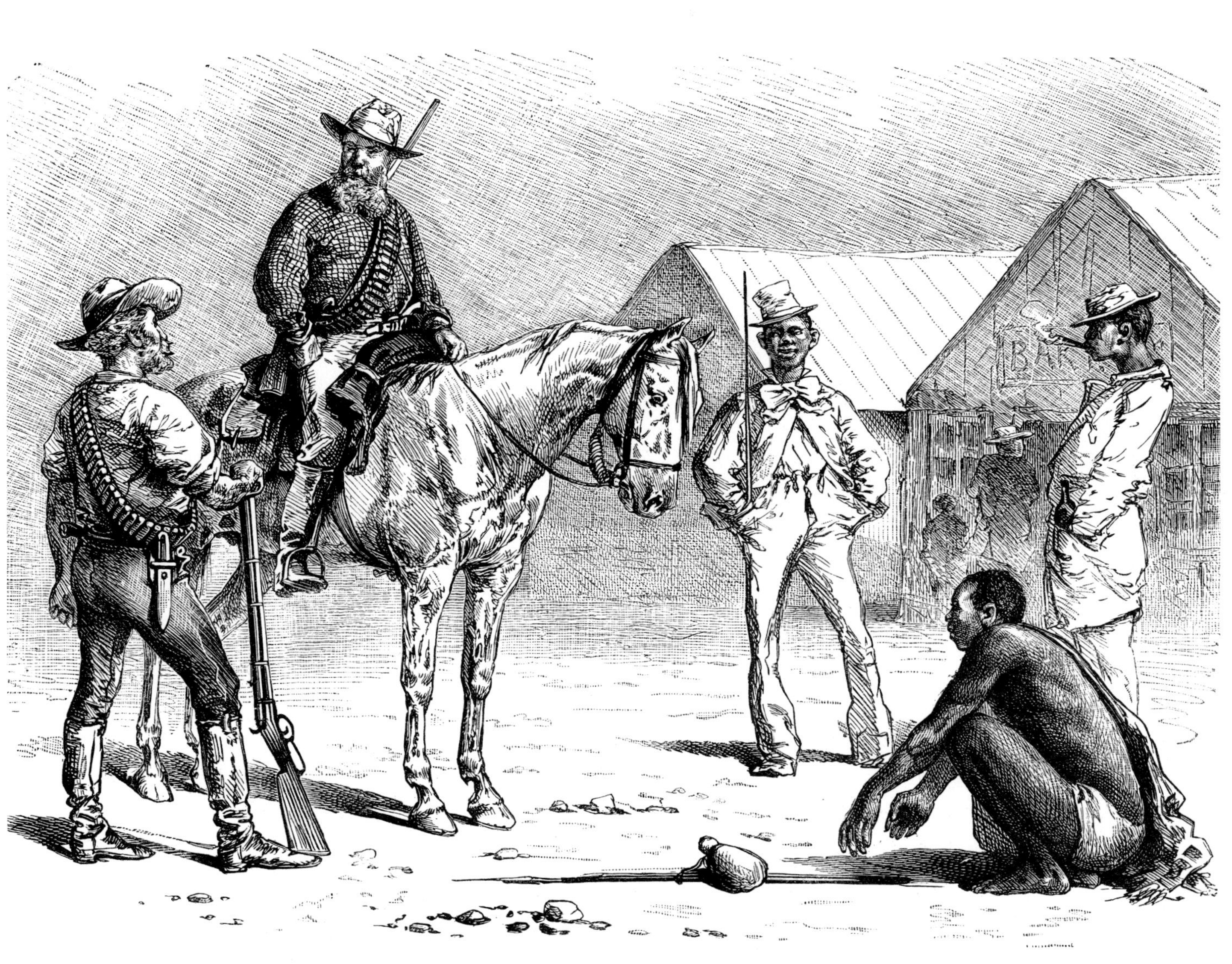

Boer colonists and black south Africans, c. 1860

Buren-Kolonisten und schwarze Südafrikaner, um 1860

Coloni boeri e negri sudafricani, ca. 1860

Colons Boer et noirs sud-africains, vers 1860

Colonos bóers y sudafricanos negros, hacia 1860

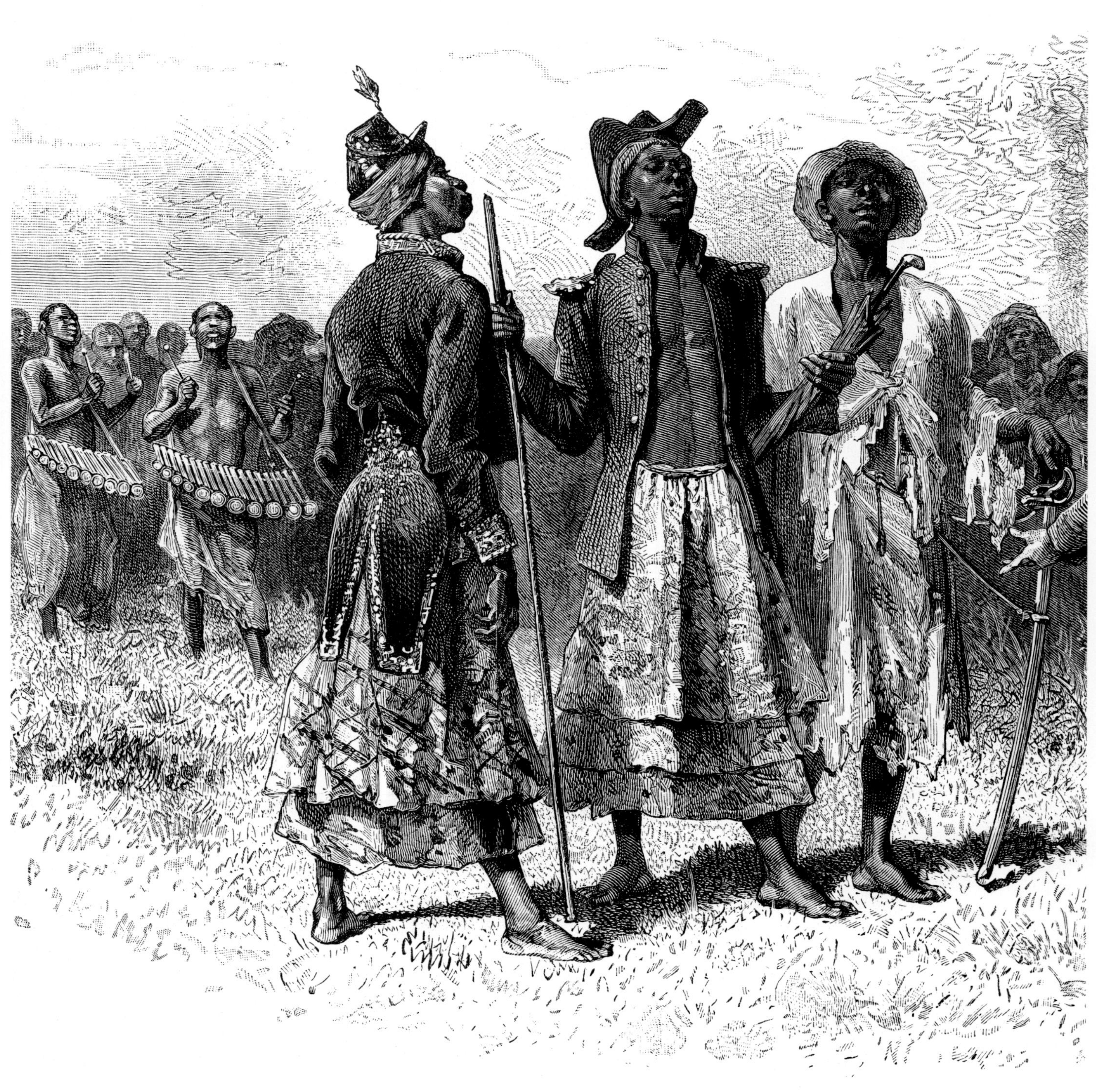

Headmen, central Angola, c. 1860

Anführer, Zentralangola, um 1860

Capitribù, Angola centrale, ca. 1860

Chefs, Angola central, vers 1860

Jefes de Angola central, alrededor del año 1860

Angola

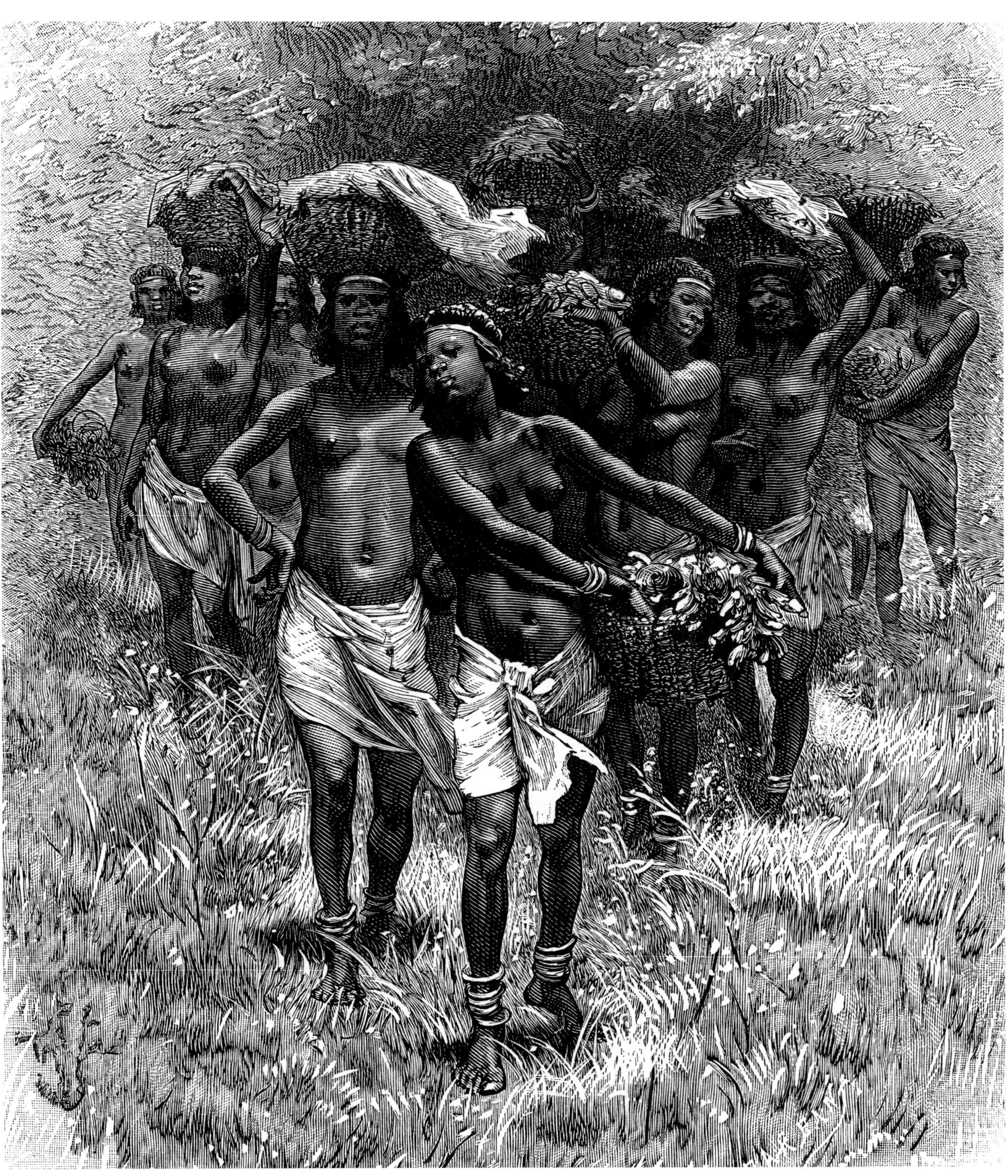

Villagers of Bié, Central Angola, c. 1860

Dörfler aus Bié, Zentralangola, um 1860

Abitanti di Blé, Angola centrale, ca. 1860

Villageois de Bié, Angola central, vers 1860

Aldeanos de Bié, Angola central, hacia 1860

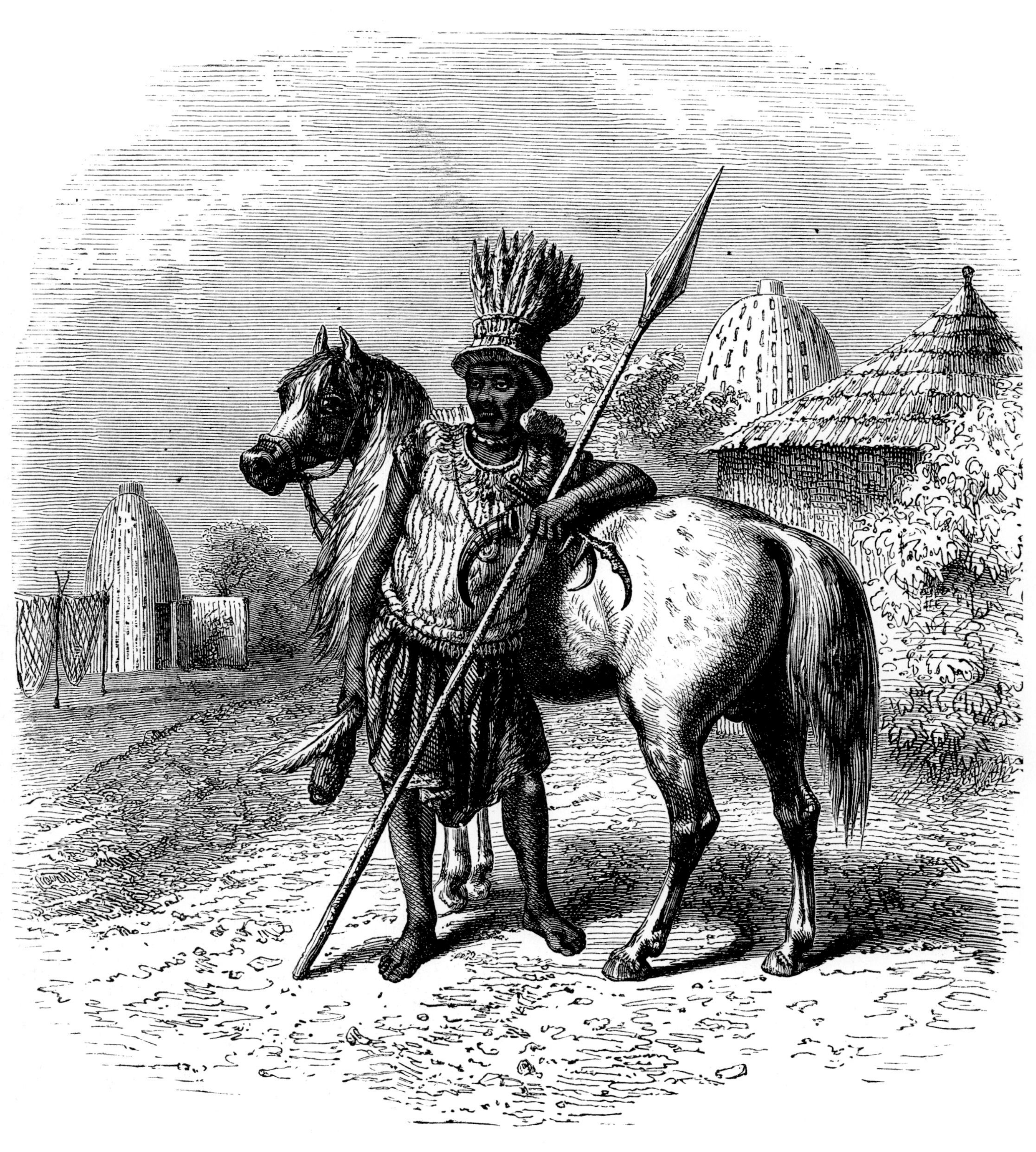

Warrior chief, c. 1880 Kriegshäuptling, um 1880 Guerriero capo, ca. 1880 Chef guerrier, vers 1880 Jefe guerrero, hacia 1880

Congo

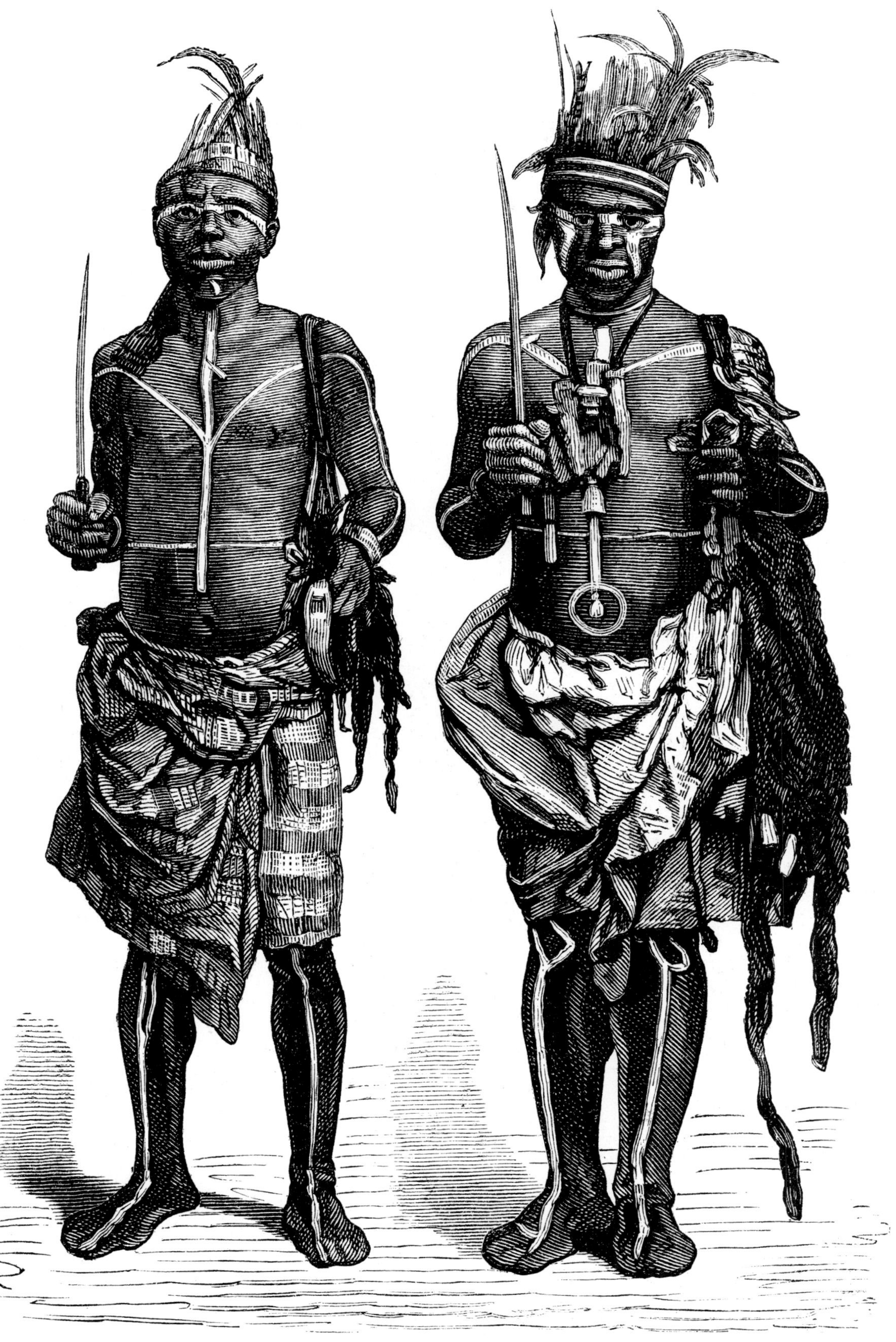

Pirates, c. 1860 Piraten, um 1860 Pirati, ca. 1860 Pirates, vers 1860 Piratas, hacia 1860

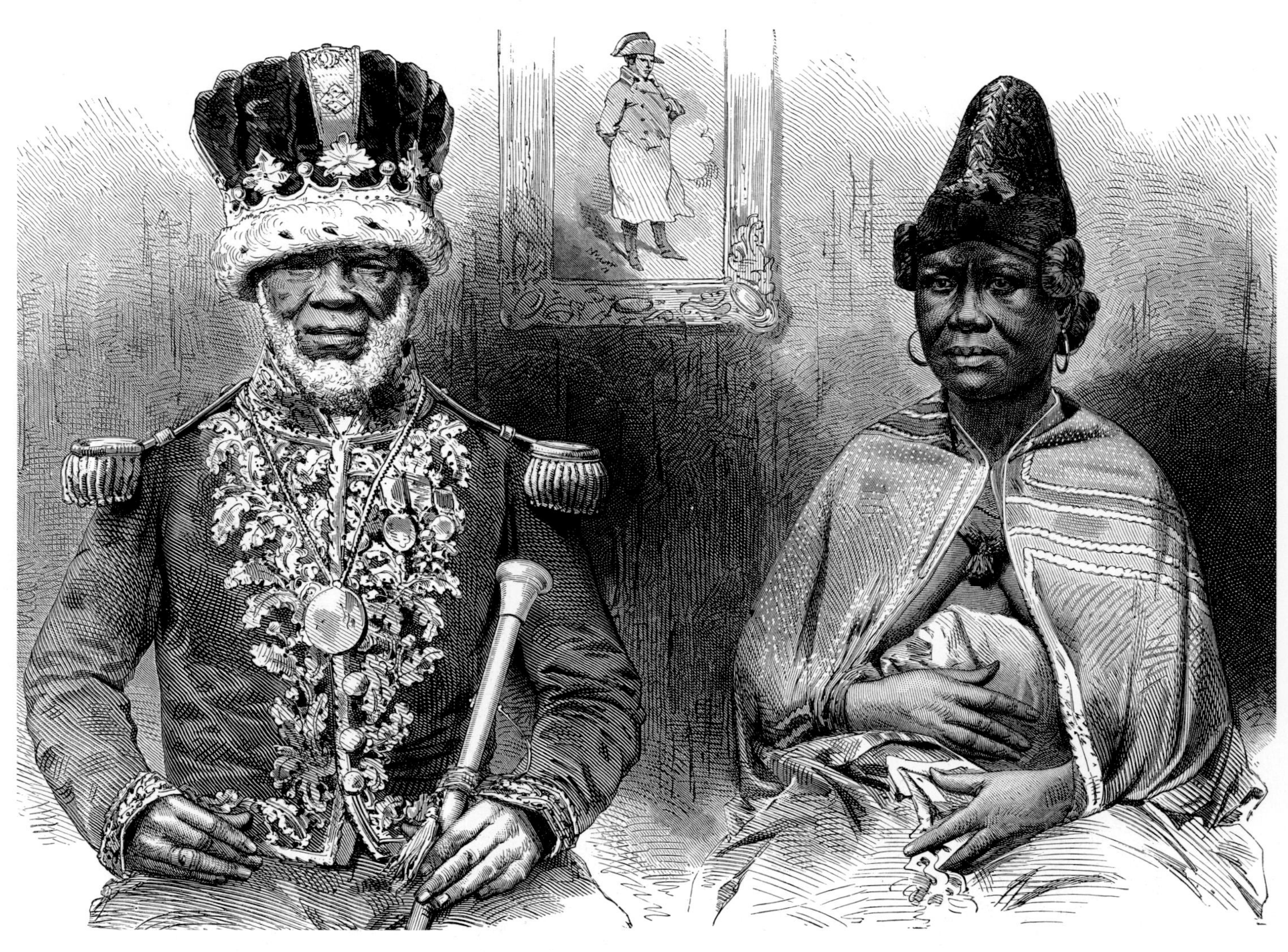

The king of Gabon with his principal wife, c. 1880

Der König des Gabun mit Hauptfrau, um 1880

Il re di Gabon con la sua principale moglie, ca. 1880

Le Roi du Gabon avec sa principale femme, vers 1880

Rey del Gabón y su esposa principal, en 1880

Gabon

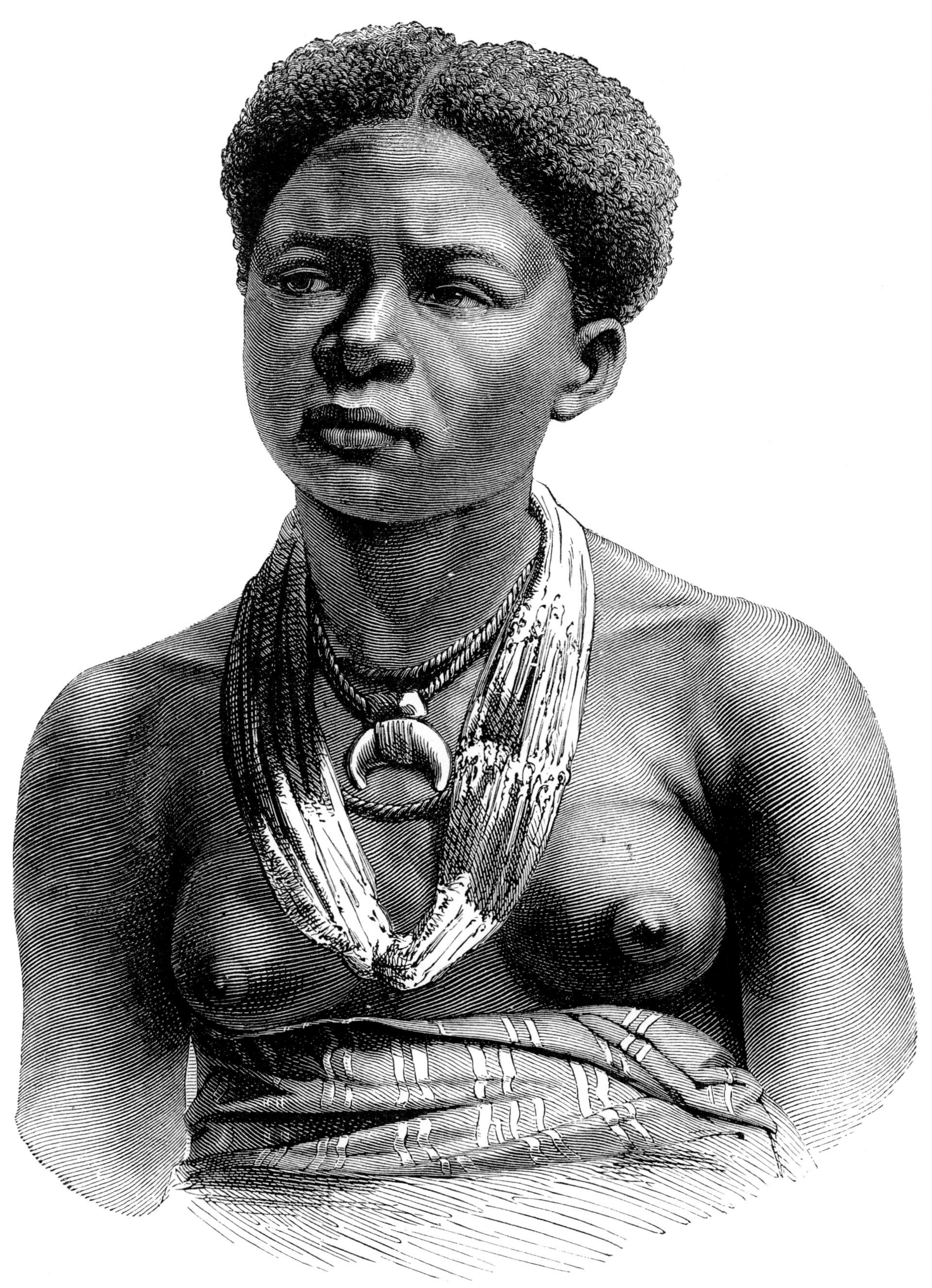

Young girl of Gabon, c. 1870

Junges Mädchen aus dem Gabun, um 1870

Giovane di Gabon, ca. 1870

Jeune gabonaise, vers 1870

Joven gabonesa, alrededor del año 1870

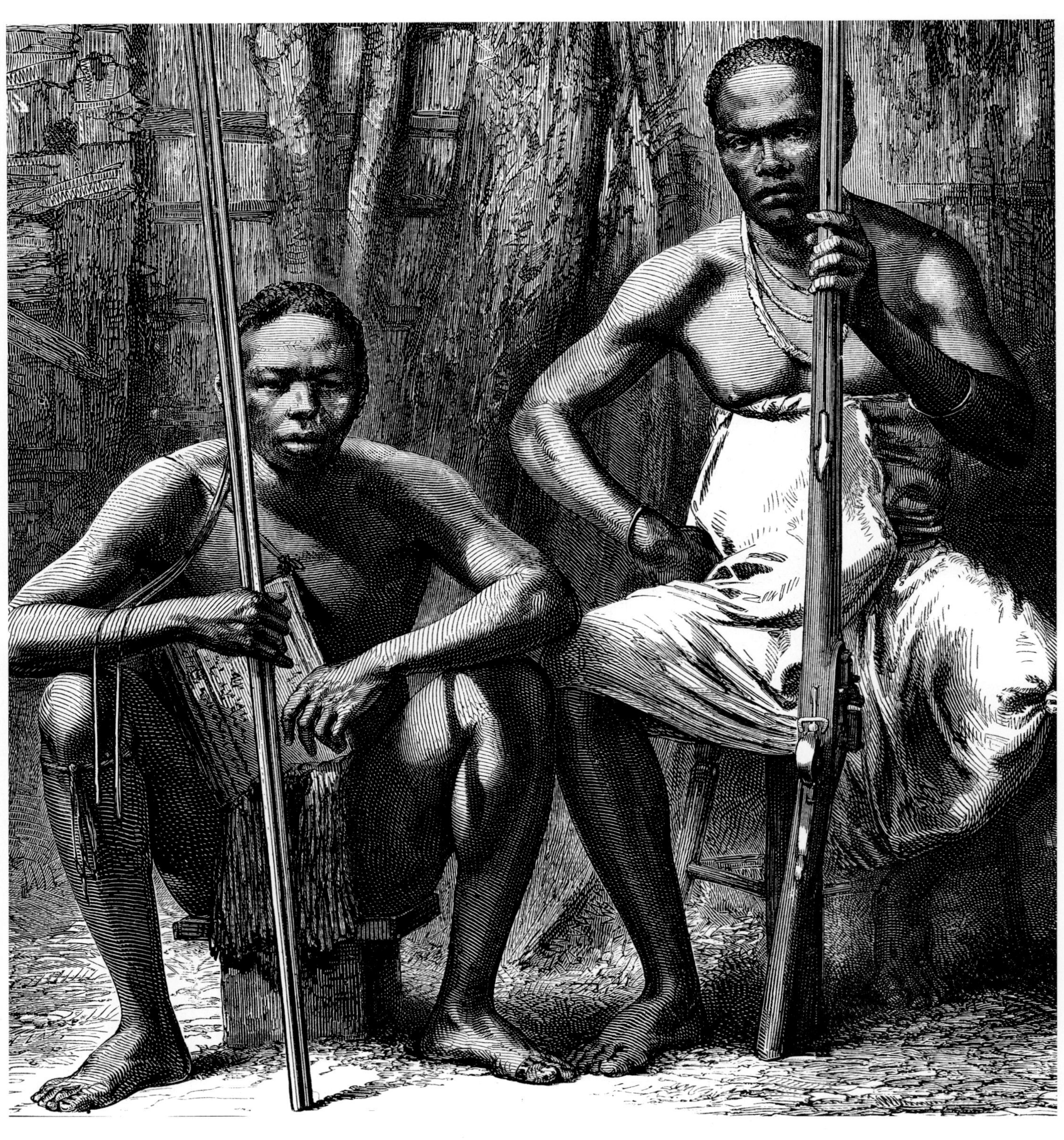

Bakalai warriors, Gabon, 1870

Bakalai-Krieger, Gabun, 1870

Guerrieri bakalai, Gabon, 1870

Guerriers bakalai, Gabon, 1870

Guerreros bakalai del Gabón, 1870

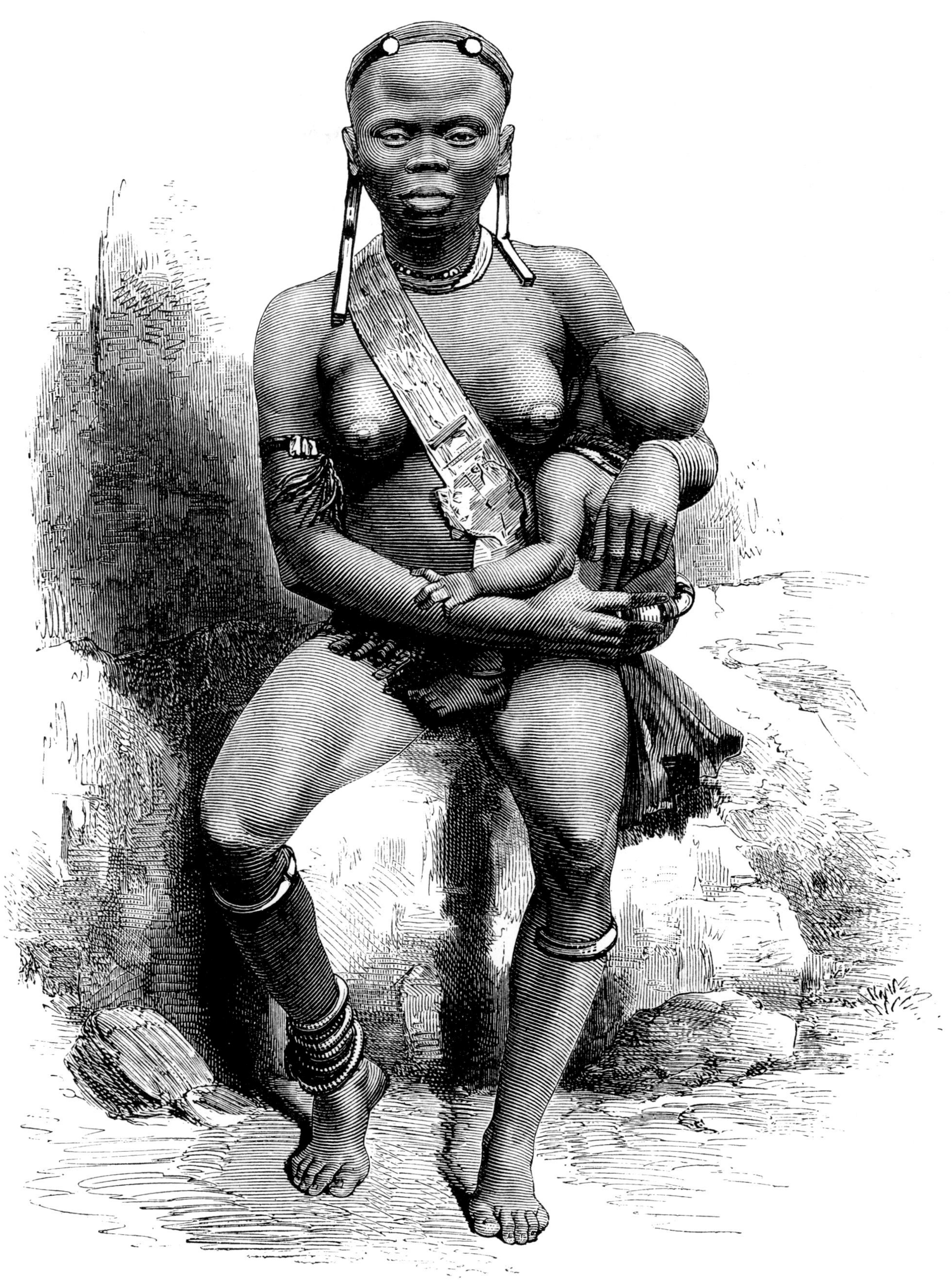

Gabonese woman with child, c. 1860

Gabunische Frau mit Kind, um 1860

Donna gabonese con bambino, ca. 1860

Femme gabonaise et son enfant, vers 1860

Mujer gabonesa con su hijo, hacia 1860

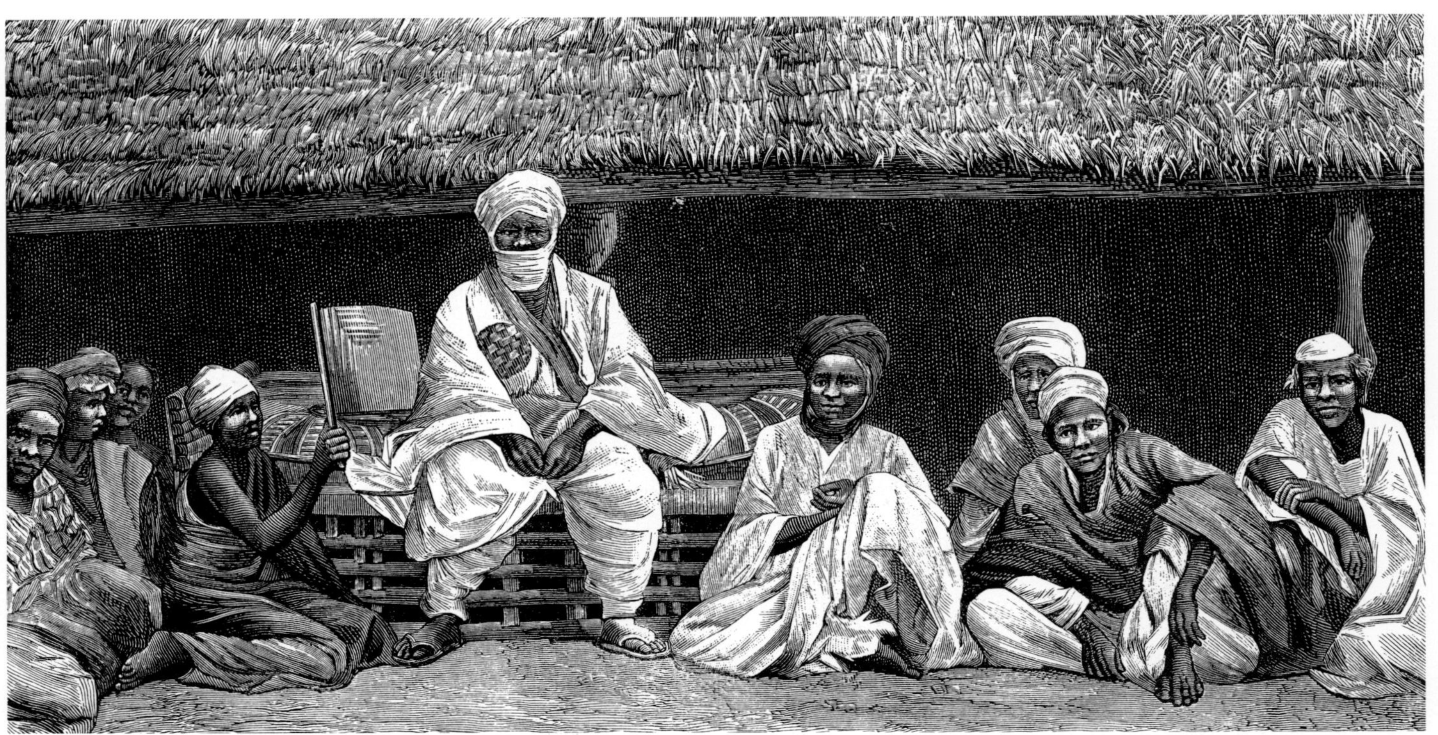

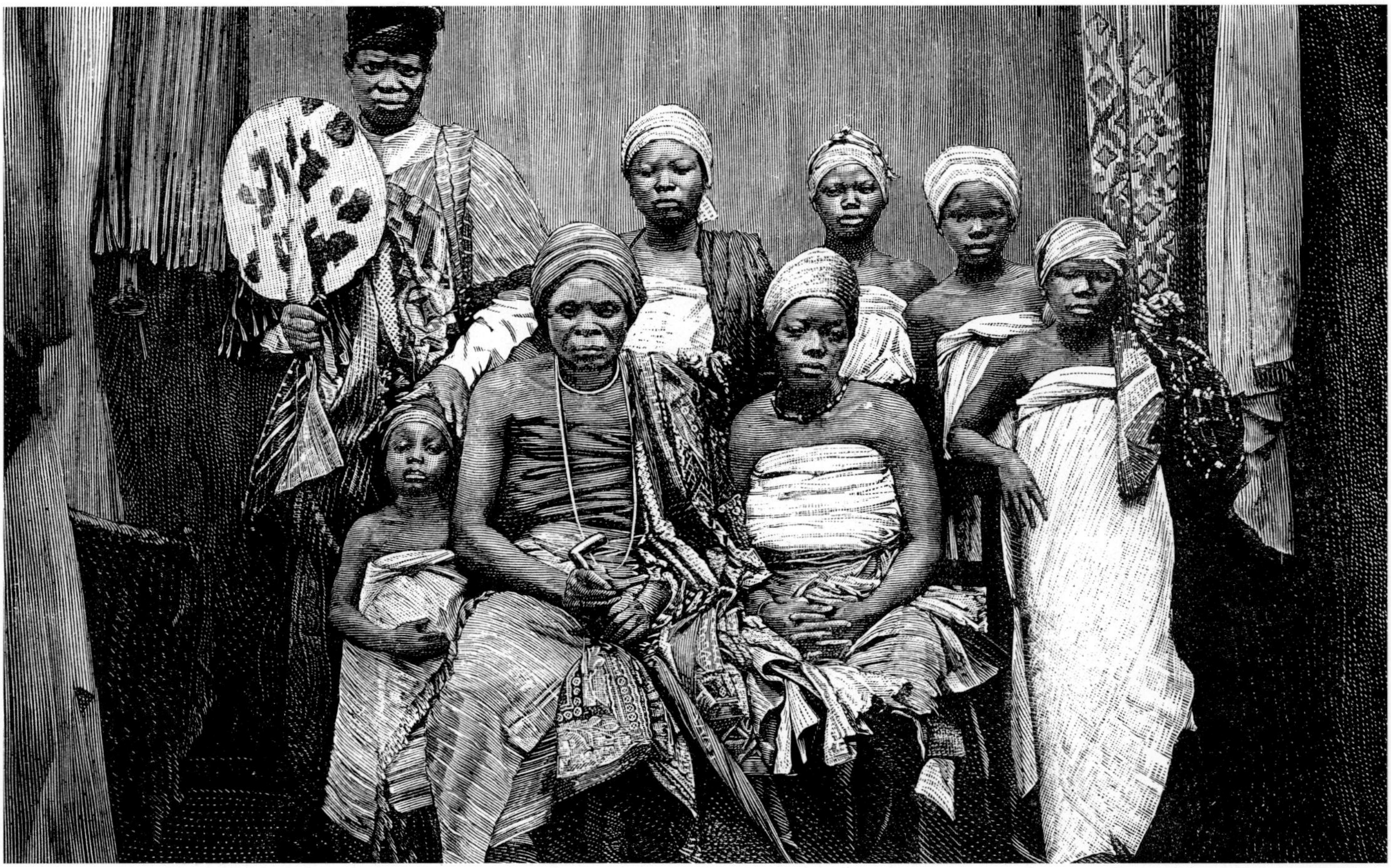

a King Maliti of Bida, present-day Nigeria, c. 1850

König Maliti von Bida, dem heutigen Nigeria, um 1850

Re Maliti di Bida, attuale Nigeria, ca. 1850

Roi Maliti de Vida, actuel Nigéria, vers 1850

El rey Maliti de Bida, actual Nigeria, hacia 1850

b Inhabitants of Abeokuta, Nigeria, c. 1850

Bewohner von Abeokuta, Nigeria, um 1850

Abitanti di Abeokuta, Nigeria, ca. 1850

Habitants de Abeokuta, Nigéria, vers 1850

Habitantes de Abeokuta, Nigeria, hacia 1850

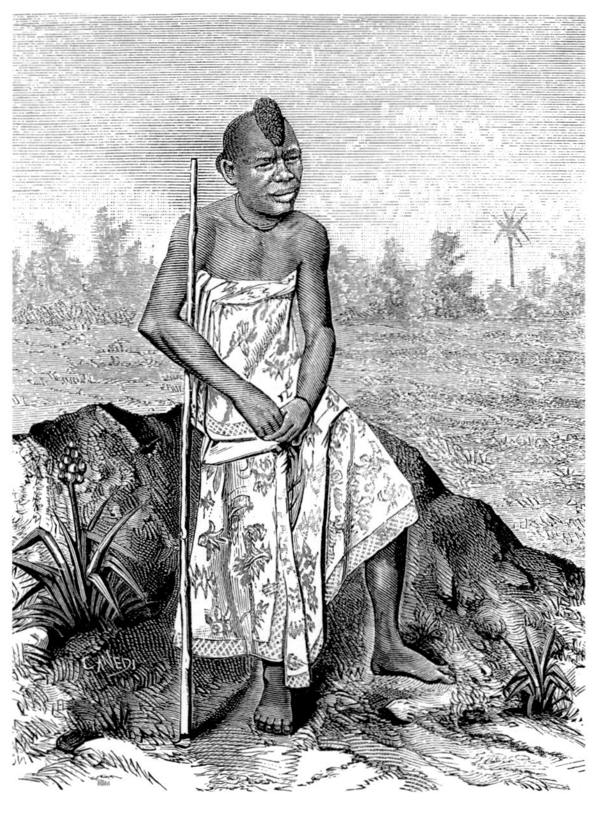

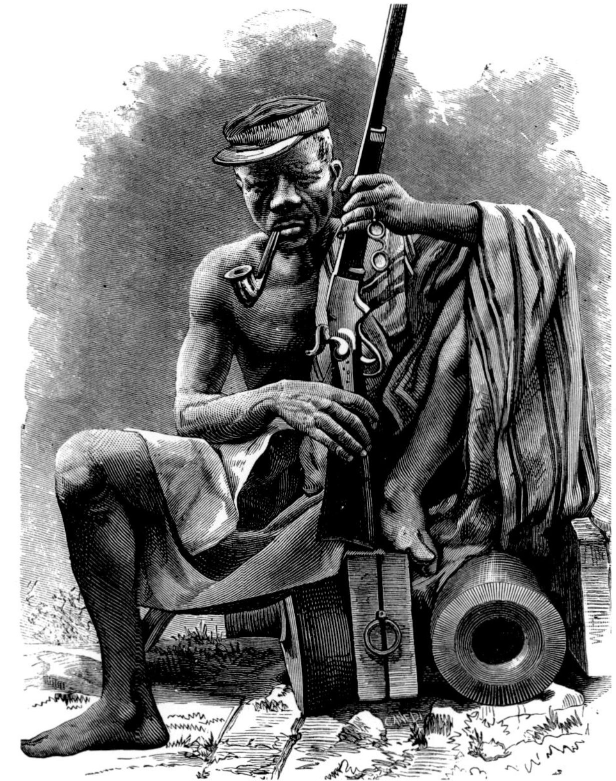

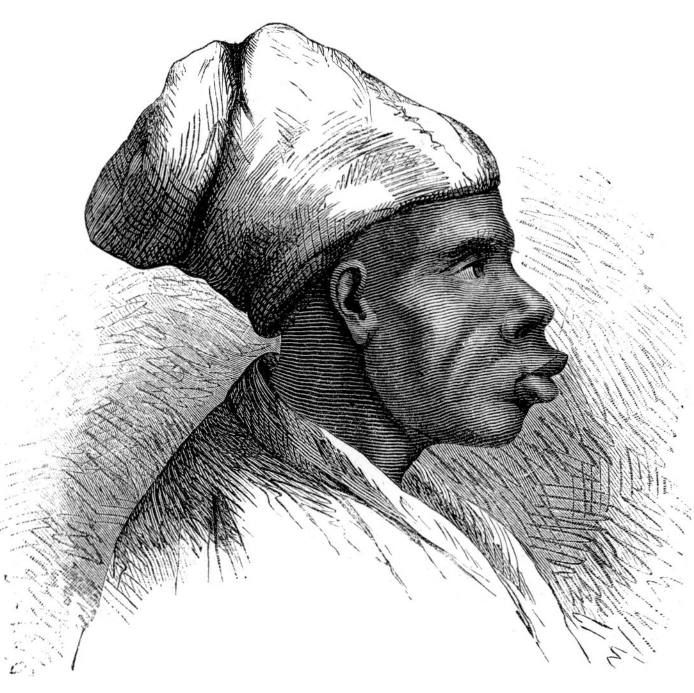

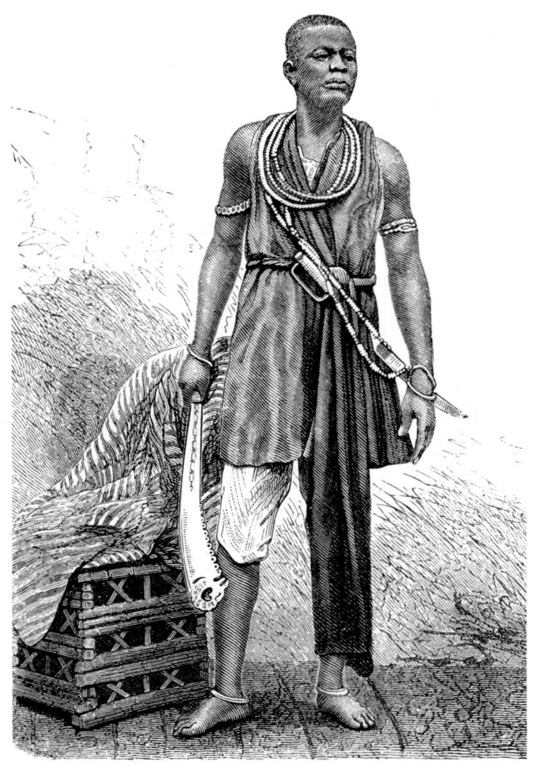

a	Medicine Man, Gabon, 1870	Medizinmann, Gabun, 1870	Stregone, Gabon, 1870	Homme-médecin, gabon, 1870	Sanador, Gabón, 1870
b	Military leader, Abeokuta	Militärführer, Abeokuta	Capo militare, Abeokuta	Chef militaire, Abeokuta	Líder militar, Abeokuta
c	Courtier, Benin, 1889	Höfling, Benin, 1889	Cortigiano, Benin, 1889	Courtisan, Bénin, 1889	Cortesano, Benín, 1889
d	Minister of trade, Benin, 1889	Handelsminister, Benin, 1889	Ministro del commercio, Benin, 1889	Ministre du commerce, Bénin, 1889	Ministro de Comercio, Benín, 1889

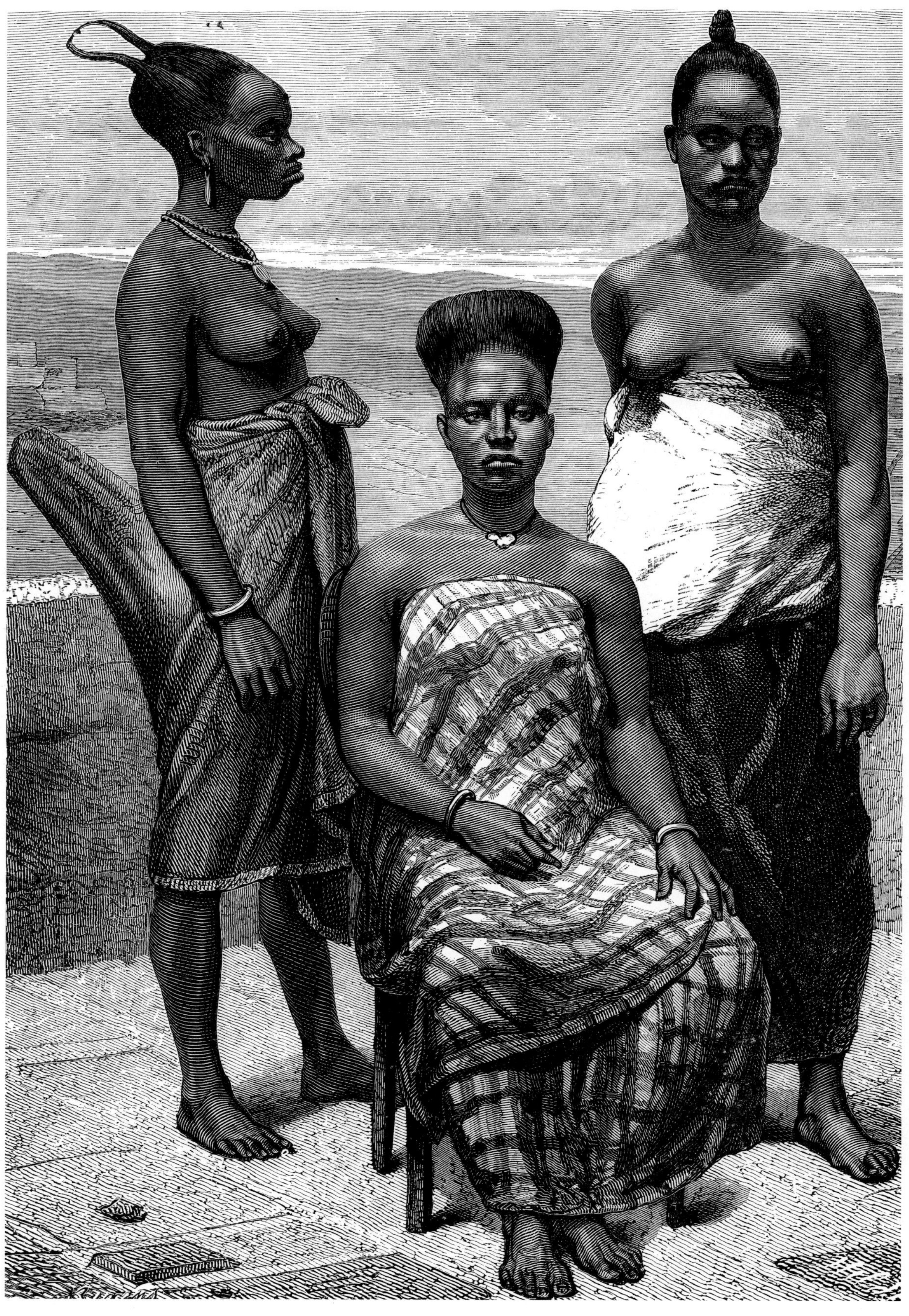

Ashanti women, 1880 Ashanti-Frauen, 1880 Donne ashanti, 1880 Femmes ashanti, 1880 Mujeres de Ashanti, 1880

Ghana

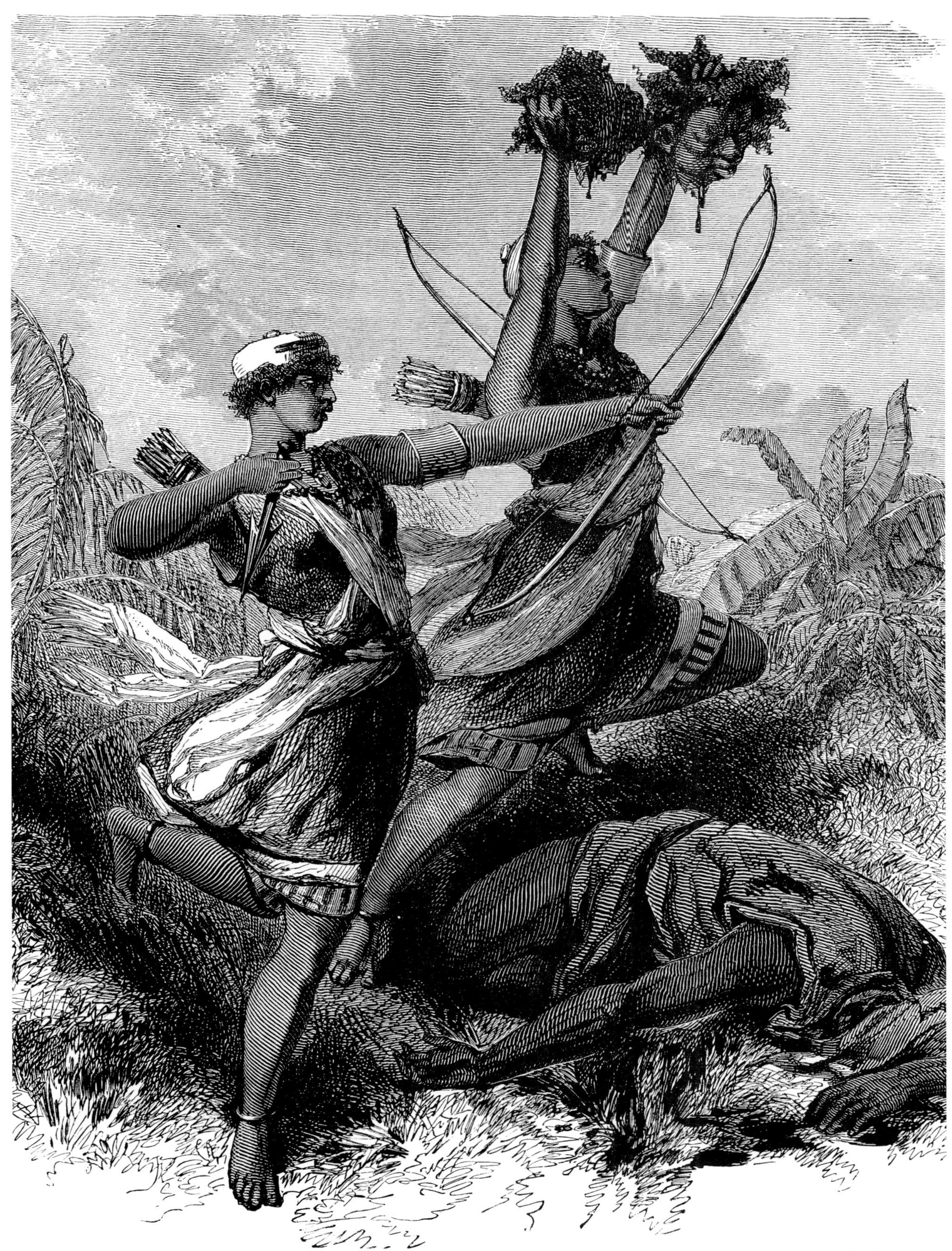

Female warriors of King Gezú of Dohomey (present-day Benin), 1870

Die Kriegerinnen des Königs Gezú von Dahomey (heute Benin), 1870

Guerriere del Re Gezú di Dohomey (attuale Benin), 1870

Guerrières du Roi Gezú du Dahomey (actuel Bénin), 1870

Guerreras del rey Gezú de Dahomey (actual Benín), 1870

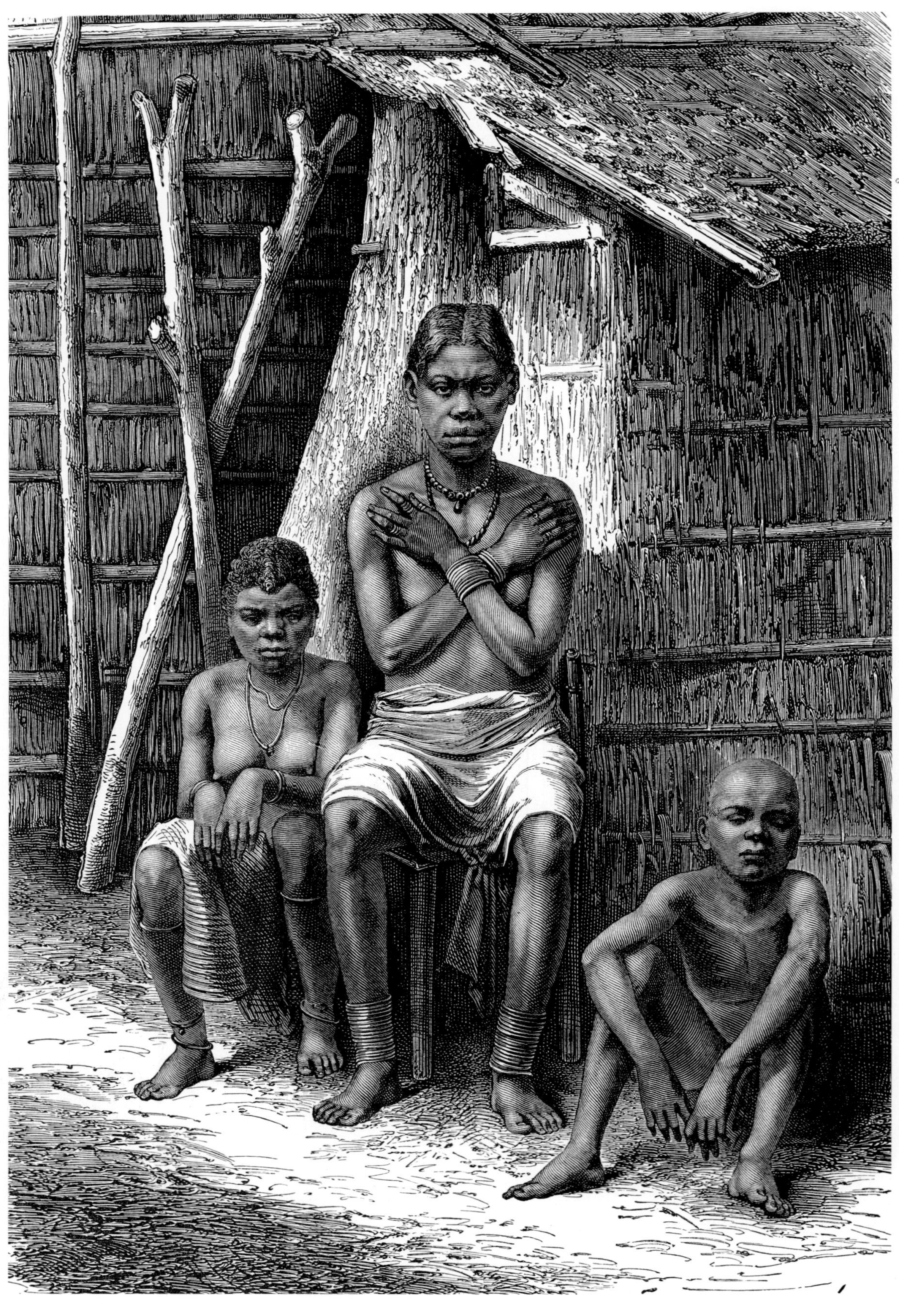

Inhabitants of Dahomey (present-day Benin), 1870

Bewohner von Dahomey (heute Benin), 1870

Abitanti di Dohomey (attuale Benin), 1870

Habitants du Dahomey (actuel Bénin), 1870

Habitantes de Dahomey (actual Benín), 1870

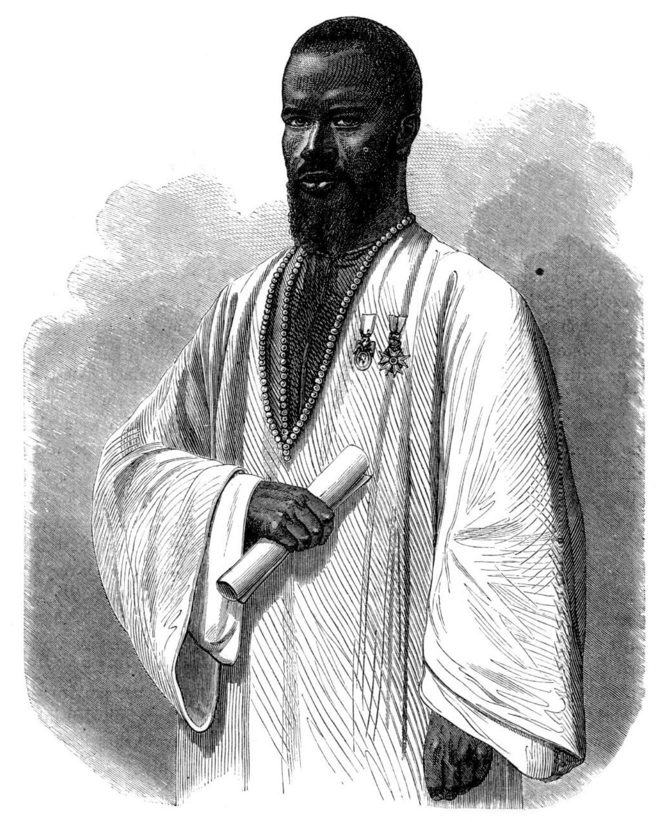

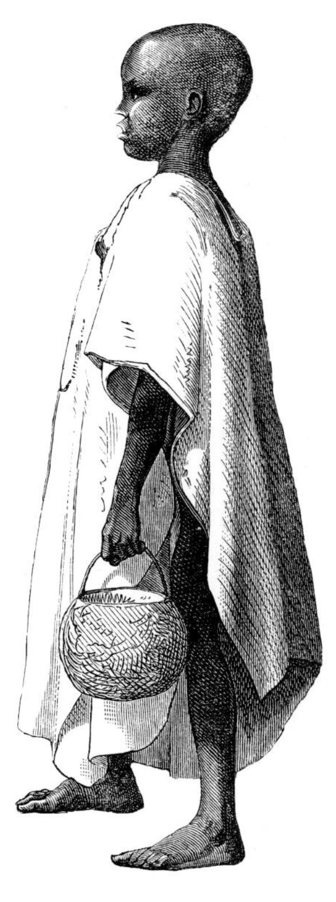

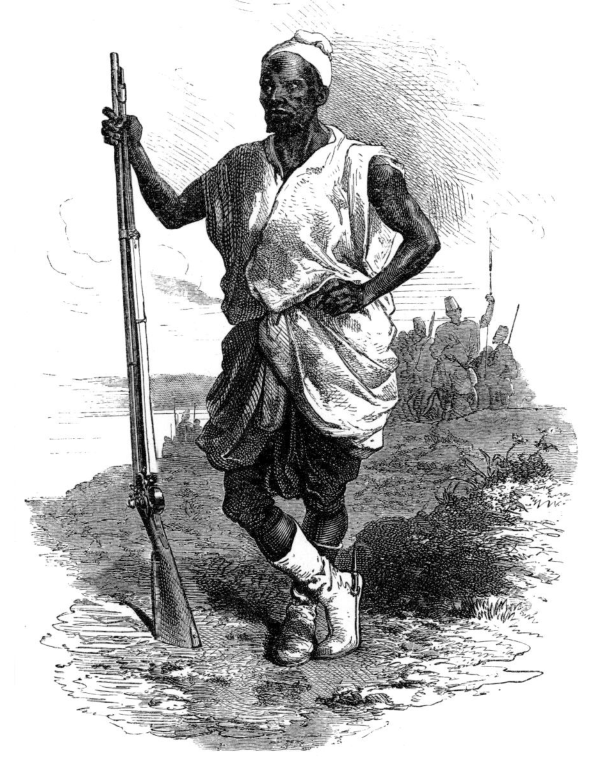

a	Senegalese official	Senegalesischer Beamter	Funzionario senegalese	Fonctionnaire sénégalais	Funcionario senegalés
b	Senegalese boy	Senegalesischer Junge	Ragazzo senegalese	Enfant sénégalais	Niño senegalés
c	Senegalese soldier	Senegalesischer Soldat	Soldato senegalese	Soldat sénégalais	Soldado senegalés

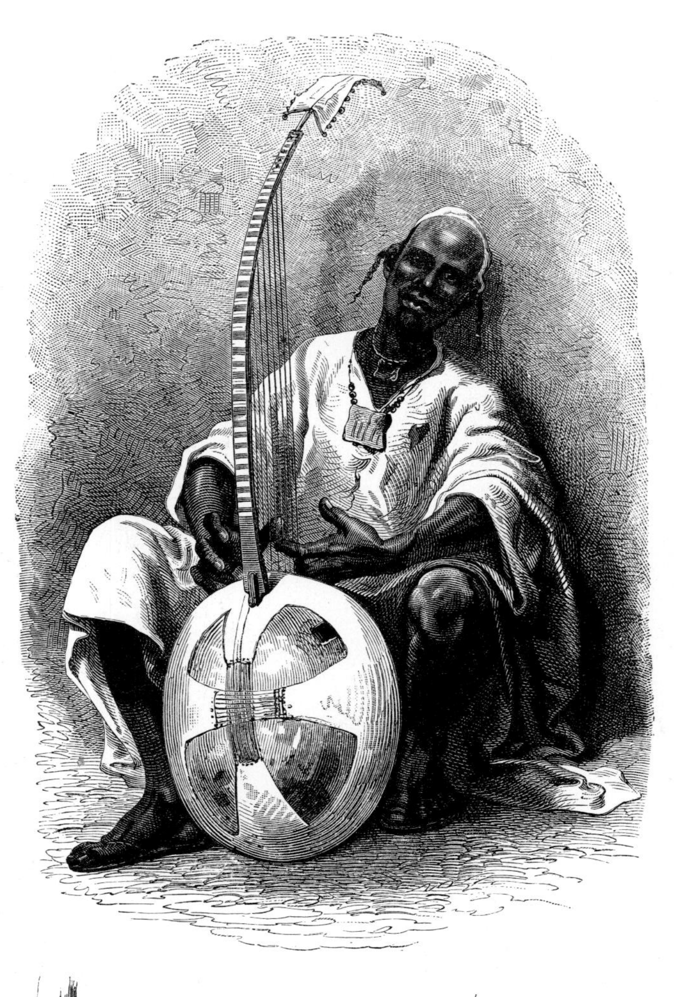

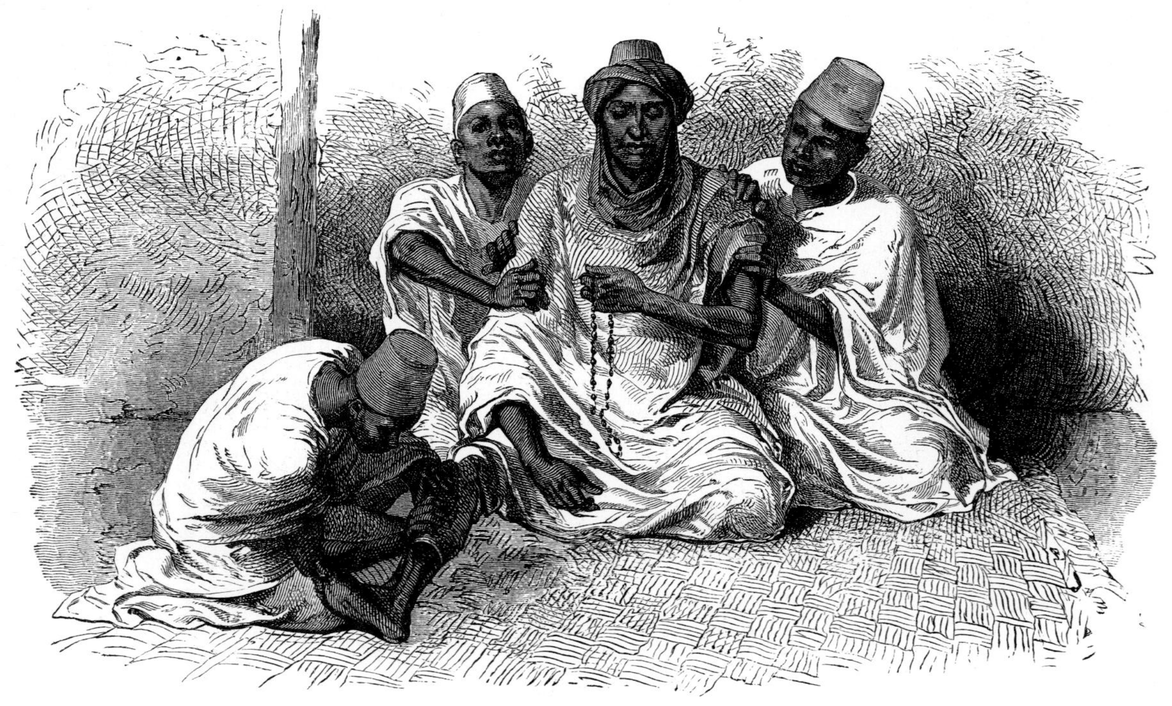

a	Musician, Dakar, c. 1880	Musiker, Dakar, um 1880	Musicista, Dakar, ca. 1880	Musicien, Dakar, vers 1880	Músico, Dakar, hacia 1880
b	Marabout with his servants, Dakar, c. 1880	Marabou (heiliger Mann) mit Dienern, um 1880	Marabut con i suoi domestici, Dakar, ca. 1880	Marabout et ses servants, Dakar, vers 1880	Morabito con sus sirvientes, Dakar, hacia 1880

Senegal

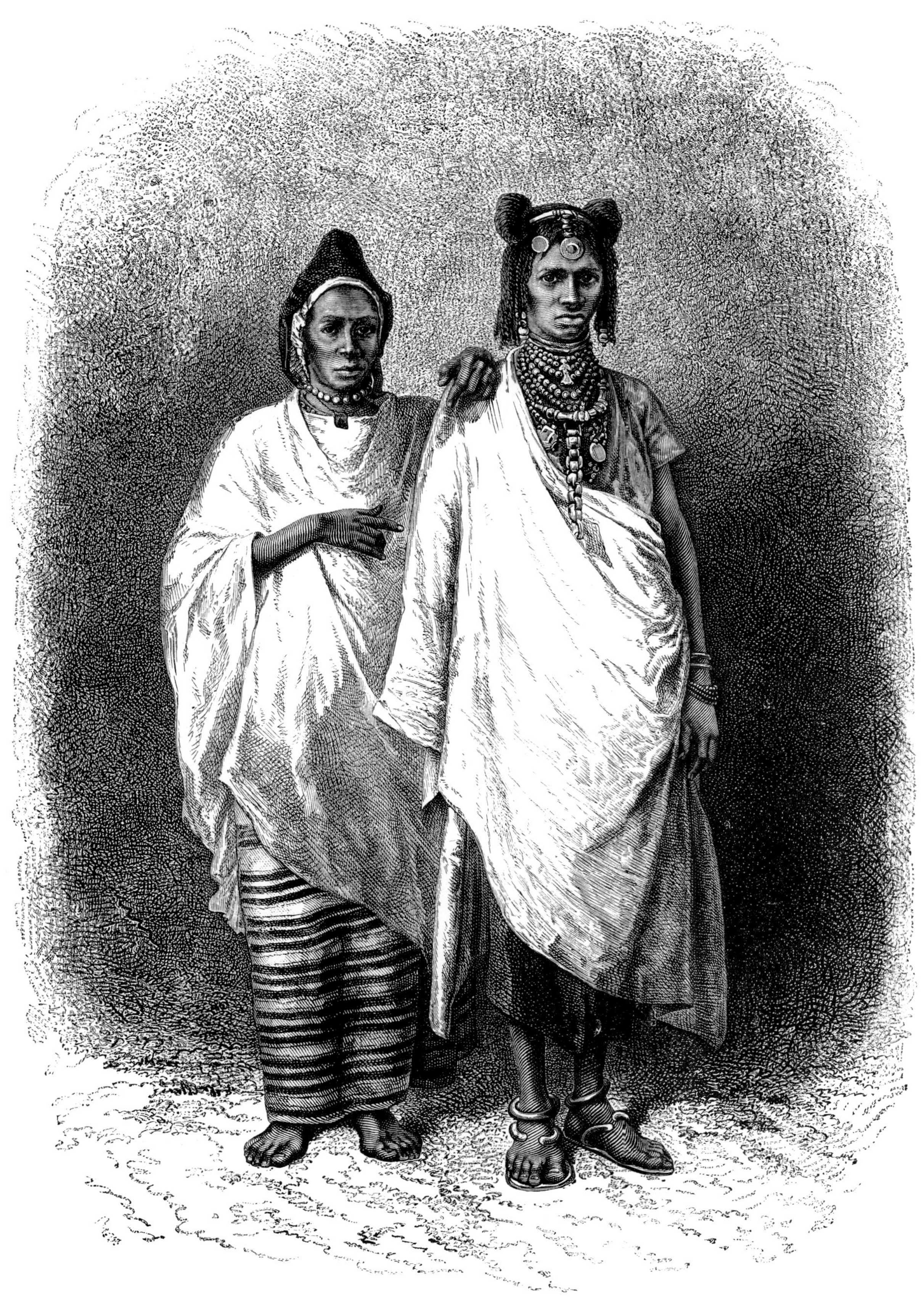

Senegalese ladies, c. 1880

Senegalesische Frauen, um 1880

Donne senegalesi, ca. 1880

Femmes sénégalaises, vers 1880

Mujeres senegalesas, alrededor del año 1880

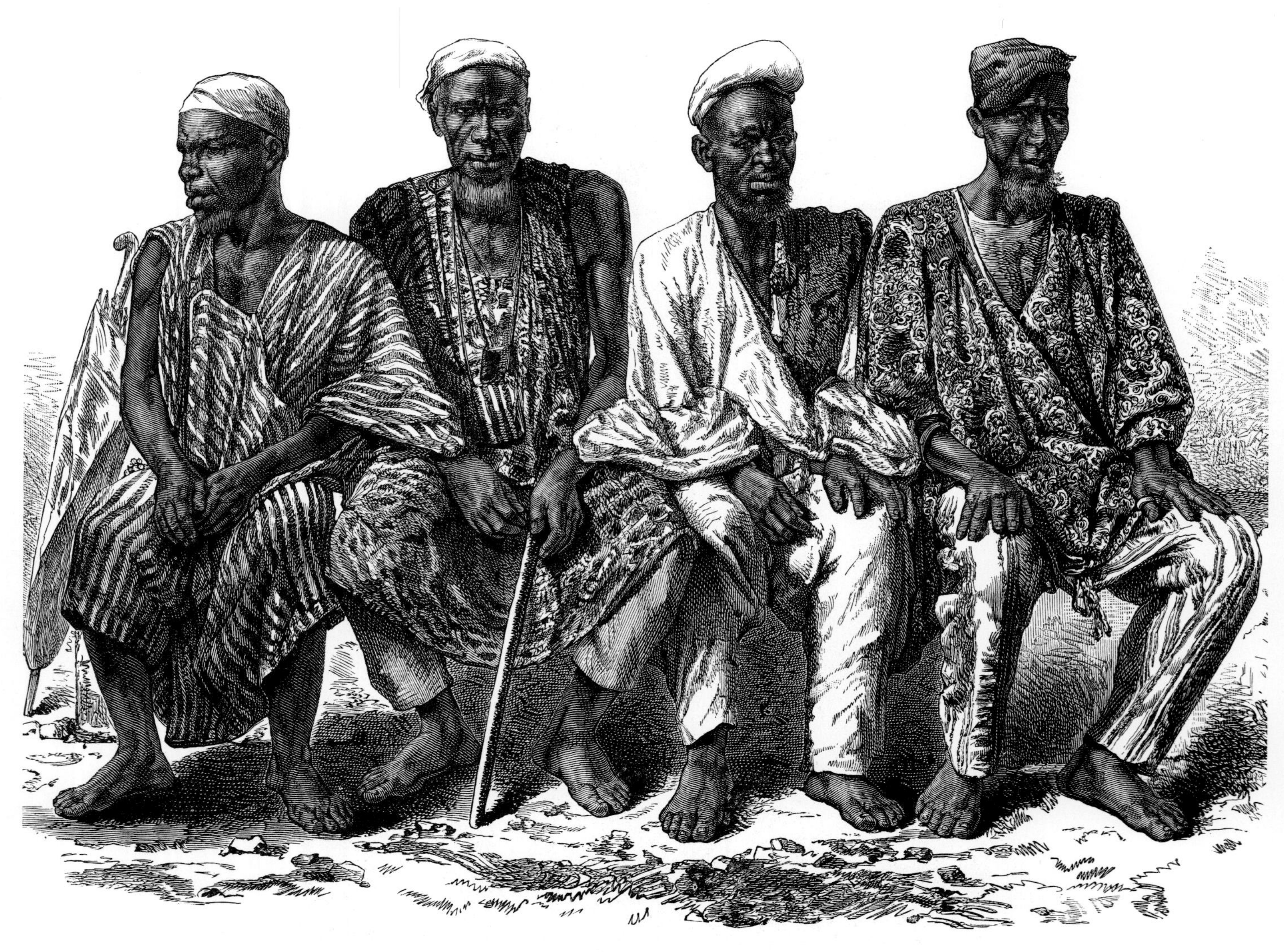

Muslim pilgrims, c. 1865

Moslemische Pilger, um 1865

Pellegrini musulmani, ca. 1865

Pèlerins musulmans, vers 1865

Peregrinos musulmanes, hacia 1865

Senegal

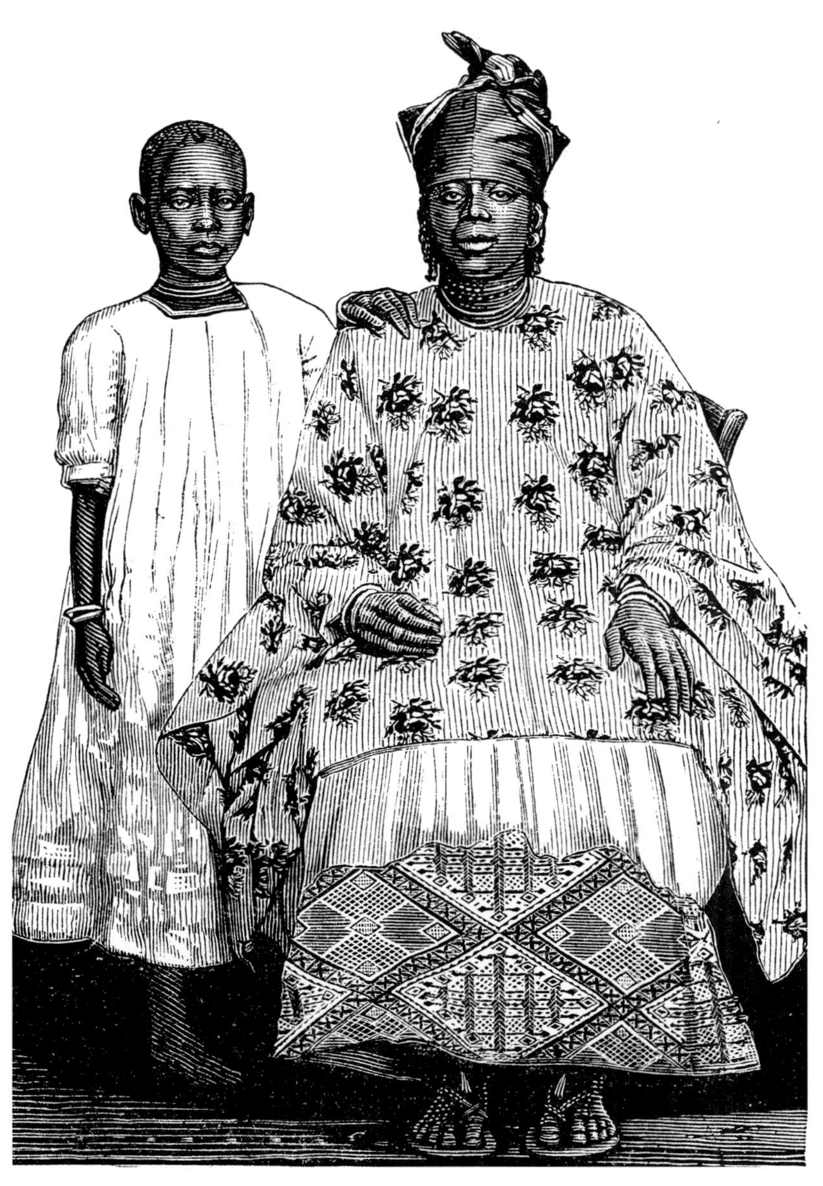

Mother and daughter, Cape Verde, c. 1875

Mutter und Tochter, Kap Verde, um 1875

Madre e figlia, Capo Verde, ca. 1875

Mère et fille, Cap Vert, vers 1875

Madre e hija, Cabo Verde, alrededor del año 1875

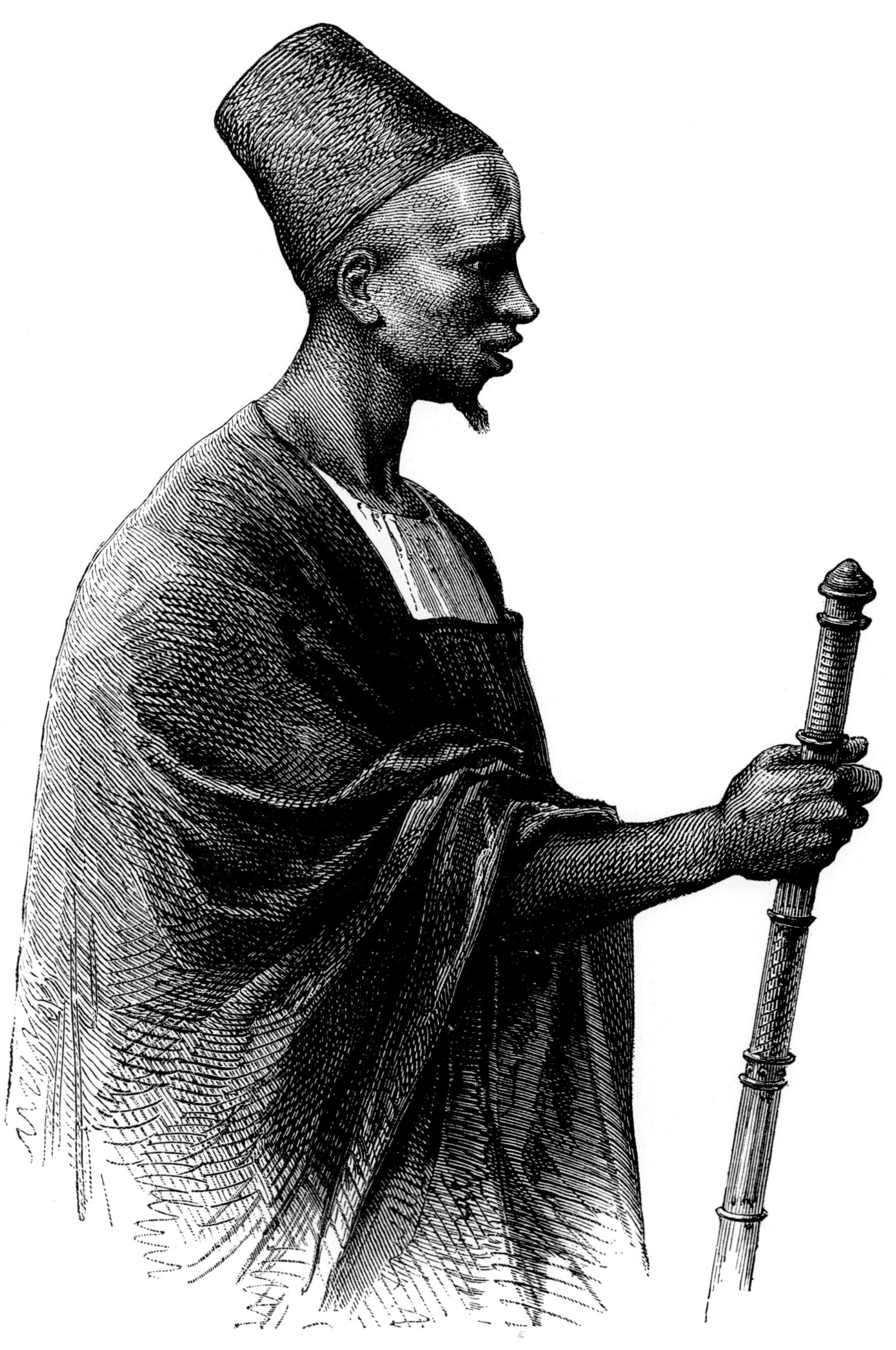

Mauretanian chief, 1900

Mauretanischer Anführer, 1900

Capo mauritaniano, 1900

Chef mauritanien, 1900

Jefe mauritano, 1900

Mauretania

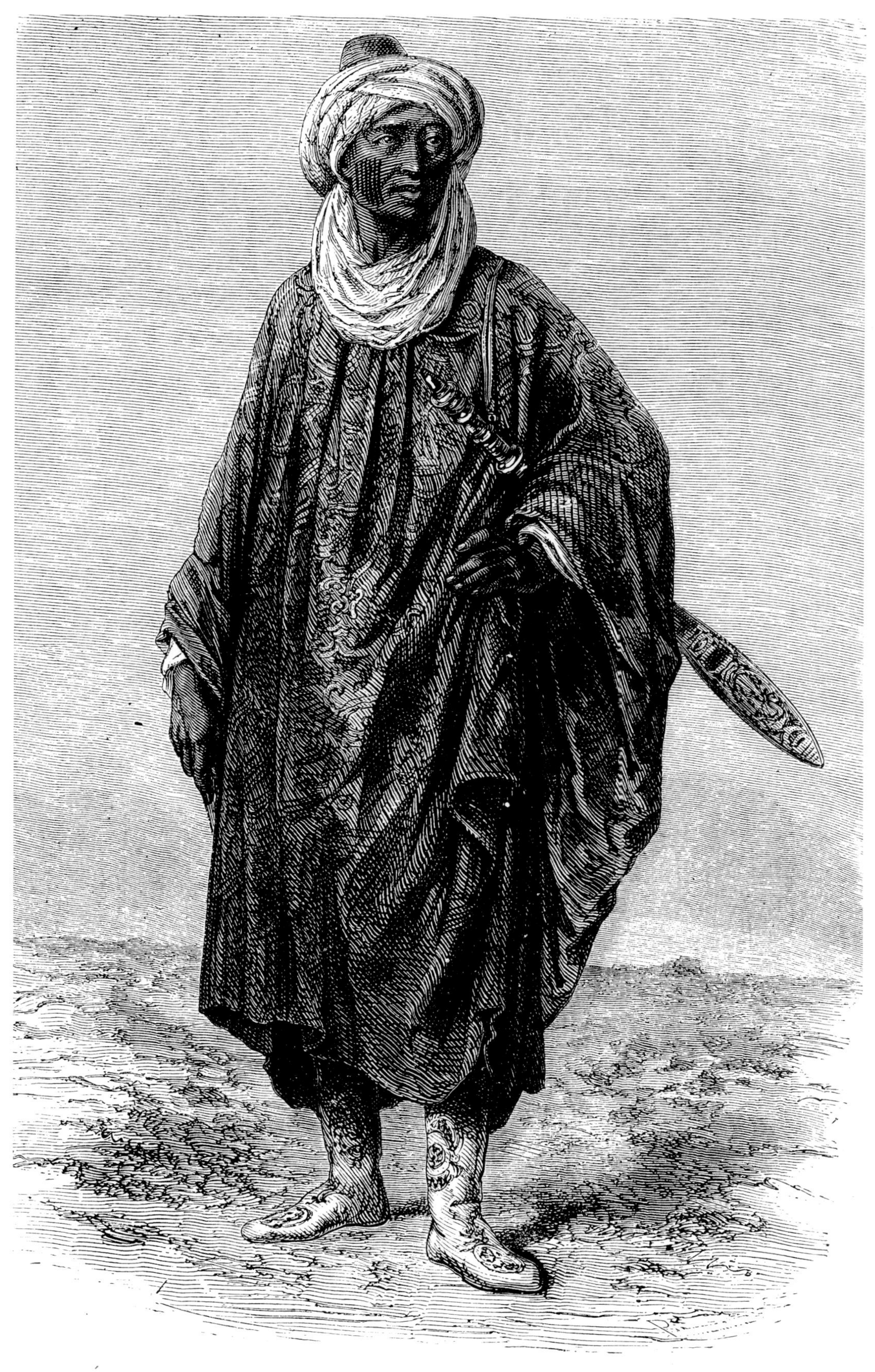

Mauretanian chief, 1880

Mauretanischer Anführer, 1880

Capo mauritaniano, 1880

Chef mauritanien, 1880

Jefe mauritano, 1880

Asia

Asien

Asia

Asie

Asia

アジア

亞洲

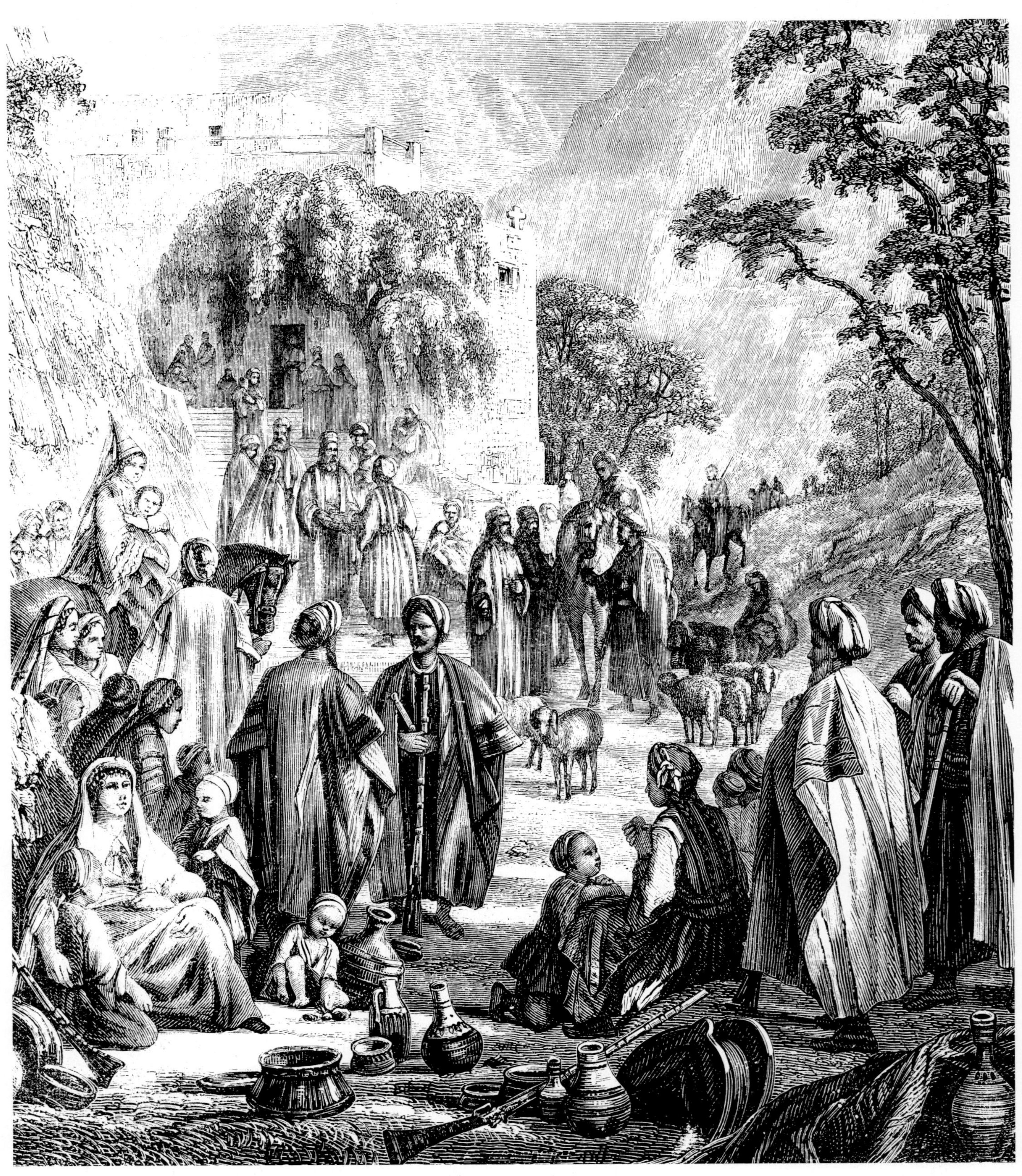

Lebanese Maronites, c. 1860

Libanesische Maroniten, um 1860

Maroniti libanesi, ca. 1860

Maronites libanais, vers 1860

Maronitas libaneses, alrededor del año 1860

Lebanon

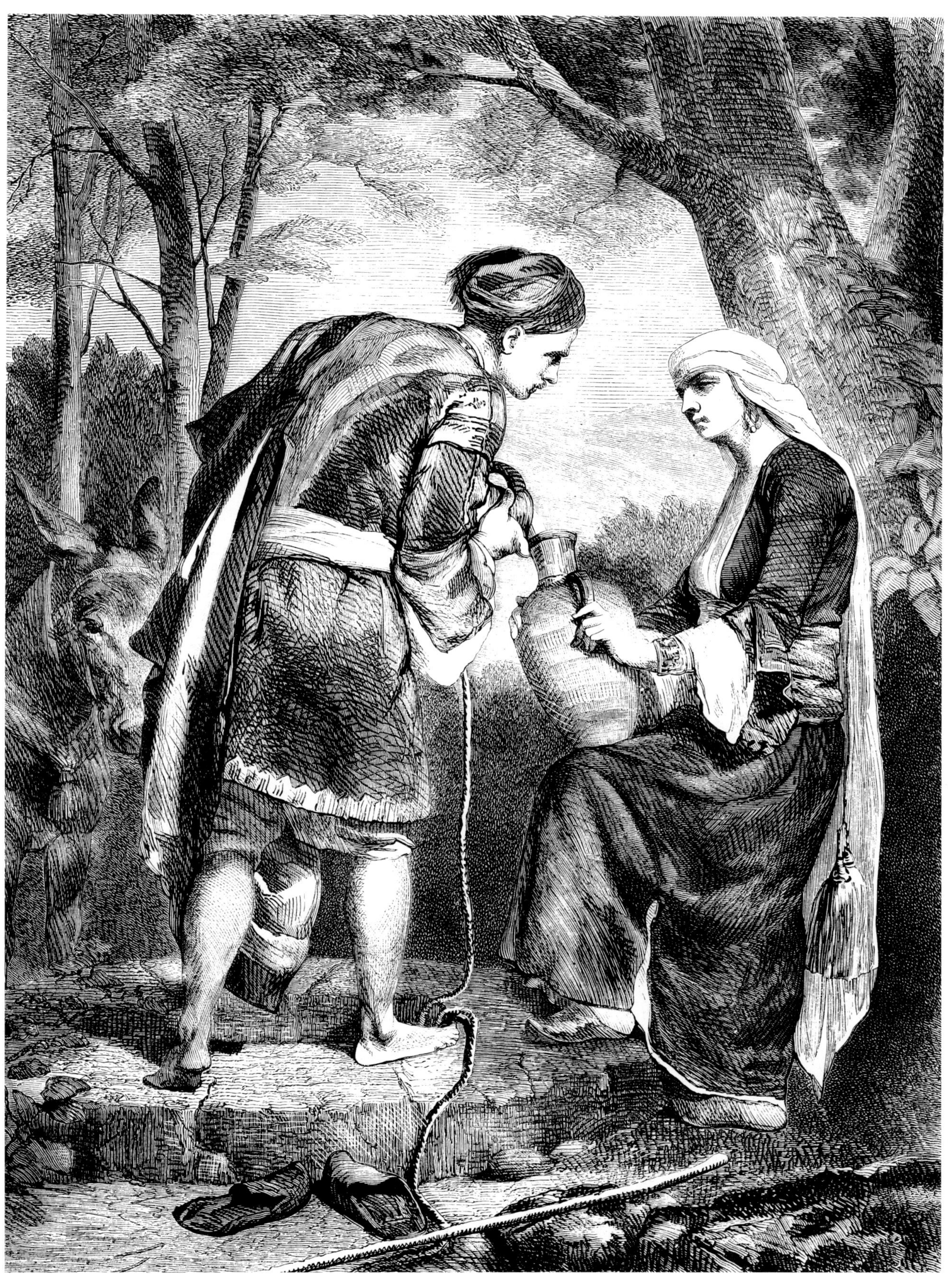

Maronite man and woman, c. 1860

Maronitischer Mann mit Frau, um 1860

Uomo e donna maroniti, ca. 1860

Homme et femme maronites, vers 1860

Hombre y mujer maronitas, hacia 1860

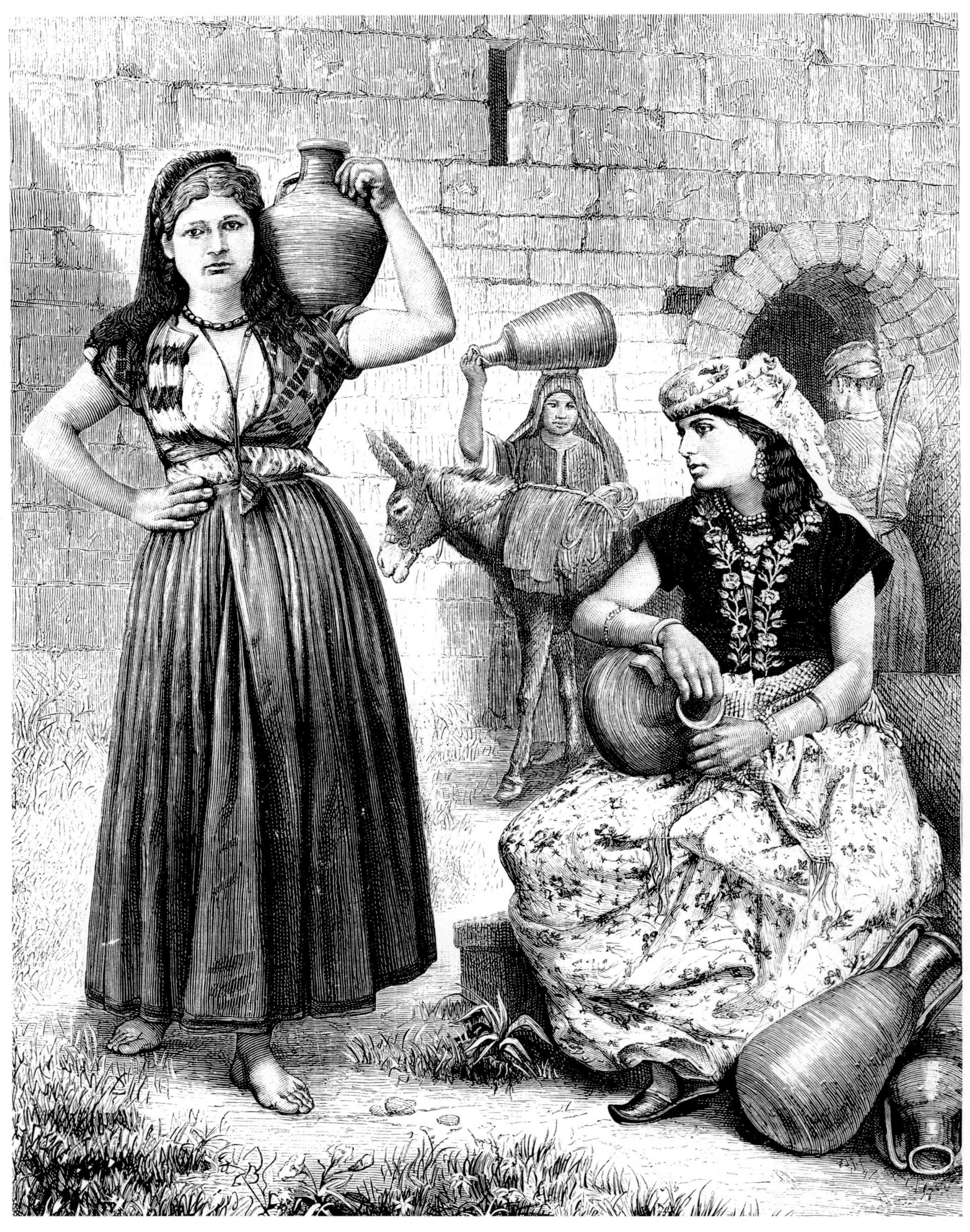

Women of Tyr, c. 1870

Frauen aus Tyros, um 1870

Donne di Tyr, ca. 1870

Femmes de Tyr, vers 1870

Mujeres de Tiro, 1870

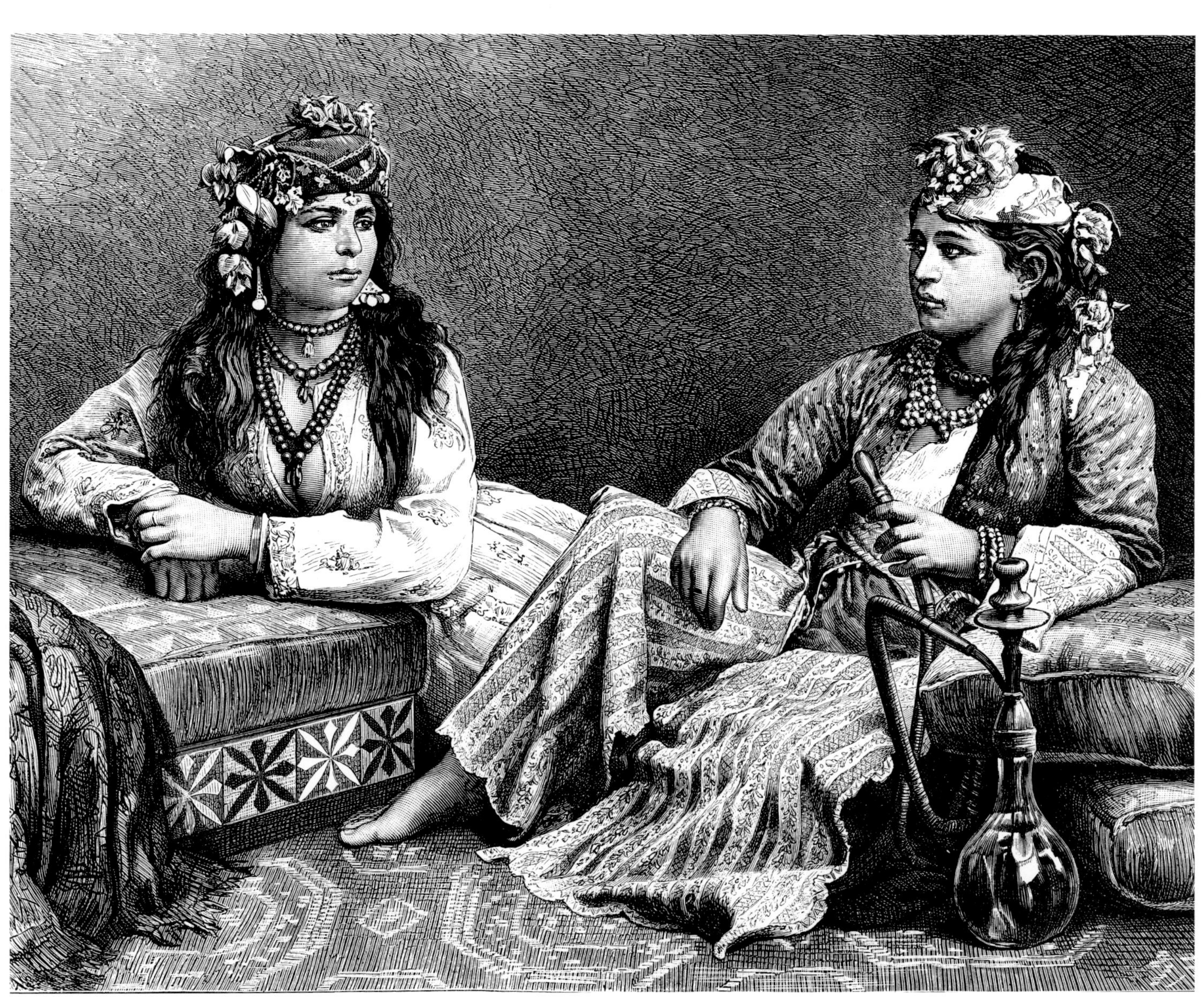

Muslim ladies in Sidon, c. 1875

Moslemische Frauen in Sidon, um 1875

Donne musulmane a Sidon, ca. 1875

Femmes musulmanes à Sidon, vers 1875

Damas musulmanas de Sidón, hacia 1875

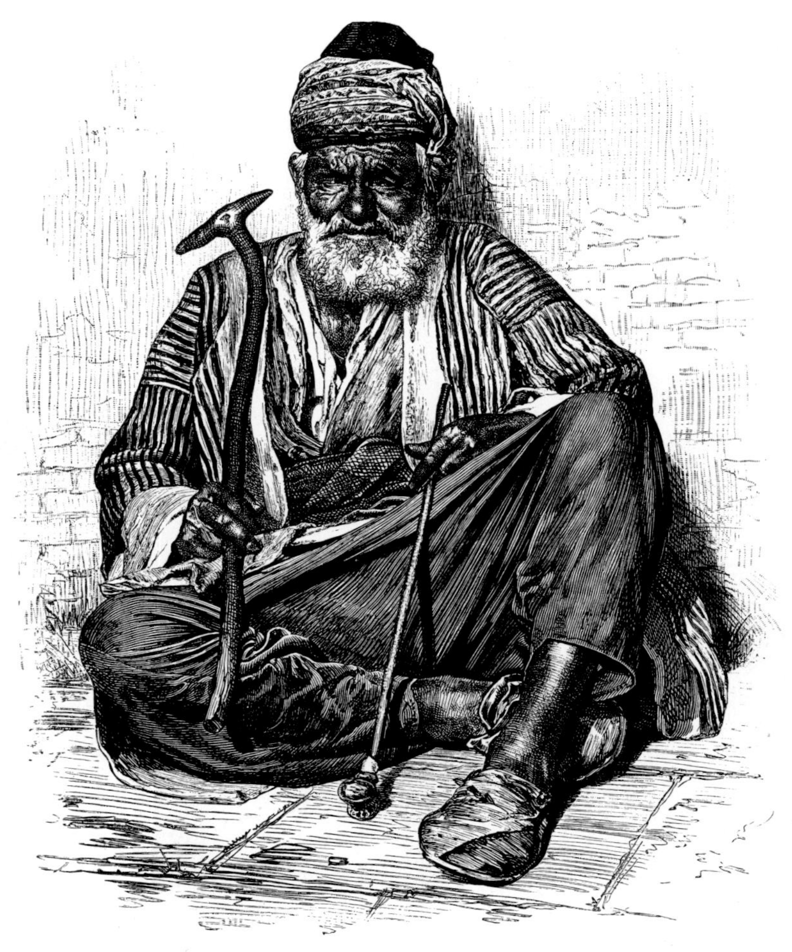

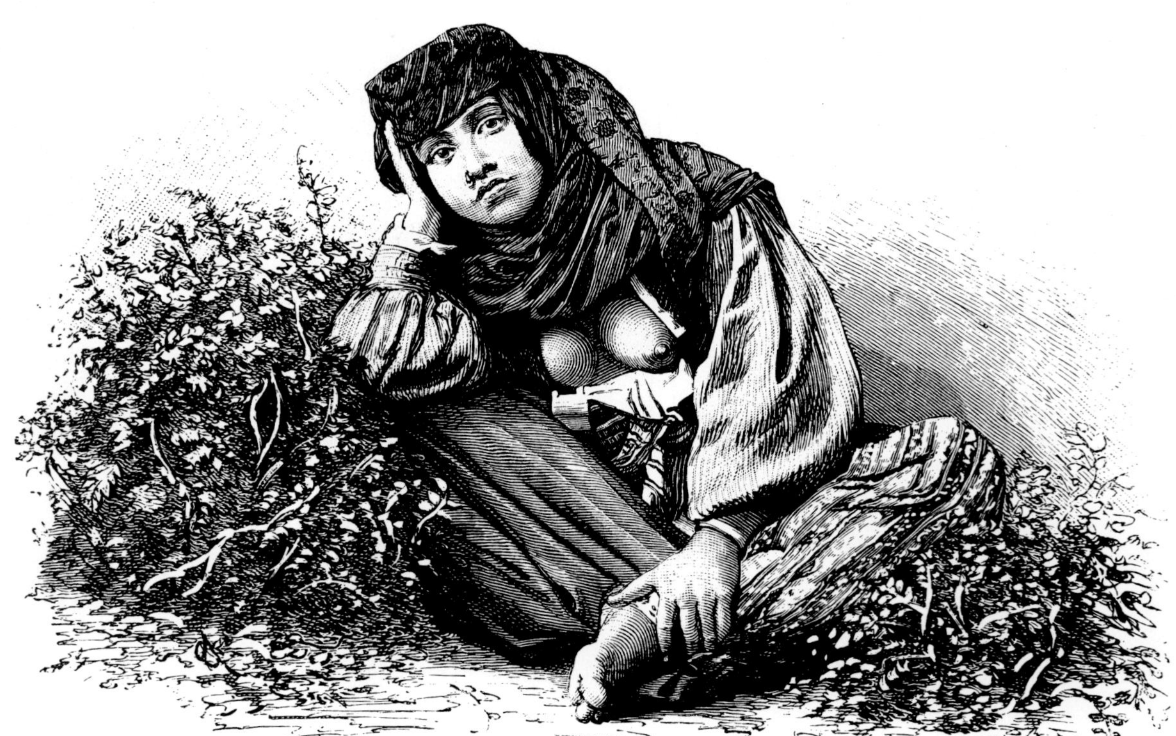

a	Man from Tyr, 1865	Mann aus Tyros, 1865	Uomo di Tyr, 1865	Homme de Tyr, 1865	Hombre de Tiro, 1865
b	Palestine woman, c. 1860	Palästinische Frau, um 1860	Donna palestinese, ca. 1860	Palestinienne, vers 1860	Mujer palestina, 1860

Lebanon/Palestine

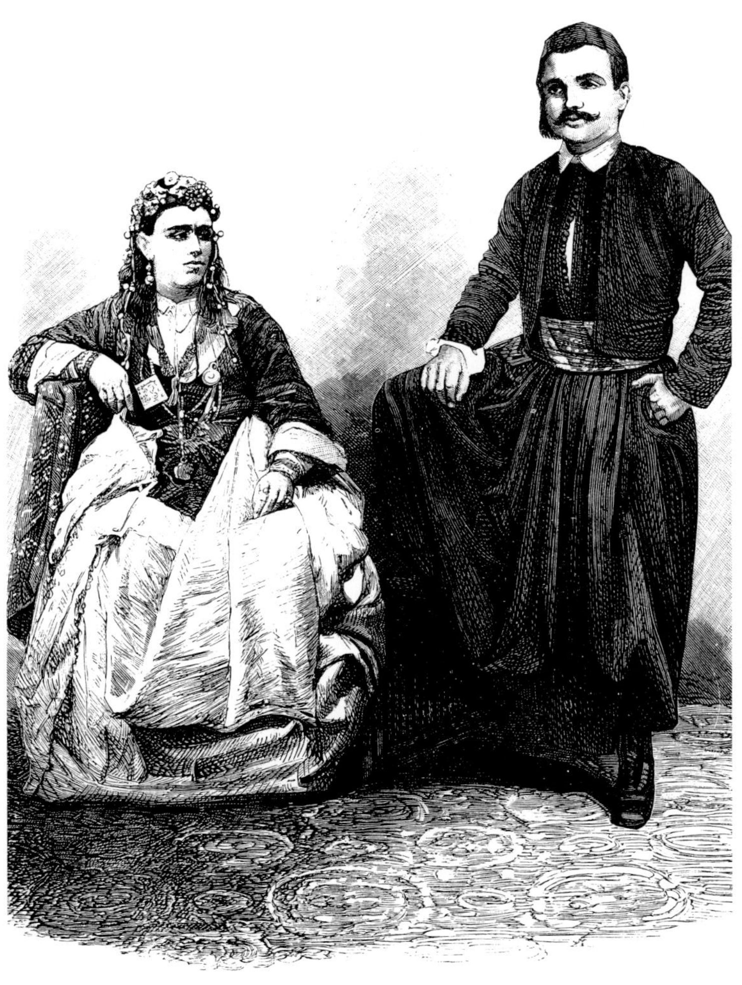

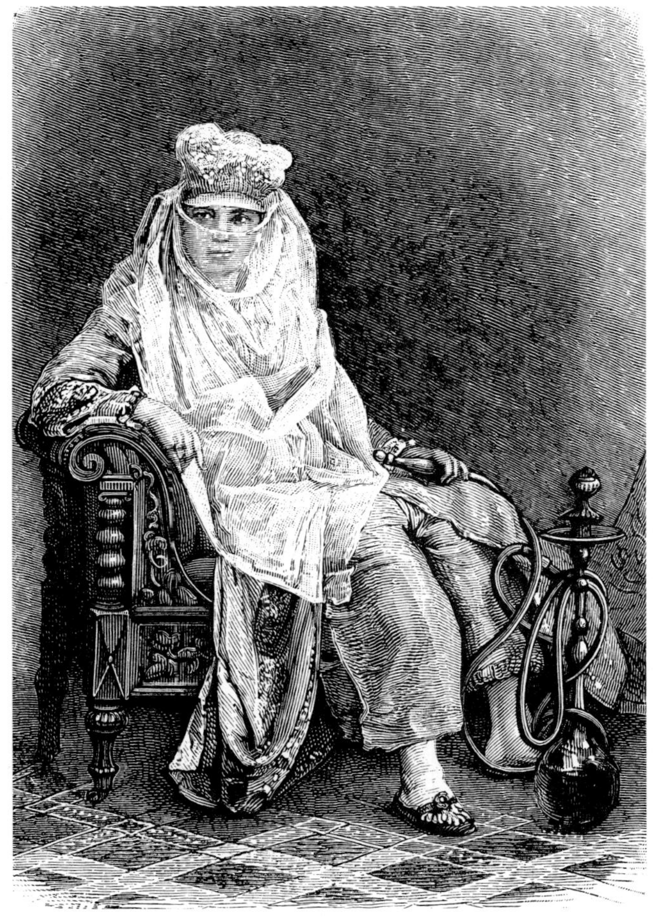

a	Muslim couple from Akko, c. 1860	Moslempaar aus Akko, um 1860	Coppia musulmana di Akko, ca. 1860	Couple musulman d'Akko, vers 1860	Pareja musulmana de Acre, hacia 1860
b	Woman from Nazareth, c. 1865	Frau aus Nazareth, um 1865	Donna di Nazareth, ca. 1865	Femme de Nazareth, vers 1865	Mujer de Nazaret, alrededor de 1865

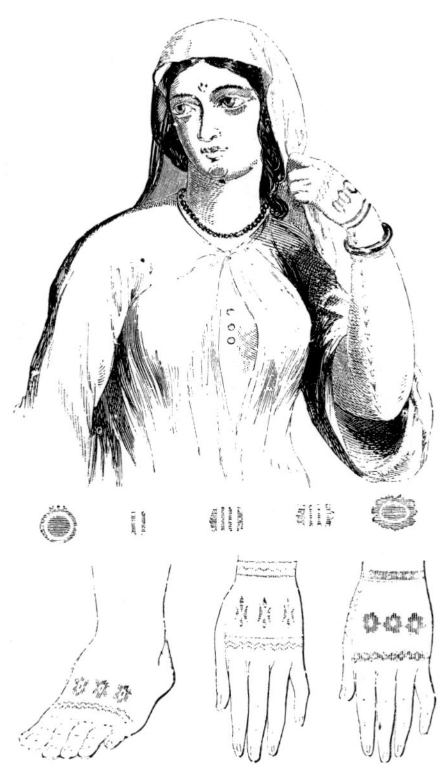

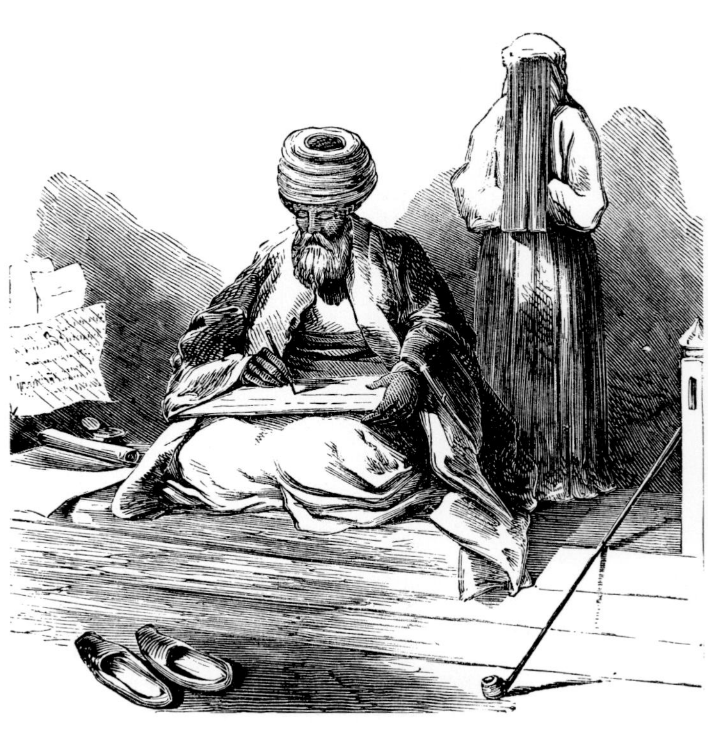

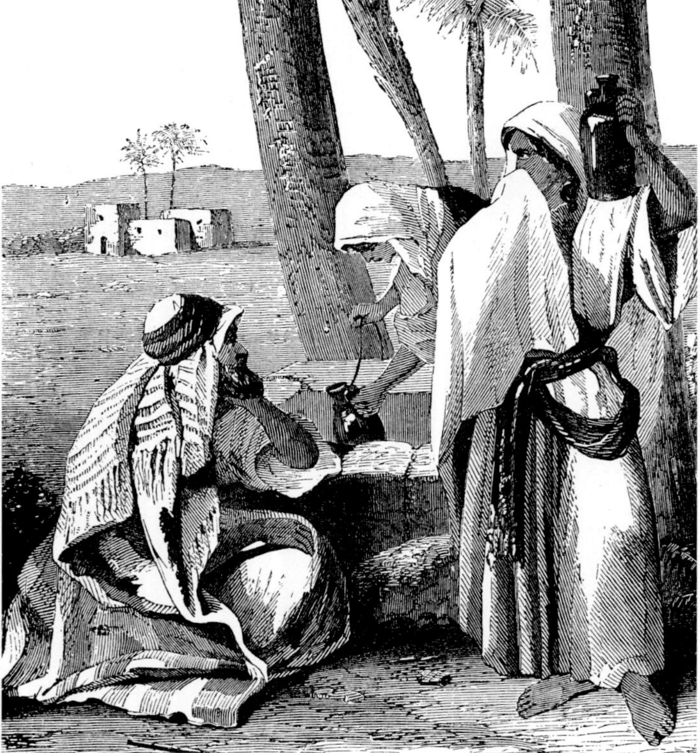

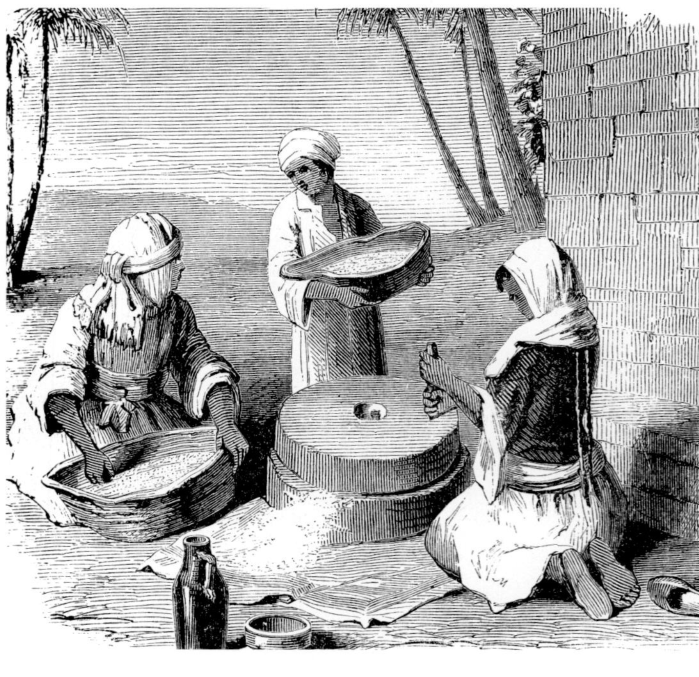

a	Female tattoos, c. 1860	Weibliche Tätowierungen, um 1860	Tatuaggi femminili, ca. 1860	Tatouages féminins, vers 1860	Tatuajes femeninos, 1860
b	Letter writer, c. 1860	Briefeschreiber, um 1860	Scrivano, ca. 1860	Écrivain public, vers 1860	Escribiente de cartas, hacia el año 1860
c	Arabs, c. 1860	Araber, um 1860	Arabi, ca. 1860	Arabes, vers 1860	Árabes, hacia 1860
d	Women grinding flour, c. 1860	Frauen beim Mehl mahlen, um 1860	Donne che macinano la farina, ca. 1860	Femmes tamisant la farine, vers 1860	Mujeres moliendo harina, hacia 1860

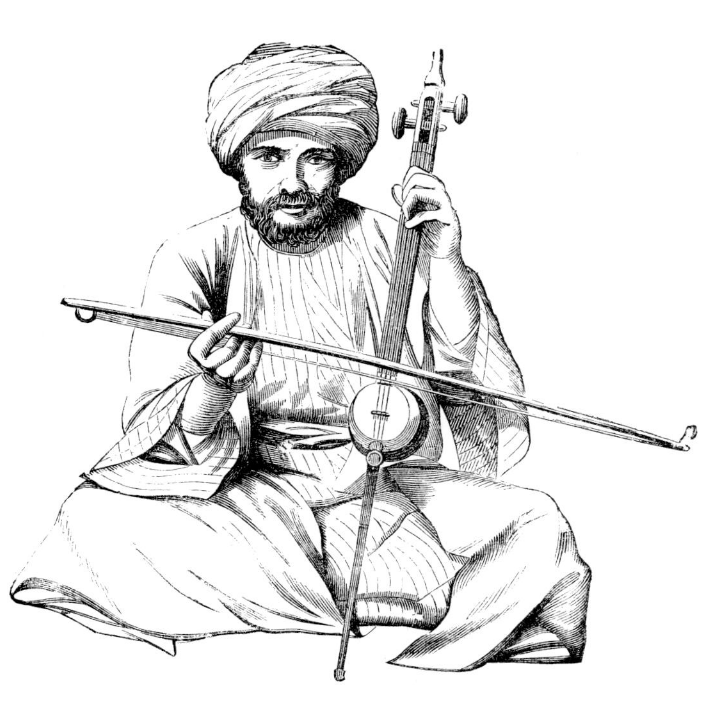

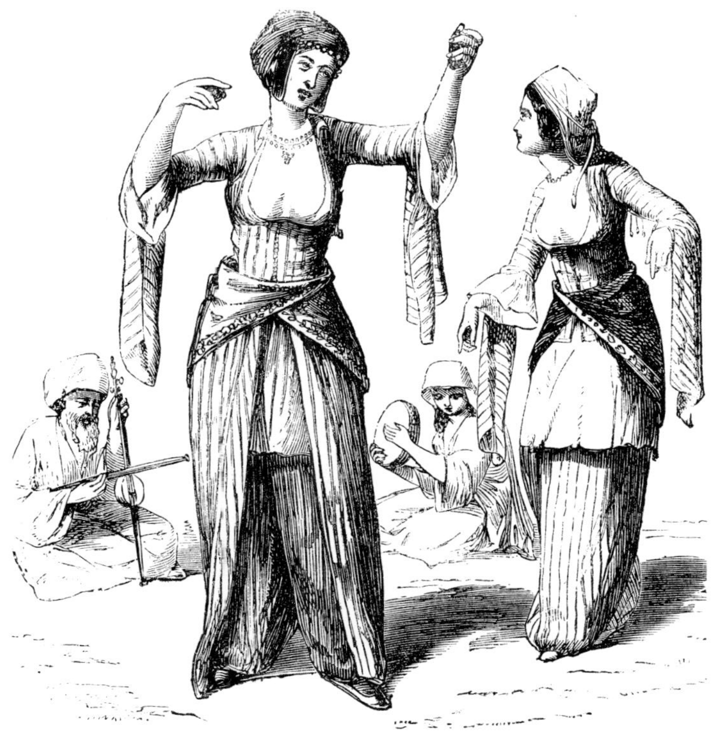

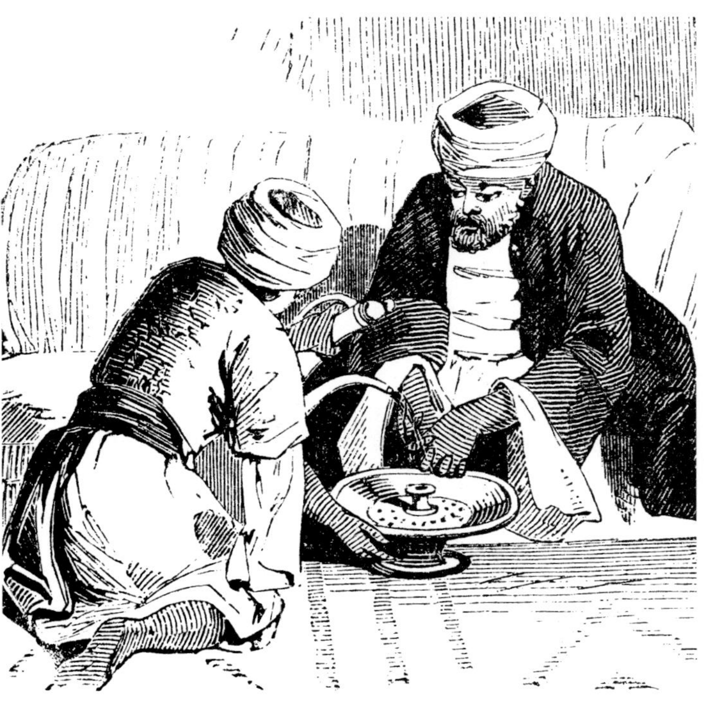

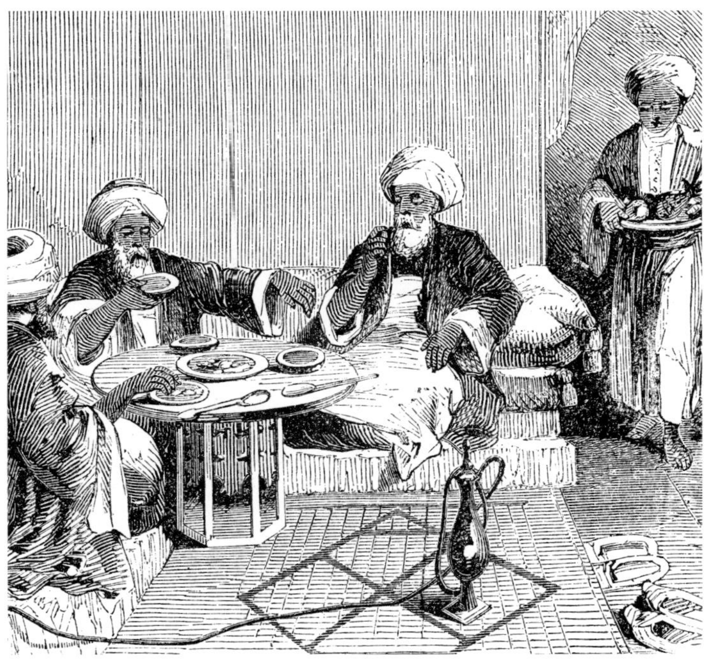

a	Musician, c. 1860	Musiker, um 1860	Musicista, ca. 1860	Musicien, vers 1860	Músico, hacia 1860
b	Dancing girls, c. 1860	Tanzende Mädchen, um 1860	Ragazze che danzano, ca. 1860	Danseuses, vers 1860	Bailarinas, hacia 1860
c	Washing hands	Beim Händewaschen	Uomini intenti a lavarsi le mani	Hommes se lavant les mains	Lavándose las manos
d	Men having dinner, c. 1860	Männer beim Abendessen, um 1860	Uomini a cena, 1860	Dîner des hommes, vers 1860	Hombres cenando, hacia el año 1860

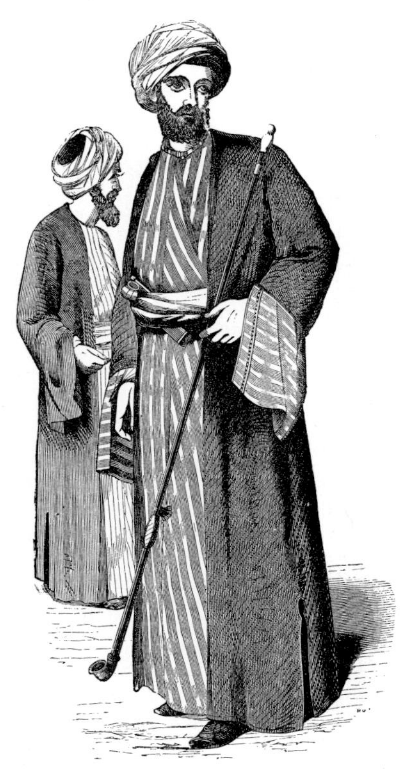

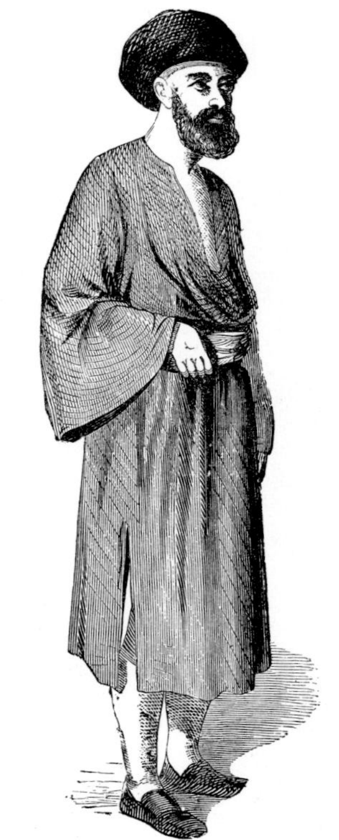

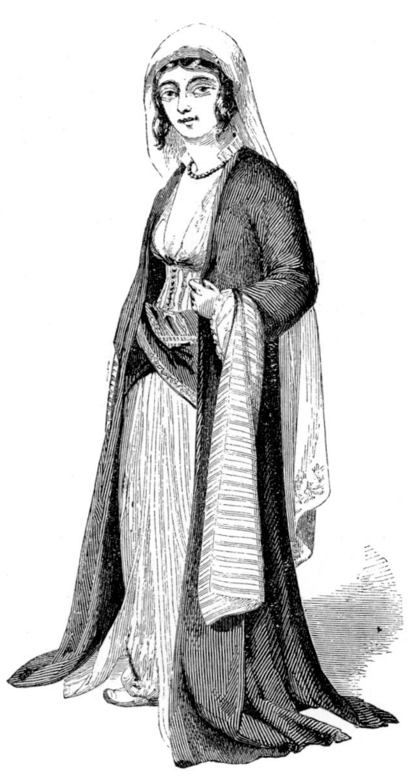

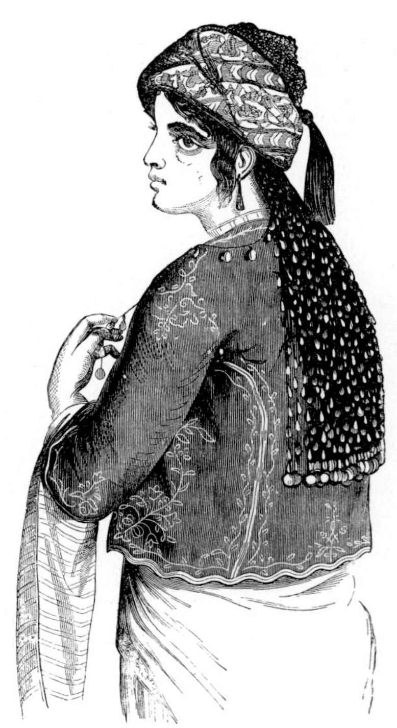

a	Syrian man, c. 1860	Syrischer Mann, um 1860	Siriano, ca. 1860	Syrien, vers 1860	Hombre sirio, hacia 1860
b	Palestine man, c. 1860	Palästinischer Mann, um 1860	Palestinese, ca. 1860	Palestinien, vers 1860	Hombre palestino, hacia el año 1860
c	Syrian lady, c. 1860	Syrische Frau, um 1860	Donna siriana, ca. 1860	Femme syrienne, vers 1860	Mujer siria, hacia el año 1860
d	Syrian girl, c. 1880	Syrisches Mädchen, um 1880	Ragazza siriana, ca. 1880	Jeune syrienne, vers 1880	Muchacha siria, hacia el año 1880

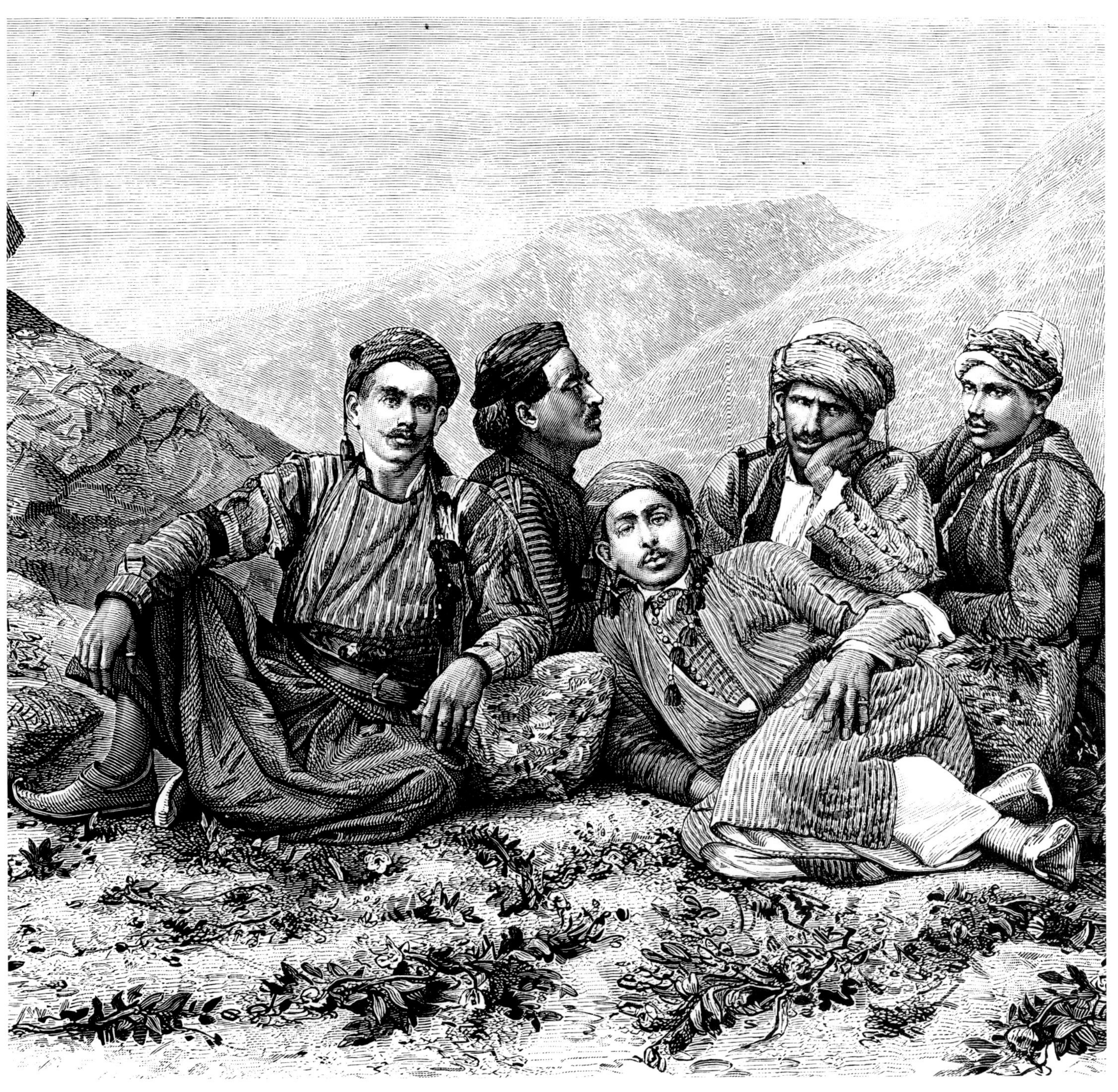

Syrian men, 1865 Syrische Männer, 1865 Uomini siriani, 1865 Syriens, 1865 Hombres sirios, 1865

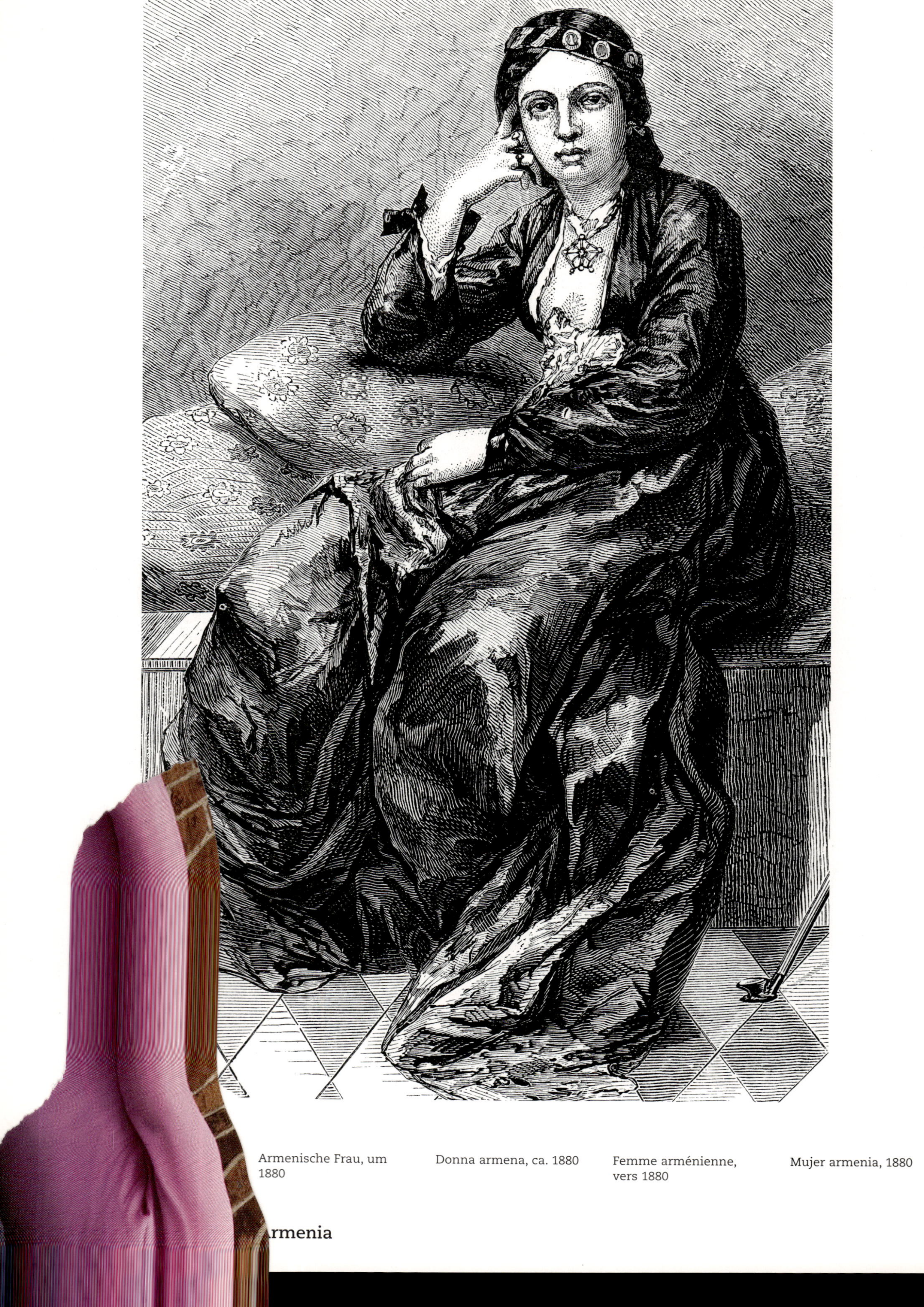

Armenische Frau, um 1880

Donna armena, ca. 1880

Femme arménienne, vers 1880

Mujer armenia, 1880

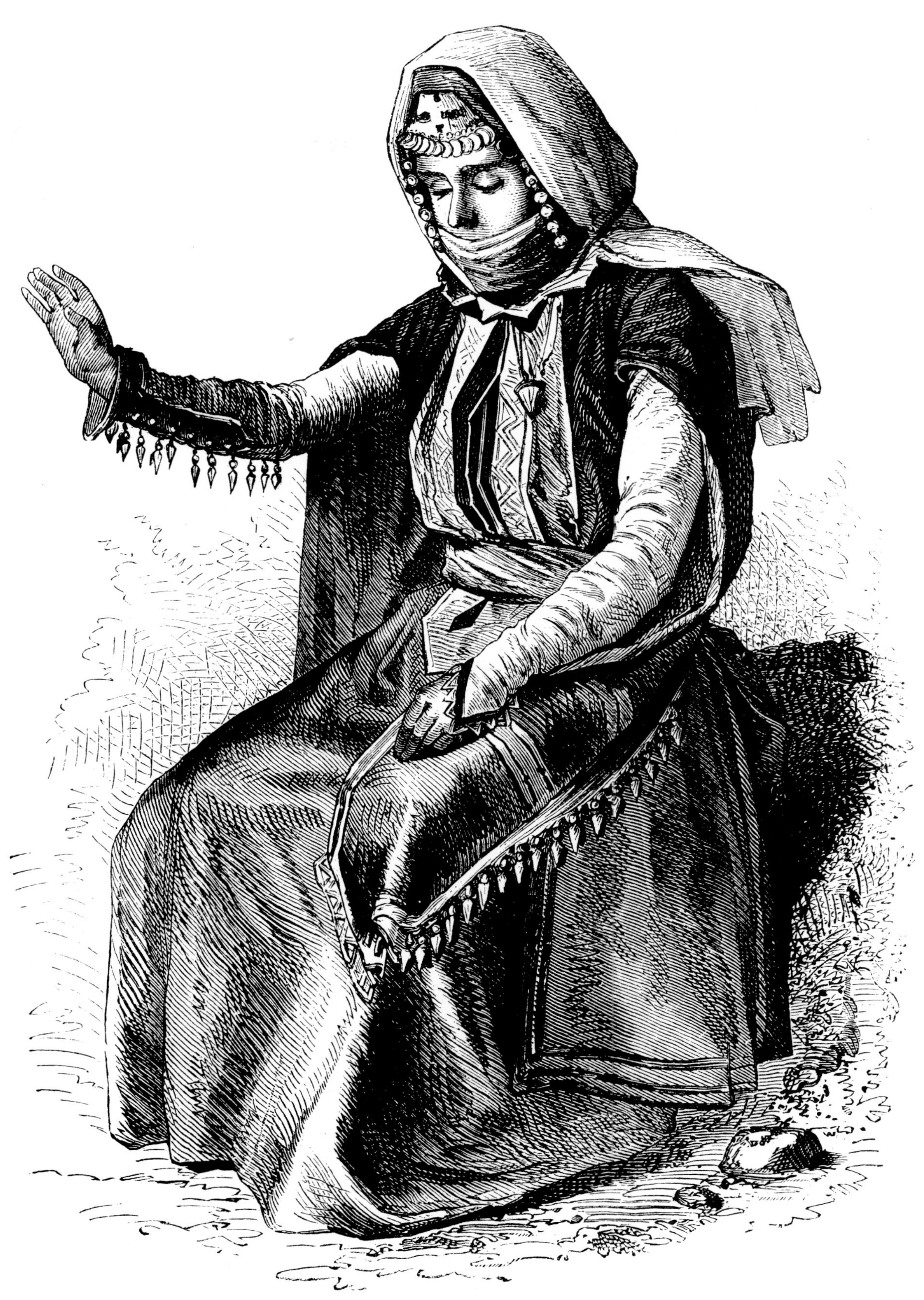

Armenian lady, c. 1865

Armenische Frau, um 1865

Donna armena, ca. 1865

Femme arménienne, vers 1865

Mujer armenia, 1865

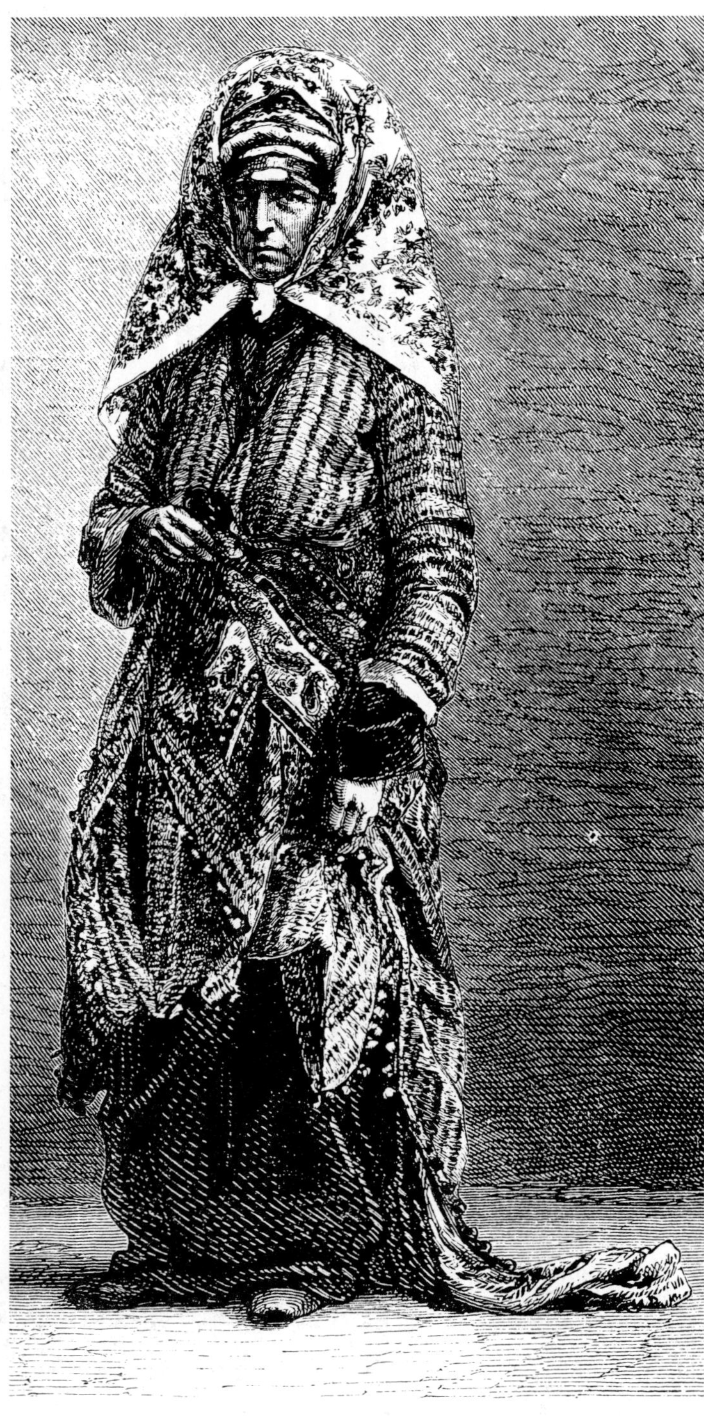

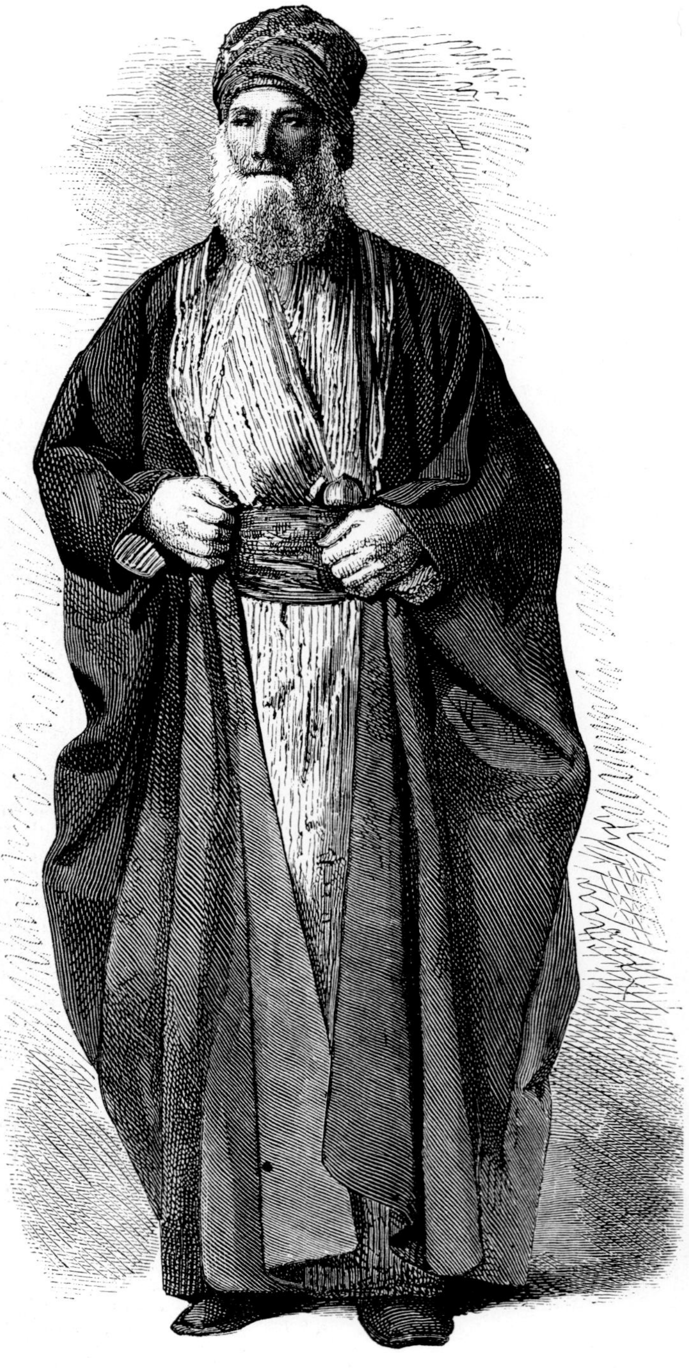

Jewish woman and man from Babylonia, c. 1860

Jüdische Frau und jüdischer Mann aus Babylonien, um 1860

Donna e uomo ebrei della Babilonia, ca. 1860

Femme et homme juifs de Babylone, vers 1860

Mujer y hombre judíos de Babilonia, hacia 1860

Iraq

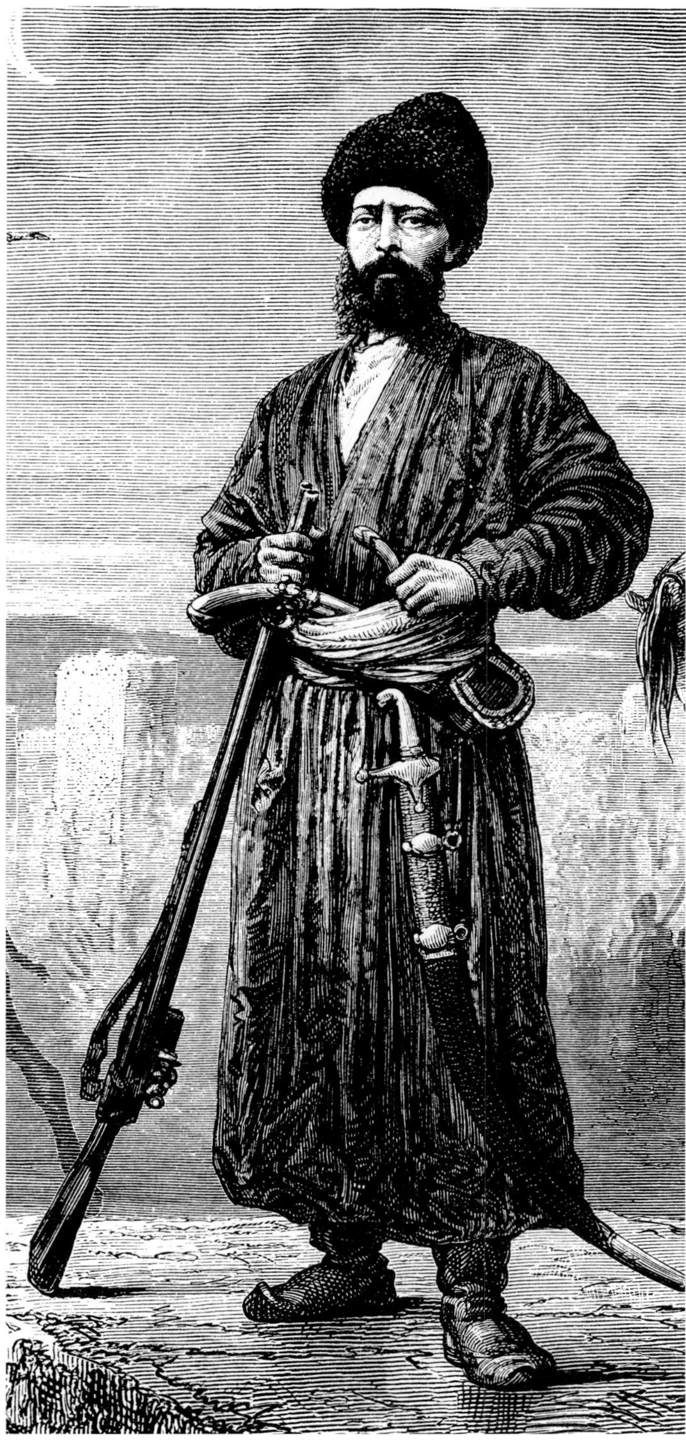

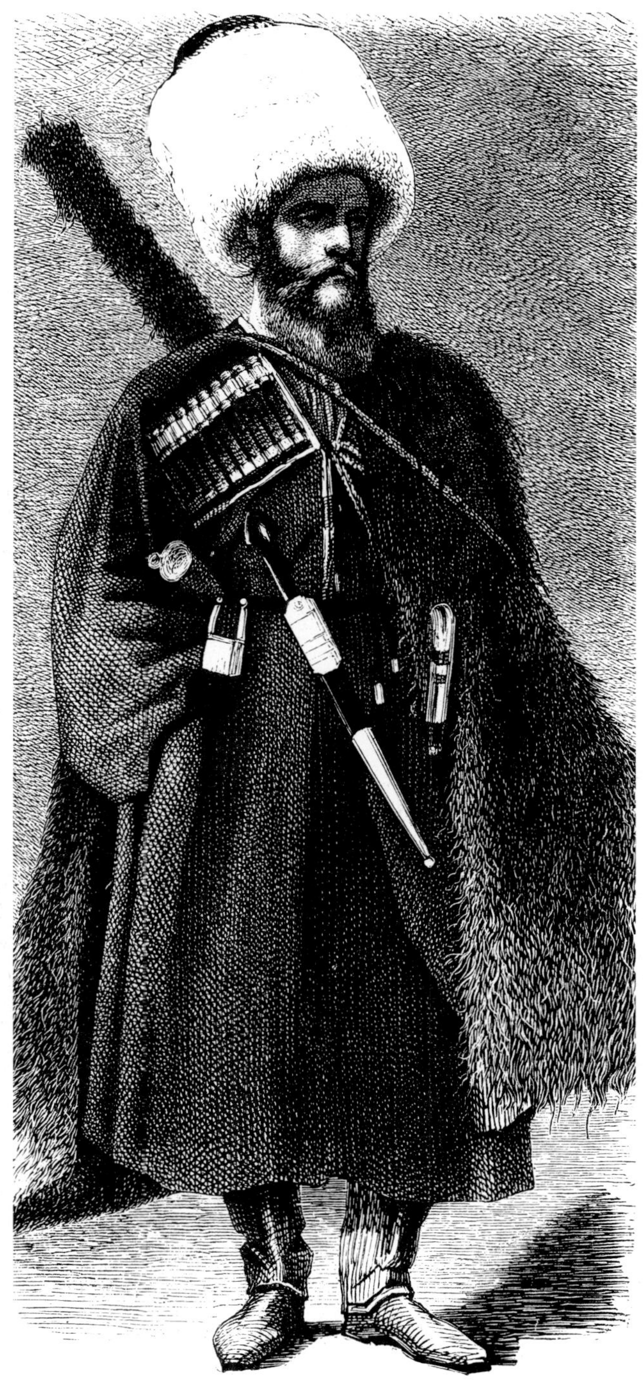

a	Turkmen officer, c. 1860	Turkmenischer Polizist, um 1860	Ufficiale turkmeno, ca. 1860	Officier turc, vers 1860	Oficial turcomano, 1860
b	Russian border officer, Kazakhstan, c. 1860	Russischer Grenzpolizist, Kasachstan, um 1860	Ufficiale di confine russo, Kazachistan, ca. 1860	Officier de frontière russe, Kazakhstan, vers 1860	Oficial de la frontera rusa, Kazajstán, 1860

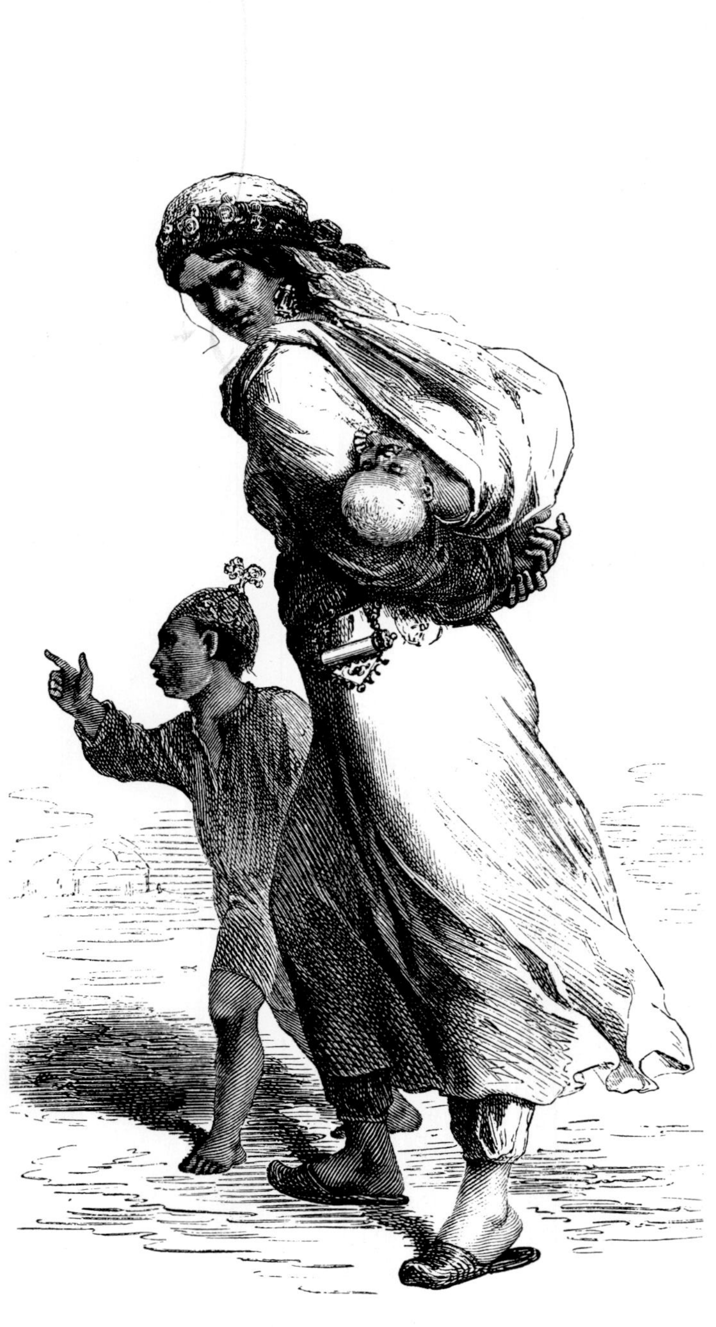

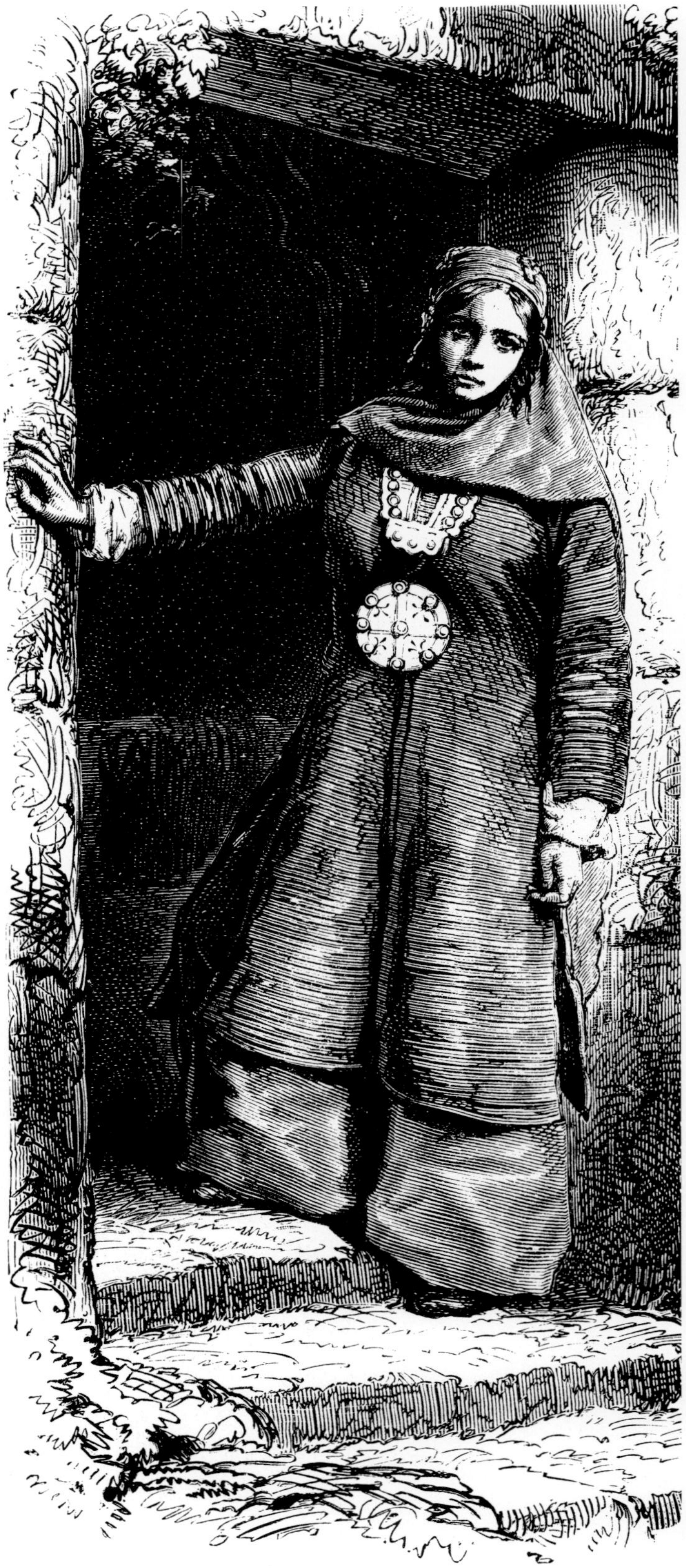

Turkmen women, c. 1860

Turkmenische Frauen, um 1860

Donne turamene, ca. 1860

Femmes du Turkmenistan, vers 1860

Mujeres turcomanas, alrededor del año 1860

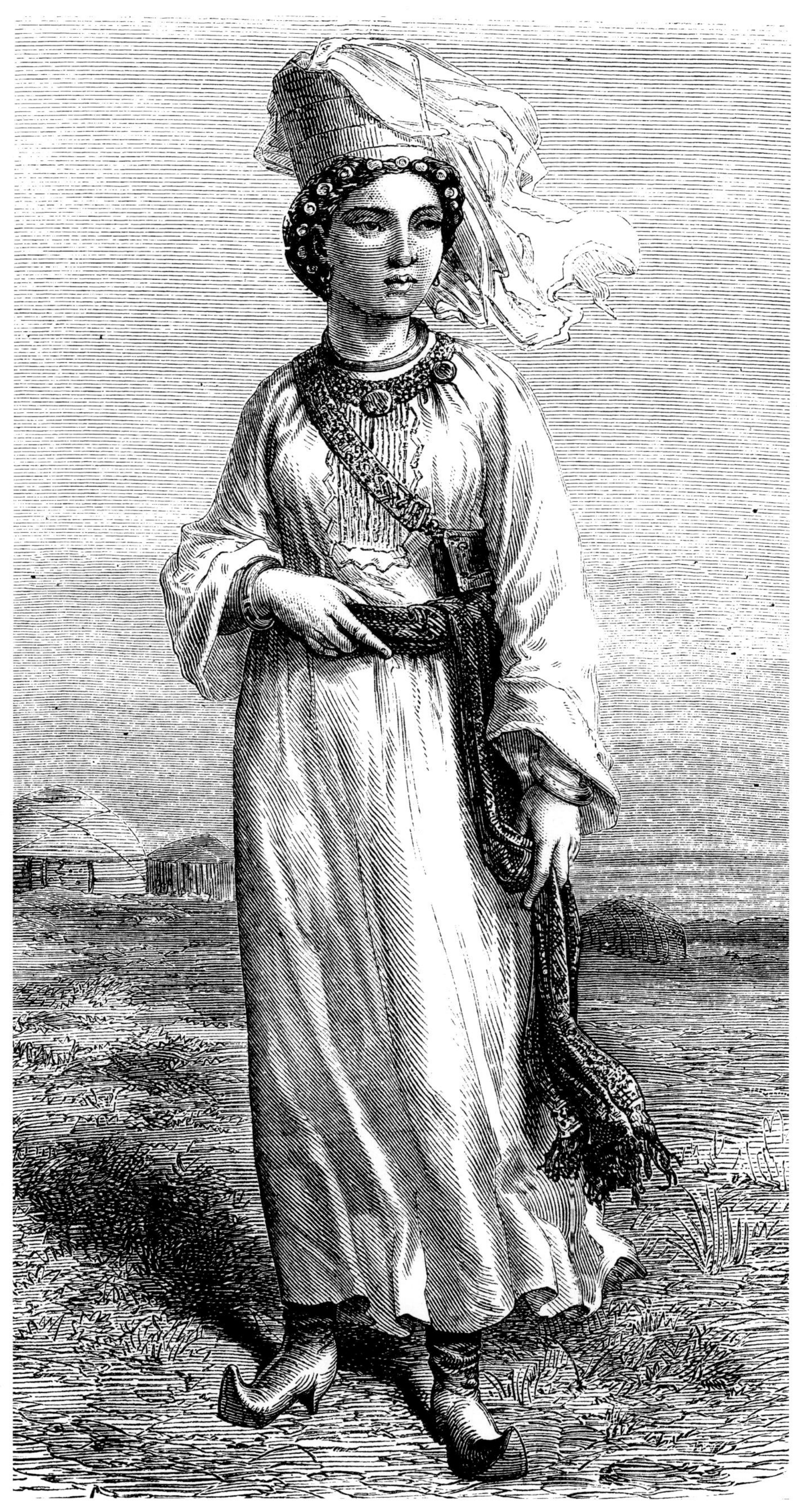

Turkmen woman, c. 1860

Turkmenische Frau, um 1860

Donna turkmena, ca. 1860

Femme du Turkmenistan, vers 1860

Mujer turcomana, 1860

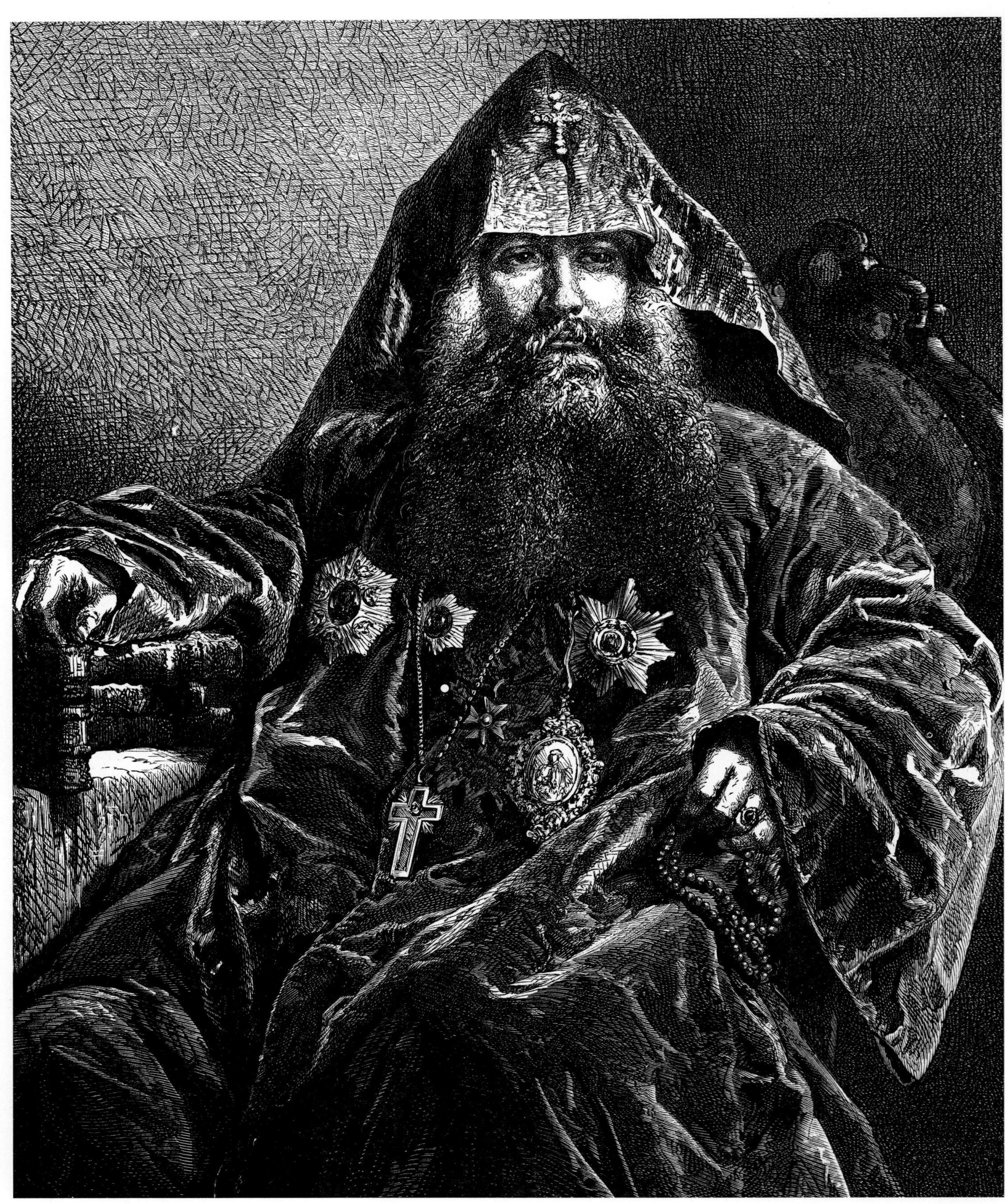

Armenian Patriarch, c. 1870

Armenischer Patriarch, um 1870

Patriarca armeno, ca. 1870

Patriarche arménien, vers 1870

Patriarca armenio, alrededor del año 1870

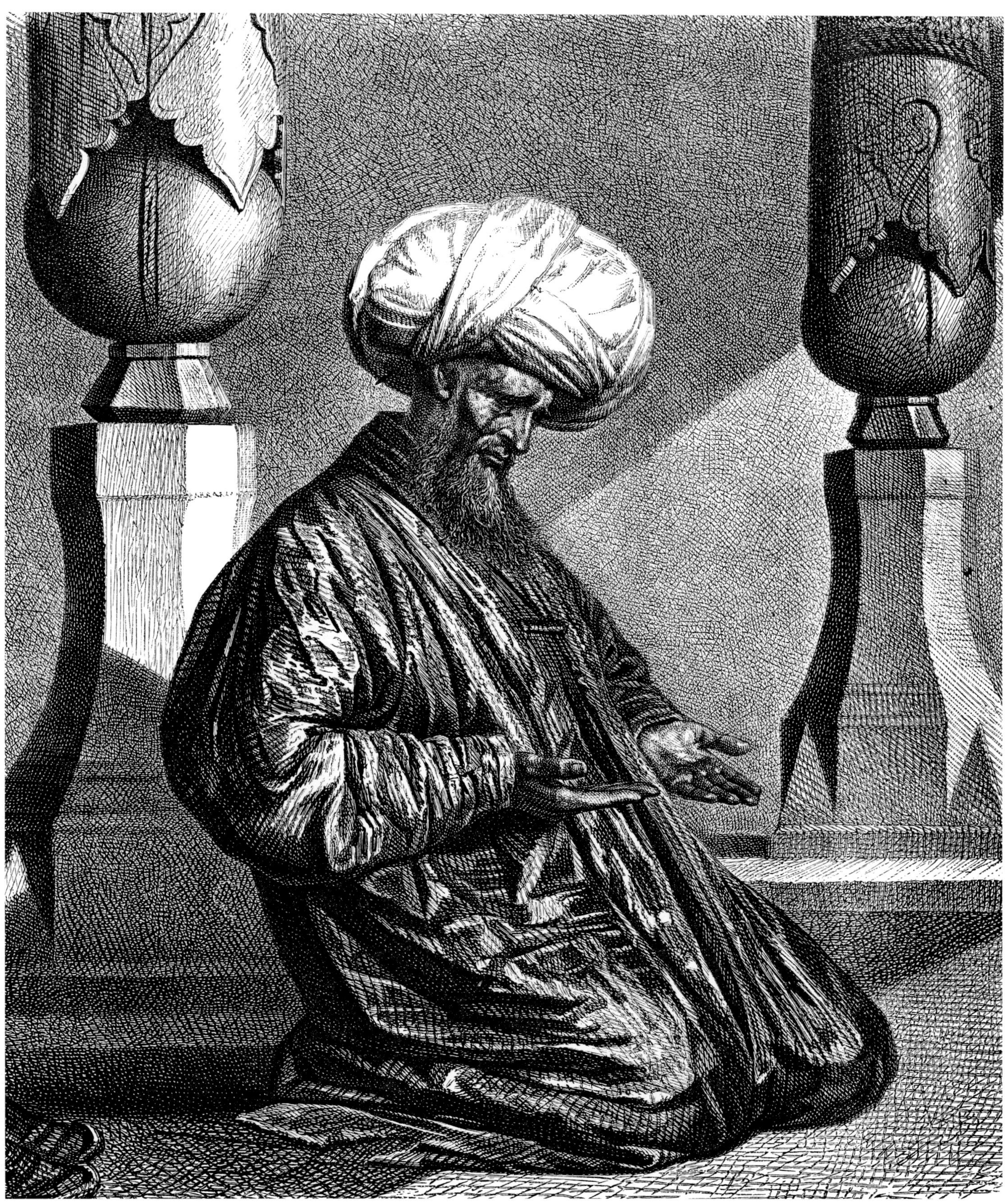

Praying muslim cleric, Samarkand, c. 1870

Betender moslemischer Geistlicher, Samarkand, um 1870

Sacerdote musulmano in preghiera, Samarcanda, ca. 1870

Ecclésiastique musulman en prière, Samarkand, vers 1870

Clérigo musulmán orando, Samarcanda, 1870

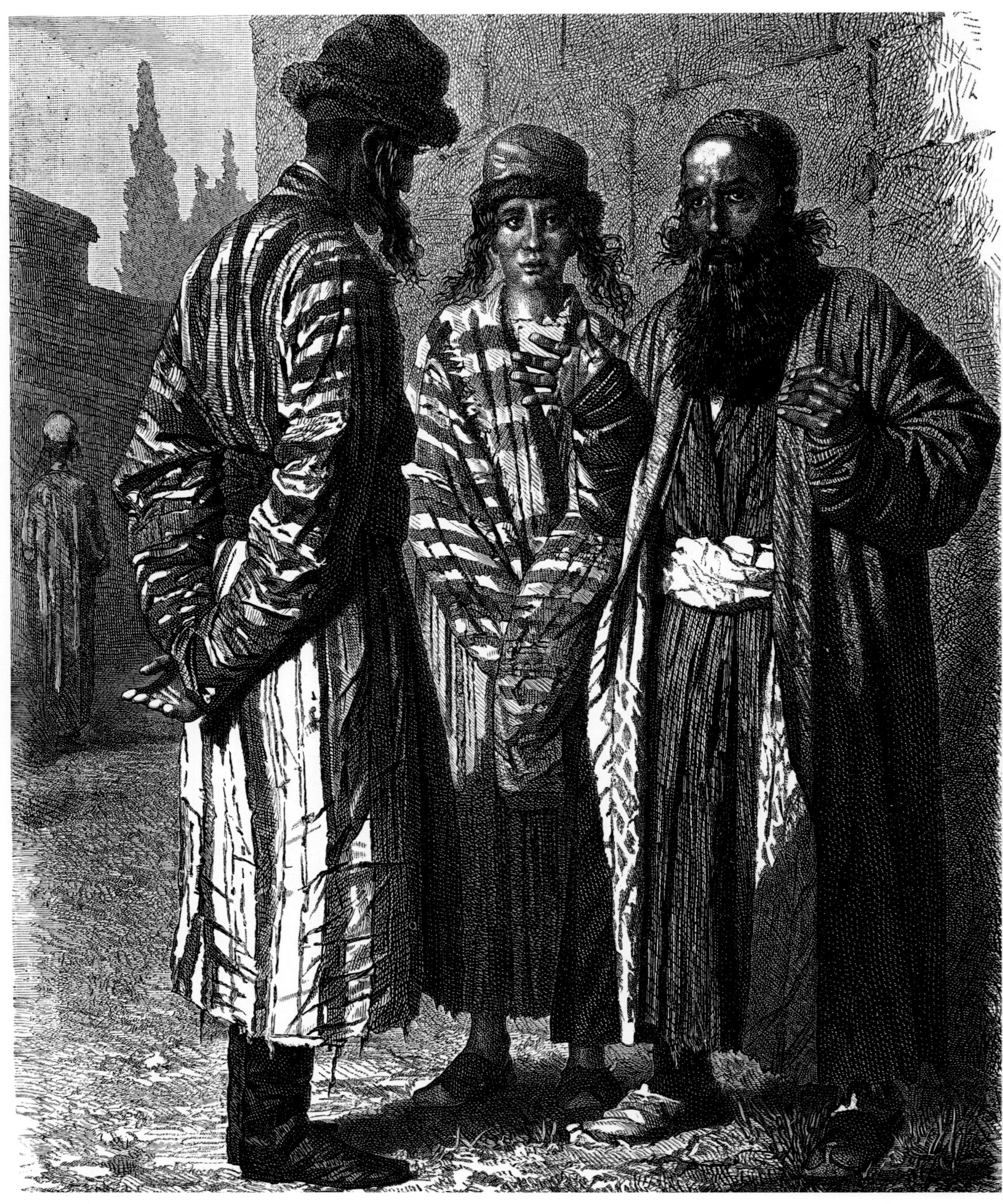

Jewish men in Tashkent, Uzbekistan, c. 1880

Jüdische Männer in Taschkent, Usbekistan, um 1880

Ebrei in Tashkent, Uzbechistan, ca. 1880

Juifs à Tachkent, Ouzbékistan, vers 1880

Judíos en Tashkent, Uzbekistán, hacia 1880

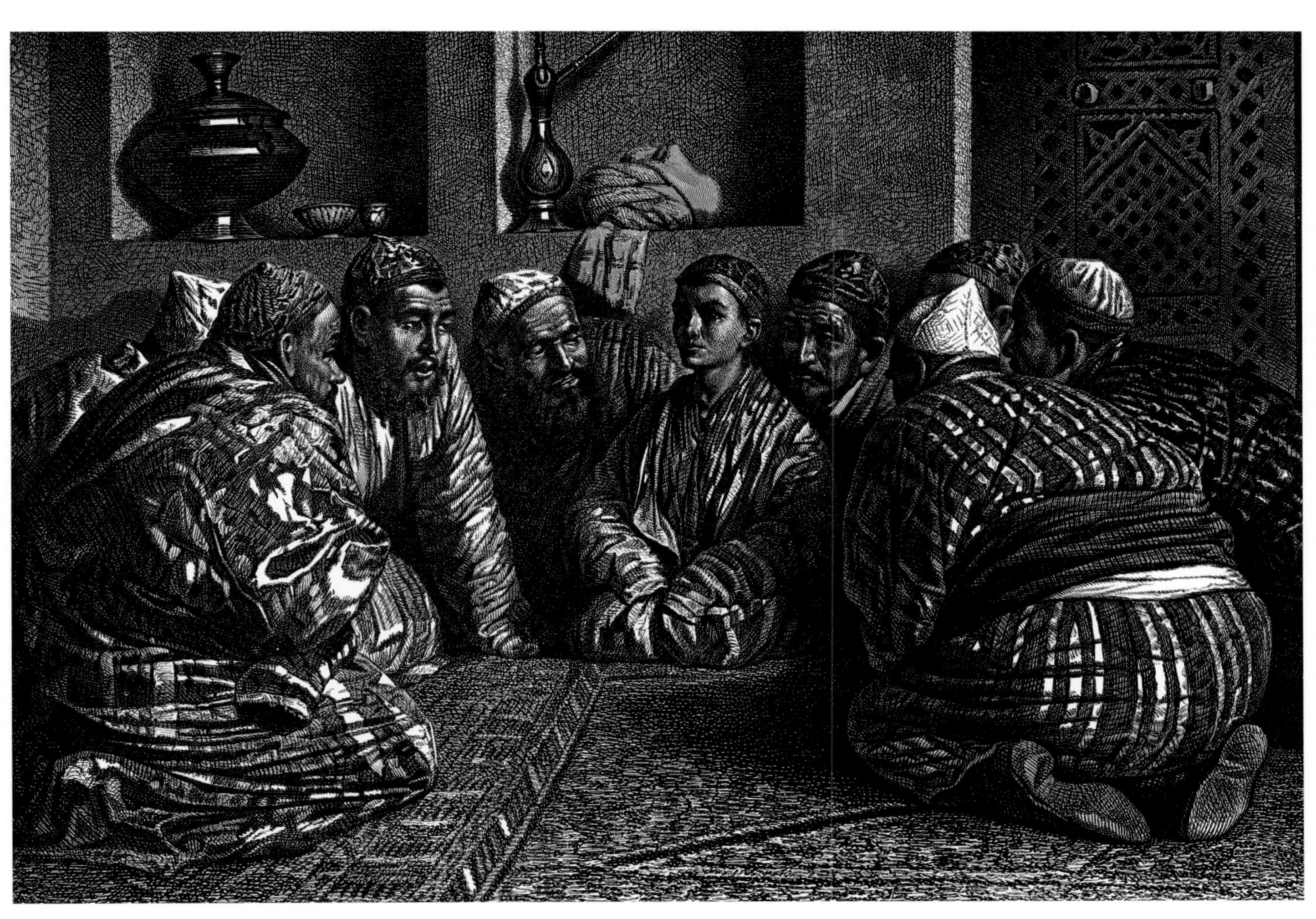

Uzbek men with a young dancer, c. 1880

Usbekische Männer mit einem jungen Tänzer, um 1880

Uzbechi con un giovane danzatore, ca. 1880

Ouzbeks avec un jeune danseur, vers 1880

Hombres uzbekos con un joven bailarín, 1880

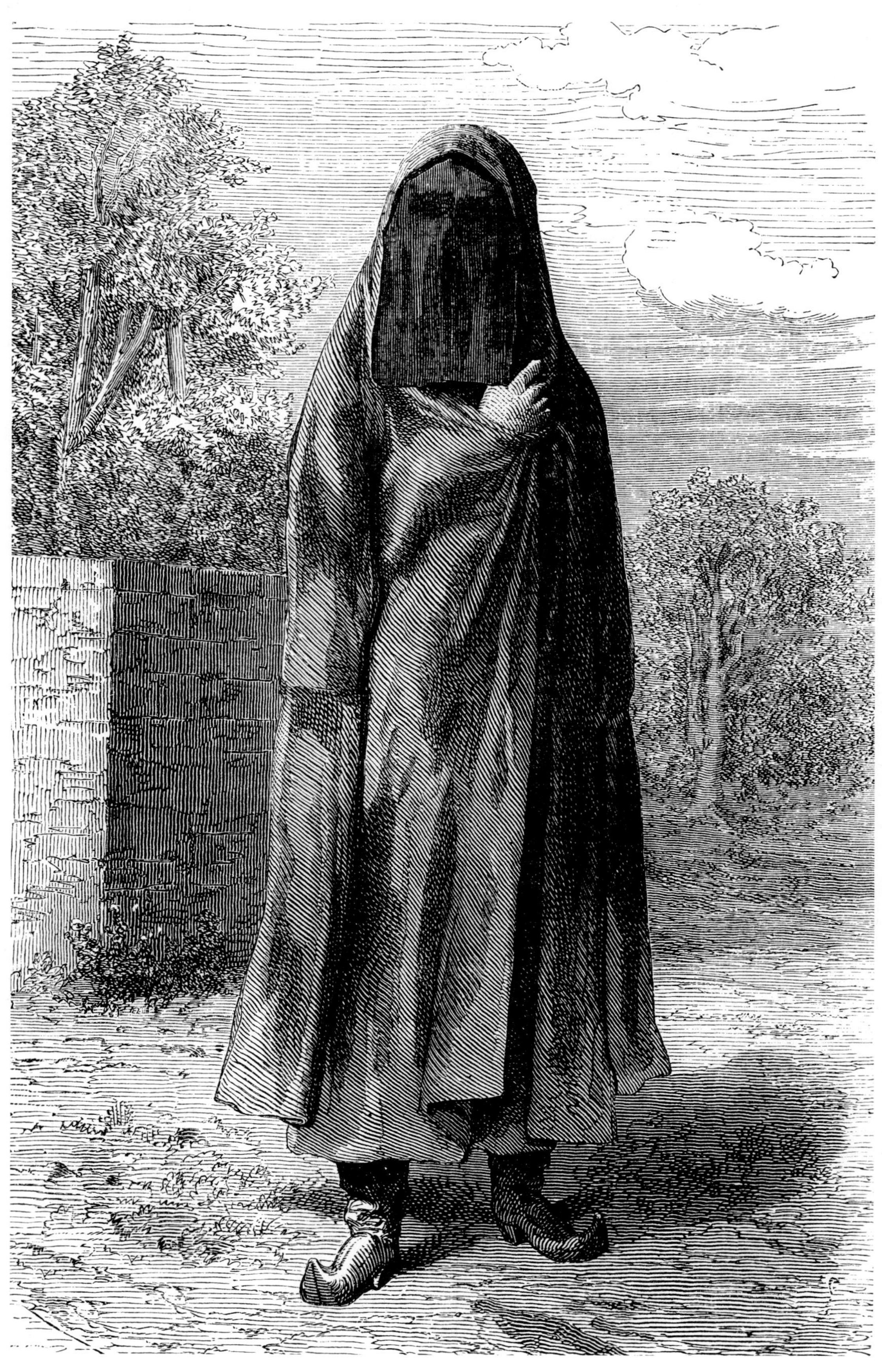

Veiled woman of Bokara, c. 1860

Verschleierte Frau aus Bokhara, um 1860

Donna di Bokara con velo, ca. 1860

Femme voilée de Bokera, vers 1860

Mujer con velo, Bokara, alrededor del año 1860

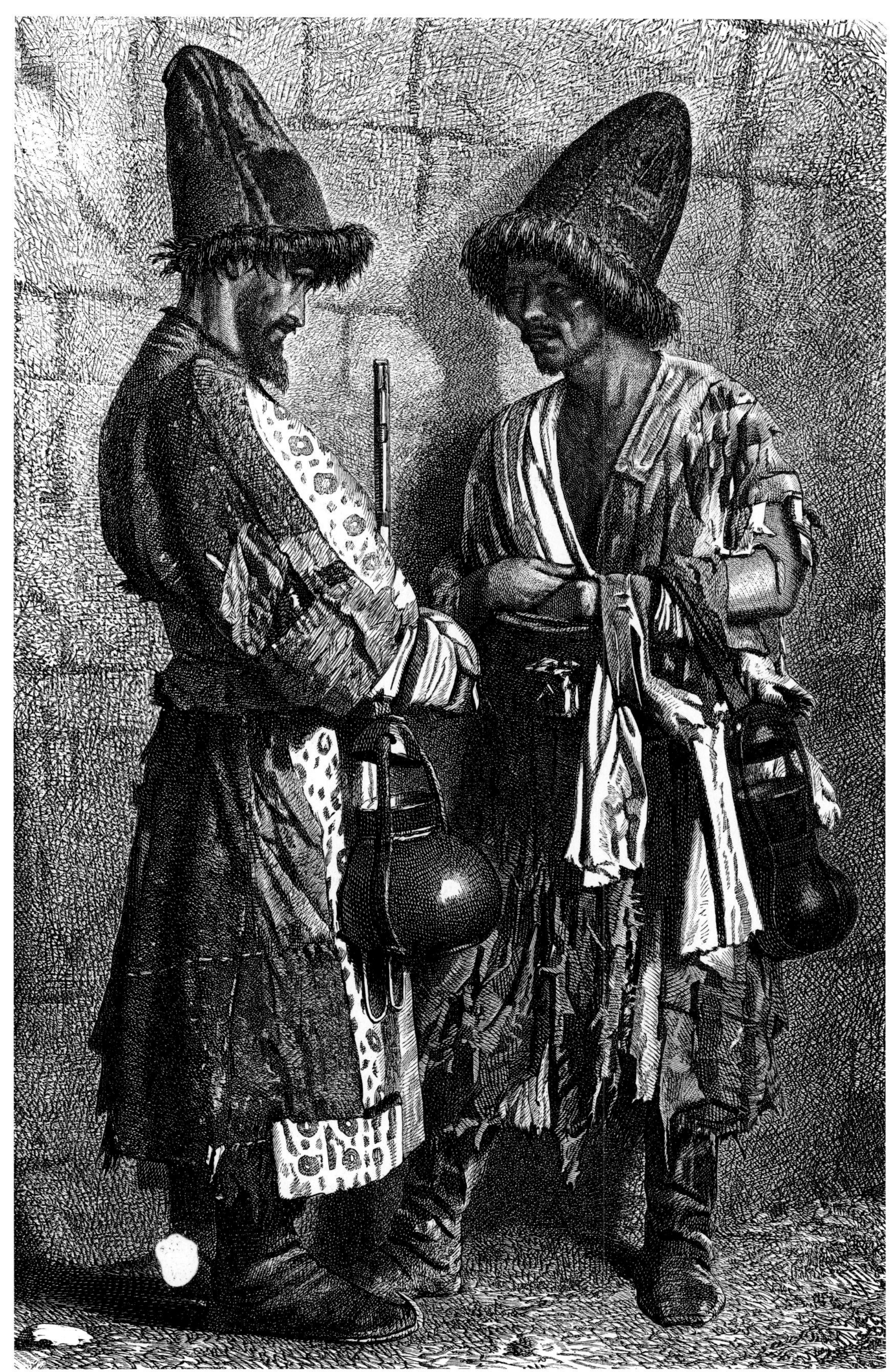

Beggars, Samarkand, Uzbekistan, c. 1880

Bettler, Samarkand, Usbekistan, um 1880

Mendicanti, Samarcanda, Uzbechistan, ca. 1880

Mendiants, Samarkand, Ouzbékistan, vers 1880

Mendigos, Samarcanda, Uzbekistán, hacia 1880

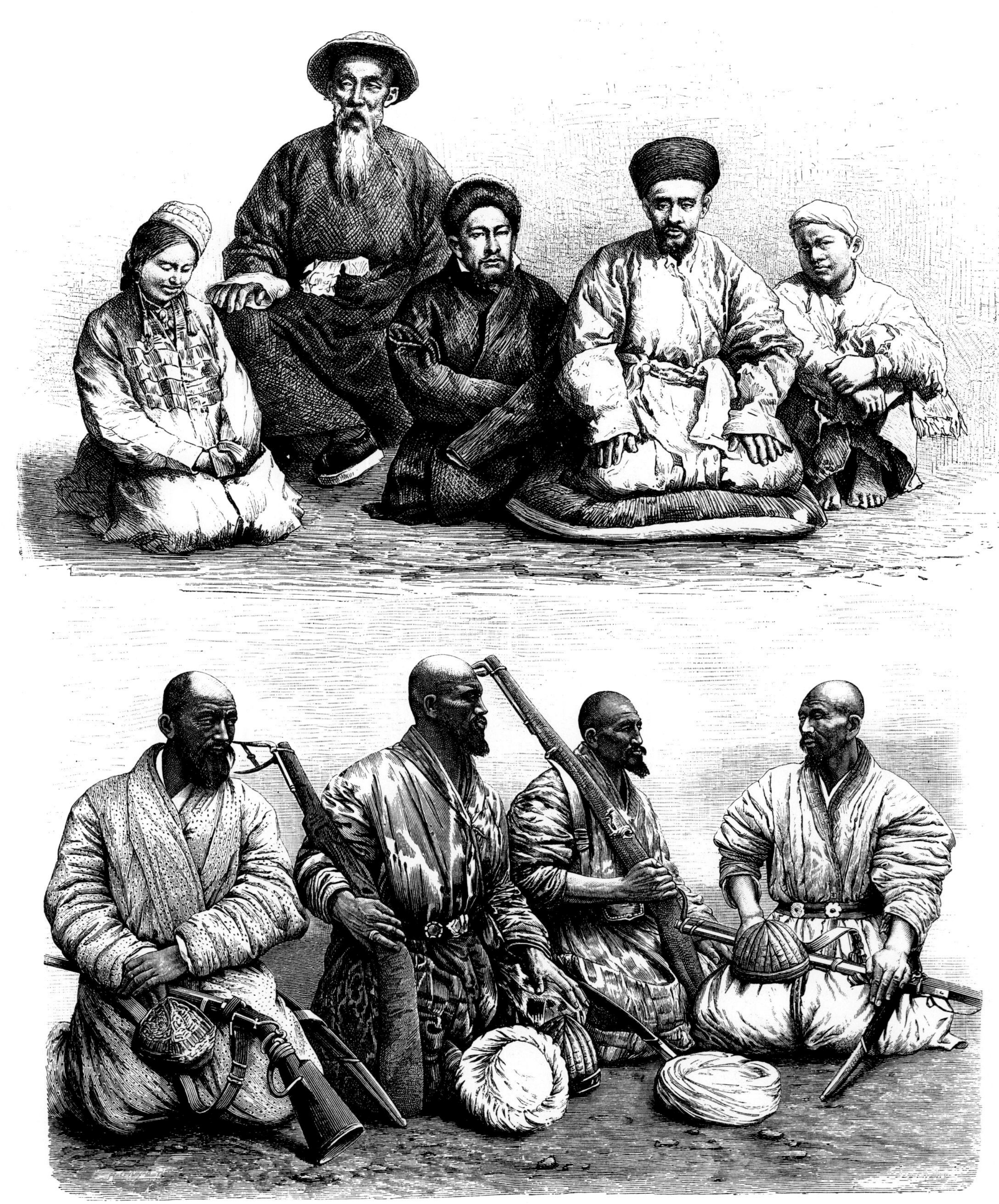

a	Kalmyks (Russian Federation), c. 1875	Kalmücken (Russische Föderation), um 1875	Kalmyk (Federazione Russa), ca. 1875	Kalmouks (Fédération russe), vers 1875	Calmucos (Federación Rusa), hacia el año 1875
b	Tajik men, c. 1875	Tadschiken ,um 1875	Uomini tajik, ca. 1875	Tadjiks, vers 1875	Hombres tayikos, 1875

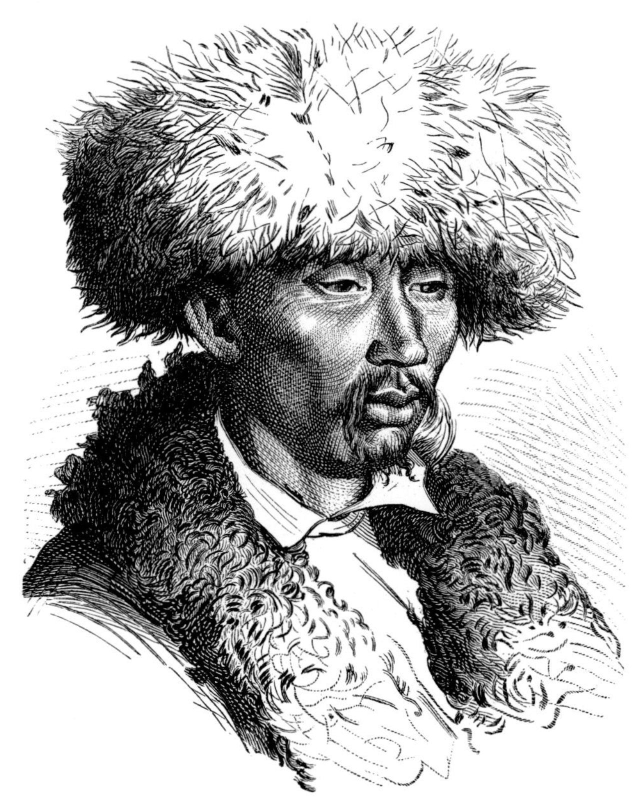

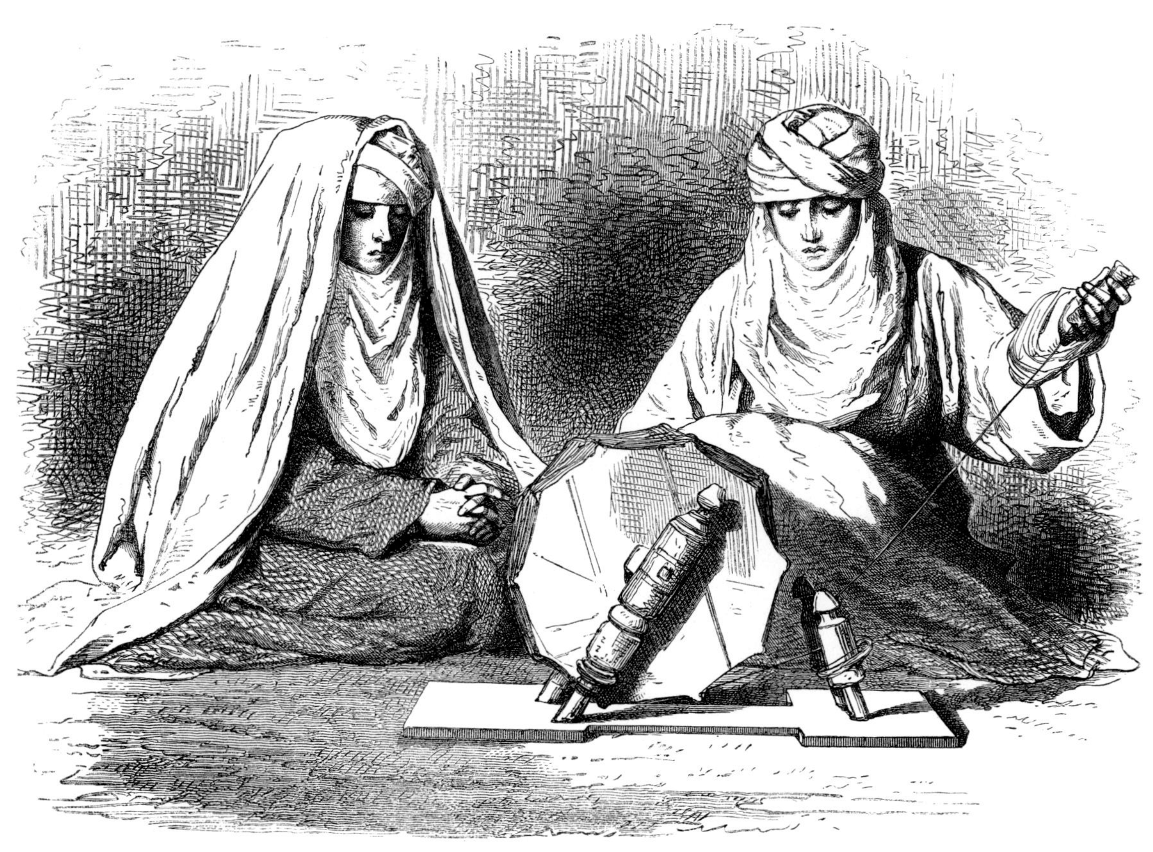

Kyrgysz man and women, c. 1860

Kirgisischer Mann und Frauen, um 1860

Uomo e donne del Kirghizistan, ca. 1860

Homme et femme du Kirghizistan, vers 1860

Hombre y mujeres kirguís, hacia 1860

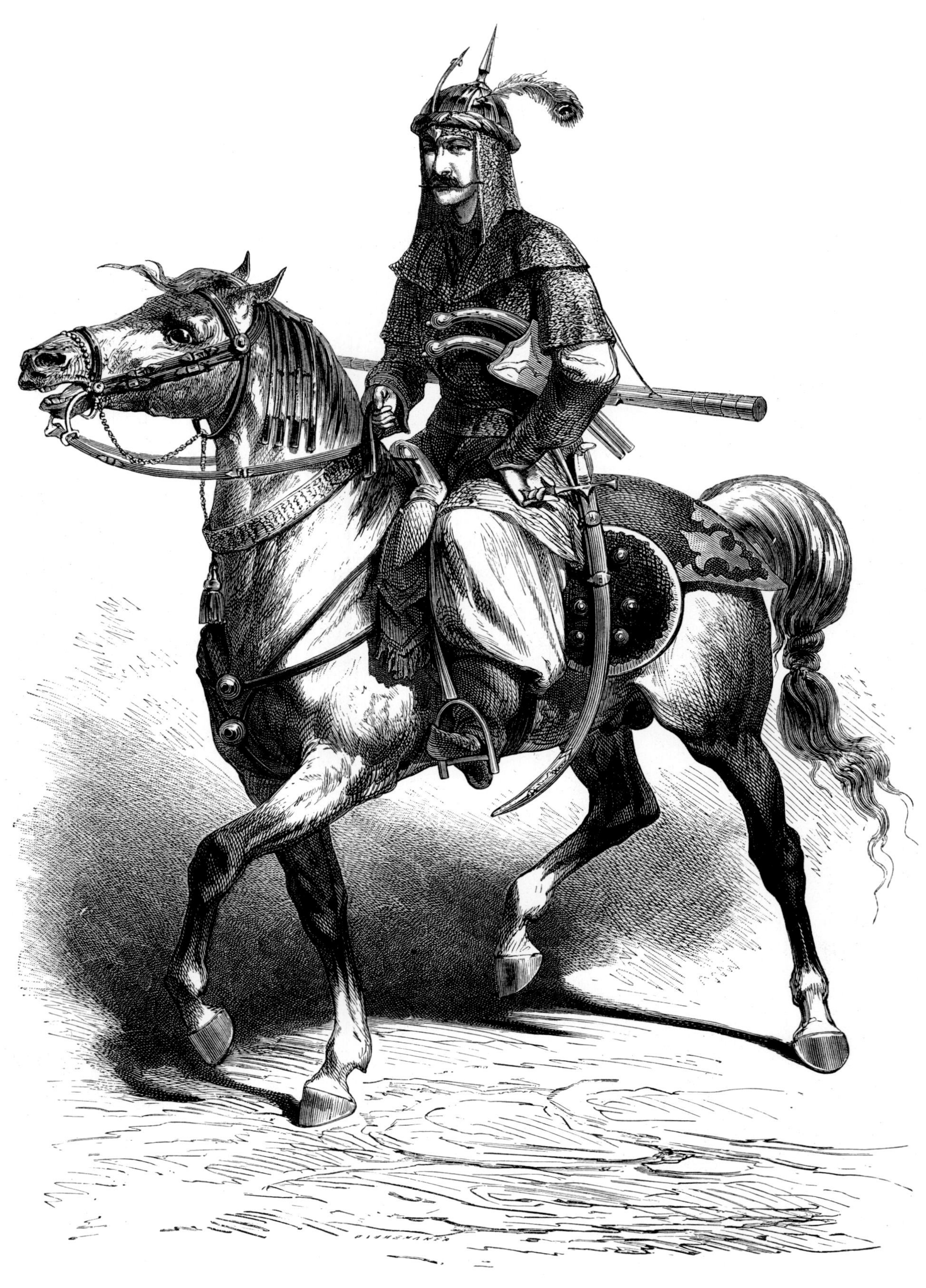

Kurdish horseman, Persia, c. 1880

Kurdischer Reiter, Persien, um 1880

Cavaliere curdo, Persia, ca. 1880

Cavalier kurde, Perse, vers 1880

Jinete curdo, Persia, alrededor del año 1880

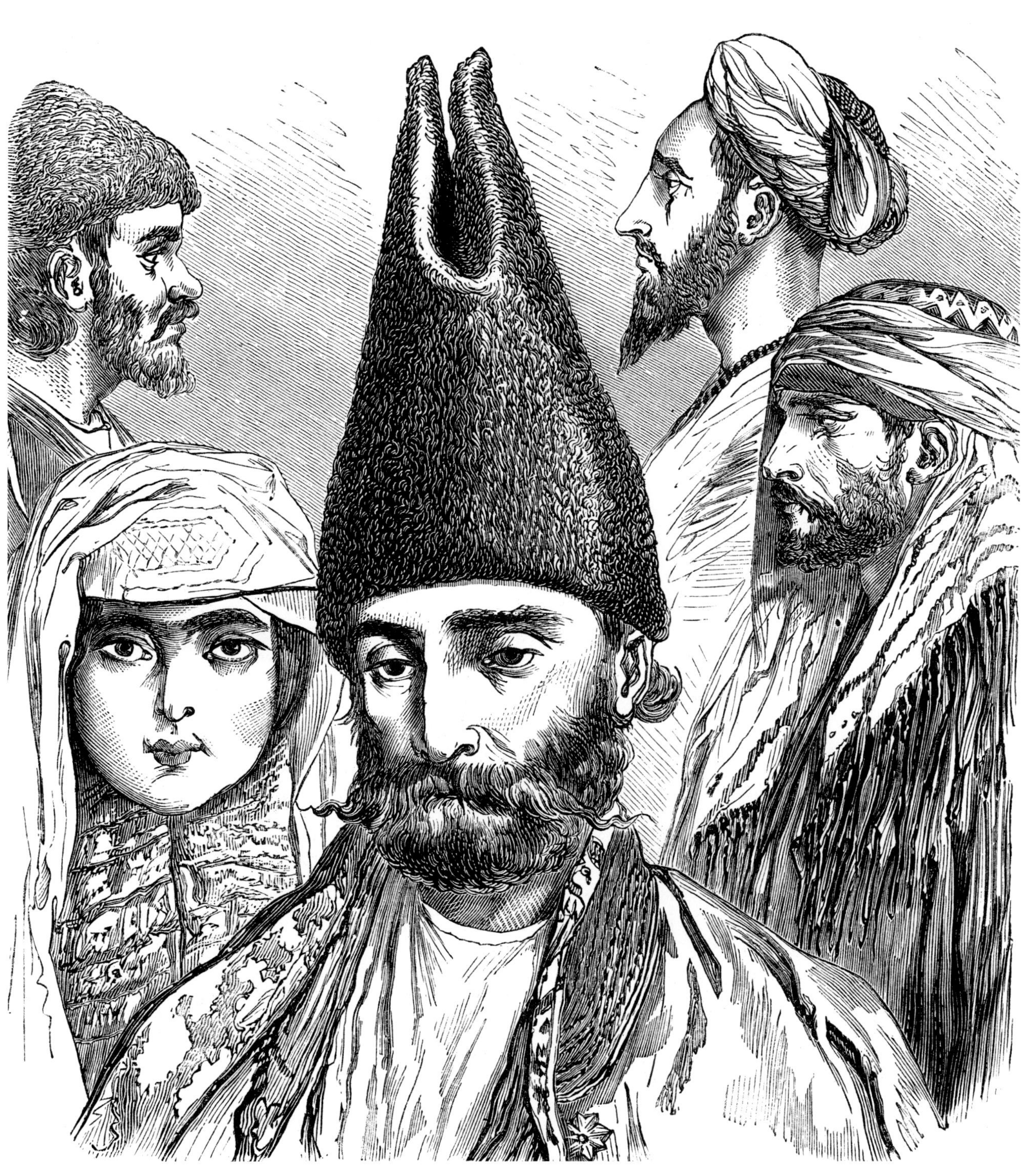

Persian men and woman, c. 1870

Persischer Männer und Frau, um 1870

Uomini e donna persiani, ca. 1870

Hommes et femme persans, vers 1870

Hombres y mujer persas, alrededor del año 1870

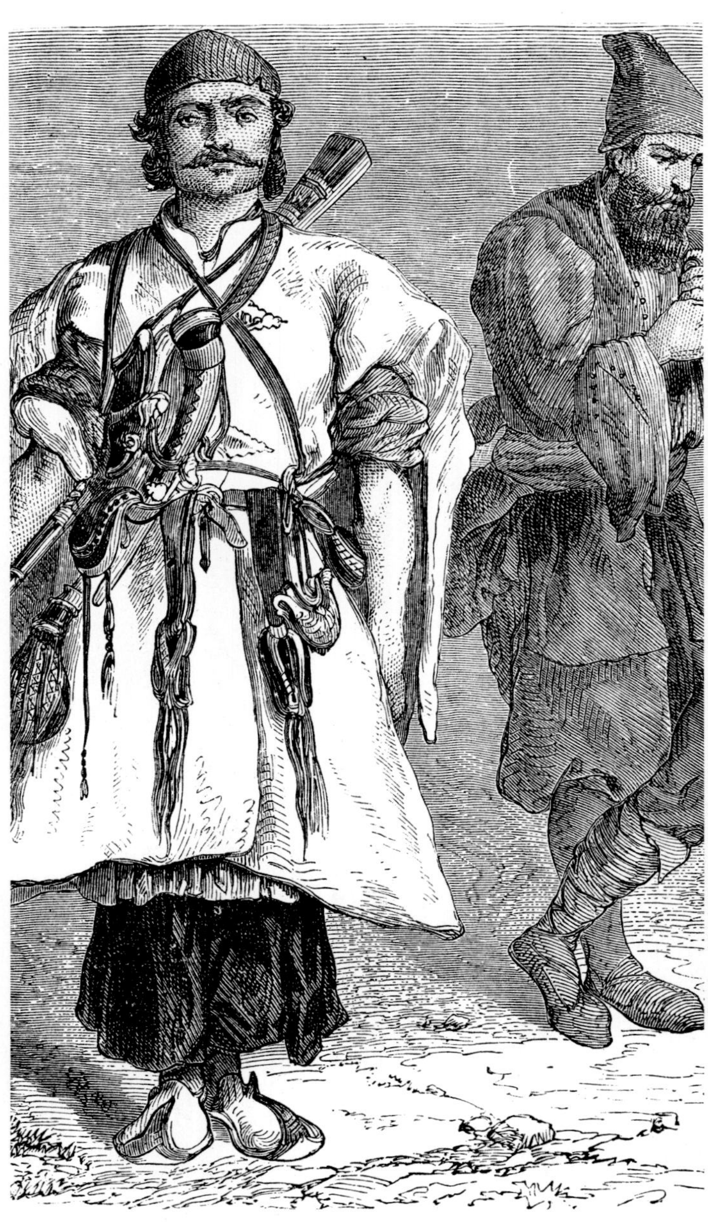

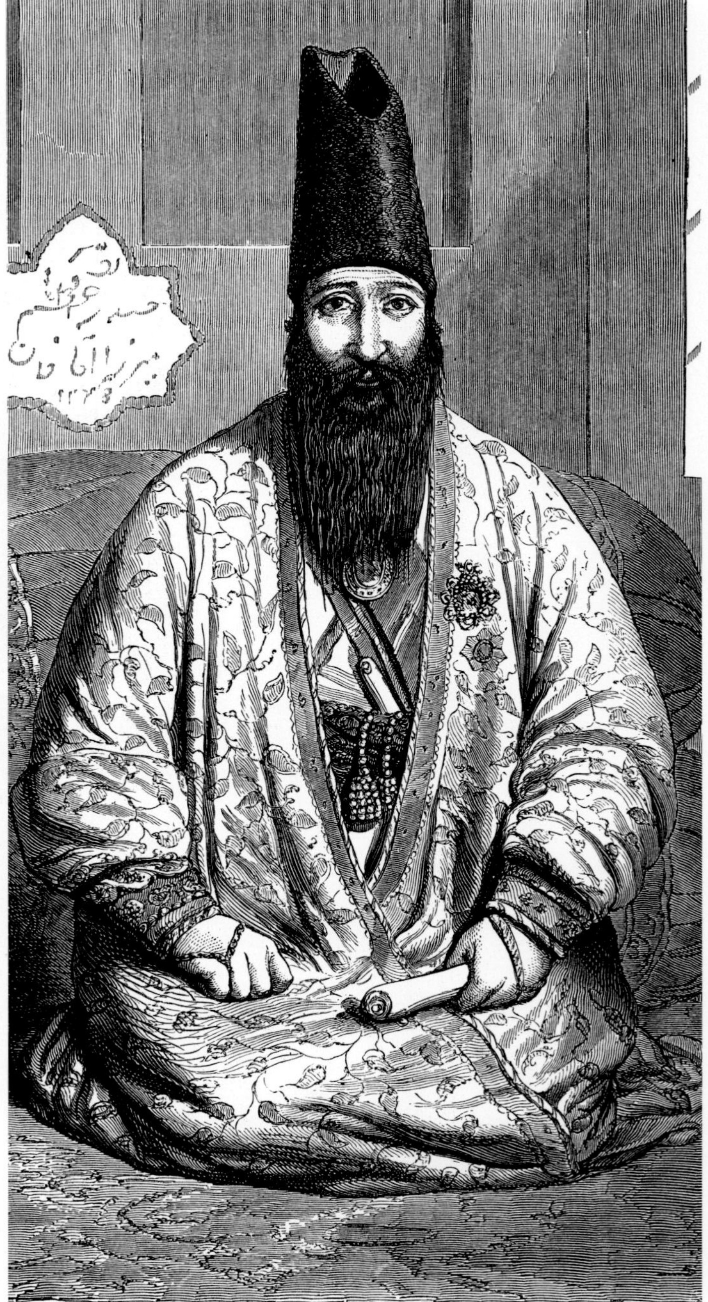

a	Persian wanderers	Persische Wanderer	Girovaghi persiani	Marcheurs persans	Nómadas persas
b	Persian scholar	Persischer Schüler	Erudito persiano	Érudit persan	Erudito persa

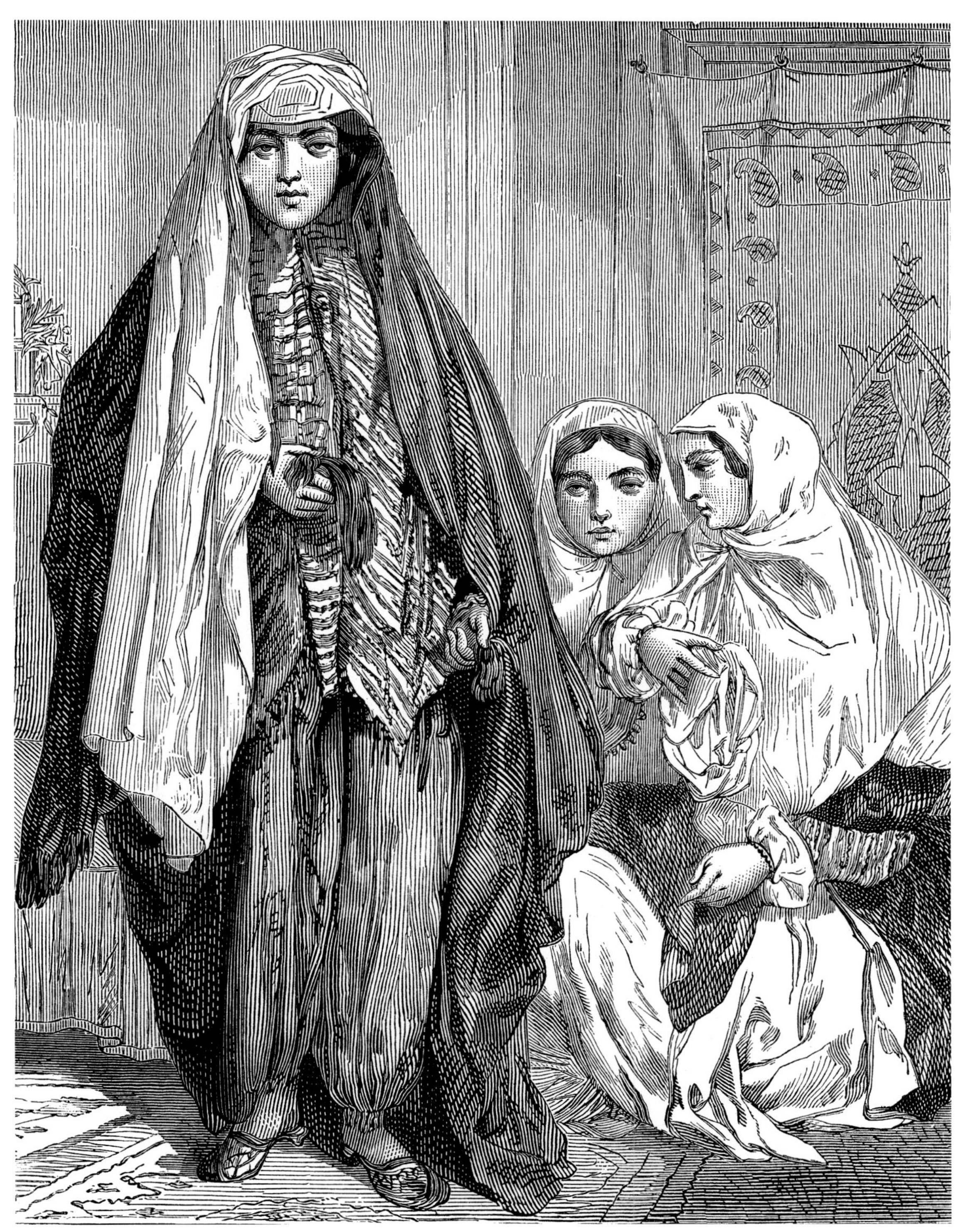

Persian ladies, c. 1880

Persische Damen, um 1880

Donne persiane, ca. 1880

Femmes persanes, vers 1880

Mujeres persas, 1880

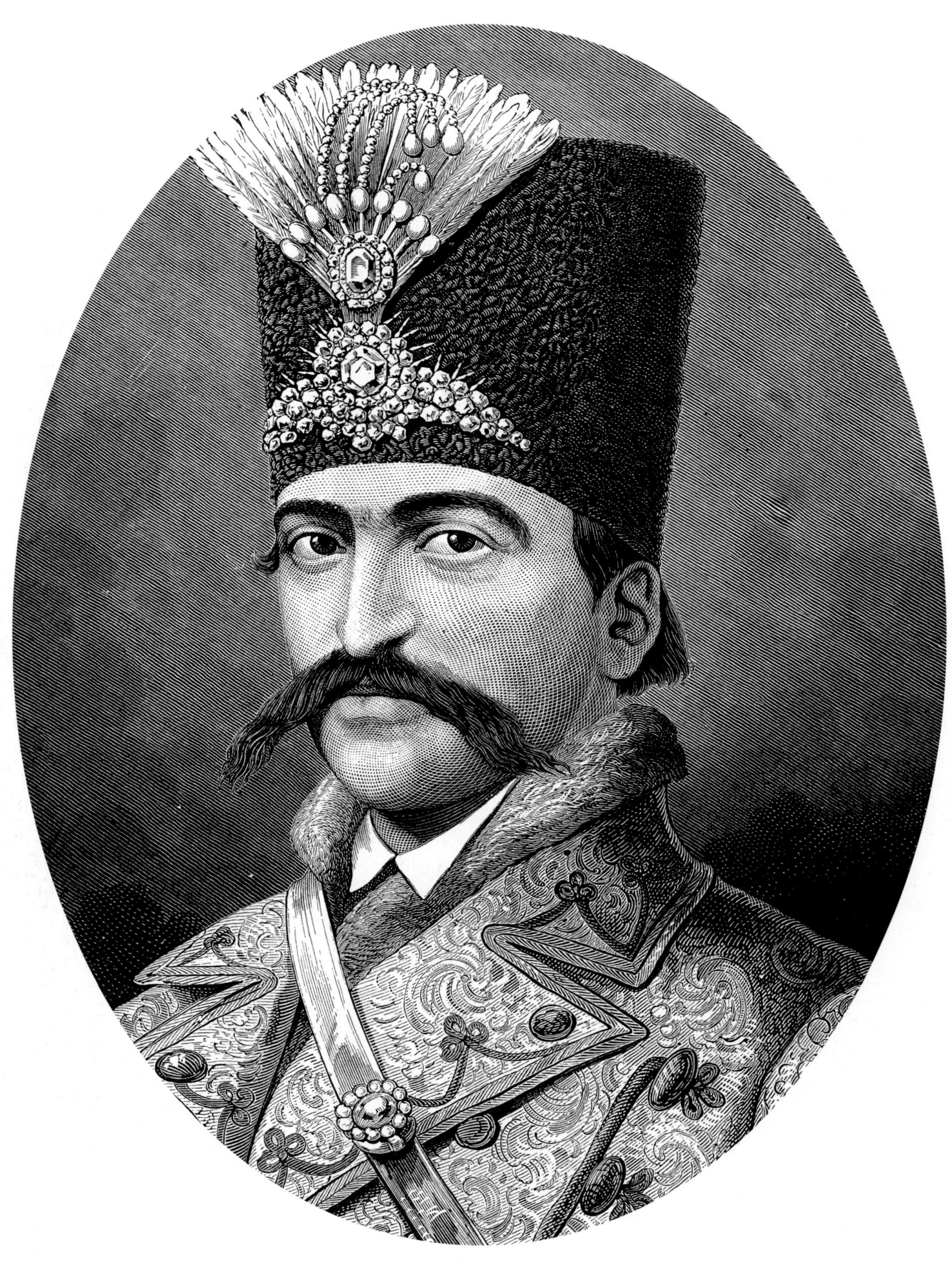

The Shah of Persia, 1880

Der Schah von Persien, 1880

Lo Scià di Persia, 1880

Le Shah de Perse, 1880

El sha de Persia, 1880

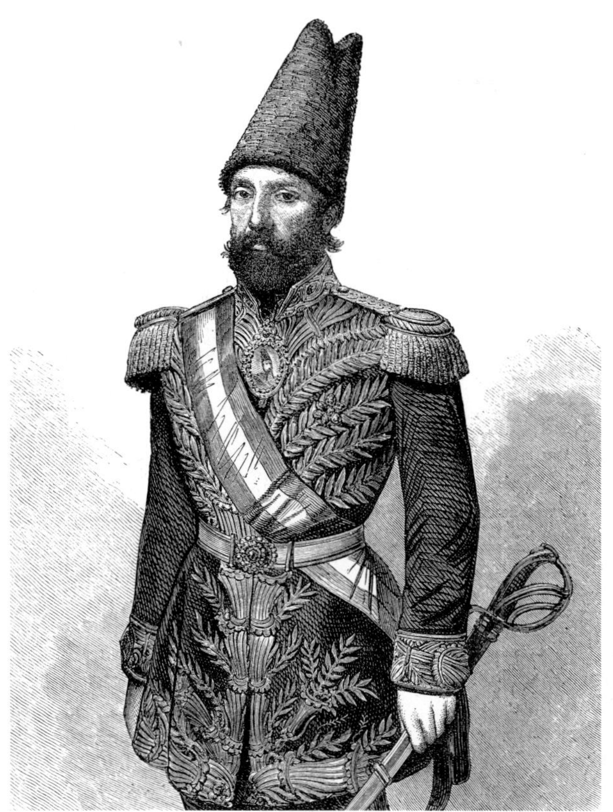

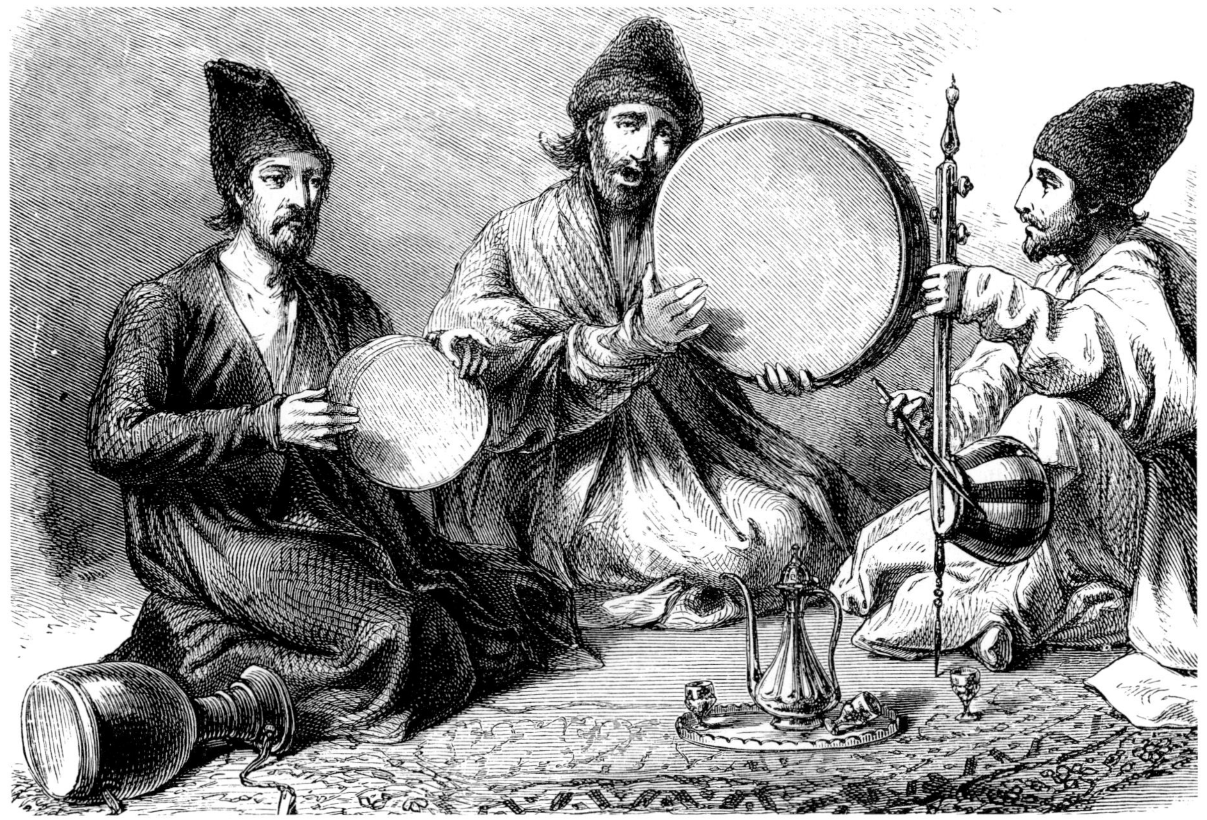

a	Governor of a Province	Der Gouverneur einer Provinz	Governatore di una provincia	Gouverneur d'une province	Gobernador de una provincia
b	Persian Musicians, c. 1860	Persische Musiker, um 1860	Musicisti persiani, ca. 1860	Musiciens persans, vers 1860	Músicos persas, hacia el año 1860

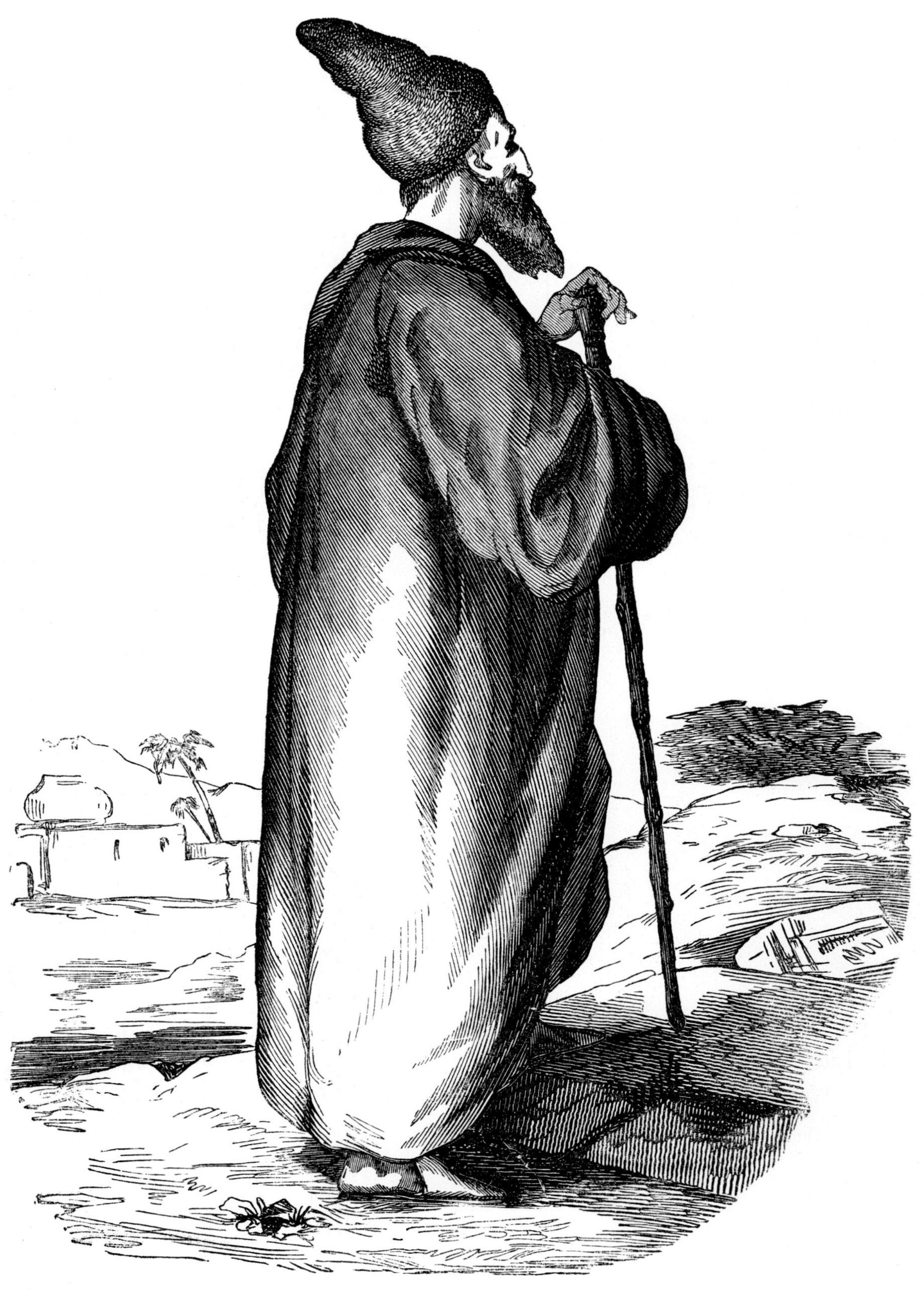

Persian, 1885 Perser, 1885 Persiano, 1885 Perse, 1885 Persa, 1885

Persia

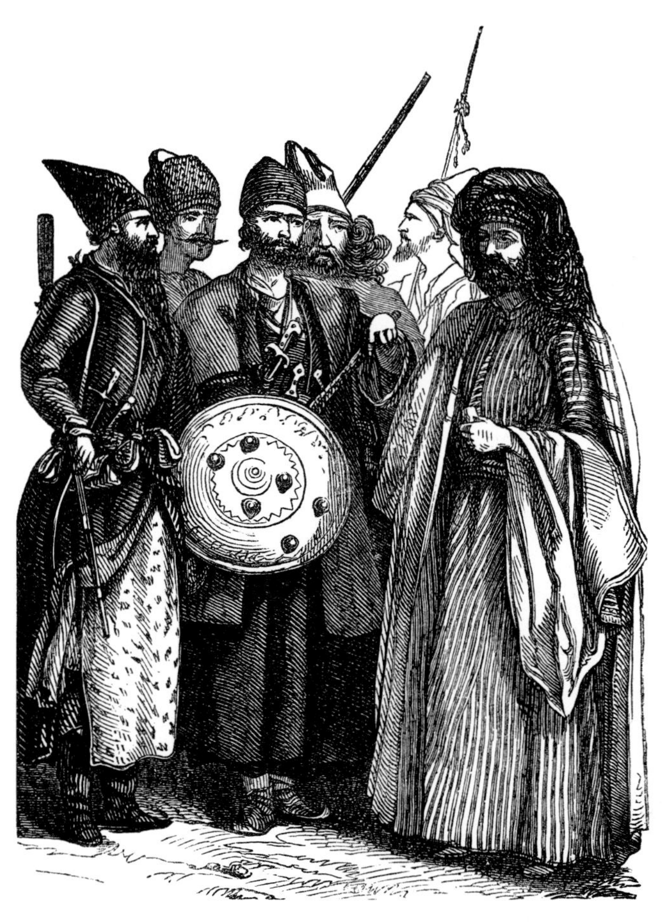

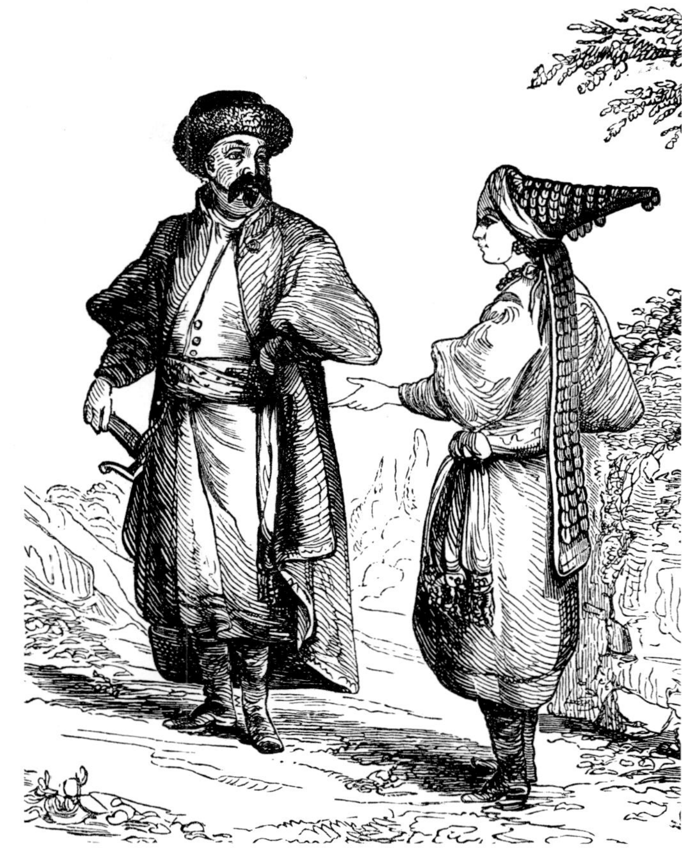

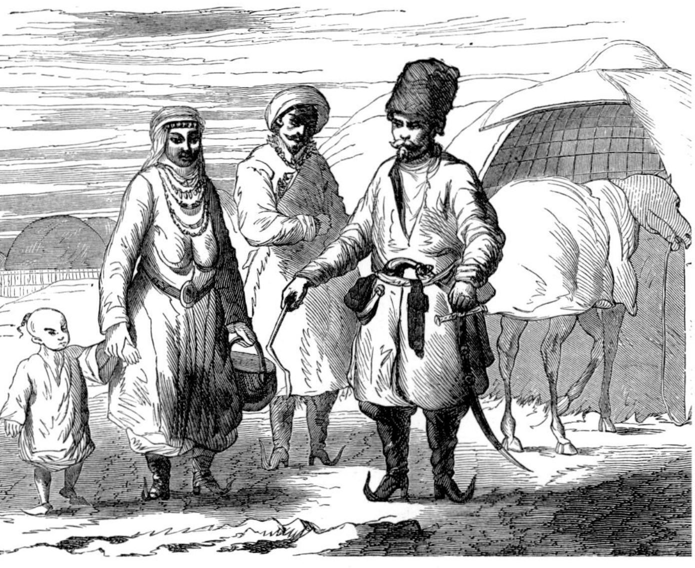

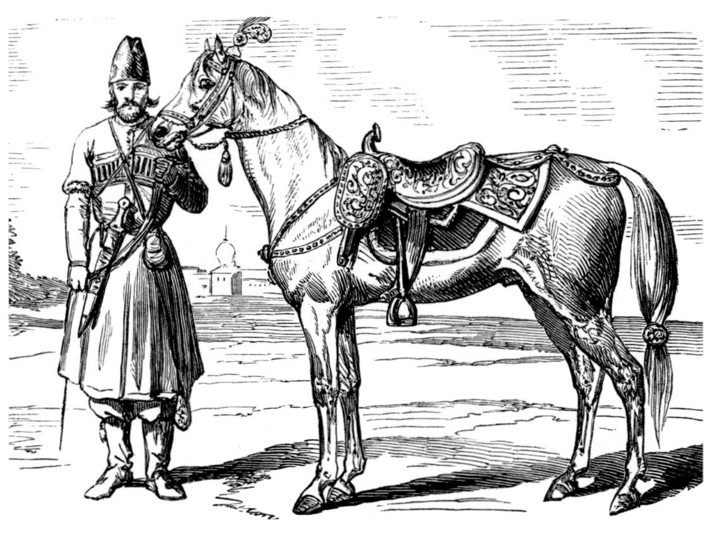

a	Persian soldiers, 1885	Persische Soldaten, 1885	Soldati persiani, 1885	Soldats persans, 1885	Soldados persas, 1885
b	Tartars from Kazan, Persia, 1885	Tataren aus Kasan, Persien, 1885	Tartari del Kazan, Persia, 1885	Tartares du Kazan, Perse, 1885	Tártaros de Kazan, Persia, 1885
c	Persian family, 1885	Persische Familie, 1885	Famiglia persiana, 1885	Famille persane, 1885	Familia persa, 1885
d	The shah's horse and keeper, 1885	Das Pferd des Schahs mit Reitknecht, 1885	Il cavallo dello Scià con il suo stalliere, 1885	Le cheval et le valet de pied du Shah, 1885	El caballo del sha y su cuidador, 1885

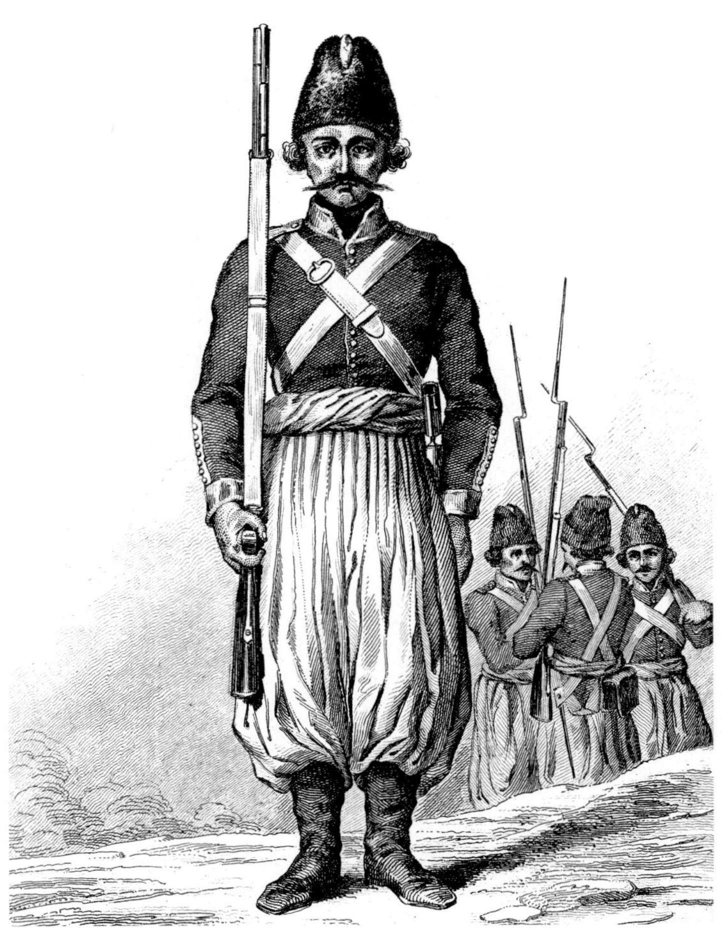

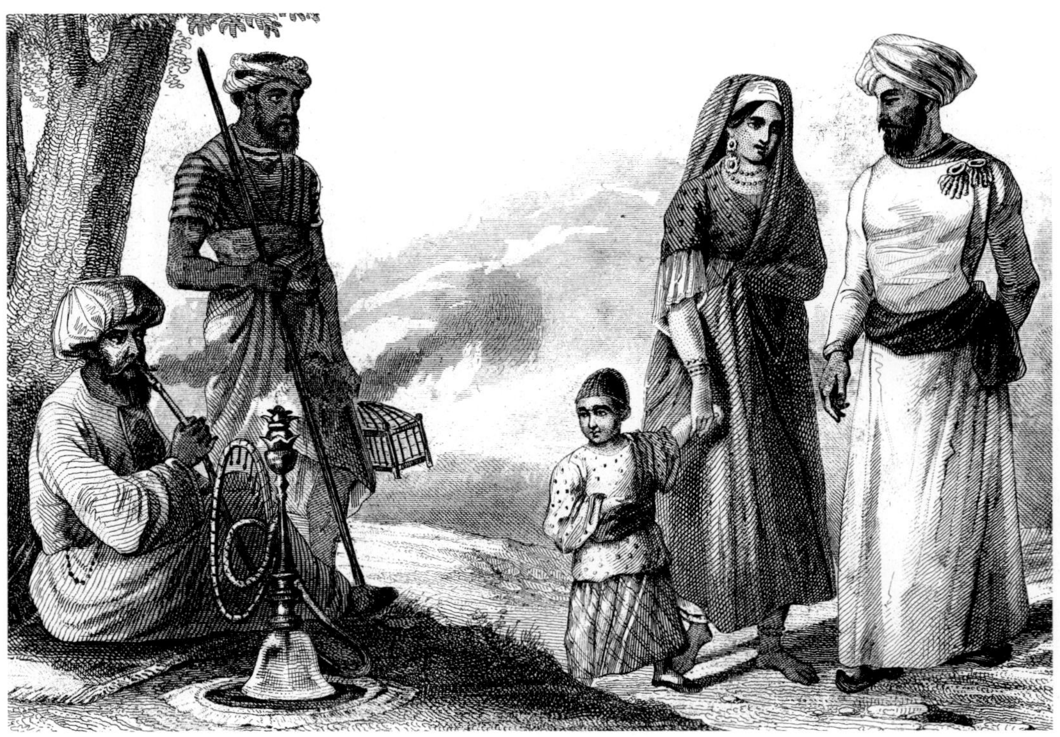

a	Persian soldiers, c. 1840	Persische Soldaden, um 1840	Soldati persiani, ca. 1840	Soldats persans, vers 1840	Soldados persas, hacia el año 1840
b	Persians, c. 1840	Perser, um 1840	Persiani, ca. 1840	Perses, vers 1840	Persas, hacia el año 1840

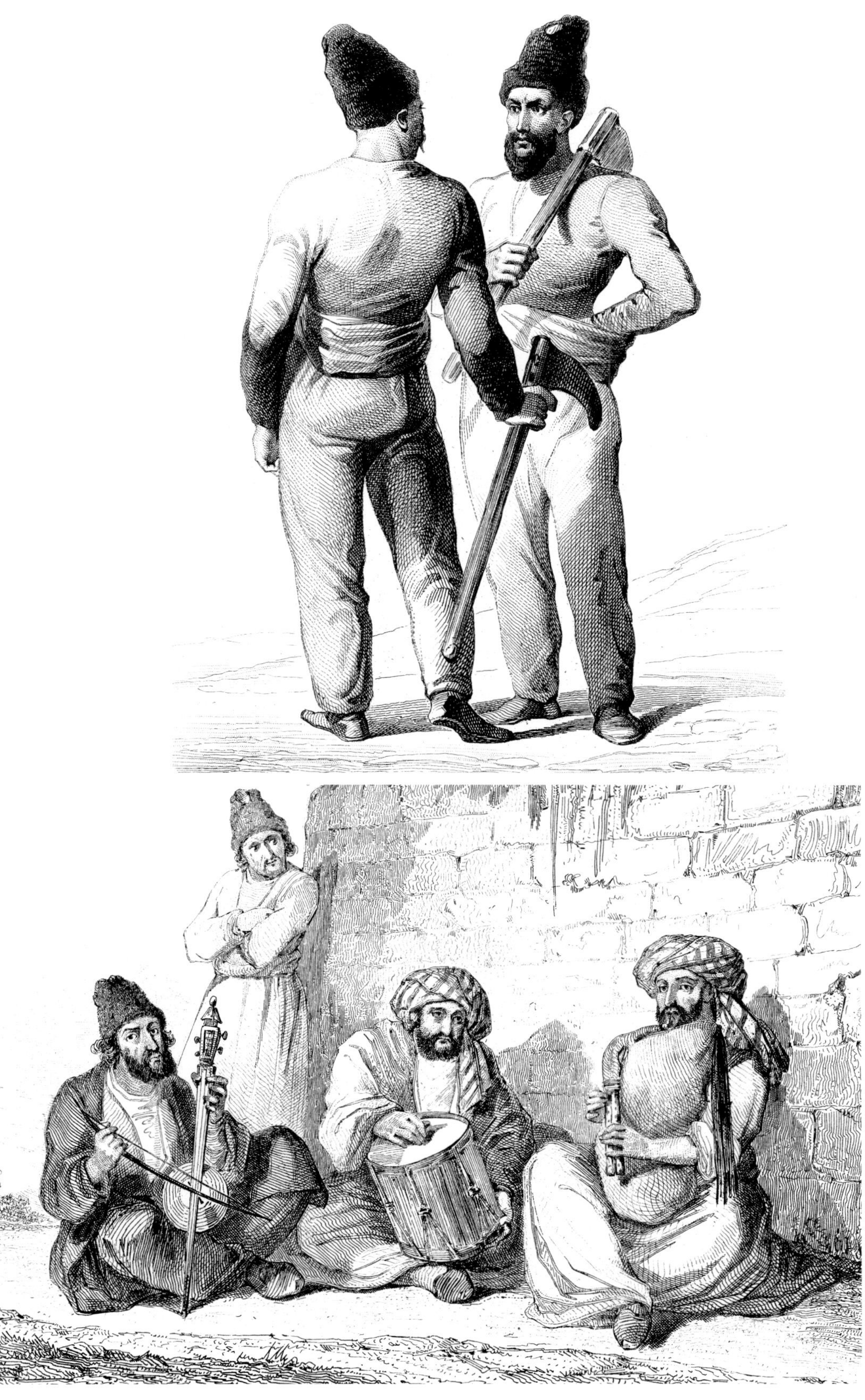

a	Persian farmers, c. 1840	Persische Bauern, um 1840	Contadini persiani, ca. 1840	Paysans persans, vers 1840	Campesinos persas, alrededor del año 1840
b	Persian musicians, c. 1840	Persische Musiker, um 1840	Musicisti persiani, ca. 1840	Mucisiens persans, vers 1840	Músicos persas, alrededor del año 1840

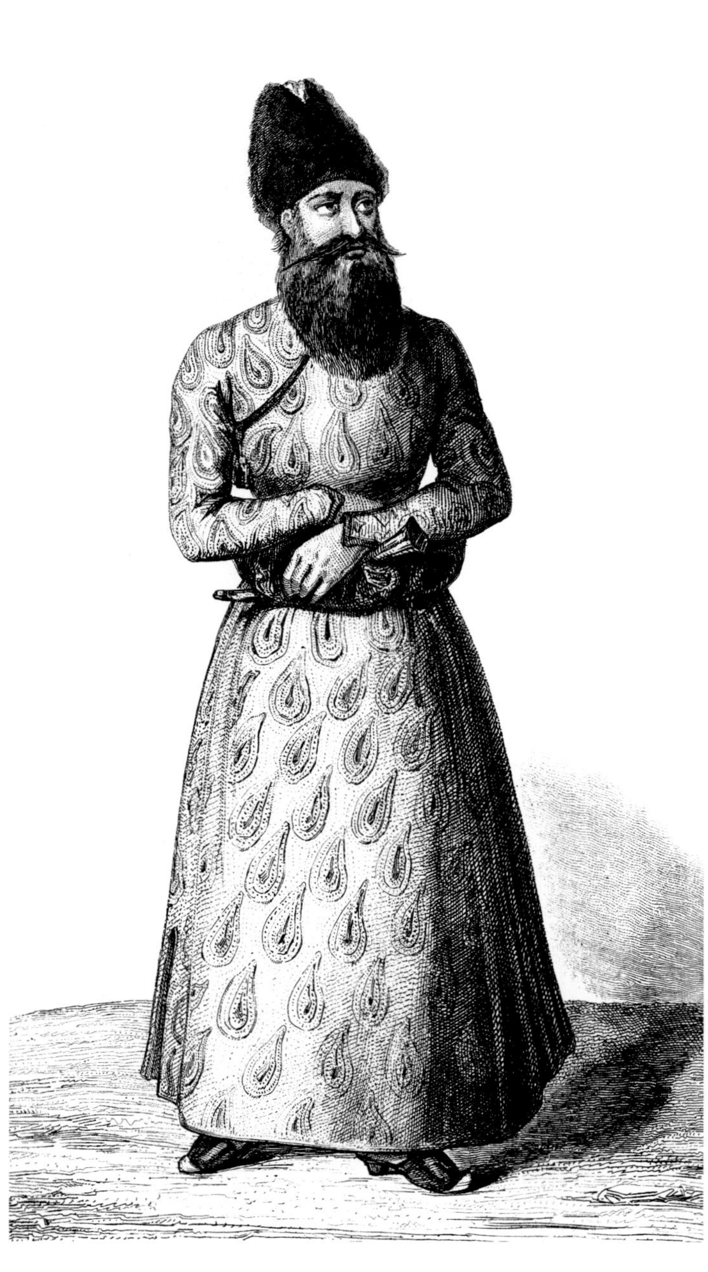

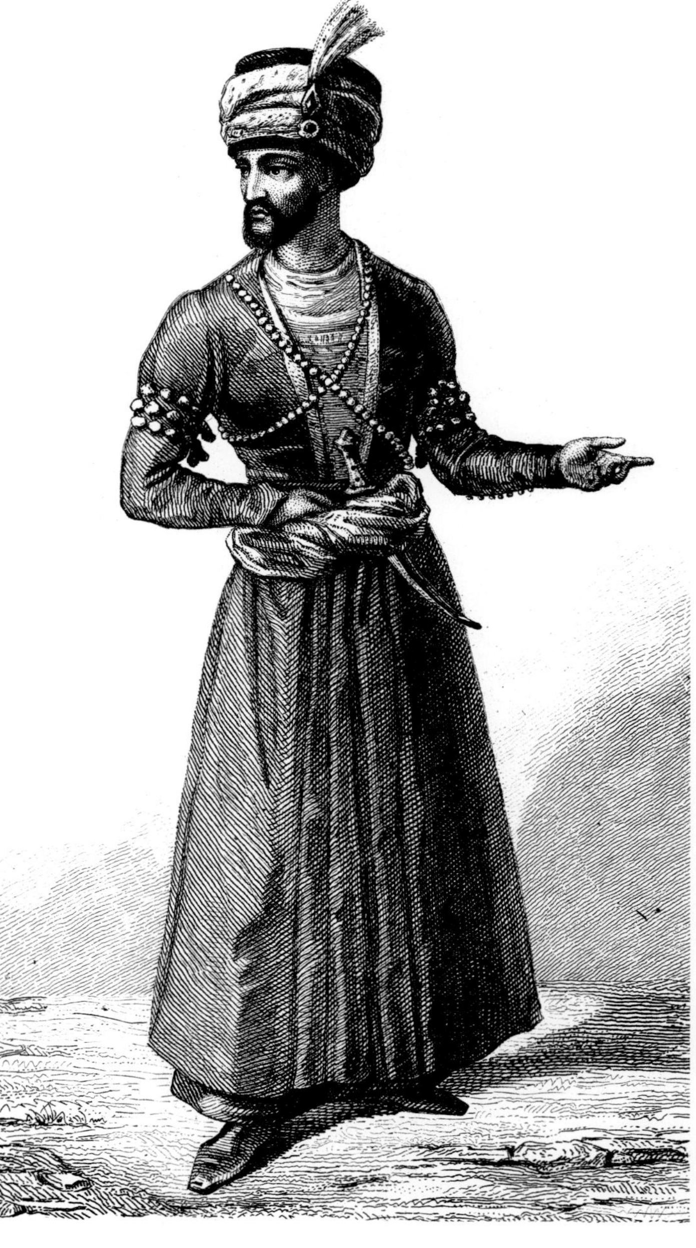

Persian Princes, c. 1840

Persische Prinzen, um 1840

Principi persiani, ca. 1840

Princes persans, vers 1840

Príncipes persas, hacia el año 1840

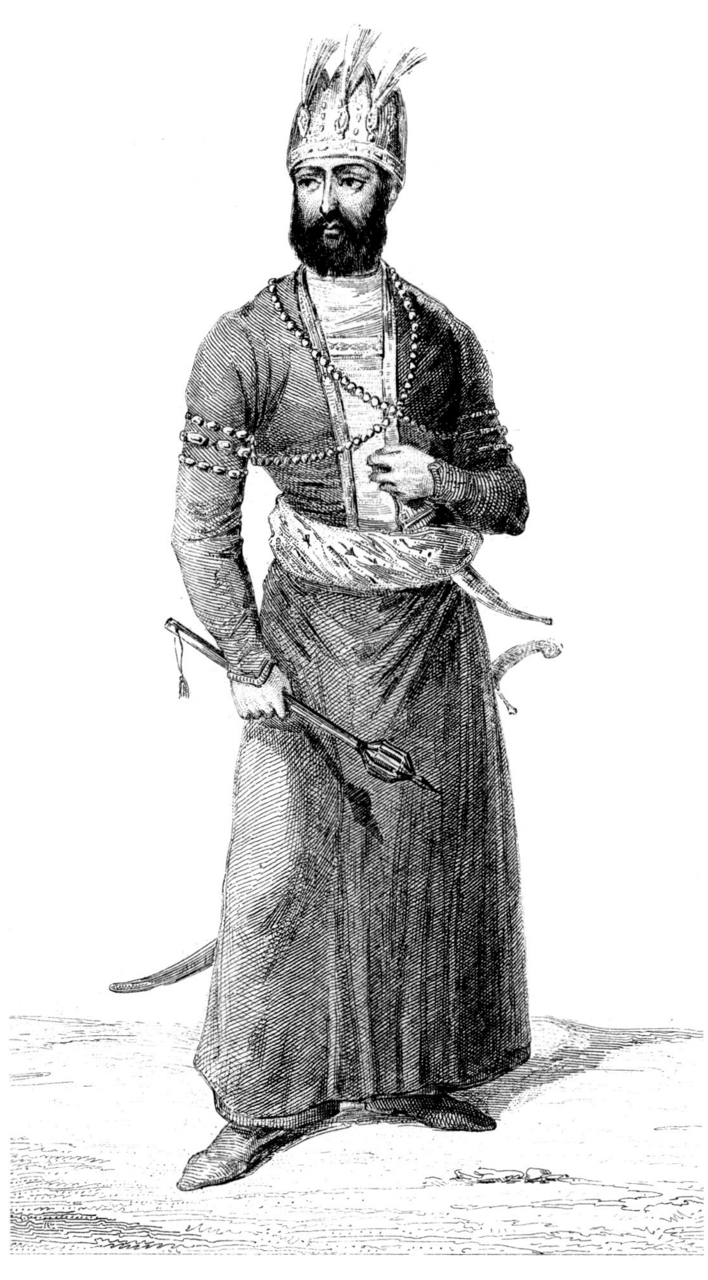

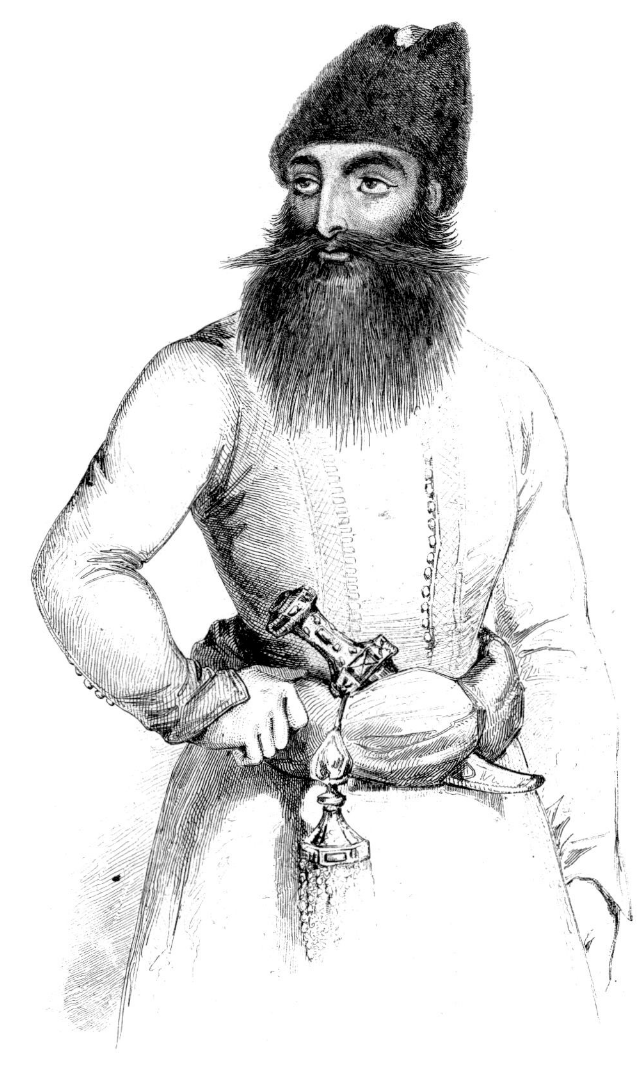

Persian Princes, c. 1840

Persische Prinzen, um 1840

Principi persiani, ca. 1840

Princes persans, vers 1840

Príncipes persas, 1840

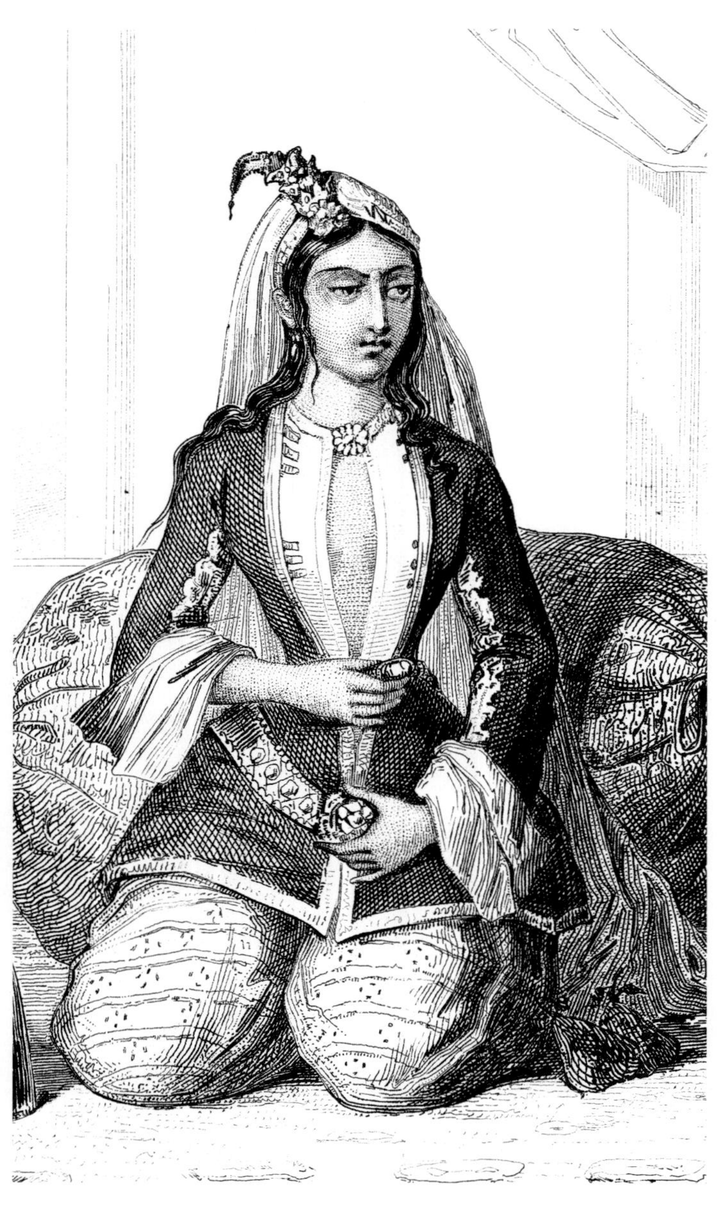

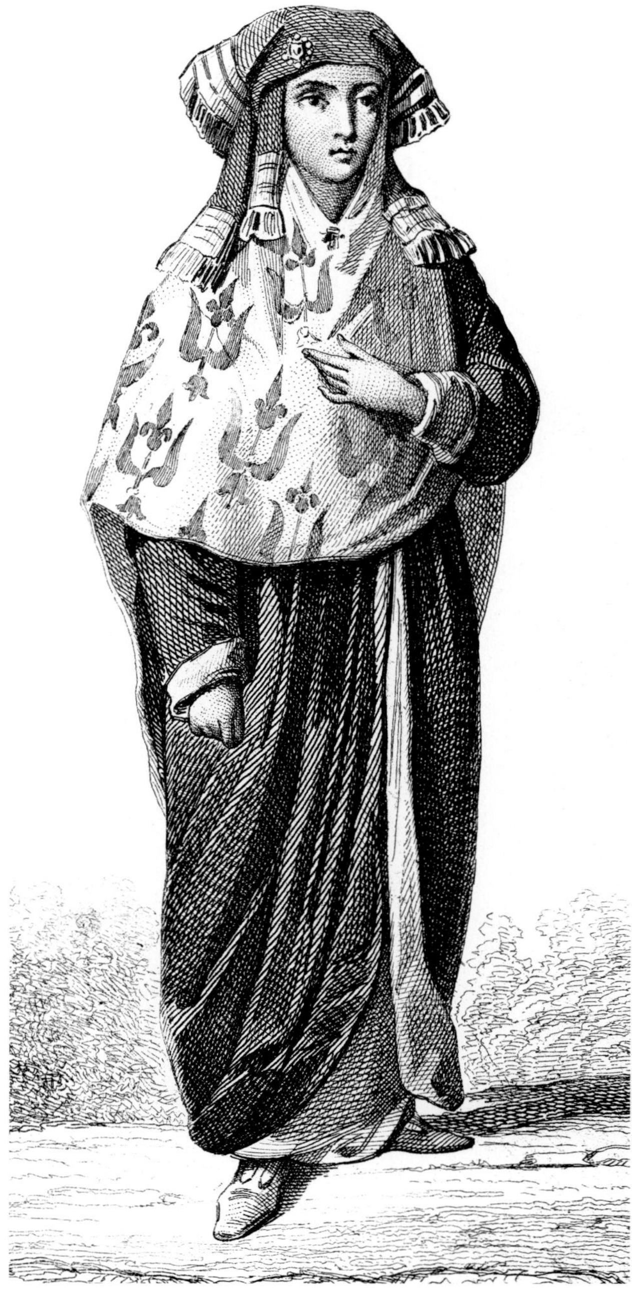

Noble ladies, 1840 Edelfrauen, 1840 Nobildonne, 1840 Femmes nobles, 1840 Damas nobles, 1840

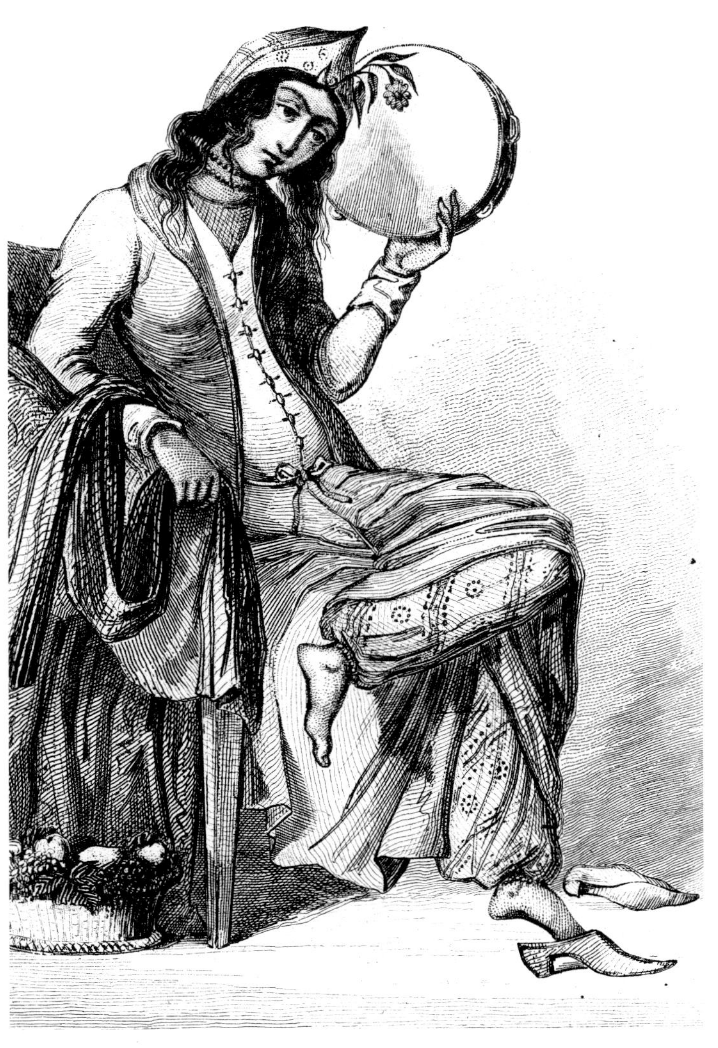

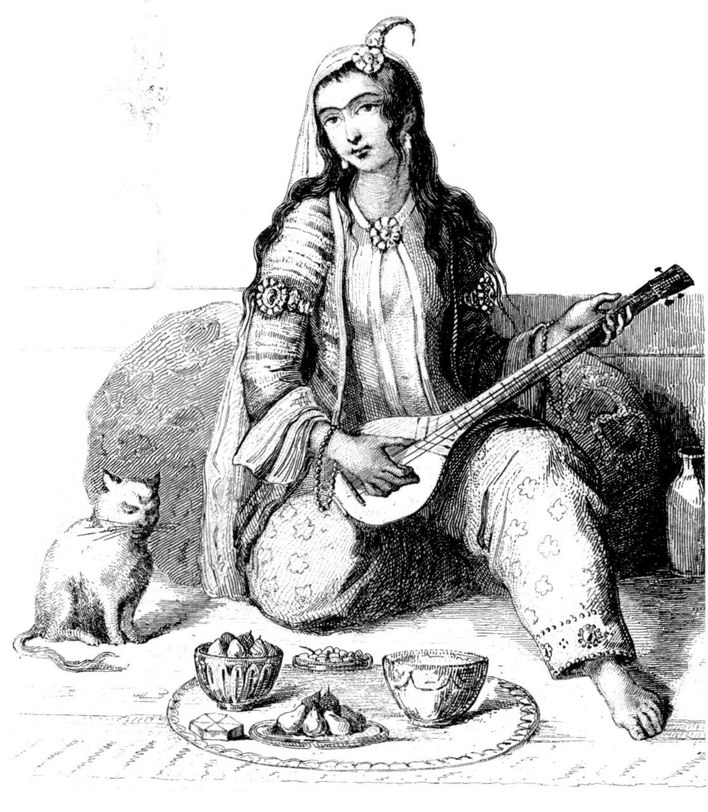

Dancing girl and harem musician, c. 1840

Tänzerin und Musikerin im Harem, um 1840

Ragazza danzante e musicista di harem, ca. 1840

Danseuse et musicienne au harem, vers 1840

Bailarina y música del harén, hacia 1840

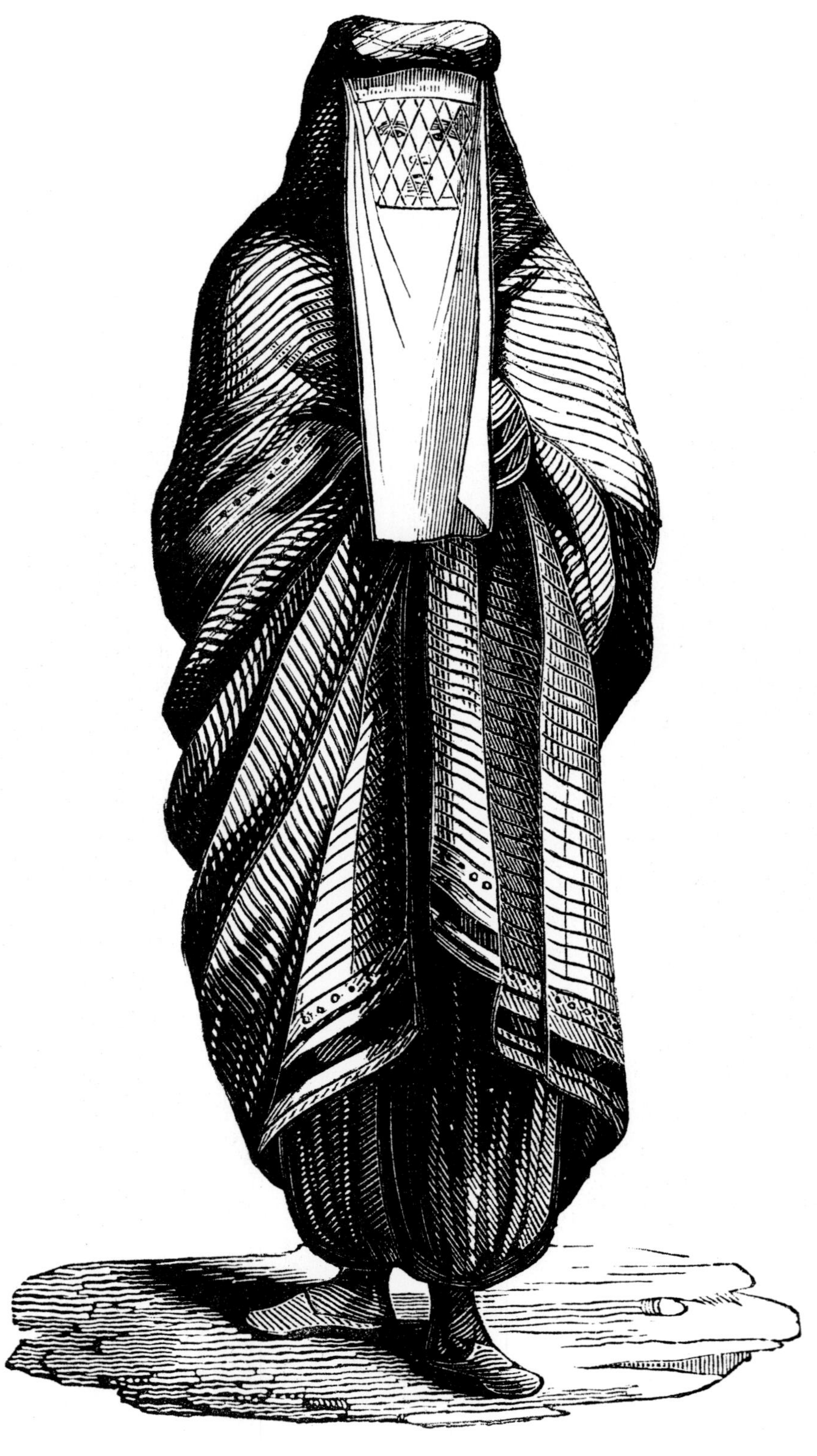

Veiled lady, 1885 Verschleierte Frau, 1885 Donna con velo, 1885 Femme voilée, 1885 Mujer con velo, 1885

Persia

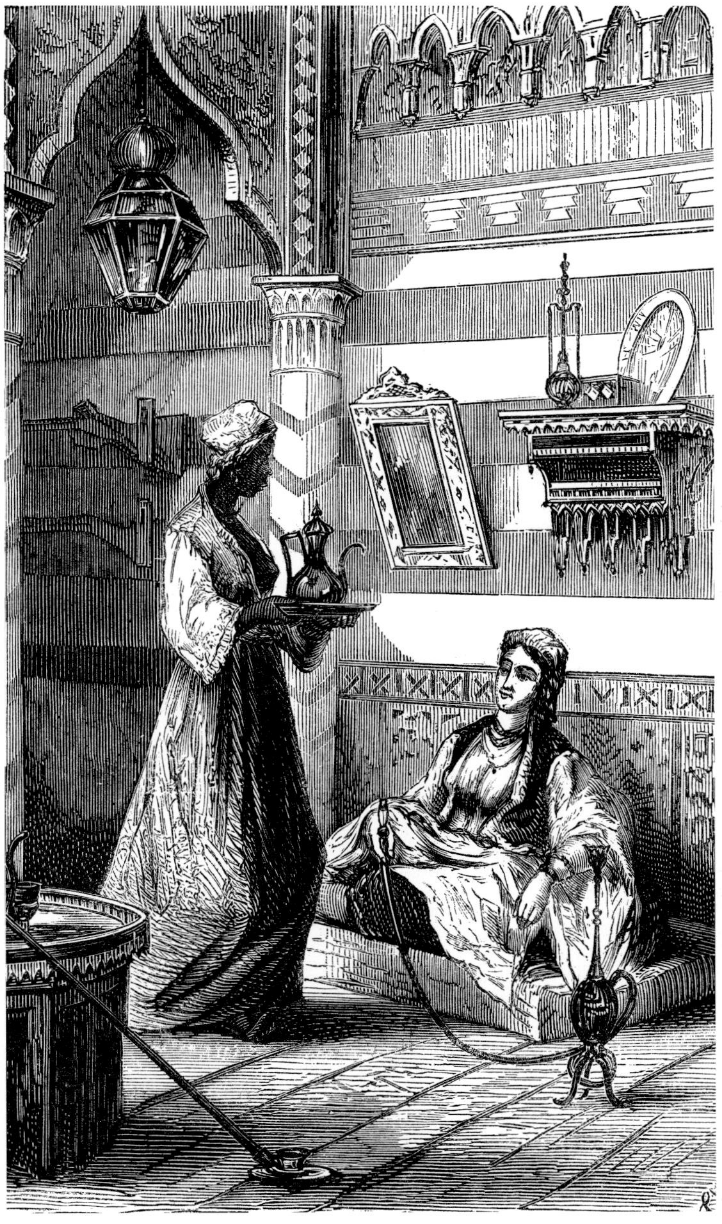

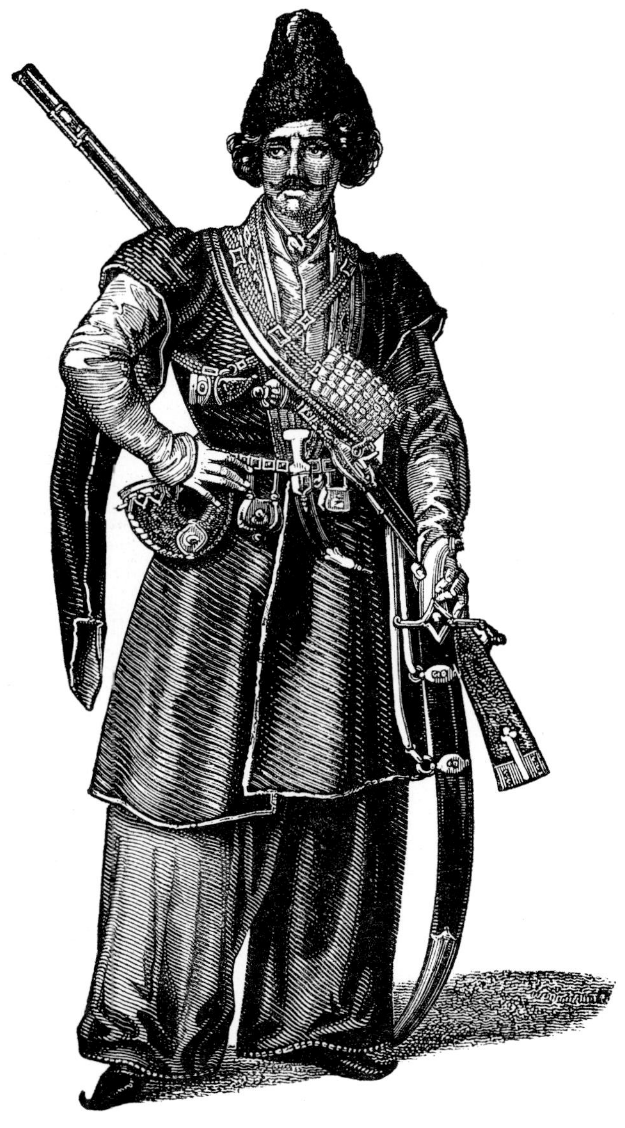

a	Persian lady with servant, 1885	Persische Dame mit Dienerin, 1885	Donna persiana con domestica, 1885	Femme persane et sa servante, 1885	Mujer persa y su sirviente, 1885
b	Persian soldier, 1885	Persischer Soldat, 1885	Soldato persiano, 1885	Soldat persan, 1885	Soldado persa, 1885

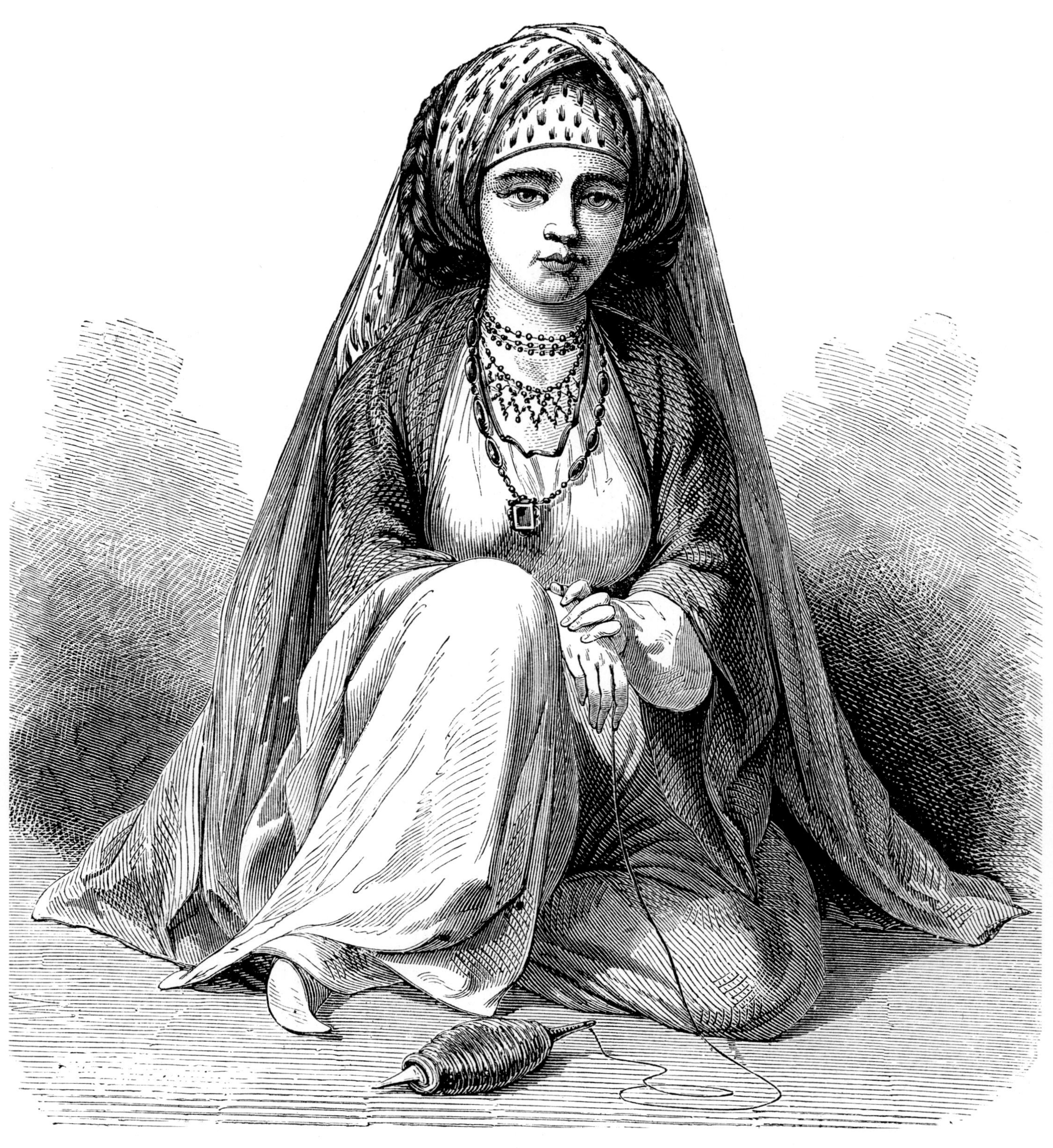

Girl from Beluchistan, Persia, c. 1860

Mädchen aus Beluchistan, Persien, um 1860

Ragazza del Beluchistan, Persia, ca. 1860

Jeune fille du Bélouchistan, Perse, vers 1860

Muchacha de Beluchistán, Persia, alrededor del año 1860

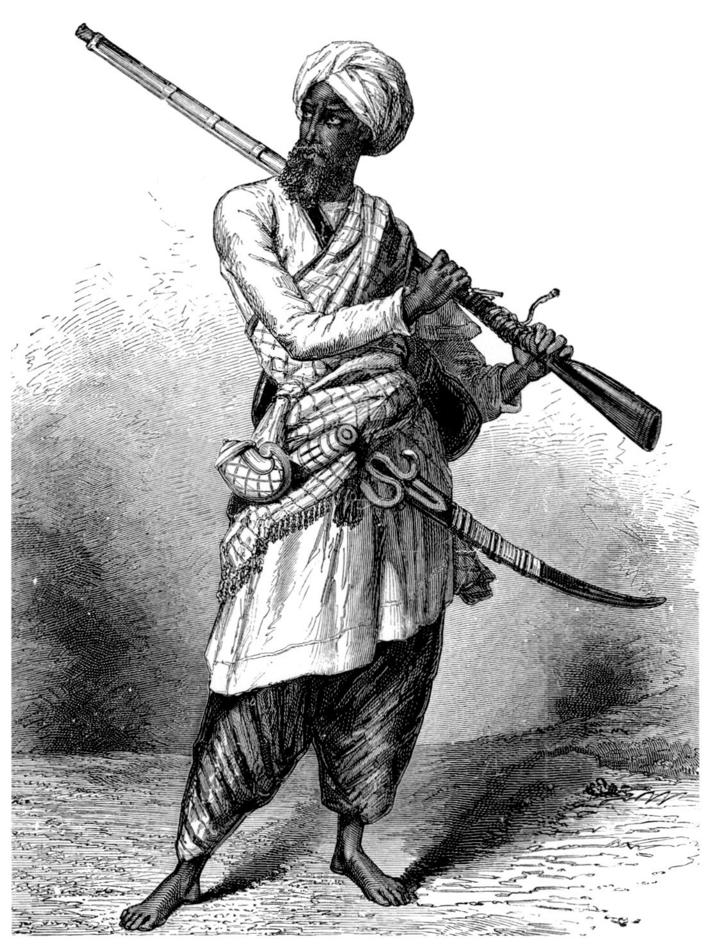

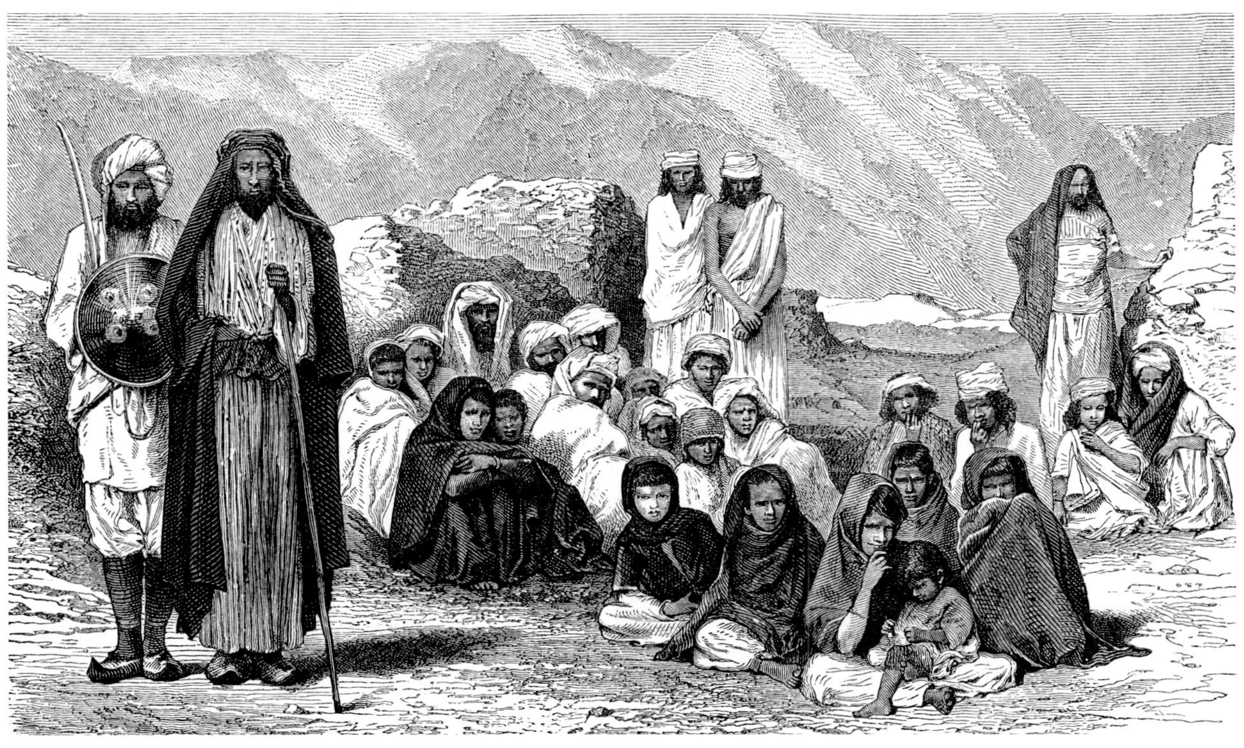

a	Afghan soldier, 1870	Afghanische Soldaten, 1870	Soldato afgano, 1870	Soldat afghan, 1870	Soldado afgano, 1870
b	Group of Afghans, 1870	Gruppe von Afghanen, 1870	Gruppo di Afgani, 1870	Groupe d'afghans, 1870	Grupo de afganos, 1870

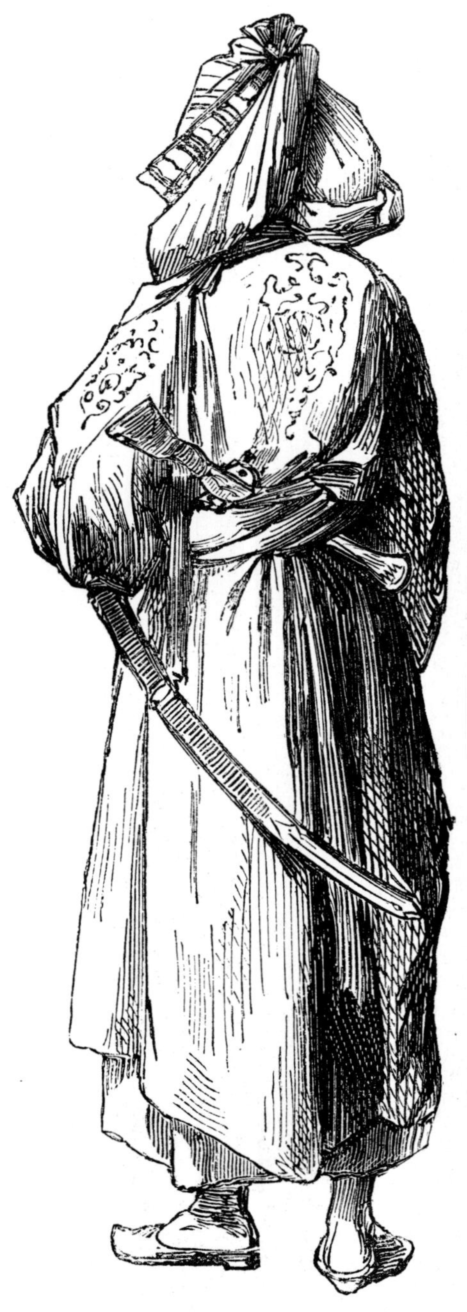

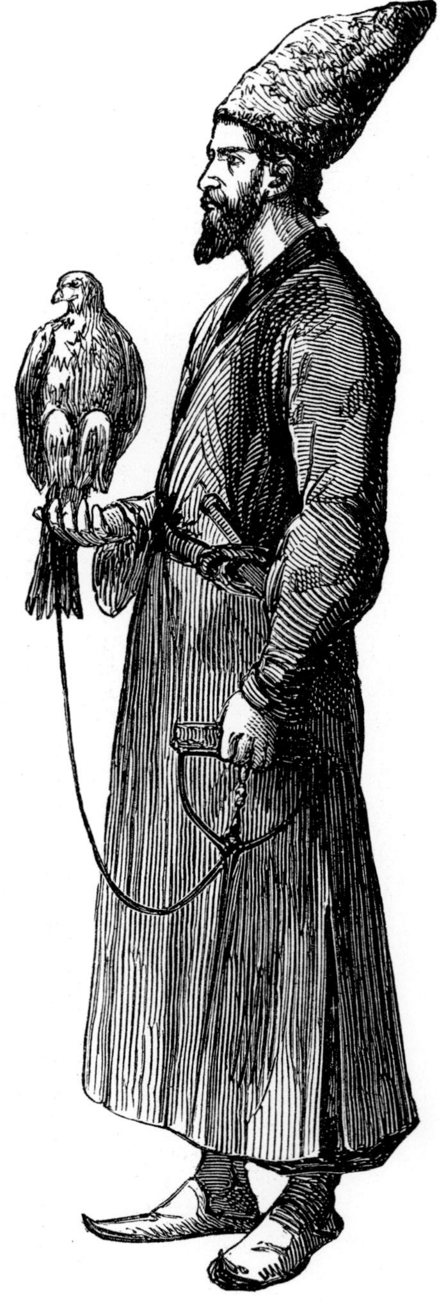

a	Afghan from Kandahar	Afghane aus Kandahar	Afgano di Kandahar	Afghan de Kandahar	Afgano de Kandahar
b	Falkoner of Ispahan	Falkner aus Ispahan	Falconiere di Ispahan	Fauconnier d'Ispahan	Cetrero de Ispahan

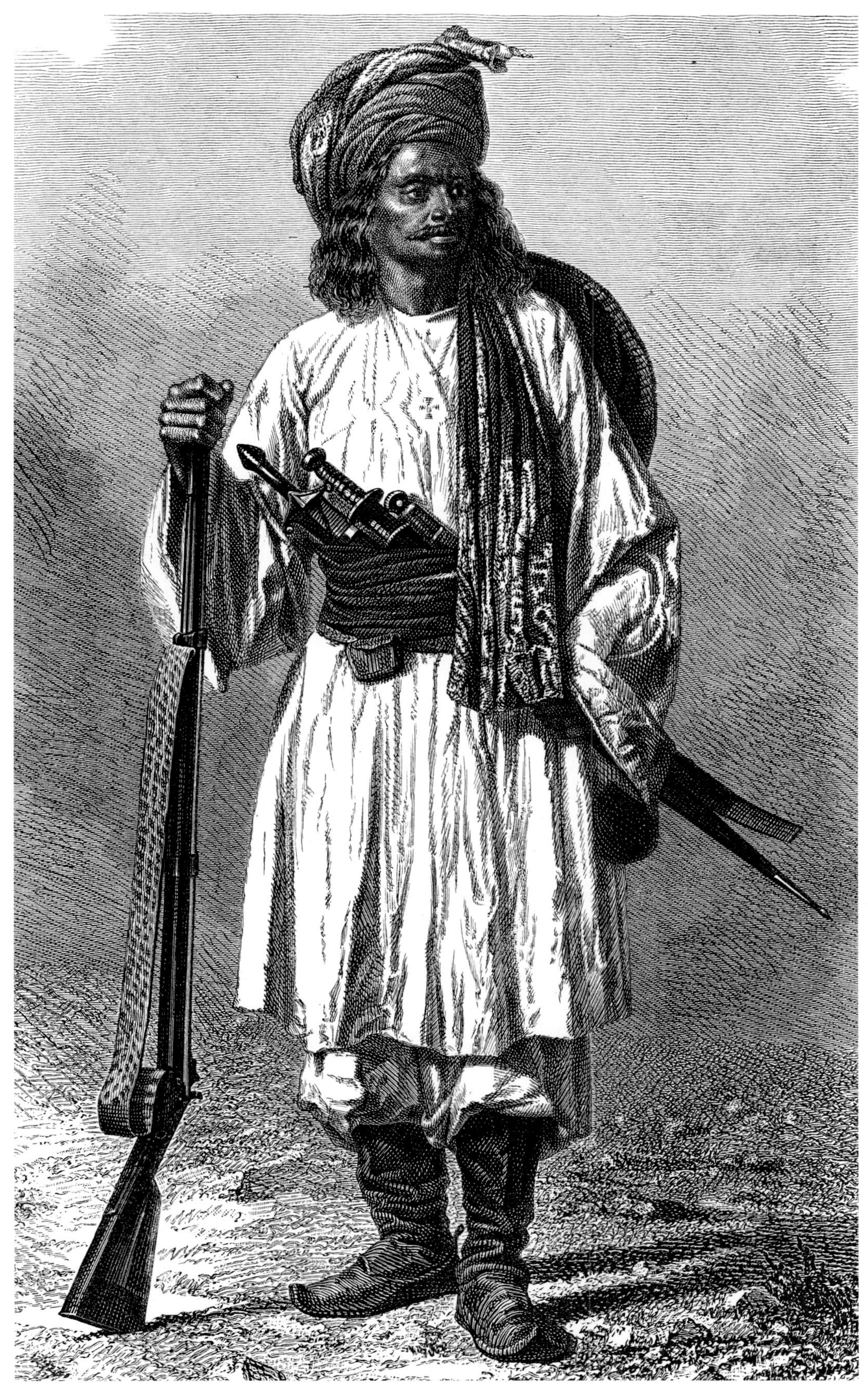

Afghan soldier, c. 1870

Afghanischer Krieger, um 1870

Soldato afgano, ca. 1870

Soldat afghan, vers 1870

Soldado afgano, hacia el año 1870

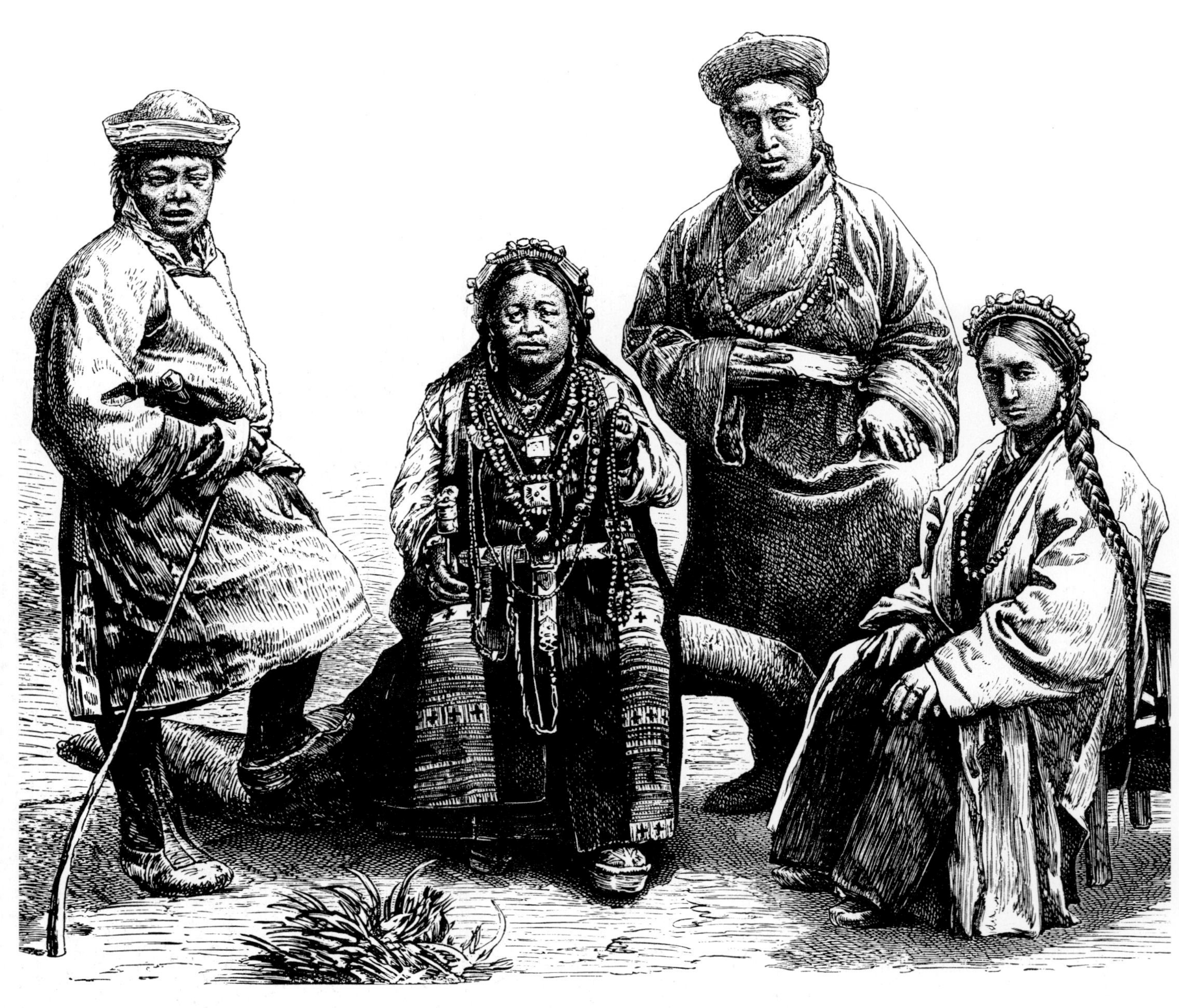

Men and women of Bhutan, c. 1860

Männer und Frauen aus Bhutan, um 1860

Uomini e donne del Buthan, ca. 1860

Hommes et femmes du Bhoutan, vers 1860

Hombres y mujeres de Bután, hacia 1860

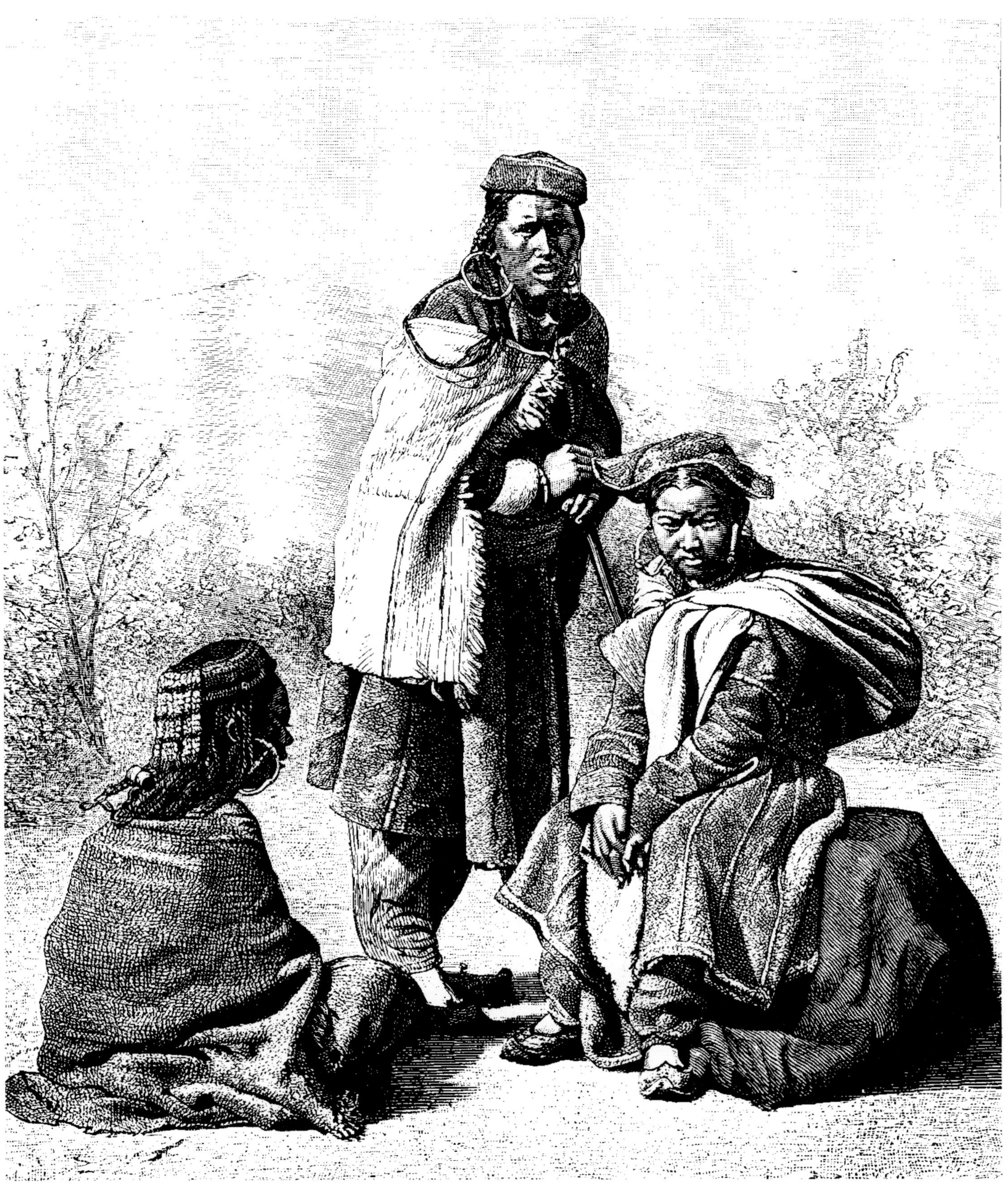

Tibetan women, c. 1870

Tibetische Frauen, um 1870

Donne tibetane, ca. 1870

Femmes tibétaines, vers 1870

Mujeres tibetanas, hacia el año 1870

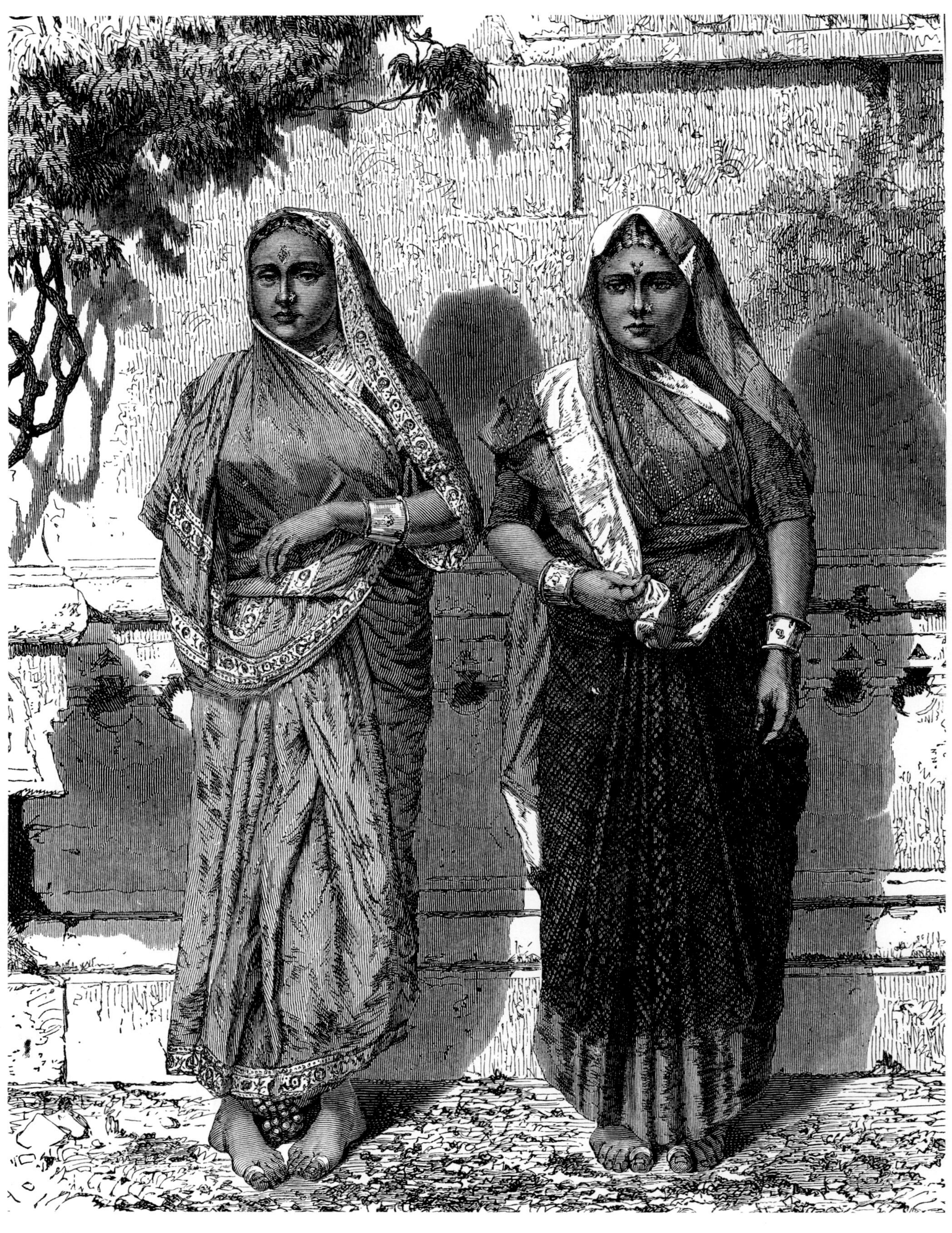

Hindu women in Bombay, c. 1870

Indische Frau in Bombay, um 1870

Donne hindu a Bombay, ca. 1870

Femmes hindoues à Bombay, vers 1870

Mujeres hindúes de Bombay, hacia 1870

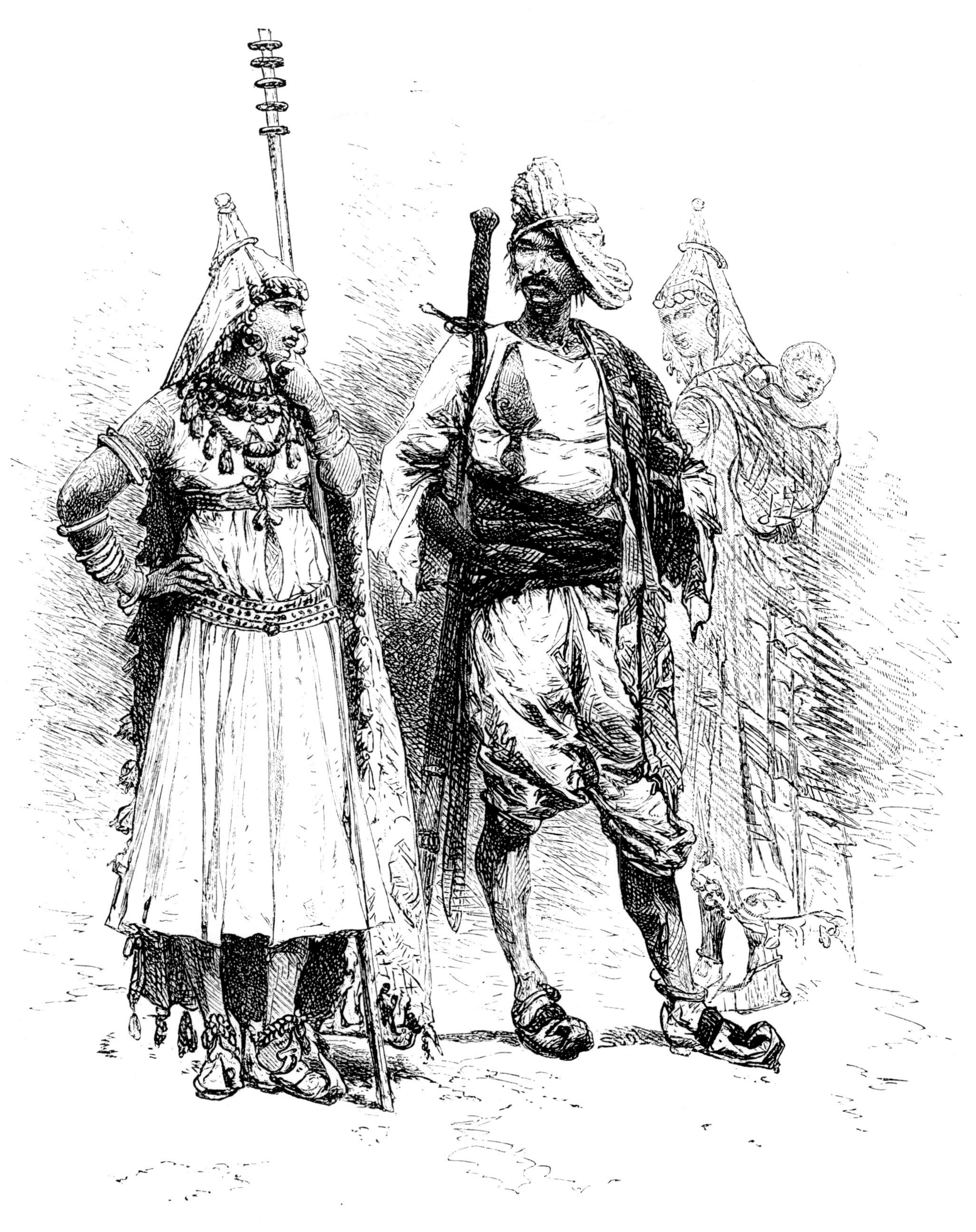

Banjari women and man, c. 1870

Banjari-Frau und -Mann, um 1870

Donne e uomo bancari, 1870

Femmes et homme banjari, vers 1870

Hombre y mujer banjari, alrededor del año 1870

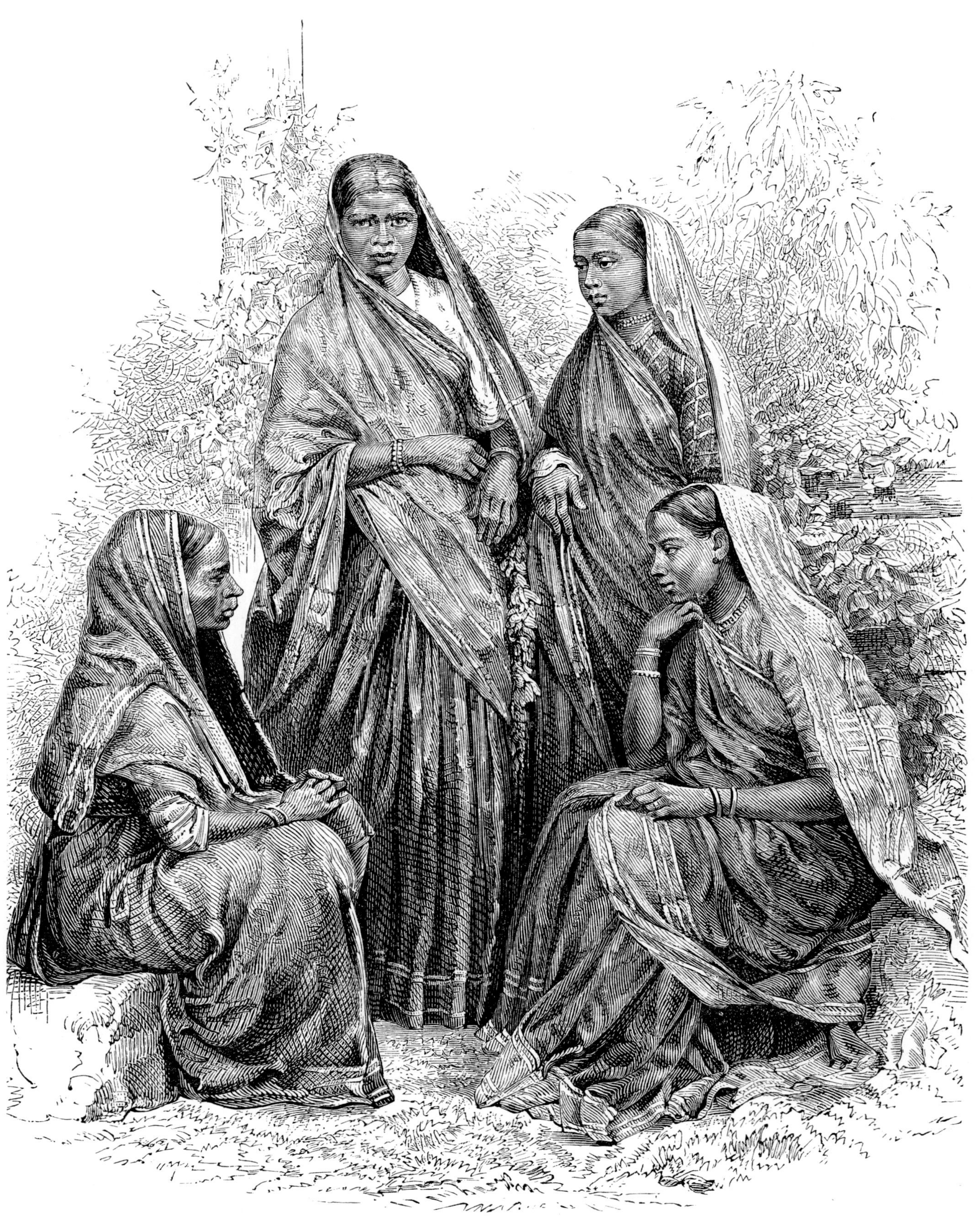

Christian converts, Bombay, c. 1890

Christliche Konvertiten, Bombay, um 1830

Convertiti cristiani, Bombay, ca. 1890

Indigènes convertis au christianisme, Bombay, vers 1890

Cristianas conversas, Bombay, hacia 1830

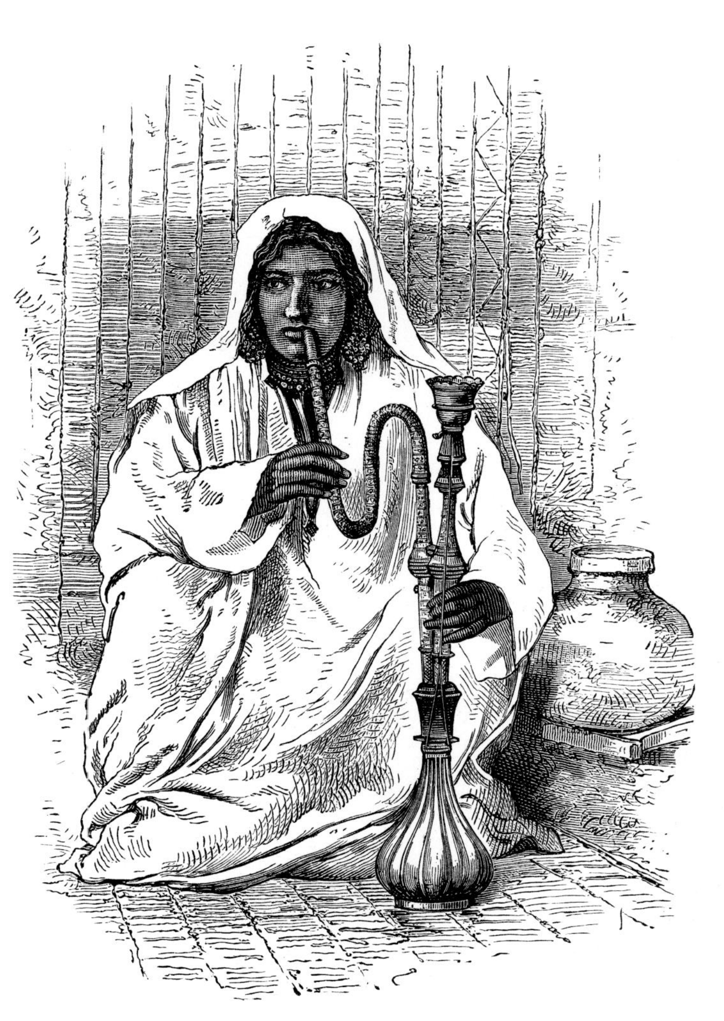

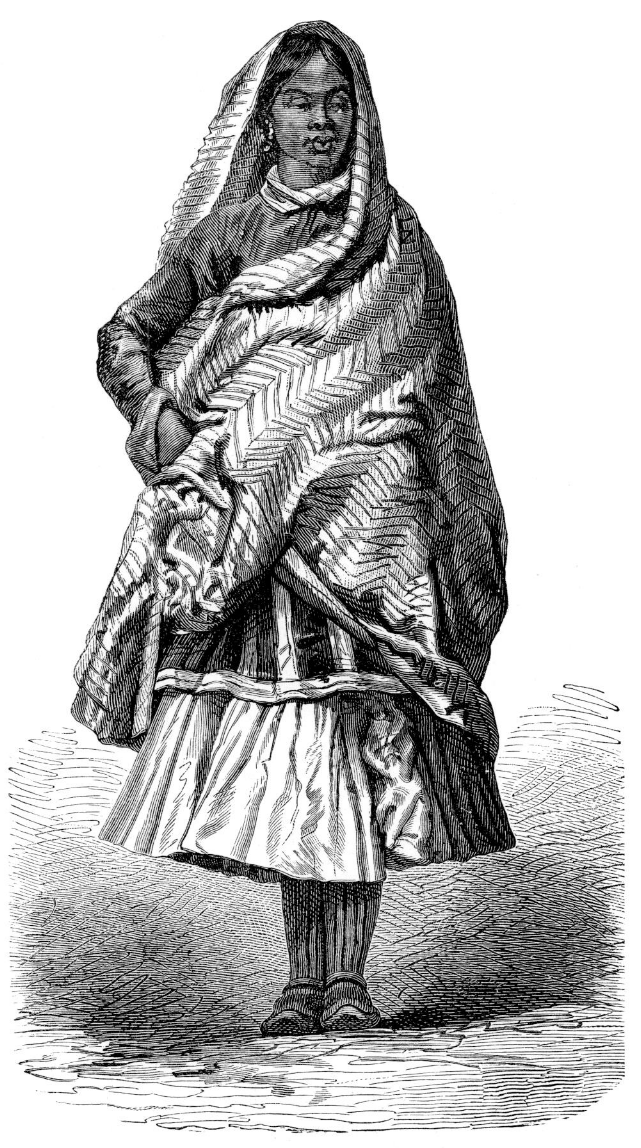

Women from Srinagar Frau aus Srinagar Donne di Srinagar Femmes de Srinagar Mujeres de Srinagar

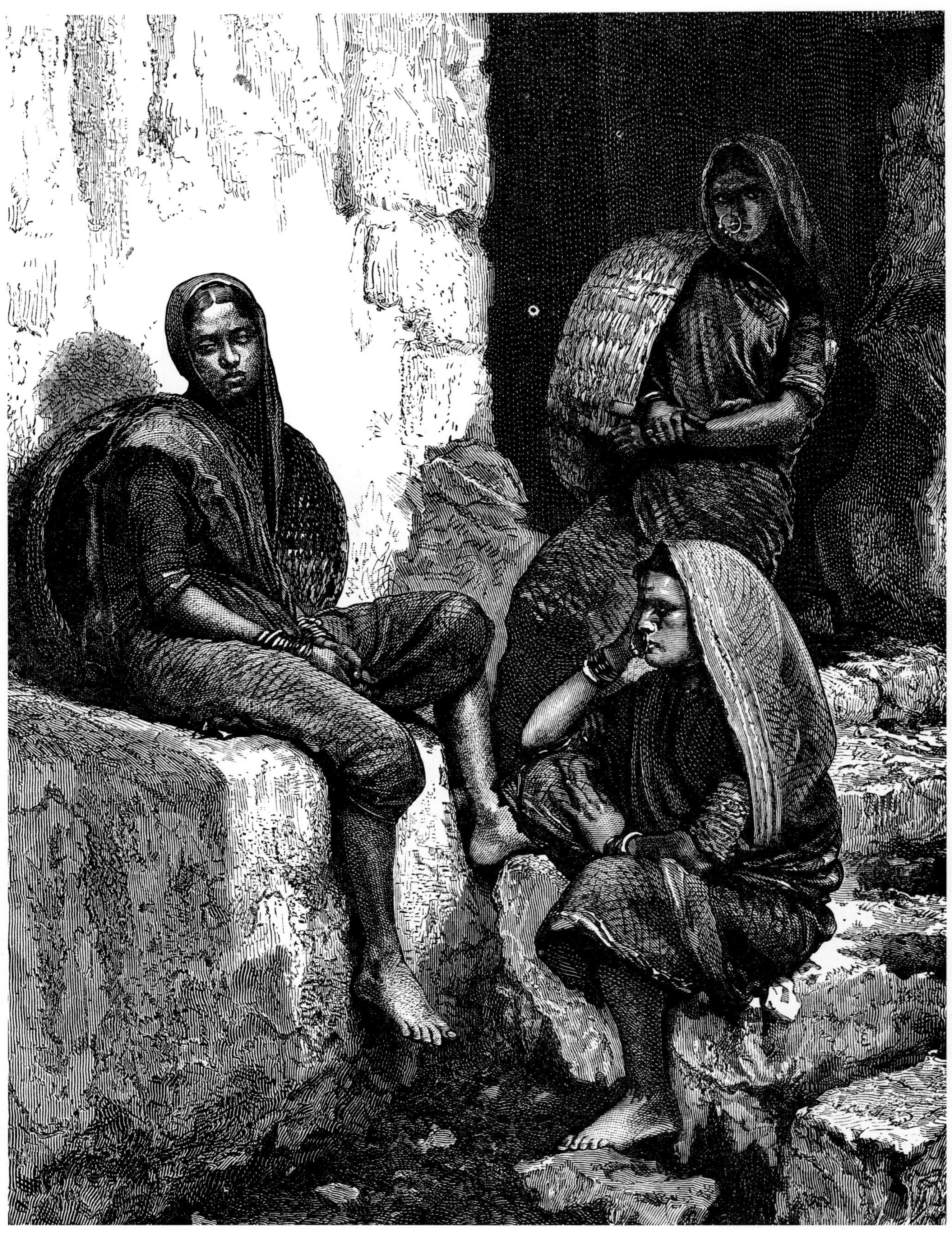

Low-caste women in Bombay. c. 1890

Frau aus der unteren Kaste in Bombay, um 1890

Donne della casta bassa a Bombay, ca. 1890

Femme de caste inférieure à Bombay, vers 1890

Mujeres de casta inferior, Bombay, hacia 1890

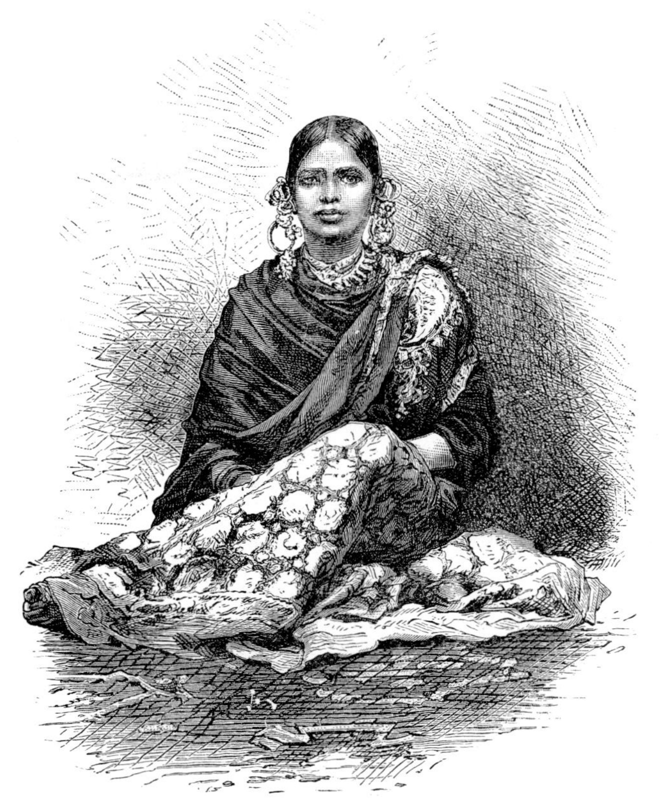

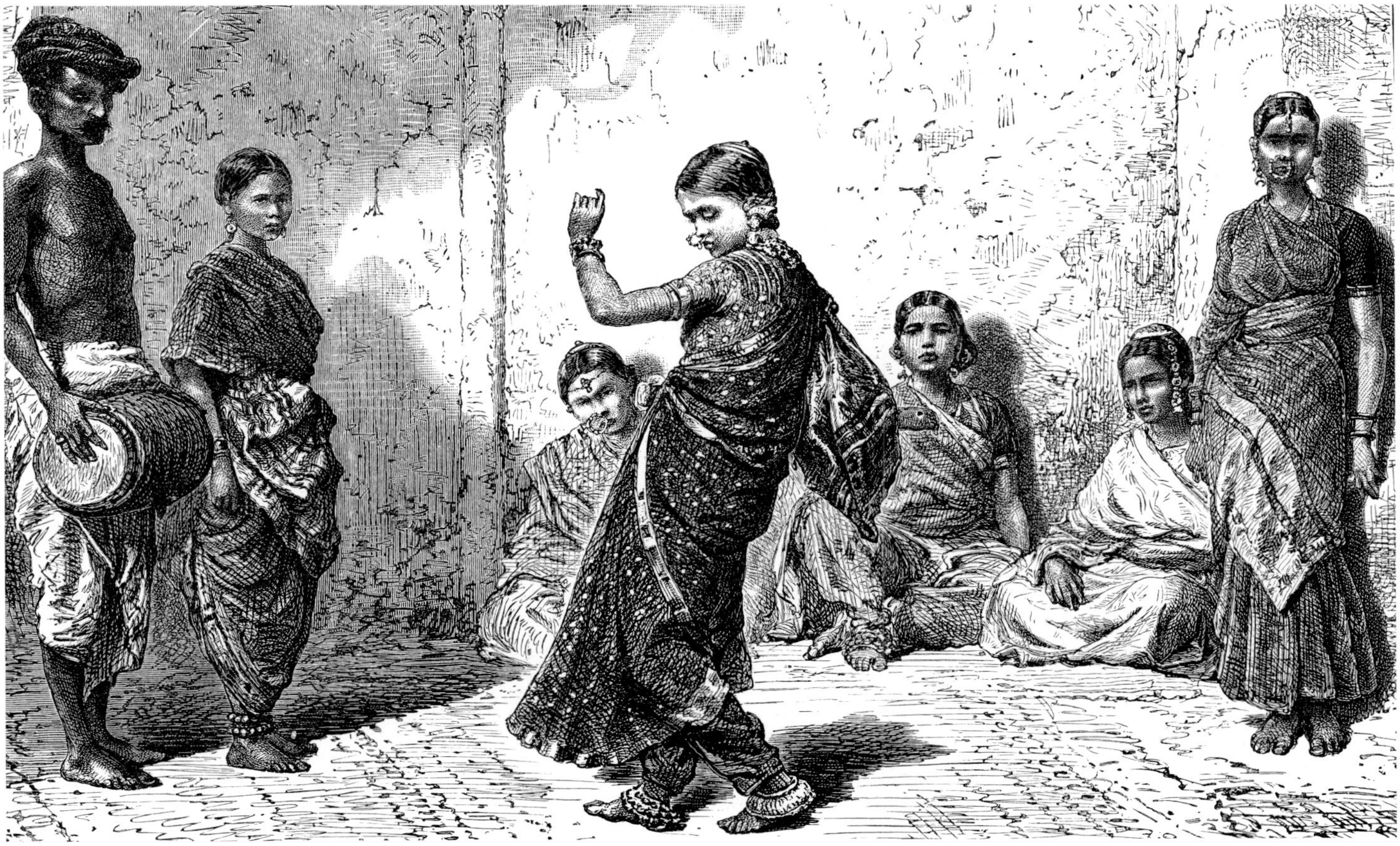

a	Dancing girl from Baroda	Tänzerin aus Baroda	Ragazza danzante di Baroda	Danseuse de Baroda	Bailarina de Baroda
b	Dancers and musicians	Tänzer und Musiker	Danzatrici e musicisti	Danseurs et musiciens	Bailarinas y músicos

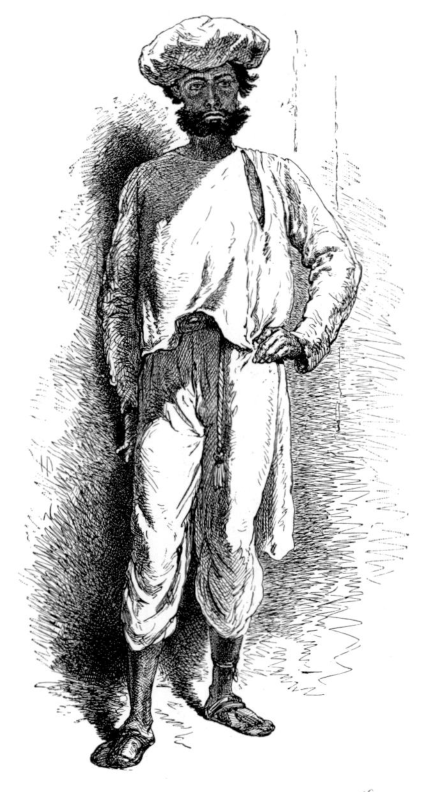

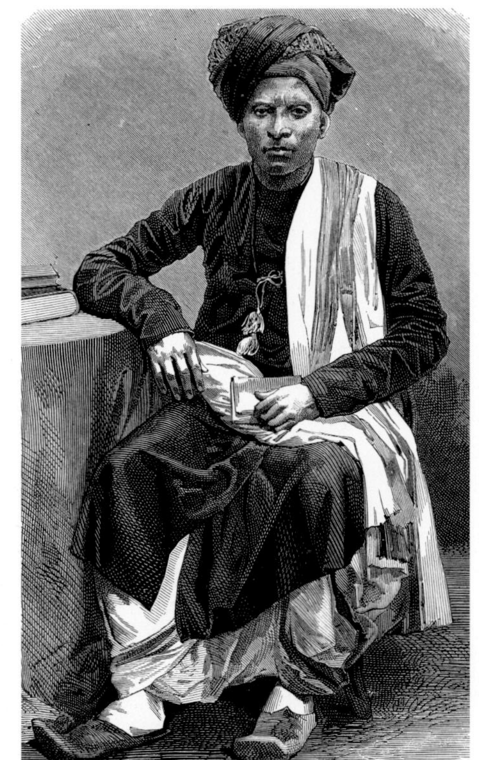

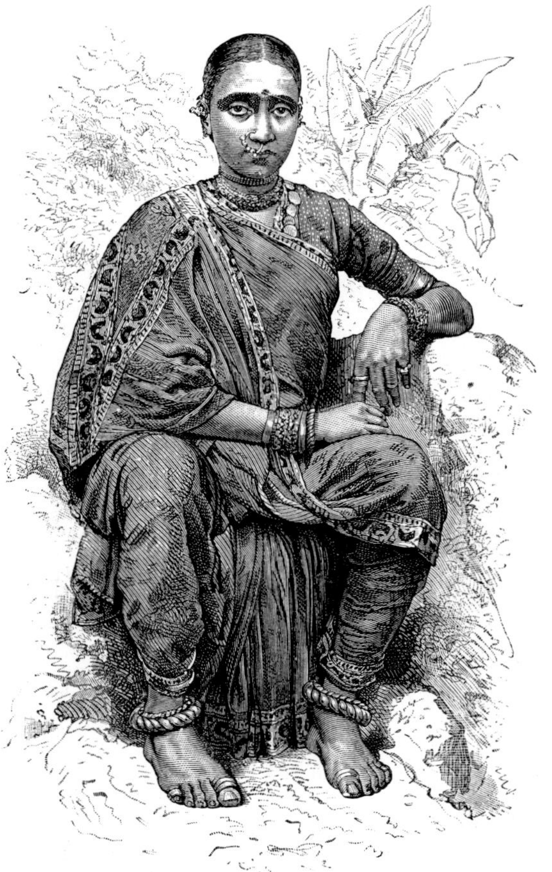

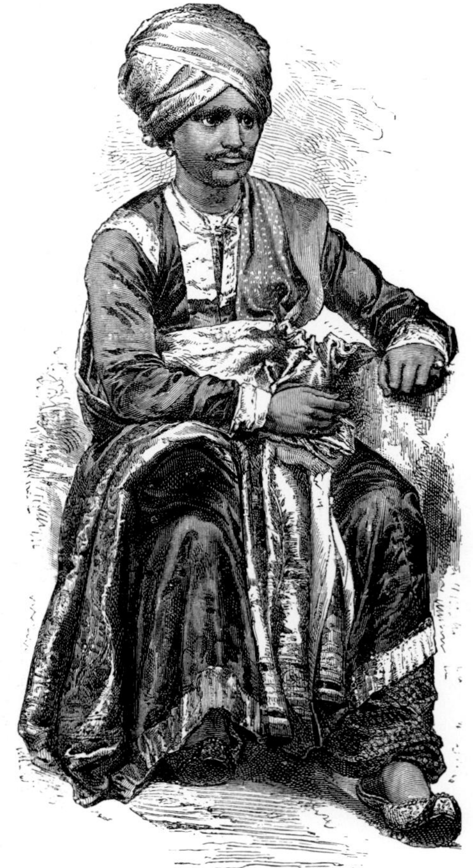

a	Coolie	Kuli	Coolie	Coolie	Culi
b	Merchant from Surat	Händler aus Surat	Mercante di Surat	Marchand de Surat	Mercader de Surat
c+d	Woman and man from Madras	Frau und Mann aus Madras	Donna e uomo di Madras	Femme et homme de Madras	Hombre y mujer de Madras

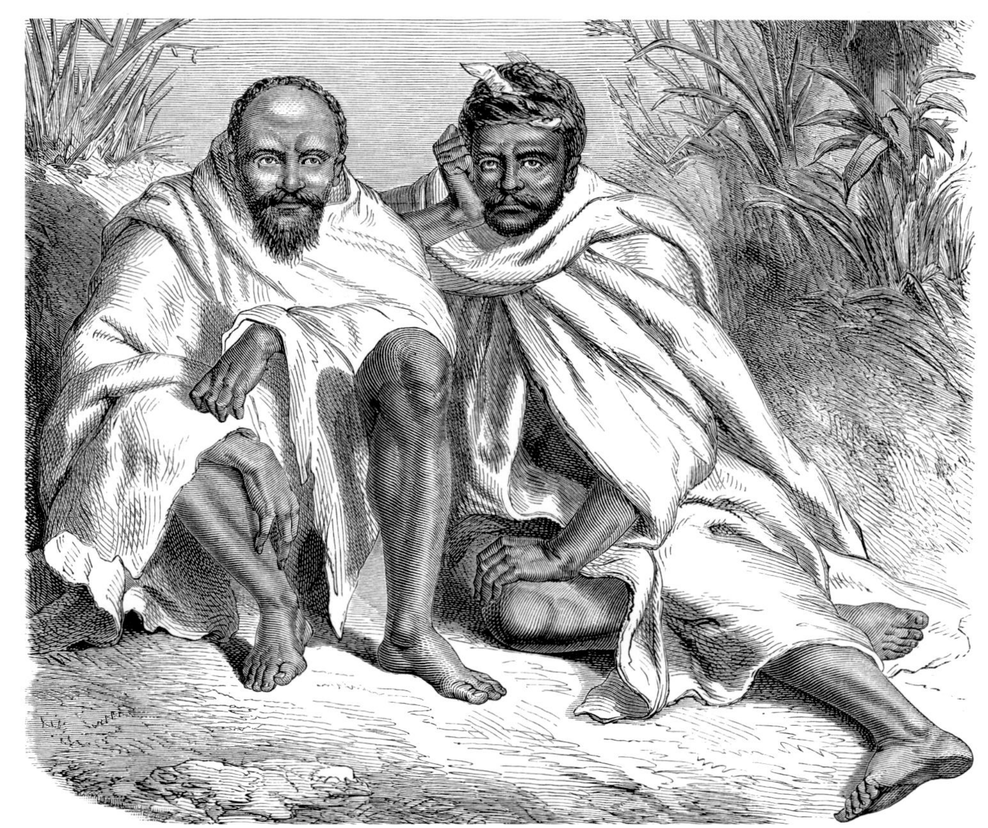

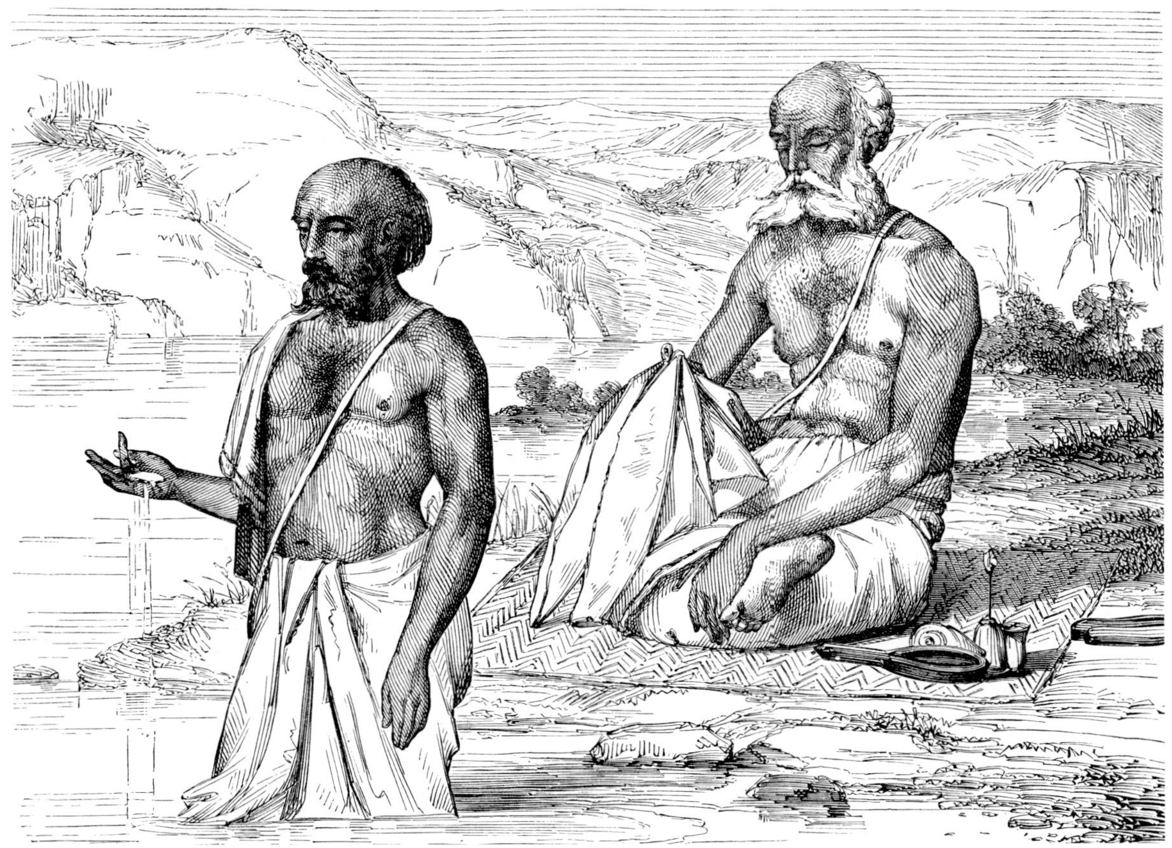

a	Men from Orissa	Männer aus Orissa	Uomini di Orissa	Hommes d'Orissa	Hombres de Orissa
b	Brahmins worshipping in Benares	Betende Brahmanen in Benares	Bramini in preghiera a Benares	Brahmanes en adoration à Bénarès	Brahmanes rindiendo culto en Benarés

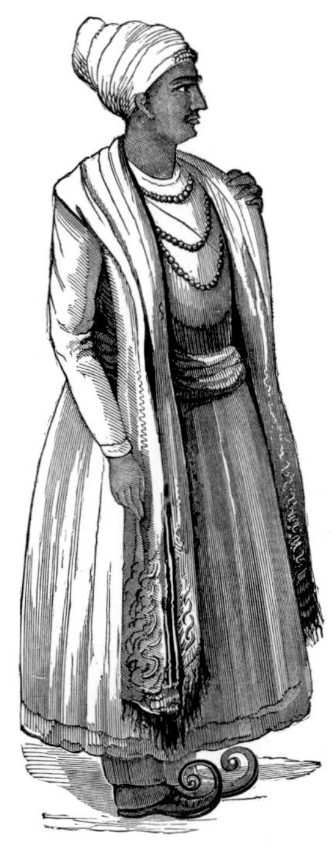

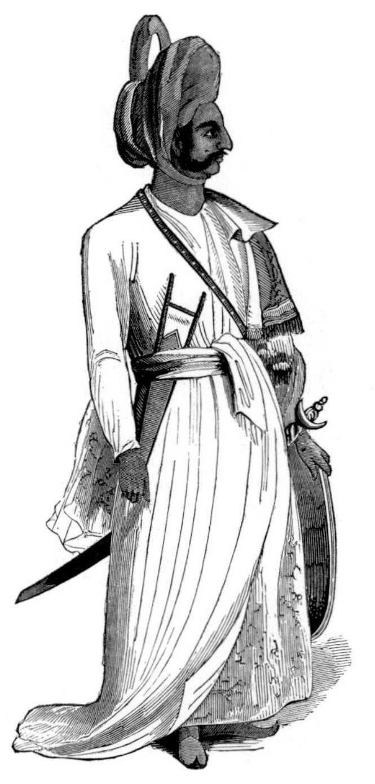

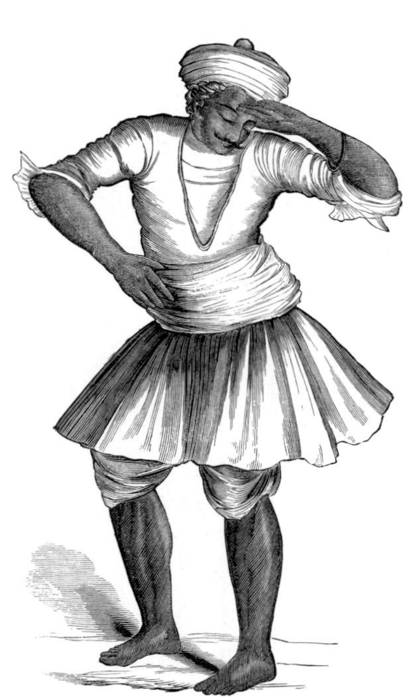

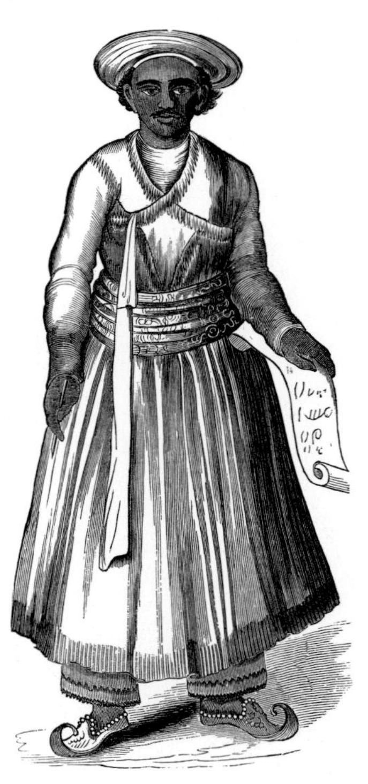

a	A Hindu merchant	Indischer Händler	Un mercante hindu	Marchand hindou	Mercader hindú
b	Indian nobleman	Indischer Adliger	Nobiluomo indiano	Noble indien	Noble indio
c	Hindu bearer	Indischer Träger	Portatore hindu	Serviteur hindou	Porteador hindú
d	Muslim of high rank from Bengal	Hochrangiger Moslem aus Bengal	Musulmano di alto rango del Bengala	Musulman de haut rang du Bengale	Musulmán de alto rango de Bengala

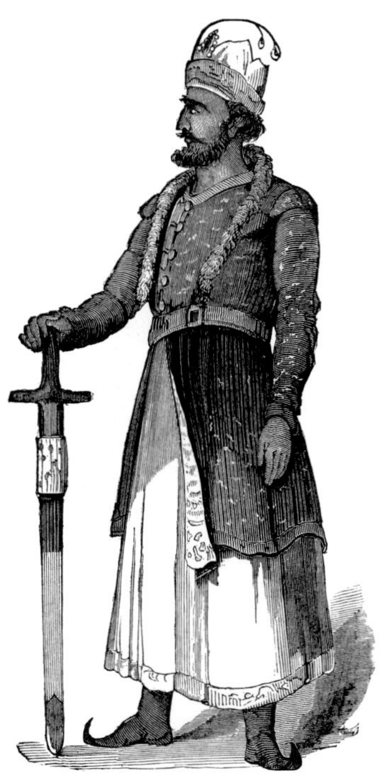
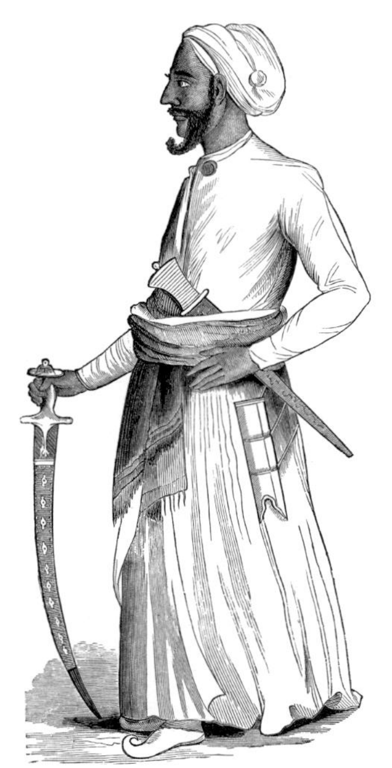
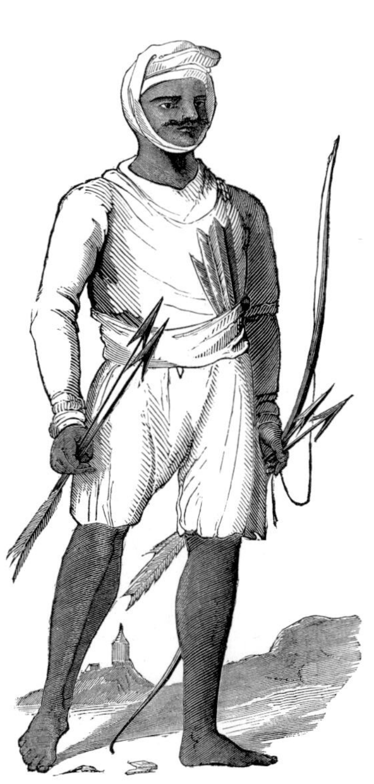
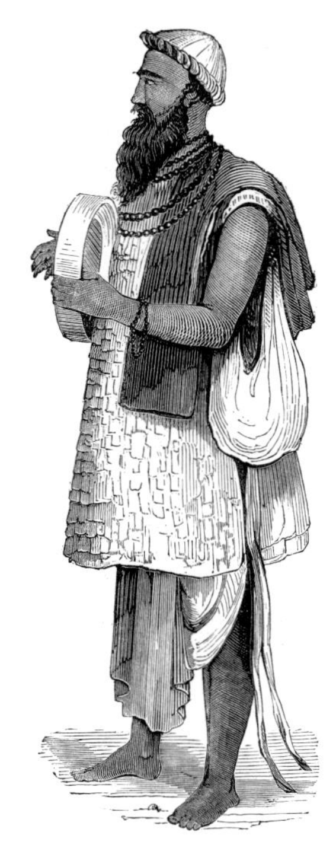

a	Baber, the founder of the Moghul empire	Baber, der Gründer des Mogulreiches	Baber, il fondatore dell'impero Mogol	Baber, fondateur de l'Empire Maghul	Babur, el fundador del imperio mongol
b	Muslim military officer	Moslemischer Militärpolizist	Ufficiale militare musulmano	Officier militaire musulman	Oficial militar musulmán
c	Soldier	Soldat	Soldato	Soldat	Soldado
d	Member of an Islamic sect of beggars	Mietglied eines islamischen Bettelordens	Membro di una setta islamica di mendicanti	Membre d'une secte islamique de mendiants	Miembro de una secta islámica de mendicantes

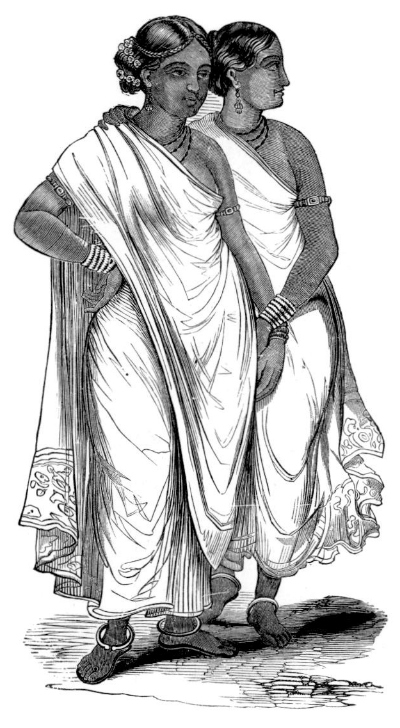

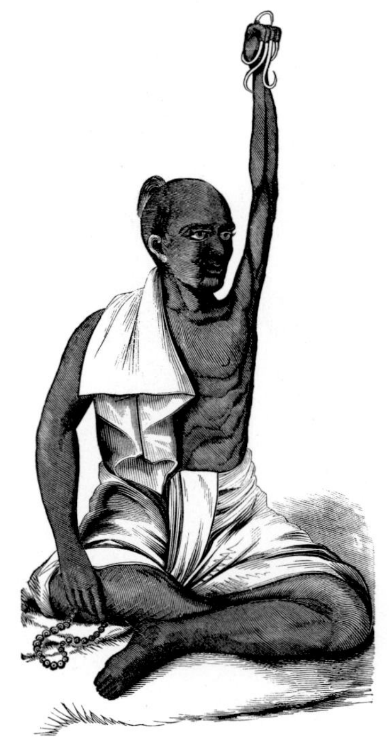

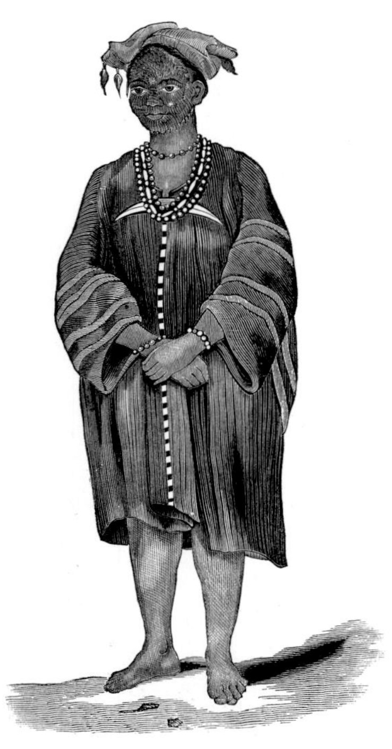

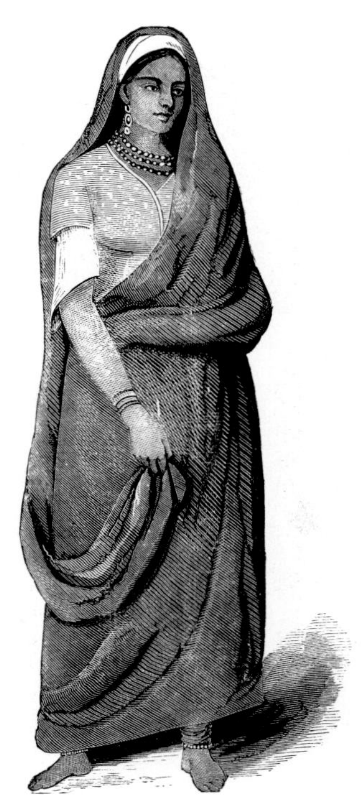

a	Hindu women	Indische Frauen	Donne hindu	Femmes hindoues	Mujeres hindúes
b	Hindu devotee	Indischer Verehrer	Devoto hindu	Adepte hindou	Devoto hindú
c	Kyan woman from Nilgiri	Kyan-Frau aus Nilgiri	Donna Kyan di Nilgiri	Femme kyan de Nilgiri	Mujer kyan de Nilgiri
d	Parsi lady from Bombay	Parsi-Dame aus Bombay	Donna parsi di Bombay	Femme parsi de Bombay	Mujer parsi de Bombay

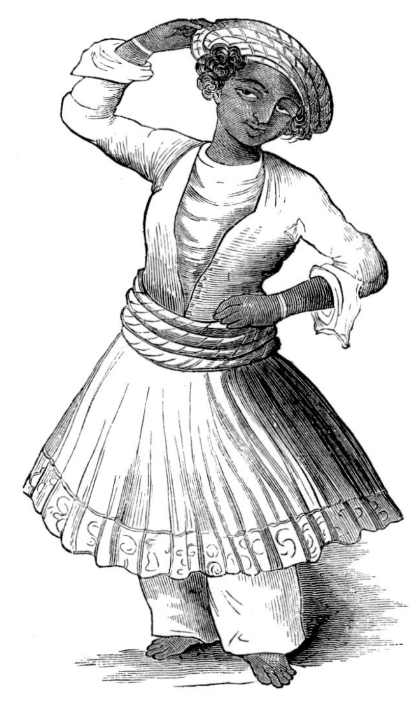

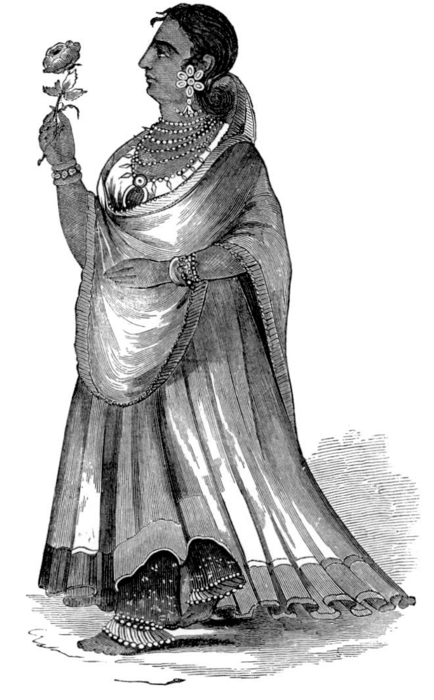

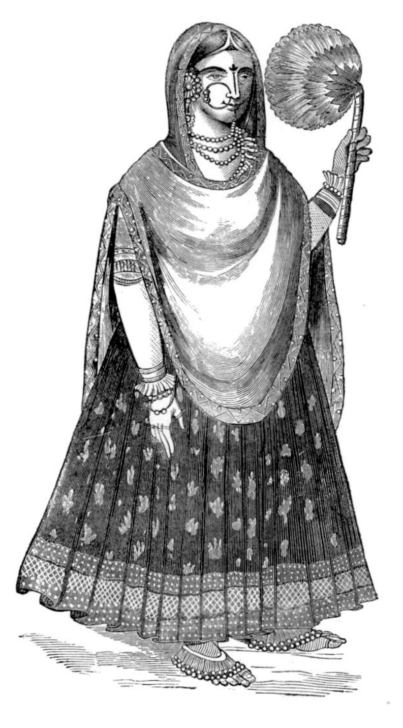

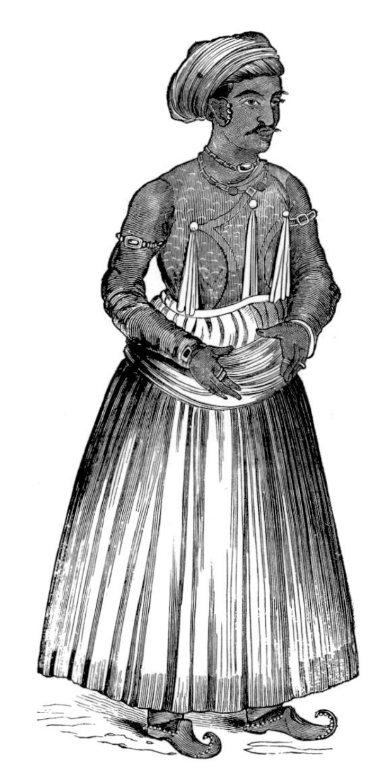

a	Dancing boy	Tanzender Junge	Ragazzo danzante	Danseur	Bailarín
b	Muslim lady from Bengal	Moslemische Frau aus Bengal	Donna musulmana del Bengala	Musulmane du Bengale	Mujer musulmana de Bengala
c	Hindu lady from Bengal	Indische Frau aus Bengal	Donna hindu del Bengala	Hindoue du Bengale	Mujer hinduista de Bengala
d	Hindu man from Bengal	Indischer Mann aus Bengal	Uomo hindu del Bengala	Hindou du Bengale	Hombre hinduista de Bengala

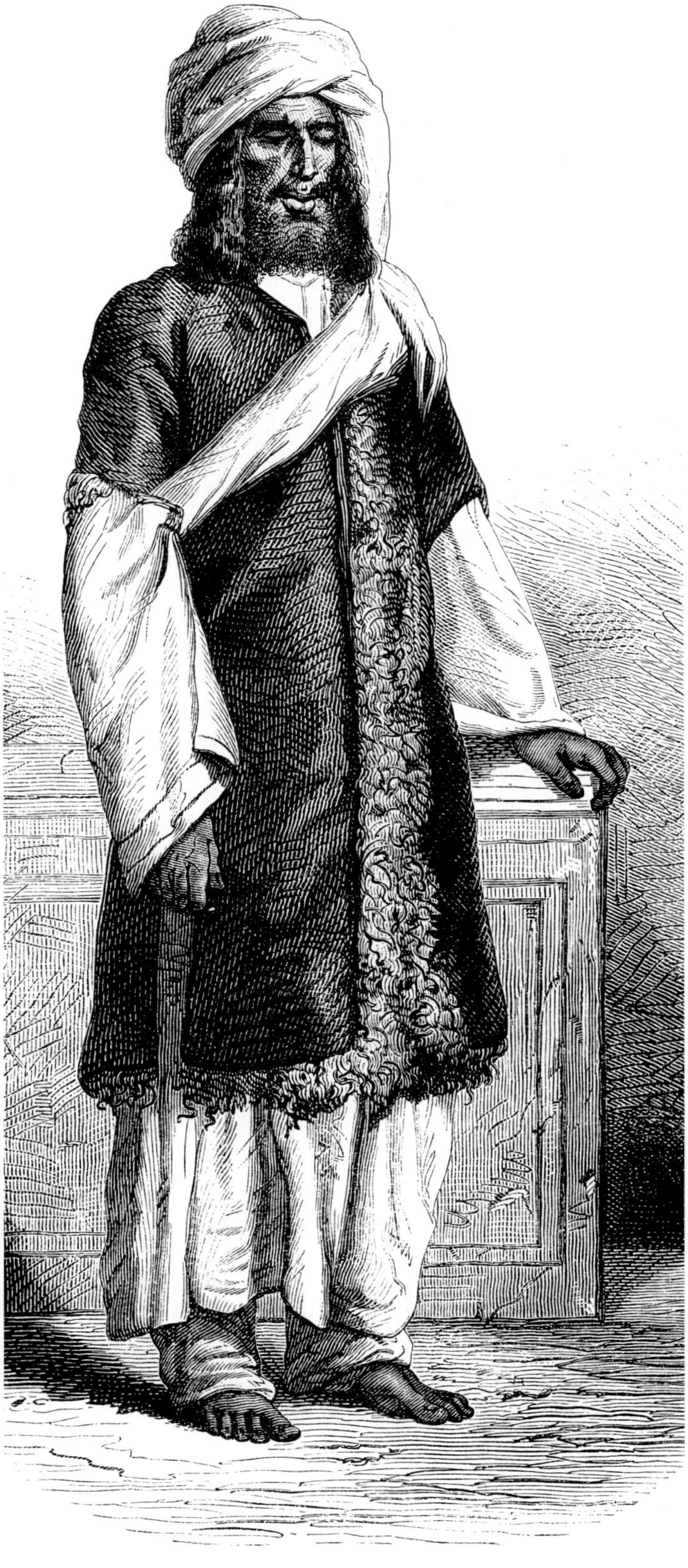

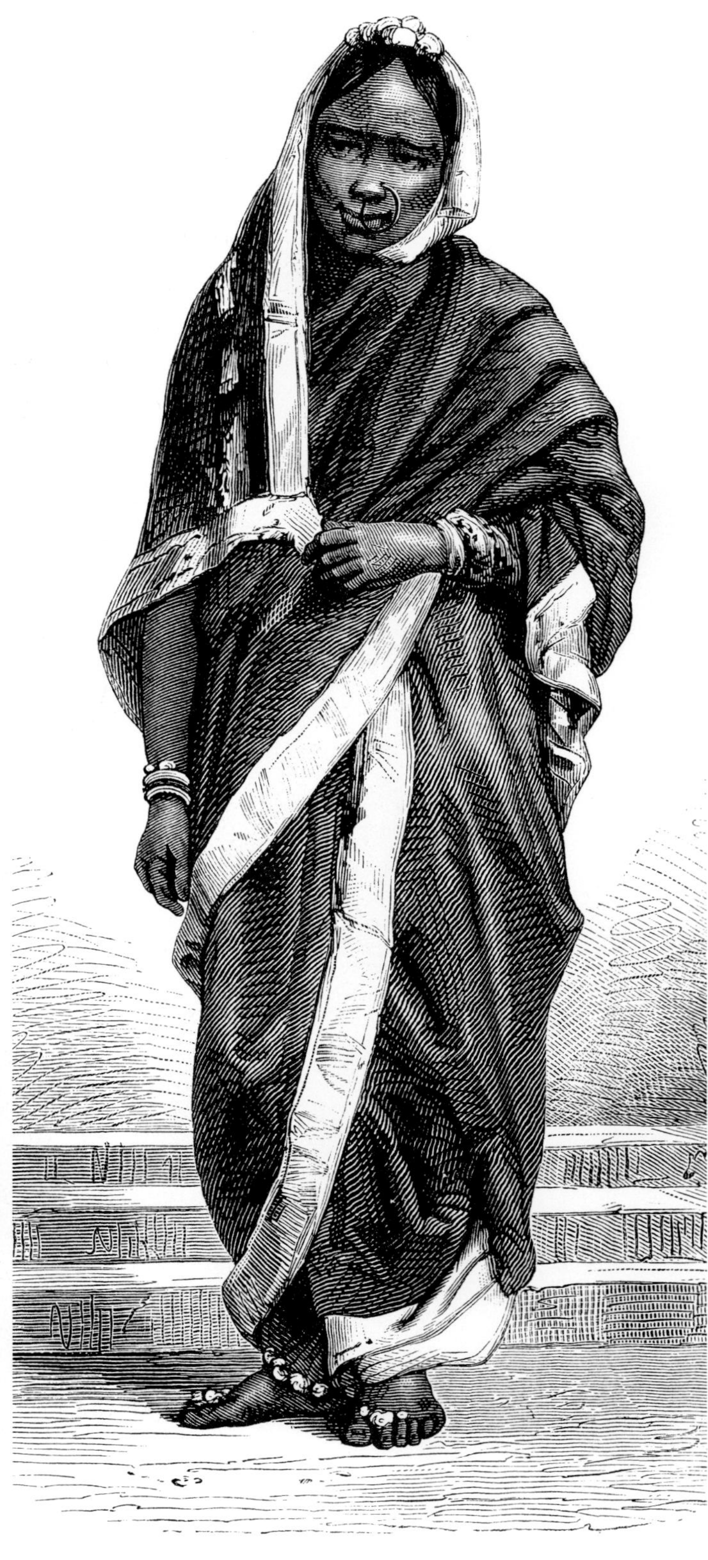

Kashmiri man and woman, c. 1865

Mann und Frau aus Kaschmir, um 1865

Uomo e donna del Kashmir, ca. 1865

Homme et femme du Cachemire, vers 1865

Hombre y mujer de Cachemira, hacia 1865

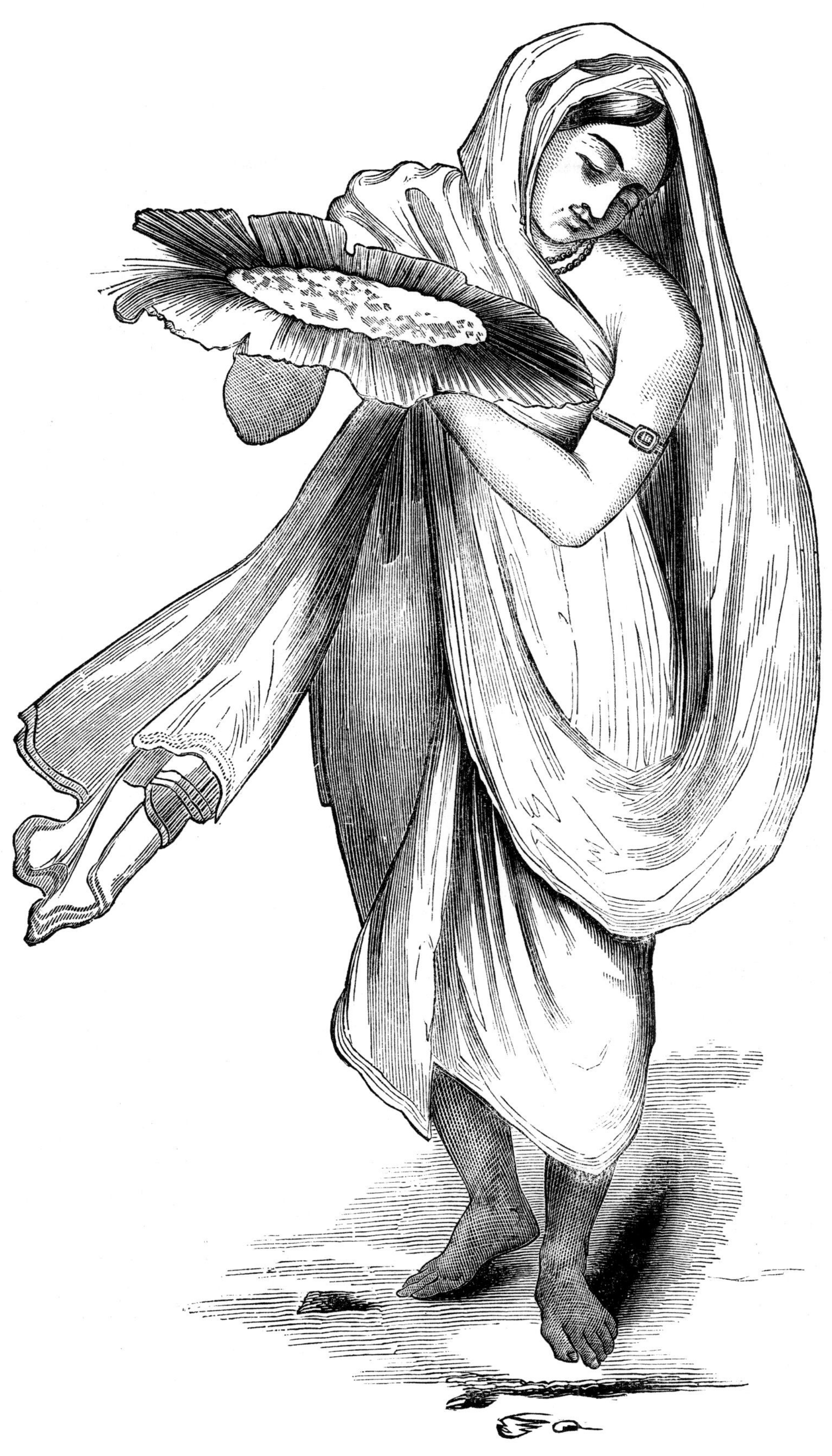

Brahmin lady carrying a rice dish, c. 1850

Brahmanenfrau mit Reisteller, um 1850

Donna bramina con piatto di riso, ca. 1850

Brahmane portant un plat de riz, vers 1850

Mujer de la casta de los brahmanes con un plato de arroz, hacia 1850

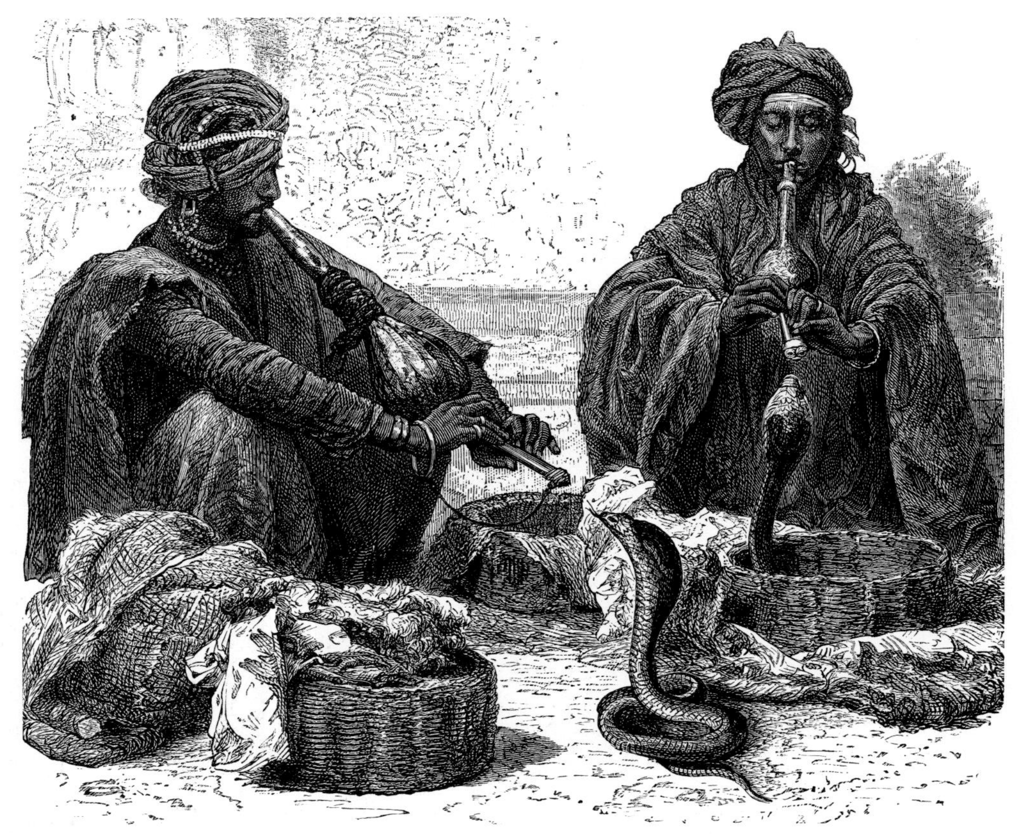

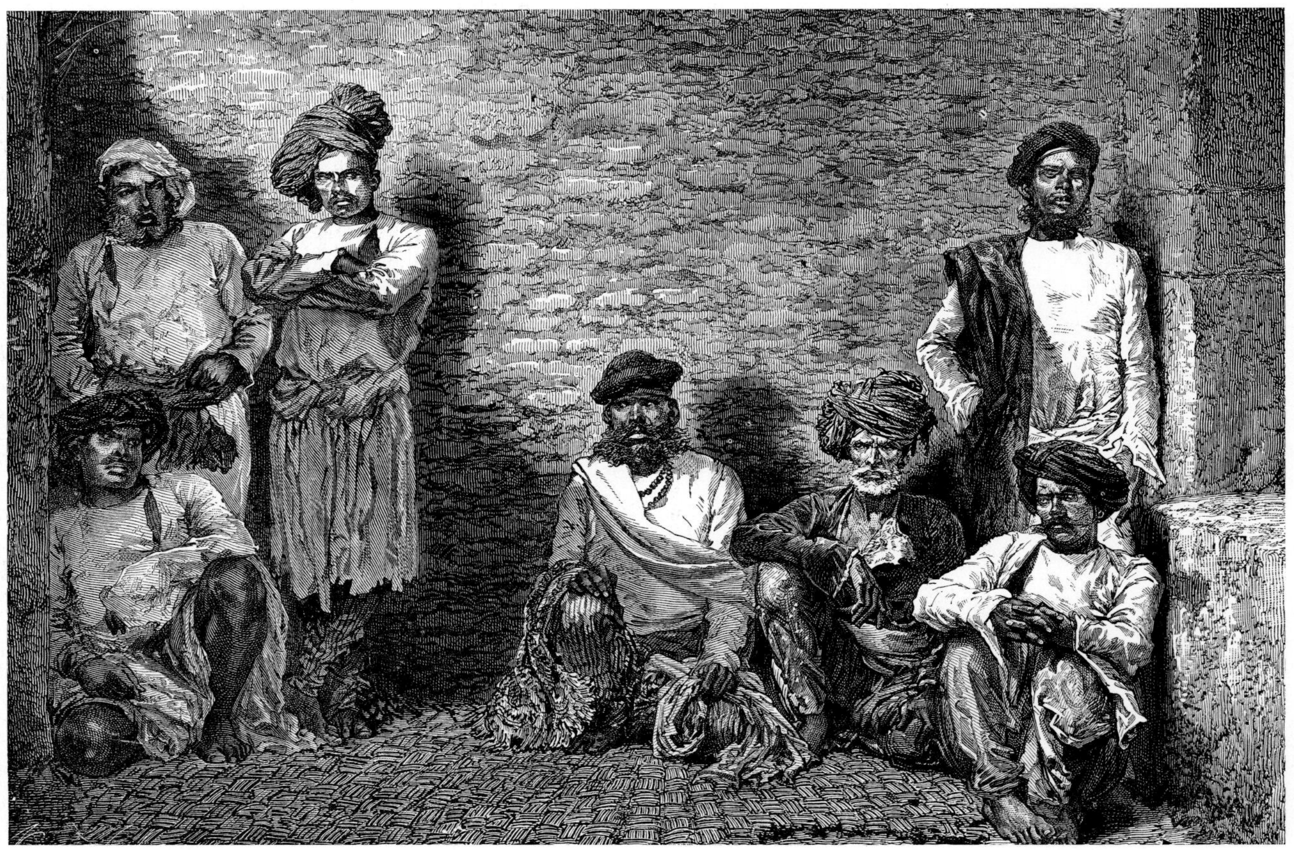

a	Snake charmers	Schlangenbeschwörer	Incantatori di serpenti	Charmeurs de serpents	Encantadores de serpientes
b	Prisoners	Gefangene	Prigionieri	Prisonniers	Prisioneros

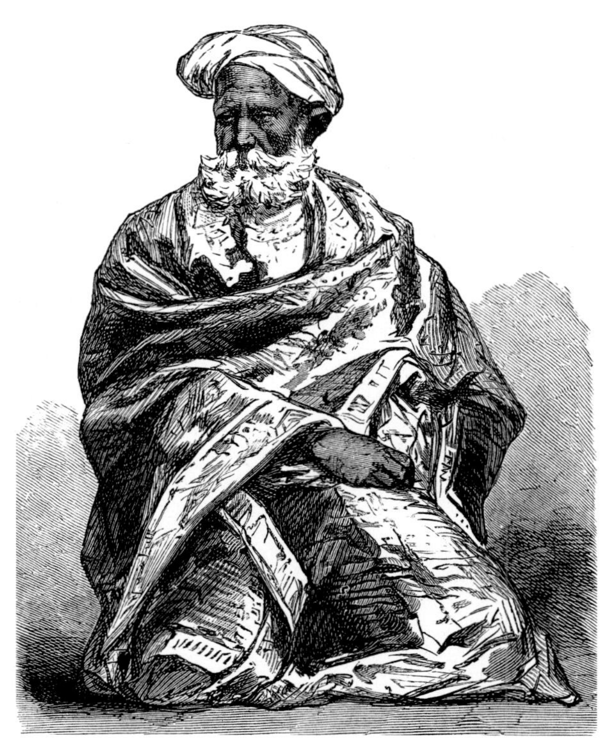

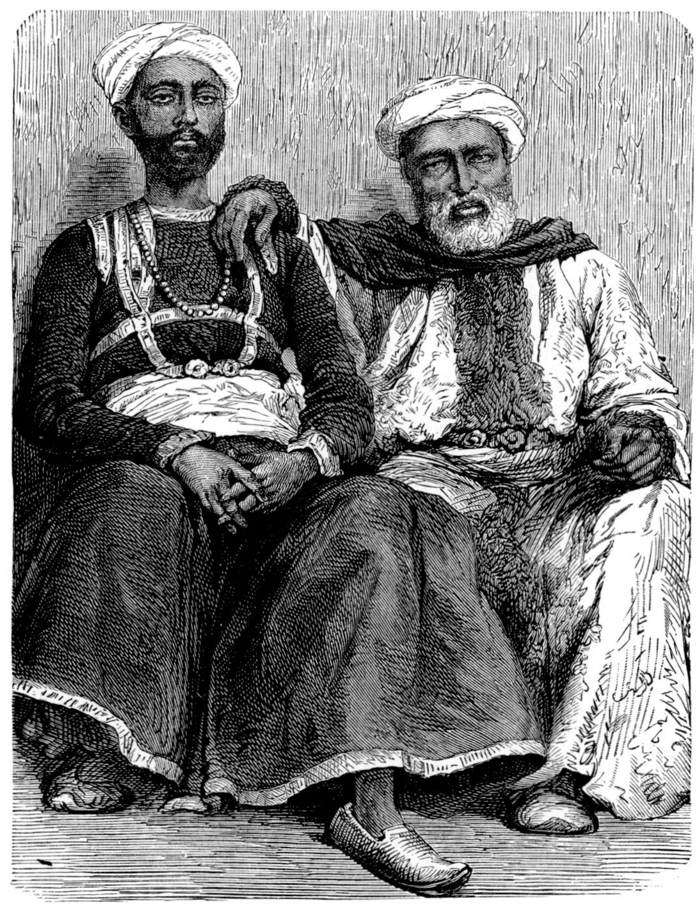

a	Sikh from the Punjab	Sikh aus Punjab	Sikh del Punjab	Sikh du Panjab	Sij del Punjab
b	Men from Hyderabad	Männer aus Hyderabad	Uomini di Hyderabad	Hommes d'hyderabad	Hombres de Hyderabad

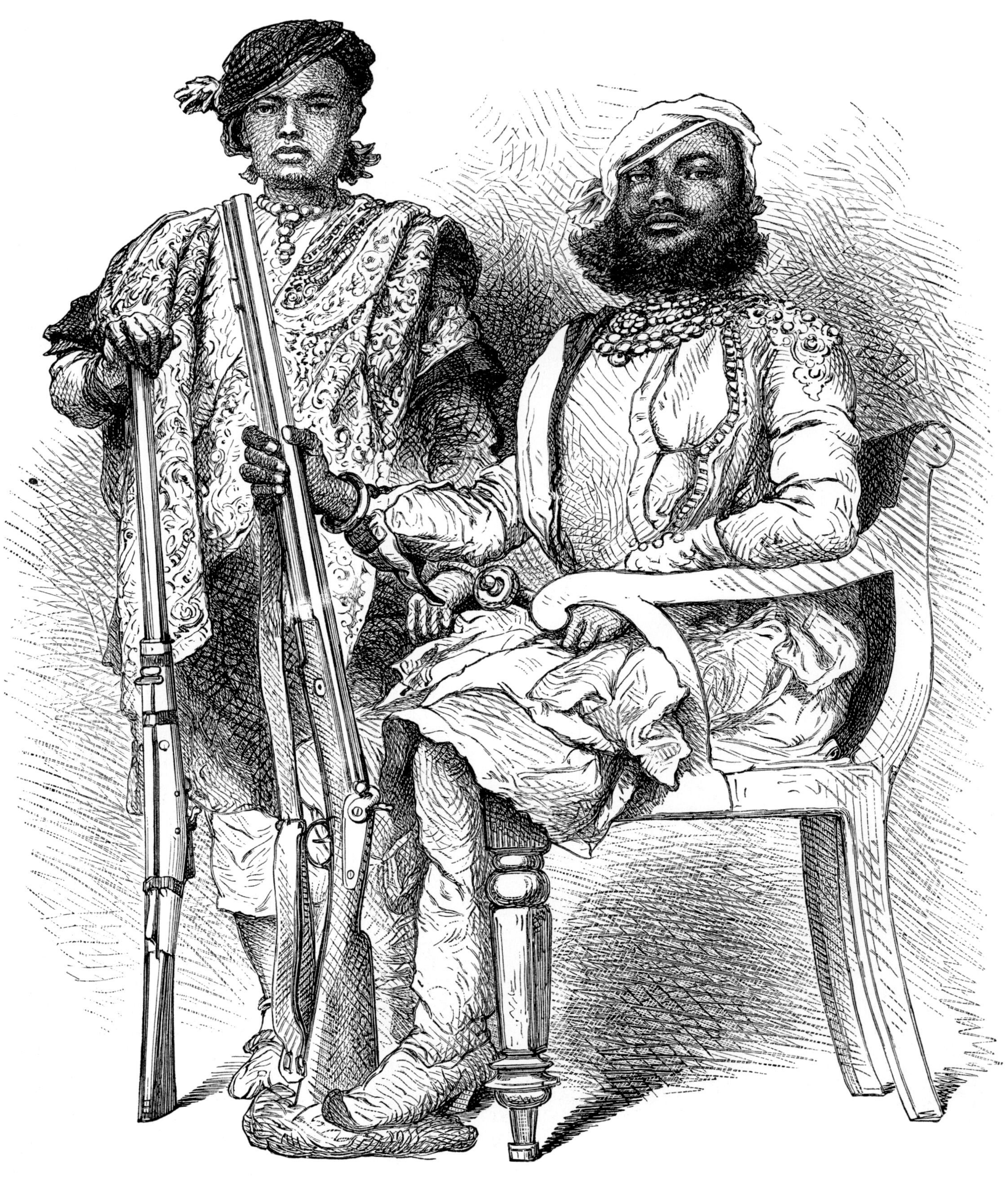

Men from Dolpur Männer aus Dolpur Uomini di Dolpur Hommes de Dolpur Hombres de Dolpur

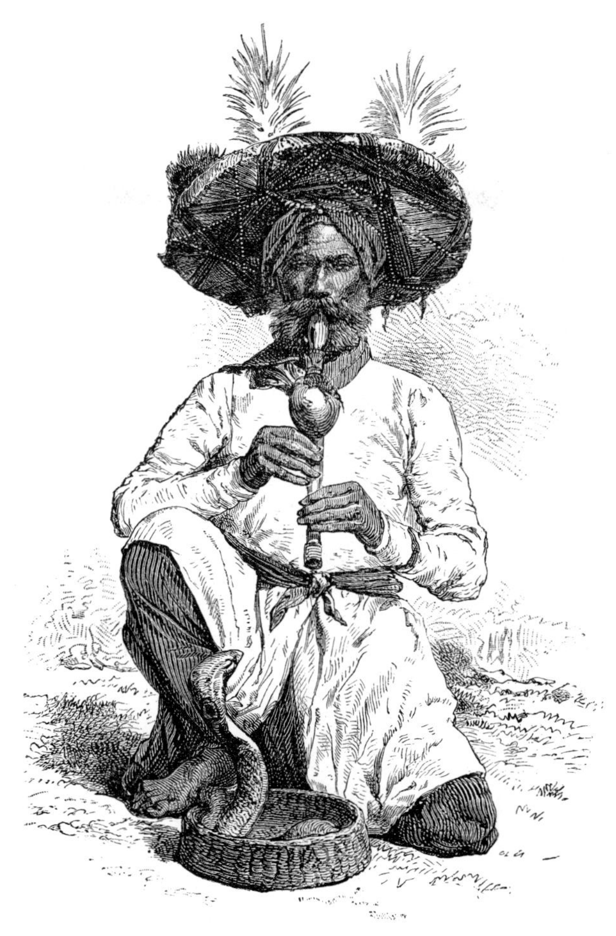

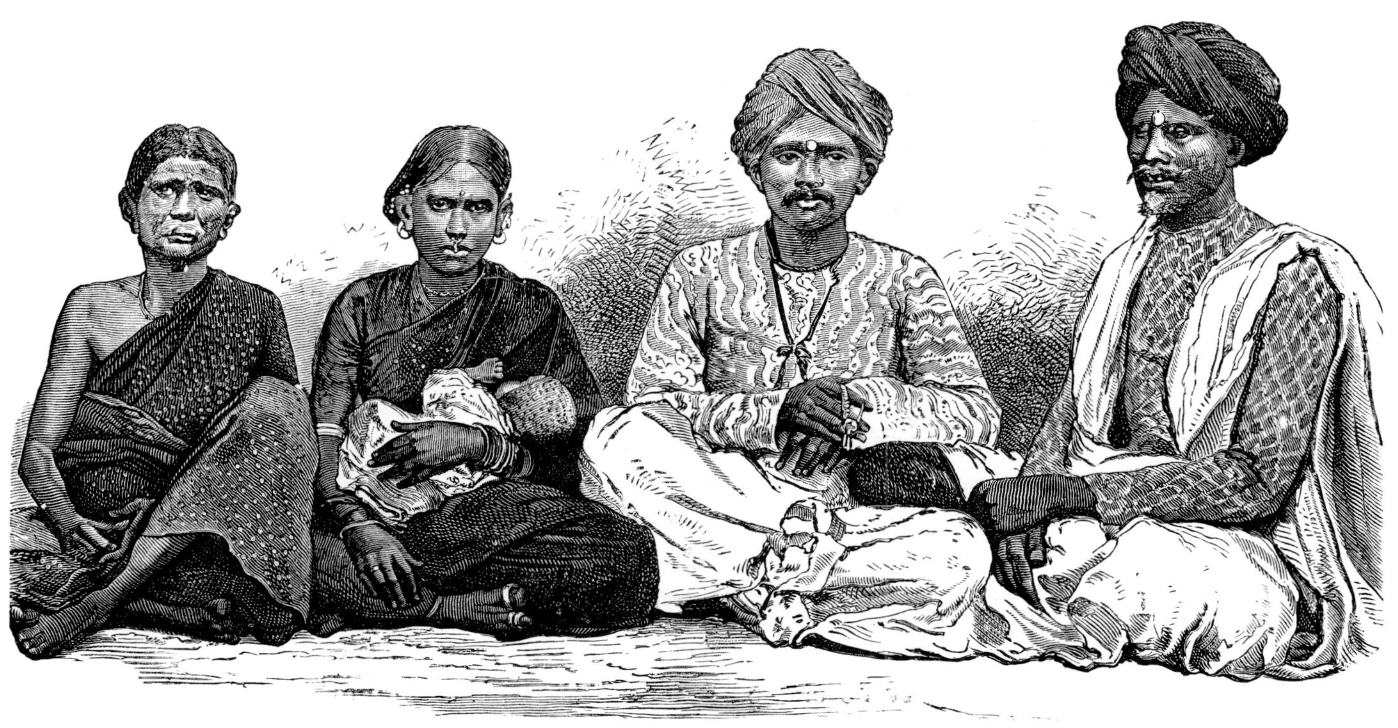

a	Snake charmer	Schlangenbeschwörer	Incantatore di serpenti	Charmeur de serpents	Encantador de serpientes
b	People from the Deccan	Menschen aus Deccan	Abitanti di Deccan	Habitants de Deccan	Habitantes del Decán

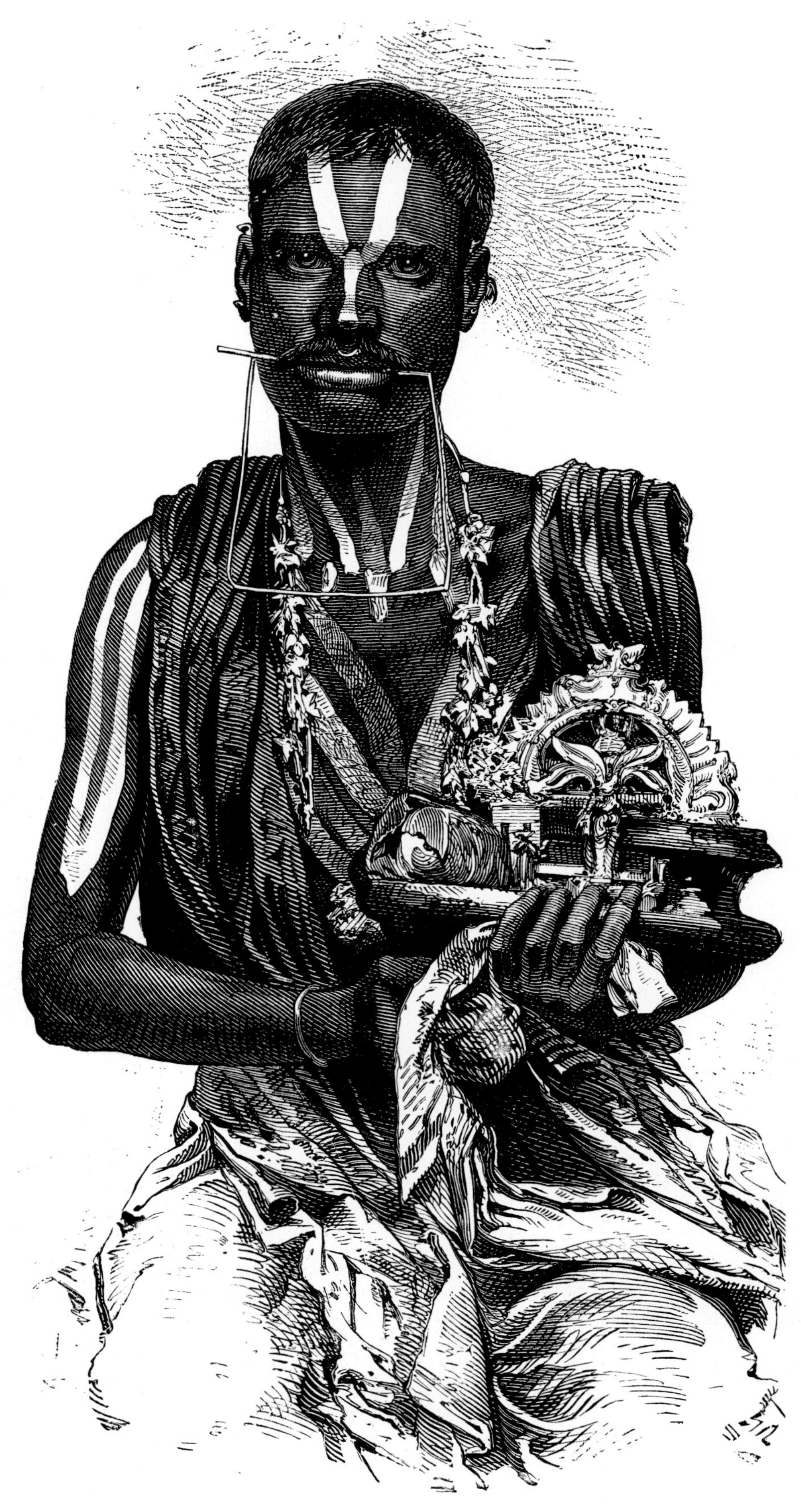

Hindu fakir | Indischer Fakir | Fachiro hindu | Fakir hindou | Faquir hindú

India

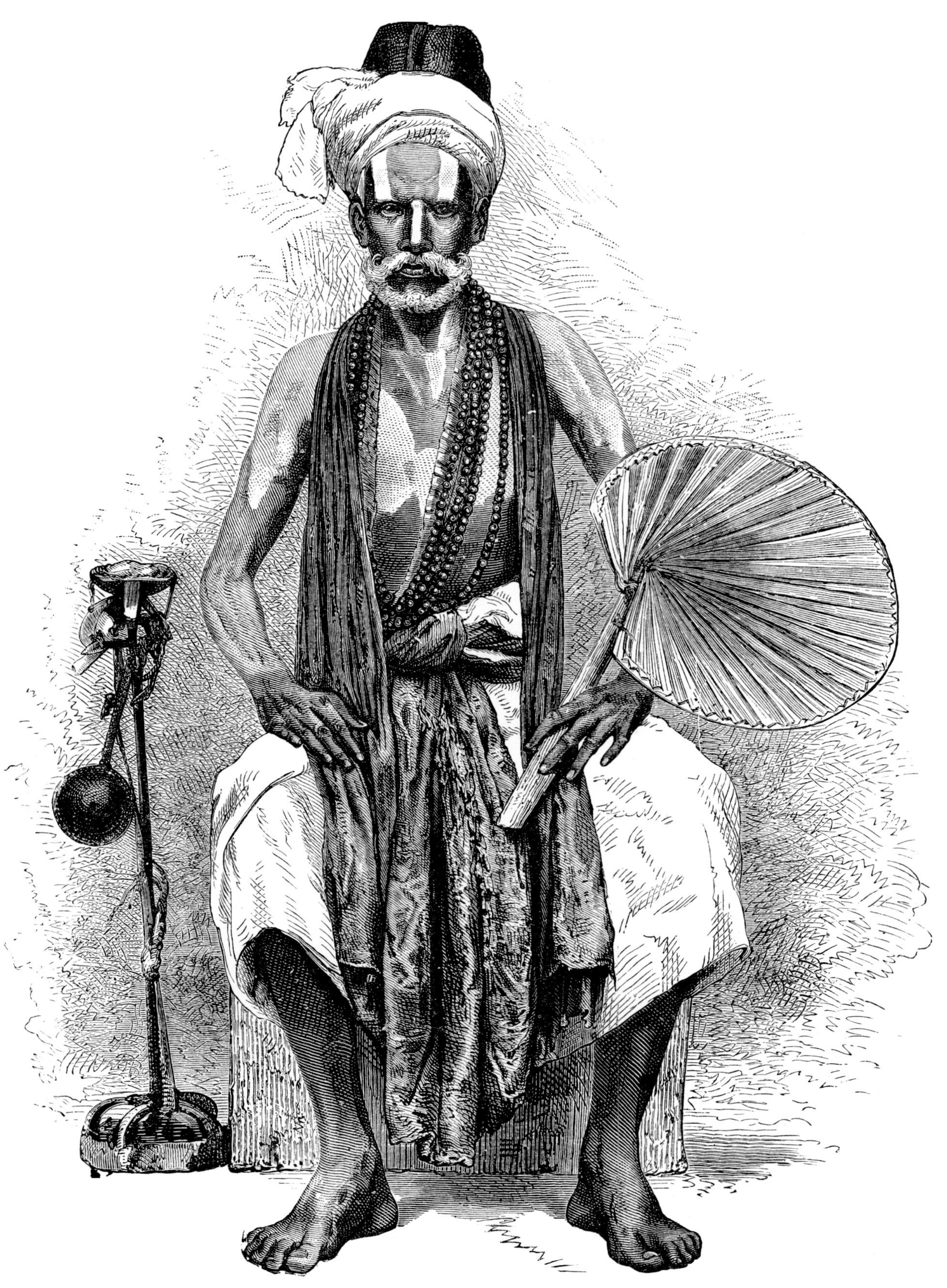

Hindu priest Indischer Priester Sacerdote hindu Prêtre hindou Sacerdote hindú

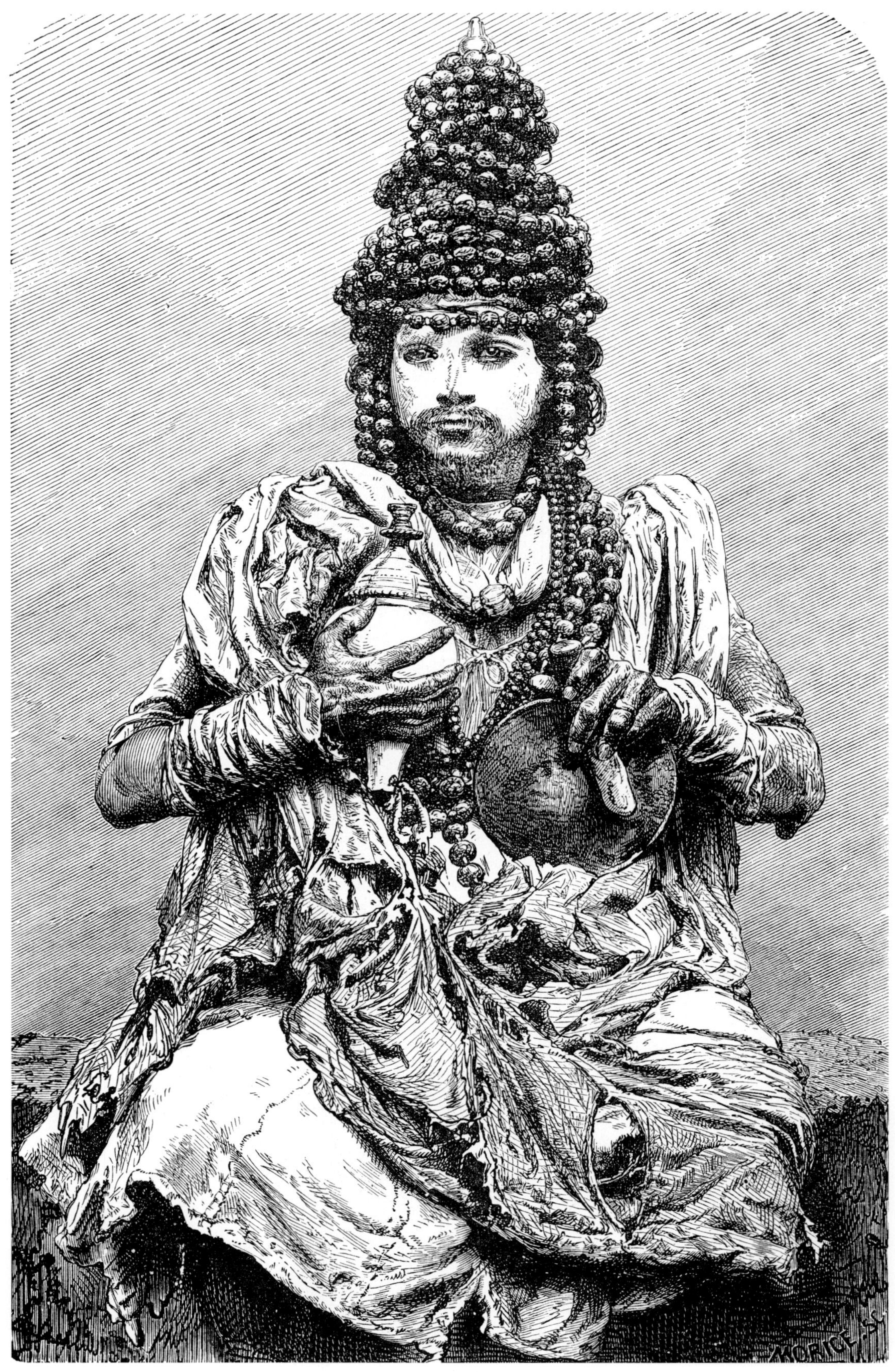

Hindu fakir | Indischer Fakir | Fachiro hindu | Fakir hindou | Faquir hindú

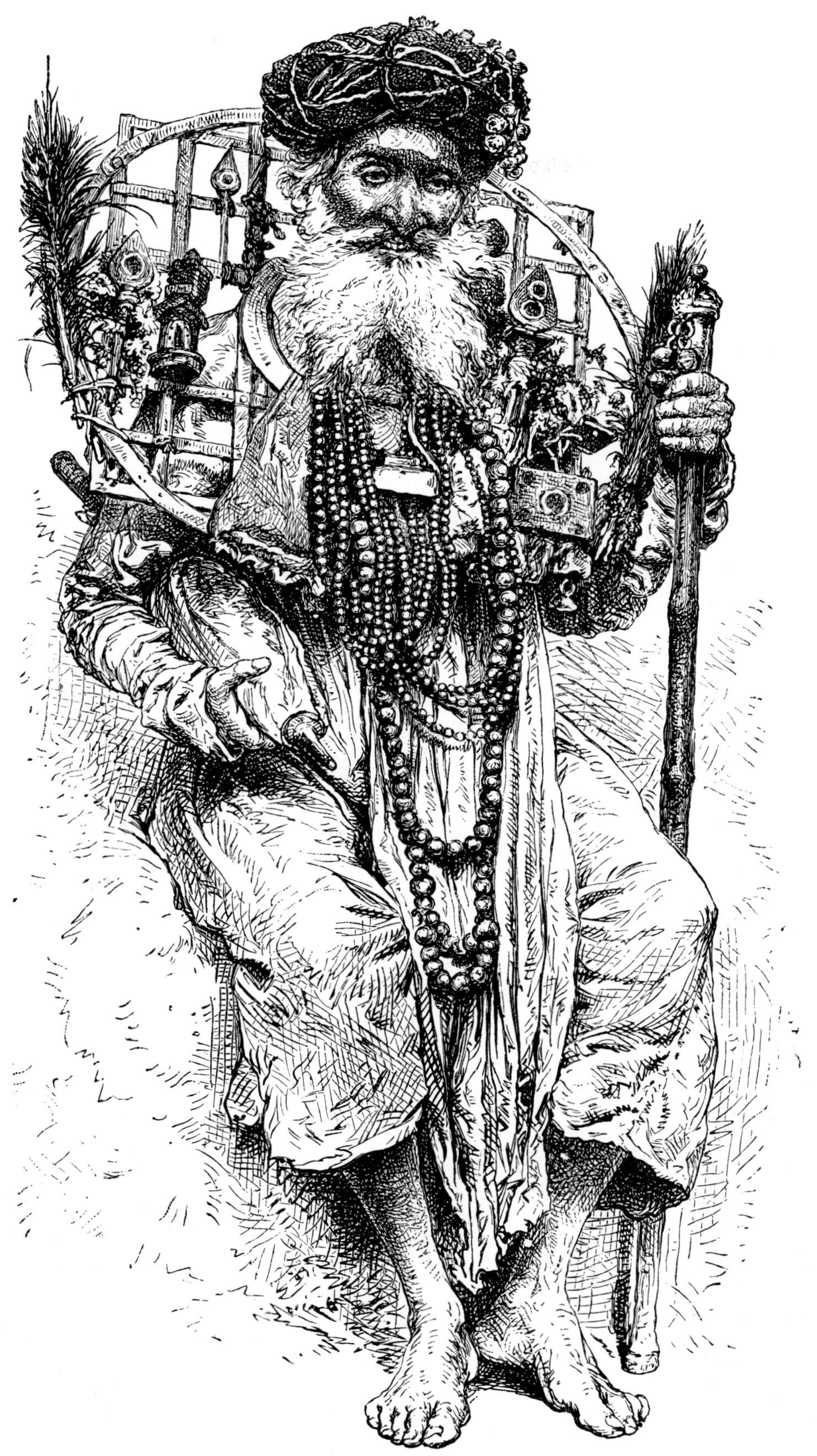

Indian fakir   Indischer Fakir   Fachiro indiano   Fakir indien   Faquir indio

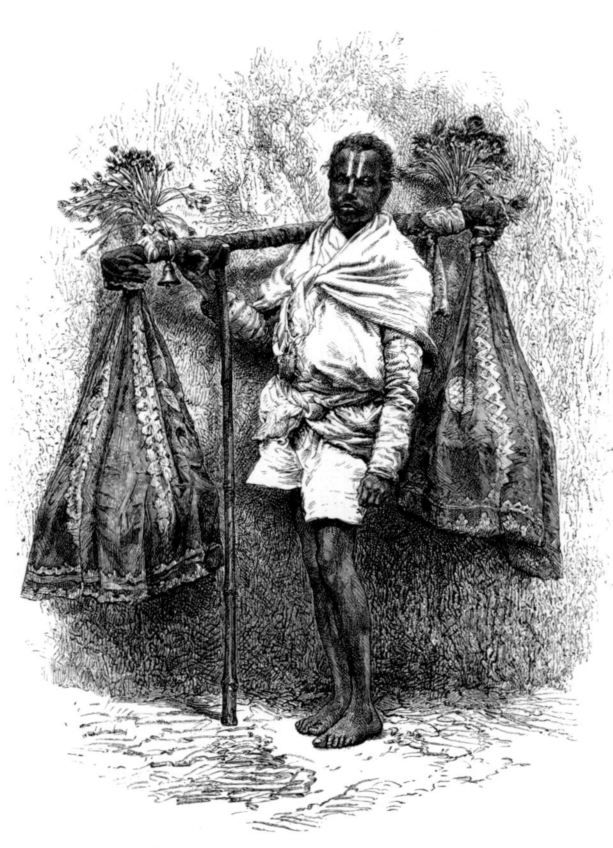

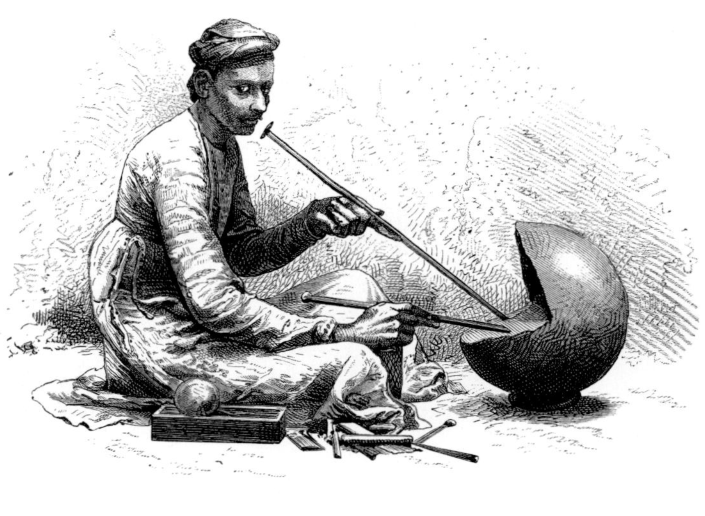

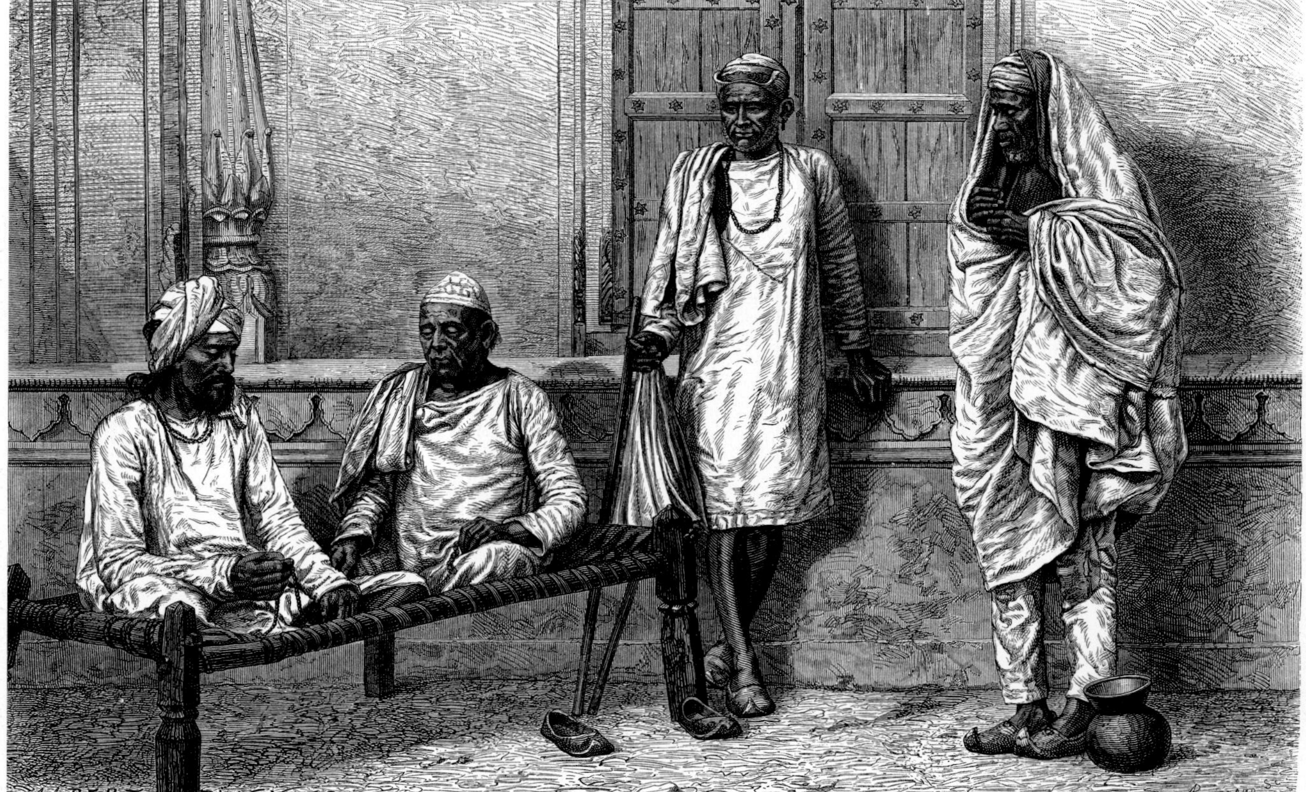

a	Fakir	Fakir	Fachiro	Fakir	Faquir
b	Goldsmith from Jaipur	Goldschmied aus Jaipur	Orafo di Jaipur	Orfèvre de Jaipur	Orfebre de Jaipur
c	Hindu clerics in Benares	Indische Geistliche in Benares	Sacerdoti hindu a Benares	Ecclésiastiques hindous à Bénarès	Clérigos hinduistas de Benarés

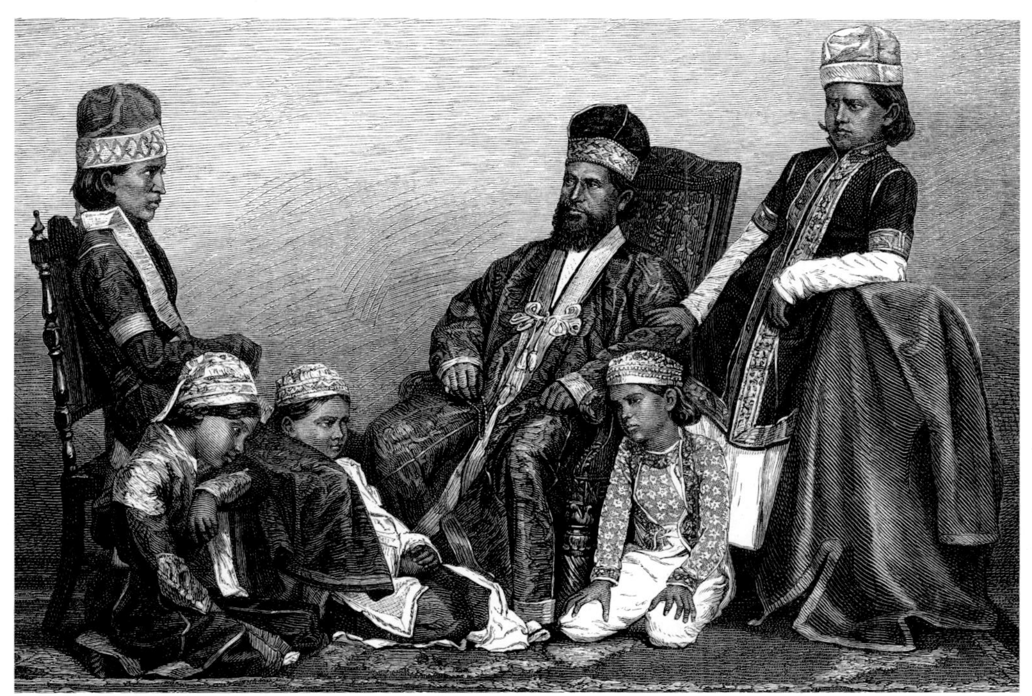

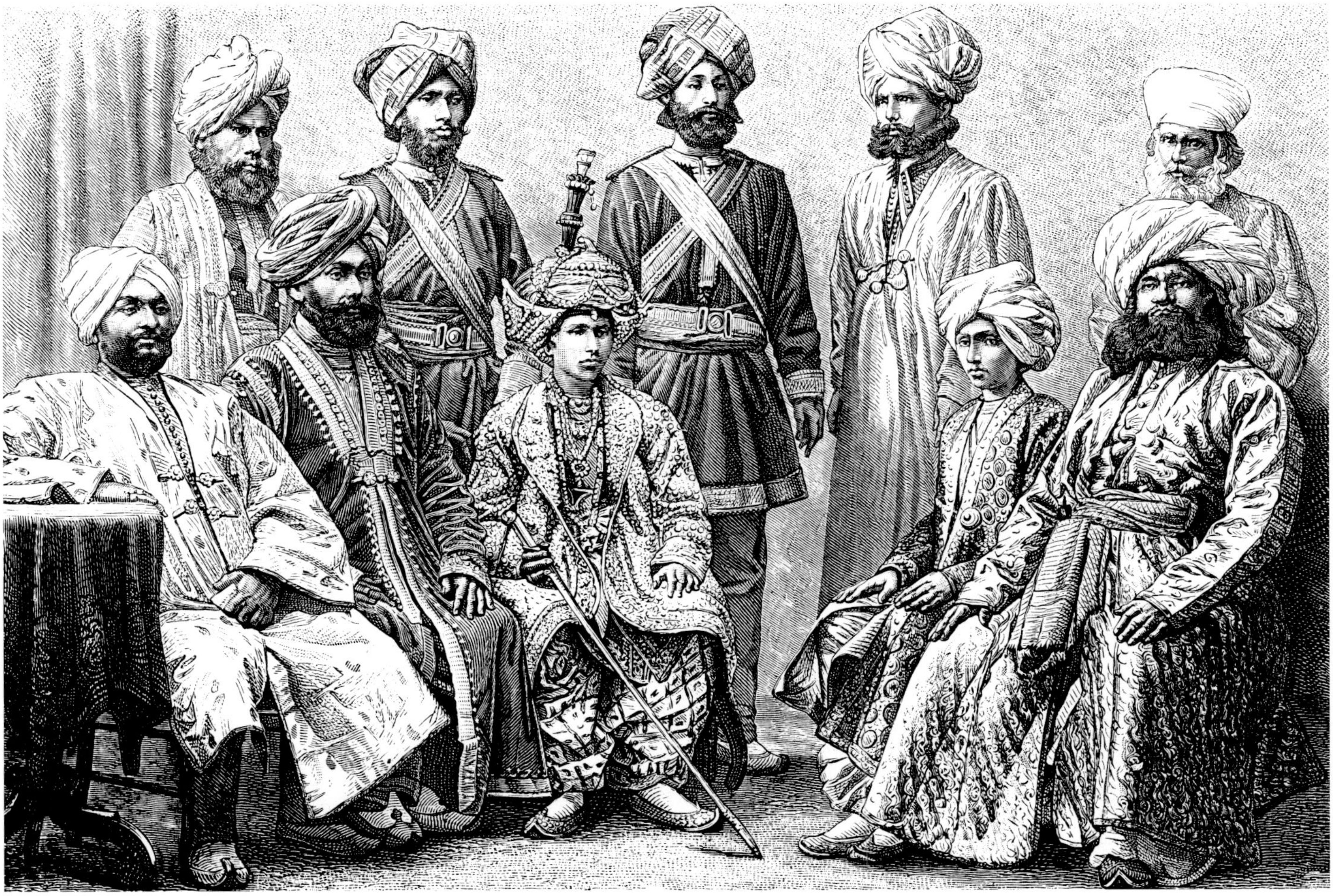

a

Nobles from Delhi

Adlige aus Dehli

Nobili di Delhi

Nobles de Delhi

Nobles de Delhi

b

The Rajah of Bahawalpur with his court, c. 1870

Der Radscha von Bahawalpur mit seinem Gefolge, um 1870

Il Rajah di Bahawalpur con la sua corte, ca. 1870

Le Rajah de Bahawalpur et sa Cour, vers 1870

Rajá de Bahawalpur y su corte, hacia 1870

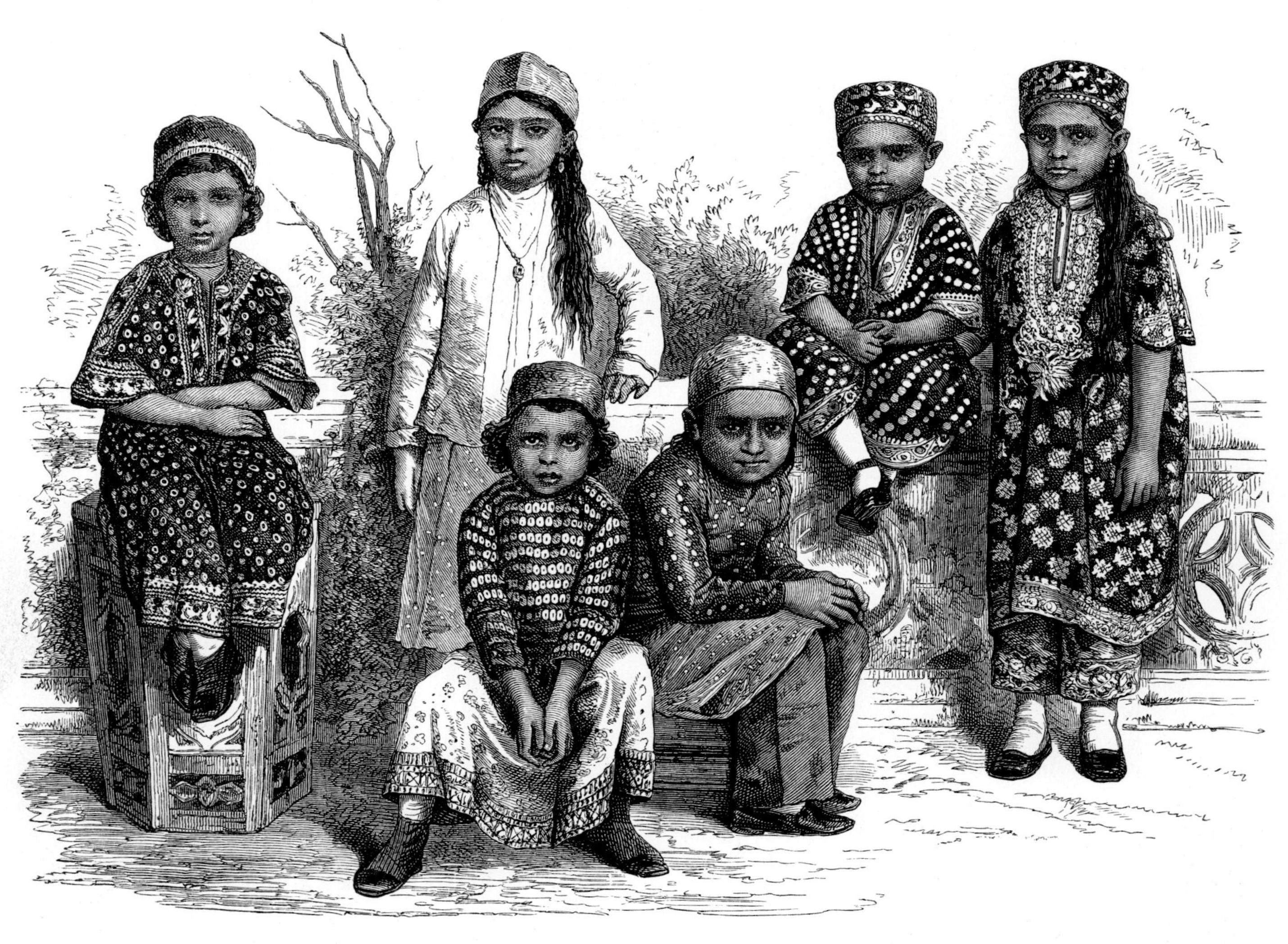

Parsi children | Parsi-Kinder | Bambini parsi | Enfants parsis | Niños parsis

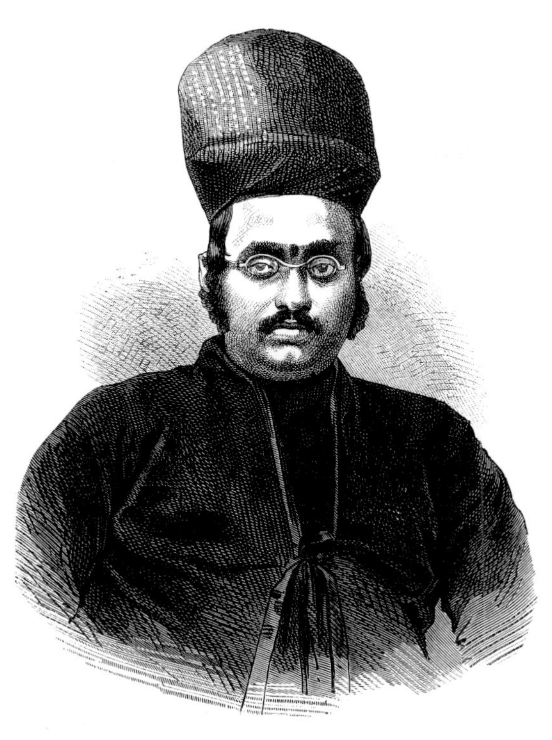

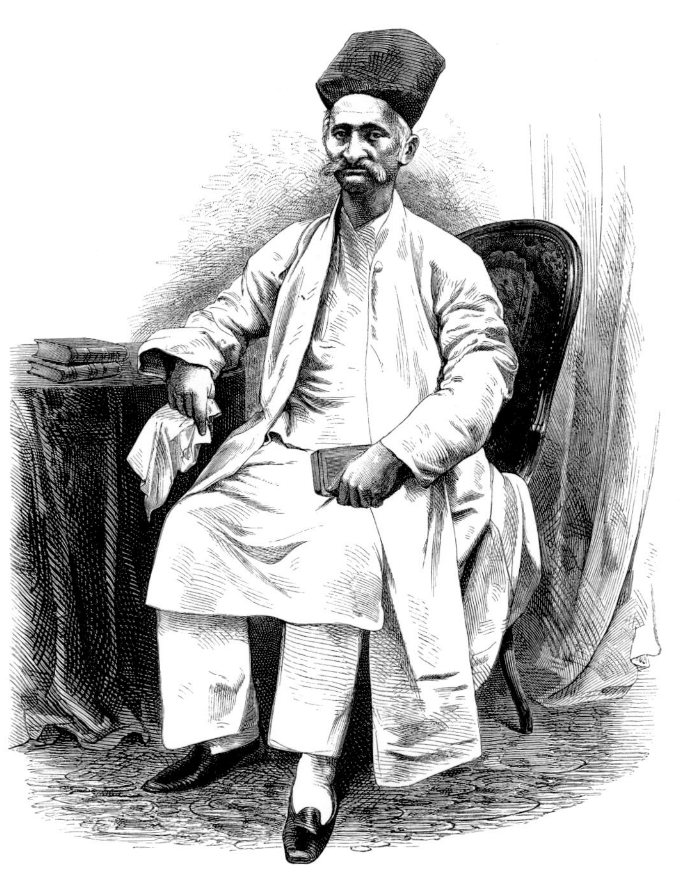

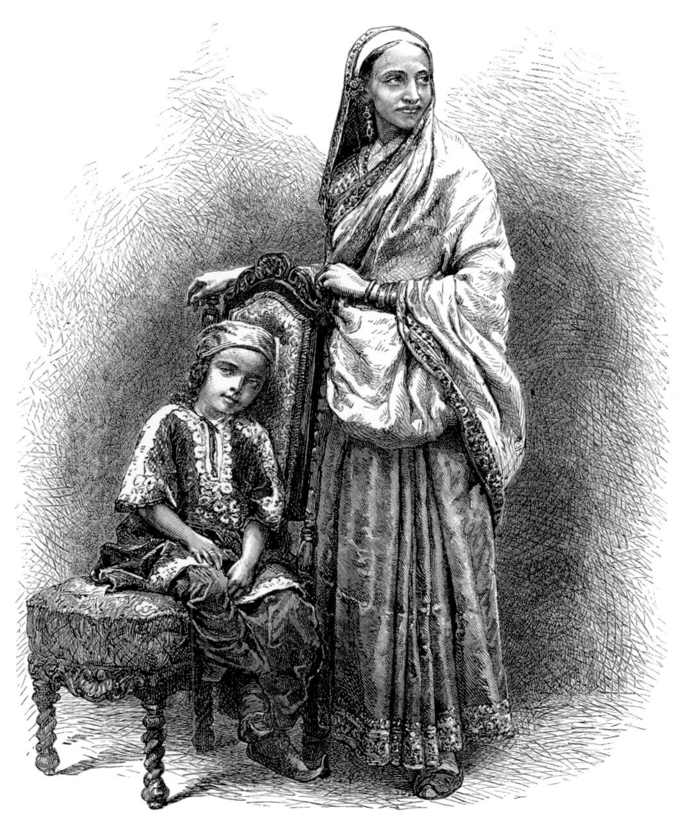

a	Parsi man, Bombay	Parsi-Mann, Bombay	Uomo parsi, Bombay	Homme parsi, Bombay	Hombre parsi, Bombay
b	Parsi lady and child	Parsi-Frau mit Kind	Donna e bambino parsi	Femme et enfant parsi	Mujer y niño parsis
c	Parsi man	Parsi-Mann	Uomo parsi	Homme parsi	Hombre parsi

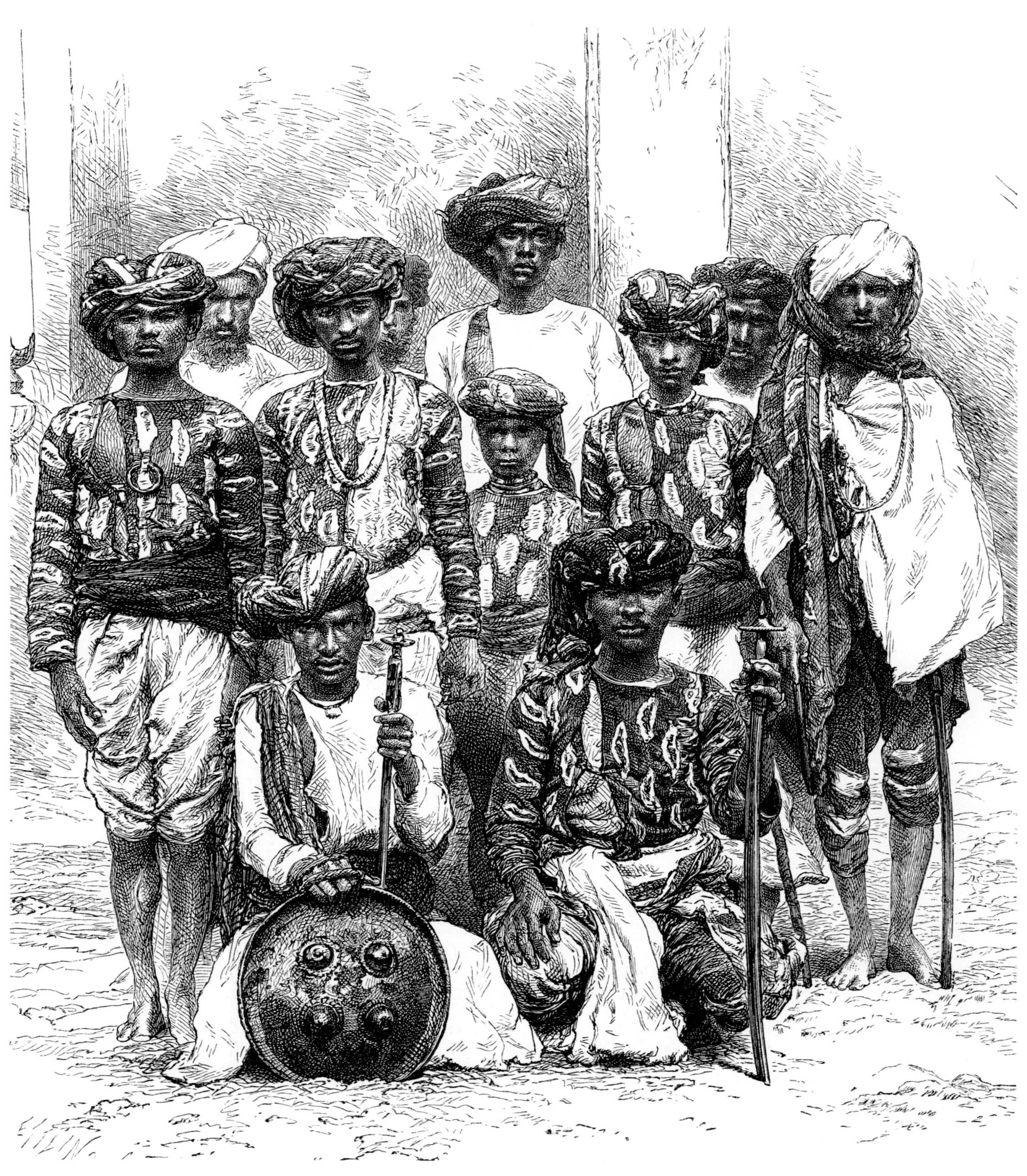

Soldiers from Hyderabad, c. 1860

Soldaten aus Hyderabad, um 1860

Soldati di Hyderabad, ca. 1860

Soldats d'Hyderabad, vers 1860

Soldados de Hyderabad, alrededor del año 1860

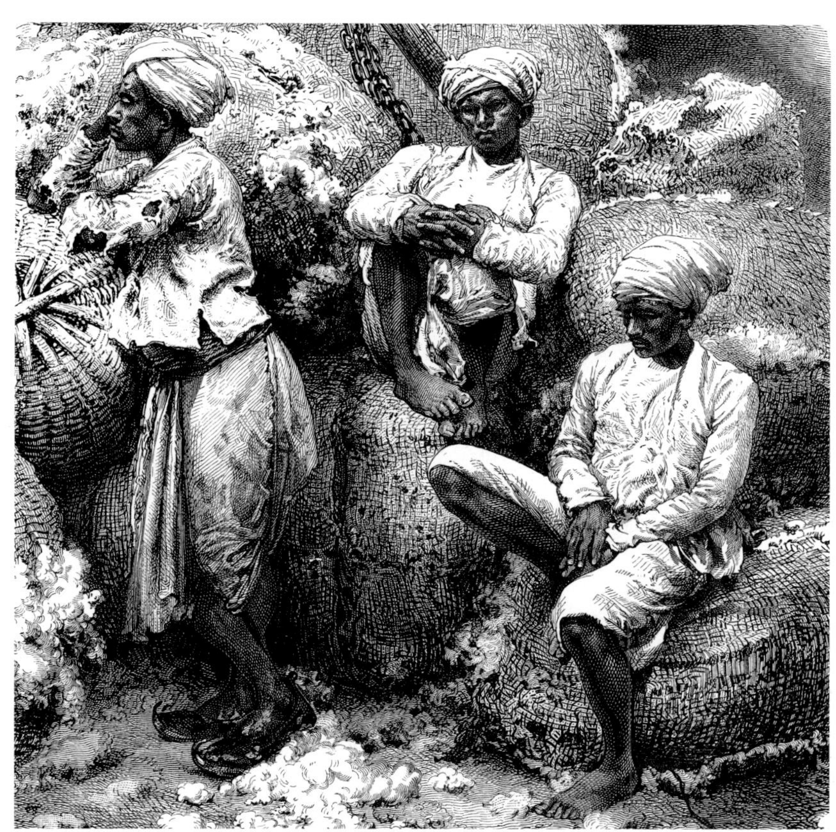

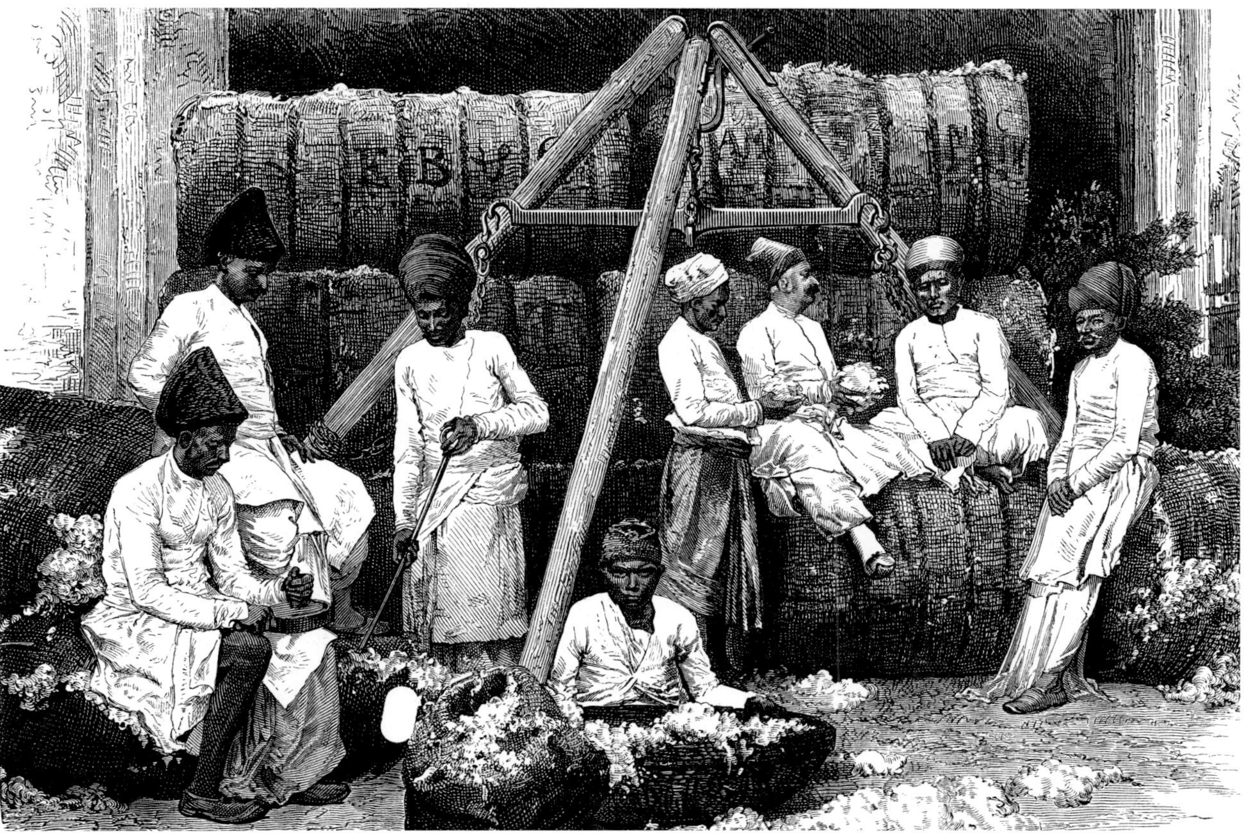

Cotton carriers and traders, c. 1870

Baumwollträger und -händler, um 1870

Portatori e commercianti di cotone, ca. 1870

Porteurs et vendeurs de coton, vers 1870

Porteadores y comerciantes de algodón, c 1870

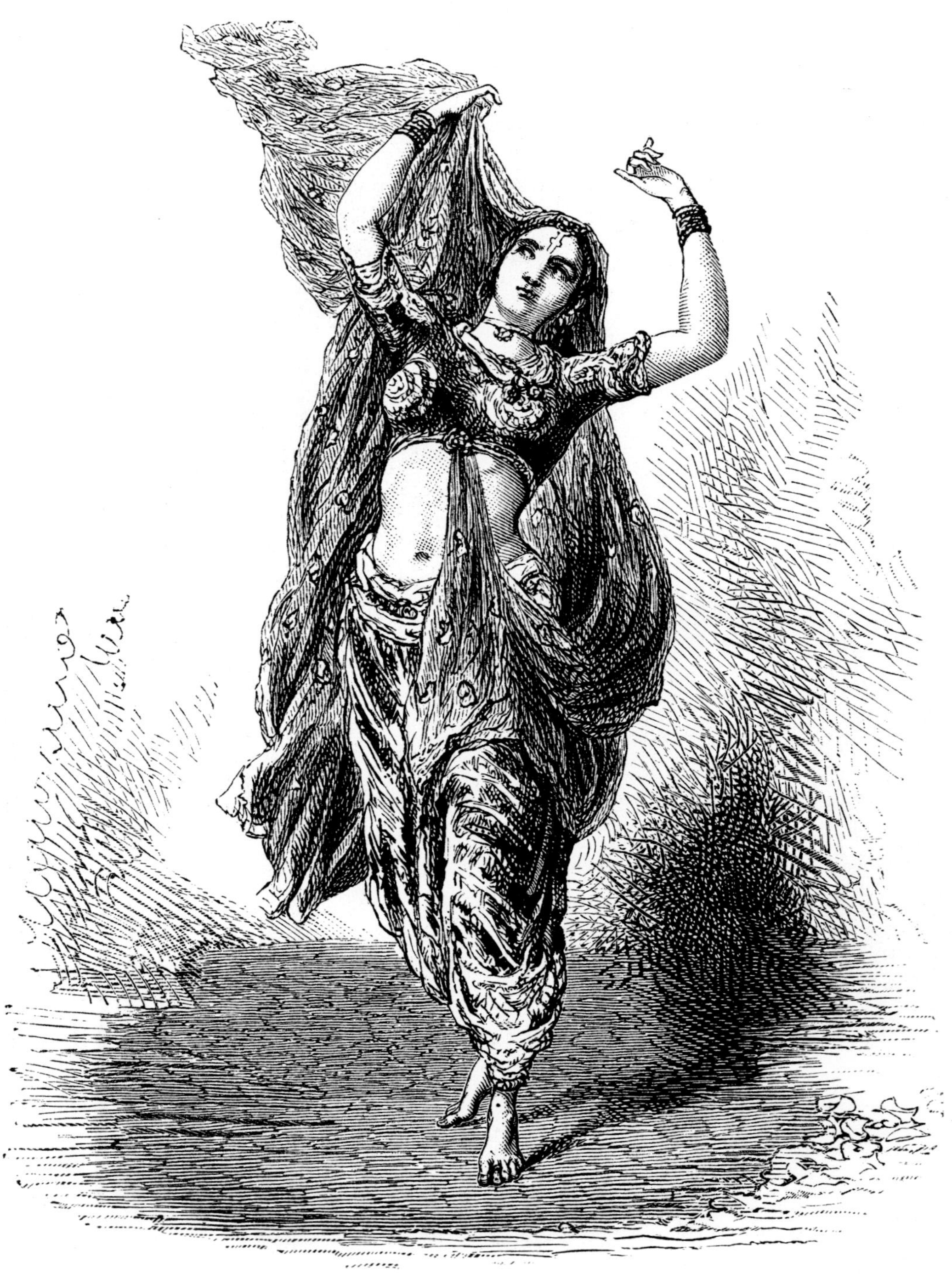

Dancing girl | Tanzendes Mädchen | Ragazza danzante | Danseuse | Bailarina

India

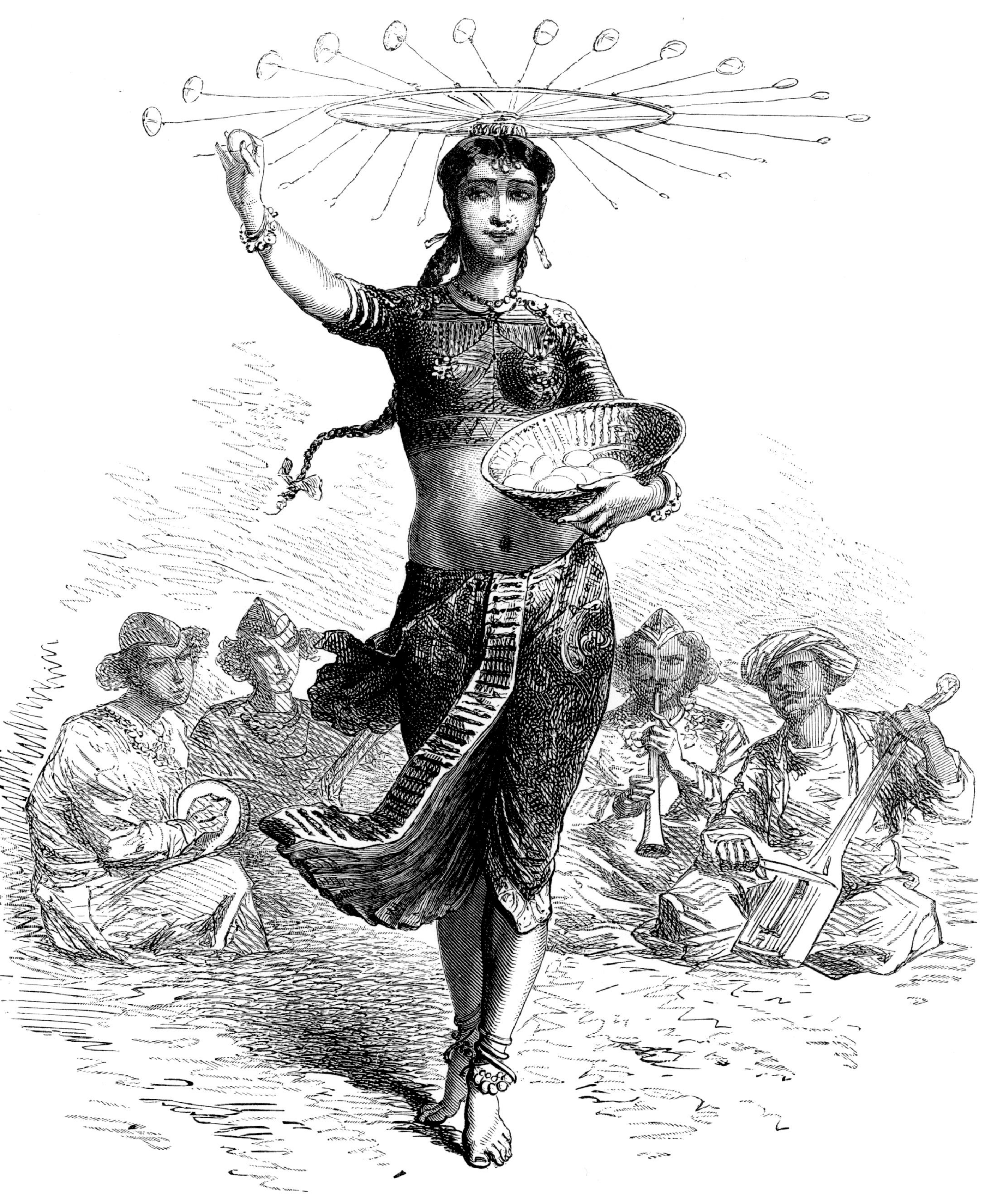

Dancing girl performing the 'egg dance'

Tanzendes Mädchen beim "Eiertanz"

Ragazza danzante nella "danza delle uova"

Jeune fille exécutant la « danse de l'oeuf »

Bailarina ejecutando la "danza del huevo"

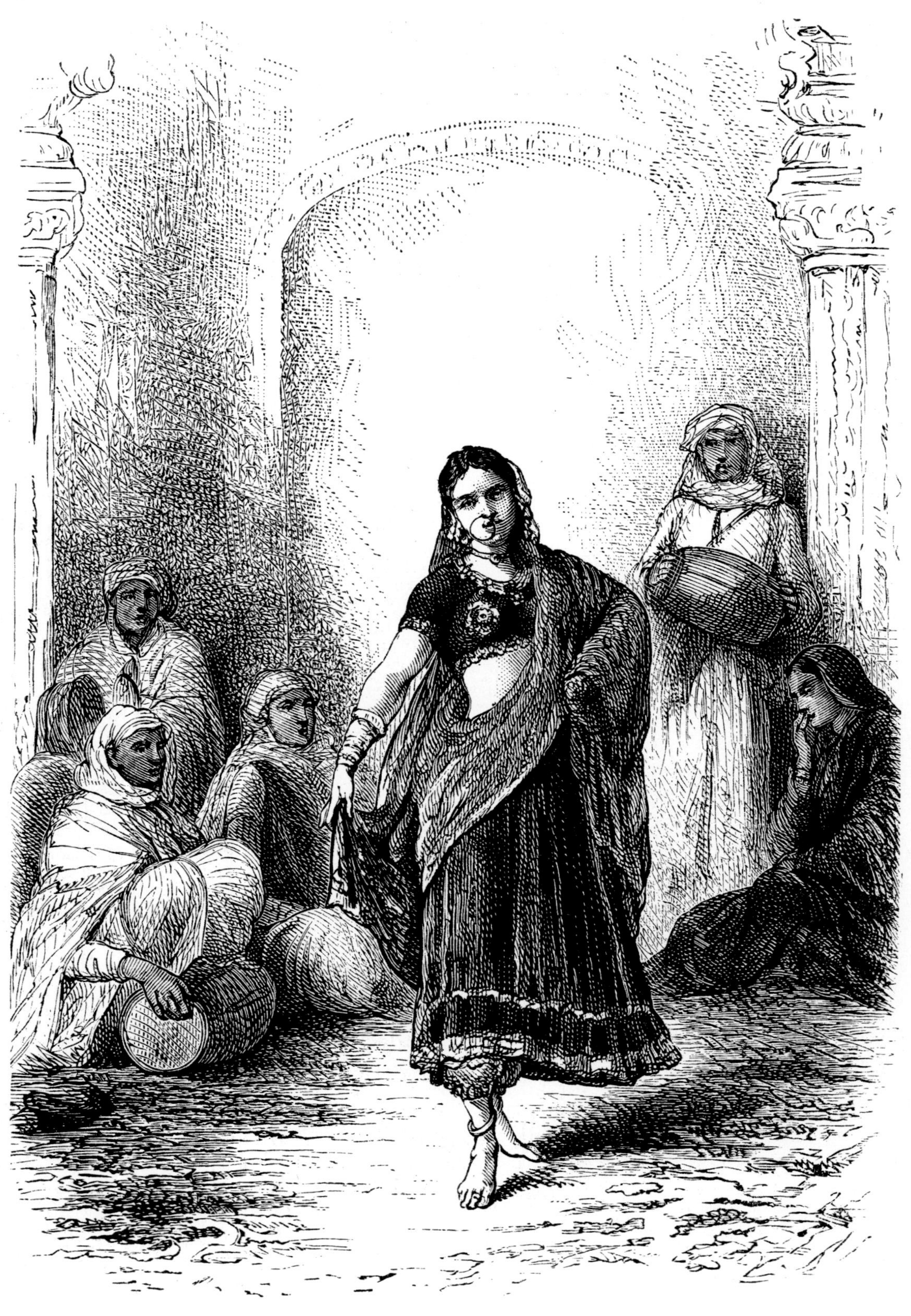

Dancing girl | Tanzendes Mädchen | Ragazza danzante | Danseuse | Bailarina

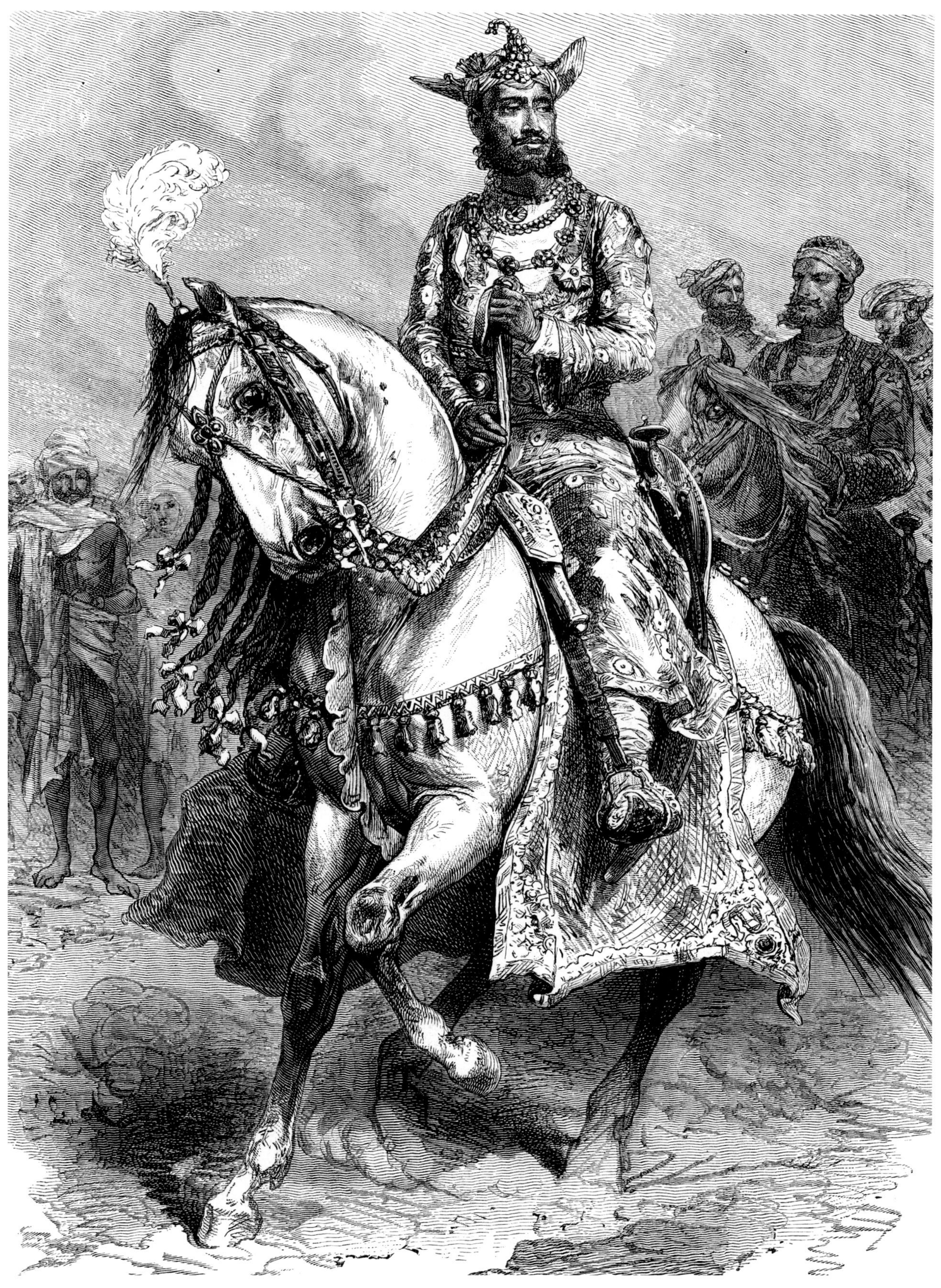

The Maharaja of Gwalior

Der Maharadscha von Gwalior

Il maharajah di Gwalior

Le Maharadjah de Gwalior

Maharajá de Gwalior

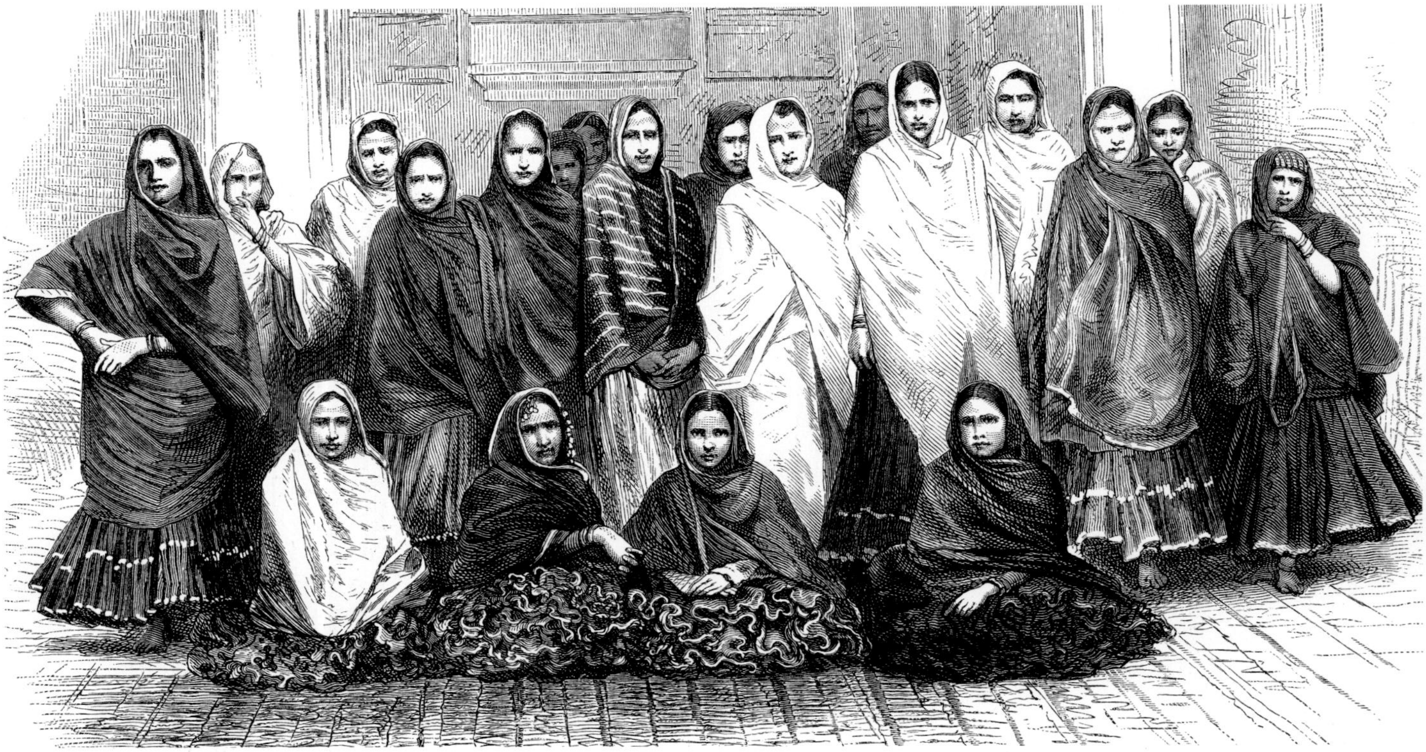

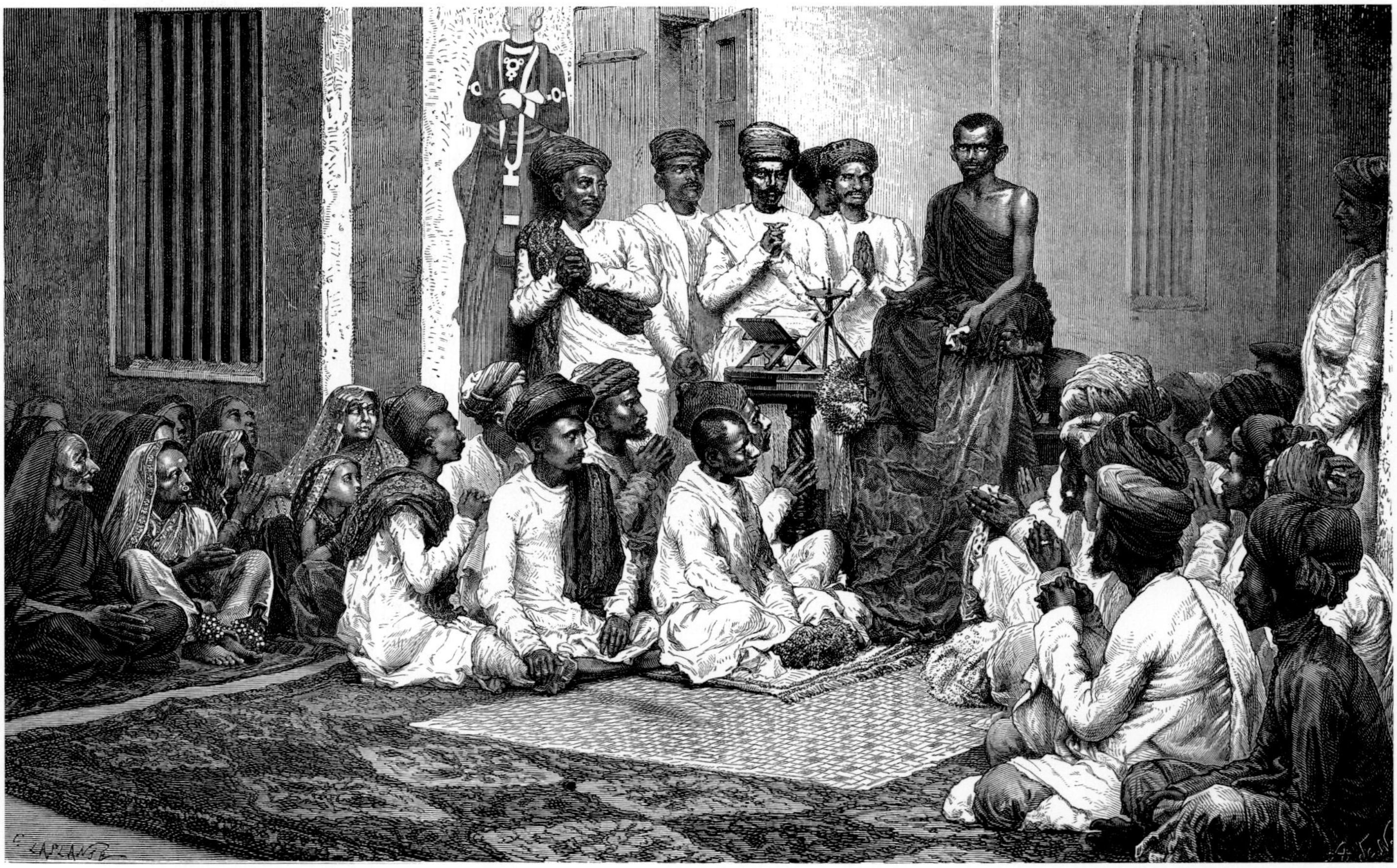

a	Court ladies	Hofdamen	Dame di corte	Femmes de la Cour	Cortesanas
b	Jain meeting, Bombay	Janistisches Treffen, Bombay	Riunione di giaini, Bombay	Rassemblement jaina, Bombay	Reunión jainista, Bombay

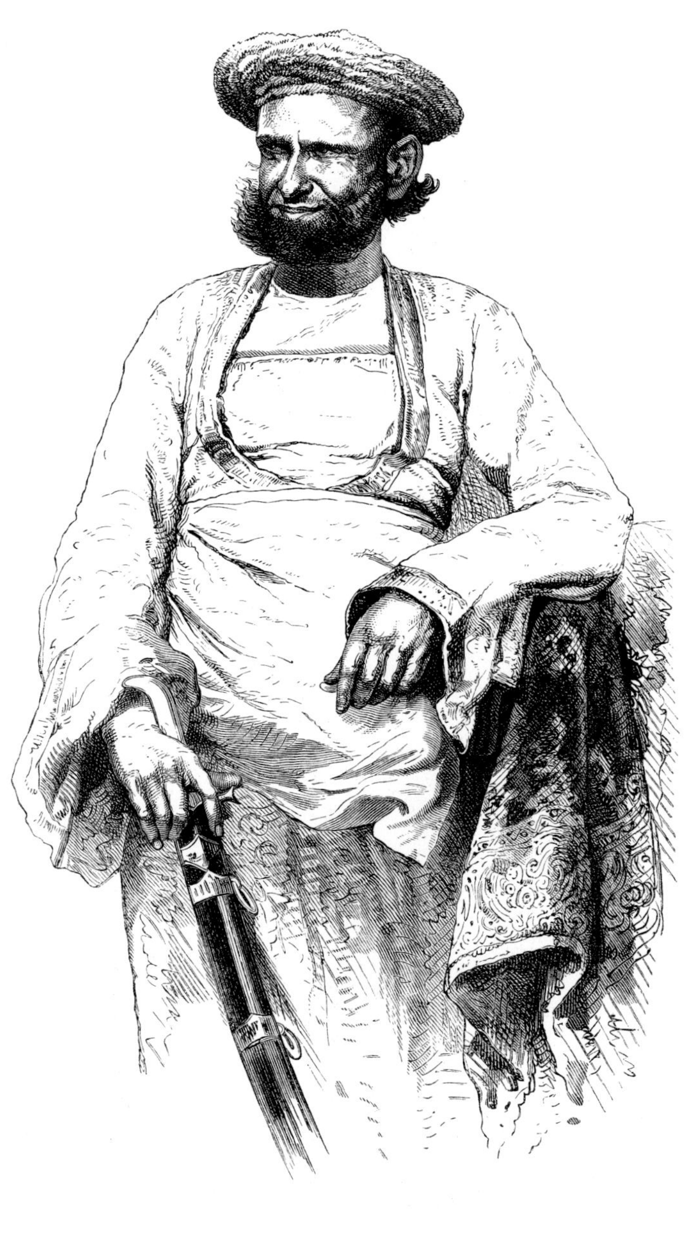

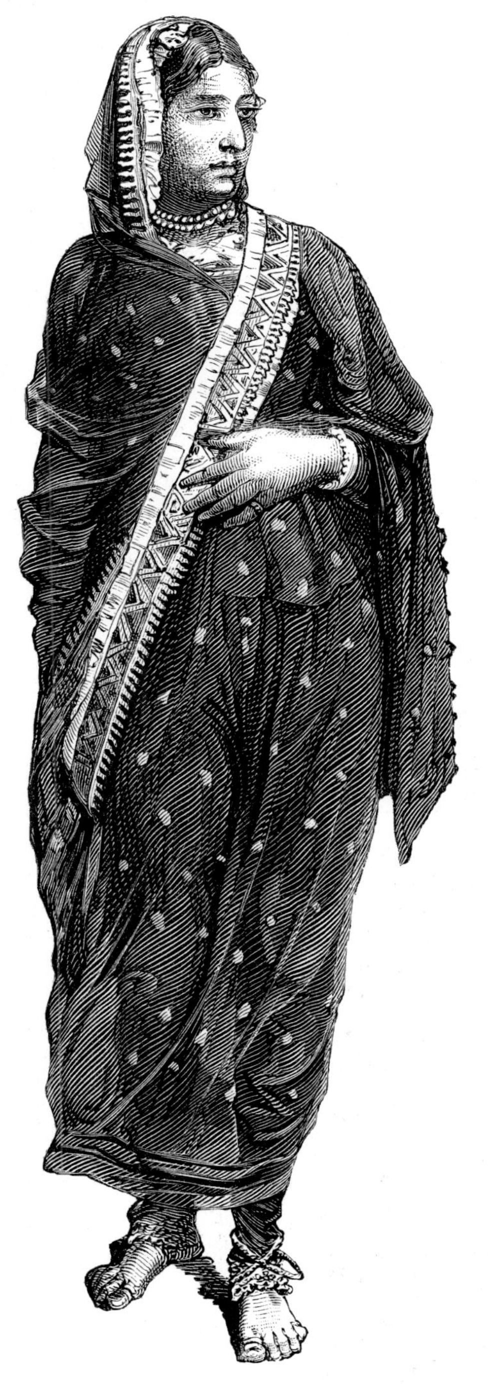

a	The Rajah of Nagode	Der Radscha von Nagode	Il Rajah di Nagode	Le Rajah de Nagode	Rajá de Nagode
b	Muslim lady from Bhopal	Moslemische Frau aus Bhopal	Donna musulmana di Bhopal	Musulmane de Bhopal	Musulmana de Bhopal

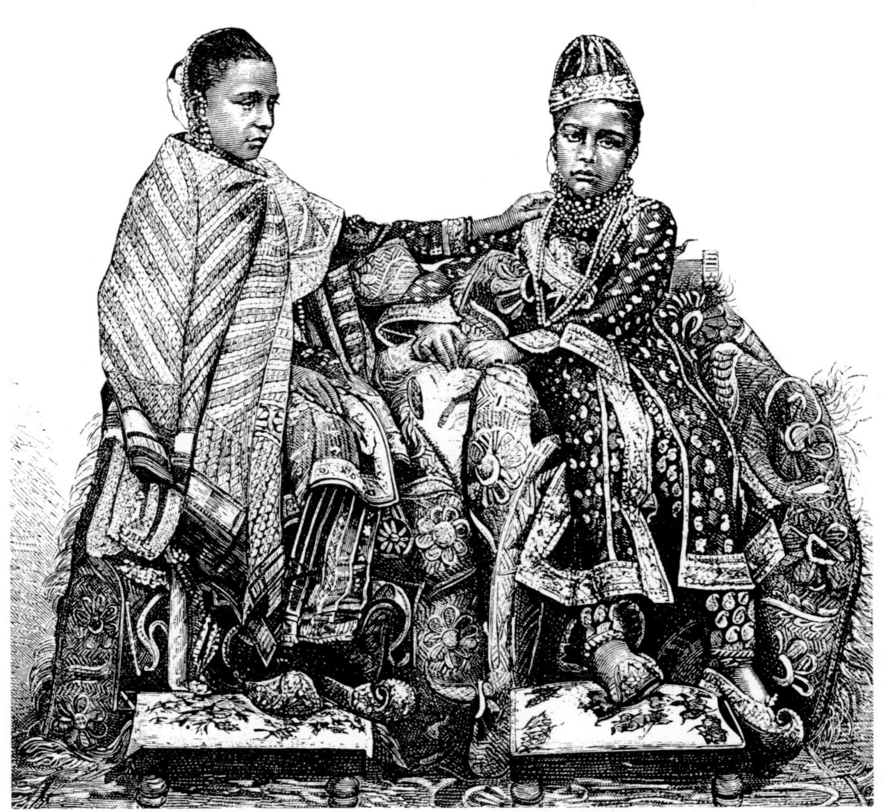

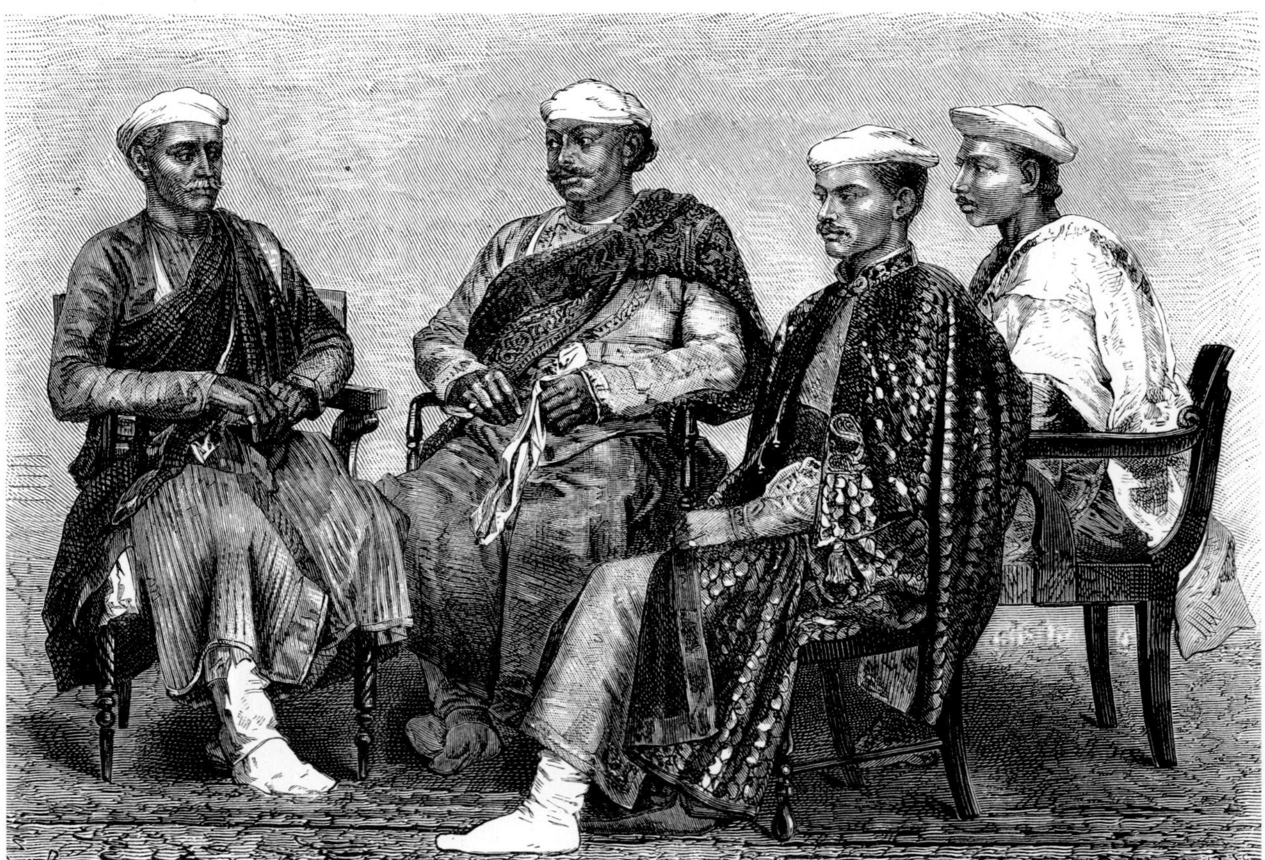

a	Princess of Bhopal, c. 1860	Prinzessin von Bhopal, um 1860	Principessa di Bhopal, ca. 1860	Princesse de Bhopal, vers 1860	Princesa de Bhopal, hacia el año 1860
b	Hindu bankers, Delhi, c. 1880	Indische Bankiers, Dehli, um 1880	Banchieri hindu, Delhi, ca. 1880	Banquiers hindous, Delhi, vers 1880	Banqueros hindúes, Delhi, alrededor de 1880

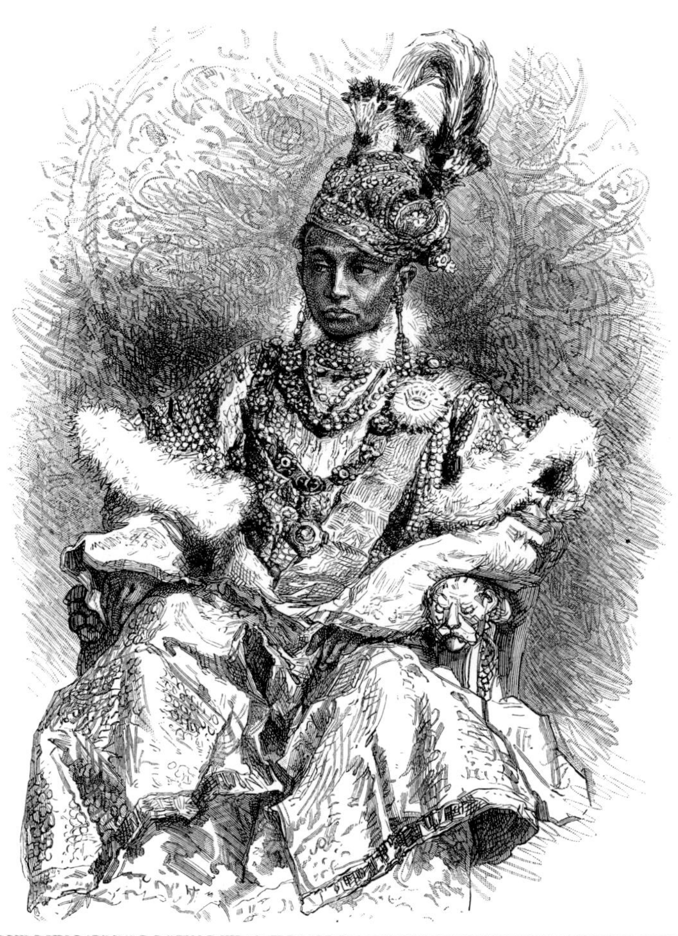

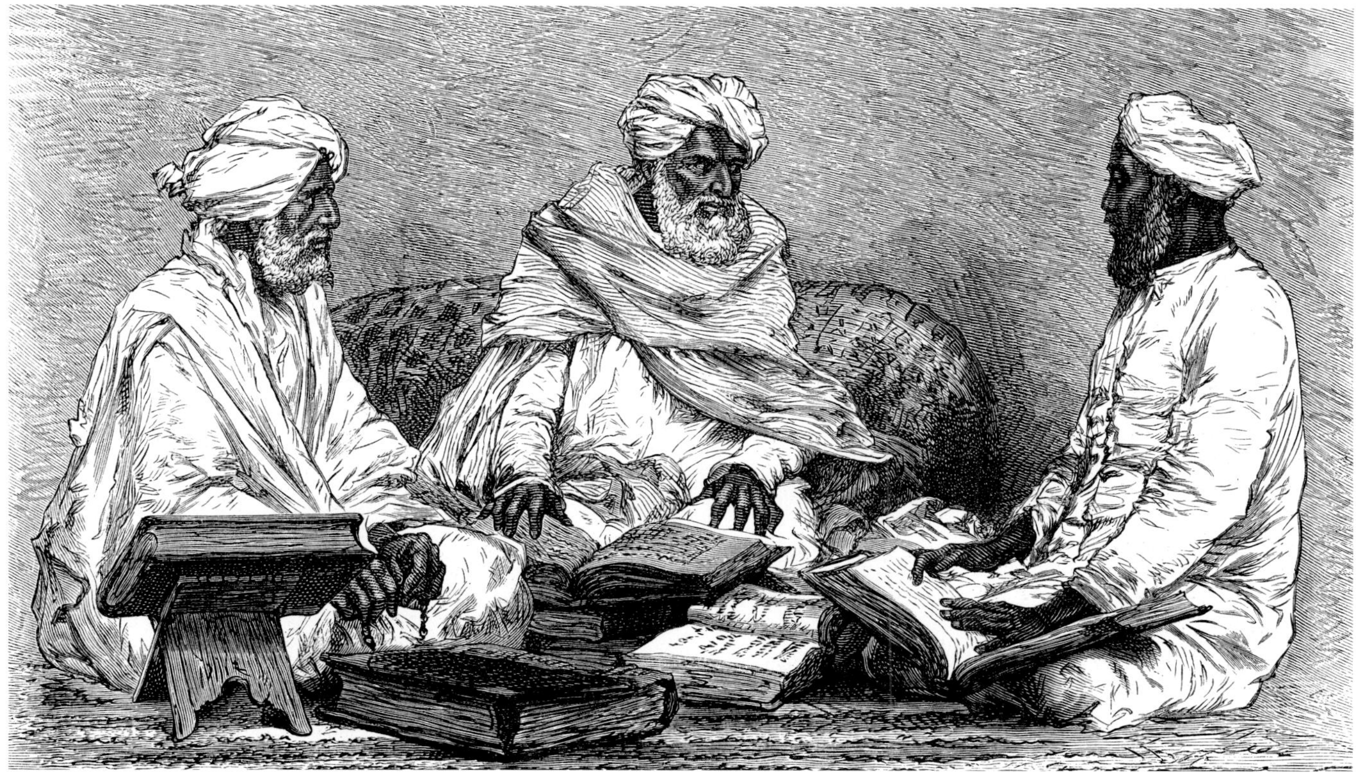

a	Princess from Bhopal	Prinzessin aus Bhopal	Principessa di Bhopal	Princesse de Bhopal	Princesa de Bhopal
b	Muslim clerics in Bhopal	Moslemische Geistliche in Bhopal	Sacerdoti musulmani a Bhopal	Ecclésiastiques musulmans à Bhopal	Clérigos musulmanes de Bhopal

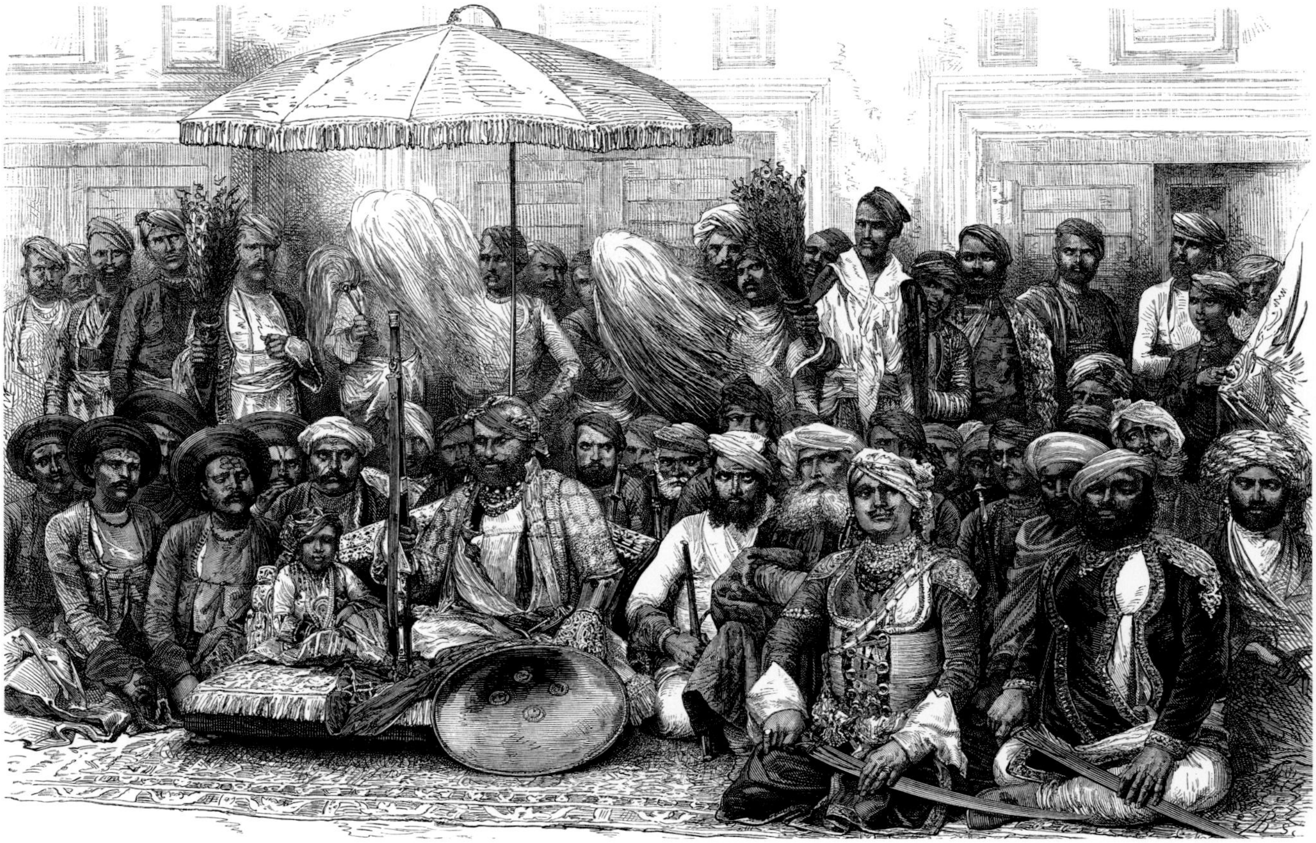

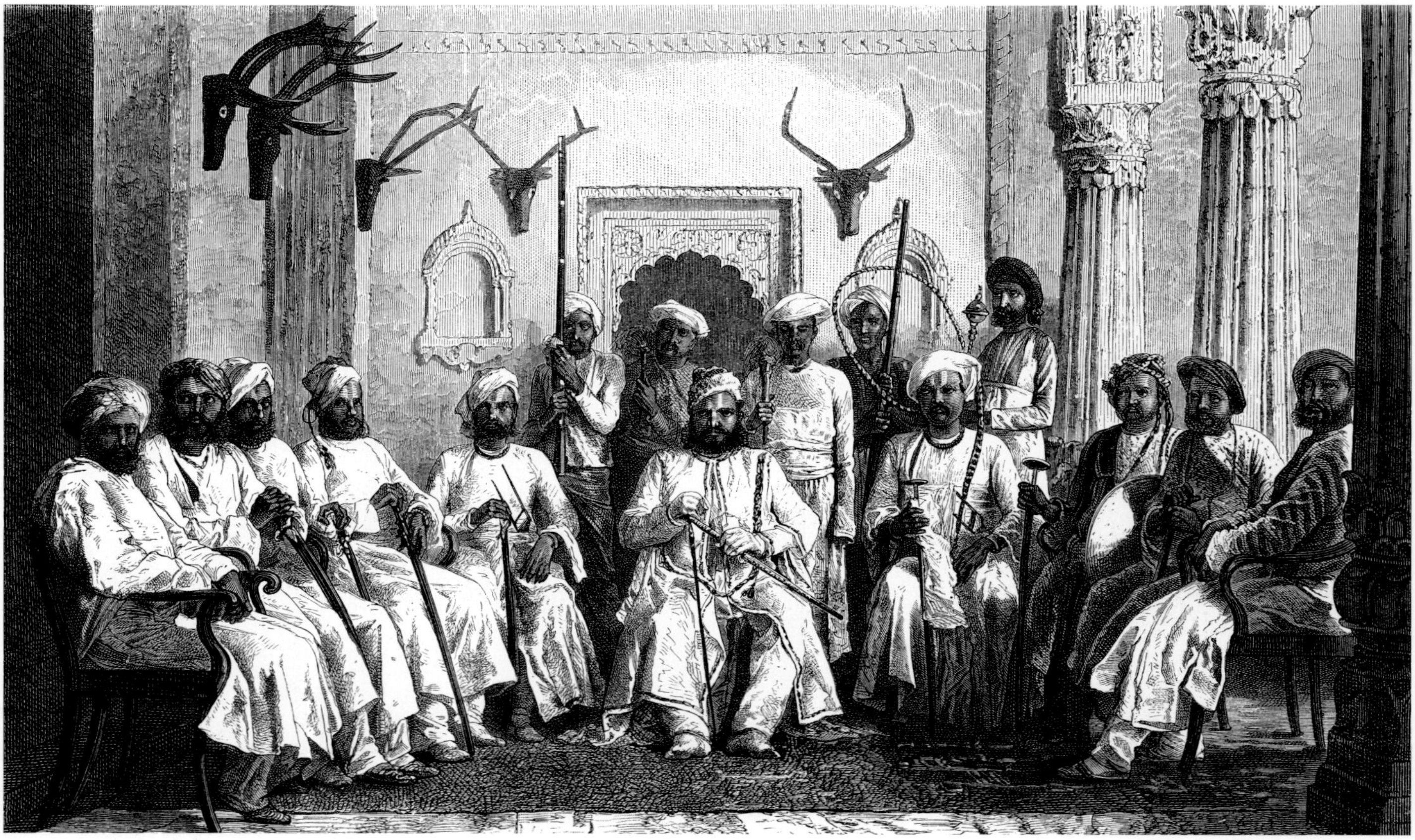

Durbars of the Maharaja of Dolpur, Punjab, and the Maharajah of Bewah

Durbar des Maharadscha von Dolpur, Punjab, und des Maharadscha von Bewah

Sala delle udienze del maharajah di Dolpur, Punjab, e il maharajah di Bewah

Durbars du Maharadjah de Dolpur, Panjab et du Maharadjah de Bewah

Durbars del maharajá de Dolpur, Punjab, y el maharajá de Bewah

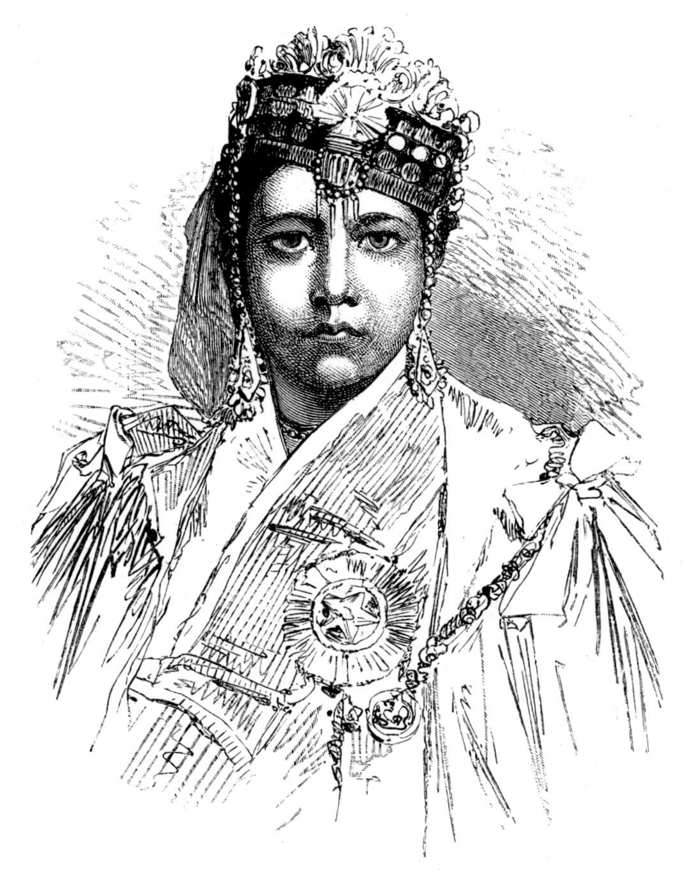

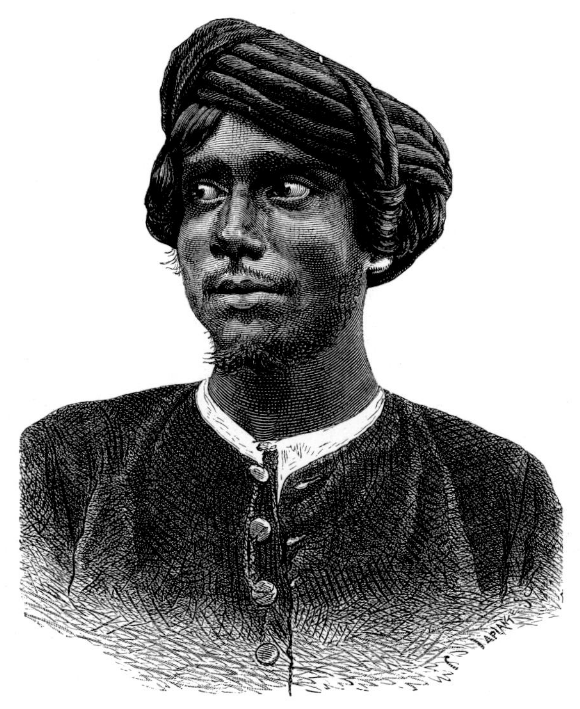

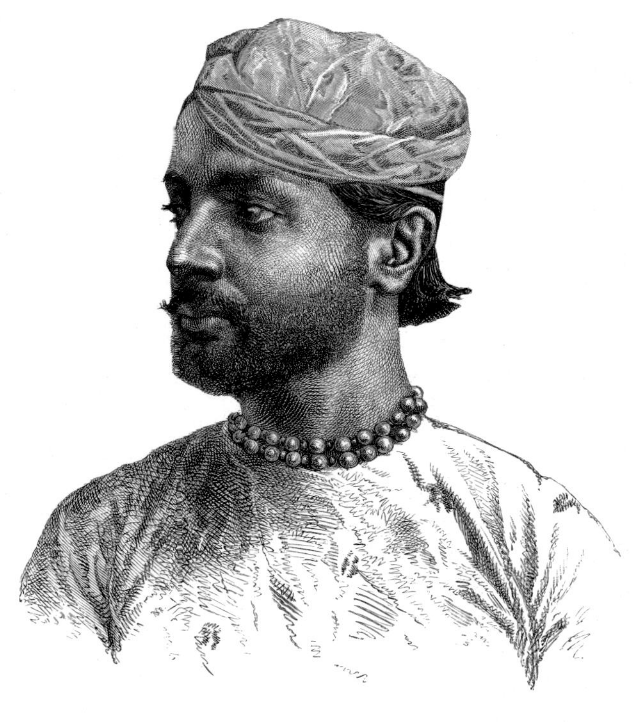

a	Princess of Bhopal	Prinzessin von Bhopal	Principessa di Bhopal	Princesse de Bhopal	Princesa de Bhopal
b	Prince from Kumari	Prinz aus Kumari	Principe di Fumari	Prince de Kumari	Príncipe de Kumari
c	Punjabi prince	Prinz aus Punjab	Principe del Punjab	Prince de Punjabi	Príncipe punjabí

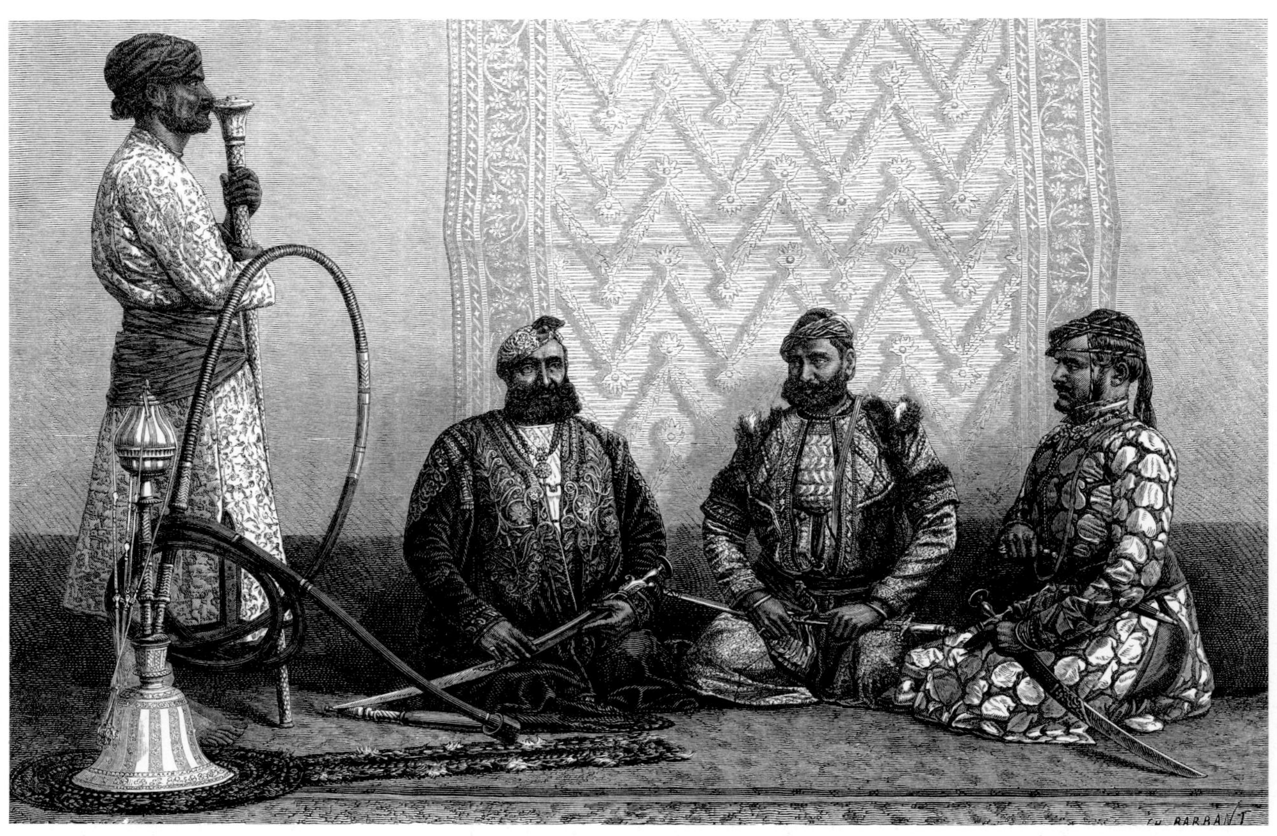

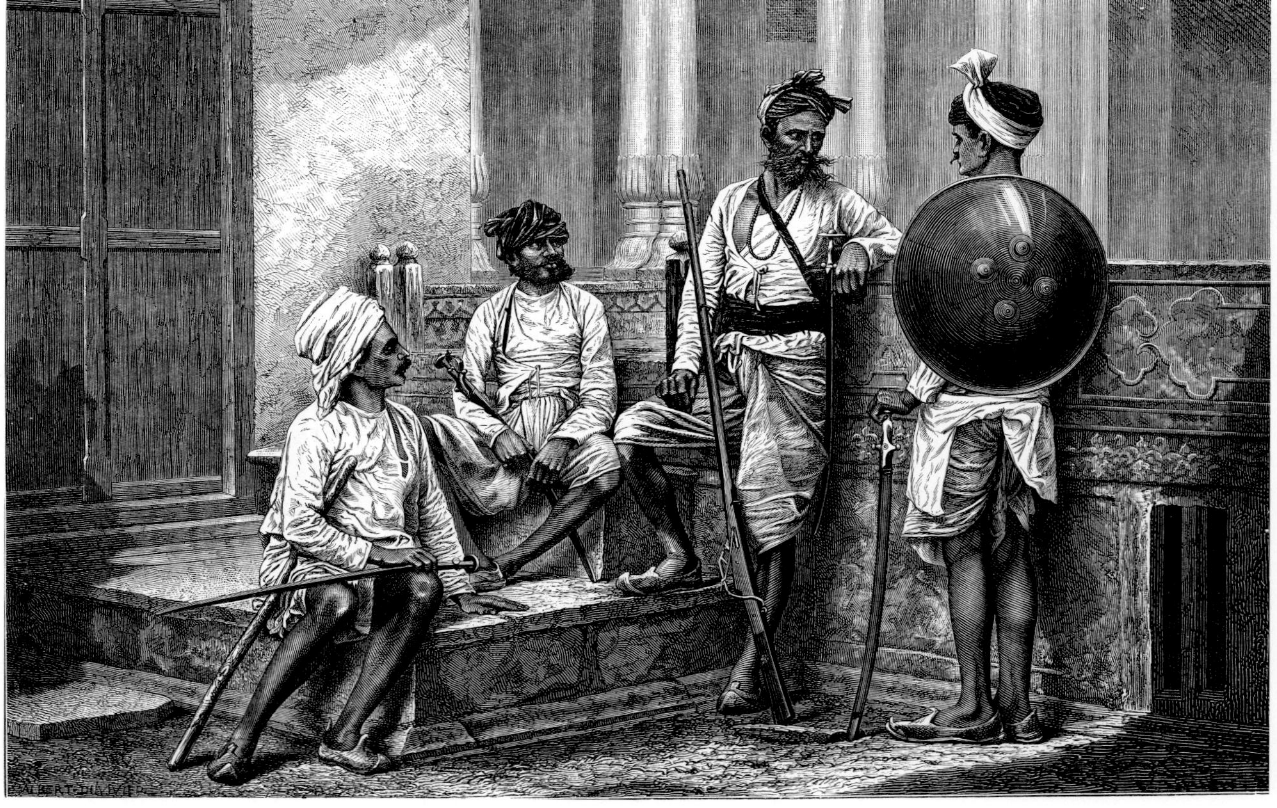

a Hindustani Princes | Indische Prinzen | Principessa hindustani | Princes hindous | Príncipes del Indostán

b Rajputs, c. 1880 | Rajiputs, um 1880 | Rajput, ca. 1880 | Rajputs, vers 1880 | Rajputs, hacia 1880

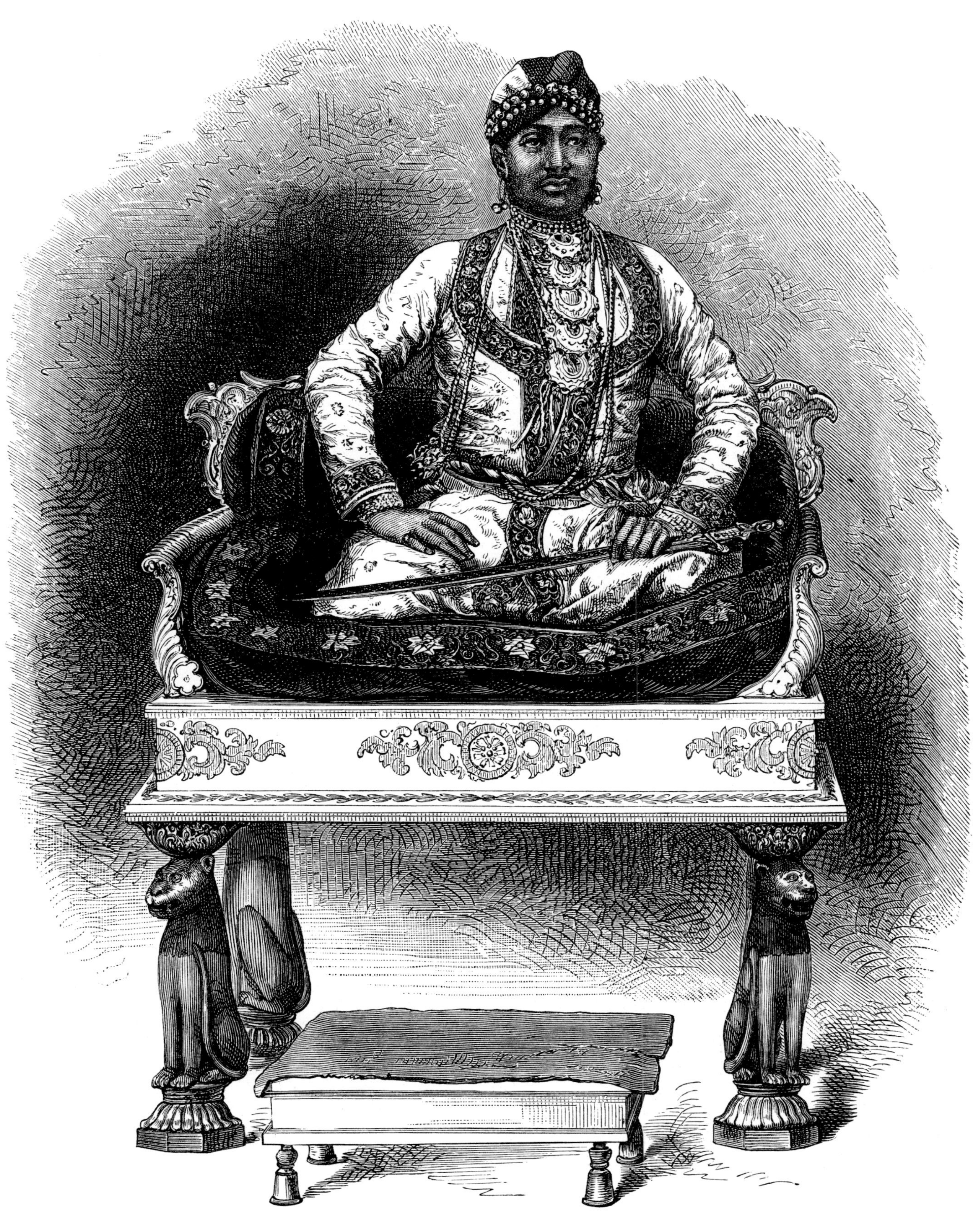

The Maharaja of Udaipur

Der Maharadscha von Udaipur

Il maharajah di Udaipur

Le Maharadjah d'Udaipur

Maharajá de Udaipur

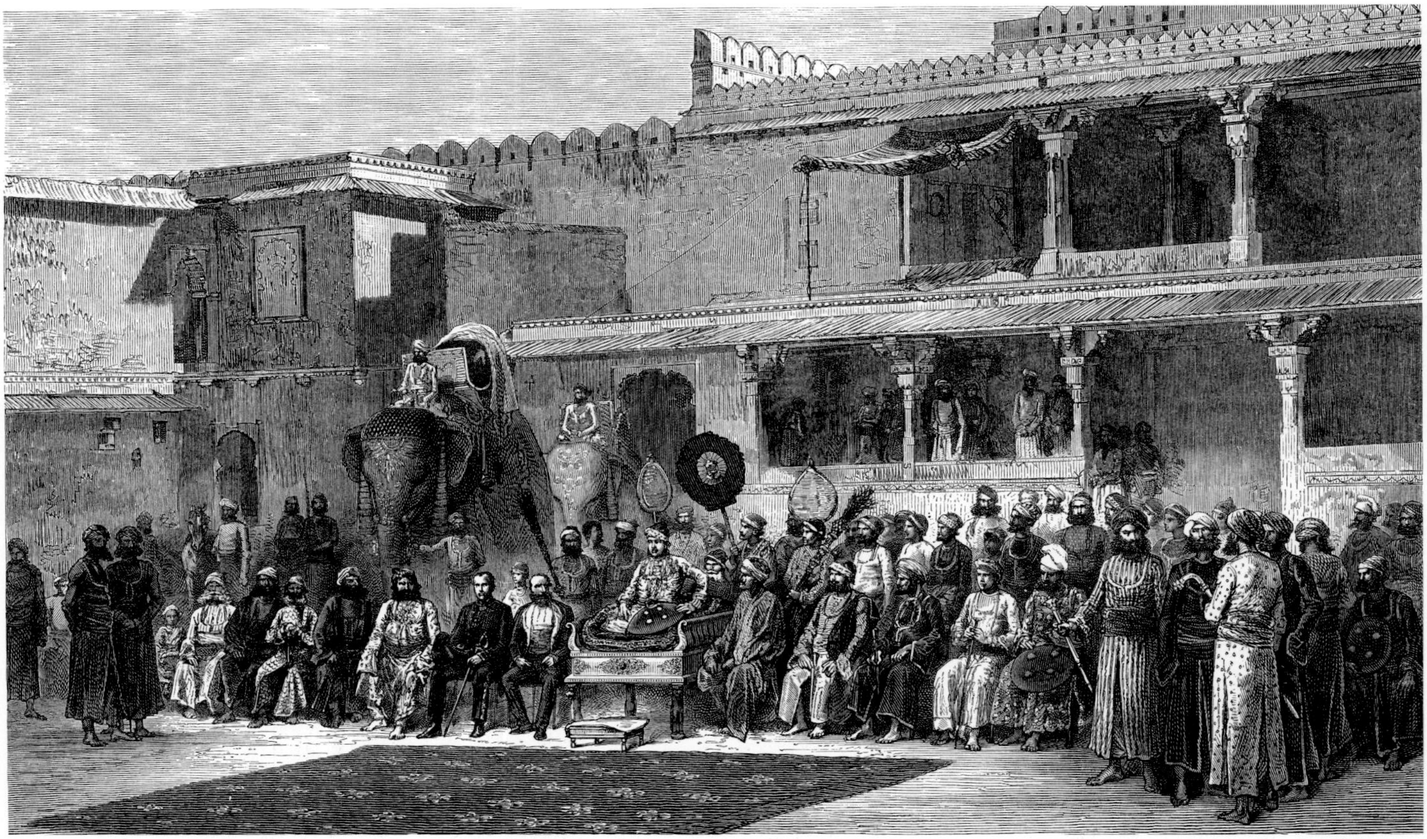

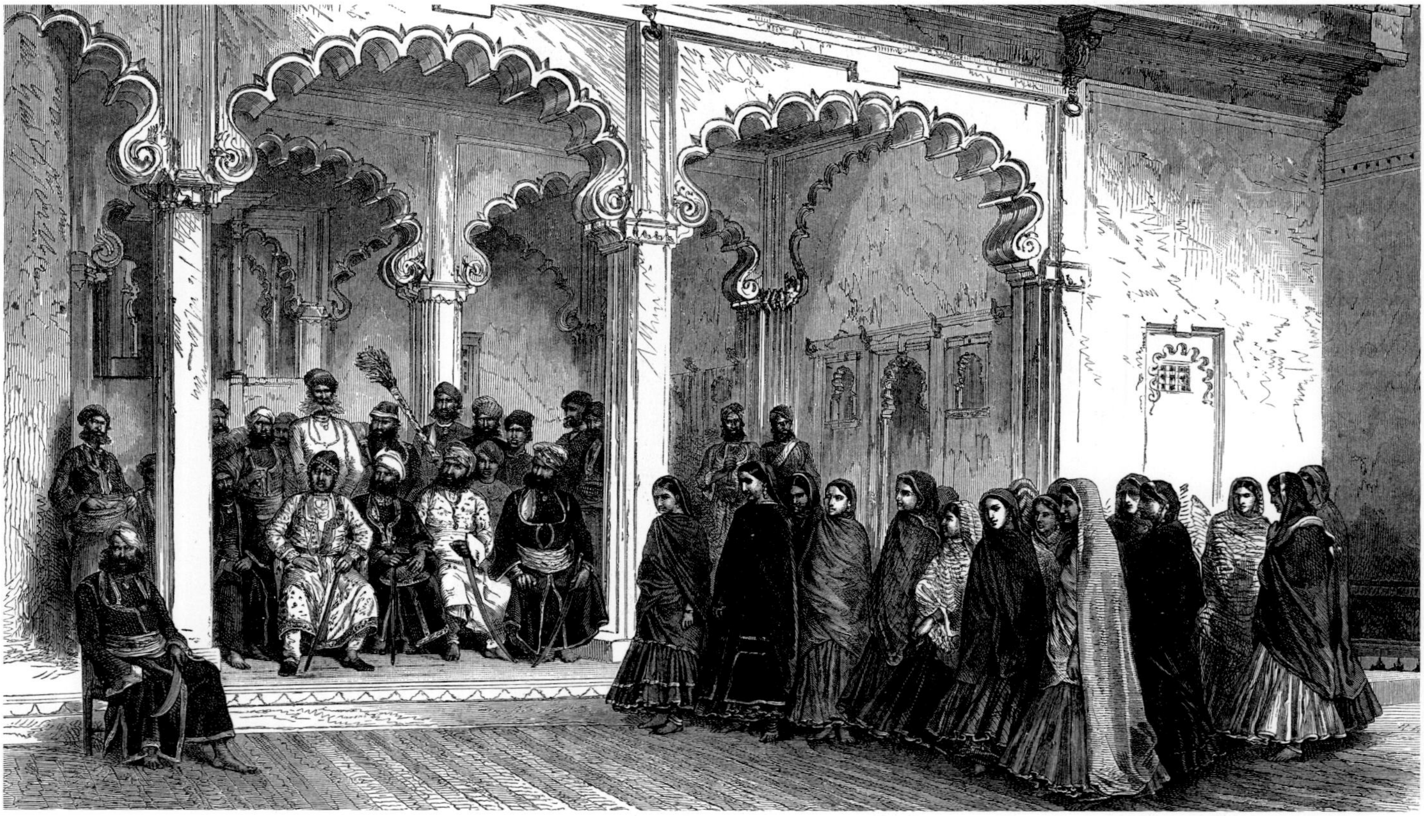

a Grand durbar of the Maharaja of Udaipur

Großer Durbar des Maharadscha von Udaipur

Sala delle udienze del maharajah di Udaipur

Grand durbar du Maharadjah d'Udaipur

Gran durbar del maharajá de Udaipur

b Performance in an Indian Palace

Aufführung in einem indischen Palast

Spettacolo in un palazzo indiano

Spectacle au Palais Indien

Representación en un palacio indio

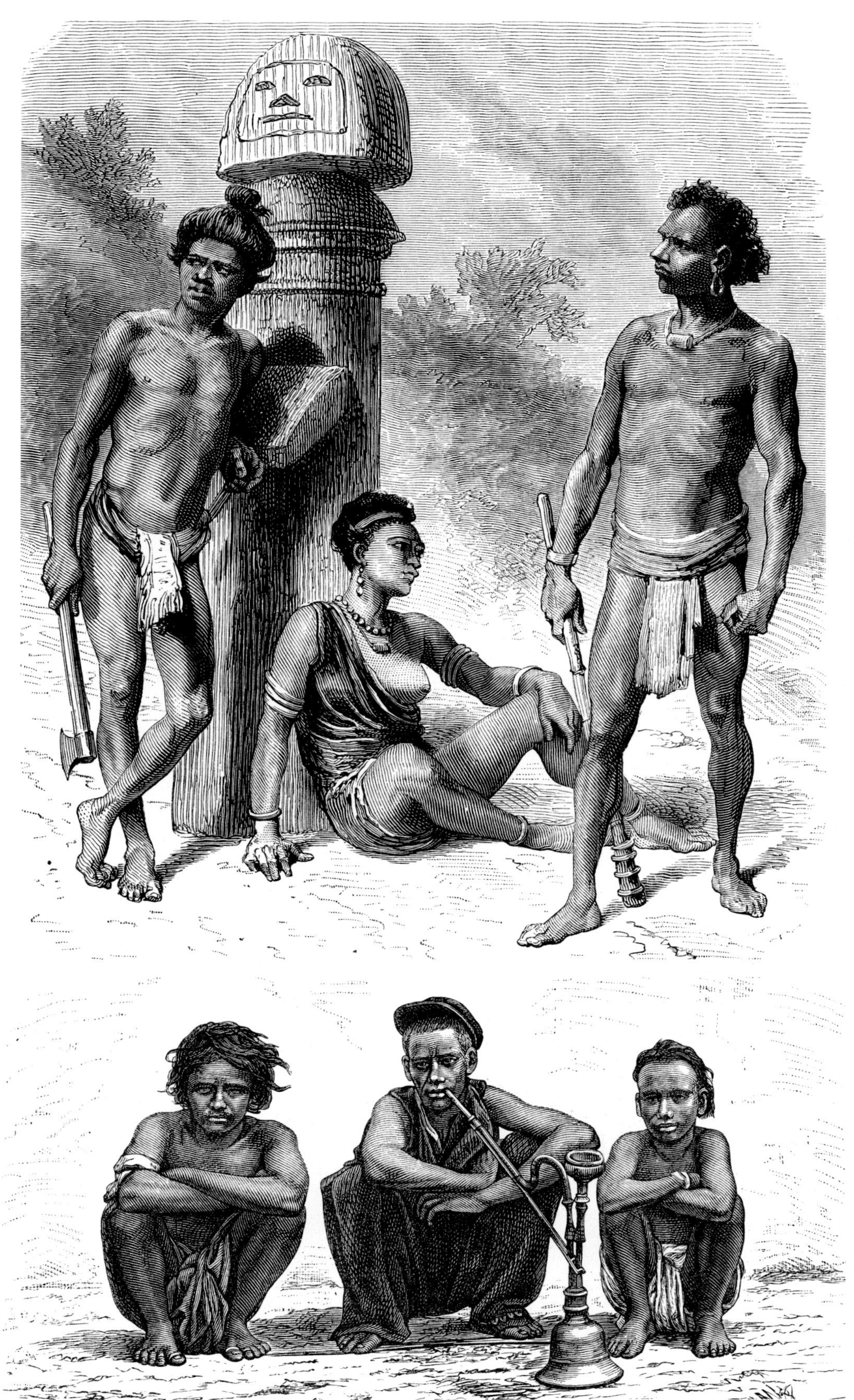

a	Workers	Arbeiter	Operai	Travailleurs	Trabajadores
b	Low-caste Bengalis	Bengalesen der unteren Kasten	Bengalesi di casta bassa	Bengalis de caste inférieure	Bengalíes de la casta inferior

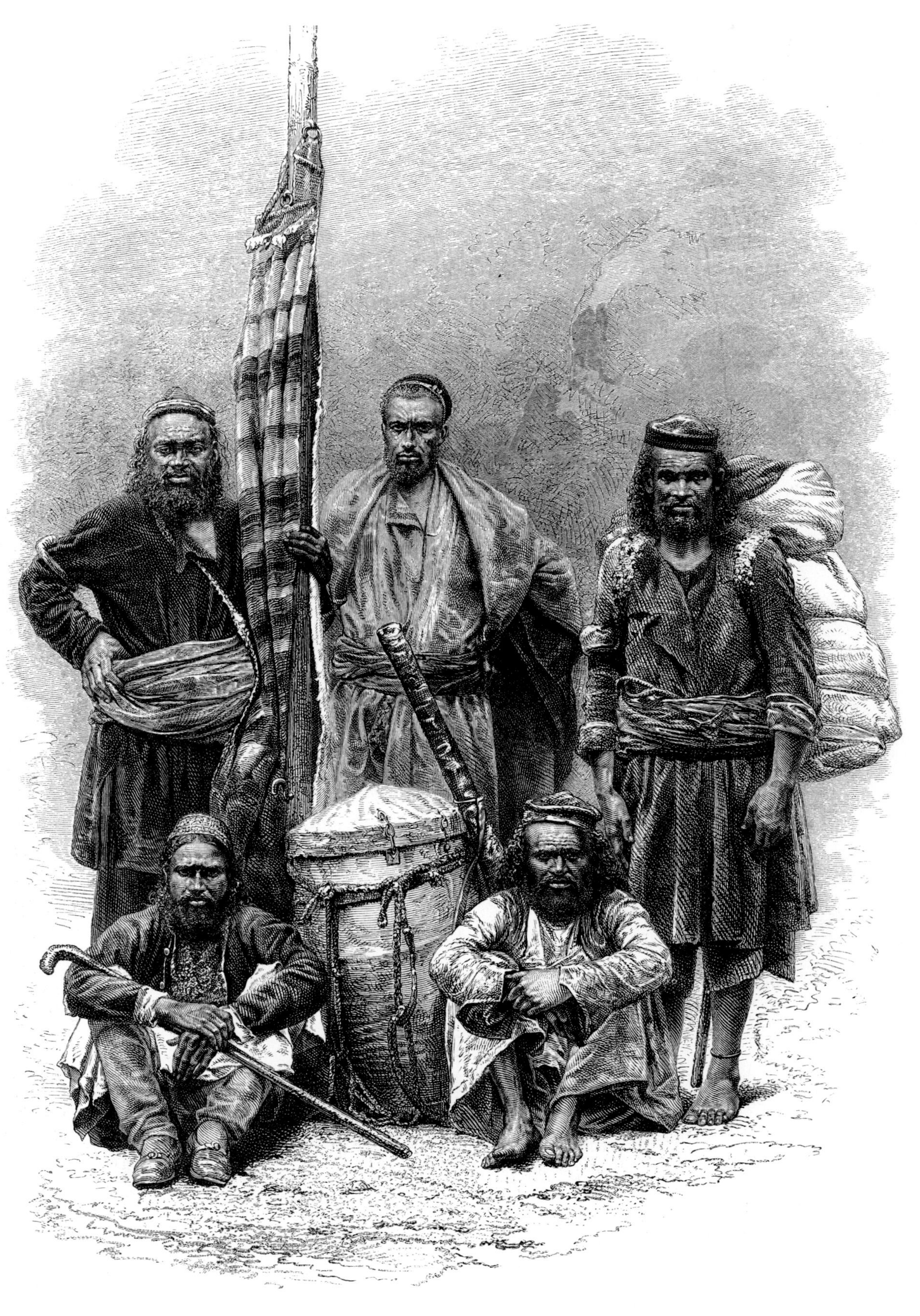

Baharis, from the western Himalayas

Bahari aus dem westlichen Himalaya

Baharis, Imalaia occidentale

Baharis de l'Ouest de l'Himalaya

Baharíes del Himalaya occidental

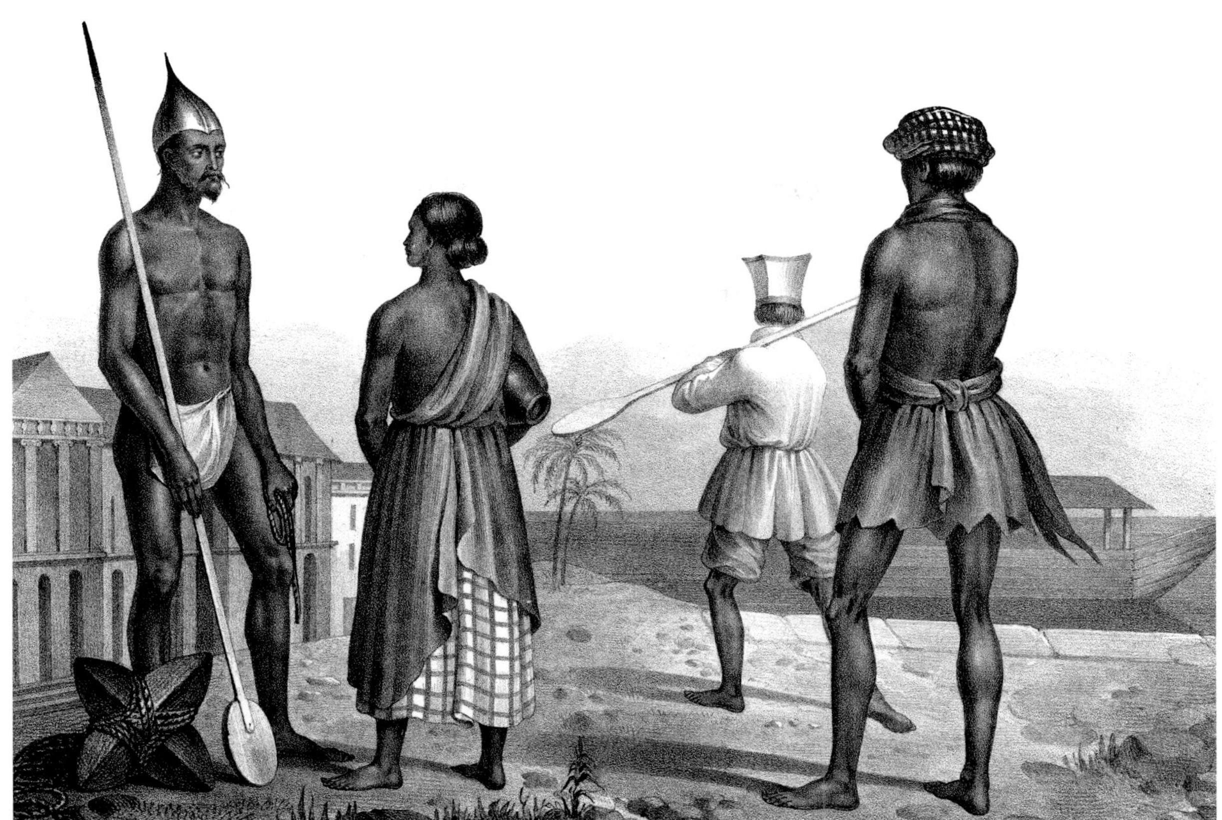

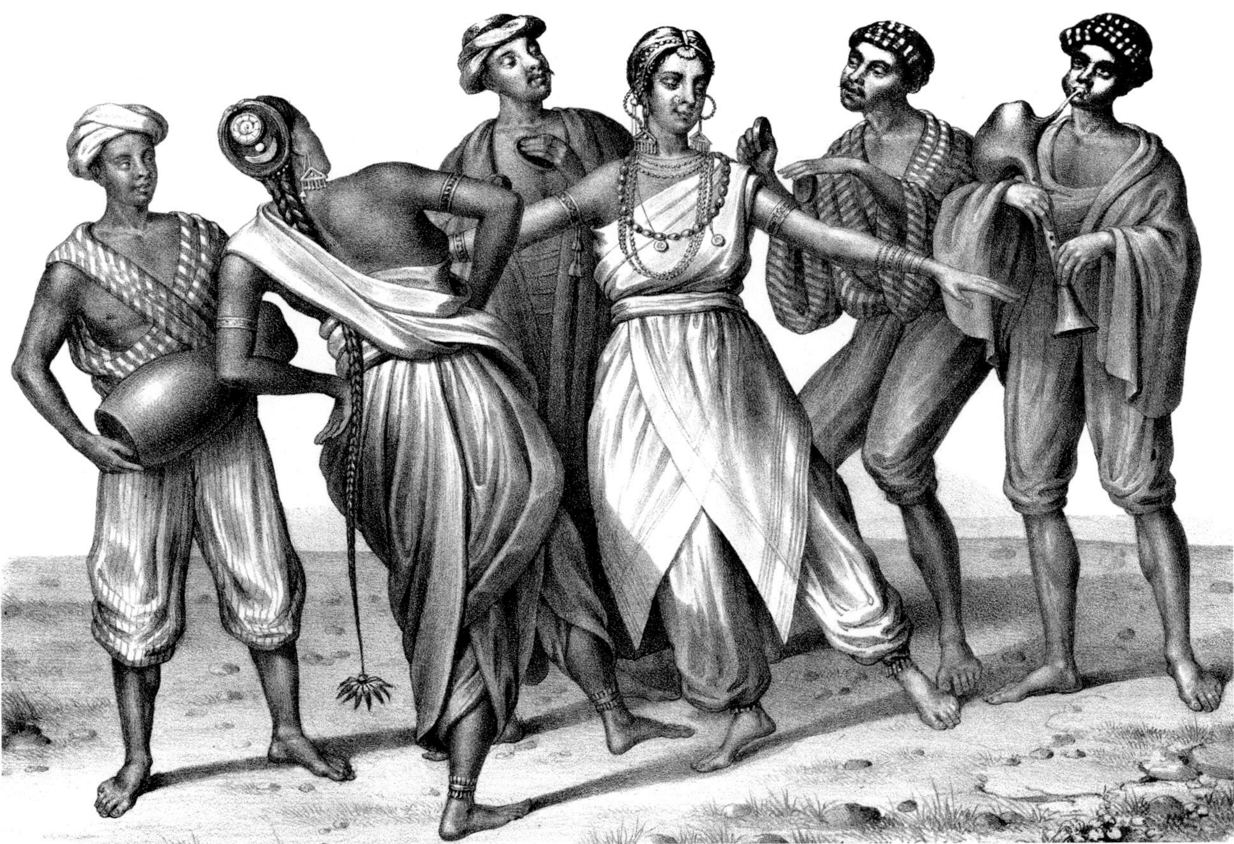

a	Workers from Madras	Arbeiter aus Madras	Operai di Madras	Ouvriers de Madras	Trabajadores de Madras
b	Musicians and dancing girl, Pondicherry, c. 1880	Musiker und tanzendes Mädchen, Pondicherry, um 1880	Musicisti e danzatrice, Pondicherry, ca. 1880	Musiciens et danseuse, Pondichéry, vers 1880	Músicos y bailarina, Pondicherry, hacia 1880

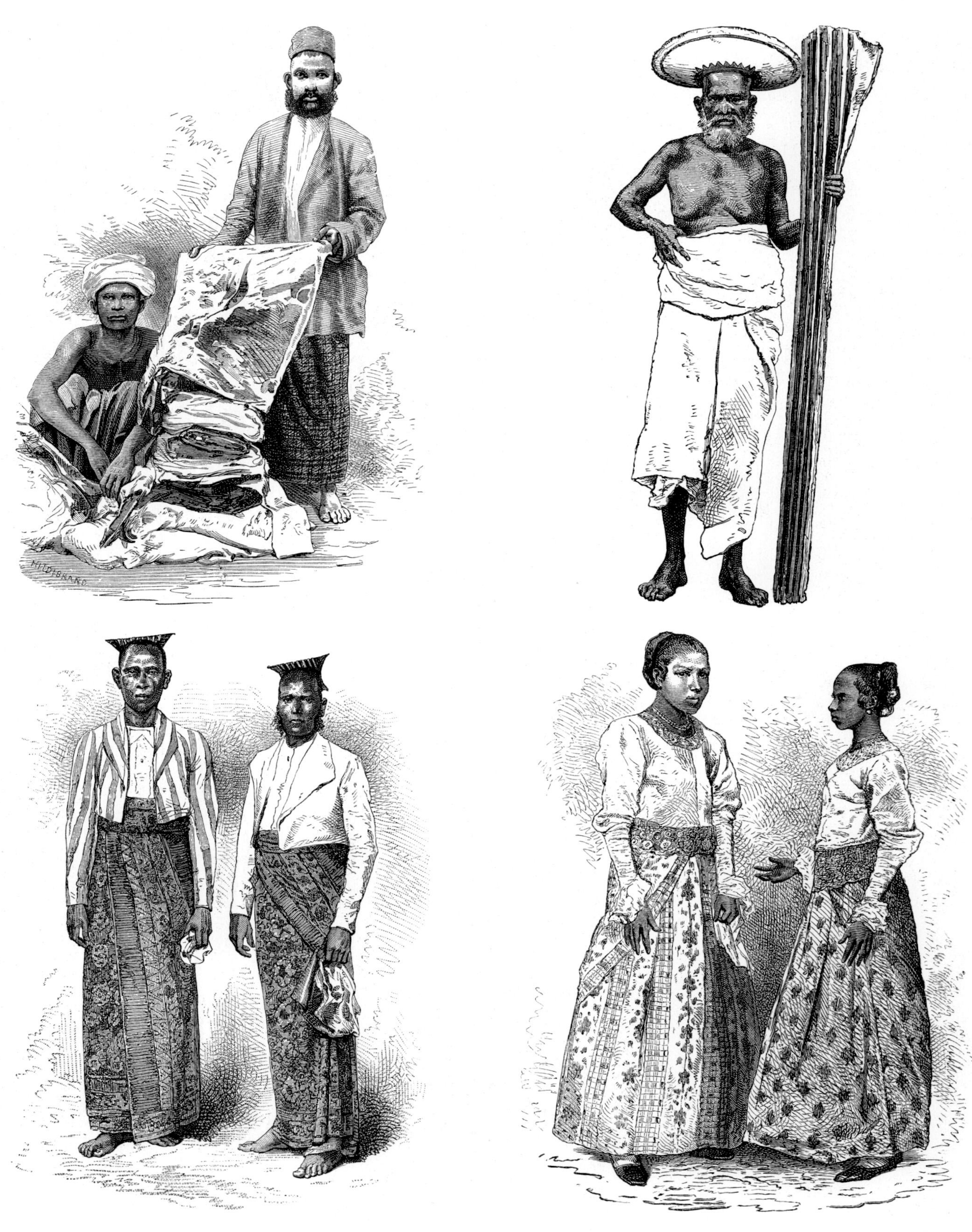

Arab trader in Sri Lanka and Sinhalese men and women, c. 1870

Arabische Händler in Sri Lanka und singalesische Männer und Frauen, um 1870

Commerciante arabo a Sri Lanka e uomini e donne singalesi, ca. 1870

Marchand arabe au Sri Lanka et femmes et hommes cinghalais, vers 1870

Comerciante árabe de Sri Lanka y hombres y mujeres cingaleses, hacia 1870

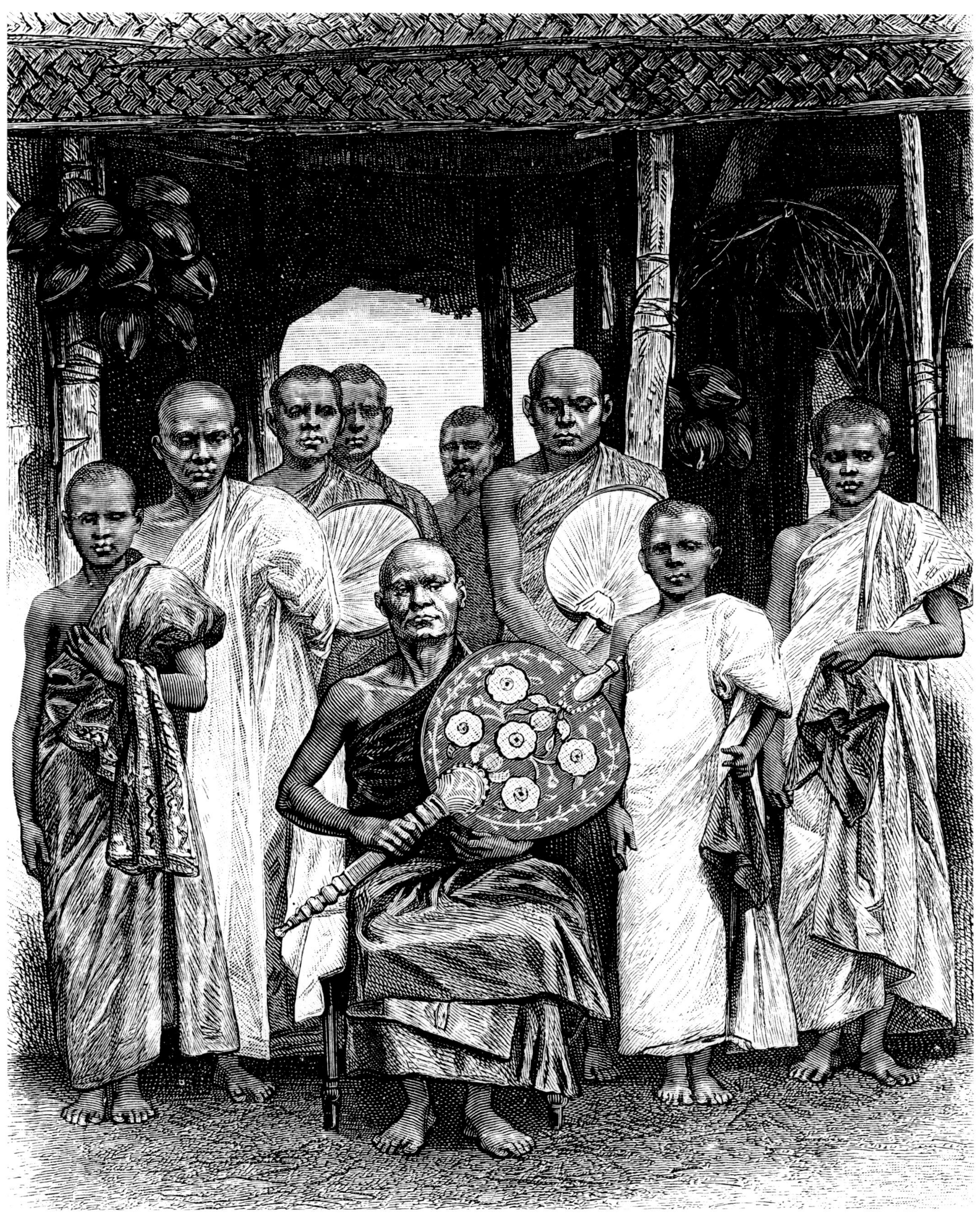

Sinhalese, 1870 Singalesen, 1870 Singalese, 1870 Cinghalais, 1870 Cingaleses, 1870

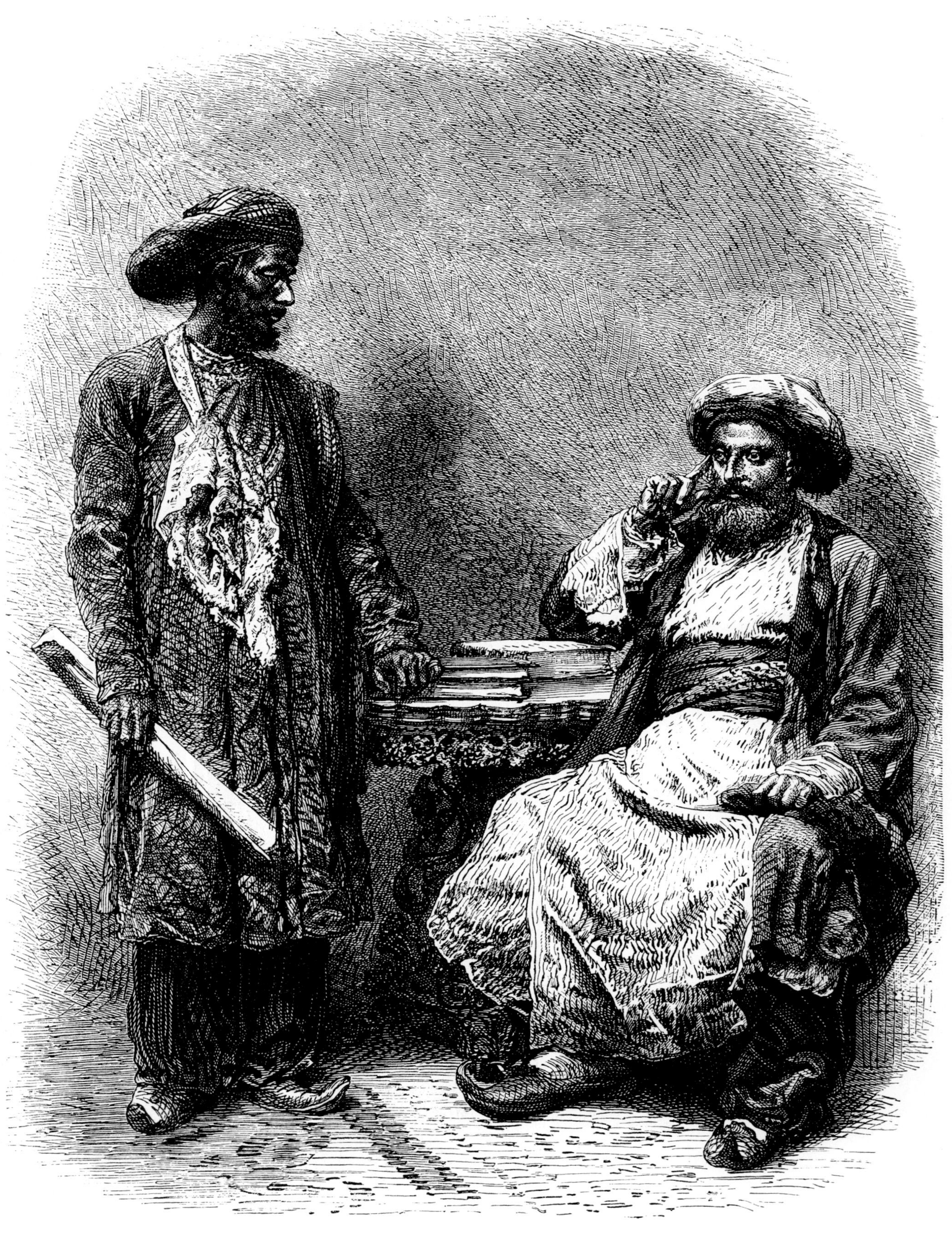

Jewish men in Colombo, c. 1860

Jüdischer Mann in Colombo, um 1860

Ebrei a Colombo, ca. 1860

Juifs à Colombo, vers 1860

Hombres judíos de Colombo, hacia 1860

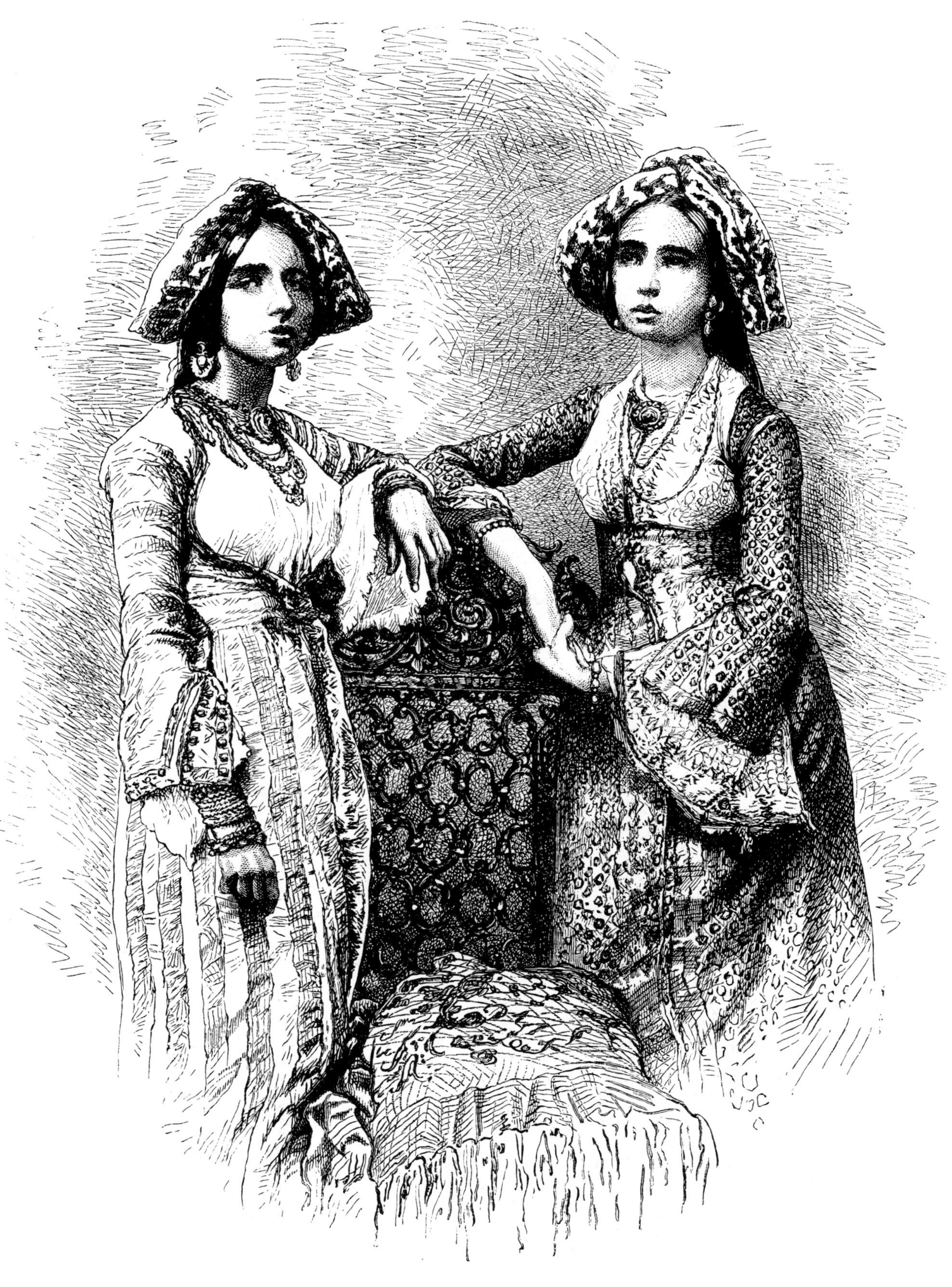

Jewish girls in Colombo, c. 1860

Jüdische Mädchen in Colombo, um 1860

Ragazze ebree a Colombo, ca. 1860

Jeunes filles juives à Colombo, vers 1860

Muchachas judías de Colombo, hacia 1860

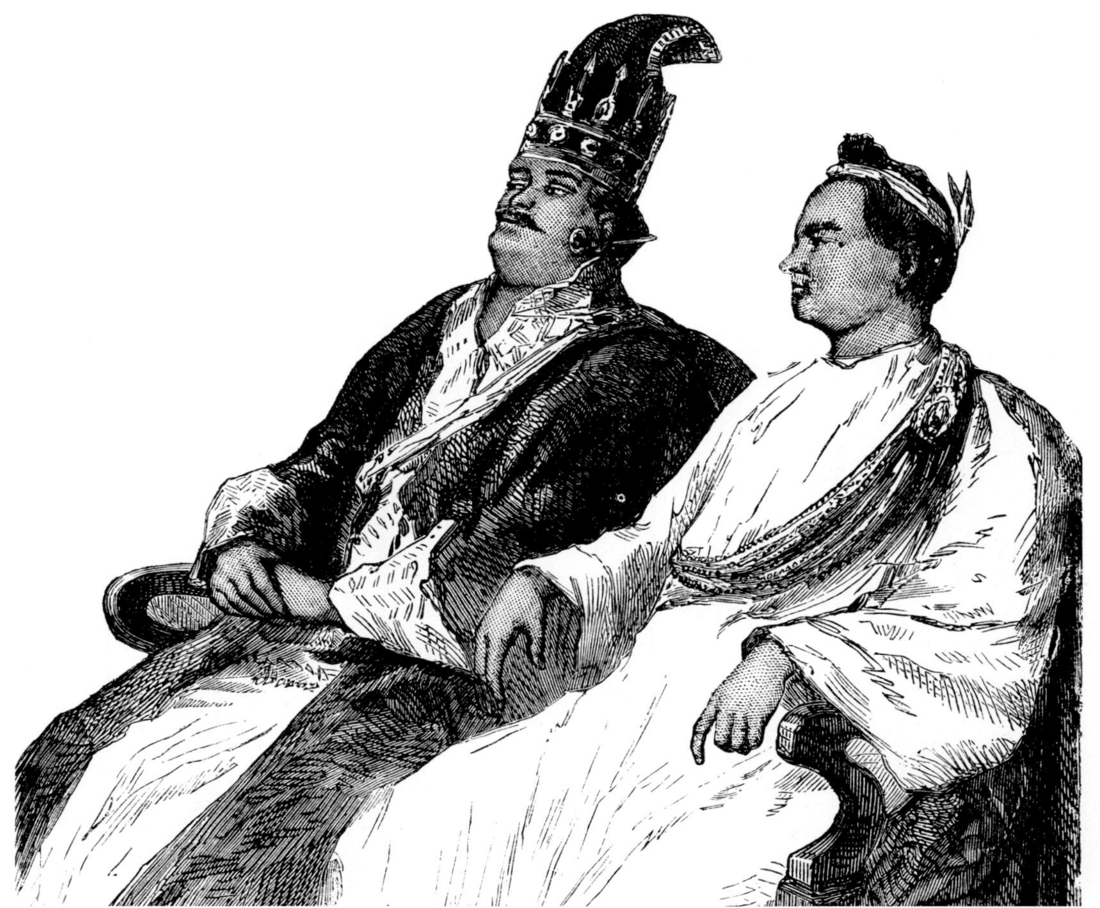

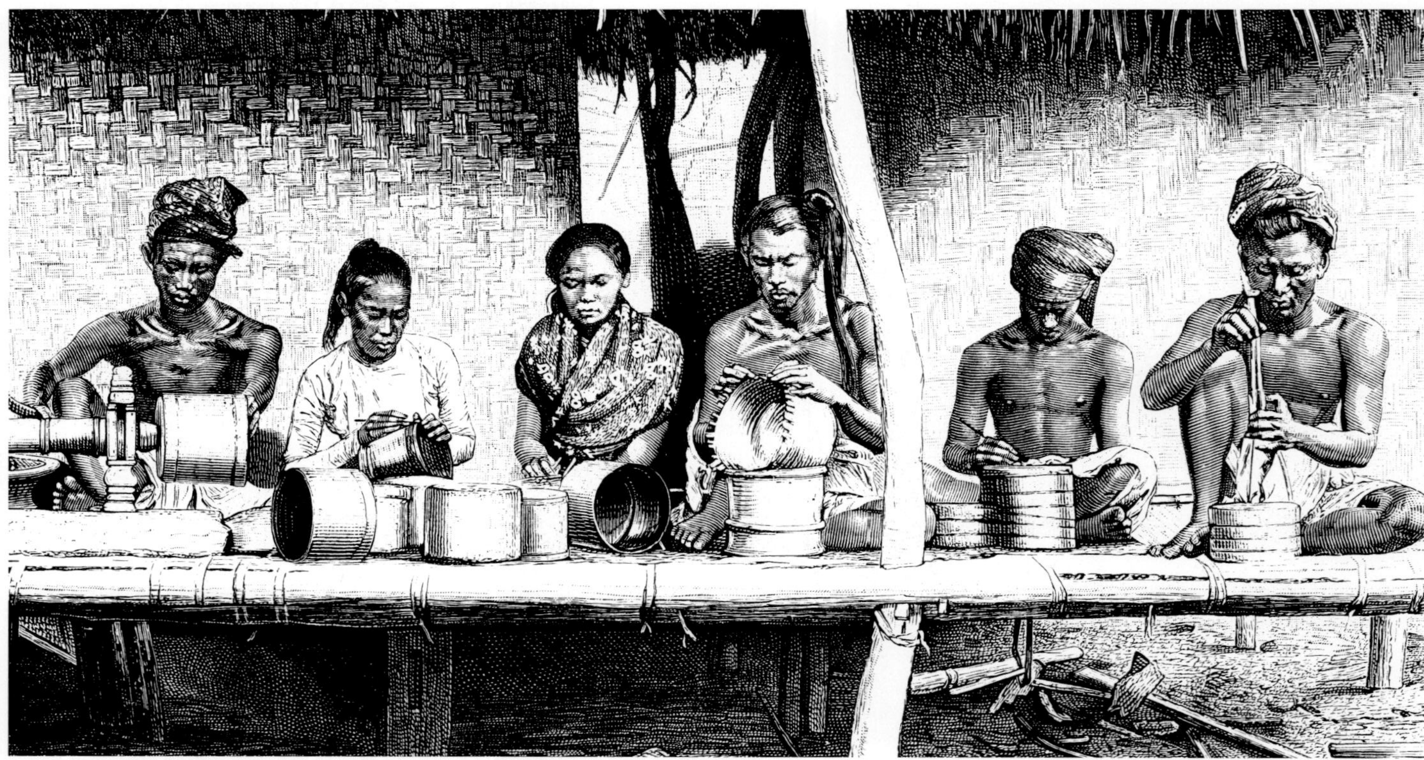

a	Burmese Nobles, c. 1860	Burmesischer Adel, um 1860	Nobili birmani, ca. 1860	Nobles birmans, vers 1860	Nobles birmanos, 1860
b	Burmese silversmiths, c. 1870	Burmesiche Silberschmiede, um 1870	Argentieri birmani, ca. 1870	Orfèvres birmans, vers 1870	Plateros birmanos, 1870

Burma

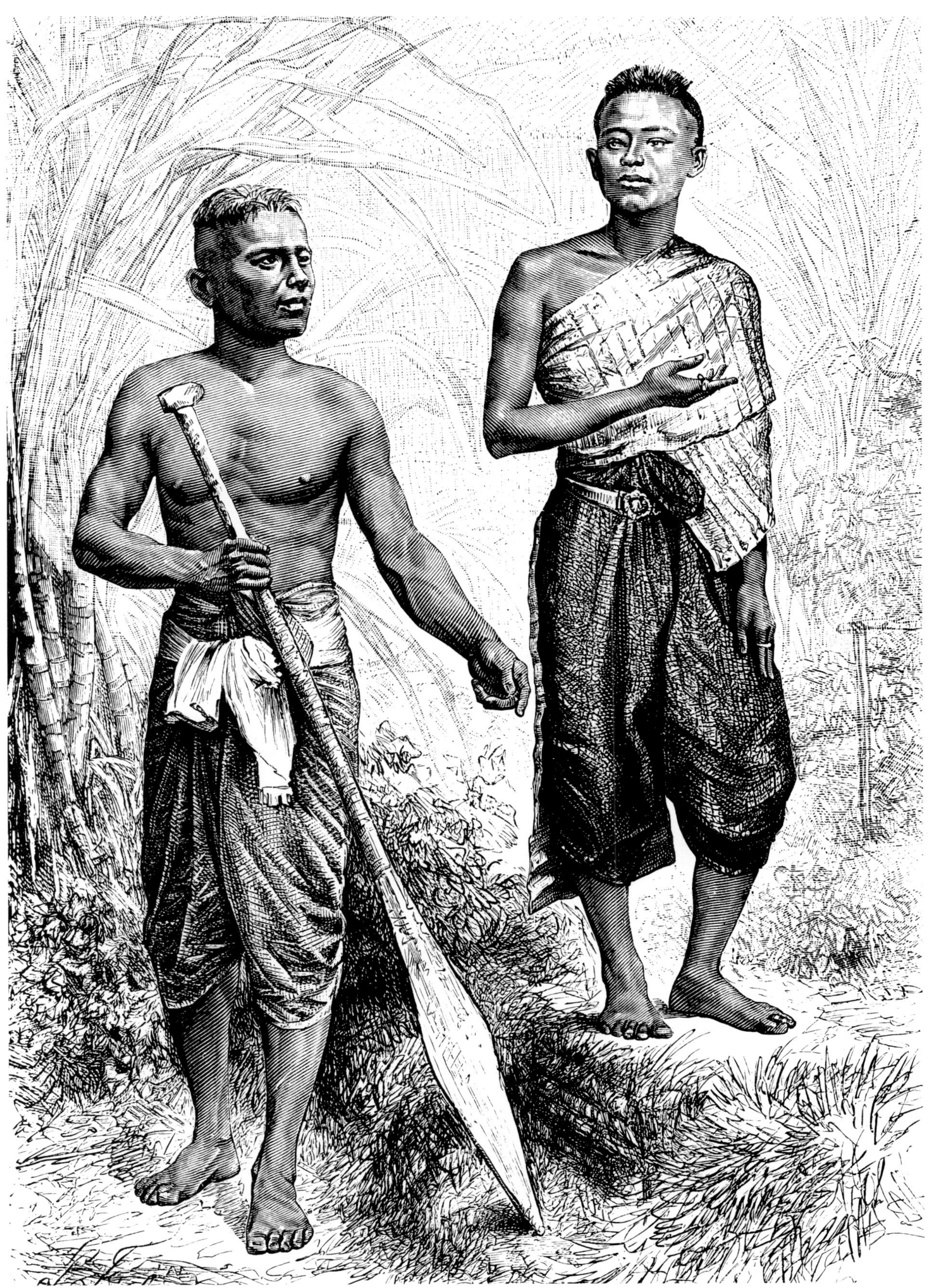

Young Thais, c. 1875

Junge Thais, um 1875

Giovani tailandesi, ca. 1875

Jeunes thaïs, vers 1875

Jóvenes tailandeses, alrededor del año 1875

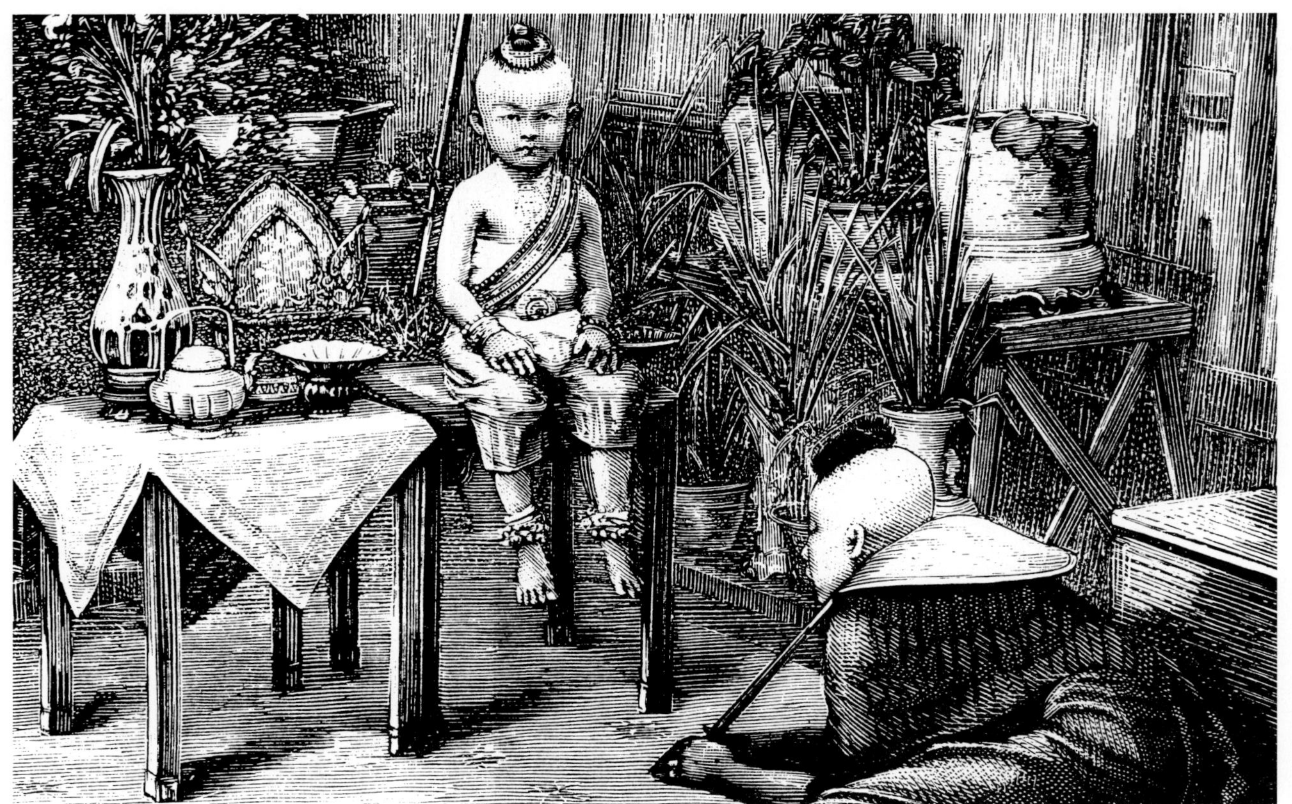

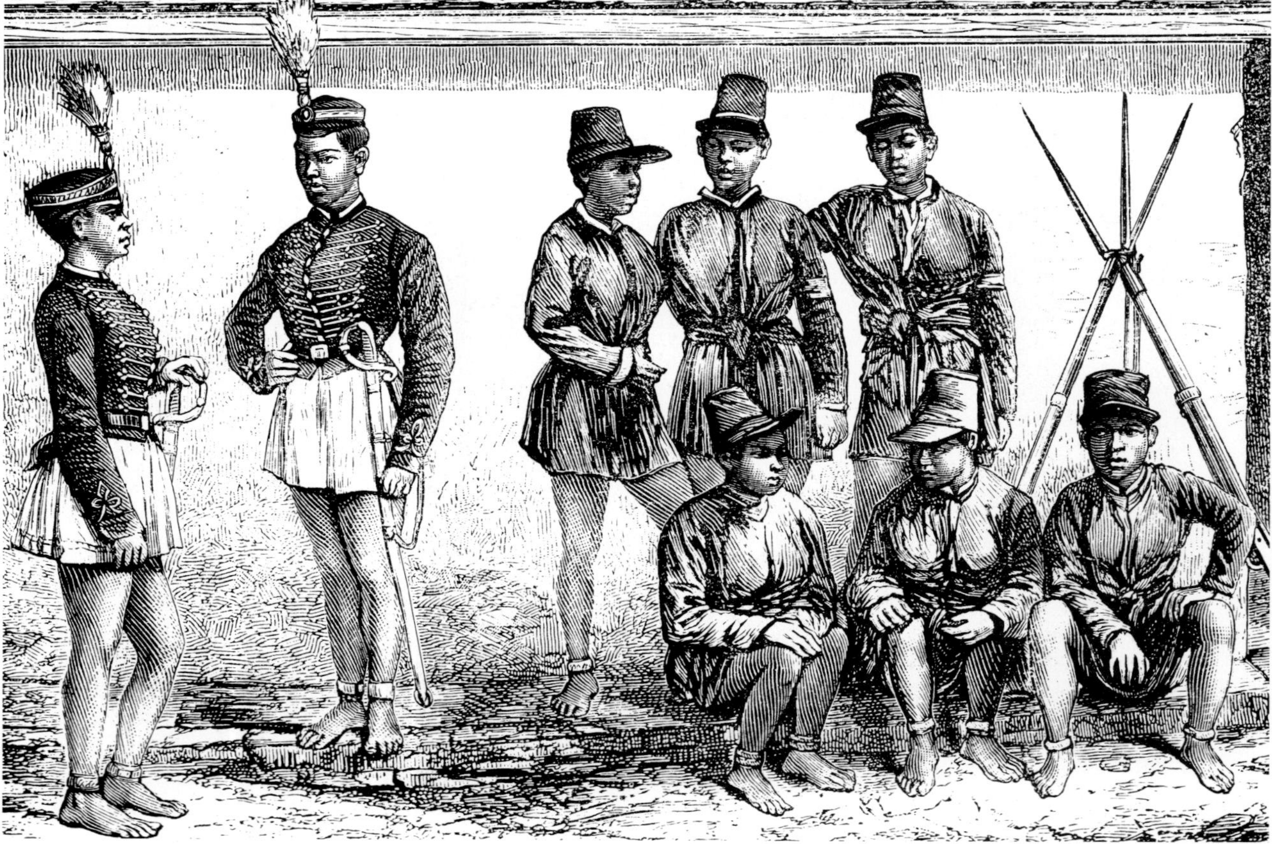

a	Thai Prince, c. 1880	Thailändischer Prinz, um 1880	Principe tailandese, ca. 1880	Prince thaï, vers 1880	Príncipe tailandés, 1880
b	Female soldiers of the Thai court, c. 1870	Soldatinnen am thailändischen Hof, um 1870	Soldatesse della corte tailandese, ca. 1870	Femmes soldats de la Cour thaïlandaise, 1870	Mujeres soldado de la corte tailandesa, 1870

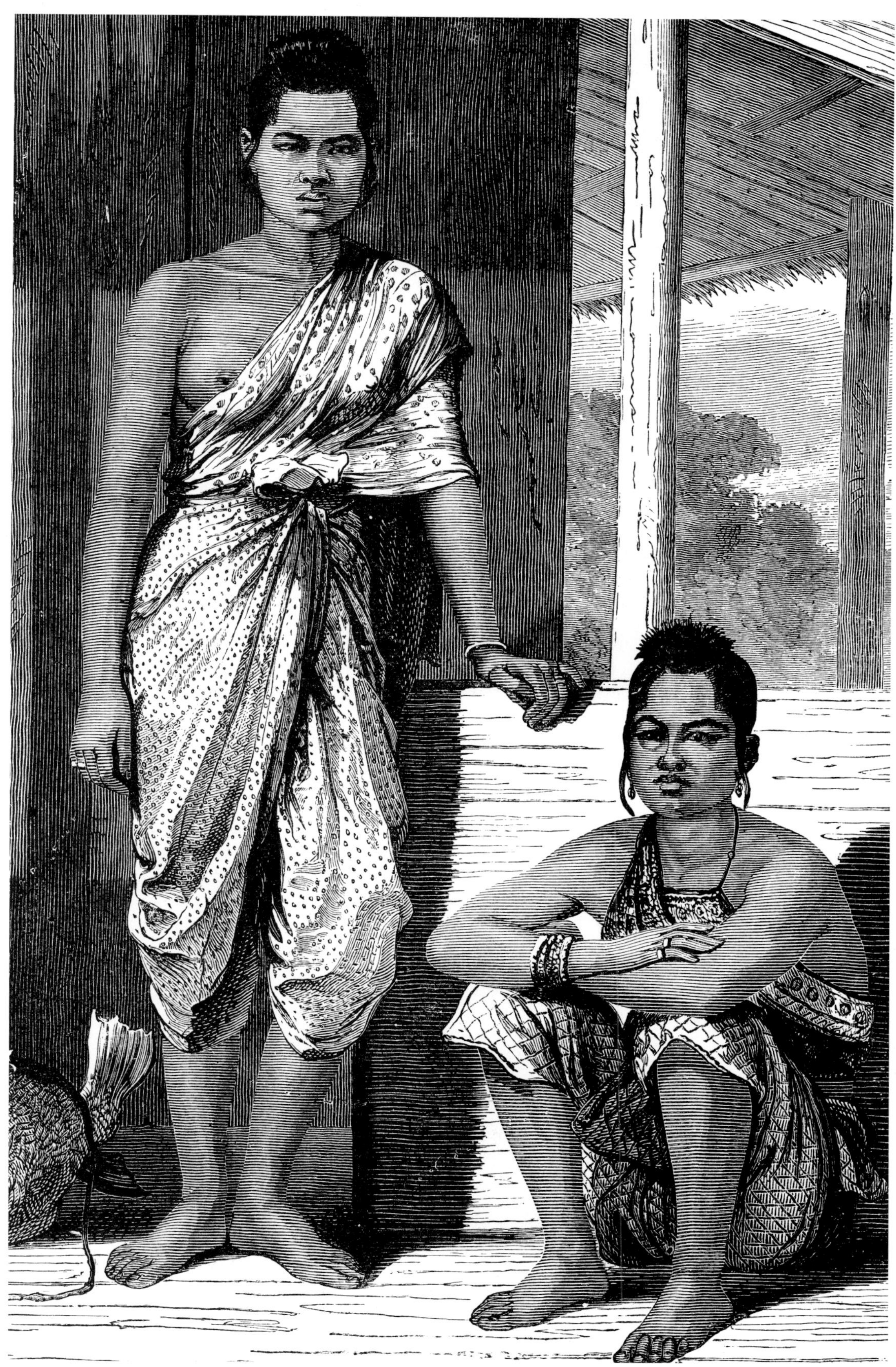

Thai women in Bangkok, c. 1870

Thailändische Frauen in Bangkok, um 1870

Donne tailandesi a Bangkok, ca. 1870

Femmes thaïs à Bangkok, vers 1870

Mujeres tailandesas de Bangkok, hacia 1870

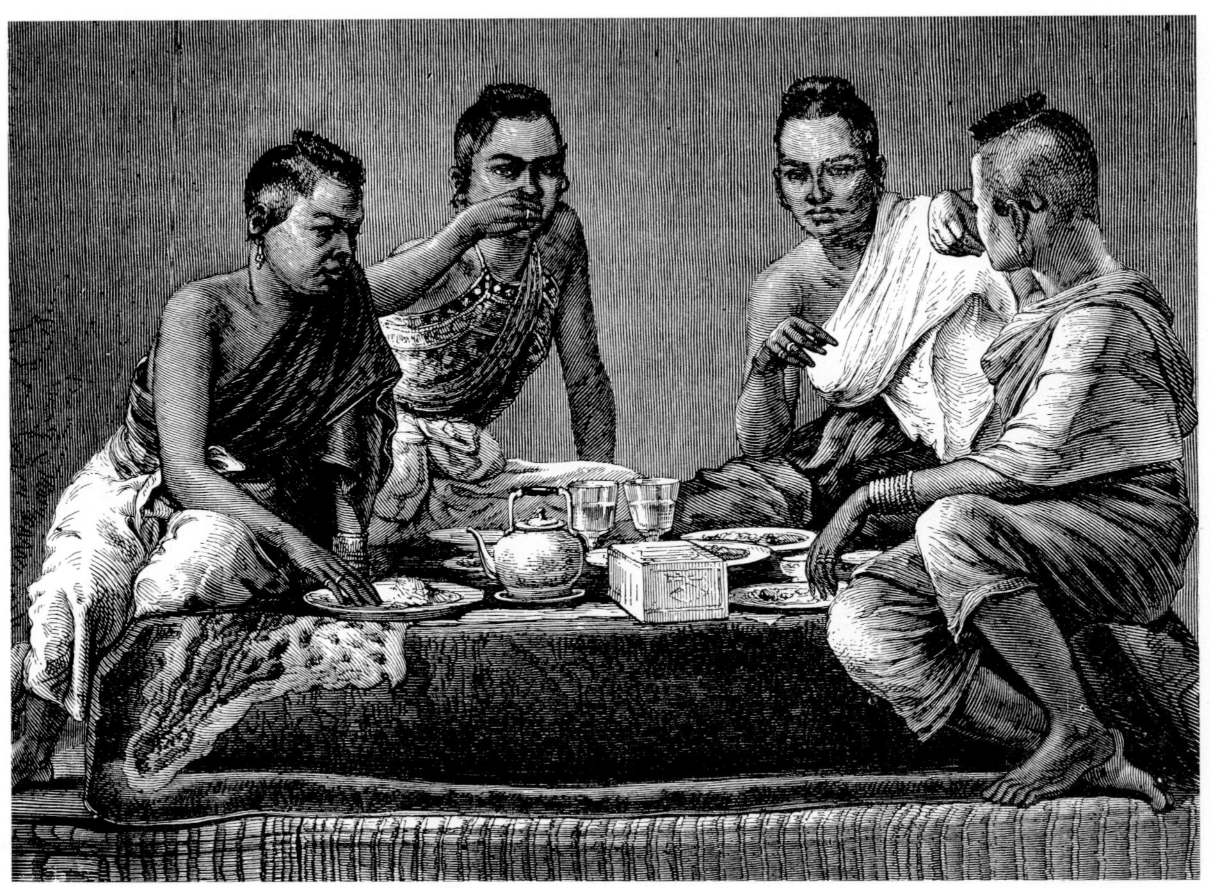

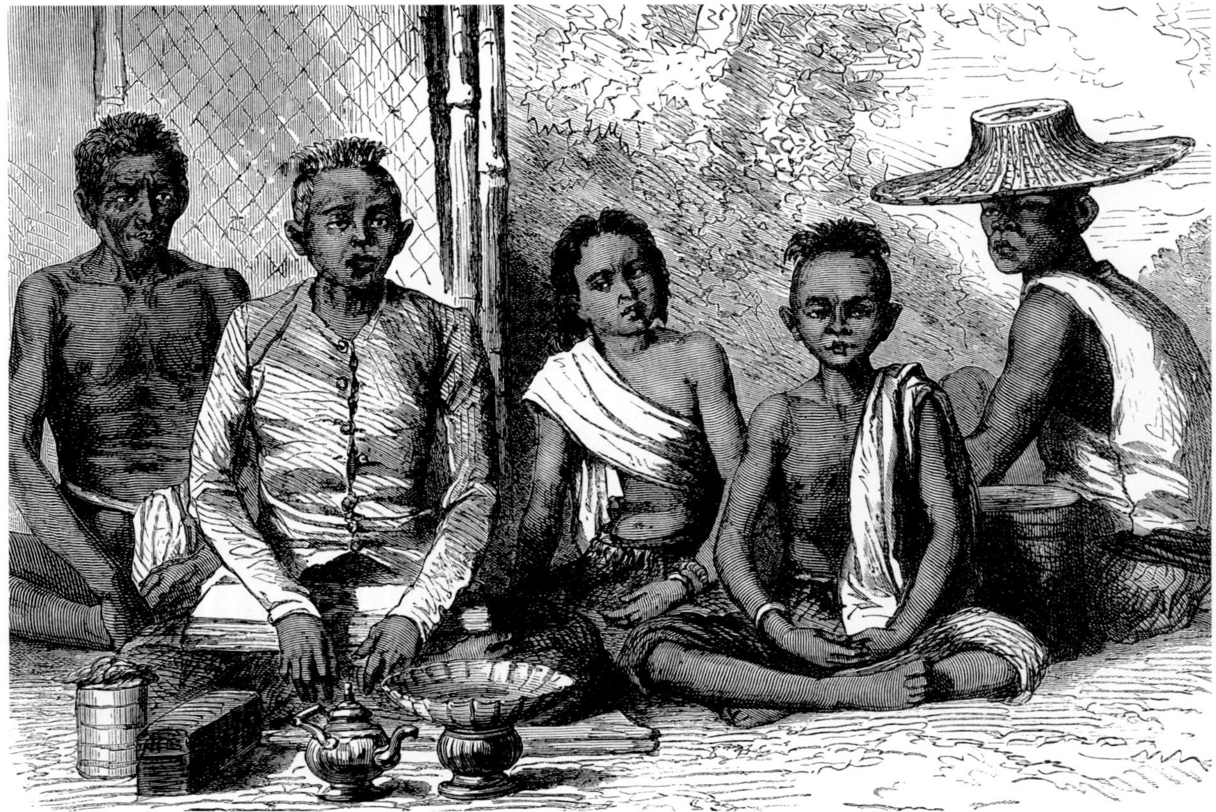

a	Siamese ladies, c. 1860	Siamesische Frauen, um 1860	Donne siamesi, ca. 1860	Femmes du Siam, vers 1860	Mujeres siamesas, hacia el año 1860
b	Laotians, c. 1870	Laotianer, um 1870	Laotiani, ca. 1870	Laotiens, vers 1870	Laosianos, hacia 1870

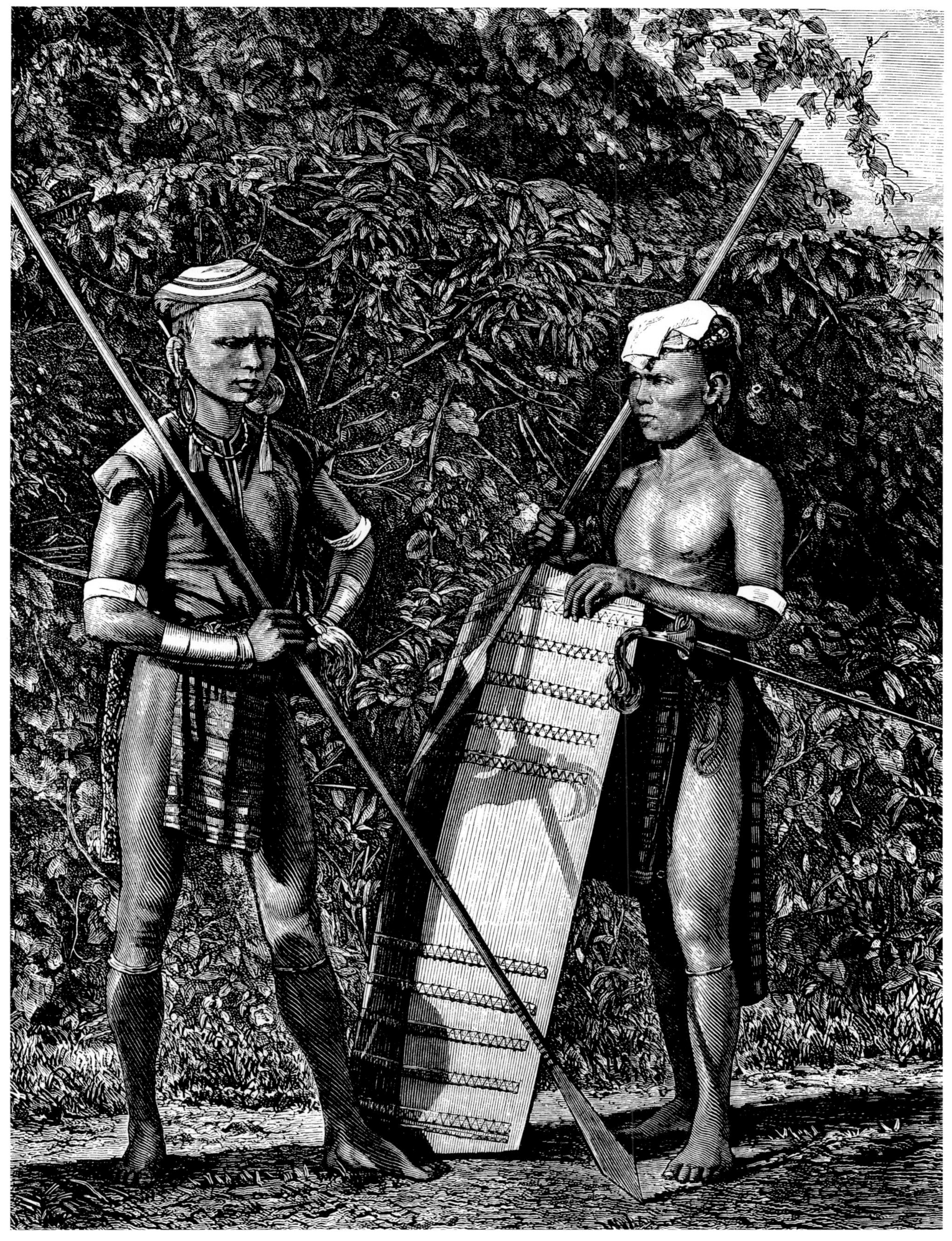

Warriors from North Borneo, c. 1860

Krieger aus Nordborneo, um 1860

Guerrieri del Borneo settentrionale, ca. 1860

Guerriers du Nord de Bornéo, vers 1860

Guerreros del norte de Borneo, hacia 1860

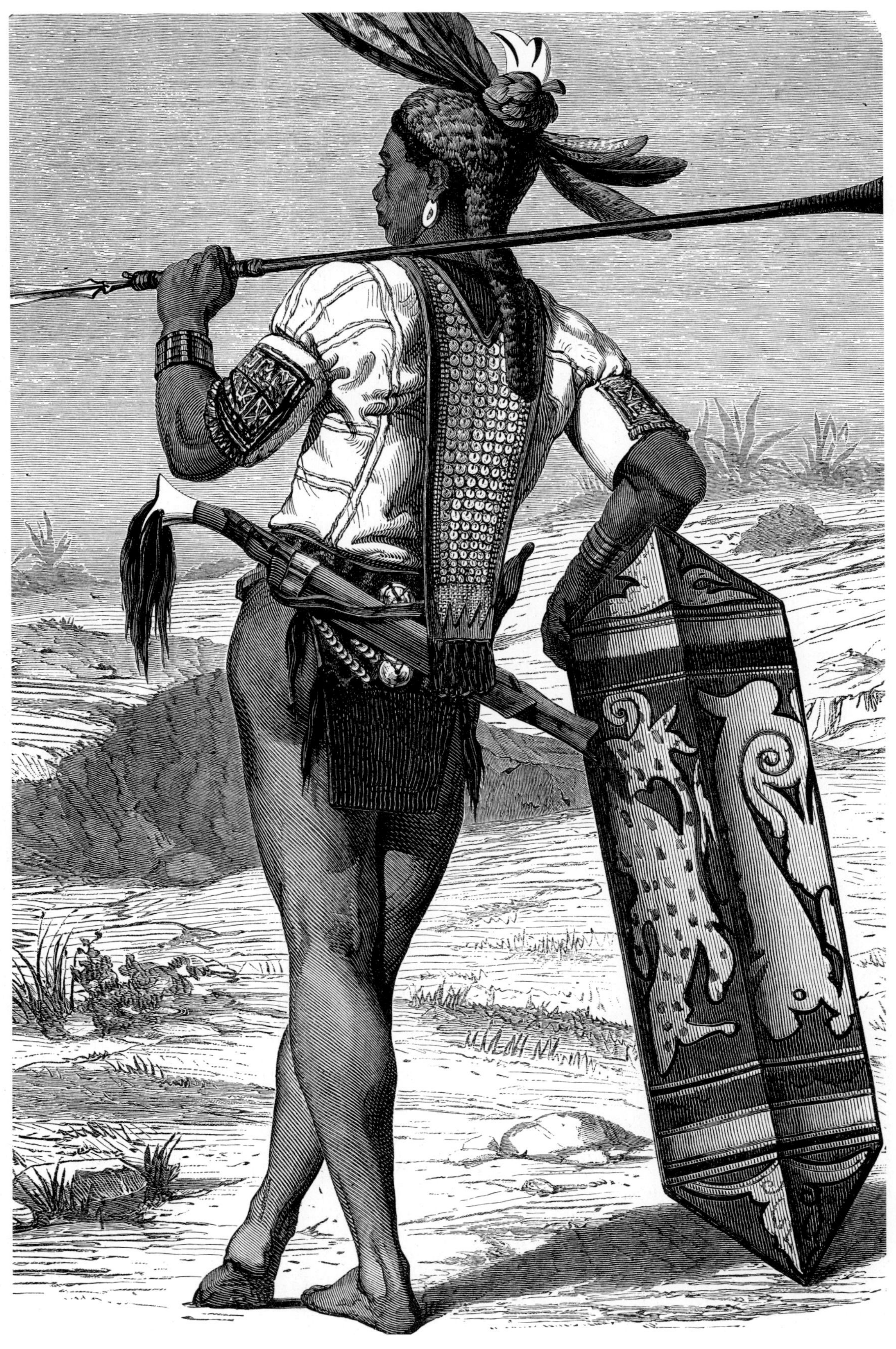

Dayak, c. 1860 Dayak, um 1860 Dayak, ca. 1860 Dayak, vers 1860 Dayak, alrededor de 1860

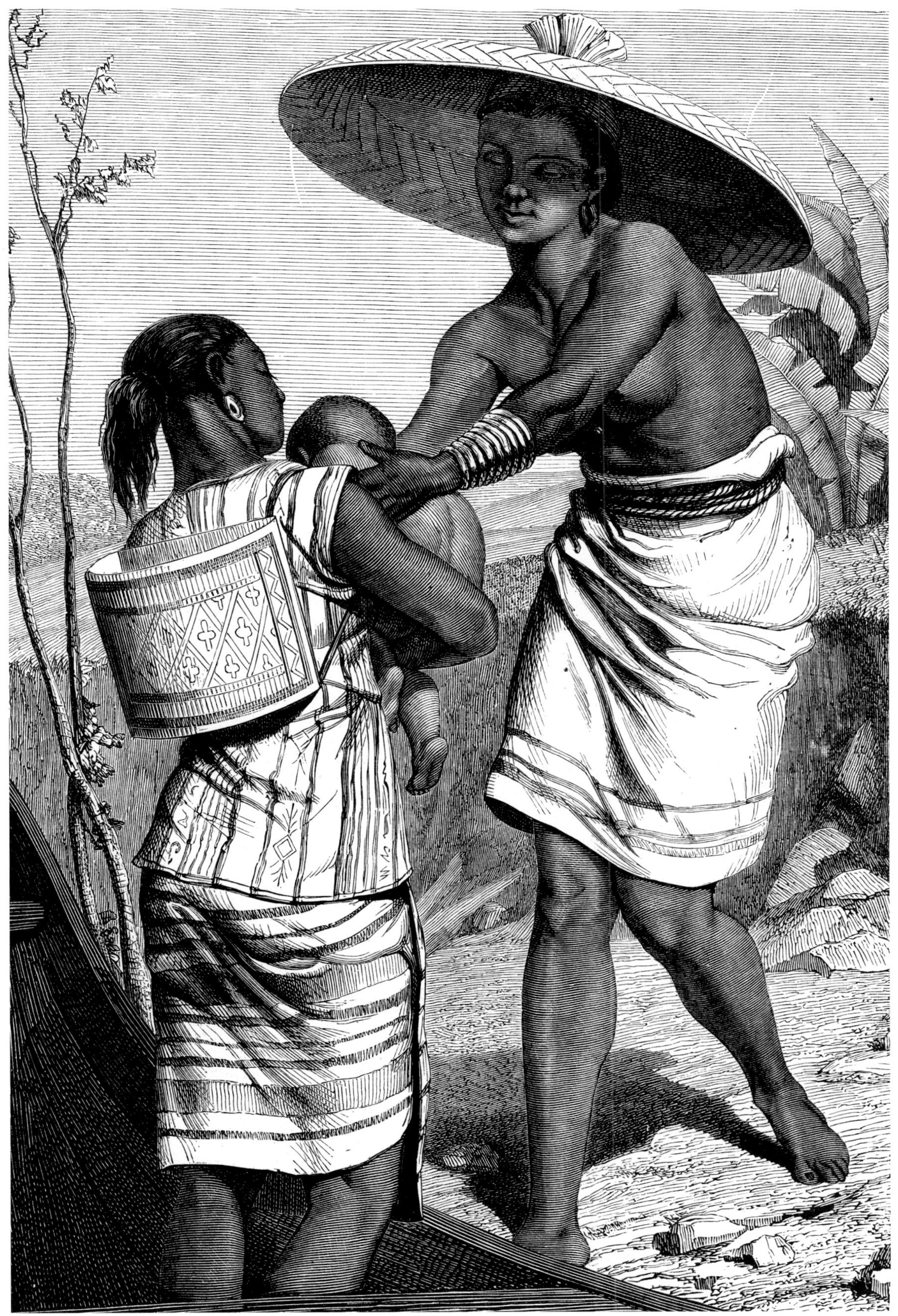

Dayak women, c. 1860 Dayak-Frau, um 1860 Donne dayak, ca. 1860 Femme dayak, vers 1860 Mujeres dayak, 1860

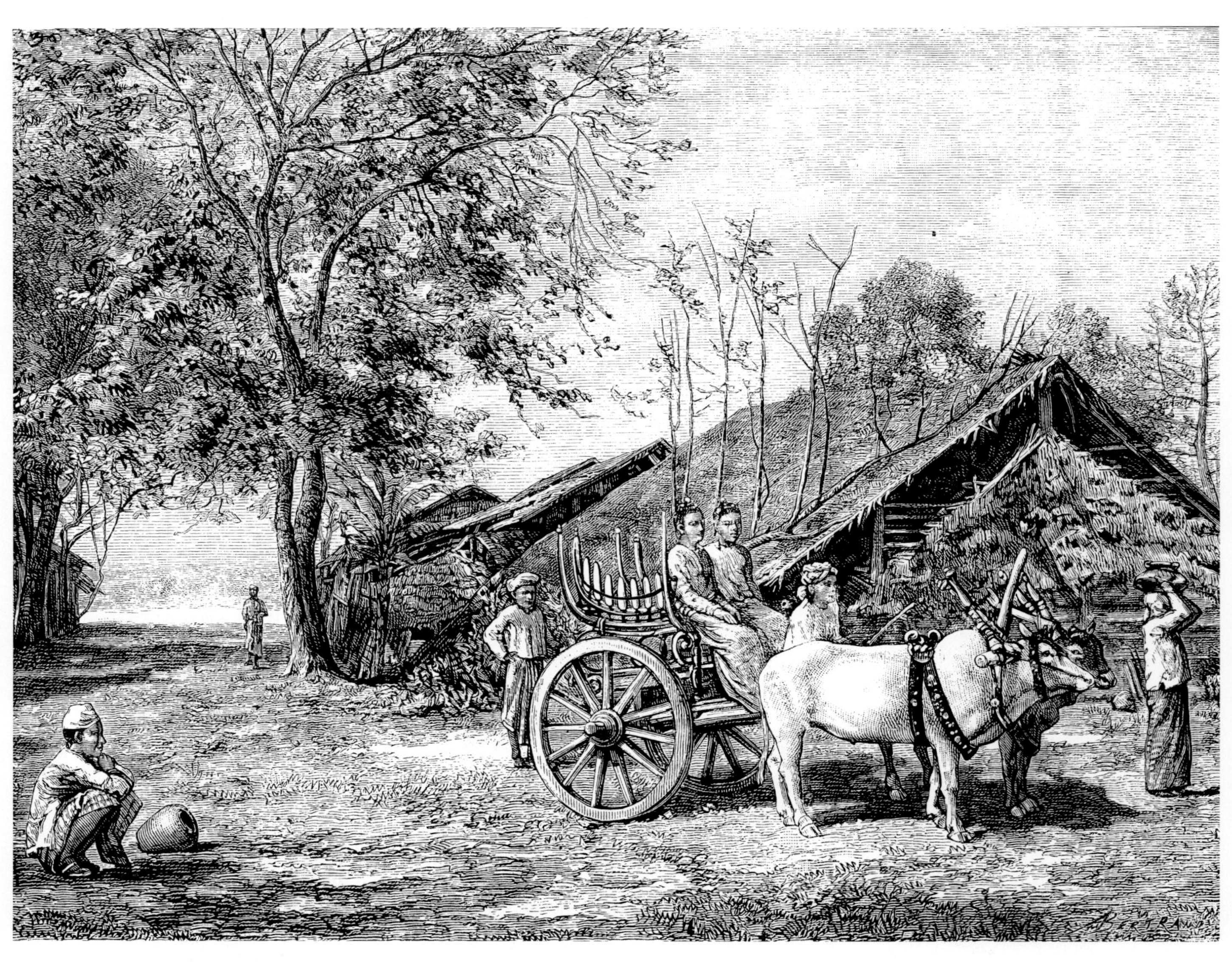

Malay village near Malacca, c. 1860

Malayisches Dorf bei Malacca, um 1860

Villaggio malese vicino Malacca, ca. 1860

Village malais près de Malacca, vers 1860

Aldea malasia cercana a Malacca, hacia 1860

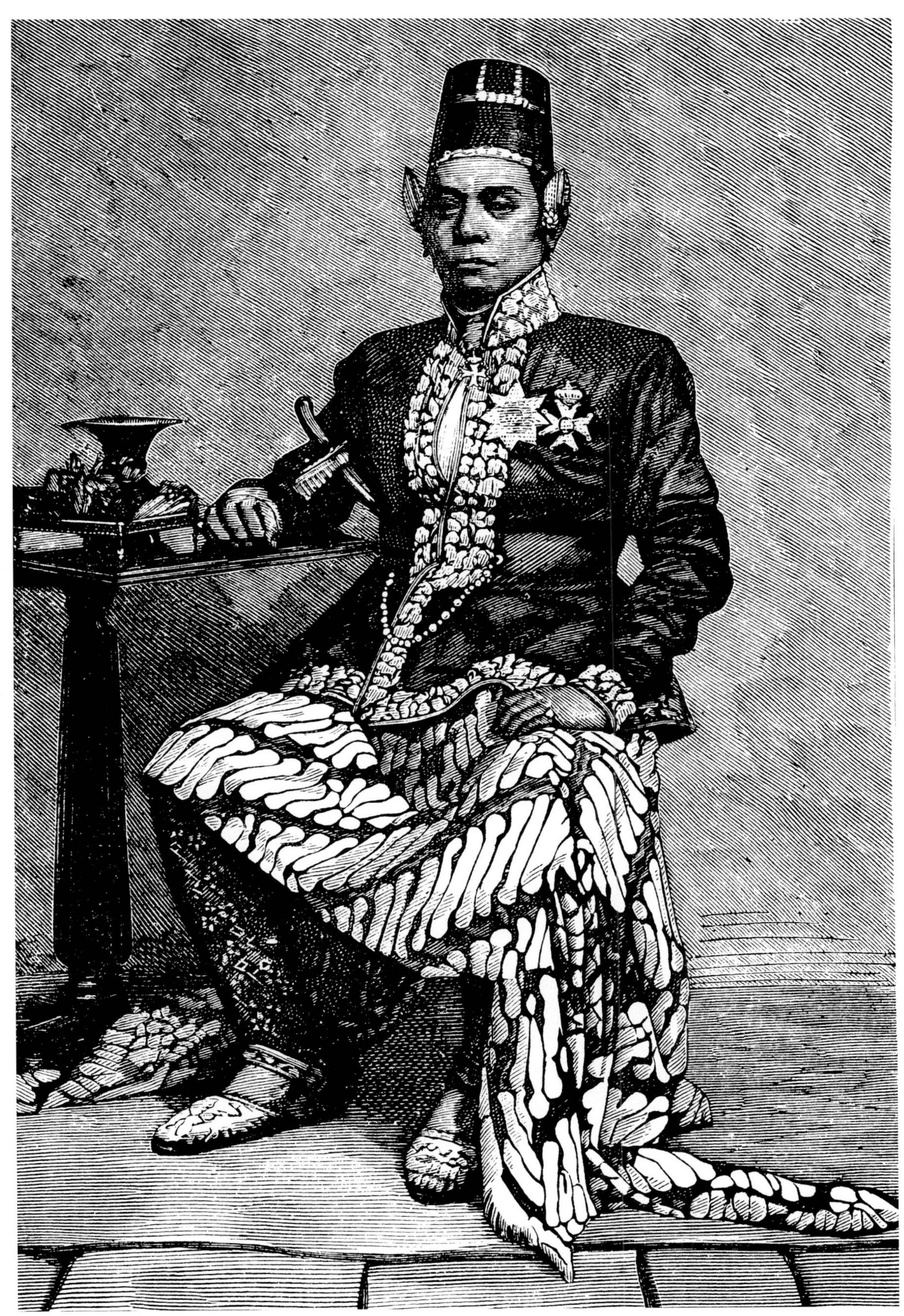

The Sultan of Jogyakarta, Java, c. 1880

Der Sultan von Jogyakarta, Java, um 1880

Il sultano di Jogyakarta, Giava, ca. 1880

Le Sultan de Jogyakarta, Java, vers 1880

Sultán de Yogyakarta, Java, hacia el año 1880

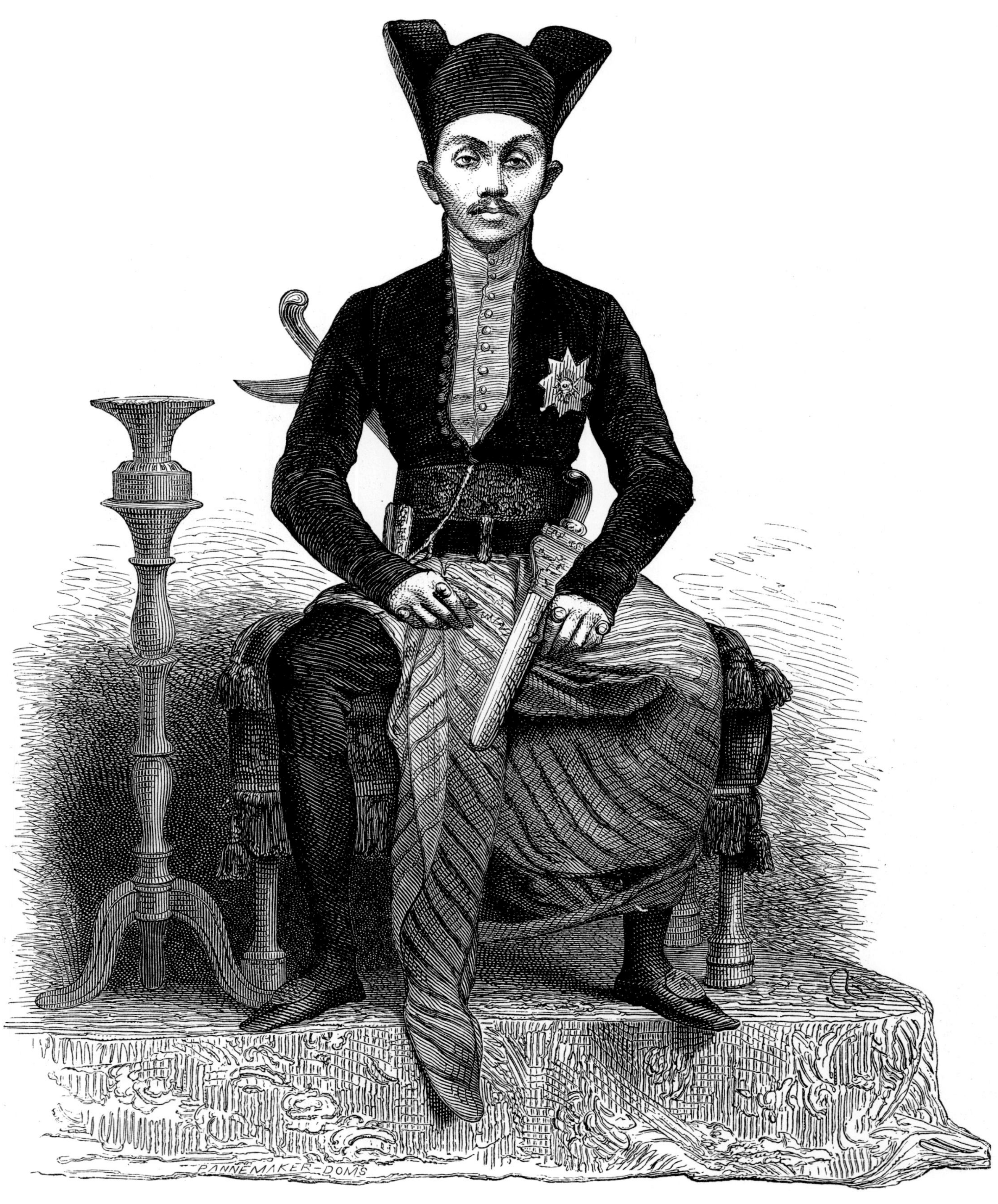

The Sultan of Surakarta, c. 1870

Der Sultan von Surakarta, um 1870

Il sultano di Surakarta, ca. 1870

Le Sultan de Surakarta, vers 1870

El sultán de Surakarta, alrededor del año 1870

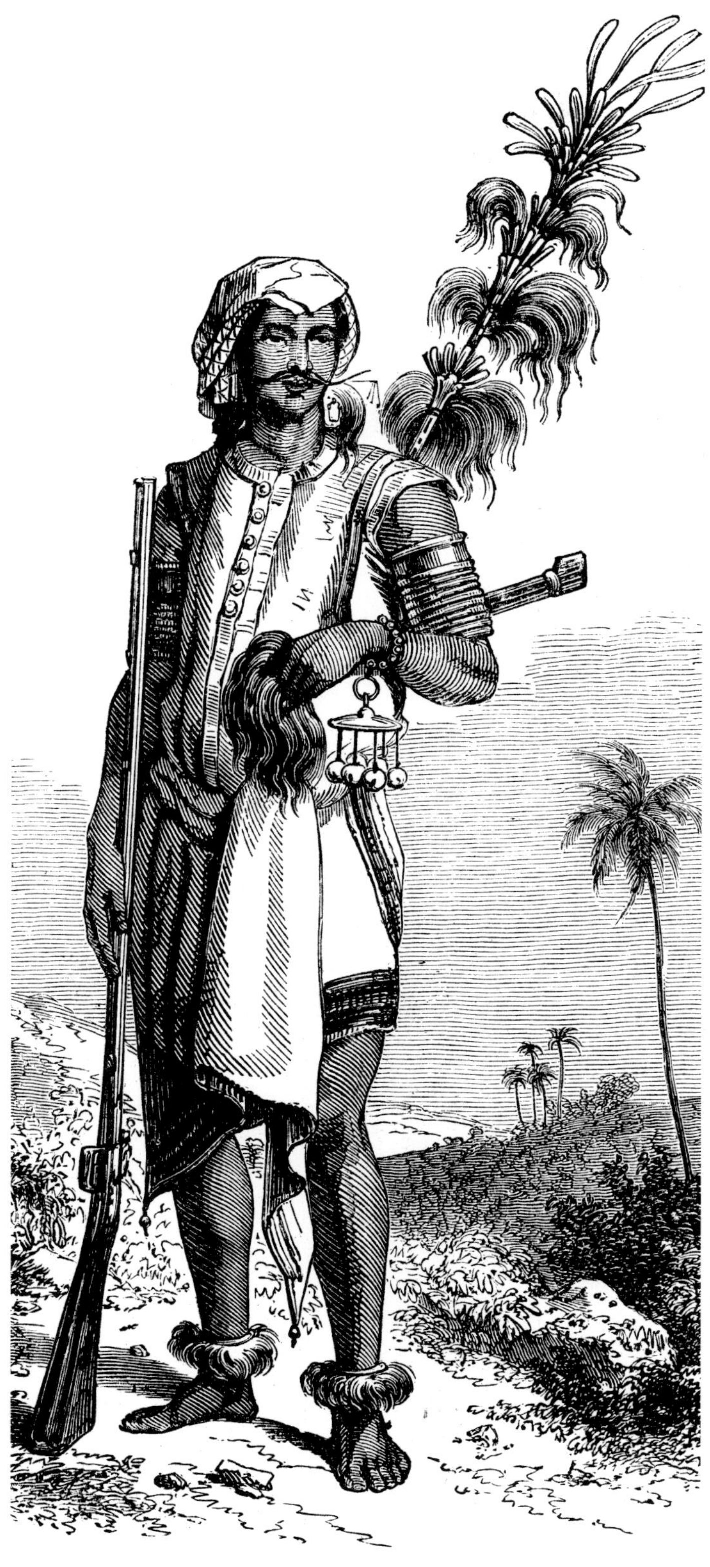

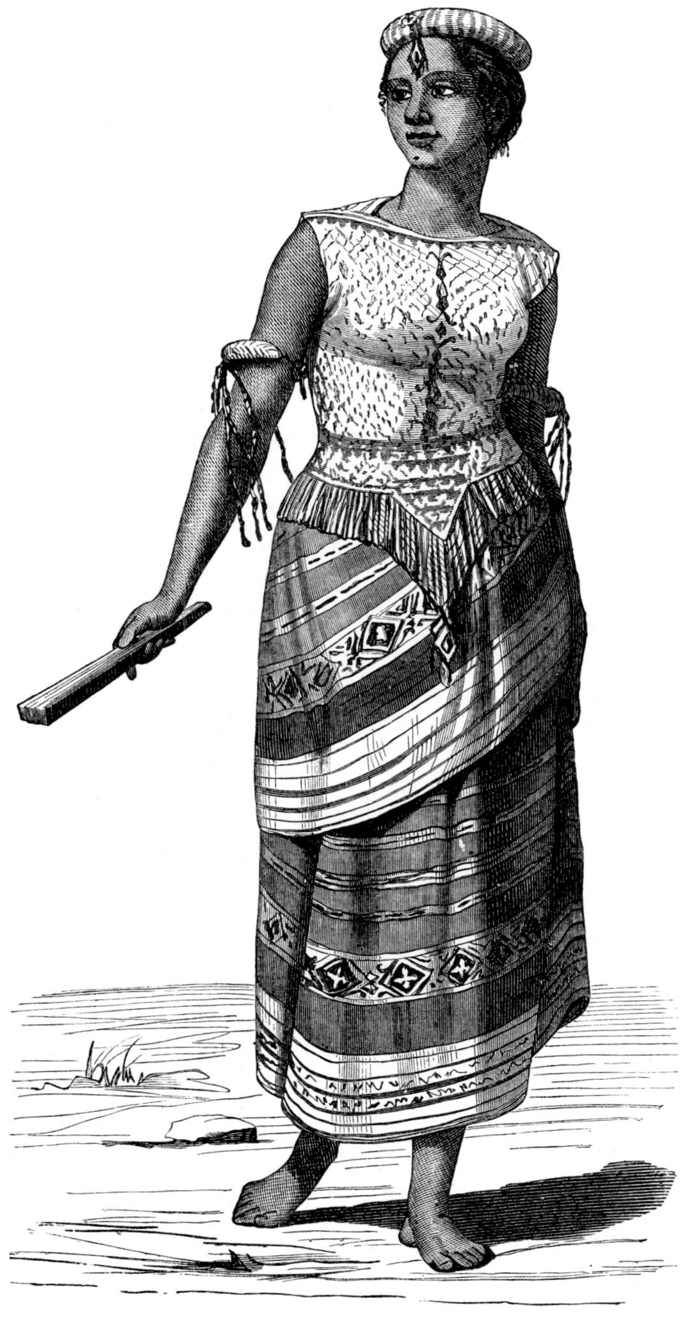

a	Chief from one of the Lesser Sunda Islands, c. 1860	Häuptling von einer der kleinen Sundainseln, um 1860	Capo di una delle Isole della Sunda minori, ca. 1860	Chef de l'une des îles de la Sonde, vers 1860	Jefe de una de las islas Pequeñas de la Sonda, alrededor del año 1860
b	Woman of Koti, c. 1870	Frau aus Koti, um 1870	Donna di Koti, ca. 1870	Femme de Koti, vers 1870	Mujer de Koti, hacia 1870

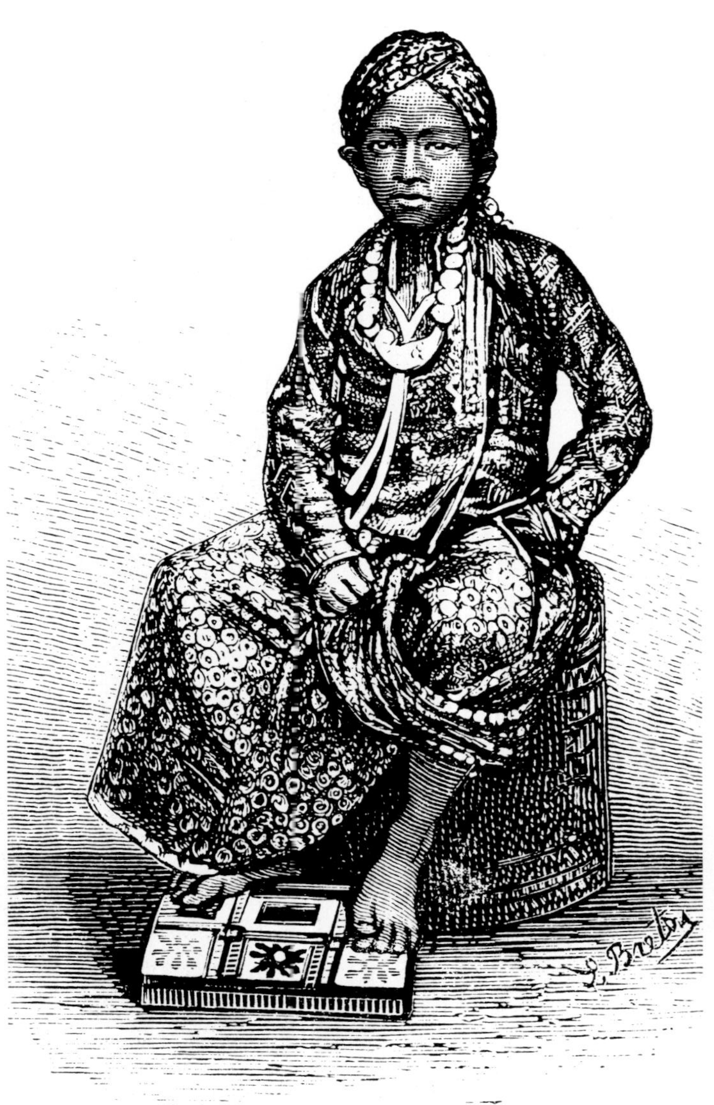

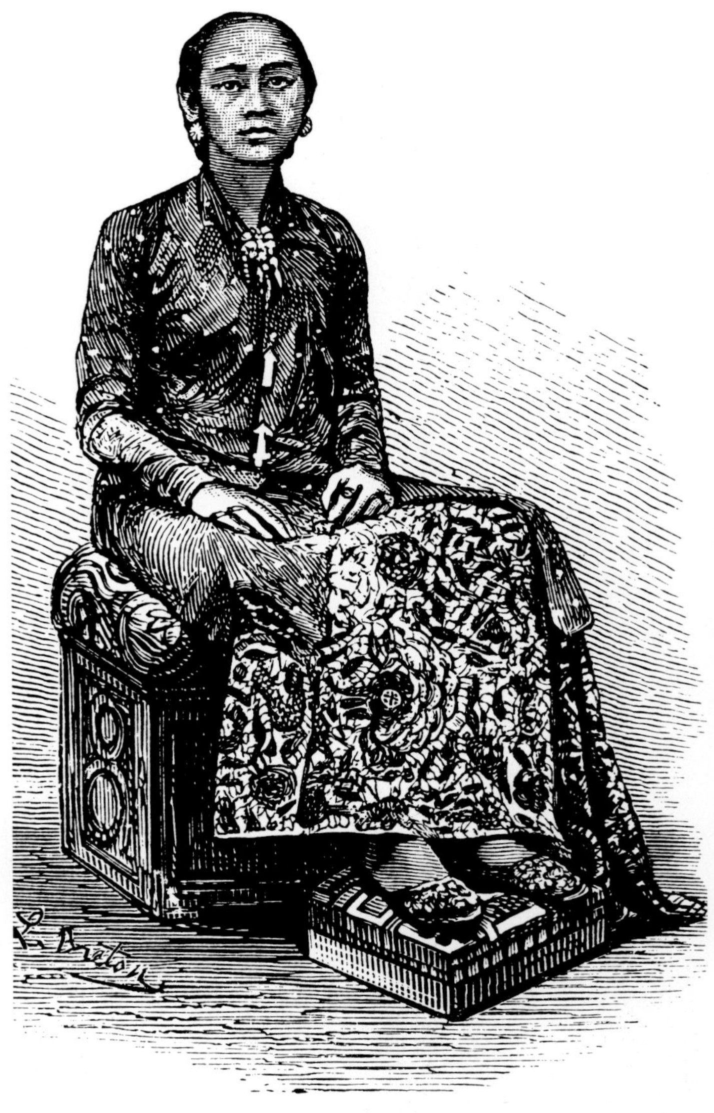

The Sultanah and a young prince of Surakarta, c. 1880

Der Sultanah und ein jüngerer Prinz von Surakarta, um 1880

Il Sultano e il giovane principe di Surakarta, ca. 1880

La Sultane et un jeune prince de Surakarta, vers 1880

La sultana y un joven príncipe de Surakarta, alrededor del año 1880

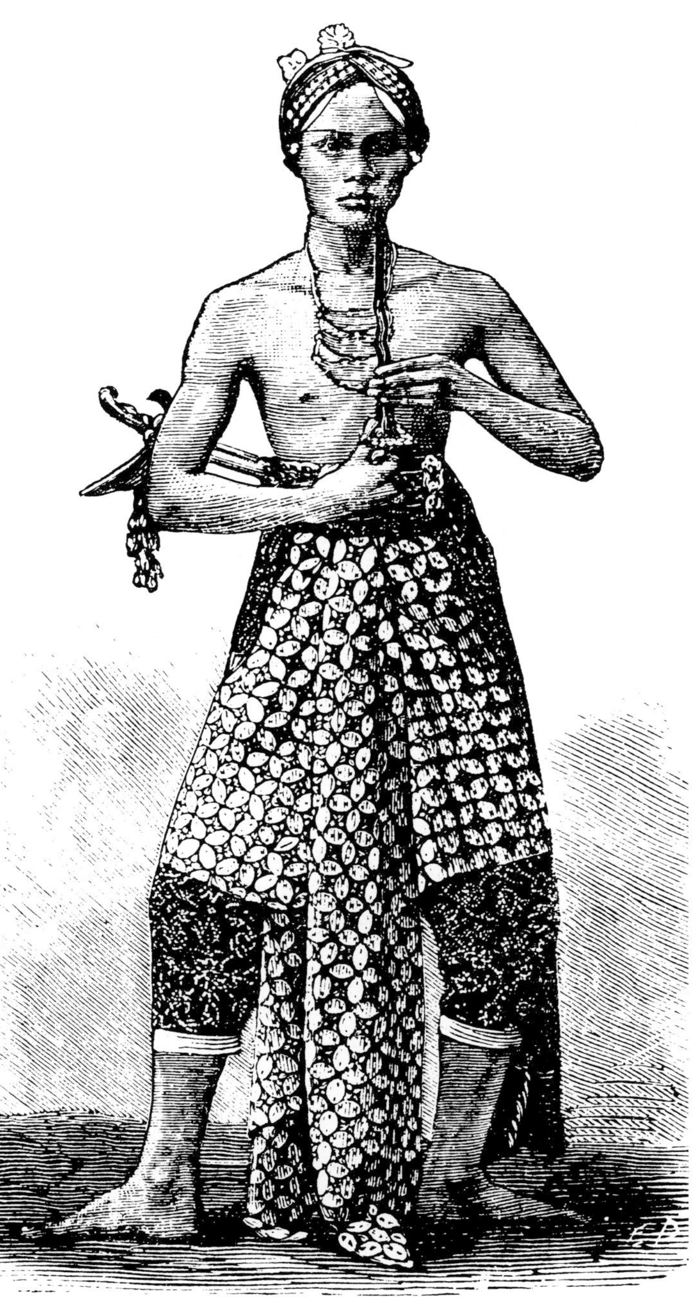

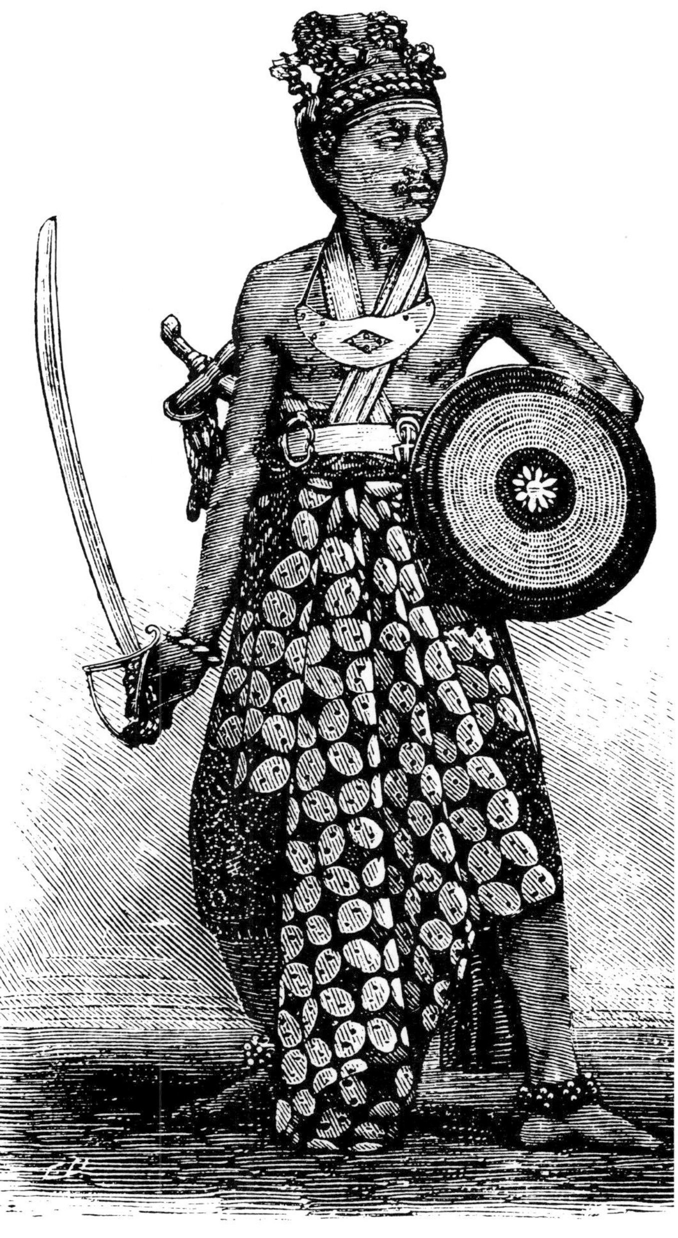

Guards of the Sultan of Jogyakarta, c. 1880

Wachen des Sultans von Jogyakarta, um 1880

Guardie del sultano di Jogyakarta, ca. 1880

Gardes du Sultan de Jogyakarta, vers 1880

Guardias del sultán de Yogyakarta, hacia 1880

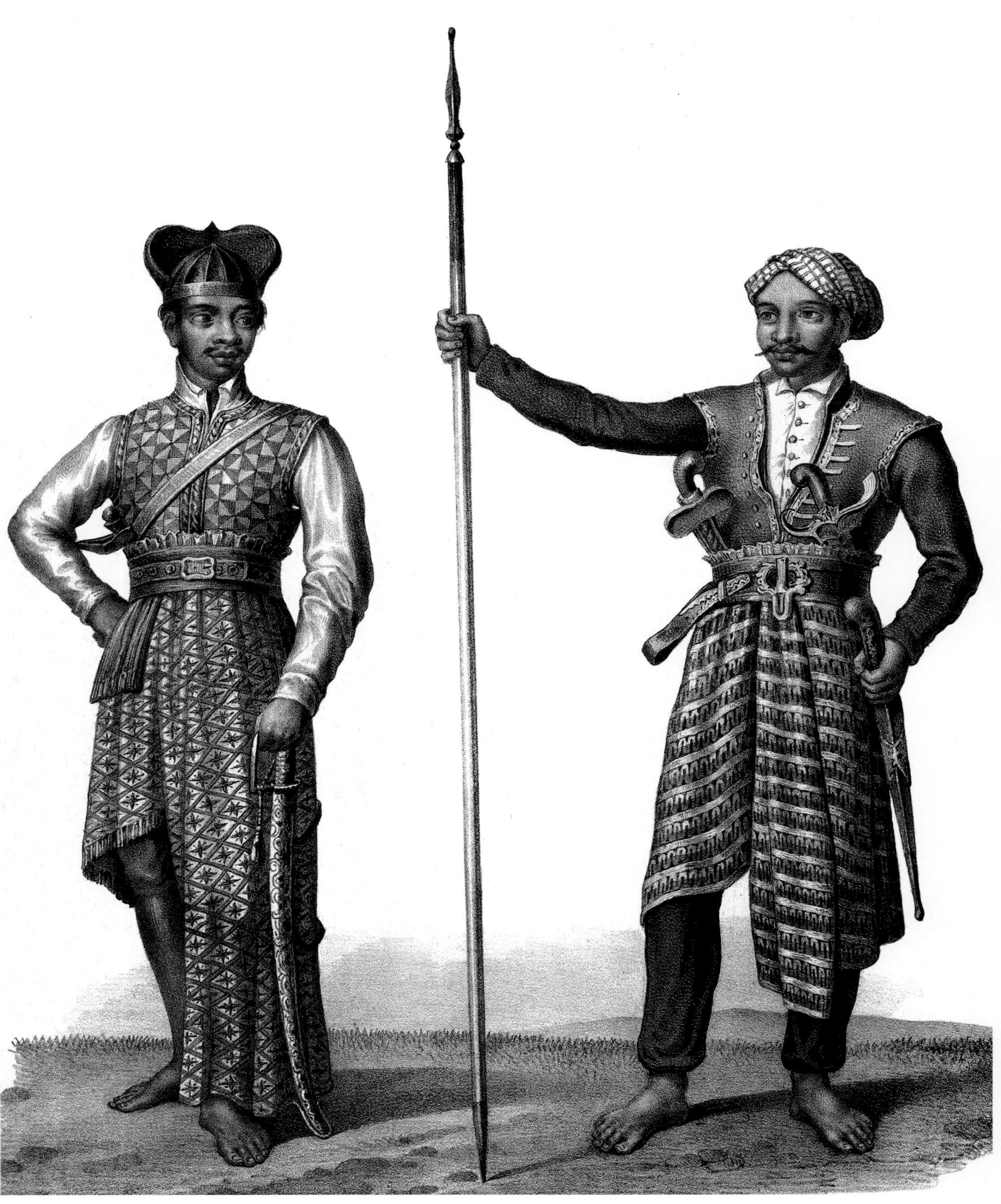

Guards of the Sultan of Jogyakarta, c. 1840

Garde des Sultans von Jogyakarta, um 1840

Guardie del sultano di Jogyakarta, ca. 1840

Gardes du Sultan de Jogyakarta, vers 1840

Guardias del sultán de Yogyakarta, 1840

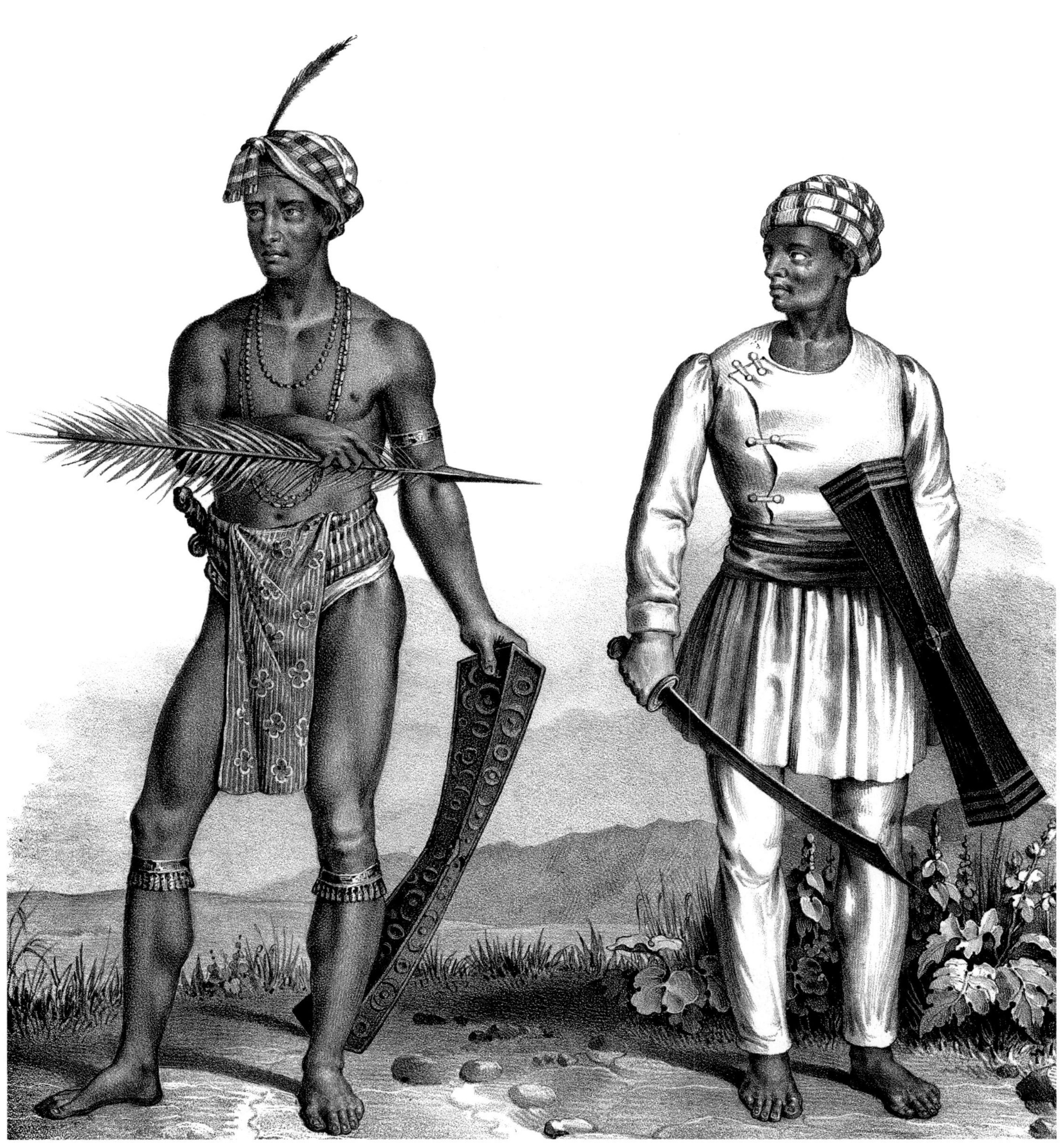

Men from North Sulawesi, c. 1840

Männer aus Nord-Sulawesi, um 1840

Uomini del Sulawesi settentrionale, ca. 1840

Homme du Nord de Sulawesi, vers 1840

Hombres del norte de Célebes, hacia 1840

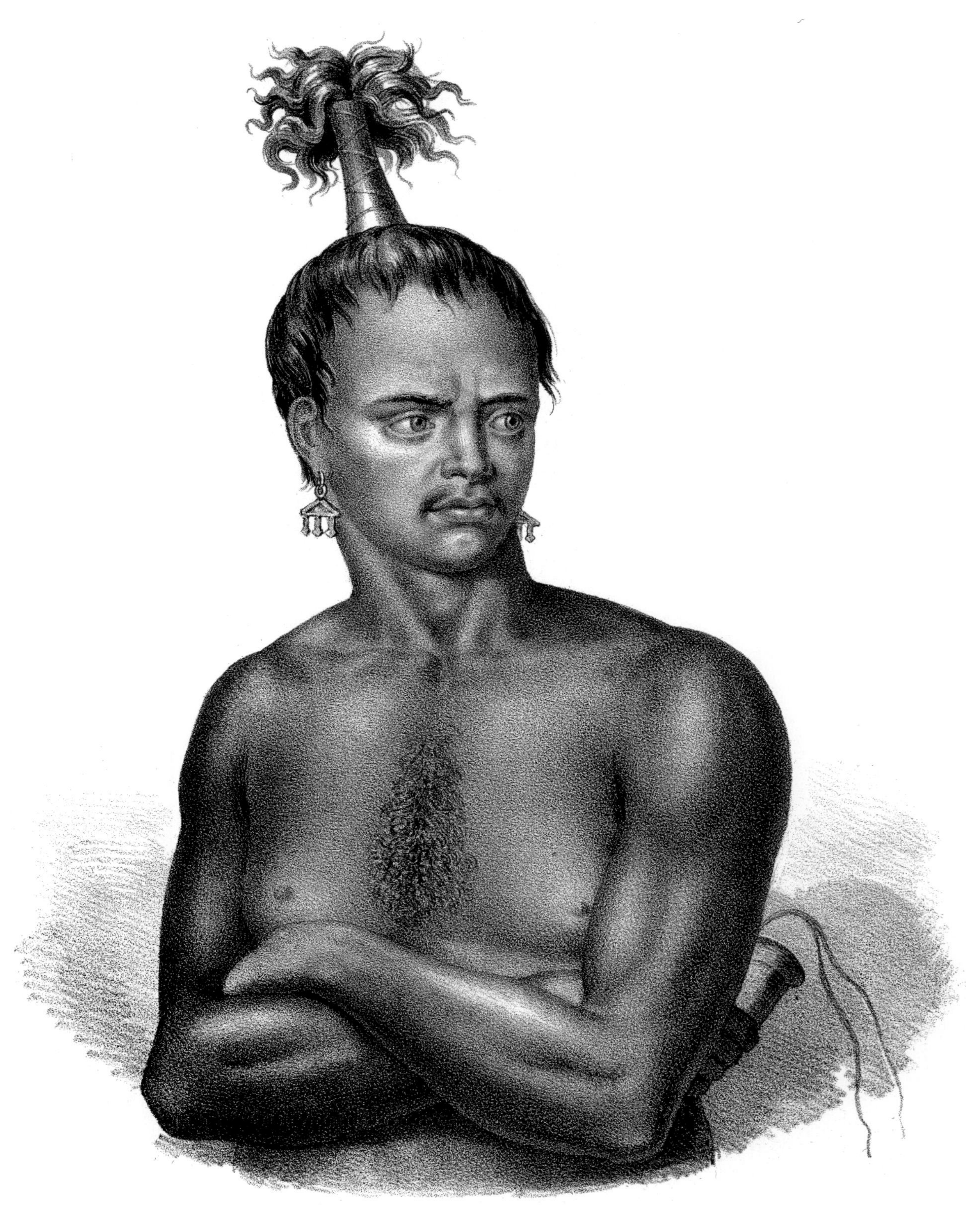

Man from the Lesser Sunda Islands, c. 1840

Mann von den kleinen Sundainseln, um 1840

Uomo delle Isole della Sunda minori, ca. 1840

Homme des îles de la Sonde, vers 1840

Poblador de las islas Pequeñas de la Sonda, alrededor de 1840

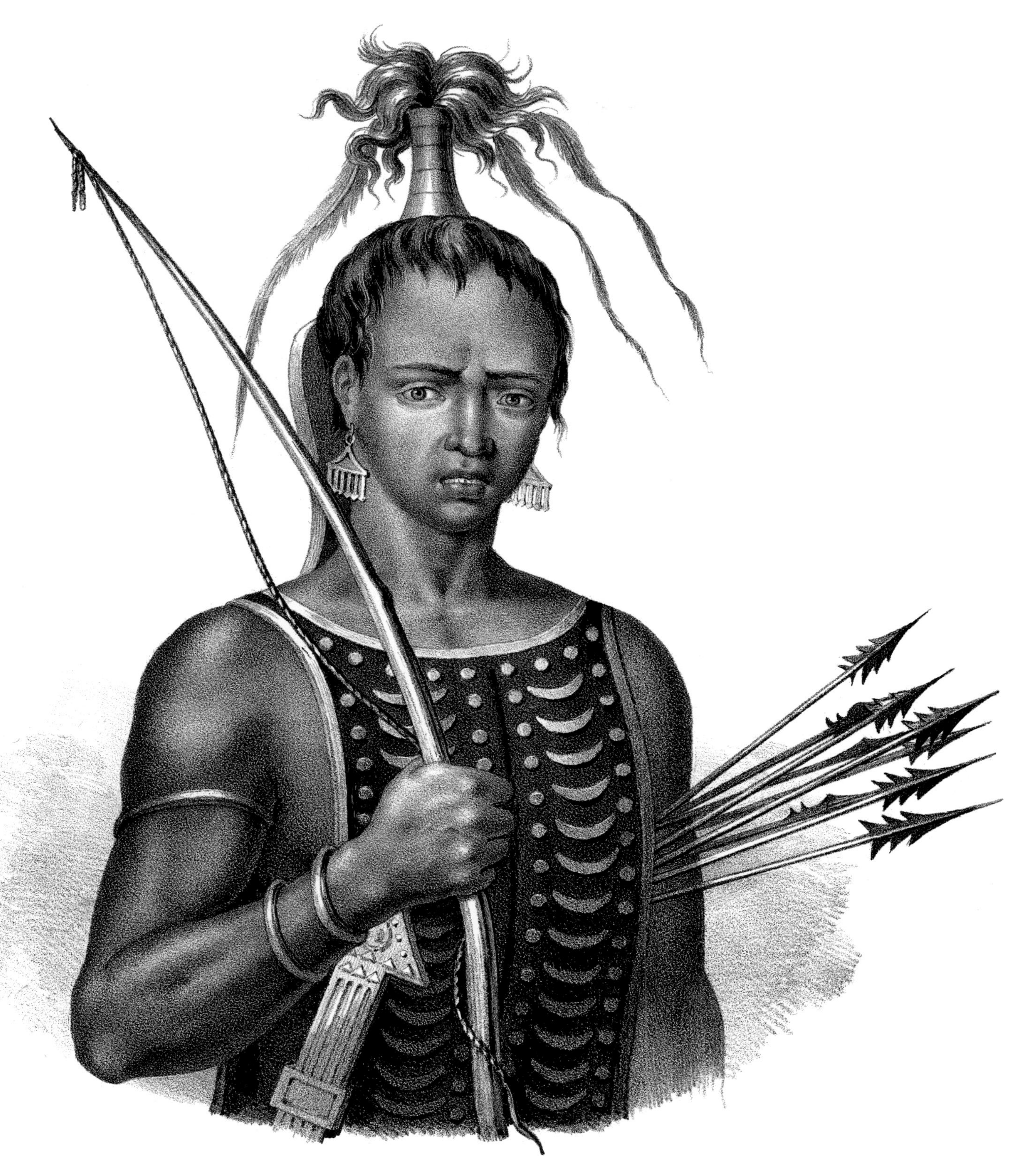

Man from the Lesser Sunda Islands, c. 1840

Mann von den kleinen Sundainseln, um 1840

Uomo delle Isole della Sunda minori, ca. 1840

Homme des îles de la Sonde, vers 1840

Habitante de las islas Pequeñas de la Sonda, alrededor de 1840

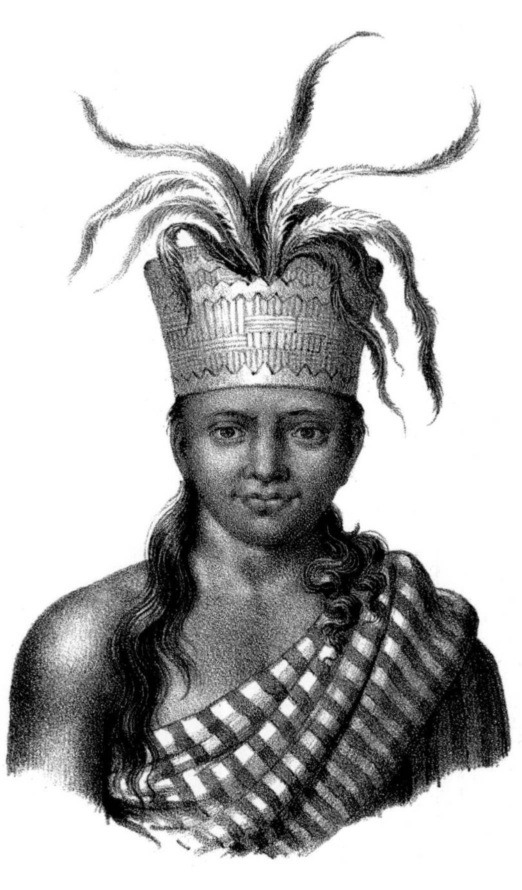

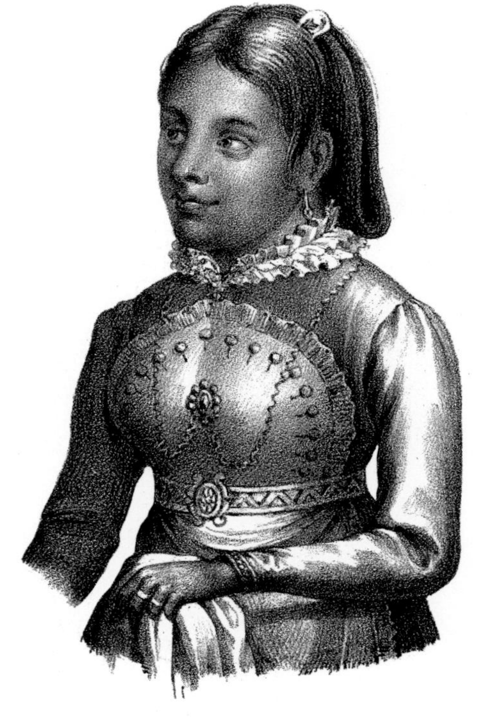

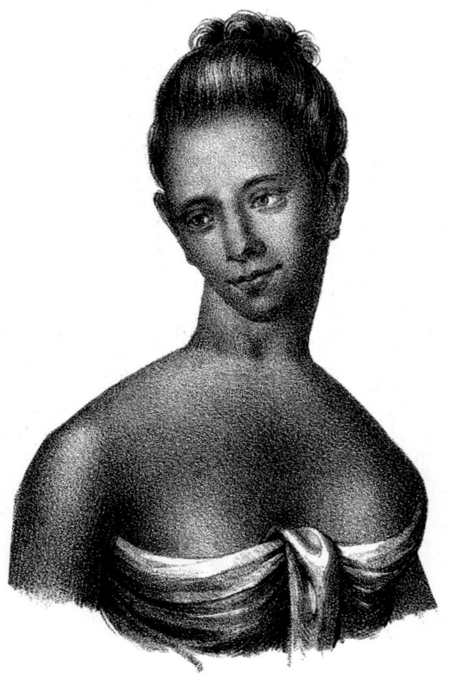

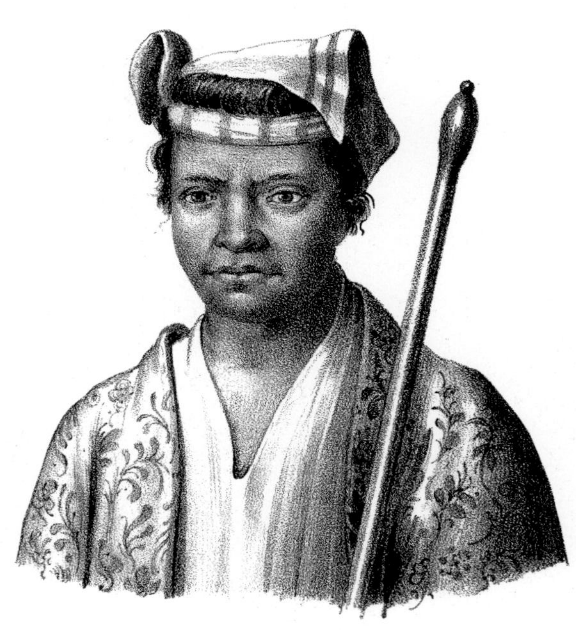

Timorese, c. 1840

Bewohner von Timor, um 1840

Abitante di Timor, ca. 1840

Habitant de Timor, vers 1840

Timoreses, hacia 1840

Timor

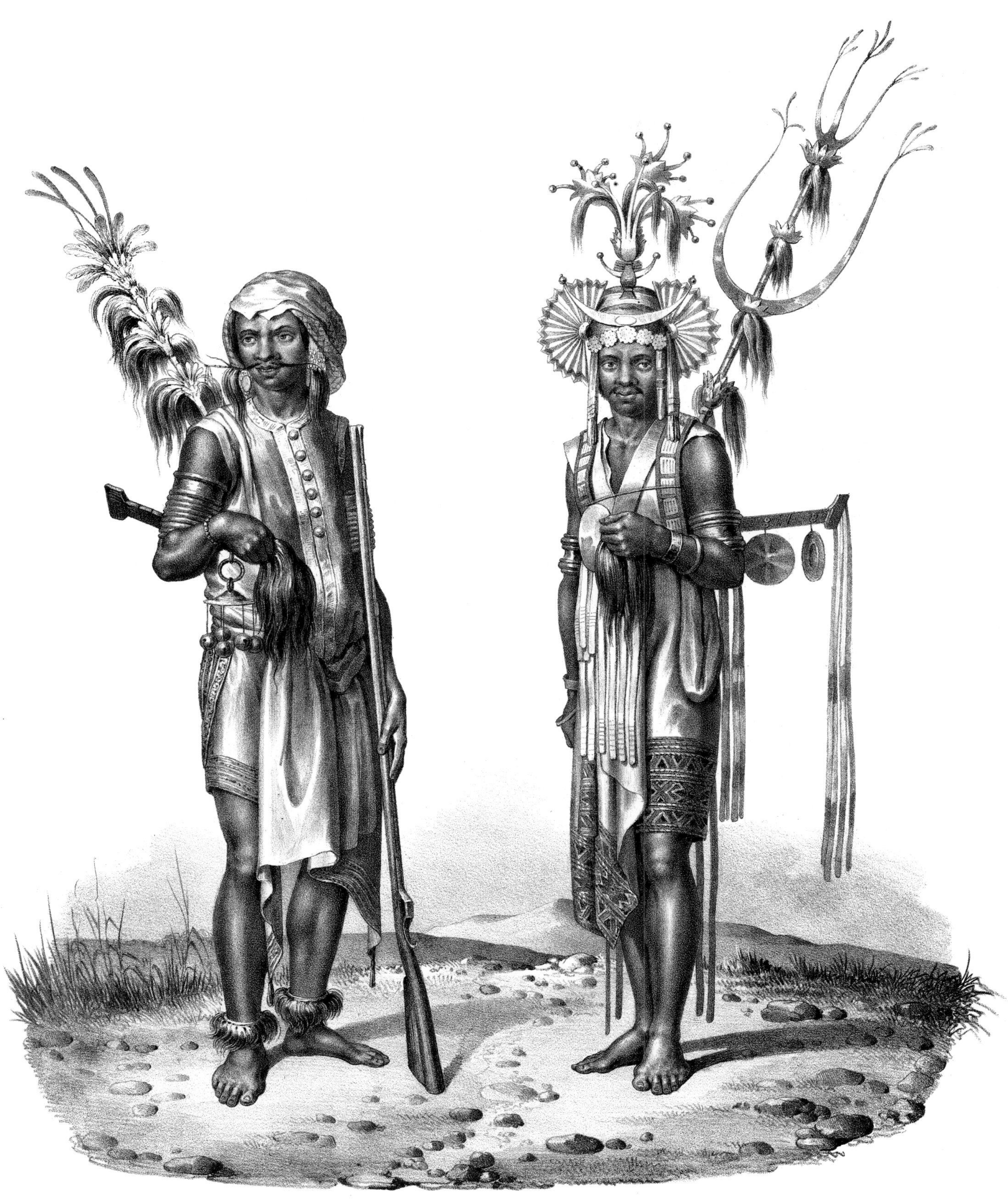

Timorese warriors, c. 1840

Krieger aus Timor, um 1840

Guerrieri di Timor, ca. 1840

Guerriers Timors, vers 1840

Guerreros timoreses, alrededor del año 1840

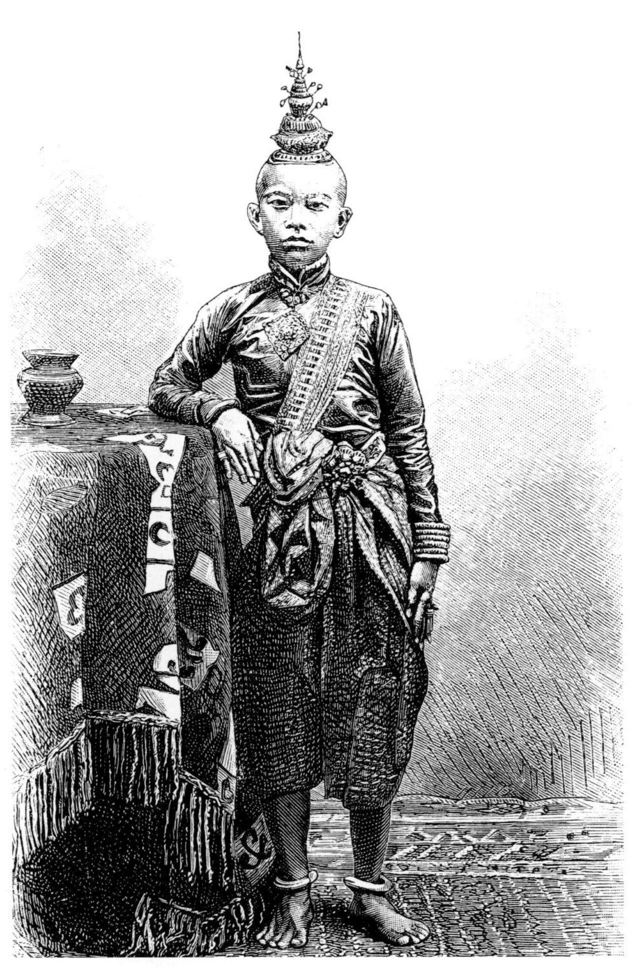

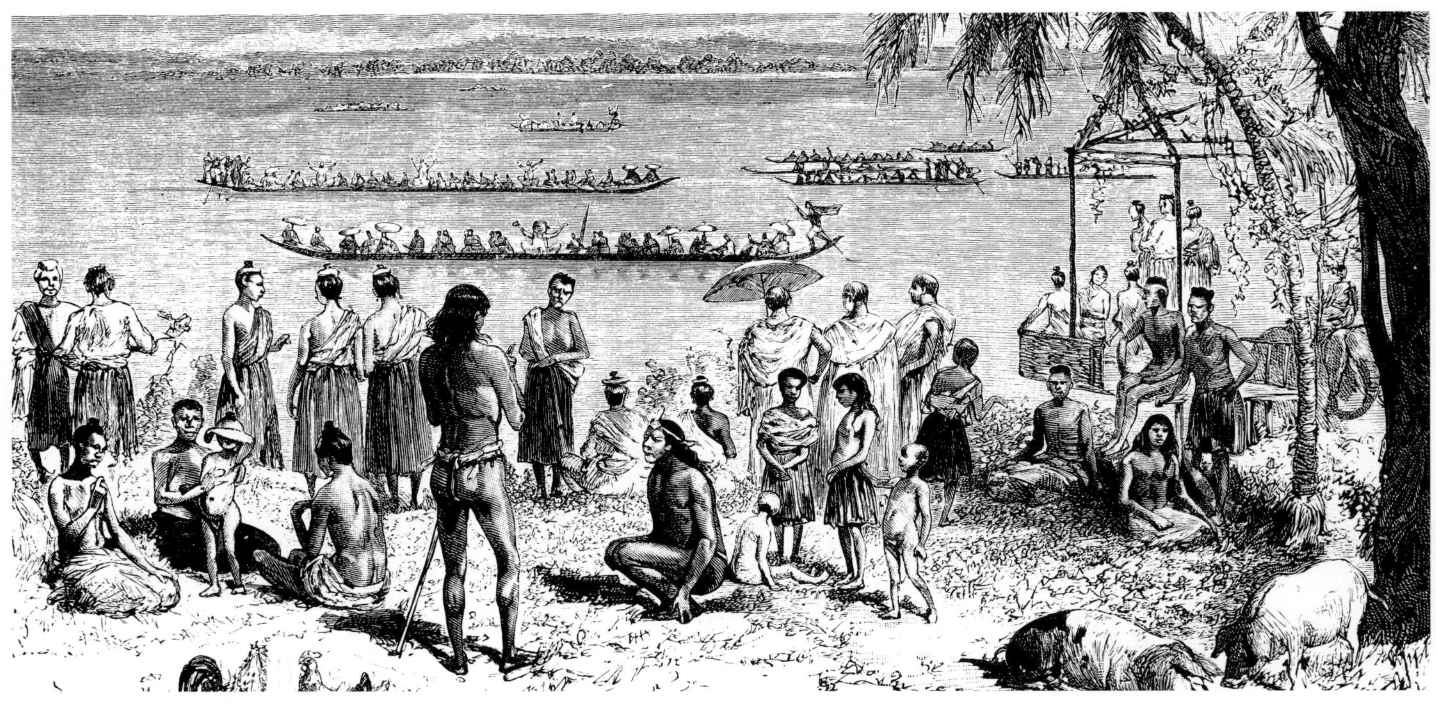

a	The crown Prince of Cambodia, c. 1880	Der Kronprinz von Kambodscha, um 1880	Il principe ereditario di Cambogia, ca. 1880	Le Prince héritier du Cambodge, vers 1880	Príncipe heredero de Camboya, hacia 1880
b	Boat race on the Mekong, Phnum Penh, 1880	Bootsregatta auf dem Mekong, Phnom Penh, 1880	Regata sul Mekong, Phnum Penh, 1880	Course de bâteaux sur le Mékong à Phnom Penh, 1880	Carrera de embarcaciones en el Mekong, Phnom Penh, 1880

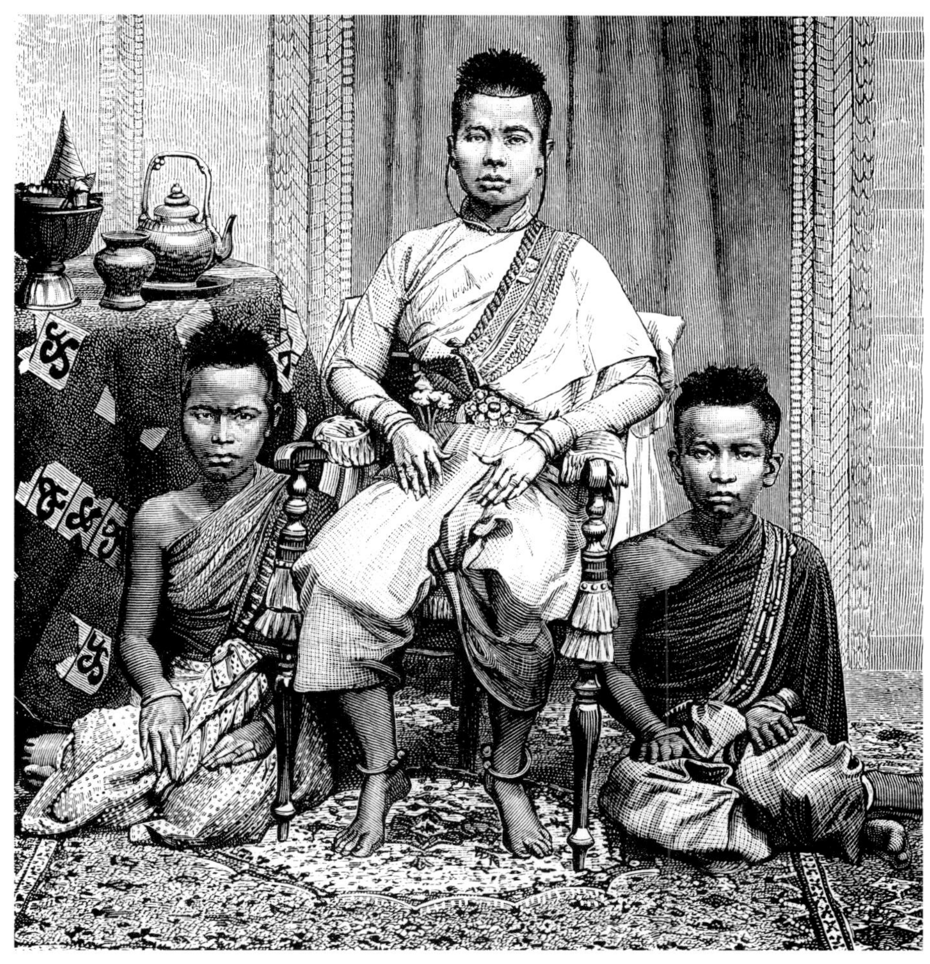

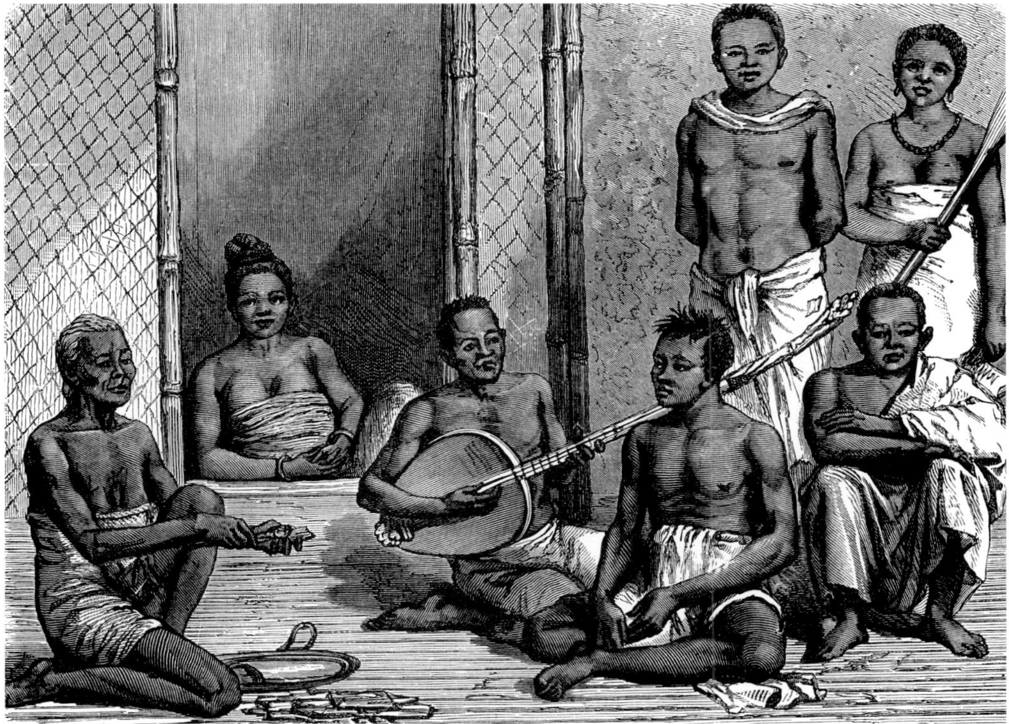

a	The Queen Mother of Cambodia, c. 1880	Die Königinmutter von Kambodscha, um 1880	La Regina Madre di Cambogia, ca. 1880	La Reine Mère du Cambodge, vers 1880	La reina madre de Camboya, hacia 1880
b	Cambodians, c. 1860	Kambodschaner, um 1860	Cambogiani, ca. 1860	Cambodgiens, vers 1860	Camboyanos, hacia 1860

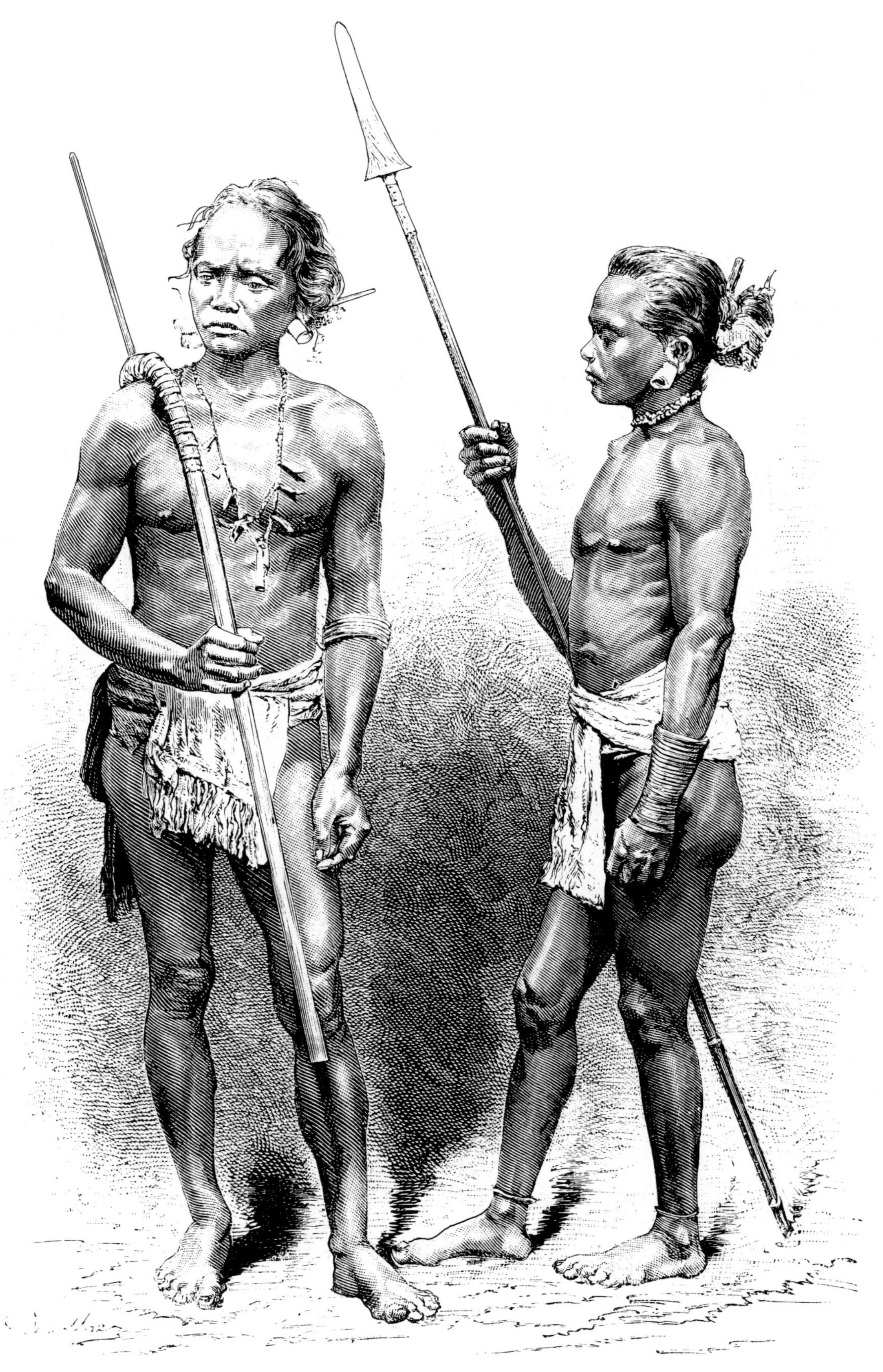

Moi warriors, c. 1860 Moi-Krieger, um 1860 Guerrieri moi, ca. 1860 Guerriers Moi, vers 1860 Guerreros moi, 1860

Vietnam

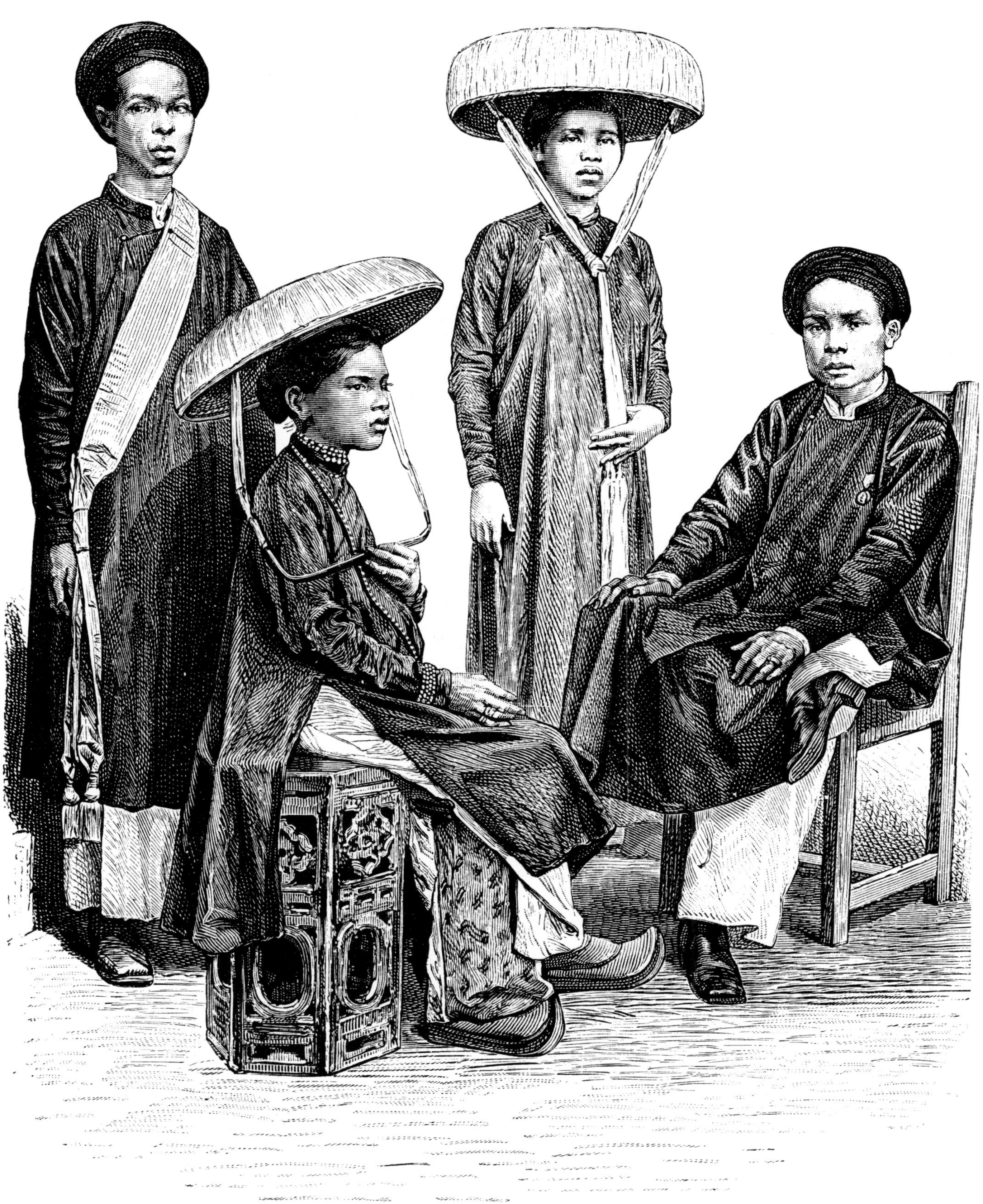

Village chiefs with their wives, c. 1870

Dorfführer mit ihren Frauen, um 1870

Capi villaggio con le loro mogli, ca. 1870

Chefs de village et leurs épouses, vers 1870

Jefes de una aldea con sus esposas, hacia 1870

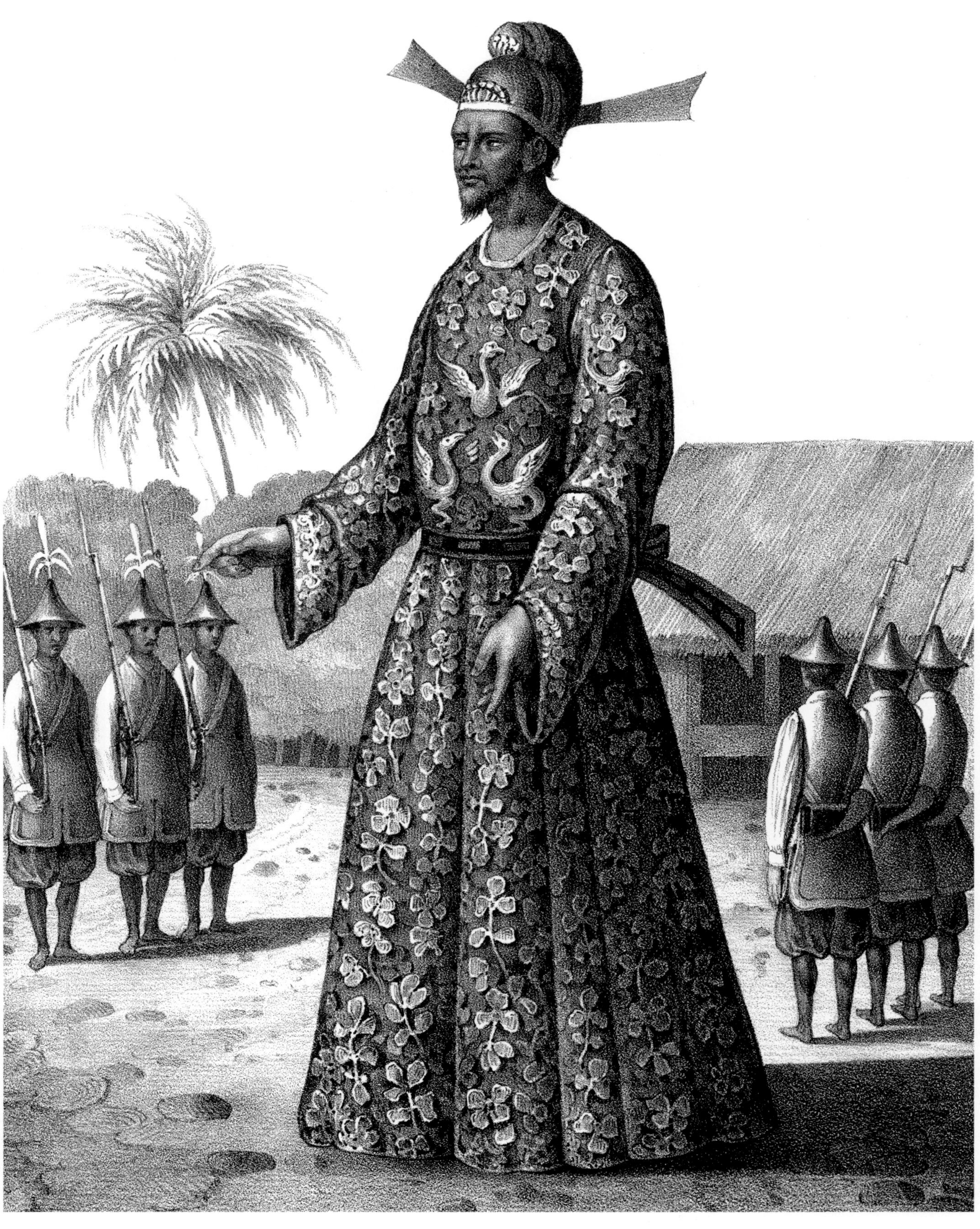

Cochin-Chinese official (present-day Vietnam), 1840

Chinesischer Beamter aus Cochinchina (heute Vietnam), um 1840

Funzionario cocincinese (attualmente Vietnam), 1840

Fonctionnaire de Cochinchine (actuel Vietnam), vers 1840

Funcionario de Cochinchina (actual Vietnam), 1840

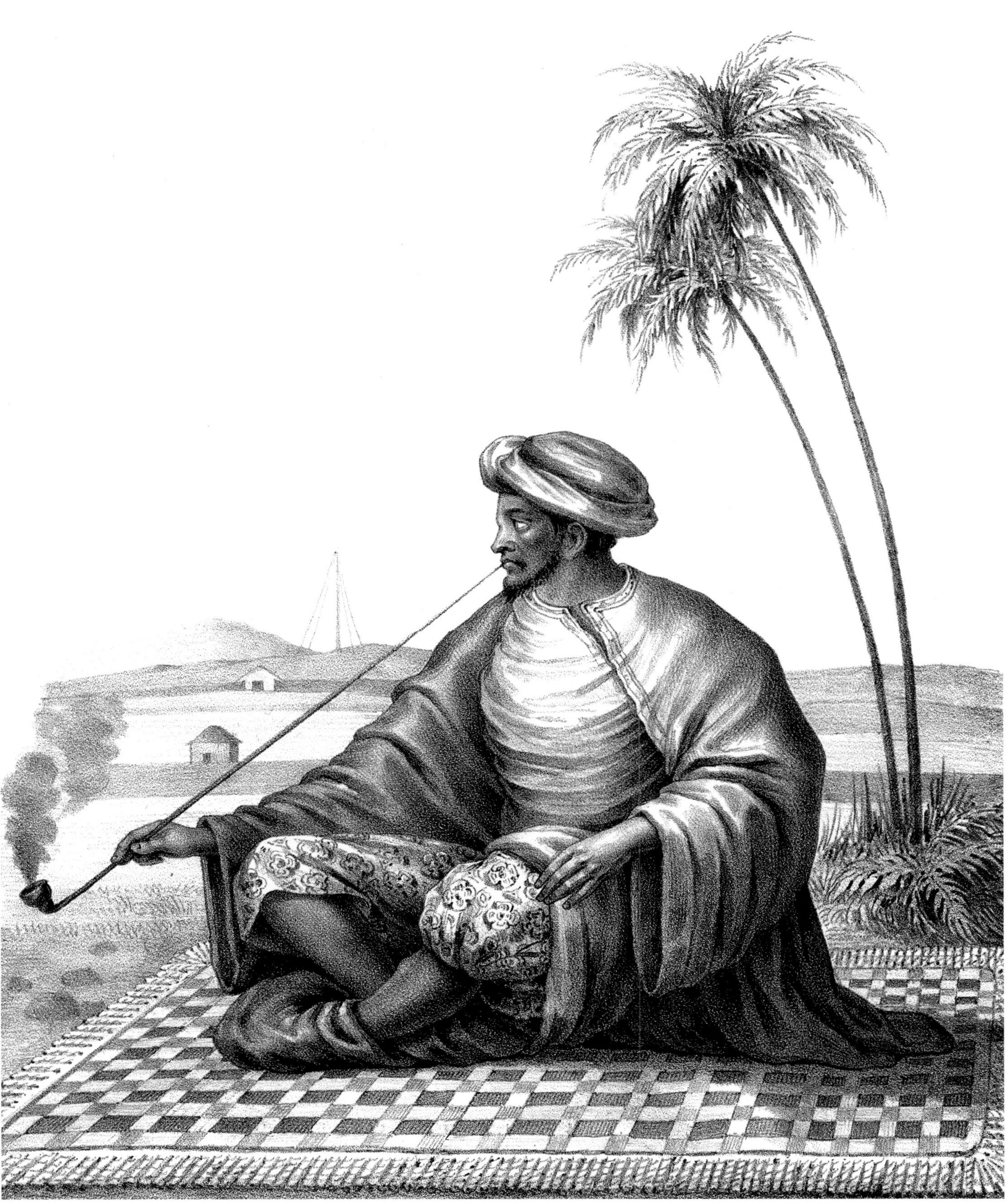

Cochin-Chinese official (present-day Vietnam), 1840

Chinesischer Beamter aus Cochinchina (heute Vietnam), 1840

Funzionario cocincinese (attualmente Vietnam), 1840

Fonctionnaire de Cochinchine (actuel Vietnam), vers 1840

Funcionario de Cochinchina (actual Vietnam), 1840

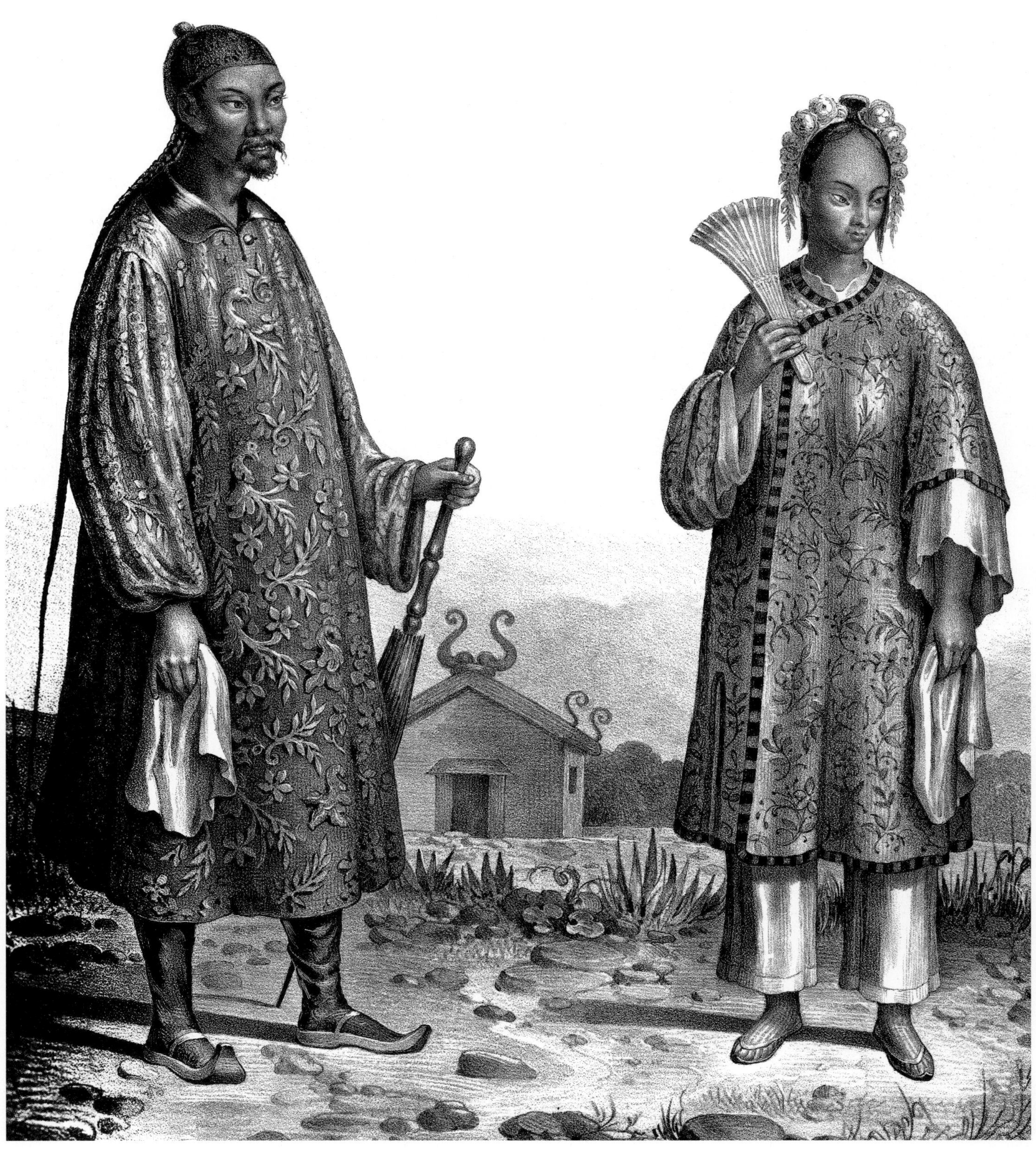

Aristocratic couple, c. 1840

Aristokratenpaar, um 1840

Coppia aristocratica, ca. 1840

Couple d'aristocrates, vers 1840

Pareja aristocrática, alrededor del año 1840

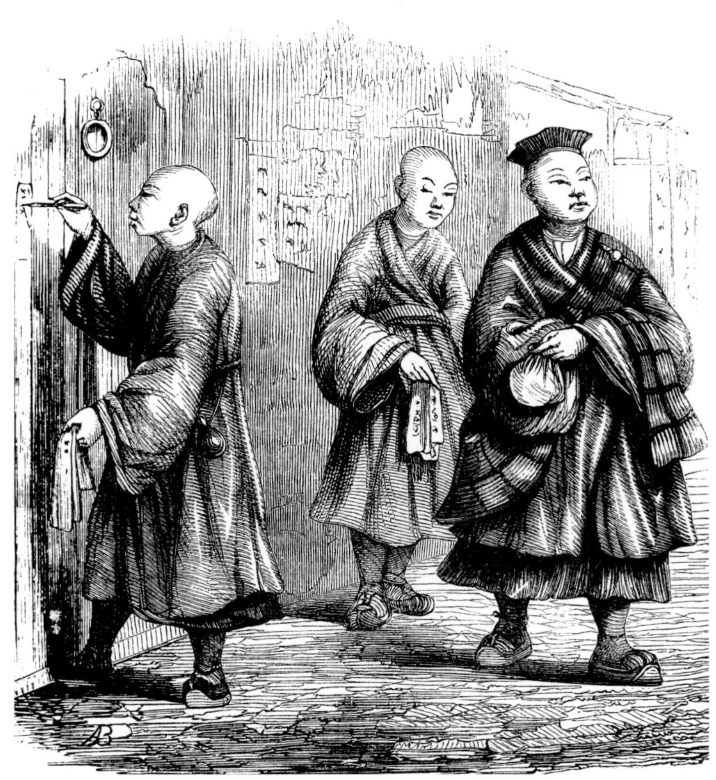

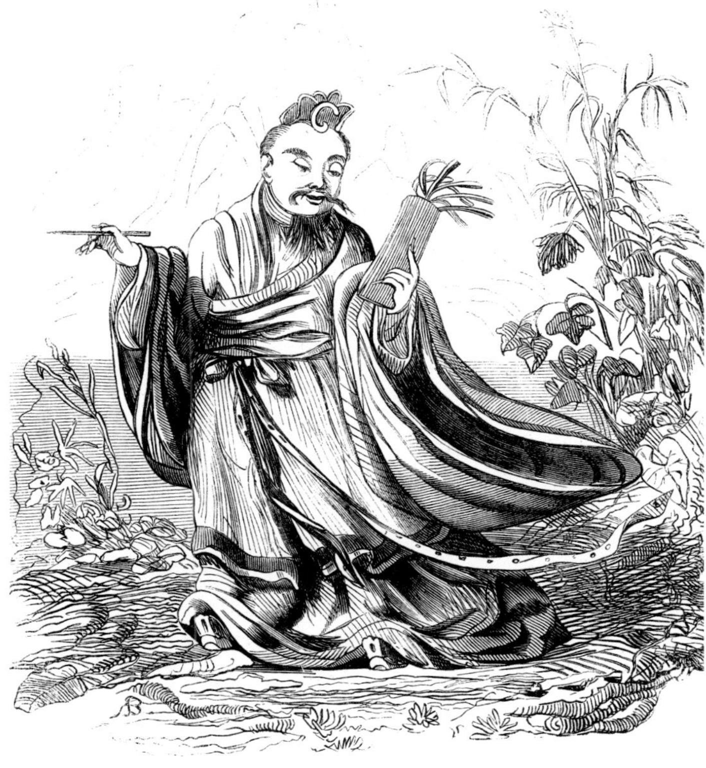

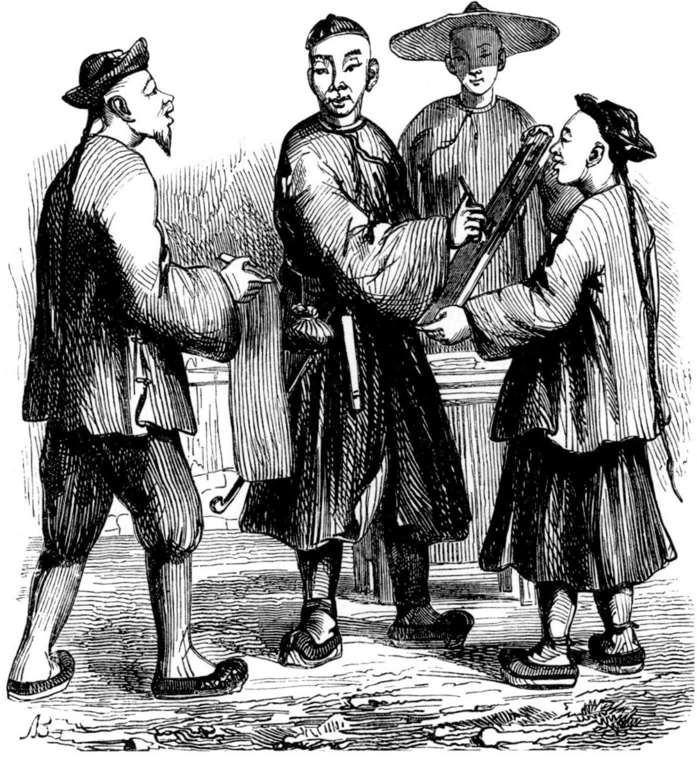

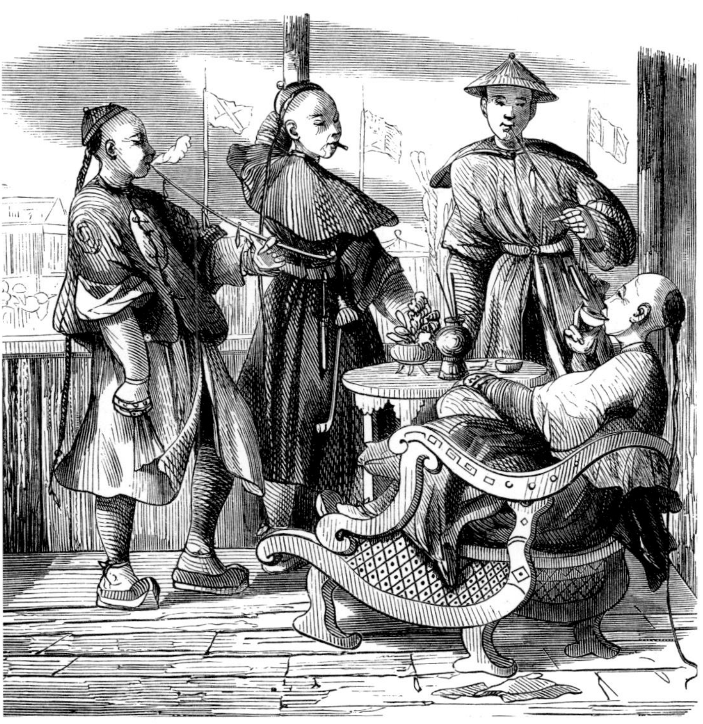

Chinese male dress, c. 1850

Chinesisches Männergewand, um 1850

Abito maschile cinese, ca. 1850

Vêtements masculins chinois, vers 1850

Trajes chinos de hombre, hacia 1850

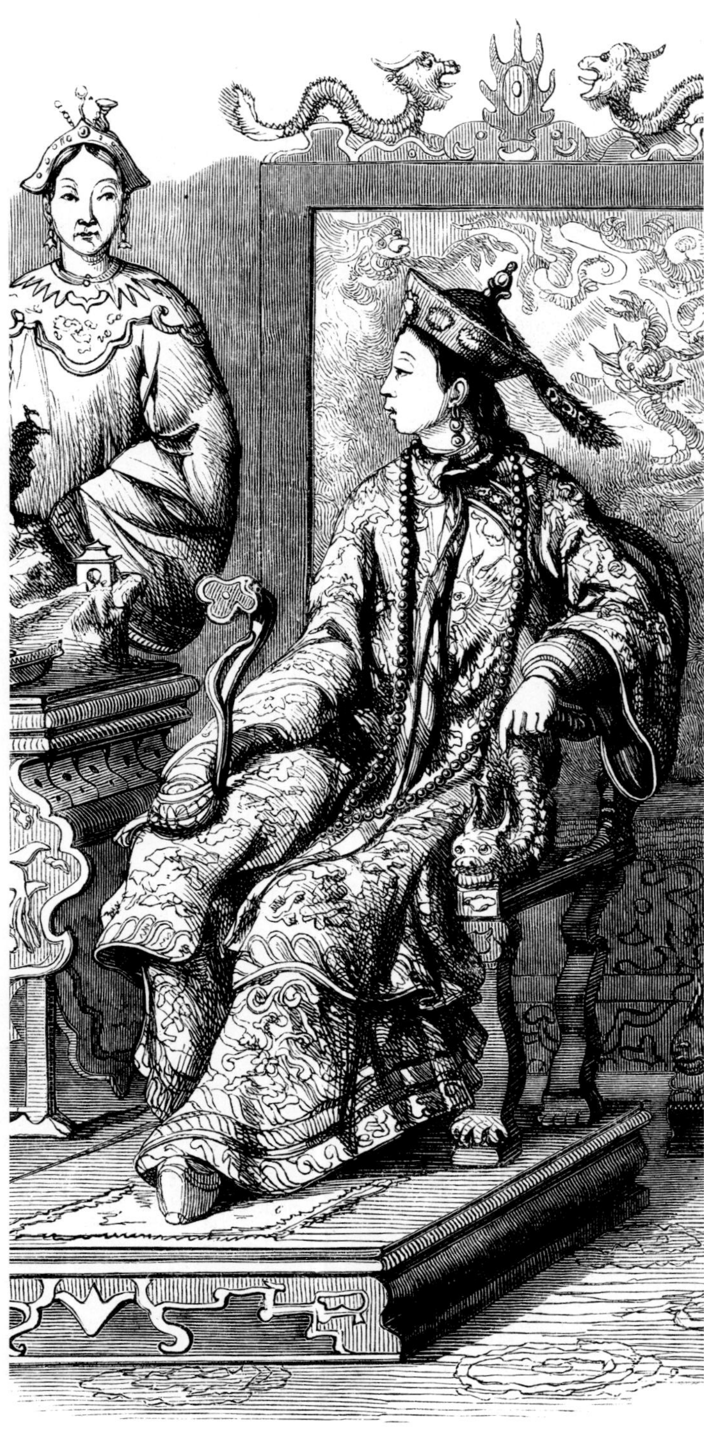

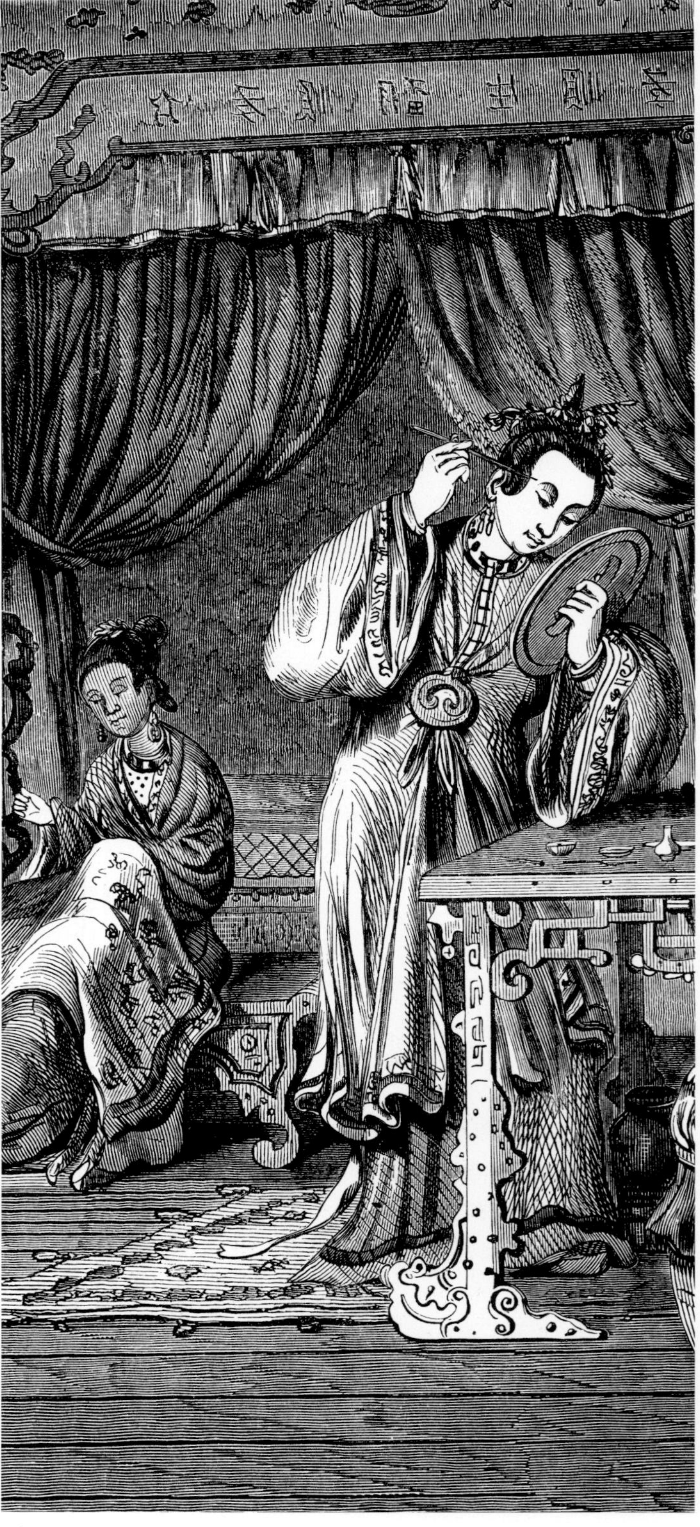

Chinese aristocrats, c. 1840

Chinesische Aristokraten, um 1840

Aristocratici cinesi, ca. 1840

Aristocrates chinois, vers 1840

Aristócratas chinos, alrededor del año 1840

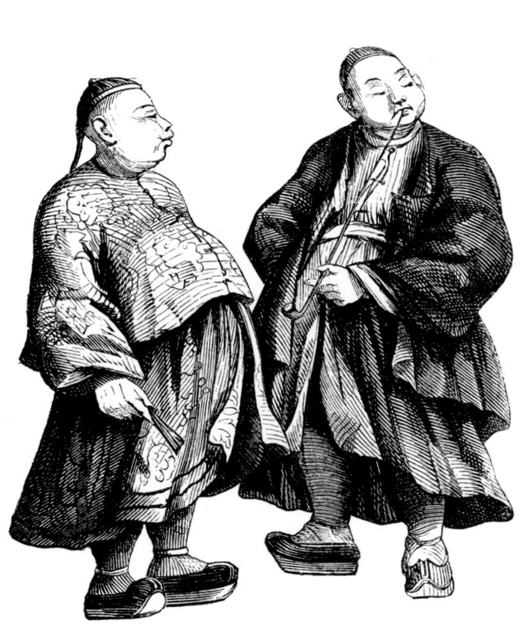

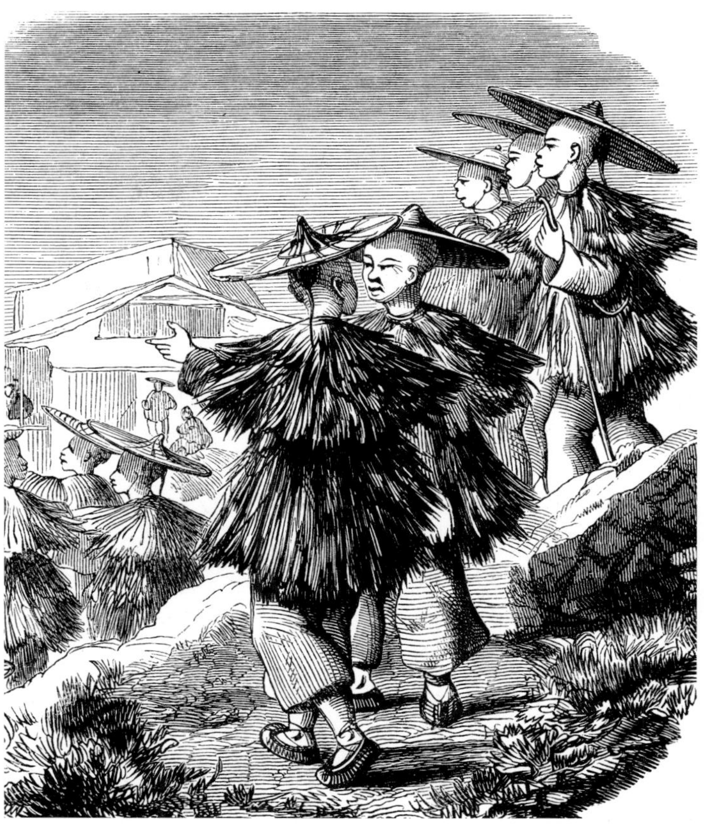

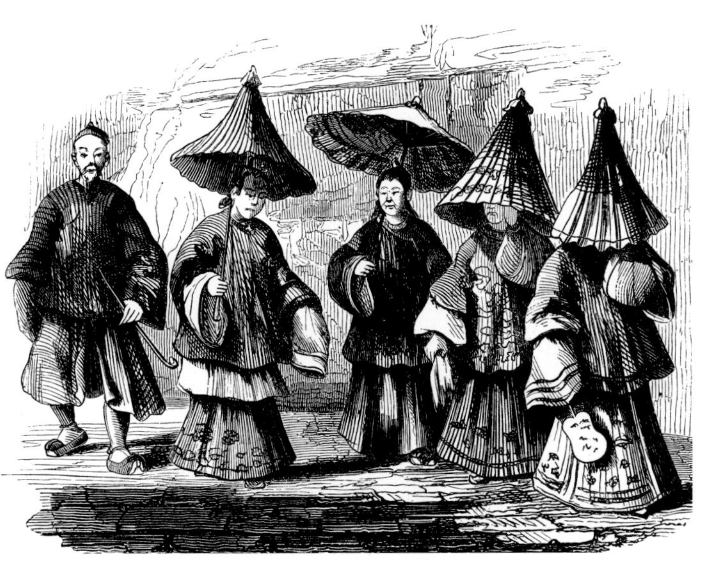

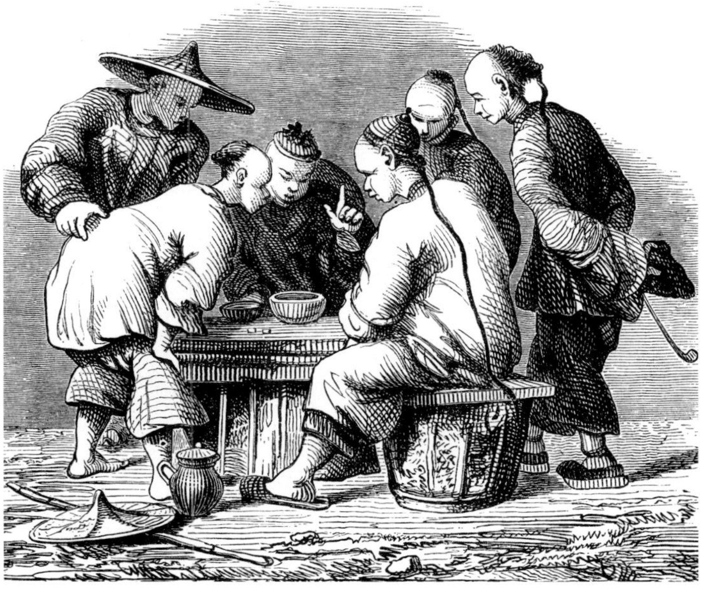

Various types of Chinese dress, c. 1850

Verschiedene Typen chinesischer Kleidung, um 1850

Vari tipi di abiti cinesi, ca. 1850

Divers types de vêtements chinois, vers 1850

Diversos tipos de trajes chinos, hacia 1850

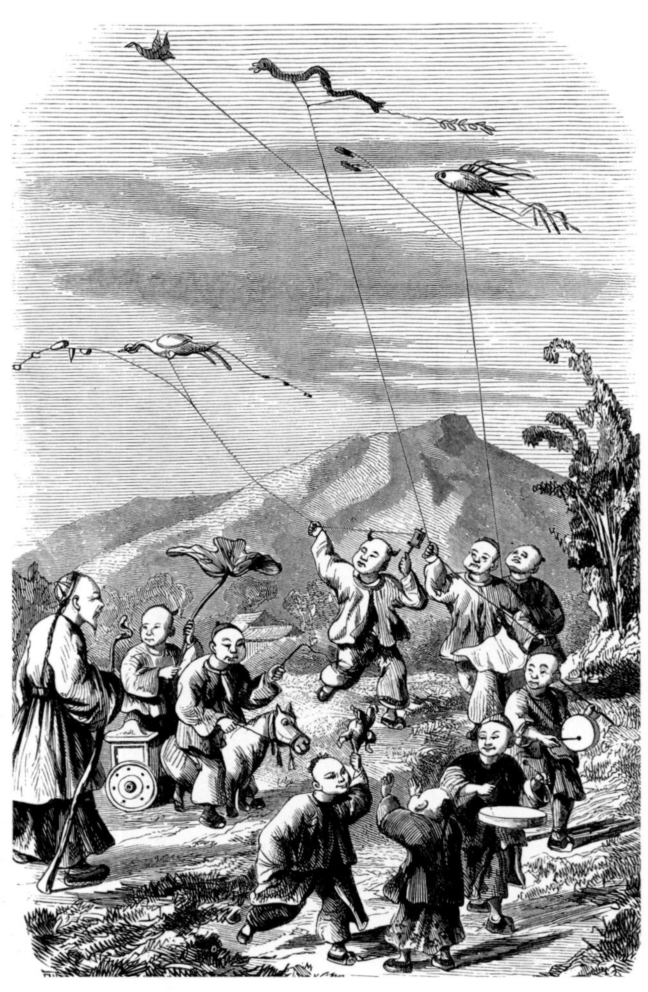

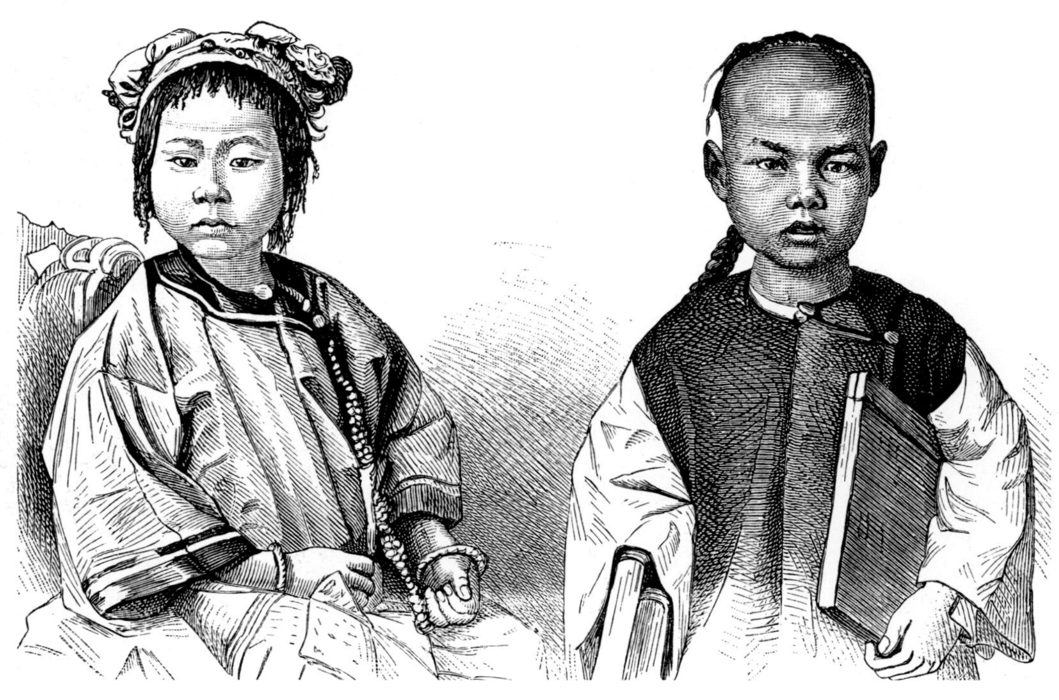

Chinese children

Chinesische Kinder

Bambini cinesi

Petits chinois

Niños chinos

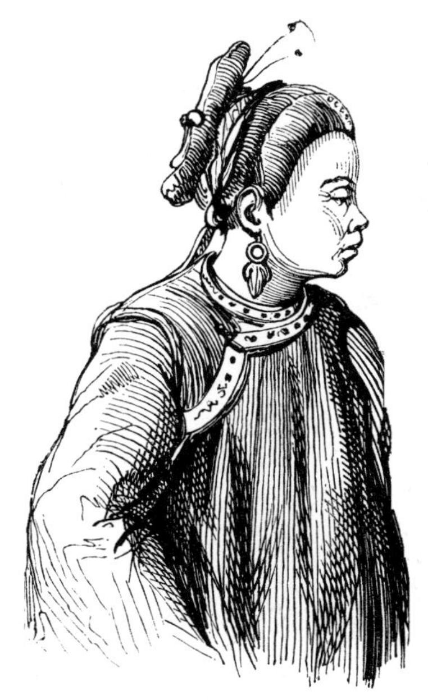

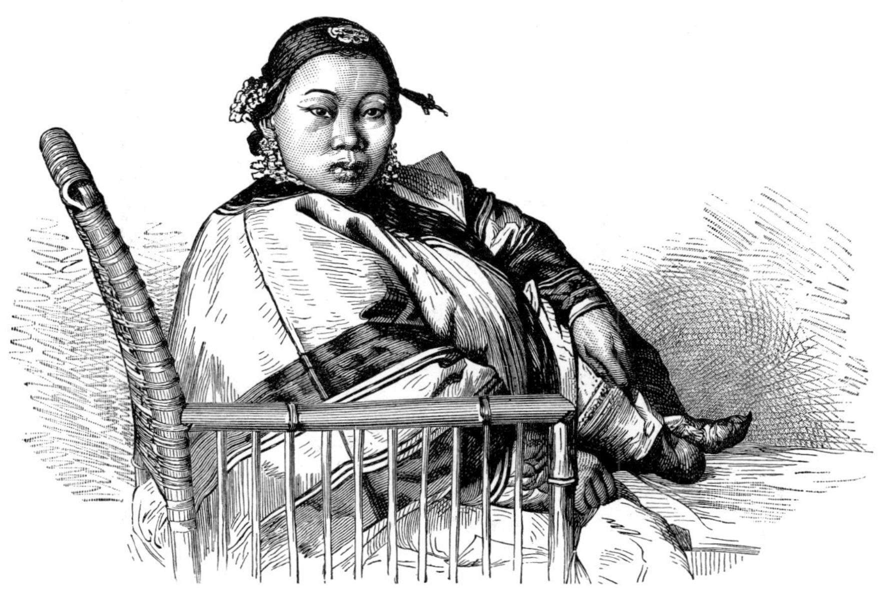

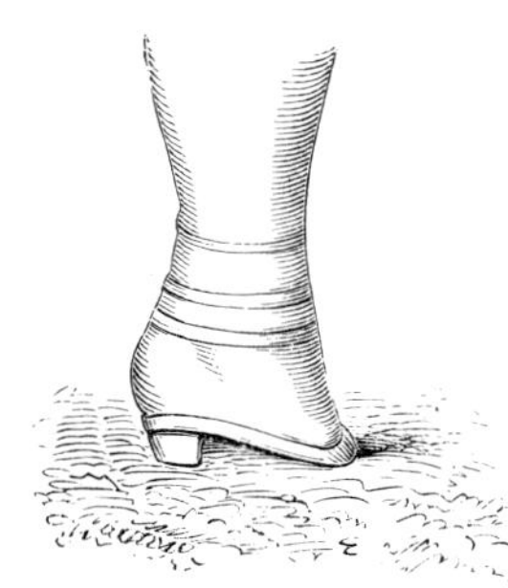

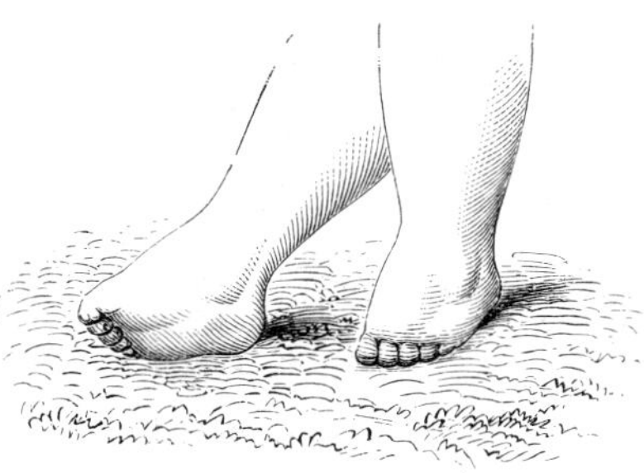

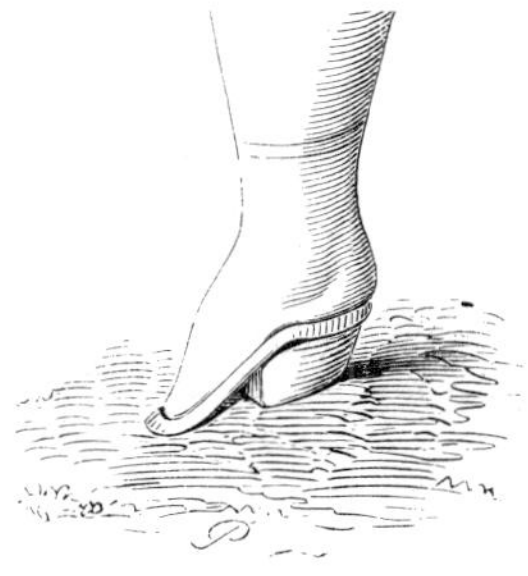

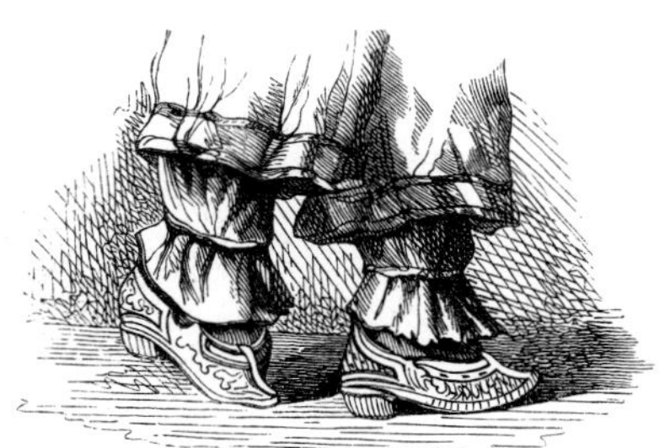

a	Chinese lady, 1880	Chinesische Frau, 1880	Donna cinese, 1880	Femme chinoise, 1880	Mujer china, 1880
b	Lady with bound feet, c. 1870	Frau mit eingebundenen Füßen, um 1870	Donna con i piedi fasciati, ca. 1870	Femme aux pieds liés, vers 1870	Mujer con los pies vendados, hacia 1870
c	Bound feet and shoes, 1900	Eingebundene Füße und Schuhe, 1900	Piedi fasciati e scarpe, 1900	Pieds et chaussures liés, 1900	Pies vendados y zapatos, 1900

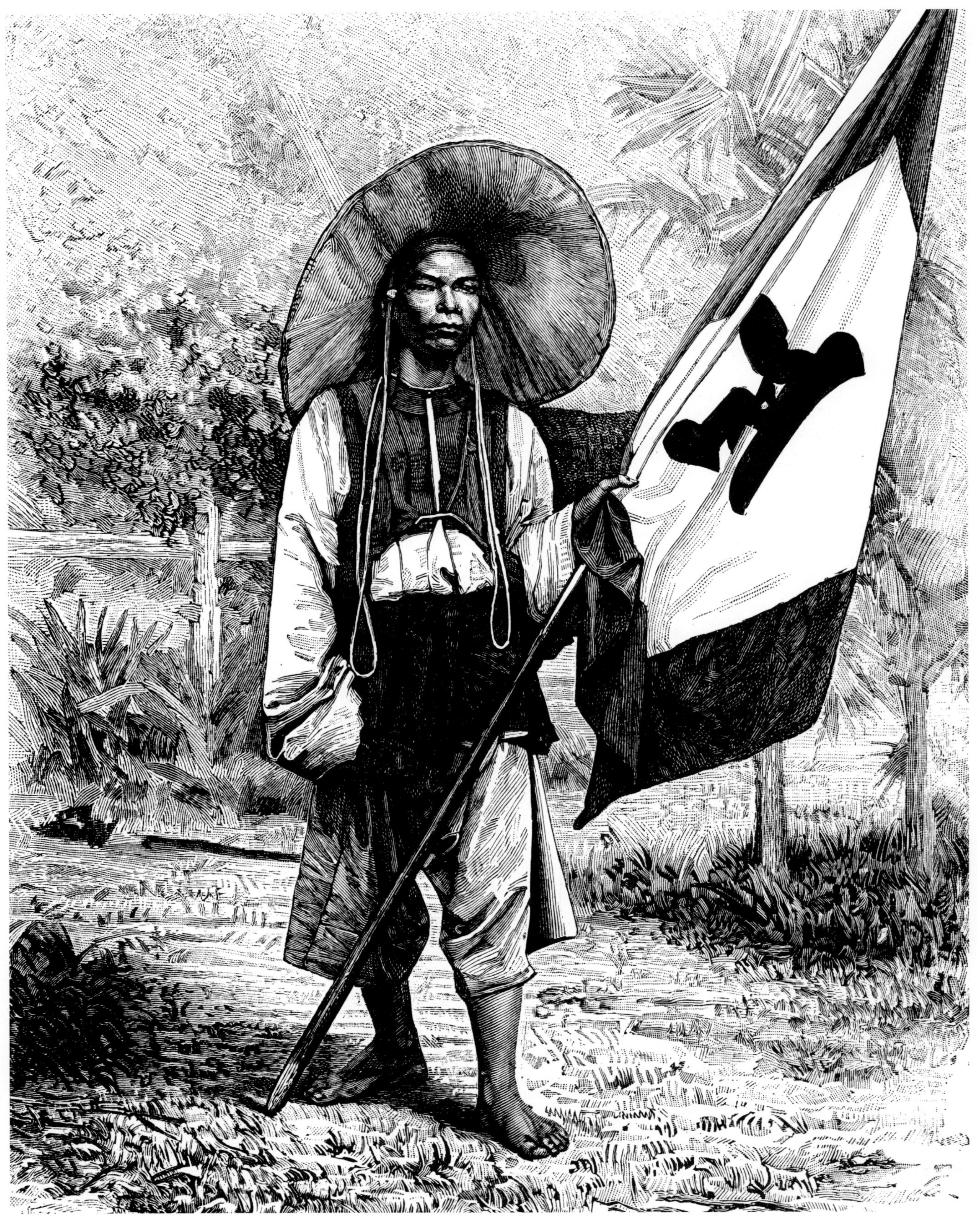

Soldier, c. 1900 | Soldat, um 1900 | Soldato, ca. 1900 | Soldat, vers 1900 | Soldado, hacia 1900

China

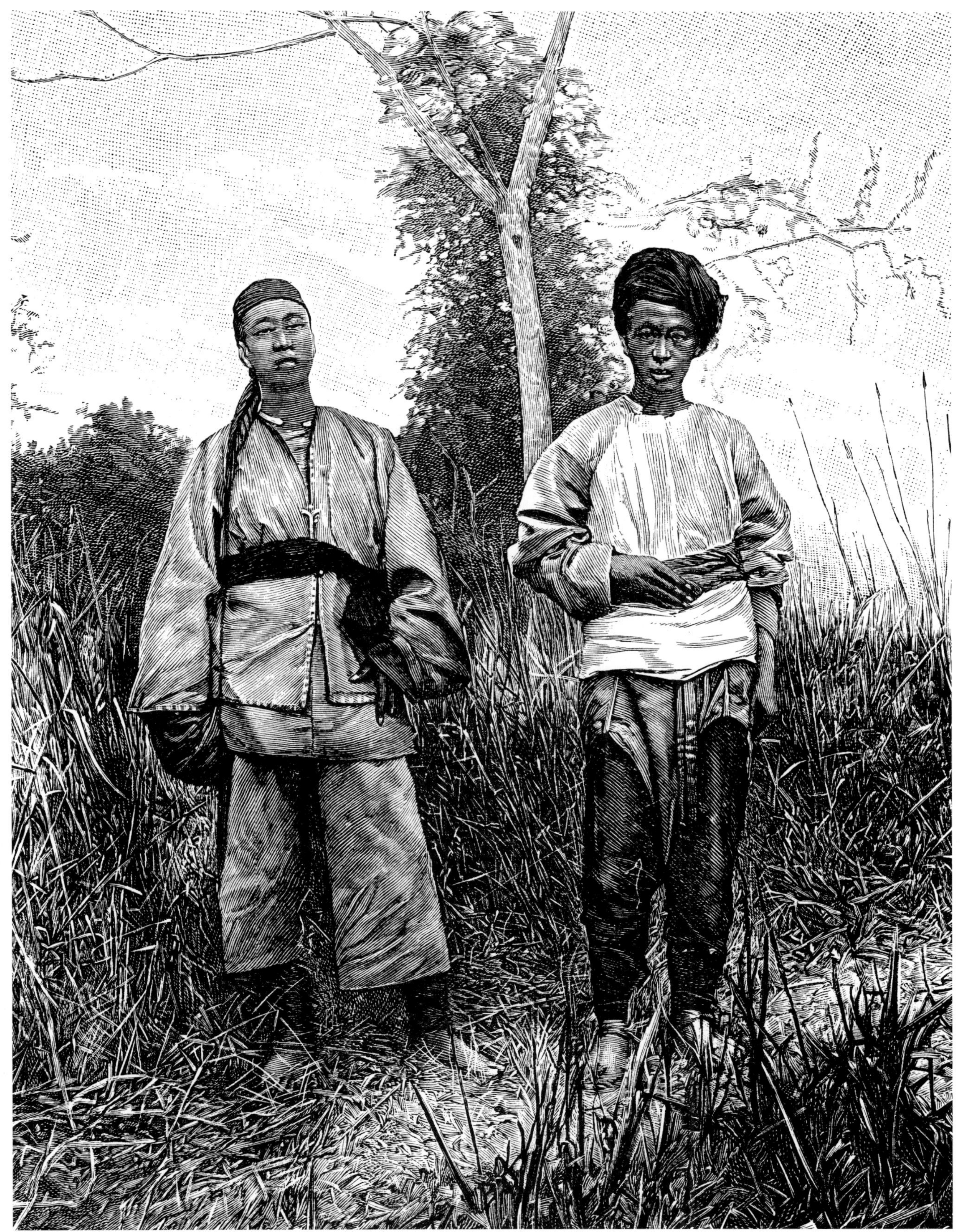

Chinese pirates, c. 1900

Chinesische Piraten, um 1900

Pirati cinesi, ca. 1900

Pirates chinois, vers 1900

Piratas chinos, hacia 1900

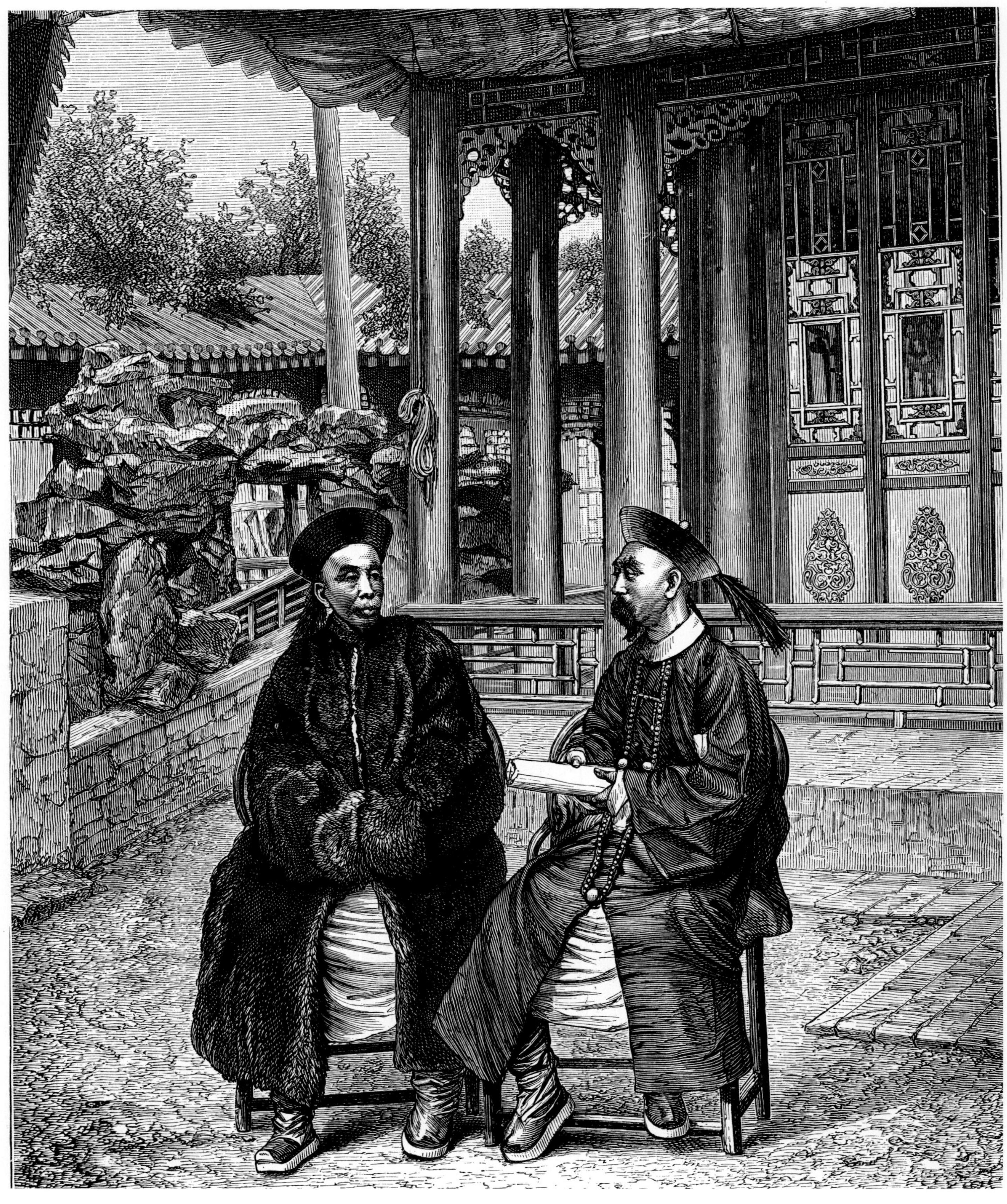

High Chinese officials, 1900

Hohe chinesische Beamte, 1900

Alti funzionari cinesi, 1900

Hauts fonctionnaires chinois, 1900

Altos funcionarios chinos, 1900

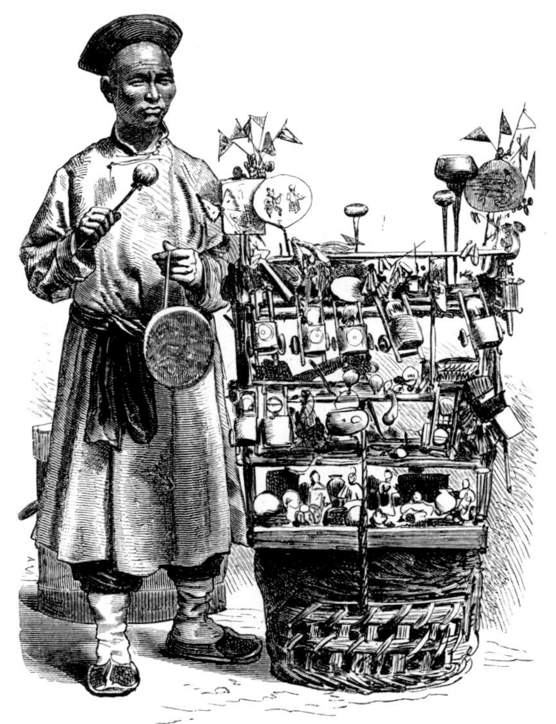

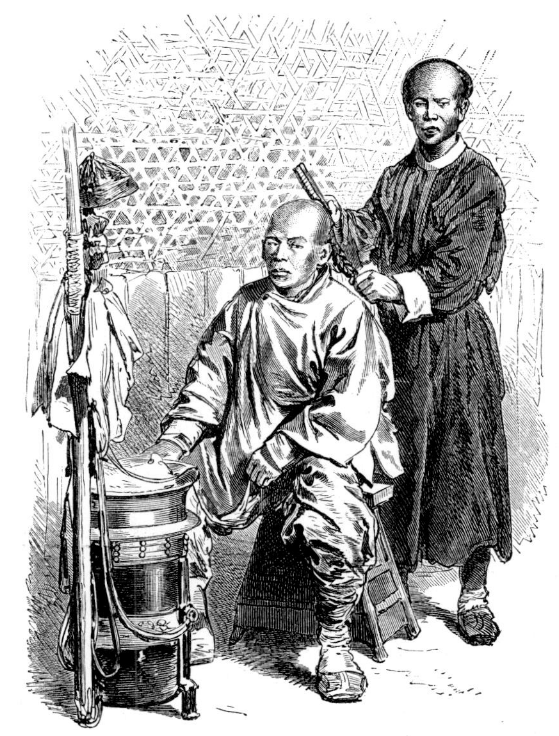

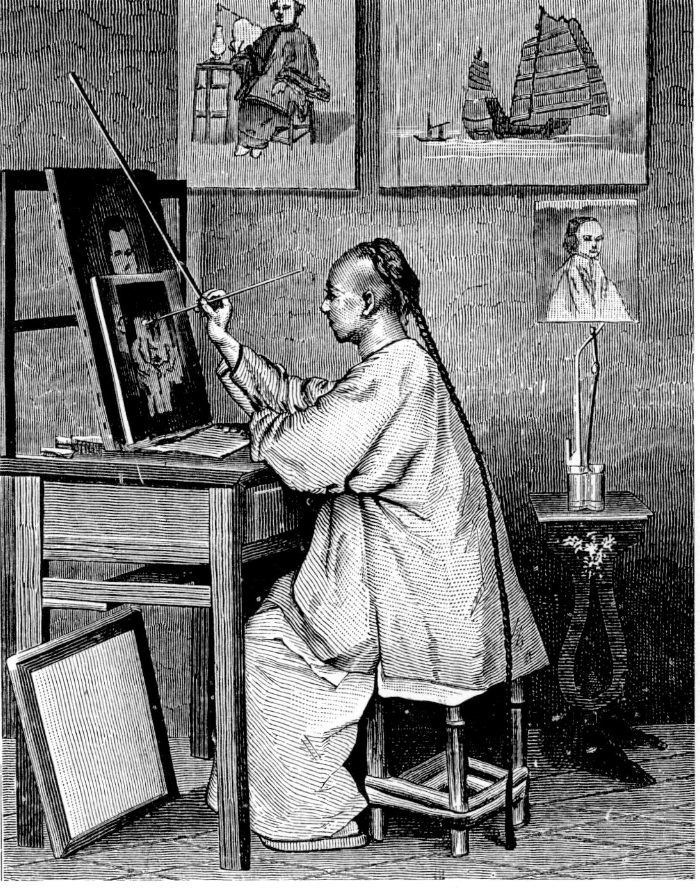

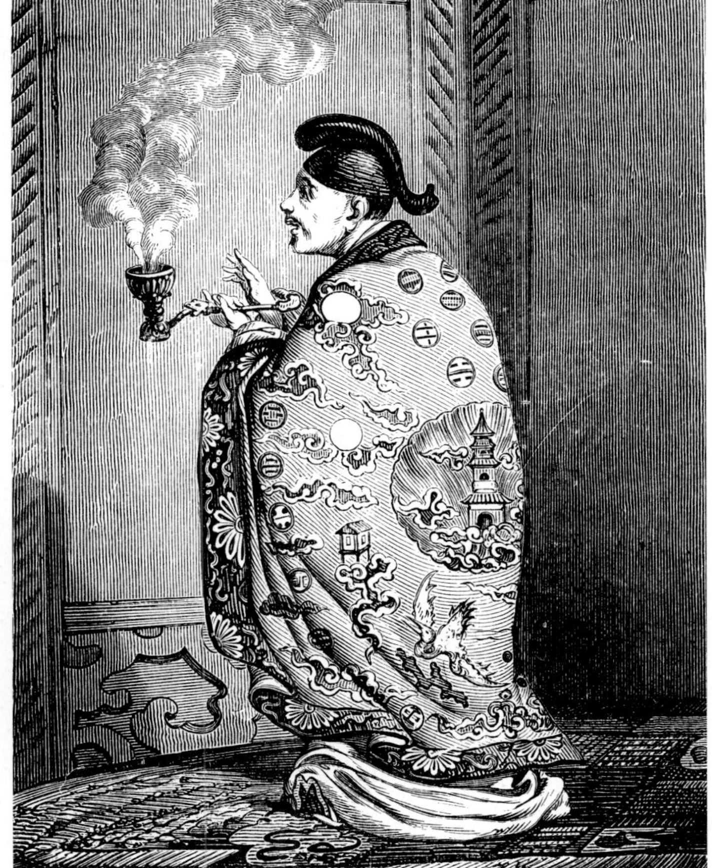

a	Toy merchant	Spielzeughändler	Mercante di giocattoli	Marchand de jouets	Comerciante de juguetes
b	Barber	Barbier	Barbiere	Barbier	Barbero
c	Painter	Maler	Pittore	Peintre	Pintor
d	Priest	Priester	Sacerdote	Prêtre	Sacerdote

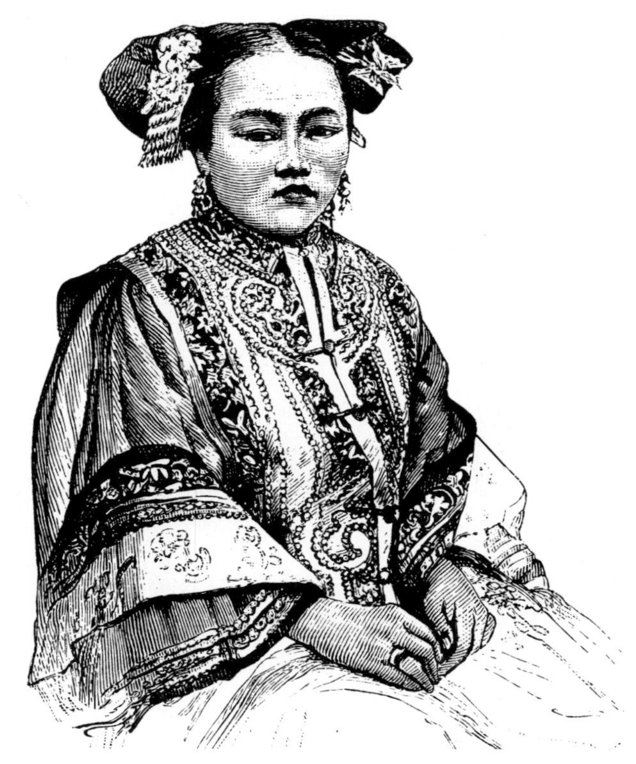

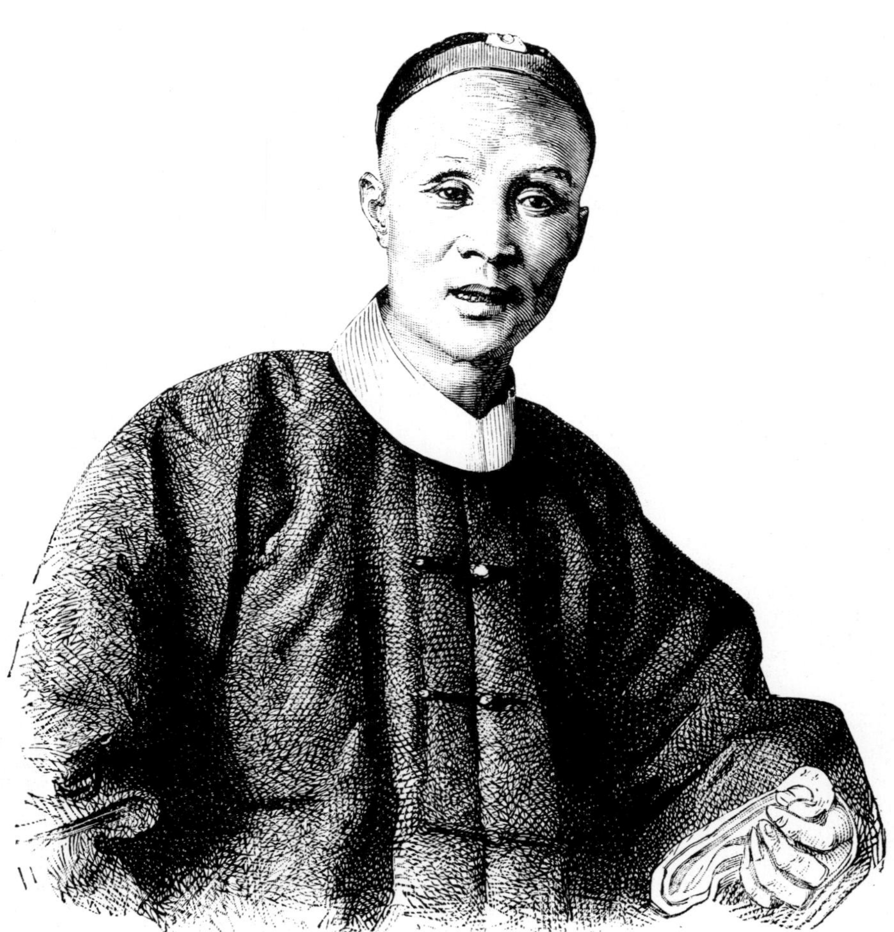

a	Manchu lady	Frau aus Manchu	Donna manciù	Femme mandchoue	Dama manchú
b	Chinese scholar, c. 1870	Chinesischer Schüler, um 1870	Erudito cinese, ca. 1870	Érudit chinois, vers 1870	Erudito chino, hacia 1870

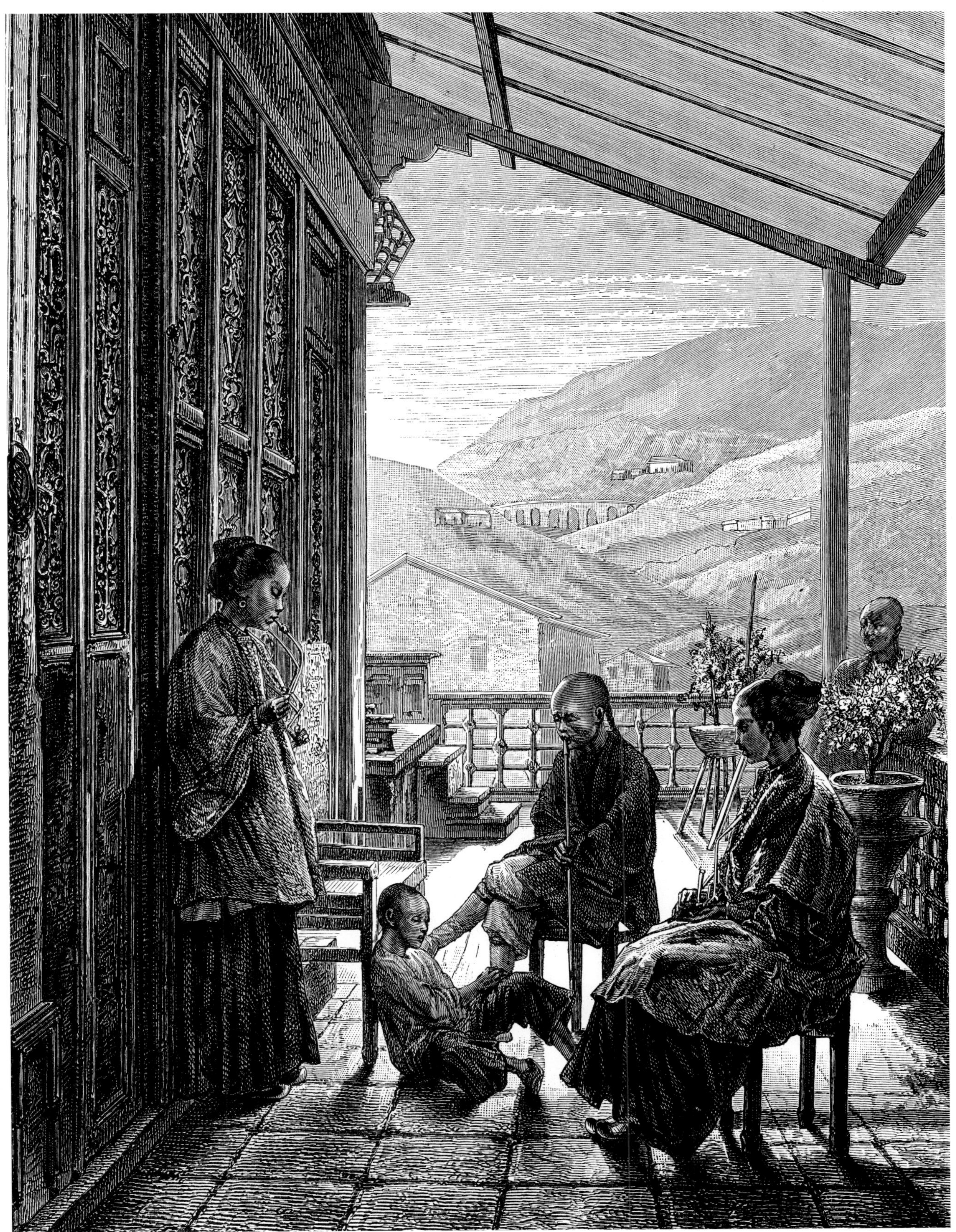

Chinese family, 1900 | Chinesische Familie, 1900 | Famiglia cinese, 1900 | Famille chinoise, 1900 | Familia china, 1900

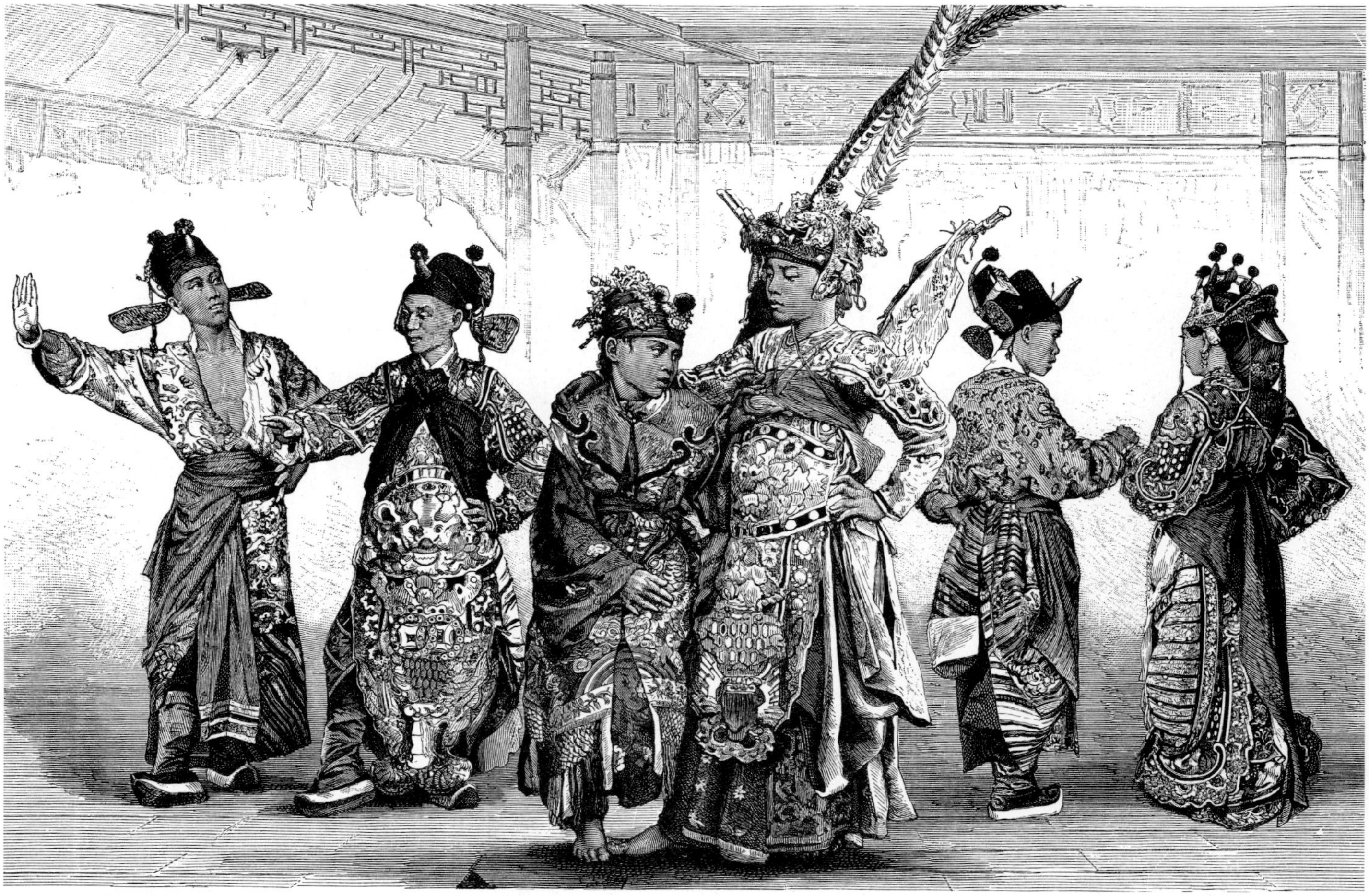

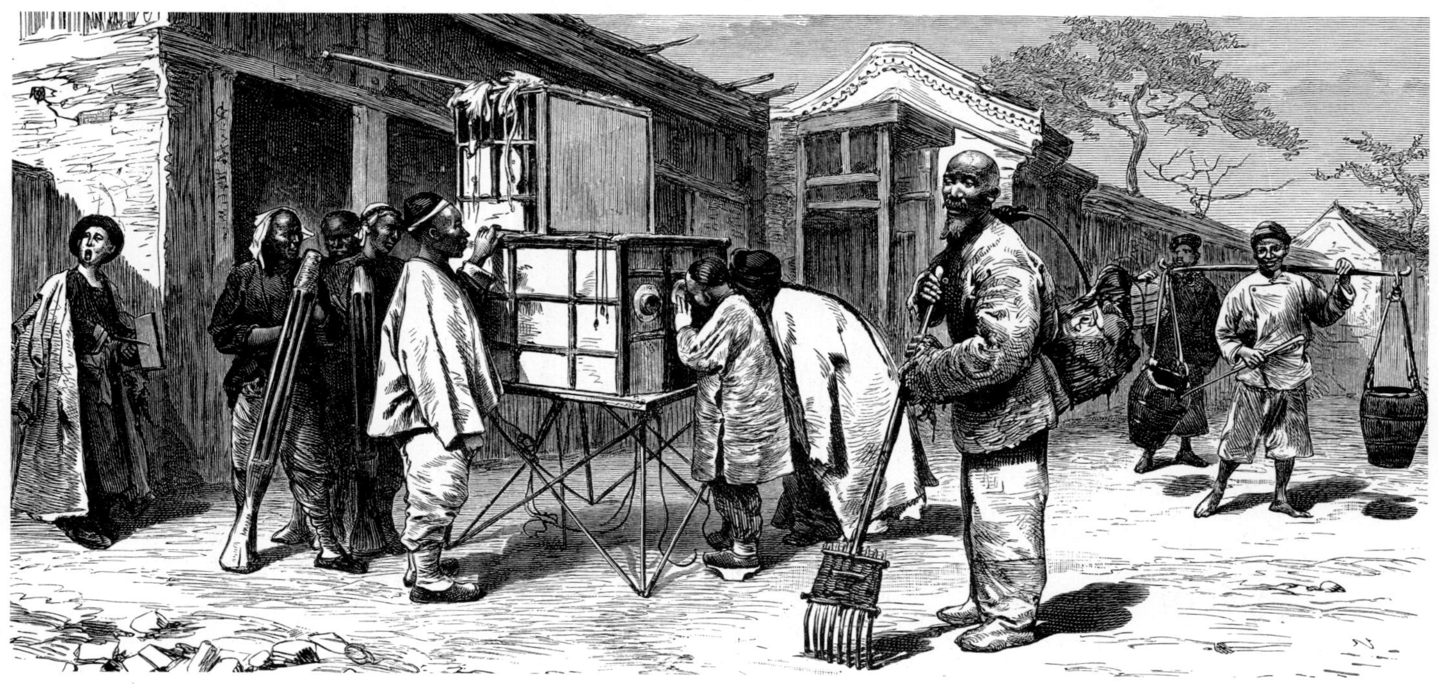

a	Chinese actors, 1900	Chinesische Schauspieler, 1900	Attori cinesi, 1900	Acteurs chinois, 1900	Actores chinos, 1900
b	Street scene in Beijing, 1900	Straßenszene in Bejing, 1900	Scena di strada a Bejing, 1900	Scène de rue à Pékin, 1900	Una calle de Pekín, 1900

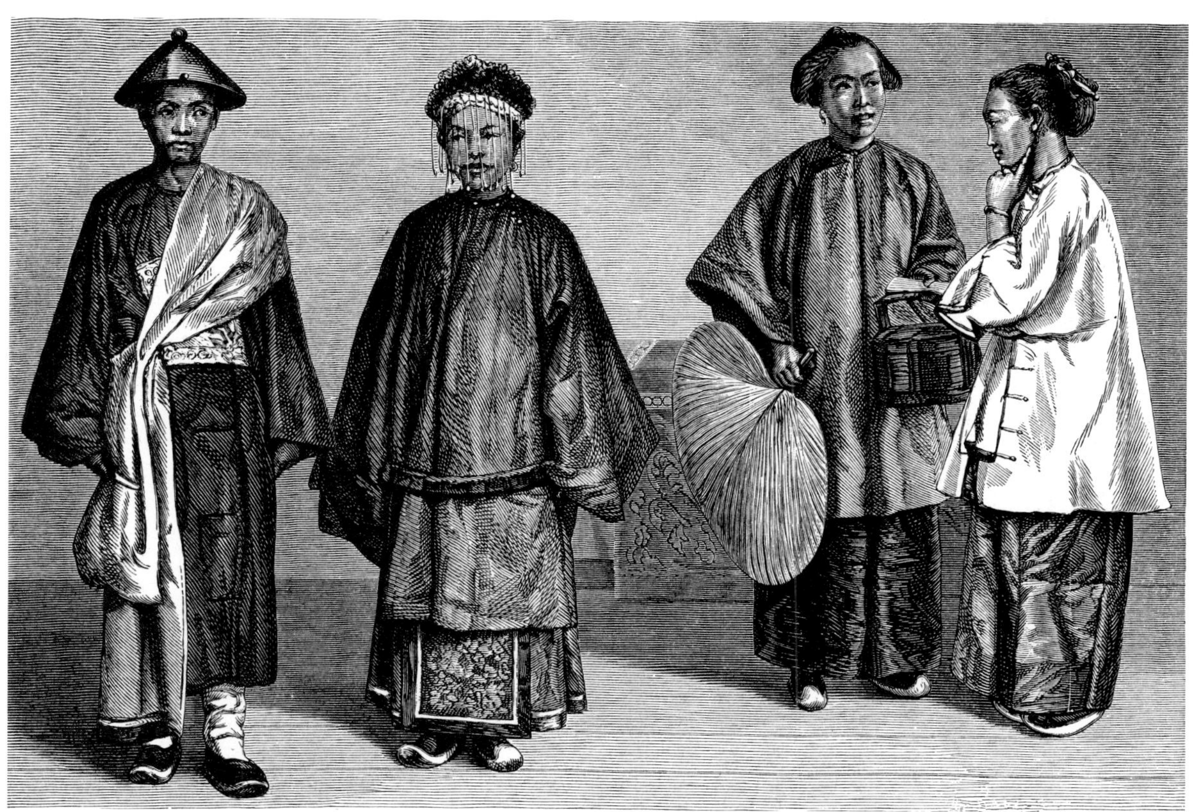

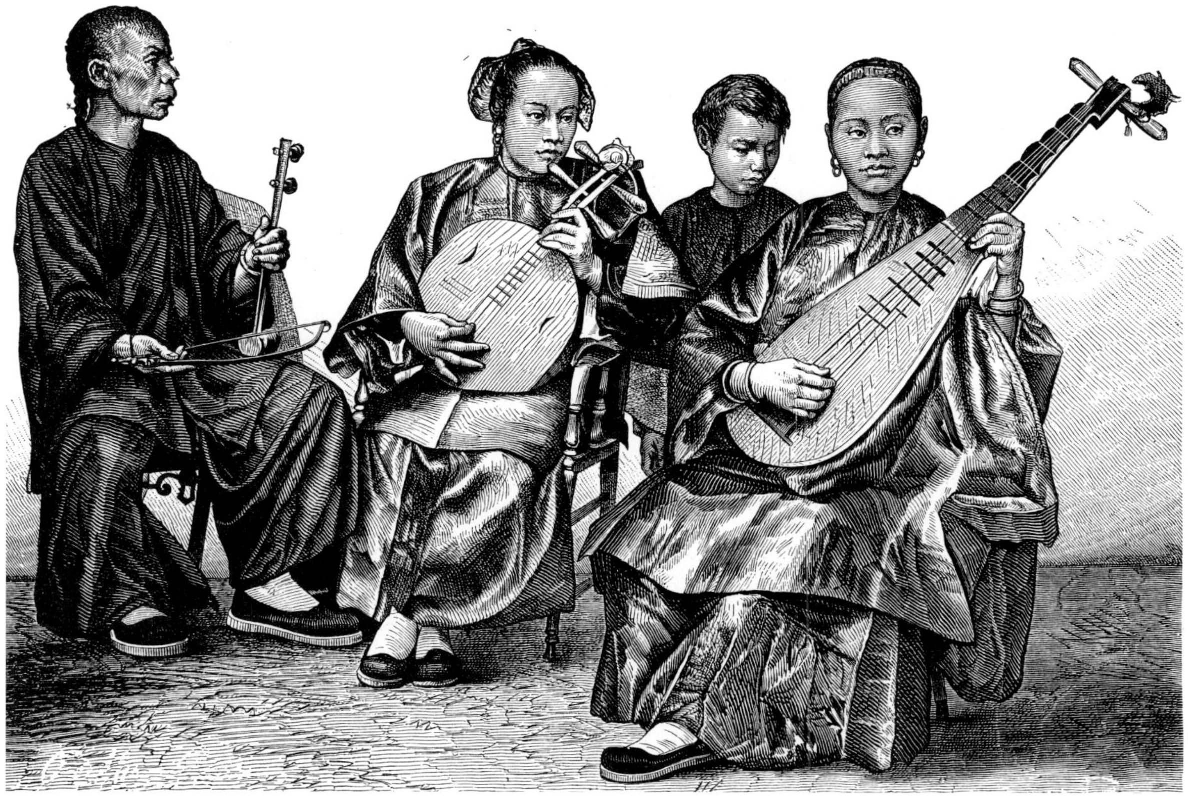

a	Bridal couple with servants, 1900	Brautpaar mit Bediensteten, 1900	Coppia di sposi con domestici, 1900	Couple de jeunes mariés et leurs serviteurs, 1900	Pareja de novios y sirvientes, 1900
b	Travelling musicians, 1900	Reisende Musikanten, 1900	Musicisti itineranti, 1900	Musiciens ambulants, 1900	Músicos itinerantes, 1900

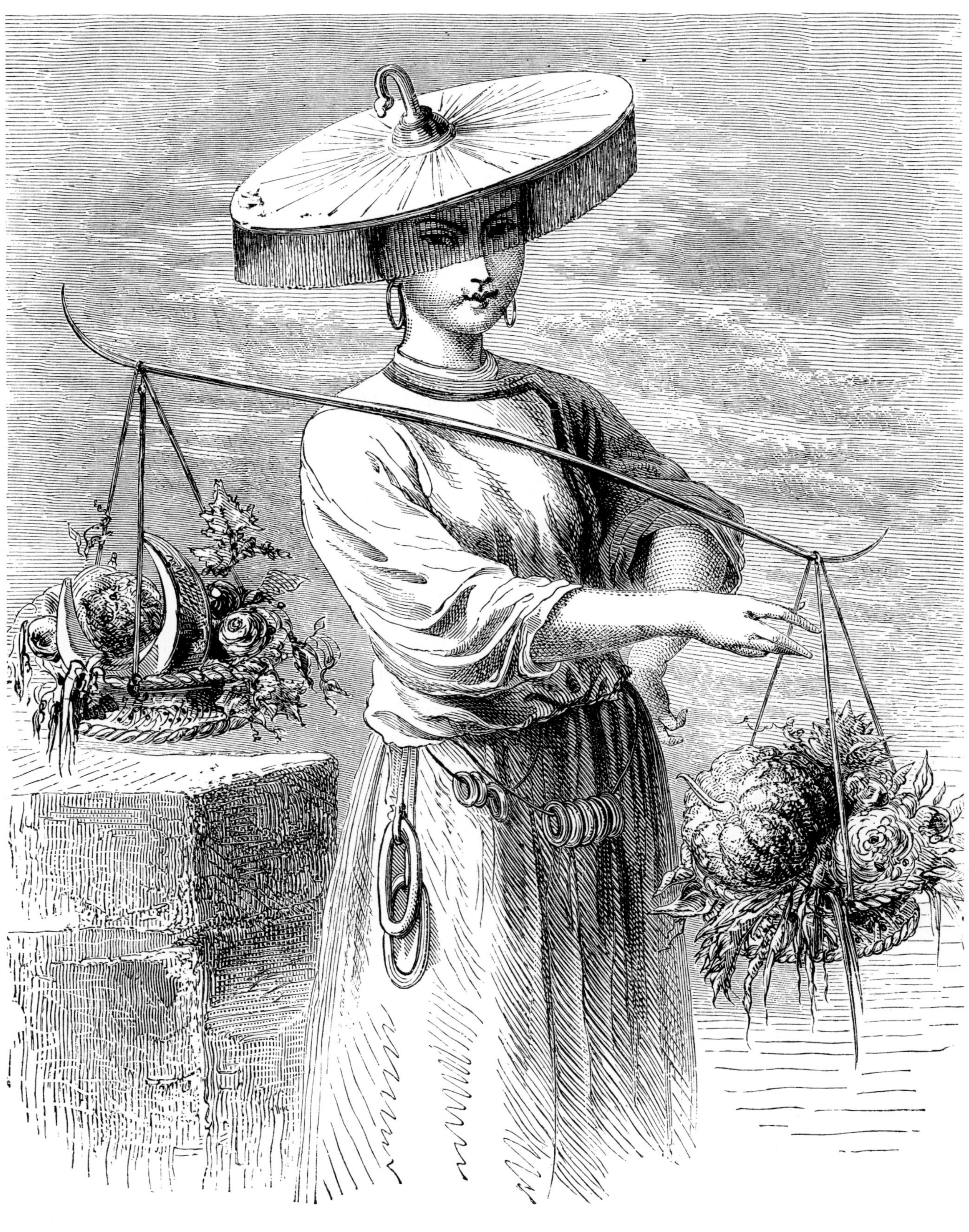

Chinese fruit seller, 1870

Chinesische Obstverkäuferin, 1870

Venditrice di frutta cinese, 1870

Marchande de fruits chinoise, 1870

Vendedora de fruta china, 1870

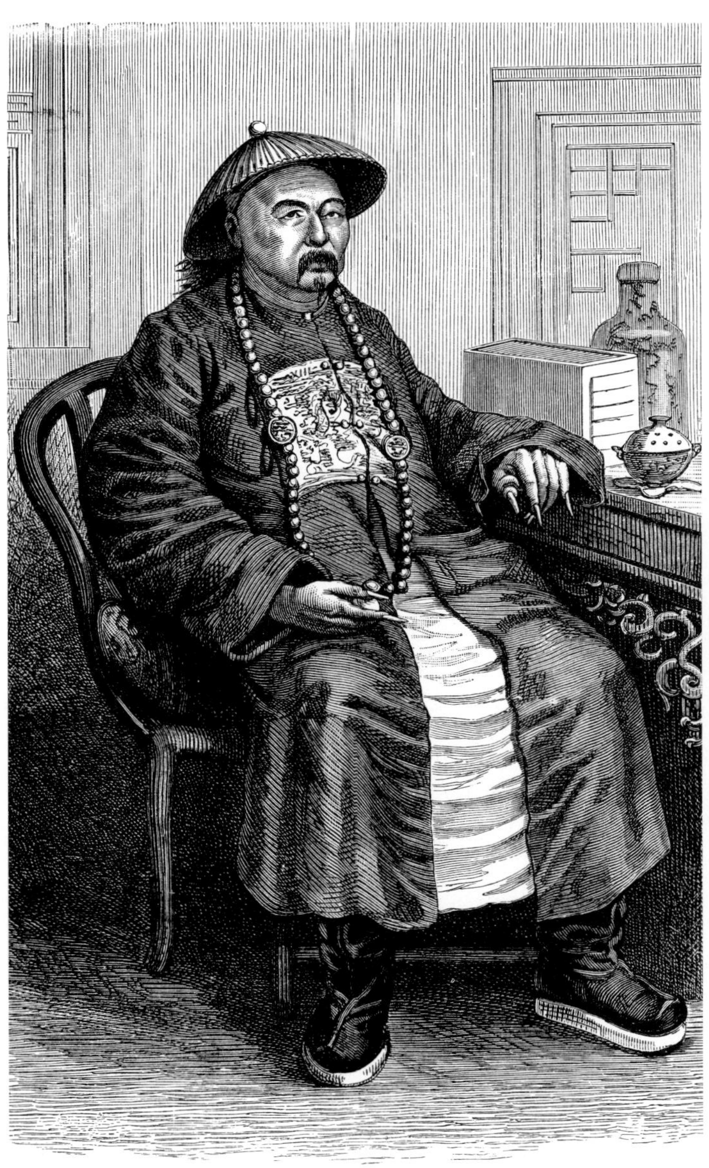

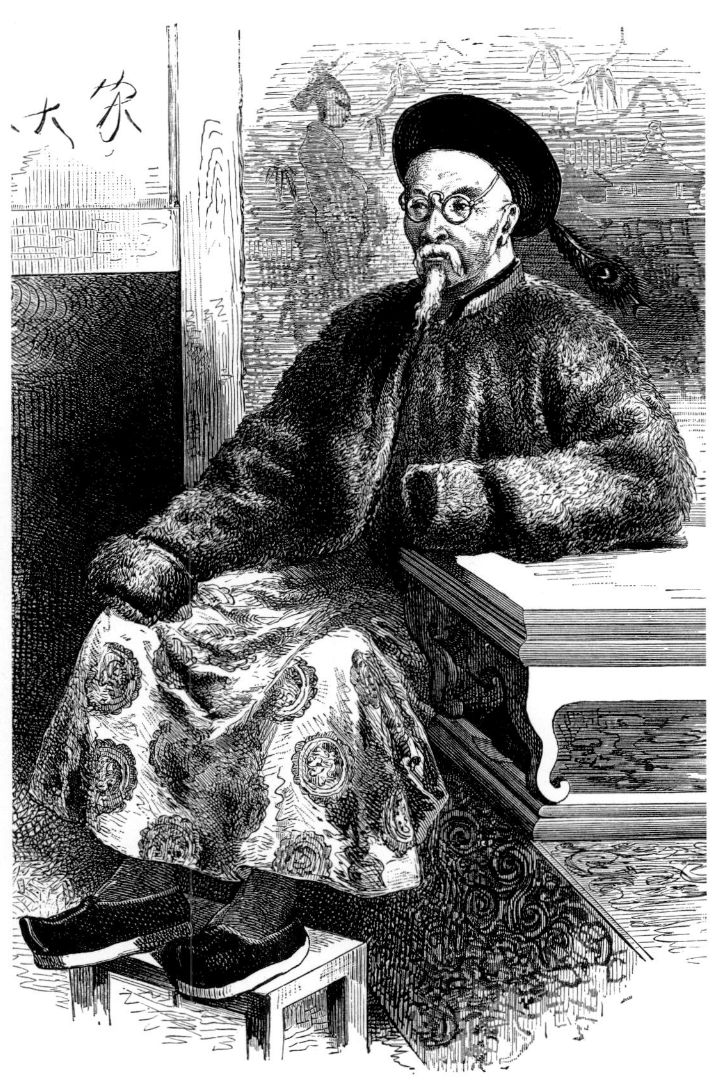

a	Governor of a province, 1900	Gouverneur einer Provinz, 1900	Governatore di una provincia, 1900	Gouverneur d'une province, 1900	Gobernador de una provincia, 1900
b	Mandarin, 1900	Mandarin, 1900	Mandarino, 1900	Mandarin, 1900	Mandarín, 1900

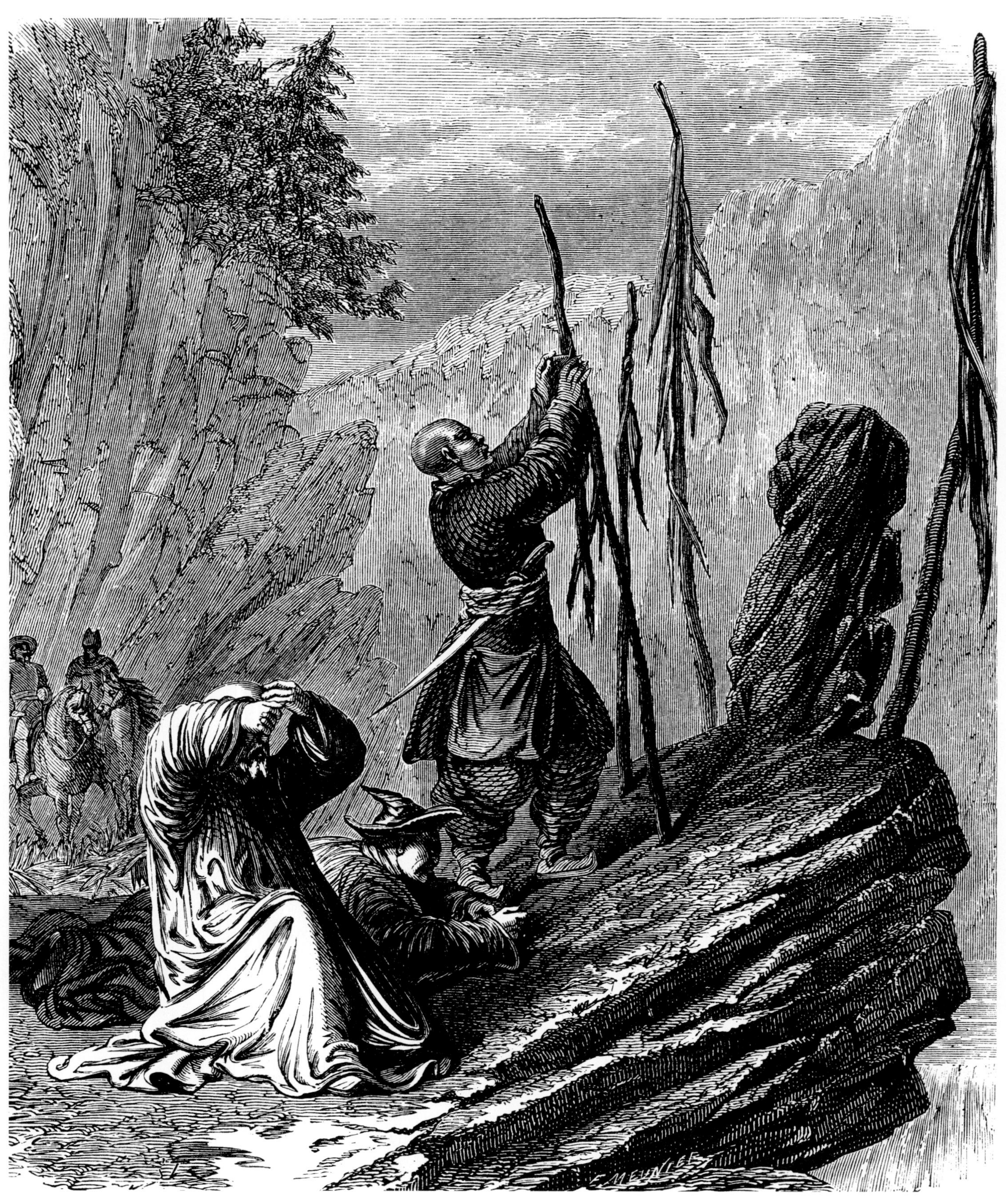

Mongolian devotees, c. 1860

Mongolische Verehrer, um 1860

Devoti mongoli, ca. 1860

Partisans mongoles, vers 1860

Devotos mongoles, alrededor del año 1860

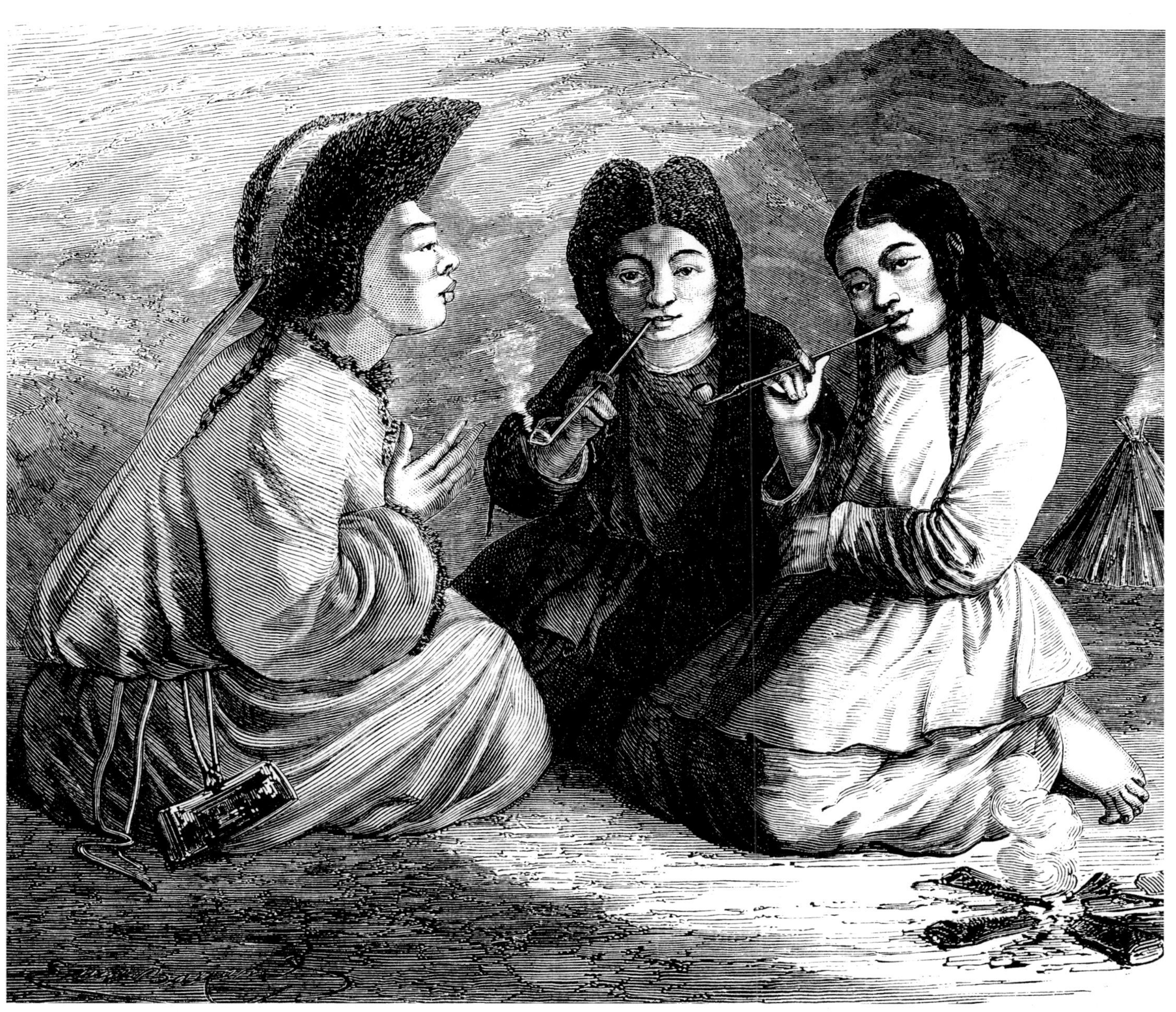

Mongolian family, c. 1860

Mongolische Familie, um 1860

Famiglia mongola, ca. 1860

Famille mongolienne, vers 1860

Familia mongola, 1860

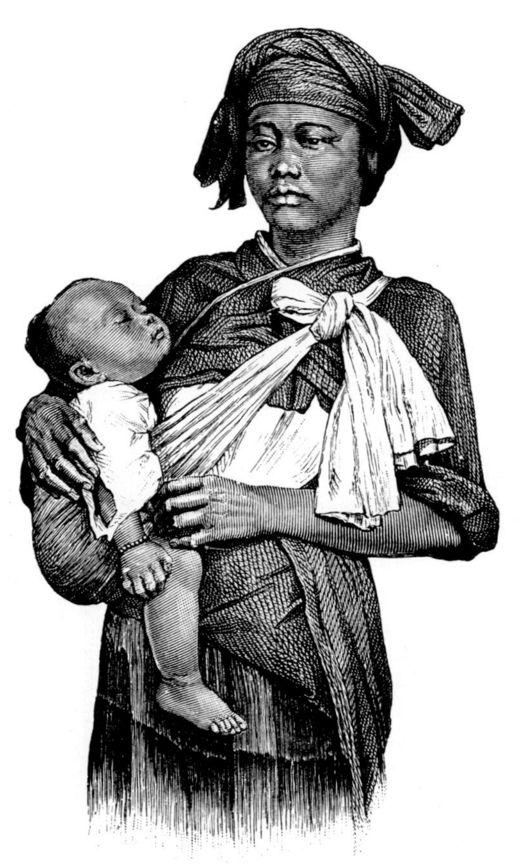

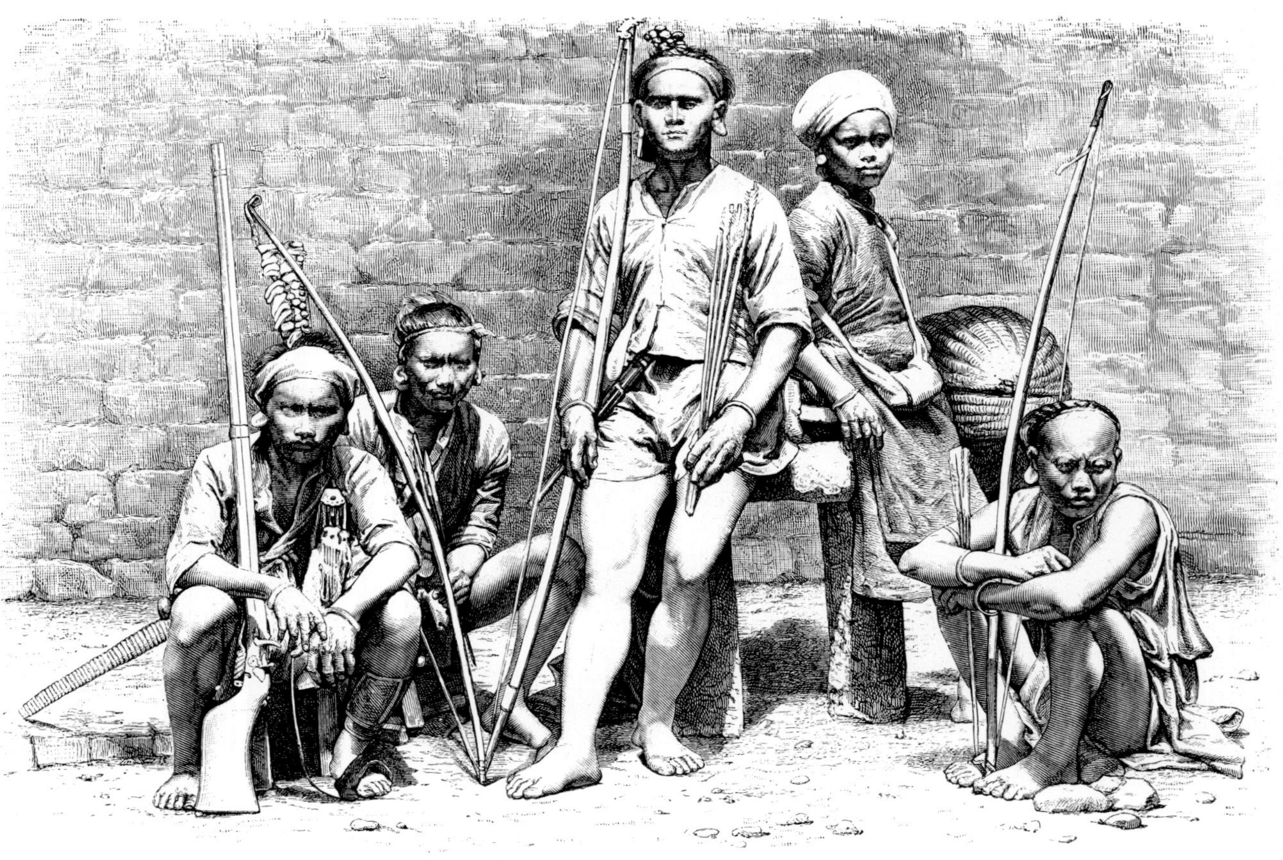

Natives of Taiwan, c. 1875

Einheimische aus Taiwan, um 1875

Indigeni di Taiwan, ca. 1875

Indigènes de Taïwan, vers 1875

Nativos de Taiwan, 1875

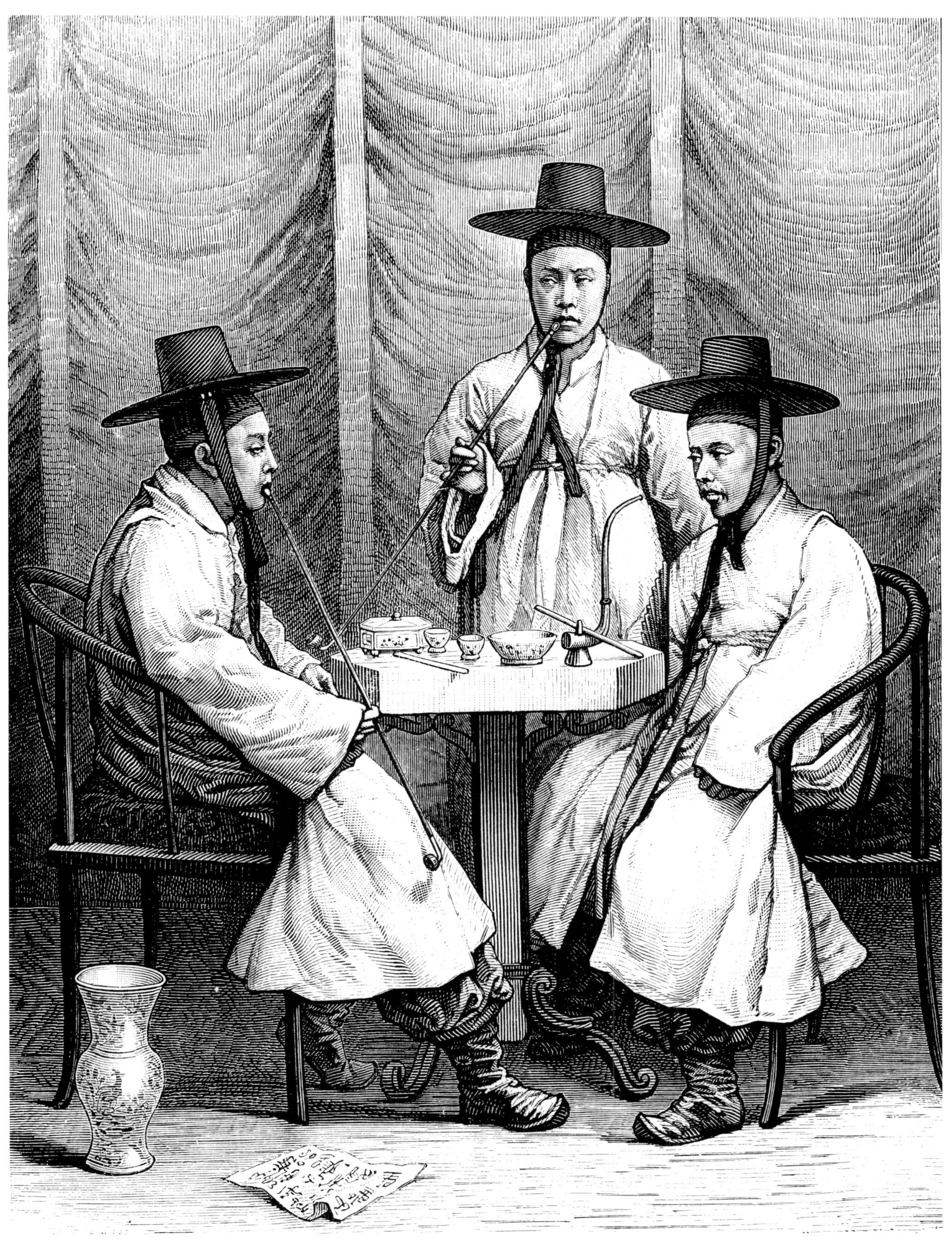

Korean gentlemen, c. 1870

Koreanische Edelmänner, um 1870

Gentiluomini coreani, ca. 1870

Gentilhommes coréens, vers 1870

Caballeros coreanos, alrededor del año 1870

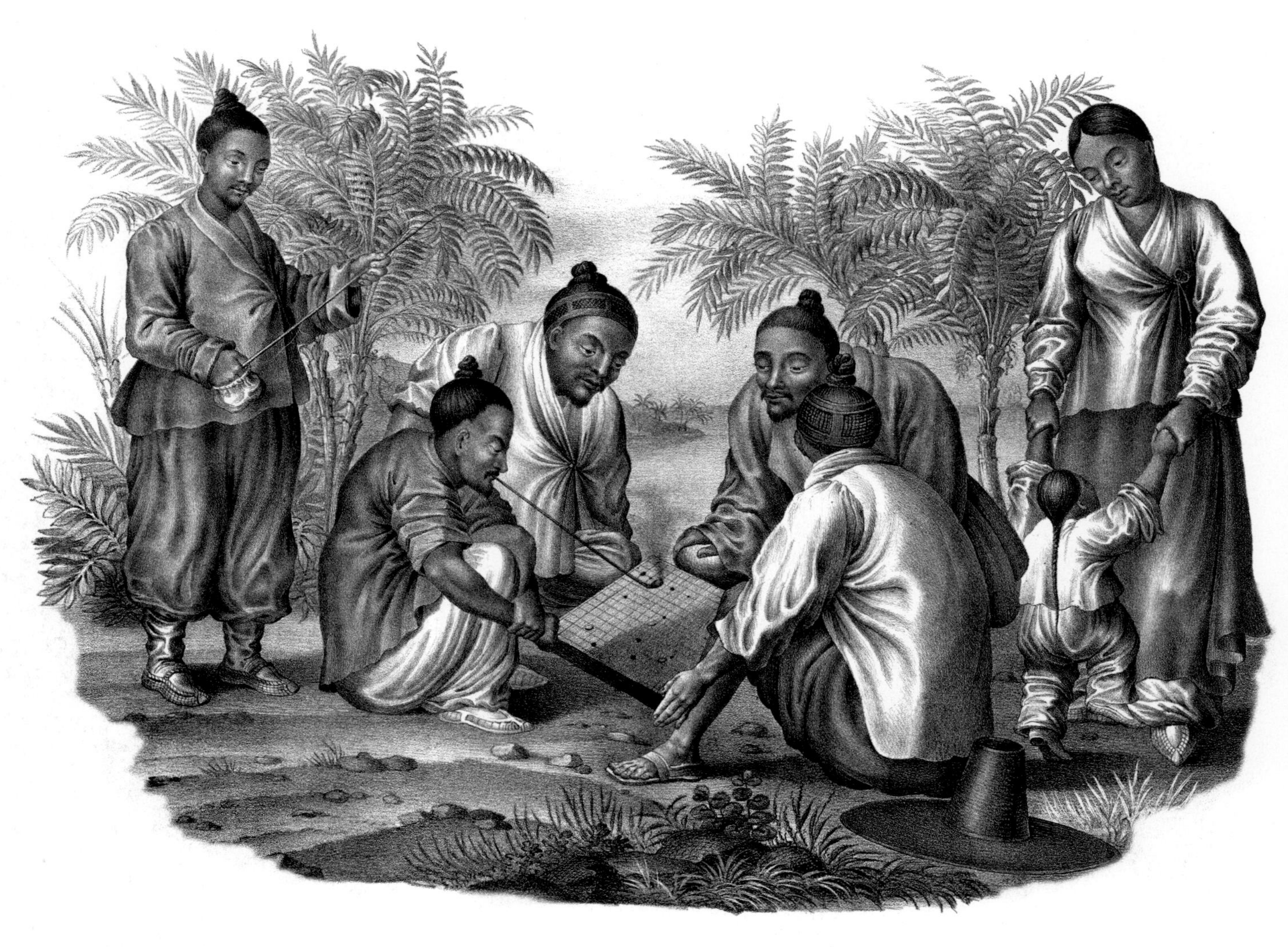

Korean fisherman's family, 1845

Koreanischer Fischerfamilie, 1845

Famiglia di pescatori coreani, 1845

Famille de pêcheurs coréenne, vers 1845

Familia coreana de pescadores, 1845

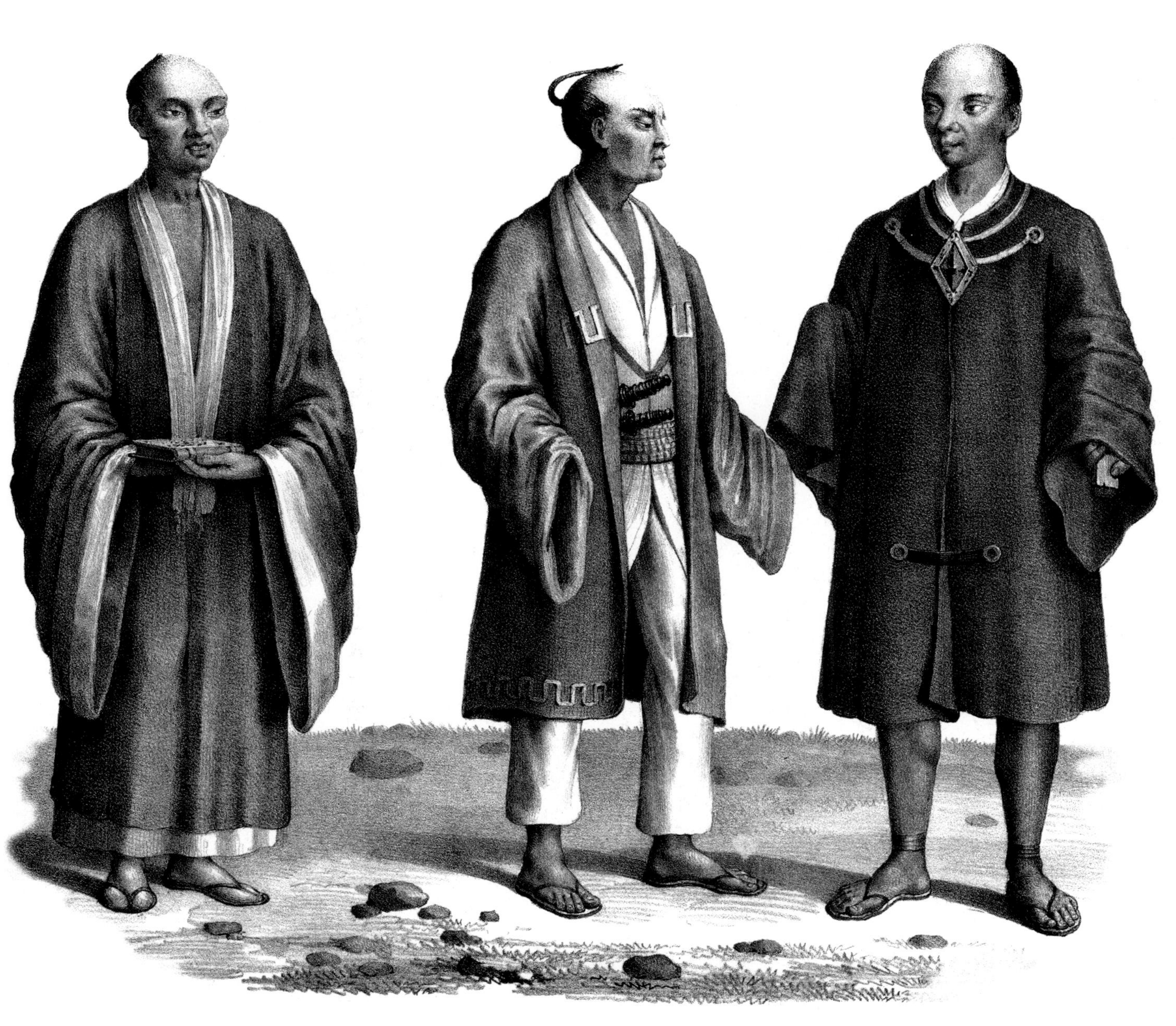

Japanese in various types of dress, c. 1840

Japaner in unterschiedlichen Gewändern, um 1840

Giapponesi in vari tipi di abiti, ca. 1840

Divers types de vêtements japonais, vers 1840

Diversos tipos de trajes japoneses, hacia 1840

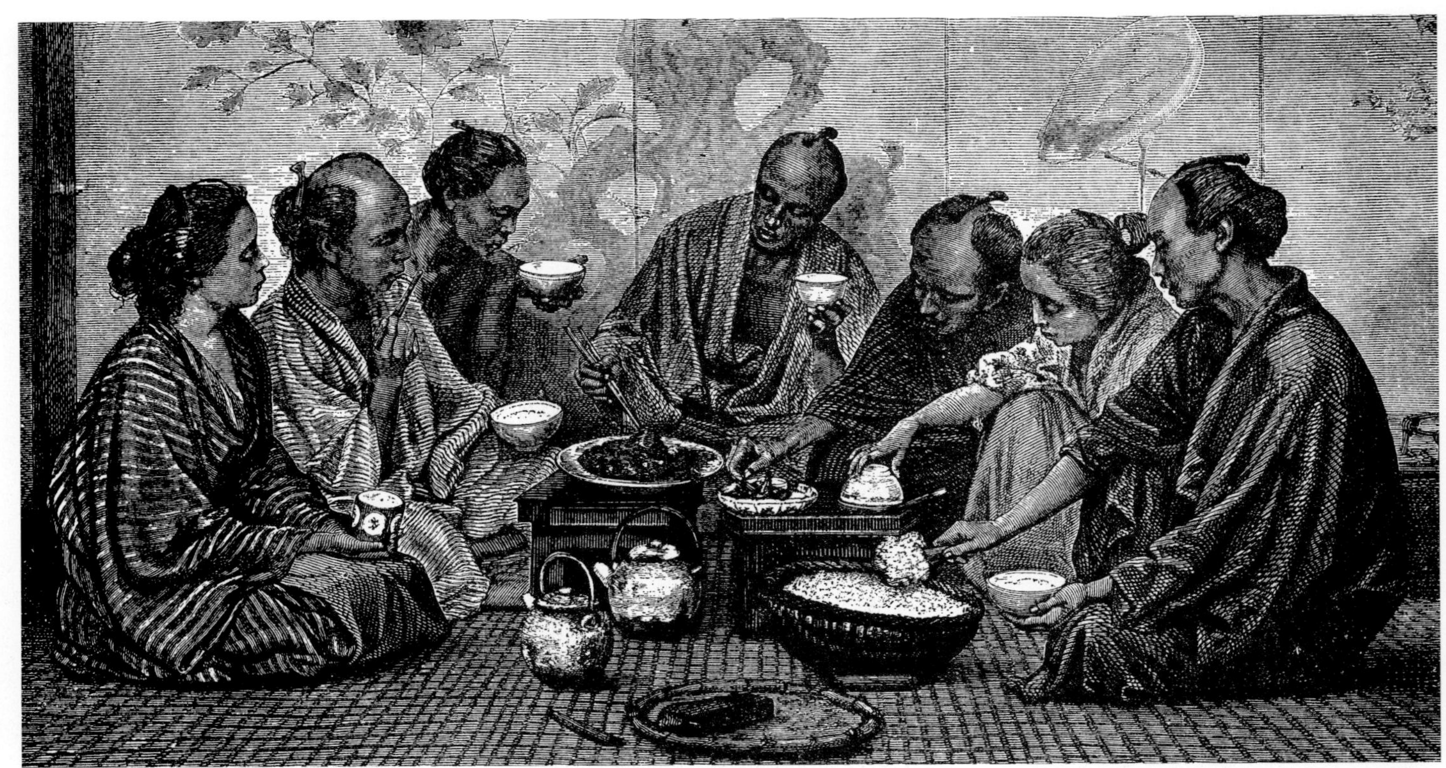

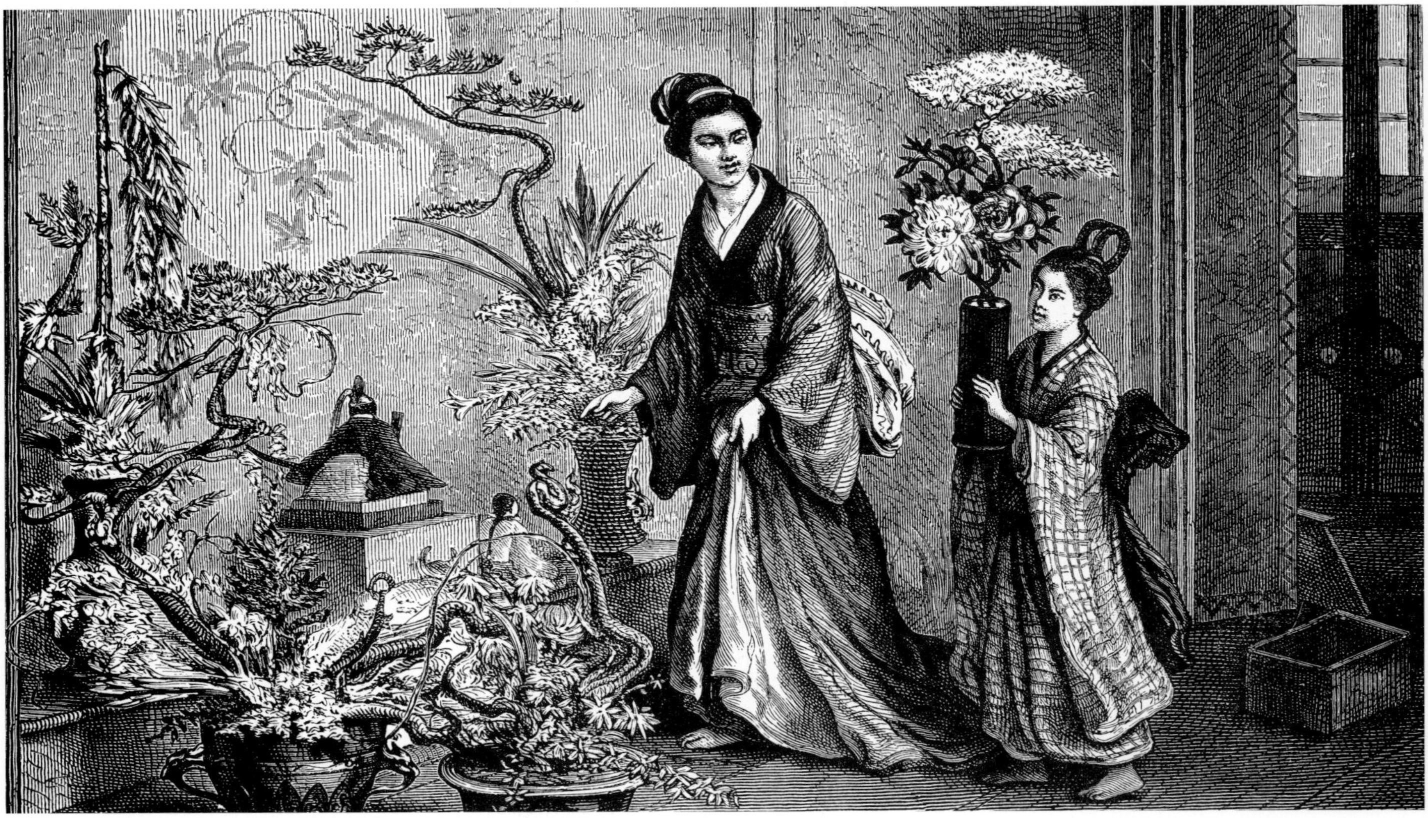

a	Middle-class family at dinner, 1880	Bürgerliche Familie beim Essen, 1880	Famiglia di ceto medio a cena, 1880	Classe moyenne à l'heure du dîner, 1880	Familia de clase media durante la cena, 1880
b	Japanese woman and girl, c. 1870	Japanische Frau mit Mädchen, um 1870	Donna e ragazza giapponesi, ca. 1870	Femme et jeune fille japonaises, vers 1870	Mujer y muchacha japonesas, hacia 1870

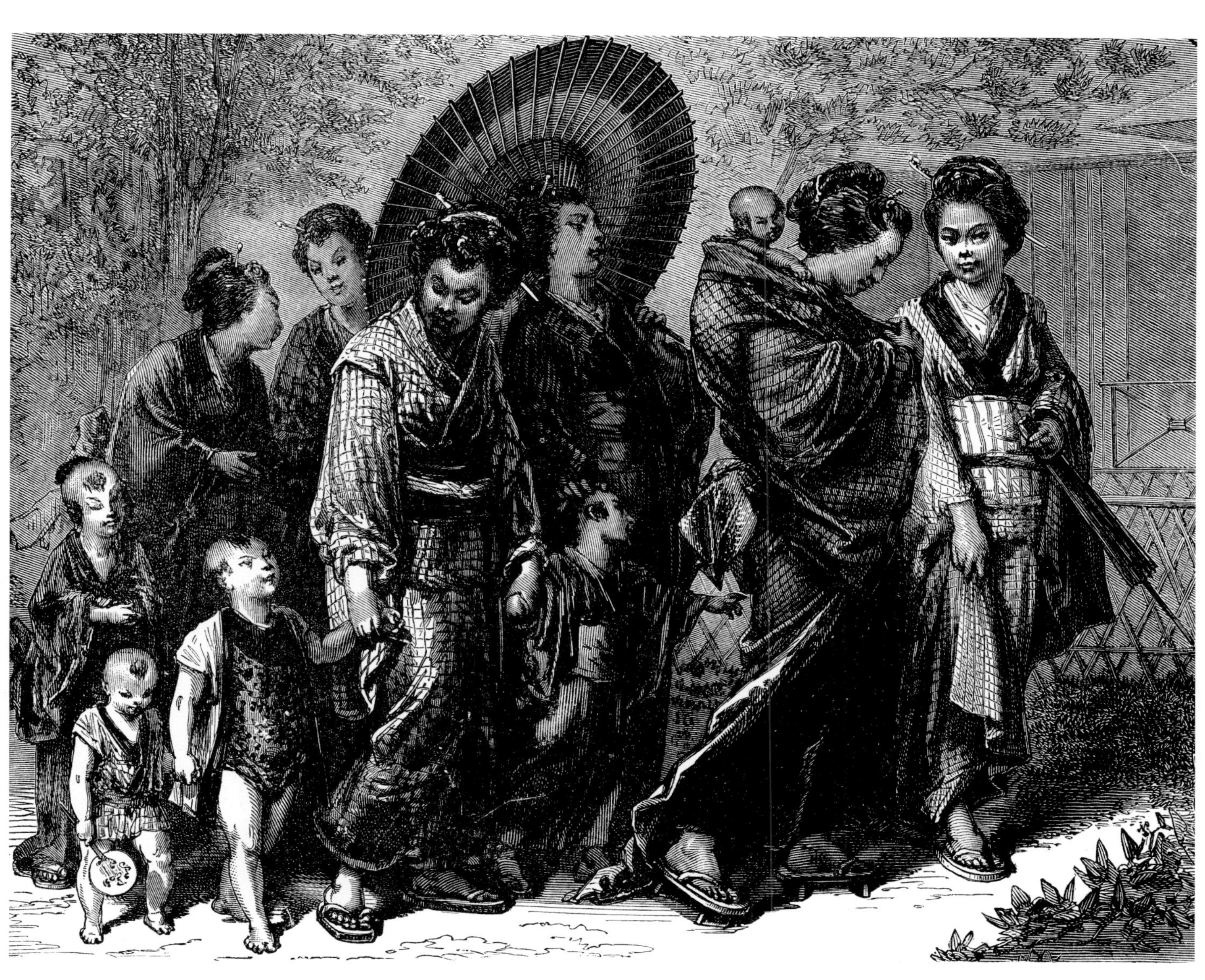

Japanese women in visiting dress, c. 1870

Japanische Frauen in Besuchskleidung, um 1870

Donne giapponesi in abito da visita, ca. 1870

Japonaise en tenue d'apparat, vers 1870

Mujeres japonesas con traje de visita, hacia 1870

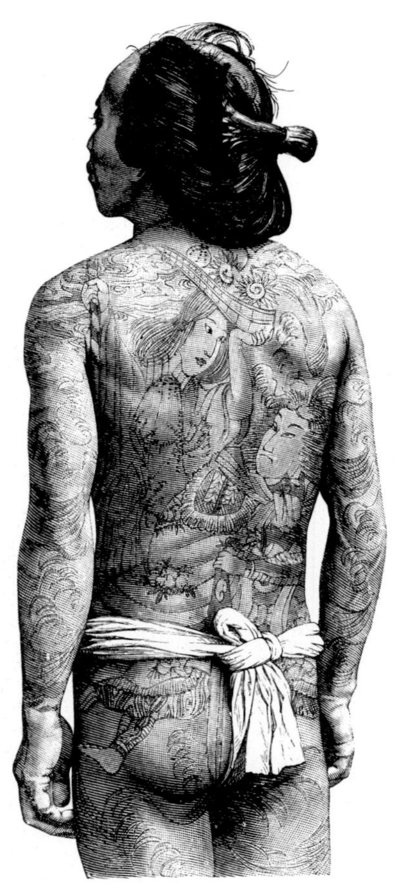

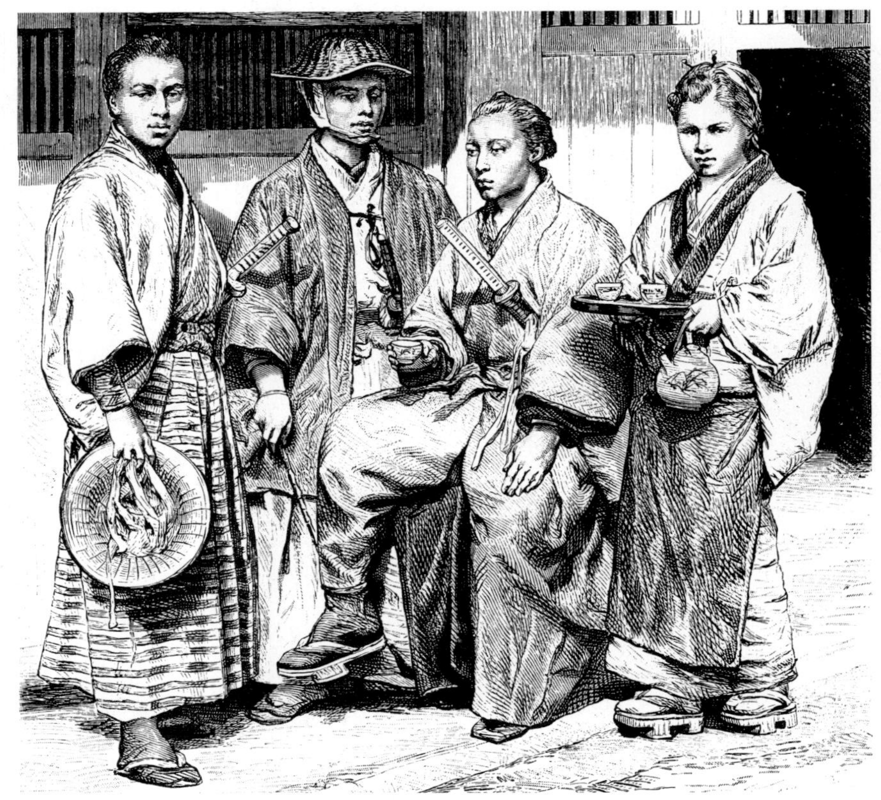

a	Tatooed man	Tätowierter Mann	Uomo tatuato	Homme tatoué	Hombre tatuado
b	Street scene in Tokyo, c. 1870	Straßenszene in Tokio, um 1870	Scena di strada a Tokyo, ca. 1870	Scène de rue à Tokyo, vers 1870	En una calle de Tokio, alrededor del año 1870

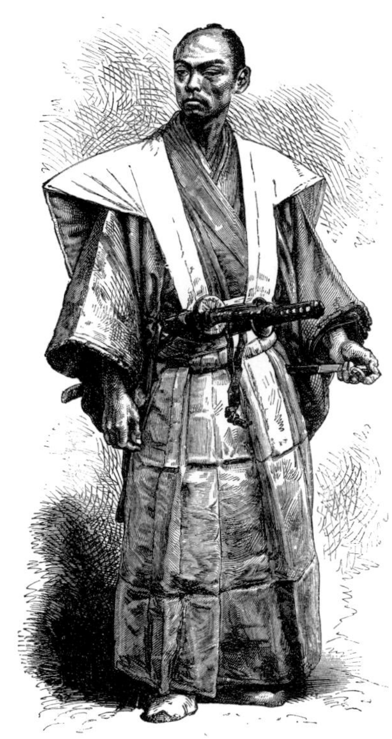

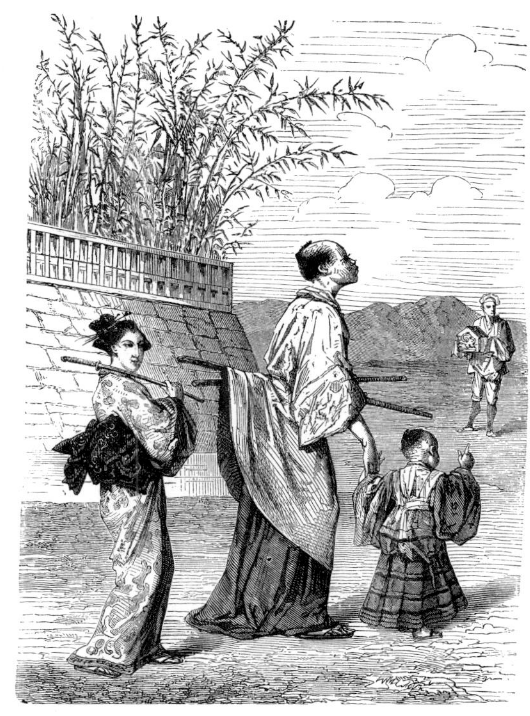

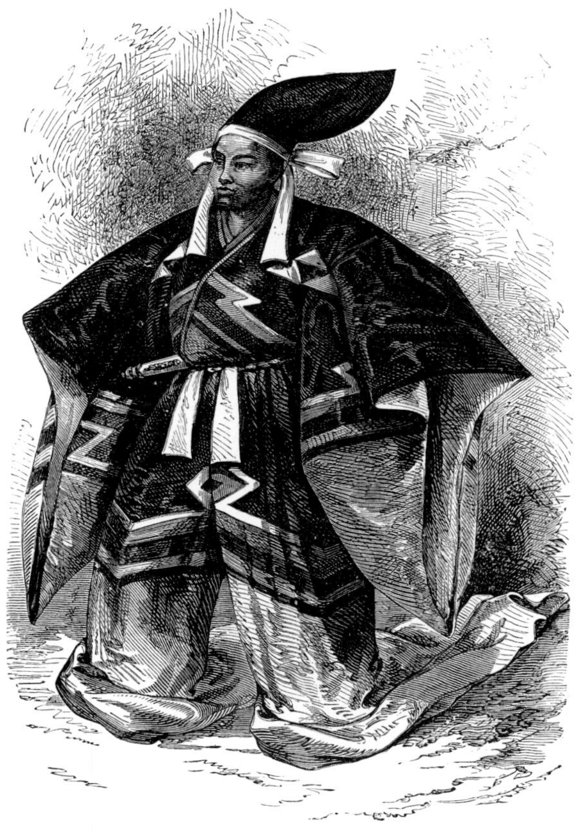

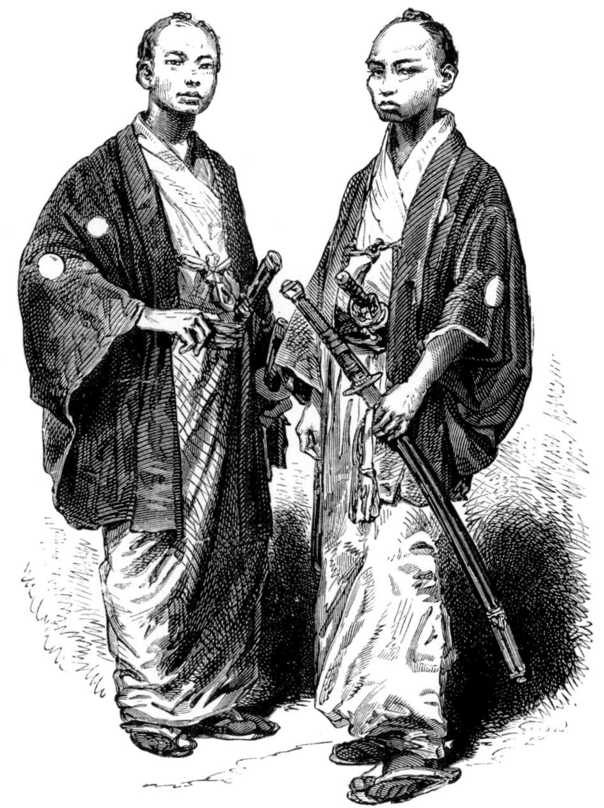

a	Government official in civilian clothes	Regierungsbeamter in Zivilkleidung	Funzionario governativo in borghese	Fonctionnaire du Gouvernement en civil	Funcionario del Gobierno con ropa de civil
b	Child Samurai	Kind-Samurai	Bambino samurai	Enfant samouraï	Niño samuray
c	High court official	Hoher Hofbeamter	Alto funzionario di corte	Fonctionnaire de la Haute Cour	Funcionario del Tribunal Supremo
d	Japanese young men	Junge Japaner	Giovani giapponesi	Jeunes gens japonais	Jóvenes japoneses

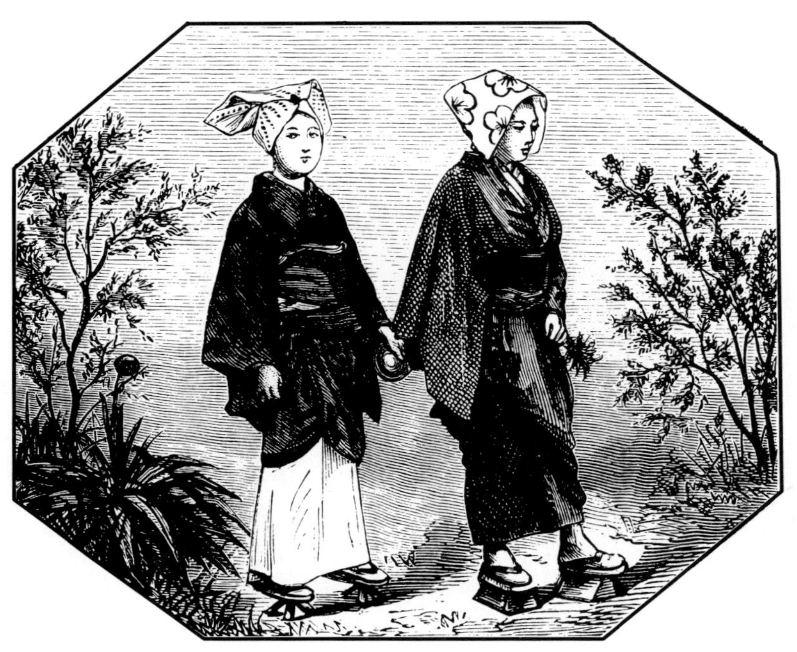

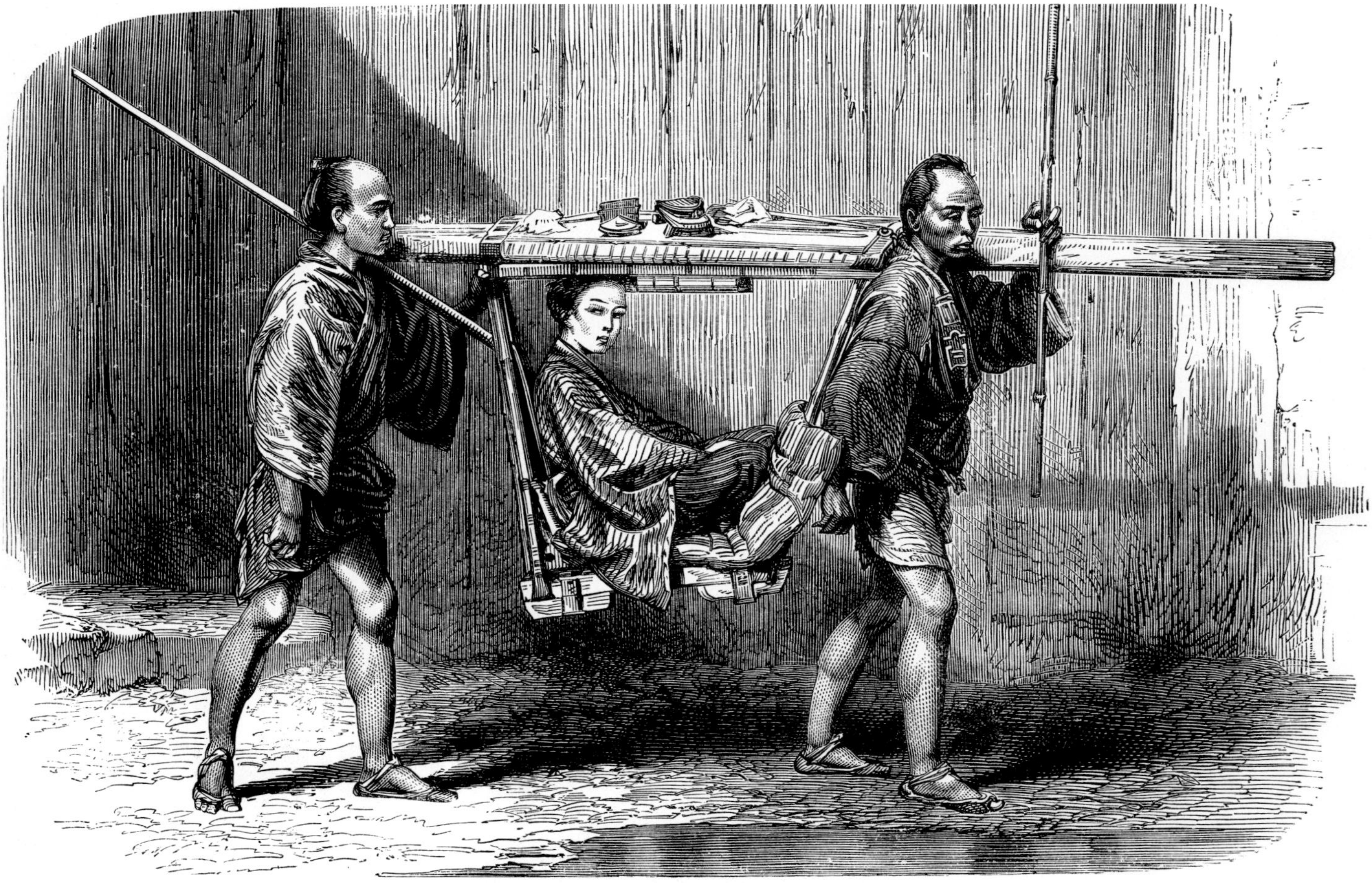

a	Girls from the countryside, c. 1880	Mädchen vom Land, um 1880	Ragazze di campagna, ca. 1880	Jeunes paysannes, vers 1880	Muchachas del campo, alrededor de 1880
b	Lady in a palenquin with bearers, Kyoto, c. 1880	Frau in Sänfte mit Trägern, Kioto, um 1880	Donna in un palanchino con portatori, Kyoto, ca. 1880	Femme au palanquin, Kyoto, vers 1880	Dama en un palanquín con portadores, Kyoto, hacia el año 1880

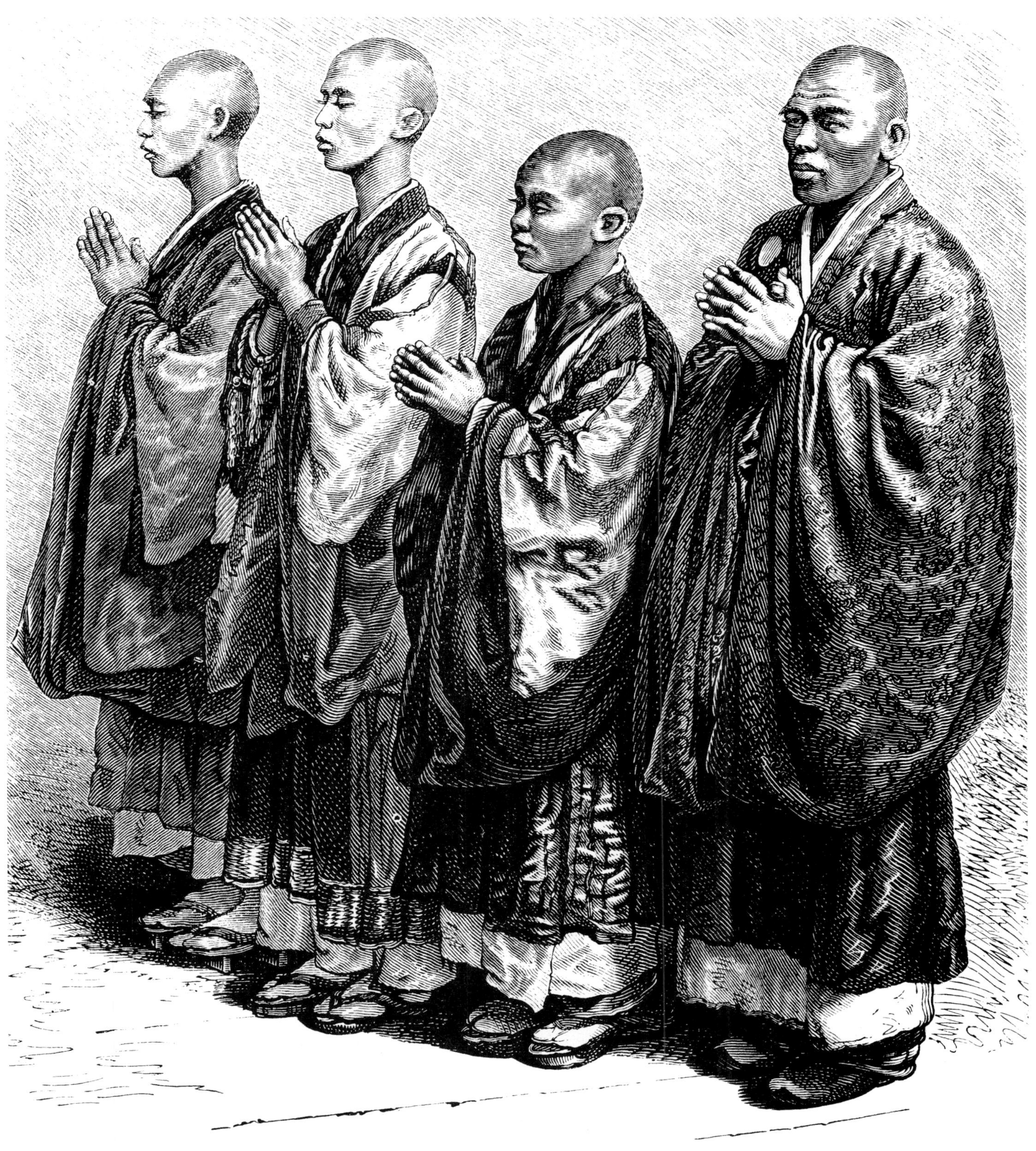

Monks, c. 1860 Mönche, um 1860 Monaci, ca. 1860 Moines, vers 1860 Monjes, hacia 1860

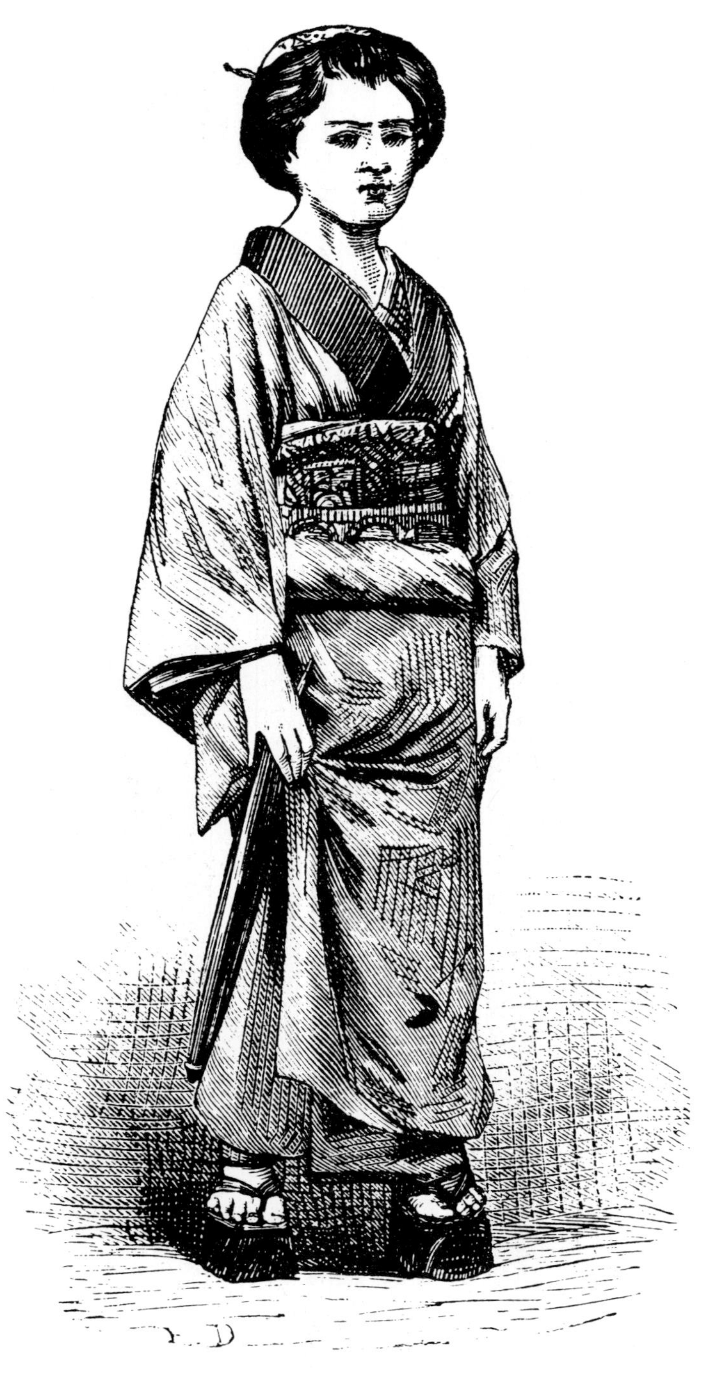

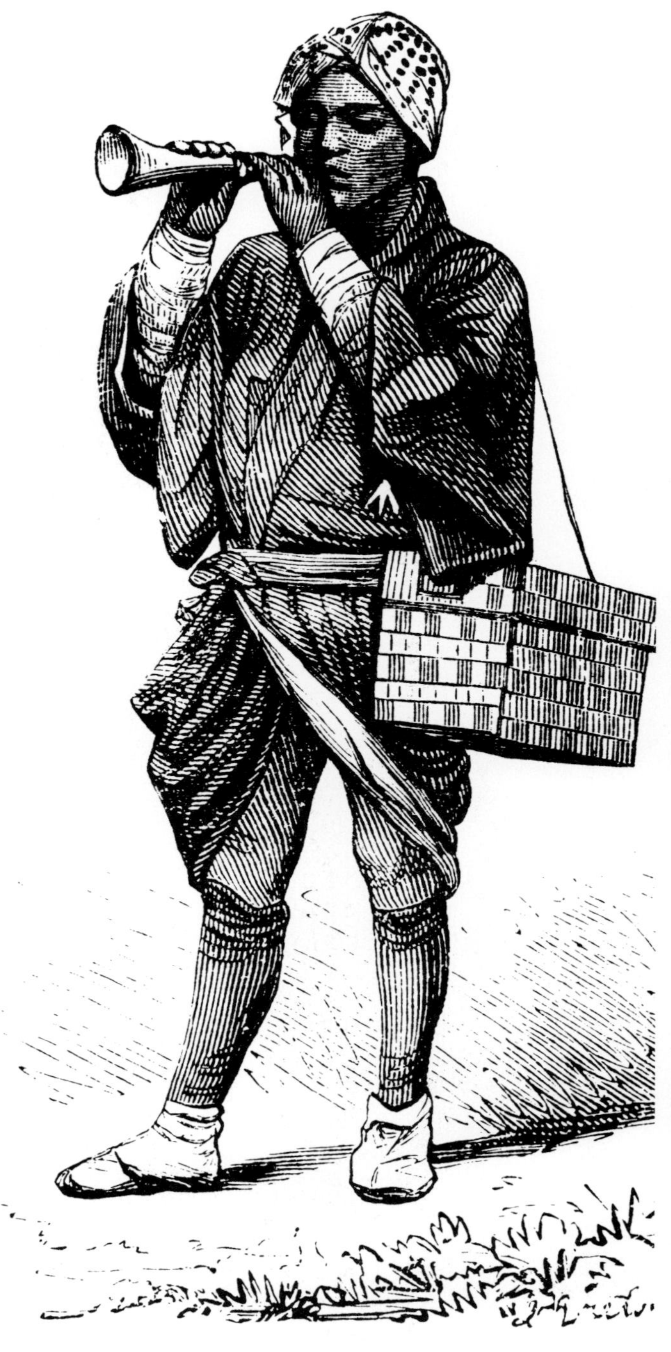

a	Young Japanese lady	Junge Japanerin	Giovane donna giapponese	Jeune femme japonaise	Joven japonesa
b	Fish vendor	Fischverkäufer	Venditore di pesce	Vendeur de poisson	Vendedor de pescado

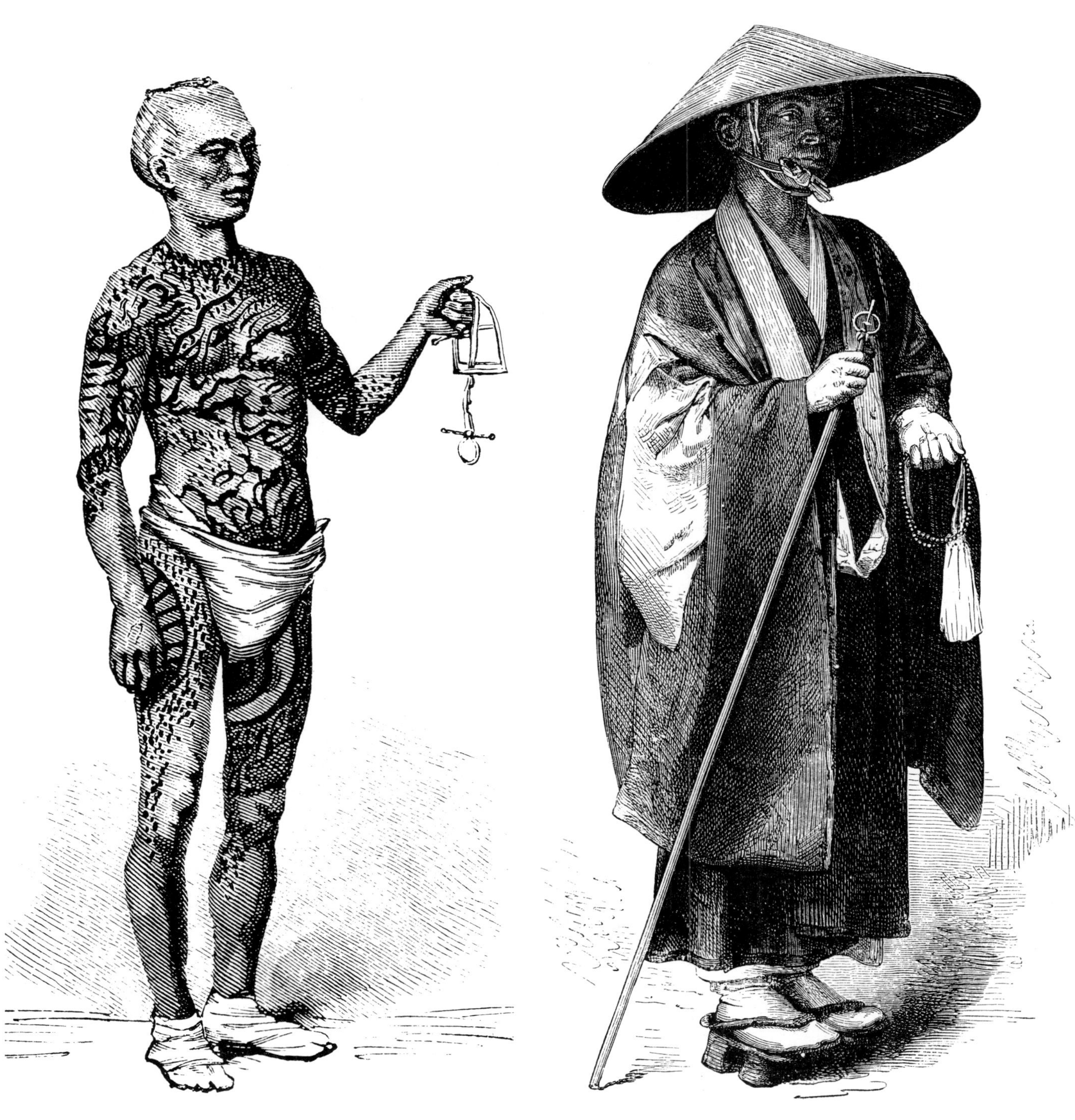

a	Tattooed Japanese groom	Tätowierter japanischer Reitknecht	Stalliere giapponese tatuato	Valet tatoué japonais	Novio japonés tatuado
b	Japanese priest, c. 1860	Japanischer Priester, um 1860	Sacerdote giapponese, ca. 1860	Prêtre japonais, vers 1860	Sacerdote japonés, alrededor del año 1860

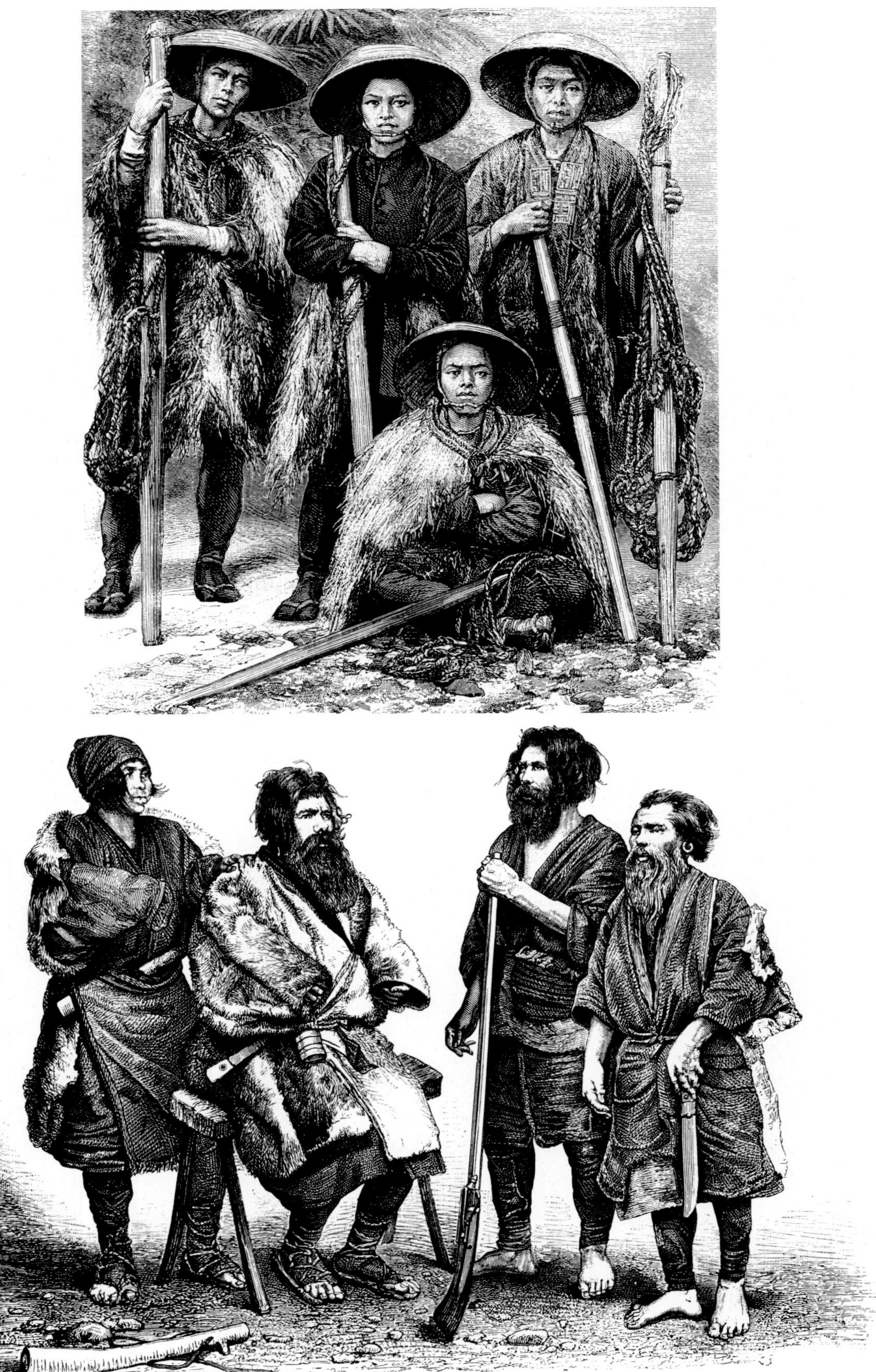

a	Japanese farmers	Japanische Bauern	Contadini giapponesi	Paysans japonais	Campesinos japoneses
b	Ainos, c. 1870	Ainos, um 1870	Ainos, ca. 1870	Ainos, vers 1870	Ainos, hacia 1870

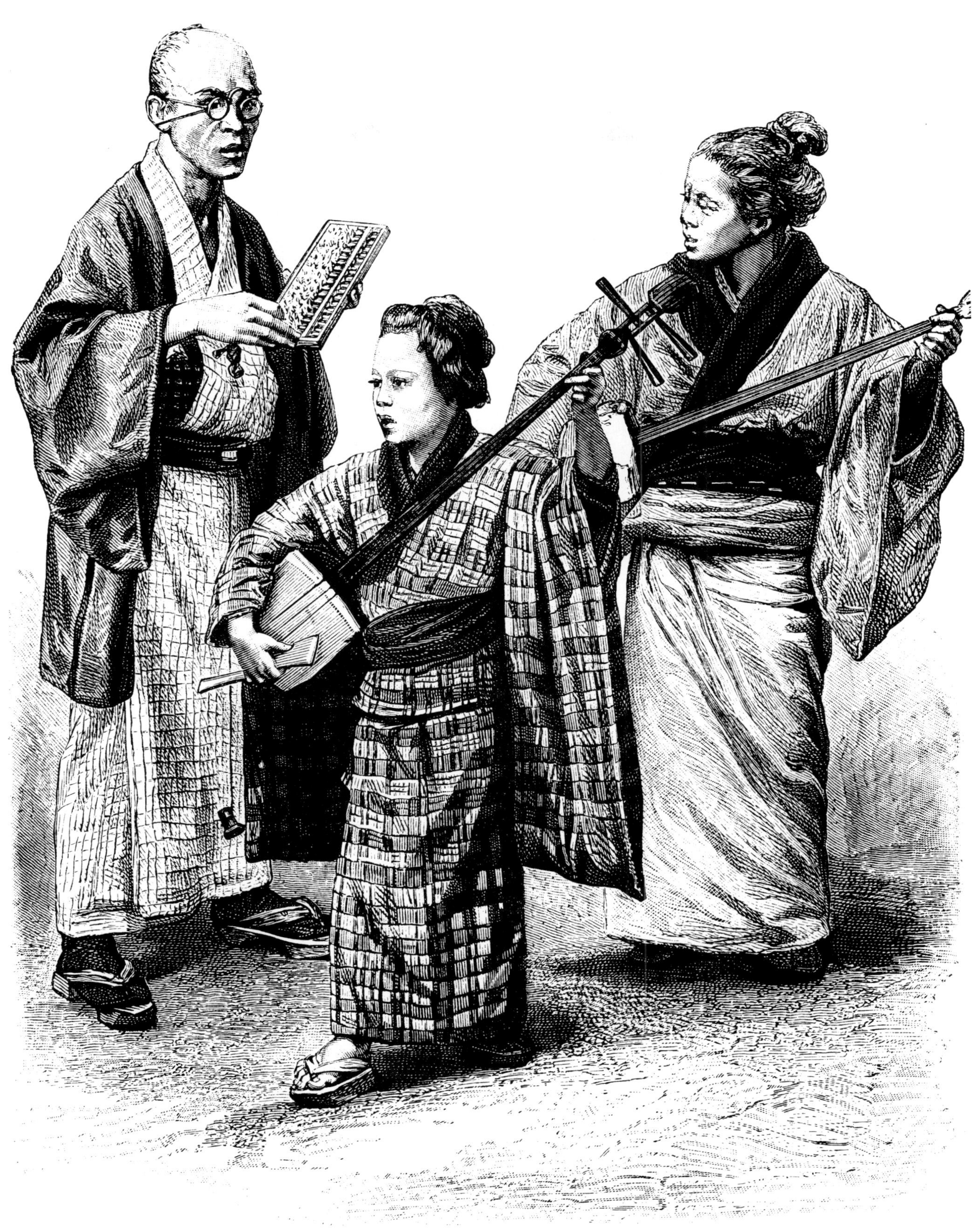

Merchant and musicians, c. 1870

Händler und Musiker, um 1870

Mercante e musicisti, ca. 1870

Marchand et musicien, vers 1870

Mercader y músicas, hacia 1870

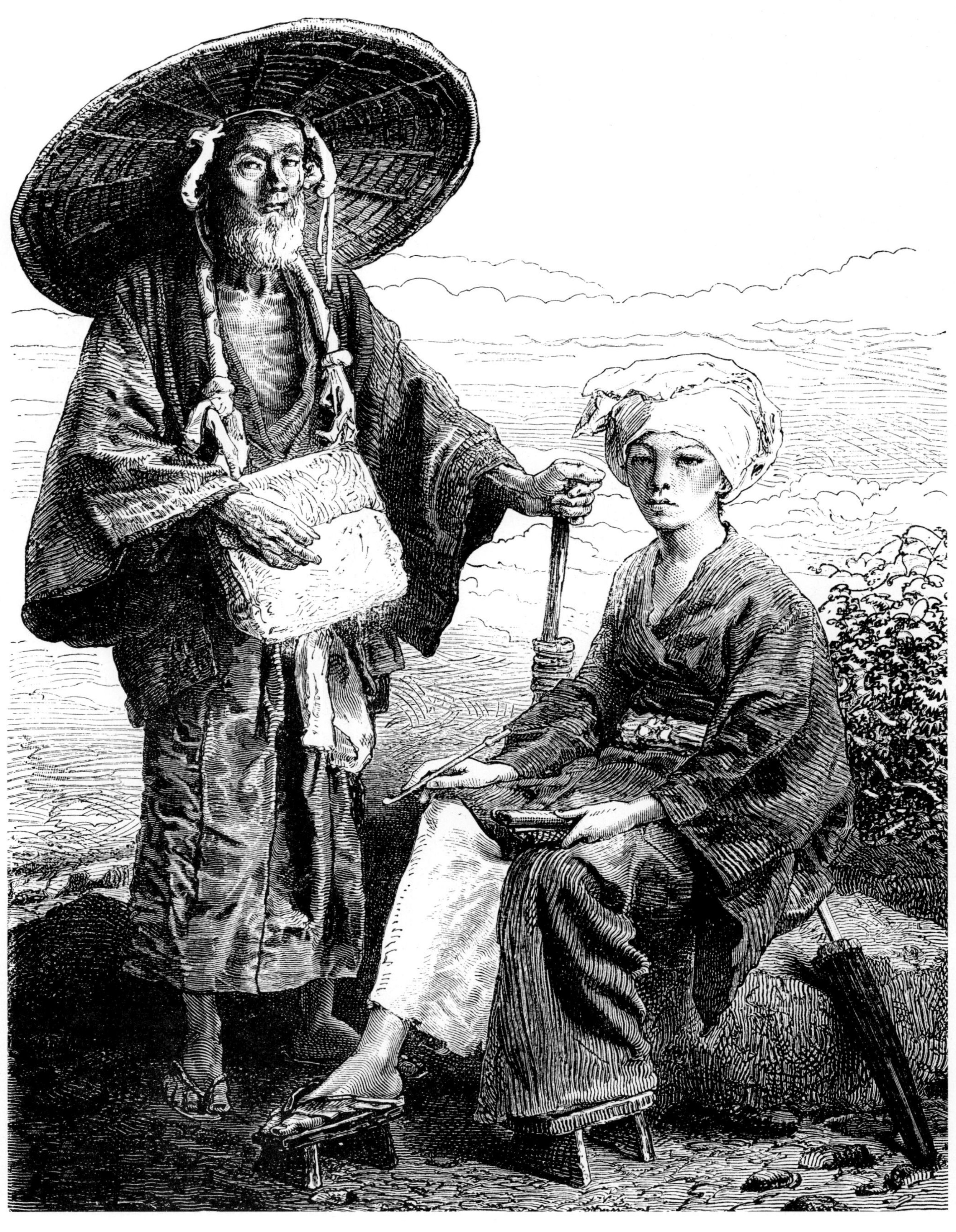

Pilgrims, c. 1860 Pilger, um 1860 Pellegrini, ca. 1860 Pèlerins, vers 1860 Peregrinos, hacia 1860

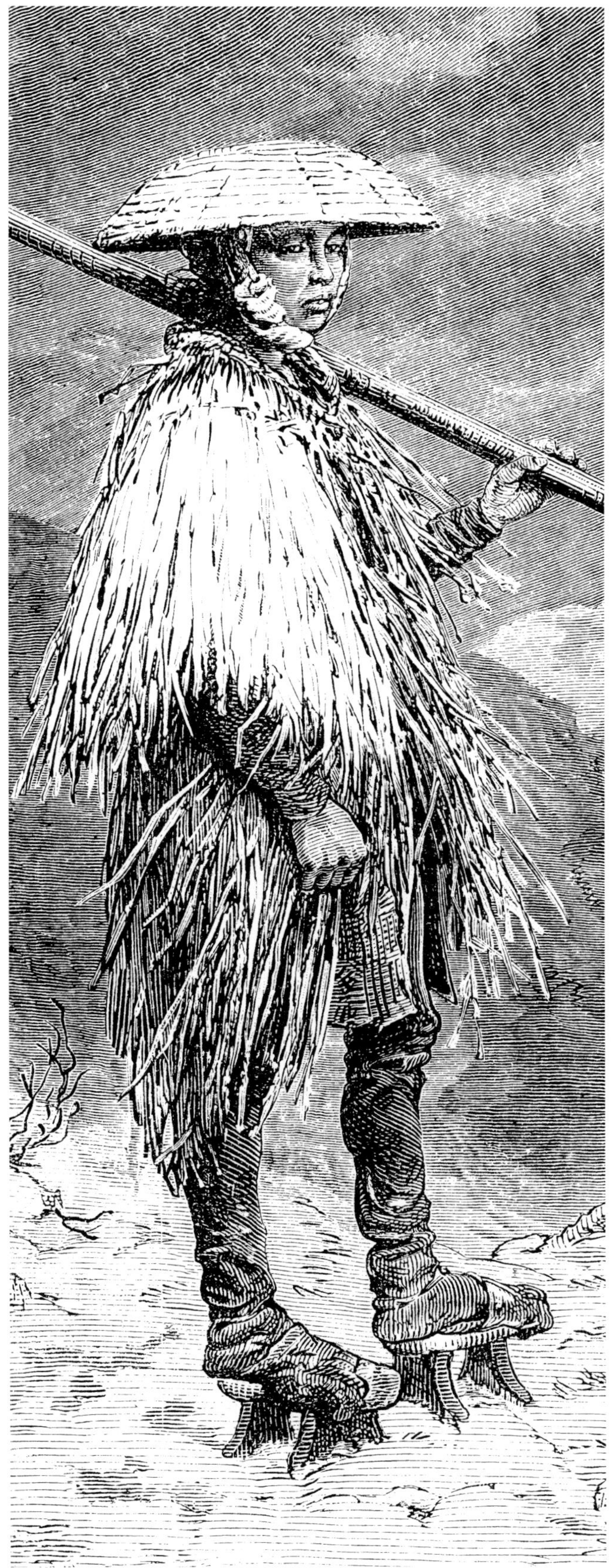

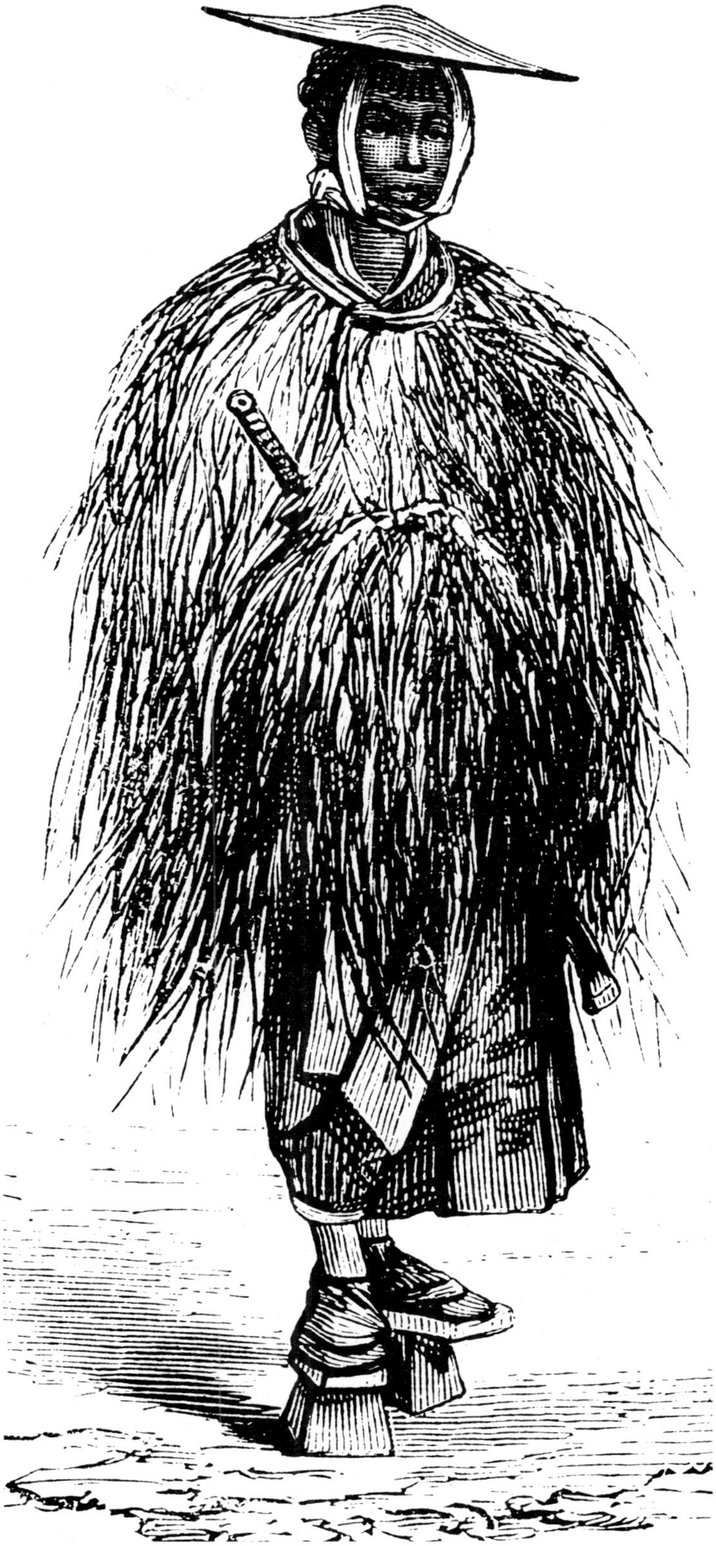

Farmer and officer in winter coats, c. 1860

Bauer und Beamter im Wintermantel, um 1860

Contadino e funzionario in abiti invernali, ca. 1860

Paysan et officier en tenue d'hiver, vers 1860

Campesino y funcionario con abrigos, hacia 1860

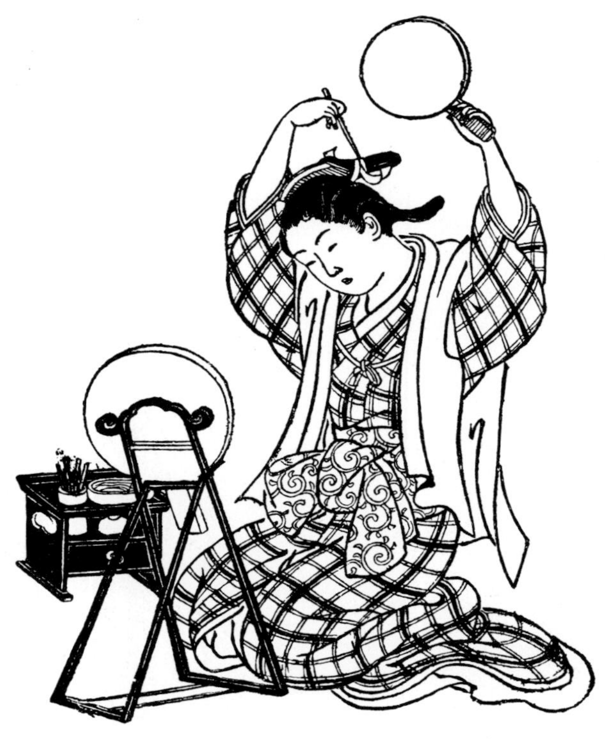

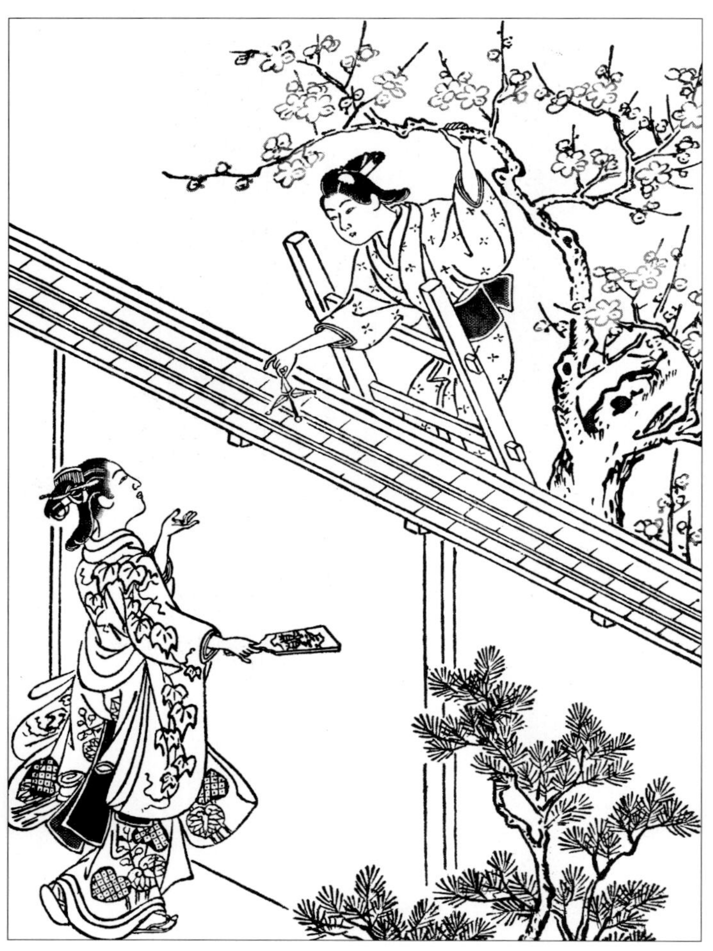

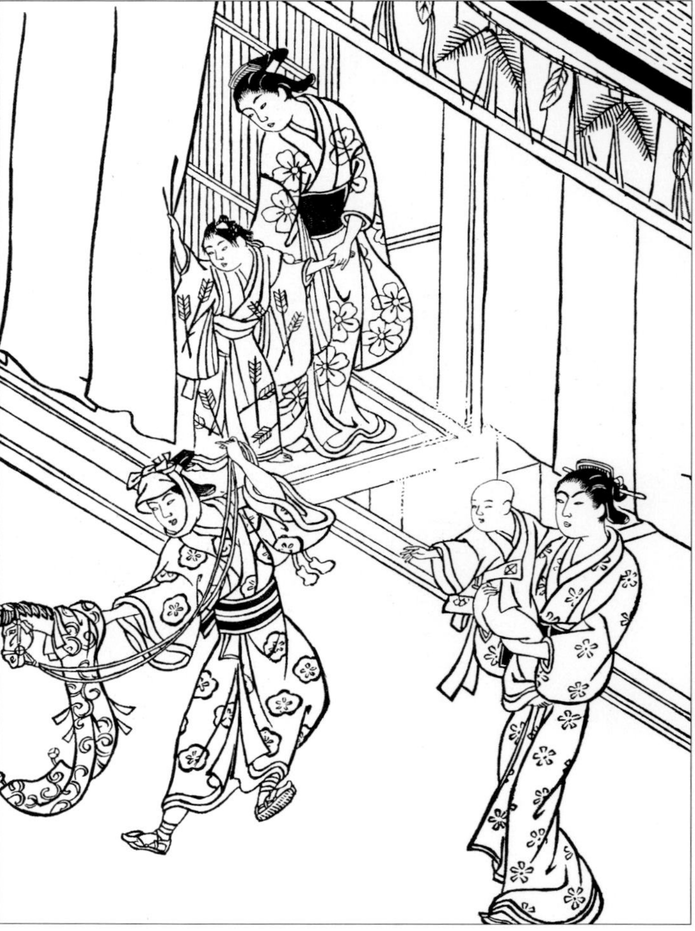

Japanese female costume

Japanische Frauentracht

Costume femminile giapponese

Costume féminin japonais

Vestidos japoneses de mujer

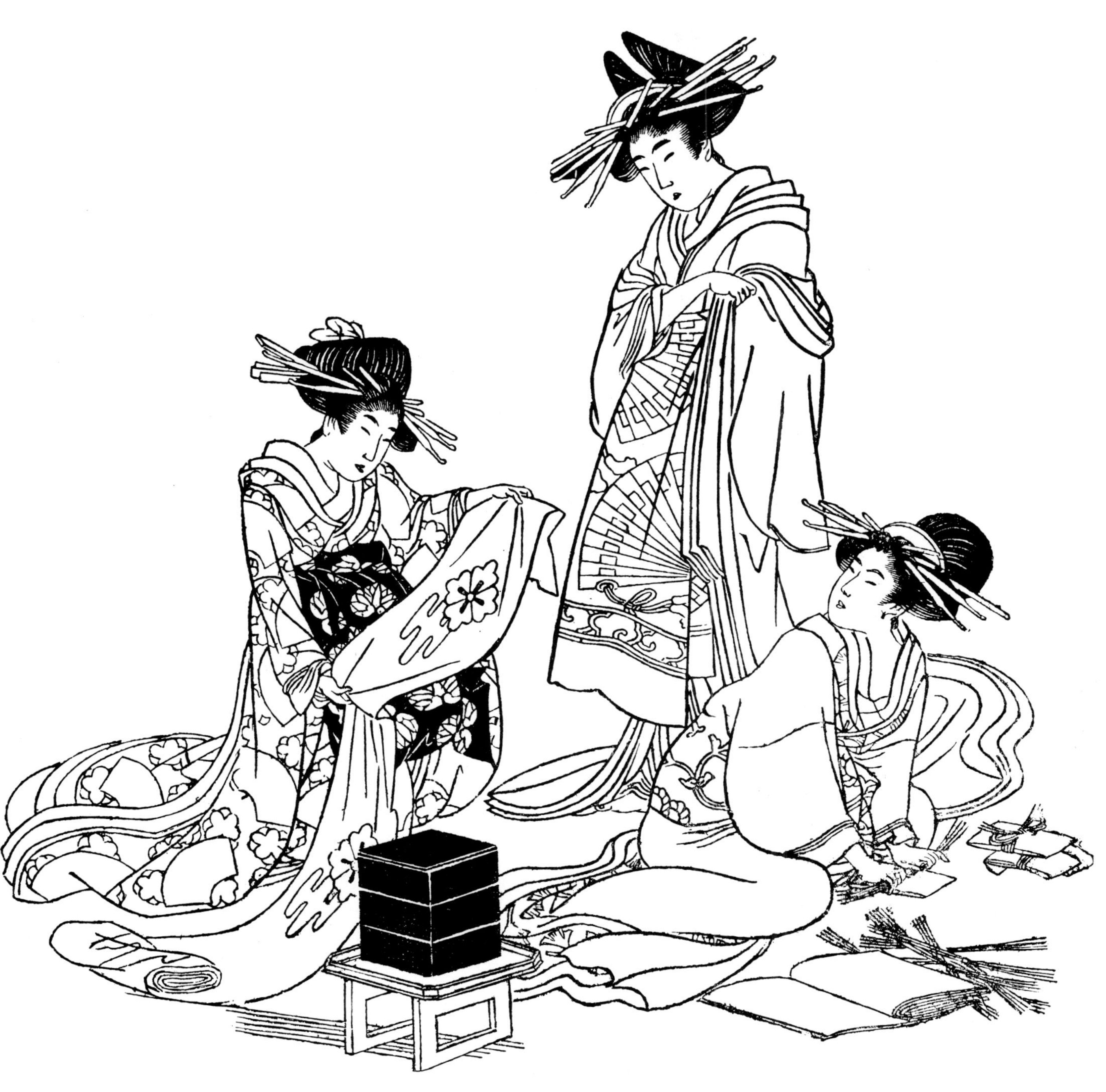

Japanese female costume

Japanische Frauentracht

Costume femminile giapponese

Costume féminin japonais

Vestidos japoneses de mujer

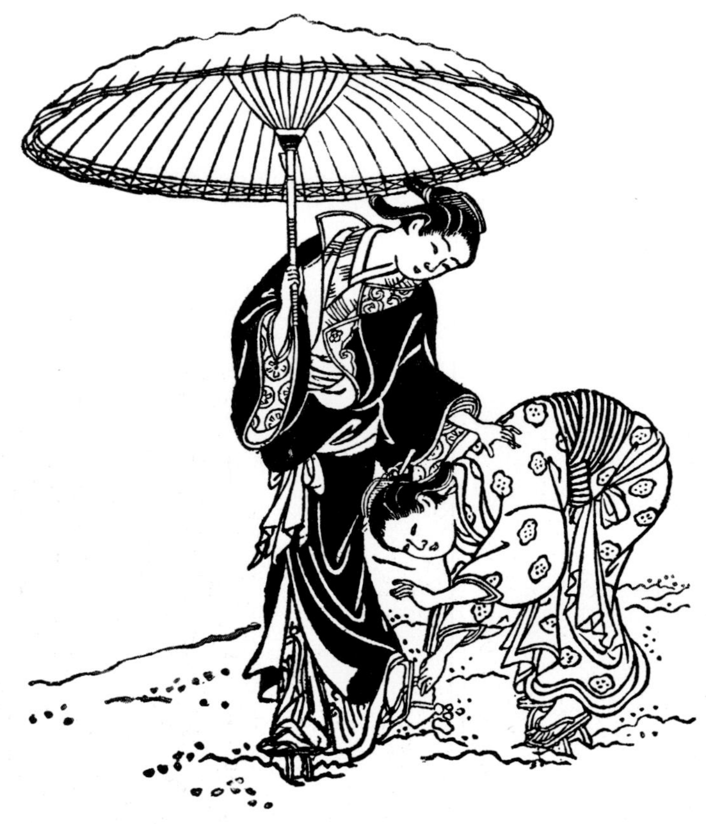

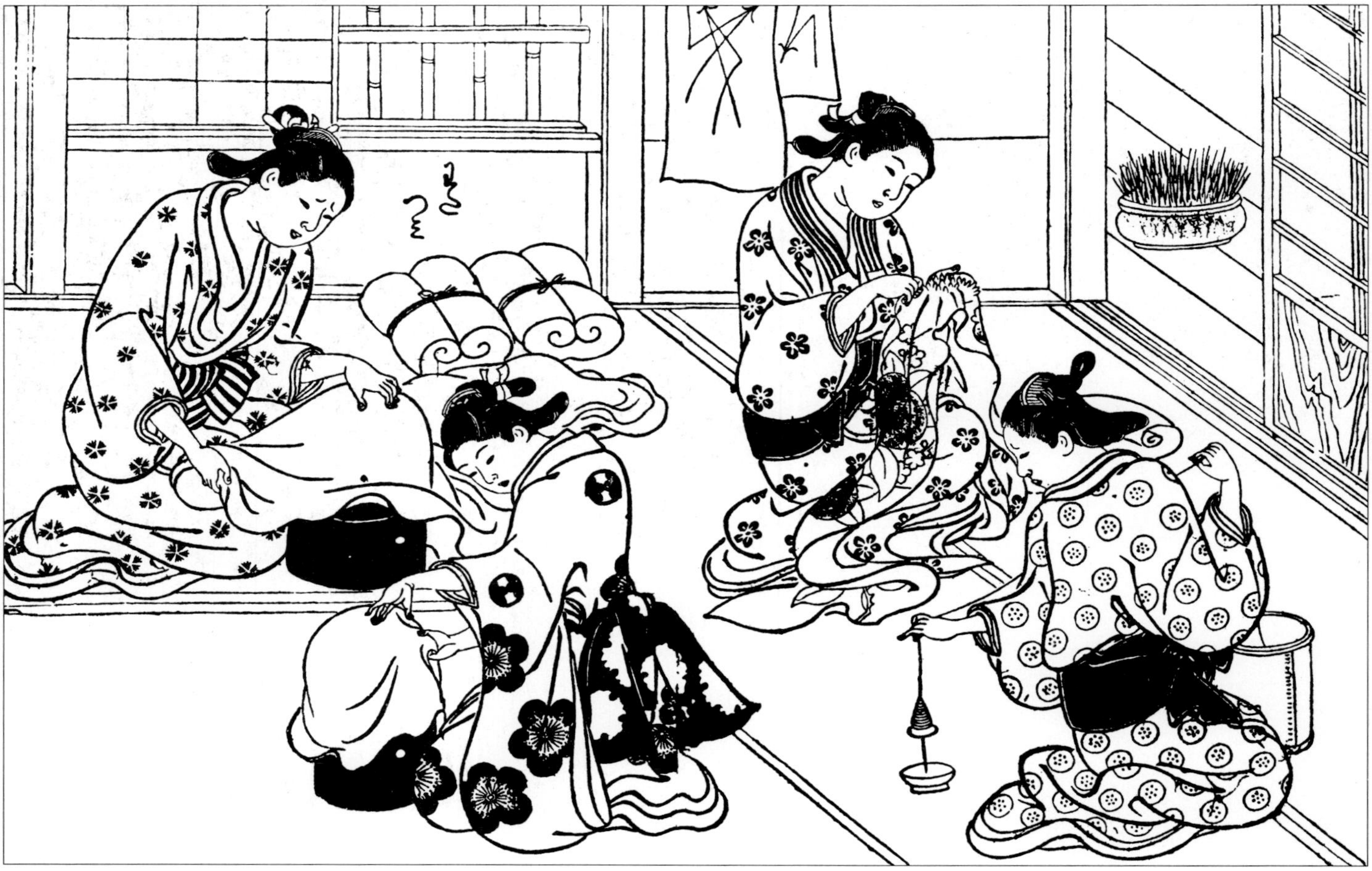

Japanese female costume

Japanische Frauentracht

Costume femminile giapponese

Costume féminin japonais

Vestidos japoneses de mujer

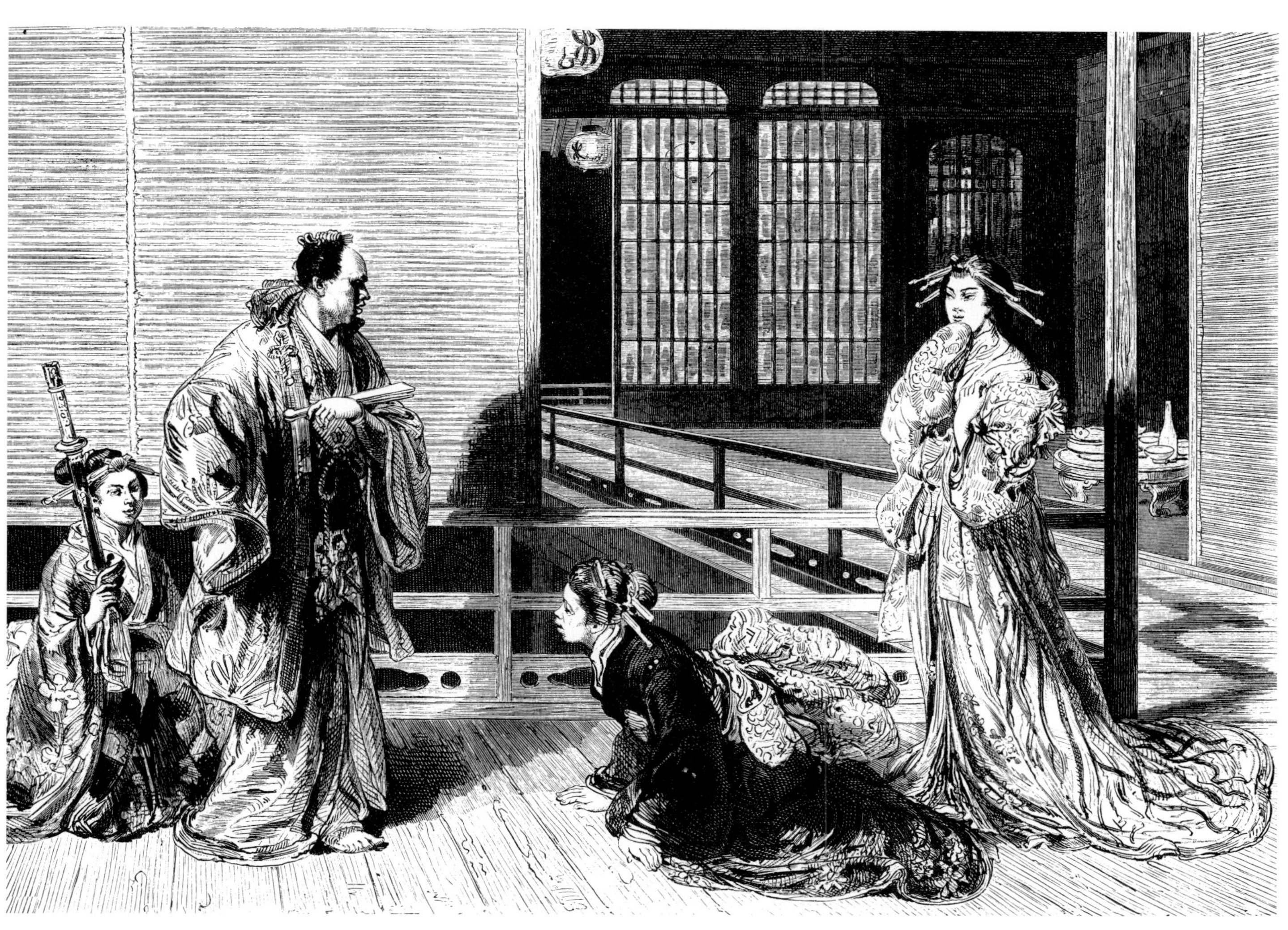

Aristiocratic couple with servants, c. 1860

Artistokratenpaar mit Bediensteten, um 1860

Coppia aristocratica con domestici, ca. 1860

Couple d'aristocrates avec leurs serviteurs, vers 1860

Pareja aristocrática y sirvientes, hacia 1860

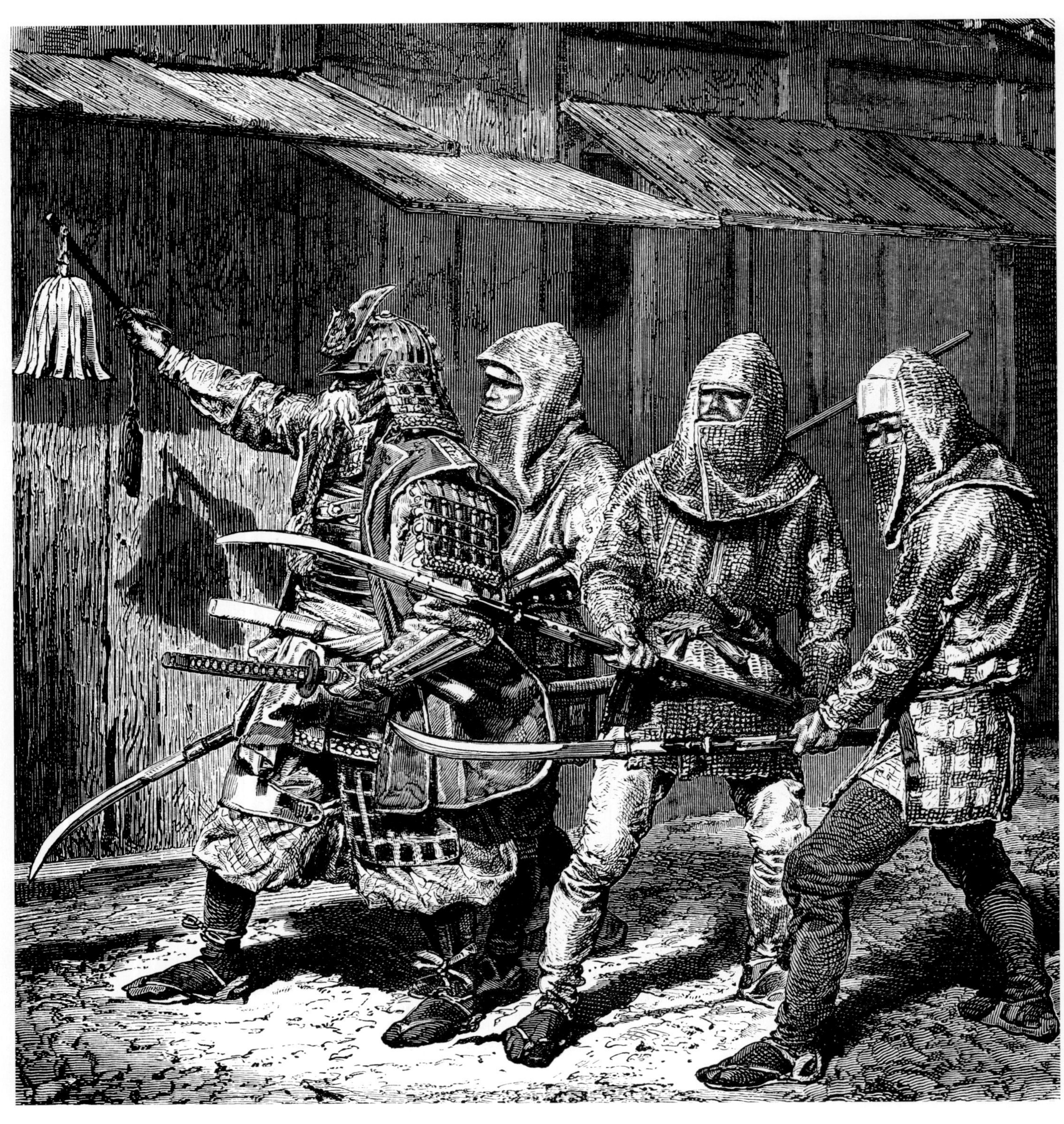

13th-century scene of officer and soldiers

Szene aus dem 13. Jahrhundert, Offizier und Soldaten

Scena del XIII secolo di ufficiali e soldati

Scène du XIIIe siècle représentant un officier et des soldats

Escena con oficial y soldados, siglo XIII

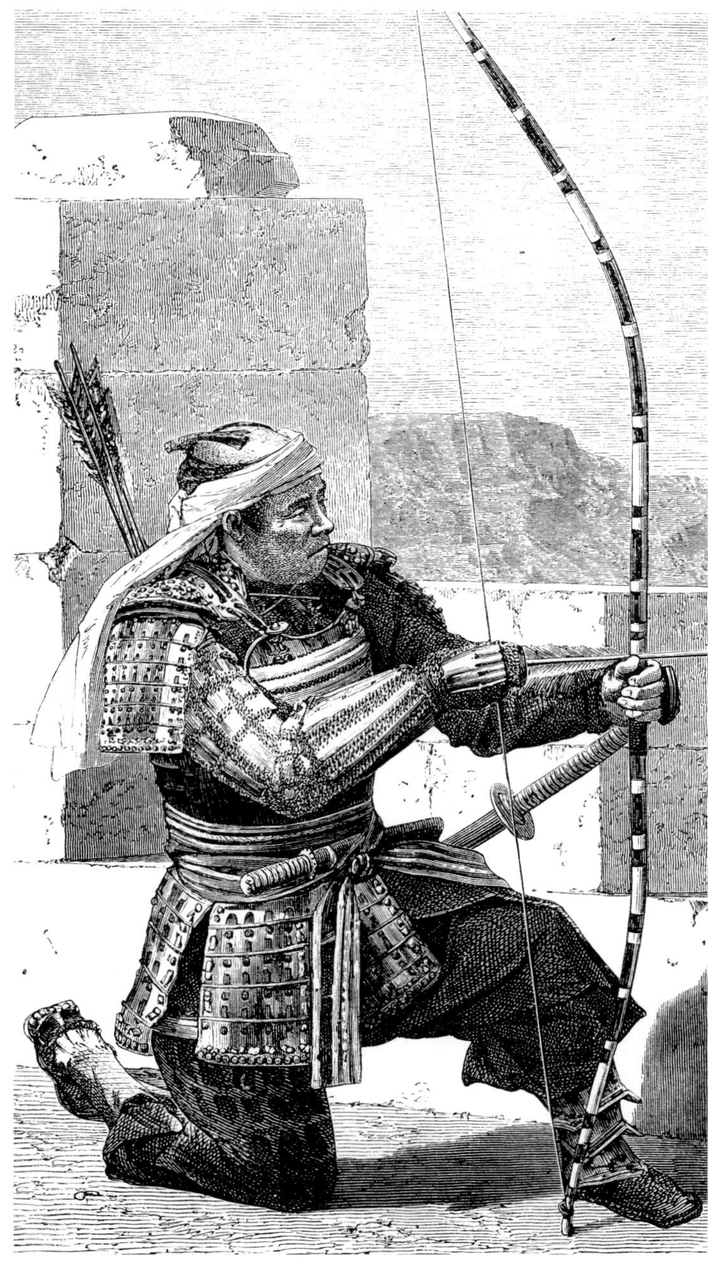

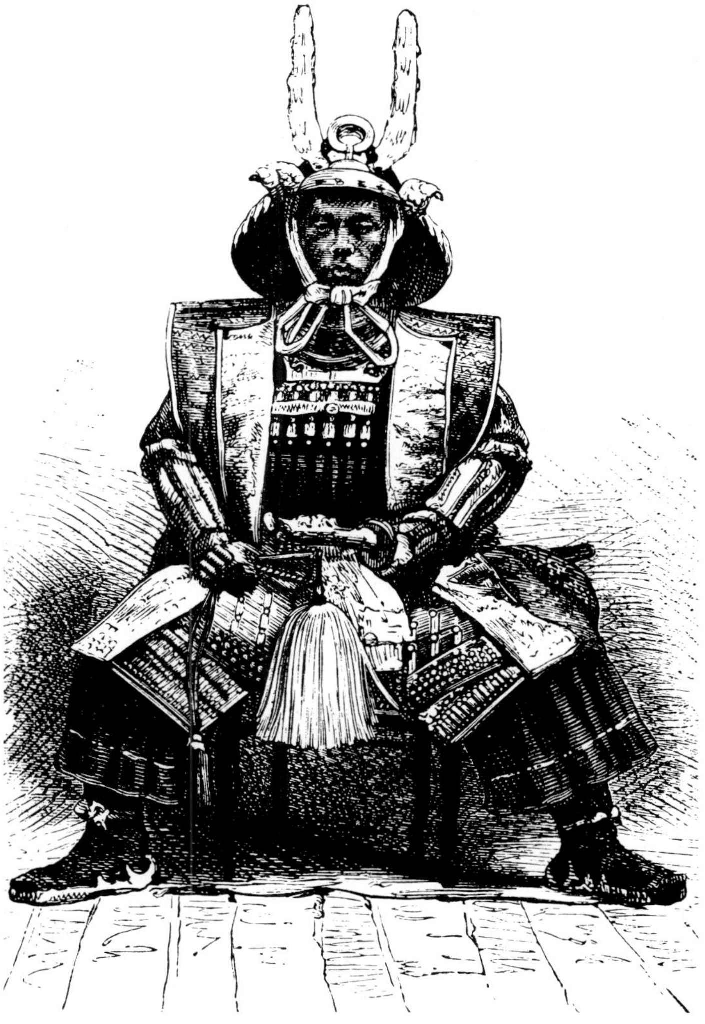

Japanese archer and officer, c. 1860

Japanischer Bogenschütze und Offizier, um 1860

Arciere e ufficiale giapponesi, ca. 1860

Archer et officier japonais, vers 1860

Arquero y oficial japoneses, hacia 1860

Pacific Islands, Australia and New Zealand
Pazifische Inseln, Australien und Neuseeland
Isole del Pacifico, Australia e Nuova Zelanda
Îles du Pacifique, Australie et Nouvelle-Zélande
Islas del Pacífico, Australia y Nueva Zelanda
太平洋諸島、オーストラリアとニュージーランド
太平洋島嶼、澳大利亞和新西蘭

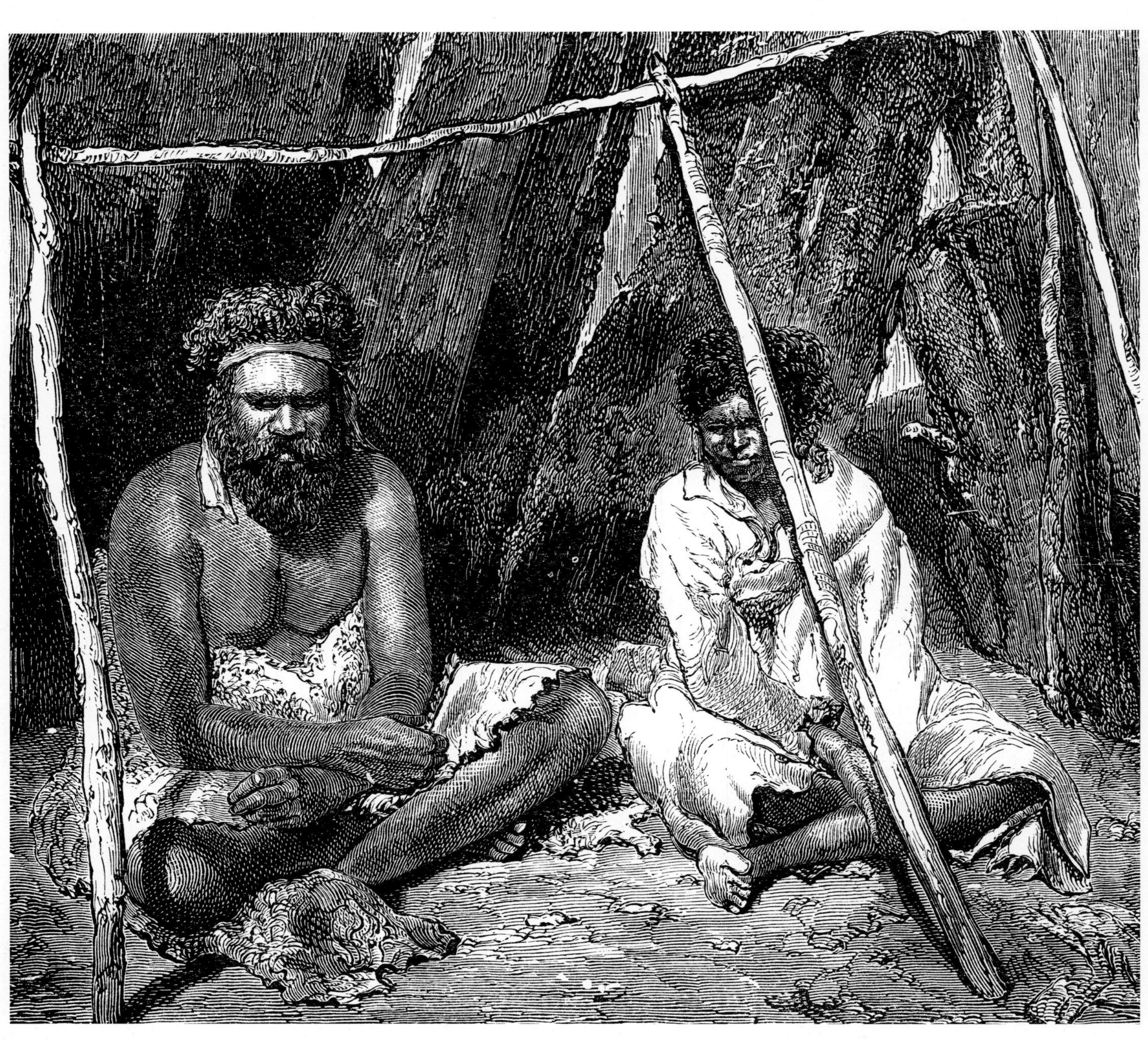

Australian Aboriginals, c. 1880

Australische Aboriginies, um 1880

Aborigeni australiani, ca. 1880

Aborigènes d'Australie, vers 1880

Aborígenes australianos, alrededor del año 1880

Australia

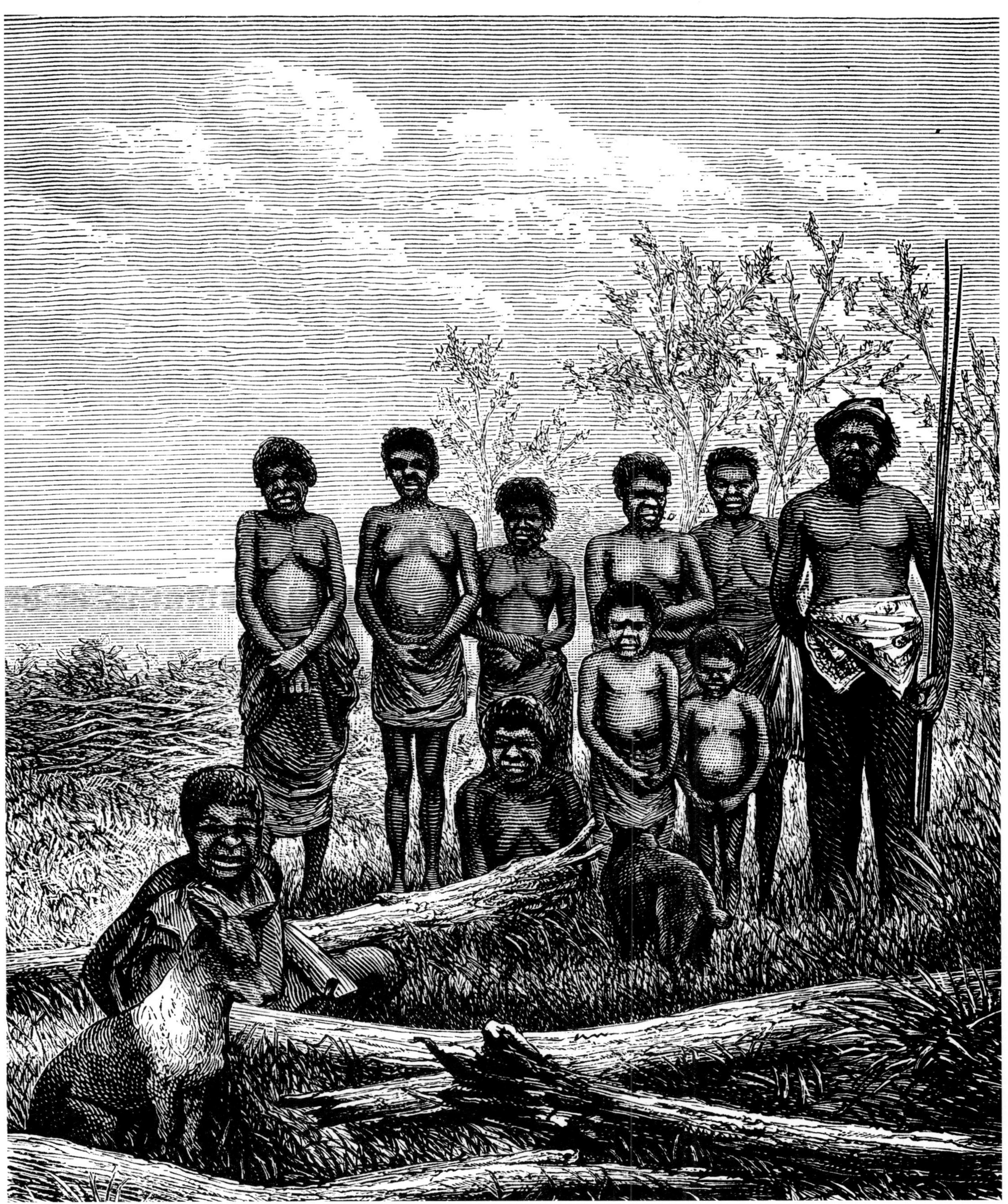

Australian Aboriginal hunters

Einheimische australische Jäger

Cacciatori aborigeni australiani

Chasseurs aborigènes d'Australie

Cazadores aborígenes australianos

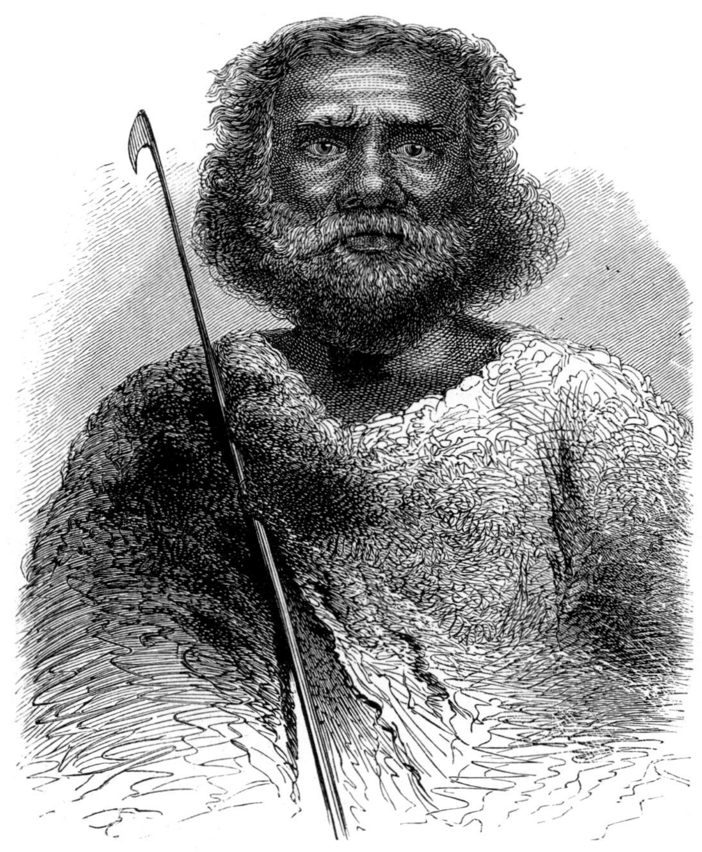

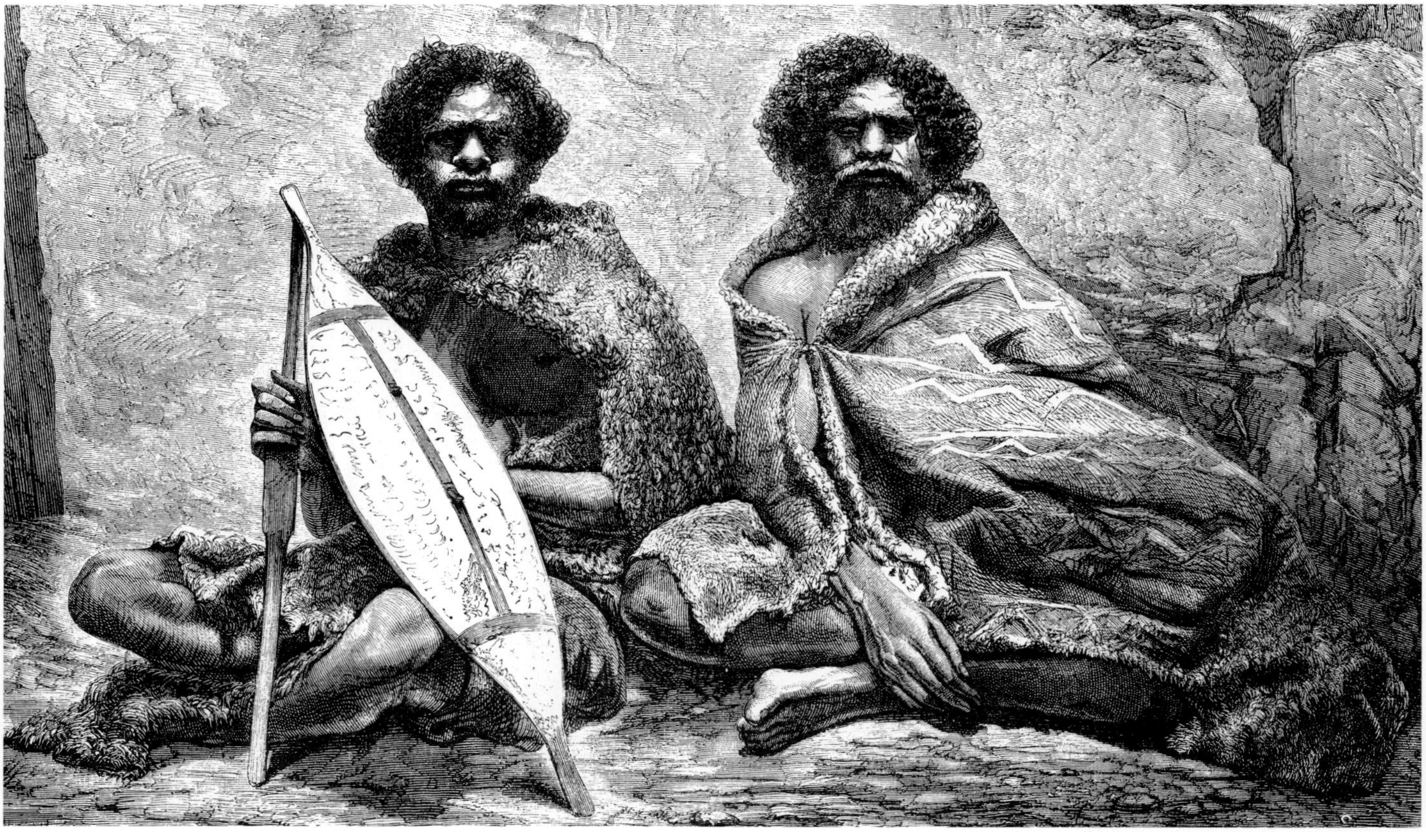

Australian Aboriginal men, c. 1860

Australische Aboriginies, um 1860

Aborigeni australiani, ca. 1860

Aborigènes d'Australie, vers 1860

Hombres aborígenes australianos, hacia 1860

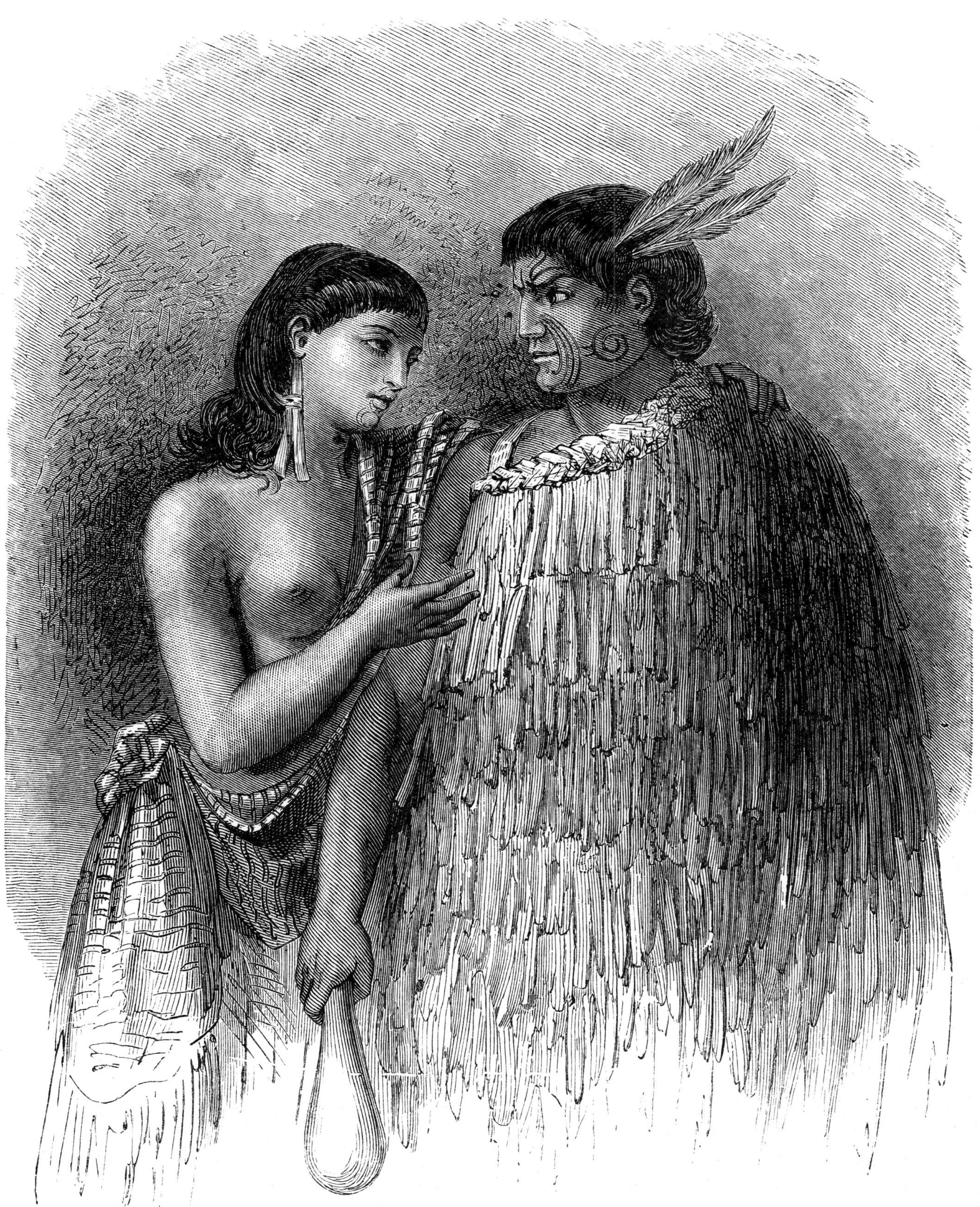

A Maori Chief with his wife, c. 1880

Ein Maorihäuptling mit seiner Frau, um 1880

Un capo maori con sua moglie, ca. 1880

Chef maori et sa femme, vers 1880

Jefe maorí con su esposa, alrededor del año 1880

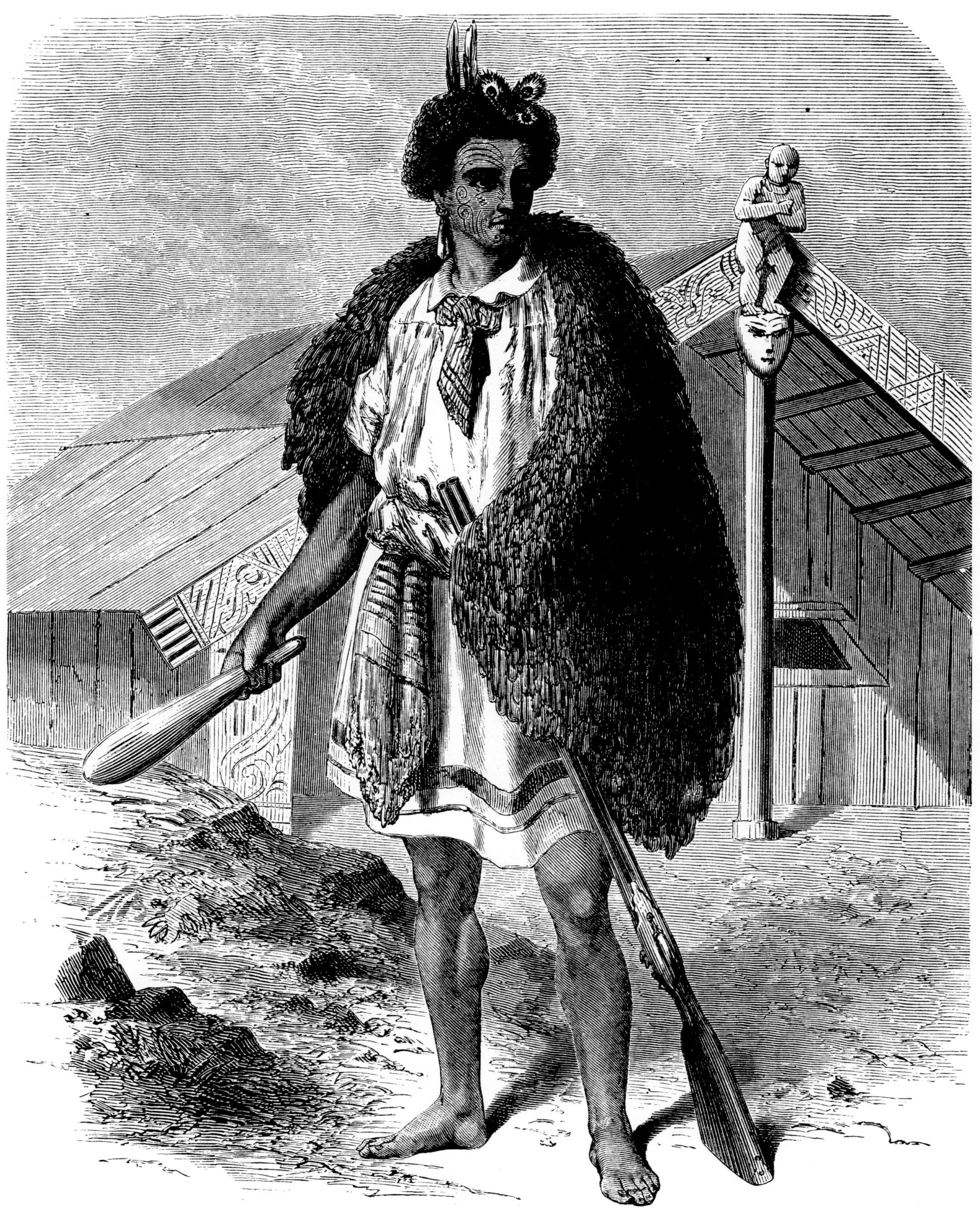

Maori chief, c. 1860 Maorihäuptling, um 1860 Capo maori, ca. 1860 Chef maori, vers 1860 Jefe maorí, hacia 1860

New Zealand

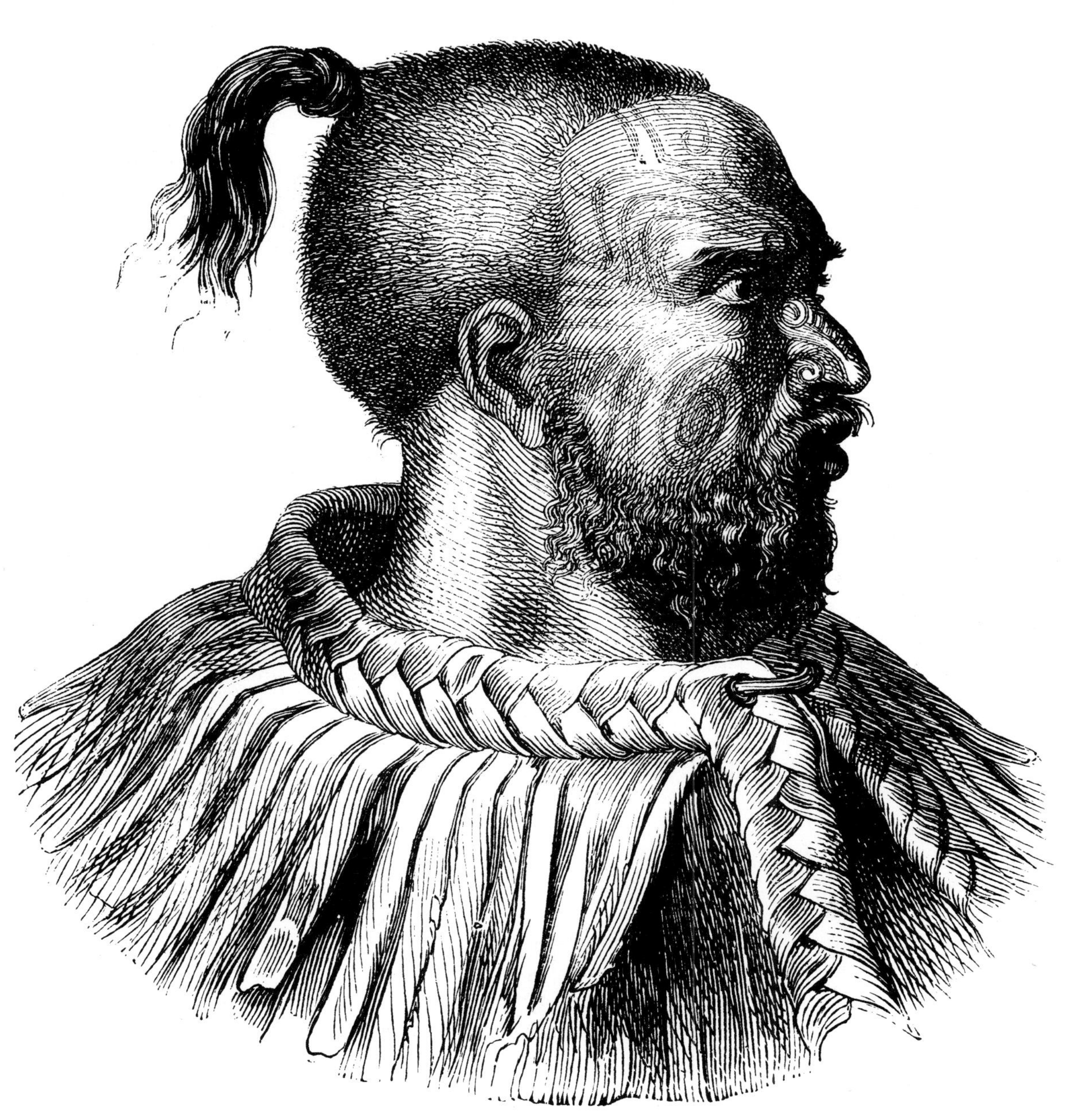

Maori chief, c. 1860 Maorihäuptling, um 1860 Capo maori, ca. 1860 Chef maori, vers 1860 Jefe maorí, hacia 1860

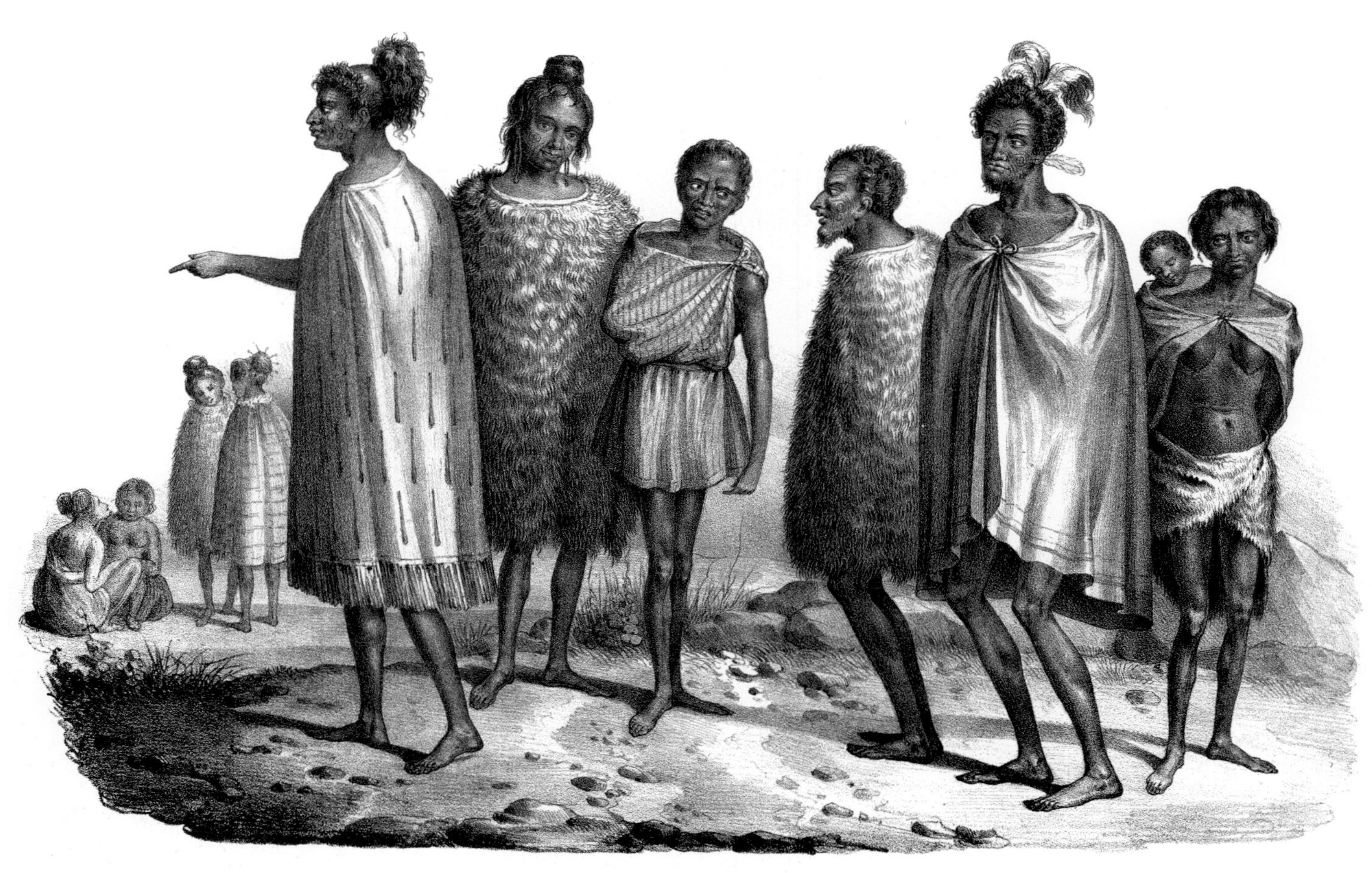

New Zealanders, c. 1840

Neuseeländer, um 1840

Abitanti della Nuova Zelanda, ca. 1840

Habitants de Nouvelle-Zélande, vers 1840

Neozelandeses, hacia el año 1840

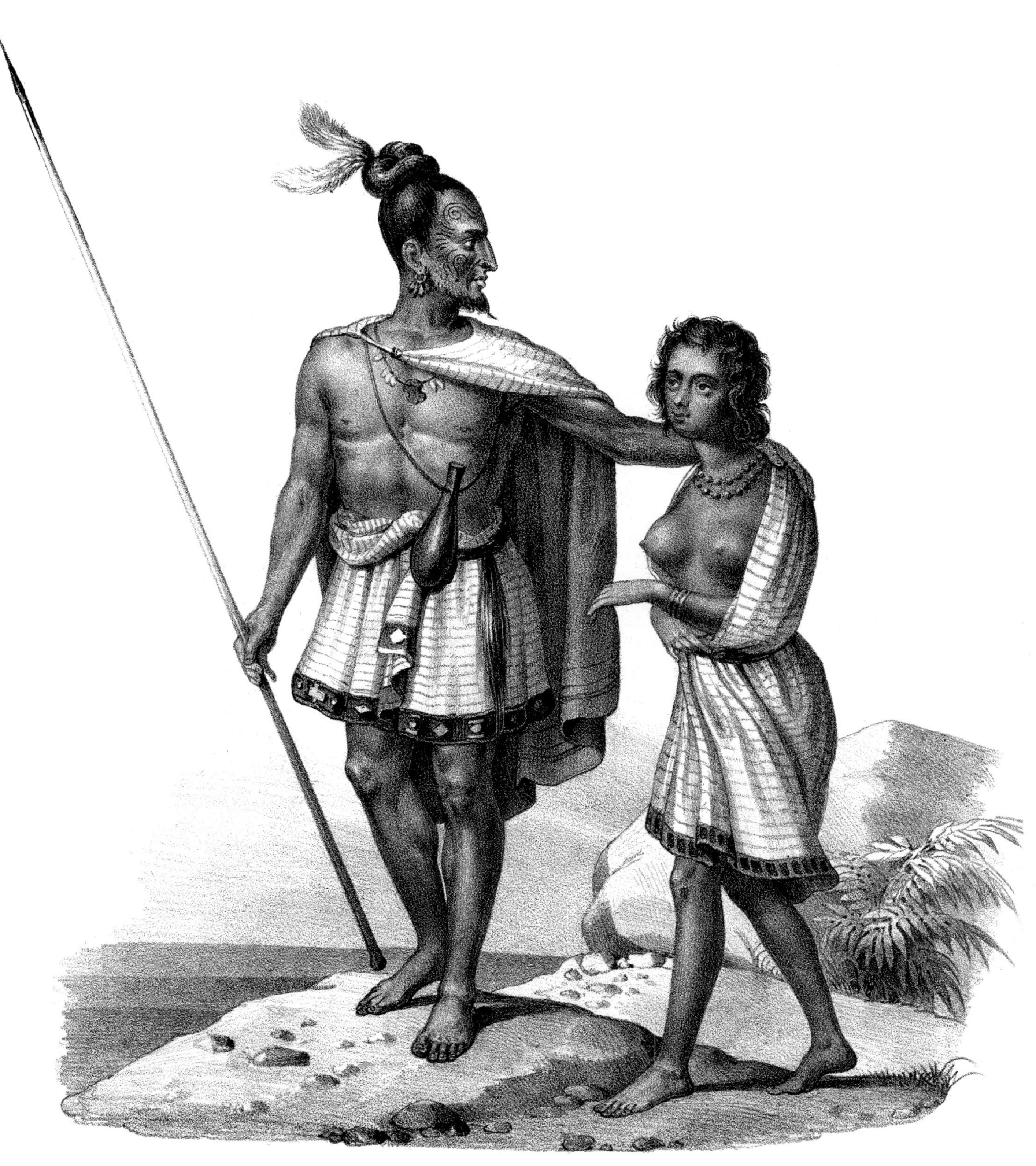

New Zealanders, c. 1840

Neuseeländer, um 1840

Abitanti della Nuova Zelanda, ca. 1840

Habitants de Nouvelle-Zélande, vers 1840

Neozelandeses, hacia el año 1840

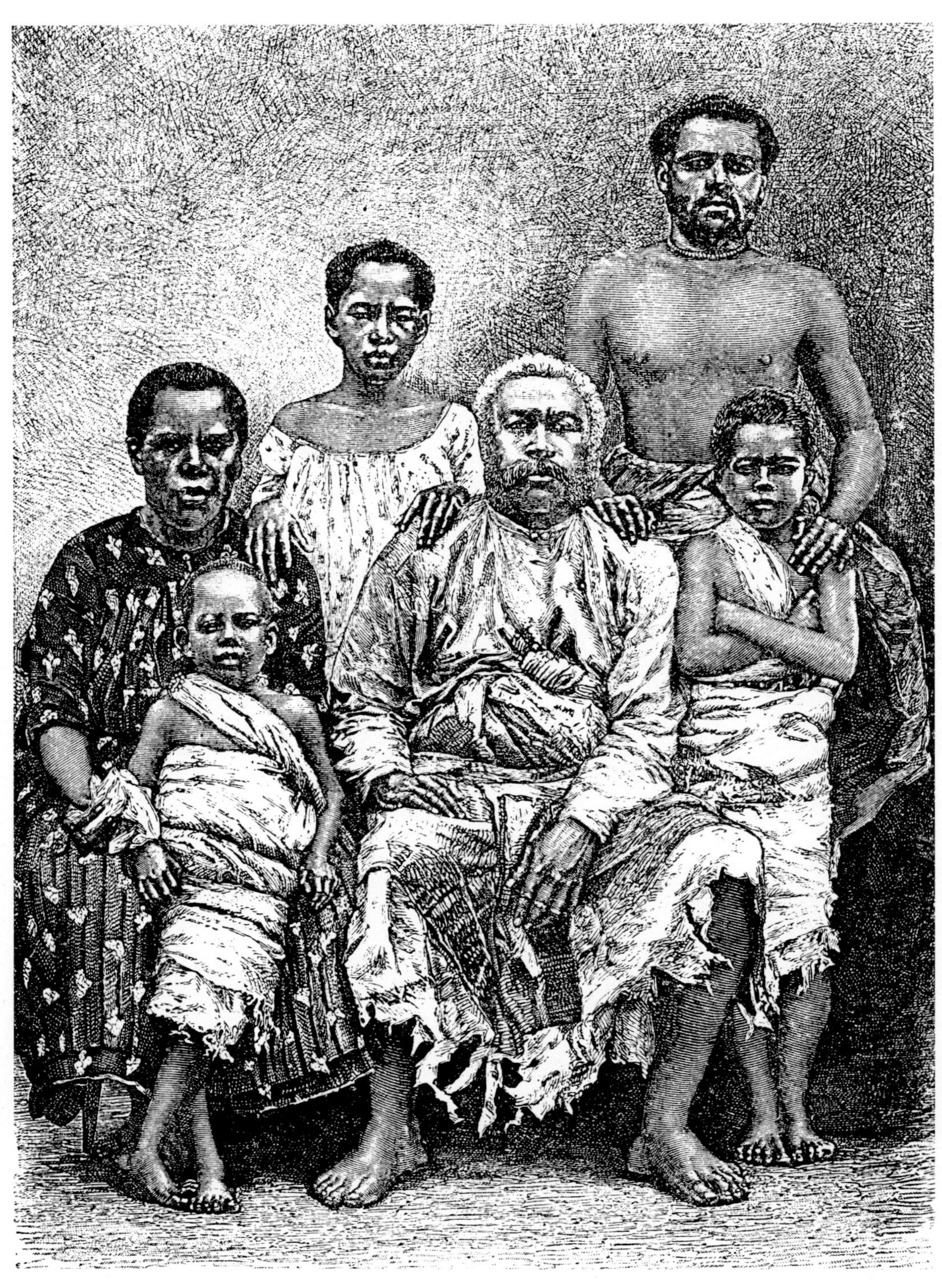

Fijian headman with family, c. 1890

Fidschianer-Häuptling mit Familie, um 1890

Capotribù delle Isole Figi con famiglia, ca. 1890

Chef fidjien et sa famille, vers 1890

Jefe fiyiano con su familia, hacia 1890

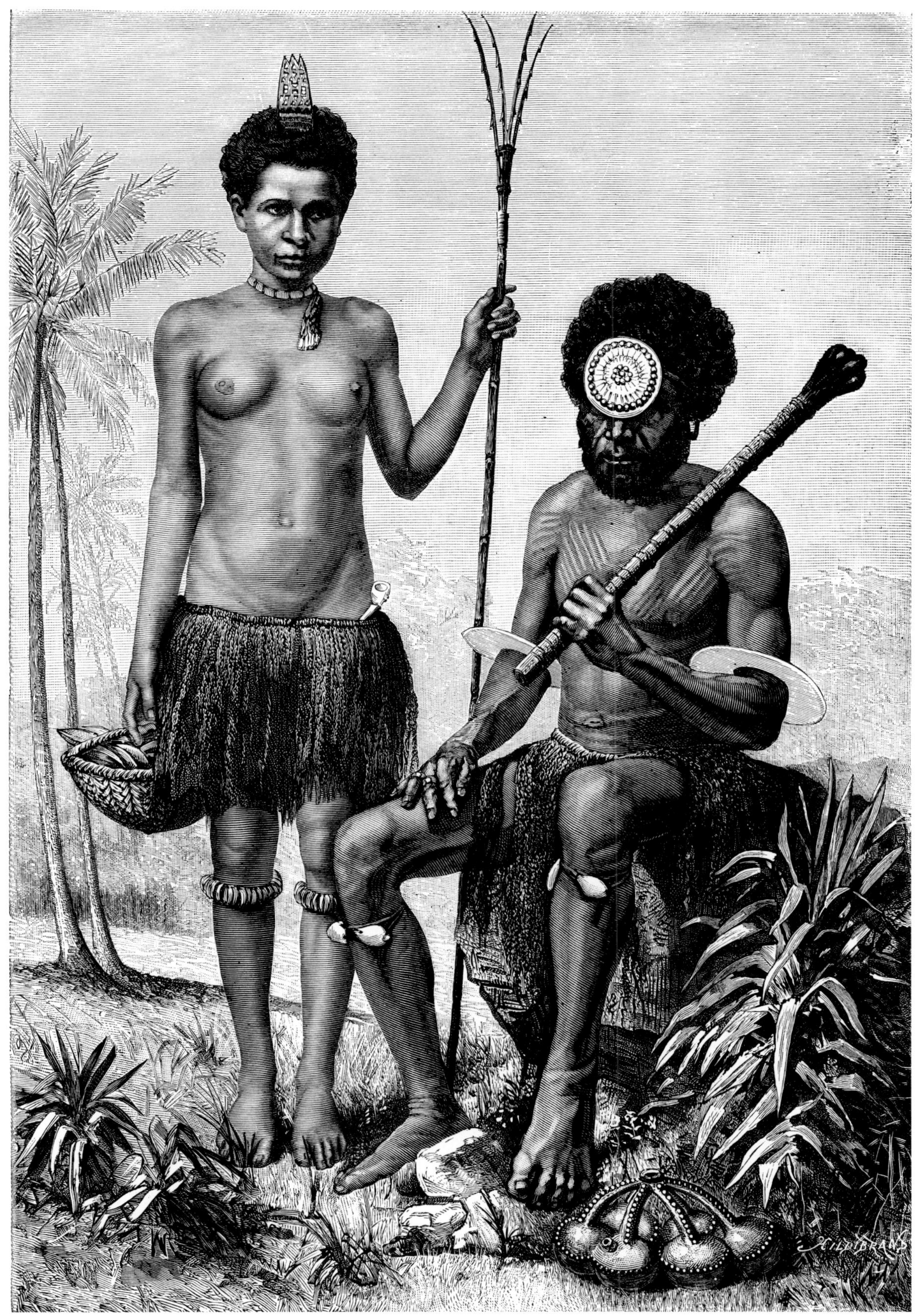

Fijians, c. 1880

Fidschianer, um 1880

Abitanti delle Isole Figi, ca. 1880

Fidjiens, vers 1880

Fiyianos, hacia 1880

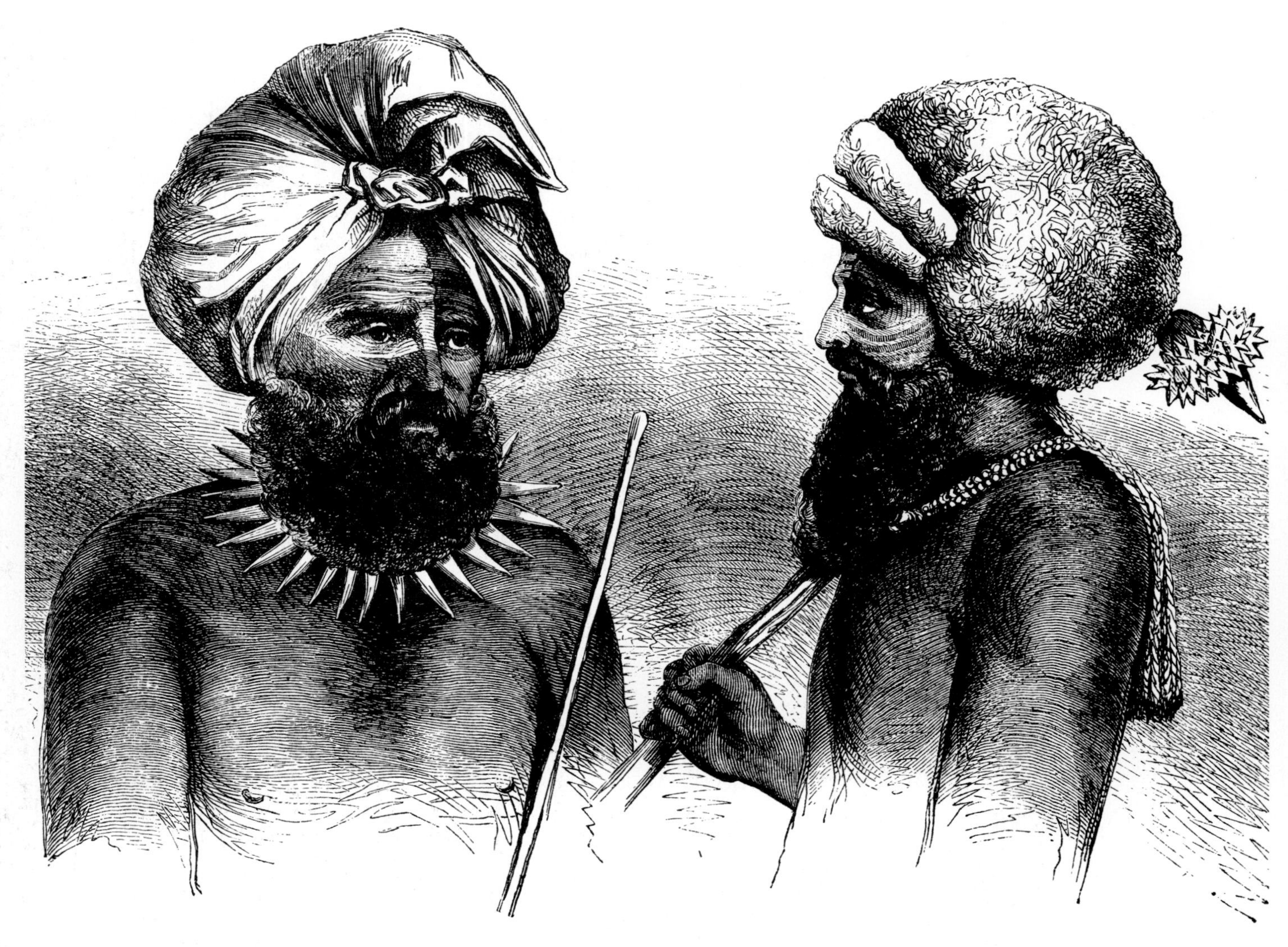

Fijians, c. 1860

Fidschianer, um 1860

Abitanti delle Isole Figi, ca. 1860

Fidjiens, vers 1860

Fiyianos, hacia 1860

Fiji

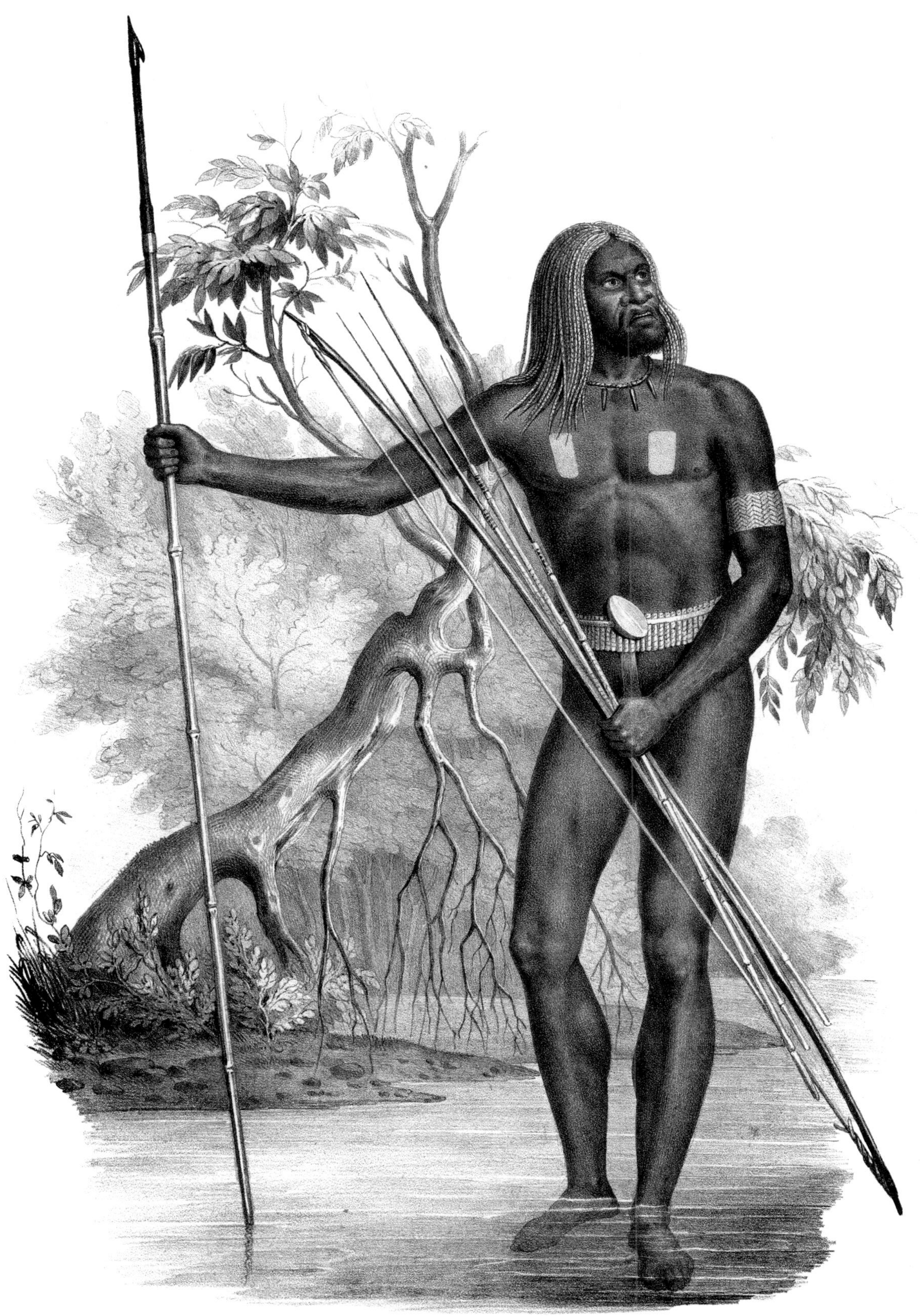

Papua warrior, c. 1880

Papua-Krieger, um 1880

Guerriero papuano, ca. 1880

Guerrier papou, vers 1880

Guerrero papú, 1880

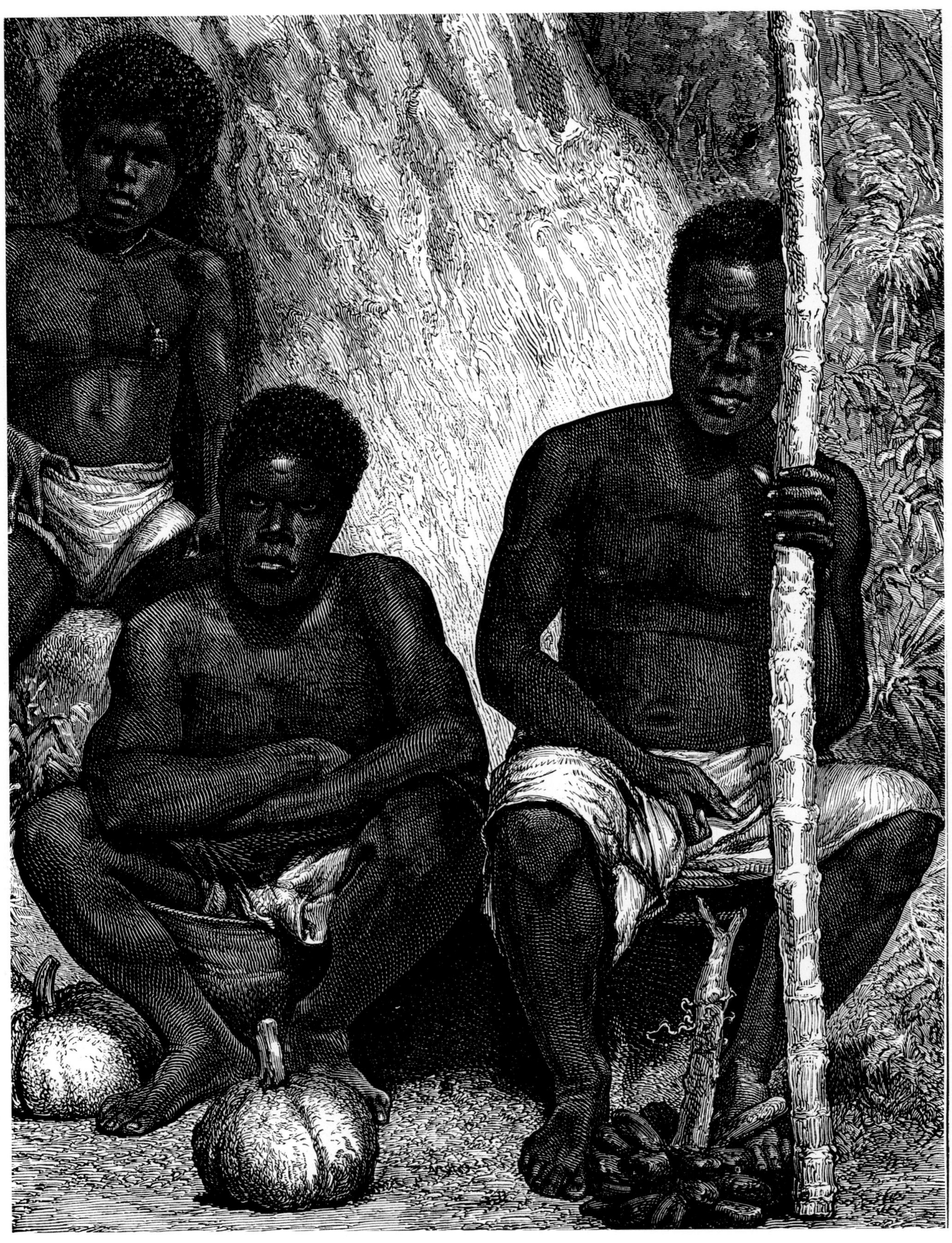

Natives from New Caledonia, c. 1880

Eingeborene aus Neukaledonien, um 1880

Indigeni della Nuova Caledonia, ca. 1880

Indigènes de Nouvelle-Calédonie, vers 1880

Nativos de Nueva Caledonia, hacia 1880

New Caledonia

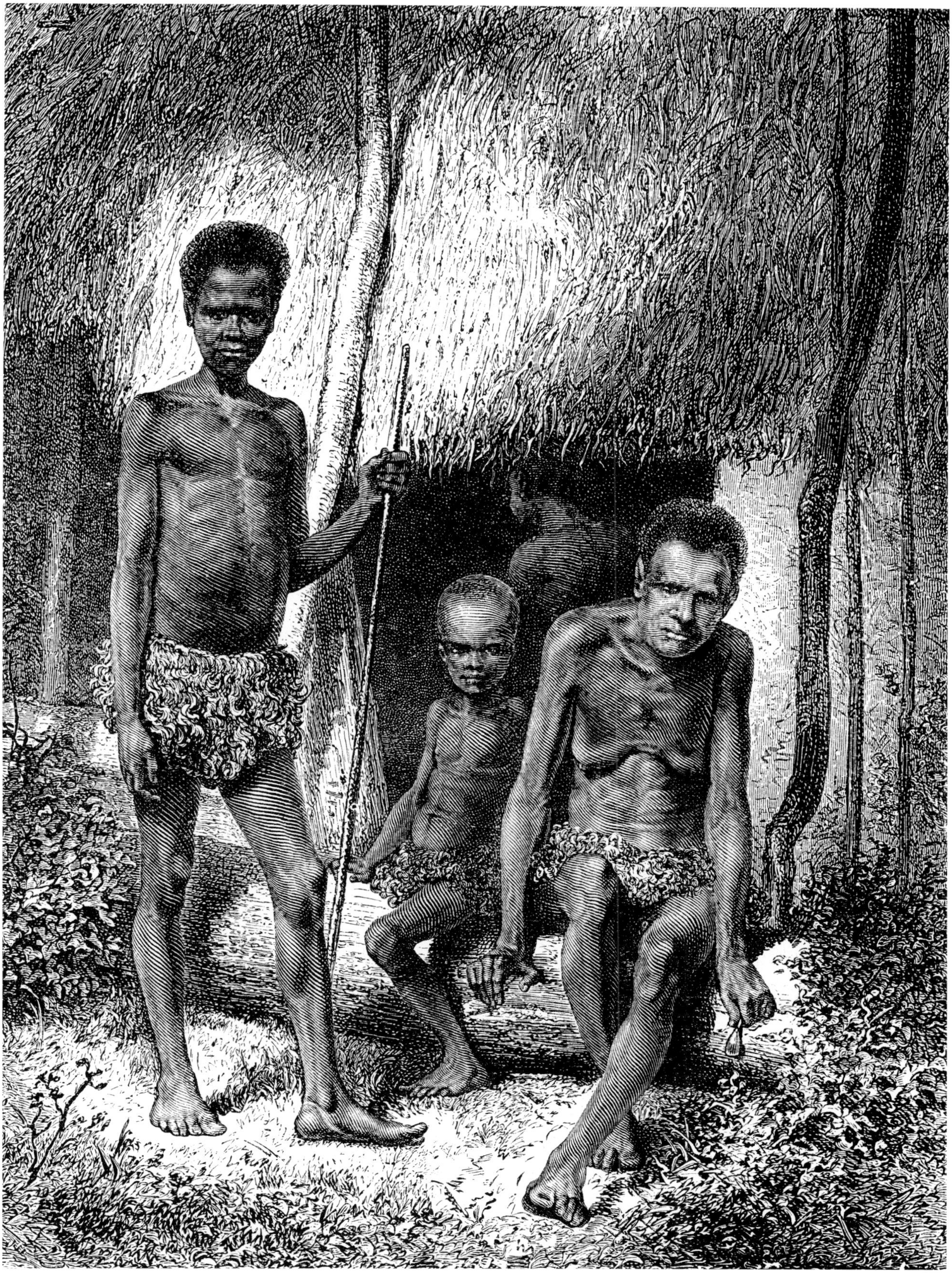

New Caledonians, c. 1880

Neukaledonier, um 1880

Abitanti della Nuova Caledonia, ca. 1880

Habitants de Nouvelle-Calédonie, vers 1880

Habitantes de Nueva Caledonia, hacia 1880

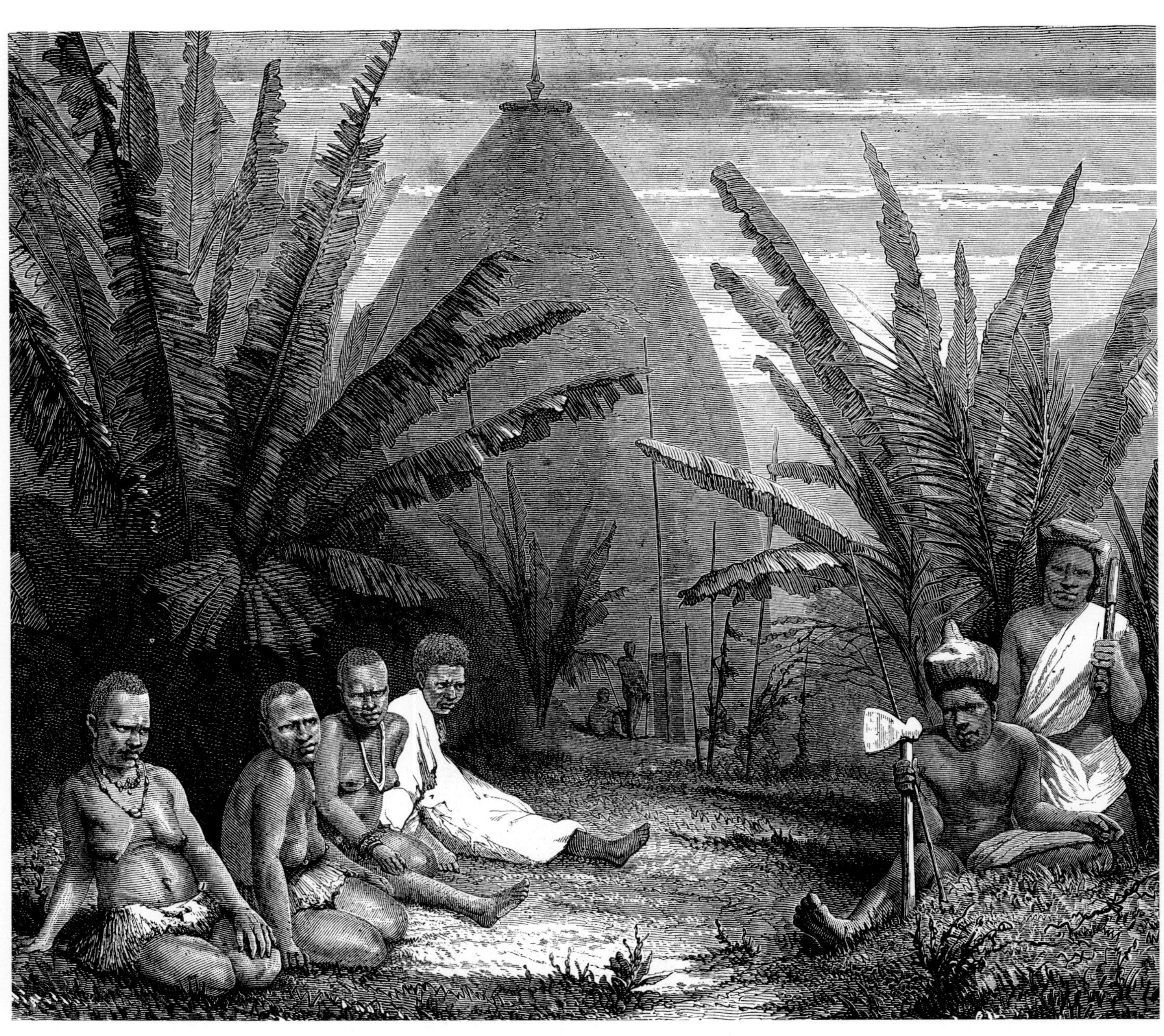

New Caledonian chief and subjects, c. 1880

Neukaledonischer Häuptling mit Untertanen, um 1880

Capo e sudditi della Nuova Caledonia, ca. 1880

Chef de Nouvelle-Calédonie et ses sujets, vers 1880

Jefe y súbditos de Nueva Caledonia, hacia 1880

New Caledonia

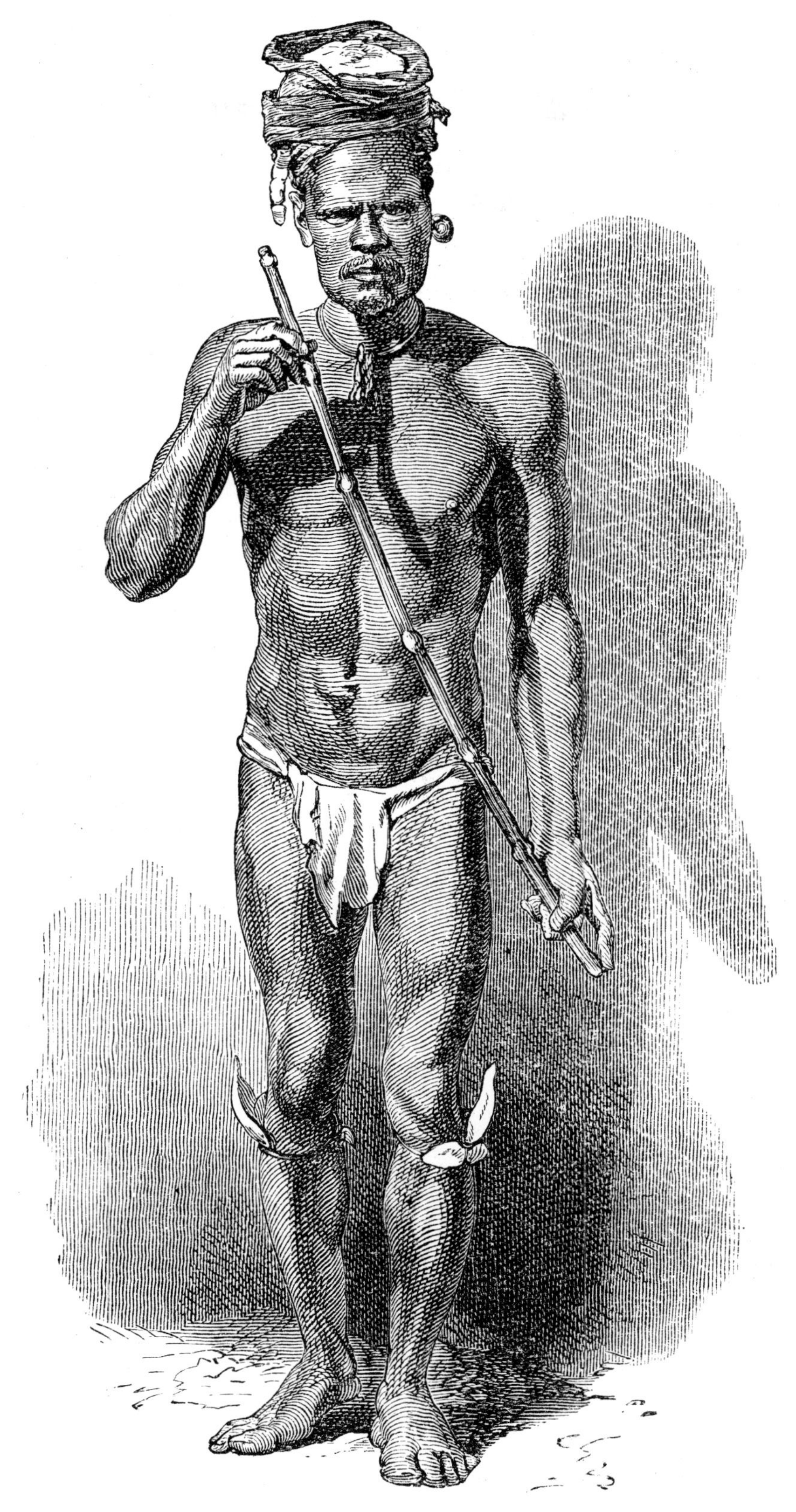

Man from New Caledonia, c. 1880

Mann aus Neukaledonien, um 1880

Uomo della Nuova Caledonia, ca. 1880

Homme de Nouvelle-Calédonie, vers 1880

Hombre de Nueva Caledonia, hacia 1880

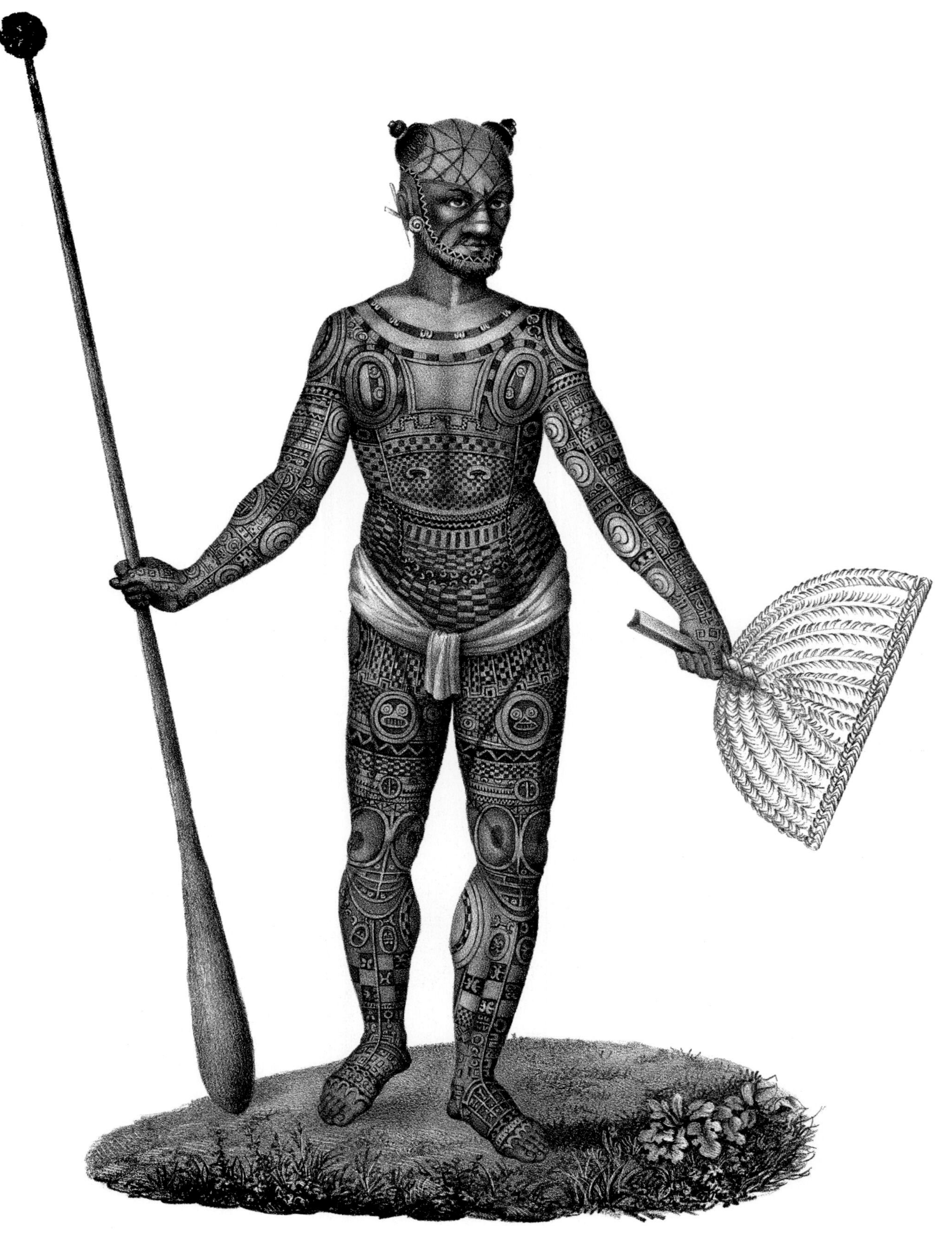

Tattooed man from Nuka Hiva, c. 1840

Tätowierter Mann aus Nuku Hiva, um 1840

Uomo tatuato di Nuka Hiva, ca. 1840

Homme tatoué de Nuka Hiva, vers 1840

Hombre tatuado de Nuku Hiva, hacia 1840

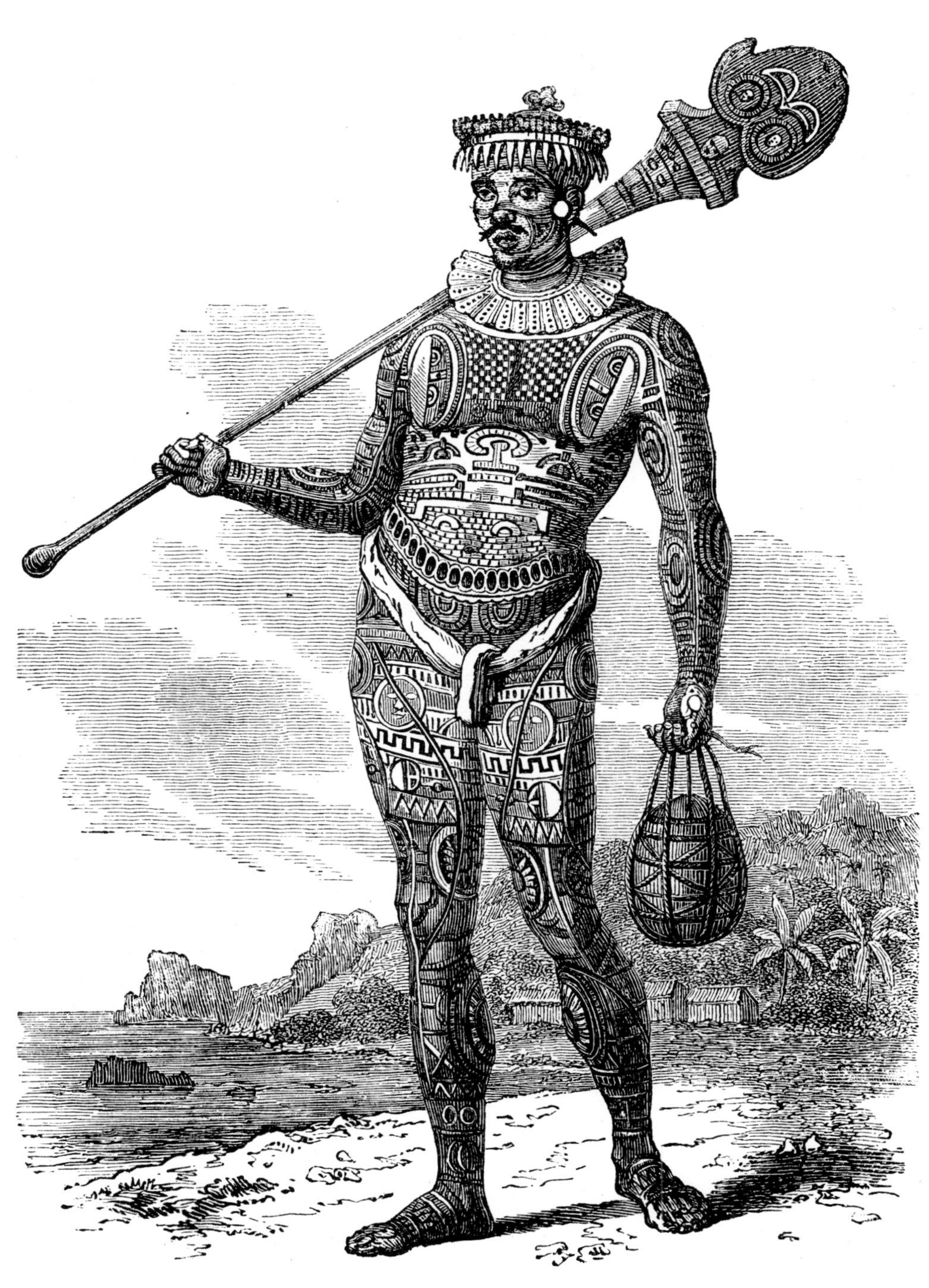

Tattooed man from the Marquesas Islands, c. 1880

Tätowierter Mann von den Marquesas-Inseln, um 1880

Uomo tatuato delle Isole Marquesas, ca. 1880

Homme tatoué des Iles Marquises, vers 1880

Hombre tatuado de las islas Marquesas, alrededor del año 1880

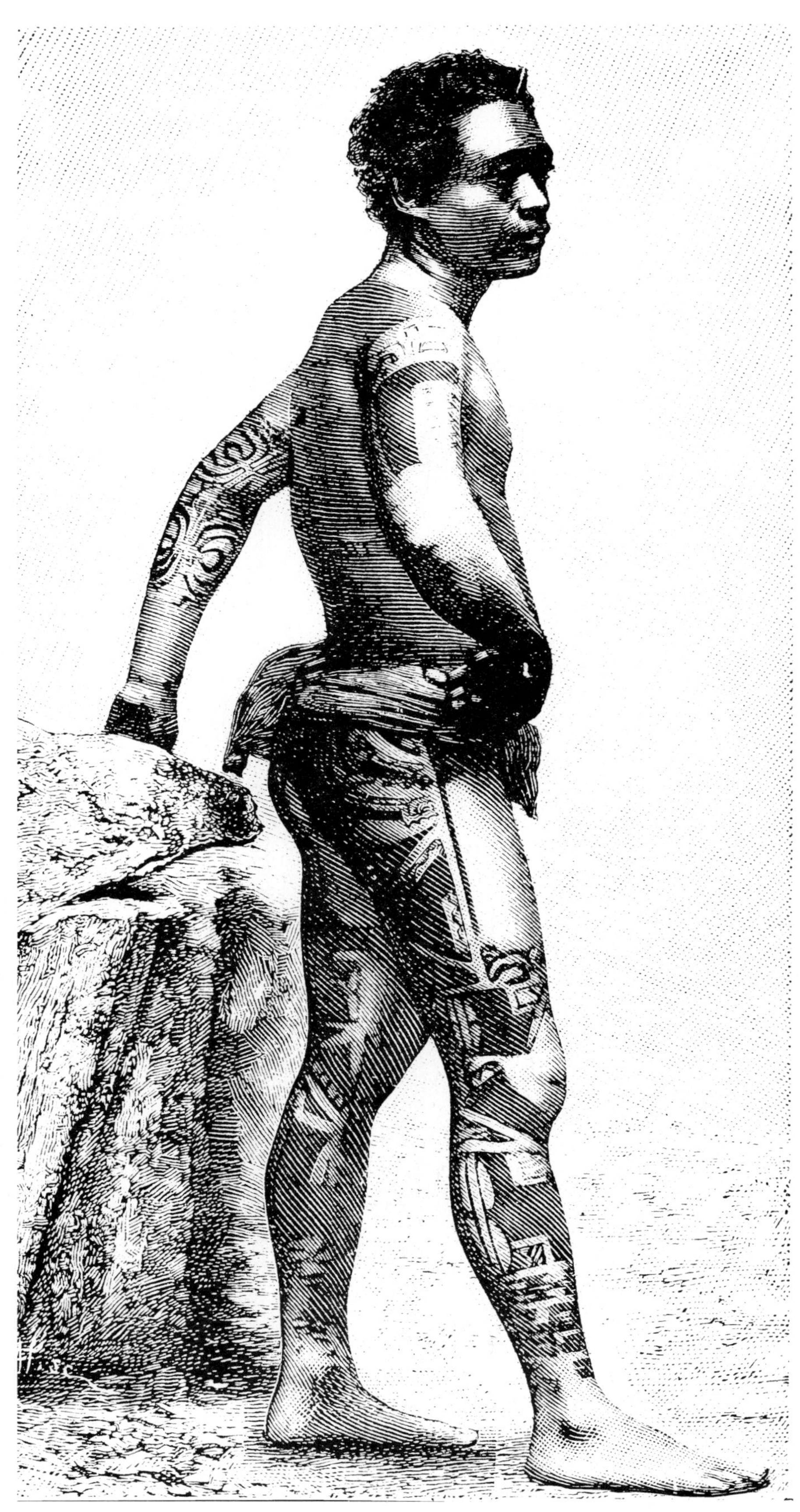

Tattooed man from the Marquesas Islands, c. 1880

Tätowierter Mann von den Marquesas-Inseln, um 1880

Uomo tatuato delle Isole Marquesas, ca. 1880

Homme tatoué des Iles Marquises, vers 1880

Hombre tatuado de las islas Marquesas, hacia 1880

Marquesas Islands

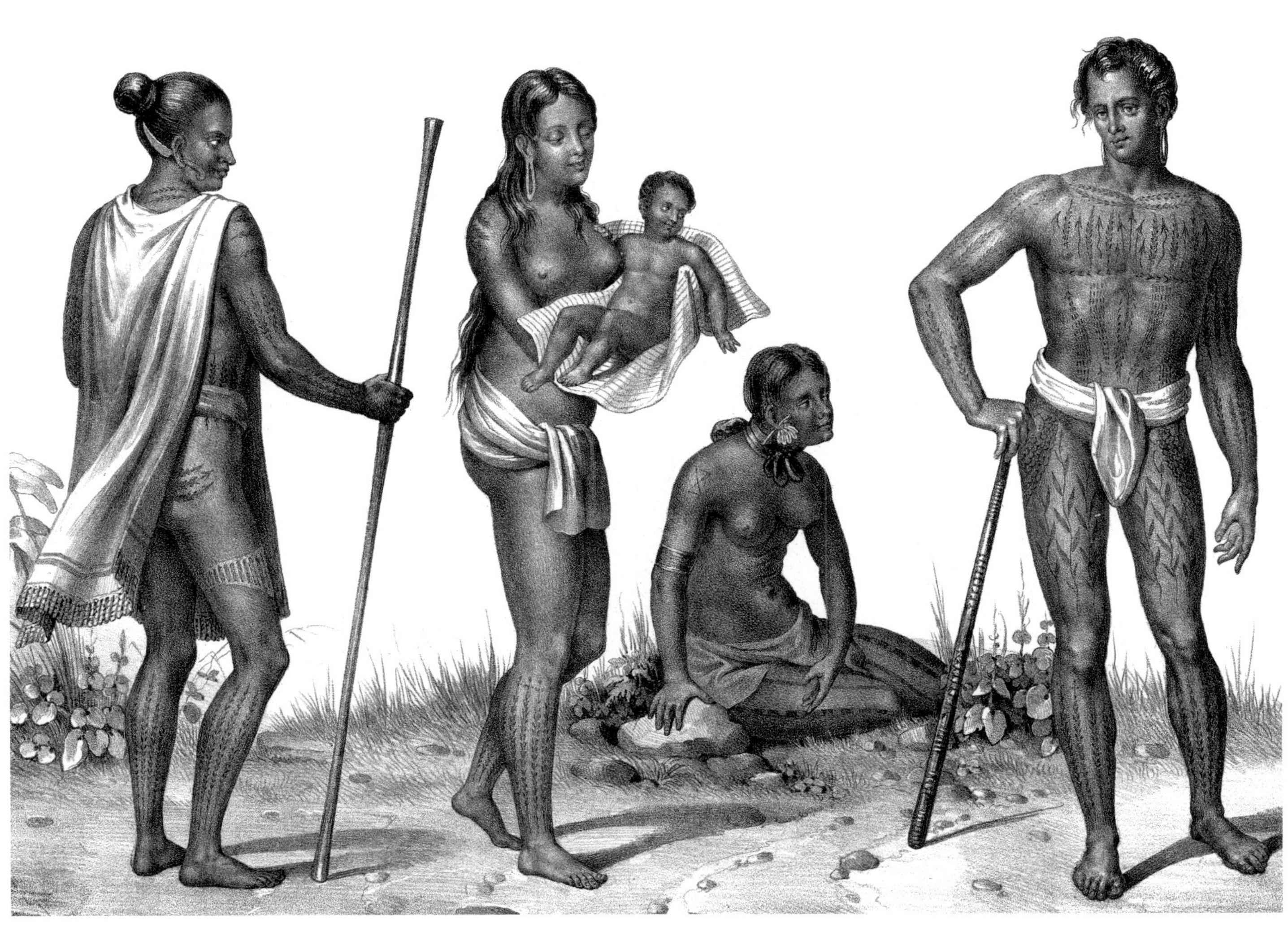

Natives of the Coroline Islands, c. 1840

Eingeborene von den Karolinen-Inseln, um 1840

Indigeni delle Isole Caroline, ca. 1840

Indigène des Iles Coroline, vers 1840

Nativos de las islas Carolinas, hacia 1840

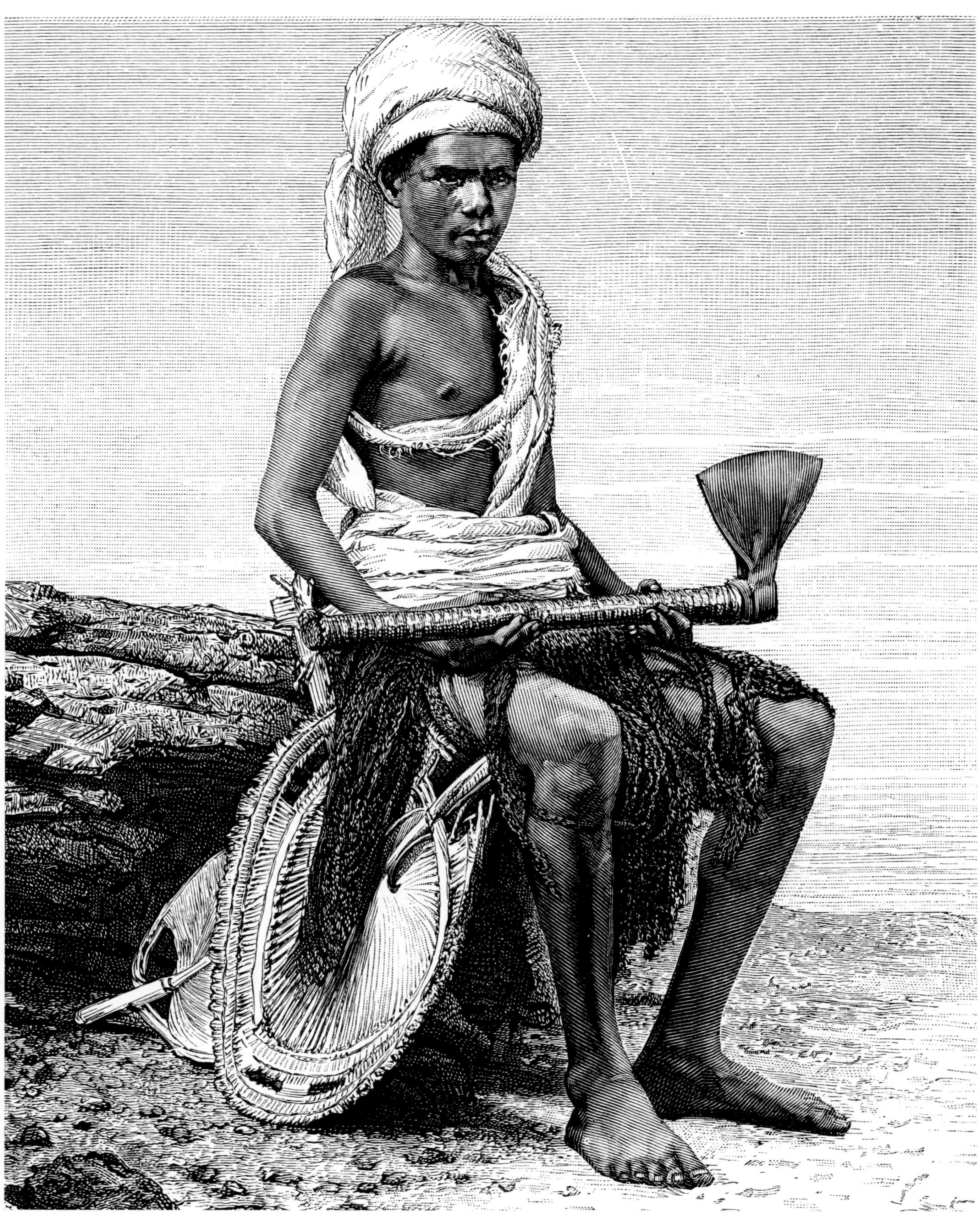

Micronesian, c. 1870

Mikronesier, um 1870

Abitante della Micronesia, ca. 1870

Micronésien, vers 1870

Micronesio, hacia 1870

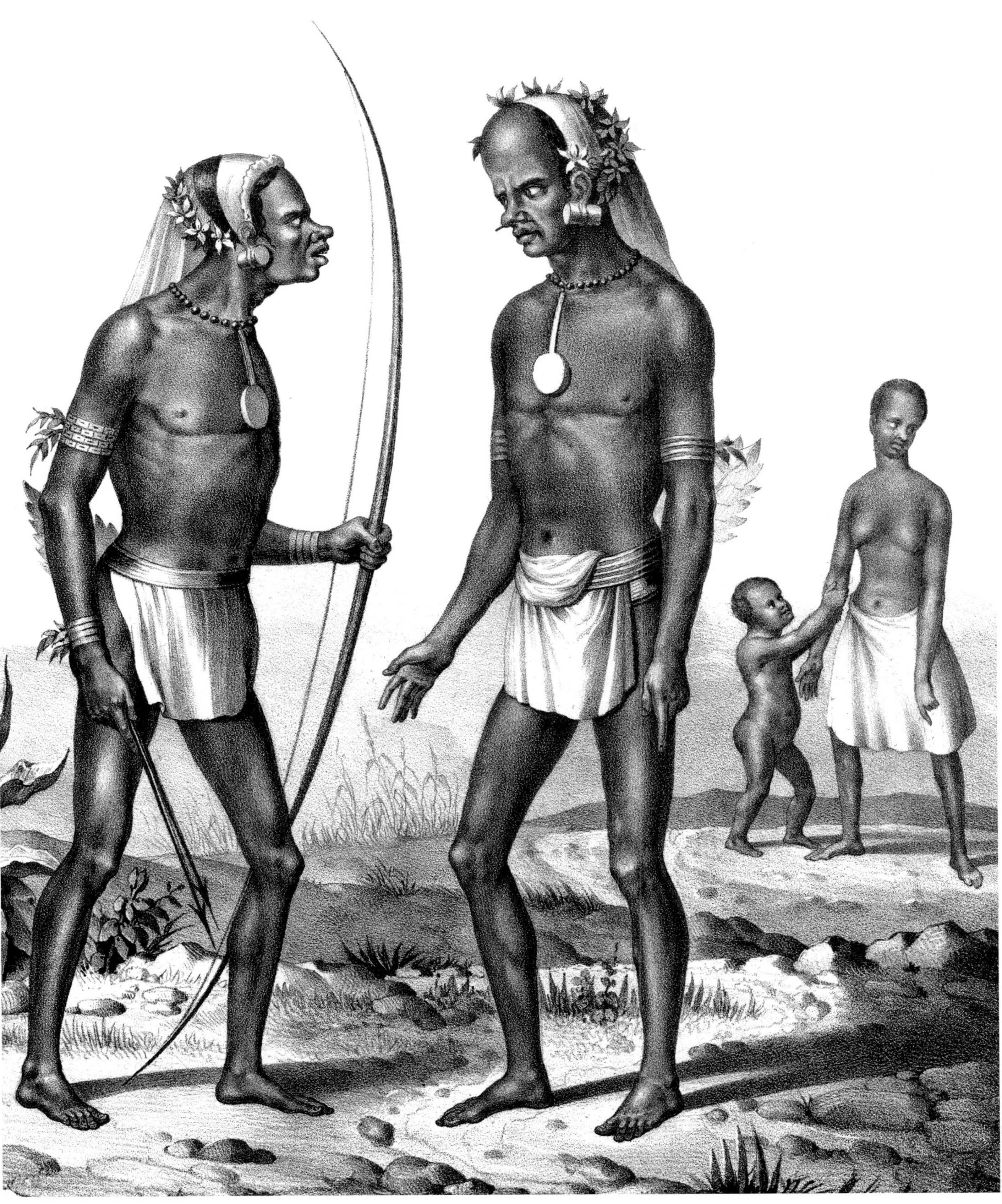

Natives of Micronesia, c. 1840

Eingeborene aus Mikronesien, um 1840

Indigeni della Micronesia, ca. 1840

Indigènes de Micronésie, vers 1840

Nativos de Micronesia, hacia 1840

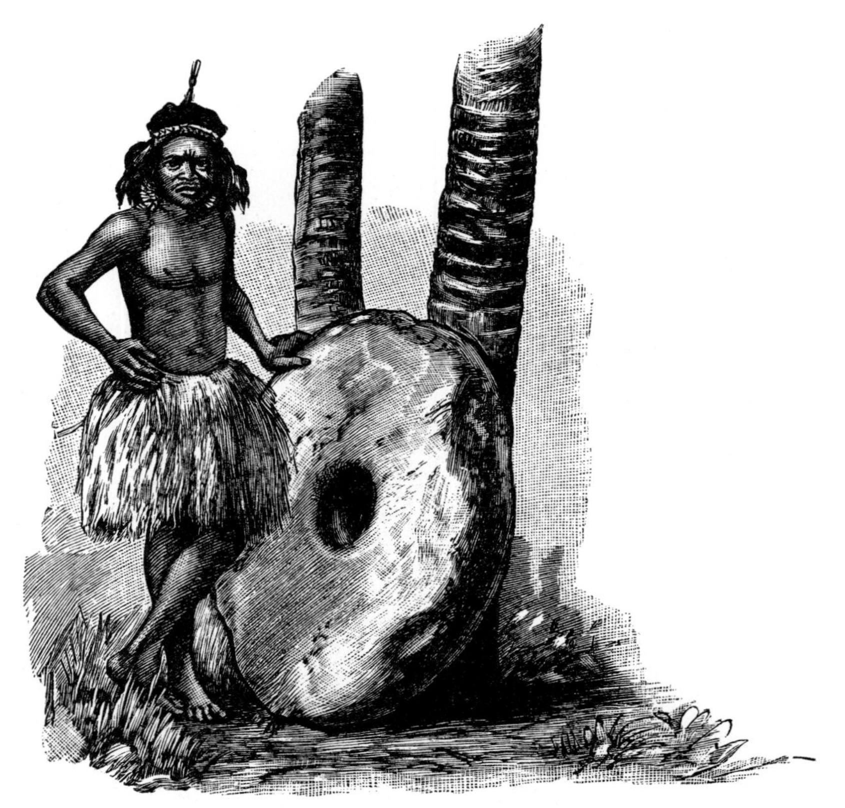

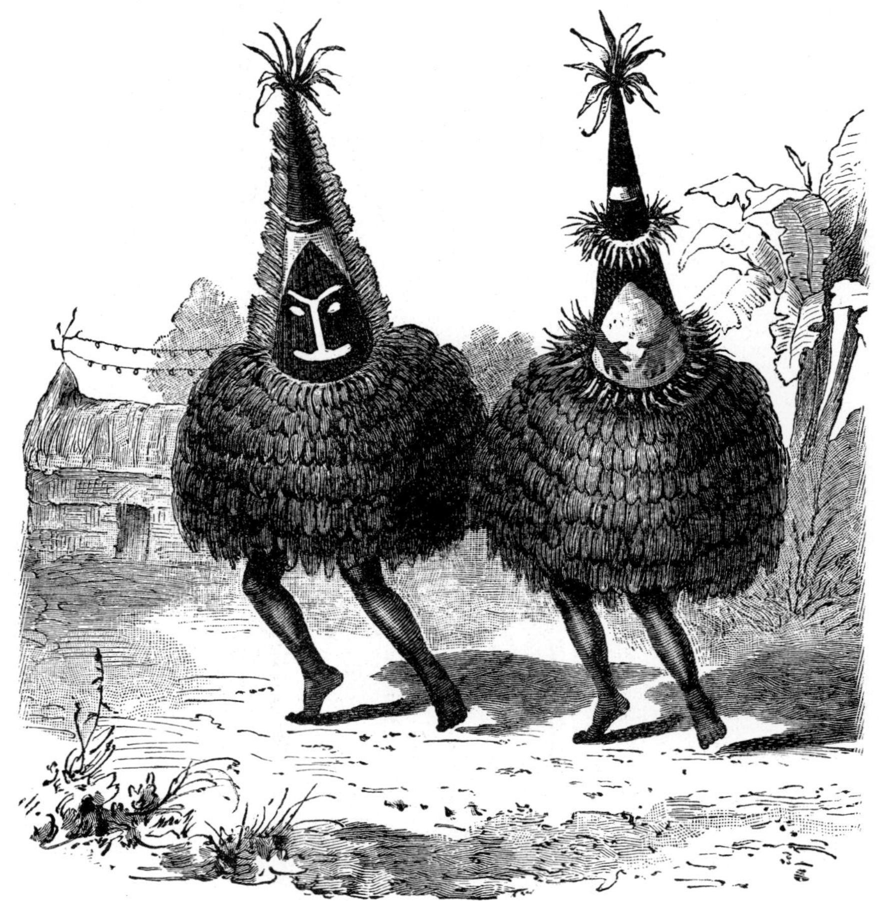

Man and dancers from Micronesia, c. 1900

Mann und Tänzer aus Mikronesien, um 1900

Uomo e danzatori della Micronesia, ca. 1900

Homme et danseurs micronésiens, vers 1900

Hombre y danzantes de Micronesia, hacia 1900

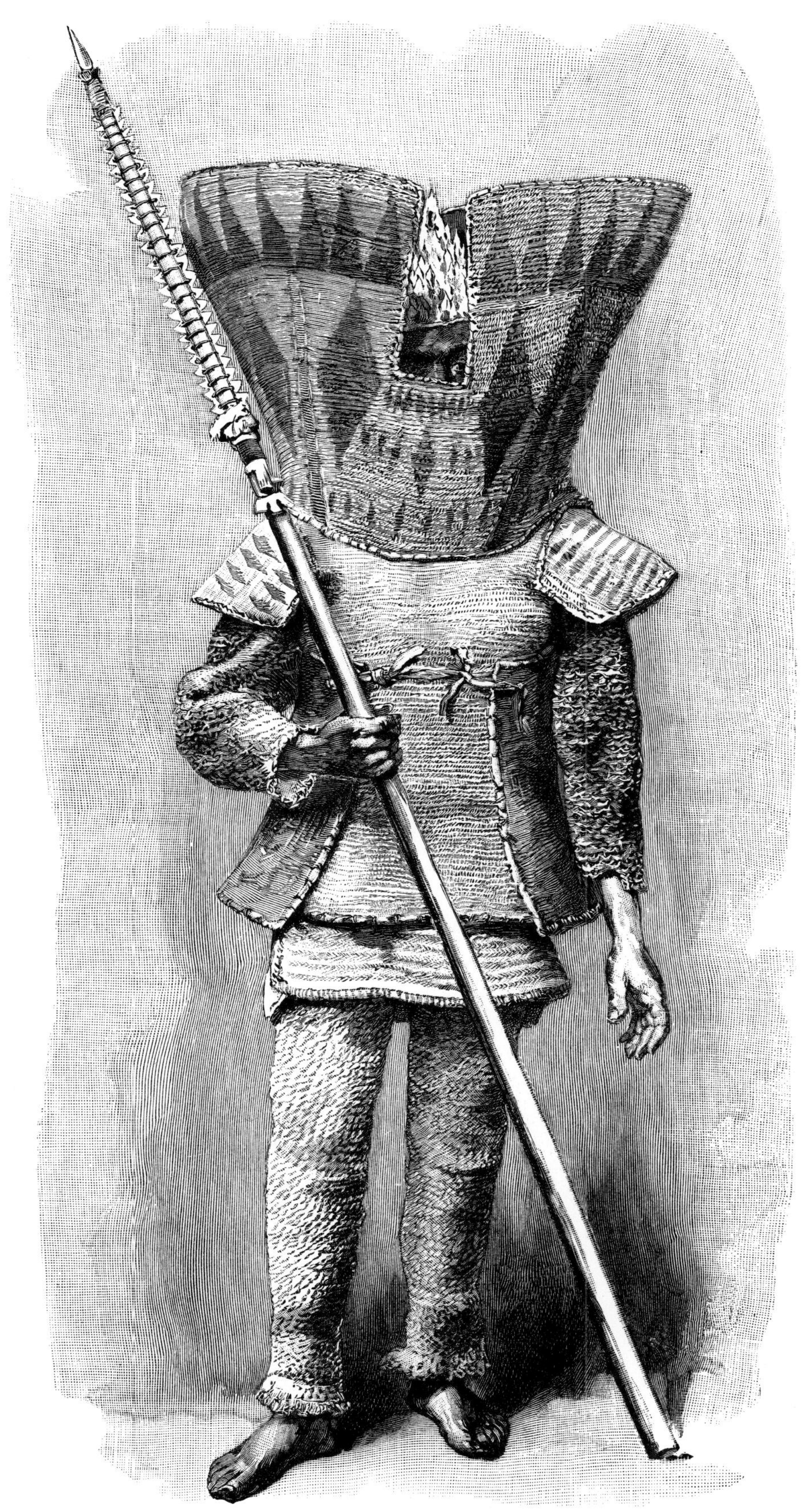

Warrior, Gilbert Islands, c. 1910

Krieger, Gilbert-Inseln, um 1910

Guerriero, Isole Gilbert, ca. 1910

Guerrier, Iles Gilbert, vers 1910

Guerrero de las islas Gilbert, hacia 1910

America
Amerika
America
Amérique
América
アメリカ
美洲

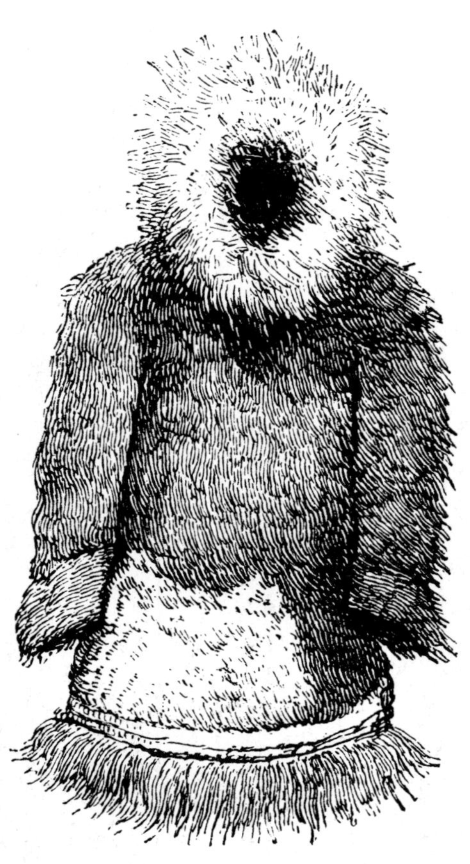

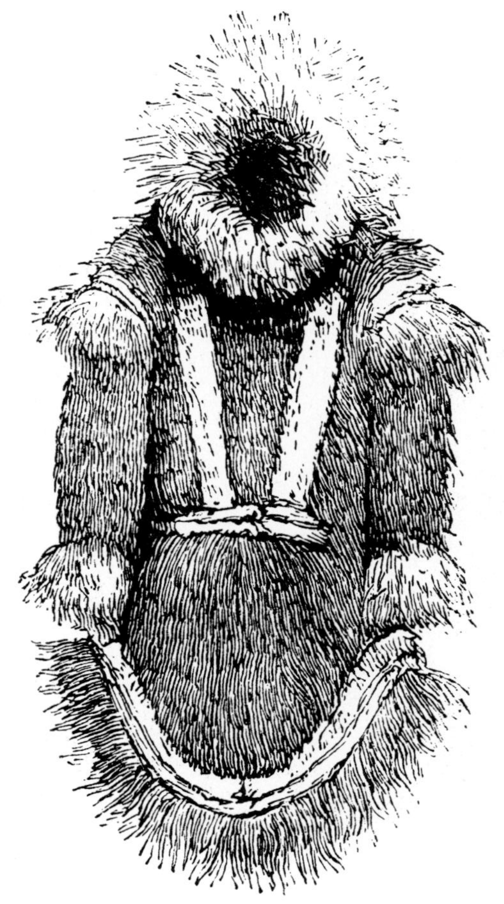

Male and female outfit from North Yukon, c. 1860

Männliche und weibliche Kleidung vom nördlichen Yukon, um 1860

Completo maschile e femminile dello Yukon del Nord, ca. 1860

Tenues homme et femme du Nord du Yukon, vers 1860

Trajes de hombre y de mujer del norte de Yukon, hacia 1860

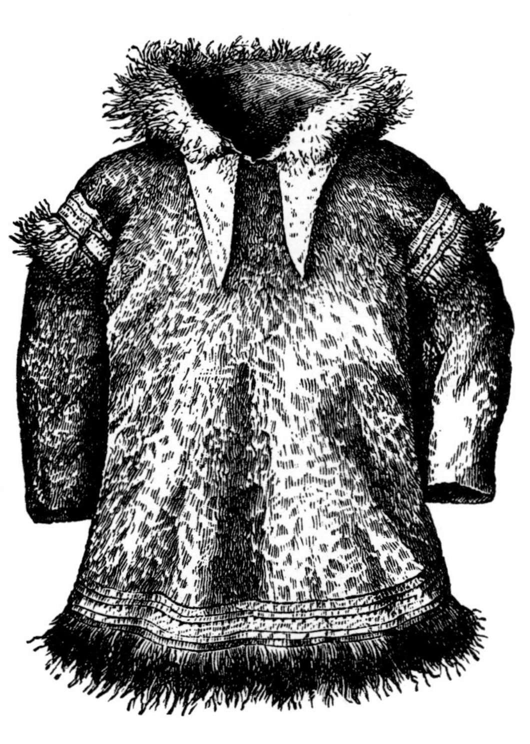

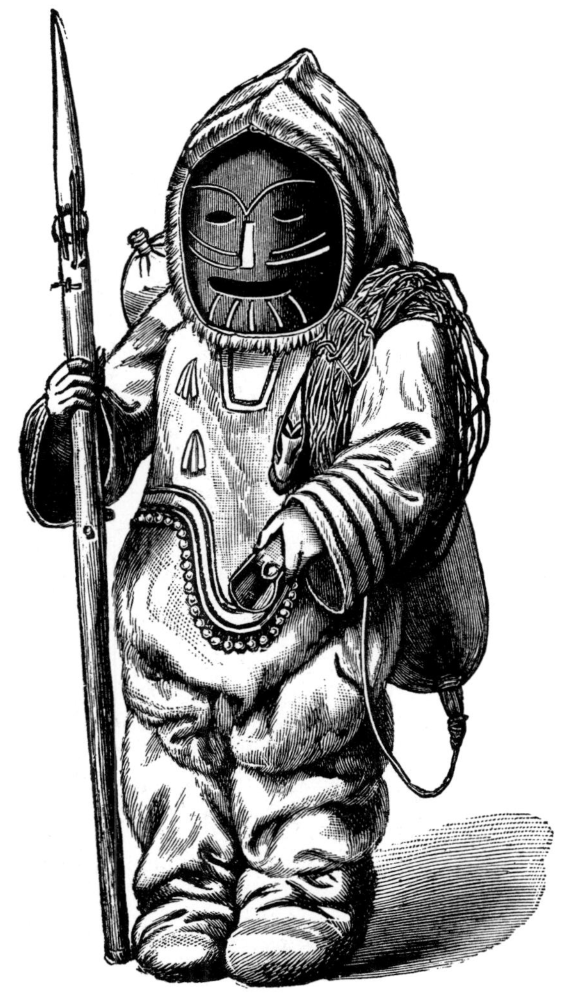

Man's jacket and masked Eskimo, c. 1900

Männerjacke und maskierter Eskimo, um 1900

Giacca maschile ed esquimese mascherato, ca. 1900

Manteau d'homme et esquimau masqué, vers 1900

Chaqueta de hombre y esquimal con máscara, alrededor del año 1900

Alaska

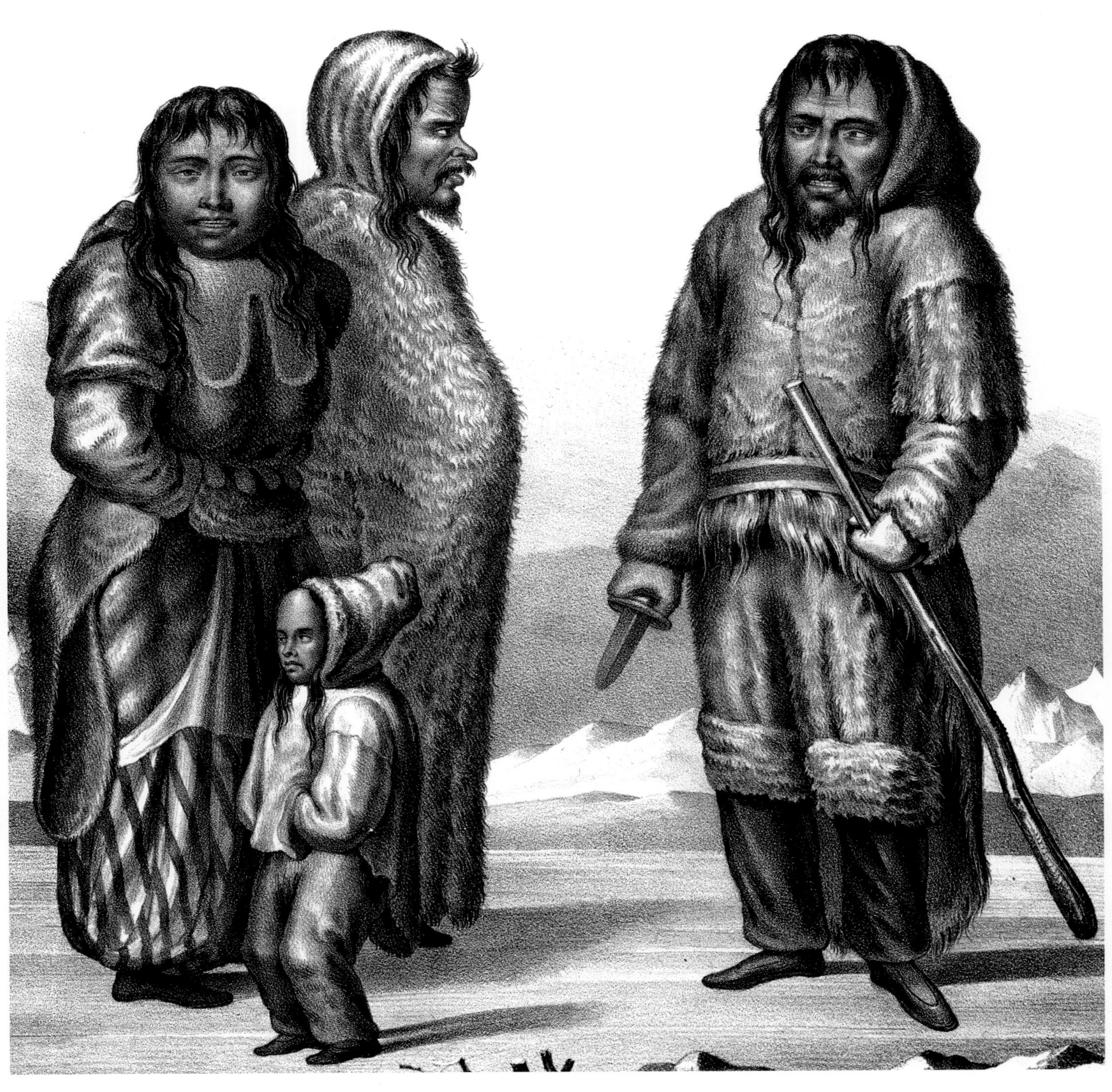

Eskimos, c. 1840 Eskimos, um 1840 Esquimesi, ca. 1840 Esquimaux, vers 1840 Esquimales, hacia 1840

Alaska

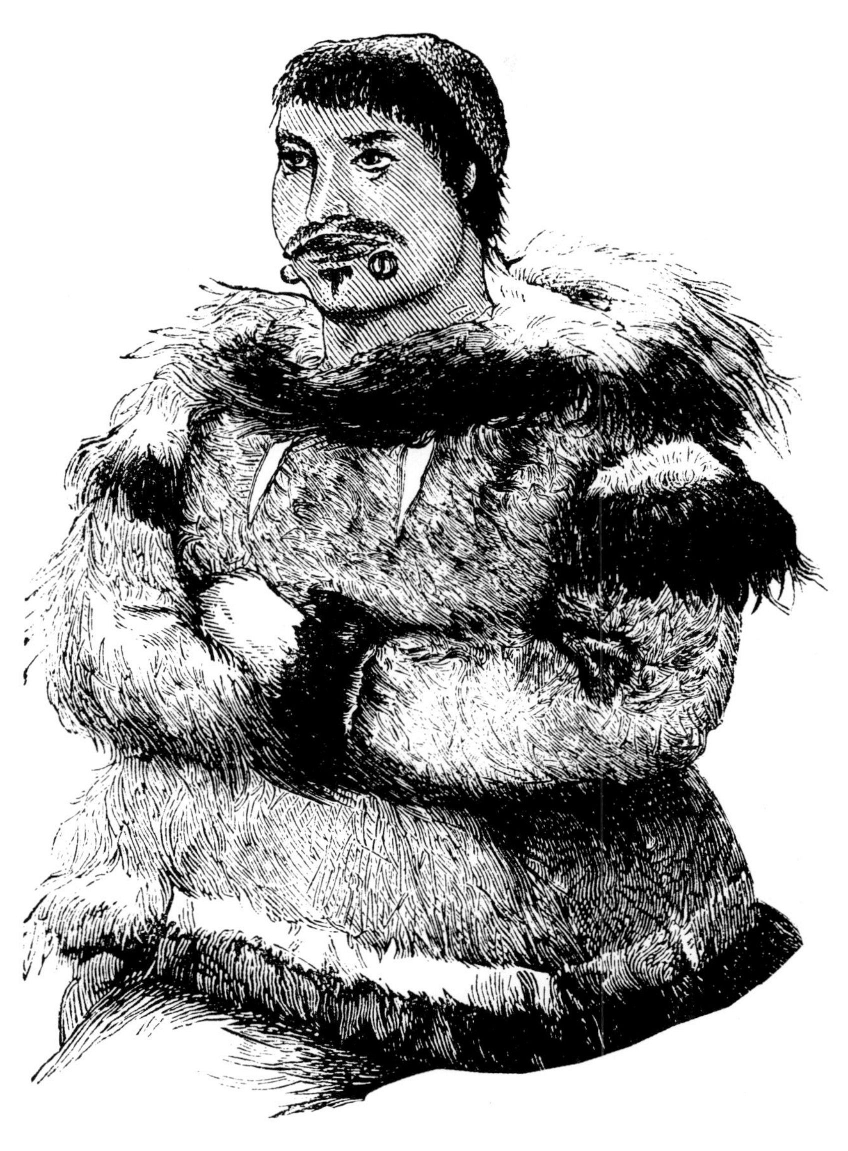

Native of North Yukon, c. 1860

Eingeborener vom nördlichen Yukon, um 1860

Indigeno dello Yukon del Nord, ca. 1860

Indigène du Nord du Yukon, vers 1860

Nativo del norte de Yukon, hacia 1860

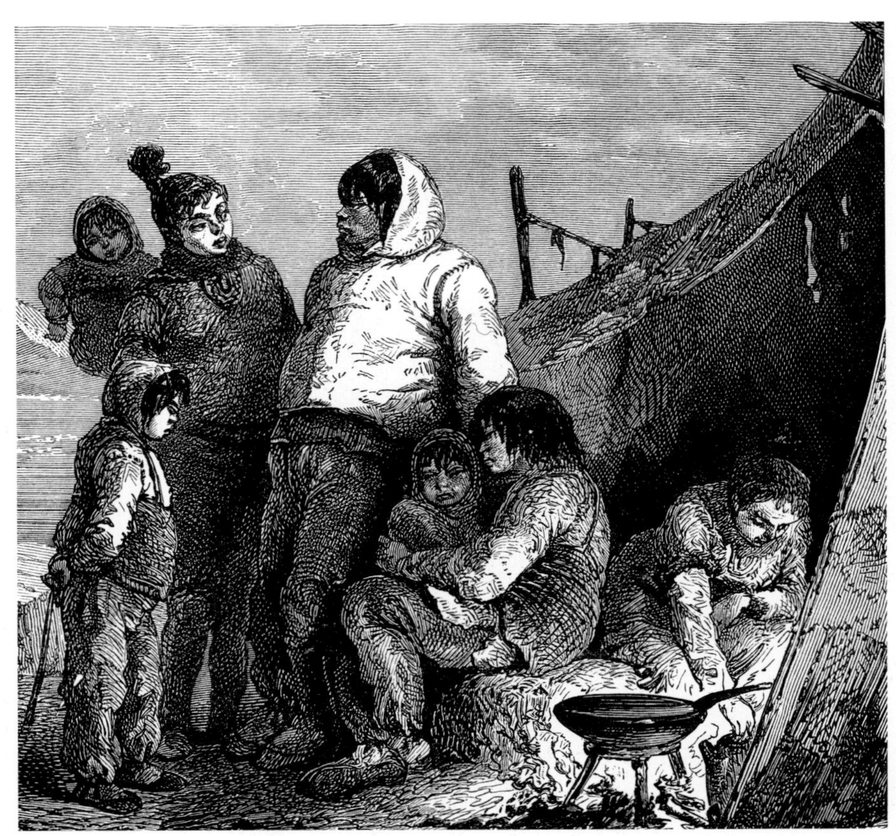

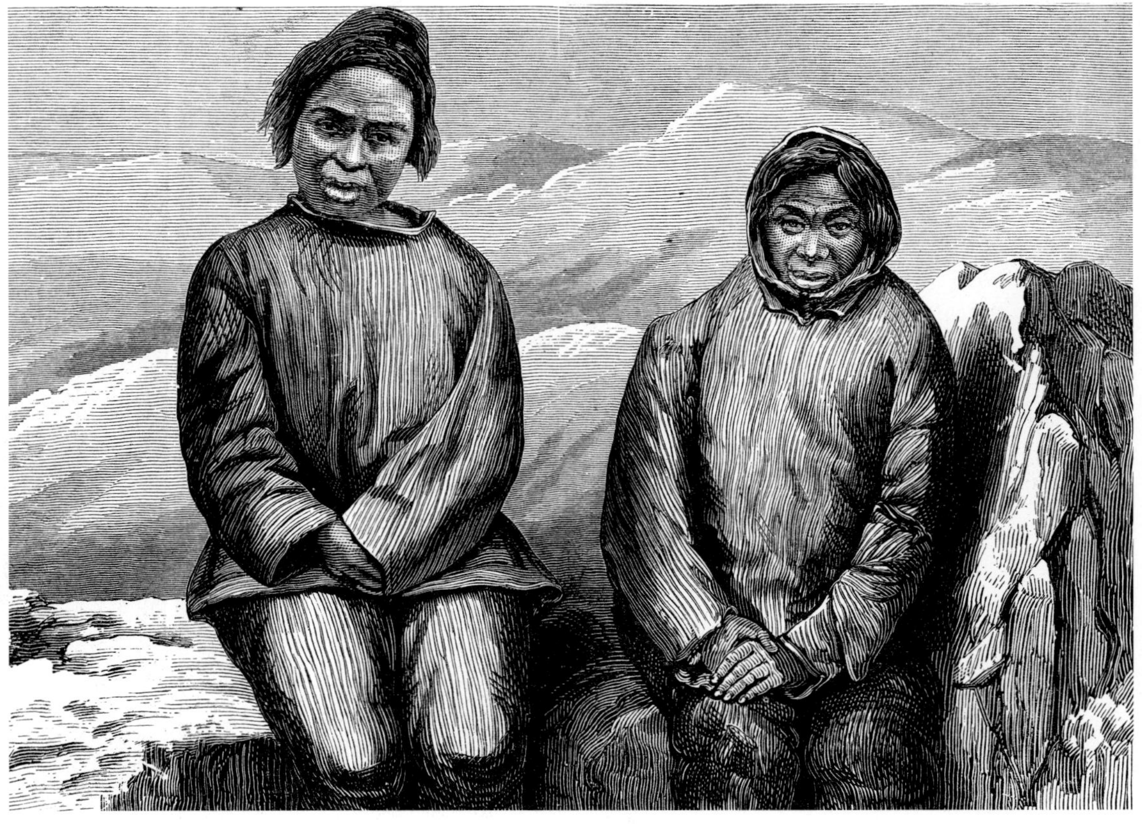

a	Eskimos in summer outfit, c. 1860	Eskimos in Sommerkleidung, um 1860	Esquimesi in completo estivo, ca. 1860	Esquimaux en tenue d'été, vers 1860	Esquimales con ropa de verano, hacia 1860
b	Eskimo men, c. 1880	Eskimomänner, um 1880	Esquimesi, ca. 1880	Esquimau, vers 1880	Esquimales, hacia 1880

Alaska

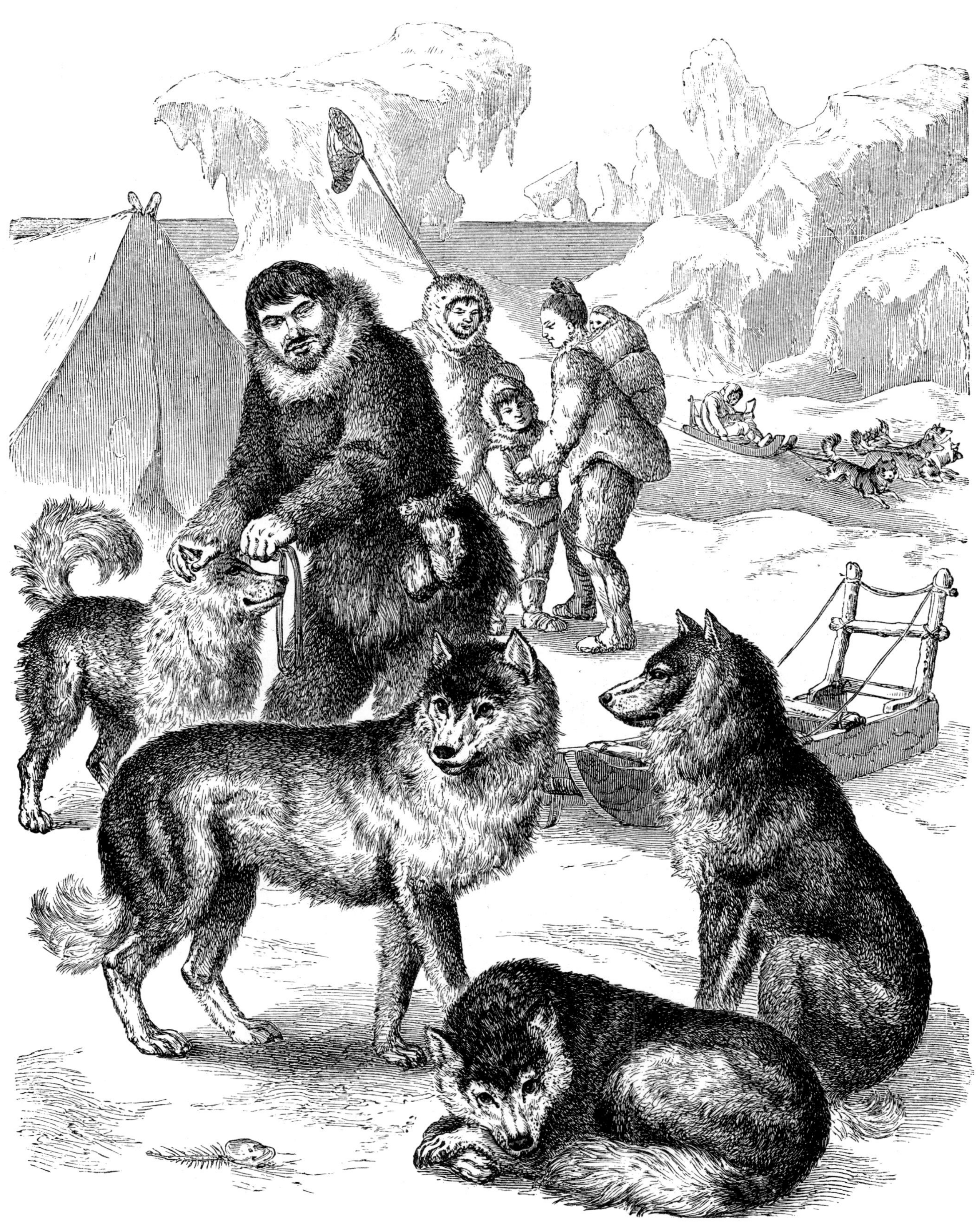

Eskimo hunter with dogs, c. 1880

Eskimojäger mit Hunden, um 1880

Cacciatore esquimese con cani, ca. 1880

Chasseur esquimau et ses chiens, vers 1880

Cazador esquimal con sus perros, hacia 1880

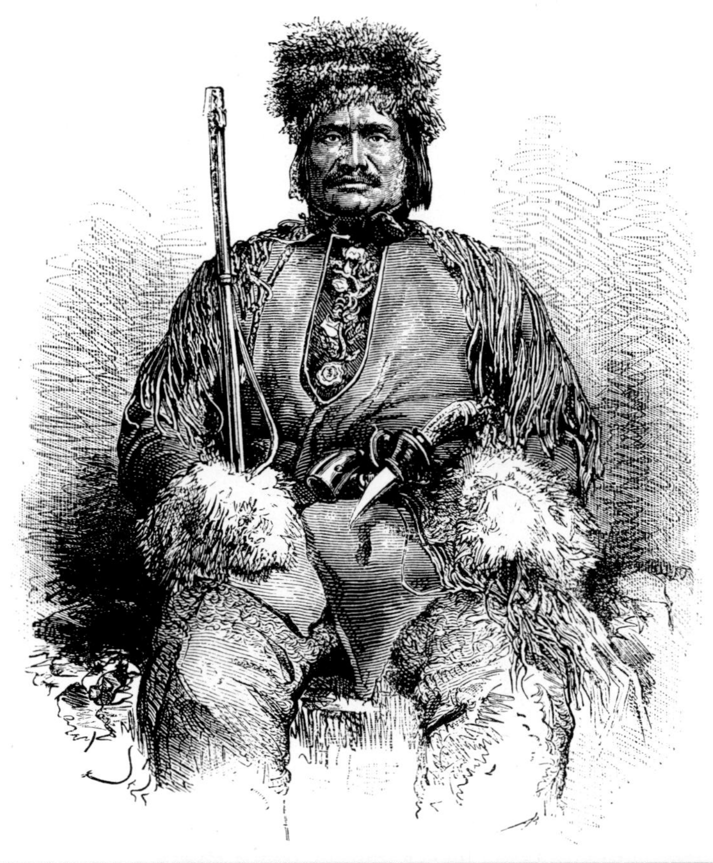

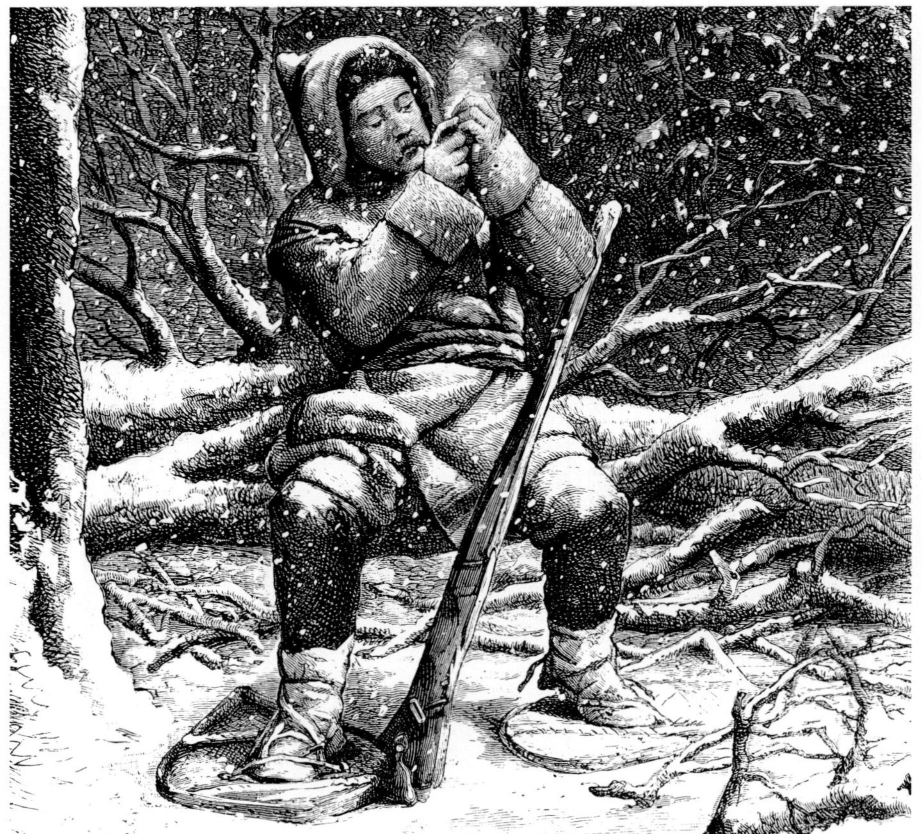

a	Franco-Canadian mestizo, c. 1885	Franko-kanadischer Mestize, um 1885	Meticcio franco-canadese, ca. 1885	Métisse franco-canadien, vers 1885	Mestizo franco-canadiense, hacia 1885
b	Canadian hunter, c. 1885	Kanadischer Jäger, um 1885	Cacciatore canadese, ca. 1885	Chasseur canadien, vers 1885	Cazador canadiense, hacia 1885

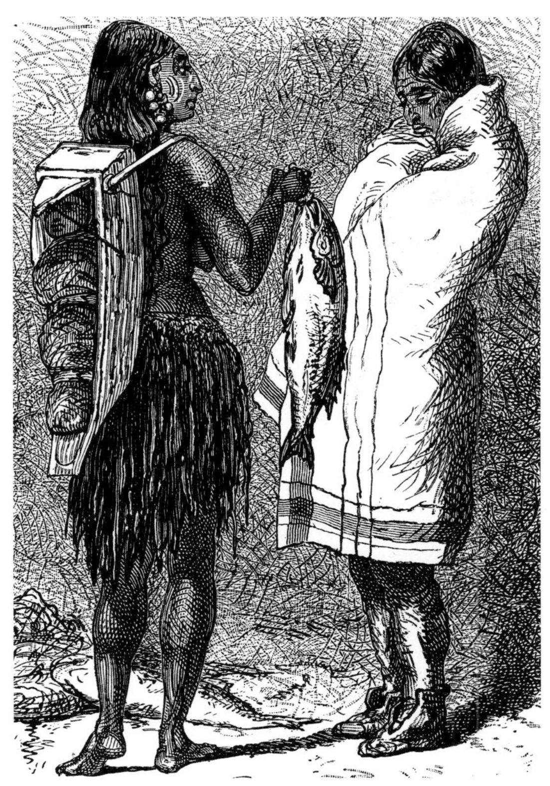

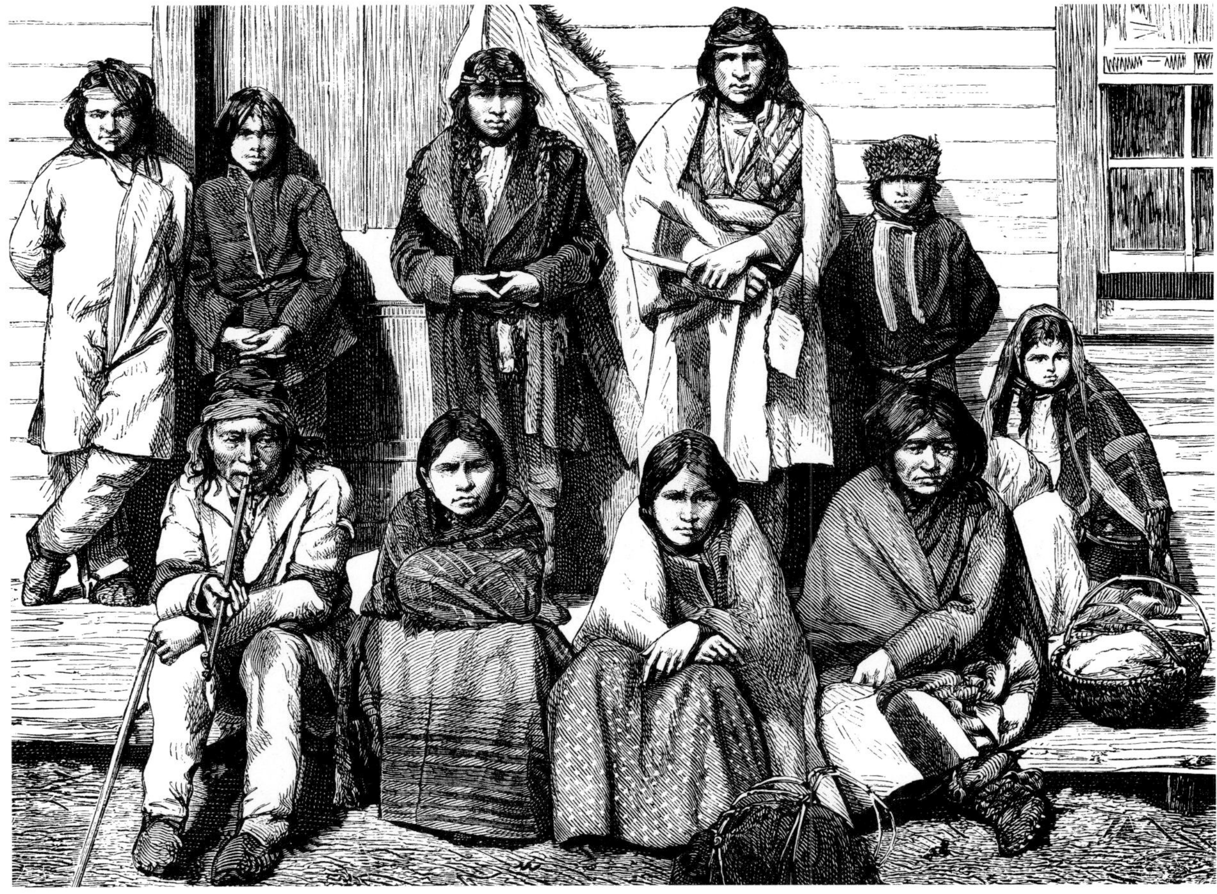

a	Native Americans from the Fraser river, c. 1880	Eingeborene Amerikaner vom Fraser River, um 1880	Indigeni americani del fiume Fraser, ca. 1880	Amérindien de la rivière Fraser, vers 1880	Nativos americanos del río Fraser, hacia 1880
b	Natives of Manitoba, c. 1885	Eingeborene aus Manitoba, um 1885	Indigeni di Manitoba, ca. 1885	Amérindien de Manitoba, vers 1885	Nativos de Manitoba, alrededor del año 1885

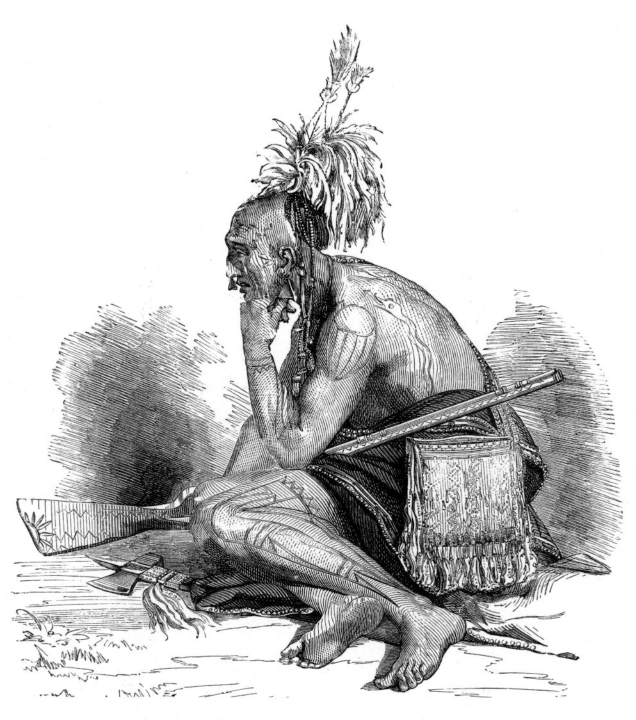

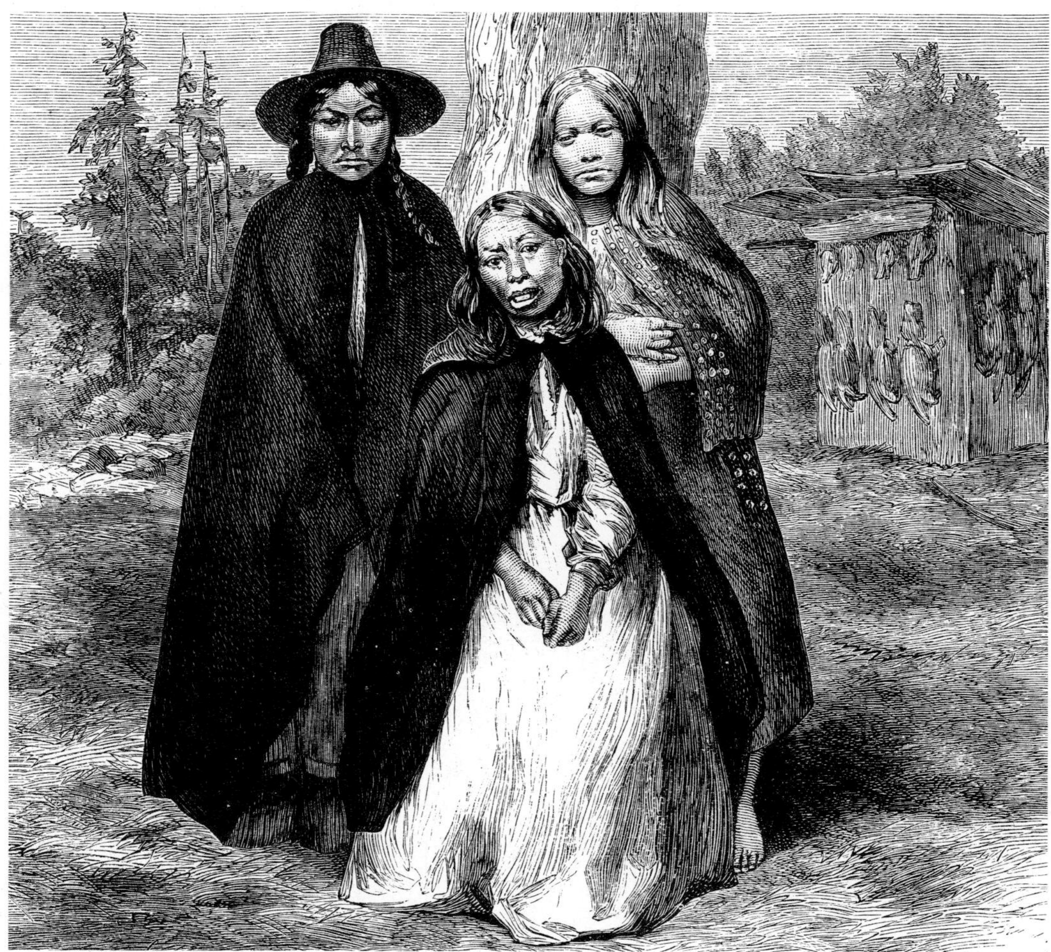

a	Native American from Eastern Canada, c. 1880	Eingeborene Amerikaner aus Ostkanada, um 1880	Indigeno americano del Canada orientale, ca. 1880	Amérindien de l'Est du Canada, vers 1880	Nativo americano del este de Canadá, 1880
b	Haidah women from Queen Charlotte Island, c. 1880	Haidah-Frauen vom Queen Charlotte Island, um 1880	Donne haidah dell'Isola della Regina Carlotta, ca. 1880	Femme haidah de Queen Charlotte Island, vers 1880	Mujeres haida de las islas de la reina Carlota, 1880

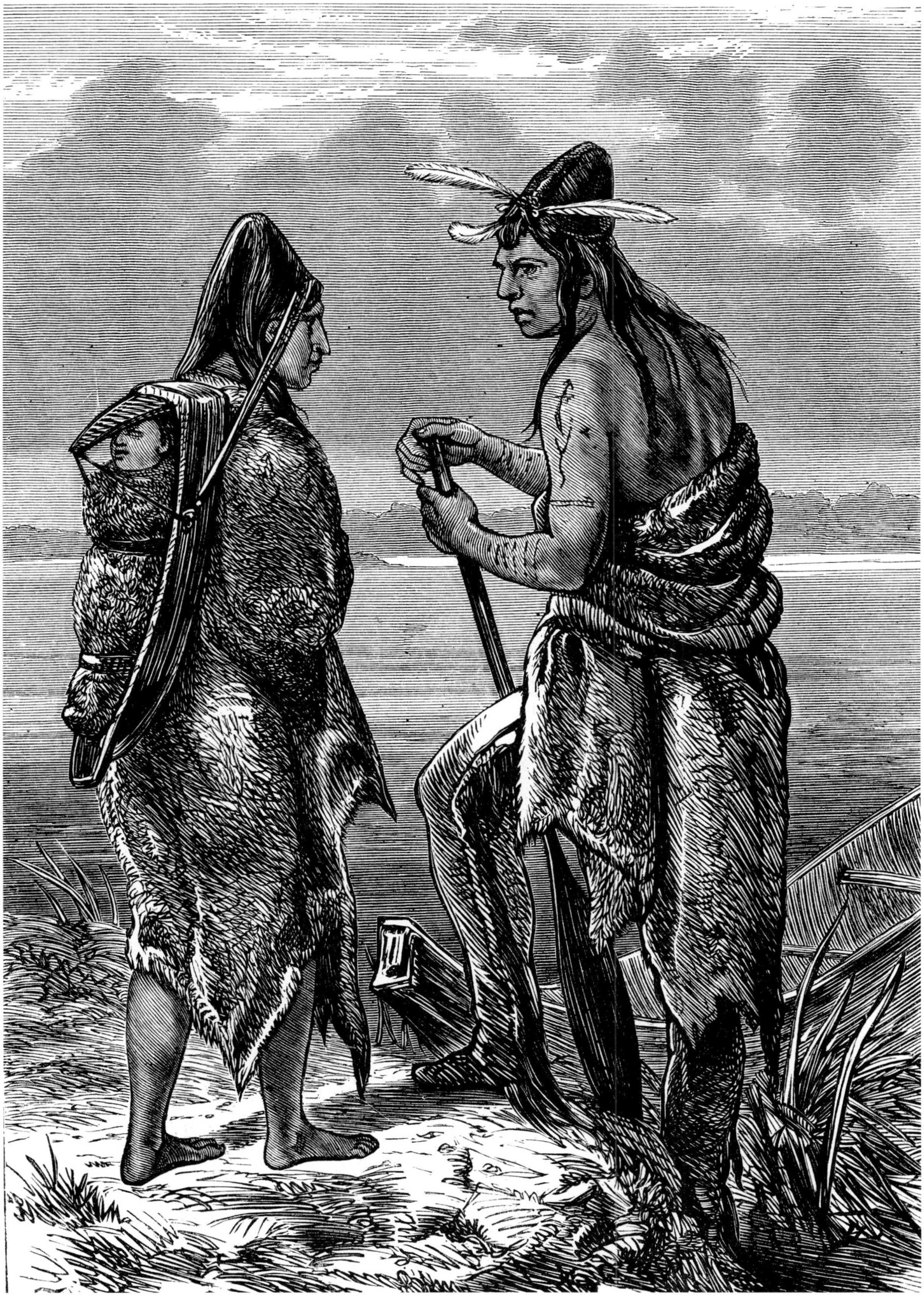

Chinook Indians, 1870s

Chinook-Indianer, 1870

Indiani Chinook, anni 1870

Indiens chinook, décennie de 1870

Indios chinuk, década de 1870

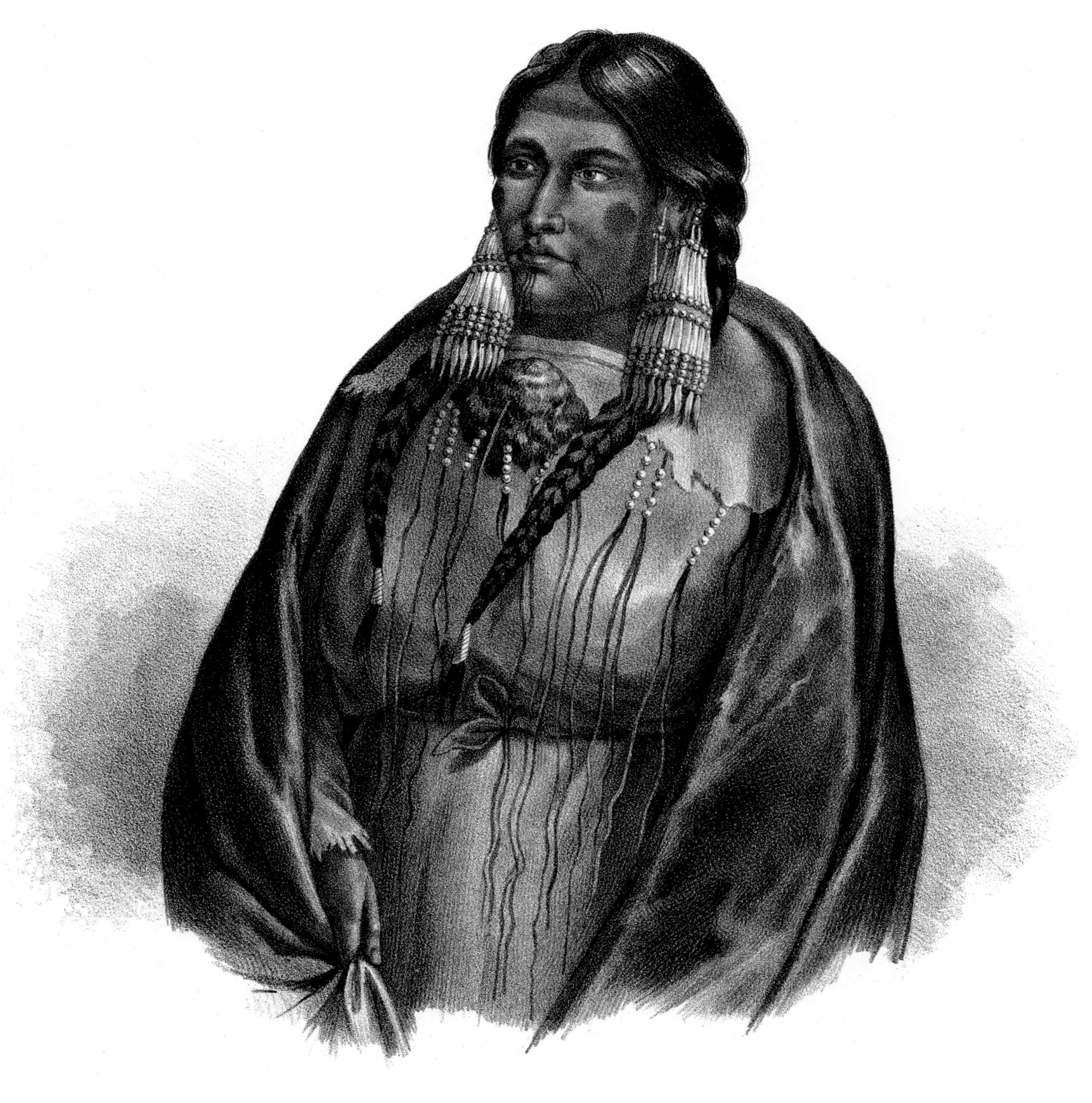

Cree lady, c. 1860 | Cree-Frau, um 1860 | Donna cree, ca. 1860 | Femme cree, vers 1860 | Mujer cree, hacia 1860

U.S.A.

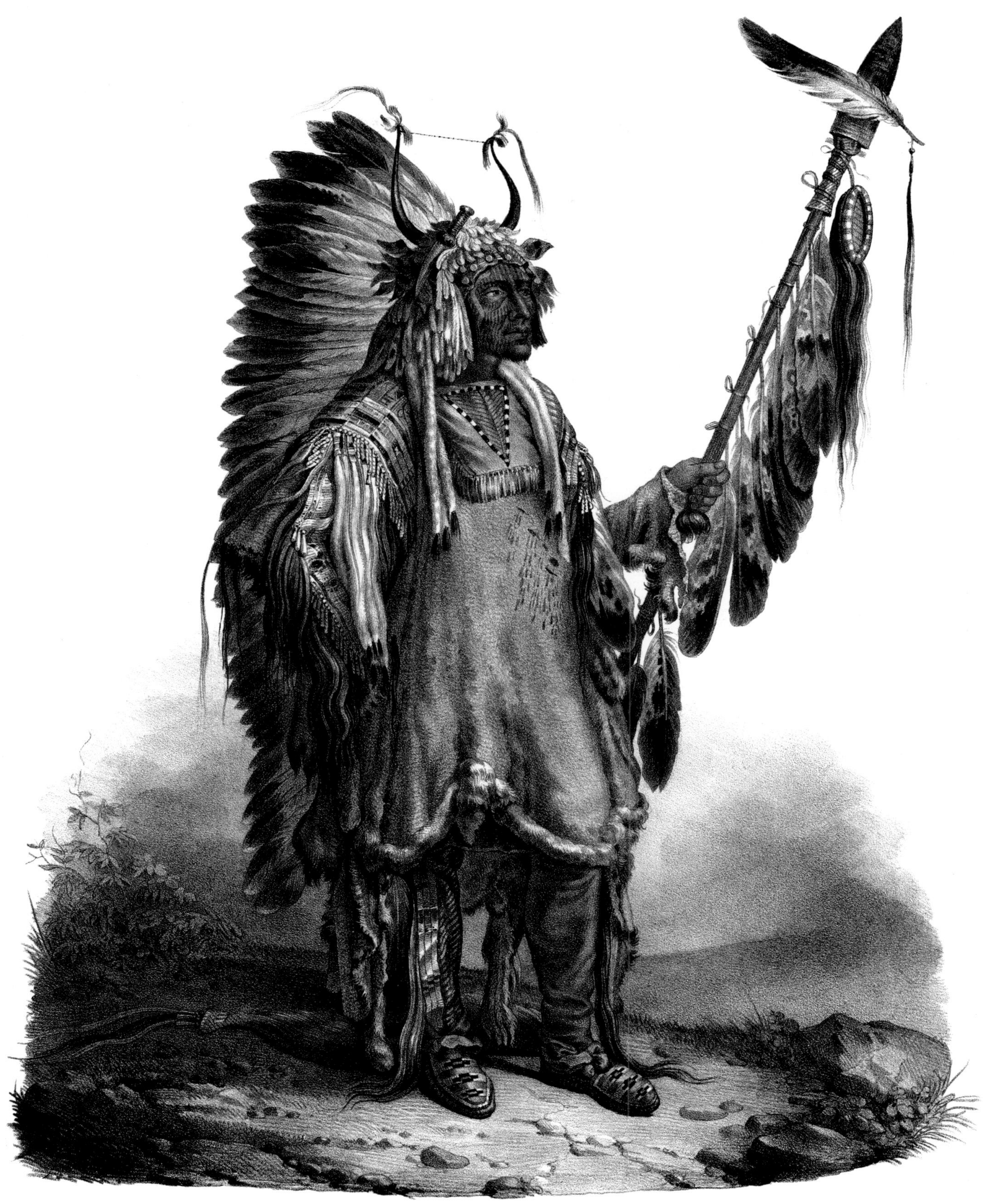

Native American chief, 1860

Amerikanischer Eingeborenenhäuptling, 1860

Capo indigeno americano, 1860

Chef amérindien, vers 1860

Jefe nativo americano, 1860

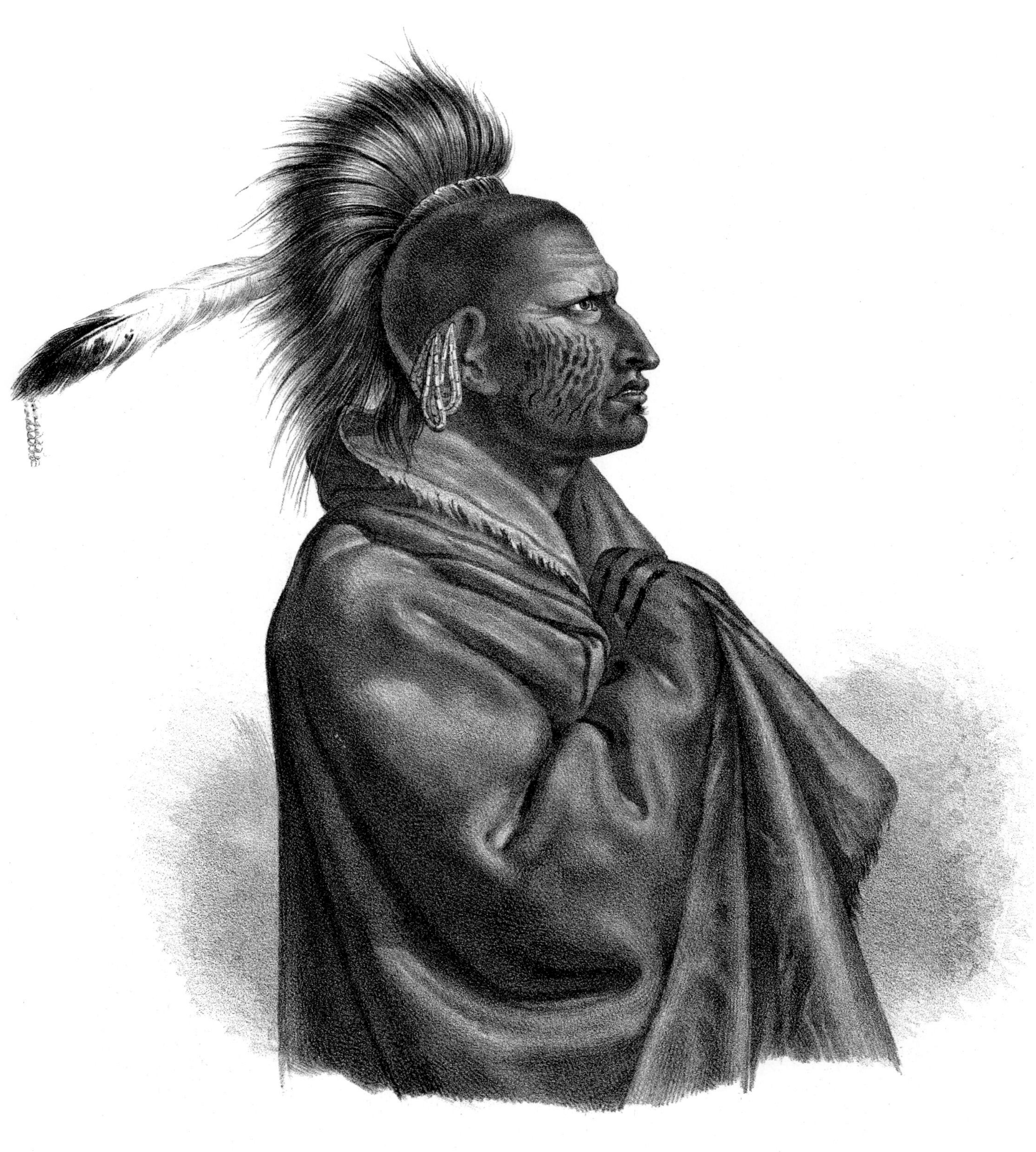

Native American chief, 1860

Amerikanischer Eingeborenenhäuptling, 1860

Capo indigeno americano, 1860

Chef amérindien, vers 1860

Jefe nativo americano, 1860

U.S.A.

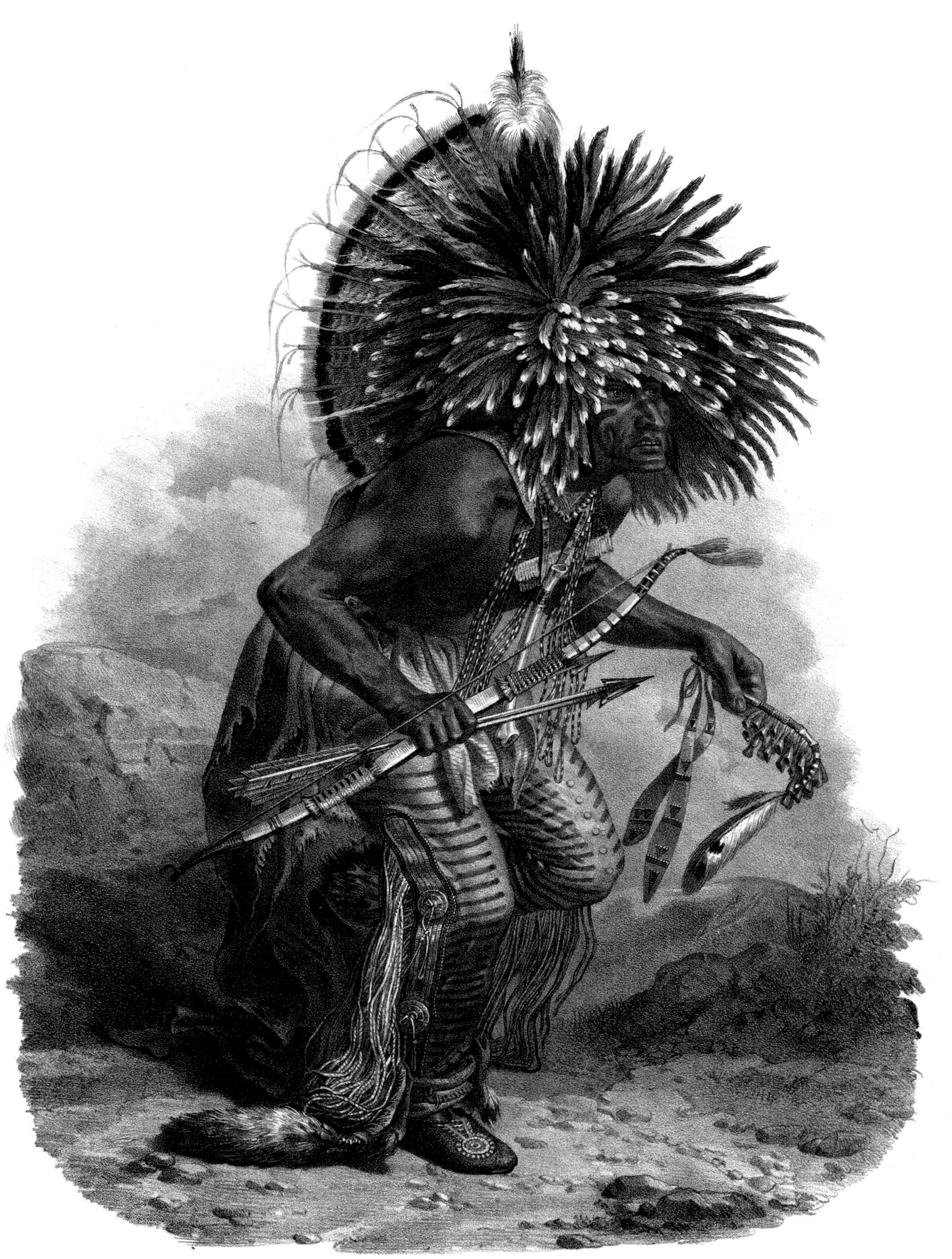

Native American performing a dance, 1860

Eingeborener Amerikaner bei einem Tanz, 1860

Indigeno americano nell'esecuzione di una danza, 1860

Amérindien exécutant une danse, 1860

Nativo americano danzando, 1860

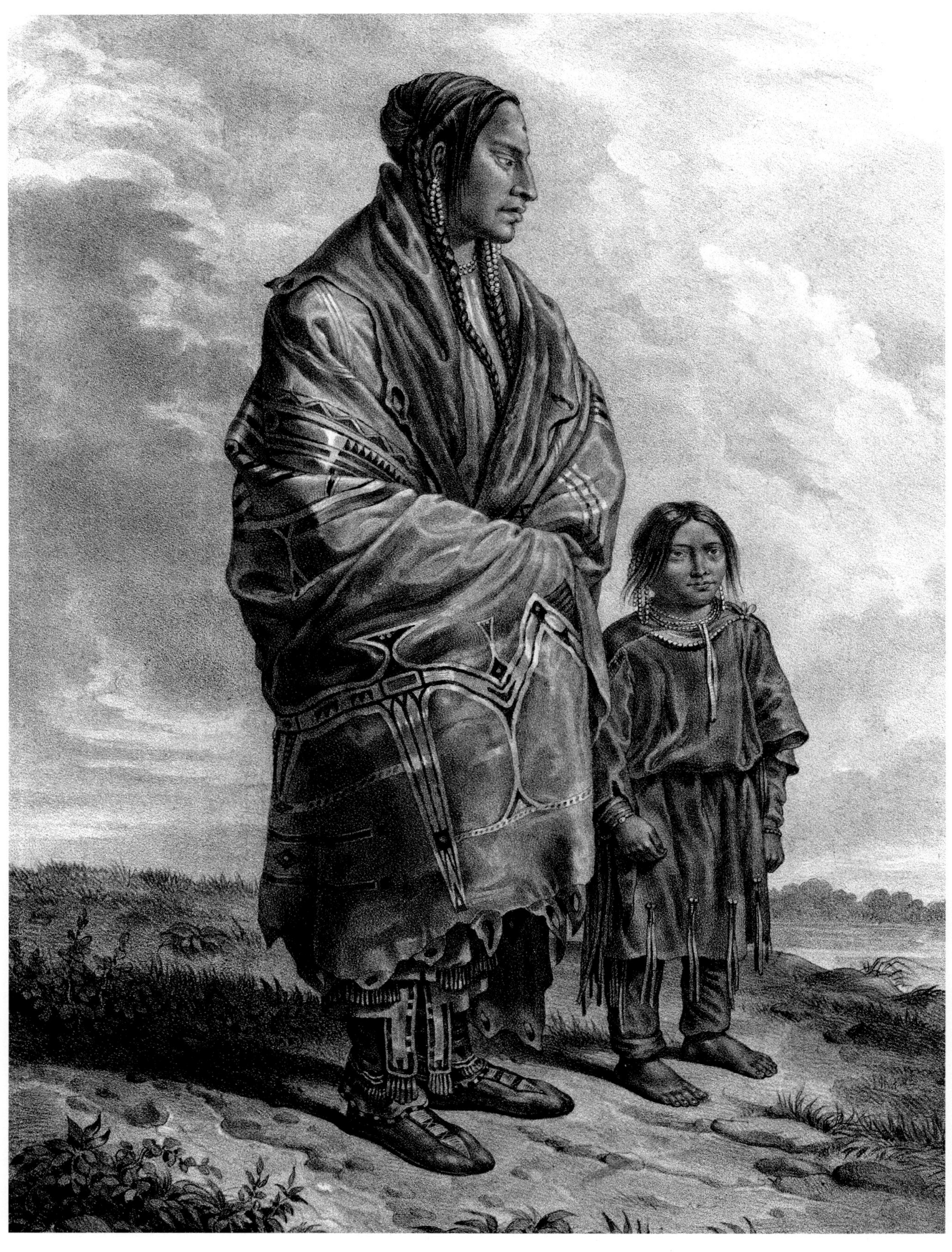

Locotah woman and child, c. 1880

Lakotah-Frau mit Kind, um 1880

Donna e bambino lacotah, ca. 1880

Femme et enfant locotah, vers 1880

Mujer y niño lakota, alrededor del año 1880

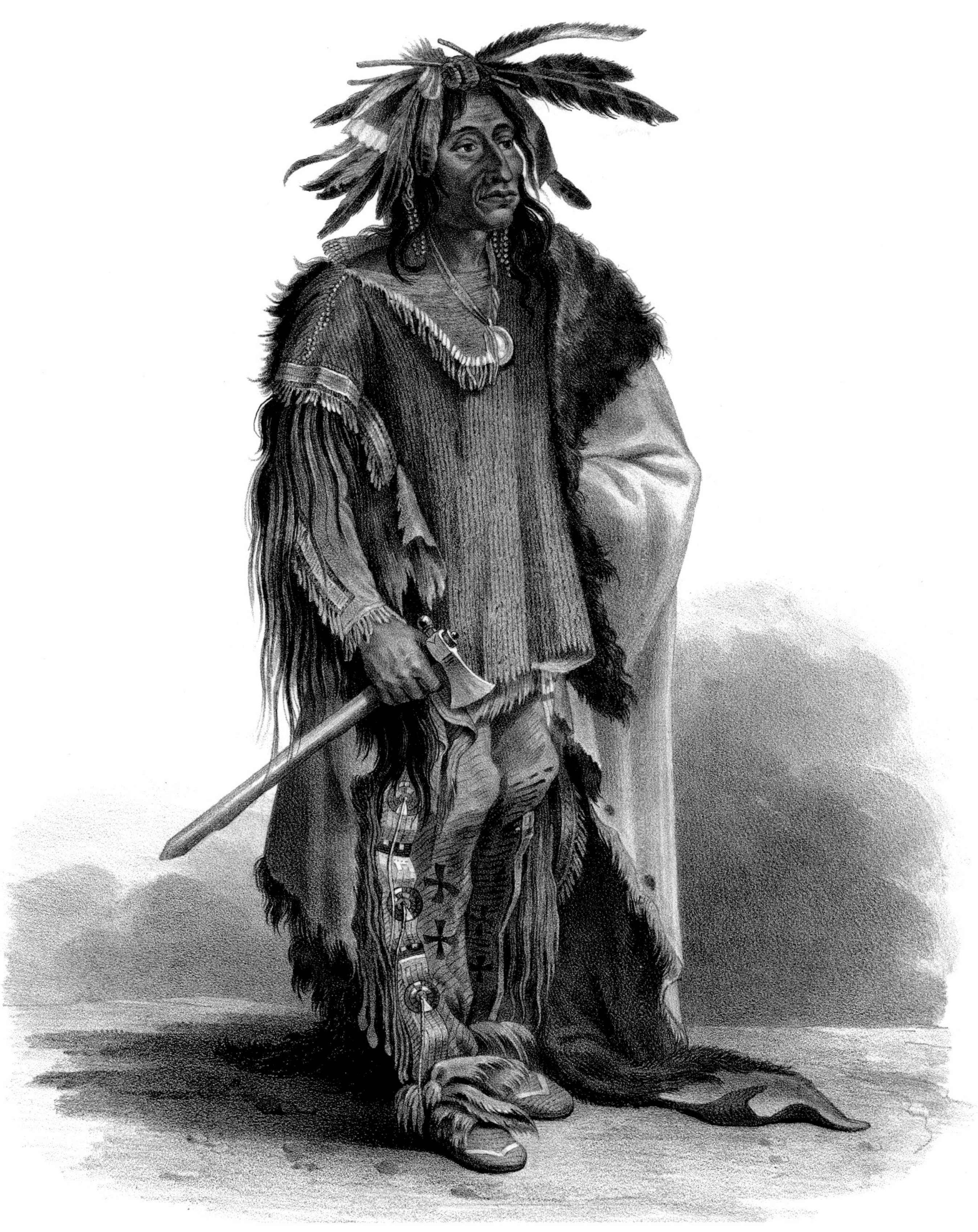

Lacotah warrior Lakotah-Krieger Guerriero lacotah Guerrier locotah Guerrero lakota

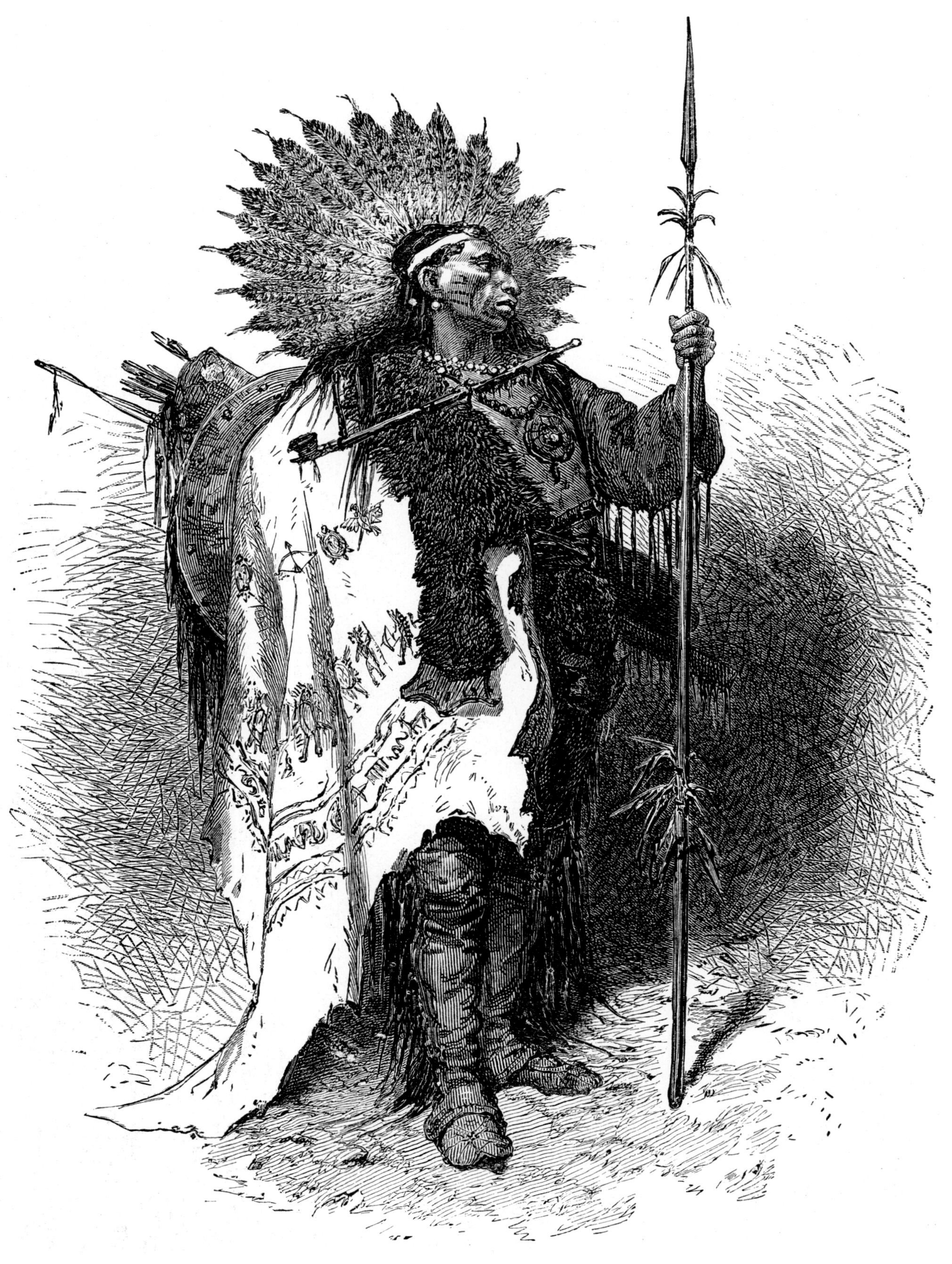

A Crow chief from the Rocky Mountains, c. 1880

Ein Crow-Häuptling aus den Rocky Mountains, um 1880

Un capo Crow delle Montagne Rocciose, ca. 1880

Chef crow des montagnes rocheuses, vers 1880

Jefe crow de las Montañas Rocosas, hacia 1880

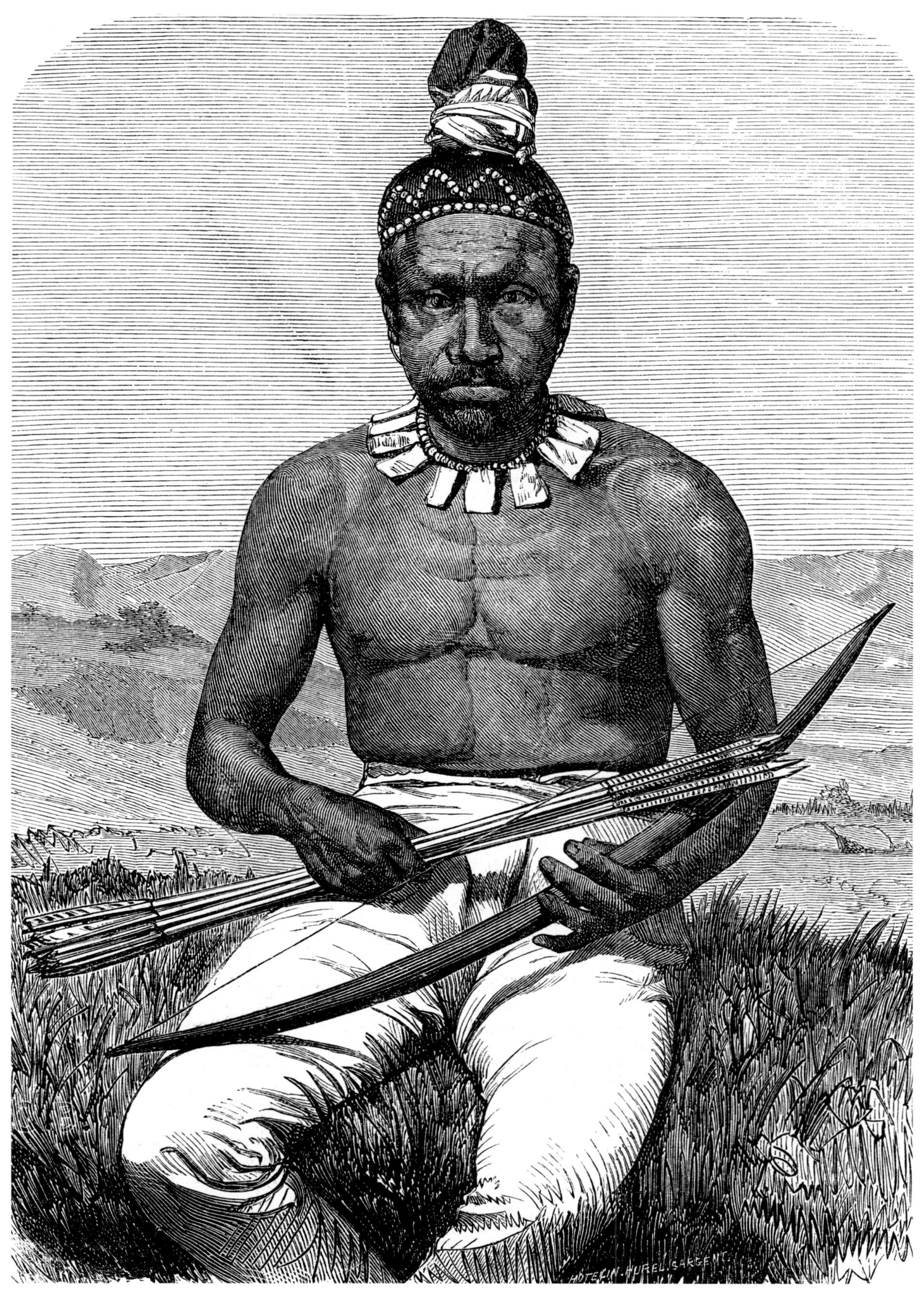

Native American from California, c. 1880

Eingeborener Amerikaner aus Kalifornien, um 1880

Indigeno americano della California, ca. 1880

Amérindiens de Californie, vers 1880

Nativo americano de California, hacia 1880

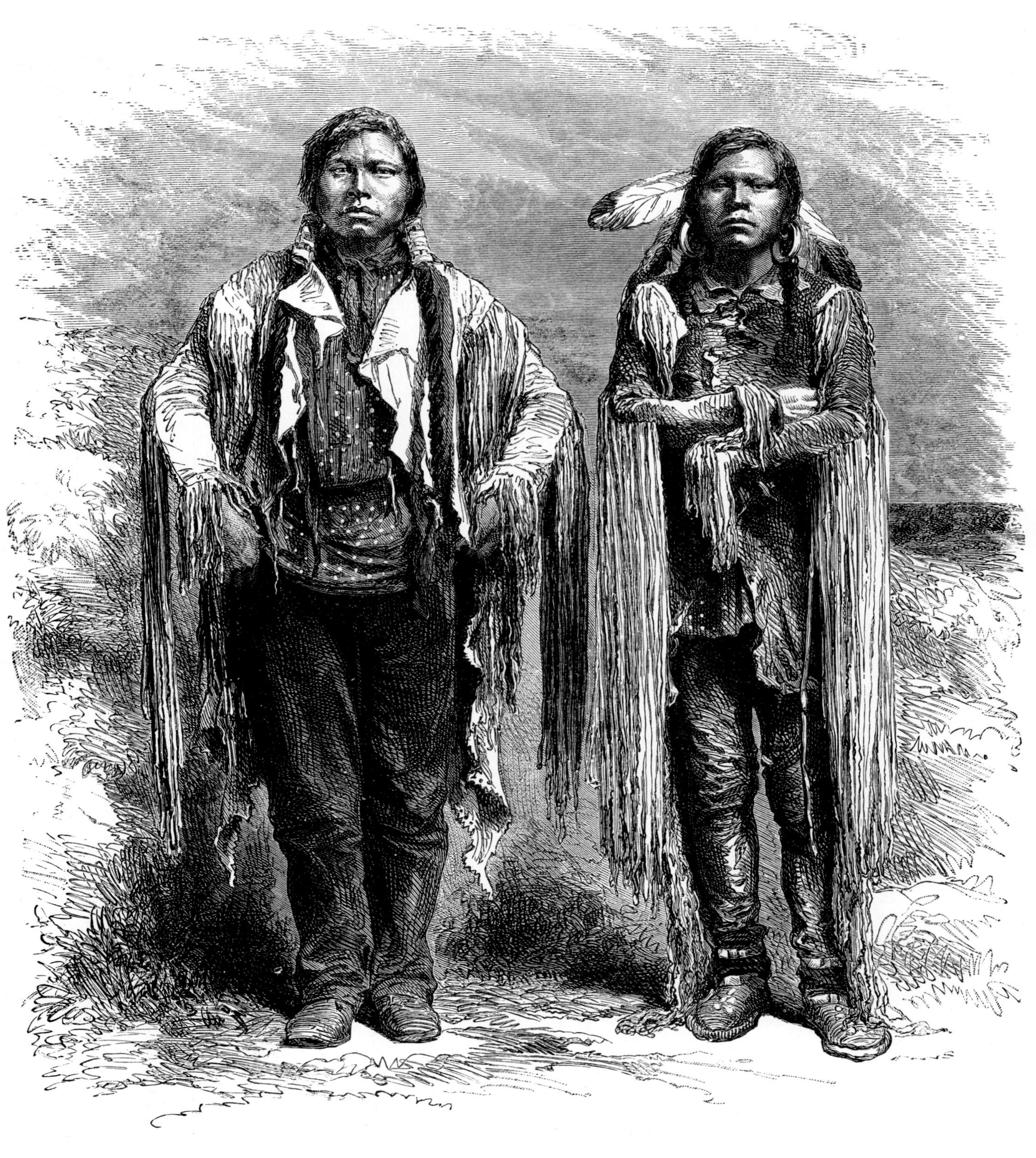

Yutes, c. 1880

Jute, um 1880

Yute, ca. 1880

Yutes, vers 1880

Utes, alrededor de 1880

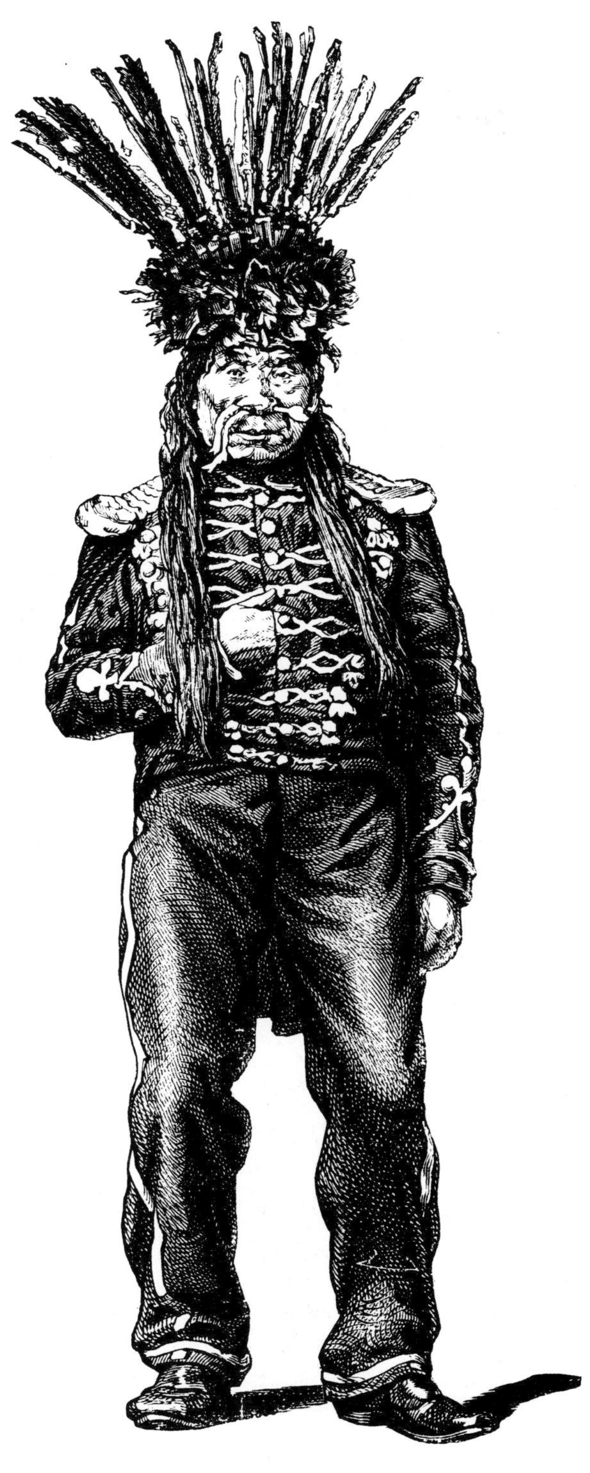

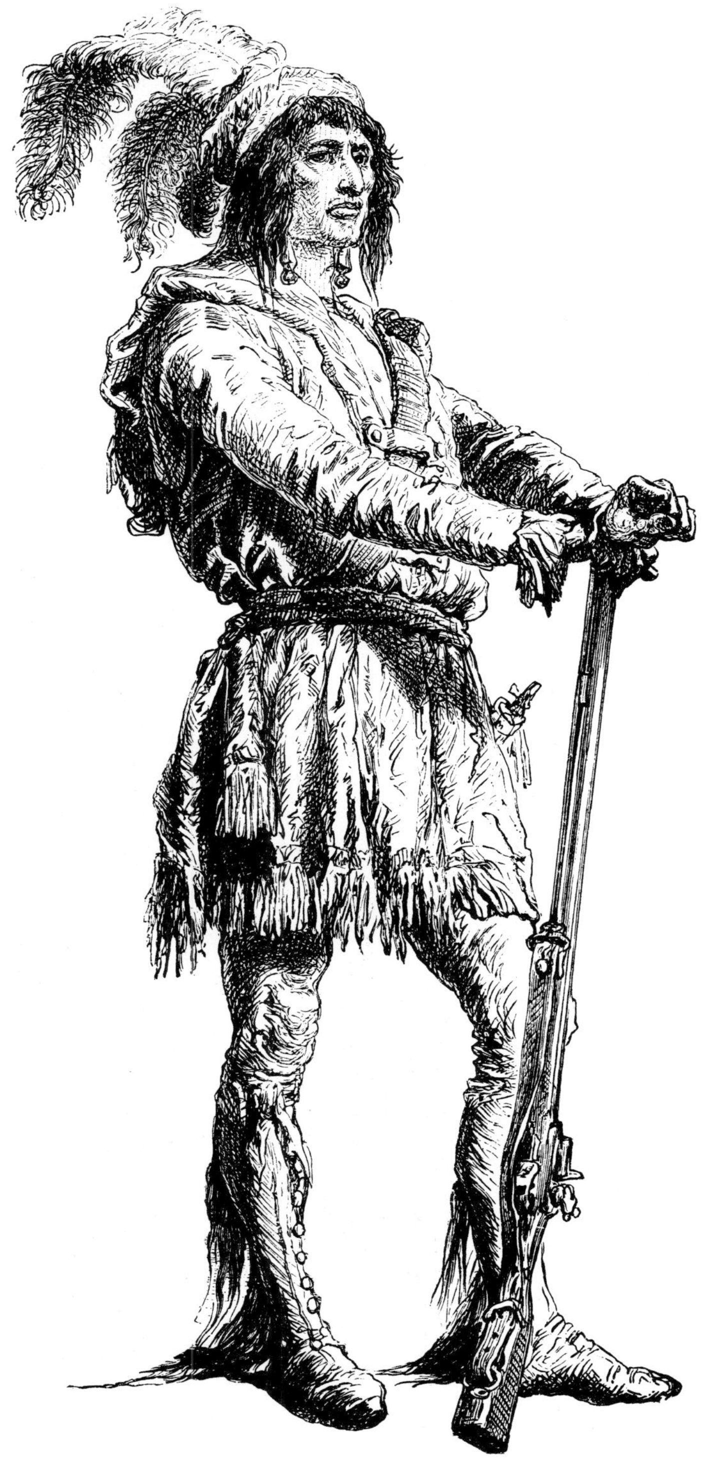

a	Yute chief, c. 1865	Jute-Häuptling, um 1865	Capo yute, ca. 1865	Chef yute, vers 1865	Jefe ute, hacia 1865
b	Seminole from Florida, c. 1885	Seminole aus Florida, um 1885	Seminale della Florida, ca. 1885	Seminole de Floride, vers 1885	Seminola de Florida, alrededor del año 1885

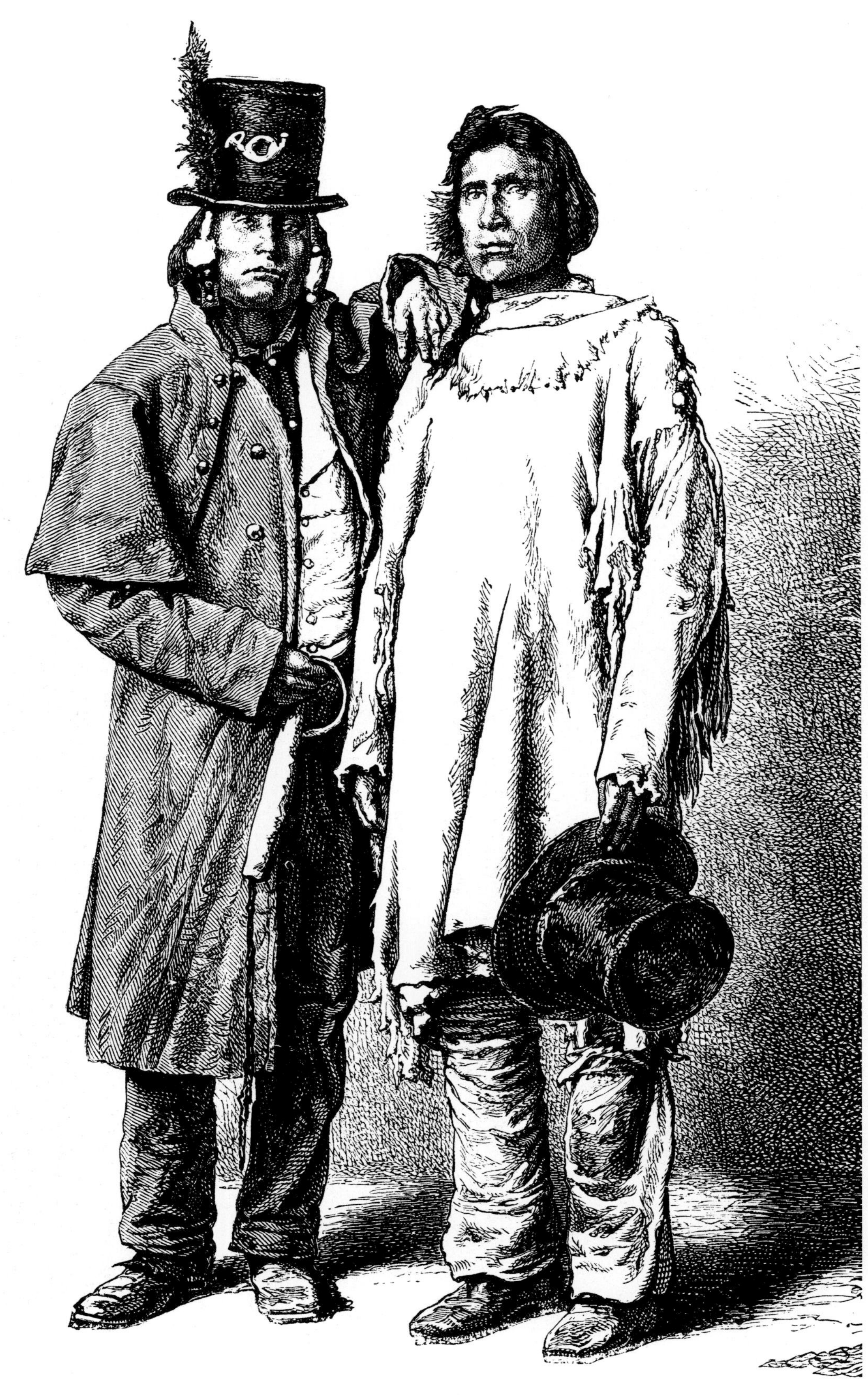

Native Americans in 'western-style' dress, c. 1885

Eingeborene Amerikaner in „westlicher" Kleidung, um 1885

Indigeni americani in abito 'stile occidentale', ca. 1885

Amérindiens en tenue «western », vers 1885

Nativos americanos con ropas "de estilo occidental", hacia 1885

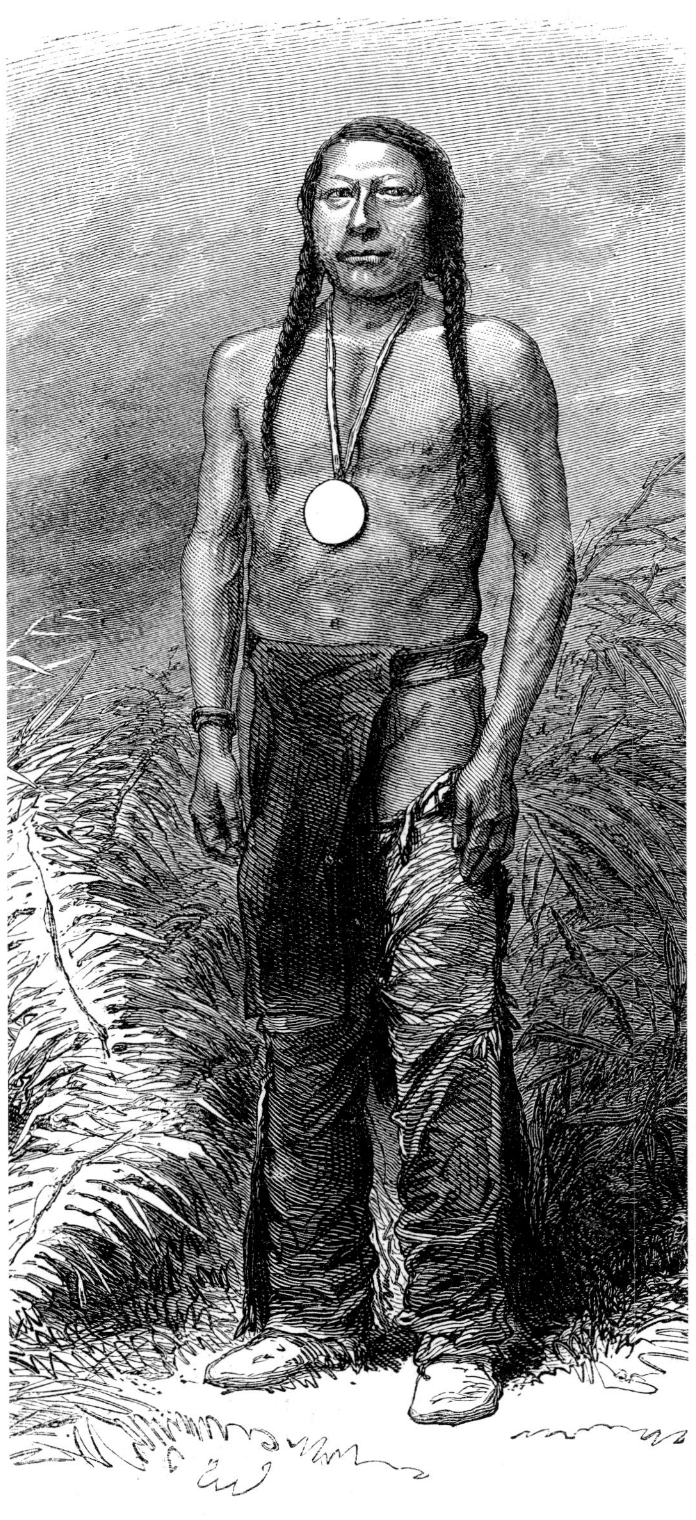

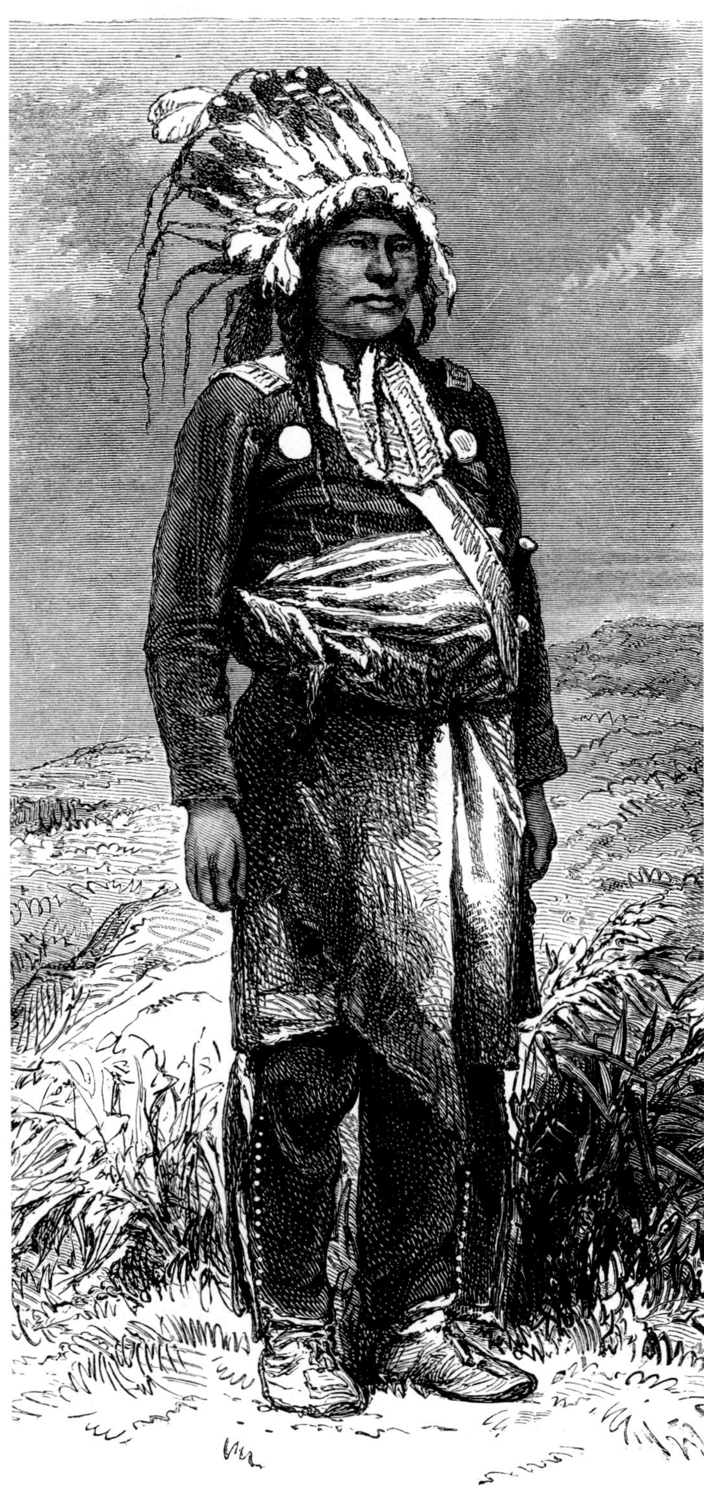

Native American chiefs, c. 1880

Amerikanische Eingeborenenhäuptlinge, um 1880

Capi indigeni americani, ca. 1880

Chefs amérindiens, vers 1880

Jefes nativos americanos, alrededor del año 1880

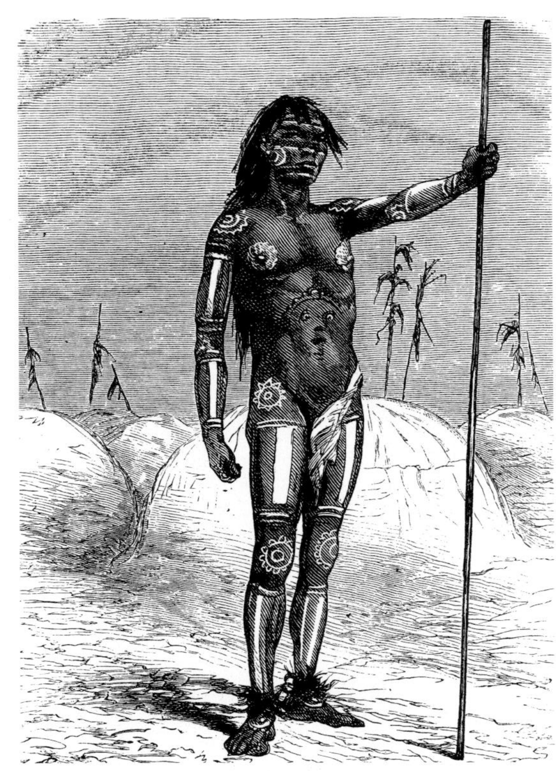

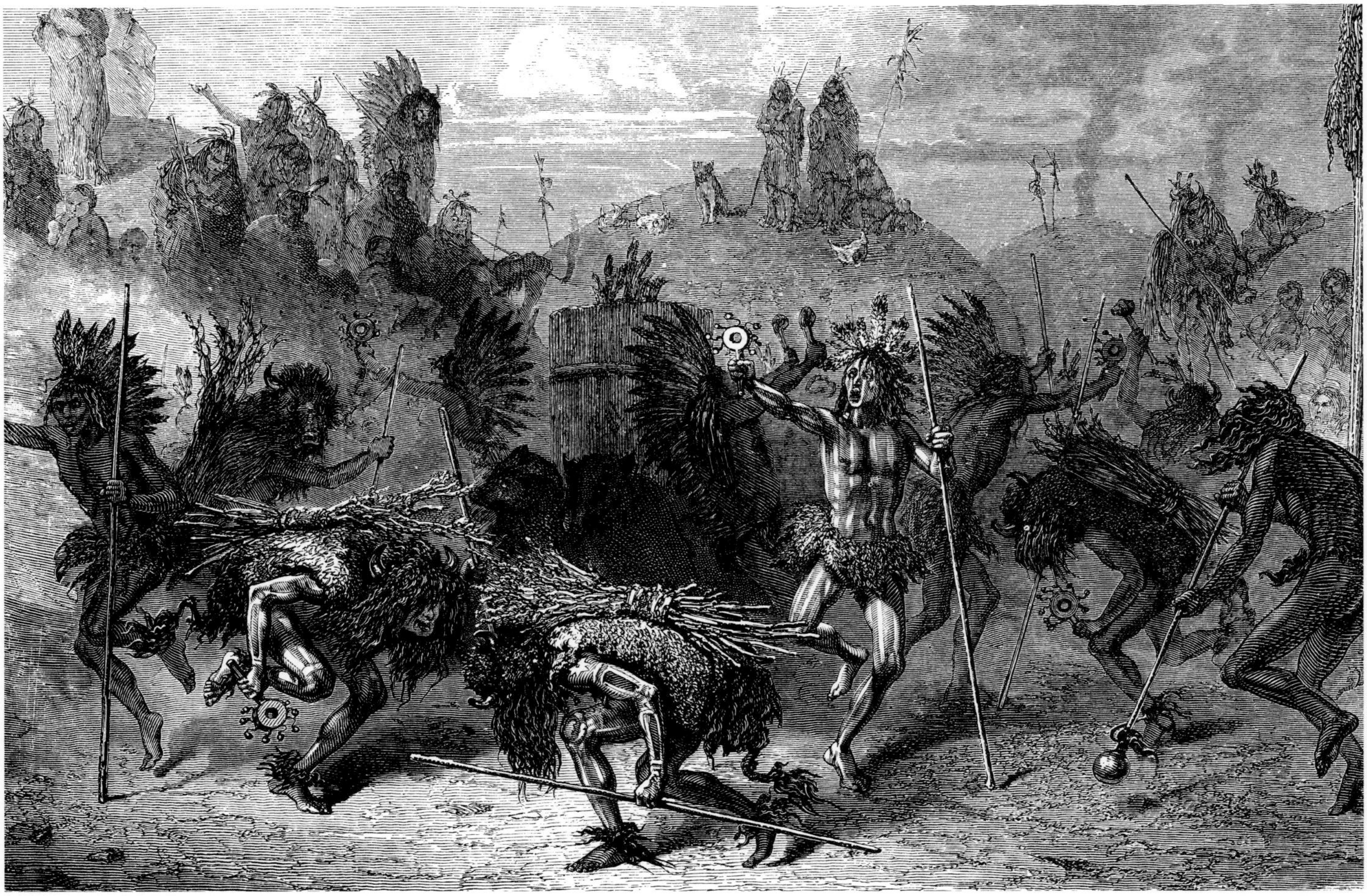

The 'Buffalo Dance', c. 1880

Der „Büffeltanz", um 1880

La 'Danza di Buffalo', ca. 1880

La « danse du buffle », vers 1880

Danza del búfalo, hacia 1880

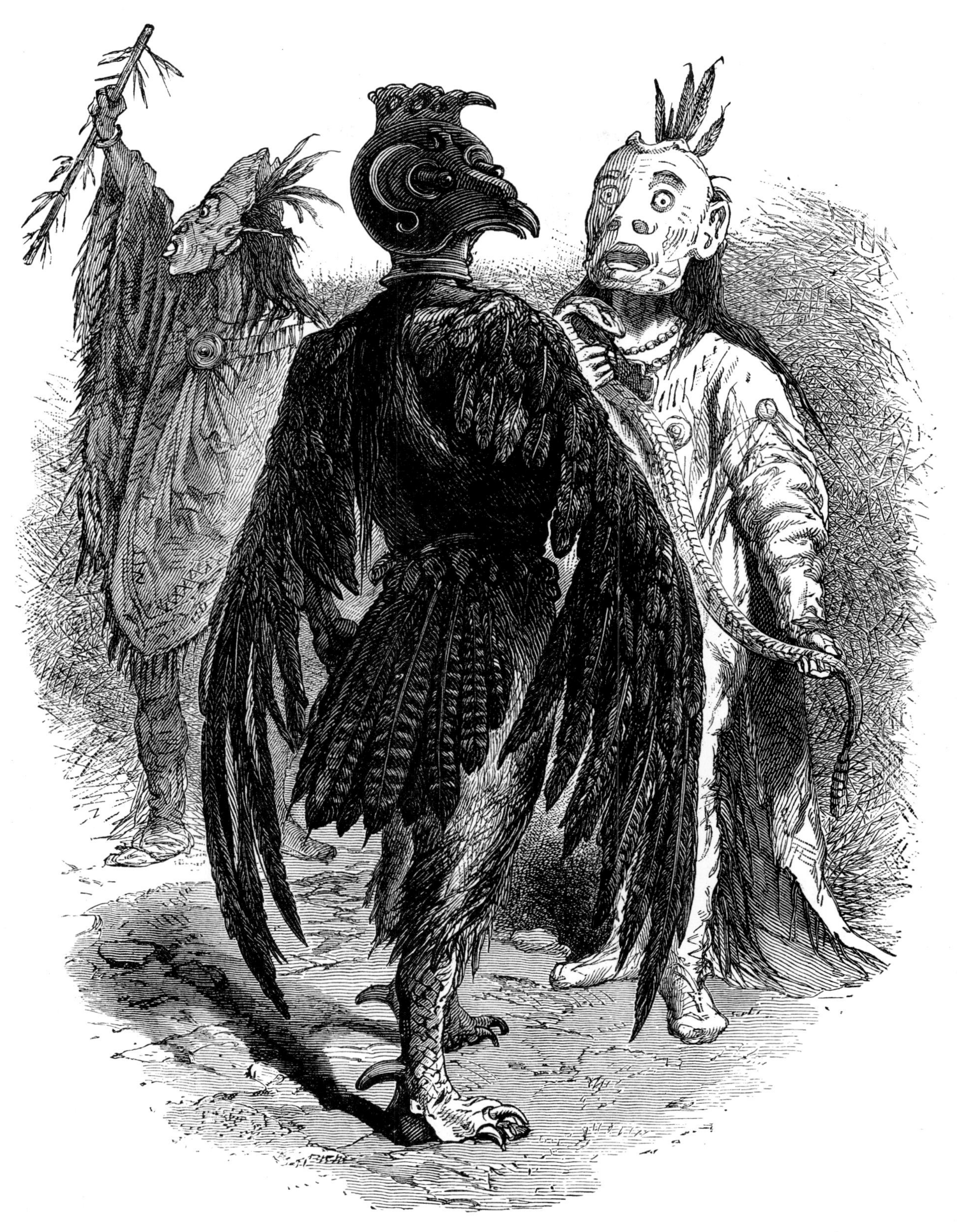

Medicine men, c. 1880

Medizinmann, um 1880

Stregoni, ca. 1880

« Hommes-médecines », vers 1880

Sanadores, alrededor del año 1880

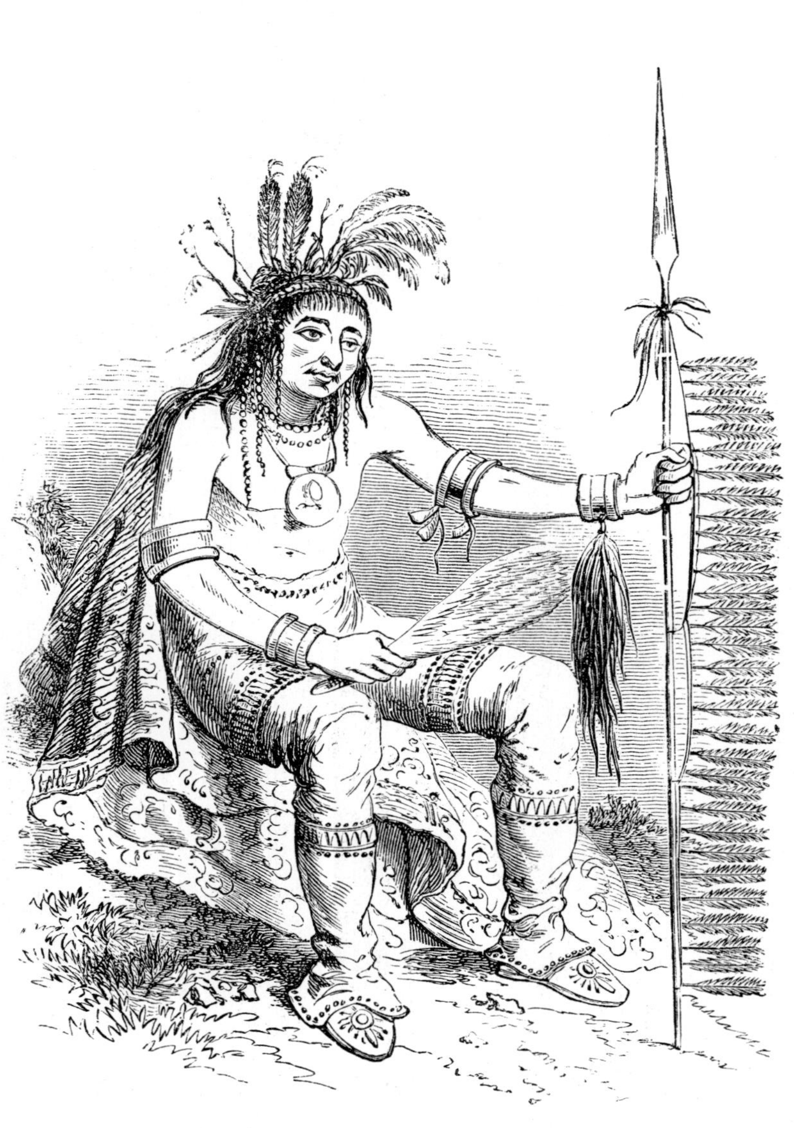

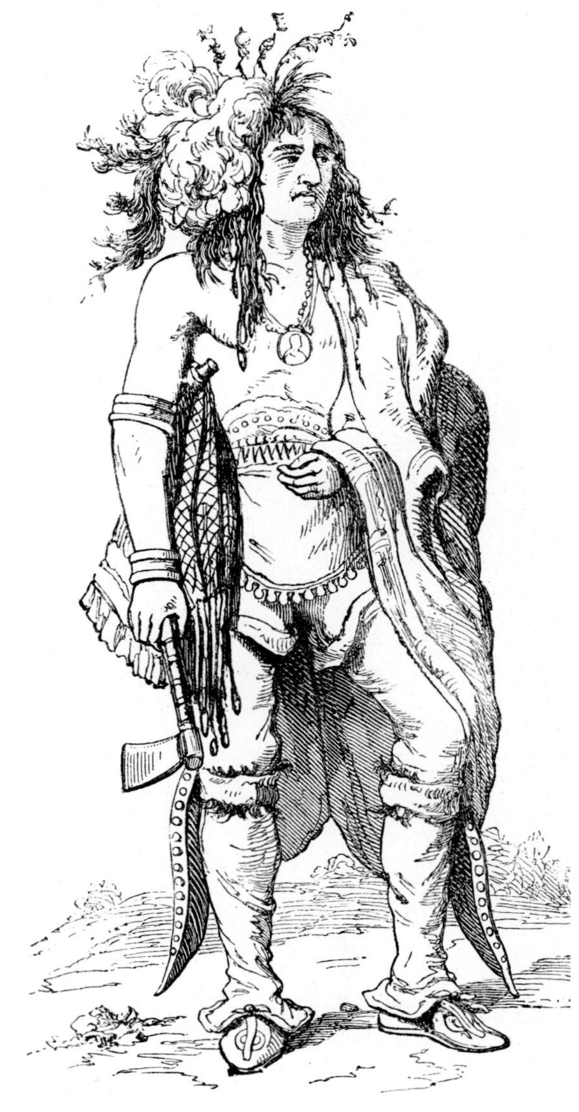

a	Chippeway Native American, c. 1880	Eingeborene amerikanische Chippeway, um 1880	Indigeno americano chippeway, ca. 1880	Amérindien chippeway, vers 1880	Nativo americano chipewa, hacia 1880
b	Iroquois Native American, c. 1880	Eingeborene amerikanische Irokesen, um 1880	Indigeno americano irochese, ca. 1880	Amérindien iroquois, vers 1880	Nativo americano iroqués, hacia 1880

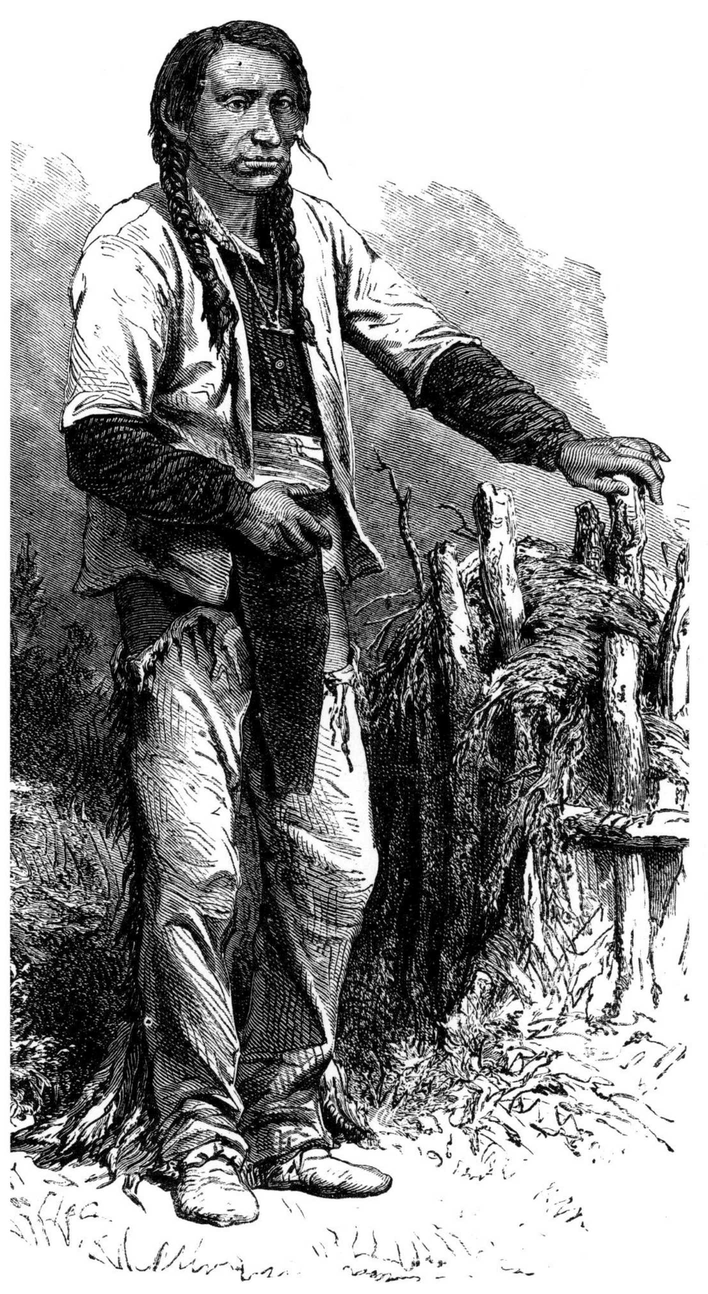

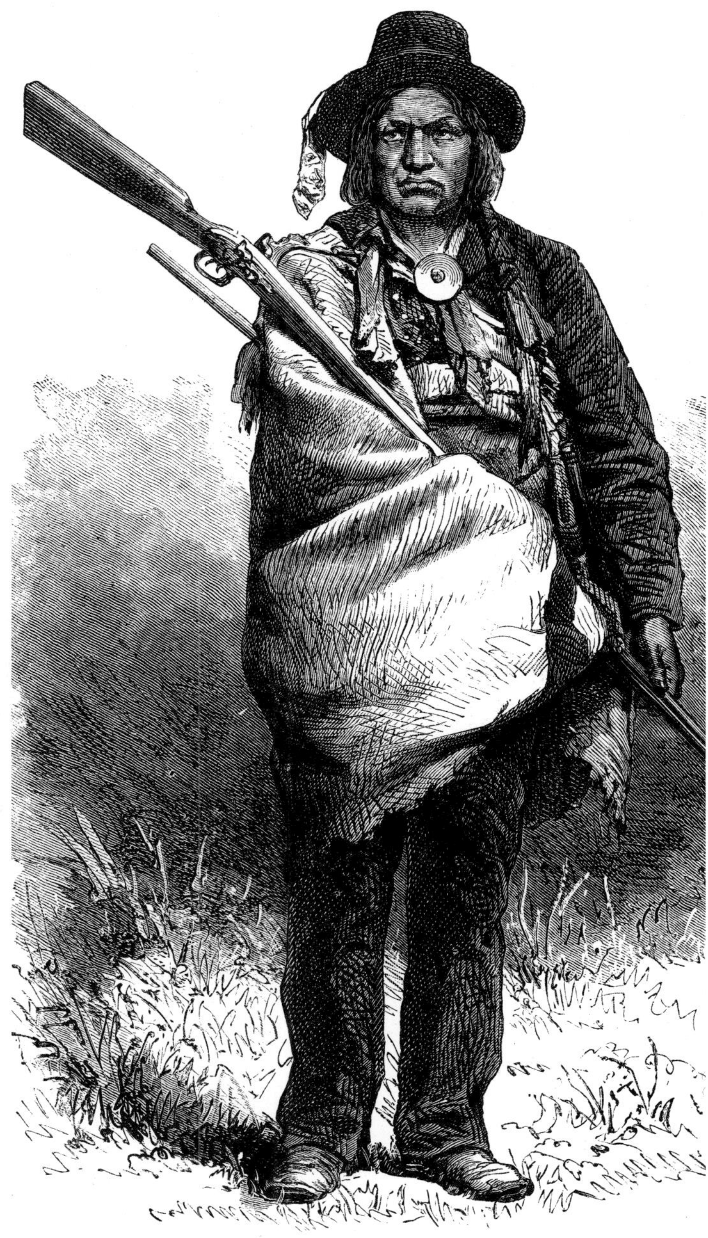

Native Americans, c. 1880

Eingeborene Amerikaner, um 1880

Indigeni americani, ca. 1880

Amérindien, vers 1880

Nativos americanos, alrededor del año 1880

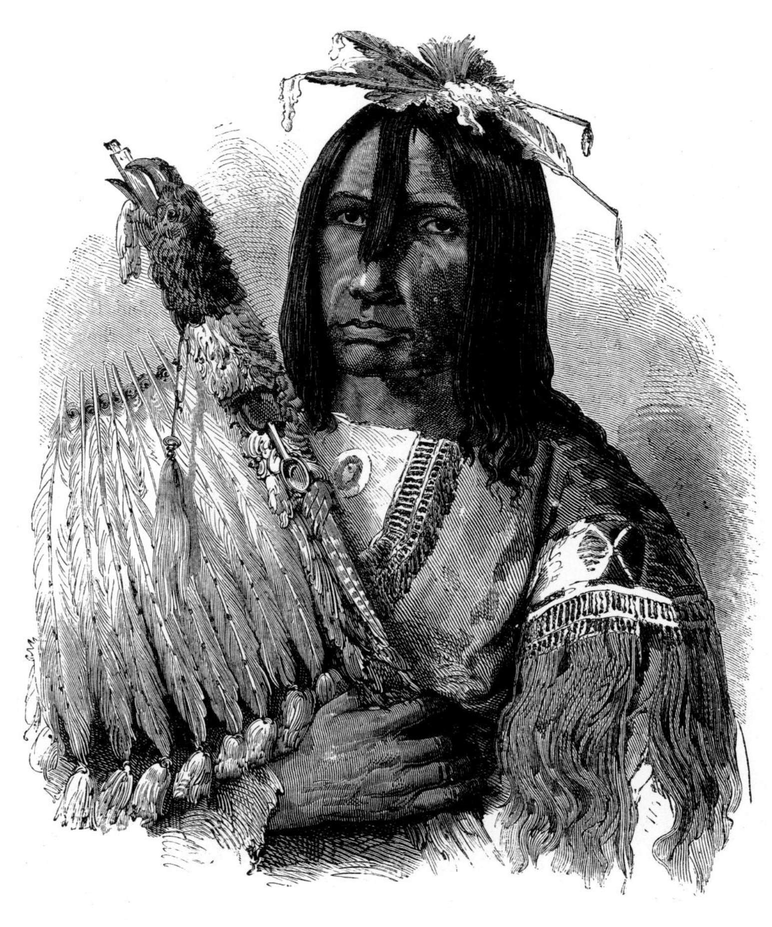

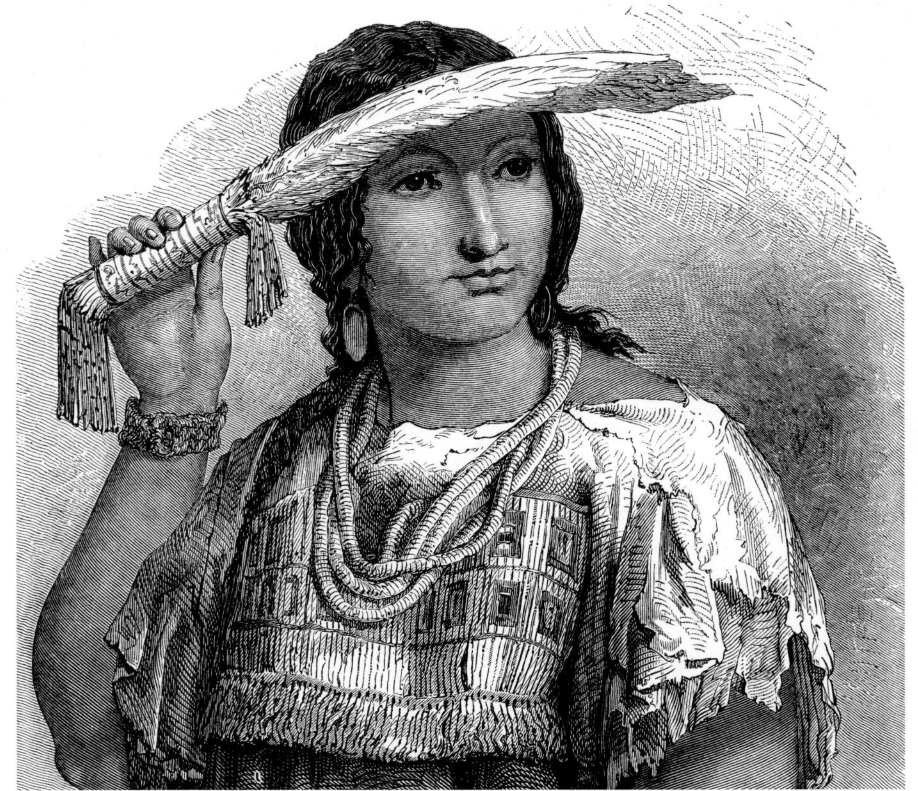

A Blackfoot chief and Sioux woman, c. 1880

Schwarzfuß-Häuptling mit Sioux-Frau, um 1880

Un capo dei piedi neri e una donna sioux, ca. 1880

Chef blackfoot et femme Sioux, vers 1880

Jefe pies negros y mujer sioux, hacia 1880

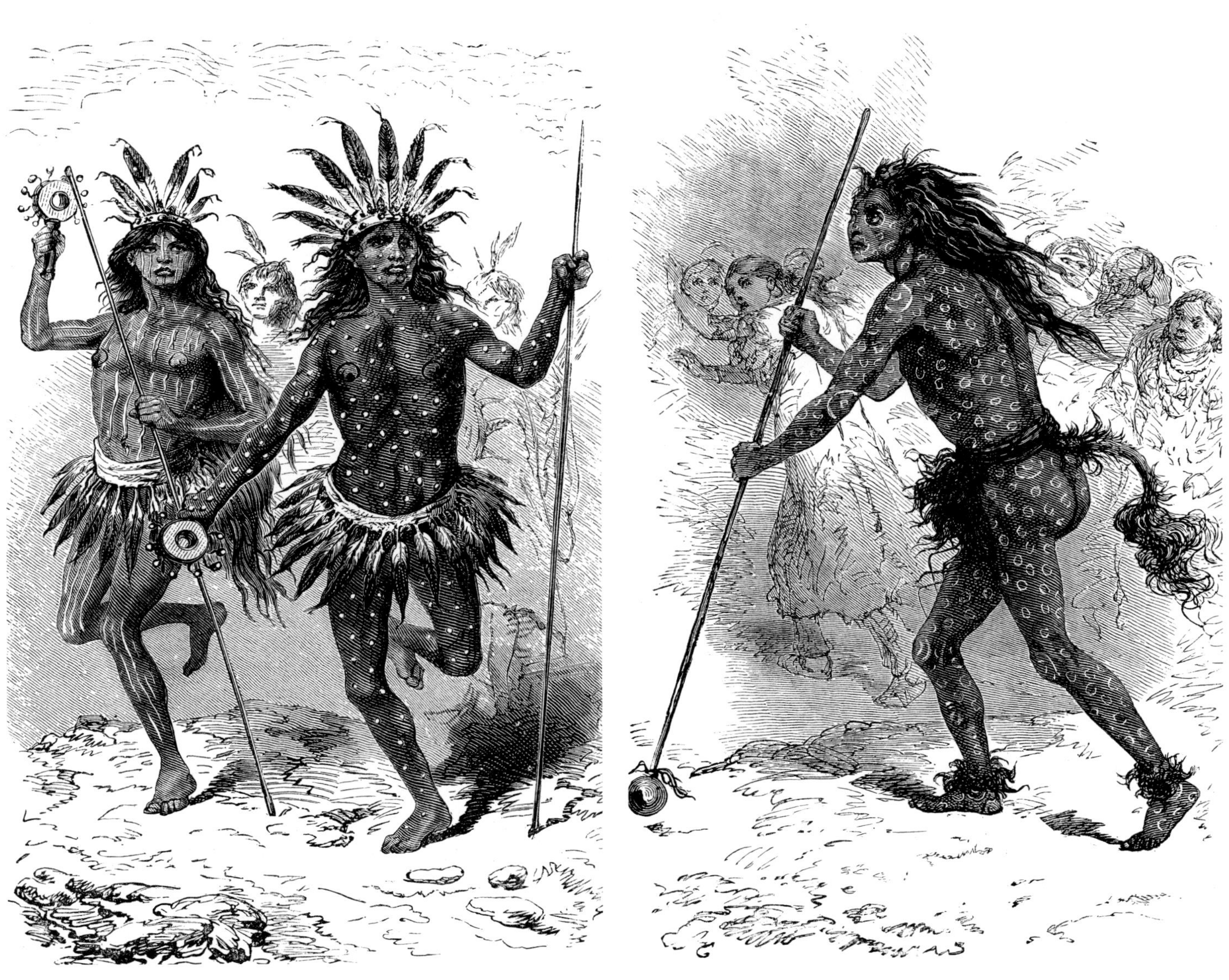

Native American dance and 'medicine man', c. 1880

Tanz der eingeborenen Amerikaner mit „Medizinmann", um 1880

Danza indigena americana e 'stregone', ca. 1880

Danse amérindienne et « Homme-médecine », vers 1880

Danza nativa americana y "sanador", alrededor del año 1880

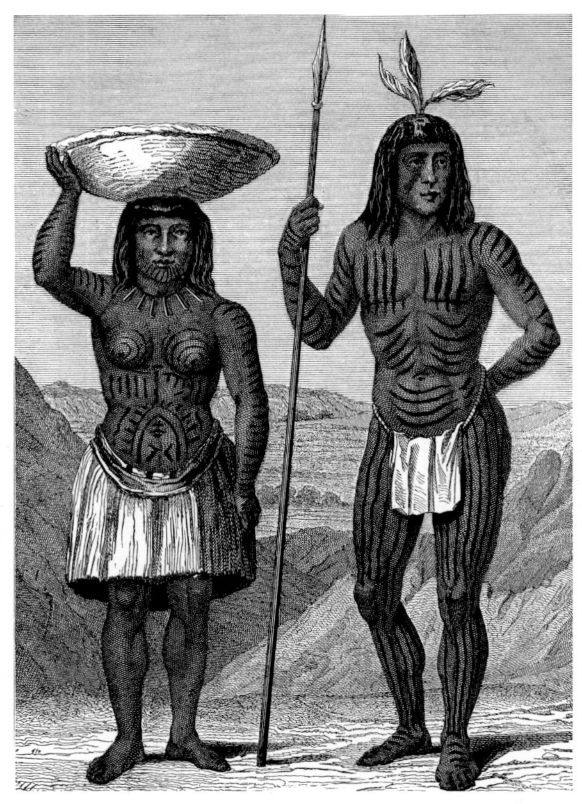

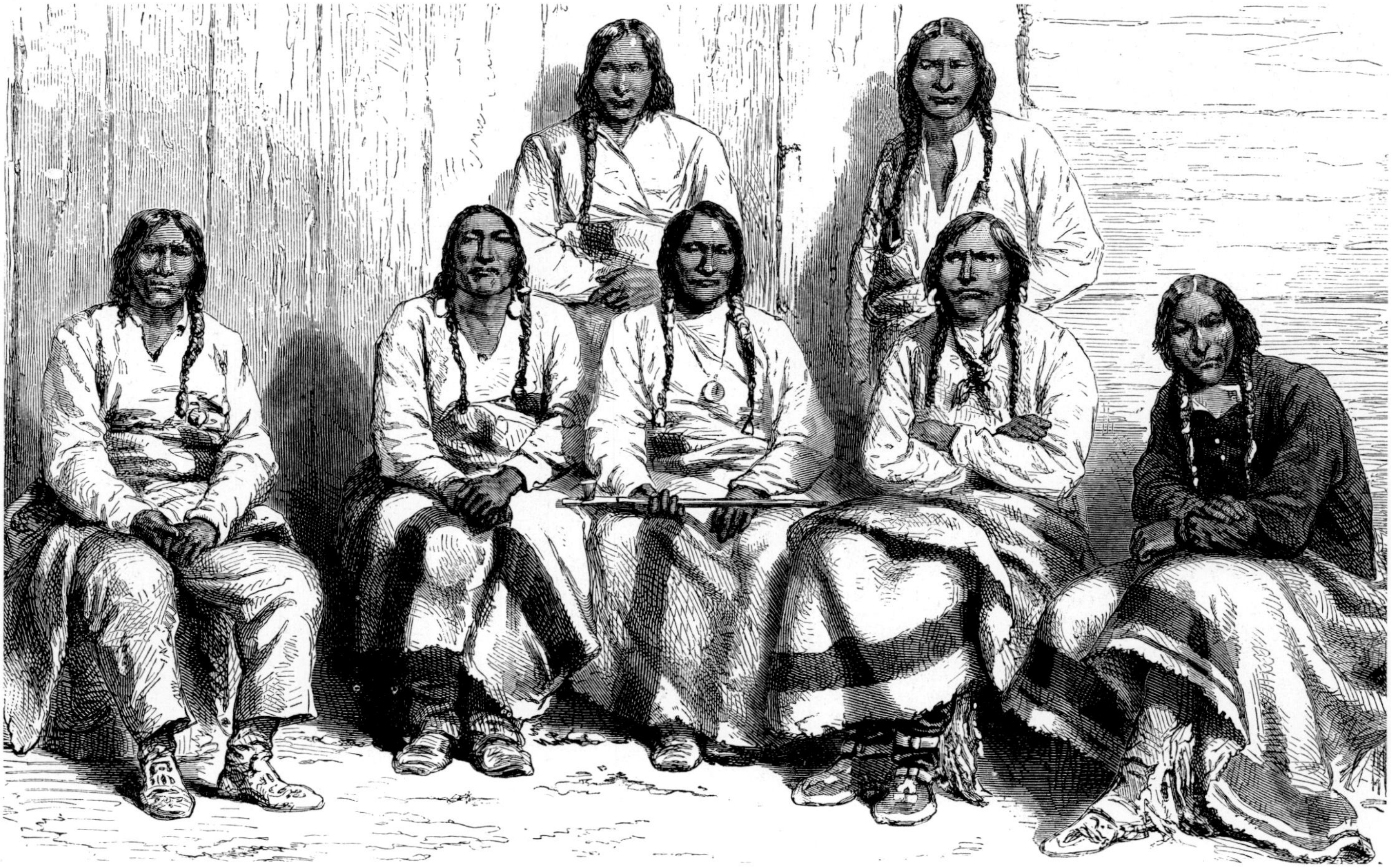

a	Mohaves from Colorado	Mohawe aus Colorado	Molavi del Colorado	Mohaves du Colorado	Mohaves de Colorado
b	Cheyennes, c. 1880	Cheyenne, um 1880	Cheyenne, ca. 1880	Cheyennes, vers 1880	Cheyenes, hacia 1880

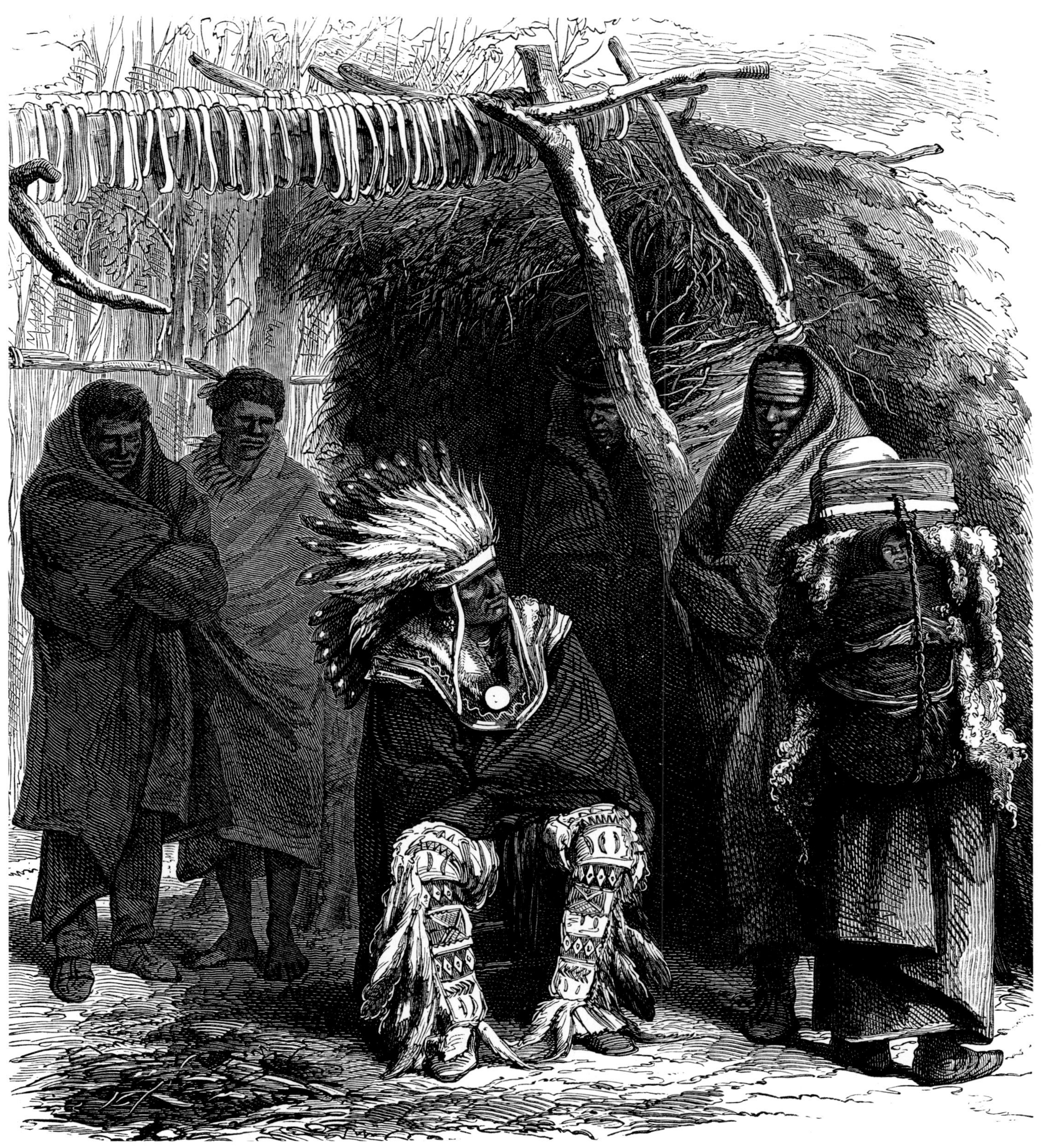

Pawnees, c. 1880 Pawnees, um 1880 Pawnee, ca. 1880 Pawnees, vers 1880 Pawnees, hacia 1880

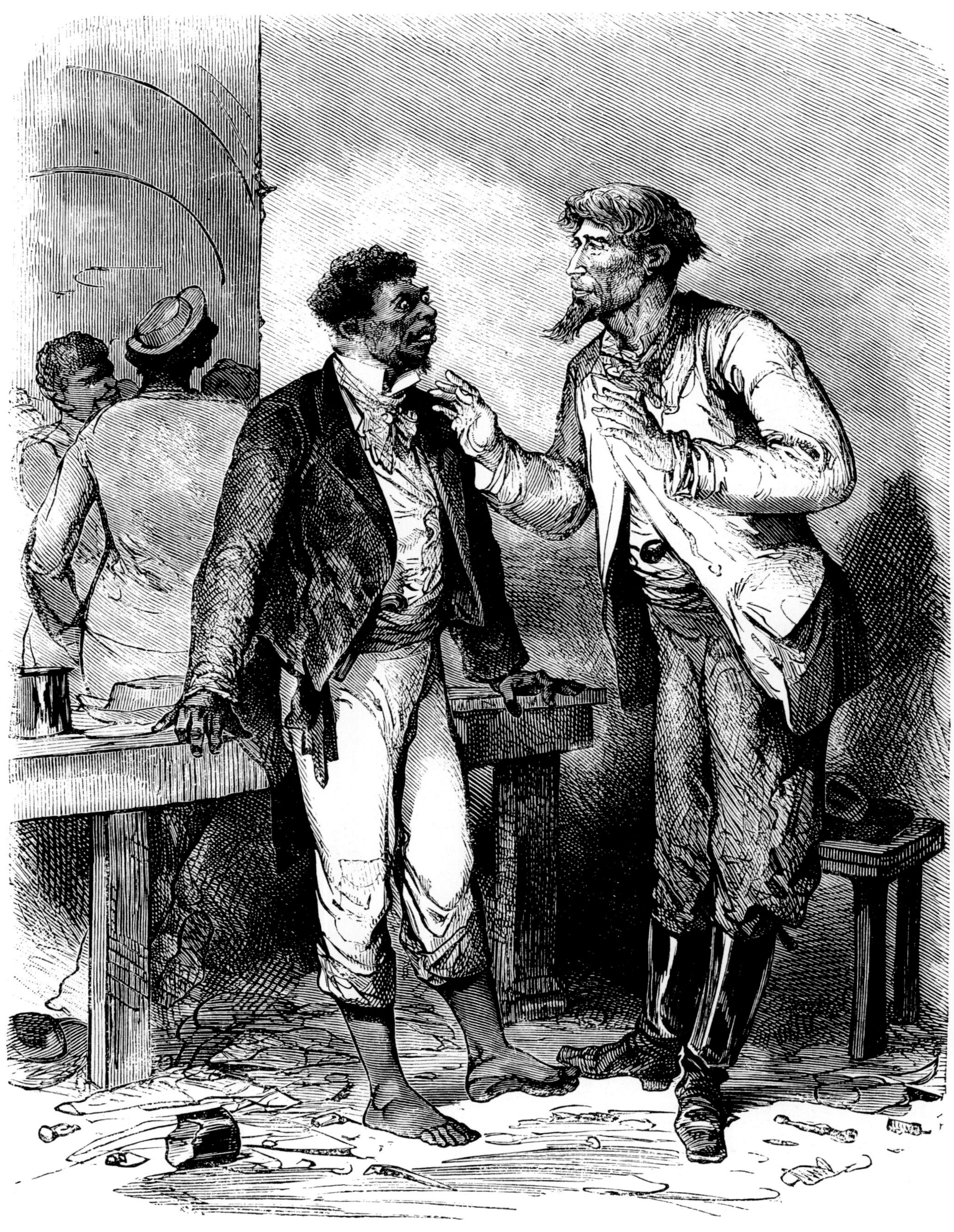

Black and white Americans, c. 1885

Schwarze und weiße Amerikaner, um 1885

Un nero e un bianco americani, ca. 1885

Américains blancs et noirs, vers 1885

Dos norteamericanos: uno de raza negra y otro de raza blanca, 1885

U.S.A.

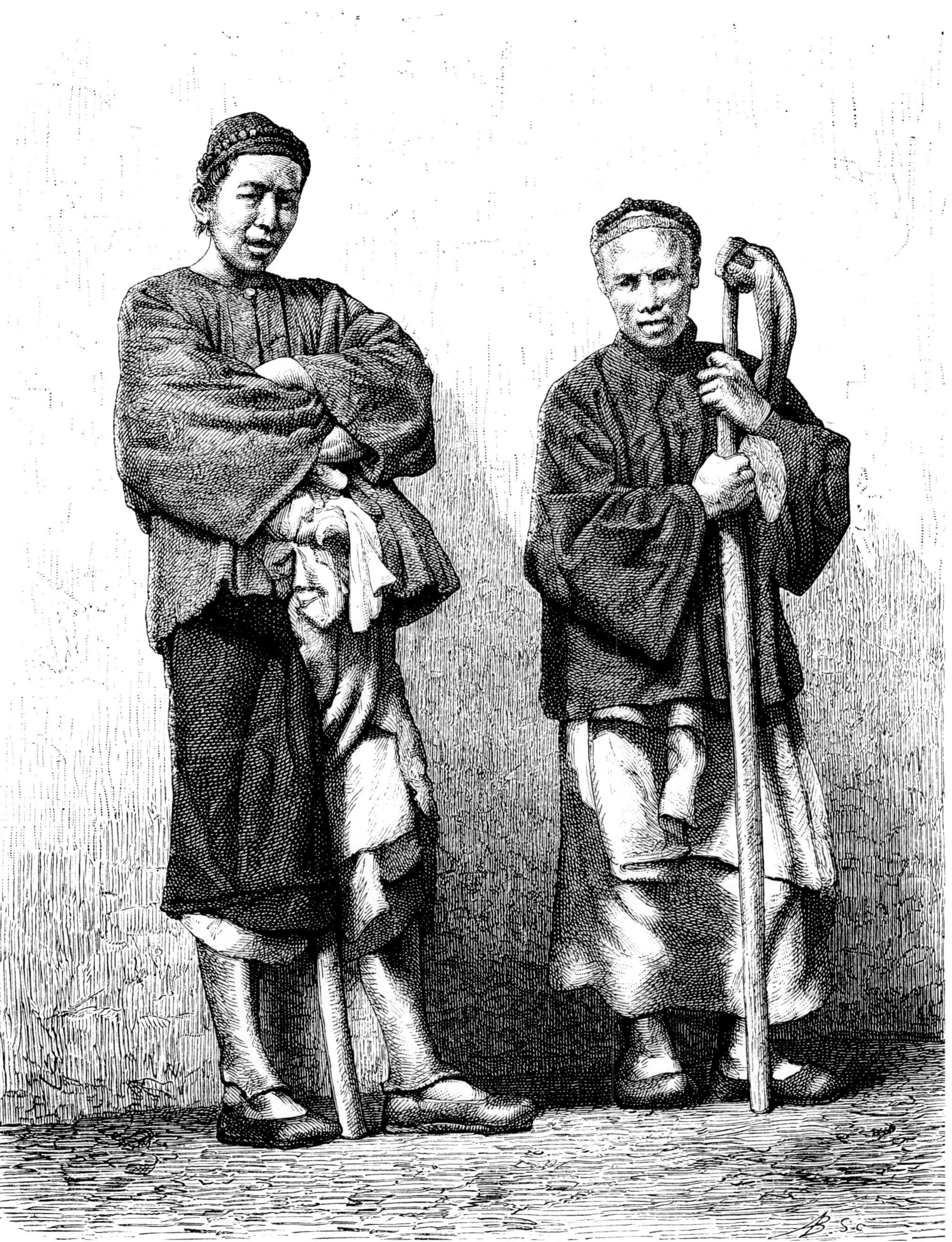

Chinese workers in North America, c. 1885

Chinesische Arbeiter in Nordamerika, um 1885

Operai cinesi nell'America del Nord, ca. 1885

Travailleurs chinois en Amérique du Nord, vers 1885

Trabajadores chinos en Norteamérica, hacia 1885

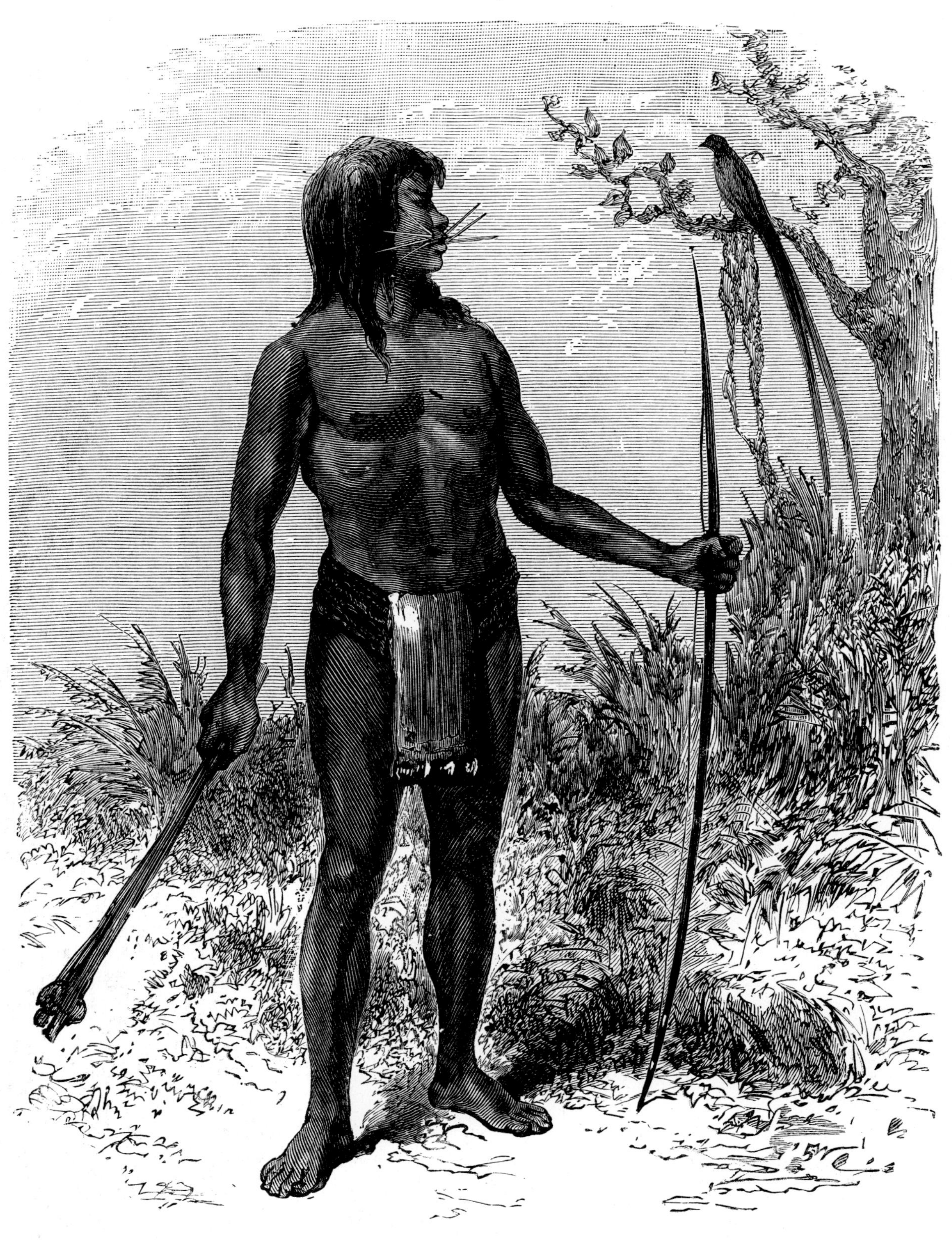

Native of the Lesser Antiles, c. 1880

Eingeborener von den kleinen Antillen, um 1880

Indigeno delle Antille Minori, ca. 1880

Indigène des Petites Antilles, vers 1880

Nativo de las Pequeñas Antillas, hacia 1880

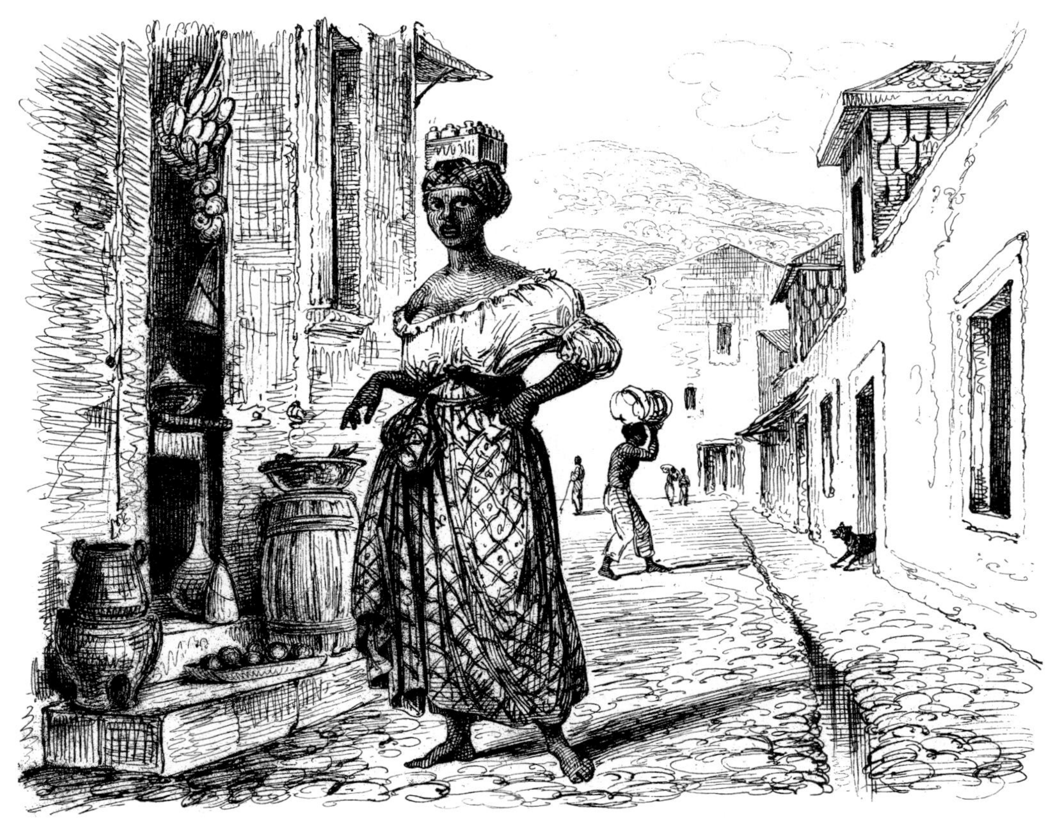

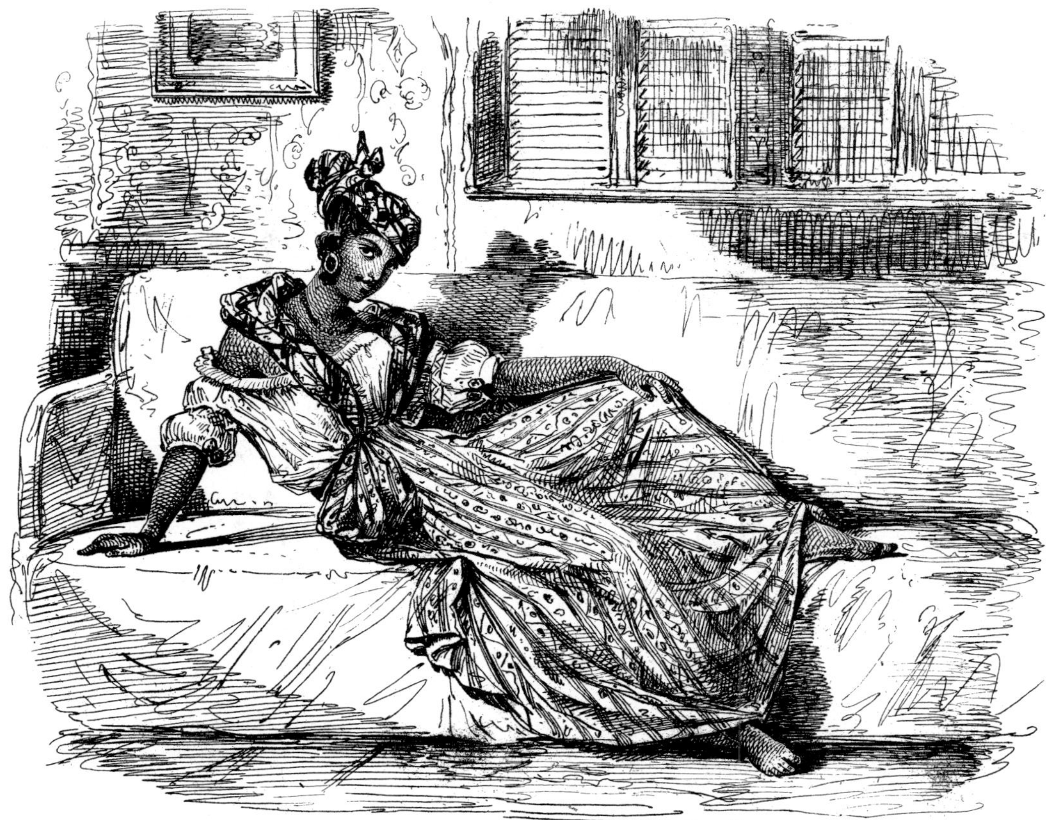

a	Street in Martinique	Straße in Martinique	Strada della Martinica	Rue de Martinique	Calle de Martinica
b	Haitian lady, c. 1870	Haitianische Dame, um 1870	Donna haitiana, ca. 1870	Femme haïtienne, vers 1870	Dama haitiana, 1870

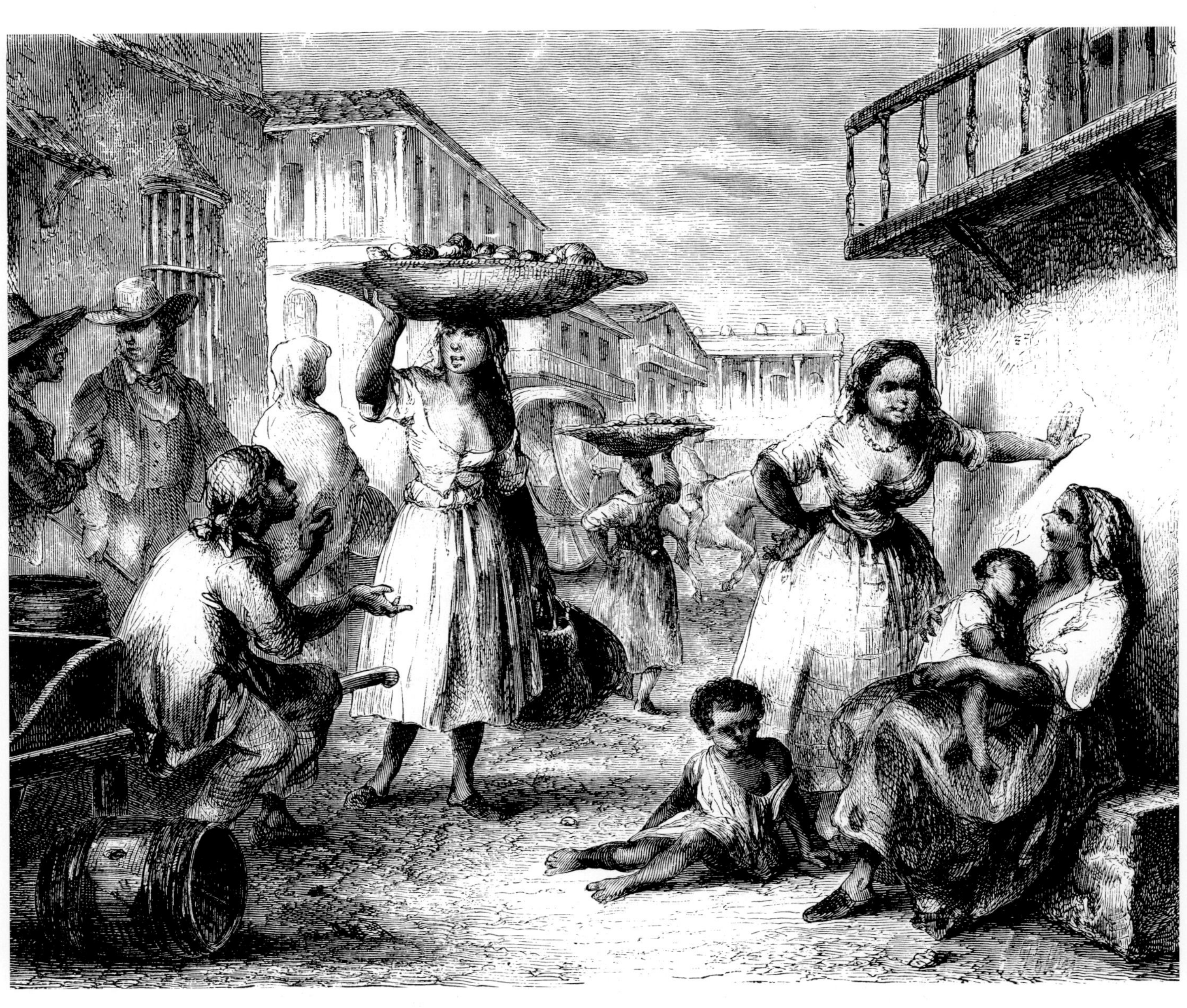

Street vendors, Havana, Cuba, c. 1885

Straßenverkäufer, Havanna, Kuba, um 1885

Venditori ambulanti, La Avana, Cuba, ca. 1885

Vendeurs de rue, La Havane, Cuba, vers 1885

Vendedores ambulantes, La Habana, Cuba, 1885

Cuba

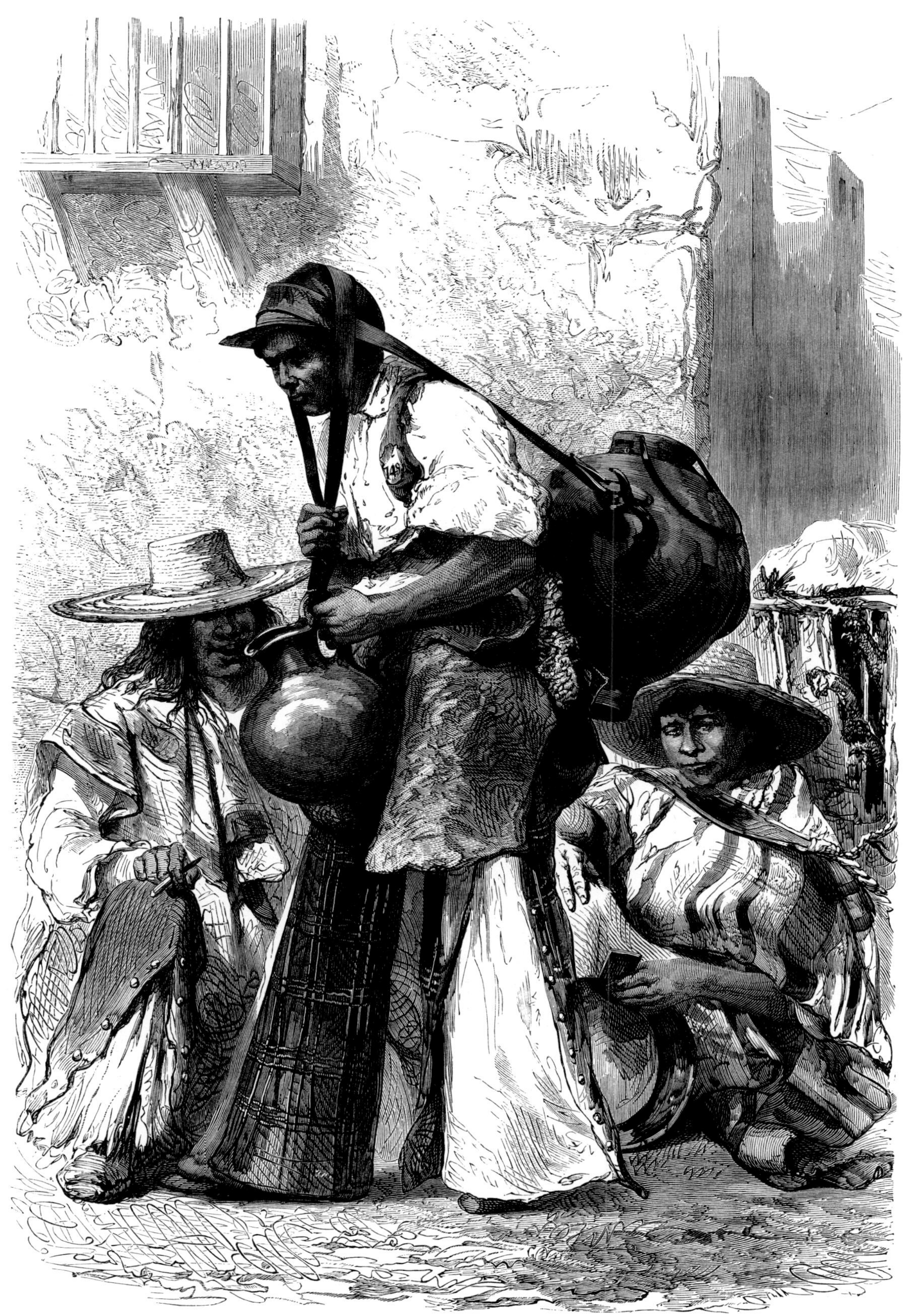

Water seller, c. 1880

Wasserverkäufer, um 1880

Venditore di acqua, ca. 1880

Vendeur d'eau, vers 1880

Aguador, hacia 1880

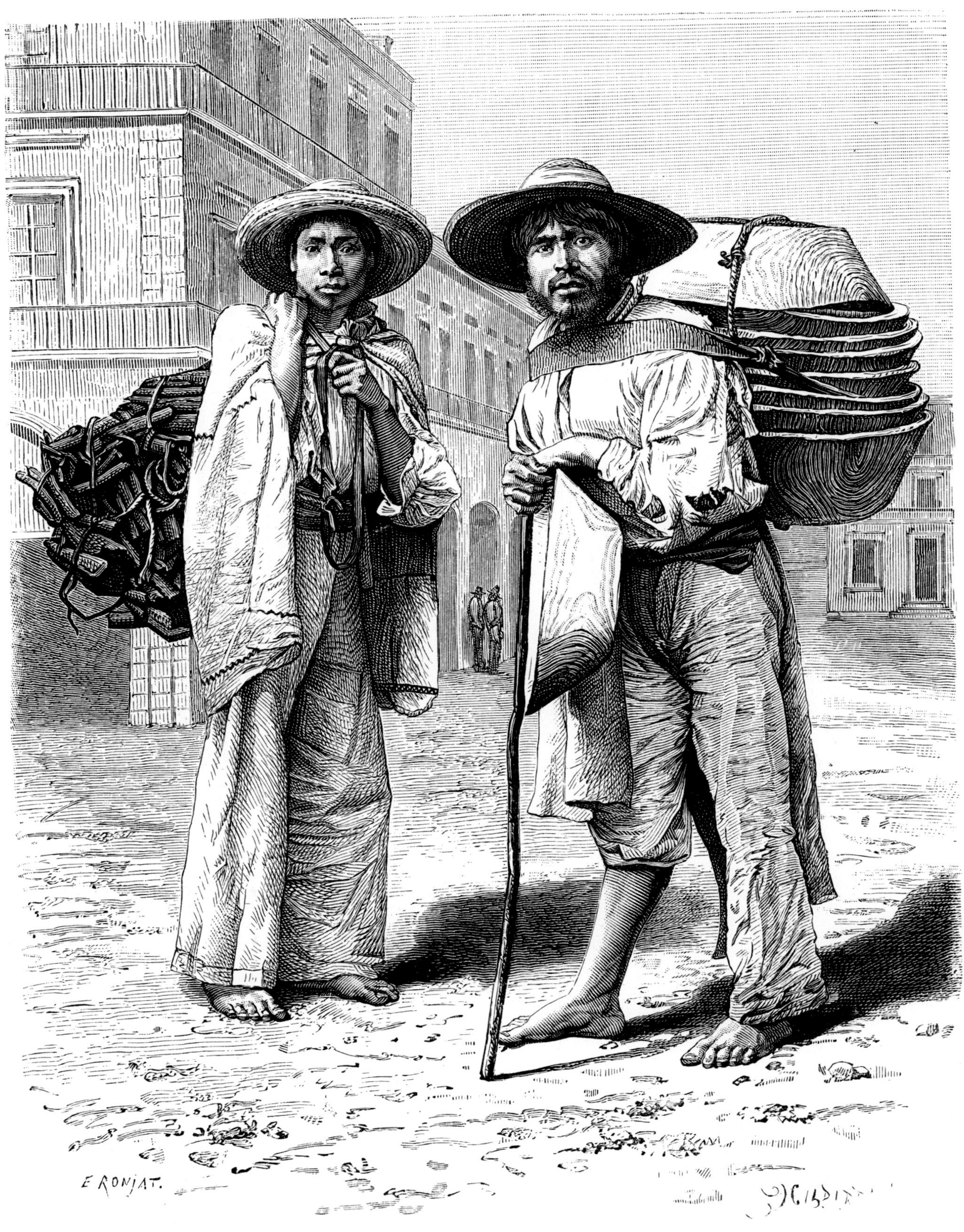

Charcoal and wooden bowl vendors, c. 1875

Holzkohle- und Holzschalenverkäufer, um 1875

Venditori di contenitori di carbone di legna e legna, ca. 1875

Vendeurs de charbon et de bols en bois, vers 1875

Vendedores de carbón y de recipientes de madera, hacia 1875

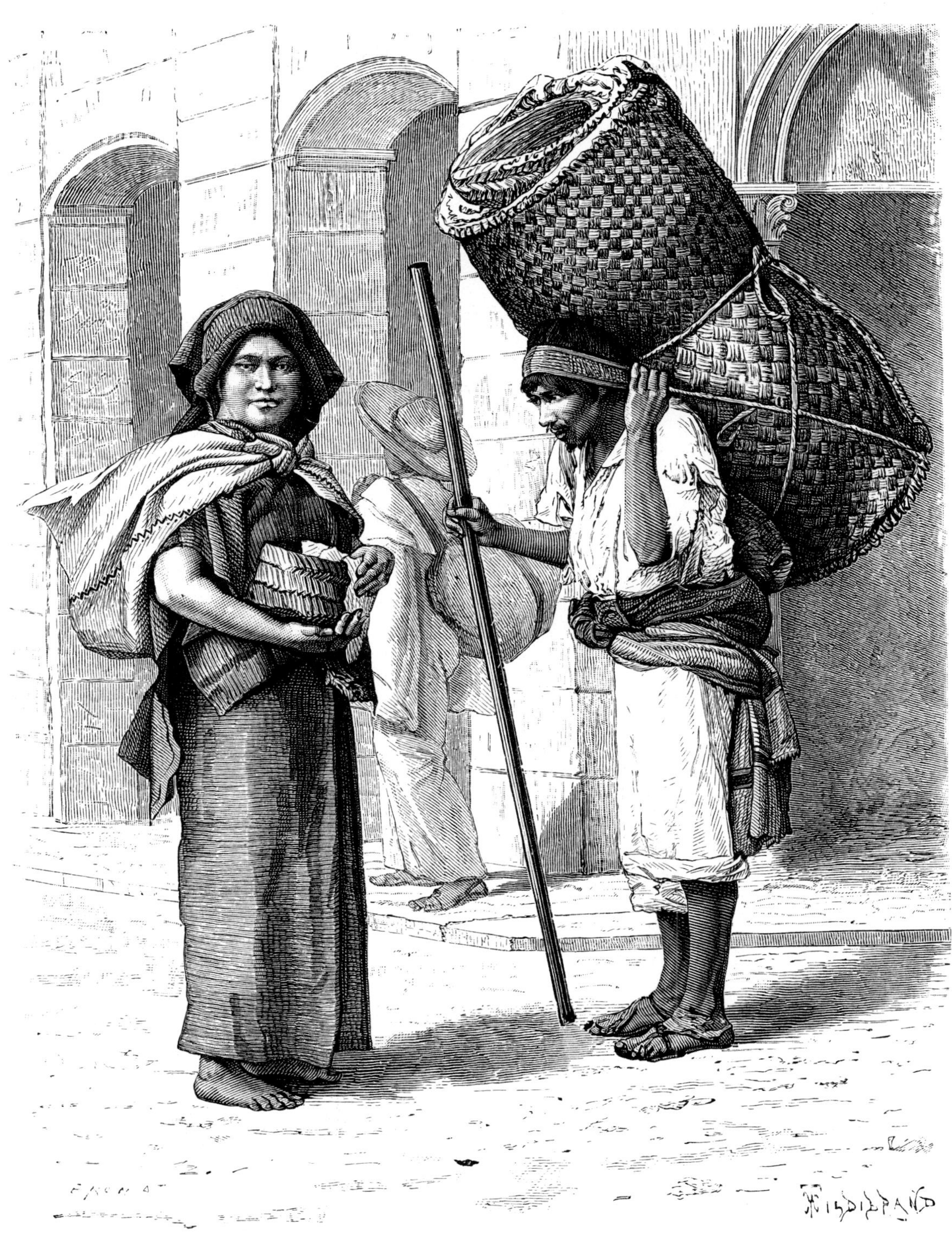

Tortilla and matress vendors, c. 1875

Tortilla- und Matratzenverkäufer, um 1875

Venditrici di tortilla e materassi, ca. 1875

Vendeurs de tortillas et de matelas, vers 1875

Vendedores de tortitas y de colchones, 1875

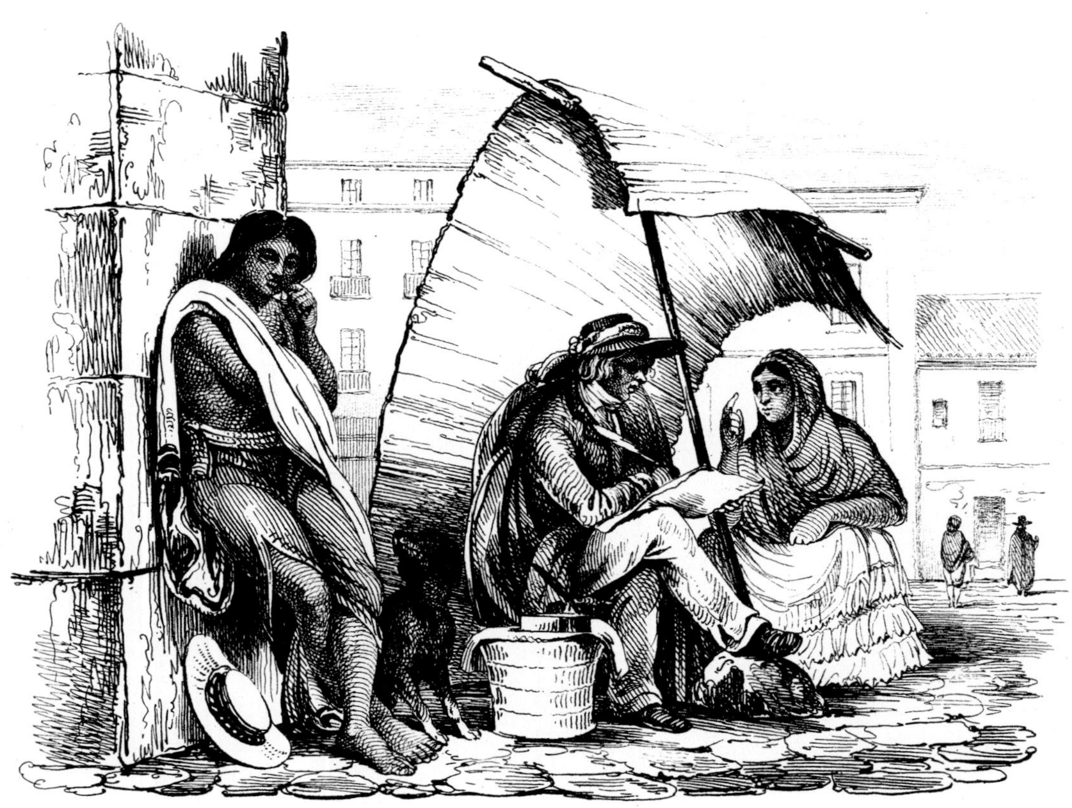

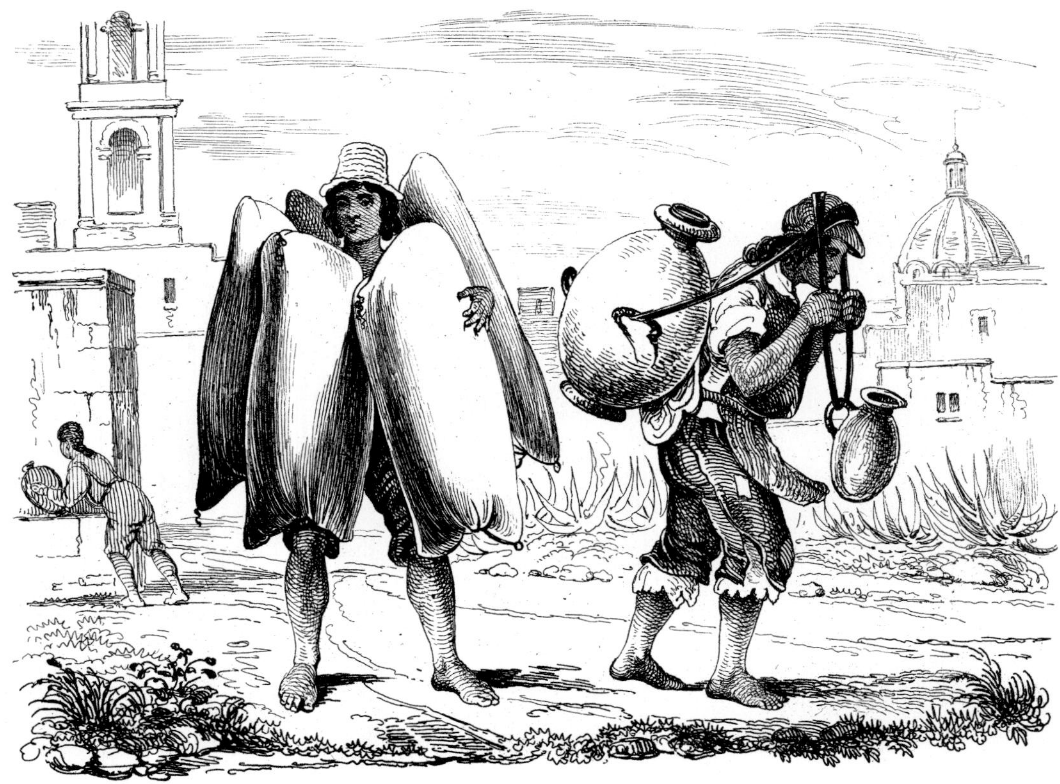

a	Street scene, Mexico City	Straßenszene, Mexiko City	Scena di strada, Città del Messico	Scène de rue à Mexico City	Una calle de México D.F.
b	Street vendor and water carrier, Mexico City, c. 1840	Straßenverkäufer und Wasserträger, Mexiko City, um 1840	Venditore di strada e portatore di acqua, Città del Messico, ca. 1840	Vendeur de rue et porteur d'eau à Mexico City, vers 1840	Vendedor ambulante y aguador, México D.F., alrededor del año 1840

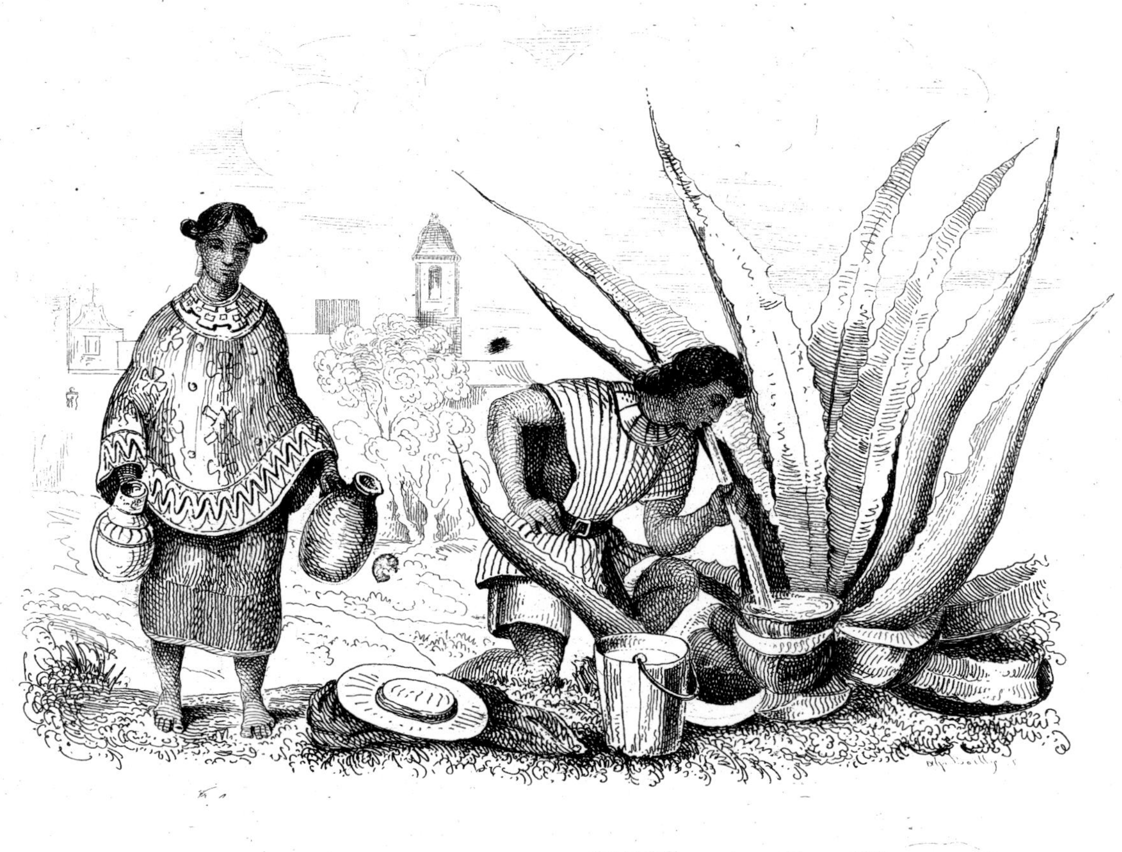

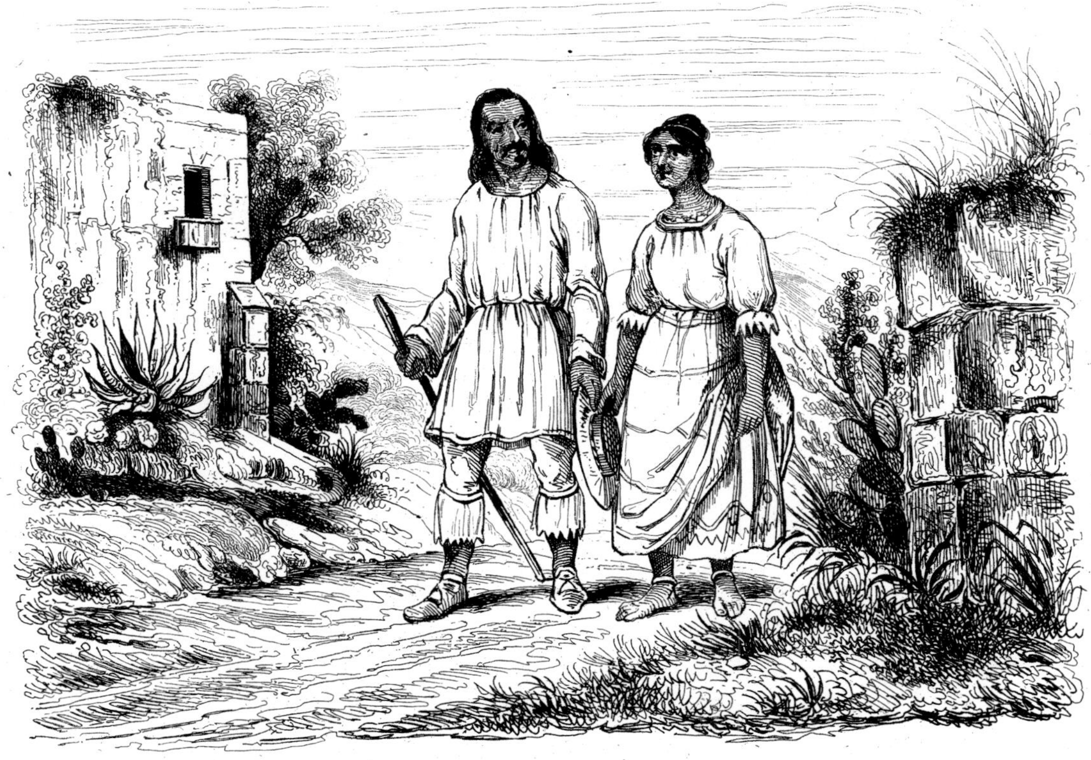

a	Natives of Southern Mexico, c. 1840	Eingeborene aus Südmexiko, um 1840	Indigeni del Messico meridionale, ca. 1840	Indigènes du Sud du Mexique, vers 1840	Nativos del sur de México, hacia 1840
b	Natives of Michoacan, c. 1840	Eingeborene aus Michoacan, um 1840	Indigeni di Michoacan, ca. 1840	Indigènes de Michoacan, vers 1840	Nativos de Michoacán, alrededor del año 1840

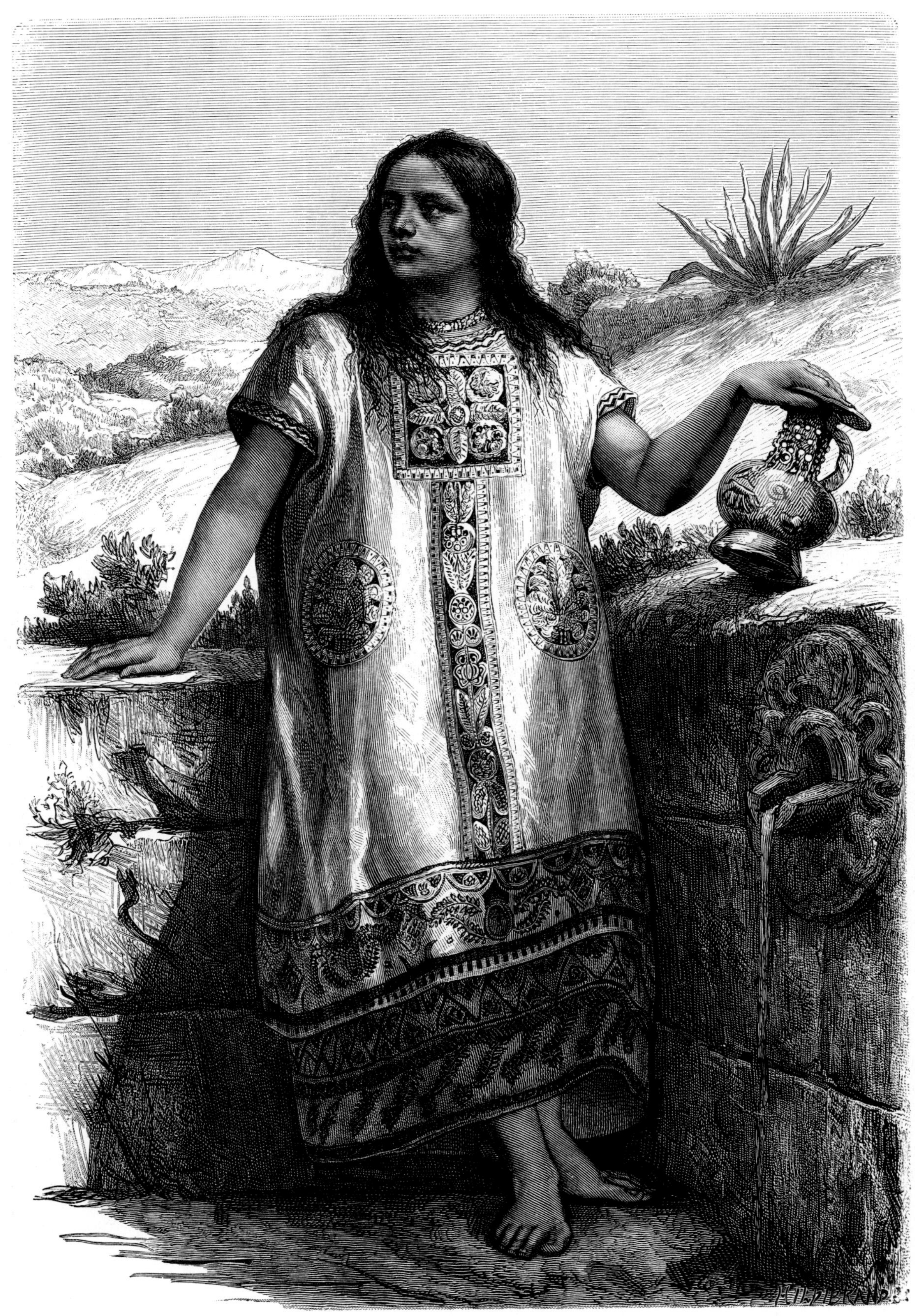

Mexican girl, with 'Tolteque-style' robe , c. 1880

Mexikanisches Mädchen mit Kleid im „toltekischen" Stil, um 1880

Ragazza messicana con abito 'stilo tolteco', ca. 1880

Jeune mexicaine vêtue d'une robe « à la mode Toltèque », vers 1880

Muchacha mexicana con vestido "de estilo tolteca", hacia 1880

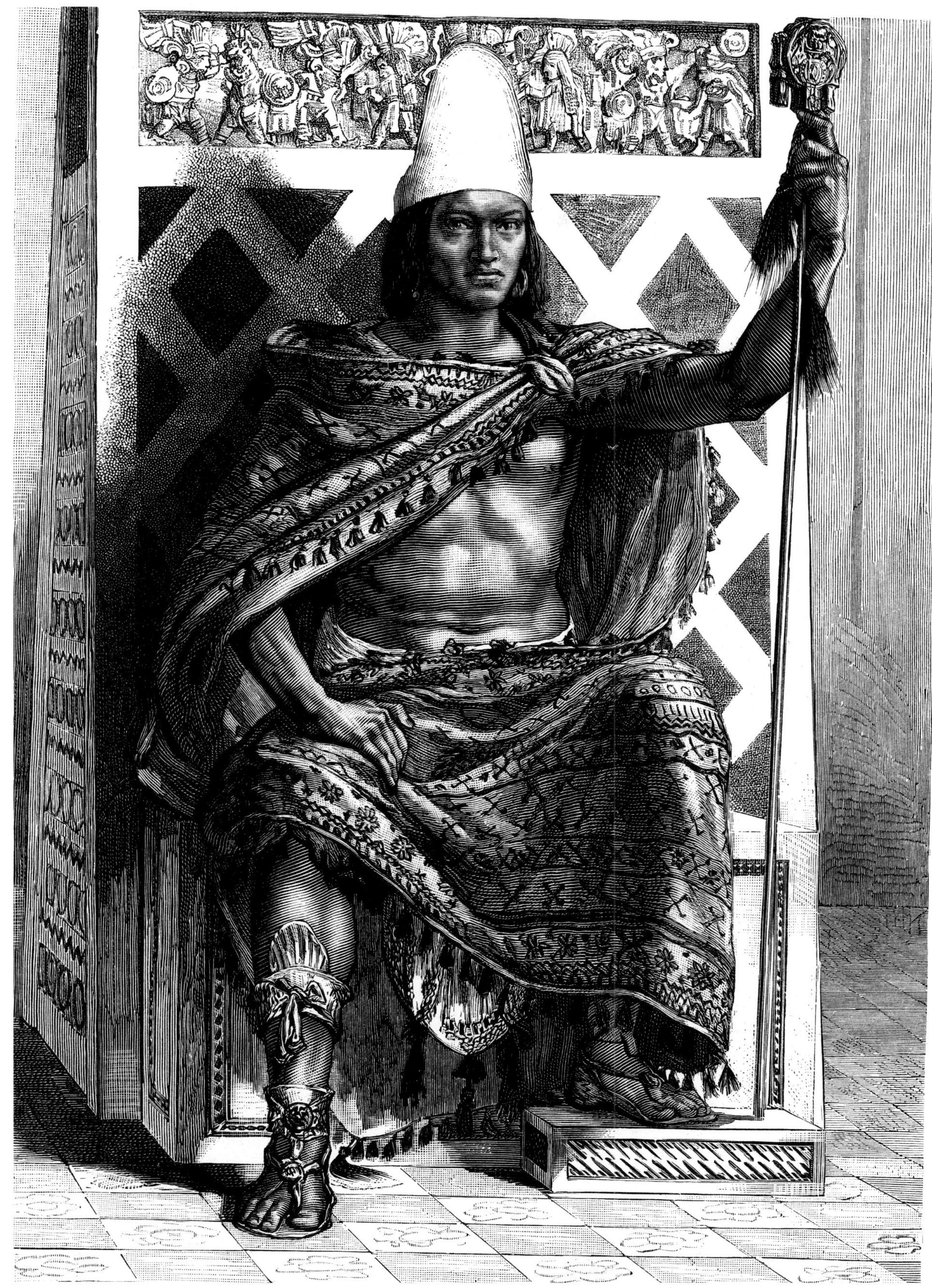

Maya king, drawing after a 19th-century painting

Mayakönig, Zeichnung nach einem Gemälde aus dem 19. Jahrhundert

Re maya, disegno tratto da un dipinto del XIX secolo

Roi Maya, dessin d'après une peinture du XIX e siècle

Rey maya, dibujo a partir de un cuadro del siglo XIX

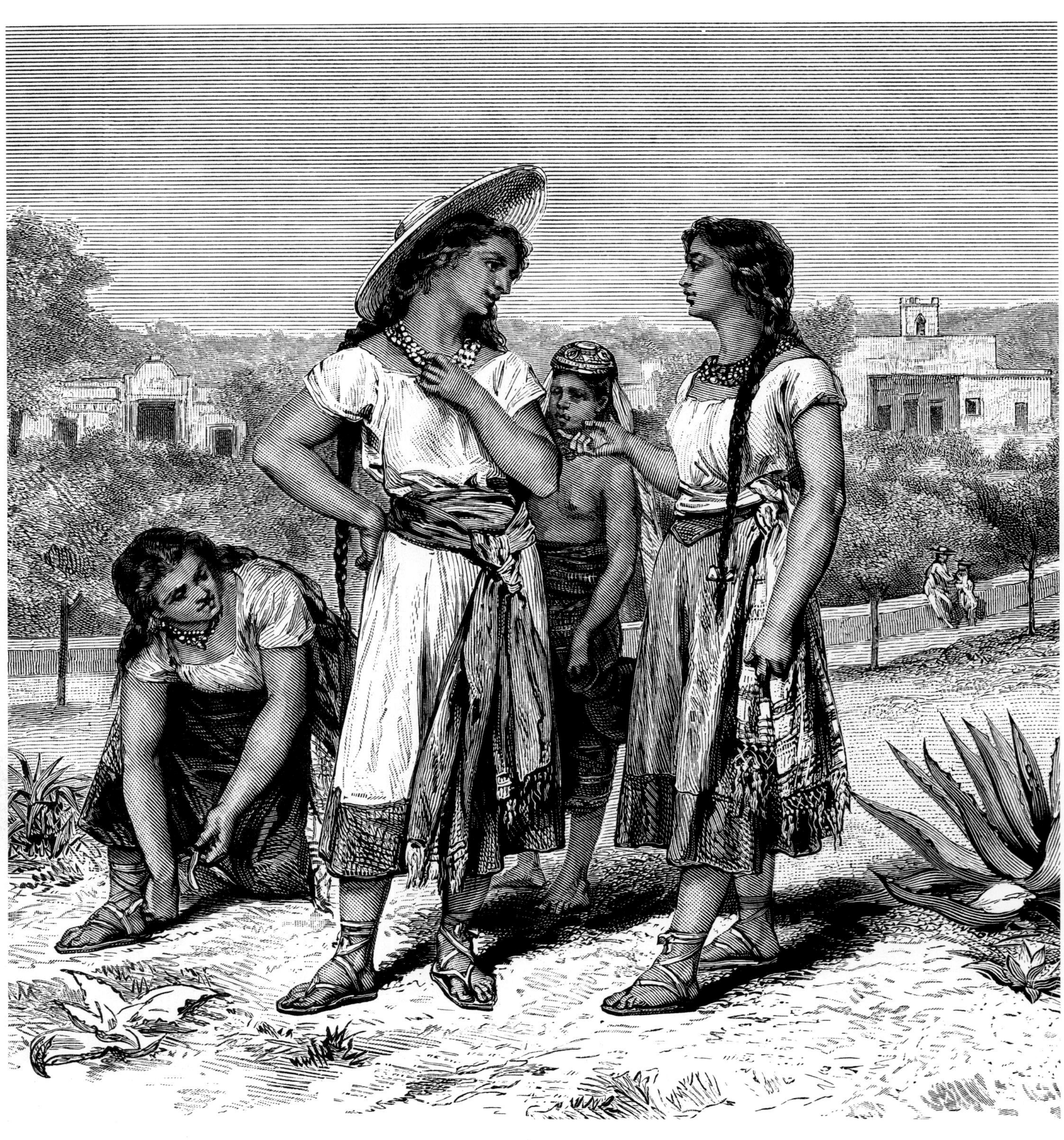

Young girls from Tuxla, c. 1875

Junge Mädchen aus Tuxla, um 1875

Giovani donne di Tuxla, ca. 1875

Jeunes filles de Tuxla, vers 1875

Muchachas de Tuxtla, alrededor de 1875

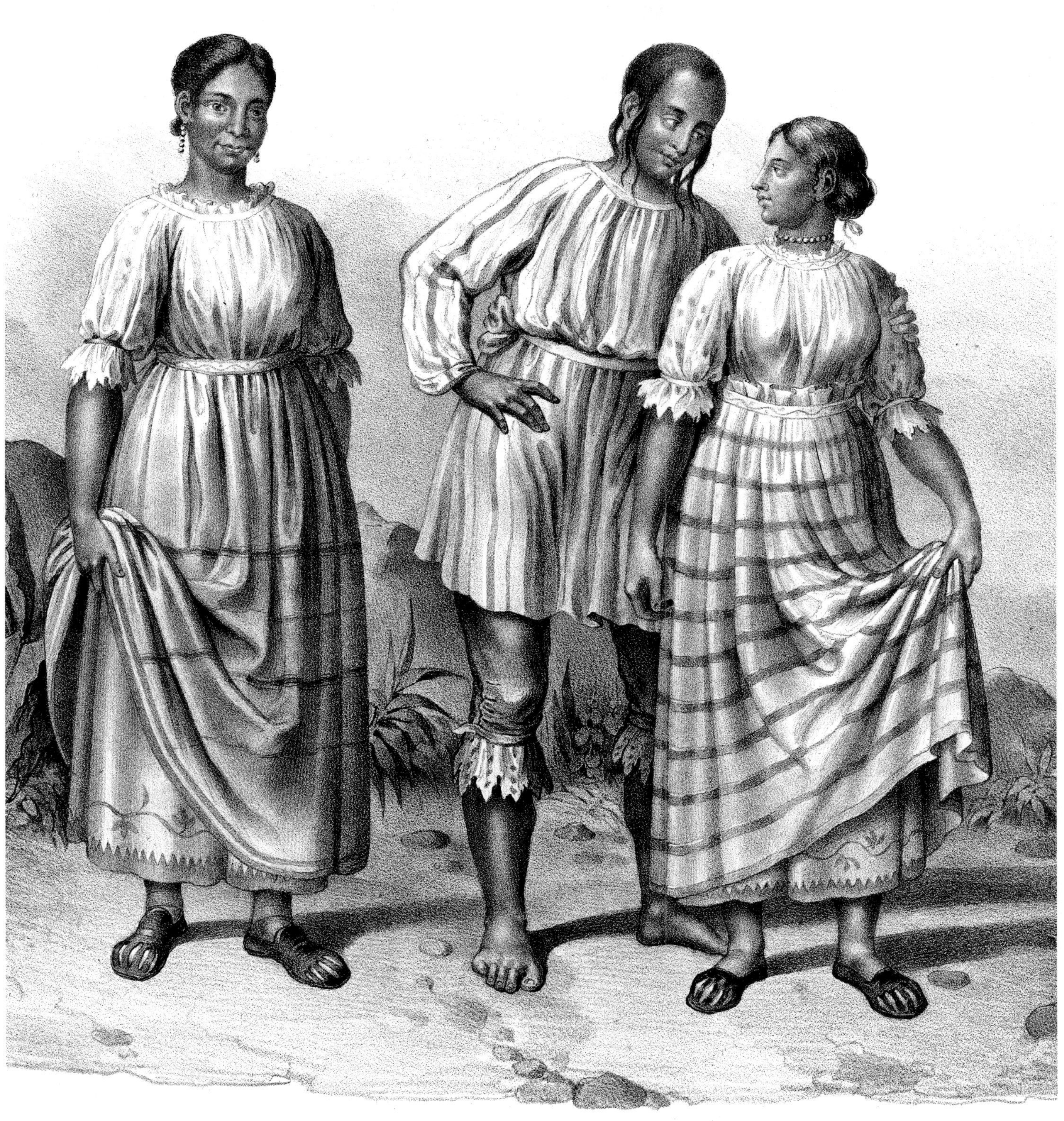

People from Michoacan, c. 1880

Leute aus Michoacan, um 1880

Abitanti di Michoacan, ca. 1880

Habitants de Michoacan, vers 1880

Habitantes de Michoacán, hacia 1880

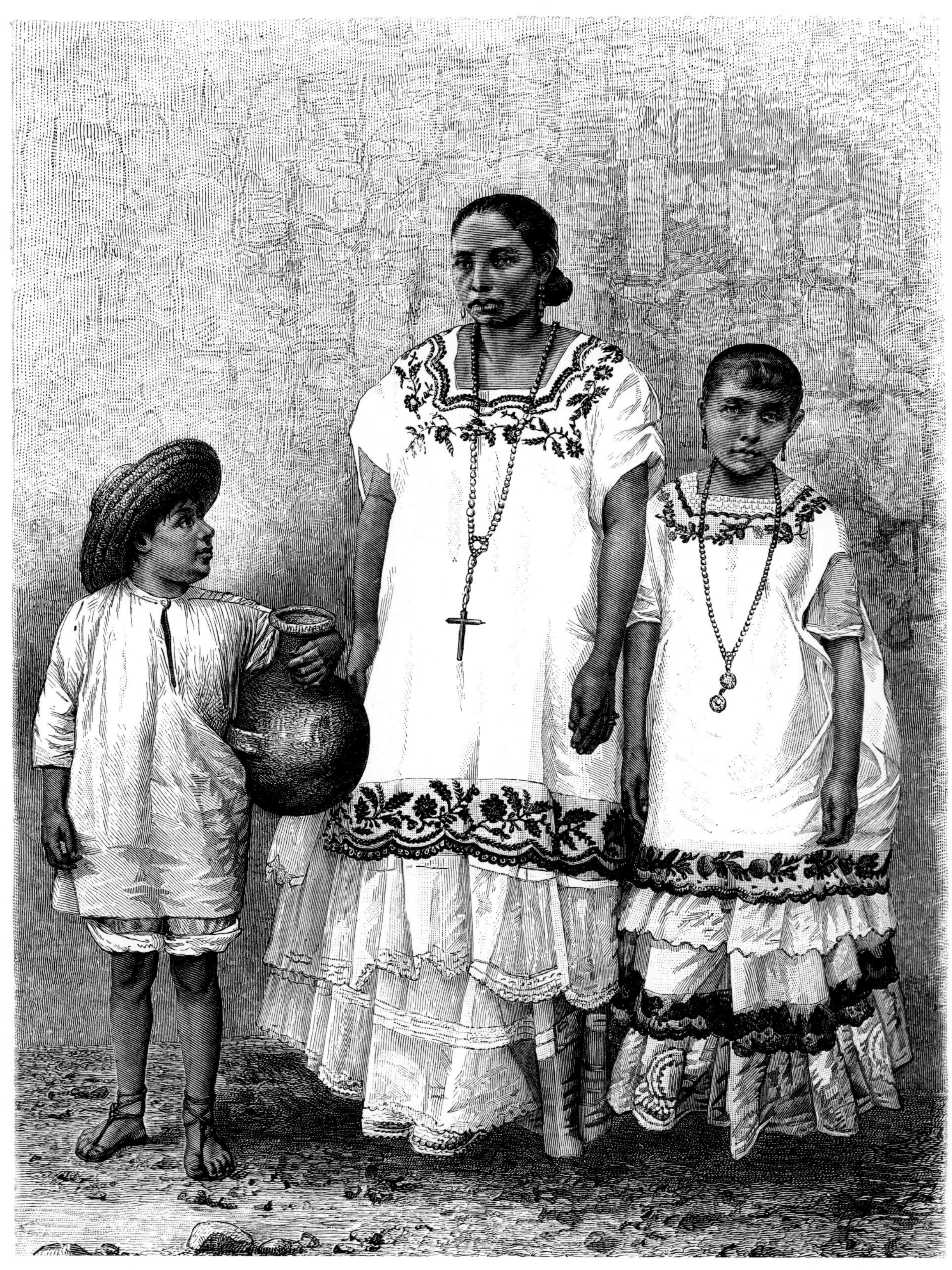

Mestizo ladies from Mérida, c. 1880

Mestizenfrauen aus Merida, um 1880

Donne meticce di Mérida, ca. 1880

Métisses de Mérida, vers 1880

Mestizas de Mérida, alrededor de 1880

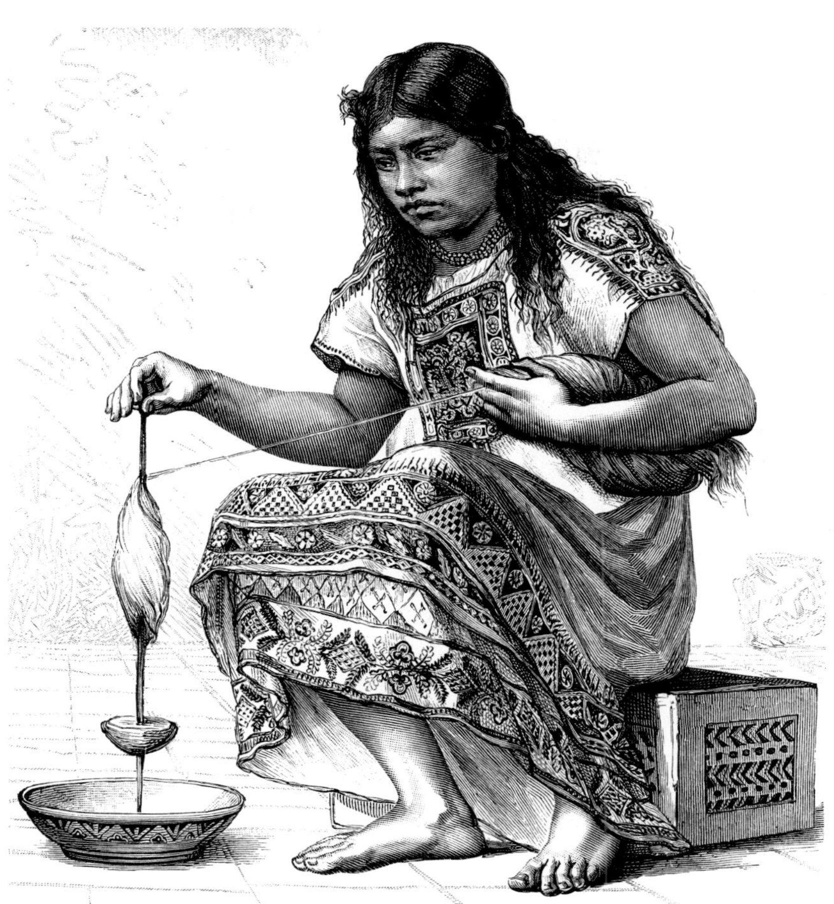

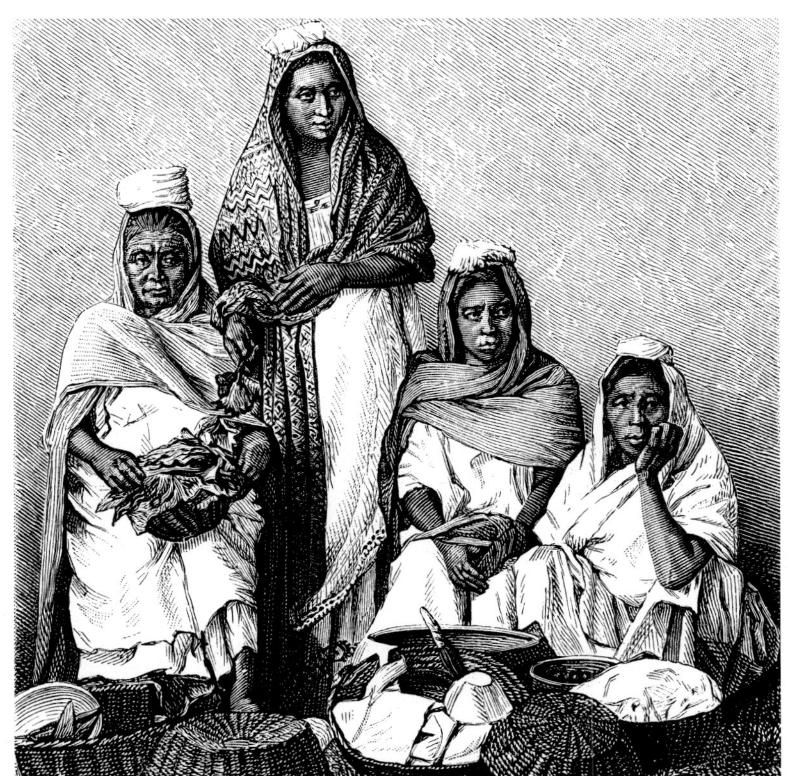

a — Mexican girl spinning cotton yarn, c. 1880 — Mexikanisches Mädchen beim Spinnen, um 1880 — Ragazza messicana mentre fila il cotone, ca. 1880 — Jeune mexicaine filant du coton, vers 1880 — Muchacha mexicana hilando algodón, 1880

b — Fruit vendors, Mérida, c. 1875 — Obstverkäufer, Merida, um 1875 — Venditori di frutta, Mérida, ca. 1875 — Vendeurs de fruits, Mérida, vers 1875 — Vendedoras de fruta, Mérida, hacia 1875

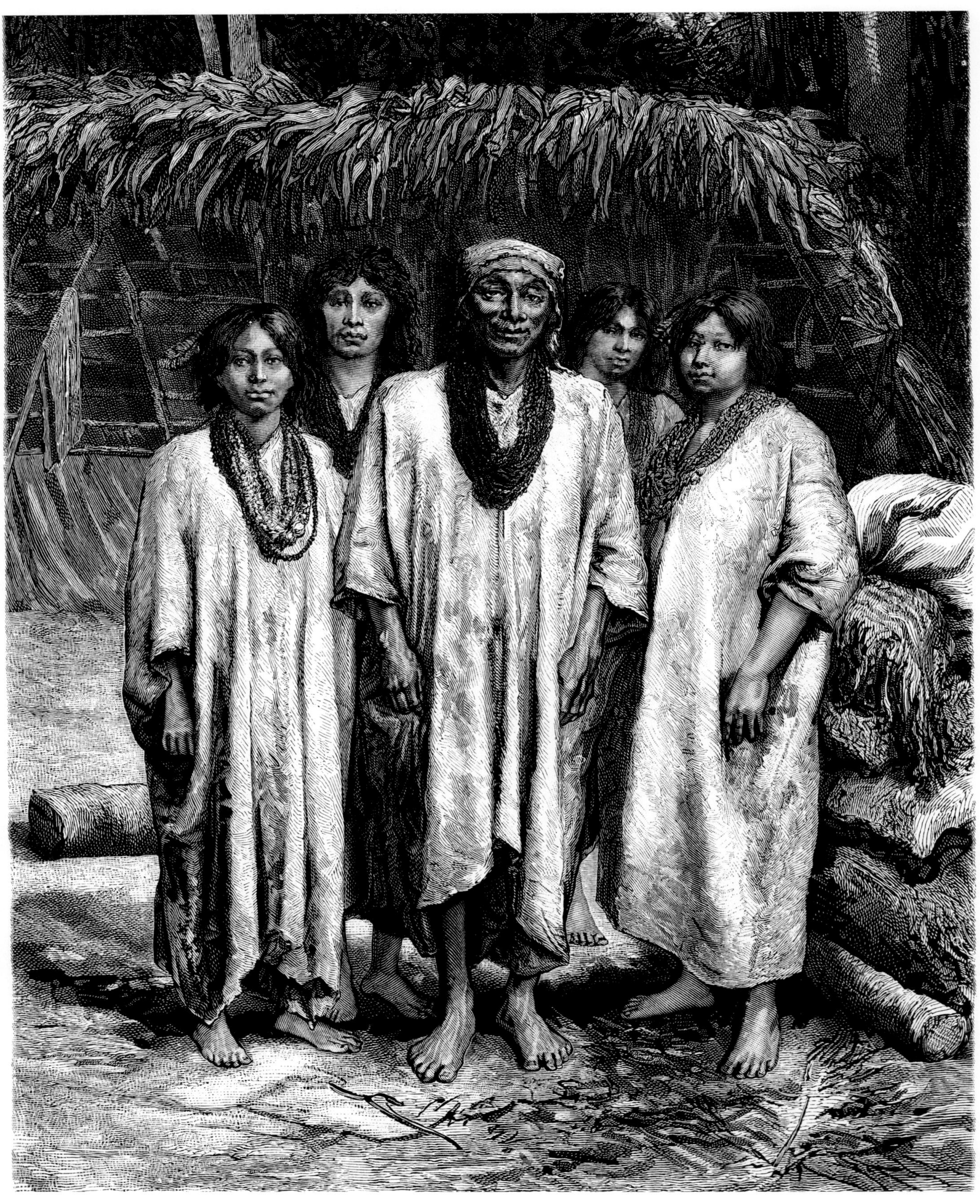

Lacandon indians, Chiapas, c. 1880

Lacandon-Indianer, Chiapas, um 1880

Indiani lacandoni, Chiapas, ca. 1880

Indiens lacandons, Chiapas, vers 1880

Indios lacandones, Chiapas, hacia 1880

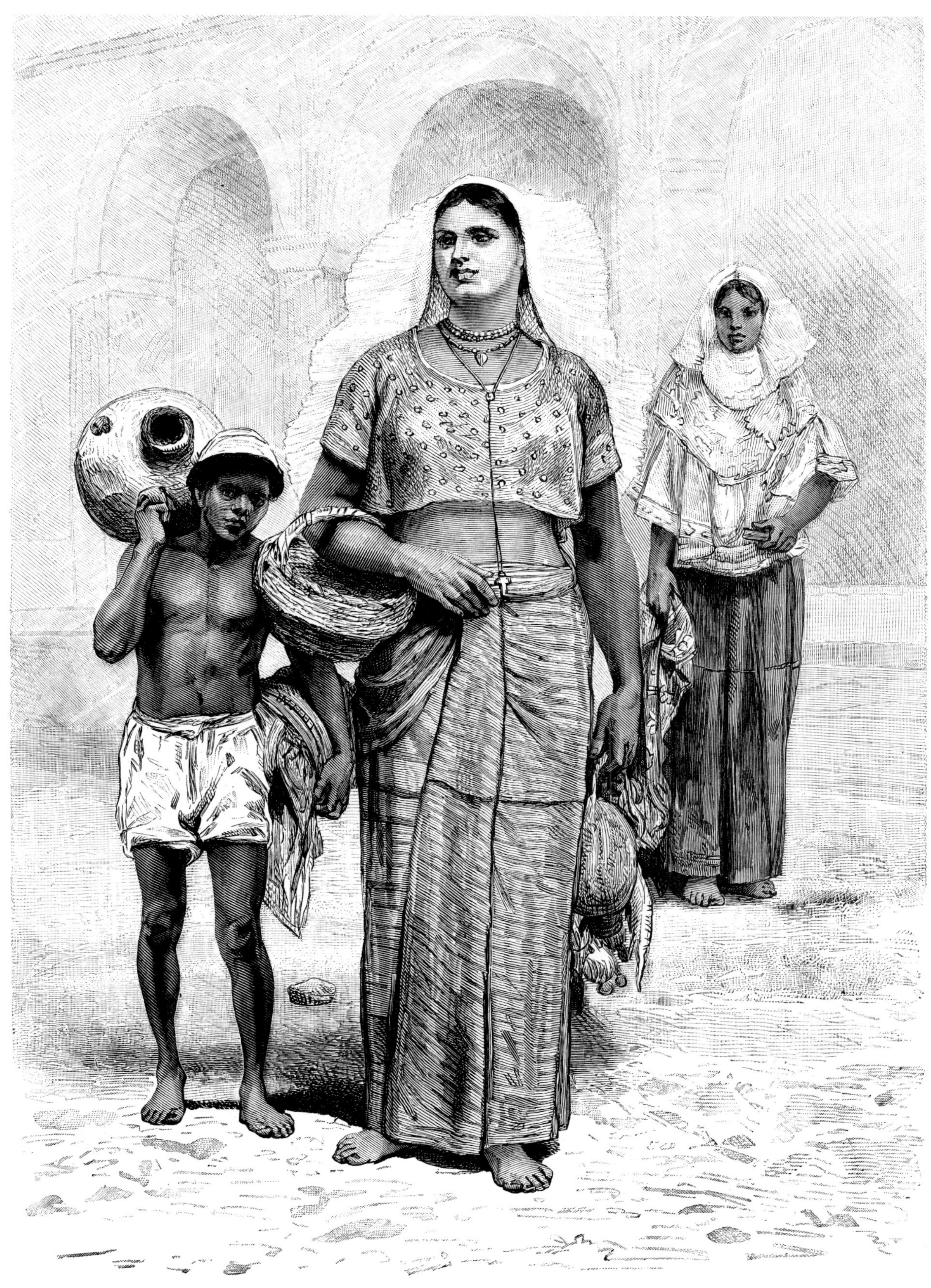

Ladies and porter in Tehuantepec, c. 1880

Frauen und Träger in Tehuantepec, um 1880

Donne e portatore a Tehuantepec, ca. 1880

Femmes et porteur à Tehuantepec, vers 1880

Mujeres y porteador, Tehuantepec, hacia 1880

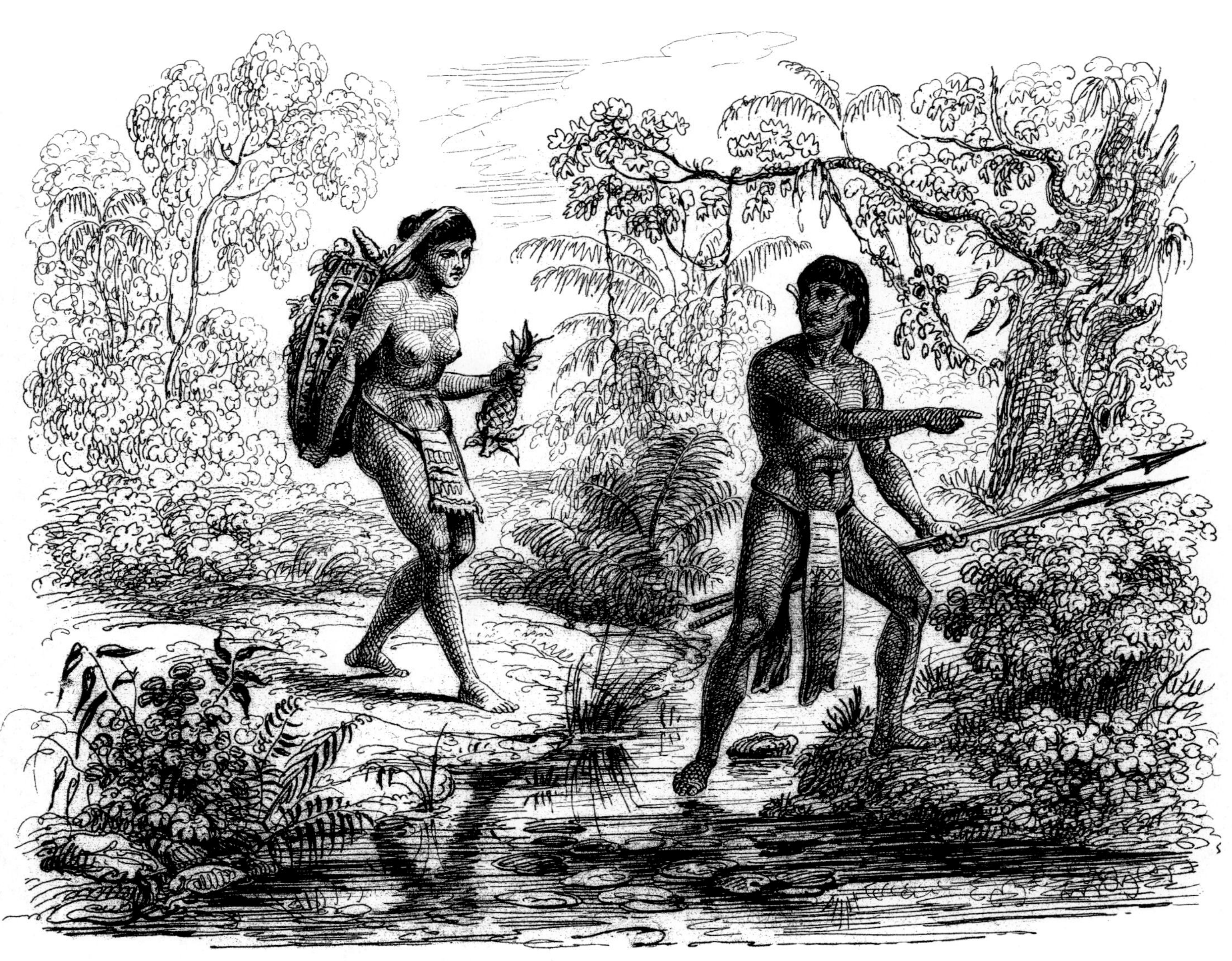

Natives of French Guyana

Eingeborene in Französisch-Guayana

Indigeni della Guyana francese

Indigènes de Guyane Française

Nativos de la Guayana Francesa

French Guyana

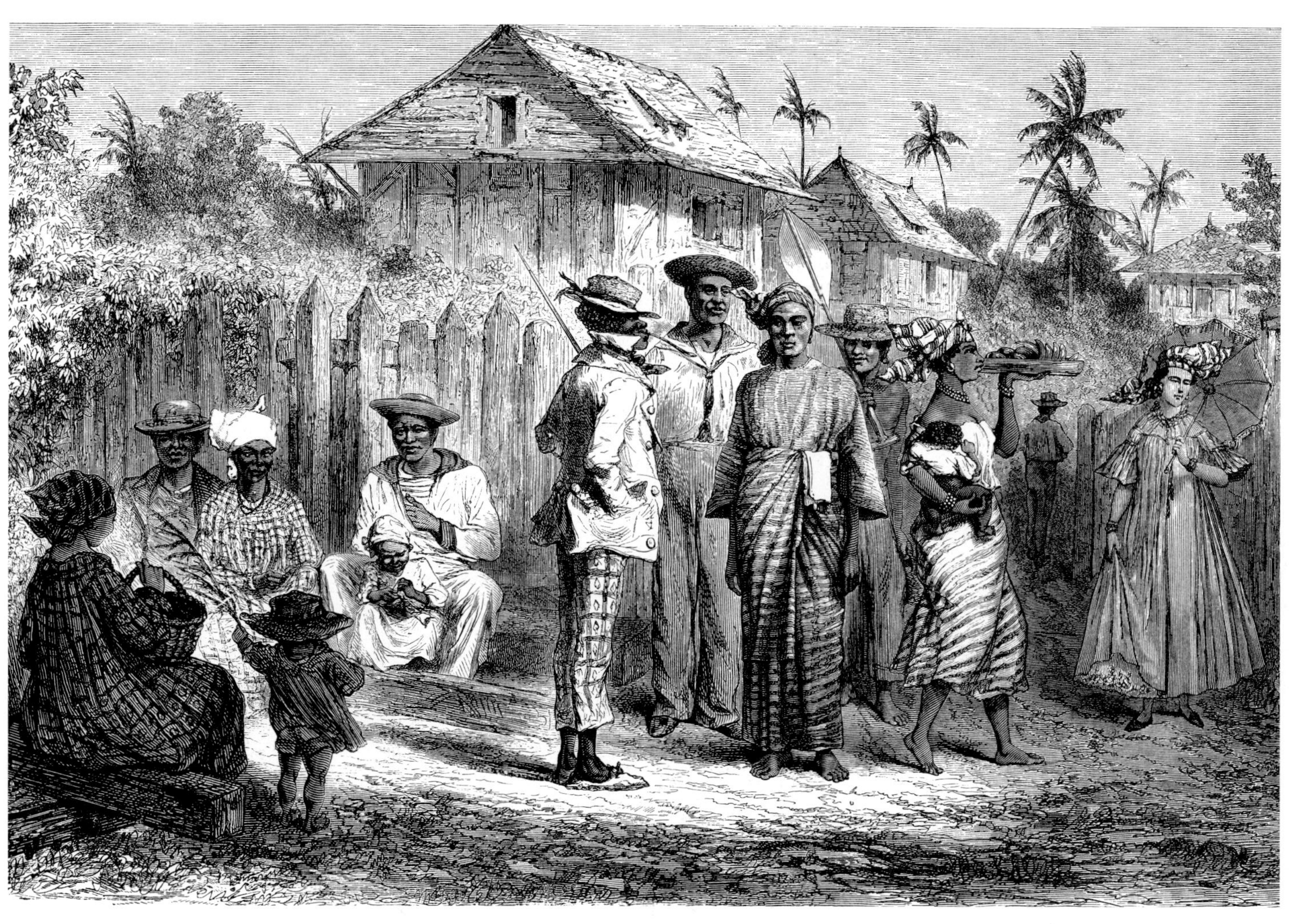

Street scene in Cayenne, French Guyana, c. 1860

Straßenszene in Cayenne, Französisch-Guayana, um 1860

Scena di strada a Cayenne, Guyana francese, ca. 1860

Scène de rue à Cayenne en Guyane Française, vers 1860

Una calle de Cayena, Guayana Francesa, alrededor del año 1860

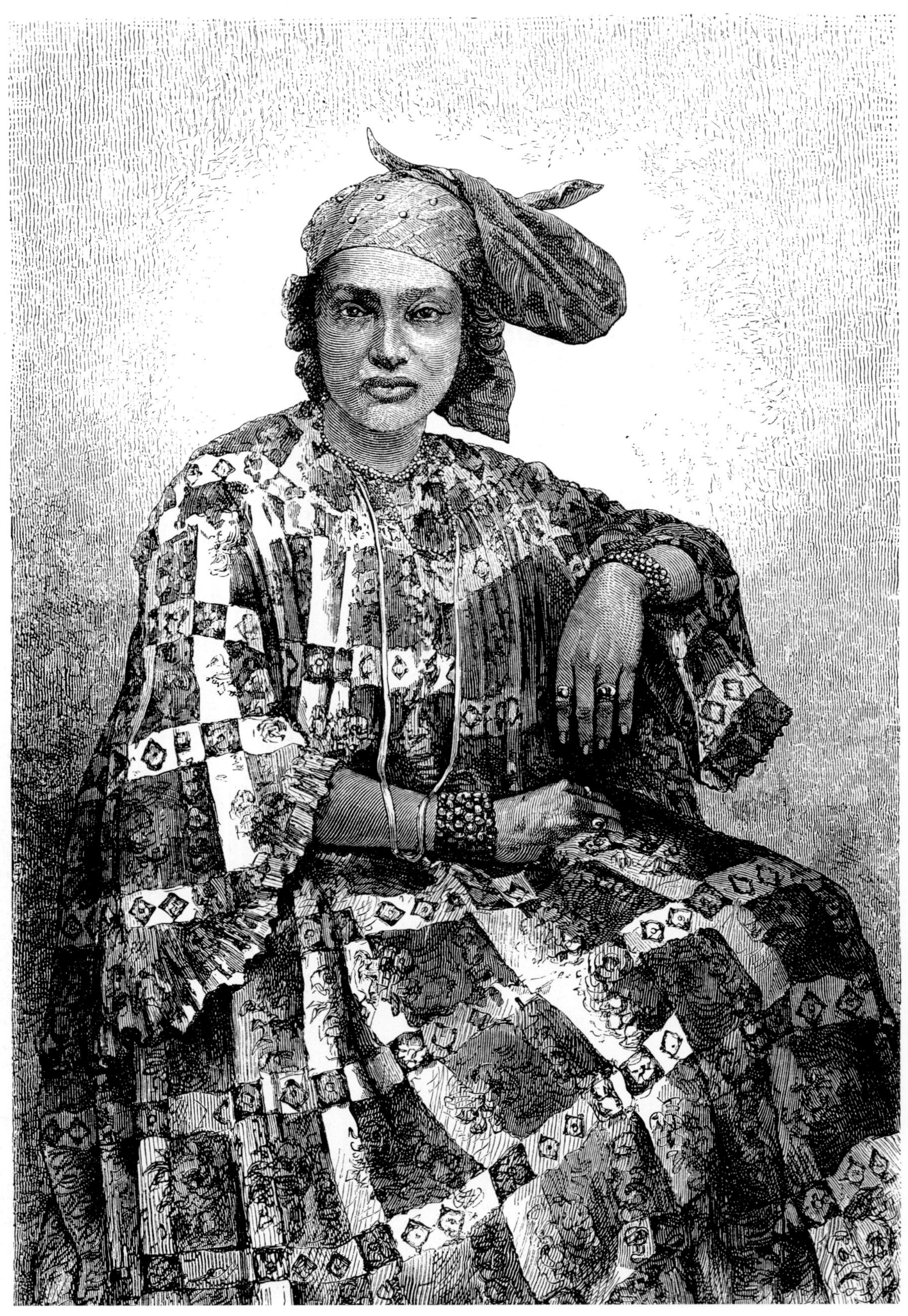

Lady in Cayenne, 1860 Dame in Cayenne, 1860 Donna a Cayenne, 1860 Femme à Cayenne, 1860 Dama de Cayena, 1860

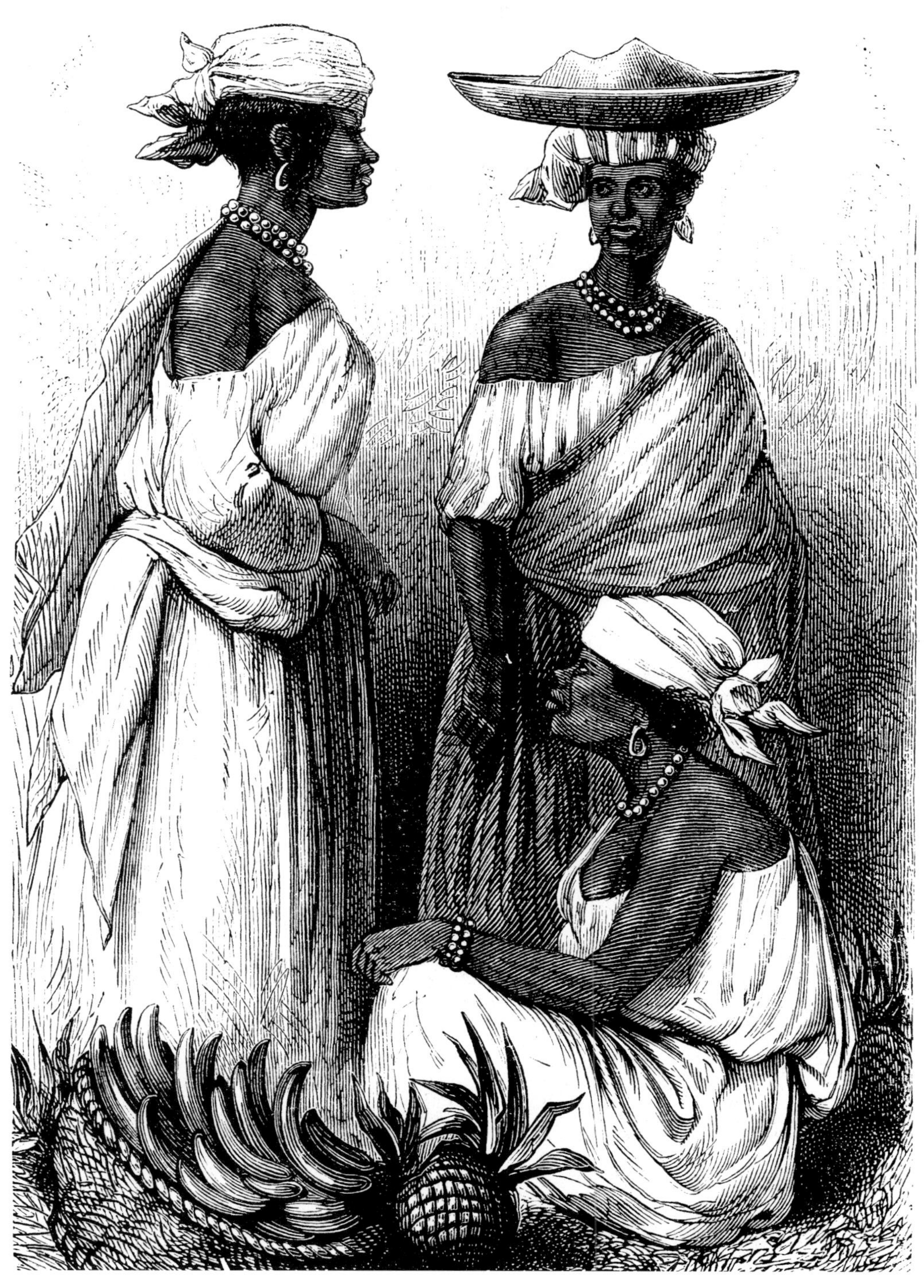

Surinamese ladies, c. 1860

Surinamesische Frauen, um 1860

Donne del Suriname, ca. 1860

Femmes du Surinam, vers 1860

Mujeres surinamesas, alrededor del año 1860

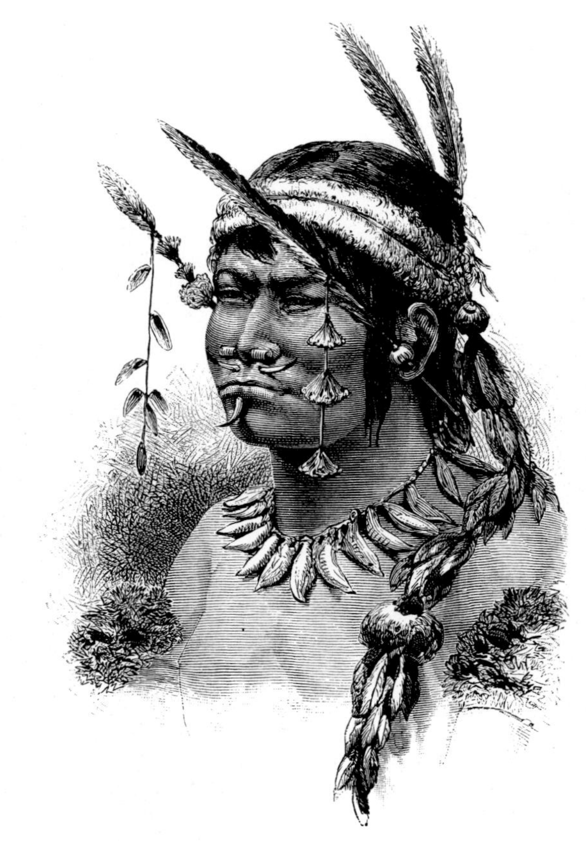

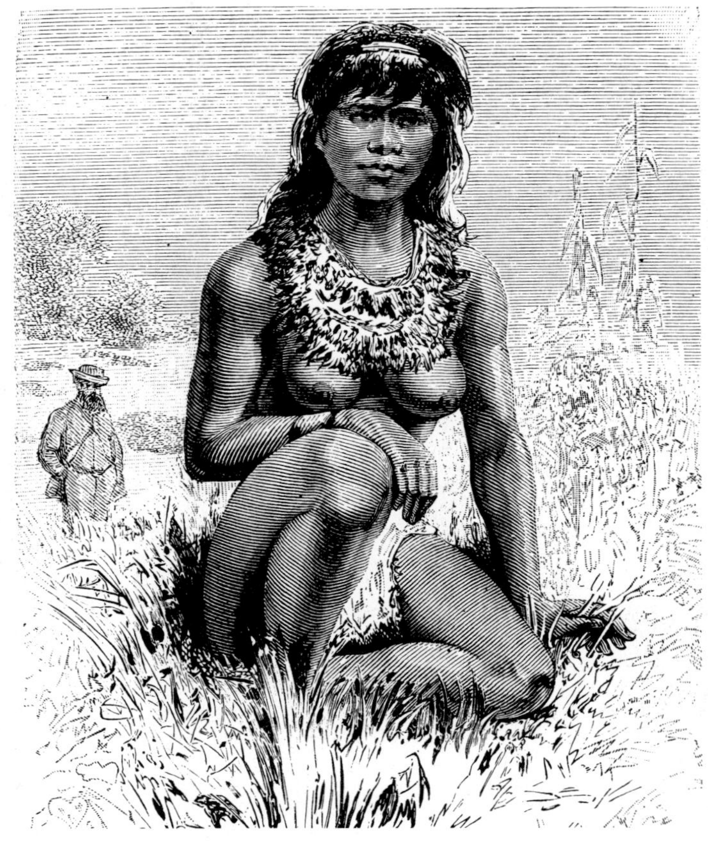

Indiginous people of the rain forrest, c. 1850

Einheimische aus dem Regenwald, um 1850

Indigeni della foresta pluviale, ca. 1850

Peuple indigène de la forêt tropicale, vers 1850

Indígenas de la selva tropical, hacia 1850

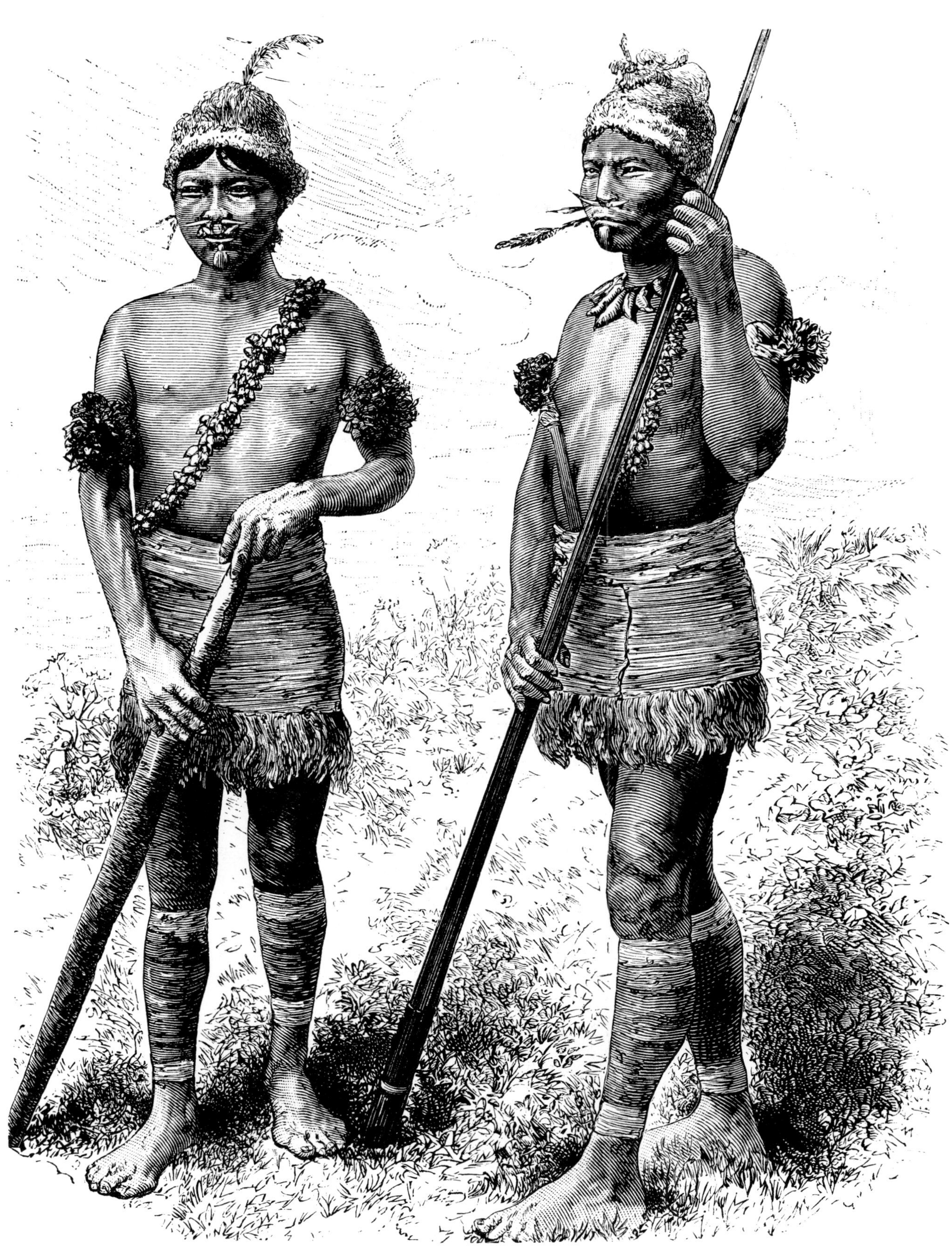

Natives of the rain forrest, c. 1860

Eingeborene aus dem Regenwald, um 1860

Indigeni della foresta pluviale, ca. 1860

Indigène de la forêt tropicale, vers 1860

Nativos de la selva tropical, hacia 1860

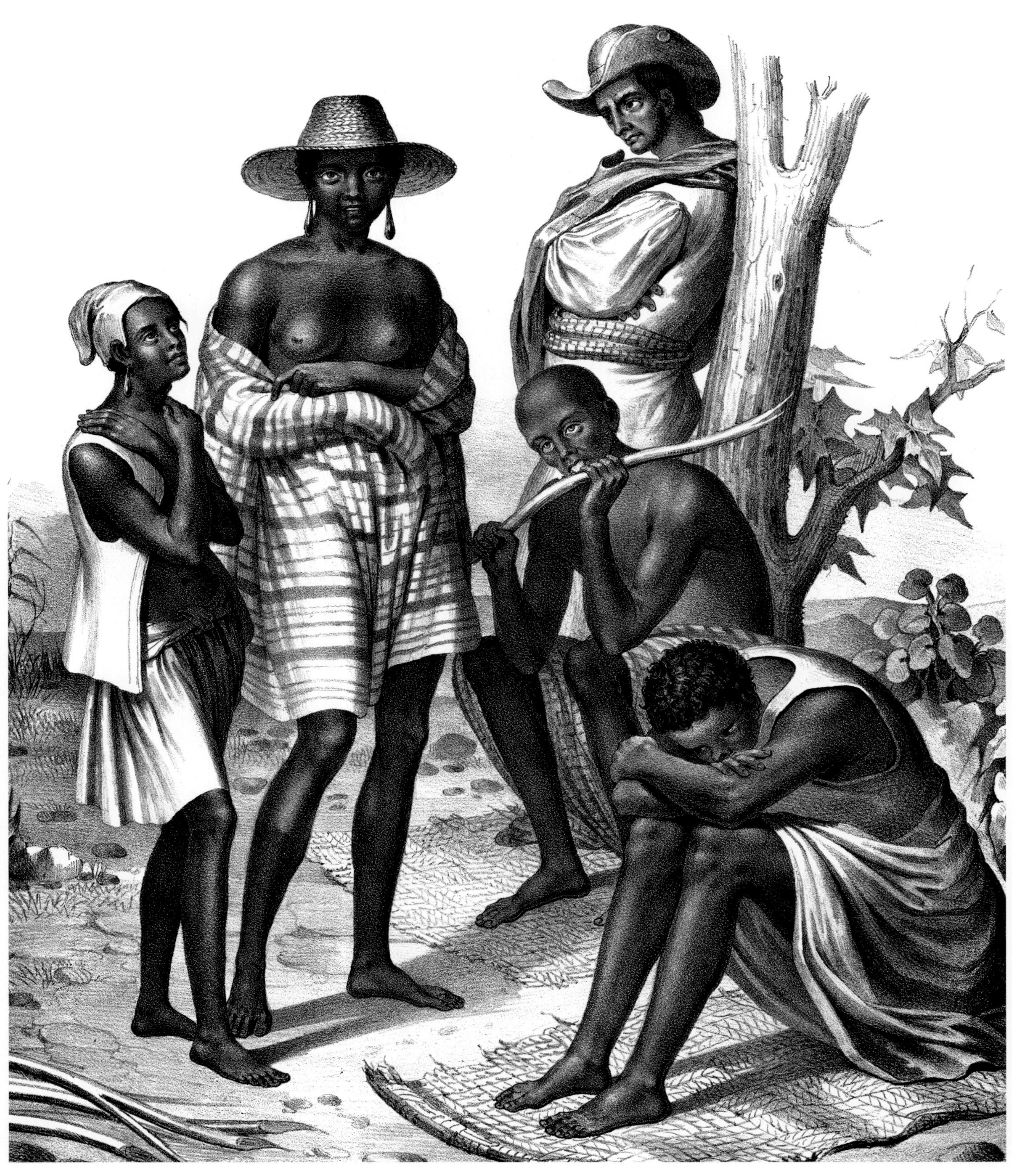

Inhabitants of Guyana, c. 1880

Einwohner von Guayana, um 1880

Abitanti della Guyana, ca. 1880

Habitants de Guyane, vers 1880

Habitantes de Guyana, alrededor de 1880

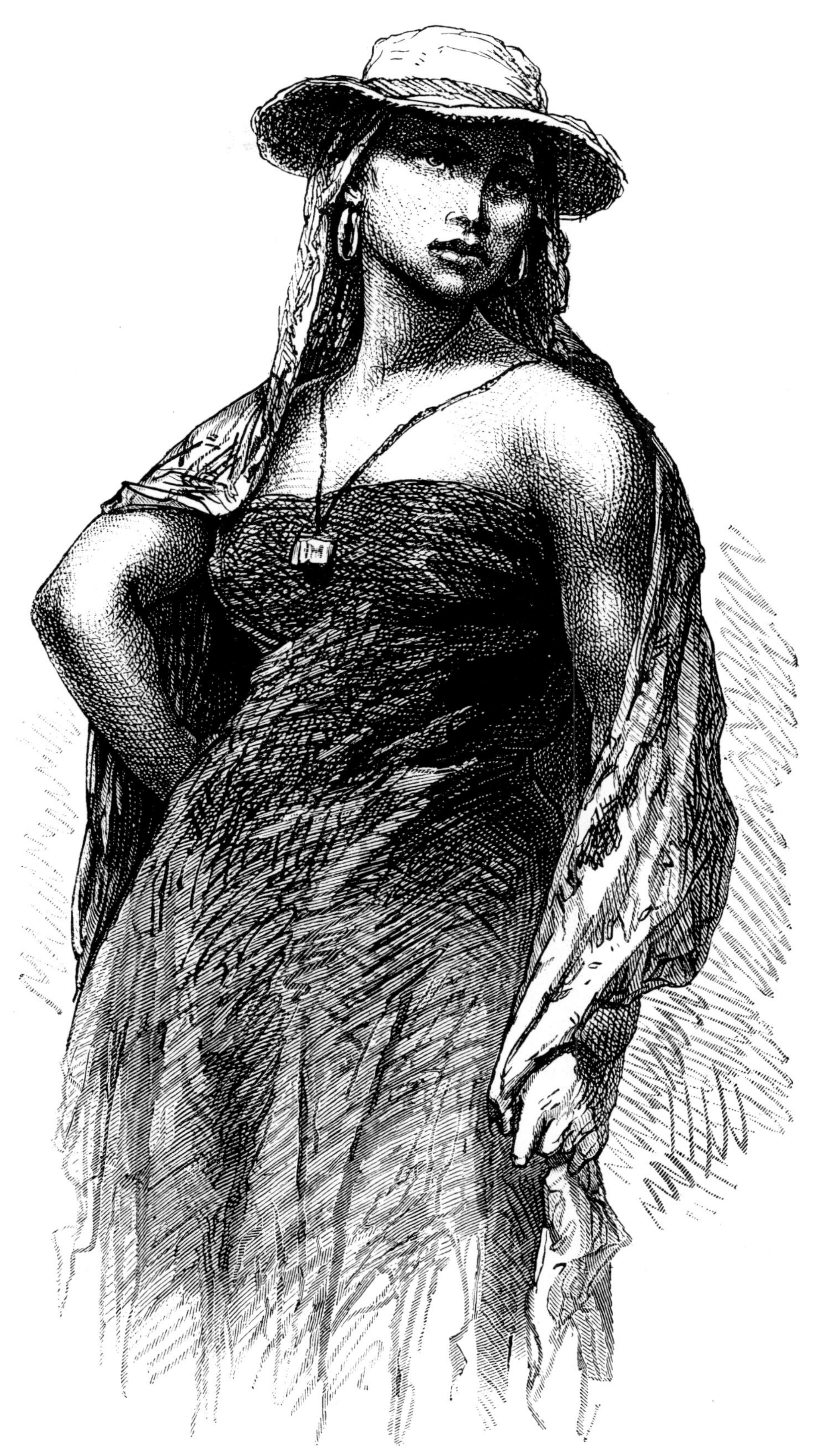

Colombian girl, c. 1885

Kolumbianisches Mädchen, um 1885

Ragazza colombiana, ca. 1885

Jeune colombienne, vers 1885

Muchacha colombiana, alrededor de 1885

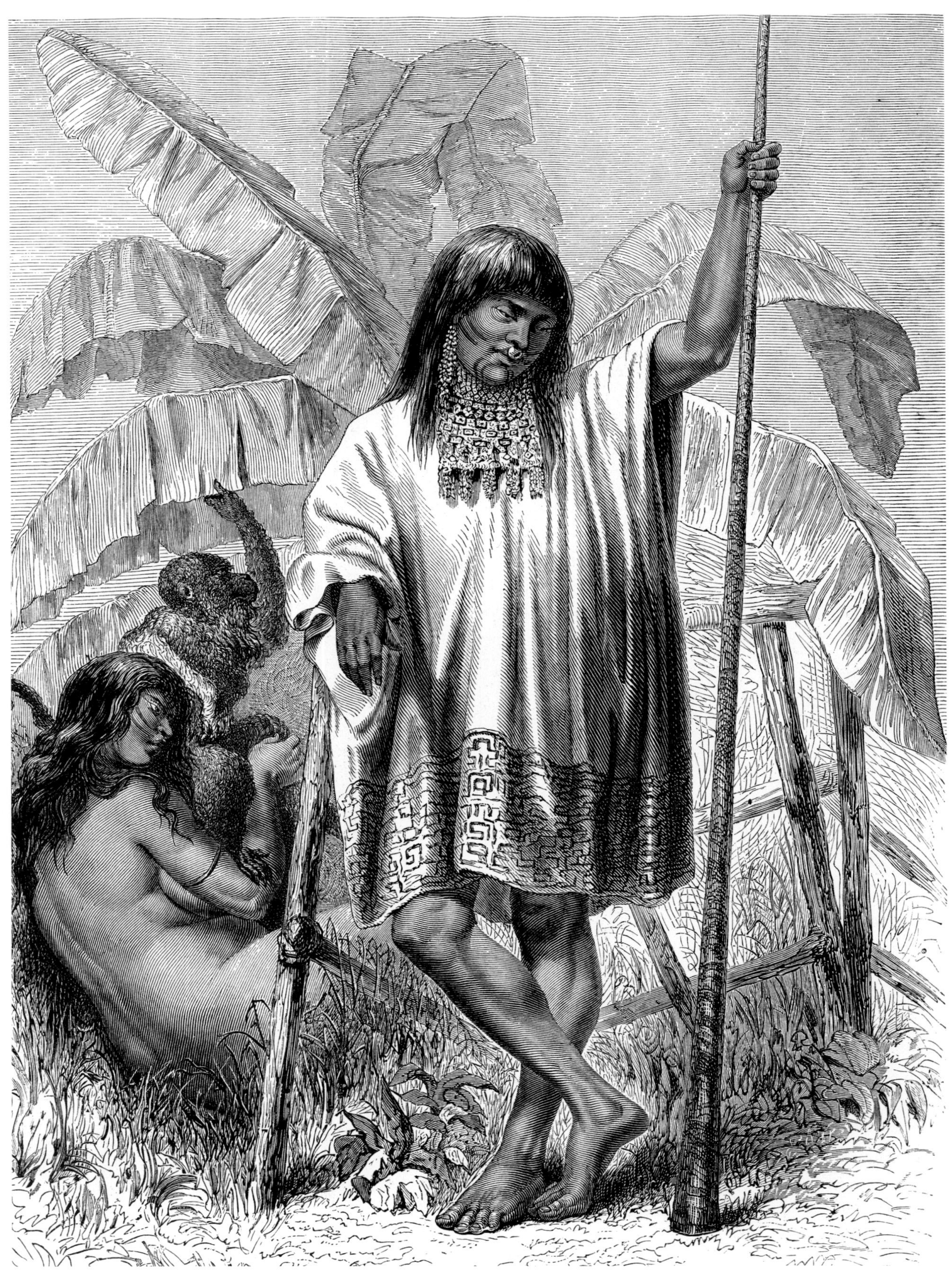

Native from the Orinoco delta, c. 1880

Eingeborene aus dem Orinoco-Delta, um 1880

Indigeno del delta dell'Orinoco, ca. 1880

Indigène du Delta de l'Orénoque, vers 1880

Nativo del delta del Orinoco, hacia 1880

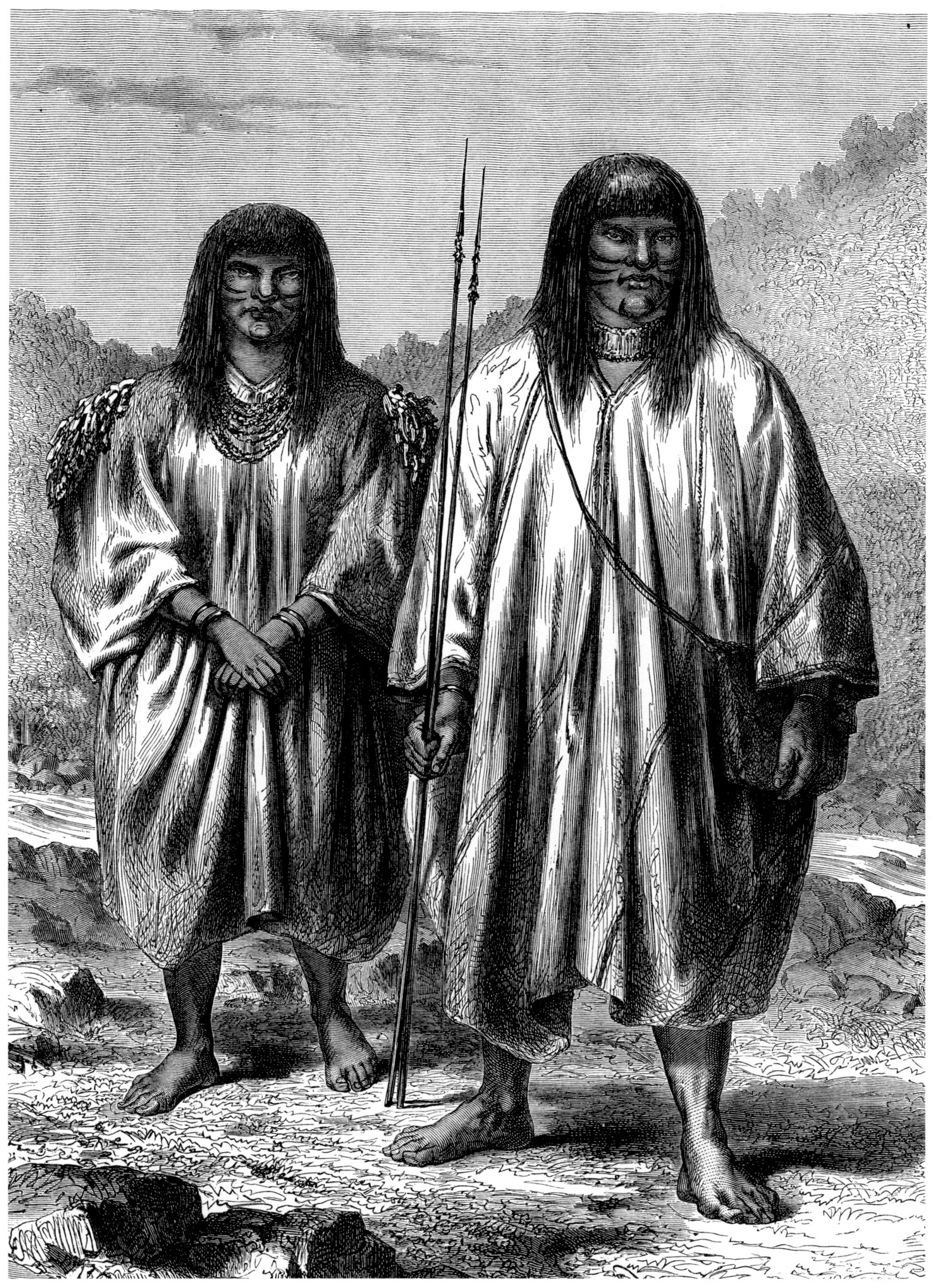

Natives from the Venezuelan interior, c. 1880

Eingeborene aus dem venezolanischen Inland, um 1800

Indigeni dell'interno del Venezuela, ca. 1880

Indigènes de l'intérieur du Vénézuela, vers 1880

Nativos del interior de Venezuela, hacia el año 1880

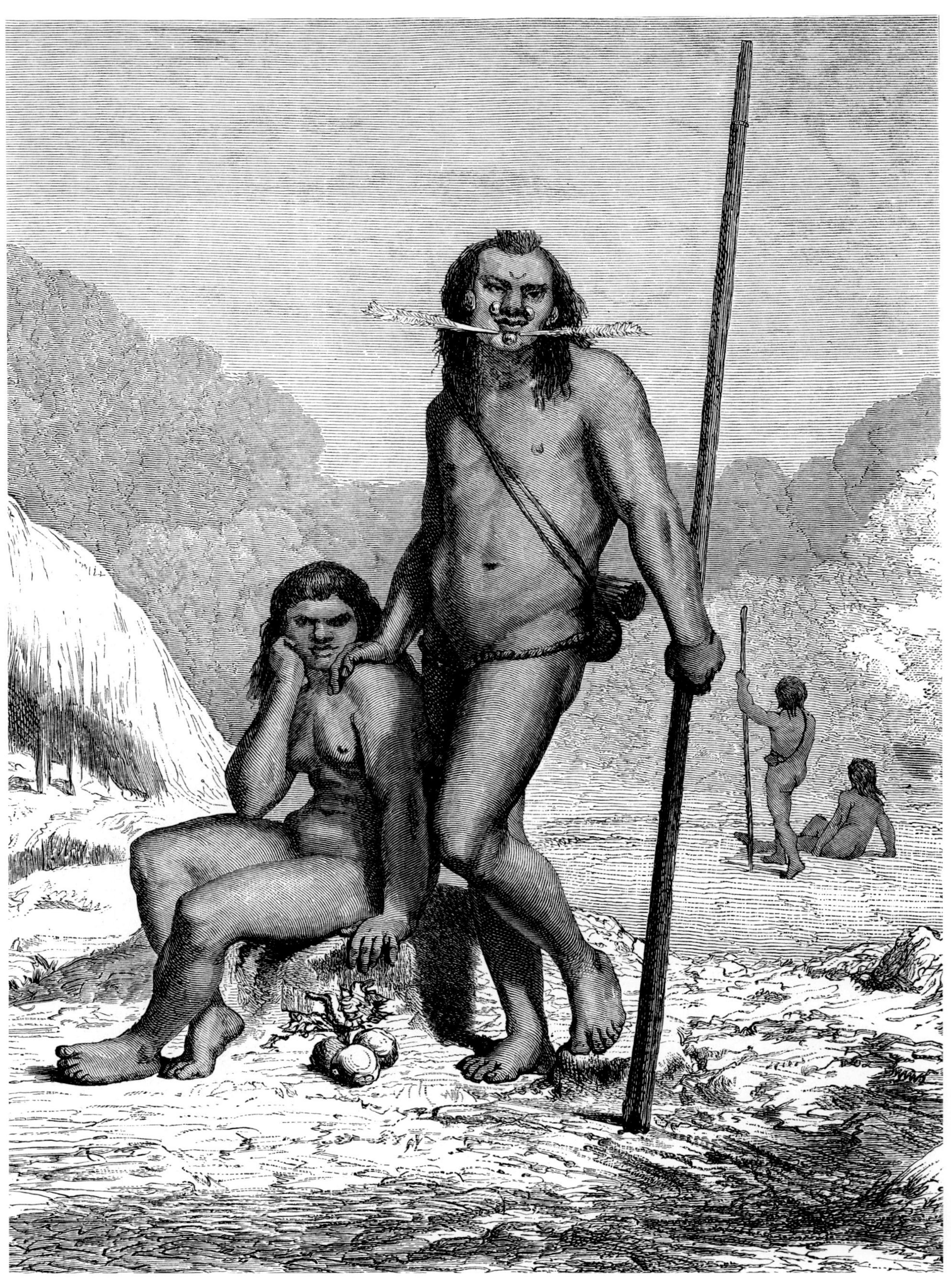

Natives from the Venezuelan interior, c. 1880

Eingeborene aus dem venezolanischen Inland, um 1880

Indigeni dell'interno del Venezuela, ca. 1880

Indigènes de l'intérieur du Vénézuela, vers 1880

Nativos del interior de Venezuela, hacia 1880

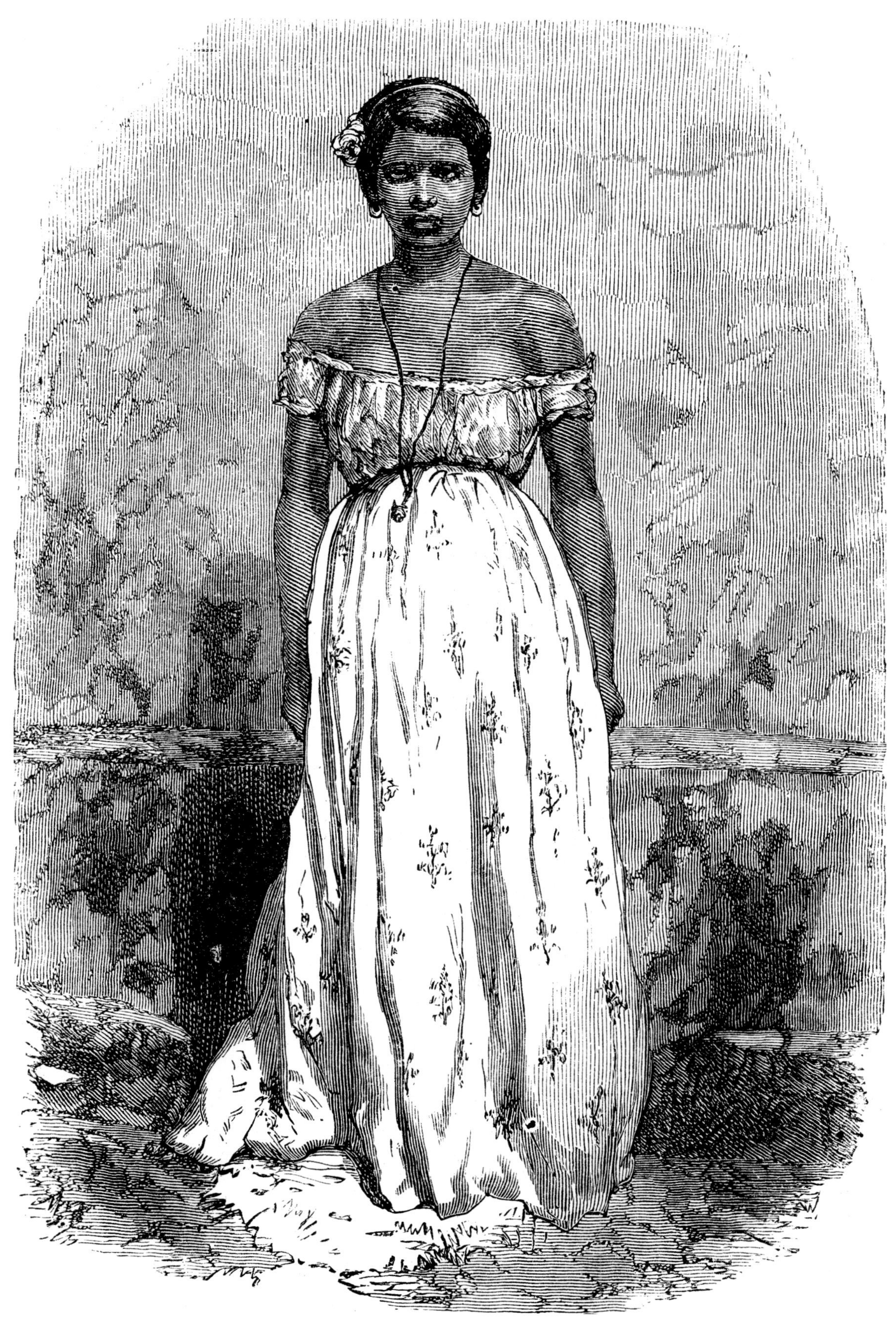

Half caste lady, Caracas, c. 1880

Mischlingsfrau, Caracas, um 1880

Donna meticcia, Caracas, ca. 1880

Femme métisse à Caracas, vers 1880

Mujer de casta media, Caracas, hacia 1880

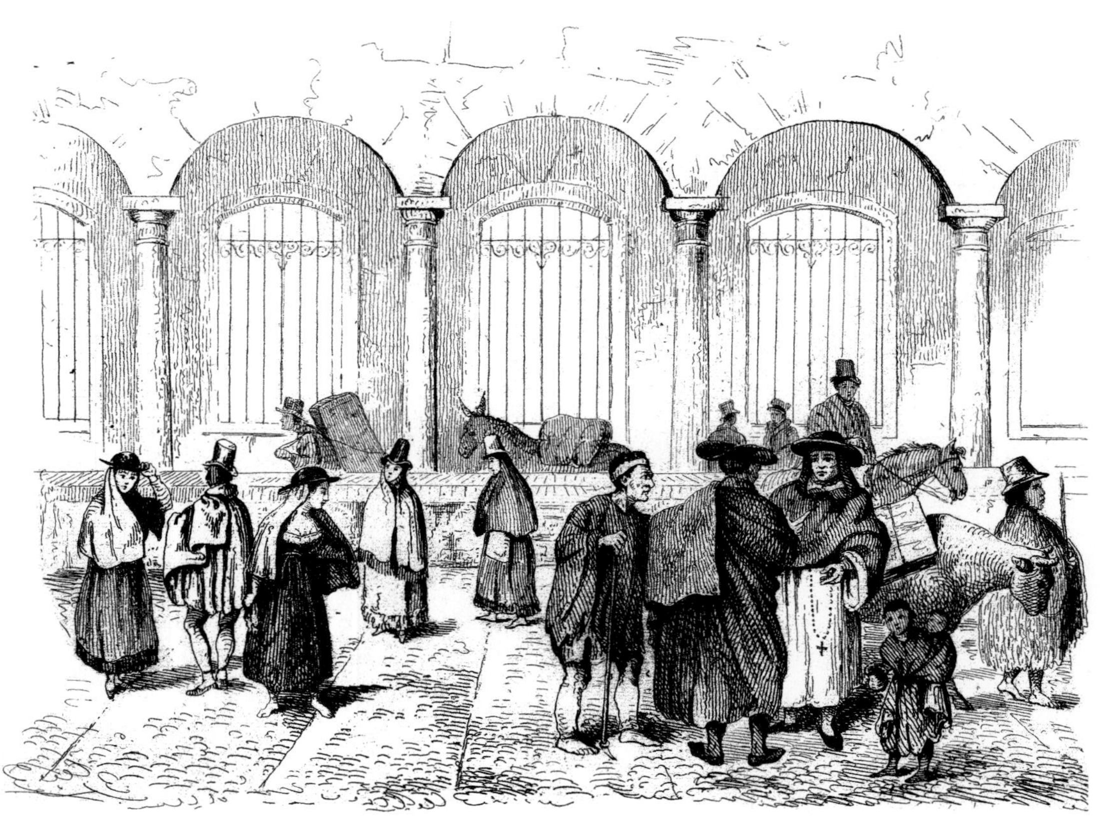

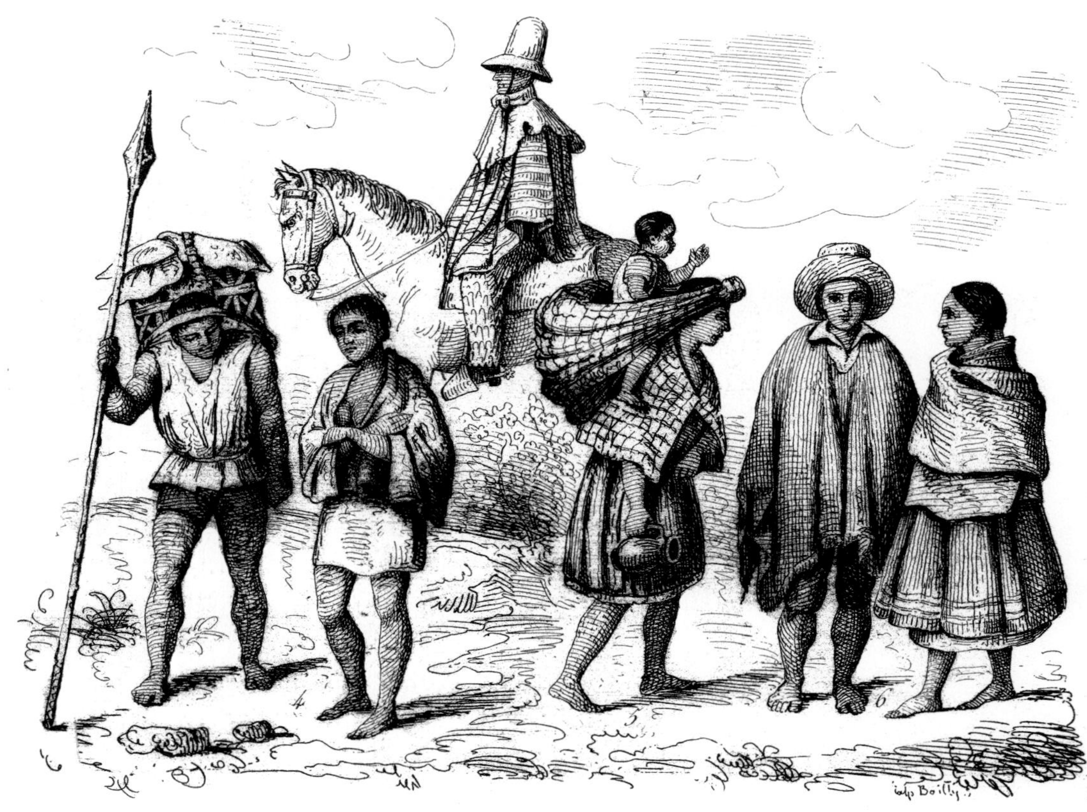

a Costume of Bogota, c. 1840

Tracht aus Bogota, um 1840

Costume di Bogotà, ca. 1840

Costume de Bogota, vers 1840

Trajes de Bogotá, alrededor del año 1840

b Inhabitants of Colombia and Equador, c. 1840

Einwohner von Kolumbien und Ecuador, um 1840

Abitanti di Colombia ed Ecuador, ca. 1840

Habitants de Colombie et d'Équateur, vers 1840

Habitantes de Colombia y Ecuador, hacia 1840

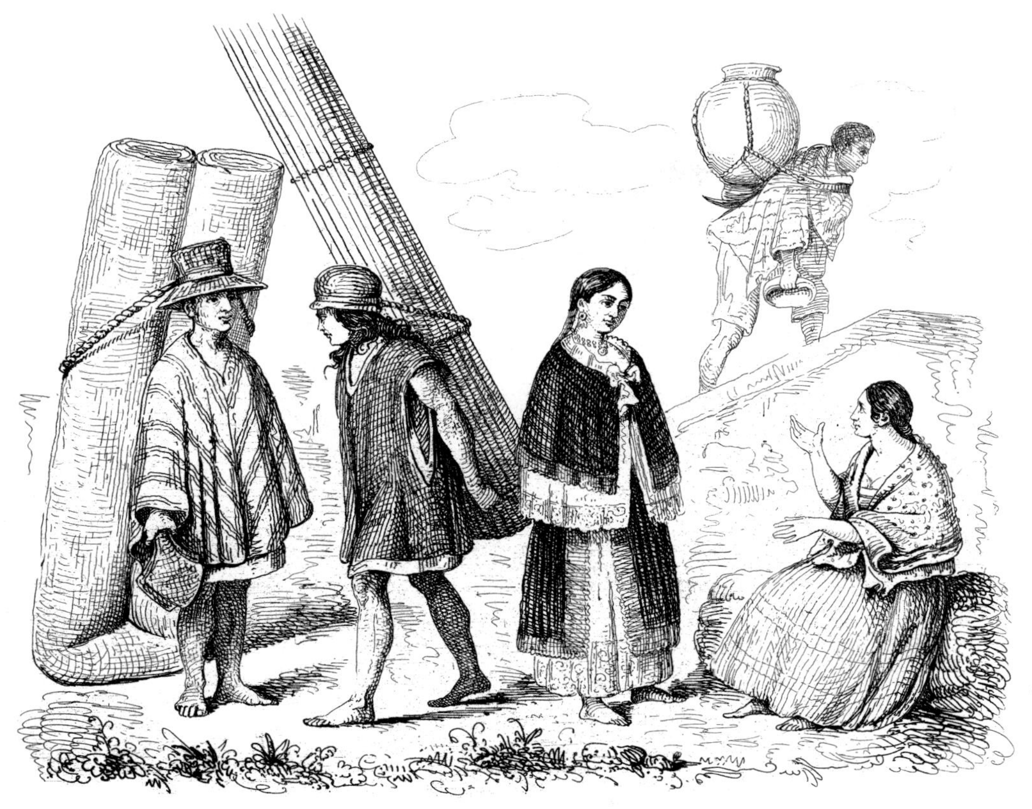

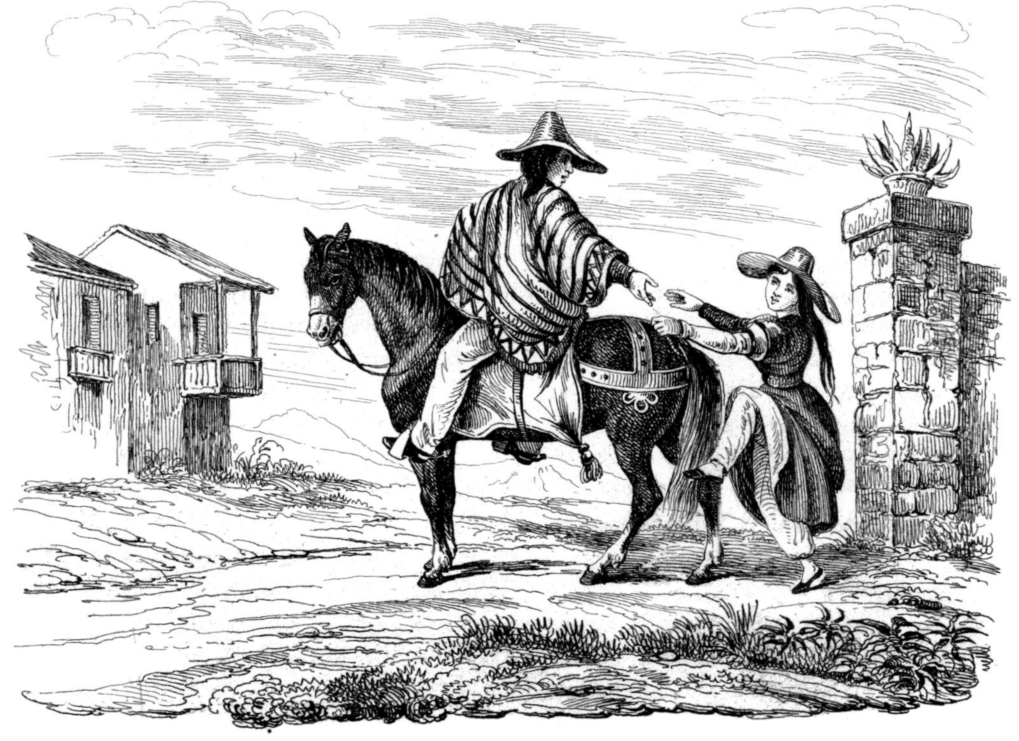

a	Costume of Quito, Equador, c. 1840	Tracht aus Quito, Ecuador, um 1840	Costume di Quito, Ecuador, ca. 1840	Costume de Quito, Équateur, vers 1840	Trajes de Quito, Ecuador, alrededor del año 1840
b	Peruvians, c. 1840	Peruaner, um 1840	Peruviani, ca. 1840	Péruviens, vers 1840	Peruanos, hacia 1840

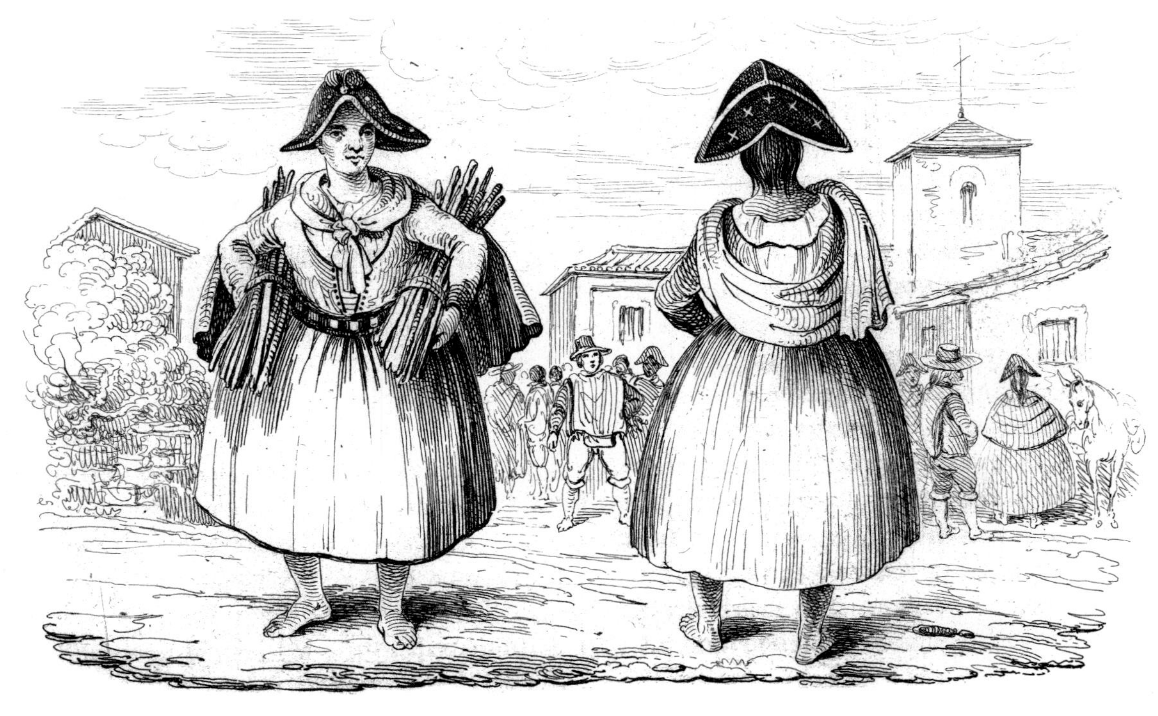

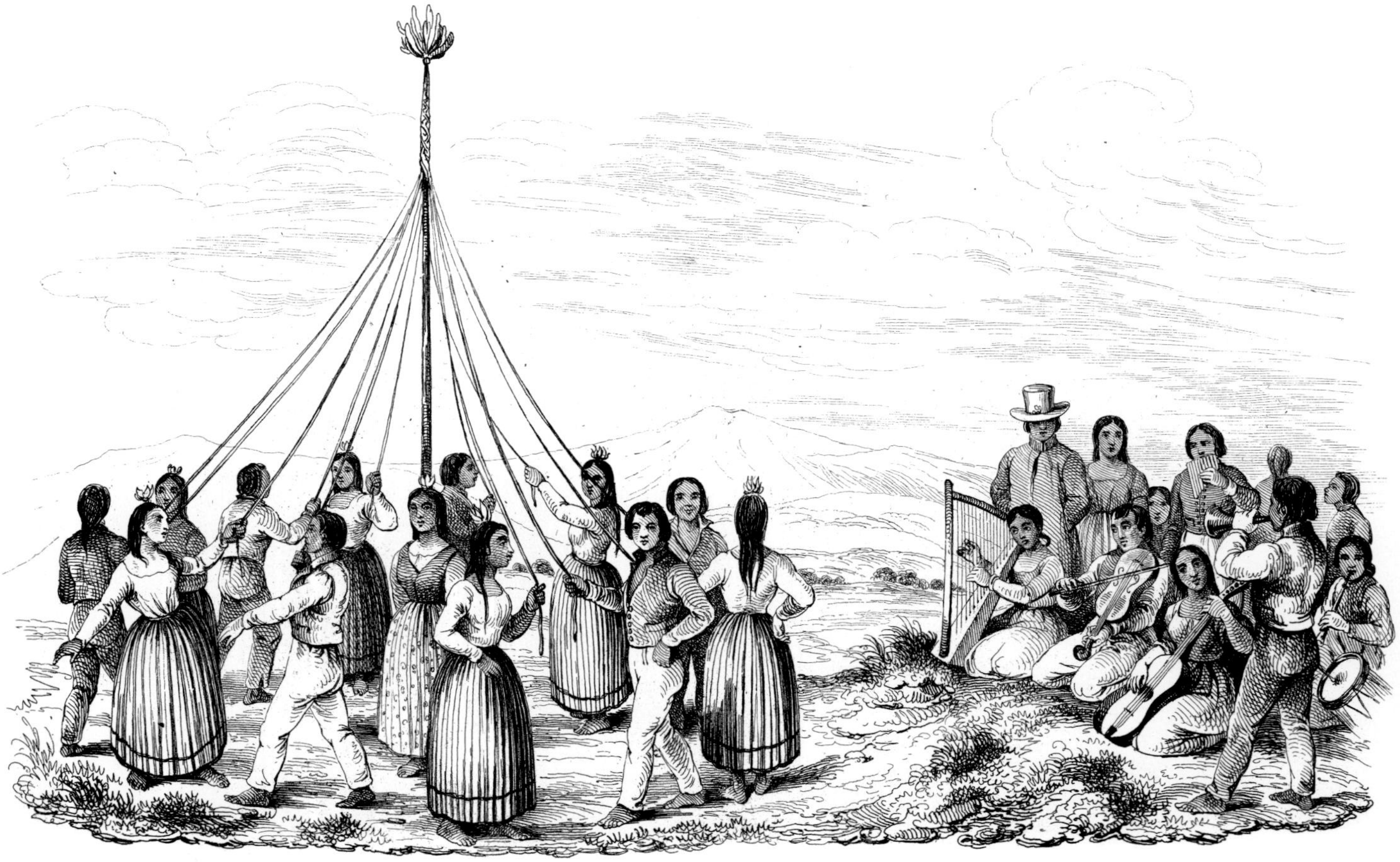

a

Market vendors in Arequipa, Peru, c. 1840

Marktfrauen in Arequipa, Peru, um 1840

Venditori del mercato di Arequipa, Perù, ca. 1840

Vendeuses sur le marché d'Arequipa au Pérou, vers 1840

Vendedoras de un mercado de Arequipa, Perú, hacia 1840

b

Miners at a dance, Peru, c. 1840

Bergarbeiter beim Tanz, Peru, um 1840

Danza di minatori, Perù, ca. 1840

Mineurs dansant au Pérou, vers 1840

Mineros durante una danza, Perú, hacia 1840

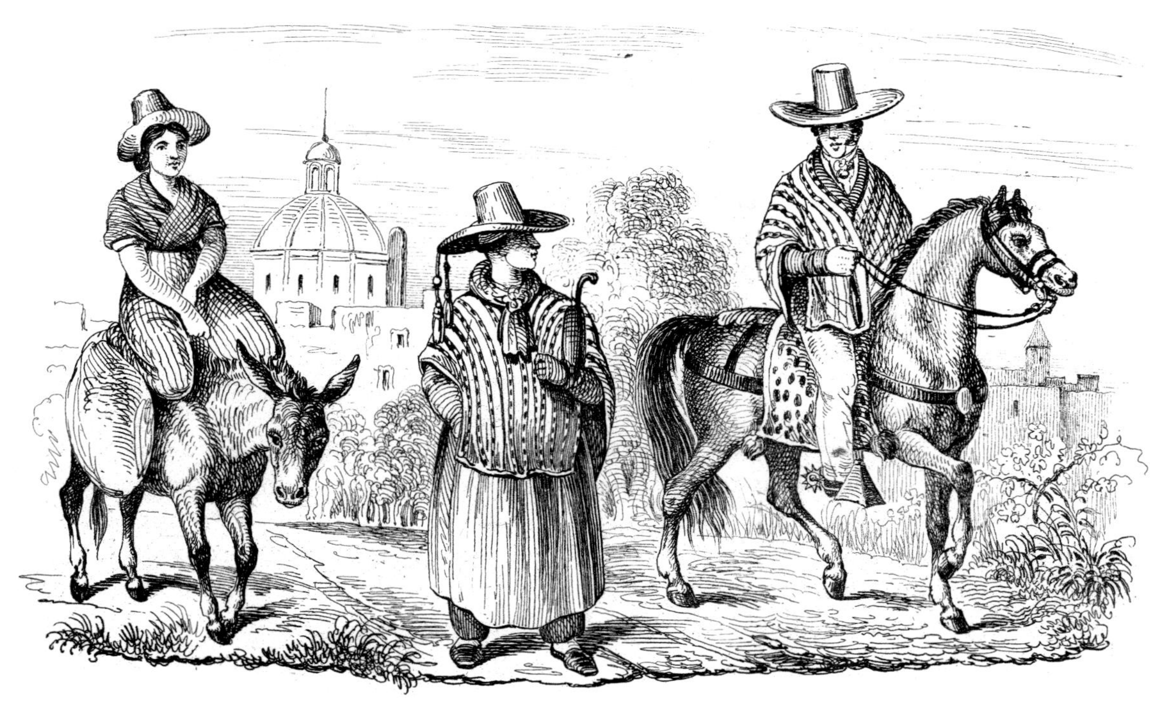

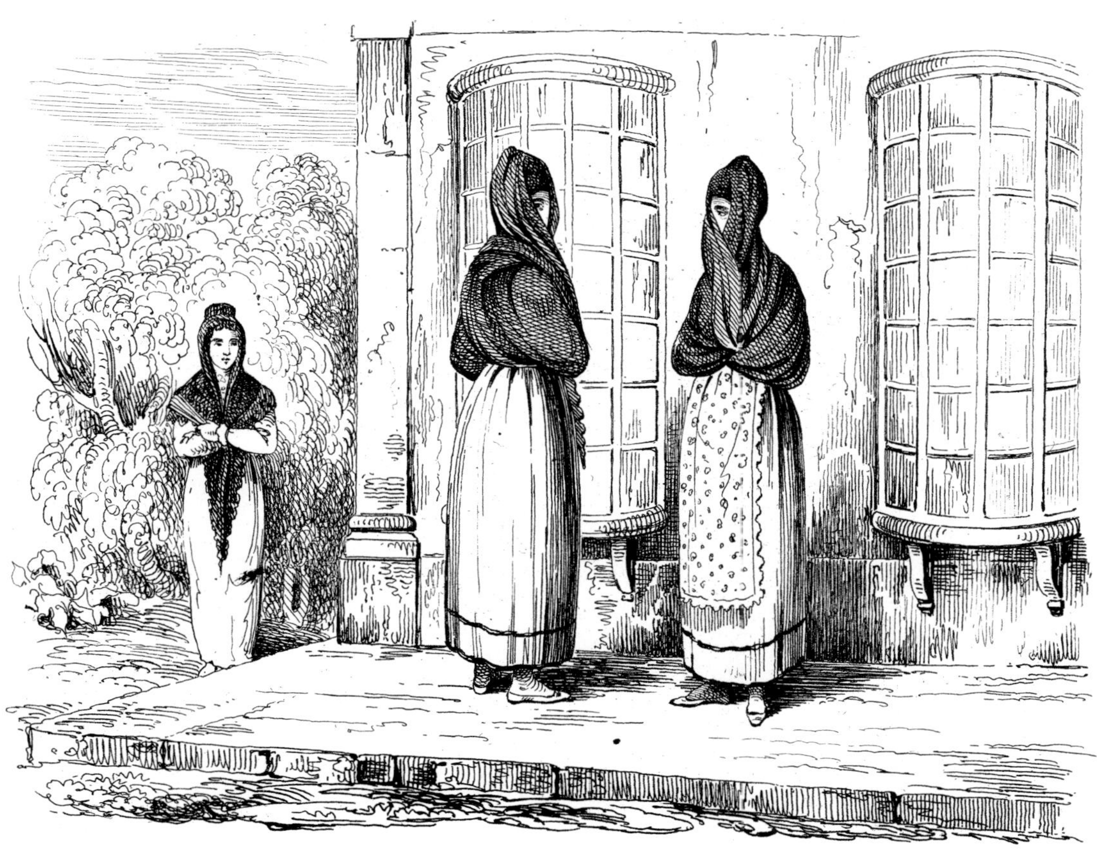

a	Farmers and land owner, Peru, c. 1840	Bauern und Landbesitzer, Peru, um 1840	Contadini e proprietario terriero, Perù, ca. 1840	Paysans et propriétaire terrien au Pérou, vers 1840	Terrateniente y campesinos, Perú, hacia 1840
b	Ladies in Lima, c. 1840	Damen in Lima, um 1840	Donne a Lima, ca. 1840	Femmes à Lima, vers 1840	Mujeres de Lima, 1840

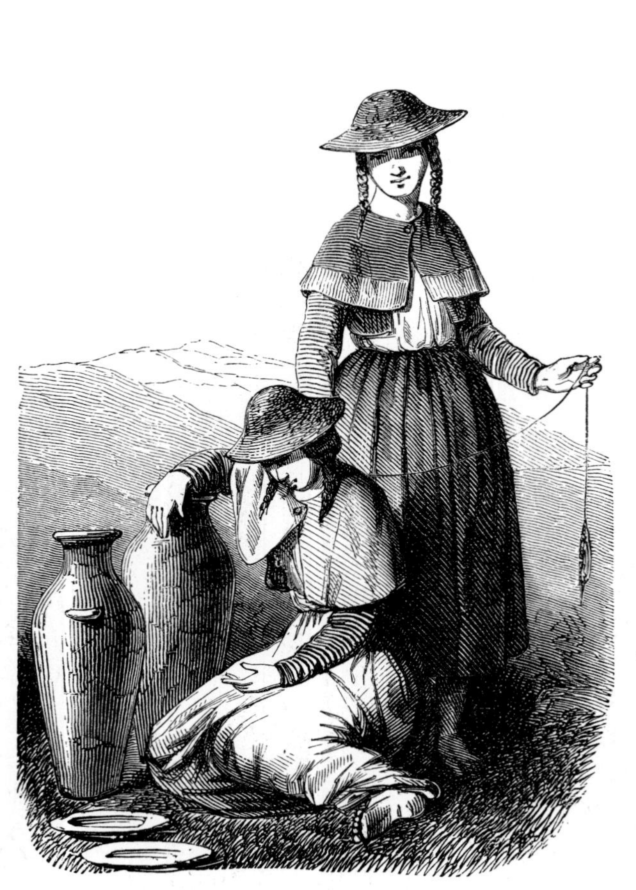

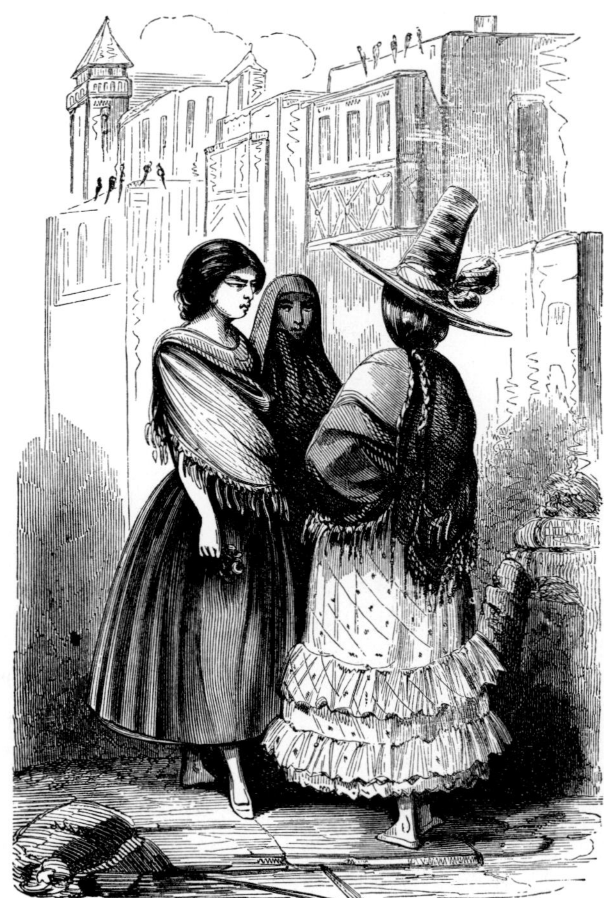

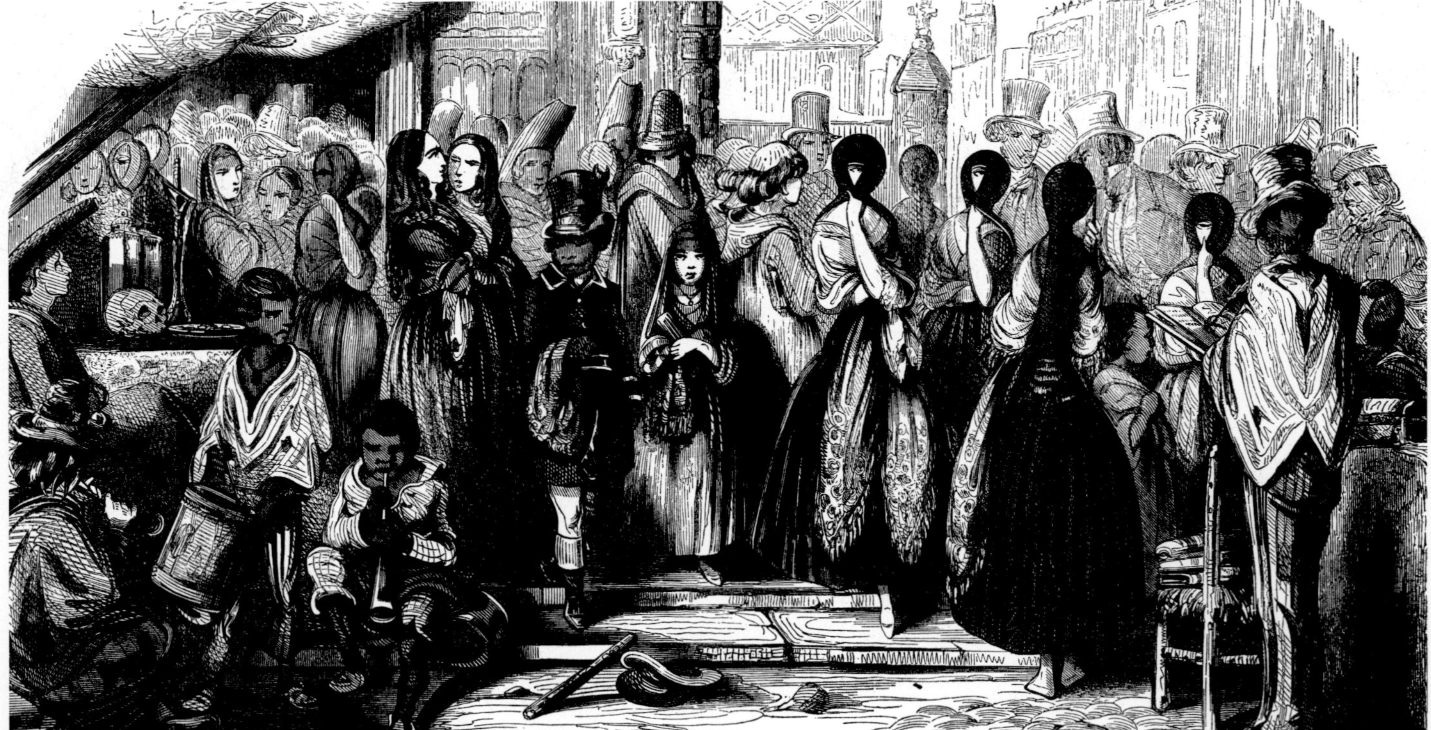

a	Corn drink vendors	Maisgetränkeverkäufer	Venditori di bibita di grano	Vendeurs de boisson	Vendedores de licor
b	Indigeneous Peruvians	Einheimische Peruaner	Indigeni peruviani	Péruviens indigènes	Indígenas peruanos
c	Lima, c. 1845	Lima, um 1845	Lima, ca. 1845	Lima, vers 1845	Lima, hacia 1845

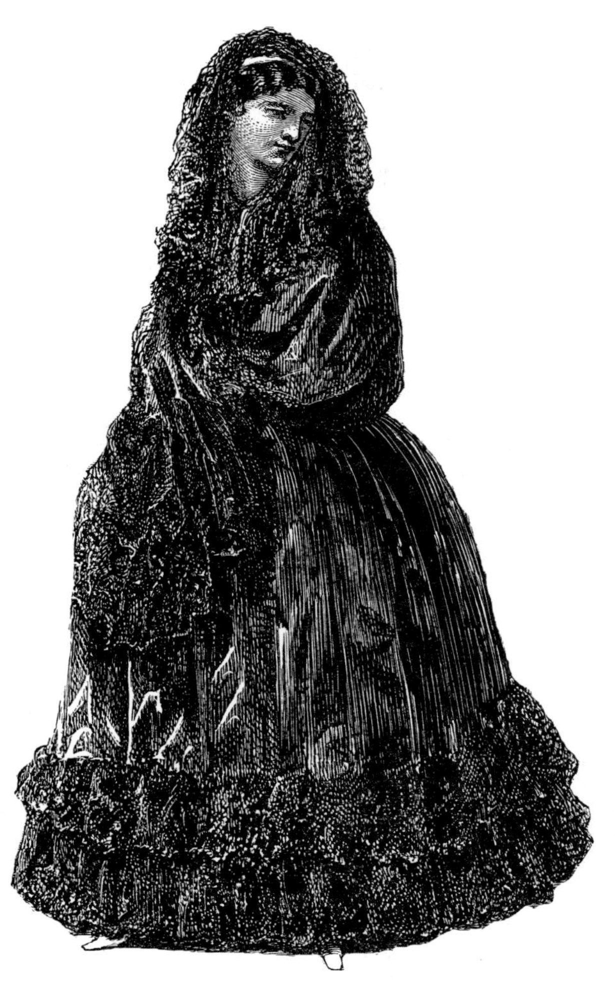

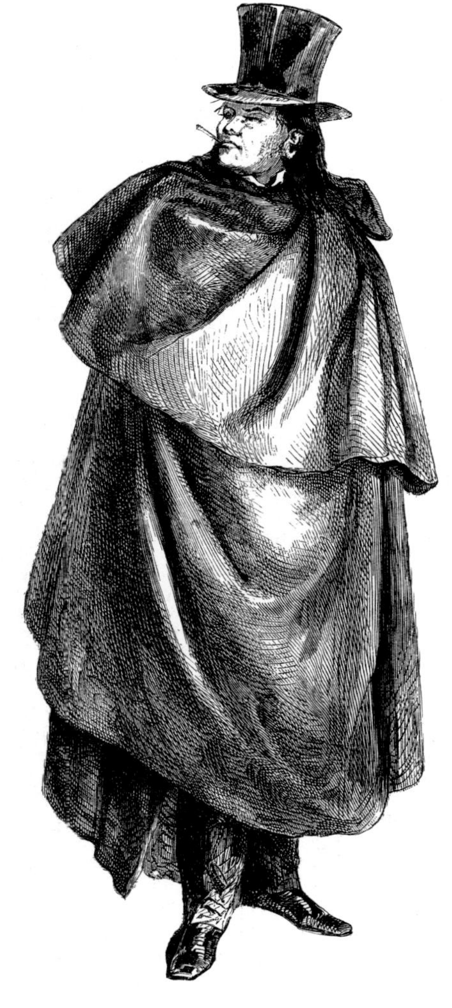

Lady and gentleman from Lima, c. 1880

Dame und Edelmann aus Lima, um 1880

Donna e gentiluomo di Lima, ca. 1880

Dame et gentilhomme de Lima, vers 1880

Dama y caballero de Lima, hacia 1880

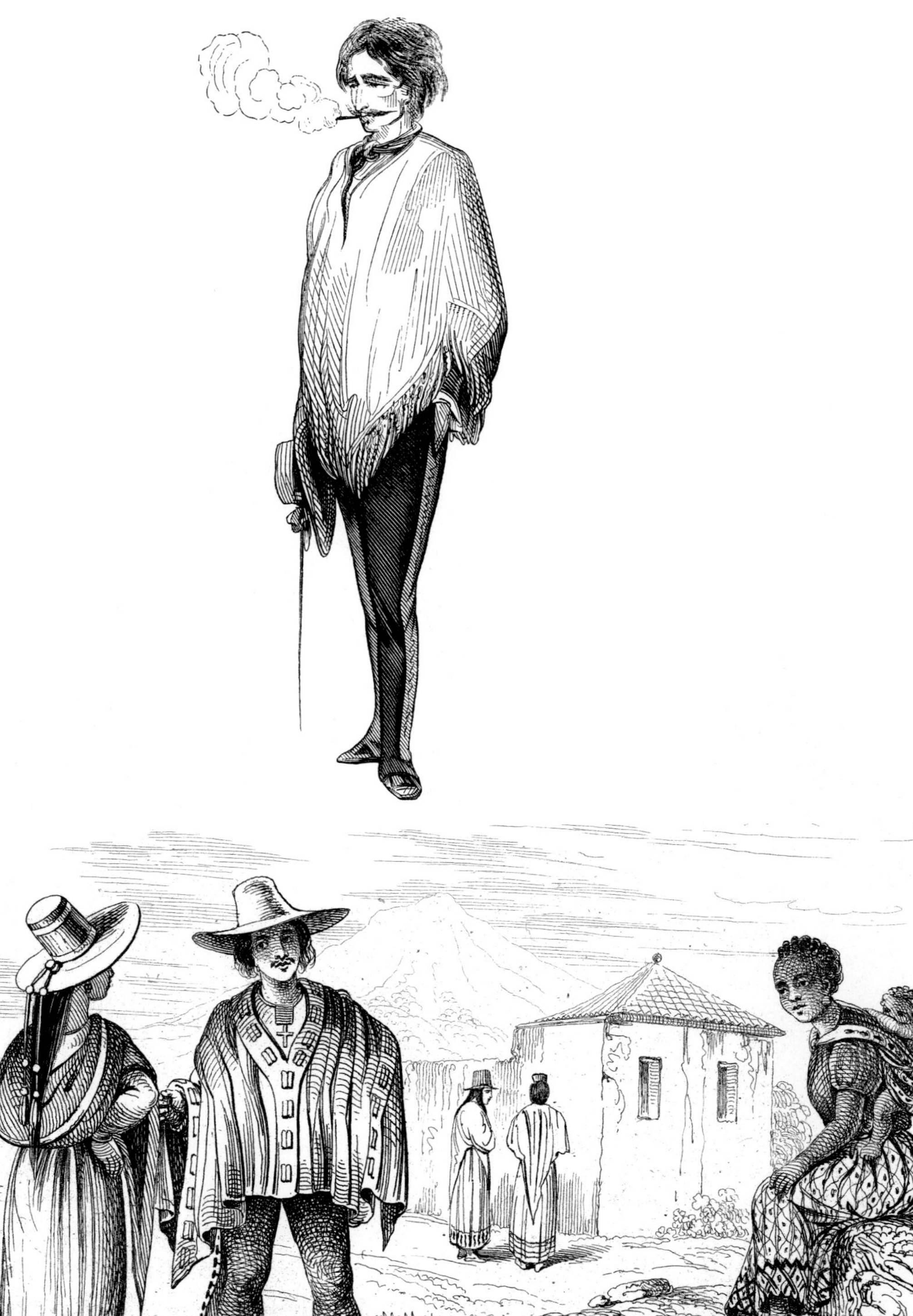

a	Gentleman from Lima, c. 1845	Edelmann aus Lima, um 1845	Gentiluomo di Lima, ca. 1845	Gentilhomme de Lima, vers 1845	Caballero de Lima, hacia 1845
b	Inhabitants of Trujillo, Peru, c. 1840	Einwohner von Trujillo, Peru, um 1840	Abitanti di Trujillo, Perù, ca. 1840	Habitants de Trujillo au Pérou, vers 1840	Habitantes de Trujillo, Perú, alrededor de 1840

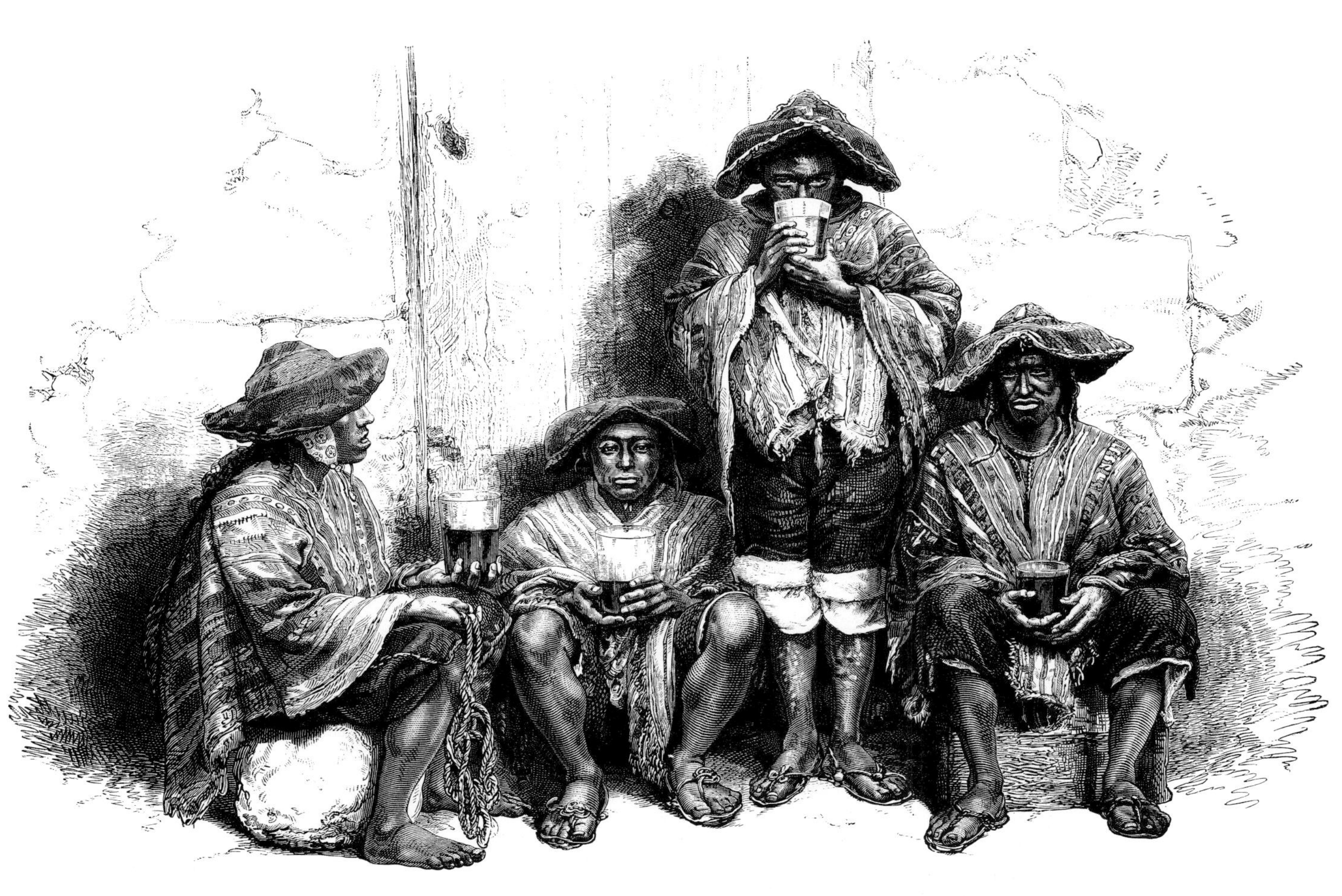

Indigeneous people from the Peruvian interior, c. 1855

Einheimische aus dem peruanischen Inland, um 1855

Indigeni dell'interno del Perù, ca. 1855

Peuple indigène de l'intérieur du Pérou, vers 1855

Indígenas del interior del Perú, alrededor del año 1855

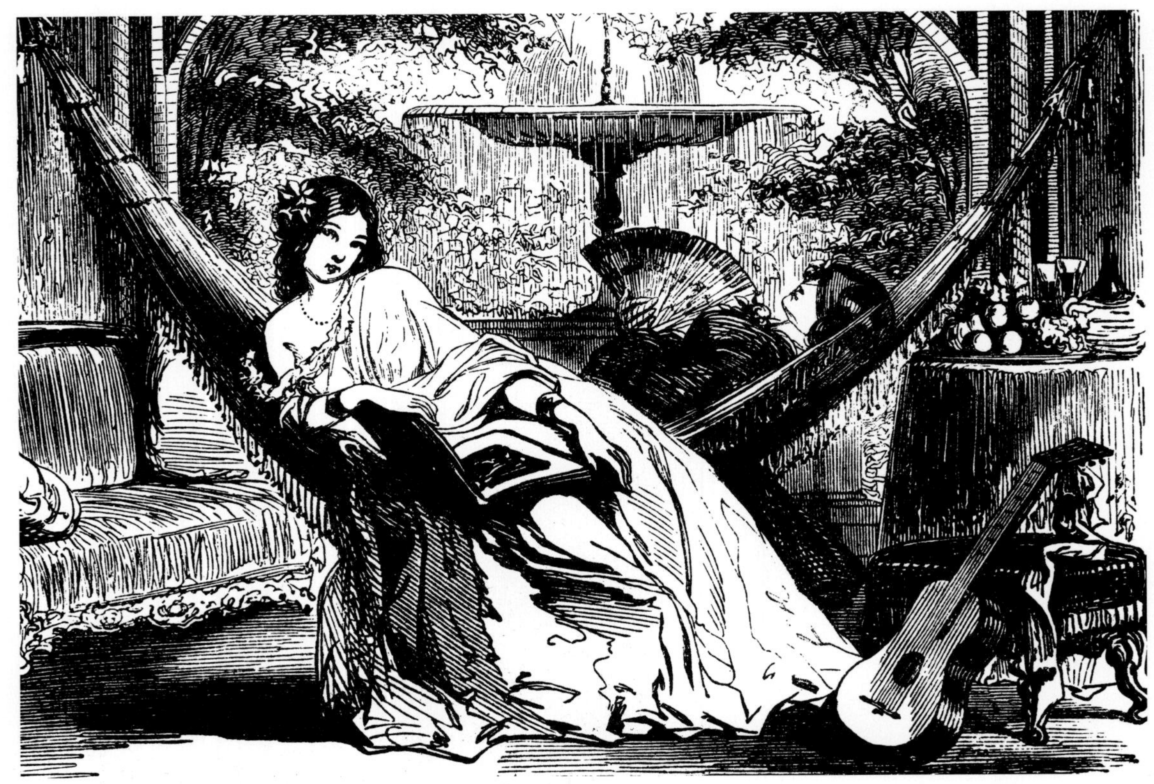

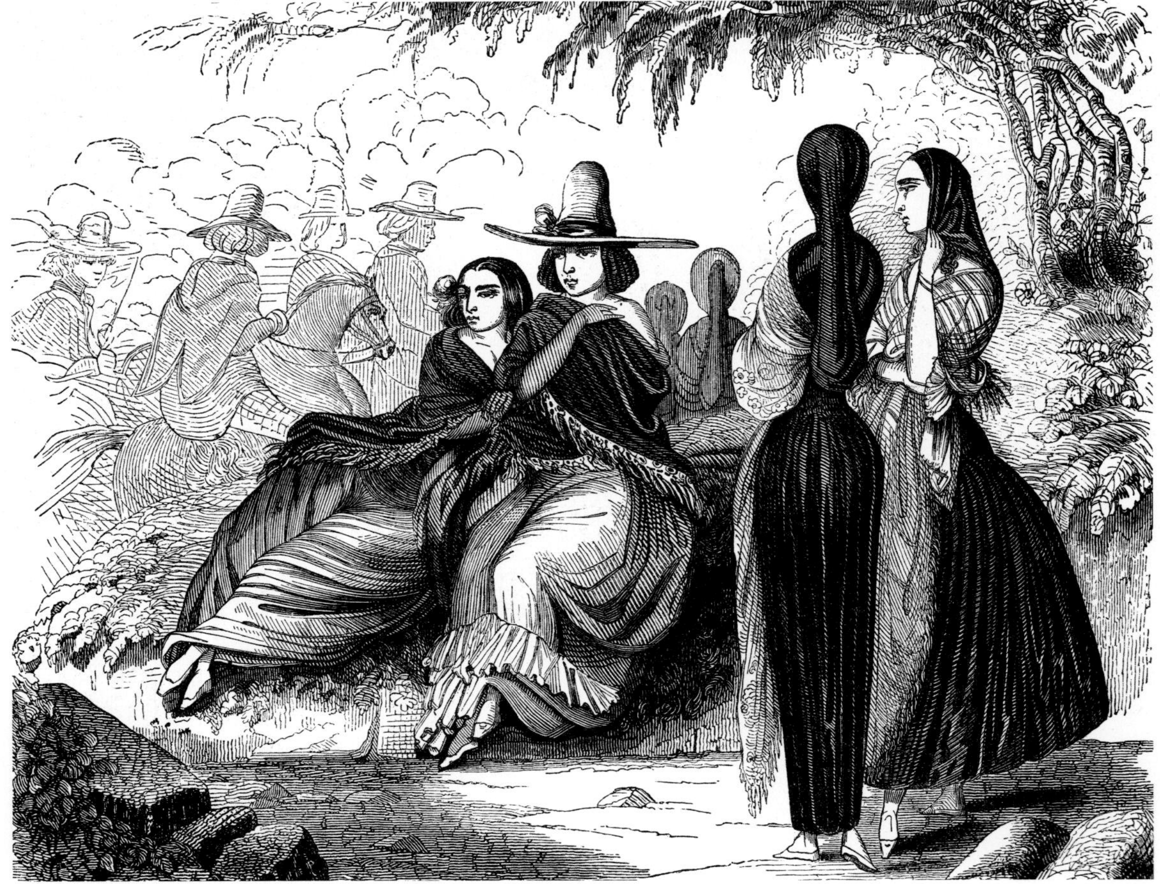

a	Lady at home in Lima, c. 1840	Dame zu Hause in Lima, um 1840	Donna a casa a Lima, ca. 1840	Femme à la maison à Lima, vers 1840	Dama en su casa de Lima, hacia 1840
b	Ladies of Lima, c. 1845	Damen aus Lima, um 1845	Donne di Lima, ca. 1845	Femmes de Lima, 1845	Damas de Lima, 1845

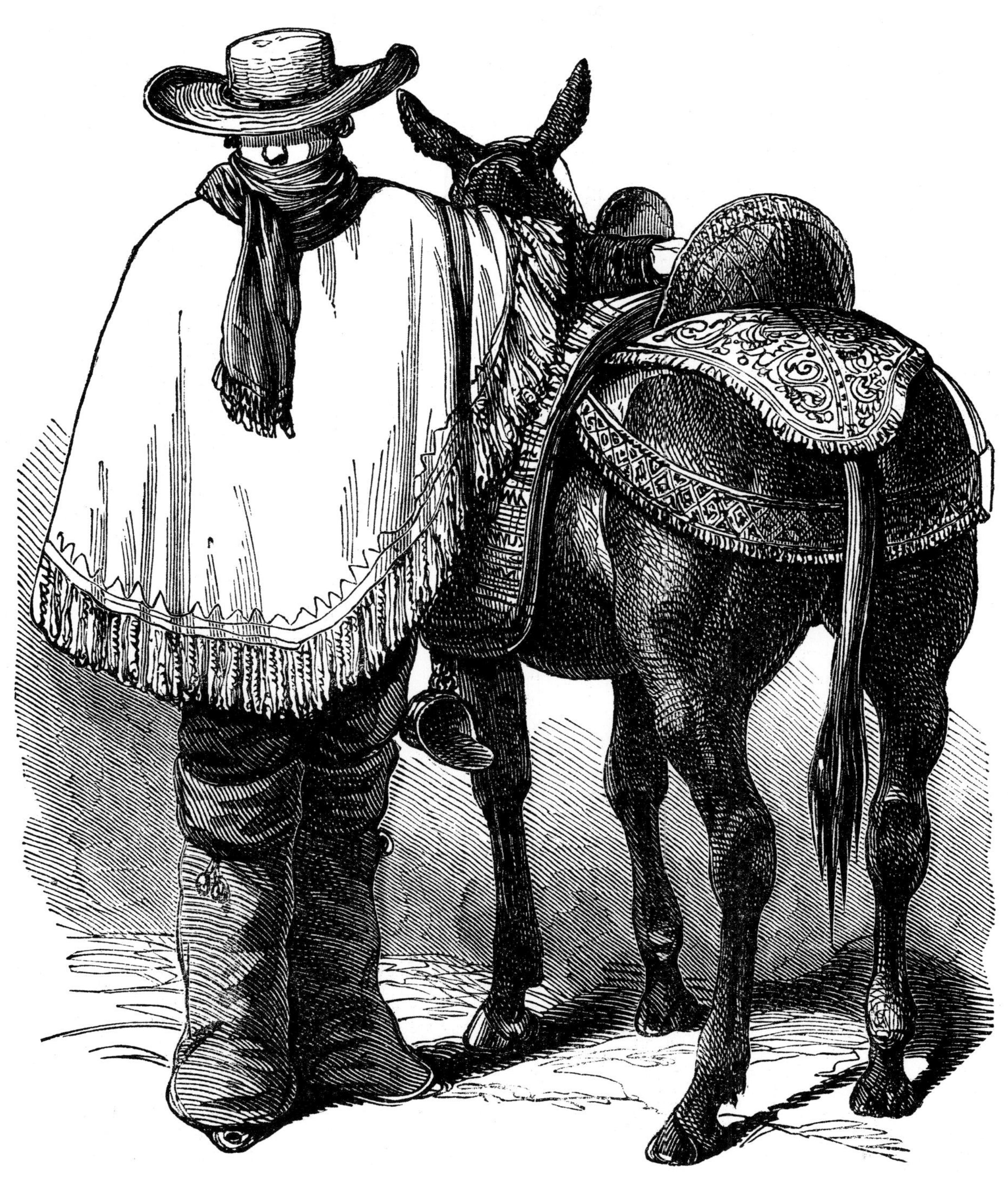

Peruvian in travel costume, c. 1845

Peruaner im Reisegewand, um 1845

Peruviano in abito da viaggio, ca. 1845

Péruvien en tenue de voyage, vers 1845

Peruano vestido con traje de viaje, hacia 1845

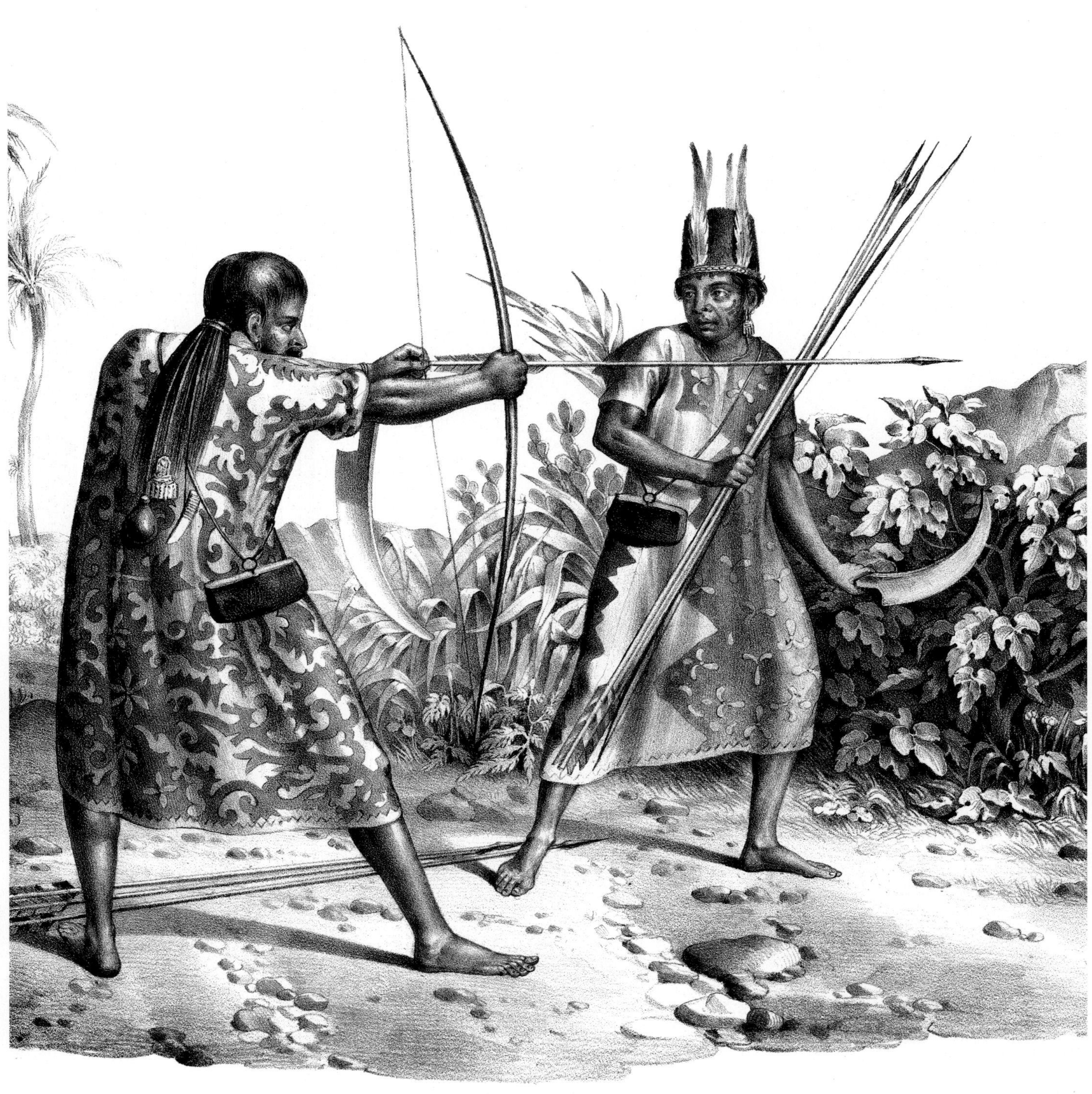

Warriors from the Peruvian interior, c. 1850

Krieger aus dem peruanischen Inland, um 1850

Guerrieri dell'interno del Perù, ca. 1850

Guerriers de l'intérieur du Pérou, vers 1850

Guerreros del interior del Perú, hacia 1850

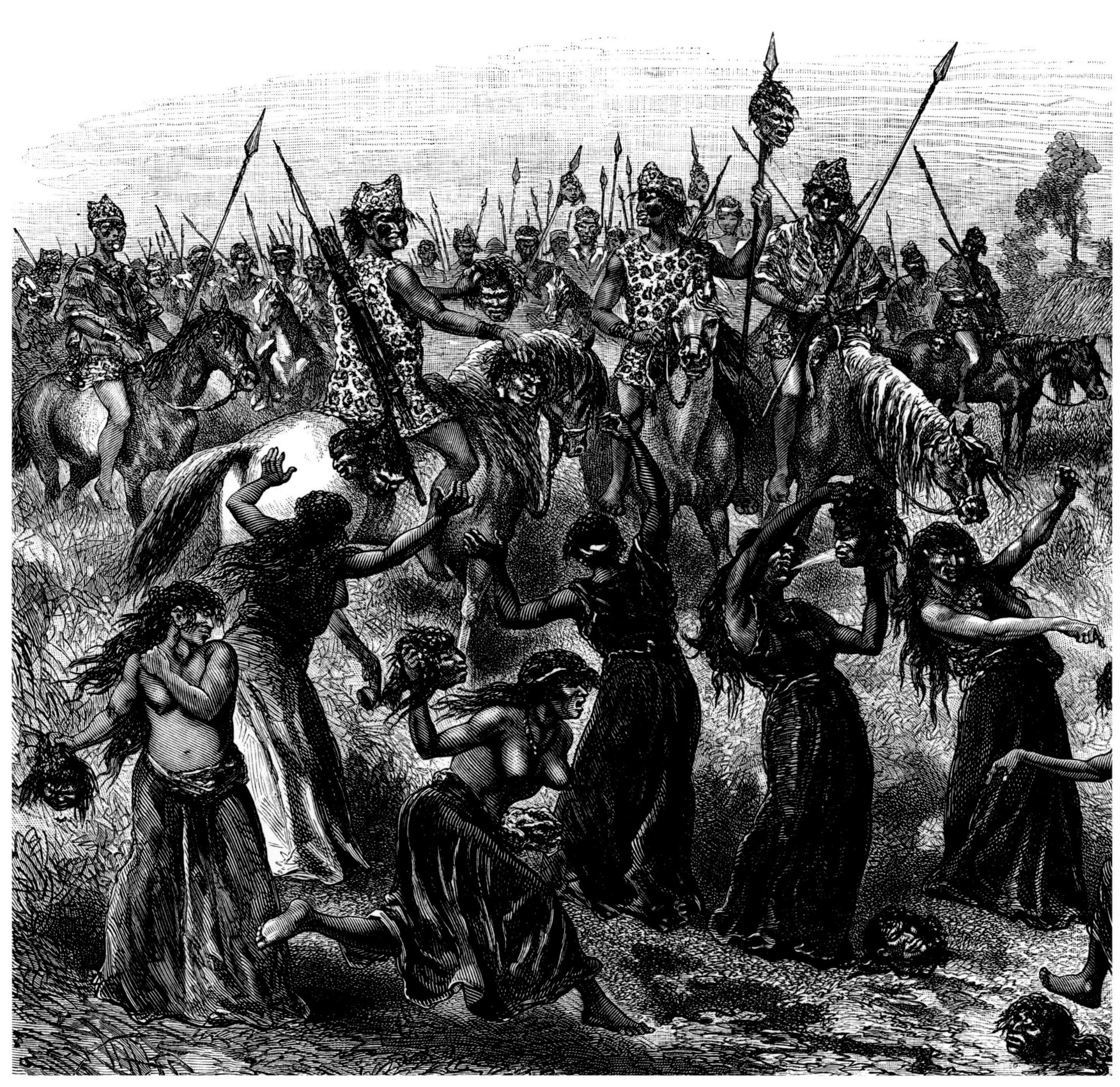

Chiriguanos after a battle, Bolivian interior, c. 1880

Chiriguanos nach einer Schlacht, Inland von Bolivien, um 1880

Chiriguani dopo una battaglia, interno della Bolivia, ca. 1880

Chiriguanos après une bataille dans les terres boliviennes, vers 1880

Chiriguanos tras una batalla, interior de Bolivia, hacia 1880

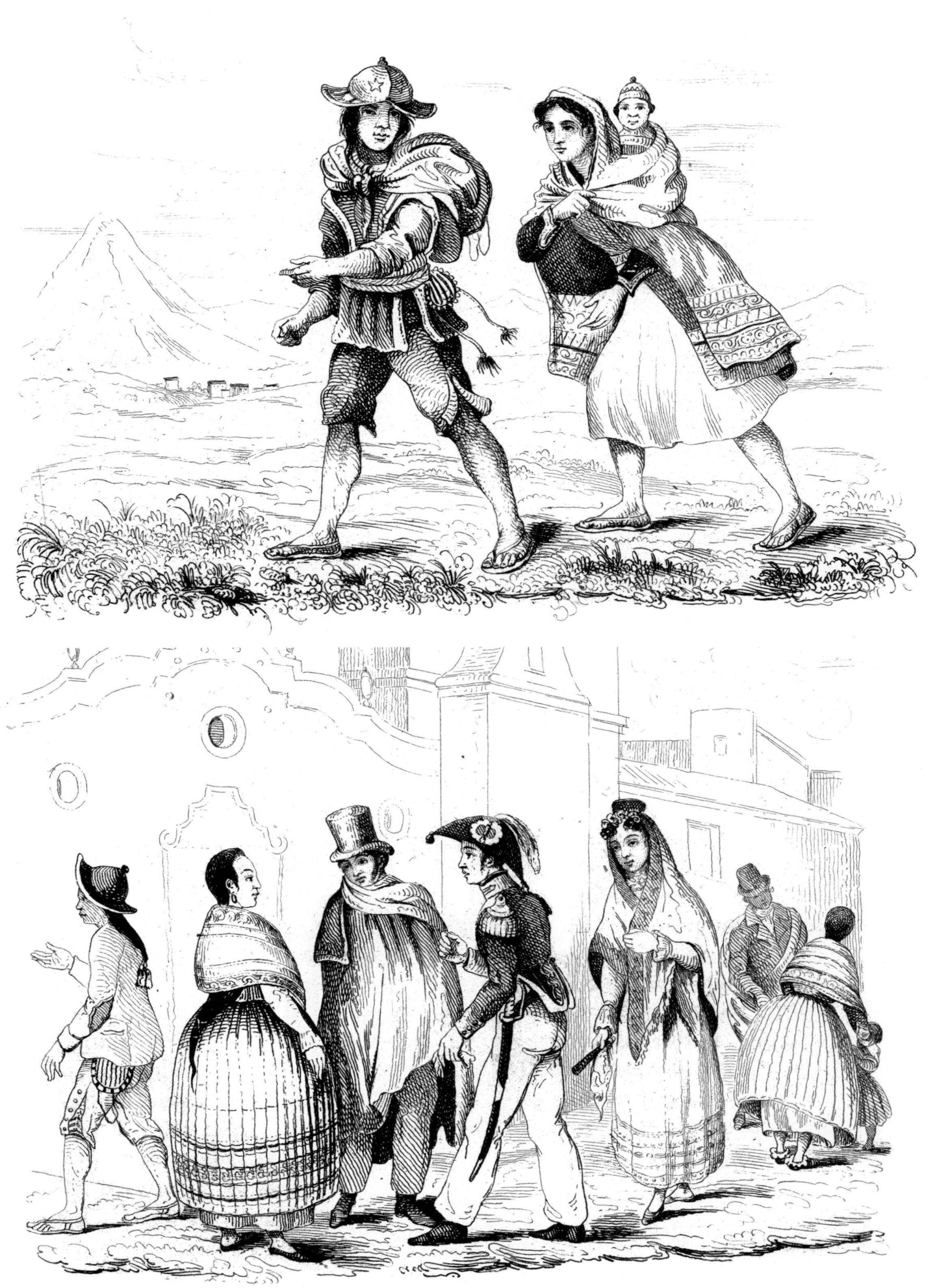

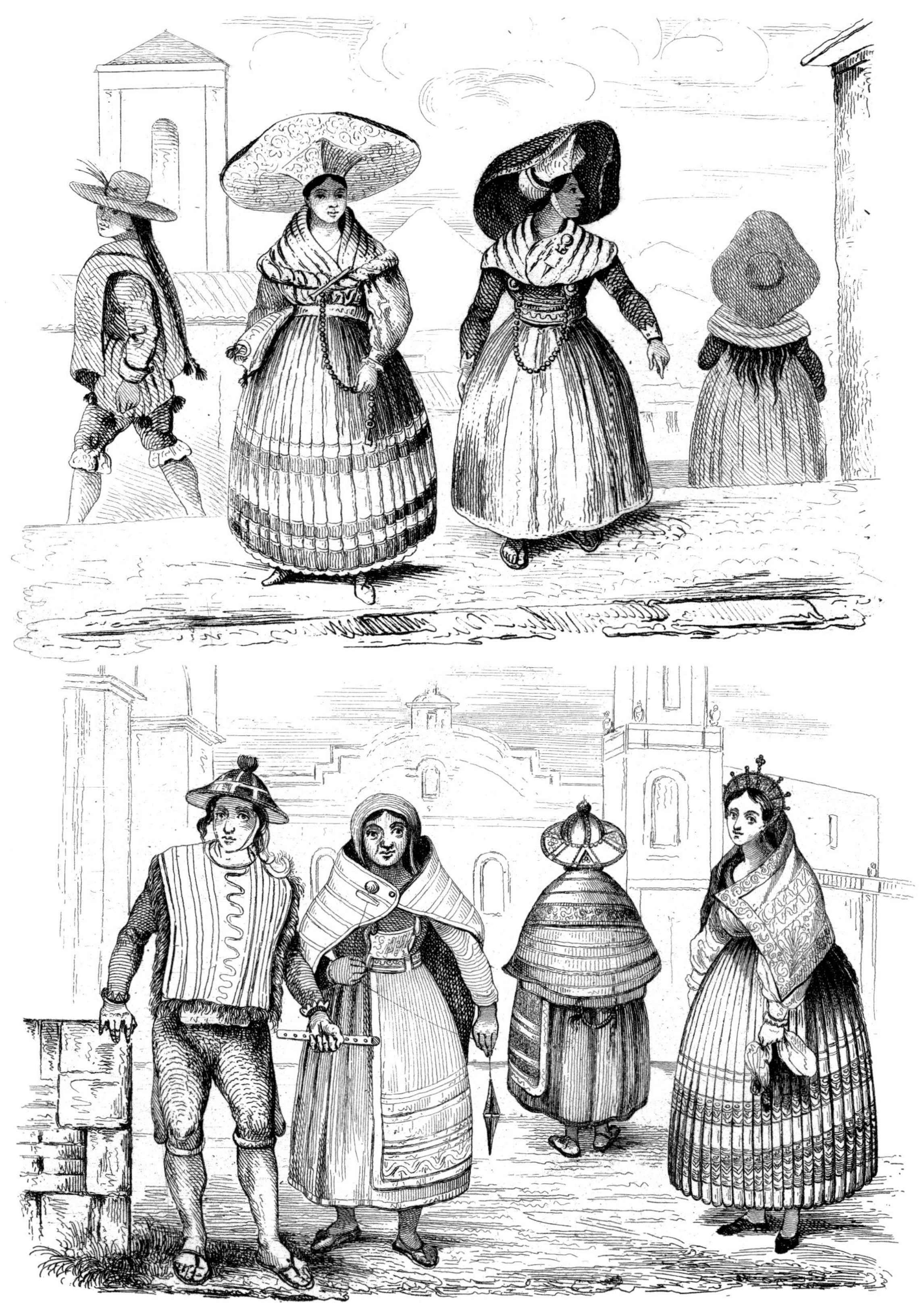

a	Street in La Paz. Bolivia, c. 1840	Straße in La Paz, Bolivien, um 1840	Strada di La Paz, Bolivia, ca. 1840	Rue de La Paz en Bolivie, vers 1840	Una calle de La Paz, Bolivia, hacia 1840
b	Sucre, Bolivia, c. 1840	Sucre, Bolivien, um 1840	Sucre, Bolivia, ca. 1840	Sucre en Bolivie, 1840	Sucre, Bolivia, hacia 1840

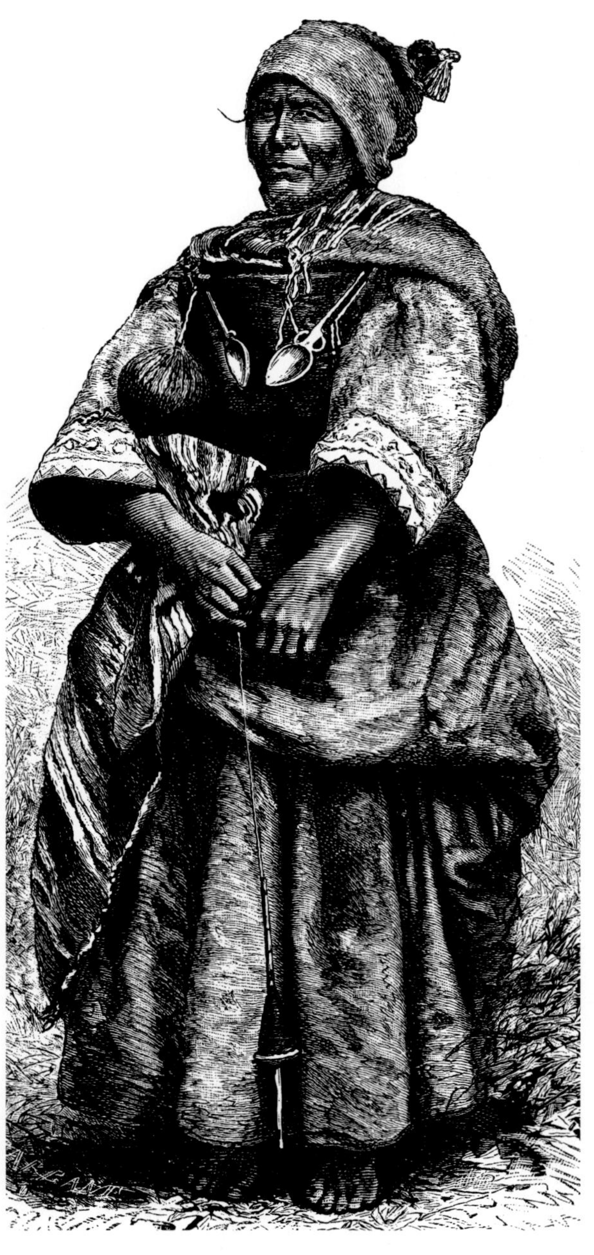

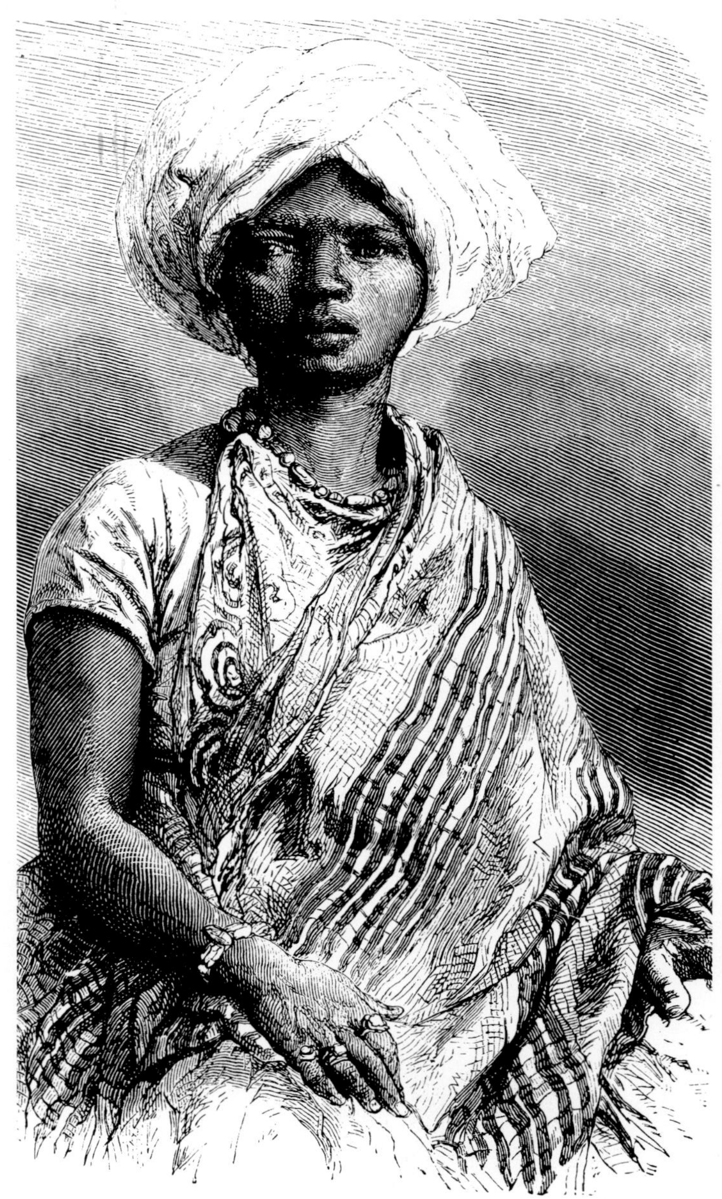

a	Aimara women, Bolivian interior, c. 1880	Aimara-Frau, bolivianisches Inland, um 1880	Donna aimara, interno della Bolivia, ca. 1880	Femme Aimara, Bolivie intérieure, vers 1880	Mujeres aimara del interior de Bolivia, 1880
b	Brazilian girl, c. 1885	Brasilianisches Mädchen, um 1885	Ragazza brasiliana, ca. 1885	Jeune brésilienne, vers 1885	Joven brasileña, 1885

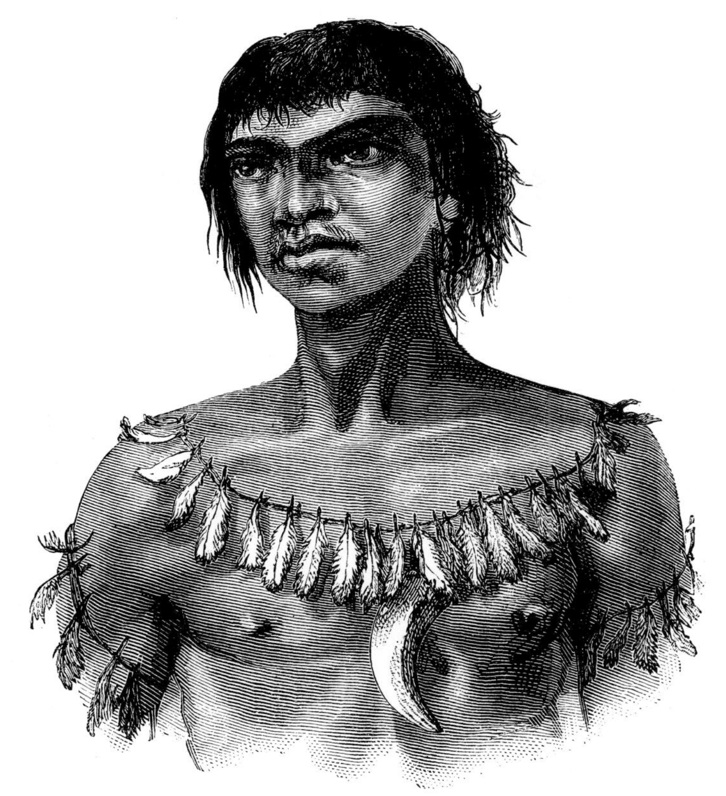

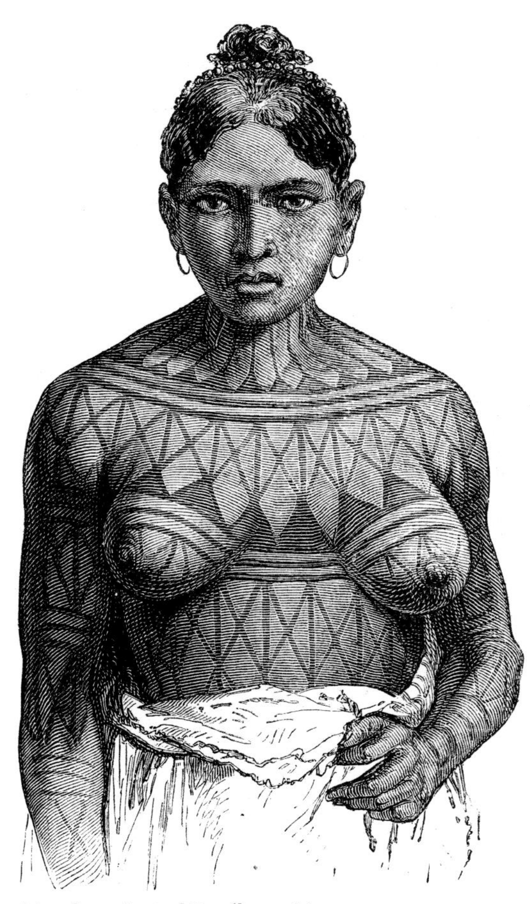

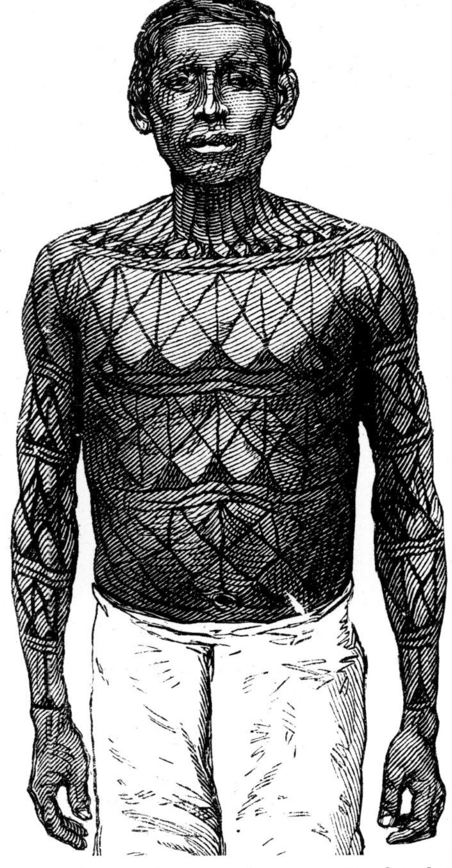

a	Man from Central Brazil, c. 1885	Mann aus Zentralbrasilien, um 1885	Uomo del Brasile centrale, ca. 1885	Homme du centre du Brésil, vers 1885	Hombre de Brasil central, hacia 1885
b+c	Mundurucus, Central Brazil, c. 1880	Munduruku, Zentralbrasilien, um 1880	Mundurucus, Brasile centrale, ca. 1880	Mundurucus, centre du Brésil, vers 1880	Mundurucúes, Brasil central, hacia 1880

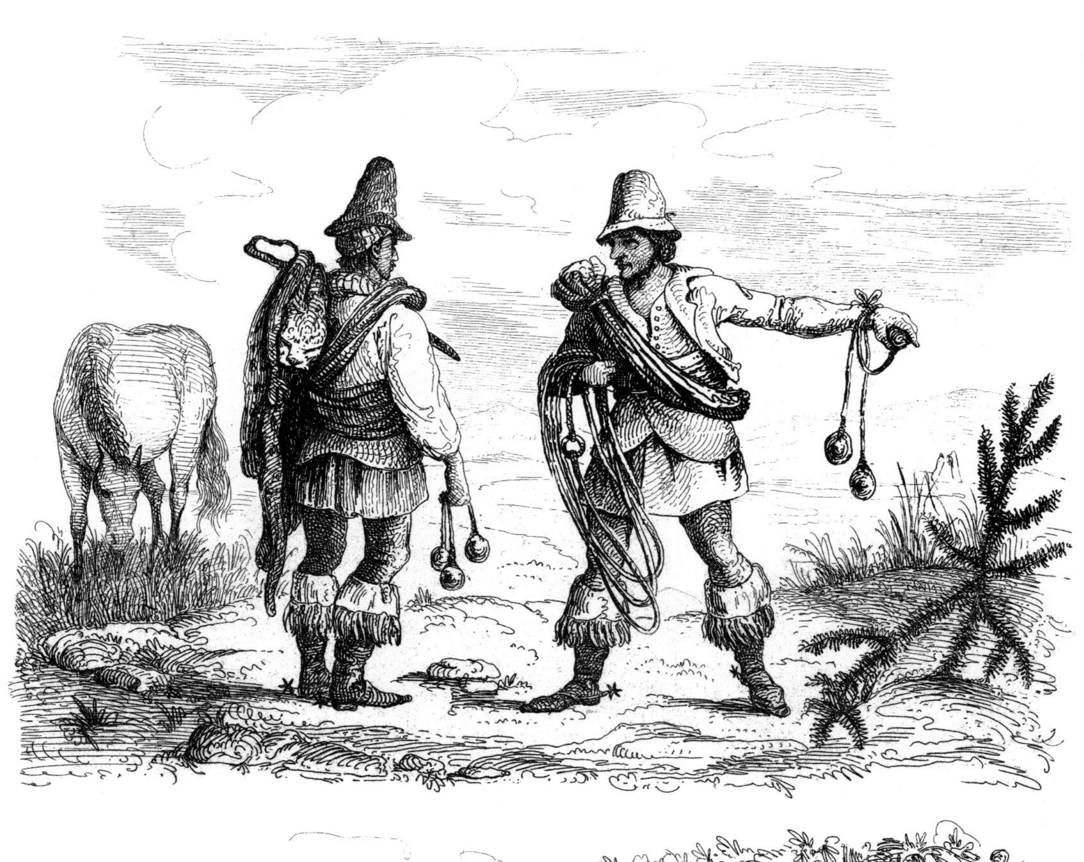

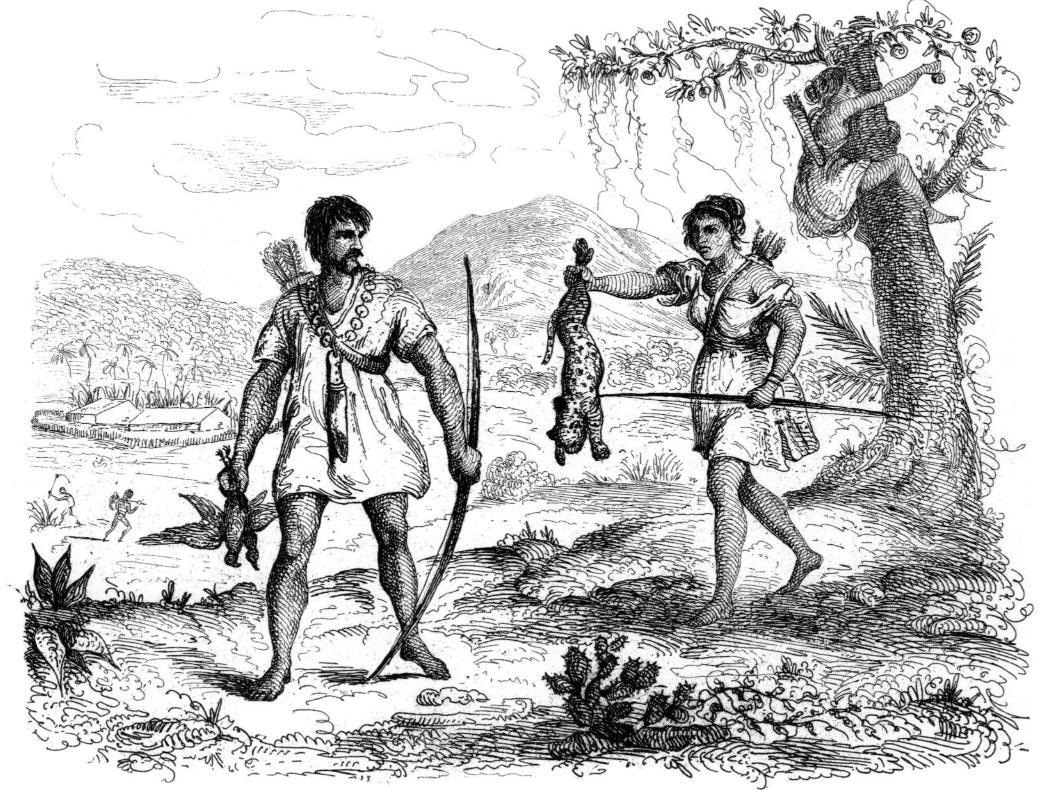

a	Charrua men in colonial dress, Sao Paulo province, c. 1840	Charrua-Mann in Kolonialkleidung, Provinz Sao Paulo, um 1840	Uomini charrua in abito coloniale, provincia di Sao Paulo, ca. 1840	Charruas en costume colonial dans la province de Sao Paulo, vers 1840	Hombres charrúa con trajes coloniales, región de Sao Paulo, hacia 1840
b	Bogre couple, Sao Paolo province, c. 1840	Bogre-Paar, Provinz Sao Paolo, um 1840	Coppia bogre, provincia di Sao Paulo, ca. 1840	Couple Bogre dans la province de Sao Paulo, vers 1840	Pareja bogre, región de Sao Paulo, hacia 1840

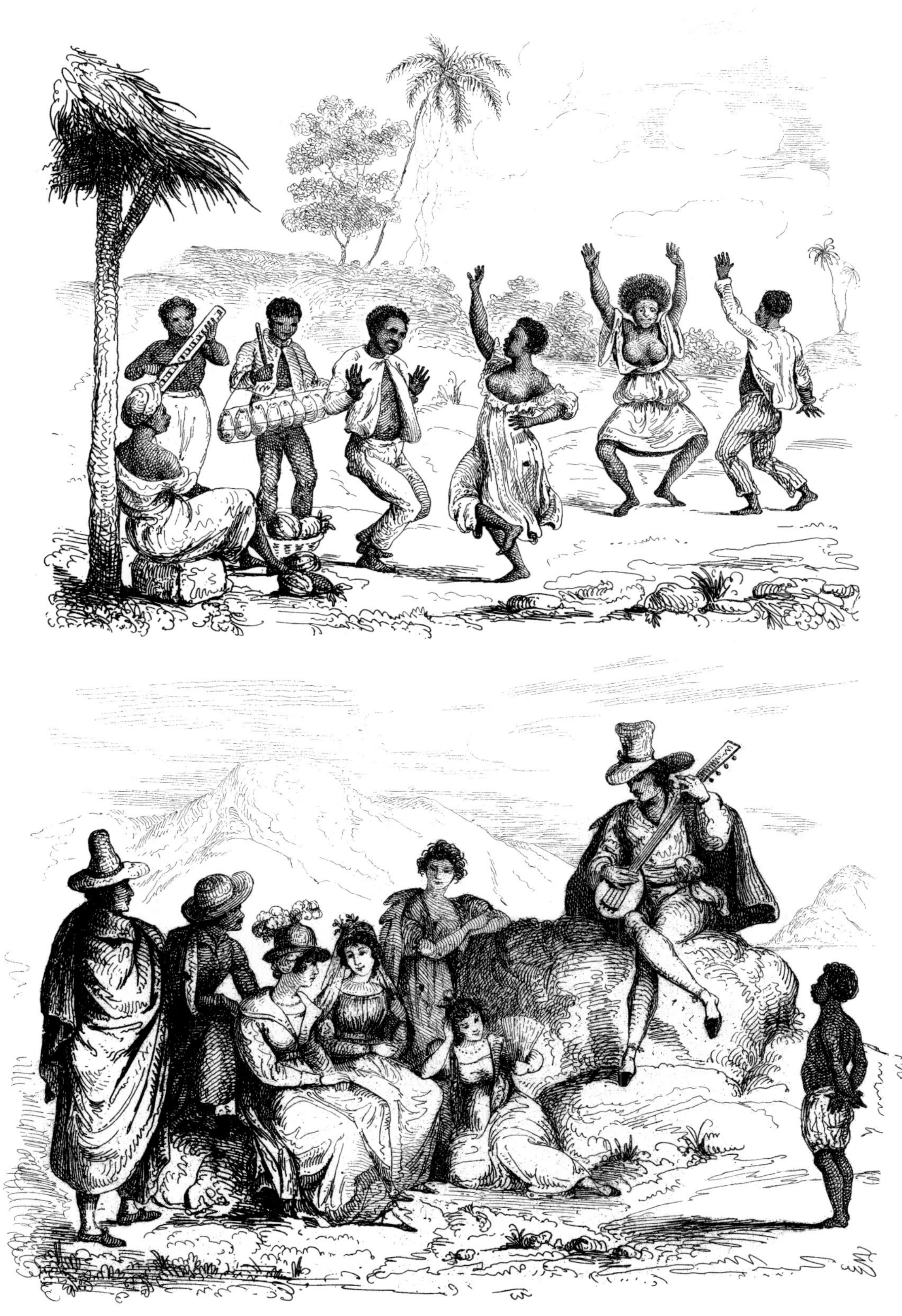

a	Musicians and dancers, Sao Paulo, c. 1840	Musiker und Tänzer, Sao Paulo, um 1840	Musicisti e danzatori, Sao Paulo, ca. 1840	Musiciens et danseurs à Sao Paulo, vers 1840	Músicos y bailarines, Sao Paulo, hacia 1840
b	Sao paulo costumes, c. 1840	Gewänder aus Sao Paulo, um 1840	Costumi di Sao Paulo, ca. 1840	Costumes de Sao Paulo, vers 1840	Trajes de Sao Paulo, hacia 1840

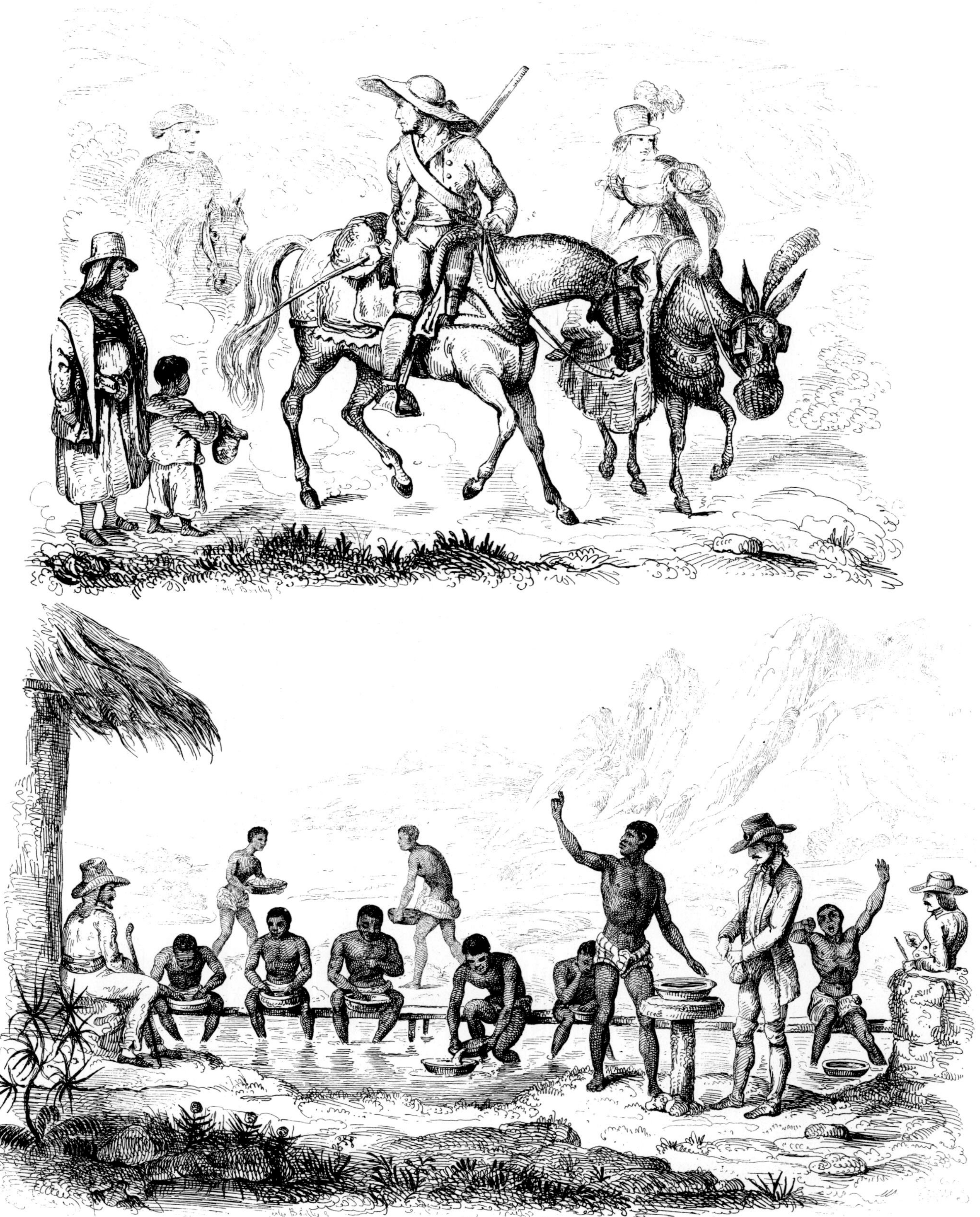

a	Inhabitants of Minas Garais province, c. 1840	Einwohner der Provinz von Minas Garais, um 1840	Abitanti della provincia di Minas Garais, ca. 1840	Habitants de la province de Minas Garais, vers 1840	Habitantes de la región de Minas Gerais, 1840
b	Diamond miners and traders, c. 1840	Arbeiter in den Diamantminen und Händler, um 1840	Minatori e commercianti di diamanti, ca. 1840	Mineurs et vendeurs de diamants, vers 1840	Mineros y comerciantes de diamantes, hacia 1840

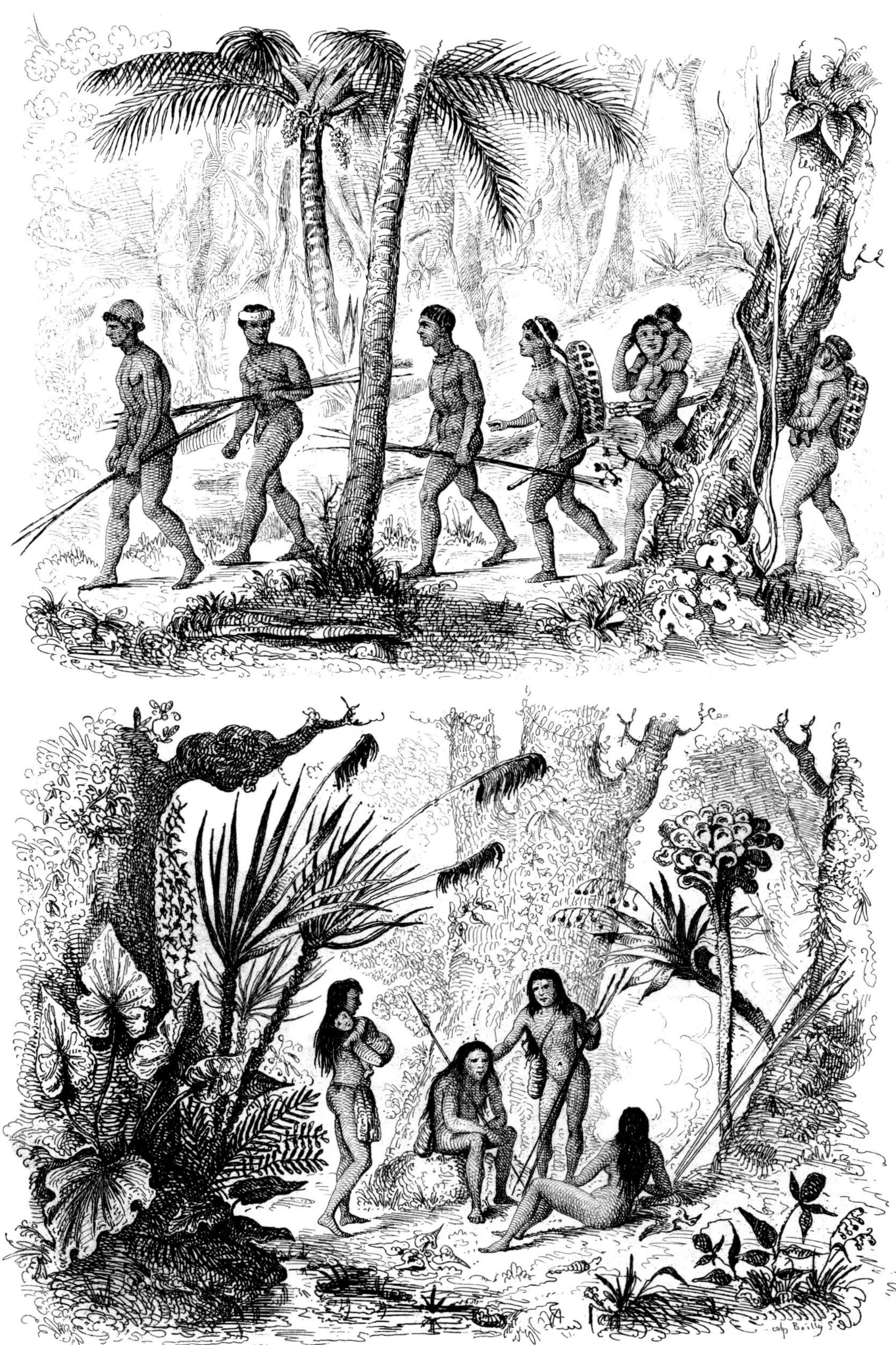

a	Members of the Puri tribe, Central Brazil, c. 1840	Mitglieder des Puri-Stamms, Zentralbrasilien, um 1840	Membri della tribù Puri, Brasile centrale, ca. 1840	Membres de la tribu Puri, centre du Brésil, vers 1840	Miembros de la tribu purí, Brasil central, alrededor del año 1840
b	Camacans, Central Brazil, c. 1840	Kamakan, Zentralbrasilien, um 1840	Camacani, Brasile centrale, ca. 1840	Camacans, centre du Brésil, vers 1840	Camacanes, Brasil central, hacia 1840

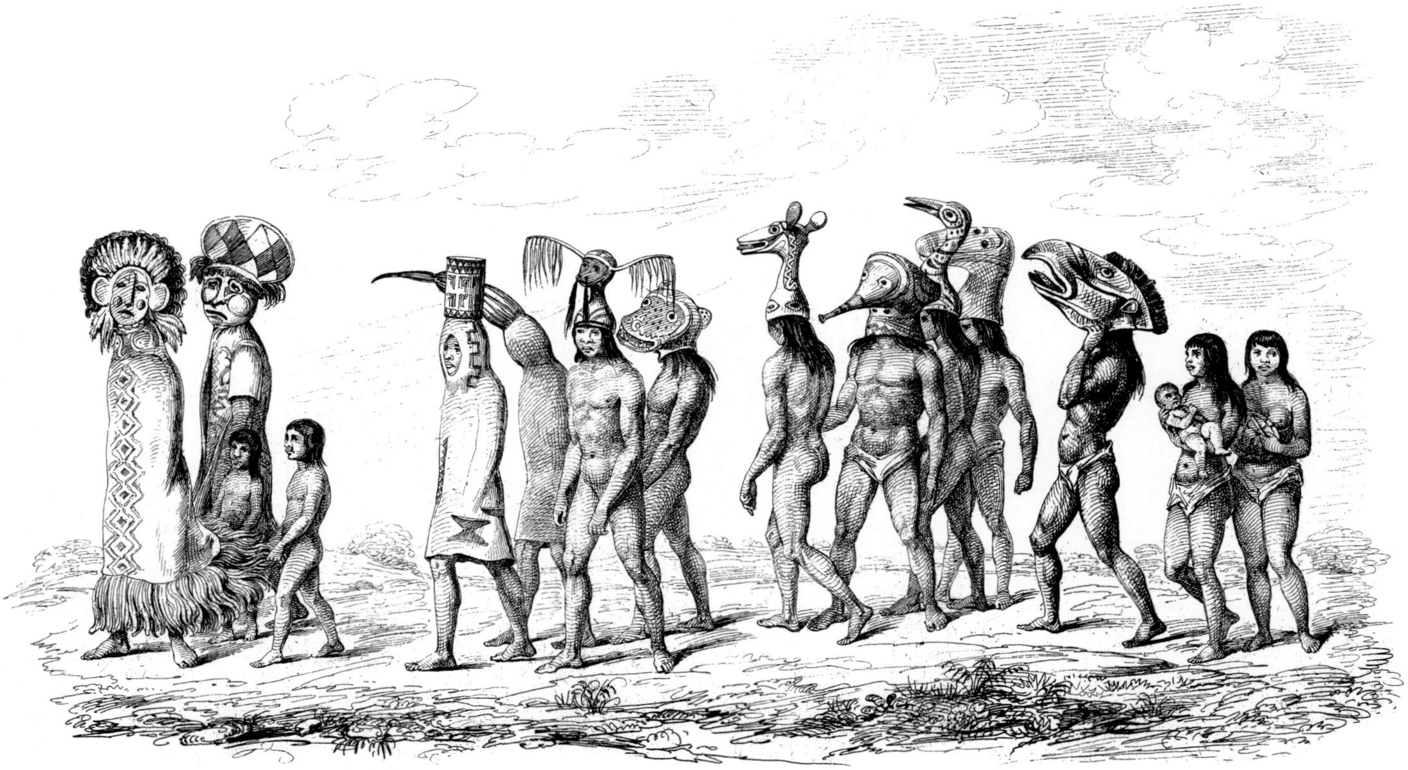

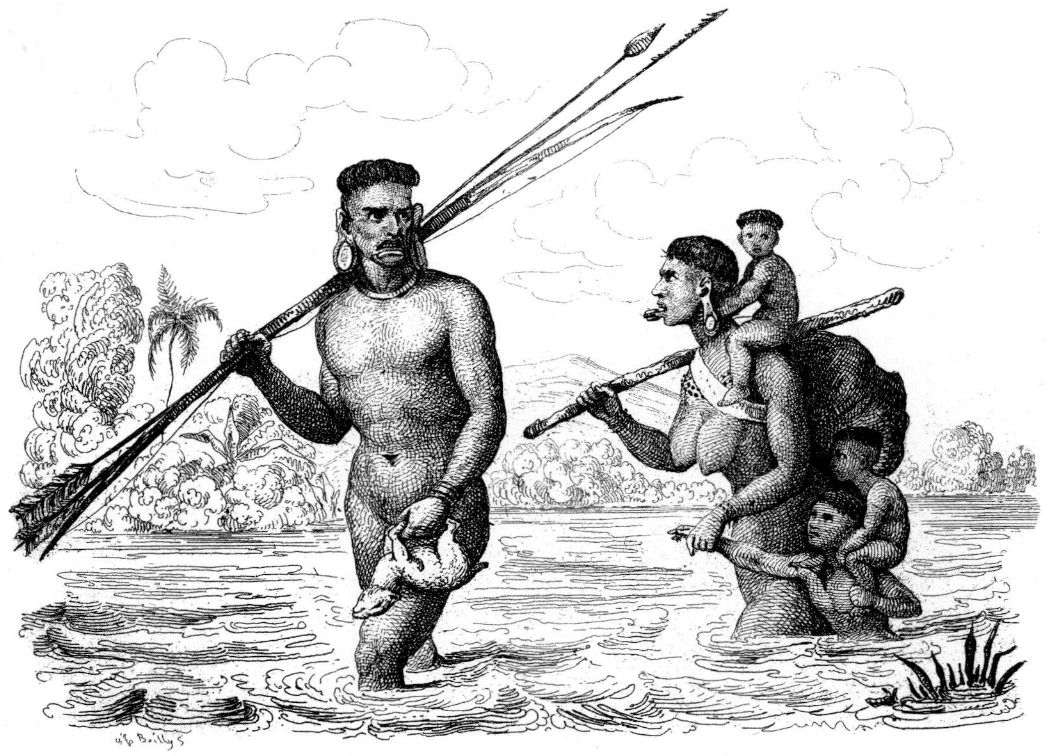

a

Dance ceremony of the Tecunas, Central Brazil, c. 1840

Tanzzeremonie der Tecuna, Zentralbrasilien, um 1840

Danza degli abitanti di Tecuna, Brasile centrale, ca. 1840

Danse cérémoniale des Tecunas, centre du Brésil, vers 1840

Ceremonia de los tecunas, Brasil central, hacia 1840

b

Botocudo family, Brazil, c. 1840

Botocudo-Familie, Brasilien, um 1840

Famiglia botocudo, Brasile, ca. 1840

Famille Botocudo, Brésil, vers 1840

Familia botocudo, Brasil, hacia 1840

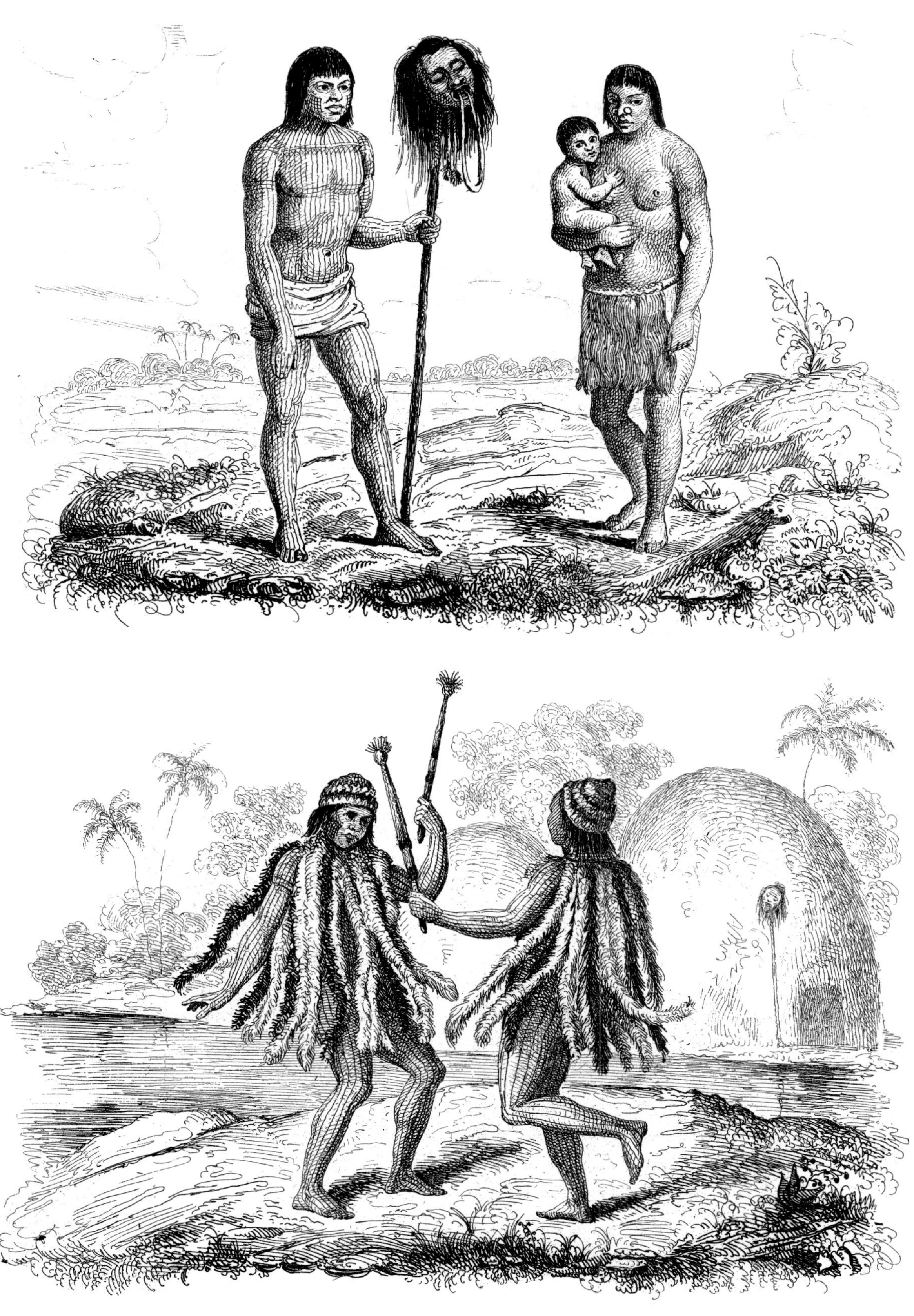

Mundurucus, Central brazil, c. 1840

Munduruku, Zentralbrasilien, um 1840

Mundurucus, Brasile centrale, ca. 1840

Mundurucus, centre du Brésil, vers 1840

Mundurucúes, Brasil central, hacia 1840

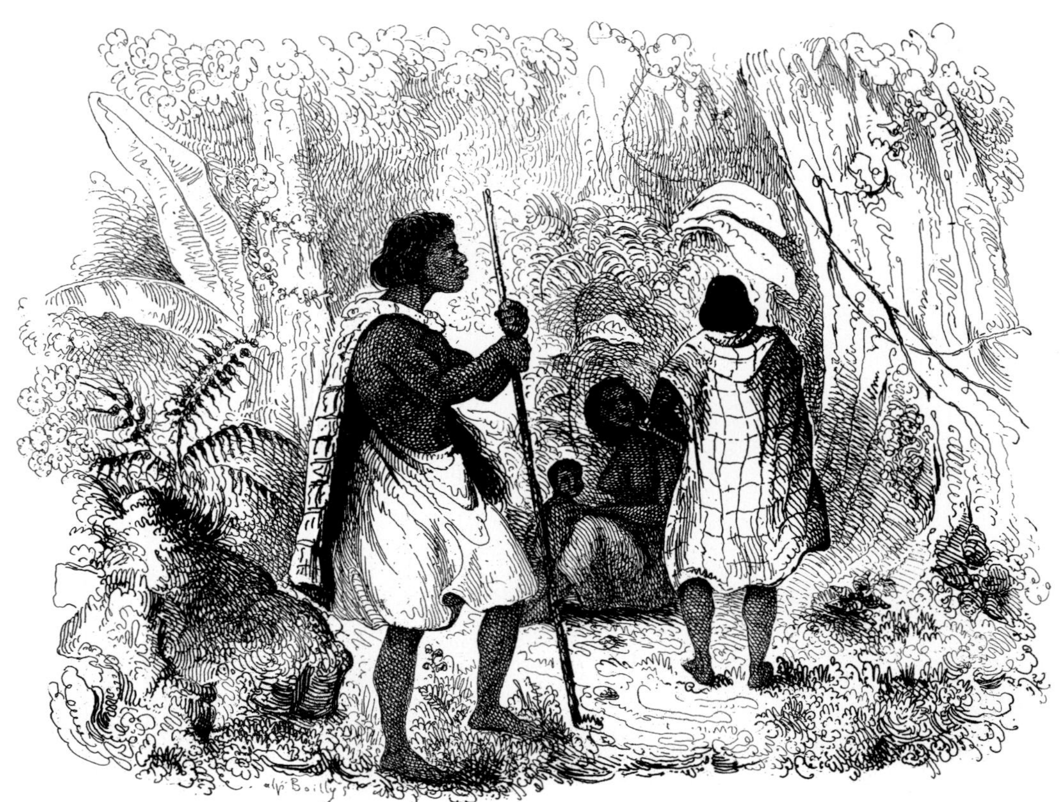

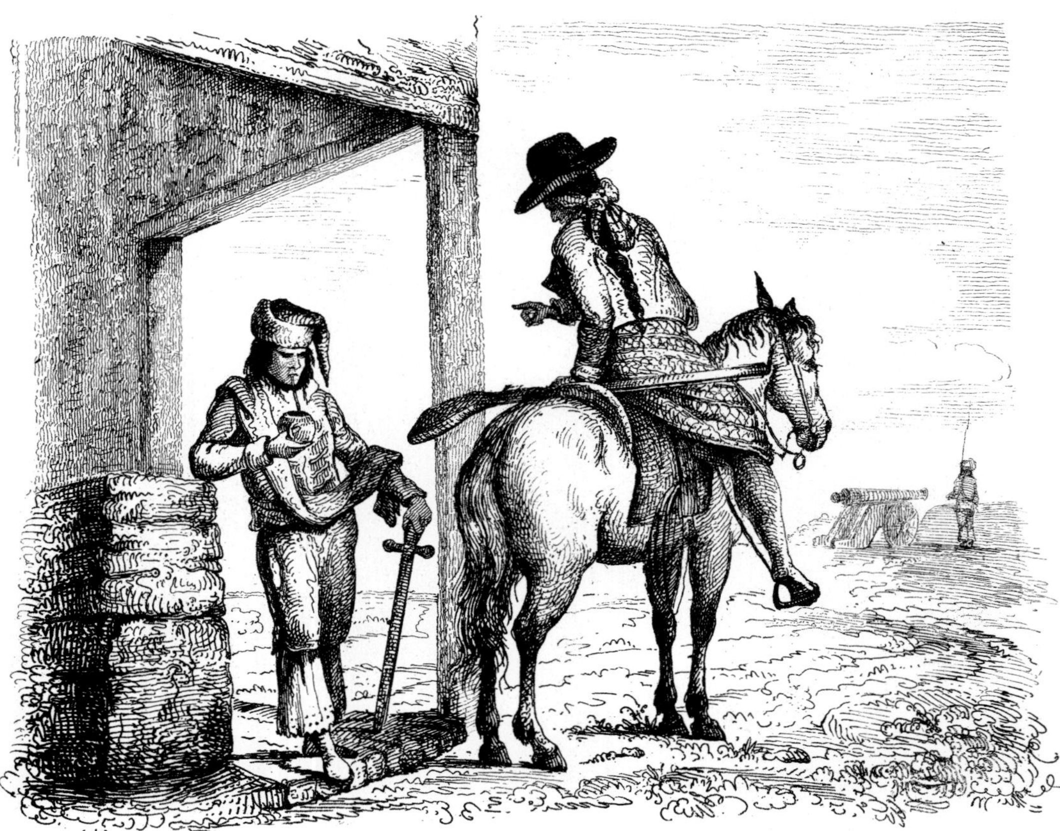

a	Inhabitants of the paraguayan interior, c. 1840	Einwohner des Inlands von Paraguay, um 1840	Abitanti dell'interno del Paraguay, ca. 1840	Habitants du centre du Paraguay, vers 1840	Habitantes del interior del Paraguay, hacia 1840
b	Militia members, c. 1840	Mitglieder der Miliz, um 1840	Membri della milizia, ca. 1840	Membres de la milice, vers 1840	Milicianos, alrededor del año 1840

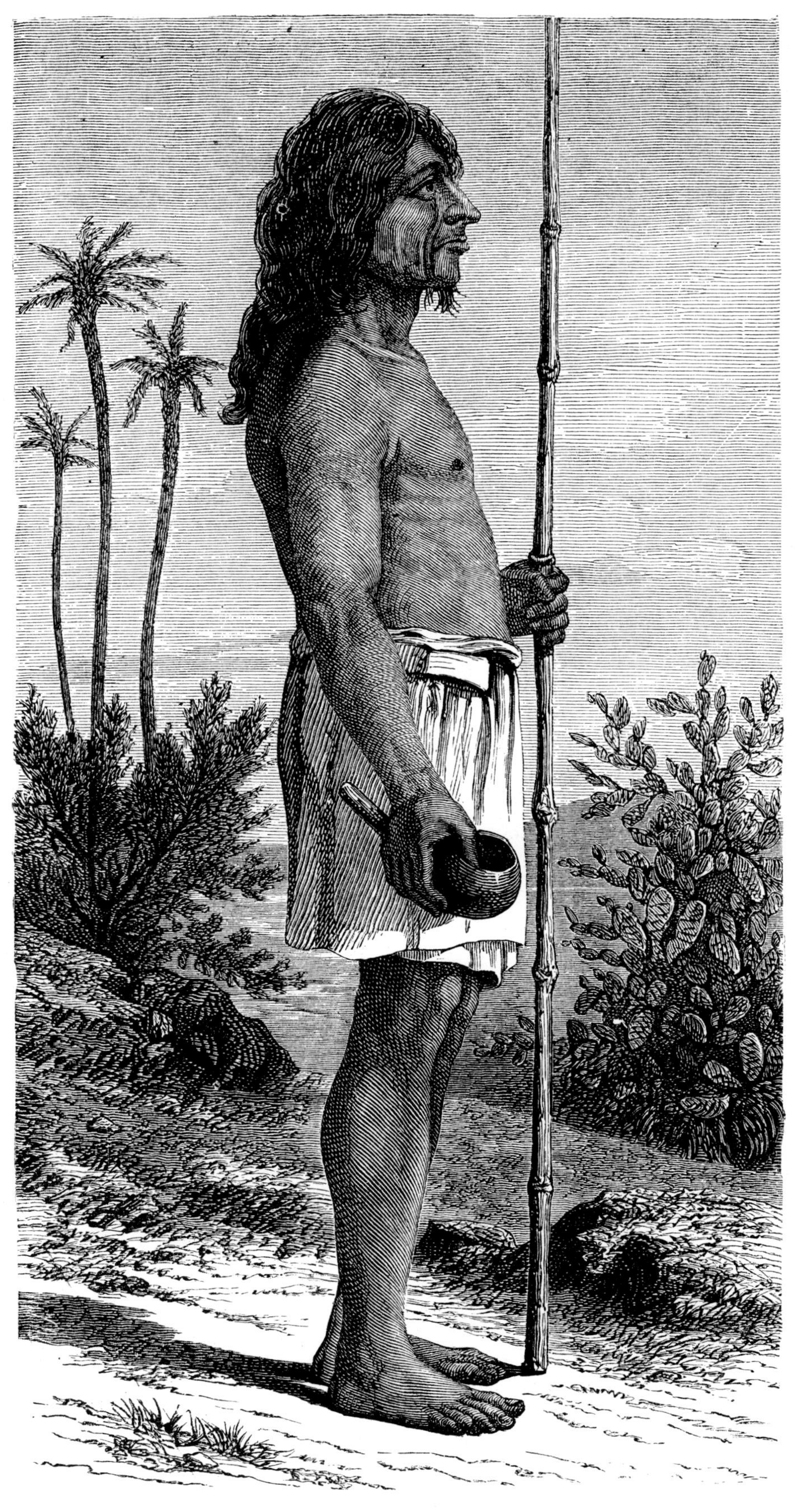

Native Paraguayan, c. 1880

Einheimischer Paraguayer, um 1880

Indigeno del Paraguay, ca. 1880

Indigène paraguayen, vers 1880

Nativo paraguayo, alrededor del año 1880

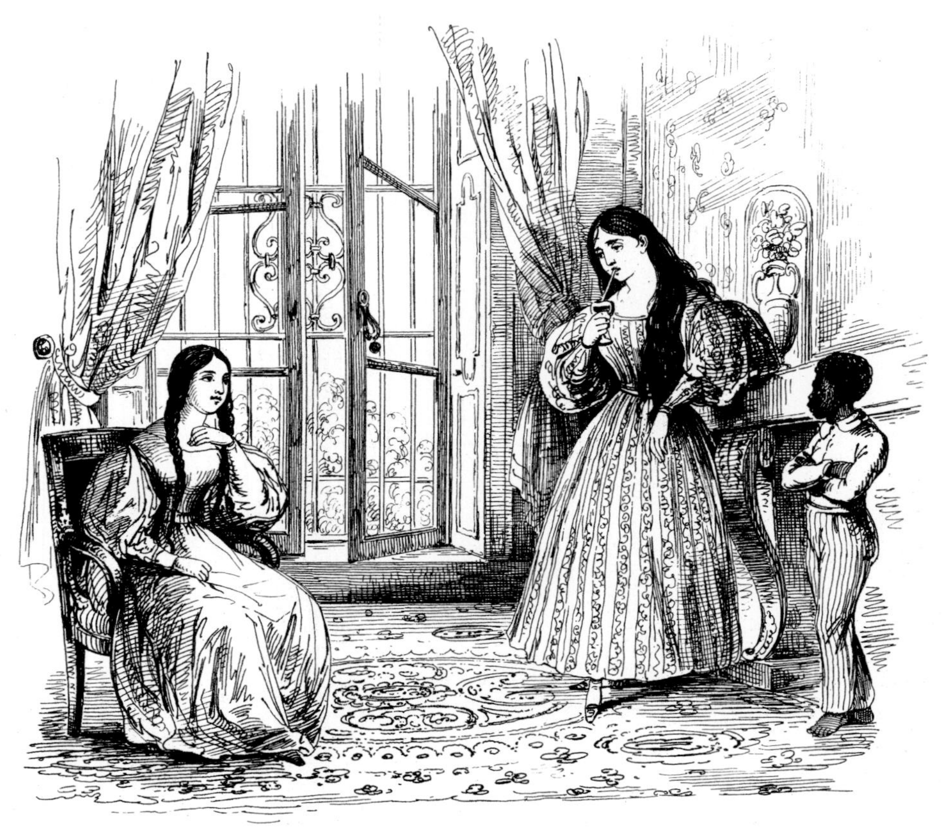

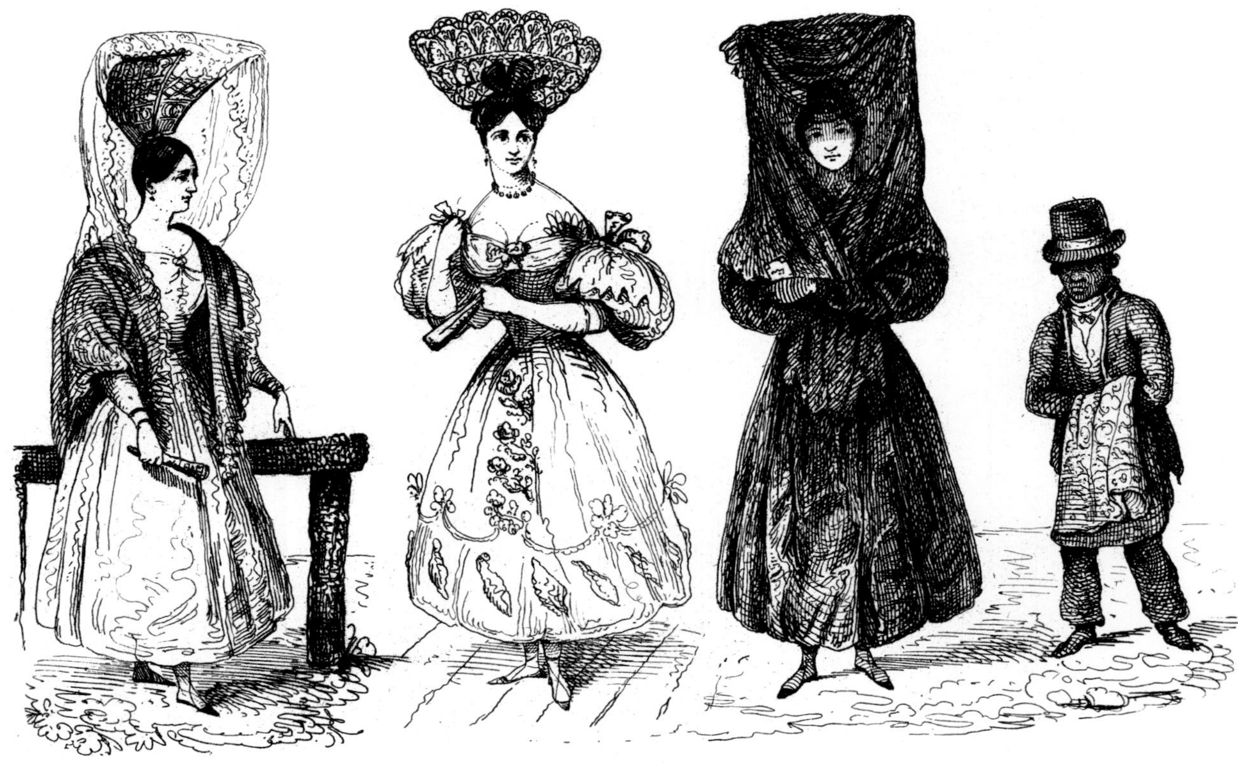

Ladies in Buenos Aires, c. 1840

Damen in Buenos Aires, um 1840

Donne a Buenos Aires, ca. 1840

Femmes à Buenos Aires, vers 1840

Damas de Buenos Aires, alrededor del año 1840

Argentina

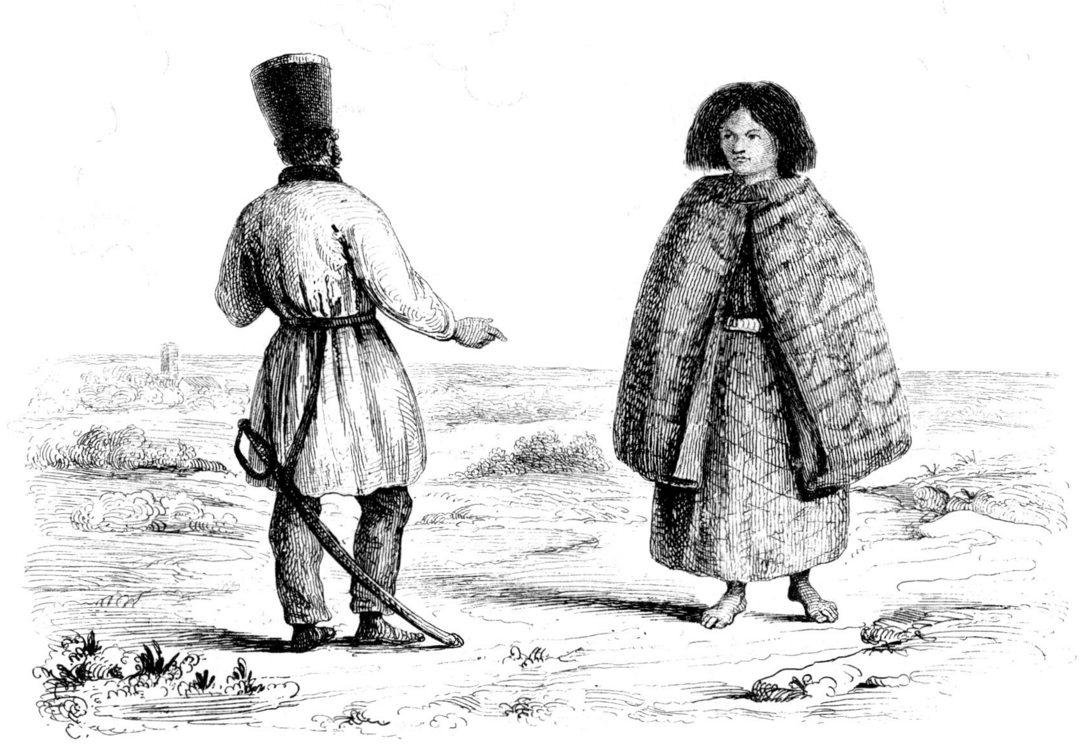

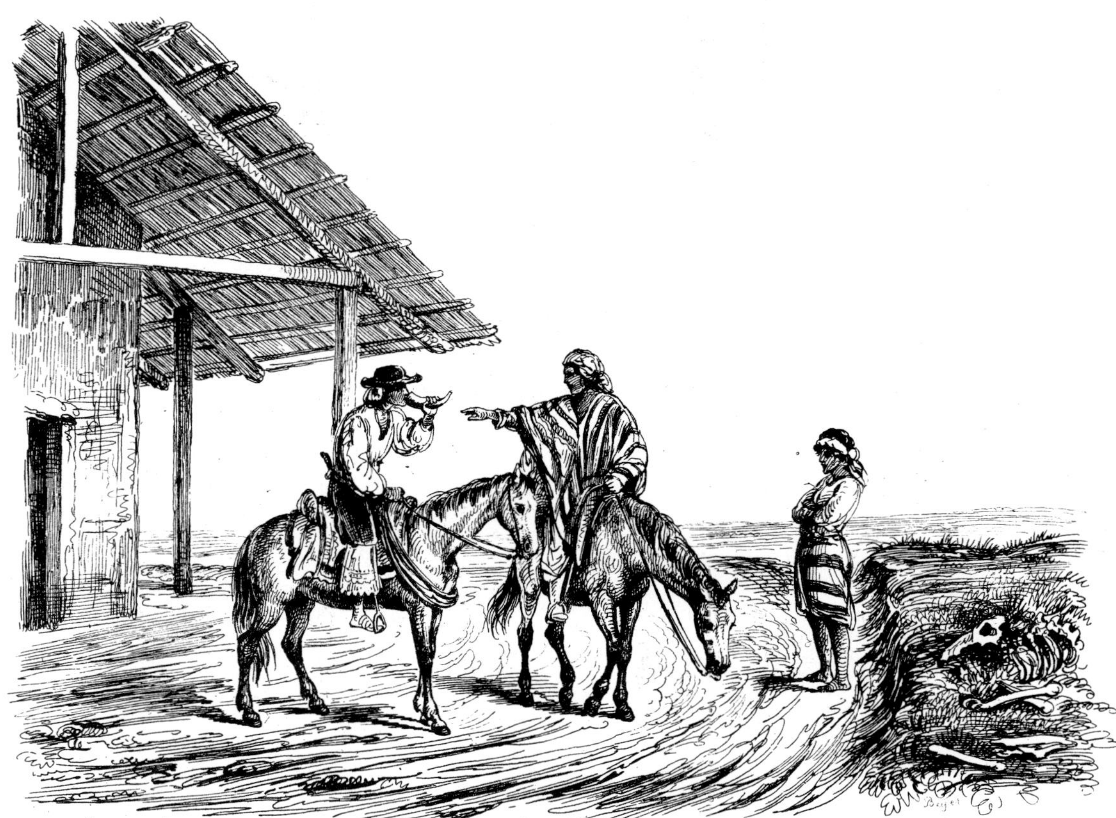

a	Soldier and local Patagonian, c. 1840	Soldat und einheimischer Patagonier, um 1840	Soldato e abitante della Patagonia, ca. 1840	Soldat et indigène de Patagonie, vers 1840	Soldado y patagón local, hacia 1840
b	Riders in Southern Argentina, c. 1840	Reiter im Süden Argentiniens, um 1840	Cavalieri dell'Argentina meridionale, ca. 1840	Cavaliers au Sud de l'Argentine, vers 1840	Jinetes del sur de Argentina, hacia 1840

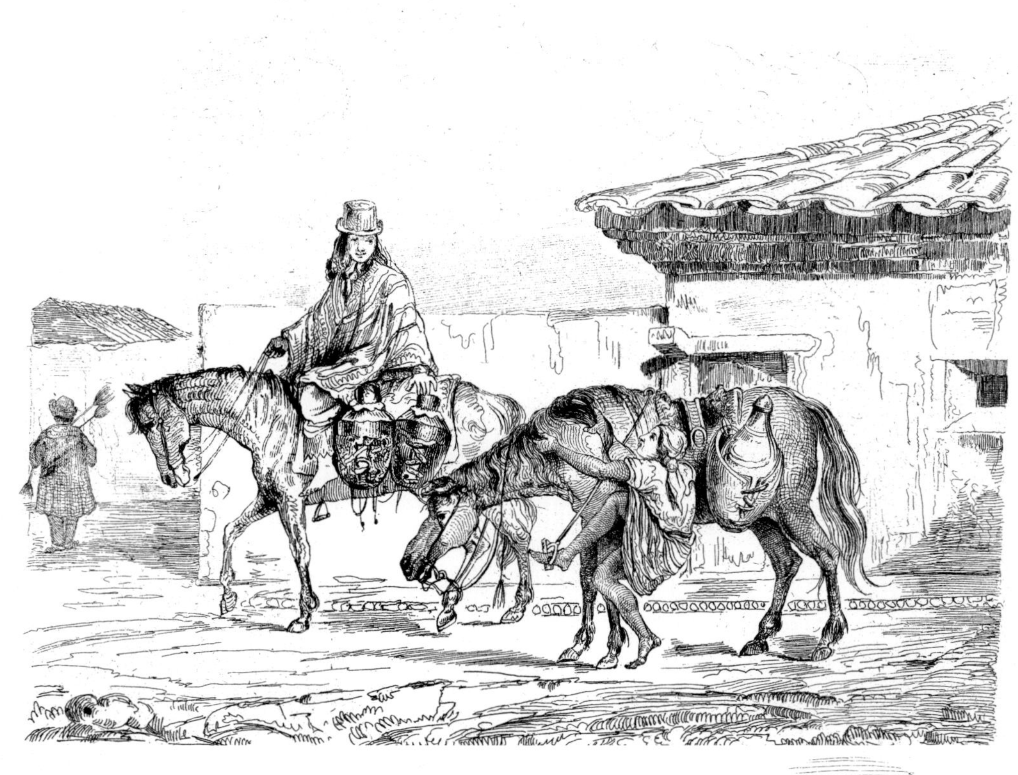

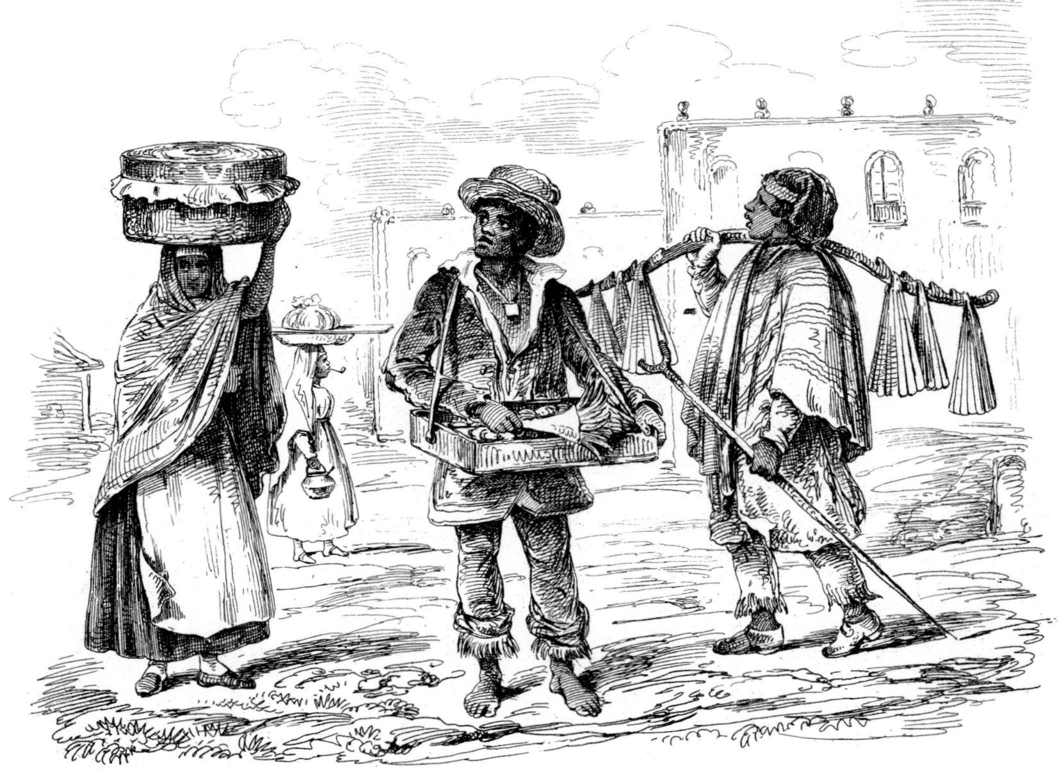

a	Milk vendor, c. 1840	Milchverkäufer, um 1840	Venditore di latte, ca. 1840	Vendeur de lait, vers 1840	Lechero, hacia 1840
b	Market vendors, Buenos Aires, c. 1840	Marktverkäufer, Buenos Aires, um 1840	Venditori del mercato, Buenos Aires, ca. 1840	Vendeurs sur le marché de Buenos Aires, vers 1840	Vendedores del mercado de Buenos Aires, 1840

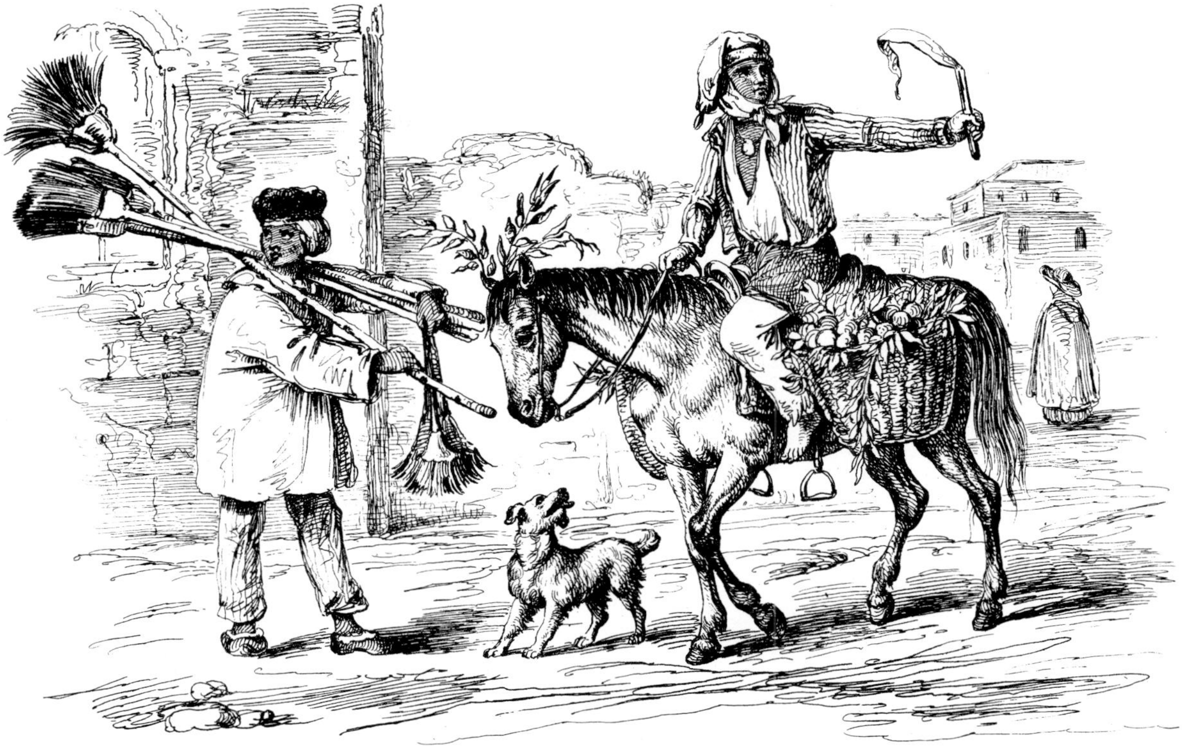

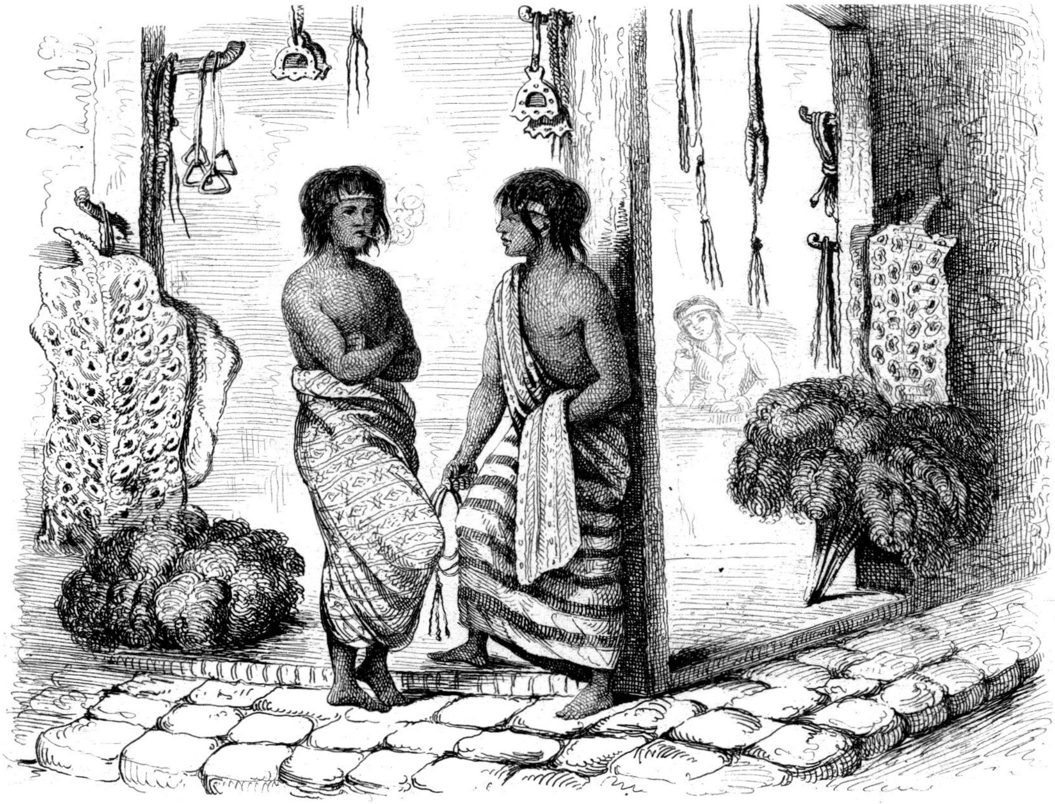

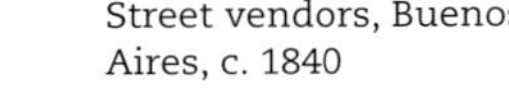

a	Street vendors, Buenos Aires, c. 1840	Straßenverkäufer, Buenos Aires, um 1840	Venditori ambulanti, Buenos Aires, ca. 1840	Vendeur de rue à Buenos Aires, vers 1840	Vendedores ambulantes, Buenos Aires, hacia 1840
b	Inhabitants of the Pampa province, c. 1840	Einwohner der Provinz Pampa, um 1840	Abitanti della provincia della Pampa, ca. 1840	Habitants de la province de la Pampa, vers 1840	Habitantes de la Pampa, alrededor del año 1840

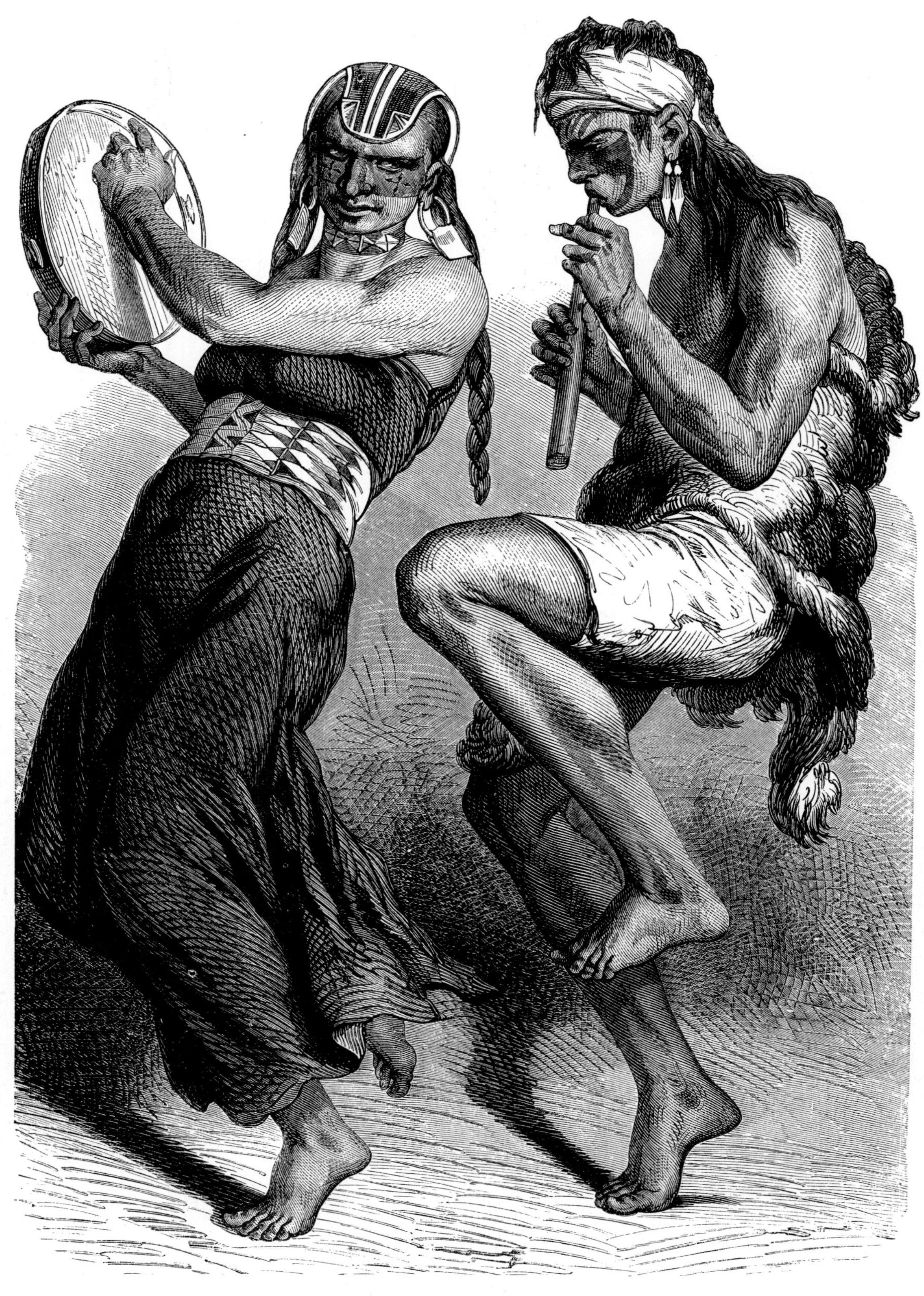

Patagonians, Southern Argentina, c. 1880

Patagonier im Süden Argentiniens, um 1880

Abitanti della Patagonia, Argentina meridionale, ca. 1880

Patagoniens au Sud de l'Argentine, vers 1880

Patagones, sur de Argentina, hacia 1880

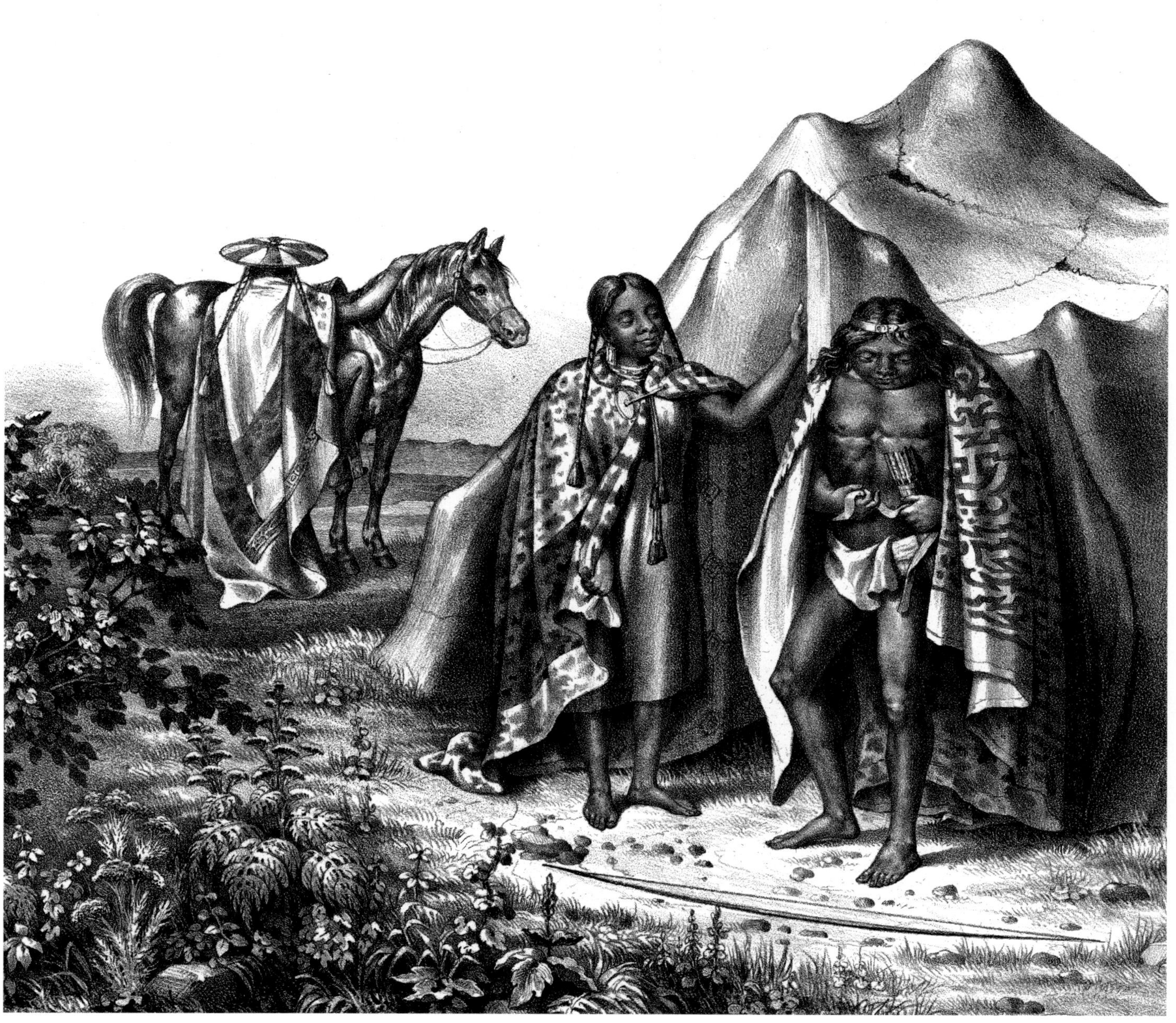

Natives of Patagonia, c. 1880

Einheimische aus Patagonien, um 1880

Indigeni della Patagonia, ca. 1880

Indigènes de Patagonie, vers 1880

Nativos de Patagonia, alrededor del año 1880

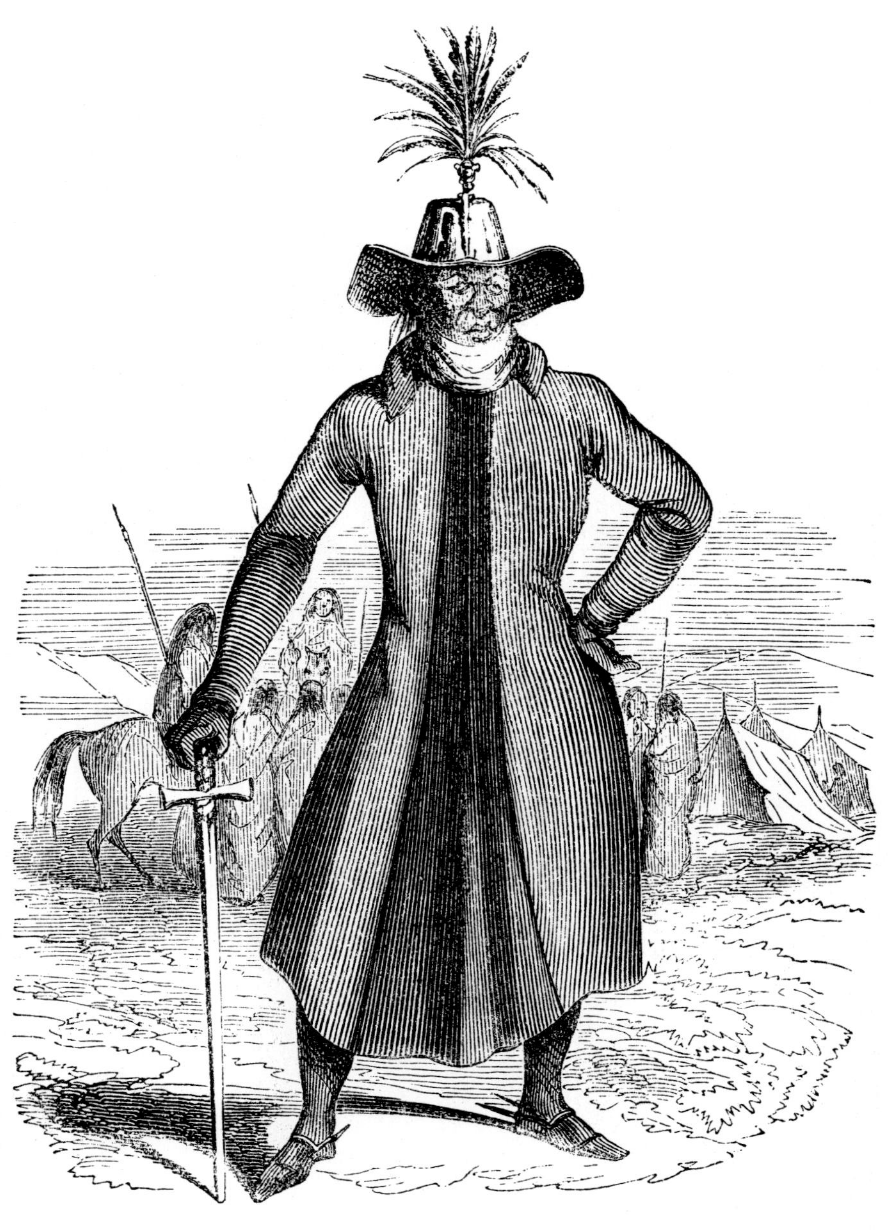

Patagonian chief in war costume, c. 1845

Patagonischer Häuptling im Kriegsgewand, um 1845

Capo paragone in costume di guerra, ca. 1845

Chef patagonien en costume de guerre, vers 1845

Jefe patagón con traje de guerra, hacia 1845

Argentina

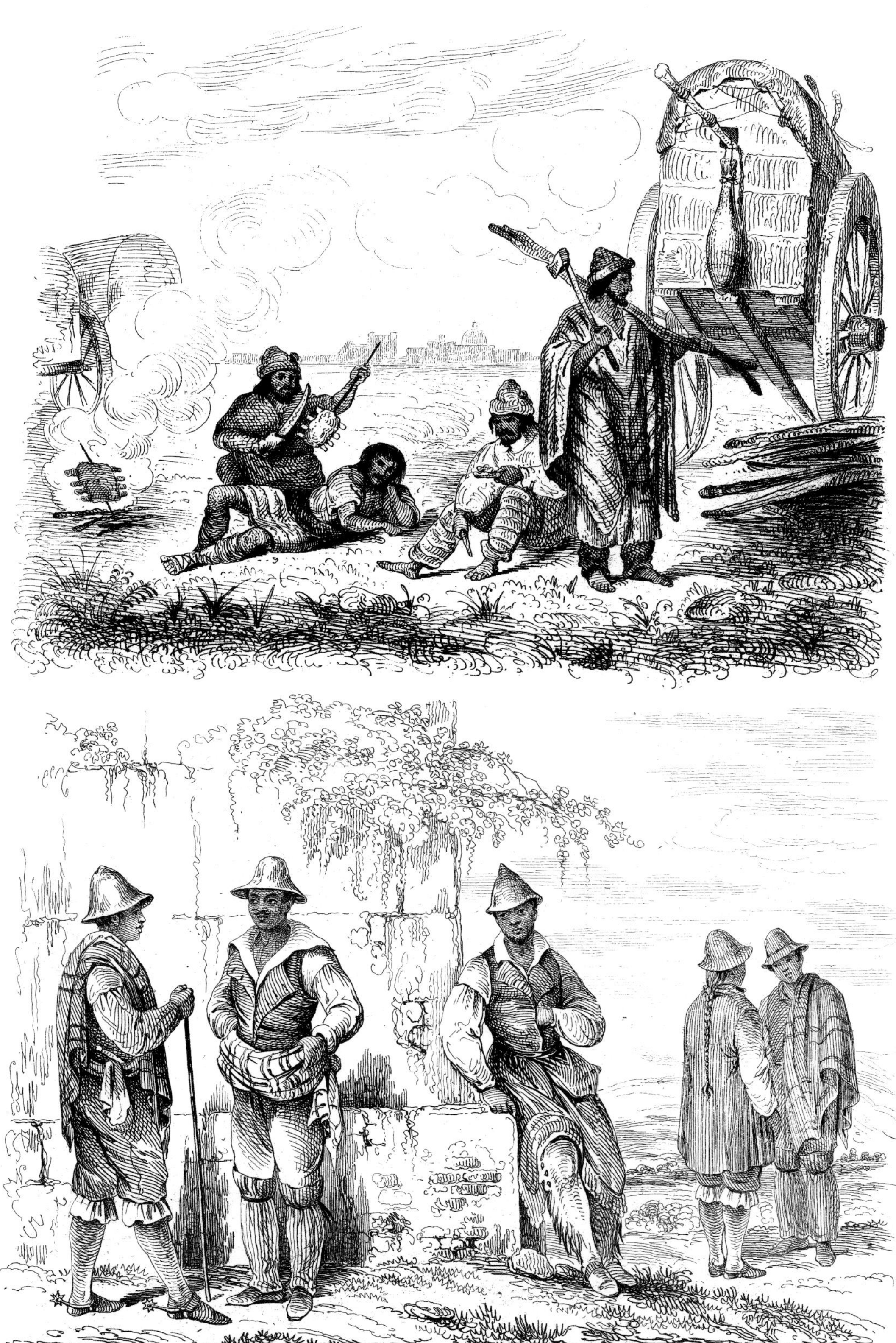

a	Carriage stop in Southern Argentina, c. 1840	Kutschstation im Süden Argentiniens, um 1840	Fermata durante un trasporto nell'Argentina meridionale, ca. 1840	Chariot à l'arrêt dans le Sud de l'Argentine, vers 1840	Parada del carro en el sur de Argentina, hacia 1840
b	Chilean costumes, c. 1840	Chilenische Kleidung, um 1840	Costumi cileni, ca. 1840	Costumes chiliens, vers 1840	Trajes chilenos, alrededor del año 1840

Index
Register
Indice
Index
Índice
索引
索 引